This is the first comprehensive history of Palestine from the Muslim conquest in 634 to that of the Crusaders in 1099. It is a translation and revised version of volume I of *Palestine during the first Muslim period* which was published in Hebrew in 1983 and presents an authoritative survey of the early mediaeval Islamic and Jewish worlds.

Professor Gil begins by reviewing the political and military events in Palestine before and after the Arab invasion. Later chapters explore the Abbasid, Ṭūlūnid, Ikhshīdid and Fatimid periods, during which time Palestine was an almost perpetual battlefield for states, armies and factions.

Against this backdrop of conflict and administrative changes, the author portrays the everyday life of Palestine and its inhabitants. He looks at the economic history of Palestine – its agriculture, transport facilities, exports and systems of taxation – as well as the religious status of Jerusalem, the nature of Islam's tolerance towards Jews and Christians and the status, leadership and customs of the Christian populace. Specific attention is paid to the history of Palestinian Jews under Muslim rule. Professor Gil details their topography, economic activities and religious life; he explores the Karaite and Samaritan communities and discusses the role of the most prominent Jewish institution, the yeshiva.

A history of Palestine, 634–1099 is based on an impressive array of sources. Professor Gil has carefully read the more than 1,000 documents of the Cairo Geniza collection and these are paralleled by Arabic, Syriac, Latin and Greek material. This monumental study will be read by students and specialists of mediaeval Islamic and Jewish history and religious studies and by anyone interested in the history of the Holy Land.

A history of Palestine, 634–1099

A HISTORY OF PALESTINE, 634–1099

Moshe Gil

Translated from the Hebrew by Ethel Broido

The right of the University of Cambridge to print and sell all manner of books was granted by Henry VIII in 1534. The University has printed and published continuously since 1584.

CAMBRIDGE UNIVERSITY PRESS

Cambridge

New York Port Chester Melbourne Sydney

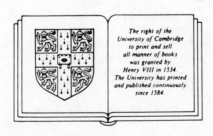

Published by the Press Syndicate of the University of Cambridge
The Pitt Building, Trumpington Street, Cambridge CB2 1RP
40 West 20th Street, New York, NY 10011–4211, USA
10 Stamford Road, Oakleigh, Victoria 3166, Australia

This is a revised edition of *Palestine During the First Muslim Period (634–1099)*

Originally published in Hebrew by Tel Aviv University in 1983

First published by Cambridge University Press, 1992
as *A history of Palestine, 634–1099*

Photoset and Printed in Great Britain by Redwood Press, Melksham

This book was published with the assistance of grants from the following:
The Memorial Foundation for Jewish Culture, the Louis and Minna Epstein Fund of the American Academy for Jewish Research, and the Taylor-Schechter Geniza Research Unit, University of Cambridge

British Library cataloguing in publication data

Gil, Moshe
A history of Palestine, 634–1099.
1. Palestine, 640–1917
I. Title
956.9403

Library of Congress cataloguing in publication data

Gil, Moshe, 1921–
[Erets-Yiśra'el ba-teḳufah ha-Muslemit ha-rishonah (634–1099). 1, Iyunim historiyim. English]
A history of Palestine, 634–1099 / Moshe Gil.
p. cm.
Translation of v. 1 of: Erets-Yiśra'el ba-teḳufah ha-Muslemit ha-rishonah (634–1099).
Includes bibliographical references and index.
ISBN 0 521 40437 1 (hardcover)
1. Palestine – History – 638–1917. 2. Islam – Palestine – History. 3. Jews – Palestine – History. I. Title
DS 124.G5513 1992
956.94'03 – dc20 90–20807 CIP

ISBN 0 521 40437 1 hardback

RB

5-8-92

CONTENTS

Preface

These studies are based mainly on the sources left to us by the three communities living in Palestine between the Arab conquest and the Crusades: the Jews, the Christians, and the Muslims. Among the Jewish sources, the Cairo Geniza documents occupy first place, owing to both their quantity and their authenticity, for these were actually written by contemporaries of the period, some of whom played important roles in the events I am dealing with. These documents, referred to in this book as 'my collection', are printed in two additional Hebrew volumes, in their Judaeo-Arabic original, with translations into Hebrew and commentaries. The reader who wishes to examine these original texts and is familiar with Hebrew and Arabic, will find them in vols. II and III of my *Ereṣ isrā'ēl ba-teqūfā ha-muslimīt ha-ri'shōnā*. Accordingly, references are made in the present book to the 'Hebrew Index' of those volumes, by which the indexes at the end of vol. III of my above-mentioned book are meant. A supplement to these volumes was published in *Te'uda*, vol. 7 (1991), containing twenty-five additional texts. In the footnotes of the present book, references to these Geniza documents are indicated by numbers in boldface type, using the same numbers as those of the documents in the above-mentioned collection. In referring to the supplement in *Te'uda*, the number is accompanied by the letter a or b, also in boldface. My collection comprises 643 documents in all. More than a third were edited earlier in their entirety and 43 in part.

The text of the present volume is arranged by numbered sections, each consisting of one or more paragraphs. The reader will find that footnotes generally correspond to entire sections rather than to smaller pieces of text. Entries in the bibliographical and general indexes refer to section numbers rather than page numbers.

A detailed description of the Cairo Geniza can be found in the first volume of Goitein's *A Mediterranean Society*. I have read most of the Geniza documents in my collection in the original but was unable to do so in a few instances, such as those located in the USSR and some of those kept in the Dropsie University Library in Philadelphia. Many of these manuscripts were examined by me by means of ultra-violet rays and with the aid of special photographic facilities.

The Muslim sources of the Middle Ages are first and foremost the chronicles; following them are the biographies, geographical literature, monographs, and so on. I also used many texts which are still in manuscript form. The interested reader may find details concerning these Arabic texts in the bibliographical index at the end of this book, and further information regarding the authors and their works is available in the well-known books by Brockelmann and Sezgin, which deal with the history of Arabic literature. Most of the information on political and military events, as well as on Muslim personalities of the period who lived in Palestine, is derived from these Arabic sources, whereas the chapters on the localities, the conditions of the dhimmīs (especially on the subject of taxes) and on the economic life of the period, are based to a large extent on information culled from Geniza documents.

As to the Christian sources, these include Byzantine writers, especially Theophanes, and Syriac literature (i.e. Christian Aramaic), which contributed its share on some vital points in the description of the political and military events. The Arabic writings of Christian chroniclers, especially Sa'īd ibn Biṭrīq and Yaḥyā ibn Sa'īd, are important from both the overall historical point of view and that of the history of the Christians in Palestine. The Greek sources of the Jerusalem Church, especially those compiled by Papadopoulos-Kerameos, provide the information (which I regret is rather poor) on the history of the Church and the Christians in Palestine during this period. The reader will undoubtedly note that these historical studies are mostly discussions focusing on the sources at the researcher's disposal. This applies to any period or subject dating from antiquity or the Middle Ages, for the student cannot presume that he is presenting a complete or continuous history, as it is obvious that wherever there is an absence of sources, there will be a void.

Research literature on Palestine – including the period under discussion – is very rich, but it is not the purpose of this book to serve as a bibliographical guide. In the following studies, I have made a point of referring to those research works which provide essential explanations and meaningful opinions. Complete details on these sources can be found in the bibliographical index. There have been attempts in the past to sum up the historical information on the period, such as M. Assaf's book on the history of Arab rule in Palestine, and Goitein's article on Jerusalem during the Arab period. Among the more specific studies, there are those of

De Goeje (the *Mémoire*) and of Caetani (*Annali*) on the Arab conquest. The papyri of Nessana, published by Kraemer, shed additional and significant light on the early Muslim period, and the works of Lammens and Shaban on the early caliphs are also worthy of mention.

In the area dealing with geography, Le Strange and the collection of sources in his *Palestine under the Moslems* are considerably helpful, as are Avi Yonah's work on the geographical history of Palestine, Dussaud on the topography of Syria, and the encyclopaedic enterprise of Z. Vilnay (*Ariel*).

In the context of the study on the status of the dhimmīs, the comprehensive article of Ashtor (Strauss) in the *Hirschler Jubilee Volume* should be mentioned, as well as Tritton's work. With regard to having recourse to the Muslim courts, one should mention, in particular, the pioneering work of J. Mann, within the framework of his series of articles on the Responsa of the Geonim, in addition to the works of Hirschberg and Goitein. The study on the masoretes of Tiberias is, to a large extent, based on the works of earlier students: Mann, Kahle, Klar, Dotan and others. Referring to the studies on the localities of Palestine, one should naturally mention the work of Braslavi and Sharon.

In the chapter dealing with economics, one should take note of the works of Cahen on matters of landed property in early Islam and of the extensive work of Goitein, *A Mediterranean Society*, which sums up the economic data contained in the Geniza. As to the identification of plants and condiments, I relied on the works of Meyerhof (the editor of Maimonides' book on medicines), Ducros, and of Zohary. With regard to textiles, the work of Serjeant should be noted. In the new book by Lombard on textiles in the Muslim world, the reader will find additional material which I have used here only minimally.

In the episode concerning Charlemagne and his connections with the caliph of Baghdad and with the Christians in Jerusalem, I had extensive research literature at my disposal which I have documented in chapter 5, note 13. As to Egyptian rule in Palestine, from Ṭūlūnid times until the end of the period being described here, the books by Wüstenfeld and Lane Poole are still authoritative on the subject, helping and serving as a serious basis for research into the events, though they do not go into detail concerning what was happening in Palestine. For enquiry into the Ismāʿīlīs – the Qarmaṭīs and the Fatimids – the studies of Ivanow, B. Lewis and Madelung, are important. Attention should also be drawn to the recent works of Bacharach in the field of monetary history and the history of the Ikhshīdids. Particular importance can be ascribed to the profound studies of Canard and especially his book on the Ḥamdānid dynasty and his articles on the Fatimids. The works of Wiet and the recent work of Bianquis also merit attention.

On questions concerning the Christians in Jerusalem, the works of Riant are worth mentioning: the methodical listing of sources dealing with the Crusaders, in which there is also a section on the period preceding the Crusades, and his research on the donation of property to the Holy Sepulchre; Vailhé, and especially his articles on the monastery of Mar Saba and on the *graptoi* brothers; also Pargoire, in his book on the Byzantine Church; Janin, and his essay on the Georgian Church in Jerusalem and a number of Jerusalem patriarchs; Amann, for his exhaustive article on the Jerusalem Church; Peeters and his articles on the Persian conquest, some of the important sources he edited and his book on the Oriental background to Byzantine hagiography; Leclercq, for his articles on holy places in Palestine, as well as his comprehensive article on Palestine.

It is now over a century since the finest students of Jewish history began probing into the Geniza documents. Were it not for these documents and the dedicated work of these researchers, we would know very little about the Jews of Palestine during this period. Foremost among them was A. Harkavy, with his notes and additions to Graetz, the Geniza sources which he edited in various places, and his outstanding contribution to the research on Karaism. Also A. Neubauer, with the sources he edited, particularly the Scroll of Aḥīma'aṣ. Similarly notable is his *Catalogue of Hebrew Manuscripts* in Oxford, which served as a guide to researchers, as did the Catalogue of the British Museum, published by G. Margoliouth. These were followed by S. Poznanski in his many articles, notably those on the Karaites and the Geonim of Palestine. S. Schechter, who rescued the Geniza, edited important texts from Palestine or relating to Palestine, in his *Saadyana* and elsewhere. H. J. Bornstein brilliantly collected the information available on the dispute of the calendar between Babylonia and Palestine in his articles and edited related fragments from the Geniza. R. Gottheil, who at the beginning of the century had already begun to deal with texts from the Geniza, collaborated with W. H. Worrell in 1927 to edit the collection of Geniza documents kept in the Freer Gallery in Washington. H. Hirschfeld edited Geniza documents, his major contribution being studies on a number of Karaite personalities. In the mid-1920s, Jacob Mann, the most important student of the Geniza in his time, began to publish his studies. Apart from his many articles, he compiled two volumes of extensive material from the Geniza pertaining to Palestine, accompanied by profound historical studies. The majority of those documents in my collection which were edited previously were mainly edited by Mann. Until today, his works form a firm basis for any additional research on the subject. A contemporary of Mann was

A. Marmorstein, who dealt mainly with the history of the Gaonate in Palestine and also edited documentary material from the Geniza, although unfortunately there were considerable misinterpretations and imprecisions in his work, which to a large extent justified the sharp criticism which came from the pen of Jacob Mann.

At the same time as Mann, S. Assaf was extensively editing Geniza documents, among them texts relating to Palestine, and one must note in particular the various kinds of deeds and letters which he included in his writings. In the framework of his articles, he also edited documents written in Arabic, whereas the scientific work this involved – that is, the deciphering and translation – was done by his colleagues at the Hebrew University, Baneth and Ashtor. The American Jewish scholar J. Starr, who died at an early age and was known primarily for his research on Byzantine Jewry, edited in 1936 a number of letters of the Maghribi Israel b. Nathan (Sahlūn). E. Ashtor (having earlier published under the name of Strauss) worked mainly on Geniza texts touching on Egypt, but also included a number of documents from Palestine in his writings, where one can find important material pertaining to the history of Palestine and its Jewish population during the period under discussion. Mention should also be made of B. Chapira, who edited documents from Palestine in some of his articles in Hebrew and French. S. M. Stern, an important scholar of Islamic culture, contributed a notable article to this special field of research, in which he edited texts dealing with the dispute of Nathan b. Abraham.

Since the 1950s, the foremost among the scholars of our day has been S. D. Goitein. As is evident from the list of works included in the bibliographical index, he studied various aspects of the subject under discussion here. He identified many texts relating to Palestine, and although he did not edit them all, he dealt with them in his many writings. Paramount in importance are the volumes of his *Mediterranean Society* and a collection of merchants' letters. He was the first of the Geniza students to base his studies on a large number of the Geniza documents written in Arabic, either in Hebrew or Arabic script (the latter being generally extremely difficult to decipher). He was also the first to organise the Geniza documents into coherent groups according to their writers, paving the way for continuous and systematic research of the documentary material in the Geniza. The significant systematic research work he carried out for many years on the history of the Jewish population in Palestine on the basis of the Geniza documents, a work which was dispersed and housed in innumerable places, is now assembled in a comprehensive collection, *Ha-yishuv* . . . Among his students, one should note J. Eliash, who in 1957/8 edited some important documents from Palestine;

N. Golb, who dealt mainly with Egypt, though his works serve to clarify details in letters from Palestine; M. A. Friedman, who in his articles and his great book on the Palestinian marriage deeds revealed their peculiarities and continuity, discussing in great detail the various terms, as well as places and personalities in Palestine, mentioned in those marriage deeds; and M. R. Cohen, who published some important articles on Ascalon, on aspects of the *negīdūt* (including information relating to Palestine), on the dispute of Nathan b. Abraham (including a Geniza letter which sheds light on the affair), and also a comprehensive book on Jewish self-government in Egypt, with a discussion on several important topics relating to Jewish personalities in Palestine shortly before the Crusaders' conquest.

Among the contemporary students of this period, one must mention A. Scheiber, who published a number of important studies, including Geniza documents relating to Palestine, chiefly from the David Kaufmann collection in Budapest. These studies were later assembled in one book, his *Geniza Studies*. Of considerable significance are the works of S. Abramson on the Geonim of Palestine and on Elḥanan b. Shemaria, which also include Geniza documents. E. Fleischer, whose major area of research is that of poetry and the *piyyūṭ*, including naturally the Palestinian poets, has in one of his articles rendered an important contribution to our knowledge of the personality of Daniel b. Azariah, the Nāsī and Gaon.

Concerning the discussion on the Karaites, apart from Harkavy and Poznanski, whom I have already mentioned, one must point to the work of S. Pinsker, who more than 130 years ago edited important Karaite texts which he copied from manuscripts, accompanied by detailed commentaries. His book *Liqqūṭē qadmōniyōt* has served as an important tool for any researcher investigating the history of Karaism in Palestine; and naturally one must mention the second volume of Mann's *Texts and Studies*, entirely devoted to the history of the Karaites, a substantial part of which deals with the Karaites in Palestine before the Crusaders' conquest. Among today's scholars, there are L. Nemoy, N. Wieder, and Z. Ankori, whose outstanding works I have mentioned in the chapter on the Karaites, each in his own right.

One must also mention in connection with the work on the Geniza documents in this book four important reference books: one is that of J. Blau, on the Judaeo-Arabic grammar of the Middle Ages, which today enables us to consider the language in which most of the documents in my collection are written, as a separate dialect with known and defined characteristics. Such matters as the turning of the Arabic *tanwīn* into a separate word, or the addition or dropping of the *mater lectionis*, and many other such points, are clarified and explained in his book. The second book is the bibliography of S. Shaked, which was of considerable help in the initial assembling of the material from the Geniza and in tracing the studies that had been made until the early 1960s. The third, the *Handbuch der jüdischen Chronologie* by E. Mahler, which helped me, by the use of its tables, to reckon the equivalents to the Hebrew dates. The fourth, G. S. P. Freeman-Grenville's small booklet, with its conversion tables of Muslim dates.

The transcription of the Arabic names and words in this book is in conformity with accepted scholarly usage. Hebrew titles and names are transcribed in a less 'orthodox' manner; both Biblical and later names and terms are transcribed according to the usage in current research, as for example in the *Encyclopaedia Judaica*. Naturally there is a certain lack of uniformity in this, which I hope will be accepted by most readers with a degree of tolerance.

I am indebted to the directors and trustees of the libraries in which the Geniza documents and the Arabic manuscripts are preserved, for permission to study and edit the texts. Foremost among them is Dr S. C. Reif, Director of the Geniza Research Unit of the Cambridge University Library (where the bulk of the Geniza materials are found), who together with his staff and other personnel of the library there helped me immensely. My gratitude goes to Professor M. Shmelzer, the Librarian of the Jewish Theological Seminary of New York, where the large collection in the name of E. N. Adler is kept; I was also rendered a great deal of assistance by him and his staff. I am also grateful to all those directors and trustees of the other libraries in which I worked and was welcomed and aided in every respect: the Bodleian Library in Oxford; the British Library; the Library of the Alliance israélite universelle in Paris; the Library of Dropsie University in Philadelphia; the Freer Gallery in Washington; the Library of Westminster College, Cambridge; and Merton College, Oxford. Special gratitude is due to the late Professor A. Scheiber, who went to the trouble of sending me excellent photographs of documents from the David Kaufmann Collection in Budapest; Dr Helena Loebenstein, also for excellent photographs of documents from the Erzherzog Rainer Collection in Vienna; and further, my thanks go to the University Library in Heidelberg for its supply of excellent photographs; the John Rylands Library, Manchester; the University Museum of the University of Pennsylvania, Philadelphia; and the Department of Manuscripts of the National Library in Jerusalem.

My special gratitude goes to the personnel of the Institute of Microfilmed Hebrew Manuscripts at the National Library in Jerusalem, where I was able to examine most of the texts from the Geniza and elsewhere, by microfilm. The writing of this book would not have been possible without the assistance of this institution. Also, I express my thanks in particular to the staff of the Library of the Tel Aviv University, where I wrote this book, amidst friendly people who were always prepared to help.

I am much indebted to Professor S. Simonsohn, Head of the Diaspora Research Institute, Tel Aviv University, who initiated and very devotedly dealt with the Hebrew edition of this book.

And last, but certainly not least, I would like to offer my heartfelt gratitude to my late teacher, Professor S. D. Goitein, who guided me towards this work and gave me his support – both by his words and his writings.

As regards the present English version, I am very grateful to the translator, Mrs Ethel Broido, who heroically supported all my remarks and inquiries; to Mrs Sheila Bahat, of Tel Aviv University, who read the manuscript and offered very valuable remarks; to Miss Ora Vaza, who prepared the general index; and to Dr Gill Thomas and Dr Susan Van de Ven, of the Cambridge University Press, for their devoted and skillful editorial work. The translation work was made possible by the assistance of Tel Aviv University, through the Haim Rosenberg School of Jewish Studies, the Diaspora Research Institute, and the Joseph and Ceil Mazer Chair in the History of the Jews in Muslim Lands.

Abbreviations

AA SS	*Acta Sanctorum*
AESC	*Annales: économies, sociétés, civilisations*
AH	hijra year
AHR	*American Historical Review*
AI	*Ars Islamica*
AIBL	Académie des inscriptions et belles lettres
AIEO	*Annales de l'Institut d'études orientales* (Alger)
AIU	Alliance israëlite universelle, Paris
AJSLL	*American Journal of Semitic Languages and Literatures*
AJSR	*Association for Jewish Studies Review*
AM	anno mundi, era of the creation
Antonin	The Antonin Geniza collection, Leningrad
AO	*Ars Orientalis*
AOL	*Archives de l'Orient latin*
b.	ben, bin, ibn, bat, bint = son or daughter of
BEO	*Bulletin d'études orientales*
BGA	*Bibliotheca geographorum Arabicorum*
BIFAO	*Bulletin de l'Institut français d'archéologie orientale*
BIRHT	*Bulletin de l'Institut de recherches et d'histoire des textes*
BJPES	*Bulletin of the Jewish Palestine Exploration Society* (Hebrew; = *Yedīʿōt ha-ḥevrā la-ḥaqīrat ereṣ isrāʾēl*)
BJRL	*Bulletin of the John Rylands Library*
BM	British Museum
BNGJ	*Byzantinisch-neugriechische Jahrbücher*
Bodl MS Heb	The collection of Hebrew (and Judaeo-Arabic) MSs at the Bodleian Library, Oxford
BSOAS	*Bulletin of the School of Oriental and African Studies* (London)
BT	Babylonian Talmud
BZ	*Byzantinische Zeitschrift*

CCM	*Cahiers de civilisation médiévale*
CCSL	*Corpus Christianorum. Series Latina*
Consist. isr.	The Geniza collection of the Consistoire israélite, Paris
CSCO	*Corpus scriptorum Christianorum Orientalium*
CSHB	*Corpus scriptorum historiae Byzantinae*
DACL	*Dictionnaire d'archéologie chrétienne et de liturgie*
DHGE	*Dictionnaire d'histoire et de géographie ecclésiastique*
DK	The David Kaufmann Collection, Budapest
Dropsie	The Geniza Collection of Dropsie University (at the Annenberg Institute, Philadelphia)
DTC	*Dictionnaire de théologie catholique*
ECQ	*Eastern Churches Quarterly*
EHR	*English Historical Review*
EI	*Encylopaedia of Islam*
ENA	The Elkanah Nathan Adler Collection, the Library of the Jewish Theological Seminary, New York
EO	*Échos d'Orient*
f.	folium
Firkovitch	The Geniza collection of A. Firkovitch, Leningrad
GAL	*Geschichte der arabischen Literatur*
GCAL	*Geschichte der christlichen arabischen Literatur*
HTR	*Harvard Theological Review*
HUC	Hebrew Union College (Cincinnati)
HUCA	*Hebrew Union College Annual*
IC	*Islamic Culture*
IEJ	*Israel Exploration Journal*
IFAO	Institut français d'archéologie orientale
IJMES	*International Journal of Middle Eastern Studies*
INJ	*Israel Numismatic Journal*
IOS	*Israel Oriental Studies*
IQ	*Islamic Quarterly*
JA	*Journal asiatique*
JAH	*Journal of Asian History*
JAORS	*Journal of the American Oriental Society*
JEA	*Journal of Egyptian Archaeology*
JESHO	*Journal of the Economic and Social History of the Orient*
JHS	*Journal of Hellenic Studies*
JJGL	*Jahrbuch für jüdische Geschichte und Literatur*
JJS	*Journal of Jewish Studies*
JNES	*Journal of Near Eastern Studies*
JNUL	Jewish National and University Library, Jerusalem

JPOS	*Journal of the Palestine Oriental Society*
JQR	*Jewish Quarterly Review*
JRAS	*Journal of the Royal Asiatic Society*
JSAI	*Jerusalem Studies in Arabic and Islam*
JSS	*Jewish Social Studies*
JTS	Jewish Theologial Seminary
MAIBL	*Mémoires de l'académie des inscriptions et belles lettres*
MGH	*Monumenta Germaniae historica*
MGWJ	*Monatsschrift für die Geschichte und Wissenschaft des Judenthums*
MIE	*Mémoires présentés à l'Institut d'Égypte*
Mosseri	The Geniza Collection of the Jewish Community in Cairo, kept by the Mosseri family
MPG	Migne, *Patrologia*, series Graeca
MPL	Migne, *Patrologia*, series Latina
MS	Manuscript
MUSJ	*Mélanges de l'Université St Joseph*
MWJ	*Magazin für die Wissenschaft des Judenthums*
OLZ	*Orientalistische Literatur-Zeitung*
PAAJR	*Proceedings of the American Academy for Jewish Research*
PEFQ	*Palestine Exploration Fund Quarterly*
PER	The collection of MSs named after Erzherzog (Archduc) Rainer, Vienna
PO	*Patrologia Orientalis*
POC	*Proche-Orient chrétien*
PT	Palestinian Talmud
PW	*Realencyclopädie der classischen Altertumwissenschaft*
QDAP	*Quarterly of the Department of Antiquities in Palestine*
RAAD	*Revue de l'académie arabe de Damas*
RB	*Revue biblique*
REB	*Revue des études byzantines*
REI	*Revue des études islamiques*
REJ	*Revue des études juives*
RH	*Revue historique*
RHC	*Recueil des historiens des croisades*
RHGF	*Recueil des historiens des Gaules et de la France*
RHR	*Revue de l'histoire des religions*
RIDA	*Revue internationale des droits de l'antiquité*
RMI	*Rassegna mensile di Israel*
ROC	*Revue de l'Orient chrétien*
ROL	*Revue de l'Orient latin*
RSO	*Rivista degli studi orientali*

SBB	*Studies in Bibliography and Booklore*
Sel.	Seleucid era
SI	*Studia Islamica*
TLZ	*Theologische Literaturzeitung*
TS	The Taylor Schechter Collection, University Library, Cambridge
ULC	University Library, Cambridge
ZA	*Zeitschrift für Assyriologie*
ZAW	*Zeitschrift für die alttestamentliche Wissenschaft*
ZDMG	*Zeitschrift der deutschen morgenländischen Gesellschaft*
ZDPV	*Zeitschrift des deutschen Palästina-Vereins*
ZfhB	*Zeitschrift für hebräische Bibliographie*

Glossary of Hebrew and Arabic terms

'alāma, a specific word, or formula, used by notables at the end of their correspondence.
alūf, a scholar appointed by the yeshiva, generally to serve as judge and leader in his community, but also a honorific title, granted by the Babylonian yeshivot.
amīr, a military commander.
av-bēt-dīn, head of the court.
dayyān, judge.
gaon (pl. *geonim*; exact spelling: *gā'ōn*), head of the yeshiva.
ḥadīth, Muslim oral tradition, generally ascribed to the Prophet.
ḥāvēr (pl. *ḥavērīm*), a scholar appointed by the yeshiva as leader and judge in his community, a title granted mainly by the Palestinian yeshiva.
heqdēsh (also: *qodesh*), the Jewish pious foundations, for the benefit of the synagogues, the poor, and so on.
kunya, the byname beginning with Abū (father of . . .).
melammēd, teacher.
midrash, traditional interpretation of a Biblical passage (often in an anecdotal style).
mumḥē, a person authorised by the yeshiva to assist the local judge.
nagid (pl. *negidim*), in the period under discussion: leader, title granted by the yeshiva to a Jewish notable who was close to the caliph's court.
nāsī (pl. *nesī'īm*), in the period under discussion: a member of the exilarchic family, which claimed descent from King David.
parnās, a community official in charge of charity, financial matters, maintenance, and so on.
piyyūṭ (pl. *piyyūṭīm*), religious poem.
rōsh (Hebrew) or *ra'īs*, *rayyis* (Arabic), head, chief, leader.
rōsh ha-gōlā, head of the Diaspora, exilarch.

rōsh ha-shānā, the Jewish New Year's day.

sijill, a decree issued by the highest Muslim state authority (usually the caliph).

talmīd, title of a scholar, correspondent of the yeshiva; less than *ḥāvēr*.

yeshiva (pl. *yeshivot*), main institution of Jewish communal leadership and learning.

Introduction

[1] As we shall see, the Muslim conquest of Palestine was not an expeditious event, at any rate not in present-day terms. It was evidently a process which began before the death of Muḥammad and at first, its principal aim was to draw the Arab tribes living under Byzantine rule into the Islamic camp – a process which lasted some ten years until the capture of Ascalon, which held out until 644. The Muslim conquest of Palestine opened an entirely new page in Palestine's history. The new element in the situation was the fact that the nomadic tribes, which for many generations had been kept at a distance from the cultivated lands and their cultures by the rulers of those lands, were now forcefully spearheading into these lands and becoming their masters. A new society was born. While the subdued population, Jews and Christians, continued to form the majority in Palestine during the period under discussion, the Bedouin constituted the ruling class under the Damascene caliphate; whereas for generations after 750, the year of the Abbasid revolt, the Muslim officials, the military, the religious personalities and legalists, ruled the country.

The most characteristic feature of this period was the undermining of internal security. These scores of generations (or more precisely, 465 years), witnessed almost unceasing warfare. The Muslim camp, which first appeared on the scene in an amazingly disciplined and united fashion, soon disintegrated. Behind the façade of the Islamic state, which stubbornly pursued its war against enemies from without, ancient inter-tribal differences arose, adding to the struggle for leadership. These quickly extended beyond the boundaries of verbal argument and political conniving and moved into the field of war and bloodshed. Later on, we shall discover, these wars took on a special significance for Palestine after the process of fragmentation of the caliphate was completed and Egypt assumed independence, ridding itself of the yoke of the central Muslim rule then located in Baghdad. The circumstances which prevailed in Palestine in ancient times were then renewed with even greater vigour, when adversaries from the North, East and South each sought to dominate it in order to prevent the likelihood of its being used as a springboard for attack by the opposing side. At the same time, Palestine once again became a permanent theatre of war between the belligerent camps, with an intensity and persistence of a kind unknown in antiquity. This led to the uprooting of the population and the destruction of the flourishing economy handed down by the Byzantines.

Apart from some ninety years during which Palestine was subject to the rule of Damascus, the country was far from the centre of government. The Damascene rulers viewed it as a region of Syria, part of al-Shām, a comprehensive term with more than one meaning which was used to denote both Syria and Palestine. True, they did not have the power to prevent inter-tribal warfare within Palestine's borders, but they did carry out building projects and attempted to improve the roads and irrigation systems. The rulers who succeeded them, however, in Baghdad and afterwards in Egypt, considered Palestine to be a neglected outlying area of interest only because of the taxes which could be extracted from the country and also for military purposes. The Christian world was interested in Palestine – particularly in Jerusalem – for religious reasons, expressing this interest in the form of pilgrimage, which continued despite difficulties and the enormous distances, as well as concern for the churches and monasteries. Nevertheless, it appears that the Christians' hold gradually declined, except in Jerusalem, and even there the Christian population became increasingly destitute. On the eve of the Crusades it was in a very sorry state indeed. Only in the Jewish mind did Palestine continue to occupy a central position. When Jews used the expression al-Shām at this time, the intended connotation was generally Palestine. The Jewish population residing in the country at the time of the Muslim conquest consisted of the direct descendants of the generations of Jews who had lived there since the days of Joshua bin Nun, in other words for some 2,000 years. During the more than four hundred years of Muslim rule, the Jewish population continued to exist despite difficulties. As to the conquest itself, it marked an important turning point in the annals of the city of Jerusalem and the history of the Jewish population in Palestine, the return of the Jews to Jerusalem and the establishment of a Jewish quarter within its confines. From a more general outlook, as the Muslim world allowed for comparatively greater freedom of movement from country to country and from region to region, we shall witness the phenomenon of Jews immigrating to Palestine from the East and the West. This immigration, which bore no ideological earmarks apart from a pure and simple attachment to the country, would at times be caused by hardship, such as the immigration from Iraq, while that of the Karaites forms a special chapter of its own.

As far back as Byzantine rule, the Palestinian sages were already arguing over the question 'whether most of Palestine is in the hands of the gentiles' or 'whether the greater part of Palestine is in the hands of Israel',[1] that is to say, to whom the major portion of the land of Palestine belongs. We may reasonably state that at the time of the Muslim conquest, a large Jewish population still lived in Palestine. We do not know whether they formed the majority but we may assume with some certainty that they did so when grouped together with the Samaritans.

An important source regarding Palestine's demographic structure during Byzantine rule are the stories of the Christian monk Bar-Ṣawmā. In the biography of this fighting monk, who was born in Samosata in Asia Minor and active in Palestine in the fifth century AD, it is told that the Jews, together with the heathens, constituted the majority in Palestine, Phoenicia and Arabia (which included the south of Palestine). There were as yet few Christians. The Jews and the Samaritans virtually governed the land and were persecuting the Christians. In the campaign against the Jews and the idol-worshippers, a band of forty monks led by Bar-Ṣawmā, and evidently with the assistance of the Byzantine army, came up against the opposition of 15,000 armed Jews. Among the synagogues that Bar-Ṣawmā destroyed was one (the source refers to a synagogue as *beyt shabe*) in the city Reqem of Gaya (Petra) 'which could bear comparison only to Solomon's temple'. In about the year 425, the Jews of the Galilee and its surroundings applied to the empress Eudocia to permit them to pray on the ruins of Solomon's temple, as Constantine had forbidden them to reside in the Jerusalem area. The author of the biography also cites the letter written by the Galilean Jews to Jews in Persia and Rome after they had received the empress' permission:

> To the great and elevated nation of the Jews, from the Priest and Head of Galilee, many greetings. Ye shall know that the time of the dispersion of our people is at an end, and from now onwards the day of our congregation and salvation has come, for the Roman kings have written a decree to hand over our city Jerusalem to us. Therefore come quickly to Jerusalem for the coming holiday of Succoth, for our kingdom is established in Jerusalem.

And indeed 103,000 Jews came and gathered in Jerusalem but were stoned from the sky, 'something that cannot be doubted', whereas the Jews complained to Eudocia claiming that it was the monks who had attacked them.[2]

[2] The relative strength of the Samaritans is evident in their rebellions,

[1] PT Demai, ii, 22 c.

[2] The stories of Bar-Ṣawmā: Nau, *ROC*, 18 (1913), 19(1914); *REJ*, 83(1927); and Honigmann, *Le couvent*, Louvain 1954, 17f, who thinks that the stories of Bar-Ṣawmā are not credible, certainly with regard to the Jews mentioned there; he sees them as figments of the author's imagination, as he lived 100 years later. But this is a very facile way of dismissing ancient sources. We must not disregard or refute their contents even if they appear legendary in character; they still retain a germ of historical truth.

which broke out generation after generation, in 484, in approximately 500, in 529, and in 555. An anti-Jewish polemical tract written at the beginning of the Muslim invasion of Palestine, entitled 'The Didaskalia [doctrine] of Jacob, the Recently Baptised', is indirect evidence of the large number of Jews in Acre and Sykamona (Haifa) at the time. Sufficiently clear reference to a dense population of Jews in southern Palestine has been preserved in Arabic sources which tell of the covenant made by Muḥammad in 630 with a number of Jewish settlements. Eilat (Ayla) is also described in Arabic sources as a city with many Jewish inhabitants. Procopius of Caesarea, writing in the middle of the sixth century, mentions the Jewish population in Eilat and its surroundings, which enjoyed a kind of autonomy there until Justinian's day.[3]

[3] The period preceding the conquest by the Muslims of important parts of the Byzantine Empire, was undoubtedly a period of decline and even of internal disintegration of the empire. The death of Justinian was followed by eras of anarchy, poverty and plagues. The chronicles describing the days of Justin II speak of the approaching end of the world. The prevailing and central event during this period was the war with Persia. In addition, the emperors were forced to wage wars against the Slavs and the Avars in the Balkan Peninsula, and also against the Longobards – Aryans by creed – in Italy, which only came to an end in 568 with the latter's victory. Justinian reached a settlement with the Persians in 561 or 562 for a fifty years' peace.[4]

[3] The subject of Acre and Haifa: Maas, *BZ*, 20(1911), 576f; see also Procopius in the First Book of the Wars, ch. xix, 3–4. Many interpret his text as applying to the island of Iotabe which he mentions. But in saying 'there the Jews lived', he means the entire neighbourhood of Aila-Eilat, which he mentions at the beginning of that narrative. Eilat (Etzion Gaver) is 'Asya, or Asya, in the Talmudic sources. See Klein, *Freimann Jubilee Volume*, 116ff; Alon, *Studies*, I, 320. Eusebius already identified it in his *Onomastikon*, see the Klostermann edition, p. 62. On the Jewish character of certain localities in Palestine, such as Tiberias, Kefar Naḥūm, Sepphoris and Nazareth, see what is written according to the sources of the Church Fathers in: Couret, *La Palestine*, 5f. He stresses that the Jews were part of the agricultural population of the country, as he puts it, together with the Greeks, the Samaritans and the Arabs. (See *ibid.*, 82, and his sources in n. 1 of that work.) The fact that Sepphoris was inhabited by Jews in the sixth century is recognisable from the Muslim tradition about Umayya, father of the family of the Damascus caliphs. He stayed in Palestine for ten years and lived with a captive who was kept by the Banū Lakhm, who was a 'Jewess from the people of Sepphoris', and had left behind a husband. She gave birth to Dhakwān, whose *kunya* was Abū 'Amr; one of the descendants of the family, 'Uqba b. Abī Mu'ayṭ, made an attempt on Muḥammad's life near the *ka'ba* in Mecca and was executed on the order of the Prophet, after having been captured during the battle of Badr; when he claimed that he was a tribesman of Quraysh, the Prophet retorted: 'You are but a Jew of the Sepphoris people'; see Ṭabarī, *Ta'rīkh*, I, 1186, 1336f; Ibn Qutayba, *Ma'ārif*, 319; Bakrī, 837; Ibn al-Athīr, *Usd*, V, 90 (*s.v.* Abū 'Amr). Mas'ūdī, *Murūj*, IV, 257f, has an additional tradition, in which al-Walīd, the son of this 'Uqba, was governor of Kūfa at the time of Caliph 'Uthmān, when 'Aqīl ('Alī's brother), shouted at him that he was but a foreigner, of the people of Sepphoris.

[4] Vasiliev, *History*, 169ff; details of the peace settlement, see Menander, *CSHB*, XII (1829), 346ff; cf. Bury, *History*, I, 467ff; II, 120 ff.

[4] Justin II (565–578) violated the treaty and refused to pay the annual tribute to the Persians which was one of its conditions (30,000 gold nomismas, or the equivalent of *ca.* 130 kilograms). The negotiations conducted between Byzantium and the Turkish tribes on the northeastern borders of the Persian empire added to the tension. Meanwhile the Byzantines were busy in Italy with the Longobards' attacks, and long, drawn-out battles were waged against the Persians, continuing well into the era of Tiberius (578–582) and Mauricius (582–602). Only during the latter's reign did the scales tip down on the side of the Byzantines, principally because of internal quarrels within the Persian royal family. The Persians were obliged to sign a new peace agreement which involved the loss of large tracts of land in Armenia and northern Mesopotamia, and the cancelling of the annual tribute mentioned earlier.

The declining security along the borders of Byzantium brought about by attacks from the Barbarian peoples, gave rise to a change in the internal governing order; new administrative bodies were formed, such as the exarchates and themai, in which the ruling power lay in the hands of the army commanders. Finally, the army took over the capital itself, Mauricius was assassinated, and the army commander, Phocas, ascended the emperor's throne (602–610). During his reign, Byzantium was torn by internal dissension, which developed into a cruel civil war between the aristocrats (the blues) and the populist party (the greens). Some sources ascribe an important role to the Jews in these events, especially the Jews of Antioch.[5]

[5] In 610, Heraclius was crowned emperor. The chronicles speak highly of him and admit to his being able and well intentioned. Many world-shaking events took place during his reign: the Persian victories, which also led to their temporary conquest of Palestine, changes within the empire, and the Muslim conquests, which deprived Byzantium of much of its Mediterranean lands.

The Persian offensive had already begun in 611, and in the course of seven or eight years the Persians conquered Antioch, the major city of the Byzantine East, Damascus and all of Syria, Palestine, Asia Minor and also Egypt. The Persian campaign brought to light the existence of connections – at least emotional and possibly also one-sided – between the Jews and the Persians. Mutual interests had already been evident about a hundred years earlier, during the war in Ḥimyar, the southern part of the Arabian peninsula. Jews and Persians then shared interests although no evidence has been preserved of actual contact or collaboration, unlike the affiliation between Byzantium and the Ethiopians and the local Christians

[5] See: Demetrius Martyr, in *MPG*, vol. 116, 1261ff; Isidor Hispalensis, in *MPL*, vol. 83, 1056A; Sa'īd Ibn Biṭrīq (Cheikho), 589ff; Theophanes, 269; *Chronicon Paschale*, in *MPG*, vol. 92, 980; Maḥbūb (Agapius), 189 (449).

of Ḥimyar. The Jews evidently enjoyed an important status in the Persian kingdom owing to their large numbers and also to the role occupied by Jewish merchants in Persia's international trade. Jewish soldiers served in the Persian army, and if we are to credit the account of Michael the Syrian, they even caused Persian commanders to put a halt to fighting on Jewish holidays.[6]

[6] There seems to be considerable exaggeration, however, in the accounts of those who describe the Persian conquest of Palestine as if it were an era of squaring accounts for the Jews; a sort of Messianic era. The *Chronicon Paschale* describes the death and destruction inflicted by the Persians in Jerusalem, without mentioning the Jews in this connection at all.[7]

[7] Antiochus Eustratios (his name dwindled to Strategios), a monk captured by the Persians in Jerusalem, describes the conquest of the city in greater detail. The patriarch Zacharias apparently intended to hand over Jerusalem peacefully but as its inhabitants opposed a settlement, it was conquered after a siege of twenty days. Antiochus places the blame for the murder of many of the city's Christians on the Jews; according to him Christians were murdered due to their refusal to accept Judaism. He also accuses the Jews of destroying the churches. Theophanes repeats Antiochus' remarks in his own chronicle, adding the story of a wealthy Jew called Benjamin of Tiberias, whom the Christians accused of having attacked them before the Emperor Heraclius when he passed through Tiberias after the Byzantine victory. Benjamin admitted his guilt and justified his actions as grounded in Jewish hostility towards Christians. He was saved from punishment by being baptised on the emperor's orders.[8]

[8] Other mediaeval chronicles merely copied and elaborated on these accounts, such as the anonymous Syriac chronicle which adds a story about the scheme which the Jews ('sons of the crucifiers') proposed to the Persian commander, namely to dig underneath the grave of Jesus in order to find the gold treasures lying underneath. From other sources it is clear that after the Persian conquest, Jerusalem and its inhabitants enjoyed a spell of serenity.

Modestus, abbot of the monastery named for the Holy Theodosius, who was the locum tenens for the exiled Zacharias, began to rebuild the city out of its ruins with contributions which poured in from the entire

6 Michael the Syrian (Chabot), II, 1.

7 *Chronicon Paschale*, in *MPG*, 92, 988.

8 See the story of Antiochus in Couret, *ROC*, 2 (1897), 147–154 (MS Paris, Ar. 262); see also Peeters, *MUSJ*, 9:3, 1923–4; Clermont-Ganneau, *PEFQ*, 1898:44; Conybeare, *EHR*, 25:502, 1910; Peeters, *Anal. Boll.*, 38:144, 1920; Milik, *MUSJ*, 37:127, 1961; see more details concerning Antiochus in Peeters, *Tréfonds*, 210; Graf, *GCAL*, I, 411; see Theophanes, 300f, 328.

Christian world, especially from the patriarch of Alexandria. In 619, while the country was still in Persian hands, Sophronius, who was to become patriarch in the autumn of 633, returned to Palestine. It is not clear whether Zacharias managed to return to Jerusalem as well, and there is conflicting information on the subject. A useful survey of sources dealing with the situation of the Jews in Palestine under Byzantine rule in the seventh century and with events which took place during the Persian conquest, including the Emperor Heraclius' policy towards the Jews, can be found in Nau's edition of the above-mentioned 'Didaskalia of Jacob', although the sources are treated by him with equal consideration and little critical discrimination. The same approach can be found today among some scholars dealing with the history of this period and its sources. Thus Stratos, who sees the Jews as responsible for whatever occurred in Jerusalem during the Persian conquest, produces an undiscerning mixture of sources together with present-day literature. For we have seen that those sources which are nearest in time and place to the events, do not mention the Jews at all. In the same manner, Hage repeats the 'information' that the Jews used to buy Christian captives in order to hand them over to be killed by the Persians. Pertusi writes in a similar vein.[9]

[9] While still engaged in the war against the Avars, Heraclius began to organise his forces for war against the Persians. It seems that an important aspect of his preparations was the pacts he concluded with tribes and peoples who were the Persians' enemies, particularly those of the Caucasus and the Khazars. Meanwhile the Persians were busy strengthening their alliance with the Avars. This war lasted some six years, from 622 until 628. One of its significant results was the defeat of the Avars in 626, when they were attempting to attack Constantinople in the wake of their collaboration with the Persians. One year later, towards the end of 627, the Persians suffered their greatest defeat near the ruins of ancient

[9] See the translation of the Syriac chronicle: Nöldeke, *Sitzungsb.* Wien, 128 (1892), No. 9, 24ff. The information regarding the Jewish revolt in Antioch that was supposed to have taken place in 610, with the approach of the Persians to the city, in Avi-Yonah, *Rome and Byzantium* (Hebrew), 1, 189, is basically erroneous. Maḥbūb (Agapius), 189(449), has information regarding this revolt as having taken place during the reign of Phocas, and it does not belong here. The town of Caesarea which the Jews handed over to the Persians, according to Sebeos (whose information is generally not correct) is not the Caesarea of Palestine, as assumed by Sharf, 49, but Caesarea in Cappadocia; cf. Avi-Yonah, *ibid.*, 224. See also Sa'īd Ibn Biṭrīq, I, 216, who repeats the account of the Jews' aid to the Persians. These sources served as a pretext for a violently anti-Semitic article by Vailhé, *Échos d'Orient*, 12:15, 1909. 'The popular belief' he says, 'disseminated almost throughout the entire world, which sees the hand of the Jews in the great calamities which spilled the blood of mankind, is not only the product of our times, and it is not only now that this strange race is ascribed a frightening role in the tragedies that befall a city or a nation . . .'; see Schönborn, 71, on the agreement and rehabilitation; see Nau, *Didascalie*, 732ff, Stratos, *Byzantium*, I, 109ff; Hage, *Syrisch-jakobitische Kirche*, 86; Pertusi, *Persia*, 619.

Nineveh, in the northern part of Mesopotamia. The Byzantine army plunged into the heart of Persia, Khusraw was dethroned and assassinated, and his heir, Kawad Sheroe, entered into negotiations with Heraclius. The Byzantines thus recovered all their lost lands and the Persians returned to the Byzantines the 'holy wood', a relic of the cross on which, according to Christian belief, Jesus was crucified. During his triumphal journey, Heraclius visited Jerusalem and together with his wife, Martina, participated in the ceremony of returning the 'holy wood'. This victory is hinted at in the Koran, in *sūrat al-rūm* (the chapter on Byzantium) xxx:1: 'The Byzantines were subdued in the nearby country, but after their defeat, they will be the victors in a few years time.'

During the Persian conquest of Jerusalem in 614, Muḥammad was already deeply engaged in his struggle against his townsmen, the people of Mecca, in an attempt to win them over to the small community of believers gathered round him. In 622, while he was fleeing to Medina with his followers, the Byzantines unleashed their war against the Persians. At the time, the latter were still reigning in Palestine, not far from Medina, and it seems that their influence was considerably felt in the Arabian Peninsula. In 628, with the return of Byzantine rule in Palestine, Muḥammad had already managed to arrange the truce in Ḥudaybiyya which prepared the ground for his conquest of Mecca. According to Muslim tradition, the Prophet was informed of the Byzantine victory on 'Ḥudaybiyya Day' and was pleased when he learned of the event. By summer's end of the same year, he organised his campaign against the Jewish farmers living in Khaybar, north of Medina. One can assume that this campaign was in some way connected with the defeat of the Persians, assumed to be the defenders of the Jews. The Byzantine victory was accompanied by a wave of persecution of the Jews throughout the Christian world. Both Christian and Muslim sources speak of Heraclius' edict of apostasy, intended to force all the Jews in his kingdom to convert to Christianity. This edict evidently suited the policy of centralisation and religious unity which Heraclius was resolutely trying to achieve, now that he was crowned with the laurels of victory. He undertook vigorous negotiations with the Monophysites in order to formulate a unified framework for the Church, for which purpose he was prepared to forego certain dogmatic precepts. They were to maintain the principle of Jesus' two natures (the divine and the human), but as a concession to the Monophysites, the Orthodox Church would have to recognise the unity of action and will (*hen thelēma*) from which stems the name of the new creed, Monotheletism. The patriarch of Constantinople, Sergius, supported the plan, as did the Monophysite patriarchs of Antioch and Alexandria. Even the pope Honorius was inclined to accept the reform and was persuaded to authorise it in his letters to Sergius. It was the Palestinian monk Sophronius, later patriarch in Jerusalem, who emphatically objected to the emperor's plan. When Heraclius made public his plan for a new religious reform in 638, there was already another pope seated in Rome, Severin, who rejected it altogether. What was worse, the Christians in the East, whom the emperor had hoped to bring back into the arms of the Church on the score of his reform, had already been or were about to be conquered by Islam. During this period of efforts to arrive at the centralisation and maximal administrative and religious unification of the empire, the persecution of the Jews became a fixed and fundamental principle of state policy.

The Romanian historian of Byzantium, Brătianu, has described the situation very aptly in 1941:

> One should stress a noteworthy fact, which sheds particular light on the similarity between the totalitarian, or at least authoritarian, regime in Byzantium in the seventh century, and those states which had, or still have today, a similar form of government: that the decline of political parties and the advent of absolute power, were in that period accompanied by a wave of acute anti-Semitism. There was nothing unusual in this, as the feeling of hatred toward the Jews was a commonplace feature of the Middle Ages, in Byzantium and elsewhere. But we are concerned here with planned and systematic persecution, which is not restricted to the Byzantine empire but attempts and also succeeds in dragging along with it the other Christian states on the Mediterranean coast.[10]

[10] Heraclius demanded of Dagobert, king of the Franks, that he compel all the Jews in his kingdom to convert to Christianity. This was indeed carried out, as it was in the rest of the empire, according to the chronicler Fredegarius. He, as well as Muslim writers, speaks of the portent revealed to Heraclius by his own reading of the stars, that a circumcised people would destroy his kingdom. As he was convinced that this portent referred to the Jews, he then issued decrees against them, unaware that the Muslims shared the tradition of having sons circumcised. Ibn Khaldūn gives a specific report about the fate of the Jews of Palestine: at first Heraclius promised the Jews security; afterwards he learned from the bishops and monks what the Jews had done to the churches, and even saw some of the destruction himself, and learned of the slaughter. He then decreed that the Jews should be killed; no one was saved except for those who hid or escaped to the mountains and deserts. As for the slaughter of the Jews of Palestine, this can also be inferred from the fact that one of the official fasts of the Coptic Church, which goes on for a week after the first

[10] See Ṭabarī, *Ta'rīkh*, I, 1009; Qurṭubī, *Jāmi'*, XIV, 5; the Prophet was pleased because the Byzantines were 'people of the Book' unlike the Persians; Brătianu, *Revue historique du sud-est européen*, 18(1941), 55f; on the return of the 'Holy Cross', see Schönborn, 86, according to whom the cross was returned only on 21 March 631, and not on 14 November 629, as was generally assumed.

day of the Carnival (that is, the great fast before Easter), is intended to beg God's pardon for the emperor Heraclius for having permitted the slaughter of the Jews of Jerusalem in 628.[11]

[11] In the light of these facts, which are undoubtedly but a very insignificant part of what actually occurred, it is not surprising that the Jews abhorred Byzantium, the kingdom known as Edom the Wicked. Daniel al-Qūmisī, the Karaite Bible commentator, writes towards the end of the ninth century AD, expounding on what is written in the Book of Daniel (xi: 30–31):

> . . . (therefore he shall be grieved, and return, and have indignation against the holy covenant: so shall he do; he shall even return, and have intelligence with them that forsake the holy covenant. And arms shall stand on his part, and they shall pollute the sanctuary of strength, and shall take away the daily sacrifice, and they shall place the abomination that maketh desolate): And he will discriminate [here the Arab root *ftn* is used], and think about the uncircumcised that are in Jerusalem . . . the daily sacrifice is that of the uncircumcised . . . the *ṣalīb* [cross] and *nāqūs* [the pieces of wood used as a bell by eastern Christians] and the Nea church . . . ; he will turn their worship into infamy and lessen their kingdom.

What Daniel al-Qūmisī meant was that the kingdom of Ishmael would abolish Christian rule over Jerusalem.[12]

[11] See Fredegarius, 153, 409; see also Mabillon, Book XI, par. 39, pp. 323ff, who speaks of the forced baptism ('which is not the thing to do') in the year 624, and *ibid.*, par. 62, on forced baptism in 627, after Dagobert submits to pressure on the part of Church circles. Ṭabarī, *Ta'rīkh*, I, 1562; Ibn 'Asākir, I, 473; Iṣbahānī, *Aghānī*, VI, 94; Ibn Kathīr, *Bidāya*, IV, 265f; Ibn Khaldūn, *'Ibar*, II, 457; Goffart, *Speculum*, 38(1963), 237, brings the story from Fredegarius as pure legend, ignoring the Muslim sources. Again, however, the historian should not belittle the significance of sources, even if they seem to be legendary in character; on the Coptic fast: *Le synaxaire arabe jaccobite*, 562; cf.*DTC*, X, 2296. According to Ibn al-Rāhib, 121, Heraclius' decrees required the apostasy of both Jews and Samaritans. The *Tōlīdā*, the Samaritan chronicle, however, tells of the crucifying of 'a great number of people from among the Samaritans' precisely by 'Khuzray [corrected reading] King of Assyria', and there it appears to have taken place four years prior to the renewed conquest of Palestine by the Byzantines, that is apparently in 624; see Neubauer, *Chronique samaritaine*, 23 (in the original text); the dates in the Samaritan chronicles are completely confused and should not be taken into account. Thus one chronicle mentions that when 'the Ishmaelites came and conquered the land of the Philistines', the great priest was Nethanel; but on the other hand, it states that the death of Abū Bakr (which happened prior to the conquest of Palestine) took place during the time of Nethanel's successor, Eleazar; see the chronicle in Adler et Seligsohn, *REJ*, 45(1902), 241; see Birmester, 13, on the Coptic fast.

[12] See TS 10 C 2 (no. 2), f.1*v* edited by Mann, *JQR*, NS 12(1921), 518, quoted here on the basis of what I read at the Institute of Microfilmed Hebrew Manuscripts, film No. 19687, which is different in some instances from what Mann has read. Mann, *Texts*, II, 9, assumed that this commentary was written by one of the pupils of Daniel al-Qūmisī. Cf. Ben Shammai, *Shalem*, 3(1981/1), 295, who shows that the commentary is by Daniel al-Qūmisī.

I
The conquest

Muḥammad and the vision of the conquest

[12] Towards the end of September 662, an event occurred which is known in Islam as the hijra. Muḥammad escaped from his tribesmen, the Banū Quraysh, who refused to accept the authenticity of his divine revelation and even persecuted him and his clan on this score. He fled from Mecca to Yathrib, which became known as al-Madīna (Medina). There, he and his followers, the Muhājirūn, found refuge with their allies, the Arab tribes who lived in this city. Muḥammad already had contacts with these tribes on an earlier occasion, when they were on their pilgrimage to Mecca and he had even concluded an agreement with them to terminate their endless violent feuding and abolish their bond with the Jews of that city.

The Muslim sources speak of the town of Yathrib as having been a Jewish city, and are quite clear that its founders were survivors from the revolt against the Romans. While agricultural pursuits were far from being the province of the Arab tribes, the Jews were the farmers *par excellence* in the northern part of the Arabian peninsula, cultivating the land in the oases. The Arab tribes of Medina had come there from the southern part of the peninsula, settling alongside the Jews, and evidently undergoing a process of transition to permanent sedentary life. The new order introduced by Muḥammad, establishing a covenant between the tribes which imposed its authority on every clan and its members, soon enabled him to attack the Jews and eventually wipe out the Jewish population of the town. Some were banned from the town, others were executed, and their property – plantations, fields and houses – was distributed by Muḥammad among his followers, who were destitute refugees from Mecca. He also used the former property of the Jews to establish a war fund, setting up a well-equipped army corps of cavalry troops, the likes of which had never before been seen on the Arabian peninsula. Muḥammad evidently believed in the capacity of this army, imbued with fiery religious belief, to perform great and sensational feats of valour.

When Muḥammad reached Medina in 622, Palestine was under Persian domination. The events of the Persian and Byzantine wars were still alive in the minds of the inhabitants of the peninsula and Muḥammad was certainly aware of what had occurred; these events are mentioned in the Koran (*sūrat al-rūm*). He understood only too well that the two major powers, Persia and Byzantium, were gradually being weakened by their continuous warring. In one of the most difficult moments endured by the young Muslim *umma* (community), when an expeditionary force from Mecca laid siege to Medina and the Muslims were compelled to surround themselves by a ditch (something that had never happened in Bedouin experience) and were complaining of the laborious digging, Muḥammad declared that he saw in the sparks that flew from the digging shovels, the palaces of Kisrā (Khusraw), as they called the Persian king, and Qayṣar (the Byzantine emperor), as the future patrimony of the Muslims. Both the Prophet and the early Muslims professed these ideas and intentions as part of a religious outlook according to which the Day of Judgment was at hand and the end of the world, that is the world of the wicked, was imminent. Muḥammad thought of himself as bringing the Word of God, a God who had chosen him to carry His message to the righteous, that is, the Muslims, and he had no doubt in his mind that the Muslims would shortly inherit the earth. Towards the end of his life, he began his first raids into Palestinian territory, which in the meantime had returned to Byzantine rule. His goal, at this stage, was evidently to induce the tribes on the Palestinian borders to join him, as we shall see below. The major conquests only began two years after his death.

The causes of the Great Jihād

It is usually assumed that the religious fervour of the Muslims was the major impetus of the conquests. It is true that initially, Islam was imbued with an ardour of an extreme and uncompromisingly fanatical nature. As I have mentioned, the Muslims viewed their war as a war of the End of Days, the realisation of an apocalyptic vision. The objective onlooker, even if reared in the school of thought which sees a socio-economic motive behind every political and military act, will have to admit that this religious zeal played a very important role. There is little doubt though that while it may not have been the chief cause, it was certainly one of the remarkable and principal determinants in the Arabs' success in their series of offensives against the Byzantines and the Persians. They invaded the territories of these two kingdoms in Asia and Africa with the brazen determination to carry out the Prophet's orders and ultimately to impose the mastery of the new religion on the entire world. This religious fervour turned the Muslim into a courageous fighter, contemptuous of death. The war was seen as the supreme effort (*jihād*, a well-known term meaning firstly 'effort'), to go the way dictated by God (*fī sabīl Allah*). Whoever falls on the way is promised a place in Paradise, and shall there enjoy the most sumptuous pleasures of this world. This belief proved that it could turn the dispersed masses of the Arab tribes, who were occupied with constant feuding amongst themselves, into a single, relatively united camp.[1]

[13] The role of the new religion in such a tremendous historical event as the conquest of a large part of the world by the Arab tribes was keenly stressed in a lecture by the British student of Islam, Watt, in 1953. In opposition to those who point to the significance of the economic and social circumstances prevailing in Mecca at the beginning of the seventh century, he drew attention to the fact that the adverse conditions of the times could have found an outlet in exploits of a fleeting or simply local nature. There were many situations in the ancient history of Islam in which the slightest weighting of the scales to the other side would have prevented the rise of an Arab empire or the continued existence, to this very day, of a world of believers in Islam numbering hundreds of millions. One can cite various battles between Muḥammad and his adversaries, which were more in the nature of experiments or feelers without any final outcome, and it is difficult to decide whether fate or more realistic factors were what finally determined the development of events. Beyond any doubt, however, one can justifiably say that without the conceptual system known as Islam, those developments would have remained outside the realm of possibility. The ideology of Islam is solely what gave the Arabs the united strength to subdue their overwhelming opponents. Even if there were many who were motivated mainly by the attraction of booty, one must remember that if these were bands of marauders who were merely interested in spoils and naught else, they could not have stood up in battle as did the Arabs. One cannot see in this ideological moment, a façade grafted upon deeper motives but rather an essential factor in this historical process.[2]

[14] One can put forward various objections to the point of view which stresses the religious moment. It is possible to claim that in fact, the true and faithful followers of Muḥammad, who genuinely and sincerely identified with Islam, were but a small group of people. This becomes evident in

1 On the relationship of Muḥammad with the Jews of Medina, see M. Gil, *IOS*, 4:44, 1974 and *idem.*, *JSAI*, 4:203, 1984.

2 Watt, *IQ*, 1(1953), 102, lecture held at the Univ. of Manchester; see Bousquet, *Levi della Vida Presentation Volume*, I, 52–60, who has relevant remarks on the importance of the religious moment and also his article in *SI*, 6:37, 1956.

the traditional Muslim texts, particularly those describing what happened after the Prophet's death. Many of the *ṣaḥāba*, the Prophet's disciples and the first followers of Islam, did not take any part in the battles in Palestine, Syria and Persia. The Bedouin, devoid of any religious inclination, were the mainstay and composition of the Muslim battalions, and they could only learn about Islam from hearsay. All they asked for was material gain and the worldly goods they saw around them – but no religious creed. Simply speaking, they merely looked for opportunities to plunder and pillage the subdued populations. Now we are only one move from the opposite approach, which sees the genuine reasons for the uninhibited Muslim offensive from inside the Arab peninsula as being purely materialistic. The Arabian peninsula, and especially Ḥijāz, was far from being a paradise. It had few natural resources and produced insufficient crops to satisfy the immediate needs of the Bedouin population, which throughout this period lived in a state of near-starvation. Indeed there was a *jihād*, an effort on the part of the Bedouin, but this was merely an effort to extricate themselves from the hardship of desert life. The quality of the land in the peninsula and the economic deprivation that resulted from it, claims one scholar, would eventually have brought about the migration of masses of Bedouin northward in the seventh century, even if a Prophet had not arisen in their midst who preached the unity of God and heralded the Day of Reckoning.[3]

[15] Facts of this kind show up here and there in the Muslim traditions, and the virtual starvation of the Muslims at the outset of their campaigns is not concealed. One of the chief Muslim commanders during the invasion of Palestine, 'Amr ibn al-'Āṣ, who was later to head the army which conquered Egypt, met a Byzantine commander in the Gaza area. The latter tried to convince him of the so-called 'family ties' that existed between the two camps – the Christians and the Muslims. 'Very well', 'Amr replied, 'then we shall take half your rivers and towns and in return, give you half of our thistles and stones'.[4]

[16] Apart from the religious and economic motives, there are some among contemporary Arab savants who perceive an ethnic motivation behind the conquests. They see Arabs everywhere: even the Canaanites and the Philistines were Arabs, according to their theories. This applies to an even greater degree to the population of Palestine and Syria in the seventh century, who were certainly Semites. Thus, according to their claims, the conquering Arab forces in the course of their battles, actually

[3] See Snouck Hurgronje, *Selected Studies*, 30.
[4] See Ibn 'Asākir, I, 461.

encountered their own people or at least members of their own race who spoke the same language.[5]

[17] This is of course a very distorted view: Semitism is not a race and only relates to a sphere of language. The populations met along the route of battle, living in cities or the countryside, were not Arabs and did not speak Arabic. We do know of Bedouin tribes at that time who inhabited the borderlands and the southern desert of Palestine, west of the Euphrates (Ḥīra) in the Syrian desert, Palmyra, and elsewhere. But the cultivated inner regions and the cities were inhabited by Jews and Christians who spoke Aramaic. They did not sense any special ties to the Bedouin; if anything it was the contrary. Their proximity and the danger of an invasion from that quarter disturbed their peace of mind and this is amply reflected both in the writings of the Church Fathers and in Talmudic sources.

The remarkable success of the Arab wars of conquest is more than comprehensible when seen against the background of the disastrous internal conditions that prevailed within the two great powers that were the object of attack. For our purposes, it is worthwhile to consider the declining state of affairs within the Byzantine empire, which to a certain extent explains its overwhelming defeat. On this subject we have data from Egypt, where documents have been preserved, relating mainly to the circumstances in the army, which undoubtedly also apply to the rest of the realm, including Palestine. Though numerically strong, the army was very badly organised. It was divided according to geographic regions and lacked a unified command. At its head stood the *duces* (*dux* in the singular, which is the *dūkās* in Talmudic literature), who divided the authoritative power amongst themselves and whose military status allowed them many rights of possession to the inhabitants' property. A universal characteristic was their indifference to matters for which they were responsible. The conditions prevalent in the army were also mirrored, to a large extent, in the social and general administrative conditions of Byzantine Egypt. A study of papyri dating from the period before the Muslim conquest shows that the status of the landed aristocracy entitled them to many privileges and they were actually not answerable to the central authorities. On the one hand, some of the Christian scholars have exaggerated the importance of this factor, trying to emphasize the degeneration and corruption which existed throughout the Byzantine empire, and clearly intending to prove that basically, this was not the victory of Islam over Christianity but the downfall of a weak and crumbling government. The Arabs themselves were well aware of this state of affairs. In this context, the remarks of ʿAmr

5 Hitti, *History*, 143: 'The native Semites of Syria and Palestine as well as the Hamites of Egypt looked upon the Arabian newcomers as nearer of kin than their hated and oppressive alien overlords.' Cf. Vasiliev, *History*, I, 209, and see the discussion below.

ibn al-'Āṣ in a letter in which he tries to convince the caliph 'Umar ibn al-Khaṭṭāb to permit him to set forth on an expedition to conquer Egypt, are typical: 'For it [Egypt] is foremost in the way of possessions and weakest in battle and warfare'.[6]

A balanced approach to this subject should take into consideration a fusion of all these factors, for we shall find the most genuine explanation for the success of the Arab conquerors in a combination of influences: the military power that derived from their unity and their attachment to the new religious vision; their strong desire to bring about a basic change in their living conditions by dominating the nearby cultivated regions; and the internal weaknesses of their enemies.

The tribes and the population of Palestine

[18] There has always been a profound contrast between the permanent inhabitants, the city and town dwellers, and the nomadic tribes. The ancient kingdoms were generally concerned with the welfare and security of the inhabitants living close to their border and in the deserts. They built fortifications along the borders for this purpose, and kept a sharp and constant watch in order to prevent nomads from penetrating and attacking the country. The reservations expressed by the local inhabitants, and one may even venture to say the fear of the Bedouin, are amply reflected in the sources, both in the Talmudic writings and in those of the Church Fathers. At the same time, we are well aware that the borders were not hermetically sealed. There is evidence of substantial and lesser incursions, and what is more, trading relations did exist, with the camel caravans from Mecca regularly making their way northward year by year in order to carry on their trading activities.

According to Arab sources, the Prophet's ancestors had close contact with certain areas of Palestine, particularly Gaza. It is told that Hāshim, the grandfather of the Prophet's father, 'Abdallah, died in Gaza (in the latter half of the sixth century) while staying there to conduct his business affairs. Of the Prophet's father as well, it is said that he used to trade in Gaza, travelling with the caravans of the Qurashites.[7]

6 Yāqūt, *Buldān*, III, 893.

7 See Ibn Sa'd, I(1), 46, 61; also IV(1), 12, in a tradition attributed to Abū 'Abdallah (evidently Muḥammad b. 'Azīz) al-Aylī saying that the Bishop of Gaza came to the Prophet when he was in Tabūk (see on the Tabūk expedition below) and told him 'In my town [Gaza] Hāshim and 'Abd Shams [Hāshim's brother] died when they came on business, and here are their moneys' (or property). See also Balādhurī, *Ansāb*, I, 58, 63f, 92, who also adds that Hāshim was twenty-five-years-old at his death; some say twenty. As to 'Abdallah, he took ill in Gaza but was brought to Medina and there he died at the age of twenty-five or twenty-eight. Ibn Qutayba, *Ma'ārif*, 71; Iṣbahānī, *Aghānī*, VI, 94: the people of Mecca had to stop their trading because of the Muslim attacks. When an armistice was

[19] Some of the writings of the Church Fathers who were active in Palestine describe Arab raids in the period before Islam and the murdering and marauding they carried out. These accounts are particularly concerned with the monasterial estates. For instance, Ioannes Moschus (who fled from Palestine because of the Persians, lived in Rome towards the end of his life and died in 620), writes about what happened to Gerontius, father of the monastery of St Euthymius. He was staying at the time in the mountains near the Dead Sea (evidently in the neighbourhood of Ein-Gedi) together with two other monks, and they witnessed an attack on a monk which led to his death on the shores of the Dead Sea at the hands of Saracens, during which one of the attackers even beheaded the monk. Gerontius adds that the Arab was punished immediately after the murderous act by the hand of God, when an enormous bird snatched him in his beak, carried him aloft and then threw him to the ground. He also tells the story of Father Nicolaus from a monastery along the banks of the Jordan, where the Saracens carried out a raid in the days of the emperor Mauricius (582–602). These were the Saracens of Names (evidently Nu'mān). He saw a group of three Arabs holding a young captive whom they had meant to have sacrificed by their priest (*hiereus*). A heavenly miracle occurred and the three began to fight among themselves until all were dead, and the captive remained in the monastery.[8]

arrived at with Muḥammad (spring, 628), trading was resumed. Abu Sufyān ibn Ḥarb (father of the Umayyads) then went to Palestine, precisely when Heraclius conquered Jerusalem again and returned the cross. Ibn Khaldūn, *'Ibar*, I, 61, quotes these comments as having been made by a poet from Gaza, Ibrāhīm b. Yaḥyā (born in 1049/50), and points out that it is not known in Gaza where Hāshim is buried, although he is buried there. Concerning trade relations between Mecca and Medina and Palestine, see also Couret, *La Palestine*, 219f and the sources he lists there.

8 See Ioannes Moschus, *Pratum spirituale*, *MPG*, 87(3), chs. 21, 155; ch. 99 also contains the story of the monk attacked by Arabs (p. 2958); see additional details on attacks by Arabs on monks, in Couret, *La Palestine*, 92f, 144f; Justinian decided to build the monastery of St Catherine after pleas from the monks in the Sinai, who suffered immensely from Arab raids (see *ibid.*, pp. 187f). Gregorius, who followed as abbot of the monastery at the time of Justin II (565–578; apparently around 575) had to withstand a heavy siege imposed on the monastery by the Arabs called Skēnētai ('dwellers in tents'), according to Euagrius, *MPG*, 86(2), 2804; see the apologetic remarks of Edelby, *POC*, 6(1956), 101, to the effect that the early forays into Palestine, Arabia and Syria were peaceful ones (!) and that the Arabs bore no resentment towards the empire and did not disturb the local population. To his credit, however, one has to note that he did add the remark: 'except when they went out on raids' ('sauf quand ils se mettaient à razzier'). As opposed to this, see the many detailed statements gathered by Constantelos, *Byzantion*, 42(1972), 327–332, from ancient Christian sources: Nilus points out that the Arabs are not interested in production, in commerce or in farming, but only in plundering and wars, like blood-thirsty wild beasts. See his remarks on the Arabs on pp. 639ff; *Narrationes*, *MPG*, 79, 627f. Methodius, Bishop of Patara (in Asia Minor) also describes the Arabs in dark colours, and points out that they do not respect either education or social institutions. The apocalypse of pseudo-Methodius also mentions that they have no respect for the elderly, for orphans, for pregnant women or priests.

[20] One of the means by which the Byzantine ruler hoped to prevent the nomadic tribes' invasion into Palestinian territory was to form alliances with those tribes who inhabited regions along the borders. These tribes assumed responsibility for the security of the area in exchange for certain benefits and subsidies. Thus in the early stages of Islam, the tribes served as a serious deterrent, as we shall soon see, in the face of the Muslims' first attempts at penetration northward. The Muslims, however, placed great emphasis on forming tribal alliances and tried to attract these tribes to their own camp.[9]

[21] The principal tribe occupying the desert area south of Palestine was that of the Banū Judhām. According to Arab sources, their land was called Madyan and its largest town was Ḥismā. Antoninus Placentinus (of Piacenza, Italy), who visited the region in *ca.* 570, mentions Arabs whom he calls Midianites, encountered in Eilat en route to Sinai. According to him, they claimed descent from Jethro, Moses' father-in-law, as it is also said, in Arab traditions, of the Banū Judhām, that they were the kinsfolk of Shu'ayb, whom some sources identify with Jethro. An important branch of this tribe were the Banū Wā'il (etymologically the equivalent of the Hebrew name Yō'ēl), a certain part of which was inclined towards Judaism, as were other clans of the Banū Judhām. A few actually converted. On the other hand, there was an element of Christian influence among some sectors of the tribe as a result of their connections with Byzantium.[10]

Antonius of Chozeba, in his study on the life of St Georgius of Chozeba (who was his teacher), describes the slaughter of the monks in Chozeba. See Vita S. Georgii Chozebitae, *Anal.Boll.*, 7:95, 1888, 129f. Maximus Confessor: 'They behave like beasts of prey though they look like human beings.' But even Constantelos feels the need to insert reservations in his article from time to time, when he points to a fact which is an exaggeration or to another which in reality applies to the Persians and not to the Arabs. This is an example of the reading of ancient texts in accordance with contemporary considerations. See further discussion of the subject in Christides, *Balkan Studies*, 10:315, 1969.

9 See Cheira, 18f, 30.

10 See Antoninus, 113f (*MPL*, 1, 72, 912f). See Hamadānī, *Jazīra*, I, 129f; Bakrī, 289, 446, 1122, 1214, 1247. Yāqūt, *Buldān*, I, 212, 267, 919f; II, 794; Ya'qūbī, *Buldān*, 33; Wāqidī, 28, 555f, 990, 1032. Hieronymus (Jerome) and his commentary on Ezek. xxv:1–3, *MPL*, 25, 244, stresses that the Midianites are 'Ismaelitai et Agareni qui nunc Sarraceni appellantur'. In his commentary on Jer. iii:2 (Lift up thine eyes . . . as the Arabian in the wilderness), *MPL*, 24, 699f, he points out that the verse refers to a thief or a raven, but it is also possible to use Arab as the interpretation: 'potest et Arabes significare quae gens latrociniis dedita usque hodie incursat terminos Palaestinae et descendentibus de Jerusalem in Jericho obsidet vias' ('for these people, who are occupied with thieving, until today steal through the borders of Palestine and rob those who go down from Jerusalem to Jericho'). See my article in *JSAI*, 4:203, 1984, in which I point out that the image of Shu'ayb developed from that of the Biblical Balaam, prophet of the Moabites and the Midianites. There I also uphold the parallel between the traditions on the spreading of Judaism amongst the Banū Judhām and some of the Talmudic traditions which speak of the proselytes, 'the sons of Jethro' or 'the children of the Kenite, Moses' father-in-law'. See PT, Bikkurim, i, 64a; BT

[22] Farwa b. ʿAmr, one of the Banū Judhām and the governor in southern Trans-Jordan on behalf of the Byzantines ('in ʿAmmān, which is in the land of the Balqā''), accepted Islam and even sent a special messenger from his tribe with a gift for the Prophet, consisting of a mule, an ass, and expensive robes of fine linen and samite embroidered in gold thread. Eventually he was arrested by the Byzantines and crucified by order of the emperor near the ʿIfrā River in Palestine.[11]

[23–24] Both the Banū Judhām and the Banū Ghassān, a large federation of tribes living in Northern Palestine and Syria, were the major Byzantine bulwark in their battle against the Arab tribes, and some of them were constant in their resistance to the faith of Islam. After the battle of the Yarmūk, records one source, the Banū Ghassān were asked to pay a land tax and a poll tax (*kharāj* and *jizya*), because they evidently preferred to remain Christians. Their leader, Jabala b. al-Ayham, absolutely refused to do so, claiming that they were Arabs, that is to say Bedouin, and therefore exempt from paying taxes. They even threatened to move to Byzantine land. The caliph ʿUmar ibn al-Khaṭṭāb, had to give way. A third alliance of tribes should be mentioned in this connection. The Banū Lakhm, whose major strength was centred in the region of the northern Euphrates but who also had branches within Palestinian territory, mixed with the Banū Judhām. According to tribal genealogical records, Lakhm were the brothers of Judhām. From the Arab sources, we get the impression that these tribes, allies of the Byzantines on the eve of the Islamic conquests, roved about the Palestinian border lands and concentrated in Arabia, that is Provincia Arabia, the separate administrative area established by Trajan in 106 and also known later by the name of Palaestina tertia (the third).[12] In an Arab source, this region is called al-Takhūm, a loan-word from Hebrew, as it undoubtedly was also called by the Jews. In Dīnawarī, we

Sanhedrin, 104a, 106; *Pesīqātā of R. Kahana* (ed. Mandelbaum), I, 36; *Sifrē Zuta* (ed. Horowitz), 263f; *Mekhilta de R. Shimon* (ed. Hoffmann), 92; *Mekhilta de R. Ishm.* (ed. Ish Shalom), 60a; see additional sources in Ginzberg, *The Legends of the Jews*, VI, 113f, in nos. 782, 783. According to certain Arab sources, the Banū Naḍīr and the Banu Qurayẓa, the major Jewish tribes in Medina, were descendants of the Banū Judhām. See my aforementioned article for a detailed discussion and sources on the entire subject of the Banū Judhām.

11 Ibn Saʿd, VII (2), 148, Ibn Hishām, 958.

12 Yaʿqūbī, *Ta'rīkh*, II, 160f, 168. The prophet negotiated with the Banū Ghassān and even sent an emissary, Shujāʿ b. Wahb of the Banū Asad, to 'the King of the Balqā' in Palestine' (the land of al-Shām), who was Ḥārith b. Abī Shamir, the Ghassānī. See Nawawī, *Tahdhīb*, I, 35. See the opinion of Ashtor, who claimed that the Byzantines set up a real buffer state for the Banū Ghassān, which covered the whole of the Ḥawrān, Phoenicia, northern Trans-Jordan and other parts of Palestine: Ashtor, *A Social and Economic History*, 12.

find the expression *takhūm arḍ al-'arab*, or 'the Takhūm, which is the land of the Arabs'.[13]

[25] Talmudic writings do not often praise the Arabs. Reservations regarding them and their customs are perceptible in a number of instances in the Babylonian Talmud and the Midrashic literature. Perhaps the sharpest expression is to be found in the Babylonian Talmud in connection with the daughter of Naqdimōn ben Guriōn 'who was picking barley grains in the dung of Arab cattle', one of the stories of the destruction of the Temple, whose moral is that 'when they do not do the will of God, He delivers them into the hands of a base people, and not only in the hands of a base people but into the power of the beasts of the base people'. There is also condemnation of the Arabs' treatment of refugees of the revolt (either the Great Revolt or that of Bar Kokhba) who fled from the Romans to Arabia.[14]

[26] Some scholars view the stories of the Church Fathers as well as some comments in the Talmudic literature with a critical eye or assume them to be unbalanced, one-sided or exaggerated, and so on. But this approach bears some bending of the historical truth. In fact, such episodes reflect the attitude of the towns and villages in Palestine quite accurately; the attitude of a sedentary population, of farmers and craftsmen, toward nomads whose source of income is the camel and who frequently attack the towns, pillage and slaughter the inhabitants and endanger the lives of the wayfarer. These sources completely contradict the argument mentioned earlier on, to the effect that the villagers and townsmen in Palestine accepted the invasion of those tribes bearing the banner of Islam with open arms because of their so-called racial affinity.

I have already described the political and military troubles endured by the Byzantine empire following the death of Justinian and afterwards. There is no questioning the fact that these difficulties contributed considerably to the success of the Muslim wars of conquest. The local Byzantine administration was inefficient as was its military command. Quite detailed information regarding this state of affairs has been preserved in Egyptian papyri and one can undoubtedly assume that there was little difference between Egypt and Palestine in terms of administration and military matters. The Arab traditions are familiar with the image of the *biṭrīq*, i.e. *patricius*, the Byzantine estate owner, who also served as commander in the army, whether in Egypt, Syria or Palestine. On hearing the news of the approaching Muslim army, the *dux* of the province of Thebes

[13] See Dīnawarī, 8: Sodom is situated between the land of Urdunn (Jordan) and the Takhūm, land of the Arabs.

[14] BT, Ket., 66b, PT, Taaniot, ii, 69b; *Lam. Rabbā* (Buber), 108; see also BT, Ket., 72b, about an Arab woman who spun in the market place, which is not fitting for a woman. The Talmudic sources dealing with Arabs were collated by Krauss, *ZDMG*, 70:321, 1916.

hastily collected whatever sums he was able to gather in taxes, and ran off with the money, leaving the region without leadership or protection.[15]

The first incursions: Dhāt Aṭlāḥ, Mu'ta

[27–28] In the eighth year of the hijra, 629, Muḥammad decided to increase his military activities and examine the possibilities of penetrating the Byzantine domain. At the end of the previous summer, in the year 628, the Muslims had taken control of the Khaybar region, situated 150 miles north of Medina – an agricultural region inhabited by Jews. Now those Jews occupying the land became tenants of the Muslims and had to hand over half the date crops. The palm trees, which were formerly their own property, now became the assets of the Muslim community. The same fate also lay in store for the Jews of Fadak, another farming region near Khaybar, and this also applied to the inhabitants of Wādī'l-Qurā (Valley of the villages) on the Palestinian border. At the same time, older members of the Islamic community who had fled from Mecca to Ethiopia some thirteen years earlier, in 615, now came and joined the Muslim camp. In the interim, Islam had accumulated considerable strength and Mecca itself would soon fall into Islamic hands. The Prophet could not ignore Byzantium's inherent weakness, despite the fact that it had just regained control of Palestine and was celebrating its victory over the

15 See Maspéro, *Organisation*, 119–132; Gelzer, *Studien*, 97ff; Bell, *JEA*, 4(1917), 106; Vasiliev, *History*, I, 210. An area on which we have little genuine information with regard to Palestine is the attitude of various Christian sects towards the conquerors, whether they were influenced by the hatred felt towards the official, that is the Byzantine Church and towards Byzantine rule itself. In this area, too, one can assume that there was some similarity to what was happening in Egypt. For this, today we have at our disposal Jarry, *BIFAO*, 62:173, 1964; *Annales islamologiques*, 6:1, 1966. He points out in his studies that the descriptions in the Muslim chronicles are simplistic. According to them, the Copts supported the conquerors, as they had suffered from religious persecution, while their opponents, apart from the soldiers, were the Greek-speaking collaborators of the Byzantines, as well as the Melekites, followers of the Byzantine Church. The conqueror of Egypt, 'Amr ibn al-'Āṣ, requited the Copts by handing over to them the churches of the Melekites. Actually, he contends, there is a difference in attitudes to the Muslims within each of the two parties, the aristocrats (the blues) and the populists (the greens). But it was precisely the blues, who had a great deal of influence at court, who asked for a policy of withdrawal, at least temporarily, in order to organise their forces properly, as Heraclius did in his war against the Persians. Apart from this, the blues were more oriented towards the West, that is, they wanted to come to some agreement with Rome in particular and were less interested in the Eastern regions. It was the greens who wanted to organise forceful opposition to the Muslim invaders, which led, according to Jarry, to the wholesale annihilation of the greens' towns by the Muslims.

Persians.[16] Muḥammad still hoped to lure the Arab tribes dwelling along the Palestinian borders to his side. At this stage, the Muslims' reconnaissance raid into Palestine is mentioned at a site called Dhāt Aṭlāḥ (apparently 'the place of the acacias'). Leading this foray stood Ka'b b. 'Umayr al-Ghifārī. This attempt ended bitterly for the Muslims: everyone taking part in the action was killed except for one wounded man who was taken for dead and afterwards succeeded in reaching the Prophet. Muḥammad wanted to despatch an expeditionary force to that site to punish the tribes who had slain his men, but when he learned that in the meantime they had evacuated the place, he abandoned the project.[17]

[29] Some weeks later, in September 629, Muḥammad again sent his cavalry to raid Palestine, this time to a place called Mu'ta. The account of this action is to be found in its most complete form in Wāqidī. As he records it, the Prophet sent al-Ḥārith b. 'Umayr al-Azdī with a letter to 'the king of Buṣrā'. On arriving in Mu'ta, he found his way barred by Shuraḥbīl b. 'Amr, a man of the Banū Ghassān, who asked him where he was heading. On being told that his goal was Palestine and that he was an emissary from Muḥammad, he was ordered to be tied up, bound and beheaded – a fate never before endured by one of Muḥammad's messengers. When Muḥammad was informed of what had befallen his messenger, he quickly organised a force of 3,000 Muslim cavalry troops, led by Zayd b. Ḥāritha. Should he fall in battle, Ja'far b. Abī Ṭālib (the brother of 'Alī), would replace him, and if he too should be killed, he was to be replaced by 'Abdallah b. Rawāḥa. Shuraḥbīl b. 'Amr soon learned of the Muslim army's advance. They camped for some days in Wādī'l-Qurā (whose inhabitants were Jews). At that point, Sadūs, Shuraḥbīl's brother, attacked the Muslims but was killed in action. Shuraḥbīl took fright and decided to entrench himself against the probable onslaught. Then the Muslims advanced until Ma'ān, whereupon they were informed that

16 Knowledge of the Byzantine victory and the death of the Persian king on 29 February 628, reached Muḥammad as already mentioned, at the time of the agreement of Ḥudaybiyya. The Persian defeat also spelled the weakening of the status of the Jews of north Ḥijāz, in Khaybar, and in other places near the borders of Palestine. The agreement signed by Muḥammad with the people of Mecca in which the latter benefited by various concessions, was aimed at giving the Muslims a free hand in subduing this Jewish region. In the Muslim sources, there is mention of an anti-Muslim pact between the Jews of Khaybar and the people of Mecca, but this became invalid with the signing of the Ḥudaybiyya agreement. See in this connection the article by M. Lecker, *JSAI*, 5:1, 1984.

17 Ibn Isḥāq, in Ibn Hishām, 983; Wāqidī, 752f; Ṭabarī, *Ta'rīkh*, I, 1601 (calling the leader of the raid: 'Amr b. Ka'b, and noting that he had a total of fifteen men with him. According to him these were the same Arabs who attacked the Muslims of the Banū Quḍā'a and their leader named Sadūs. The Banū Quḍā'a were made by the Muslims the target of their attack at Mu'ta, as we shall see below. Even before that, evidently in the summer of 628, there were Muslim actions against the Banū Judhām in southern Trans-Jordan (see below); cf. Caetani, II, 79.

Heraclius (Wāqidī evidently refers to the Byzantine army rather than the emperor himself) had moved southward and was encamped in 'Moab, which is the land of the Balqā'' with a force of some 100,000 men of the Bahrā, Wā'il, Lakhm and Judhām tribes, headed by a member of the Balī tribe named Mālik b. Rāfila. The Muslims waited two days before writing to the Prophet to inform him of these new circumstances. In order to raise their spirits, 'Abdallah b. Rawāḥa reminded them how they had withstood, a handful against many, in their earlier battles. With the onset of the battle, the Muslim commanders Zayd b. Ḥāritha and Ja'far b. Abī Ṭālib were killed one after the other, and subsequently the third commander, 'Abdallah b. Rawāḥa, also fell. According to some traditions, Khālid b. al-Walīd was put in command, eventually becoming one of the most important commanders in the campaign of the conquest of Palestine. He had only joined the Muslim ranks a short time earlier. Withdrawal was inavoidable. Returning from Mu'ta to Medina, they were greeted by shouts of derision and were accused of desertion. But Muḥammad stood by them, stating that they had withdrawn their forces (in order to reorganise their troops) and had not deserted. As we have seen, the battle took place in the neighbourhood of Moab, and there are sources which claim that it was fought in *mashārif al-balqā'*, or the hills of Moab.[18]

[30] The assault on Mu'ta is also described by the Byzantine writer Theophanes. He speaks of four commanders appointed by Muḥammad to lead the attacking forces. He also mentions the place Moukheōn Kōmē, which may mean 'Village of the Moukhaians' with Theodore in charge (*bikarios*). In this version, Theodore learns well in advance that the Muslims are about to attack (a similar account can also be found in Arab sources) from someone named Koutaba, who was a 'Korasenos'. Evidently the person mentioned was an Arab named Qutayba of the Quraysh tribe, who knew and could enlighten them as to the exact time the Muslims were intending to launch an attack, and thus Theodore stole a march on the Muslim forces and took the offensive at a site called

18 See Wāqidī, 755–769. He tells here of the incident of al-Nu'mān, son of Pinḥas the Jew, who was in the presence of the Prophet when he appointed the three commanders, and told him that if he was indeed a prophet, the three would be killed; for when the prophets of the children of Israel appointed commanders and designated 'if so-and-so is killed', all the commanders were killed, even if a hundred had been appointed. Ibn Isḥāq, in Ibn Hishām, 791–802, adds that apart from the 100,000 unbelievers, tribesmen, there was a similar number of regular Byzantine soldiers. Ṭabarī, *Ta'rīkh*, I, 1610–1618; Ibn Sa'd, II(1), 92; IV(1), 27: Ja'far b. Abī Ṭālib was killed in the battle of Mu'ta, in the Balqā'; Mas'ūdī, *Tanbīh*, 265; Ibn Sayyid al-Nās, *'Uyūn*, II, 153; Nawawī, *Tahdhīb*, I, 265: 'Abdallah b. Rawāḥa was killed in the battle of Mu'ta and did not leave any heirs. Suyūṭī, *Khaṣā'iṣ*, II, 70–72; Ibn Kathīr, *Bidāya*, IV, 244. The Balqā', it appears from the sources, is southern Trans-Jordan. Ya'qūbi quotes a tradition indicating that this name derives from a man named Bāliq, who met Joshua bin Nun there. See *Ta'rīkh*, I, 47; on Ja'far b. Abī Ṭālib see Ibn Sa'd, IV(1), 27. Cf. on the raid on Mu'ta: Caetani, II, 80–90.

Mothous. We learn further from Theophanes that the Muslims intended to wield their swords against the Arab tribes on that very spot. Those tribes were about to offer up a huge sacrifice in honour of their gods on that very day. Which goes to prove that Christianity had taken only a marginal and superficial hold on these tribes who lived under Byzantine rule.[19]

Muḥammad and the Palestinian tribes

[31] The Mu'ta affair stresses the fact that Muḥammad's goal during his last years was to compel the tribes along the Palestinian borders to accept Islam and consolidate around him. He decided to adopt towards those tribes outside the Arabian peninsula, particularly those under Byzantine control, the same policy that he had successfully applied to the Arabian peninsula; that of cruel campaigns accompanied by rebuke and chastisement while proposing peace and security to those who joined his ranks. However, this policy did not produce notable results during his lifetime, and these tribes, such as the Ghassān, Quḍā'a, Judhām and others, remained loyal to their Byzantine masters. It was only after Muḥammad's death that his vision of taking over the palaces of Byzantium and Persia materialised.[20]

[32] The first cracks in the surface of these tribes' loyalty to the Byzantines had apparently begun to appear during the Prophet's lifetime. As we have seen, the traditions preserved the memory of Farwa b. 'Amr of Judhām, whom the Byzantines had placed in a position of authority and who lost his life by converting to Islam. Evidently Islam had infiltrated into his tribe here and there, but on the whole it was rejected by most of the tribesmen. Rifā'a b. Zayd, a member of the clan of Ḍubayb, who belonged to the Judhām, appeared before Muḥammad in the summer of 628 (after the armistice with Quraysh and before the campaign against Khaybar), bringing the Prophet the gift of a slave and accepting Islam with all

[19] In Mas'ūdī, *Tanbīh*, 265, the name of the commander is Thiadux (see there different versions in the notes, but it seems that the original version had Theodoros and this was evidently taken from Theophanes). This is one of the rare occasions in which the Muslim chronicles (at least Mas'ūdī) compared their own information with that found in the Byzantine sources, just as Theophanes also knew what was said in the Muslim sources, in addition to his own. See Theophanes, 335; cf. De Goeje, *Mémoire*, 4–8, who speaks of the interpretation of the name of the place in Theophanes and mentions that he possibly intended Ma'ān.

[20] See what the traditions say about the Prophet during the digging of the trench in Medina (the *khandaq*): when his pickaxe strikes a stone and the sparks fly, he sees in them the future conquests in Yemen, in Byzantine and Persian regions (Ibn Hishām, 673; Wāqidī, 450; Ṭabarī, *Ta'rīkh*, I, 1469). In Ṭabarī, the version is that the Prophet saw in these sparks the red palaces or fortresses of Byzantium, resembling the teeth of dogs (red, perhaps because of the name applied to Byzantium by the Jews – Edom).

his heart. In return the Prophet gave him a letter addressed to his tribesmen, confirming that he was being sent to call them to join with God and His Messenger, and to inform them that they had an interim of two months to consider the matter. In the meantime, it seems that Muḥammad sent additional emissaries to the tribes in Palestine. One of these, Diḥya b. Khalīfa al-Kalbī, on his return from the Palestinian area (according to the traditions, it was on his return from Qayṣar, the Byzantine emperor, but the intention here is obviously to the place he returned from, i.e. a Byzantine domain, and it is certainly unlikely that he would have been on a mission to the emperor), was attacked by tribesmen of Judhām. The Prophet then sent Zayd b. Ḥāritha to attack the area inhabited by the Judhām tribe, which is Ḥismā in southern Trans-Jordan. The Muslim force consisted of 500 cavalry troops, and they took captives and spoils. Afterwards the two sides made peace and the captives and spoils were returned, but this does not mean that the tribe converted to Islam, for as we shall see in subsequent events, this, the largest of the tribes living along the Palestinian borders, was still on the side of the Byzantines.[21]

Dhāt al-Salāsil

[33] The defeat at Mu'ta may have placed the Muslim camp in an inferior position, as a result of the humiliating military setback. In order to prevent a decline in the prestige they enjoyed among the tribes, Muḥammad hastened to organise a new force made up of 300 cavalry troops and attack the southern region of Trans-Jordan. In general, his target was Dhāt al-Salāsil, which was in the hands of the Banū 'Udhra, a branch of the Judhām. This force was meant to attack the Banū Balī and the Banū Quḍā'a specifically ('Udhra was also the name of the place, and is frequently mentioned as belonging to the Judhām area. As to Balī, they were part of Quḍā'a; but the sources are sometimes inconsistent, and the placing of the tribes is not always clear). 'Amr b. al-'Āṣ was appointed to head the force. He had been one of the most important figures in and commanders of Mecca, and in the past had participated in actions against the Muslims; but some time prior to this he had converted to Islam. Through his grandmother, he had family connections with the Banū Balī, and the Prophet's intention was, apart from the military operation, that he would try to induce the Palestinian border tribes to come over to Islam. On reaching Dhāt al-Salāsil, 'Amr sensed that his forces would not withstand the opposition and he asked for assistance. The Prophet sent 200 more cavalry troops to his aid, under the command of Abū 'Ubayda ibn al-Jarrāḥ. These

21 Ibn Hishām, 962f; 975ff; Ṭabarī, *Ta'rīkh*, I, 1740–1745; Wāqidī, 557–560; Watt, *Muḥammad at Medina*, 108f, changes the order and places the campaign of Zayd b. Ḥāritha before the visit of Rifā'a b. Zayd.

two armies contained some of the most important personalities in the Muslim camp, such as Abū Bakr, ʿUmar ibn al-Khaṭṭāb, Saʿd b. Abī Waqqāṣ, and others. The local tribes fled in panic as the Muslim forces advanced. It appears that there was much in this campaign to encourage those who had joined Islam; and at the same time there was in this almost unbridled advance into Byzantine territory evidence of the unusual military deterioration of the empire.[22]

Tabūk

[34] At the beginning of 630, Mecca was in the hands of the Muslims. This was the most important stage in the consolidation of the Arab tribes and their unification under the Islamic banner. Tribes which for generations had fought with one another were now under a single leadership and shared a common awareness of a mission conferred on them by God: to inherit the earth from the wicked, or in other words, from Byzantium and Persia. The presence of constant tension from the increasing preparations for war was a vital necessity in the Muslim camp at the time. If the enormous quantity of contained energy implanted in the armed cavalry troops, members of the tribes, standing at the ready for Muḥammad's command, were to be consumed and wasted on local infighting and trivialities, it would quickly lead to the division of the camp and the return of civil wars. And so Muḥammad started energetic preparations for an enormous campaign against Byzantium. This expedition was afterwards known as the Tabūk campaign. The development of events is described in Wāqidī as follows. There were close connections between Medina and the region of Palestine, thanks to the farmers (the Nabateans, as the source calls them), who used to come to Medina to trade. It was from them that the Muslims learned what was happening in Byzantine territory. On orders from the Byzantines, evidently, the farmers began to spread rumours of large concentrations of the Byzantine army, who also had the support of the Arab tribes (Lakhm, Judhām, Ghassān, ʿĀmila), and that Heraclius was also stationed nearby in Ḥimṣ. The Prophet started on a large scale recruiting exercise among the tribes who had joined Islam through loyal envoys sent to each tribe. While formerly he would conceal his intentions, making a secret of the target of the next assault and spreading a smokescreen over his actions for this purpose, this time he changed his usual practice and openly declared his intention and even demanded that the tribes contribute appreciable sums to finance the

[22] Ibn Hishām, 984f; Ṭabarī, *Taʾrīkh*, I, 1604f; Wāqidī, 769–774; see a survey of the expedition to Dhāt al-salāsil in Caetani, II, 100f.

campaign. Abū Bakr wanted to serve as an example to others and donated 4,000 dirhams, which he claimed was two-thirds of his fortune. Other heads of the Muslim community also contributed generously, both in money and food, especially dates. The women, too, donated some of their ornaments, expensive finery and precious jewels. There were Muslims who wept at the thought that they could not arm themselves at their own expense to join the campaign and others had to supply them with what was needed. The traditions speak of an army of 30,000-strong going out to battle. On their route, they passed through the Jewish settlements of Wādī'l-Qurā, who honoured the Prophet by serving him with their typical dishes, according to the Muslim sources, which was the *harīs* (or *harīsa*); only that according to the traditions of the descendants of these Jews (and they continued to dwell there for many generations), the Prophet imposed on them an annual tax of 40 *wasq*s of dates (a *wasq* is *ca.* 200 kilograms, or the load that a camel can bear).[23]

[35] The Prophet and the Muslims remained in Tabūk for twenty days; the entire campaign lasting two months, from approximately mid-October to mid-December 630. Taking into consideration that Heraclius had abandoned his plans to attack, the Prophet decided to return to Medina as well, on the advice given him by ‘Umar. One can assume that the withdrawal was really caused by the low morale that was spreading through the Muslim camp, hints of which one can sense in the traditions that have been preserved. At this juncture, it should be pointed out that there were individuals within the Muslim camp itself who from the very outset were opposed to the expedition into Byzantine territory. The texts describe the reservations, evasiveness and even open opposition to this campaign.[24]

23 The people of Wādī'l-Qurā (written Wādī al-qry, as in Arabic) are mentioned in a list of books from the Geniza: ‘Queries from people of Wādī'l-Qurā to Sherira Gaon and Hayy Av (= father of the court), of blessed memory’, i.e. sent towards the end of the tenth century. See: Ginzberg, *Geonica*, II, 54, 61; similarly in Harkavy, *Responsa*, 94: ‘These were the queries asked by the people of Wādī'l Qurā of our Master Sherira, Head of the Yeshiva, of blessed memory, and of Av, of blessed memory.’ The opening of the first query has been preserved. It is interesting that agricultural matters are being discussed, from which we learn that the Jews of the area were still living on their own land (the query referred to the possession of date palm trees, a matter dealt with in the Mishna, Bava Batra, v:6; in the PT, *ibid.*, v, 15a; in BT, *ibid.*, 81a–82a, 124a). In a letter from Solomon b. Judah written in around 1020, a certain Isaac from Wādī'l-Qurā is mentioned, who ‘has to be excommunicated for what he has done to his family in Rabbat Benē ‘Ammōn (‘Ammān), for he deserted his wife, like a living widow for some four years now’: this same Isaac supplied the finances for commercial ventures, travelled to Egypt and returned ‘to his land’, that is to Wādī'l-Qurā, and since then, there is no trace of his whereabouts. See **58,** a, ll. 20–25; on the *wasq*, see: Hinz, 53.

24 Wāqidī, 989–1022; Ibn Hishām, 893–906; Ṭabarī, *Ta'rīkh*, I, 1692–1705. See a detailed review of the Tabūk campaign in Caetani, II, 238–253, 257ff.

The treaties with towns in the south of Palestine

[36] Muslim tradition associates the Tabūk campaign with an important turning point in Muḥammad's attitude towards the Jews and the Christians. While previously the Prophet had adopted a hard line towards the Jews in Medina – which was expressed in dispossession, eviction and even annihilation (Banū Qurayẓa), dispossessing the Jews in the towns in the northern part of the Arabian peninsula, depriving them of their property and turning them into tenants – he now altered his policy. During his own stay along the borders of Palestine, on land populated by Jews and Christians, he seems to have sensed that a wiser policy would be to convince them to acquiesce, to relinquish any intention of maintaining a military force and to rely on Muslims for their personal security and that of their possessions in exchange for the payment of taxes laid down according to special treaties. Letters of protection have been preserved which Muḥammad issued to four towns during his stay in Tabūk, one in the northern Ḥijāz on the coast of the gulf of Eilat, Maqnā, and three others in Palestine: Eilat, Jarba and Adhruḥ.

The following is the version of the letter to the people of Eilat:

To Yuḥanna b. Rūba and the worthies of Ayla, Peace be with you! Praised be Allah, there is no God save Him. I have no intention of fighting you before writing to you. Thou hast to accept Islam, or pay the tax, and obey God and His Messenger and the messengers of His Messenger, and do them honour and dress them in fine clothing, not in the raiment of raiders; therefore clothe Zayd in fine robes, for if you satisfy my envoys, you will satisfy me. Surely the tax is known to you. Therefore if you wish to be secure on land and on sea, obey God and his Messenger and you will be free of all payments that you owed the Arab [tribes] or non-Arabs, apart from the payment to God [which is] the payment of his Messenger. But be careful lest thou do not satisfy them, for then I shall not accept anything from you, but I shall fight you and take the young as captives and slay the elderly. For I am the true Messenger of God; put ye your trust in God and his books and his messengers and in the Messiah son of Maryam, for this is God's word and I too, put my trust in Him, for he is the Messenger of God. Come then, before a calamity befalls you. As for me, I have already given my envoys instructions with regard to you: give Ḥarmala three *wasq*s of barley, for Ḥarmala is your well-wisher, for if it were not for God and if it were not for this, I would not be sending you messengers altogether, but rather you would be seeing the army. Therefore if you obey my messengers, you will have the protection of God and of Muḥammad and all that stand at his side. My messengers are Shuraḥbīl and Ubayy and Ḥarmala and Ḥurayth b. Zayd who is one of the sons of the Banū Ṭayy'. All that they decide with regard to you shall be according to my wishes, and you will have the protection of God and of Muḥammad the Messenger of God. And peace will be with you if you obey me. And the people of Maqnā thou shall lead back to their land.[25]

[25] Ibn Sa'd, I(2), 28–29, see also p. 37: Yuḥannā was king and bishop. According to Wāqidī, 1031, Yuḥannā was son of Ru'ba, king of Ayla. Ṭabarī, *Ta'rīkh*, I, 1702: 'the owner of

[37] And this is the wording of the letter to the people of Adhruḥ, as Wāqidī copied it:

In the name of God, the merciful, the compassionate. From Muḥammad the Prophet to the people of Adhruḥ; They [will live] securely by virtue of the letter of security from God and from Muḥammad. They are due to pay 100 dinars, good and weighed, on every Rajab. And if one [of them] flees from the Muslims, out of fear and awe – for they feared the Muslims – they shall live securely until Muḥammad will visit them before he leaves.[26]

[38] And the letter to the people of Maqnā:

To the sons of Ḥanīna, who are Jews of Maqnā, and the people of Maqnā, near Ayla. Your request has reached me [which was sent] when you returned to your village. With the arrival of this letter your security is ensured and you are granted God's protection and that of his Messenger; God's Messenger forgives you the wickedness you have done and for all the sins you have committed. Therefore you are granted God's protection and that of his Messenger; no one will do you injustice or harm, for it is the Messenger of God himself who gives you protection from what he himself will not do to you. Your arms belong to the Messenger of God; as well as all the slaves that are with you, and the rings, apart from what the Messenger of God, or the envoy of the Messenger of God, will allow you to keep. And from now onwards you will owe a quarter of your date harvest and a quarter of your fishing yield, and a quarter of the yarn spun by your women. Except for these you will be free of any levy or impressment. If you will listen and obey, the Messenger of God will respect the honourable amongst you and forgive the sinners amongst you. And for the information of the believers and the Muslims: anyone coming to the people of Maqnā who is concerned with their well-being will benefit; and anyone who intends doing them harm will suffer harm. There will be no chief over you other than one of you or one of the Messenger of God's people. And peace.[27]

Ayla' [ṣāḥib], similarly also Balādhurī, *Futūḥ*, 60. According to Wāqidī, the tax levied on the people of Ayla was 300 dinars annually, for there were 300 men there. See also Ibn Sa'd, *ibid.*, 377; Ibn Hishām, 902; Mas'ūdī, *Tanbīh*, 272 states that Yuḥannā was bishop of Ayla. See further Abū 'Ubayd, *Amwāl*, 200; Dhahabī, *Ta'rīkh*, I, 331. The letter of protection was preserved by the people of Ayla, as was the Prophet's coat, which he gave them as a gift. The first of the Abbasid caliphs, al-Saffāḥ, bought them for the sum of 300 dinars; Diyārbakrī, II, 127; Ibn 'Asākir, I, 421; Ibn al-Athīr, *Kāmil*, II, 280; that Ayla was the seat of a bishop at the beginning of the seventh century is evident from a letter preserved among the papyri of Nessana, from Mōusēs (Moses), the Bishop of Ailanē (the district of Ayla) concerning Victor, the son of Sergius, of Nessana. The letter accompanied a package sent to the churches of St Sergius in Nessana and its environs: *Nessana*, 146 (51).

26 Wāqidī, 1032; the editor corrected the version, so that it was given the opposite meaning, that is, 'if someone would flee from the Muslims to them' (to the people of Adhruḥ), which belies common sense. A similarly distorted version is to be found also in Ibn Sa'd, I(2), 37, and this served as the basis for the 'correction'. See also Mas'ūdī, *Tanbīh*, 272.

27 Ibn Sa'd, I(2), 28. Certain expressions were already unfamiliar in Ibn Sa'd's time, and he tried to explain them in the continuation to the version of the treaty, not quite accurately. See the subject of the treaty in Balādhurī, *Futūḥ*, 59f; who states that he was told by an Egyptian that he had seen the letter of protection to the people of Maqnā in the original,

[39] It is distinctly stated of the people of Maqnā, Jarba and Adhruḥ that they were Jews. As to the people of Eilat, it appears that Yuḥanna b. Ru'ba represented the Christians as well as the Jews living there. One should especially note the phrase in the letter of security (towards the end) to the people of Maqnā in which they are promised a leader from amongst themselves, although the matter is qualified by the possibility mentioned there that their leader could be an envoy of Muḥammad. We find in these treaties the paradigm of letters of security that the leaders of the Muslims were to issue during the great conquests as well. Here can be found certain key words for the first time: letter of security (*amān* or *amana*); tax (*jizya*; this word afterwards took on a specific meaning, that of poll-tax); protection (*dhimma*); giver of protection (*jār*). One should note that the root *'mn* in Arabic expresses the idea of security, and that the meaning of the word *mu'min*, which is translated above as believer and which is characteristic of the Muslims, at the time was linked to the idea of security, something like 'the participants of the security pact [under the protection] of God and his Messenger'. Only at a later stage did it acquire the meaning of the Hebrew word *ma'amīnīm* (believers). The new policy towards the Jews and the Christians was also evident in the Koran. In chapter ix (*sūrat al-thawba*, the repentance, verse 29): 'Fight ye those who were given the Book, who do not trust God nor the Last Day, and do not forbid what God and his Messenger have forbidden, since their religion is not the religion of truth; [fight them] until they are lying down and pay the tax according to their ability' [or their profits].[28]

[40] From such precedents, the basic legal outlook of Islam towards non-Muslims developed, becoming an integral part of Muslim martial law. They were obliged to (1) accept Islam (although theoretically Islam

written on red parchment, with the script already faded; it was he who copied the version and dictated it to Balādhurī, who has the version: Banū Ḥabība, while that in Ibn Sa'd was: Banū Janba. See the matter of the treaties (letters of protection) also in: Ḥalabī, III, 160; Daḥlān, II, 374f; Ibn Kathīr, *Bidāya*, V, 16f. See also Hirschberg. *Israel Ba-'arāv*, 152ff, on the subject of the treaties, and also the parallel notes on p. 304. As to the name of Jewish inhabitants of Maqnā, the versions have been interchanged: Janbā, Ḥabība, Ḥanīna, all clearly one name which was distorted because of the similarity of the letters in Arabic writing; this has already been noted in: Sperber, Die Schreiben Muḥammads an die Stämme Arabiens, *Mitteilungen des Seminars für orientalische Sprachen zu Berlin*, 19(2):1, 1916. The version *Ḥanīna* is also found in a fake letter of protection preserved in the Cairo Geniza, whose author most certainly copied the names from an Arabic source. On this subject, see the article by Goitein, *KS*, 9:507, 1931–33.

[28] Ibn Sa'd, I(2), 38: The people of Maqnā were Jews who lived on the coast, and the people of Jarba and Adhruḥ were Jews as well. On the passage from the Koran, see: Kister, *Arabica*, 9:272, 1964. It is said of this passage that 'it was brought down', meaning that God revealed it to the Prophet, before the Tabūk campaign, See *ibid.*, 278. However there is also a tradition that ascribes it to a period after Tabūk. See Ibn Qayyim al-Jawziyya, *al-Manār*, 102f.

does not recognise forced Islamisation), or (2) accept the status of protected people (defined for the first time in letters such as those quoted above), or (3) be killed (with the exception of women, children and slaves). Arabs, that is tribesmen, were in principle left with the choice between the first and third possibilities (though in practice there were exceptions).[29]

The expedition of Usāma b. Zayd

[41] The two raids across the Palestinian border which followed the defeat in Mu'ta, the attacks on Dhāt al-Salāsil and on Tabūk, did not seem to the Prophet sufficient to erase the shame and loss of prestige in the eyes of the northern tribes. The tribes of the Palestinian border region had still not learned their lesson. Some two and a half years after the attack on Tabūk, in May 632, Muḥammad invited Usāma b. Zayd b. Ḥāritha to the mosque and ordered him to act as commander of the army which was to invade Palestine again, and in the words of Ibn Isḥāq 'to spur on his horses to the Takhūm of al-Balqā' which is in Palestine', that is, the border area of Moab. Zayd b. Ḥāritha, the father of Usāma, a man who was very close to the Prophet (his freed slave) had commanded the army in the campaign of Mu'ta, as we have already seen, and was slain in battle. In addition to the Balqā', he was also ordered to descend upon the Dārūm. Some weeks later, the Prophet began to suffer from the disease which was to end his life. Already ill, he again announced with stubborn determination from his seat (the *minbar*) in the mosque that Usāma should head the expeditionary force, and rebuked those who thought that he did not merit this honour as being too young for the appointment, while the best commanders of the Muslim army, from Mecca and from Medina, were available. And thus Usāma did set up the expeditionary forces camp in Jurf, about four miles from Medina. The Prophet's orders to Usāma were unequivocal: he was to go out to the very place where his father had fought and fallen together with the other Muslim commanders: 'Attack the people of Ubna early in the morning and destroy them by fire!' He stipulated that children and women were not to be killed (they were to be taken captive) and handed him the battle flag. This raid also attracted the foremost Muslims, among them 'Umar ibn al-Khaṭṭāb and Abū 'Ubayda b. al-Jarrāḥ. Usāma managed to visit the Prophet before going into battle. He was exceedingly weak and even unable to speak, but he was still able to lift his hand to the heavens, afterwards pointing to Usāma, as a sign that he was praying for him.

The following day, as the army was preparing to leave, the Prophet

[29] See Schacht, *Introduction*, 130.

died. It was a Monday, towards evening, on 8 June 632. After Muḥammad's death became known, rumours were heard of the first tribal secession from Islam. The Muslims began to hesitate as to the necessity of setting out for Palestine. Abū Bakr, however, insistently repeated the Prophet's last instructions: carry out the campaign of Usāma's army! He also ordered 'Umar ibn al-Khaṭṭāb not to join the campaign as planned because he needed him in Medina, and Usāma agreed. And so Usāma went out at the head of an army of 3,000 men, of whom some 1,000 were cavalry troops. Abū Bakr, the caliph who had just taken up his position, accompanied them part of the way. At a distance of two days journey from Ubna, Usāma learned from a spy he had sent there that the inhabitants were relaxed and had no suspicion whatsoever of the approach of the Muslim army. Usāma therefore hurried to reach Ubna and launched a surprise attack, with the Muslims shouting their war cry: *Ya manṣūr amit* (Oh ye victor, kill!). They slaughtered the local population mercilessly, destroying, burning, and taking as many captives as they could. At the same time, Usāma rode astride his father's horse and succeeded in slaying his father's killer.

Ibn Hishām and Wāqidī's versions of what occurred at Ubna differ. Ṭabarī relates that Usāma was ordered that the attack should take place in the region of Trans-Jordan (al-Urdunn), at Ābil al-Zayt (Ābil of the Olives). One may assume that the attack took place somewhere in the neighbourhood of Moab and it is certainly unlikely that Ubna (probably a distortion), can be identified with Yavne, as some have asserted. Nor is the actual site of Ābil al-Zayt known.[30]

The great invasion

[42] Abū Bakr's absolute determination to fulfil the Prophet's orders and carry out the planned attack in the Moab area no matter what the outcome, indicates that he perceived, clearly and correctly, that Islam would stay alive only if the momentum of war continued. There were already troublesome signs of disintegration which were becoming increasingly blatant. Even in the circles of the most faithful – the people of Medina and Muḥammad's allies and his first disciples – there was growing bitterness and rancour, particularly as none of them had been chosen to be

[30] Ibn Hishām, 970, 999, 1006; Wāqidī, 1117–1127; Ṭabarī, *Ta'rīkh*, I, 1794f, 1797, 1810, 1845–1851. Muqaddasī, *Āqālīm*, 174: Dārūm means the region around Bayt Jubrīn. See the discussion on the site of the attack: De Goeje, *Mémoire*, 17ff; Ya'qūbī, *Buldān*, 329, and Mas'ūdī, *Tanbīh*, 273, who identify Ubna with Yavneh, and the latter also adds that Usāma attacked Ashdod (Azdūd) apart from Yavneh (Yabnā). See the detailed survey in Caetani, II, 490ff; 587–591.

the Prophet's replacement (*khalīfa*), but rather a man from the Muhājirūn people of Mecca, of the Quraysh tribe. It was therefore helpful for Abū Bakr to keep the unsatisfied elements out of town for a certain time by keeping them absorbed in the war effort led by Usāma.[31]

[43] The process of secession, the *ridda*, consisted mainly of the dissolution of the Muslim alliance and the forfeiting of obligations it had imposed on the tribes. Also, in various corners of the peninsula, local prophets were appearing on the scene and in this way, religion and politics were interwoven. In practical terms, the secession was expressed by the refusal to pay the *ṣadaqa*, the tax levied on the tribes as a contribution to the war fund, and non-compliance to the dictates of the envoys from Medina. After the army returned from its campaign in Palestine, a large force was organised under the command of Khālid ibn al-Walīd, and he put down the centres of insurgence one after the other and achieved his principal victory in routing Maslama (Musaylima, as the Muslims called him, a pejorative diminutive), a prophet who had emerged in the centre of the peninsula. There are various opinions with regard to the final suppression of the secession, but it seems that this happened in the main before the spring of 633; some centres of rebellion continued to exist for about another year.[32]

[44] Once he had restored the tribes to compliance and renewed the rule of Islam on the peninsula, Abū Bakr decided that the time had come to invade Palestinian territory. This occurred when he returned from his pilgrimage in the year 12, that is, February–March 634. Two large forces were sent to Palestine. The first was under ʿAmr b. al-Āṣ, who was ordered to pass through Eilat by the *muʿraqa* (by way of the mountains; which appears to be the correct interpretation of this word) to the coastal region. The second force was under a triad of commanders: Khālid b. Saʿīd b. al-ʿĀṣ, Abū ʿUbayda b. al-Jarrāḥ, and Shuraḥbīl b. Ḥasana. Khālid b. Saʿīd belonged to the clan of Umayya, from which the caliphs of Damascus were descended. He was one of the first to join Islam. Abū ʿUbayda was also a veteran of Islam, from the clan of Balḥārith, of Quraysh, and participated in the first *hijra* (to Ethiopia). He was one of Abū Bakr's most loyal adherents, as he was of ʿUmar, while Shuraḥbīl b. Ḥasana belonged to one of the 'southern' tribes (as is also indicated by his name, which was typical of the south), and it is not clear to which of them he belonged – perhaps Kinda, Tamīm or Lakhm. Ḥasana was the name of

31 See De Goeje, *Mémoire*, 20; a very detailed survey of the outset of the invasion, including Khālid b. al-Walīd's expedition from the Euphrates to the Ḥawrān. See Caetani, II, 1119–1236.

32 See the article Abū Bakr, in *EI*² (by W. M. Watt); the story of the *ridda* can also be found in any history of early Islam.

his mother, while 'Abdallah was his father's name. He too was one of the first followers of Islam and took part in the *hijra* to Ethiopia.

The second force was under orders to charge through the Tabūk region into Moab (al-Balqā'). Each of the three commanders stood at the head of a force of 3,000 fighters (some say 5,000). Khālid Ibn Sa'īd was the first to wield success in battle, when advancing according to Abū Bakr's orders through Tayma. He had to recruit additional fighters *en route*, on condition that they did not take part in the secession. Indeed, many groups of warriors joined him. The Byzantines were informed of the approach of this army and organised an opposing force amongst the Bahrā, Kalb, Salīḥ, Tanūkh, Lakhm, Judhām, and Ghassān tribes. Khālid wrote and informed Abū Bakr of this but the latter answered with a letter of encouragement and demanded that he continue to advance. And in fact as he advanced, the tribes in the Byzantines' service dispersed, while his own strength was being reinforced by these very tribes *en route*, many of whom joined Islam. In the neighbourhood of Ābil (evidently Ābil al-Zayt), he was attacked by a Byzantine commander (*biṭrīq*), named Bāhān. In one version Khālid overcame and slew him (but this is not correct, as we shall meet up with Bāhān [or Māhān] later on), and scattered his army to the winds. Whereas in another version, Bāhān delayed Khālid b. Sa'īd's advance considerably and even dealt him a serious setback at a place called Marj Ṣuffar (the valley of birds), east of the Sea of Galilee. Khālid's son Sa'īd was killed in this battle. Reinforcements sent by Abū Bakr, mostly tribesmen from Yemen and the centre of the peninsula, under the charge of 'Ikrima b. Abī Jahl and al-Walīd b. 'Uqba, succeeded, with great difficulty, in preventing the complete collapse of the Muslim offensive. Another factor which helped to improve the situation at that moment was the advance of the forces under Shuraḥbīl b. Ḥasana.[33]

[33] Ṭabarī, *Ta'rīkh*, I, 2108f; Balādhurī, *Futūḥ*, 107f; see Gibb's article on Abū 'Ubayda b. al-Djarrāḥ in *EI*²; on Khālid b. Sa'īd see Ibn al-Athīr, *Usd*, II, 90ff; on Shuraḥbīl b. Ḥasana, see *ibid.*, II, 391f; Balādhurī, *Ansāb*, I, 214; Ibn Qutayba, *Ma'ārif*, 325. Balādhurī, *Futūḥ*, 118ff, discusses the battle at Marj Ṣuffar as if it were a later occurrence, and according to him, it was Khālid b. Sa'īd himself who was killed on the morning after his betrothal, and not his son; and it seems that Ṭabarī's version is more reliable. De Goeje, *Mémoire*, 78–81, defends Balādhurī's chronology, and assumes that the battle at Marj Ṣuffar indeed took place after the conquest of Bet Shean, Peḥal (Pella), and Tiberias, during the advance to Damascus. Nöldeke, *ZDMG*, 29(1876), 425f, n. 3, tries to prove that Marj Ṣuffar is relatively near Damascus. Cf. also Dussaud, *Topogr.*, 318–322. This argument, however, does not contain enough to deny most of the Muslim sources which place this campaign in the days of Abū Bakr, and one cannot deny the possibility that a Muslim cavalry unit may have advanced, at an earlier date, to the Ḥawrān region. Ibn Kathīr, *Bidāya*, VII, 10, refers to a source according to which Māhān, the Byzantine commander, tried to handle the Muslims diplomatically: he says that Māhān knew they were driven into their campaign by suffering and hunger; he offered each ten dinars and food and clothing, adding the promise that in the future he would treat them similarly – all on condition that they return

[45] At the same time, Abū Bakr decided to accept 'Umar ibn al-Khaṭṭāb's advice, who for some time had been asking him to get rid of Khālid b. Sa'īd in the command. The reason for this, according to the sources, was that 'Umar doubted his loyalty, especially as it had taken him two months to swear his allegiance to the new caliph. It appears that already at this stage, the Umayyads had set their hearts on achieving the central role in the leadership of the Muslim camp, and this is precisely what 'Umar hoped to prevent. Nevertheless, in place of Khālid b. Sa'īd Abū Bakr appointed Yazīd b. Abī Sufyān, who came from another branch of the Umayyads, and who seemed more trustworthy (this was Yazīd the brother of Mu'āwiya, who afterwards became caliph).[34]

[46] Abū Bakr was particularly attentive to Yazīd b. Abī Sufyān, recently appointed by him to lead the major force intended to go into action in Palestine. He accompanied him part of the way on foot, while Yazīd rode on his horse. Sources ascribed to Abū Bakr the issuing of an order of the day to the forces going out to conquer the north, but there are no identical views as to whom the order was given; whether to Usāma b. Zayd or to Yazīd b. Abī Sufyān. Some ascribe similar instructions to the Prophet; these are as follows:

ten precepts have I for you, remember them in my name. Do not betray. Do not embezzle or behave craftily. Do not disable. Do not kill a small child or an elderly person or a woman. Do not uproot palm trees and do not burn them. Do not fell a fruit-bearing tree. Do not slaughter sheep, steer, or camel, unless it be for eating. When on your way, you will encounter those who have shut themselves up

to their homes. The Muslims naturally rejected his offer with contempt. Cf. *ibid.*, VII, 5: Heraclius writes to his administrators in Palestine and suggests they come to some compromise with the Arabs, by which the latter will receive half the taxes of al-Shām (Syria and Palestine), while the mountainous regions (?Jibāl al-Rūm) will remain in the hands of the Byzantines. Māhān's name is written in various forms, such as Ahān, Bāhān, cf. Ibn 'Asākir, I, 452; in a Byzantine source from the first half of the fifteenth century: Blanēs, see Klein-Franke, *BZ*, 65(1972), 5 (1.5). De Goeje, *Mémoire*, proposes Baanes (Bāhān). Perhaps this is the name Makhaōn, see: Preisigke, *Namenbuch*, 210. According to Sa'īd Ibn Biṭrīq, II, 13, Māhān was the commander appointed by Heraclius over the Arab tribes, such as Ghassān, Judhām, Kalb, Lakhm, etc.; Ibn Kathīr, *Bidāya*, VII, 6 states that Māhān was an Armenian. See the discussion (comparatively recent) in Stratos, 64, who claims that his name was Vahan or Vaanes, and that he was a Persian, son of Shahrbaraz, the Persian commander who led a rebellion in 630 and wanted to become king of the Persians; Vahan escaped and fled to Heraclius after his father was killed. See also a further note, *ibid.*, 209. Shaban, *Islamic History*, 25, tries to emphasise the fact that at the head of the great invasion Abū Bakr appointed mainly people of Quraysh ('Amr b. al-'Āṣ, Khālid b. Sa'īd, Yazīd b. Abī Sufyān); these were people who knew southern Palestine well, and also north of this region, due to the widespread commercial transactions they had conducted previously.

[34] On the subject of the ousting of Khālid b. Sa'īd, see Ṭabarī, *Ta'rīkh*, I, 2079f; Balādhurī, *Futūḥ*, 108.

in monk's cells, do them no harm and permit them to devote themselves to their chosen paths. You will encounter people bearing vessels, offering you all kinds of foods. Invoke God over every dish. When you meet people who have shaven their heads in the middle and left a sort of halo around, strike them with spears.

A remnant of these instructions turned up in the Muslim traditions, and was included in the *ḥadīth* collections in the form of a taboo (in the Prophet's name) on *qazʿ* – this being the name given this type of tonsure.[35]

[47] Considerable contradictions in the sources appear regarding the time when the conquests began. But it appears that in principle, we have to accept the description which places the drive northwards immediately after the suppression of the attempted secession. While Abū Bakr and his aides and the entire Muslim camp were still basking in the aura of victory and prestige which had spread far and wide as a result of putting down the rebels, the caliph wanted to take immediate advantage of the situation by invading the region which would confront them with the least opposition, and that was the area of which the Arab tribes were in charge. Indeed we have seen how the tribes of Trans-Jordan receded with the approach of the

[35] Ṭabarī, *Ta'rīkh*, I, 1850; the Prophet's words to Usāma b. Zayd, according to Wāqidī, when charging him with the mission of revenging the death of his father, are somewhat similar in content but not precisely the same. See Wāqidī, 1117; cf. the shortened version of Yaʿqūbī, *Ta'rīkh*, II, 82; and see in the anonymous Syriac chronicle, 240, a version translated from the Arabic original, in which the killing of the 'people of the haircut' is omitted. See De Goeje, *Mémoire*, 23, the discussion on the significance of the last two passages. There is no doubt that the intention was to order the killing of people with these particular haircuts, who were, according to De Goeje, *ibid.*, Christian priests, differentiating them from the monks. But it is possible that the reference here is to the Manichaean priests, who were especially abhorred by the Muslim leadership. Hinting at the circle (hair? or band?) around the head, see in the picture of Mani, with the Manichaean seal, in Adam, *Texte*, 105, and others which are similar, *ibid.*, in continuation, 108. On the other hand, the type of haircut described here was indeed common among the Christian priests; although from the decisions of the fourth Council in Toledo (which met at precisely the same time as the events described here, in 633), one can understand that there was also a 'haircut of the heretics': 'Omnes, clerici vel lectores sicut levitae et sacerdotes, detonso superius toto capite, inferius solam circuli coronam relinquant', that is, all the priesthood, readers, the Levites and the Priests, should shave the upper part of their pates, leaving a round circle of hair, in order to differentiate themselves from the: 'ritus haereticorum: qui . . . in solo capitis apice modicum circulum tondent' ('a custom of the heretics who . . . shave the tops of their heads and nothing else'); see Mansi, X, 630; cf. the detailed discussion in Leclerq, Tonsure, *DACL*, XV (2), 2430–2443. Maḥbūb (Agapius), 179 (439), mentions the decree issued by the Emperor Mauricius in the eleventh year of his reign, 593, that the Jews of Antioch, who were to be evicted from the city, should shave their heads in the middle, in order to have some mark of identification. The matter is therefore complex, and there is no way of identifying these tonsured individuals to whom the caliph is referring. *Qazʿ*, see, for instance, in Bukhārī, *Ṣaḥīḥ*, *k. al-libās, bāb al-qazʿ*; cf. Goldziher, *MGWJ*, 29(1880), 356.

advancing Muslim army and how many of them joined the ranks of the Muslims.[36]

[48] This is completely in accord with what Theophanes and Nicephorus, the patriarch of Constantinople, tell us from the Byzantine angle. According to these writers, the Byzantine governor delayed the payment of thirty gold livres which he owed the Arabs who were responsible for the security of the desert borderlands. When they came to ask for their due, the eunuch in charge of finances replied, 'My master has dificulty enough in paying his own soldiers; how then can he pay such dogs?' This led to the Arabs' abandonment of the Byzantines and joining of the Muslims descending on Gaza. Similar information is conveyed by Sa'īd Ibn Biṭrīq, who mentions that Māhān, Heraclius' governor of the Arab tribes, wrote to Manṣūr, the governor of Damascus, that he should pay the tribes' envoys whatever was owing to them. When these envoys arrived in Damascus, Manṣūr told them: 'The emperor does not want such a large army, for the Arabs are only good for forays, and if they will have to contend with an army that will force them to do battle, their entire armies will be slain. And this is an army which requires large sums of money and Damascus does not have enough to give them.' There were those who claimed that Manṣūr said this intentionally, so that the loyal tribes would disperse and Damascus would fall to the Muslims. Behind this incident, one can also discern the weakness of Byzantium. Although the Byzantines had just then defeated the Persians, their treasuries had been emptied as a result of the ceaseless wars. One can also discern the shifting trend in the Arabs' state of mind, concurrent with Islam's early victories in the border area of Palestine. However, when the Muslims actually first encountered the Byzantine army on the battlefield, somewhere in central Trans-Jordan, and headed by Bāhān, they suffered an overwhelming defeat which the Muslim sources tend to make light of or do not always mention. This was the reversal at Marj Ṣuffar, and it appears to have occurred in the summer of 634.[37]

[36] See De Goeje, *Mémoire*, 25–29, and his notes on the conflicting texts. He himself doubted the veracity of the description in Ṭabarī (according to Sayf; this is most of the description given above): he is inclined to accept the traditions in Balādhurī, which shift the battle of Marj Ṣuffar to Muḥarram, in the year AH 14 (March AD 635), and claim that Khālid (and not his son), was killed in that battle. But it seems that precisely the somewhat unusual version of Sayf is the correct one, while the others tried to lend greater stature to personalities who later became more accepted in Islam, particularly Abū 'Ubayda b. al-Jarrāḥ.

[37] Theophanes, 335. Nicephorus, 26f. Cf. De Goeje, *Mémoire*, 29, and see Sa'īd Ibn Biṭrīq, II, 114; cf. also Caetani, II, 1113f.

The expedition of ʿAmr ibn al-ʿĀṣ

[49] The right wing of the Muslim offensive which pushed eastward in Trans-Jordan was forced to come to a standstill, and perhaps even to withdraw southward to the border region, having evidently been repulsed. At the same time, the left wing advanced under ʿAmr ibn al-ʿĀṣ, via the ʿArāvā into the coastal region. According to the tradition in Balādhurī, 'the first battle between the Muslims and their enemies was fought at a village in the neighbourhood of Gaza called Dāthin, against the governor (*biṭrīq*) of Gaza. A battle raged until God gave the victory to His followers, routing His enemies and disbanding their troops'. But prior to this, it seems that there was an encounter in the ʿArāvā region, when six Byzantine commanders with 3,000 men opposed the Muslims. On that occasion the Muslims overcame the Byzantines. One of the latter's officers was killed, and the Muslims pursued them until Dubya, or Dābya, as Balādhurī puts it. Ṭabarī says in his parallel version that the pursuit lasted until Dāthina, and he is evidently correct.[38]

[50–51] This battle is described in an anonymous Syriac chronicle as follows:

In the year 945, on Friday the 4th of Shevat (the fourth of February 634 was actually a Friday), at the ninth hour, there was a battle between the Byzantines and the Arabs of Muḥammad in Palestine, 12 miles from the town of Gaza. The Byzantines fled and abandoned the commander (the *patricius*, in Arabic sources: *biṭrīq*) in the Jordan, and the Arabs slew him. Some 4000 poor villagers from Palestine were killed, Christians, Jews and Samaritans and the Arabs destroyed the place completely.

The fact that the Samaritans fought alongside the Byzantines against the Muslims is mentioned in other Syriac chronicles as well. According to these, the forces opposing the Muslim army consisted of 5,000 fighters, recruited by the patricius Sergius from among the Byzantines and the Samaritans (Shamrāʾē). The Muslims were victorious and first of all killed

[38] See Balādhurī, *Futūḥ*, 109. Dābya is certainly a distortion of the name Dāthina. The name Dāthin (or Dāthina) is parallel etymologically to the Hebrew Dōshen, and this may have been the name of the place. For we find *dōshnāh shel Yerīḥō* (see *Sifrē* on Num., par. 81 [ed. Horowitz, 77] and its parallels). It is not unlikely that a place called Dōshna near Jericho is intended, despite the fact that the Arab sources say it is in the vicinity of Gaza; hence one can assume that ʿAmr advanced through the ʿArāvā until the region of the Dead Sea and from there veered westward. This assumption is supported by the Syriac source which is quoted below, according to which the Muslims captured the Byzantine commander 'in the Jordan'. The meaning of the word *ʿarābā* (in the Arab sources) was not clear to Yāqūt, the Muslim geographer of the Middle Ages, and some modern scholars are also puzzled by it, but it is merely the ʿArāvā whose meaning we have become accustomed to. See De Goeje, *Mémoire*, 30f. Cf. Ṭabarī, *Taʾrīkh*, I, 2108; Ibn Kathīr, *Bidāya*, VII, 4. See in Saʿīd ibn Biṭrīq, II, 10, instead of Dāthin: 'Tādūn, a village in the Gaza area, near Ḥijāz'. In Theophanes, 332: Dathesmos.

all the Samaritans. The patricius Sergius managed to escape, but the Arabs caught him and had him executed. We find contrary information about the Samaritans in Balādhurī, according to whom the Samaritans served as spies and informers to the Muslims.[39] The Byzantine commander was also called Sergius, according to Theophanes; he went out of Caesarea to face the Arabs at the head of a small force, some 300 strong, but the Arabs defeated him and he was killed. The Arabs already dominated Hēra at the time (it is not clear where this is) as well as the entire Gaza district (*khōra Gazēs*).[40]

[52] The expedition of ‘Amr ibn al-‘Āṣ is reflected also in a Christian source I have already mentioned above, which it seems is actually a product of the time, that is, the Didaskalia of Jacob. Justus of Acre (Ptolemais), son of Samuel, argues with Jacob; while setting out his arguments, he recalls that he received a letter from his brother Abraham from Caesarea, telling of a false messiah who has appeared among the Arabs (*en mesō Sarakēnōn*) and that they have killed Sergius, the *candidatus*. According to Justus, the Prophet who appeared within the ranks of the Arabs is an omen of the true Messiah who has yet to come; but one of the sages of Sykamina (which is Haifa), denied this, for it is not the manner of prophets to come mounted and with the sword.[41]

39 BM Or 14, 643, fol. 50*v*, printed in Land, *An.Syr.* I, 17, and see his Latin translation, *ibid.*, 116, and its copy in De Goeje, *Mémoire*, 30. It is possible that in writing ‘Yarden’ the chronicler who apparently already wrote under Islam, meant northern Palestine, i.e., jund Urdunn. De Goeje's assumption that there was a distortion here of the Syriac text has no basis; nor has that which Caetani, II, 1144, n. 2, writes in his wake. The anonymous Syriac chronicle, 241f, contains a long description of the battle with Sergius, according to which most of the fighters in the Byzantine forces were Samaritans, in all, 5000 men. A similar version can be found in Michael the Syrian (Chabot), II, 413 (French translation; 411f, in the original). See also Bar Hebraeus (Bedjan), 99f; see Budge's English translation, 93. And see further Balādhurī, *Futūḥ*, 158, and cf. Lammens, *Yazīd*, 385.

40 Theophanes, 336. Caetani's assumption, in II, 1143, that Hēra is perhaps Ḥīra, and that the subject being dealt with is the war with the Persians and Khālid ibn al-Walīd, is not convincing. See the description of the raid on Gaza (within the context of the first raids): Pernice, *Eraclio*, 272ff; this description is arbitrary to a large extent, and is evidently not based on a study of the sources themselves.

41 See the words of Justus, in the Bonwetsch edition, 86; cf. Krauss, *Zion* (ha-me'assēf), 2(1927/8), 30; Crone and Cook, 3ff; Constantelos, *Byzantion*, 42(1972), 351f; Maas, *BZ*, 20(1911), 576; the ‘candidate’, a Roman administrative position, was in this period the commander of a Byzantine elite military unit; Liudprand mentions the *candidati* in the same breath as the *spatharii*; see Leclercq, Candidator, *DACL*, II(2), 1842; see various interpretations of this term: Du Cange, *Gloss.*, s.v. See also the list of *spatharokandidatoi*: Beneševič, *BNGJ*, 5(1926/7), 133; see also Bury, *Imperial Administration*, 22; The candidate wore a special gold chain; see *ibid.*, 113. It is obvious that they were a select body, apparently commanders in the cavalry units. See what is said in Procopius, *Wars*, VII, xxxviii, 5 (Loeb V, 20–22) on Asbadus, who succeeded in becoming one of Justinian's guardsmen because he was considered a candidate and was the commander of the cavalry units which served as a garrison. The word ‘candidatus’ is derived from the white colour of their dress.

The expedition of Khālid ibn al-Walīd

[53] Until now, we have seen how the Muslim tribes pushed forward towards southern Palestine, largely owing to the weak defense put up by the opposition led by those Arab tribes which were faithful to Byzantium, as well as by a small Byzantine garrison which could not withstand the onslaught of the Muslim cavalry. But it seems that both the army in the field as well as the caliph knew well that this advance was insufficient to conquer all of *al-Shām*, or Syria and Palestine. They estimated accurately that in order to fortify and consolidate their initial achievements, they had to gather additional forces and try to finally overthrow the Byzantines' power of resistance. With this necessity in mind, and particularly in view of the increasing rumours that were reaching them about the concentration of Byzantine forces and their preparations to go into action, the Muslim leadership headed by the caliph Abū Bakr decided to enter on a rather unusual course, a very daring and dangerous one. Abū Bakr ordered Khālid ibn al-Walīd, the commander of the major Muslim forces who at that time were fighting the Persians in Iraq, to go to the assistance of the tribes struggling in Palestine. This move indicated that priority was being given to the Byzantine front, and this would clearly endanger the Persian campaign. There was also the risk to the forces that were to move from Iraq to Syria through the desert, without any pause to prepare themselves adequately for such a campaign, something which had never been attempted before.

According to the description of Ibn Isḥāq, Abū Bakr wrote to Khālid, who was stationed in Ḥīra near the Euphrates, ordering him to depart for al-Shām with the pick of his men and leave the weaker elements behind in Iraq. Khālid thought this a plot connived at by 'Umar ibn al-Khaṭṭāb (who harboured resentment towards Khālid, as we shall see below), in order that he should not be recognised as the conqueror of Iraq. Despite what he had been told of the difficulties awaiting him *en route*, particularly the lack of water, Khālid did not give way, and using the best methods of preparing the camels for long treks without water, according to the extensive experience of the Bedouin in these matters, he managed to bring his men through the desert successfully as far as Buṣrā in the Ḥawrān, via Tadmur, in a pattern forming an arc whose outer curve faced northward.

The traditions contradict one another as to the number of fighters, fluctuating from 500 to 3,000; one of the versions even mentions 9,000. Buṣrā was taken after a siege and submitted voluntarily (by *ṣulḥ*), and a tax (*jizya*) was levied on its inhabitants. 'And this was the first city taken in *al-Shām* in the days of Abū Bakr.' In the region of Damascus, Khālid first met up with the great tribe, Banū Ghassān, who were Christians. He found them near Marj Rāhiṭ, celebrating Easter, which that year fell on

24 April. It ensues that Khālid's forces penetrated into Palestine through the Galilee at the beginning of May 634.[42]

Ijnādayn

[54–55] According to Balādhurī, the Byzantine army at this stage totalled 100,000 men. Arab sources mention the names and ranks of some of the Byzantine commanders. Sergius, governor of Caesarea; Theodore (or Theodorikos), the brother of the emperor (and the sources stress that he was a full brother on both the mother's and the father's side) who was the chief commander; Georgios son of Theodore; Arṭabūn, which is evidently a distortion of *tribunus*; a man who held the title of *qinqilār*, or *qubqulār* (evidently *cubicularius*); *fiqār*, or *vicarius*; and *drunjār* or *drungarius*. Bāhān, who has already been mentioned at the start of the war, is mentioned again. As to the Muslims, their numbers were far less than those of the Byzantines. The right wing was situated eastwards of Trans-Jordan, with the three commanders I have already mentioned above, Abū 'Ubayda, Shuraḥbīl and Yazīd, and they seem to have moved westward. 'Amr ibn al-'Āṣ was then somewhere in the south, between the neighbourhood of the Dead Sea and somewhere south of Gaza, while Khālid, it seems, was based in the Galilee. One can estimate that the entire Muslim

[42] See Caetani, II, 1193–1236, especially the table, *ibid.*, 1222f; see the description of the desert crossing in Ṭabarī, *Ta'rīkh*, I, 2122ff; Ibn al-Athīr, *Kāmil*, II, 408; the campaign through the Syrian desert was led by a man of the Banū Ṭayy', Rāfi' b. 'Umayra, who hesitated at first, and claimed that even a single horseman would not dare to take this route across the desert let alone an entire army with the logistics involved. The fighters were ordered to provide themselves with enough water for five days; twenty choice she-camels were deprived of water and then permitted to drink as much as they could, and every day, *en route*, four of them were slaughtered and the horses were then allowed to drink from the contents of their bellies. On the fifth day, the people and the horses were left without water, and then, in an almost miraculous way, Rāfi' managed to discover a spring which he remembered from childhood, under a zyzyphus tree, although this very tree had already been felled by someone. See in De Goeje, *Mémoire*, 37–50, a detailed discussion on the various contradictory versions concerning the details of Khālid's route and the number of fighters he had with him. On the conquest of Buṣrā, see Ṭabarī, *Ta'rīkh*, I, 2125; his version according to which Khālid had already met the three commanders of the army fighting in Palestine, Abū 'Ubayda, Shuraḥbīl and Yazīd, in Buṣrā and they all participated in the siege on the town, is not really credible. At the time, these three were far off in the south of Palestine. Discussion of the dates: De Goeje, *ibid.*, 39f. Ṭabarī, *Ta'rīkh*, I, 2109, has another version in which Khālid left Ḥīra on Rabī' II, but Rabī' II, in the 13th year started on 4 June, and this contradicts the fact that the raid on the Banū Ghassān occurred during Easter. Evidently there is some error here, and the correct version would be that Khālid arrived from Ḥīra at the beginning of June 634. See also Ya'qūbī, *Ta'rīkh*, II, 151, who within the framework of Khālid's exploits (also found in other sources), tells of taking captive twenty young Jews from the synagogue, in an undefined place on the Euphrates. See further: Pernice, *Eraclio*, 275f.

army numbered no more than 40,000 fighters. The decisive battle took place on the 28th of Jumādā I in the year AH 13, which is the 30th of July, AD 634, or two months after Khālid reached Palestine, in a place called Ijnādayn, which most of the Muslim sources say is situated between Ramla and Bayt Jibrīn. The site has still to be identified. One explanation is that the name Ijnādayn, which seems to mean 'two armies', is the equivalent of *legionum*, that is Lajjūn, or Megiddo. In favour of this supposition is the fact that Megiddo is a critical point strategically and it is reasonable to assume that the united Muslim forces, whose columns advanced from the north (Khālid) and the south ('Amr, Abū 'Ubayda and the rest) actually met up with the Byzantines at this crucial juncture, which the latter had to defend with all their might. However, we do not have enough data to take a definite stand on the matter. At any rate, the Muslims scored a smashing success which now enabled the tribes to dominate all of Palestine. Heraclius at the time, was stationed in Ḥimṣ, according to Arab sources, and when he learned of the defeat he hurried towards Antioch, as if he wished to avoid the dangerous site.[43] After the

[43] As to the date, some place it earlier and some later, but the preferable version is 28 Jumādā I; see De Goeje, *Mémoire*, 51. Also see *ibid.*, 52–60, the discussion on the site of Ijnādayn and his assumption, which seems unfounded, that the Arab sources confused the battle of Ijnādayn with that of the Yarmūk, for Ijnādayn, according to one source, is near Hebron and Hebron is near Yarmūt (a Biblical location [Jarmuth] mentioned also by Eusebius in his Onomastikon; see de Goeje, *ibid.*, 59, n. 2). See Ṭabarī, *Ta'rīkh*, I, 2087 who gives the name of the emperor's brother as Tadhāriq. The Byzantine army concentrated in Jilliq (or Jallaq?), in northern Palestine. Jurja b. Tūdhra was sent to oppose Yazīd b. Abū Sufyān. The *durāquṣ* (droungarios?) was sent against Shuraḥbīl b. Ḥasana; the *fiqār* (vicarius?) ibn Nasṭūs was sent against Abū 'Ubayda. See *ibid.*, 2125: Qubqulār (perhaps it was qunqulār). As for the date, see *ibid.*, 2126. See also Balādhurī, *Futūḥ*, 113f; Ya'qūbī, *Ta'rīkh*, II, 150f; Khalīfa ibn Khayyāṭ, I, 103f; Ibn 'Asākir, I, 478ff, Ibn Kathīr, *Bidāya*, V, 54f; Ibn Ḥubaysh, 127, points out explicitly that the battle of Ijnādayn took place twenty-four days before the death of Abū Bakr (22 Jumādā II) and this confirms the date mentioned above. Dhahabī, *Ta'rīkh*, I, 375: Ijnādayn is situated between Ramla and Jarash. Ibn Kathīr, *Bidāya*, VII, 5f, mentions among the Byzantine commanders Jurja b. Būdhīhā (evidently he is Tūdhrā, which is Theodore, in Ṭabarī), who was in charge of the central sector of the army, according to him. The name of the cubicular, who was one of Heraclius' eunuchs, was Nasṭūras. See further on the date, Ibn al-Athīr, *Usd*, I, 37 (s.v. Abān v. Sa'īd); Ibn 'Abd al-Barr, *Istī'āb*, I, 64 (as mentioned); on the battle, see also: Mawṣilī, *Wasā'il*, 217; Yāqūt, *Buldān*, I, 136. On the Byzantine offices mentioned in Muslim sources in the account of this battle: Droungarios, see Bury, *Imperial Administration*, 41f; Beneševič, *BNGJ*, 5(1926/7), 125, who explains that he was a commander of a *moira*, which is a unit of some 1000 to 3000 men; cf. Sophocles, *Greek Lexicon*, s.v.; also Ibn Khurdādhbih, 111, who says that the ṭaranjār (droungarios) commanded over 1,000 men. See also Guilland, I, 563–587: 'Le drongaire et le grand drongaire de la Veille' (an article of the same name was first printed in *BZ*, 43 [1950], 340–365), according to whom the droungarios was one of the commanders of one of the four army corps of the Byzantine army, namely that which was called *viglē, vigiliae*. There were also the droungarios of the navy, see 'Le drongaire de la flotte': *ibid.*, 535–562; *BZ*, 44(1951), 212–240; it is difficult to tell to which droungarios the Arab sources are referring (Guilland does not mention them). As to the cubicularios, see *ibid.*, 269–282, Titres des eunuques (*REB*, 13, 1955, 50–84); the bearers of the rank

victory at Ijnādayn, the Muslims conquered most of the cities in Palestine one after the other; Gaza, Sebastia, Nābulus, Lod, Yavne, Emmaus, Bet Guvrin, Jaffa and Rafiaḥ.[44]

Additional conquests

[56] On the 23rd of August, 634, the caliph Abū Bakr died and 'Umar ibn al-Khaṭṭāb, his right-hand man and closest aide throughout the period of his caliphate, became caliph in his place. Towards the end of the summer, as we have seen, the conquest of most of the cities of Palestine had come to an end. Evidence of this could be heard in the sermon held by the Jerusalem patriarch, Sophronius, on Christmas Day that year. In his words, the Arabs ('the Saracens') 'plunder cities, despoil the fields, burn the villages, destroy holy monasteries'. Out of fear of the Arabs, the Christians celebrating in Jerusalem were not permitted to visit Bethlehem, as was their annual custom on this day, and they remained shut securely behind the city walls.[45]

[57] Remnants of the Byzantine army concentrated in the Jordan Valley in the neighbourhood of Bet Shean after their downfall in Ijnādayn. There they attempted to stave off the Muslims' advance northward and eastward, towards Tiberias and the northern Trans-Jordan. They dammed off the irrigation canals with the intention of creating large quagmires, but despite the difficulties and the losses suffered while trying to cross the marshes with their horses, the Muslims succeeded in breaking through to the east and taking over Fiḥl (Pella) after a battle, evidently in the middle of January 635. Immediately afterwards, Tiberias capitulated to the Muslims together with all the towns in the area. The conditions of the surrender of these localities (such as Tiberias and Bet Shean) were that half the inhabitants' houses should go to the Muslims, they would pay a dinar poll-tax annually and they would hand over to the Muslims a quantity of wheat or oats equivalent to the number of seeds planted on each unit of land.

were eunuchs considered of high status, even of nobility, who accompanied the emperor on his military expeditions; and he mentions (based on Nicephorus of Constantinople) Marianus the cubicular appointed by Heraclius to halt the advance of the Arabs into Egypt.

44 Balādhurī, *Futūḥ*, 138. He points out that Sebastia and Nābulus were taken on conditions of *amān*, that is, personal and property security in exchange for the payment of taxes. In Bet Guvrin, 'Amr took over an estate called 'Ajlūn, named after a client whom he had there. Emmaus was called by the Byzantines Nikopolis, and the fact that the Arabs called it 'Imwās, proves that it was called by its ancient name by the people of Palestine. It appears that later on it was the main base of the Muslim army in Palestine, which we can surmise from the fact that the name was also used for the greatest plague that broke out among the Muslim army, *ṭā'ūn* 'Imwās. See: Vincent et Abel, *Emmaus*, 356f.

45 See Sophronius' sermon: De Goeje, *Mémoire*, 174f, and also Schönborn, 90f.

Concurrently, Shuraḥbīl conquered all the towns of Urdunn (which is *Palaestina secunda* in the Arab sources) and their citadels, including Sūsīta (Sūsiya), Afēq (Afīq), Jarash, Bayt Ra's, Qedesh (Qadas), and all of the Golan, Acre, Tyre, and Sepphoris (Ṣafūriyya).[46]

(58) At about the same time, Ḥimṣ, in Syria, was captured and Damascus lay under siege. Panic was rife in Damascus when the taking of Tiberias and the other cities in northern Palestine, in the Ḥawrān and in the Golan, became known. The siege on Damascus began on the 16th of Muḥarram of the year AH 14, the 12th of March AD 635, and continued for half a year, until the 10th of September. We shall not go into the many details of the victory over Damascus, but it will suffice to point to the fact that there are hints of betrayal within the city itself, apart from the pressure exerted by the Muslims, and in this connection the name of Manṣūr b. Sarjūn (Sergius), the governor of the town, is mentioned, for he seems to have secretly hoped for the Muslims' triumph. Here too, the name of Māhān, or Bāhān, arises, as the chief Byzantine commander; Nasṭās (Anastasius) is also mentioned, as is Theodore the Sakellarios. There is an interesting episode concerning the great church of St John in Damascus; according to the terms of settlement, the church was divided in half and

[46] De Goeje, *Mémoire*, 70ff; Suyūṭī, *Ta'rīkh*, 131; Ibn Sa'd, IV(1), 144; the battle of Fiḥl occurred in Dhū'l-Qa'da of the year 13 (December 634 – January 635). According to Ṭabarī, *Ta'rīkh*, I, 2158, the people of Bet Shean were prepared to fight the Muslim army, commanded by Shuraḥbīl b. Ḥasana, but in the meantime, they learned of the setback in Fiḥl. Although a few of them put up some resistance to the Muslims and lost their lives in the process, the remainder of the inhabitants of Bet Shean surrendered to the Muslims by a peace pact (*ṣulḥ*); see the same also in Ibn Ḥubaysh, 138. For the terms of the surrender see Ṭabarī, *ibid.*, 2159; on the opening of the dams in the Bet Shean valley, *ibid.*, 2145: Bet Shean from that time was given the cognomen 'the marshy one' (*dhāt al-radgha*). It should be noted that the traditions on the conquest of Fiḥl and the events in the Bet Shean area are recounted in the name of Ibn Ḥumayd, by Salama and Ibn Isḥāq, and that these are traditions taken from a very early commentary on the Koran by Sa'īd ibn Jubayr al-Asadī, a man from Kūfa who was one of the first commentators, and who was killed by al-Ḥajjāj in 714 (see Sezgin, I, 28ff). According to Khalīfa ibn Khayyāṭ, I, 117, all the towns in the area were taken in battle, with the exception of Tiberias, which surrendered willingly by *ṣulḥ*; see also *ibid.*, 103f. See also Ya'qūbī, *Buldān*, 328; Tiberias yielded to Abū 'Ubayda of its own accord, whereas the remainder of towns in the Urdunn had been captured earlier by Khālid b. al-Walīd and 'Amr ibn al-'Āṣ. See Ya'qūbī, *Ta'rīkh*, II, 159f; cf. Ibn Ḥubaysh, 138f; Ibn 'Asākir, I, 486, 525; Dhahabī, *Ta'rīkh*, I, 377; II, 10; see also Ibn al-'Imād, I, 28. Balādhurī, *Futūḥ*, 116, notes that the condition laid down for the peaceful surrender of Tiberias was that houses unoccupied because their owners had fled, would be handed over to the Muslims and that a site would be allotted to the Muslims for a mosque; but the people of Tiberias afterwards defaulted on the contract with the help of remnants of the Byzantine army, and then Abū 'Ubayda sent 'Amr ibn al-'Āṣ to them, along with 4,000 men and they surrendered for the second time, under the same conditions. Some say that this occurred under the command of Shuraḥbīl. See also Yāqūt, *Buldān*, III, 509. Modern scholars speak of the Dekapolis conquest; whereas actually in the list of captured towns (the most complete list is contained in Balādhurī), only a few are towns of the Dekapolis.

the west side was allotted to the Christians while the east side was given to the Muslims.[47]

The battle of the Yarmūk

[59] The emperor Heraclius, who according to the Arab sources was in Antioch at the time (635), began with supreme effort to organise a counter-attack. According to Ibn Isḥāq, Heraclius first of all gathered together those Arab tribes who were opposed to Islam – the Lakhm, Judhām, Balqīn, Balī, 'Āmila, Quḍā'a and Ghassān – in addition to which he also had army units of Armenians. Heading the army stood 'Heraclius' eunuch', the Sakellarios Theodore. Georgios (Jurja) was in command of the Armenians, while Jabala b. al-Ayham, of the Banū Ghassān, led the Arab tribes still loyal to the Byzantines. This army numbered 100,000 men; some claim that it comprised as many as 200,000 men. Some sources mention that Bāhān was still in charge of the army. Opposing them was the Muslim army, with a mere 24,000 fighters. Although it is not mentioned specifically, there must have been Aramaic-speaking recruits from the local populations and Greek-speaking Byzantine soldiers in this conglomerate army of the Byzantines, for it is clear that it was not marked in any way by its uniformity or its unity.[48]

47 De Goeje, *Mémoire*, 82–103; Ibn 'Asākir, I, 493–526; see *ibid.* on p. 501, the tradition according to which 'a monk' (here certainly meaning Manṣūr) handed over the town to Khālid ibn al-Walīd, while another section of the Muslim army broke into the town forcibly. See Ṭabarī, *Ta'rīkh*, I, 2151ff, on the siege; according to one of his versions, the siege lasted only seventy days; but *ibid.*, 2155, the tradition according to Wāqidī mentions that the siege went on for six months. Afterwards members of the family of Manṣūr b. Sarjūn acted as chief administrators for the Umayyad caliphs; his son, Sergius (Sarjūn), was a major official of 'Abd al-Malik, see Balādhurī, *Futūḥ*, 193; cf. Ṭabarī, *Ta'rīkh*, II, 205, 228, 239, 837. The anonymous Syriac chronicle, 248, calls him John the diakonos, son of Sargūn. See also on Manṣūr b. Sarjūn, Sa'īd ibn Biṭrīq, II, 14f, according to whom Māhān became a monk on Mount Sinai out of fear of punishment for the fall of Damascus, and who wrote a commentary on the sixth chapter of psalms (*al-mazmūr, zabūr Da'ūd*). See a short summary of this family's matters in Stratos, 61, n. 214. See a fragment from MS BM Add 14461, edited by Nöldeke, *ZDMG*, 29(1876), 77f, from a Syriac chronicle, which has the date on which the Byzantines fled Damascus as 10 August (Av), which is earlier by a month from that given in the Muslim sources. See also Theophanes, 337f, who mentions Bāhān and the Sakellarios as those who stood at the head of the defence of Damascus. On the church of Damascus, see De Goeje, *ibid.*, 96f; cf. in addition to the sources he refers to: al-Badrī, 53.

48 See Ṭabarī, *Ta'rīkh*, I, 2347, and cf. *ibid.*, 2389f, an unclear description of a trial attack by the Byzantines in an unknown place which he calls Marj al-Rūm (valley of the Byzantines), evidently north of Damascus, under the command of the Byzantine Shanas (or Shanash), who fell in battle. See Balādhurī, *Futūḥ*, 135ff, where he speaks of a Byzantine army of 200,000 men, 'Byzantines, people of al-Shām (Syria and Palestine), people of al-Jazīra (northern Mesopotamia) and Armenia'; see in Caetani, III, 553, traditions on 300 or even 400 thousand Byzantine fighters. See also Khalīfa ibn Khayyāṭ, I, 118; Ibn 'Asākir, I, 529, 531; Dhahabī, *Ta'rīkh*, II, 10; Ibn Kathīr, *Bidāya*, VII, 7. The Sakellarios is described

[60] In view of the tremendous concentration of forces organised by the Byzantines in preparation for their great counter-attack, the Muslim leaders decided to shorten their front. After consultation with the caliph through letters, they executed a complete withdrawal and actually left Syria, both in the north (Ḥimṣ) and in the south (Damascus). According to the tradition preserved by Balādhurī, it is told that the Muslims returned the taxes which they had levied on the inhabitants of Ḥimṣ, saying: 'It is impossible for us to be your helpers and defenders, therefore take care of yourselves.' Then the people of Ḥimṣ are said to have retorted:

Your protection and sense of justice are preferable to injustice and violence; therefore we shall stand together with your leader and protect the town from Heraclius' armies. The Jews of Ḥimṣ even swore on the Torah that they would not permit Heraclius' governor to enter Ḥimṣ, and even locked the gates of the city, placing a guard at the gates. This was how the Christians and the Jews behaved in the cities which had submitted earlier to the Muslims.

The narrator adds that after the Muslims were triumphant and defeated the Byzantines, they were again received by the inhabitants of the towns with great joy and song. Adversely, we have the Syriac Chronicle telling of the destruction of Ḥimṣ and its environs by the Muslims.[49]

[61] The Muslims then concentrated their forces in the southern part of the Golan and to the east of the Sea of Galilee while the Byzantines advanced from the region of Antioch southward. According to Theophanes, the first confrontation between the armies at the start of the battle

in the sources as the person in charge of the emperor's personal affairs, and he frequently bears the title *praepositus sacri cubiculi*, and was principally in charge of the emperor's treasury, the *sacellum*, from which the name of the office derives. See in Guilland, I, 357, in the chapter Le préposite (= *Byzantinoslavica*, 22[1961], 241–301); cf. Beneševič, *BNGJ*, 5 (1926/7), 117, where the patrikios sakellarios is mentioned (*ho patrikios kai sakellarios*); Sophocles, *Greek Lexicon*, s.v., translates it: bursar; cf. also Bury, *Imperial Administration*, 41f, 76–85, Du Cange, *Gloss*, s.v.: an officer in charge of the treasury (*fisci custos*).

49 Balādhurī, *Futūḥ*, 137; Abū Yūsuf, 81. The marked difference between the strength of the Byzantines and that of the Muslims, is mentioned by the Karaite commentator Yefet ben 'Alī (in the middle of the tenth century) in his commentary on Dan. xi:25–26: 'and he shall stir up his power and his courage against the king of the south', etc.; in his view, the Bible speaks of the battle between 'Umar ibn al-Khaṭṭāb and the Byzantines who were in Palestine, at Marj 'Imwās near Jerusalem, and although the Muslim army was also large ('with a great army'), the Byzantine army was still greater ('a very great and mighty army'); the Byzantine king's men betrayed him when they saw the Muslims advancing ('for they shall forecast devices against him') and a great many of them were killed ('and many shall fall down slain'). Then Palestine was captured from the Byzantines by the *ṣāḥib al-Islām* – 'until this very day'. See his commentary on Daniel, 124. See De Goeje, *Mémoire*, 108–118, the discussion about the problem of whether the capture of Damascus occurred before the battle of the Yarmūk or afterwards. He demonstrates that the Muslims captured Damascus twice, as is also described here. The Syriac source: in the MS BM Add 14, 461, Nöldeke, *ZDMG*, 29(1876), 77f, see lines 8–9. See further on the evacuation of Syria by the Muslims: Ibn Ḥubaysh, 143f.

of the Yarmūk was on Tuesday the 23rd of July 636. While that part of the Byzantine forces under the Sakellarios suffered a defeat, the army commanded by Baanes (Bāhān) rebelled against the emperor and crowned the Sakellarios in his place. There was a general withdrawal and the Arabs used this opportunity to launch an attack in the midst of a sandstorm brought on that day by a wind from the south, and therefore the Byzantines, who came from the north, were unable to see the enemy facing them. Most of the Byzantine army was wiped out in the region's valleys and ravines during their flight, together with their commanders.

The date of the event, according to Muslim sources, is Rajab in the year 15. Ibn al-Kalbī cites the 5th as the date, but there are also other versions, less reliable, which place the battle of the Yarmūk much earlier, even in the year AH 13 (AD 634), apparently confusing this battle with that of Ijnādayn. If we accept Ibn al-Kalbī's date, we find that the battle took place on the 13th of August, 636, that is three weeks after the date given by Theophanes. A Syriac source tells of a Byzantine defeat in Gabītha in which 50,000 soldiers were killed on the 20th of August. As Theophanes speaks at one and the same time of the battle in Gabītha and the other in Iermoukha (Gabītha is Jābiya in the Golan, which evidently was a concentration point for the Byzantines), Nöldeke assumed, quite correctly, that the Syriac source was actually referring to the battle of the Yarmūk. We see, therefore, that the dates ascribed to the battle of the Yarmūk move between the 23rd of July (Theophanes) and the 20th of August (the Syriac source).[50]

50 Theophanes, 332, 338; one can surmise that what he is describing was an uprising of the Armenians; cf. Ya'qūbī, *Ta'rīkh*, II, 160; Balādhurī, *Futūḥ*, 135: 70,000 Byzantines and others who had joined forces with them were killed; Muslim women also participated in the battle. Ṭabarī, *Ta'rīkh*, I, 2347ff; Ibn 'Asākir, I, 528f, 533, 537; on pp. 538–545 he includes traditions that describe the course of the battle. Bāhān gave a heartening address to his men and then ordered his left flank to launch an attack, under the command of the droungarios (*dirnījār*). Opposing them were mainly the tribes of Yaman, which made up the right flank of the Muslims, and though the pressure on them was heavy, they withstood it. But they eventually had to withdraw towards the centre in view of the tremendous waves of Byzantine soldiers attacking them, apart from some 500 fighters who stubbornly continued to fight until those who had withdrawn returned and replaced them. Finally, the outcome of the battle was decided by the Muslims' left flank, under Khālid ibn al-Walīd. See more versions in Ibn Kathīr, *Bidāya*, VII, 4–16; in his account, the battle of the Yarmūk takes place in the days of Abū Bakr; cf. Ṭabarī, *Ta'rīkh*, I, 2155; see also his story of the unusual tactics of Khālid ibn al-Walīd, who divided his cavalry in two, one half to the left flank and the other to the right flank, in order to strengthen both of them. See the Syriac source, as in the previous note, from line 20; cf. Nöldeke, *ibid.*, 79; Theophanes, 332. See also Sa'īd ibn Biṭrīq, II, 14: the Byzantines under Māhān were stationed in a large wadi called Wādī Ramād in the Golan, known also by the name al-Yaqūṣa (this name, Yaqūṣa or Waqūṣa, is also mentioned in other sources) thinking that the wadi protected them, while the Arabs were ensconced opposite them. At this point, Manṣūr, the governor of Damascus, betrayed the Byzantines by coming to their position

[62] Heraclius, who was awaiting the results of the battle in Antioch, sailed to Constantinople as soon as he learned the bitter truth, and according to Muslim sources exclaimed: 'Peace be with you, O Syria! My beautiful country [meaning the land of al-Shām] from now on you belong to the enemy!' Damascus, Ḥimṣ and all the other Syrian cities were now again in the hands of the Muslims, who recaptured them immediately after the victory of the battle of the Yarmūk and the devastation of Byzantine power.[51]

The dismissal of Khālid ibn al-Walīd

[63] After the battle of the Yarmūk there was widespread internal dissension within the Muslim camp which led to the dismissal of Khālid ibn al-Walīd from the command of the army which had fought in Palestine. The traditions vary and contradict one another with regard to this affair: some describe Khālid's dismissal as having occurred at the beginning of 'Umar's caliphate. These traditions speak of 'Umar's resentment towards Khālid because of the latter's behaviour during the *ridda* battles, whereas the more reliable traditions stress the central role which Khālid played during the battle of the Yarmūk. It is not likely that 'Umar would oust such an accomplished and experienced warrior from the central command before knowing whether the final outcome was entirely in favour of the Muslims. Apparently the real reason behind his discharge lay in differences over the spoils, and the traditions refer to this very frankly. According to one of the traditions quoted in Ṭabarī, for instance, 'Umar learned (for nothing was hidden from him) about a gift of 10,000 dinars

at the head of a great number of people from Damascus at night, bearing torches, and the Byzantines thought that these were Arabs and that they were being attacked from the front and from the rear, so they took to their heels in panic, and thus met their end. *Futūḥ* (ascribed to Wāqidī), I, 205f: the traitor to the Byzantines was Abū Ju'ayd, one of the leaders of Ḥimṣ, who lived in a town called Zirā'a. The Byzantine soldiers mistreated his wife and murdered his children; for which he took his vengeance on them by provoking a stampede within the ranks of the Byzantine army stationed in Wādī Yaqūṣa. Later on, we find Abū Ju'ayd mentioned also in connection with the capture of Jerusalem. See the comprehensive discussion and survey of the sources relating to the battle of the Yarmūk in Caetani, III, 549–613. See appreciation of Khālid ibn al-Walīd's strategic talents in Canard, *Settimane-Spoleto*, 12(1964), 50ff; the strategic withdrawal in the face of Heraclius' forces, the evacuation of southern Syria and Damascus and the counter-movement on the Yarmūk are evidence of his excellent organising ability and his skill at manoeuvring on the battlefield. Khālid's qualities as an outstanding commander were already evident during his march from Iraq to Syria through the desert, a feat which has no parallel. See also the interesting discussion *ibid.*, 309–335.

51 Balādhurī, *Futūḥ*, 137. Various versions of the farewell speech in Ibn Ḥubaysh, 142f; cf. Ṭabarī, *Ta'rīkh*, I, 2395f; Sa'īd ibn Biṭrīq, II, 16. The anonymous Syriac chronicle, 251: he said: *sāzū sūriyā = sōsou Syria*).

which Khālid had given Ash'ath b. Qays, leader of the Kinda tribe. At that moment, 'Umar ordered his dismissal, even if what he had given Ash'ath came out of his own pocket. This action is understandable against the background of 'Umar's general policy of struggling with intense energy against corruption in the division of the spoils. He also exerted considerable effort in trying to restrict occurrences of theft and the abuse of local populations. To pursue this policy, he travelled from Medina to Jābiya, where the headquarters of al-Shām was stationed. In place of Khālid, he appointed Abū 'Ubayda ibn al-Jarrāḥ to the high command. Khālid expressed his disappointment and bitterness on his dismissal 'now that al-Shām was as quiet as a camel', but did not dare to rise up against 'Umar.[52]

[64] One can mention three focal points associated with the internal struggle echoed in the issue of Khālid's dismissal. First is the frictions and contradictions between the various tribes of the peninsula who had been

52 Ṭabarī, *Ta'rīkh*, I, 2526; see *ibid*, 2148, the versions of Sayf ibn 'Umar and of Ibn Isḥāq, which antedate Khālid's dismissal and relate it to 'Umar's grudge against him; *ibid.*, 2401f: 'Umar came to al-Shām four times; he was shocked on coming to Jābiya to see Khālid ibn al-Walīd's cavalry wearing silk. He descended from his horse and started throwing stones at them and reprimanded them severely. *Ibid.*, 2149: after he was summoned to Medina, 'Umar demanded of Khālid, 'Oh, Khālid, take the money of God from under your bottom', and confiscated 40,000 dirhams, of which half he found on his person. Ya'qūbi, *Ta'rīkh*, II, 168: 'Umar ordered the spoils to be divided equally between all the tribes, with the exception of Lakhm and Judhām (that is, inhabitants of Palestine), and said, 'I shall never admit of any equality between those who have gone through all the hardships of the road and those who have merely stepped outside their doorway'. See also Ibn al-Athīr, *Kāmil*, II, 500f; Ibn 'Asākir, I, 556; Nawawī, *Tahdhīb*, I, 201: Zayd b. Thābit (who had been the Prophet's secretary) was appointed to take charge of the division of spoils taken in the battle of the Yarmūk; Ibn Kathīr, *Bidāya*, VII, 44, on 'Umar's visit to al-Shām, and see *ibid.*, 58, other versions, according to which he only visited Jābiya three times, but some say, only twice. *Ibid.*, 16: immediately after the ousting of Khālid from the command, Abū 'Ubayda took over arranging matters concerning the spoils, the main object being to deduct the fifth due to the Muslim treasury according to law and send it to Medina. *Ibid.*, 12: a version which describes the dismissal of Khālid as having occurred at the height of the battle of the Yarmūk. 'Abd al-Jabbār, *Tathbīt*, I, 230: 'Umar's policy aroused opposition among the Muslims. See Ibn al-Athīr, *Usd*, I, 53: They heard 'Umar ibn al-Khaṭṭāb say in Jābiya in a sermon: 'I herewith apologise to you for what Khālid ibn al-Walīd did. I ordered him to dedicate this property to the welfare of the Muhājirūn (the Muslim refugees from Mecca), but he gave it to the evil-doers, to the notables and to those of slick tongues. I therefore discharged him and appointed Abū 'Ubayda ibn al-Jarrāḥ'. Lammens, *Mo'āwia*, 5, explains the deposing of Khālid after the battle of the Yarmūk by the fact that he belonged to the Banū Makhzūm, wealthy people of Mecca (who were loyal allies of the Umayyads), and therefore 'Umar mistrusted him and plotted against him. On Abū 'Ubayda, see 'Azīzī, I, 492f; II, 13, 16, 245: his name was 'Āmir b. 'Abdallah b. al-Jarrāḥ; the Prophet said about him that he is the most loyal in this *umma* (that is, of the Muslims). See the article Abū 'Ubayda in *EI*[2] (Gibb); he was one of the first Muslims and took part in all the battles. It is possible that 'Umar saw in him a suitable successor. See a comprehensive discussion on the question of Khālid's dismissal: De Goeje, *Mémoire*, 65–70, 124–131; Caetani, III, 937.

gathered together within the Muslim camp. These tribes had diverse origins and previously had had little in common. A large portion of the army which fought in Palestine and Syria consisted of tribes who came from every part of the Arabian peninsula, but the main core consisted of men from Mecca, Medina, Ṭā'if and members of the tribes of northern Ḥijāz. There were also those tribes, or clans from the northwest of the peninsula, which were Yamanīs (southerners) by extraction, such as Balī, and those assembled around 'Amr ibn al-'Āṣ in particular. The second focal point is the animosity between all these tribes, the Muslims who came from afar, and the local Arabs in the conquered lands, who enjoyed the fruits of victory, while those who had come from some distance were concentrated in Jābiya, the central camp of the Muslim army. The third focal point is arguments concerning attitudes to and the treatment of local populations. There were those who wished to exploit the victory until the very end, to confiscate all property, completely enslave the population, and distribute the houses and lands among the Muslims. These were the aspirations in a setting of vandalism, plunder and massacre. 'Umar intended to solve these problems at their very roots and thus dismissed Khālid, who according to the traditions, typified the craving for spoils and riches and even discriminated between the Muslims themselves, apparently showing a partiality for the local tribes and his own retainers. The man who influenced 'Umar with regard to restraining the Muslims and changing their approach to the local populations was Mu'ādh b. Jabal, who according to Muslim tradition, was a man of understanding and a sort of expert on the economy and finances. He said to 'Umar:

> if the land shall be divided [that is to say, become the private property of the Muslims, including the local population], the portion meted out to people [to each of the Muslims] will be tremendous and they will waste it, and everything will become the property of one man or woman [that is, will fall into the hands of a few]; afterward the successors of the Muslims will follow [that is, their descendants] and they will find nothing. Consider the matter in such a way that will satisfy the first and the last generation.

Thus 'Umar arranged living conditions of the population under Muslim rule in such a manner as to preserve their personal liberty and property, according to conditions to be discussed further on.[53]

[53] Abū 'Ubayd, *Amwāl*, 59; Balādhurī, *Futūḥ*, 151f; Abū'l-Fidā', *Mukhtaṣar*, I, 160: 'Umar ibn al-Khaṭṭāb was the first to organise a census of the tribes and to fix the allowances of the Muslims, in the year AH 20 (AD 641). Abū Zur'a (MS), 11f: 'Umar came to Jābiya in the year 18 [AD 639], and arranged a general convention at which all the commanders handed over to him all the property they had collected; he introduced order into the army units and bases and fixed the allowances and payments; cf. Shaban, *Islamic History*, 26, 41.

The capitulation of Jerusalem

[65] In the autumn of the year 636, Palestine was under Muslim control, with the exception of Jerusalem and Caesarea. The latter was the capital of Palaestina prima, a fortified port with a large army stationed there. Hence the Muslims delayed attempting to capture it for a further five years. Jerusalem was also a stronghold and the approaches to it were difficult. It was manned by a Byzantine garrison and armoured units made up of the local inhabitants. The two cities were virtually in a state of siege although nowhere is it stated specifically that the Muslims had actually encircled them. But the roads were all cut off and impassable and while Caesarea still maintained its sea lanes, Jerusalem was completely severed from the rest of the country after the battle of the Yarmūk. We have already seen how Sophronius, the patriarch of Jerusalem, complained in his Christmas sermon in the year 634 that the people of Jerusalem could not reach Bethlehem for fear of the Arabs.

The Muslim traditions contradict one another with regard to the date on which Jerusalem was captured. In Ṭabarī, at one point, the year AH 15 (AD 636) is mentioned and in another, the year 16 (637). Balādhurī says that the city surrendered in the year 17 (638). This information complies with the account of Theophanes, who says that the city was under siege for two years (that is, after the battle of the Yarmūk). Further evidence that the city was indeed taken in 638 is the fact that the patriarch Sophronius is said to have died of sorrow shortly after the surrender of the town. Sophronius was appointed patriarch in the autumn of 633 and it is said that he kept the position for four years. He died in March 638.[54]

[54] On the presence of the Byzantine army in Jerusalem, see Ṭabarī, *Ta'rīkh*, I, 2398: Arṭabūn stationed an immense army in Ramla (he probably meant Lod, as Ramla had not as yet been founded), and also an immense army in Jerusalem (Īliyā). On the question of the date see Ṭabarī, *ibid.*, 2406: the year AH 15 (in the version of the treaty, to be discussed below, according to Sayf b. 'Umar); *ibid.*, 2360, he mentions a date which is not clear, perhaps the end of the year AH 15 (evidently according to Ibn Isḥāq: see *ibid.*, 2346, and 2350 at the bottom of the page); Khalīfa ibn Khayyāṭ, I, 124: the year 16; Balādhurī, *Futūḥ*, 139; Theophanes, 339; Ibn al-Athīr, *Kāmil*, II, 501: some say that Jerusalem was conquered in the year AH 16. On Sophronius, see Sa'īd ibn Biṭrīq, I, 12f: Sophronius was active in Alexandria against the patriarch Cyrus who supported the Monotheletism (see sec. 9 above) of Heraclius (in the words of Sa'īd, he was a Mārūnī, accepting the stand of Mārūn). Afterwards, he left for Constantinople and there met the patriarch Sergius, who eventually decided to support Cyrus rather than Sophronius. Sophronius left for Jerusalem; he won the support of the monks and the population in the city and they elected him patriarch, for there was no patriarch in Jerusalem in those days; that is, in the second year of 'Umar's caliphate (635). Cf. also Couret, *ROC*, 2(1987), 126f; see Schönborn, 83ff: Sophronius reached Jerusalem in the autumn of 633 and was immediately appointed patriarch, for the post was available. He was eighty-eight when he died (born in Damascus in January 550), see *ibid.*, 54; but see also Le Quien, *Oriens Christianus*, III, 278, and therein various opinions regarding the year of Sophronius' death, ranging from 636 to 644; and see further details on Sophronius, *ibid.*, 264ff, 272 (the letter in which he complains of the

[66] The sources do not provide us with many details on the fall of Jerusalem. They generally stress that the siege lasted a long time and that the inhabitants of Jerusalem were prepared to hand over the city only to the caliph himself. Thus 'Umar came and received its capitulation. Other sources state that a delegation of Jerusalemites came to Jābiya and that the details of the surrender were finalised there. Others point out that it was not 'Umar himself who took on the task, but that he sent an army unit to Jerusalem headed by a man from al-Shām, Khālid b. Thābit b. Ṭā'in b. al-'Ajlūn al-Fahmī. This force started to assail the people of Jerusalem, but immediately afterwards, negotiations began and 'Umar, in Jābiya, confirmed the conditions of the treaty determined by Khālid b. Thābit.[55]

Arabs' assaults). See also *Annales Cavenses*, 186, which has an impossible date for the conquest of Jerusalem – 633. Dhahabī, *Ta'rīkh*, II, 20 tells us that in the year AH 16 'Umar came to al-Shām and conquered Jerusalem. *Futūḥ* (ascribed to Wāqidī), I, 216f, claims that the siege of Jerusalem took place in the winter and lasted for four months; Bar Hebraeus, *Chronicle* (Bedjan), 103 (cf. Budge, 96) says that in the year AH 15, 'Umar came to Palestine and Sophronius, the bishop of Jerusalem, came out to greet him; Ibn Khaldūn, *'Ibar*, II, 949 reports the year AH 15, and some say AH 16. See the discussion on this subject in De Goeje, *Mémoire*, 154ff, and Caetani, III, 920–959.

55 See Ya'qūbī, *Ta'rīkh*, II, 167: Abū 'Ubayda wrote to 'Umar about the prolonged resistance of the Jerusalemites while some claim that it was the people of Jerusalem themselves who demanded that 'Umar grant them the *ṣulḥ*. 'Umar came first to Jābiya and from there to Jerusalem and arranged the matter of the *ṣulḥ*. Khalīfa ibn Khayyāṭ, I, 124, has a similar version in the name of Ibn al-Kalbī, according to whom Khālid ibn al-Walīd also participated in the campaign against Jerusalem, at the head of the Muslim avant-garde. On Khālid ibn Thābit see Balādhurī, *Futūḥ*, 139; Ibn 'Asākir, V, 29; he was called al-Fahmī, evidently because he was a client of the Banū Fahm, a tribe that lived along the shores of the Red Sea, see Caskel, II, s.v.: and see Ibn al-Athīr, *Lubāb*, II, 229: al-Fahmī, since he belonged to a clan of Qays 'Aylān, and see on this tribe Caskel, II, s.v. Qais b. an-Nās; Yāfi'ī, I, 73; Subkī, *Shifā'*, 47; see the long and very elaborate description of the taking of Jerusalem: *Futūḥ* (ascribed to Wāqidī), I, 213ff: see also Constantinus Porphyrog. (Moravcsik), 82: 'Umar captured Jerusalem craftily by promises given to Sophronius, bishop of Jerusalem, a wise and zealous man, that the churches would not be harmed; and this occurred after a siege which lasted two years. Goitein, *Yerushalayim*, 4(1952/3); 83 (= *Ha-yishuv*, 7) treats the information doubtfully with regard to 'Umar's coming to Jerusalem. In his opinion, one should regard this information in the light of the tendency to enhance and elaborate on the circumstances of the taking of Jerusalem; he also assumes that one could find certain Jewish influences in these sources, such as the midrash to Is. x:34, 'and Lebanon shall fall by a mighty one'. Jerusalem will only be surrendered to a king, who is worthy of being called 'a mighty one' (BT Gittin 56b). Busse, *Judaism*, 17(1968), 444f suggests the possibility that 'Amr ibn al-'Āṣ was the true conqueror of Jerusalem, but that it was ascribed to 'Umar. This he deduces from a passage in Balādhurī which says that 'Amr ibn al-'Āṣ stopped the siege of Caesarea in order to conquer Jerusalem. There is some logic to the assumption that the traditionists exaggerated the role of 'Umar in the surrender of Jerusalem in order to glorify the event; however, this is an insufficient reason to utterly invalidate the historical value of these traditions, especially in view of the fact that 'Umar's visits to Palestine and Syria are described in these traditions not merely in connection with the conquest of Jerusalem, as has already been mentioned. See the opinion of Noth, *Quellenkritische Studien*, 161, who suggests giving credence to the tradition on 'Umar's involvement in the matter of the treaty, although there is place for doubt as to whether the fact that the refusal of the people of Jerusalem to surrender to any other but him is what brought him from Medina to Jābiya.

[67] In 638 Islam had already reached the heights of its victories and now had only to bring events to a successful conclusion. The man whose role it was to stand at the head of these tremendous happenings came to receive the surrender of Jerusalem, the city of David, the capital of the Children of Israel, the city which Christianity had chosen as the living symbol of its victory. Muslim tradition takes great pains to present 'Umar's coming to Jerusalem as a demonstration of humility, modesty and austerity, evidently with a didactic purpose in mind. The caliph did not lose his head in the wake of the many victories and triumphs; he behaved as an orthodox Muslim should behave, disdaining the vanities of this world and exhibiting those simple habits in keeping with the best of Bedouin tradition. He entered the city riding on a camel, wrapped in a cloak made of camel-hair. Men of the Muslim army, tribesmen, who had now spent four years in settled and cultivated lands, in Palestine and in Syria, were embarrassed by the sight of their supreme commander appearing in such a manner before a conquered people. They demanded that he dress in clothes suitable to the circumstances and that he ride on a horse, and not on a camel. 'Umar refused the first request but accepted the second and entered Jerusalem on a horse, but held onto the reins of a camel. 'For this makes me into another person' he said; 'I fear lest I grow too great in my own eyes and nothing favourable will come out of such a change.' Theophanes' description of 'Umar's entry into Jerusalem is evidently influenced by this story, but it took on a derisive and hostile tone. The caliph's entrance wearing worn clothing made of camel-hair appeared to him like the wearing of a pretentious, hypocritical, mask. 'Umar asked to see the temple built by King Solomon in order to turn it into a prayer site for his own 'blasphemies'. The patriarch Sophronius cried out when he saw him: 'So here is the abomination of desolation prophesied by Daniel and here he stands in the holy place . . . this knight of righteousness', continues Theophanes, 'wept over the Christian people'. In Theophanes' version, it was the patriarch who suggested that 'Umar change his clothes and asked him to accept a cloak and garments of linen. But 'Umar refused to wear them. After much convincing, he agreed, but only until his own apparel would be washed. Then he returned Sophronius' garments and continued to wear his own clothes.[56]

[68] In Ṭabarī, in the context of a passage concerning the conquest of Jerusalem which he copied from Sayf ibn 'Umar, a version of a letter of

[56] See Maqdisī, *Muthīr* (Le Strange), 297: 'Umar entered Jerusalem through the gate of the Prophet Muḥammad (i.e., from the south). In Ṭabarī, *Ta'rīkh*, I, 2407f, there is a similar story which speaks of a horse and a mule (or just any beast of burden). Theophanes, 339; Constantinus Porphyrog. (Moravcsik), see the previous note (as in Theophanes), cf. De Goeje, *Mémoire*, 157f; Busse, *Judaism*, 17(1968), 447.

protection (*amān* or *ṣulḥ*) had been preserved, which 'Umar gave to the people of Jerusalem, who were all Christians. According to Ṭabarī, this document was written in Jābiya. This is what the letter says:

In the name of God the merciful and compassionate. This is the covenant given by God's slave 'Umar, commander of the Believers, to the people of Jerusalem: He grants them security, to each person and his property; to their churches, their crosses, to the sick and the healthy, to all the people of their creed. We shall not station Muslim soldiers in their churches. We shall not destroy the churches nor impair any of their contents or their property or their crosses or anything which belongs to them. We shall not compel the people of Jerusalem to renounce their beliefs and we shall do them no harm. No Jew shall live among them in Jerusalem. The people of Jerusalem are obliged to pay the same tax we impose on the inhabitants of other cities. The inhabitants of Jerusalem must rid themselves of the Byzantine army and any armed individuals. We ensure the safety of these people on their departure from Jerusalem, both of their persons and of their property, until they reach their asylum. To those who wish to remain in Jerusalem, we ensure their safekeeping but they are obliged to pay the same tax that the other inhabitants of Jerusalem must pay. To those inhabitants of Jerusalem who wish to join the departing Byzantines in person and with their property, to vacate their churches and abandon their crosses, we pledge to ensure the safety of their persons and that of their churches and crosses, until they reach their destinations. Those villagers who are present [in Jerusalem] since the murder of so-and-so, should depart with the Byzantines, if they wish to do so, or return to their families; nothing will be collected from them before the harvest.

An analysis of this version of the 'covenant' reveals certain general principles in common with those which the Prophet contracted with the Jews during the Tabūk expedition, which we have mentioned earlier, but it also reveals other distinctive principles. The recurring principles may be summarised as follows: (1) security of person and property, (2) security of the houses of worship, their property and contents; as well as freedom of worship, and (3) the obligation to pay taxes to the Muslims. The distinctive principles appearing in this covenant are (1) the ban on Jews' residing in Jerusalem, (2) assurance of the personal safety of Byzantines or other armed individuals, and also that of any inhabitant of Jerusalem who decides to leave the city, until they reach an area under Byzantine dominion, (3) permission to members of the Byzantine army or Byzantine officials to remain in the city on condition that they pay the same taxes as the remainder of the city's inhabitants, and (4) the safety of refugees currently living in Jerusalem should they wish to return to their villages, and the promise that they would not be obliged to pay the taxes until after the harvest.[57]

[57] Ṭabarī, *Ta'rīkh*, I, 2405f. The letter of protection in the original is called *amān*. Jerusalem is called Īliyā; 'the sick and the healthy' are not to be understood literally but as a figure of speech meaning, 'to everyone without exception'. The tax is called *jizya*, a term which as yet did not mean specifically poll-tax, as it did later; 'armed men' is a liberal and

[69] Goitein claims that this version of the covenant is not plausible and that one cannot rely on the source in which it has been preserved, namely the account of Sayf ibn ʿUmar, from which Ṭabarī copied. Goitein questions Sayf's authenticity on other subjects as well, where his versions show bias and differ from those of other traditions. He goes on to mention a number of other traditions dealing with the surrender of Jerusalem, which contain no trace of a covenant with its inhabitants, or a ban on Jews' abiding in the city. We shall examine a number of other sources which tell of the surrender of Jerusalem.

The traditions about Khālid b. Thābit in Balādhurī and in Ibn ʿAsākir portray him as the conqueror of Jerusalem and make reference to an agreement which was reached (according to Balādhurī in exchange for payment and only referring to within the walled city) and which ʿUmar authorised afterwards. Elsewhere in his chronicle Ibn ʿAsākir quotes another and strange version from Wāqidī, according to which the agreement was made with the Jews who were in Jerusalem, twenty in number, their leader being Joseph bin Nūn (!). According to this agreement, the inhabitants of Jerusalem had to pay *jizya* and in return were promised security of their persons, property and their churches, on condition that they would not revolt nor harbour rebels. Apparently the idea of the twenty Jews relates to another matter, which is that of the twenty Jews who later served on the Temple Mount. Theophanes, in his account of ʿUmar's visit to Jerusalem, mentions the fact that Sophronius, patriarch of Jerusalem, handed over the city in exchange for a *logos*, which in this context, undoubtedly means a promise. Yaʿqūbī evidently knew the story found in Ibn ʿAsākir, and the substance of the covenant he mentions is similar, but he claims that there was a difference of opinion with regard to the *ṣulḥ* in Jerusalem. Some say it was made with the Jews, but the prevailing opinion is that it was made with the Christians. The Christian Saʿīd ibn Biṭrīq, who elsewhere relates that it was forbidden for Jews to abide in Jerusalem from the time of Constantine and afterwards, brings up the subject of the covenant and a version of it, in which the safety of person, property and the church is included, without mentioning the ban on Jews living in Jerusalem at all. We find in Musharraf information about

approximate translation of the word *luṣūt*, evidently identical with the Hebrew word *lisṭīm*, both taken from the Greek: *lēstēs*, robber. But it is not likely that the Christians in Jerusalem would ask for a clause to be included in the pact giving protection to robbers, therefore the meaning here is evidently: inhabitants who are not in the army but who participated in the defence of the city. Villagers (literally: people of the soil) were apparently refugees from the villages who sought refuge in Jerusalem when the Muslims took large stretches of Palestine. The letter apparently mentioned some murder that frightened the population and drove many of them to seek refuge in Jerusalem, but the copyist of the letter was not interested in copying the name of the victim (or victims) and wrote, the murder of so-and-so (*fulān*).

a letter sent by Abū 'Ubayda to the people of Jerusalem in which he tries to convince them to turn to Islam. Muṭahhar b. Ṭāhir al-Maqdisī notes that 'Umar concluded the *ṣulḥ* with the people of Jerusalem, which according to him entailed the security of the churches and the assurance that the monks would not be exiled. Ibn al-Athīr, who generally copied from Ṭabarī, points out with regard to Jerusalem only that a *jizya* was imposed on its citizens. The same applies to al-Makīn, and although Ṭabarī is also his principal source, he only mentions the beginning of a version of the agreement and does not mention the Jewish matter at all. The Christian chronicler Agapius (Maḥbūb) of Manbij tells how the patriarch Sophronius goes out to greet 'Umar on his arrival in Jerusalem from Medina and receives a covenant from him, bearing his seal, but only mentions the Jewish aspect: that of the absence of any protection for any Jew living in Jerusalem, and that, if found there, they would be punished physically and their property affected. Similarly Michael the Syrian indicates only 'that no Jew is permitted to live in Jerusalem', as is the case with Bar Hebraeus.

Although there is some doubt as to the authenticity of Sayf's information (which was copied by Ṭabarī), and although contradictions appear in his accounts, it appears that we cannot disregard him altogether. The version itself seems to be reliable; it is possible that the passage in which the year (15) is incorrect, was added by Ṭabarī, or perhaps by Sayf himself. The names of the witnesses mentioned therein, all of whom were important figures in the Muslim command, seem artificial; but the language of the covenant and its details appear authentic and reliable and in keeping with what is known of Jerusalem at that time. We have seen that most of the Muslim sources ignore the details of the pact, apart from the fundamentals – security and taxes. On the other hand, as one might anticipate, the subject of the Jews appeared important to almost all the Christian chroniclers, for here was a ban forbidding the Jews to live in Jerusalem. The question still remains as to how this Jewish aspect could be adapted to the historical fact (proven by a number of sources) that the Jews indeed settled in Jerusalem shortly after the conquest. I shall attempt to find some explanation for this contradiction.[58]

[58] Goitein, *Melila*, 3–4 (1949/50), 158ff; see also his article *Yerushalayim*, 4(1952/3), 84ff. An important argument against the reliability of Sayf ibn 'Umar is his inaccuracy with regard to the year of the conquest of Jerusalem. See on this matter the remark of Noth, *Quellenkritische Studien*, 57, that the chronological frameworks are generally the work of editors (in this case, Ṭabarī); therefore the essential value of the genuine tradition remains intact even though the chronological sequence is not correct. See Balādhurī and Ibn 'Asākir, above in n. 55; cf. also Ibn A'tham, I, 296: the *ṣulḥ* was attained through the mediation of a tribesman of Palestine (certainly this is what he meant by *musta'riba*) sent by 'Umar whose name was Abū'l Ju'ayd. The agreement contained a stipulation on the payment of the *jizya* and permission to remain in the city. The Jews are not mentioned

The completion of the conquest

[70] The most difficult areas to conquer were principally the cities along the coast, which were surrounded by walls on all sides facing the land. The Muslims were unable to attack them from the sea, having only land forces. This refers mainly to Tripoli, Caesarea and Ascalon. Apparently, Hebron also held out longer than the other cities in the country. We have no information about Hebron from Muslim sources, but from a comparatively later Christian source, contained in a manuscript from the fifteenth century, is the story of two monks from Hebron at the time of the Crusades. Most of the text is concerned with the discovery of the graves of the patriarchs, which occurred (as we know from Arab sources) in the year

here. According to him, the *amān* is still with the Christians in Jerusalem 'until this very day'. Cf. the anonymous Syriac chronicle, 225: the agreement was made with Abū Ju'aydad (!), who was one of the two heads of the city of Jerusalem, the other being the bishop Sophronius. See also *Futūḥ* (ascribed to Wāqidī), I, 226: Abu Ju'ayd (who was involved in the battle of the Yarmūk) was the one who advised the Christians not to rebel against the Muslims. He proved to them that it was the Muslims who were truly the righteous mentioned in the Bible and the New Testament (*injīl*) – as after the Christians displayed the valuables in their possession, on his advice, none of the Muslims laid a hand on them. See a similar story in al-Ḥimyarī, 151; in connection with the valuables, Stratos, 134ff, points to the fact that during the taking of Jerusalem, most of the church treasures were no longer in their place, but had been removed after the battle of the Yarmūk via Caesarea to Constantinople, together with the Holy Cross, and he notes the fact that they were displayed in the Church of St Sophia in Constantinople during the last three days of Easter week. See Maqdisī, *Muthīr*, 298: 'Umar sent a man of the Banū Jadhīla and it was he who conquered Jerusalem; see the additional tradition in Ibn 'Asākir, II, 323; Theophanes, 339; Ya'qūbī, *Ta'rīkh*, II, 167f; Sa'īd ibn Biṭrīq, I, 133, and II, 17; Musharraf, fol. 18; Maqdisī, *Bad'*, V, 185; Ibn al-Athīr, *Kāmil*, II, 501; Agapius (*PO* VIII), 215; the anonymous Syriac chronicle, 255: 'that no Jew shall live in Jerusalem'; Michael the Syrian (Chabot), 419, text; II, 425, translation; Bar Habraeus, *Chronicle* (Bedjan), 103, cf. the translation (Budge), 96; 'Ulaymī, 224, has an exact copy from Ṭabarī; De Goeje, *Mémoire*, 155, finds it only natural that a ban on living in Jerusalem should have been applied to the Jews at that time. Logically, this was probably a concession, obtained by negotiations, to the Christians' demands and their hatred of the Jews. An atmosphere of conciliation towards the Christians was also noticeable, in his opinion, in the fact that the covenant had no clauses to humiliate or restrain the Christians, such as are found in other letters of surrender of that time. Meinardus, *Copts*, 11, gives information from an anonymous source about the 'Umar pact, in which Latins, Copts, Syrians, etc. are mentioned; of course, this information lacks any foundation whatsoever. Ṭabarī has another tradition, also taken from Sayf ibn 'Umar, in which the commanders of the army fighting in the battles around Jerusalem were: Abū'l-A'war, who was active in the north ('in charge of Urdunn'), 'Alqama ibn Ḥakīm, Masrūq b. 'so-and-so' (evidently he was not of Arab origin), Abū Ayyūb al-Anṣārī, who is Khālid b. Zayd b. Kulayb. Abū Ayyūb was an important figure in the Prophet's day, see Ibn al-Athīr, *Usd*, V 143f; he was from the family of the Banū al-Najjār, one of the first to adhere to Islam, and afterwards a retainer of 'Alī. It is said that he was of the lineage of a *ḥabr* (a Jewish sage), see Samhūdī, I, 189, cf.; Kister, *IOS*, 2 (1972), 233, n. 141; Gil, *JSAI*, 4(1984), 211. As to Abū'l-A'war, he is 'Amr b. Sufyān al-Sulamī, who received the surrender of Tiberias, see Ṭabarī, *Ta'rīkh*, I, 2093, 2159; Ibn al-Athīr, *Usd*, IV, 108f; V, 138.

AH 513, that is AD 1119–1120. In this Christian manuscript there is a passage dealing with the Muslim conquest of Hebron:

When they [the Muslims] came to Hebron they were amazed to see the strong and handsome structures of the walls and they could not find any opening through which to enter; then Jews happened to come, who lived in the area under the former rule of the Greeks [that is, the Byzantines], and they said to the Muslims: give us [a letter of security] that we may continue to live [in our places] under your rule [literally – amongst you] and permit us to build a synagogue in front of the entrance [to the city]. If you will do this, we shall show you where you can break in. And so they did.[59]

[71] As to the cities of the coast, according to Balādhurī, 'Irqa, Jubayl and Beirut were easily taken shortly after the conquest of Damascus, evidently at about the end of the year 636. Balādhurī has it that the Byzantines attacked and took over the coastal cities again towards the end of 'Umar's caliphate, or at the beginning of 'Uthmān's time, that is in 644; Mu'āwiya returned and recaptured them, rebuilt them and stationed garrisons which lived off the taxes from the neighbouring countryside. Only Tripoli remained a hard nut to crack. In the days of 'Uthmān (*ca.* 645), Mu'āwiya decided to capture it (Balādhurī explains that it was a city made up of three cities). He cut it off from the sea, put up a fortress a number of miles from the town and called it Sufyān, and completely blockaded the city. The entire population concentrated in one of the city's citadels. They wrote to the emperor requesting that he send ships to evacuate them to areas under his dominion. The ships actually arrived and embarked with the population in the course of one night. According to Ibn 'Asākir, the inhabitants of the city set fire to the city as they were leaving. Only one Jew who had managed to escape the fire remained, and it was he who told the Muslims what had occurred. According to Ibn 'Asākir, Mu'āwiya then placed a large number of Jews from al-Urdunn, that is, the north of Palestine, in the city's citadel (which according to Balādhurī's interpretation served as a port in his time).[60]

59 See the treatise of the Canonicus Hebronensis in *RHC* (Occ.), V, 309; see the introduction *ibid.*, LXIII; see the discussion on this source in Riant, *AOL*, 2(1–1884), 411–421. This story is further proof that there actually was a synagogue in Hebron during the Muslim occupation. This synagogue existed until the Crusaders' conquest, and this is also confirmed by the Geniza documents, see below; the story is attributed to two monks, Eudes and Arnoul. See also Vincent, *Hebron*, 159, 167f, 178. The fragment was also edited by Assaf and Mayer, *Sefer ha-yishuv*, 6, which has a literal translation. *Circa regionem illam morati fuerant* does not mean: 'who had remained under Greek rule in that area'; *portam facere* does not mean 'to erect the gate' but is an idiom. Vincent translates here: 'indiquèrent aux conquérants le point à dégager pour se créer une entrée'.

60 See Balādhurī, *Futūḥ*, 126f; Ibn 'Asākir, V, 183ff. *A'ṭāhum al-qaṭā'i'*, I translate: he allotted them (the garrisons) the income from the land taxes. Afterwards, these sources say, the Christians were given permission to return and to settle in the town again, under the *biṭrīq*

[72] Caesarea was under siege more than once, evidently already in the year 13, in Jumādā I, or July 634. But the Muslims despaired of capturing it at the time and this persisted until Mu'āwiya finally took it in Shawwāl of the year 19, or October 640. According to the tradition in Balādhurī, Mu'āwiya found in Caesarea 700,000 mercenaries, 30,000 Samaritans, 200,000 Jews, 300 markets, and 100,000 men guarding the walls of the city nightly. The town was captured with the help of a Jew called Joseph, 'who came to the Muslims at night and showed them how to creep in through an underground trench in which the water reached up to one's knees'; for this, he received an *amān* (letter of security), for himself and for his *ahl* (an expression that has various meanings: perhaps 'his family', or 'his people' or perhaps meaning to say 'the Jews'). It is quite possible that the sources, in referring to the capture of Caesarea, are influenced by the information on the conquest of Caesarea in Cappadocia by Maslama b. 'Abd al-Malik in 729. He took captive the inhabitants of the city and sold them as slaves; the exception was the Jews, as they were the ones who handed over the town to him.[61]

(*patricius*), whose name was Buqanṭar, and these Christians undertook to pay taxes. But some fifty years later, in the days of 'Abd al-Malik, they rebelled, killed the governor, took prisoners among the Muslims and the Jews, and took flight aboard ships. Afterwards they returned with Byzantine reinforcements and attempted to capture the town but their plan failed. They were subdued and their leader was crucified by 'Abd al-Malik. There is also (*ibid.*) the interesting information that the Muslims usually kept a full garrison in the town only on days when it was possible to sail, whereas when the 'sea was closed', that is to say, during the winter months, it would be taken away from there. Cf. also Ibn al-Shaddād (MS Leiden 3076), 100b, who copied from Balādhurī and Ibn 'Asākir.

61 Balādhurī, *Futūḥ*, 141; the date is confirmed by Abū Ma'shar (died in 786), who was a contemporary of Ibn Isḥāq (younger than him) and a Medinan who later moved to Baghdad; see on him Sezgin, I, 291f; Wāqidī (quoted by Ṭabarī) also gives this date. See the account of Abū Ma'shar in Ṭabarī, *Ta'rīkh*, I, 2579, who also cites other opinions: of Ibn Isḥāq – the year 20 (641), and of Sayf ibn 'Umar – the year 16 (637). It seems that if we divide the numbers in Balādhurī into a hundred, we shall arrive at numbers near the actual ones. Ya'qūbī, *Ta'rīkh*, II, 172: there were 80,000 fighters in Caesarea, and he has the year as AH 18 (AD 639). See further, Khalīfa ibn Khayyāṭ, I, 134; Sa'īd ibn Biṭrīq, II, 20. In the seventh year of 'Umar's reign (641); according to Yāqūt, *Buldān*, IV, 214, the siege of Caesarea lasted seven years less one month. The man who showed the Muslims how to get in was a certain Linṭāk, who was their hostage (it does not say that he was a Jew), and the event occurred on Sunday when everyone was in church. Bar Hebraeus (Bedjan), 104b; (Budge), 97: the siege lasted five months (from December until May). A total of seventy-two shooting machines bombarded the attackers from the walls. Only after penetrating the walls while others were scaling the battlements on ladders, did the Muslims succeed in overcoming the defenders, who had been unable to descend from the walls into the town for three days. Seven thousand Byzantine soldiers (one-hundredth of the number given by Balādhurī), fled from Caesarea by sea. Caesarea in Cappadocia: Chabot, *REJ*, 29(1894), 292, following an anonymous Syriac chronicle which he ascribed to Dionysius of Tel-Maḥrē, patriarch of the Jacobites (died in 845); Noth, *Quellenkritische Studien*, 24, 150, points to the uniformity of pattern ('typology') in the descriptions of the conquest of cities in Islamic traditions: Damascus, Caesarea, Babel (Babylon) of Egypt (afterwards Fustat), Alexandria, Tustar, Qurṭuba: (a) the traitor reveals the weak spot in the defence, (b) the

[73] There is a difference of opinion with regard to Ascalon, as to whether it was taken by 'Amr ibn al-'Āṣ or Mu'āwiya. Here too the resistance lasted longer than usual due to the assistance lent by the Byzantines to the town's defenders from the sea. The traditions are generally in accord that the city was conquered only in 644. Balādhurī has it that at first Ascalon was captured by 'Amr ibn al-'Āṣ, but there was an uprising with the help of the Byzantines and Mu'āwiya conquered it anew and stationed a garrison there.[62]

[74] During this period of the consummation of the conquests in Palestine, the Muslims suffered a cruel blow in the form of an undefined plague, known by the name of 'The Emmaus plague'. Many people died as a result, among them some of the most important of the Muslim commanders, Abū 'Ubayda ibn al-Jarrāḥ, Mu'ādh b. Jabal, Yazīd b. Abī Sufyān (Mu'āwiya's brother) and others. The plague occurred in the year AH 18 (AD 639). 'Umar tried to save Abū 'Ubayda's life, and in a letter ordered him to return to Medina, but the latter, understanding his intention, refused to go. When 'Umar learned of the deaths of Abū 'Ubayda and Yazīd, he appointed Mu'āwiya, Yazīd's brother, as commander in charge of the province (*jund*) of Damascus, and Shuraḥbīl b. Ḥasana in charge of the province of Urdunn.[63]

The attitude of the population towards the conqueror

[75] We have already discussed the episode of Ḥimṣ and the conflicting accounts of this episode in the Muslim traditions and the Syriac-Christian

population is occupied with something, such as a festival, etc., (c) the vanguard storms ahead on ladders; (d) the sounding of the *takbīr* (*allāhu akbar*) to proclaim victory, (e) the entrance gates are opened to the Muslim army from within. According to Ibn 'Abd al-Ḥakam, 76, Caesarea was conquered in the same year Heraclius died, which was the year 20 (641), and see the year of his death in Vasiliev, *History*, I, 193; Stratos, 150ff, argues that the exact date of Heraclius' death was 11 February, 641. In Suyūṭī, *Ta'rīkh*, 132, the date of the conquest of Caesarea is the year AH 19 (AD 640).

[62] Balādhurī, *Futūḥ*, 142ff; Ṭabarī, *Ta'rīkh*, I, 2798 (according to Sayf ibn 'Umar): Ya'qūbī, *Ta'rīkh*, II, 170: Sa'īd ibn Biṭrīq, II, 20; Ibn al-Athīr, *Kāmil*, III, 77.

[63] Ṭabarī, *Ta'rīkh*, I, 2516ff; Balādhurī, *Futūḥ*, 139f, mentions the ages of the dead: Abū 'Ubayda, fifty-eight, Mu'ādh b. Jabal, thirty-eight (he died in the vicinity of Uqḥuwāna in the Urdunn region); Shuraḥbīl b. Ḥasana (contrary to the information in Ṭabarī concerning his appointment by 'Umar), sixty-nine. Ya'qūbī, *Ta'rīkh*, II, 172: 25,000 died; Ibn Qudāma, 140, Mu'ādh b. Jabal died after he was appointed commander to replace Abū 'Ubayda in a town between Ramla and Jerusalem, at the age of thirty-three; Tha'ālibī, *Thimār*, 546f, has a sort of play on words on the subject – saying that the people of al-Shām are famous for their submissiveness to the rulers (*ṭā'a-ṭā'ūn*) and the plagues (*ṭā'ūn*). Vincent et Abel, *Emmaus*, 357, point out that from the fact that the famous plague was named after Emmaus (while it was known that it raged throughout Palestine and Syria), one can understand that this place must have been the major concentration point for Muslim troops at the time.

chronicles. We have also seen the description by a Syriac source of the slaughter of the local population in this region. In addition, we have taken note of the Muslim sources that speak of the aid rendered by the Jews to the Muslims in the conquest of Hebron and Caesarea, and the episode of the Jews in Tripoli. One should take note that the latter sort of information is found only in the Muslim traditions. Naturally, it is impossible to learn the real truth in this case, but one can assume that the local population suffered immensely during the course of the war and it is very likely that many villages were destroyed and uprooted in the frontier regions, and that the lot of these local populations was very bitter indeed. It appears that the period of the conquest was also that of the destruction of the synagogues and churches of the Byzantine era, remnants of which have been unearthed in our own time and are still being discovered. This assumption is based both on what is said in a few Christian sources I have mentioned and on Muslim sources describing 'Umar's visits to al-Shām. There is no doubt that one of the main purposes of these visits was to establish order and put an end to the devastation and slaughter of the local population.[64]

[76] One should recall that the Muslim invasion of Palestine occurred only some five or six years after the tremendous upheaval of the wars between Persia and Byzantium, that is, after the defeat of the 'kingdom of Edom' and then its victory. One can assume that great messianic hopes were aroused among the Jews of Palestine and that they wove what was happening into the pattern of events of the days of redemption as foretold by the prophets of Israel and the book of Daniel. The Muslims certainly did not appear to them as the instruments of salvation, but only as its harbinger. The Muslim conquests were perceived as an essential stage determined in advance by Providence for the coming of the Messiah.

Evidence of these moods can be found in 'The Mysteries of Rabbi Shimon Bar Yoḥai'; though written some generations after the conquests, it contains some basic ideas which were perhaps prevalent among the

[64] As to the attitude of the Jews towards the Muslims, the Arab sources themselves were inclined to laud themselves on the good relationship between the Muslims and the subdued population, and the Christian sources attempted, for their own reasons, to describe the Jews as allies of the Muslims; we can see an element of this in the story of the taking of Hebron as related by monks of the Crusaders' period; cf. Ghévond, 2; this Armenian chronicler who lived in a distant land, some ten generations after the Muslim conquest, claims to know of the Prophet's command before his death that the Muslims should ask for the aid of the Jews, and that the latter would show them the way to conquer the world. The Jews welcomed this idea, for God had promised Abraham's heirs that they would dominate the world. As they themselves had transgressed and were excluded from ruling, then at least the Arabs, themselves also of the seed of Abraham, would gain supremacy. The Armenian bishop Sebeus also describes a sort of cabal between the Jews and the Arabs against the Christians, see his chronicle in a French translation (Macler), 102ff. One need not ascribe any historical significance to this kind of story.

Jews of Palestine during the conquests. The kingdom of Edom was seen as the kingdom of the wicked. The secrets were revealed to Rabbi Shimon Bar Yoḥai 'when he was hidden from the emperor, king of Edom, in a cave'. One is speaking here, naturally, of 'Mysteries of the End'. At the beginning one finds a homily based on 'and he looked on the Kenites' (Num., xxiv:21):

As soon as he saw the Kingdom of Ishmael was coming, he began to say: Was it not enough for us what the wicked Kingdom of Edom has done to us; now [there comes] also the Kingdom of Ishmael? Immediately Maṭaṭrōn, the *sar ha-pānīm* [Prince of the Presence (?)], retorted, saying to him: do not fear, man, the Almighty only brings the Kingdom of Ishmael in order to save you of this wicked one, and he appoints over them a prophet of His wish, and will conquer the Land for them; they will restore it to its grandeur; and a great fear will befall the Children of Esau.

This idea, the perception of Muḥammad as a prophet sent by God to the Arabs, merits some attention, particularly if it also reflected the attitude of the Jews at the time of the conquest, something whose truth can never be ascertained. The archetype of the prophet sent to the gentiles is, of course, Balaam. In the midrash it is also stated: 'just as He [the Almighty] placed angels and sages and prophets in Israel, so did he do similarly for the nations of the world'. The treatise on the argument between Jews and Christians in Palestine (the Didaskalia of Jacob the recently baptised), speaks of the rumour that spread among the Jews of Palestine about the rising of a prophet from among the Arabs. Arab sources also tell of Jews who agreed that Muḥammad was really the messenger of God, but only to the Arabs.[65]

[77] This midrash of the 'Mysteries of Shimon Bar Yoḥai' sees the

65 See the midrash in Jellinek, *Bēt ha-midrāsh*, III, 78ff, edited from the Salonika edition, 1743, re-edited by Even Shemuel; see his *Midreshē ge'ullā*², 187ff (a version adapted by the editor, which deprives it of any scientific value). See the introductions to these two editions. Parallel versions can be found in 'The prayer of Rabbi Shimon Ben Yoḥai'. See in Jellinek, *ibid.*, IV, 117ff, and in Even Shemuel, 268ff; also in 'The Midrash on the Ten Kings' edited by Ḥ. M. Horovitz, *Bēt 'eqed ha-agādōt*, 38ff (and see the parallel fragment on pp. 51f). The Kenite, Jethro's tribe, is identified in the Targum with Benē Salmā'a, which was a by-name for the Arabs in the Byzantine period; see Urbach, *Eretz Israel*, 10(1970/71), 60, n. 13; Gil, *JSAI*, 4(1984), 217f; it is natural that the midrash identifies the Kenite here with Ishmael. Crone and Cook, 37, surmised that in the passage from 'The mysteries of Rabbi Shimon Bar Yoḥai' where the Kenite is mentioned, a different source was inserted into the midrash, therefore one must differentiate between Kenites and Ishmaelites; but this has no foundation. The nature and timing of the midrash has been extensively treated in research literature, see the bibliography in Baron, *SRHJ*, III, 274, n. 27; see particularly the opinions of Graetz (Hebrew), III, 433, n. 16; Baer, *MGWJ*, 70(1926), 162f, n. 6; Steinschneider, *ZDMG*, 28(1874), 636f, 639, 642, draws attention to Byzantine elements in the midrash; Lewis, *BSOAS*, 13(1949–51), 309; see pp. 321ff, where he claims that the Kenite means Rome and Byzantium, and in its later sections, the Crusaders; but this is not correct. See also his article in *A. Abel Memorial Volume*: 197, where he tries to prove that the *piyyūṭ*, 'On that day', edited by Ginzberg, *Ginze Schechter*, II, 310ff refers to the

mission of Islam as the disabling and elimination of the Byzantine empire. But later on, it compares this mission with that of the Messiah himself, and has an interpretation of Is., xxi:6–7 ('And he saw a chariot with a couple of horsemen, a chariot of asses, and a chariot of camels'), as 'why does he put before a chariot of camels, a chariot of asses? [It should] not [be] a chariot of asses, a chariot of camels but: a chariot of camels a chariot of asses. Once he started he rides a camel; when his kingdom has grown under his rule, he rides an ass; in other words: since he rides an ass, the conclusion is that they are a salvation for Israel, equal to the salvation of the one who will ride an ass' (i.e., the Messiah). Interestingly enough, echoes of this Jewish exegesis reached Muslim writers. Thus Bīrūnī says in the eleventh century,

> Such or similar to this is the interpretation of the saying of Isaiah [Īsha'yā] the prophet: God ordered him to place a scout on a watch-tower who shall say what he observes ['what he shall see he will say']; and he [the scout] said: I see a rider on an ass and a rider on a camel; and one of the two stood up and shouted: Babylon has fallen and all its wooden idols are broken (Is., xxi:9). And the interpretation of these tidings is [the coming of] the Messiah [that is to say, Jesus] who is riding the ass, and Muḥammad, who is riding the camel.[66]

[78–79] The manner of viewing Islam can be seen in the term 'little horn', which the Jews customarily applied to the Muslim rule, according

conquest of Palestine by the Muslims. The contents of the piyyūṭ: the coming of the Messiah, son of David; cosmic changes; the war between the east and the west; the west is victorious; King Joktan wages war and wins; the Jews are redeemed, 'the kings of Edom disappear'; Antioch rebels; Tiberias (Maaziah) and Samaria 'will be consoled'; Acre and the Galilee 'will meet mercy'; war in the Acre valley; 'Gaza and its surrounding towns will be stoned'; Ascalon and Ashdod will panic; the Jews leave the city; for forty days 'they will not have a grain to eat'; the Messiah arrives. In my opinion, this *piyyūṭ* has no reliable foothold on which to determine its date. See further on the midrash under discussion: Ashtor (Strauss), *Zion*, 4 (1938/9), 51 (on 'the prayer of Rabbi Shimon Bar Yoḥai); Urbach, *Eretz Israel*, 10(1970/71), 58–63. On Balaam and his metamorphosis in the Arab tradition see Gil, *JSAI*, 4(1984), 215ff. The midrash on the prophets of the nations, see in *Ba-midbar Rabba*, xx (at the beginning). The *Didaskalia*, see the Bonwetsch edition, 86; in fact, the source calls the prophet of the Arabs *planos prophētēs* (false prophet); see 'Abd al-Jabbār, *Sharḥ*, 577; Ṭiḥāwī, *Sharḥ*, III, 214: it is not enough for a Jew to declare that there is no God but Allah, and that Muḥammad is his messenger, in order to become a Muslim, for it is possible that he is attached to the view which says that Muḥammad is God's messenger only to the Arabs. On the readiness of some Jewish sects (Abū 'Īsā al-Iṣfahānī, 'Anan) to admit Muḥammad's divine mission to the Arabs, see Qirqisānī, I, 52 (Book I, 11.2), III, 283f (Book III, 13.2); Maqrīzī, *Khiṭaṭ*, III, 372; cf. Poznanski, *REJ*, 44(1902), 178.

[66] Bīrūnī, 19, see also Karājilī, 91; Ibn Ẓafar, *Khayr al-bishr*, 17; Ibn al-Jawzī, *Wafā'*, I, 61. Another interpretation is found in a letter attributed to the emperor Leo III (717–741) to caliph 'Umar ibn 'Abd al-'Azīz (717–720): the riders are but one person. The ass is the Jewish nation (and the reasons for this are provided there, but they are self-evident); the camel is the Midianites and the Babylonians, who make frequent use of this animal. The writer hints that the rider is actually Satan himself, who in the course of riding these animals (that is, the Jews and the pagans) instilled false belief (that is, Islam) among the Arabs. See a version of the letter as in Ghévond, the Armenian chronicler (*ca.* 900), in Jeffery, *HTR*, 37(1944), 327ff. Cf. Von Grunebaum, *Medieval Islam*², 17f.

to Daniel, vii:8.[67] Between the horns which symbolise in this book the gentile kingdoms, this is the last horn before 'the Ancient of Days' will sit on the seat of judgment; that is to say that Muslim dominion was conceived as the last stage before the Day of Judgment and salvation. The Christians saw in 'Umar on his entry into Jerusalem 'the abomination of desolation', also based on the book of Daniel. On the other hand, a Muslim tradition tells how 'Umar asked the bishop of Jerusalem: 'Do you really find me in the book?' and the bishop replied: 'yes'. 'And how do you find me?' The answer came: 'I find you a horn, a horn of iron, true and strong' (perhaps suggested by Mic., iv:13).[68]

[80] It seems that the atmosphere of the End of the Days which the Muslim forces felt in Palestine is reflected in the tradition of the *dajjāl*, a sort of apocalyptic creature who must be killed before the coming of the Day of Judgment. Some traditions attribute the victory over the *dajjāl* and his slaughter to Jesus, and others to 'Umar ibn al-Khaṭṭāb. He abides in Palestine near the gates of Lod. In the tradition of Ṭabarī, a Jew foretold to 'Umar, when he met him near Jābiya, that God will grant him Jerusalem and that the Arabs under his command will kill the *dajjāl*, who is located less than ten cubits from the gates of Lod. The *dajjāl* belongs to the tribe of Benjamin. In another version of the tradition, Ṭabarī relates, in continuation, that the Jew was from the Jews of Damascus. This other version also mentions that the Jews said of the *dajjāl* that he was from the tribe of Benjamin. The explanation of the gate of Lod can be found in the work of al-Musharraf b. Murajjā, a Jerusalemite of the eleventh century, who explains that it does not mean 'the gate of the church near Ramla' (St George of Lod) but the western gate of the city of Jerusalem (David's gate, the western one, which is near *miḥrāb Da'ūd*). The term *dajjāl* is evidently borrowed from the Syriac, *meshīḥā daglā*, a false messiah; as for example in the Syriac translation of Mat., xxiv:24; in the Greek original it is *pseudokhristoi*.[69]

[67] This expression is found mainly in Karaite writings, which apply 'the little horn' to the number of hijra years. See, for instance, the fragments of the Karaite calendar, ed. Gil, *ha-Tustarīm*, 86ff, and the Hebrew Index.

[68] See Ibn al-Athīr, *Jāmi'*, IV, 482; al-Ṭabarī al-Muḥibb, II, 38, attributes these words not to the bishop but to Ka'b al-Aḥbār who even interprets the meaning of the iron horn as always being innocent in the eyes of God. See also Ḥalabī, *Sīra*, I, 239; Zamakhsharī, *Khaṣā'iṣ*, 61, who ascribes these words to 'Abdallah b. Salām, a Jew of Medina who accepted Islam.

[69] Ṭabarī, *Ta'rīkh*, I, 2402f; cf. Ṭayālisī, 170; in which the killing of the *dajjāl* is ascribed to Jesus, and is told in the name of Mujammi' b. Jāriya, one of Muḥammad's opponents in Medina; see Musharraf, 79b–80a. Musharraf's version contradicts what Muqaddasī, *Āqālīm*, 176, wrote some two generations earlier: '[in Lod] there is a magnificent church, where alongside its gate Jesus will kill the *dajjāl*. See also: Bīrūnī, 212; Ibn al-Faqīh, 95, 117, who quotes a conversation between a Muslim and the people of Lod: the Muslim claims that the church of St George was built for King Solomon by the devils (*al-shayāṭīn*)

The episode of the Temple Mount and the return of the Jews to Jerusalem

[81] The Muslim traditions ascribe special significance to Caliph 'Umar's visit to the Temple Mount. Most of them add to his entourage on this visit Ka'b al-Aḥbār, a Jew from the southern part of the Arabian peninsula who joined the Muslims, turned to Islam and was considered an authority on matters of the Jews and their Torah. According to the Muslim tradition (and there is no reason to doubt it), the Byzantines turned the Temple Mount into Jerusalem's refuse dump from the time of Helena, the mother of Constantine. One should remember that Jerusalem was not foreign to the consciousness of the Muslim conquerors. The first *qibla* (the direction turned to in prayer), taken by Muḥammad in Mecca was towards Jerusalem, and even during his stay in Medina, he continued for some time (it is generally thought to be sixteen months but there are different versions) to turn towards Jerusalem while praying, until God 'sent down' the order to turn the *qibla* in the direction of Mecca (Koran ii:139); he then even made changes in his mosque in Medina, which since

while the people of Lod (that is, the Christians) reply that everything that seems sumptuous to the Muslims, they ascribe to the devils; obviously this building was constructed much earlier than the birth of Solomon by many generations. Ibn 'Asākir, I, 215, 217, 606–619; Yāqūt, *Buldān*, IV, 592f; Ibn al-Athīr, *Kāmil*, II, 501; Qurṭubī, *Tadhkira*, 232; the tradition of Jesus killing the *dajjāl* in his text is linked by him with the war of the End of the Days carried on by 'Urwa al-Sufyānī (with the hope of regaining the glory of the Umayyads) who will be defeated. His army will be dispersed and he will be found on the highest tree alongside the Sea of Galilee; cf. Sha'rānī, *Mukhtaṣar*, 197; Qurashī, 508; Ibn Ḥajar al-Haythamī, *Ṣawā'iq*, 165; Samarqandī, *Bustān*, 100: the *dajjāl* has still not been born; he will appear at the End of the Days, masses of Jews will follow him, until Jesus will arrive and kill him at the gate of Lod in Jerusalem. See the collection of traditions relating to Jesus' struggle with the *dajjāl* in Suyūṭī, in the supplement to Ṭabarānī, *Mu'jam*, II, 210f; in Samhūdī, *ibid.*, I, 87, who quotes from Ibn Zabāla (who finished his book in 814, see Samhūdī, *ibid.*, 7, 252), the killing of the *dajjāl* will take place in the vicinity of the basalt plateau (*ḥarra*) east of Medina; 'then their faces will shine on the Day of Resurrection like the light of the full moon'; these words are attributed to Ka'b al-Aḥbār as he found them in the *tawrāh* (there is perhaps some influence of Zech., xiv:4–7); 'Azīzī, III, 246, 485; Jesus will kill the *dajjāl* at the gate of Lod. Modern scholarship relates this tradition to the church of St George in Lod, where this saint who killed the dragon was venerated. Gutschmid, 184, attempted to prove that this veneration had ancient roots, going back to the time of Persian rule. Cf. Baedeker, *Palestine and Syria*, 136; Couret, *La Palestine*, 235; Steinschneider, *ZDMG*, 28(1874), 343: a tradition on Jesus and the *dajjāl* which mentions the eastern tower near Bāb Jayrūn in Damascus (The Gate of Jayrūn is also mentioned in 'The Mysteries of Rabbi Shimon Bar Yoḥai'). See the discussion on the *dajjāl* and the church of St George in Lod, in Nöldeke, *Sitzungsberichte* (Wien), 128(1893), 27, n. 2, who quotes Muqaddasī and Ibn al-Faqīh. It is possible to point to a certain parallelism between the tradition of the killing of the *dajjāl* at the gate of Lod and the Talmudic tradition of the stoning of Ben Stada in Lod; see *Tosefta*. Sanh. i:11 (Zuckerm, 431) and in the PT, *ibid.*, vii, 25d; see Nau, *ROC*, 6(1901), 525, 531, and the parallels he mentions on the origin of Jesus and the matter of Pantir, with regard to the letter of Jacob of Edessa which he edits there (without linking it to the Muslim tradition of the *dajjāl*); cf. Bell, *Origin*, 202.

then has been called also the *masjid al-qiblatayn*, the mosque with two directions of prayer. According to the story of Rajā' b. Ḥayawa (one of the most important Palestinian personalities in the days of the Umayyads, at the beginning of the eighth century), as Ṭabarī has copied it, 'Umar ordered Ka'b to be brought to him when he was approaching the Temple Mount. Afterwards he came to the *miḥrāb Da'ūd* (apparently meaning the Temple Mount). As it was already night, he began to pray there; at dawn he prayed with his men and read the *sūrat ṣād* (xxxviii), and *sūrat banī Isrā'īl* (xvii); in the first one the religions which preceded Islam are mentioned, as are David, whom God made caliph over the earth, Solomon, Abraham, Isaac, Jacob and Ishmael. The other chapter tells of the night journey of the Prophet, and this is known as *sūrat al-isrā'* (of the night journey). Afterwards he consulted Ka'b as to the question of where the most suitable place to pray should be. Ka'b told him that it should be behind the rock (that is, north of the *ṣakhra*) so that the prayer facing Mecca would at the same time face the rock as well. 'Umar immediately rejected this suggestion, censuring Ka'b on trying to imitate the Jews. 'For I have noticed that you have already removed your shoes', to which Ka'b replied: 'I wanted to stick to the ground with my feet.' 'Umar decided then to put up the prayer house in front of the rock, as the most proper place, 'for we were not directed about the rock but about the *ka'ba*'. In what follows, Ka'b explains to 'Umar that the entrance to the place and the evacuation of the refuse from the Temple Mount, is the fulfilment of the five-hundred-year-old prophecy which foretold of the rise of Jerusalem and the fall of Constantinople. According to Muhallabī's version, written two generations after Ṭabarī, it was the Jews (and not only Ka'b) who came to 'Umar and informed him of the actual site of the 'rock' because Constantine's mother, Helena, turned it into the outlet for the town's sewage and refuse. 'Umar ordered the Muslims to clean up the place and the Jews helped them to do so.

A Muslim tradition also accredits to Muḥammad a similar position of principle with regard to Jerusalem: 'Some say that when he was in Mecca, he would pray in the direction of Jerusalem thus, that the *ka'ba* would be behind his back . . . but others claim that he always [also] faced the *ka'ba* . . . and that when he was in Mecca he would face both *qibla*s [at the same time] for the *ka'ba* was between him and Jerusalem'. In Ibrāhīm b. 'Alī al-Wāsiṭī's words: 'When the Prophet prayed while he was still in Mecca, he would face in the direction of Jerusalem in such a way that the *ka'ba* was in front of him as well.' Theophanes, the Byzantine chronicler, confirms this in principle; on his arrival in Jerusalem, 'Umar went into the question of where Solomon's temple stood, and on that spot, built a prayer house for his abominations.

The subject of the Temple Mount being turned into a refuse dump is also mentioned in the commentary to Lam., i:17 ('Jerusalem is as a menstrous woman among them') by the Karaite Salmon b. Yeruḥim: 'That is, what Edom have done when they destroyed the second temple, for all the days of their stay here [in Jerusalem] they would discard thereupon [the site of the temple] the menstrual cloths and the refuse and all kinds of filth.' The subject of the refuse disposed of on the site of the Temple Mount spoken of by Salmon b. Yeruḥim is also mentioned in Musharraf. The Byzantine women would send their menstrual cloths to Jerusalem in order that they be thrown on the rock.[70]

70 The matter of changing the *qibla* appears in all the biographies of the Prophet. See for instance Ibn Sa'd, I(2), 3f; III(2), 146f; Balādhurī, *Ansāb.* I, 271: Muḥammad changed the *qibla* at noon, on Tuesday the 15th of Sha'bān of the 2nd year of the hijra (11 February AD 624) but some say: sixteen months after the hijra. Samhūdī, I, 240, 259; see the story of 'Umar and Ka'b on the Temple Mount in Ṭabarī, I, 2408ff, and a fuller version in Ibn 'Asākir, I, 557; Wāsiṭī, 45f; Muhallabī, 54; Ḥimyarī, 149f; an amended version is found in the work of the Christian chronicler Sa'īd ibn Biṭrīq, II, 17f; the patriarch Sophronius suggests to 'Umar to pray in the church of St Constantine but 'Umar refuses in order not to give the Muslims a pretext and a precedent for confiscating it from the Christians; and it was the patriarch who suggested building the mosque on the rock itself, the place where Jacob spoke to God and called it the gate of heaven (Gen., xxviii:17), and the Children of Israel called it the Holy of Holies and the centre of the earth; as to the matter of the refuse on the Temple Mount, it is perhaps also possible to relate to what was said in *Bereshit Rabba* xxxii (ed. Theodore and Albeck, 296), about Rabbi Jonathan whom a Samaritan told that it was better for him to pray with them in Shechem than in that *Beytā qīqaltā*; and it is possible that by *qīqaltā*, he meant refuse: cf. Safrai, in: *Perāqīm*, 388f, and see his parallel versions. More detailed information is to be found in Jerome in his commentary on Is. lxiv:11 (Our holy and our beautiful house, where our fathers praised Thee, is burned up with fire: and all our pleasant things are laid waste): 'et Templum in toto orbe celebratum in sterquilinium urbis novae quae a conditore appelabatur Elia (sit)' ('and the Temple which earned reverence throughout the world has become the refuse dump of the new city whose founder called it Aelia [that is, Hadrianus, Aelia Capitolina]'). See *MPL*, 24, 626; *CCSL*, A73, 740; cf. Prawer, *Cathedra*, 17(1980/81), 51. Sa'īd ibn Biṭrīq does not conceal the fact that the place was made a refuse dump by Helena and explains it in the desire of the Byzantines to fulfil the words of the New Testament on the destruction of the Temple. According to him, Sophronius was the one who helped 'Umar clear away the refuse: and he continues: 'and there were people who said: let us fix it (the prayer site) thus, that the rock should be the *qibla*, but 'Umar refused and said: we shall fix the prayer site so that the rock will be behind it'. See also: Bakrī, 827; Muqaddasī, *Muthīr* (Le Strange), 297, quoting Shaddād b. Aws, one of the early Muslims who settled in Jerusalem (I shall speak of him below): the patriarch wished to show him the Church of the Holy Sepulchre which he claimed was the site where David prayed (*masjid Da'ūd*), but 'Umar did not believe it. Afterward he claimed that the church of Zion was the site where David prayed, but 'Umar still refused to believe him. The rock was covered with refuse which the Byzantines placed there to annoy the Jews. 'Umar took off his outer clothing and started to work on cleaning up the place together with all the Muslims; see similar versions in Musharraf, 21a. On the manner of Muḥammad's praying see Ibn Sayyid al-Nās, *'Uyūn*, I, 236; see these traditions also in Ibn Qayyim al-Jawziyya, *Badā'i'*, IV, 168; on p. 171 he includes a tradition that Moses would also pray near the rock, facing 'the Holy House' (i.e., Mecca), with the *ka'ba* as his *qibla* while the rock is in front of him. See also what he says regarding the Samaritans of his time (the first half of the fourteenth century), who claim that the Jews falsified the

[82] These descriptions of 'Umar's visit to the Temple Mount are related to a question I shall deal with below, and that is the sanctity of Jerusalem to Islam. At this point I shall concentrate on the presence of Ka'b together with 'Umar on the Temple Mount, according to certain traditions, and also on the presence of the Jews. These traditions, though they are legendary in the main, undoubtedly preserved the basic fact of expressing the Jews' involvement and interest, to the extent that it enabled them to reach some understanding with the Muslims with regard to everything concerning the situation of Jerusalem and the status of the Temple Mount. The Jewish point, that is, the connection between the Jews and figures from the past, such as Moses, David, and Solomon on the one hand, and the specifically Jewish character of the place on the other, was certainly present in the Muslims' mind during the conquest, and thereafter also generated the traditions surveyed above. The Jews felt that the injunction against their entry into Jerusalem, not to speak of their settling there – which was maintained more or less consistently for slightly more than five

true *qibla*, which is the mountain in Shechem. See further: Ibn Kathīr, *Bidāya*, II, 96; VII, 54ff, who speaks of 'Umar's and Ka'b's visit on the Temple Mount, and adds: 'the throwing of the refuse on the Temple Mount was the Byzantine reprisal against the Jews for throwing refuse on the site of the crucifixion, hence the place (of the Church of the Sepulchre) is called *al-qumāma* (the refuse) and the church was also called thus. Abū 'Ubayd, *Amwāl*, 154; Wāsiṭī, 17; and following him, Ibn Faḍlallah al-'Umarī (Cairo 1924), 139: Ka'b bribed a Jewish scholar to show him the site of the rock and afterwards prayed near *bāb al-asbāṭ* ('gate of the tribes' in the north-eastern corner of the city), for according to him, King Solomon faced the whole of the Temple Mount; see other parallels in the editor's note 4, in Wāsiṭī; cf. also Silafī, *Faḍā'il*, 41b–43b. In al-Subkī, *Shifā'*, 47, Ka'b became a Muslim at that very time. Cf.: *Futūḥ al-Shām* (ascribed to Wāqidī), I, 227f; Abū' l-Fidā', *Buldān*, 241; 'Ulaymī, 226f; Abū'l-Fidā', *Mukhtaṣar*, I, 38, who quotes al-Muhallabī (see above): Ka'b turned to Islam during 'Umar's time and earned respect and attention from 'Umar because of his knowledge of the matters of the *isrā'īliyyat* (the traditions relating to the Jews) but many of the traditions ascribed to him are inaccurate and full of sin; his full name was Ka'b b. Māti', and his *kunya* was Abū Isḥāq; he was from Ḥimyar, from the clan of Dhū Ra'īn. He had a stepson, the son of his wife, whose name was Tubay' b. 'Āmir al-Ḥimyarī, who settled in Palestine and died in the year AH 101 (AD 720) in Alexandria. On Ka'b himself, it is told that he said that if it were not for his love for Palestine, he would have settled in Egypt. He studied with a certain Abū Muslim the Galilean, from the mountains of the Galilee, about whom it was said by some that he was a Jew and by others that he was a Christian monk. See Dhahabī, *Ta'rīkh*, III, 100, 220; IV, 95; Ṭabarī, *Muntakhab*, 116: Ka'b died in the year AH 32 or 34 (AD 652/3 or 654/5). See Theophanes, 339; and copied from him, Constantine Porph. (Moravcsik), 82 (ch. xix); the Syriac chronicle (Baethgen), has a similar version among events of the year AH 16; also Bar Hebraeus (Bedjan), 103 (Budge), 96; Salmon b. Yeruḥim, *Commentary on Lamentations* (Feuerstein), XLIV: see also what Sahl b. Maṣlīaḥ says in his introduction to his Book of Precepts, edited by Harkavy in *MWJ*, 6(1879), 181 (omitted from the version of the introduction in *Ha-mēlīṣ* because of censureship, see below): 'By God's grace, He did not hand over His Temple to the uncircumcised [i.e., the Christians], in order not to have idols put in them, so the Jews should not be ashamed. Since it is not right to bow before a site where foreign gods [version: idols] are placed'. See some of the traditions about 'Umar's uncovering of the rock, on Ka'b, etc., in Vogt, *Biblica*, 55(1974), 57f. Musharraf, fol. 21a; cf. Busse, *JSAI*, 5(1984), 89.

hundred years (AD 135–638) – had come to an end. That embargo was certainly close to the heart of the Christians for it suited their views of the waning of Judaism and its debasement. For the Fathers of the Church, the separation of the Jews from Jerusalem and the obliteration of any remnant of their earthly temple became an integral part of their creed's body of law. The most genuine expression of this viewpoint was that of Jerome, who wrote towards the end of the fourth century, in a manner reflecting the actual situation as well as the satisfaction and exultation at the disappearance of the Jews, who were considered the enemies of Christianity. They are included in his commentary on Zeph., i:15 ('That day is a day of wrath, a day of trouble and distress, a day of wasteness and desolation, a day of darkness and gloominess, a day of clouds and thick darknesss'):

Until this very day those hypocritical tenants (*coloni*) are forbidden to come to Jerusalem, because of the murder of the prophets (*servorum*), and the last of them – the Son of God; unless [they come] to weep, for then they are given permission to lament over the ruins of the city in exchange for a payment. Just as they purchased the blood of the Messiah, now they are purchasing their own tears; therefore even the lamentation is not given them for naught. On the day that Jerusalem was taken and destroyed by the Romans, one could see this people, women dressed in rags and the old bearing their tatters and their years, gather for a time of mourning, proving by their bodies and their dress the meaning of the wrath of the Lord. Then a rabble of the wretched gathers, and while the wood of the crucifix of the Lord shines and glows and celebrates His resurrection, and the symbol of the cross is topmost on the Mount of Olives, the children of this wretched nation are bemoaning the destruction of their temple, but are not worthy of compassion.[71]

[83] Karaite commentators of the tenth century mention in a number of instances the drastic change effected by the Muslims in their capture of Jerusalem. Thus Daniel al-Qūmisī writes at the end of the ninth century in his commentary on the Book of Daniel, xi:32: 'For before he came [the king of Ishmael, who defeated the king of the south, that is the Byzantine emperor] they could not come to Jerusalem; and they would come from the four corners of the earth to Tiberias and Gaza to see the temple; but now with his coming he brought them to Jerusalem and gave them a place and many of Israel settled there; and afterwards Israel come from the four corners of the earth to Jerusalem to preach and to pray . . .' In this same strain, Sahl b. Maṣlīaḥ writes in the introduction to his Book of Commandments:

. . . and after they left the place, it was more than five-hundred years in ruins,

[71] See *MPL*, 25, 1418f; quoted also in Schürer, I, 699, 703f. Cf. what the pilgrim of Bordeaux (333) has to say about the pierced stone on the Temple Mount, which the Jews visit every year, anoint it (with oil) and howl and wail and tear their clothing: Tobler et Molinier, I, 17: on the perforation in the ṣakhra see Wāsiṭī, 75, and the corresponding references in editor's note 3; on the ban on Jews residing in Jerusalem, see also Sa'īd ibn Biṭrīq, I, 133; according to whom the ban was imposed by Constantine.

inhabited by hyenas, and not one of Israel could come. There were Jews from the east who came to the city of Maaziah [Tiberias] to pray there. From the west they would come to the city of Gaza. From the land of the south they would come to the city of Zoar. And in the days of the little horn, God opened the gates of his compassion to His people and brought them to His Holy City and they settled there and they built places to read and to interpret and to pray at all times and to keep watchers therein at night...

Similarly, his contemporary Salmon ben Yeruḥim, in his Arabic commentary to Ps. xxx: wrote '... as we know, the temple remained in the hands of the Romans for more than 500 years and they did not succeed in entering Jerusalem; and anyone who did and was recognised [as a Jew] was put to death. But when the Romans left it, by the mercy of the God of Israel, and the kingdom of Ishmael was victorious, Israel was permitted to come and to live...'[72]

[84] Until now we have seen that the Karaite commentators confirm what we know from the Christian sources, that it was forbidden to Jews to enter Jerusalem, and they point out that the Muslims changed this situation when they captured the city. The author of the 'Mysteries of Rabbi Shimon Bar Yoḥai' also writes: 'The second king who will rise from Ishmael [that is to say, 'Umar ibn al-Khaṭṭāb] will be a lover of Israel and will repair their cracks and the cracks of the temple'. A Jewish chronicle, a fragment of which is preserved in the Cairo Geniza, also confirms that it was 'Umar who gave permission to the Jews to settle in Jerusalem and on the basis of his decision seventy Jewish families came from Tiberias and settled there. This was preceded by bargaining between the Jews and the

[72] Daniel al-Qumisī, see TS 10 C 2 (No. 2), f. 1v (see above, chapter 1, n. 12). See the introduction by Sahl b. Maṣlīaḥ to the Book of Precepts edited by Harkavy in *Ha-mēlīṣ*, 1879, p. 640 (= *Me'assēf Niddāḥīm* No. 13) and see the reprint of that series, 199. 'Little horn' means the kingdom of Islam (see above, note 67). Harkavy edited the introduction on the basis of manuscripts which he found in the Firkovitch collection and pointed out in the above version some *variae lectiones*: Holy boundary (instead of: Holy city); they built houses (instead of: they built places; places as parallel to the Arabic word *mawāḍi'* which means places, but also dwelling places). On the particular meaning of 'night watchers' see: Wieder, *Judean Scrolls*, 96–103, see especially his comments on the three foundations: *Miqrā, Derāshā* (= to interpret!), *Tefillā, ibid.*, 103. Salmon b. Yeruḥim: see the manuscript from the Firkovitch collection, II, No. 1345, edited by Neubauer, *Aus der Petersburger Bibliothek*, VII, 109, and following him, Mann, *Jews*, I, 46, n. 1, and his corrected reading in *Texts*, II, 18. Writing about the period in which the Byzantines ruled and the ban on Jews to reside in Jerusalem Salmon b. Yeruḥim uses the expression תק ונייף. The Arabic word *nayyif* means an addition to round numbers, and this can generally be any number from three to nine. The historical number is 638 (the Muslim conquest), minus 135 (the suppressing of the Bar-Kokhba revolt), equals 503; cf. Sahl b. Maṣlīaḥ: 'more than five hundred' (this seems to be a translation from the Arabic, which was in the original as in Salmon). This expression תק ונייף shortened to תק ונ, is evidently what produced the information of the alleged 550 years of Byzantine rule, mentioned in some *piyyūṭīm*, including that of Samuel 'the third' b. Hosha'na, and this, it seems, is the solution to this problem, which was discussed by Fleischer, *Zion*, 36(1971), 110.

patriarch, in the presence of the caliph; the Jews requested residence permits for Jerusalem for two hundred families while the patriarch was only ready to agree to fifty, until 'Umar decided on the number he thought fitting. Also in a letter from the yeshiva of Jerusalem to the communities in the diaspora [evidently those in Egypt], written in the middle of the eleventh century, we find the passage: 'And from our God there befell His mercy upon us before the kingdom of Ishmael; at the time when their power expanded and they captured the Holy Land from the hands of Edom, and came to Jerusalem, there were people from the Children of Israel with them; they showed them the spot of the temple and they settled with them until this very day . . .'[73]

[85] In these latter sources, we not only find the confirmation of the information in the Karaite commentaries with regard to the renewed settlement of Jews in Jerusalem shortly after the conquest, but also an interesting point found also in the Muslim traditions on the participation of the Jews in disposing of the refuse on the Temple Mount and the appointment of a number of Jews to be responsible for its cleanliness. The fragment of the letter quoted above and the fragment of the Jewish chronicle also confirm the episode of the Jews assisting in uncovering the rock. It is worth adding the words of the Jewish chronicle on how the cleaning of the Temple Mount proceeded: 'Taking part were all the Muslims in the city and in the district and participating with them were a group of Jews; afterwards they were ordered to evacuate the rubbish from the sanctuary and to clean it; and 'Umar watched them all the time. Whenever a remnant was revealed, he would ask the elders of the Jews about the rock, namely the *even shetiyyā* ('the foundation stone'), and one of the sages would mark out the boundaries of the place, until it was uncovered . . .' Indeed these statements correspond to what was said in the Muslim chronicles, in which that 'one of the sages' was Ka'b al-Aḥbār, as we have seen above. In addition, the letter from the yeshiva mentions afterwards that those Jews who came to Jerusalem immediately after the Muslim conquest 'took a pledge upon themselves', that is, they promised to be responsible for the cleanliness: 'to clear away its refuse and to clean its drains' . . '[74]

[73] Jellinek, *Bēt ha-midrāsh*, III, 79; cf. 'the prayer of Rabbi Shimon Bar Yoḥai', *ibid.*, IV, 120, and see **1,** a, lines 11–19; b, lines 1–10, 16–17; **420,** III, lines 10–13.

[74] See **1,** a, lines 1–9; naturally it is possible that the Jewish chronicle and the letter from the yeshiva drew on what was said in the Muslim sources, just as it is possible that the Muslim tradition was influenced by what was common knowledge among the Jews. See in the letter from the yeshiva, **420,** III, line 34. One cannot conclude from these sources that there were Jews in the ranks of the Muslim army, as does Dinur, *Isrā'ēl ba-gōlā*, I (1), 22, n. 22, to which he has already been replied by Assaf, *Meqōrōt*, 17; also Crone and Cook, 156, n. 29, exaggerate in seeing here proof of general Muslim-Jewish collaboration.

[86] This matter of the responsibility for cleanliness is confined in the Muslim sources to the area of the Temple Mount. According to these sources, the Mosque al-Aqṣā had ten, and later twenty Jewish servants, who were exempt from paying the poll-tax; they were in charge of the sanitation until the Caliph ʿUmar ibn ʿAbd al-ʿAzīz (717–720) replaced them with slaves from the Muslim treasury (*khums*). Salmon ben Yeruḥim evidently meant exactly the same thing when he wrote that at the time of the renewed settlement in Jerusalem, the Jews were allotted 'buildings in God's House', and they even prayed there during this period. Afterwards, however, there were complaints against them to the 'King of Ishmael' for their vile actions, and he ordered them to be evicted from there and placed near one of the gates of the Temple Mount; elsewhere he complains that the Muslims placed servants in the house of God who were of foreign nations.[75]

[87] One must add Theophanes' story to the information I have given, with regard to the renewal of Jewish presence in Jerusalem during ʿUmar's time, after an absence of more than 500 years. According to Theophanes, the shrine (*naos*) which ʿUmar began to build in Jerusalem would constantly collapse. They could not discover the reason for this until ʿUmar asked the Jews and they told him that his temple was only collapsing due to the cross that was standing opposite the temple, on the Mount of Olives. Actually after the cross was removed, the shrine no longer caved in. For the same reason, he adds, the enemies of the Messiah have removed many crosses. Theophanes was one of the sworn enemies of the Iconoclasts. His story is intended to prove the power of the cross, though in a roundabout manner we also learn that there were Jews in Jerusalem at that time. According to him, these miraculous events occurred during the reign of Constantine II, who ruled after Heraclius for only a few months in 641.

As I have already mentioned above, there is a clear contradiction between the information that I have summarised until now with regard to the renewed settlement of Jews in Jerusalem shortly after the conquest, at

[75] See Wāsiṭī, 43f; Muhallabī, 54; see Musharraf, 24b, who tells that the Dome of the Rock had 300 servants who were bought (by ʿAbd al-Malik) from the *khums* of the treasury. Whenever one of them died they would replace him. There were also ten Jewish servants who were exempt from poll-tax, and when their offspring increased, their number grew to twenty, and they would clean up after the people who came to visit there when the caravans came, in winter and summer. They would also clean the pool of purification outside. Further on, he tells that the Jews were also taking care of the glass panes of the lanterns and the other glass objects, of the candlewicks, etc. In continuation, he again tells (fol. 88b) that the Jews were in charge of lighting the candles on the Temple Mount. See also ʿUlaymī, 250. According to Ḥimyarī, 151, *anbāṭ* (farmers, villagers) from Palestine were given the task of cleaning the Temple Mount. Muqaddasī, *Āqālīm*, 171, explains that slaves of the treasury (*akhmās*) had been on the Temple Mount from the time of ʿAbd al-Malik. See also Maqdisī, *Muthīr* (Le Strange), 303ff; Abū ʿUbayd, *Amwāl*, 154; Salmon b. Yeruḥim, in Mann, *Texts*, II, 18; his commentary on Lamentations, MS Paris 295, 55b.

any rate, during the days of 'Umar ibn al-Khaṭṭāb, and the wording of 'Umar's treaty with the Christian population of Jerusalem, in which it is specifically stated that Jews are not permitted to settle in Jerusalem. We have seen how Goitein, in his attempt to overcome this contradiction, expressed doubt as to the authenticity of the treaty's version as transmitted by Sayf ibn 'Umar. But there seems to be little justification for this very stringent attitude towards a source that has been preserved for more than a thousand years. 'Umar's guiding line appears to have been to adopt the most decent attitude possible towards the local population and enable it to continue to pursue its customary mode of life and to earn its living in its own fashion and from then on, also to nourish the Arab tribes. It was then natural that, at a time when he wished to persuade Jerusalem to surrender, he would submit to the demands of the Christian inhabitants of the city to maintain the former legal status with regard to the Jews. However, perhaps three years later (if we accept the presence of the Jews according to Theophanes, in 641), 'Umar acknowledged the importance of the Jews in Palestine, comprising still a sizable population and economically the most important, and their request to settle again in Jerusalem was granted. In his own fashion, he secured the Christians' agreement to change that situation, despite the treaty. Here we must attach considerable importance to the information that has been preserved in the Jewish chronicle, according to which 'Umar decided on this new step only after he consulted the opinion of the patriarch as to the number of Jews that should be permitted to reside in Jerusalem. In the end, his decision was something of a compromise between the opinions of both sides. From the point of view of the Muslims' specific interest, he certainly did not see any fundamental reason to deny the Jews' request in this matter. And why was he obliged to give preference to the Christians with regard to permission to live in Jerusalem and to carry out their religious duties and precepts there? On the contrary, he was certainly aware that it would be more astute to prevent the Christians from being the sole non-Muslims living in this city, whose significance was very obvious to him. For the Jews' claim to their prior historical connection with the holy places was in conformity with Muslim tradition; to them the city was that of the ancient Children of Israel, of David and of Solomon, their kings and prophets. The presence of the Jews in the city would serve to weaken the validity of the exclusive hold which the Christians had achieved in the course of the three hundred years in which they ruled the Holy City. As we shall see further on, the Muslims, at the time, still did not attribute any sanctity to the city from their own standpoint, and at any rate, did not see it as a centre of Muslim ritual, and all they wanted was to lay the foundations of their rule and strengthen it, in Palestine generally and in Jerusalem in particular. For this purpose, it was worthwhile to draw the Jews closer, to reduce the Christians' exclusive tighthold on the city, and to lessen the strength of their claims to historical rights in it, for the Christians saw the ousting of the Jews from Jerusalem as a victory and an additional justification for their creed. The treaty with the Christians and the permission granted to Jews to reside in Jerusalem are not then historically opposed, nor do they exclude one another, in spite of some time difference between them; and both should be considered historical facts.[76]

[76] Theophanes, 342; to be more precise, it was Constantine III ('the Second' was generally applied to the son of Constantine the Great); see Schwabe, *Zion (ha-me'assēf)* (1926/7), 102f, and *ibid.* also a Hebrew translation of the passage. See the story, copied from Theophanes, in Michael the Syrian, book 9, ch. 8 (Chabot, II, 431); cf. Vasiliev, *History*, 193; Ostrogorsky, *History*, 130. The passage belongs to events which Theophanes describes under the year 6135 of the creation. Theophanes used the era of Panodoros, an Egyptian monk, who counts from the creation to the death of the archbishop Theodoros (AD 412) i.e., 5904 years. His era starts on 29 August 5493 BC; however Theophanes accepted the correction of Anianus, according to whom the era started on 25 March, 5493 BC; see on Theophanes' era: *Realencyclopaedie für protestantische Theologie und Kirche*, XXI, 923f; Dölger, *BZ*, 31(1931): 350; Breyer, *Bilderstreit*[1], 17; an interesting parallel to Theophanes' story is to be found in the Karaite Sahl b. Maṣlīaḥ's introduction to his Book of Precepts (see Harkavy, *Me'assēf*, 199): 'and we heard that in the days of Hadrian the wicked, God made a sign when he was building the temple to place an image in the temple, and the building fell. And they returned and built it a secord time and when they brought the image into the building, it fell again. And they built it a third time and it fell after its completion; a reminder of the words: they shall build but I will throw down (Mal., i:4); and so he abandoned it and took Zion and the house of the forest of Lebanon' (1Ki., vii:2; 2 Chr., ix:16, 20. The house of the forest of Lebanon was the house of King Solomon; with these words he meant two centres of Christianity in Jerusalem: the area of the Church of the Holy Sepulchre and Zion, which is the Nea; for it is not likely that he could discriminate between pagan Rome and Christianity). 'And he built altars within and put up images and their abominations just as one did in the generation of Jeremiah in the temple . . .' (this motif, of Jews by whose initiative Christian ritual objects are destroyed, repeats itself in Theophanes again elsewhere, 401f: a Jew of Laodicea in Phoenicia came to Caliph Yazīd and promised him forty years rule if he would rid the churches of the images. But with the help of Jesus and that of the Mother of Christ, Yazīd died in that same year [723; see more of this below, sec. 97]).

2

ISLAM STRIKES ROOTS

Events in Palestine to the end of Umayyad rule

In the days of Mu'āwiya

[88] We have little knowledge of what went on in Palestine during the rule of the 'rightly guided' caliphs or 'al-Rāshidūn': Abū Bakr, 'Umar ibn al-Khaṭṭāb (killed in 644), 'Uthmān ibn 'Affān (killed in 656), and 'Alī ibn Abī Ṭālib (killed in 661). During 'Uthmān's rule, serious schisms appeared in the Muslim camp, and open rivalry between the Hāshimids from which Muḥammad stemmed, and who were centred round 'Alī ibn Abī Ṭālib, and the Meccan aristocracy, which centred round the Umayyads. A rebellion developed which led to the assassination on 17 June 656, of the caliph 'Uthmān, who supported the Umayyads. 'Alī was declared caliph and was immediately forced to fight those who conspired against him. Opposition to 'Alī was led by two veterans and leaders of Islam, Ṭalḥa and Zubayr, together with 'A'isha, the beloved wife of Muḥammad and daughter of Abū Bakr. 'Alī's victory over the rebels at the 'Battle of the Camel' near Baṣra in Iraq on 9 December 656 did not restore stability to his reign. Mu'āwiya ibn Abī Sufyān of the Umayyads, who as we have seen above was appointed military commander in al-Shām and governor of the area on behalf of the caliph 'Umar (after the plague of Emmaus), refused to recognise the new caliph or to pledge loyalty to him. Thus Palestine was in fact under the governorship of the person who was considered the head of the uprising – Mu'āwiya. Alongside him stood 'Amr ibn al-'Āṣ, who had been governor of Egypt and had been dismissed by 'Uthmān. During the rebellion against 'Uthmān, with the help of tribes in Egypt, 'Amr found refuge in Palestine, in the neighbourhood of Sab' (which is Beersheba), on 'Amr's estate in 'Ajlān. He and Mu'āwiya met in Jerusalem and formed an alliance, and indeed 'Amr fought alongside Mu'āwiya in the battle of Ṣiffīn at the end of July 657. It was his idea to hold leaves of the Koran on the lances, an act which convinced 'Alī's followers, who were close to victory, to agree to an armistice and arbitration. This took place at Adhruḥ in Trans-Jordan (in the neighbourhood of Petra). 'Amr represented Mu'āwiya and actually

managed to get rid of 'Alī as caliph. Afterwards, 'Amr seized Egypt while the war between Mu'āwiya and 'Alī resumed; only after another armistice did the war of the tribes come to an end with an attack on 'Alī's life, and his death on 25 January 661 from the wounds inflicted during the attack. Half a year earlier, Mu'āwiya had been proclaimed caliph by his followers in Jerusalem. He was given complete support by the tribes in Palestine, both by the Urdunn tribes under the command of Sufyān b. 'Amr al-A'war al-Sulamī and by the tribes of jund Filasṭīn headed by Maslama b. Mukhlid.

The sources enumerate the tribes in Palestine and their commanders: leading the infantry of jund al-Urdunn was 'Abd al-Raḥmān b. Qays al-Qaynī, and over the people of jund Filasṭīn was al-Ḥārith b. Khālid al-Azdī. The Banū Quaḍā'a, who lived in Urdunn, also supported Mu'āwiya and were headed by Ḥubaysh b. Dalaja (or Dulja) al-Qaynī; the Banū Kināna of Filasṭīn were headed by Shurayk al-Kinānī; the Madhkhij tribe of Urdunn was headed by al-Mukhāriq b. al-Ḥārith al-Zubaydī; the tribes of Lakhm and Judhām, then in Filasṭīn, were led by Nātil b. Qays al-Judhāmī; the Banū Hamadān of Urdunn were led by Ḥamza b. Mālik al-Hamadānī (Ṭabarī and Balādhurī report him as Ḥassān b. Mālik b. Baḥdal), and the tribe of Ghassān from Urdunn was led by Yazīd b. al-Ḥārith b. Abī' l-Nams.

The father of Sufyān (the head of the Urdunn tribes), 'Amr b. Sufyān, that is Abū'l-A'war al-Sulamī (we have seen above that he participated in the battles of conquest in Palestine), was the one who accepted the surrender of Tiberias and was afterwards in charge of the army in Urdunn, an appointment he received from the caliph 'Uthmān. According to the chronicle of Michael the Syrian, it was he who introduced the systematic payment of taxes (in the year 669 or 674; it seems that the former is probably correct) imposed on the Christian villages. According to Ya'qūbī, it was the father who was the commander during Mu'āwiya's war against 'Alī, so it appears that both father and son functioned on behalf of Mu'āwiya during this period.[1]

[89] Of those mentioned above, the two outstanding figures among the

[1] The Mu'āwiya-'Amr pact in Jerusalem: Ibn Sa'd, IV(2), 2f; Dhahabī, *Siyar*, III, 94f; tribes of Palestine: Naṣr b. Muzāḥim, 206f, 226; Dīnawarī, 172 (who has Maslama b. Khālid instead of b. Mukhlid); Khalīfa ibn Khayyāṭ, I, 222 (who has: Shurayṭ al-Kinānī, instead of Shurayk; al-Ḥārith b. 'Abd, instead of b. Khālid. We have confirmation that he was indeed called al-Ḥārith b. 'Abd in the papyri of Nessana, for in some of them he is mentioned between October 674 and February 677; see *Nessana*, 33); Ibn 'Asākir, III, 439, points out that some say b. Khālid and some say b. 'Abd. On p. 451 he calls him: al-Ḥārith b. 'Abdallah. On Abū'l-A'war see: Ṭabarī, *Ta'rīkh*, I, 2159, 2398, 3057f; Ibn al-Athīr, *Kāmil*, III, 186; Michael the Syrian, II, 450, and in the Syriac source: 433 (the translation refers to 435 by mistake). Cf. Lammens, *Mo'āwia*, 48ff, who also has details on the tribe of Abū'l-A'war, Sulaym, a large and rich tribe based in the region of the holy cities in Ḥijāz,

leaders who supported Mu'āwiya in Palestine were Ḥubaysh b. Dulja of the Quḍā'a tribe and Nātil b. Qays, leader of Judhām. Considering the relatively important place these figures occupy in the sources one can conclude that both tribes, the Quḍā'a and the Judhām, held central positions in the Palestinian arena. Ḥubaysh b. Dulja played a leading role later, as well, in command of the army which Caliph Marwān sent against the rebels led by 'Abdallah ibn Zubayr in the year 684. As to Nātil b. Qays, leader of the Banū Judhām, he was evidently omnipotent in Palestine and dominated its financial administration. He afterwards betrayed the Umayyads and went over to 'Abdallah b. Zubayr, causing a split in the tribe, as we shall see. He was killed in the year 66 of the hijra, which is the year AD 685/6.[2]

[90] While the tribes in Palestine were loyal to Mu'āwiya, there was danger looming from the south as Mālik b. al-Ḥarith, also called al-Ashtar, one of the most fanatical of 'Alī's supporters, was *en route* to Egypt. The chances that al-Ashtar would dominate that country were very likely. Thus Mu'āwiya bribed the *dihqān* (a Persian term, which is used in Arab sources to mean 'owner of the place', that is, the local leader) of al-'Arīsh, promising him exemption from taxes for a period of twenty years. The *dihqān* then poisoned al-Ashtar, who was, as I have said, on his way to Egypt.[3]

[91] The extent to which the tribes in Palestine were deeply involved in the struggle between 'Alī and Mu'āwiya can be perceived from the story told by al-Ash'ath (who is Abū Muḥammad Ma'dikarib b. Qays), head of the Banū Kinda, one of the moderate tribes among 'Alī's followers, concerning the outcome of the battle of Ṣiffīn: 'indeed I saw the tents and the courtyards in Filasṭīn; not a tent nor courtyard nor building nor camp of tents but had tied to them a man's hand or leg' (in place of pegs).[4]

Mecca and Medina. Ya'qūbī, *Ta'rīkh*, II, 226; Ḥassān b. Mālik: Ṭabarī, *Ta'rīkh*, II, 468; Balādhurī, *Ansāb*, V, 125. In the same war, Mu'āwiya promised Ayman b. Khuraym, the leader of the Banū Asad, that he will appoint him governor of jund Filasṭīn, if he would come over to his side together with his tribe and fight 'Alī; but Ayman refused. It is said that Ayman was a poet and also an outstanding war-lord. See Ibn Sa'd, VI, 24f; Ibn Abī'l-Ḥadīd, I, 435.

[2] On Ḥubaysh b. Dulja: Ṭabarī, *Ta'rīkh*, II, 579; Ibn Ḥabīb, *Muḥabbar*, 481; according to Ya'qūbī, *Ta'rīkh*, II, 298f, he took part afterwards in the famous battle at Medina, the battle of the Ḥarra, in 682, at the head of 1000 fighters. See about him also in Ibn Qutayba, *Ma'ārif*, 416; Khalīfa ibn Khayyāṭ, I, 329; Ibn 'Asākir, IV, 40ff; Ibn al-Athīr, *Kāmil*, IV, 190f; Nātil b. Qays, Ṭabarī, *Ta'rīkh*, II, 468; Mas'ūdī *Tanbīh*, 307; *idem*, *Murūj*, V, 225: Nātil b. Qays was killed in Palestine in the battle of Ijnādayn, between the caliph's army and the tribes loyal to 'Abdallah ibn Zubayr. See also Ya'qūbī, *Ta'rikh*, II, 304ff, 321; Khalīfa ibn Khayyāṭ, I, 332; Ibn Ḥazm, *Jamhara*, 420f; Iṣbahānī, *Aghānī*, XVII, 111; Sibṭ ibn al-Jawzī, *Kanz*, 5: Nātil (see versions: Nā'il, Nābil) ruled in Filasṭīn, in the coastal area and in Jerusalem; Ibn al-Athīr, *Kāmil*, IV, 145.

[3] Mas'ūdī, *Murūj*, IV, 422; cf. Wüstenfeld, *Statthalter*, I, 24.

[4] Naṣr b. Muzāḥim, 339.

[92] The followers of Mu'āwiya pronounced him caliph in Jerusalem in the year AH 40, or AD 661, according to the Arab sources. A Syriac source states that Mu'āwiya then came to the Church of the Golgotha in Jerusalem, and also visited Mary's grave in Gethsemane. According to this source, the event occurred during Ṣafar-Rabī' I of the year AH 40, that is July AD 660, while 'Alī was still alive; whereas according to the Arab sources, it occurred after his assassination. It appears that Mu'āwiya visited Palestine quite often because its tribes were a reliable buttress to his rule. He chose to settle in al-Ṣinnabra (evidently south of the Sea of Galilee, near the mouth of the Jordan – Khirbat al-Karak). Later caliphs would also come there. Following the period of severe warfare which had raged within the Muslim camp, it seems that Palestine enjoyed a period of comparative serenity in Mu'āwiya's time. One indication of this may be the relatively high taxes which were collected during those days of the two junds of Palestine: in Filasṭīn, 450,000 dinars were collected and in Urdunn, 180,000 dinars were collected annually. Mu'āwiya and his son Yazīd evidently visited Jerusalem frequently. Three Iraqis made attempts on Mu'āwiya's life in the mosque in Jerusalem but it is not known exactly when.

Yazīd, Mu'āwiya's son and heir to the caliphate, stayed in Jerusalem at the time of his father's death, in April 680. Two or three years later, it is stated that he was staying in Tiberias. This was at the height of a bitter struggle which he had to conduct against his enemies, for the tribes in the north of Palestine (Urdunn) were then his loyal supporters.[5]

The war of the Zubayrids

[93] One can undoubtedly speak of a special connection which both Mu'āwiya and his son Yazīd, who reigned after him, enjoyed with the

[5] Ṭabarī, *Ta'rīkh*, II, 4; Ibn Kathīr, *Bidāya*, VIII, 16; *Chronicon Maron.*, 71: this source tells that while the Muslims were gathering in Jerusalem to pronounce Mu'āwiya caliph, there was a severe earthquake during which Jericho and a large number of churches were destroyed, among them the church of St John the Baptist on the Jordan. Much harm was also suffered by the monastery of St Euthymius. According to Syriac sources, the earthquake occurred on 9 June 659; according to Theophanes, 347: in the month of Daisios in the year 6150, in the second indiction, in the 17th year of Constans. Before that, on page 346, it is mentioned that 'Uthmān was murdered in the 14th year of Constans, which is AM 6147. 'Uthman was assassinated in AD 656; hence AM 6150 here is actually AD 659 while Mu'āwiya was pronounced caliph in 661. Cf. also Nau, *ROC*, 4(1899), 324; Nöldeke, *ZDMG*, 29(1875), 85; see *ibid.*, p. 91 the text, and p. 95 the translation. Nöldeke points out there the difference in times between the Arab sources and the Syriac one. Al-Ṣinnabra, see Yāqūt, *Buldān*, III, 419: it is situated opposite the Afēq pass (*'aqabat Afīq*) three miles from Tiberias. Al-Ṣinnabra is Sennabris in Greek sources, Sinnabrī in the Talmudic sources. See Lammens, *Mo'āwia*, 380; Mayer, *Eretz-Israel*, 1:169, 1950/1: Bar-Adon, *Eretz-Israel*, 4:50, 1955/6. The taxes: Ya'qūbī, *Ta'rīkh*, II, 288; the attempted murder in Jerusalem, see Dhahabī, *Siyar*, III, 94f; Yazīd in Jerusalem: Damīrī, *Ḥayawān*, I, 105; cf. Qaramānī, I, 119.

tribes of Palestine. They were the major political and military support of the Damascene ruler, and this was certainly reflected in the caliph's attitude towards them, expressed in the form of subsidies and regular allowances. The tribes expressed their loyalty through the participation of 5,000 fighters of the Banū Judhām, under the command of Rawḥ b. Zinbā', and of 1,000 fighters from the Banū Kināna, under the command of Ḥubaysh ibn Dulja in the battle of the Ḥarra, which was the slaughter of the regime's opponents in 682 in Medina. The almost continuous struggle for power within the caliphate left its mark on the tribes in Palestine and atrocious inter-tribal battles frequently took place on its soil. In 680–692 the tribes of Palestine actively participated in the war between the two brothers, 'Abdallah and Muṣ'ab, the sons of al-Zubayr (al-Zubayr was the Prophet's cousin and one of his closest aides) and the Umayyads. The two brothers succeeded in capturing Ḥijāz and also parts of Iraq.

These events developed rapidly immediately after the assassination of Ḥusayn, the son of 'Alī ibn Abī Ṭālib, in Karbalā' on 10 October 680. 'Abdallah ibn al-Zubayr then placed himself at the head of the opposition to the Umayyads, and started preaching against them from his base in Mecca. After the submission of Medina, Mecca became the centre of opposition to the reigning caliph and the siege which Yazīd's army imposed on Mecca almost succeeded in obtaining its surrender, when the news of Yazīd's death in November 683 arrived. From that point onwards, 'Abdallah ibn al-Zubayr met with increasing success and he enjoyed the support of important sectors of the Muslim world, including Egypt. The Palestinian tribes played a fateful role in the course of events within this context. The Banū Hamadān, led by Ḥassān b. Mālik b. Baḥdal, succeeded in organising a strong alliance of tribes, which called themselves 'southerners' or Banū Kalb; and these stood staunchly by the Umayyads and were the major factor in their victory over ibn al-Zubayr's 'Syrian' champion, al-Ḍaḥḥāk b. Qays al-Fihrī, head of the rival alliance of the 'northerners', or Banū Qays. Al-Fihrī had been appointed governor of Damascus on ibn al-Zubayr's behalf. This victory was achieved by the 'southerners' after a hard and gory battle in Marj Rāhiṭ, east of Damascus, in July 684.

In these events, the Banū Judhām fulfilled an important role. At that time, they moved from jund Urdunn to jund Filasṭīn, that is, they moved southward, under the leadership of Rawḥ b. Zinbā', and replaced the Banū Hamadān, who seem to have weakened somewhat and moved to Urdunn in place of the Judhām, and who were led by Ḥassān (or Ḥamza) b. Mālik

Tiberias: Ṭabarī, *Ta'rīkh*, II, 492. See in Lammens, *Yazīd*, 107, n. 2, references to more sources, some of which claim that at the time of his father's death, he was in Ḥimṣ or elsewhere.

b. Baḥdal. Ḥassān was the uncle of the new caliph Yazīd (his mother's brother). Both tribes, together with their leaders, remained faithful to the Umayyads and pledged their loyalty to Yazīd, son of Mu'āwiya, on the death of his father. But within the Banū Judhām a radical change was taking place under the leadership of Nātil b. Qays; he had snatched command of the tribe and went over to the side of 'Abdallah ibn al-Zubayr, while Ḥassān b. Mālik, head of the Urdunn tribes, remained loyal to Yazīd although the tribes there had stringent complaints against Yazīd's two sons, 'Abdallah and Khālid, who had been appointed by him to take charge of Urdunn. Hence a rupture was created between the tribes of the two junds – Urdunn and Filasṭīn. The tribes of jund Filasṭīn sided, together with the Banū Judhām led by Nātil b. Qays, with 'Abdallah ibn al-Zubayr. When in the course of the struggle the scales began to come down in favour of the Umayyads, in the days of the caliph Marwān, Nātil b. Qays (the source refers to him as *ṣāhib Filasṭīn*, the chief of Filasṭīn), fled from Palestine to Ibn al-Zubayr in Mecca. Another point of dissension arose with the death of Mu'āwiya II, son of Yazīd, who was caliph from November 683 until June 684. The tribes of Palestine, especially in Urdunn, under the leadership of Ḥassān b. Mālik, favoured the appointment of Khālid b. Yazīd in opposition to Marwān b. al-Ḥakam, who was pronounced caliph after Mu'āwiya II. When Khālid's mother (the widow of Yazīd and later married to Marwān) murdered Marwān, the tribes renewed their support of Khālid, but to no avail, and 'Abd al-Malik b. Marwān became caliph in April 685. At that time, however, the sons of al-Zubayr were still a serious threat to the Umayyads and although most of the tribes of al-Shām supported the Umayyads, the tribes of Filasṭīn, led by Nātil b. Qays, were a worrying exception. At this point, 'Abd al-Malik enjoyed the help of Rawḥ b. Zinbā' and his son Ḍib'ān, leaders of a branch of the Banū Judhām who had remained faithful to the Umayyads. 'Abd al-Malik was then also forced to defend himself against a Byzantine offensive initiated by the emperor Justinian II Rhinothmetos, son of Constantine IV Pogonatos (Mas'ūdī calls him Lāwī ibn Flanṭ). But 'Abd al-Malik succeeded in maintaining his composure, managed to appease the emperor by grants of money (1,000 dinars per week) and gifts, and defeated the tribes of Filasṭīn led by Nātil b. Qays; according to Mas'ūdī the defeat took place at Ijnādayn. Nātil b. Qays was killed in that battle. 'Abd al-Malik then sent a force of 6,000 fighters under Ṭāriq b. 'Amr (a client or *mawlā* of the caliph 'Uthmān b. 'Affān), who had formerly been the governor of Medina, to set up a temporary line of defence against the sons of Zubayr in the region between Eilat and the border of Ḥijāz (Wādi'l-Qurā). Evidently the information regarding the Byzantine raid on Caesarea and Ascalon belongs to the beginning of 'Abd al-Malik's rule (*ca.*686; Balādhurī states that this occurred during the time of Ibn Zubayr). The Byzantines destroyed these two ports and exiled their inhabitants, and it is quite possible to conceive of this as pertaining to that war which was initiated by Justinian II. Afterwards, ʿAbd al-Malik stationed two special garrisons on permanent alert in these two cities.[6]

[94] Rawḥ b. Zinbāʿ the Judhāmite became one of the favourite companions of the victorious ʿAbd al-Malik. Some sources mention that he was much younger than his rival Nātil ibn Qays, the supporter of ʿAbdallah ibn Zubayr. It is said that Rawḥ was very gifted and that his rank was like that of a wazīr (an office that was as yet non-existent). ʿAbd al-Malik said of Abū Zurʿa (that is Rawḥ) that in obedience he was a Shāmī (a man of al-Shām), in shrewdness he was an Iraqi, in knowledge of legal matters (*fiqh*) he was a Ḥijāzī, and in calligraphy he was as good as a Persian. He died in the year AH 84, or AD 703. We shall find his sons, Ḍibʿān and Saʿīd involved in later events.[7]

Muḥammad ibn al-Ḥanafiyya

[95] While the struggle between the Zubayrids and the Umayyads was at its height, a strong movement of the followers of the ʿAlids was afoot which had its centre in Kūfa in Iraq, under the leadership of Mukhtār. This movement centred round the personality of Muḥammad ibn al-Ḥanafiyya, the son of ʿAlī from another woman (not from Fāṭima, ʿAlī's wife and the daughter of the Prophet, but rather from Khawla, whom the Muslims captured from the Banū Ḥanīfa), despite the fact that he himself did not take an active part in the movement's actual leadership. Muḥammad ibn al-Ḥanafiyya almost fell victim to the suspicions of ʿAbdallah ibn Zubayr, who ruled Mecca at the time, that he was setting himself up as a rival. An army sent by Mukhtār freed Muḥammad from the prison into

6 See note 2 above; on the Banū Judhām and Banū Hamadān, see Ṭabarī, *Ta'rīkh*, II, 468f, 474, 481, 577; Yaʿqūbī, *Ta'rīkh*, II, 298f, 321; Masʿūdī, *Murūj*, V, 224f; *Tanbīh*, 307; Khalīfa ibn Khayyāṭ, I, 332; Sibṭ ibn al-Jawzī, *Kanz*, 5; Iṣbahānī, *Aghānī*, XII, 80; XVII, 111; Ibn ʿAsākir, VII, 40f; Ibn al-Athīr, *Kāmil*, IV, 145, 151; Ibn Abī Ḥadīd, II, 368. Ḥassān b. Mālik was not the only member of the Banū Kalb who had relations through marriage with the Umayyads, which continued for several generations. See on this: Lammens, *Moʿāwia*, 310ff; and *ibid.*, 286ff, on the family of Baḥdal (ibn Unayf) and on Ḥassān, his grandson, important personalities in the Banū Kalb. See there also on the special link they had with the Banū Quḍāʿa, another important tribe which joined the supporters of the Umayyads. The destruction of Caesarea and Ascalon: Balādhurī, *Futūḥ*, 143 (garrisons: *rawābiṭ*).

7 Ṭabarī, *Ta'rīkh*, II, 1164; Balādhurī, *Ansāb*, I, 36f; Yāfiʿī, I, 175; Thaʿālibī, *Laṭā'if*, 61, 159 (praise of Abū Zurʿa); Dhahabī, *ʿIbar*, I, 98 (Head [*sayyid*] of the Judhām; commander [*amīr*] of Filasṭīn); Ibn Kathīr, *Bidāya*, IX, 55; Ibn ʿAsākir, V, 337f, who adds that Rawḥ had a house in Damascus and that his father, Zinbāʿ, was of the *ṣaḥāba*, that is, of the Prophet's circle; Ibn al-ʿImād, I, 95; Ibn Khaldūn, *ʿIbar*, III, 126. See also Lammens, *Moʿāwia*, 214, n. 8 (*dāhiya*, a term used frequently at that time, meaning astute). See on the conflict between Rawḥ and Nātil b. Qays also: Lammens, *Yazīd*, 310ff.

which 'Abdallah had thrown him. Apparently, this occurrence caused Muḥammad to leave the peninsula. He then reached Eilat accompanied by a large group of his partisans. The people of Eilat welcomed him gladly. 'Abd al-Malik, when news of Muḥammad's arrival in Eilat reached Damascus, was uneasy about his proximity. After consultation with Rawḥ b. Zinbā' the Judhāmite and Qabīṣa b. Du'ayb, he wrote him a letter in which he demanded that Muḥammad either leave the place or pledge his loyalty to him. In return for a declaration of loyalty, he promised to grant Muḥammad a hundred ships, which would await him at the port of Qulzum (today, Suez) laden affluently. Muḥammad ibn al-Ḥanafiyya then preferred to leave the city, for he wanted to maintain absolute neutrality between the camps who were still fighting at that time, that is the Umayyads and the Zubayrids. He moved to Medina and there he remained until 'Abdallah ibn Zubayr's final downfall in October 692. He died three months later. According to an anonymous chronicle of the ninth century AD, Muḥammad's base in Palestine was in Kudād, a distance of some two miles from Ḥumayma (in the region of Moab), which was also the base of the Abbasids.[8]

The sons of al-Muhallab

[96] In the days of al-Walīd b. 'Abd al-Malik (705–715), his brother Sulaymān ruled in Palestine. It was here that the sons of al-Muhallab, who had been one of the important commanders in the service of the Umayyads, found refuge. After the death of al-Muhallab, the sons were hounded angrily by al-Ḥajjāj ibn Yūsuf, against a background of inter-tribal rivalry. They and their retinue were taken in by Wuhayb b. 'Abd al-Raḥmān and Sufyān ibn Sulaymān, both notables of the Banū Azd, a distinctly Yamanī tribe, similar to the sons of al-Muhallab, who were also Yamanīs. These two were retainers of Sulaymān ibn 'Abd al-Malik. Al-Ḥajjāj ibn Yūsuf accused the sons of al-Muhallab of embezzling money and obtained an order from Caliph al-Walīd to his brother Sulaymān that he should send them to Damascus. And so Sulaymān sent them (it is not clear whether he sent both brothers or merely the eldest Yazīd), accompanied by his own son, all three in chains. Then al-Walīd took pity on them, however, and released them.[9]

[8] See the article Muḥammad b. al-Ḥanafiya (by F. Buhl) in *EI*[1]; here the episode of Eilat is not mentioned at all. See about this matter: Ibn Sa'd, V, 79f; on p. 85 he mentions another date of Muḥammad's death: the year AH 81, which is AD 700; *Akhbār al-dawla al-'abāsiyya*, 107, 197; Dīnawarī, 309; Kudād, see another version: Kurār ḥumayma (status constructus); Ṭabarī, *Ta'rīkh*, II, 1975.

[9] Ṭabarī, *Ta'rīkh*, II, 1211f; according to him this takes place in the year AH 90, which is AD 709; in Ibn Khaldūn, '*Ibar*, III, 140: the year AH 86 (AD 705): in the long run, the sons of

Religious unrest

[97] The twenties of the eighth century were stormy ones as far as inter-faith relations were concerned. Within the Byzantine empire during the reign of Leo the Isaurian (714–717), the Iconoclastic movement was astir. The sources of the period contain claims that it was the Jews who incited the emperor to act against the worship of icons and crosses. On the other hand, it is stated that in the days of Leo there was an edict of forced baptism against the Jews. I have already mentioned that Theophanes wrote that a Jew of Laodicea came to Yazīd and proposed to him to rid the Christian churches under his dominion of all images, and that as a result, he would enjoy undisturbed rule for forty years. According to Theophanes this occurred in the seventh year of Leo's reign, that is 723, during the days of Yazīd II, son of ʻAbd al-Malik. Yazīd actually issued decrees against the worship of icons. According to other information in Theophanes, a man of Christian origin named Beser was taken and held in captivity in Syria by the Muslims (that is, the Umayyads), and accepted Islam. After he was freed from captivity, he returned to Byzantium, became a Christian again, and influenced Leo to introduce decrees against the worship of images. Another Christian source, on the other hand, tells the name of the Jew who swayed Yazīd to order the destruction of all images worshipped by Christians throughout his domain. He was the leader of the Jews in Tiberias ('leader of the mad Jews, a magician and seer, a tool of the soul-destroying devils') called Tessarakontapekhys ([the man] of forty cubits). But Yazīd died in the same year and did not manage to achieve the destruction of the images. It is difficult to guess who is behind this description; it should be remembered that Tiberias was then still the centre of the Jews of Palestine and the seat of the Sanhedrin. It would be interesting to juxtapose against it the story from an anonymous Muslim chronicle, according to which one said that the *biṭrīq* (*patricius*) who represented the emperor Leo in negotiations with the Muslims, was a clever man known by the nickname 'the man of forty cubits'.

At the same time, there was evidently considerable religious turbulence within the Islamic world itself. According to some sources, a false prophet appeared in Jerusalem during the rule of ʻAbd al-Malik, a certain al-Ḥārith b. Saʻīd (or b. ʻAbd al-Raḥmān b. Saʻīd), who was said to be a *mawlā* (client) of Marwān b. al-Ḥakam (the father of ʻAbd al-Malik). He attracted many followers in Jerusalem. ʻAbd al-Malik sent a special unit of forty men from Farghāna (a district on the river Sir-Darya in Central Asia) to Jerusalem, led by a man of Baṣra; the composition of the unit perhaps

al-Muhallab did not escape the verdict of fate – they rebelled and were executed in August 720.

indicates that 'Abd al-Malik did not trust the local people for this purpose. Al-Ḥārith was caught, brought to Damascus, and there crucified.[10]

The uprising of the tribes in Palestine in 744

[98] Serious events closely related to inter-tribal affairs began to occur in the Umayyad caliphate during the spring of 744. It is important to note, in connection with our subject, that Palestine served as the principal arena for these events. The story as it appears in Ṭabarī, told by Rajā' ibn Rawḥ ibn Salāma, who was the great grandson of Rawḥ ibn Zinbā' the Judhāmite, runs as follows. At the head of the tribes in the Filasṭīn region stood Sa'īd and Ḍib'ān, the sons of Rawḥ ibn Zinbā'. After the murder of Caliph al-Walīd II (who was the grandson of 'Abd al-Malik and the son of Yazīd II) by Yazīd his cousin (son of al-Walīd I and grandson of 'Abd al-Malik), in April 744, Sa'īd b. Rawḥ wanted to dismiss Sa'īd b. 'Abd al-Malik, who was the governor of Filasṭīn, on behalf of the assassinated caliph, Walīd. Despite the fact that Sa'īd behaved well as governor of the region, the tribes preferred Yazīd b. Sulaymān b. 'Abd al-Malik, who was the leader of the Sulaymān family. This family lived within the domain of jund Filasṭīn and enjoyed the affection of the local tribes. Sa'īd b. Rawḥ then wrote to Yazīd b. Sulaymān on behalf of the tribes and proposed that he come (evidently from Damascus to Palestine) in order to be made

[10] On the forced baptism see Theophanes, 401; on the Jew from Laodicea and on Beser, *ibid.*, 402. It appears to be an Arab name, Bishr. Cf.: Becker, *Islamstudien*, I, 446, and see the parallel in Ṭabarī, *Ta'rīkh*, II, 1463f. A Jew prophesied to Yazīd ibn 'Abd al-Malik that he would reign forty years; some say that the name of that Jew was Abū Māwiya: another Jew said about him that he lied, since in fact he saw (in a dream?) that he would reign forty reeds (*qaṣaba*) each reed being a month, and instead of that he said: years. It is interesting that this number – forty – is also woven into traditions and information on 'the man of forty cubits'. On the forced baptism cf. also: Agapius of Manbij (Maḥbūb), 244; Elias of Nisibis, in Baethgen, to the year 101 (= 719–720); Michael the Syrian, IV, 457; Cedrenus, *MPG*, 121, 869. This is also the time of the appearance of Jewish sects, of Abū 'Īsā al-Iṣfahānī and of Severus; which is a topic of its own, and it is not known whether it has any connection to the history of Palestine. The Jew from Tiberias: Mansi XIII, 197ff (Council of Nicaea, 787). The parallel between the sources was first discerned by Brooks, *JHS*, 19(1899), 26–30, who added also the information in Theophanes regarding the brother-in-law of the empress Irene (799) whose name was Serantapēkhos, which is the name of the Tiberias Jew in the Latin version of the proceedings of the council of Nicaea in Mansi, *ibid.* (Sarantapekkos). See in Brooks, *ibid.*, also the Muslim source (from *al-'uyūn wa'l-ḥadā'iq*). Starr, *Speculum*, 8:500, 1933 excludes any possibility of historical truth in the Jewish aspect of the story and assumes that only is there the tendency to ascribe to the Jews the anti-Christian decrees in the Muslim world. This view is perhaps too extreme. Crone, *JSAI*, 2(1980), 76ff, tries to prove by these sources on Bishr, etc., the existence of Judaeo-Christian sects; but the matter is very obscure and the sources themselves say nothing about it. The matter of al-Ḥārith b. Sa'īd: Ibn 'Asākir, III, 442ff; Dhahabī, *Ta'rīkh*, III, 147f, notes the time: the year AH 79, which is AD 698; according to Ibn Kathīr, *Bidāya*, IX, 27, he was a zindīq, an appellation given generally to Manichaeans, but sometimes, in orthodox Islam to schismatics of any description.

governor in jund Filasṭīn, while to Sa'īd ibn 'Abd al-Malik he wrote that he should vacate his position since the tribes preferred another. Sa'īd ibn 'Abd al-Malik was then in Beersheba. In order to lend greater cogency to his letter, Sa'īd ibn Rawḥ mobilised the tribes. Sa'īd ibn 'Abd al-Malik was taken aback at the size of the force facing him and fled to the new caliph, Yazīd ibn al-Walīd, to be followed by the tribes, led by Yazīd ibn Sulaymān, going out to fight the caliph. This rebellion, which as mentioned began in jund Filasṭīn, quickly spread to jund Urdun. The tribes there took on a new leader, Muḥammad ibn 'Abd al-Malik, and at the head of the tribes of Filasṭīn there stood, as mentioned, Sa'īd and Ḍib'ān, the sons of Rawḥ ibn Zinbā' the Judhāmite. The caliph Yazīd sent an army against them under the command of his cousin, Sulaymān ibn Hishām ibn 'Abd al-Malik. Sulaymān preferred to negotiate, and with the help of envoys and mediators he succeeded in convincing the brothers Sa'īd and Ḍib'ān, the sons of Rawḥ, to submit to the caliph Yazīd's authority and to pledge their allegiance to him. Muḥammad ibn 'Abd al-Malik, the leader of the Urdunn tribes, also agreed to accept the new caliph's authority. It seems that the most convincing argument was the distribution of benefits and various offices to the tribesmen. For instance, Ḍib'ān was promised that he would be appointed governor of jund Filasṭīn for life. One can say in summation that there was an outbreak of general rebellion within the Palestinian tribal framework and their refusal to accept the authority of the new caliph lasted until they were promised, on his part, various favours and benefits for their leaders. But the atmosphere among the tribes continued to be antagonistic to the caliph. The official responsible for collecting taxes in Urdunn on behalf of the new caliph, Muḥammad ibn Sa'īd ibn Ḥassān, encountered opposition when he requested that people come to his office in Tiberias. He was obliged to ask for help from Sulaymān ibn Hishām in that he should place an armed force at his disposal to overcome the opposition of the local tribes. Sulaymān hesitated to fulfil his request, and only after Muḥammad applied to the new caliph and obtained a written order to Sulaymān, did the latter comply with his request. He then placed a force of 5,000 men at his disposal, under the command of Muslim ibn Dhakwān. The army set forth at night and quartered its men in villages in the neighbourhood of the Sea of Galilee, while Muḥammad ibn Sa'īd ibn Ḥassān went out with a group of fighters in the direction of Tiberias. This time the tribesmen realised that there was no point in prolonging their opposition, with the army beginning to dominate the area and to treat the tribes' property as if it were their own. They expressed their anger with the two leaders of the rebellion against the new caliph, Yazīd ibn Sulaymān and Muḥammad ibn 'Abd al-Malik by robbing their homes, and even took their mounts and their arms. Afterwards they dispersed and each man returned homeward to his family. From then onward, Sulaymān ibn Hishām felt that he controlled the situation and that there were many roads open to him. He advanced with his army to al-Ṣinnabra south of the Sea of Galilee and the tribes of Urdunn came there and pledged their loyalty to the new caliph Yazīd before Sulaymān. From there, Sulaymān sailed with his men to Tiberias and they all prayed together, for it was Friday, and there too all those present swore an oath of loyalty to Yazīd.

Despite the fact that it is not clearly stated or spelled out in any detail, it appears that one of the reasons for the rupture between Yazīd and the tribes was the problem of the Jews and the Christians. Evidently Yazīd strongly objected to the tribes' extortion of non-Muslims and told them quite distinctly, 'I will not tolerate your behaviour which causes the poll-tax payers to exile themselves from their country and see no future ahead of them.' The tribesmen saw in this a favouring of the non-believers and Yazīd was accused openly of being *qadarī* and *ghaylānī*, that is to say, one of the disciples of Abū Marwān Ghaylān, a Jerusalemite who was one of the chief heralds of the school of free will and seemed to be under the influence of Christianity.[11]

[11] See Ṭabarī, II, 1831ff; Ibn al-Athīr, *Kāmil*, V, 294. When these sources use the term *ahl* or *nās* the tribes are always intended. See also: Ibn Kathīr, *Bidāya*, X, 13; Abū'l-Fidā', *Mukhtaṣar*, I, 206; Ibn Khaldūn, *'Ibar*, III, 232; on the loyalty of the Palestinian tribes (especially Sa'īd b. Rawḥ b. Zinbā') to Sulaymān b. 'Abd al-Malik and his son Yazīd see the comments of Bosworth, *IQ*, 6(1972), 47f. The treatment of non-Muslims: Ṭabarī, *Ta'rīkh*, II, 1834f; Yazīd accused of being ghaylānī and qadarī: Dhahabī, *Ta'rikh*, IV, 289; V, 179; similar criticism of the attitude to the dhimmīs can be found in what was said by Caliph Marwān ibn Muḥammad; he points his finger at the tribes (evidently the tribes of Palestine): 'You only want to rob the property of every dhimmī you encounter'. See also, Ibn al-Athīr, *Kāmil*, V, 309. Ghaylān, of the leaders of the qadariyya in Damascus, was executed in Hishām ibn 'Abd al-Malik's day (724–743; see Ṭabarī, *Ta'rīkh*, II, 1733), after a kind of religious disputation between him and Maymūn b. Mihrān. 'Abd al-Malik's grandson, Marwān b. 'Abdallah, and the latter's son, fell victim to the anger of the Damascene crowd and were murdered after being accused of belonging to the qadariyya, who favour free will. The caliph Yazīd was also accused of having appointed officials from among the followers of Ghaylān, among them Manṣūr b. Jumhūr, made governor of Iraq (see Ṭabarī, *ibid.*, 1828, 1874); Dhahabī, *Ta'rīkh*, IV, 289, calls Ghaylān: Ghaylān al-Qudsī, that is, he was a Jerusalemite. According to him there was a sort of cross-examination going on in the presence of the caliph Hishām ibn 'Abd al-Malik, by the cadi al-Awzā'ī: Ghaylān refused to repent despite all the warnings, and so he had his limbs torn off and was crucified. Dhahabī, *Ta'rīkh*, V, 289, points out that Yazīd was probably inclined to Ghaylān's views (he does not refer to Ghaylān the man, for Ghaylān himself was executed before this). See also Ibn Sa'd, V, 395; according to 'Ubāda b. al-Ṣāmit (see on him below), the Prophet himself had already foretold the appearance of Ghaylān, who will create a schism among the Muslims, worse than that created by Satan. See *ibid.*, VII(2), 177f, on Maymūn b. Mihrān, who was one of the officials of the caliph 'Umar ibn 'Abd al-'Azīz, and it appears that the disputation between him and Ghaylān was conducted in letters; it seems that Ghaylān admonished Maymūn for being in the service of the caliphs ('Umar ibn 'Abd al-'Azīz and Yazīd ibn 'Abd al-Malik), and Maymūn expressed his regrets about it. See also the article Ghaylān b. Muslim in *EI*[2] (by C. Pellat), and the article on Ghaylān's movement by Van Ess, *SI*, 31:269, 1970.

The uprising of the tribes in Palestine in 745

[99] About half a year later, Palestine again erupted, this time during the reign of Marwān II, ibn Muḥammad ibn Marwān, who became caliph at the end of November 744. At the same time, at the head of the tribes of Urdunn stood his cousin, al-Walīd ibn Mu'āwiya ibn Marwān, and at the head of the jund Filasṭīn tribes stood Thābit ibn Nu'aym al-Judhāmī. The latter had been appointed on behalf of the former caliph, Ibrāhīm ibn al-Walīd, to be responsible for the *dīwān* Filasṭīn, that is, to handle the registration of the tribes and to execute the payment of allowances and subsidies. The Palestinian tribes at that point joined the uprising which broke out in northern Syria, in Ḥimṣ. Leading the rebellious tribes in Palestine was the same Thābit ibn Nu'aym. He descended on Tiberias but al-Walīd ibn Mu'āwiya managed to hold his ground; after a battle that lasted a few days, the caliph sent reinforcements under Abū'l-Ward Majzāh b. al-Kawthar, of the tribal federation of the Banū Kilāb, to help the beleaguered fighters in Tiberias. The population of Tiberias (apparently the non-Muslims) also went out to fight against Thābit ibn Nu'aym, and his men were scattered to the winds. His three sons, Nu'aym, Bakr and 'Imrān, were caught, while he himself managed to escape. His sons were executed and the same fate awaited him when he was later caught together with another son, Rifā'a. Marwān then appointed a man from the Banū Kināna as governor of jund Filasṭīn, al-Rumāḥis ibn 'Abd al-'Azīz. The disturbances evidently continued throughout the winter until the summer of 745. Immediately afterwards, another insurrection broke out in northern Syria, this time headed by Sulaymān ibn Hishām. This rebellion, drowned in rivers of blood, once again included the tribes of Palestine, and during its course, as Theophanes tells us, Marwān destroyed the walls of Jerusalem, as he did in Ḥimṣ, Damascus and other cities.[12]

Ḥumayma – the end of the Umayyads

[100] Only some five years separated these events from the end of the reign of the Umayyads. Feverish activities were already underway in the

[12] Ṭabarī, *Ta'rīkh*, II, 1892, 1894; III, 46; Balādhurī, *Futūḥ*, 209; Mas'ūdī, *Tanbīh*, 326; Ibn al-Athīr, *Kāmil*, V, 330f; al-Rumāḥis – evidently the correct version, and not al-Dumāḥin as in the editor's note in Ibn al-Athīr, *ibid.*; Dhahabī, *Ta'rīkh*, V, 32; Ibn Kathīr, *Bidāya*, X, 23; Abu'l-Fidā', *Mukhtaṣar*, I, 207; Ibn Khaldūn, *'Ibar*, III, 244; Theophanes, 422; Breyer, 64; on Thābit ibn Nu'aym see also: Jahshiyārī, 71; on al-Rumāḥis see also: Fīrūzābādī, *Muḥīṭ*, II, 220: al-Rumāḥis b. 'Abd al-'Uzzā; he was in charge of the police (*shurṭa*) of the caliph Marwān ibn Muḥammad. Ibn 'Asākir, V, 328: he moved afterwards (that is, after the Abbasid coup) to Andalus and was in the service of the Caliph 'Abd al-Raḥmān. These events were the result of the serious polarisation which occurred among the tribes after the murder of al-Walīd, between 'north' and 'south'. The tribes of 'the north' (Muḍar) supported Marwān while the tribes of 'the south' (Yaman) opposed him. Cf. Nagel, *Untersuchungen*, 150.

underground of both sides of the revolution, Khurāsān in the east and Ḥumayma in Palestine, in the region of Moab. Ḥumayma was situated some fifty kilometres southeast of Ma'ān in Trans-Jordan. 'Alī ibn 'Abdallah, the grandson of 'Abbās, the uncle of the Prophet, settled there in the year 690 or thereabouts; he fortified the place and it became a centre for the descendants of the Abbasids. According to the tradition (which undoubtedly has no historical authenticity), Abū Hāshim 'Abdallah, the son of Muḥammad ibn al-Ḥanafiyya, transferred his rights as *imām* and leader of the Muslim world, while he was on his deathbed, to Muḥammad ibn 'Alī of the Abbasids, the son of the above-mentioned 'Alī. From that time, Muḥammad ibn 'Alī was the leader of the Abbasids; he was the father of the two first Abbasid caliphs: Abū'l-'Abbās al-Saffāḥ and Abū Ja'far al-Manṣūr.[13]

[101] As is known, the centre of the insurrection moved to Khurāsān, under the leadership of Abū Muslim, who united all the streams and the sects of the Umayyads' enemies into one movement. From Khurāsān the rebelling armies spearheaded westward; on 2 September 749 they conquered Kūfa. In the meantime, the Abbasids joined the revolution under Abū'l-'Abbās, the elder son of Muḥammad ibn 'Alī. Marwān suffered his final defeat in January 750, on the Great Zāb river, to the east of the Tigris. The last act took place in Palestine, at Abū Fuṭrus, which is Antipatris (Rōsh ha-'ayin), where the Umayyads were slaughtered. The sources generally speak of the killing of eighty of the Umayyads, the execution being supervised by 'Abdallah ibn 'Alī, Abū'l-'Abbās al-Saffāḥ's uncle.[14]

[13] See: *Akhbār al-dawla al-'abbāsīya*, 185; Ibn 'Abd Rabbihi, IV, 475f (on the circumstances of the arrival of 'Abdallah ibn Muḥammad ibn al-Ḥanafiyya to his cousin the Abbasid, Muḥammad ibn 'Alī ibn 'Abdallah ibn 'Abbās at Ḥumayma); Ibn Khallikān, III, 278; VI, 315; Ibn al-Athīr, *Kāmil*, V, 53; cf. Lammens, *Mo'āwia*, 127f; he points to the fact that Ḥumayma was near Adhruḥ and the villagers who lived in Adhruḥ were *mawālī*, converted to Islam, who were clients of the Hāshimids, and this is perhaps why the Abbasids settled just in Ḥumayma. That Adhruḥ was inhabited by Christians we can learn from the colophon of an Arabic manuscript in the Monastery of St Catherine in the Sinai, from the year AH 288 (AD 901), saying that the *anbā* (father) Mūsā b. Ḥakīm al-Qasīs (the priest) al-Adhruḥī ordered the book (a collection of religious sayings). See Oestrup, *ZDMG*, 51(1897), 453, and see also in Lammens, *ibid.* See further Shaban, *Abb. Rev.*, 150f; the article Ḥumayma (by D. Sourdel) in *EI*².

[14] Ṭabarī, *Ta'rīkh*, III, 47ff (he writes that the governor and official of the treasury at the time in jund Filasṭīn was a man of the Banū Judhām, an offspring of Rawḥ b. Zinbā', al-Ḥakam ibn Ḍib'ān); Ya'qūbī, *Ta'rīkh*, II, 425f; Mas'ūdī, *Murūj*, VI, 75f; *al-'Uyūn wa'l-ḥadā'iq* (De Goeje), 203f; Ibn Qutayba, *Ma'ārif*, 372; Dhahabī, *Ta'rīkh*, V, 297; Ibn al-Athīr, *Kāmil*, V, 425; Ibn al-'Adīm, *Zubda*, I, 54; Ibn 'Asākir, III, 134; Ibn Kathīr, *Bidāya*, X, 45 (92,000 men were killed in one day near 'a river in Ramla'); Ibn Taghrī Bardī, I, 258, 324 ('a large group of the supporters of the Umayyads were imprisoned in Egypt by Ṣāliḥ b. 'Alī, another uncle of the Abbasid caliph, governor of Egypt, and in the end, they were executed in 'Qalansawa in the land of Filasṭīn'); see also *ibid.*, II, 7; Ibn Khaldūn, '*Ibar*, III,

Natural disasters

[102] Until now, we have seen to what extent Palestine was involved in the military and political events of the Umayyad period. The tribes living in Palestine during that era and who were an important element in the military and political system set up by the Umayyads were a permanent and active factor in these events. Before dealing with other aspects of life in Palestine during this period, we must outline some of the misfortunes and disasters that befell Palestine that were not of man's doing.

I have already mentioned above the earthquake that occurred in 659, some two years before Mu'āwiya was pronounced caliph in Jerusalem, evidence of which has been preserved in Theophanes and in Syriac sources. In the year AH 80, or AD 699/700, a severe plague hit al-Shām, which prevented the usual summer raid on Byzantine areas. One year later, we are told of the Dome of the Rock having been hit by lightning. In AH 86, or AD 705, a calamitous plague once again broke out in al-Shām, known as the plague of the girls, because its first victims were women. Further plagues were recorded in AH 115, AD 733, and in AH 116, AD 734. A Christian source (and there are no parallels in Muslim sources) informs us of a severe earthquake which affected all of Palestine (including *Iordanē*) and Syria, in which myriad people were killed and many monasteries destroyed, particularly in Jerusalem. A very devastating earthquake occurred in the year AH 130 (beginning 11 September AD 747), during which the eastern and western sides of the Dome of the Rock collapsed. Many of the *anṣār* (people of Medina), who were living in Jerusalem, were killed during this earthquake, especially as a result of the caving in of the house of Shaddād b. Aws. All his sons were killed in that earthquake. The people of Jerusalem fled from the city and remained in the fields for forty days. We also have information about this earthquake from Christian sources. According to Michael the Syrian, Tiberias was then completely destroyed, with the exception of the home of one man whose name was 'Īsā. Thirty Jewish synagogues in the town were also laid waste and the Jewish bath-houses were also destroyed. According to Ibn Muqaffa', the quake took place on the 16th of January, and Agapius also mentions the month of January. Kedrenos mentions the 18th of January, but he is off the mark with regard to the year. It is possible that this earthquake determined the setting of a fast called 'the fast of the Sabbatical year'. Indeed, the year of the earthquake, AM 4508, was a Sabbatical year. It is possibly to this earthquake that the poem *yōṣēr ra'ash shevī'ī*, written by a poet named Samuel, refers. It recalls the earthquake and its disastrous effects in Ti-

271, 283. See also Moscati, *Archiv Orientalni*, 18(3): 88, 1950 (who does not say anything new).

berias and Ramla ('in the Shefēlā, in the Valley of the Sharon'). Many were drowned at the time, and it is not clear where 'little children and women, teachers of the Bible and the Mishna' suffered this fate. Its superscription reads the 23rd of Shevat, which in that year (AD 748) fell on the 28th of January (Sunday), and this differs from what is stated in some of the Christian sources. The difference is not great and it possibly stems from a mistake in the copying of the Christian sources.[15]

The religious status of Jerusalem

[103] A most important development in the status of Jerusalem occurred during the Umayyad period, and this was its transformation into a Muslim holy place. We have seen that there was a different relationship to the city at the time of its conquest, when 'Umar decided that the Muslims would pray with their backs towards the rock on the Temple Mount, so as not to behave in the manner of the Jews. Even if we assume that there is no historical truth in this story, it at any rate reflects the basic approach of the Muslims during the first generations of the occupation. This *qibla*, Jerusalem, was the first direction which the Prophet faced, but he himself ruled it out after the hijra. 'Umar ibn al-Khaṭṭāb, his heir and the fulfiller of his testament, loyally continued the tradition laid down by the Prophet,

[15] The plague in the year 80: Khalīfa ibn Khayyāṭ, II, 360; Ibn Kathīr, *Bidāya*, IX, 27 (who has: in the year 79). The incidence of the lightning: Dhahabī, *Ta'rīkh*, III, 227. 'The plague of the girls': Ibn Kathīr, *Bidāya*, IX, 61 (*ṭā'ūn al-fatāyāt*); and on other plagues: *ibid.*, 309, 312. The earthquake in 738: Papadopoulos-Kerameos, III, 4 (he is perhaps mistaken; actually it is the earthquake of the year 747/8 which is meant); the earthquake in 747/8: Wāsiṭī, 84; Maqdisī, *Muthīr* (Le Strange), 304; Dhahabī, *Siyar*, II, 330; Ibn Taghrī Bardī, I, 311. Pseudo-Dionysios (Chabot), 47 (text), 42 (translation), points out that the earthquake occurred in 1059 Sel., which is AD 747/8, 'in the land of the west'; Agapius, 521 (he claims that more than a hundred thousand people died in Tiberias then); Elias of Nisibis, 171 (text); 82 (translation): the quake was in the year AH 131; a village in the neighbourhood of Mount Tabor moved from its place four miles without any damage having been caused; Severus (Evetts), 393f: the quake occurred on the 21st of Ṭūba, the day of the death of St Mary (the Dormition, i.e., 16th of January, cf. *DTC*, X, 2302), and Egypt was not affected apart from Dumyāṭ (Damietta); it was felt from Gaza to the border of the Persian regions. Theophanes, 651, and following him Cedrenus, II, 7, set the time of the earthquake in the sixth year of Constantine V (Copronymus), which is 746, and pointed out that it was felt in Palestine as far as the River Jordan, and in all of Syria; thousands of people were killed and many monasteries and churches were destroyed, particularly in the desert region around Jerusalem. Cf. Zonaras, III, 268; some of the above references are mentioned by Creswell, *Early Muslim Architecture*², 374, n. 3. Michael the Syrian, II, 510 (p. 466 in the original), does not mention an exact date, but the quake is mentioned in the framework of events that took place after 740 (contrary to what is said in Assaf and Mayer, *Sefer ha-yishuv*, 10, n. 8). The piyyūṭ: Zulay, *Yedī'ōt*, 3(1936/7), 156–162; the connection between the piyyūṭ and the earthquake of 748 was first suggested by Margaliot, *BJPES*, 8(1940/41), 97–104, and see there the fragment from the poet Pinḥas, who also mentions 'the fast of the earthquake of the sabbatical year'. See also *idem*, *Tarbiz*, 29:339, 1959/60.

signifying that Jerusalem was not holy to the Muslims, and that only the Jews were still wholeheartedly attached to its sanctity.

The new status of Jerusalem and the renewed recognition of its sanctity were not the result of scholarly discussions or new theological interpretation. They were born with the Dome of the Rock, an idea conceived by the ruler, Caliph 'Abd al-Malik, and translated by the best architects and builders of the time into a language of pillars and arches bearing all the splendour that the imagination could possibly envision.

'Umar built his first mosque only as a place of prayer (and the meaning of the Arabic word *masjid* is place of prayer for the Muslims) on the Temple Mount out of respect and recognition of the tradition of the Children of Israel, which linked this place with the memory of the ancient prophets, the predecessors of Muḥammad and his heralds. We have seen that the view attributing the building of the Mosque to 'Umar is confirmed both in the Arab traditions and by Theophanes, the Byzantine chronicler; while on the other hand, the author of 'the Mysteries of Rabbi Shimon Bar Yoḥai' was imprecise when he attributed to 'Umar the achievement of 'Abd al-Malik two generations later. 'The second king who will arise from Ishmael' will, according to his words, 'hollow out Mount Moriah and make it entirely into a plain and build there a place of bowing down on the foundation stone, as it is said: and thou puttest thy nest in the rock.' Arculf, a Gallic bishop (it is not clear whether he was from the south of France or from Wales), who visited Palestine one or two generations after the conquest, gives us a description of the mosque put up by 'Umar. In his words, this is what the Muslims built on the Temple Mount: '. . . *quadrangulam orationis domum quam subrectis tabulis et magnis trabibus super quasdam reliquias construentes, vili fabricati sunt opere* . . .' (they built a house of prayer in the form of a square made of wooden planks and large beams which they constructed over the remnants [of ruined buildings], a work of inferior quality). It is obvious that this structure was of a type similar to that of the Prophet's mosque in Medina. According to Muslim tradition, the Prophet, when he first decided to build a mosque in Medina, asked that the building should be simple, like the 'booth of Moses' '*arīsh Mūsā*, for in any case the end of the world was imminent.[16]

16 'The mysteries of Rabbi Shimon Bar Yoḥai': Jellinek, *Bēt ha-midrāsh*, III, 79; the Biblical quotation is from the verse 'And he looked on the Kenites, and took up his parable, and said, strong is thy dwellingplace, and thou puttest thy nest in a rock' (Num., xxiv:21). Arculf: in Tobler et Molinier, I, 145. On the Prophet's mosque see the traditions gathered and interpreted by Kister, *BSOAS*, 25:150, 1962. On the resemblance of the ancient mosque of 'Umar on the Temple Mount, according to the description of Arculf and the mosque of the Prophet in Medina: Abel, *DACL*, VII(2), 2304; on the parallel between Arculf's description and the Muslim traditions on the building of the mosque in 'Umar's days (or according to his orders): Riess, *ZDPV*, 11(1888), 208. Musharraf, 23a, says that 'Umar appointed Salām b. Qayṣar to pray at the head of the believers in Jerusalem (in other

[104] It was during his reign as caliph that ʿAbd al-Malik had the Dome of the Rock constructed, a building that was in complete contradiction to the modesty of the period of the conquest. The work of construction evidently began in 688. ʿAbd al-Malik appointed three people to be responsible for putting up the structure: Rajāʾ b. Ḥayawa, Yazīd b. Salām and his son, Bahāʾ b. Yazīd. The last two were clients (*mawālī*) of ʿAbd al-Malik (they were, possibly, originally Christians). ʿAbd al-Malik informed all the districts under Muslim rule of his decision to build the mosque, and all his subjects consented to the plan. He gathered expert builders from all over his domain. Before they started on the actual construction, they set up a model for the caliph according to their designs, near the building site. The income from the collection of taxes (*kharāj*) in Egypt for the course of seven years was invested in the building. In the building process, the caliph was represented by his son Saʿīd, called Saʿīd the Good. The building work lasted four years, from 688 to 692. The Christian chronicler Saʿīd ibn Biṭrīq attributes the construction of the Dome of the Rock to ʿAbd al-Malik's son al-Walīd. In his version, the latter ordered the removal of the dome of the church in Baʿlabakk, a dome of gilded brass, and its replacement on the building he put up in Jerusalem. But it seems that this information is not credible, and the Muslim sources are reliable in ascribing the erection of the Dome of the Rock to ʿAbd al-Malik. It is possible, however, that the information with regard to al-Walīd refers to the building of the al-Aqṣā mosque. A Jewish midrash tells that ʿAbd al-Malik b. Marwān '... shall build the house of the God of Israel', a version that appears somewhat strange to us today, but is certainly intended to say: 'shall build on the site where the house of the God of Israel stood'. The clearest proof that it was indeed ʿAbd al-Malik who built the Dome of the Rock is the passage on the upper rim of the central arches, on the outer southeastern side, where the date AH 72 (AD 692) is inscribed, even though the name ʿAbd al-Malik was replaced by that of the Abbasid caliph al-Maʾmūn.[17]

sources: Salāma). From the above-mentioned descriptions in the Muslim traditions it emerges that the first mosque on the Temple Mount was built to the south, evidently on the site where the al-Aqṣā mosque was subsequently erected.

[17] Wāsiṭī, 81ff; Musharraf, 23b; Maqdisī, *Muthīr* (Le Strange), 297ff; ʿUlaymī, 240ff (according to him, one started to build in the year AH 66, that is AD 685/6); Ibn al-ʿArabī, *Muḥāḍara*, II, 366ff; Saʿīd ibn Biṭrīq, II, 42; Ibn Khaldūn, *ʿIbar*, III, 148; he probably copied from Ibn Biṭrīq and shortened it: he built the Dome of the Rock on the site of a Christian church which he destroyed. Donner, *ZDPV*, 93(1977), 4, did not understand Saʿīd ibn Biṭrīq correctly, as if he said that ʿAbd al-Malik 'enlarged the mosque by including the rock within it'; actually he merely says that he built a magnificent mosque with the rock at its centre. The midrash: Bodl MS Heb f 24 (Cat. Neubauer 2642), in Wertheimer, *Battē midrāshōt*, II, 30 (Jerusalem 1893/4); cf. Levi, *REJ*, 67(1914), 178. The Arab sources mentioned above note that ʿAbd al-Malik also ordered a treasury building to be constructed (apparently to house the money intended for the Dome of the Rock), and perhaps

[105] In establishing this splendid building, 'Abd al-Malik undoubtedly wished to convey a message to the Muslims as well as to non-believers. Since he considered Palestine, and within it, Jerusalem, part of the area which served as the principal and most loyal base of his reign, he devoted considerable attention to the place and most certainly wished to emphasise, first of all, the religious significance of Jerusalem in the eyes of the Muslims. Arab sources of the Middle Ages tried to attribute to him radical and far-reaching tendencies. As the Ḥijāz was in the hands of the Zubayrid rebels, 'Abd al-Malik wanted to divert the hearts of the believers from Mecca and substitute the Dome of the Rock for the Ka'ba. On the other hand, however, the same sources point out that it was the magnificence of the Christian churches in Jerusalem that motivated 'Abd al-Malik to construct a building which would supersede them in beauty and splendour and demonstrate the superiority of Islam. According to Muqaddasī, when he asked his uncle whether al-Walīd would not have done better if the Muslims' money spent on building a mosque in Damascus was spent on the building of roads and public works and defence, his uncle explained to him that al-Shām was a Christian country with beautiful churches, attractive to the eye and which have become famous, like the Church of the Holy Sepulchre, or the church in Lod and the church in al-Ruhā (Edessa). So the Muslims put up a mosque which would put these in the shade and attract Muslim attention – one of the wonders of the world: 'For it is clear that when 'Abd al-Malik saw the beauty of the Dome of the Tomb [in the text: *qubbat al-qumāma*, dome of the refuse] and its form, he was afraid lest it arouse respect in the hearts of the Muslims and he erected this dome on the rock'. The tradition which crystallised in the time of the Umayyads is interesting, according to which a true caliph is only one who governs over the two mosques of Mecca and Jerusalem.[18]

it is the building which is still standing to the east of the Dome of the Rock, which is the *qubbat al-silsila*. The inscription 'Abd al-Malik: Kessler, *JRAS*, 1970, 9; Creswell, *Early Muslim Architecture*², 69; regarding the date it is worth noting a seventeenth century source: the Italian Franciscan Morone da Maleo, who was the appointee (*custos*) of the Holy See in Palestine (1651–1657), and in his book *Terra Santa nuovamente illustrata*, 1669–1670, I, 81, quoted in Italian an inscription from the Dome of the Rock, according to which the mosque was built by 'the great king, son of Marwān (*il re grande figlio de Mesuan*[!]) in the 65th year of the hijra (*de' Saraceni*)', that is AD 684/5, which is, of course, an error, for only in that year (towards the end) did 'Abd al-Malik become caliph. See the version in Clermont Ganneau, *Rec.*, II, 400, and see a detailed discussion in Sharon, *Baneth Memorial Volume*: 245.

18 Muqaddasī, *Āqālīm*, 159; Ibn Taymiyya, *Majmū'a*, II, 61: 'Abd al-Malik wanted to attract people to a religious visit (*ziyāra*) to Jerusalem instead of the *ḥajj* to Mecca. See also Ya'qūbī, *Ta'rīkh*, II, 311; and so also the Christian Sa'īd ibn Biṭrīq, II, 39: 'Abd al-Malik forced people to go on pilgrimage to Jerusalem and did not permit them to go on pilgrimage to Mecca, because of 'Abdallah ibn al-Zubayr. The tradition on the two mosques: 'Ulaymī, 213f; cf. Hirschberg, *Rocznik Orient.*, 17(1951/2), 319f (in Hirschberg's opinion the story of 'Umar's visit to Jerusalem and his interest in the Temple Mount

[106] The Dome of the Rock has caught the attention of many of those who deal with the history of Muslim art, hoping to discover the identity and ethnic kinship of its builders and to clarify the architectural tradition to which they adhered. Different and conflicting opinions have been expressed on this subject. Some attribute the building to Roman tradition, but most scholars ascribe it to the Byzantine art of building and claim that the executors were architects and craftsmen brought from Byzantium, pointing to the architectural similarity to the group of buildings of the Church of the Holy Sepulchre in particular. Of the most recent studies on the subject, that of Grabar is the most outstanding, particularly in terms of his analysis of the artistic motifs that appear in the interior ornamentation. These represent, according to Grabar, images of authority and conquest, especially the crowns; in this he finds parallels in Persian and Byzantine art, and also explicit examples of the use of the symbolism of the victor. Both these symbols and the verses from the Koran inscribed on the walls of the building are directed to a non-Muslim population and express three basic ideas: the principles of the Muslim creed; the stature of Muḥammad and the universal nature of his mission; and the reverent standing Islam also reserves for the earlier prophets – Jesus and the others. Therefore, Grabar finds in all this a direct appeal to the 'peoples of the book'. Profound and exhaustive discussions on these questions can also be found in the writings of Creswell, who in 1924 already defined the connections between the Dome of the Rock and Christian-Byzantine architectural concepts found chiefly in three structures: the Church of the Holy Sepulchre, the Church of the Ascension on the Mount of Olives, and the

interlinked with the need to maintain Mecca's stature expresses a similar tendency). Goitein challenged the view that was common to many scholars which gave too much credit to the alleged intention of 'Abd al-Malik to establish a holy place which would compete in sanctity with the *ka'ba* due to political circumstances (the revolt of the Zubayrids); see his article: *JAORS*, 70:104, 1950, and also the chapter on the sanctity of Jerusalem and Palestine in ancient Islam: *Studies*, 135–148; opposing him Caskel, *Felsendom*, 24ff, maintained the contrary opinion, arguing that what Muqaddasī wrote on the competition with the Christians only refers to the building style, the splendour; the motivation, however, was political, that is the domination of Mecca by the Zubayrids; but the verse he quotes, p. 28, does not prove anything, and contrary to his opinion, one cannot interpret the name Quraysh as meaning the Zubayrids, being a rather poetic parallelism to the Umayyads mentioned in continuation. Crone and Cook, 19, see the placing of the Dome of the Rock on the place of the Jewish temple as an expression of the severance of the connection between Islam and Judaism (a very strong connection, according to the view they are trying to prove). Creswell, *Early Muslim Architecture*², 66f argues fervently in favour of the argument that the building of the Dome of the Rock, was indeed motivated by political reasons. Whereas Baer, *OLZ*, 68(1973), 120f, in a critical review on Creswell's book, goes to the defence of Goitein. Poliak, *Dinaburg Jubilee Volume*, 165, maintains the far-fetched supposition, that does not seem well-founded, that the special status of the rock was the result of Jewish propaganda. It was mainly the Jews who had converted to Islam, who, in his opinion, had spread the idea that the foundation stone was the centre of the world and therefore obviously the most holy of places.

Cathedral of Buṣrā. He expressed and developed his views in detail in the second edition of his book on ancient Muslim architecture. A wide canvas of comparisons with Christian buildings with centuries of tradition behind them is discussed by Echouard in an article he published in 1972. He refers to buildings intended to be used in the rituals of the saints, generally built around the grave of that saint and intended to receive the masses who came to pray to him, and he gives comparative descriptions of various churches of this type, such as the church of St Simeon (Stylites) in northern Syria, of St Vitale in Ravenna, and others.[19]

[107] A central point in all of these architectural discussions on the Dome of the Rock is its octagonal form. An attempt was made, with some justification, to compare this aspect of the mosque to Christian structures, but it seems to me that the basis of this type of building is, in this case, a specifically Muslim concept. It is a description of Paradise, which the Muslim tradition claims (in the name of the Prophet) has eight openings. Indeed, the tradition attributed to the Prophet declares that the rock (on the Temple Mount) belongs to Paradise.[20]

[108] Another important step in the process of investing Jerusalem and the Temple Mount with holiness was the building of the al-Aqṣā mosque. The Muslim sources have not generally preserved any detailed information on its construction. Some of them attribute it to ʿAbd al-Malik and others to his son al-Walīd (705–715). It now appears that the time of its construction can be determined more precisely with the aid of papyri preserved in Egypt (in Aphrodito, upper Egypt) which deal with shipments of workers and the supplies from Egypt for the building of the mosque in Jerusalem. These papyri, to the extent one can discern from the dates listed in them, are from a period of about ten years, from 706 to 717, which is the period of Walīd and Sulaymān, the sons of ʿAbd al-Malik. One can surmise, therefore, that the building of the mosque began in the days of Walīd (and it is not unlikely that building had already begun during

19 See the brief summary of various views on the architectural tradition which can be revealed in the Dome of the Rock in Briggs, 36f; and see Grabar, *AO*, 3:33, 1959; Creswell, *Origin*; *idem*, *Early Muslim Architecture*², 67–123, and see especially his survey of the various approaches, 101–109. See also the article on the mosaics of the Dome of the Rock by M. Van Berchem in Creswell's book, 213–322; Echouard, *BEO*, 25:37, 1972. A somewhat unusual approach is that of Strzygowski, *Der Islam*, 2:79, 1911, who tried to prove that the building style is basically Persian.

20 The tradition on the eight openings of Paradise occurs in many places, for example: Ibn Māja, I, 512 (no.1604); Muslim, I, 227; Nasāʾī, *Sunan*, I, 78; ʿAzīzī, II, 216. The rock belongs to Paradise: it seems that the more ancient form of the *ḥadīth* refers to what the Prophet said of a species of dates from Medina, *al-ʿajwa*, that they are from Paradise; afterwards the rock was added; *al-ʿajwa waʾl-ṣakhra*; see Ibn Māja, II, 1143 (no. 3456); Ibn al-Athīr, *Nihāya*, II, 254. At the End of the Days, the Paradise will move to Jerusalem: see Yāqūt, *Buldān*, IV, 592; and see more traditions on the connection between the *ṣakhra* and Paradise in Wāsiṭī, 67ff, 78.

the reign of 'Abd al-Malik, who died in October 705). Unlike the Dome of the Rock, which despite its many renovations has been preserved basically as it was built, with most of the ancient inscriptions intact, there have been many alterations in the al-Aqṣā mosque and nothing remains that can tell us of its early history.[21]

[109] The construction of the two magnificent mosques on the Temple Mount was contrary to the spirit of early Islam, which denied the sanctity of the place on the one hand, and considered that more modest structures should suffice, on the other. This was evidently the turning point in determining the religious status of Jerusalem and the Temple Mount. 'Abd al-Malik and his sons turned the Temple Mount into a magnet which drew thousands of visitors from the Muslim world who were on their way to Mecca, and this is where the process of sanctification began, a process which increasingly produced its own momentum. These caliphs laid the physical foundations which, from then on, lent a renewed spiritual aura to the Temple Mount, and around which traditions were created and these, in the manner of Muslim traditions, naturally related to the commentaries of the Koran and the *ḥadīth*, and were rumoured to have come from the Prophet himself. A kernel of the tradition brought about in this way can be found in *sūrat al-isrā'* (the chapter of the night journey) which is xvii, verse 1: 'Praised be He who took his slave for a night journey, one night, from the holy *masjid* [i.e. the *ka'ba*] to the furthermost *masjid* whose surroundings We blessed [it is God speaking here, pluralis], in order to show to him [to the slave, i.e. Muḥammad] some of Our signs'. According to the *ḥadīth* traditions that developed around this verse, it was the angel Gabriel who carried Muḥammad, mounted on al-Burāq, a winged beast of burden, from Mecca to Sinai, from there to Bethlehem (some say to Hebron as well), and from there to Jerusalem. There Gabriel put him down alongside the gate of the mosque, and tied al-Burāq to the iron ring that all the prophets had always, from time immemorial, tied their horses to. Even older traditions interpret the expression *al-masjid al-aqṣā* ('the furthermost mosque'): the house of prayer in heaven, and they tie in the *isrā'*, the night journey, with the *mi'rāj* (the ladder), that is the ascension of the Prophet to heaven. There Muḥammad prayed in the company of the other prophets: Abraham, Moses, Jesus and all the rest.

The Koran itself contains nothing specific, in this chapter, which links

[21] The papyri were originally edited by Bell in *Der Islam* between 1911 and 1928, and they are included in his publication: *Greek Papyri in the BM*, IV (The Aphrodito Papyri); see No. 1366 (of 710); 1403 (the palace of the caliph [aulē toū amiralmoumnin] and the mosque in Jerusalem [masgida Hierosolymōn] are mentioned therein); 1414 (as the previous one); 1433 (706/7); 1435 (715/6); 1439; 1441 (706); 1451 (701/2 or 716/7). See an analysis of the art and mosaics of al-Aqṣā: Hamilton, *Structural History of the Aqsa Mosque*; Creswell, *Early Muslim Architecture*², 373–380.

the idea of 'the furthermost mosque' with Jerusalem in particular. There is no doubt that the identification of the furthermost mosque with the mosque at the south of the Temple Mount was born relatively later, after the two magnificent buildings were built there. It is interesting that the Koran itself, when speaking of Palestine, calls it *adnā al-arḍ*, the very close land, the nearby (xxx:1), and this certainly does not fit in with the placing of the furthermost mosque in Jerusalem. A profound study of the development of the interpretations of the term *al-masjid al-aqṣā* has been written by Guillaume. He points to the fact that this term is to be found in an ancient tradition on the pilgrimage journey of Muḥammad from Medina to Mecca, in the eighth year of the hijra (when Mecca, of course, was already in Muslim control). While passing through al-Ja'rāna (between the two cities, some fifteen kilometres from Mecca) 'he was in the state of purification' (*iḥrām*) between 'the furthermost mosque' and 'the nearby mosque'; evidently speaking of the two mosques in Ja'rāna. Naturally it is impossible to reach solid conclusions on such an obscure subject, and there is more than one possible explanation for the birth of the expression 'the furthermost mosque'. In my view, a reasonable assumption would be that the expression was already essentially theological on its first appearance, in the Koran. It seems to me that it is connected with one of the basic ideas of Islam as expressed by Muḥammad, namely the idea of the chain of prophecy, or successive revelation. Muḥammad saw himself, as we know, as the last link in a chain, sealing the prophecy. This idea is not Muḥammad's invention, and a number of early Christian sects subscribed to the idea in their way, for they saw Jesus as the last of the prophets. So did the Manichaeans, who saw Mani as the seal of prophecy. The Manichaean theology (which had considerable influence on Muḥammad's views; this is a subject which should be dealt with separately) connected the idea of the last link in the chain of prophecy and divine revelation with the 'congregation at the very end' in which the revelation occurs. Saint Nilus, at the beginning of the fifth century, ridicules the Manichaeans and accuses them of inventing silly stories: *epi tēs ekklēsias tēs en tē eskhatia* ('on the congregation at the furthermost end'). It would appear that this is the *fons et origo* of 'the furthermost mosque' in the Koran and the meaning of the 'night journey', which was to bring Muḥammad into that framework (which was the Muslim community, the Arabs) in which the Word of God would be revealed to him as it was revealed to the former prophets, his predecessors; a revelation which would be final and the last of its kind and would occur in 'the furthermost mosque', the end of the chain. To an Arab traditionist who lived two generations after the erection of the Masjid al-Aqṣā, Ḍamra b. Rabī'a (died in 817), it was already clear that the *isrā'* was necessarily to Palestine (al-Shām, in his language), for God did not send any prophet but from there, and if he was from some other place, he would be brought there during a night journey. Mas'ūdī, writing in the first half of the tenth century, no longer has any doubt that *masjid al-aqṣā* in the Koran is the temple built by Solomon, 'whose neighbourhood was blessed by God'.[22]

[110] The circle of sanctity widened and included the whole of Jerusalem. A rich literature of traditions attributed to the Prophet was created, containing praise of Jerusalem, and known as the *faḍā'il al-quds*: eulogies of Jerusalem. The date when these traditions were first collected is not known, but it is not unlikely that it was in approximately the second quarter of the eighth century, although the first work known to us dates from the beginning of the eleventh century.[23]

[111] The praises for which Jerusalem warranted that every Muslim should come and visit it and the Temple Mount, touch on the great value of the prayers said in this place. Masjid al-Aqṣā is the first of the mosques in the world after the ka'ba mosque in Mecca, and later than it by only forty years (the intention is to Solomon's temple). One prayer in Jerusalem is worth five-hundred times more than in any other place (and there are other estimations). One should note that all of Palestine merits praise. In the Koran it is called *al-arḍ al-muqaddasa* (v:24), the sanctified land. The Koran was 'handed down' (by God) in three places, said the Prophet: in

[22] There is a verb in Arabic which means 'to travel by night'; its root is *sry*, and the word *isrā'*, night journey, derives from it. See Guillaume, *Andalus*, 18:323, 1953. In the same article he also quotes traditions which assert that the *mi'rāj*, the ascension to heaven, took place in Mecca on the roof of the Prophet's house and not in Jerusalem. The tradition on Ja'rāna, see: Wāqidī, 858f; Samhūdī, II, 184. According to another tradition the location of the *mi'rāj* was Kūfa; see al-Burāqī, 68. See on the subject of the chain of prophecy: Friedländer, *JQR*, NS 3(1912/3), 246–254; Andrae, 98; Buhl, 212f; on the claims of Mani that he is the seal: Bīrūnī, 207; and see also Polotski, *PW*, Suppl. VI, 266f. The letter of Nilus: *MPG* 79, 357. Ḍamra ibn Rabī'a: Ibn 'Asākir, I, 154 (quoted also in Goitein, *BJPES*, 12 [1945/6], 124, n.43); Hirschberg, *Rocznik Orient.*, 17(1951/2), 341; see Mas'ūdī, *Murūj*, I, 111. On Ja'rāna see also Zarkashī, *A'lām*, 63, 180; Caskel, *Felsendom*, 19f, challenges the views of Guillaume and of others who agree with him, and claims that the furthermost mosque in the Koran meant Jerusalem from the very outset. See the comprehensive discussion on the various Muslim traditions relating to the furthermost mosque: Kister, *Le Muséon*, 82:173, 1969. According to the diary of al-Ḥasan b. Aḥmad al-Bannā', of Baghdad (in the eleventh century), the followers of Abū Ḥanīfa in Baghdad (in 1069) claimed that the three holy places (to which they go on pilgrimages and religious visits), are Mecca, Medina and 'that place', meaning the grave of Abū Ḥanīfa. The Ḥanbalīs shouted at them: 'You have forgotten that there is a place in the world called Jerusalem!' See al-Bannā', 290, and the translation, 302. See a general discussion on the matter of the sanctity of Jerusalem to Islam, in the article of Lazarus-Yafeh, *Herzog Jubilee Volume*, 117.

[23] See a general survey of this literature of *faḍā'il al-quds*: Sivan, *IOS*, 1:263, 1971, and see there additional references. The manuscript of Abū Bakr Muḥammad b. Aḥmad al-Wāsiṭī was edited by I. Hasson, Jerusalem, 1979. Two other treatises written before the Crusades are of al-Musharraf b. al-Murajjā ibn Ibrāhīm al-Maqdisī (mid-eleventh century), and of his pupil, Abū'l-Qāsim Makkī b. 'Abd al-Salām al-Rumaylī al-Maqdisī, which was not completed (see on these personalities below).

Mecca, Medina and in al-Shām, and one of the traditionists adds: that is to say, in Jerusalem. Jerusalem is the locale of Abraham, Lot, Jesus; it is one of the places in which God permitted the creation of buildings for His name to be mentioned. From there, He lifted Jesus to heaven and it is there that he will be put down again. At the End of the Days, all the mosques in the world (including the ka'ba) will gather together and come to Jerusalem. 'The rock' in Jerusalem is the place where one will blow the trumpet on the day of the resurrection of the dead, just as it was the first place to appear above the water after the flood; it is the place closest to heaven. The *dajjāl* and other apocalyptic creatures have no access to the rock. Adam, Isaac, Abraham (in this order!) commanded that they be buried there, and for that purpose, Jacob and also Joseph were brought there. In Jerusalem people would be separated in terms of those who were to go to Paradise and those who were to go to the fires of Hell. It is interesting that most of these traditions are conveyed in the name of Muqātil b. Sulaymān, a native of Khurāsān (Balkh) who lived in Baṣra and Baghdad. It is said that he incorporated into his commentaries on the Koran many Jewish and Christian traditions. He died in 767, and was therefore living at about the time the two mosques were being built on the Temple Mount.

There is also another passage of the Koran which according to its commentary recalls Jerusalem, in the *sūrat al-tīn* ('the chapter of the figs'), xc:1: [God swears by] 'the figs, the olives, the Mount Sinīn, and this the secure city'. It is said that 'olives' is an appellation for Jerusalem.[24]

[112] A tradition attributed to Muḥammad b. Ka'b, one of the offspring

[24] Shiblī, *Wasā'il*, 25a–34b. See in Zarkashī, *I'lām*, 286, a collection of traditions on the value of prayers in Jerusalem. A man who performs his needs should not do so in the direction of Mecca nor in the direction of the ṣakhra (a tradition attributed to the Prophet, *ibid.*, 293). 'Ajlūnī, II, 282: he who dies in Jerusalem, it is as if he died in heaven. The value of the prayer in Jerusalem: *ibid.*, I, 291; see a similar collection of ḥadīths in Nuwayrī, I, 325–339; praises of the holy land; of al-masjid al-Aqṣā; of Jerusalem; of the religious visits (*ziyāra*) there; of prayers said there; of the houses, of the sojourn and the passing away in Jerusalem; the graves of the Prophets, miḥrāb Da'ūd, the Silwān (Siloam) spring; the traditions on the ascent of the Prophet from Jerusalem to heaven, etc. The number of prayers in Jerusalem and their relative value according to the faḍā'il literature has its parallel in ancient Eastern Christianity: to visit seven times the Qarṭāmīn monastery is like going to Jerusalem; see Vööbus, *History of Asceticism*, II, 319. 'Azīzī, III, 343: The advantage of visiting Jerusalem before the pilgrimage to Mecca; *ibid.*, 388: the Prophet said: Whosoever does not come to Jerusalem to pray, should send there oil for lighting. Subkī, *Shifā'*, 49, complains (middle of the fourteenth century) that few come to Jerusalem, although its praises are famous and prayers there are doubly valued. 'The descent' of the Koran in three places: Ibn 'Asākir, I, 154, and see the supplementary fragment in the old edition (Badrān), I, 36 (omitted by the editor of the new edition, al-Munajjid). Ibn Sa'd, I (1), 107; the Temple Mount is the site of Jacob's dream, see: al-Maqdisī, *Bad'*, IV, 87; and see the collection of traditions in Yāqūt, *Buldān*, IV, 591f; and the treatise of Ibn al-Firkāḥ, *Bā'ith al-nufūs* (which also contains a collection of praises of Jerusalem). Muqātil b. Sulaymān, see: Ibn Ḥajar, *Tahdhīb*, X, 279–285, cf. Sezgin, I, 36f. *Sūrat al-tīn*: see Ibn al-Jawzī, *Mawḍū'āt*, I, 249; Silafī, *Faḍā'il*, 113; Ibn Bābawayh, *Ma'ānī*, 350 (this Shiite writer gives Jerusalem the honour of being

of the Banū Qurayẓa, of the Jews of Medina, tells that God promised Jacob that some of his descendants would become kings and prophets until He would send the *ḥaramī* Prophet (that is, from the *ḥaram*, or Mecca), who will be the last of the prophets (the seal), whose people would build the sanctuary (*haykal*) of *bayt al-maqdis*; hence the building of the mosque on the Temple Mount is the realisation of the word of God.

It appears that during subsequent generations, a special feeling of reverence developed among the Muslims in Jerusalem, as described by one of the city's inhabitants, Muqaddasī, at the end of the tenth century: 'You have no more honourable than the people of Jerusalem, because it has no breach and no outcry. They do not drink wine in public, there is no drunkenness, it has no house of abomination, either hidden or apparent, and its people are God-fearing and honest. And there was once an *amīr* [a governor of the city] about whom rumour had it that he used to drink; so the people broke into his house and dispersed those who were assembled there.'

The ideas of sanctity were extended, apparently towards the end of the Umayyad period, to other parts of Palestine as well. First was Hebron, the site of the graves of the patriarchs, and primarily the city of Abraham and his place of prayer – Masjid Khalīl Allah, for Abraham was called a friend (*khalīl*) in Muslim tradition (as in the Jewish tradition, 'the seed of Abraham, thy friend' [2 Ch., xx:7], 'the seed of Abraham my friend', [Is., xli:2], and also in the Talmuds and Midrash), and hence the name of the city among the Arabs, (*madīnat*) al-Khalīl, the city of the friend. Eventually other traditions developed, such as the one saying that Adam, who was also a prophet according to Islamic tradition, he, too, is buried in Hebron, as are Joseph and another forty anonymous saints. According to some traditions, the Prophet alighted in Hebron during his night journey from Mecca to Jerusalem – there even was a shoe of the Prophet kept in the mosque at Hebron.[25]

'the olives'; but Mount Sinīn, which the traditions generally say is Mount Sinai, he interprets as: Kūfa; Ibn 'Asākir, I, 205f. See a collection of praises of Palestine also in Shazarī, 26ff; Suhaylī, *Ta'rīf*, 10a: 'the sanctified land' (in the Koran) is Jerusalem and its environs; the *qibla*: Muqaddasī, *Āqālīm*, 151. Muqaddasī is proud of the fact that al-Shām was the first *qibla*.

25 Muqaddasī, *Āqālīm*, 7; *ibid.*, 34, again notes that Jerusalem is the place worthy of God-fearing people. On the graves of the patriarchs, see the traditions in Tadmurī, 65 (in the name of Muqātil ibn Sulaymān, see the previous footnote). Despite his doubts, he arrives at the conclusion that one has to believe that Abraham and the other patriarchs are buried there, as tradition (*naql*) states. According to him, *ibid.*, 61a, the first to be buried there was Yarid (that is, Jared); he also tells the story of Ephron the Hittite, and a story from the time of al-Rāḍī, the Abbasid caliph (934–940), on the discovery of a Greek inscription on Rachel's tomb containing details of the graves in the cave, whose each one was, see 63b, and in the Matthews edition: 181f; according to him one had to use the services of one of the elders of Ḥalab, the only one who was able to read the inscription. See also Ibn

[113] Ascalon also won a certain aura of sanctity by a tradition ascribed to the prophet, according to which it was one of the two bridal cities (*al-'arūsayn*), the second being Damascus (though some say Gaza). It is said that the Prophet promised Ascalon that it would enjoy peace and prosperity throughout the rule of Islam. It was allotted a special role in the resurrection of the dead: 70,000 people would rise up again there who would have to give no account of their deeds. Jericho is also mentioned in the ḥadīth literature. The traditions interpret the saying in the Koran 'Enter this city' – so the Children of Israel were ordered; *sūrat al-baqara* (the chapter of the cow) ii:55, as having been aimed at Jericho, though most of the interpreters say it was Jerusalem, and others say it was Bet Shean. A ḥadīth conveyed in the name of Ka'b al-Aḥbār says that whoever wishes to earn his livelihood and be well-off and God-fearing, should settle in Bet Shean. Its dates are mentioned in the ḥadīth attributed to Tamīm al-Dārī; it is said of the place that it is the 'tongue' of the country. Its spring, 'Ayn al-fulūs, comes from Paradise and is one of the two springs mentioned in *sūrat al-Raḥmān* (lv:50); the other is the Siloam spring (Silwān).[26]

[114] This process of lending special godliness to certain locations is well known in the Islamic world. There is an extensive literature of *faḍā'il* (praises) containing traditions, generally ascribed to the Prophet, concerning the special holy qualities of certain places. With regard to Palestine, we can follow an interesting course of development, from the denial of the sanctity of the *ṣakhra* (the rock) and of Jerusalem to the bestowing of special sanctity upon them. It is quite possible to envision the stages of this process as well as its principal motivations. Without going so far as to deny the primacy of Mecca and the *ka'ba* and of Medina, a religious aura

al-Faqīh, 101; Subkī, *Shifā'*, 111: the Prophet descended during the *isrā'* also near Abraham's grave, and also near Jesus' grave (in Bethlehem!); *ibid.*, 106, he vigorously defends the custom of visiting the grave of Abraham and those of the other prophets in Palestine. On the shoe of the Prophet see also: Dozy, *Vêtements*, 421ff; according to one tradition the shoe was found in Damascus, together with the original version of the Koran from the days of 'Uthmān (Goldziher, *Muhammedanische Studien*, II, 362f; Mez, 327). See also the article al-Khalīl (by M. Sharon) in *EI*², who has more references. In 'Ulaymī, 64f, it is said about Ibrāhīm ibn Aḥmad al-Khalanjī (perhaps a relative of Muḥammad b. 'Alī al-Khalanjī, see below) apparently the appointee over Palestine on behalf of the Abbasids, that the concubine (*jāriya*) of the caliph al-Muqtadir (908–932) requested of him, during her stay in Jerusalem, to look after Joseph's grave; he went there with a number of workers, and they dug until they uncovered Joseph, and arranged his grave alongside those of the other patriarchs, behind Solomon's courtyard(?), opposite Jacob's grave; see the English translation of this fragment in Le Strange, *Palestine*, 325.

26 See the tradition on the '*arūsayn* in 'Azīzī, II, 313; Ibn 'Asākir, I, 86; Yāqūt, *Buldān*, III, 674; cf.: Gruber, 61; and the article 'Asḳalān (by R. Hartmann) in *EI*². Jericho: Mawṣilī, *Nihāya*, 53a; Suhaylī, *Ta'rīf*, 3b. Bet Shean: Ibn 'Asākir, I, 211; II(1), 125; see also: Sam'ānī, II, 396; 'Imād al-Dīn, *Tadhkira*, 46: Bet Shean is one of the places in which there are *abdāl*

emerged around Jerusalem and Palestine during the second half of the Umayyad era, to be distinguished from the period of conquest and the first generations thereafter. This aura of sanctity was the direct consequence of the great building enterprise of 'Abd al-Malik and his sons, who turned the Temple Mount into a centre of attraction to visitors from all over the Muslim world. It is interesting to note that there was an awareness of this change among the Muslims of the Middle Ages, the clearest reflection being the antagonistic and disrespectful remarks openly expressed by more than one of the Muslim men of letters about the process of sanctification, in which they saw a dangerous innovation and perversion from the true creed. Reservations of this kind could also be found in the description, mentioned above, contained in some Muslim chronicles of 'Abd al-Malik's decision to build the Dome of the Rock, as if it sprang from a wicked desire to deny the sanctity of Mecca. Ya'qūbī makes some very explicit comments on the subject, which he attributes to 'Abd al-Malik '... the mosque in Jersualem will take the place for you of the ka'ba mosque, and this rock, which according to the tradition the Prophet put his foot on as he was ascending to heaven, will take the place of the ka'ba' (a stone for a stone!). Further on he adds that therefore 'Abd al-Malik built a dome over the rock, hung silk curtains therein, placed servants there and demanded that people encircle it (carry out the *ṭawāf*) just as they encircle the ka'ba.

Refuting the holiness of the *ṣakhra* evidently continued for a long time. Even after the Dome of the Rock was already standing on its site, we find that one of the greatest scholars of al-Shām in the middle of the eighth century, 'Abd al-Raḥmān b. 'Umar al-Awzā'ī, used to pray in Jerusalem with his back to the *ṣakhra*. True, everyone praying in the al-Aqṣā mosque has his back to the *ṣakhra*, which is to the north, as he is facing southward to Mecca. But the fact that this has been recorded is evidence that this was a demonstrative act. Unfortunately it is impossible to determine whether this happened after the Abbasid revolution or earlier, during the days of Umayyad rule.

Ibn Taymiyya, writing in about 1300, argues that it is impossible to perform the *ṭawāf* around the rock in Jerusalem, and that it is unacceptable to turn the rock into a *qibla* due to the presence of a *naskh* (uprooting, that is, the heavenly command to change the former rite of facing Jerusalem to that of facing Mecca). He even provides evidence from the act of 'Umar, who refused to take advice to build the mosque to the north of the rock,

(something like the 'lamed-waw', the thirty-six Jewish righteous; in Bet Shean there are two, and some say four).

and built it to the south in order that the Muslim facing Mecca would stand with his back to the *ṣakhra*. This whole matter of the sanctity of the *ṣakhra* began, according to him, from the period of 'Abd al-Malik's war with the Zubayrids, when he wished to divert the attention of the Muslims from Mecca and attract them to the *ziyāra* (visiting of holy places) in Jerusalem. All the alleged traditions, he writes, dealing as it were with the footsteps of the Prophet or the cradle of 'Isā (Jesus), are merely deceptions. The only place fit to pray in Jerusalem is the mosque of 'Umar (that is, al-Aqṣā); and he stresses in particular the ban on visiting Christian churches, such as the Church of the Holy Sepulchre (al-qumāma – 'of the refuse') and churches in Bethlehem, Mount Zion and elsewhere. Ibn Qayyim al-Jawziyya, shortly after Ibn Taymiyya, also denies absolutely the holiness of the *ṣakhra*. All the traditions about it, he states, are lies and inventions. The *ṣakhra* is merely the *qibla* of the Jews, and to them, its status as a place is like the status of the sabbath with regard to time. Among the learned Muslims in the Middle Ages, there was cognisance of the fact that the extensive publicising of the traditions about the sanctity of Jerusalem could be ascribed to the war with the Crusaders, when the whole Muslim world was trying to awaken the sympathies of people towards Jerusalem.

Opposition to the idea of the sanctity of Ascalon or Hebron is also to be found in the writings of these two learned men. Another scholar, Ibn al-Jawzī, decided that all the traditions ascribed to the Prophet and which speak in praise of Ascalon were false. The famous cadi and writer 'Iyāḍ, who lived during the first half of the twelfth century, claims that none of the *ṣaḥāba* (the Muslims contemporaries of the Prophet), nor anyone of the subsequent generations, either before or after the conquest of Palestine, would customarily perform the *ziyāra* of Abraham's grave nor of any other prophet's grave in Palestine. Ibn Taymiyya also looks back at the first generations and points out that nothing of the kind existed; that there was no precedent for praying over graves or building mosques over them. Abraham's grave, he writes, was closed and enclosed and it would not have occurred to anyone to pray there, and whoever came to Jerusalem would pray in the al-Aqṣā mosque and return to his home without visiting the *maghārat al-khalīl* ('the cave of Abraham', i.e., of the patriarchs). Only with the Crusaders' domination of the cave, Ibn Taymiyya adds, was the gate opened and the place turned into a church, and when the Muslims recaptured the place, some of them turned it into a mosque, but the scholars (*ahl al-'ilm*) deny this, and all the traditions that tell of the Prophet descending during the *isrā'* (the night journey) on any other place than the al-Aqṣā mosque are fake. However, reliable sources from the tenth and eleventh centuries give evidence of the fact that Hebron attracted Muslim visitors even before the Crusaders' period.[27]

The achievements of the Umayyads

[115] We have already found that there was a special relationship between the Umayyads and Palestine, and that the tribes of Palestine were an important foundation of Umayyad power and the governmental system it established. Shreds of information that were preserved in the chronicles speak of caliphs and their families visiting Jerusalem and other places in Palestine. Yazīd II, son of 'Abd al-Malik, lived in Irbid in Trans-Jordan (Arab sources: in the Balqā') at the end of his days and died there in January 724. His predecessor, Sulaymān b. 'Abd al-Malik, was very attached to Palestine. When he was proclaimed caliph, he was staying in Palestine and delegations came to Jerusalem to pledge their loyalty (to convey the *bay'a*). Before he became caliph, while still governor of jund Filasṭīn, he would sit in one of the domed buildings on the Temple Mount, near the *ṣakhra*, and there he would receive people in audience and there his orders would be written. When he became caliph, he had it in mind to make Jerusalem his official seat.[28]

[116] Sulaymān b. 'Abd al-Malik is also the caliph to whom the building of Ramla is attributed. Apparently, the building of the town started before he became caliph, for it is said that at the time of the death of his brother,

[27] Ya'qūbī, *Ta'rīkh*, II, 311; on al-Awzā'ī see: 'Ulaymī, 259; Ibn Khallikān, III, 127ff (he was an inhabitant of Beirut); see the article al-Awzā'ī (by J. Schacht) in *EI*², which has more sources about him. Al-Awzā'ī is also mentioned in a Samaritan chronicle: ''Eved ha-raḥūm [the slave of the Merciful i.e., 'Abd al-Raḥmān] ha-Wazā'ī[!], the judge of Damascus, who lived in Beirut', etc. see in Adler et Seligsohn, *REJ*, 45(1902), 244. Ibn Taymiyya, *Majmū'a*, II, 61ff; cf. Kister, *Le Muséon*, 82(1969), 195f. Ibn Qayyim al-Jawziyya, *al-Manār*, 86–91; *ibid.*, 99, he adds something to the list of aberrations from the right customs of the proper Islam: the prayer in mid-month Sha'bān is an innovation introduced after the year 400 (that is, in the eleventh century); it was introduced in Jerusalem; this is confirmed by Muqaddasī, *Aqālīm*, 183, who counts among the things for which Jerusalem excels the night which ends the reading of the Koran in the al-Aqṣā mosque and 'also the night of the middle of Sha'bān in Īliyā'; Zarqashī, *I'lām*, 296, quotes a ḥadīth ascribed to the Prophet, which links the *ḥajj* to Mecca with the ziyāra and notes: 'some say they only have heard about this ḥadīth after the victory of the Sultan Ṣalāḥ al-Dīn (that is, after Jerusalem was reconquered from the Crusaders); Zarqashī recalls in contrast to this another ḥadīth in favour of the ziyāra to Jerusalem, in the name of Musharraf ibn Murajjā, of the generation before the Crusaders conquest. See what Ibn al-Jawzī has to say on the traditions about Ascalon: *Mawḍū'āt*, II, 52ff; the opinion of 'Iyāḍ, see: Subkī, *Shifā'*, 106 (who argues with him and speaks in favour of this ziyāra); see Ibn Taymiyya, *Tafsīr*, 167; similarly also Ibn Qayyim al-Jawziyya, *al-Manār*, 94. For sources on religious visits to Hebron, see chapter 3, note 80.

[28] Yazīd: Mas'ūdī, *Murūj*, V, 446; Ibn al-'Adīm, *Zubda*, I, 47; Ibn Kathīr, *Bidāya*, IX, 231; Sulaymān: Maqdisī, *Muthīr* (Khālidī), 45; 'Ulaymī, 249; Ibn al-Athīr, *Kāmil*, V, 11. 'Umar II ibn 'Abd al-'Azīz acted in the same way, and was sitting on the Temple Mount, see Ibn 'Abd Rabbihi, *'Iqd*, IV, 434.

the caliph al-Walīd (on 24 February 715), Sulaymān was in Ramla. The city achieved quite a reputation in the Muslim world. According to Koran commentators, it is possible that 'the hill that was a haven and has a spring', to which God brought Mary and Jesus (*sūrat al-mu'minīn*, xxiii:52) was Ramla. It is interesting that the Muslim traditions on the conquest of Palestine sometimes mention Ramla, although the city was not founded until some three generations later. Possibly this is the result of some confusion in defining dates or in the use of the name Ramla instead of Filasṭīn (for Ramla was the capital of jund Filasṭīn); but it is also possible that a town called Ramla (by the Arabs) actually existed near Lod before the Muslim era. It is perhaps the *ḥōlīt ha-meḥōz* (*ḥōl* meaning sand, like Arabic *raml*), mentioned in the *Tosefta*, 'Arākhīn, ii:8. A Christian chronicle which describes the renovation of the Christian churches after the Persians devastated them tells that the monk Modestus, who collected money for the renovations, also went down to Ramla to obtain money. From the Muslim traditions, it evolves that the Muslims did not maintain regional administrative institutions in Caesarea, which was formerly capital of *Palaestina prima*, evidently out of fear of Byzantine attacks from the sea. The tradition I have mentioned earlier on the stay of Sulaymān b. 'Abd al-Malik, when he was governor of jund Filasṭīn, on the Temple Mount, teaches us that the affairs of the region were at first handled in Jerusalem. However, it seems that the genuinely non-Muslim surroundings were not congenial to the Muslims; on the other hand, they undoubtedly wished to dominate the coastal roads, and when they realised that Lod was also not suitable as capital of the region, again because of the non-Muslim population, it was decided to lay the foundations of (or develop) Ramla.

The building of the city began with its fortress. Afterwards they erected a building known by the name of *dār al-ṣabbāghīn* (the house of the dyers, and the meaning here is: textile dyers) which also contained a pool. They also built a canal known as *barada* ('middle of the eye'?) and also dug wells for drinking water. Then they built a mosque there and at the same time, permitted anyone who wished to do so, to build himself a house. Sulaymān b. 'Abd al-Malik, who was then governor of jund Filasṭīn, as aforementioned, appointed one of his officials, a Christian whose name was al-Biṭrīq b. Nakā, or Bakār, to supervise the building work. Until about 840 the Umayyad caliphs, and after them the Abbasids, maintained the wells and canals at their own expense, until the Abbasid caliph al-Mu'taṣim (833–842) transferred this responsibility to the governors of the province.

The founding of Ramla led to the decline of Lod, for Sulaymān began to destroy Lod and forced its people to move to Ramla in its place. Those who refused were punished and prevented from receiving supplies. One chronicle reveals the reason for this; it was an act of revenge for the people of Lod refused to permit his adviser, Ibn Biṭrīq, to build himself a house (meaning, probably: an administrative building) on land which was the property of the church of St George. Sulaymān also considered transferring the pillars of the church from Lod to Ramla, for the building of the mosque, but the patriarch appeased him. With the help of the Byzantines, Sulaymān was induced to use pillars in building the mosque in Ramla, which were specially hewn for this purpose in the same cave in *al-Dārūm* from which the pillars in Lod were hewn, and this was a secret cave known only to the Byzantines.

Muqaddasī writes, towards the end of the tenth century, that Ramla could be considered one of the best of the cities of Islam, if it were not for the quality of its water, which was poor owning to the saltiness of the wells. He also points out its central position for commerce, due to its proximity to both the Mediterranean and the Red Sea, and to its connection to them by adequate roads. According to him, Ramla served as a warehouse for the Egyptians, and the sources state further that the city was a *ribāṭ*, like other seaports along the coast of Palestine, that is, a military base for units in a state of permanent readiness.

In May 789, during the days of the Abbasid caliph Hārūn al-Rashīd, a pool was built in Ramla which exists until this very day, known particularly for its very unusual pointed arches. The ancient residential section of the city was apparently built around the mosque, known as the 'white mosque'. Many central figures in the political life of the Muslim world chose to live in Ramla, especially at the time when Palestine became subject to Egypt; that is, in the ninth century.

The building of Ramla created a new administrative centre. It became the capital of jund Filasṭīn and actually the most important city in Palestine. One can assume that the Jews of Lod moved to Ramla, as did the rest of the population, and they formed the basis for the relatively large Jewish population living in Ramla afterwards, according to the sources from the eleventh century.[29]

[29] Sa'īd ibn Biṭrīq, I, 217 (Modestus in Ramla); 'Azīzī, II, 323: some say that the hill (in the Koran) is Ramla, some say Damascus, some Fustat; Ibn 'Asākir, I, 200f: some say it is Ramla and some say it is Jerusalem. Ṭabarī, *Ta'rīkh*, I, 2399: 'Amr sends an army (during the conquest) against Ramla, under the command of al-Tadhāriq; *ibid.*, II, 1281: on the day of al-Walīd's death loyalty to Sulaymān ibn 'Abd al-Malik was sworn, and he was then in Ramla (Saturday, the 24th of February, 715). See in: Ya'qūbī, *Ta'rīkh*, II, 351; Balādhurī, *Futūḥ*, 143; Ibn al-Faqīh, 102; Shazarī, 29a, the traditions on the building of Ramla and the ruin of Lod. Dimashqī, 201: in the long run, Ramla was destroyed by earthquakes while Lod was rebuilt. Yāqūt, *Buldān*, II, 817ff, mentions alongside the traditions on the building of Ramla, the reason for Sulaymān's anger with the people of Lod; he also has the name of the one who refused to hand over the land he wanted: Ibn al-Biṭrīq. Jahshiyārī, 48:

[117] Fragmentary information, of considerable importance however, informs us that the Umayyads took pains to reclaim the ruins of the country and persevered in its settlement and development enterprises, in addition to the aforementioned construction works on the Temple Mount and Ramla. An impressive remnant from the days of their reign is Khirbat Mafjar near Jericho, a splendid unfinished palace attributed to the caliph Hishām ibn ʿAbd al-Malik (724–743), though it is impossible to pinpoint with any certainty the identity of the builder.

The Umayyads invested great efforts in developing a Muslim fleet and in renovating seaports in Palestine and Syria. Restoration and fortification works were carried out in Tyre, Acre, Caesarea, Jaffa and Ascalon. Arab army units were garrisoned at these ports. Muʿāwiya stationed carpenters and artisans and set up shipyards in the coastal towns. Acre became the chief naval base in his day and it was from here that the army set out in 647 to conquer Cyprus. Acre was also the site of the shipyard of the jund Urdunn but during ʿAbd al-Malik's time, the shipyard was transferred to Tyre, which then became the major naval base. Muʿāwiya also adopted a policy of settlement in the ports. In the year AD 662/3, he moved Persian army units who had come over to the Muslim camp during the conquest of Persia and who were stationed in Baʿlabakk, in Ḥimṣ and in Antioch, to the seaports of jund Urdunn: Tyre, Acre and others. The Umayyads viewed the coastal cities as *amṣār* (singular *miṣr*) that is, fortified frontier towns; their collective appellation was *al-sawāḥil* (from *sāḥil* meaning coast), and their inhabitants enjoyed special privileges, such as granting rights to the tribes and individuals settled there to collect taxes. The fortified towns along the coast and other vital places were called *rawābiṭ* or *ribāṭāt* (singular: *ribāṭ*), and the army units stationed there were called *murābaṭa*, from a root meaning to bind, an expression for permanent

it was Ibn Biṭrīq who asked for the land for himself and was refused, and then advised Sulaymān to build Ramla; and see there also the story of the pillars. See also: Ibn Taghrī Bardī, I, 240; *Futūḥ* (ascribed to Wāqidī), 6, and there the information that Ramla already existed in the days of the Children of Israel. See on the antiquity of Ramla, Ish-Shalom, *Ḥafīrōt*, 195ff. Muqaddasī, *Āqālīm*, 36, 164f, describes Ramla. He mentions some of its streets (*durūb*): *Bi'r al-ʿaskar* (the well of the army), and *masjid ʿanaba* and also roads leading to Jerusalem, to Lod, to Jaffa, to Fustat, and to Dājūn, and called by their names. See also: Samʿānī, VI, 169. On the white mosque and the supposed residential quarter see: Rosen-Ayalon, *IEJ*, 26(1976), 119; on the pool of Ramla: Creswell, *Short Account*, 228ff. He quotes the inscription saying that the pool was built in Dhū'l-ḥijja 172 (May 789), that is, in the days of Hārūn al-Rashīd. According to him, what makes it singular is the great number of sharply pointed arches, the most ancient known to us. See also El'ad, *Cathedra*, 8(1977/8), 165 and n. 64; the conjecture on the Jews moving from Lod to Ramla, see: Assaf, *Meqōrōt*, 10; a Samaritan chronicle, the *Tōlīdā*, points out that Ramla was a new city: 'in his days (of the great priest ʿAqbūn) a new city was built, called al-Ramla'. See Neubauer, *Chronique samaritaine*, 23. As to the date in this chronicle: the earlier date it mentions is 634. Afterwards it counts terms of priesthood which amount to 155 years, that is, the building of Ramla should have been in 789, which makes no sense.

readiness. We know that the Muslims launched raids on Byzantine areas, and it appears that these seaports served as their departure points. Less is known about the Byzantines' contra-raids, though undoubtedly they happened quite often, an example being the aforementioned occurring during the insurrection of the Zubayrids. Palestine advanced in the development of its seaports and ship-building compared with the state of these matters during the Byzantine period, when Alexandria was evidently the major supplier to the empire's navy. According to a tradition in Balādhurī, there was a *ṣinā'a* (ship-yard) only in Egypt, until the year AH 49 or AD 669. Then Mu'āwiya ordered the artisans (ship-builders) and carpenters to be assembled and have them placed in the sea-ports.[30]

[118] As Palestine was close to the centre of government, it appears that the Umayyads were accustomed to using it as a place of exile for tribes and leaders who caused them trouble in other parts of the caliphate, particularly in Iraq. It is said that Mu'āwiya purged Kūfa of 'Alī's supporters, including Qa'qā' b. 'Amr b. Mālik, of the Banū Tamīm, one of the heroes of the war against the Persians who participated alongside 'Alī in the 'Battle of the Camel' and who was exiled to Jerusalem. The transfer of the Jews, who were then considered loyal, was undoubtedly a similar course of action, and they were encouraged to settle in Tripoli on the Syrian coast.[31]

[119] We learn of the Umayyads' concern for the agriculture of the country from the canal they dug in jund Urdunn. No details are available concerning the canal or its site, except that it was in the north. It was excavated in the days of Walīd II, in around 743, as is evinced in Ṭabarī. Ṭabarī quotes a witness of Walīd's last hours before he was killed; al-Muthannā b. Mu'āwiya tells: '. . . I came to Al-Walīd; I came in through the back entrance of the tent-camp. He ordered a meal and it was brought to him . . . Then he addressed someone who sat alongside him and spoke to him, but I could not hear what he said. I asked the man sitting between us what they had spoken of, and he said he was enquiring about the water

[30] See a summarising review of Khirbat al-Mafjar: Hamilton, *Khirbet al-Mafjar*. The author assumes that the palace was built by the caliph Walīd ibn Yazīd (February 743–April 744), but tribal wars and inner dissension prevented its completion. See: Baramki, *QDAP*, 5:132, 1936; 8:51, 1939; Schwabe, *QDAP*, 12:20, 1946. Baramki describes in his article (the second) an Arabic inscription written by 'Abdallah b. 'Umar for the caliph Hishām; Schwabe describes ten inscriptions he found in the digs there, and which include many Greek names, among them that of Theophilos, who in his opinion may have been a Jew (a name mentioned also in the Aḥīma'aṣ Scroll), but of course this is only a conjecture. See on the building works of the Umayyads also: Strika, *Rendiconti*, ser. 8, 23:69, 1968, and the bibliography therein, especially on p. 69, no. 1. On the ports and the transfer of the Persians: Balādhurī, *Futūḥ*, 117f, 126ff, 143f. See also: Fahmy, 52ff; Eickhoff, 130; El'ad, *Cathedra*, 8(1977/8), 156–163.

[31] The purge of Kūfa: Ṭabarī, *Ta'rīkh*, I, 1960. On Qa'qā' see: Ibn al-Athīr, *Usd*, IV, 207.

canal he is digging in Urdunn, to know how much still had to be excavated there'. The 'Mysteries of Rabbi Shimon Bar Yoḥai' speak of '... a great king who will rule for nineteen years [undoubtedly 'Abd al-Malik] ... who will plant orchards and rebuild ruined cities [the coastal towns mentioned above] and will dig ditches for waterways to irrigate his plantations', and further, 'another king will make way for the water of the Jordan and bring workers from afar to dig and make conduits for the water of the Jordan and irrigate the land and the earth they have dug will fall upon them and kill them; and their chiefs, when they heard of it, will come to the king and kill him ...' Walīd was indeed killed by Yazīd, who became caliph in his stead. The reason given by the midrash for Walīd's murder is interesting – suggesting that it was due to the catastrophe that occurred during the digging. As Braslavi has shown, it is possible that there is a hint of this in Yazīd's sermon after he became caliph, in which he promised that he would be thrifty with the state's money and refrain from waste and disparity in the distribution of allowances to the tribes; he also pledged not to continue with building projects or the digging of canals.[32]

[120] That the Umayyads were responsible for the renovation and improvement of the roads in Palestine one can see from some milestones that have been discovered to date which bear the name of Caliph 'Abd al-Malik. Two were found in the neighbourhood of Abū Ghosh and Bāb al-Wād; on one the distance of seven miles from Jerusalem was inscribed, and on the other, eight miles. A third stone, discovered in Koziba in the Judaean hills, indicated the distance from Damascus (although only the number 100 was preserved). The stones are of white marble, 39 × 57 centimetres. A fourth stone was found in the Sea of Galilee, near Ṣemaḥ, and it commemorates the paving of the road in the pass of Afēq, in the days of 'Abd al-Malik, under the supervision of Yaḥyā b. al-Ḥakam (the caliph's uncle, brother of Marwān).[33]

[121] During the reign of the Umayyads, the Muslims began to mint

32 Ṭabarī, *Ta'rīkh*, II, 1803, 1834; Ibn al-Athīr, *Kāmil*, V, 292; Jellinek, *Bēt ha-midrāsh*, III, 79, see Graetz (Hebrew), III, 436; Steinschneider, *ZDMG*, 28(1874), 638; Graetz and Steinschneider did not know the passage in Ṭabarī. The connection between what is said in the 'Mysteries of Rabbi Shimon Bar Yoḥai' and the passage in Ṭabarī was first noted by Braslavi: Braslavski, *JPOS*, 13:97, 1933. See the Hebrew version: Braslavi, *Le-ḥeqer*, 53ff; contrary to Braslavi's opinion (following Graetz), there is nothing in the 'Mysteries' that can serve as proof for the time of its writer, for all those details could have been found in the Arabic chronicles; the bitterness against Walīd was not necessarily born out of the caving-in of the trench, as Braslavi believed, but was caused by his policy towards the tribes and his prodigality on building projects; and not as Braslavi would have it, the *nesī'īm* in the 'Mysteries' were not the Umayyad leaders but the heads of the Yamanī (Kalb) tribes which joined Yazīd in his war against Walīd.

33 See Lagrange, *RB*, 3:136, 1894 on the stone marking eight miles from Jerusalem; he proves that the Arabic mile was 2,500 metres long (3,000 cubits) and similarly in Samhūdī, II, 358, and this is missing in Hinz, *Masse*, 63. See also Lagrange, *RB*, 6:104, 1897, and the

their own coins, which replaced the Persian and Byzantine coins which had been used until that time. According to the information on this in Ibn al-Athīr, the mintage of coins began in the year AH 76, or AD 695. Previously the Muslims exported papyrus from Egypt which was exchanged for dinars from the Byzantines. The papyrus would be stamped with a cross and Christian sayings for the Byzantines, but later they began to be imprinted with Muslim versions. The Byzantine emperor threatened that if they would continue to do this, the Byzantines would mint coins stamped with insults to Muḥammad. It was at this point that the Muslims began to mint their own coins, at first in Iraq (Wāsiṭ), at a mint whose operation was committed by al-Ḥajjāj ibn Yūsuf to a Jew named Sumayr. The finds of coins indicate that there was an intensive production of coins in Palestine in the following places: Jerusalem, Bet Guvrin, Ramla, Ascalon, ʻAmmān, Gaza, Lod, Yavne, Tiberias, Bet Shean, Sepphoris, and Tyre. Some of these coins were already in existence during the Byzantine era, and it appears that they were again in use during the days of the Damascene caliphs after ʻAbd al-Malik. The inscriptions on the coins were Īliyā Filasṭīn, ʻAsqalān Filasṭīn, and the like. From the mint of Bet Shean, coins were found with Greek inscriptions, but appear to have been gradually replaced by Arabic. There were among those coins from Bet Shean some with the Greek inscription 'Skythopolis' together with the Arabic, 'Baysān', or 'Baysan'.[34]

The administrative division

[122] The administrative division of Palestine was determined in general terms immediately after the conquest and it was developed during the Umayyad period. By and large, this division followed along the lines that existed in the days of the Romans and the Byzantines. During the Byzantine era, Palestine was divided into three parts: *Palaestina prima*, *Palaestina secunda*, *Palaestina tertia*. These are explicitly mentioned in an imperial order of 23 March 409, included in the Theodosian Code. The first part

inscription on the stone saying: 'the building of this road was ordered by *amīr al-mu'minīn* ʻAbd al-Malik, of blessed memory; from Īliyā to this mile there are eight miles'. See there also on the stone from the monastery of Koziba. See Vincent, *RB*, 12:271, 1903, on the stone marking seven miles from Jerusalem; see also *Répertoire d'épigraphie arabe*, nos. 15, 17; Van Berchem, *MIE*, 3(1900), 418f. On the stone in the Sea of Galilee see: Sharon, *BSOAS*, 29:367, 1966; Sharon finds here proof that the road from Damascus to Jerusalem passed to the south of the Sea of Galilee. Cf. also Björkman, *Der Islam*, 15(1926), 97: the Crusaders used all the milestones they could find, for their buildings.

34 See Ibn al-Athīr, *Kāmil*, IV, 416; Ibn Taghrī Bardī, I, 177; Walker, *Catalogue* (1956), I, xviiif, lxxiii–lxxvi; lxxixf, 22, 23f; II, lxviii; 1f, 203, 205, 240, 266; see also a coin from Ascalon from the time of the Umayyads: Stickel, *ZDMG*, 39(1885), 40; 40(1886), 81; and coins from Tiberias and Gaza, evidently from the time of Walīd: *Monete cufiche* (Museo di Milano), 37, and see also Nassar, *QDAP*, 13:121, 1948.

included the coastal area, Judaea and Samaria, and its capital under the Byzantines was Caesarea. This sector was called jund Filasṭīn shortly after the Muslim conquest and its capital undecided until Ramla was built. The second sector contained upper and lower Galilee, and the western part of Peraea (the land stretching east of the Sea of Galilee); this would shortly be called jund Urdunn after the conquest, and its capital was transferred from Bet Shean to Tiberias. The third sector, which included areas of Edom and Moab (*Palaestina Salutaris, Arabia Petraea*) and the entire *'Arāvā*, no longer existed as a separate region and was partly absorbed into the jund Filasṭīn and partly into the jund Dimashq.

Jund Filasṭīn covered the stretch from Rafiaḥ (Rafaḥ) to Megiddo (or Lajjūn; the Byzantines had called it Maximianopolis), and from Jaffa (Yāfā) to Jericho (Rīḥā, or Arīḥā). According to some sources, Bet Shean also belonged to jund Filasṭīn. Jund Urdunn included the Jordan valley (which is the *ghawr*) along its entire length, to Eilat in the south and up until Bet Shean in the north (some say: including Bet Shean), that is to say, also Ṣō'ar and Jericho, also including the Galilee, northern Samaria, the entire area of the Sea of Galilee and part of the coast from 'Atlīt northward, including Acre and Tyre. The border between Ḥijāz and Palestine was the place called Wādī' l-Qurā, 'valley of the villages'. The Muslim sources emphasise the point that the Jews were not evicted from there when 'Umar ibn al-Khaṭṭāb evicted all the Jews from the Ḥijāz, as this valley was part of al-Shām and not Ḥijāz.

In the ninth century, jund Filasṭīn included the districts (*kuwar*; singular: *kūra*) of Ramla, Jerusalem (Īliyā), 'Imwās, Lod, Yavne, Jaffa, Caesarea, Nābulus (Shechem), Samaria (Sebastia), Bet Guvrin (Bayt Jibrīn; in the days of the Byzantines – Eleutheropolis), the Dead Sea (Baḥr Lūṭ), Ascalon, and Gaza. In the eleventh century, we find that the chief administrator of Muslim rule, the governor, was still stationed in Ramla, which was the capital of Filasṭīn, while Jerusalem was under one of his subordinates; the Gaon Solomon ben Judah refers to him (at the end of 1042) as 'the governor in the holy city', whereas he uses the following formula when writing about the governor of Filasṭīn: '. . . and over all, the great governor in Ramla'. Daniel ben Azariah mentions (*ca.* 1055) 'the *al-qāṣīn* [the chief, the commander] who is in Jerusalem' (perhaps he meant the cadi). The district, *kūra*, was divided into sub-districts, which were called *iqlīm* (pl.: *āqālīm*). One should take note that these terms were a direct heritage from the Byzantine administration, as the papyri found in the excavations of Nessana go to prove, for in them we find *min kūra ghazza min iqlīm al-khalūṣ* as against *klēmatos Elousēs khōras Gazēs*.

As to jund Urdunn, it included the following districts: Tiberias,

Samaria, (Sāmira – one part of Samaria; the other part, Sebastia, belonged to jund Filasṭīn, as aforementioned), Bet Shean, Fiḥl, Bayt Ra's, Gādēr (Jadar), Avēl, (Ābil), Sūsīta (Sūsiya), Sepphoris (Ṣafūriyya), Acre, Qedesh Naphtali (Qadas), and Tyre.[35]

[123] As one can see from these lists, the Arabs applied their own names to places in Palestine, some of which were genuinely Arabic but most of which were born out of different pronunciations of the original names. Palestine was part of al-Shām. Muqaddasī speaks of *iqlīm al-Shām*. The term undoubtedly originated in Ḥijāz, and referred to the large area that stretched to the north of the Arabian peninsula. Sometimes we find expressions of the fact that in al-Shām there were actually two different units, Syria and Palestine, and then the dual *Shāmān* is used. Salmon ben

[35] *Codex Theodos.*, VII–4, 30; there is a clear reminder of the Byzantine heritage in the expressions *al-shām al-ūlā* (the first), *al-shām al-thāniya* (the second), that is, jund Filasṭīn and jund Urdunn, as explained by Ibn 'Abd Rabbihi, VI, 251. He adds that Bet Shean is between the two. See Ibn Khurdādhbih, 78f; Ya'qūbī, *Buldān*, 327f; Ibn Ḥawqal, 168ff; Iṣṭakhrī, 55ff; Muqaddasī, *Āqālīm*, 154f, 186; Ibn al-Faqīh, 103, 116. cf. Abel, *Géogr.*, II, 171–178; Le Strange, *Palestine*, 28–35; Grohmann, *Ḥirbet Mird*, XLIIIff. See also Ibn Shaddād, *Barq*, 107a; Mas'ūdī, *Murūj*, II, 395: the border of Filasṭīn starts at the place known by the name 'al-Shajara' (the tree), which is the tip of the land of Egypt and the border between it and al-Shām, and is a well-known place between al-'Arīsh and Rafaḥ; cf. Ibn Taghrī Bardī, 37: the southern border of Filasṭīn – two trees between Rafaḥ and al-'Arīsh; *ibid.*, 57: Egypt begins at Eilat (written in the fifteenth century). One must remember that many of the Arab chroniclers lived far from Palestine and were not always precise; thus for instance Ibn Sa'd tells: I(1), 21, about Abraham who settled in Beersheba, which is Sab', a place between Jerusalem and Filasṭīn. Possibly in saying Filasṭīn, he intended Ramla, as is also noted by Nāṣir Khusraw, 19 (text), 65 (translation): the town of Ramla is called Filasṭīn, both in al-Shām and in the Maghrib (and vice-versa, one can assume that not infrequently when meaning jund Filasṭīn, they said Ramla). Wādī'l-Qurā, see for instance: Balādhurī, *Futūḥ*, 34; Samhūdī, II, 388f–389. Solomon b. Judah: **132**, ll.12–14; Daniel b. Azariah: **357**, b, l. 21. See: *Nessana*, No. 60, lines 2–3 of the Arabic part (p. 180), of the year 674 (October–November); No. 61, lines 2–4 (p. 182) of the year 675 (August); No. 62, lines 2–4 (p. 184), of the year 675 (October). At a later period, the term *iqlīm* was used, meaning a much wider geographical area and instead of the term *jund* one used *sawād*: see for instance: Maqdisī, *Bad'*, IV, 72: Jerusalem is the *sawād* of Ramla. As to Bayt Ra's, in Gilead, it is Beyt Reyshā, i.e. Kapitolias (see Avi-Yonah, *Ge'ōgrāfya hīsṭōrīt* [Hebrew], 161); Gādēr, see *ibid.*, 159f; Avēl, *ibid.*, 157f, and see the map *ibid.* facing p. 150. Yāqūt, *Buldān*, I, 776, in the entry Bayt Ra's, says it is the name of a village in *Bayt al-maqdis*, by which he may have meant either Jerusalem or Palestine. And he continues 'and some say it is a district (*kūra*) in Urdunn'. The latter is undoubtedly correct, and one should not deduce from him that there was at some time a village by this name near Jerusalem. It is worth mentioning in particular some border regions described by the Muslim geographers and which are part of what has been assembled by Le Strange, *Palestine* on pp. 30–35: the 'Jifār' is the area of northern Sinai, from lake Tinnīs in the Delta, to the border of Palestine; the 'Ghawr', its main city was Jericho, is the area of 'the people of Lot' and the Dead Sea, being the valley which starts from the Sea of Galilee southward, and as we have seen, part of it belonged to jund Filasṭīn and another part (from Bet Shean northward) to Urdunn; 'al-Ḥūla' is according to Yāqūt the region between Tyre and Bāniyās; 'al-Balqā', is the region of Ammon and its main city, 'Ammān; 'al-Sharāh', is the region of Moab, and its main city Adhrūḥ. Ṣo'ar (Zughar, Zoar) was considered the border of the Sharāh, which stretched between Moab (Ma'āb) and Zoar, see Bakrī, 699.

Yeruḥim explains in his commentary on Ps., xlviii:2 (Beautiful for situation [*nōf*], the joy of the whole earth, is mount Zion, on the sides of the north): Zion is on the sides of the north, that is to say northward (*shām*) from Nōf (or Memphis, which is in Egypt) since in his words, from Egypt one goes to al-Shām, northward, for Palestine (*balad bayt al-maqdis*) is to the north of Egypt.[36]

[124] It is already clear from the foregoing discussion that by the name Filasṭīn the Muslims meant only a part of Palestine. The name is naturally not an Arab one, but a distortion of the name of the country in Greek and Latin. To the ancient writers it was obvious that this name was taken from that of the Philistines, who were the inhabitants of the coastal strip in Biblical times. As they were ethnically close to the Greeks, the Philistines were well-known to them, unlike the Israelites, who lived in the interior. Epiphanius, one of the writers of the early Church (who died in May 402) could explain that: 'the seed of Abraham is widespread in the land of Canaan, that is, in the Jewish land [Ioudaia] and in the land of the Philistines [Philistiaia], that which is now called Palaistine'. Also among the Jews there was the awareness that Filasṭīn is none other than that 'land of the Philistines', and sometimes we find this expression, land of the Philistines, in letters from the Geniza, in the eleventh century AD, when the writer is referring to jund Filasṭīn. An Arabic translation of the Bible renders Gen., xxvi:15: For all the wells ... the Philistines had stopped them: 'Sadhā al-filasṭāniyūn'. A Samaritan chronicle, in speaking of the

[36] Muqaddasī, *Āqālīm*, 151f: one says al-Shām because it is the beauty spot (*shāma*) of the *ka'ba*; some say because those who go there turn left (that is, going from Ḥijāz, facing eastward) – *tashā'um*; some say because of the spots (*shāmāt*) on its earth: red, white and black. The Iraqis call al-Shām everything beyond the Euphrates. Ibn al-Faqīh, 92: al-Shām is the region between Kūfa and Ramla, and between Bālis (a city on the Euphrates, see: Le Strange, *Lands*, 107) and Eilat. Badrī, 13ff, quotes a series of explanations for the name, and among them that it was the name of one of the sons of Canaan. Mas'ūdī, *Murūj*, III, 139ff: because it is to the left of the ka'ba; some say it is because of its bad luck (*shūm*), etc. Some say: after Shem, the son of Noah. See Dimashqī, 192: after Shem, the son of Noah, as the *sīn* became *shīn* (in Arabic he is called Sām); Sijistānī, *Gharīb* (MS India Office), 111a. *Shāmān*, see for instance: Sibṭ ibn al-Jawzī, *Mir'āh* (MS BM Or 4619), 189b; Jawālīqī, *Khaṭā'*, 146, emphasises that the spelling is al-Shām, without a *hamza*, the *alif* being a *mater lectionis*. See Salmon ben Yeruḥim, *Commentary on Psalms*, ad locum; cf. *Kitāb al-sab'īn lafẓa*, ed. Allony, *Goldziher Memorial Volume*, II, 27: 'beautiful for situation the joy of the whole earth . . .' (i.e., that Palestine is [like] the most beautiful boughs of a tree in the world); the '*Arūkh*, VIII, 97b, referring to the expression in BT, Men. 33b: *pitḥē shīma'ē* (a kind of door that is exempt from the *mezūzā*, according to Rabba): 'in Arabic, one says *balad al-Shām*, which is the Land of Israel'; cf. *Ōṣar ha-ge'ōnīm* to Erubin, p. 86. From this and from many other places, it is clear that among the Jews the most common meaning of al-Shām was Palestine. Cf. Bacher, *JQR*, 8:564, 1905/6; Vilnay, *Zion*, 5(1940), 75; Goitein, *Leshonenu*, 30(1965/6), 211. And see TS AS 161.69, a fragment from an Arabic commentary on the Talmud, line 6: *al-talmūd al-shāmī*, that is, the Palestinian Talmud; and against this, line 9: *fī talmudnā* – in our Talmud – that is, the Babylonian.

Muslim conquest, says that 'the Ishmaelites came and captured the land of the Philistines'.[37]

[125] As to Jerusalem, we find that its ancient name among the Arabs in the period preceding Islam and also in the first generations of Islam, was Īliyā. This name undoubtedly came from the Roman name of the city after the rebellion of Bar Kokhba, being called after Hadrian: Aelia Capitolina. It seems that the Arabs began to use the name Īliyā at a very early period. Under later Byzantine rule we do not find it in Greek sources. Theophanes, who wrote at the beginning of the ninth century, does not mention this name at all, whereas Muslim writers were still using it in the tenth century. Indeed, Muslim writers tried to interpret the name in many ways, such as that it derived from Elijah (Ilyās), or that its meaning was 'the house of God'; or that it was the name of the woman who built Jerusalem. But there were those who knew that it was the name of a Roman emperor. Some time after the conquest, also the name Bayt al-Maqdis began to come into use, a name which could be taken for a shorter version of Madīnat Bayt al-Maqdis, city of the temple. Only later, principally starting from the eleventh century, do we find that the name al-Quds was in use, supplanting all the other names. It was at that time that the claims were first heard that it was forbidden to use the name Īliyā, as it was a heathen name. Other names were also known to Arab writers: Yerūshalayim, Urshalim, Shalēm, and Zion or Ṣahyūn, which Bakrī emphasises should be written Ṣihyūn. The term *bayt al-maqdis* became open to various other meanings. Sometimes it meant the Temple Mount and sometimes (in most cases) the city of Jerusalem, but at times also the whole of Palestine. The Karaite Sahl b. Maṣlīaḥ evidently means Palestine when he says in his letter to Jacob b. Samuel: 'Know that I came from the *beyt ha-miqdāsh* to warn'. Ibn 'Asākir says of 'Ubāda b. al-Ṣāmit: 'he died in *bayt al-maqdis* in Ramla'.[38]

Muslim personalities in the Umayyad period

[126] We can now examine more closely the figures who actually held the reins of government in Palestine in the political field, that is the

[37] Epiphanius, *MPG*, 41, 209; see the fragment of the Arabic translation: TS AS 70.119; the Samaritan chronicle: Adler et Seligsohn, *REJ*, 45(1902), 241.

[38] Mas'ūdī, *Tanbīh*, 128: after the name of Īliyā Adhriyānūs, and this is what it is called to this day; in *Murūj*, II, 305 he points out that the city was built by Antoninus (in the printed version: Abṭūlis) and it is he who first called it Īliyā. Bakrī, 217, 235, 844: Īliyā = the house of God; so also Suhaylī, *Ta'rīf*, 10b; Khafājī, II, 293: Īliyā in Syriac (the language of Adam) means the house of God; Abū'l-Fidā', *Mukhtaṣar* (following al-Muhallabī): Jerusalem was rebuilt gradually after Titus destroyed it and called it Īliyā, which means: House of the Lord. Wāsiṭī, 21: it is forbidden to say Īliyā, only *Bayt al-maqdis* (in the name of Ka'b al-Aḥbār), and see in the notes 2 and 4 on p. 22, additional references listed by the editor.

administration and the army (though it is generally difficult to differentiate between them), in the legal arena and in the religious and spiritual spheres.

In the first rank, we find the caliph's families. Naturally, the Umayya clan, both the Sufyānids (Muʿāwiya's branch) and the Marwānids (the branch of Marwān ibn al-Ḥakam and of his son ʿAbd al-Malik), preferred their brothers and sons to others and entrusted to them the governing of Palestine. The most striking case, which we came across during the discussion on the building of Ramla, was that of Sulaymān b. ʿAbd al-Malik, who even before he became caliph was already governor of Palestine, at first on behalf of his father ʿAbd al-Malik and afterwards on behalf of his brother al-Walīd. Similarly, we find ʿAbd al-Malik's grandsons occupying positions in Palestine and involved in the wars of the tribes in 744–745. The last Umayyad caliph, Marwān, also appointed his relative al-Walīd b. Muʿāwiya b. Marwān as governor to jund Urdunn, in accordance with the tribes' wishes however. ʿAbd al-Malik himself appointed his brother, Abū ʿUthmān Abān as governor of jund Urdunn (at the same time as he appointed his own son Sulaymān to govern jund Filasṭīn). ʿAbd al-Malik's son, al-Walīd, left his brother Sulaymān in his position in jund Filasṭīn, and appointed his own son, ʿUmar, to govern over jund Urdunn. In the former branch of the Umayyad dynasty as well, the Sufyānids, we find Caliph Yazīd b. Muʿāwiya appointing his son Khālid to govern the two junds of Filasṭīn and Urdunn.[39]

[127–130] Apart from the members of the caliph's families, the sources

See also: Ibn al-Faqīh, 96, who adds that it is the name of the woman who built Bayt al-maqdis; Maqdisī, *Bad'*, IV, 87: Īliyā, that is to say, al-Khiḍr (a figure in Muslim tradition identified with Elijah). Ibn ʿAsākir, I, 13, also knows that it is the name of a Roman emperor. Yāqūt, *Buldān*, IV, 592: one must not call Jerusalem Īliyā, because it is the name of the woman who built the city; one should say Bayt al-maqdis (in the name of Kaʿb al-Aḥbār). Jawālīqī, *Khaṭā'*, 155: one should write an *alif* (*hamza*) at the end of the word: Īliyā'; and he quotes for this purpose a verse by al-Farazdaq. Zarkashī, *Aʿlām*, 277f, has a lengthy discussion on the names of Jerusalem, and adds: Bayt al-quds, Urshalīm, and other strange names which are evidently distortions of distortions, such as Bābūsh, evidently Yābūs (=Jebus) in the original. See Sahl b. Maṣliaḥ, in Pinsker, *Liqqūṭē qadmōniyōt*, II, 30. Ibn ʿAsākir, I, 110, also uses the term al-Quds for Palestine when, in the name of Kaʿb al-Aḥbār, he says that the best part of God's world is al-Shām, and the best part of al-Shām is al-Quds, and the best part of al-Quds is the mountain of Nābulus; see examples of the use of 'Bayt al-maqdis', or 'Bēt hamiqdāsh', in the sense of Jerusalem or Palestine, in Assaf, *Meqōrōt*, 40f, n. 53. For names of Jerusalem see Goitein's article, *Zlotnik Jubilee Volume*, 62; see on the matter of Arabic names for places in Palestine: Vilnay, *Zion*, 5: 73, 1940. On ʿUbāda ibn Ṣāmit, see Ibn ʿAsākir, VII, 208.

39 Khalīfa ibn Khayyāṭ, II, 394, 417 (on the governors of ʿAbd al-Malik and Walīd); Balādhurī, *Ansāb*, IV(B), 65. On Abān b. Marwān, see also: Ibn Qutayba, *Maʿārif*, 354. See: Shaban, *Islamic History*, 115ff, who deals with this policy in appointing governors, particularly with reference to the Marwāni branch. These Umayyads who were appointed governors were mostly under the aegis of al-Ḥajjāj ibn Yūsuf and his favourites, and the offices which they held served those who eventually became caliphs as an excellent school for their future careers.

mention others who filled governing roles in Palestine. These were generally heads of tribes who took part in the conquest, or who lived (or had settled) in Palestine. It seems that the first of those mentioned was a certain 'Ubayd, who was the governor of Jerusalem on behalf of 'Umar, and occupied this position when the plague of 'Imwās was raging (639).[40] Evidently he was put in charge of what was afterwards jund Filasṭīn. The man responsible for governing jund Urdunn was apparently residing in Bet Shean in the period immediately after the conquest. To this post, 'Umar ibn al-Khaṭṭāb appointed Abū'l-Ḥarr Ḥuṣayn b. Mālik ibn al-Khushkhāsh Abū'l-Qalūṣ, a man of the Banū Tamīm, from the 'Anbar clan. He seems to have maintained this position for forty years.[41] Another governor placed in office in jund Filasṭīn by 'Umar was 'Uwaymir b. Sa'd, a Medinan of the Banū Aws, of the clan of 'Amr b. 'Awf. He settled in Palestine and died there. 'Uwaymir was one of the most important Muslim commanders during the wars of conquest. Most sources mention that he governed the junds Ḥimṣ and Qinnasrīn (northern Syria). One source stresses his decent behaviour towards the dhimmīs: on seeing a group of dhimmīs being taken into custody for not paying the *kharāj*, he ordered them to be freed.[42]

In the days of Caliph 'Uthmān, 'Alqama b. Ḥakīm, of the Banū Kināna, governed jund Filasṭīn. While in Urdunn, Abū'l-A'war 'Amr b. Sufyān, of the Banū Sulaym, a clan of the Qays 'Aylān, was in charge. Responsible for the remainder of jund Filasṭīn, after the deposal of Khālid ibn al-Walīd, was 'Alqama b. Mujazziz (or Muḥarriz), who was one of the highest commanders during the conquest. 'Umar appointed him governor of Jerusalem and also responsible for half of jund Filasṭīn, while 'Alqama b. Ḥakīm was in charge of the other half and was stationed in Ramla (which had not yet been founded; the intention may possibly be Lod). 'Alqama b. al-Mujazziz came of the Banū Murra, and they too were a branch of the Banū Kināna.[43]

[131–133] The next governor of jund Filasṭīn was Maslama b. Makhlad.

[40] Ulaymī, 253.

[41] Ibn 'Asākir, IV, 371; Ibn al-Kalbī (Caskel), 81; Ibn Ḥazm, *Jamhara*, 209, calls him Ḥusayn b. al-Ḥarr and mentions that he was governor of Meyshan (Maysān) for forty years, and one can easily see that this is a mistake and that it is Bet Shean which is being spoken of, and not Meyshan, which is in Iraq.

[42] See Ibn Ḥazm, *Jamhara*, 334; perhaps Balādhurī was referring to him in *Ansāb*, IV(A), 137, when speaking of the Anṣārī (that is, one of the first Muslims in Medina) 'Amr b. Sa'īd, whom Mu'āwiya appointed governor of jund Filasṭīn. See also: Ibn al-Athīr, *Usd*, IV, 144f (called also 'Umayr); Sahmī, 86.

[43] Ṭabarī, *Ta'rīkh*, I, 2526, 2866, 3058; Ibn al-Athīr, *Kāmil*, II, 501, 535; Ibn 'Asākir, I, 545; Ibn Khaldūn, '*Ibar*, II, 949; Ibn al-Kalbī (Caskel), 36, 44, see *ibid.*, II, 154 ('Alqama b. Muḥarriz). Ibn al-Athīr, *Usd*, IV, 14, quotes the lineage of 'Alqama b. al-Mujazziz and the tradition that he was killed in a campaign against the Ethiopians organised by 'Umar ibn al-Khaṭṭāb.

(Naṣr b. Muzāḥim speaks of *ahl Filasṭīn*; by *ahl* he and other writers always mean the tribes. The governor was appointed primarily to stand at the head of the tribes, which implicitly meant at the head of the army stationed in the area and in this way, was in fact, the ruler of the place.) This appointment was apparently connected mainly with the organisation of the tribes in Palestine during the war against ʿAlī, when these tribes and their leaders stood staunchly by Muʿāwiya.[44] Afterwards, in the year AH 38, or AD 658/9, Muʿāwiya appointed Shumayr al-Khathʿamī as governor of jund Filasṭīn, while in jund Urdunn, he left the aforementioned Abū'l-Aʿwar, that is ʿAmr ibn Sufyān al-Sulamī, in the position he occupied.[45] The local governor in Jerusalem during Muʿāwiya's time was Salāma (or Salma) b. Qayṣar, and it is said that his descendants continued to live in Jerusalem.[46]

[134–137] In 682, during Yazīd b. Muʿāwiya's reign, before the campaign against Medina (the battle of al-Ḥarra), the caliph appointed Ṭarīf b. Ḥābis, known by the nickname Ibn Khushkhāsh al-Hilālī, to stand at the head of the tribes of jund Filasṭīn.[47] At about the same time, in 683–684, a governor is mentioned in the papyri of Nessana by the name of Abū Rāshid.[48] Coming originally from Palestine, Saʿīd b. Yazīd of the Banū Azd, began to govern Egypt in 682. It was said that he was not very effective there and that ʿAbdallah ibn Zubayr removed him from his post in less than two years.[49] Afterwards, in the days of ʿAbd al-Malik, we come across a position that is generally not mentioned, *ṣāḥib al-Balqā'*, which means the governor of Balqā', southern Trans-Jordan. This may possibly indicate not only an administrative division in geographical terms but also the formation of a local tribal grouping that is not clear to us. That governor was ʿUmar b. Muḥammad, of the Banū Thaqīf, who was an uncle of al-Ḥajjāj b. Yūsuf.[50]

44 Naṣr b. Muzāḥim, 206; Khalīfa ibn Ḥayyāṭ, I, 222. According to Ibn Abī'l-Ḥadīd, I, 649, it was ʿAlī who appointed Maslama b. Makhlad, and not Muʿāwiya. Dīnawarī, 172: Maslama b. Khālid. It is likely that this Maslama b. Makhlad is the same as Meslem, the governor mentioned in the papyri of Nessana, between 682–689 (see: *Nessana*, 33, 170, line 10: Meslem *despotos*). But perhaps that governor is Muslim b. ʿUqba. Ibn Ḥazm, *Jamhara*, 435: he was one of Muʿāwiya's retainers, and was a descendant of the family of Ḥimyar b. Sabā, that is, from Yaman (from those who claim descent from Qaḥṭān).

45 The Banū Khathʿam clan, a southern tribe, see Ibn al-Kalbī (Caskel), 224. Ibn al-Aʿwar was from the Banū Sulaym, a clan of the Qays ʿAylān, see Ibn Ḥazm, *Jamhara*, 264; Yaʿqūbī, *Ta'rīkh*, II, 226.

46 Ibn al-Athīr, *Usd*, II, 326; Maqdisī, *Muthīr* (Khālidī), 34.

47 Ibn ʿAsākir, *Ta'rīkh*, VII, 57. From the Banū Khushkhāsh we later on find Khālid b. Yazīd, who was cadi in Trans-Jordan (in Balqā'), see: Ibn Ḥajar, *Tahdhīb*, III, 125f.

48 *Nessana*, 33.

49 Ibn Taghrī Bardī, I, 157; cf. Lane-Poole, *History*, 46.

50 *Akhbār al-dawla al-ʿabbāsiyya*, 156; cf. Ibn al-Kalbī (Caskel), 118. Khalīfa ibn Khayyāṭ, II, 394, turns things around and calls him: Muḥammad b. ʿUmar.

[138–139] The leaders of the Banū Judhām also governed in Palestine at that time. These were Nātil b. Qays and Rawḥ b. Zinbā' and his sons, who have already been mentioned in describing the political and military events of the time. In the days of Marwān b. Muḥammad, the last Umayyad caliph, the names of the following governors of Palestine appointed by him are mentioned: al-Rumāḥis b. 'Abd al-'Azīz of the Banū Kināna, in jund Filasṭīn; Tha'laba ibn Salāma, of the Banū 'Āmila, in jund Urdunn. They later fled together with the caliph when the Abbasid army pursued him.[51] Al-Ḥakam b. Ḍib'ān b. Rawḥ, of the Banū Judhām, remained head of the tribes of Filasṭīn instead of al-Rumāḥis, but after a short time was also obliged to flee, to Ba'labakk; where the people of the new regime caught him and had him put to death.[52]

[140] In addition to the people I have already mentioned and of whom it is explicitly told that they were appointed to govern in Palestine and over the tribes living there, the names of some personalities who were involved in the political life of Palestine and who were active in various administrative positions are known to us. At the head of the Christian tribe Ghassān, one of the most important of the tribes in Palestine, stood Jabala b. al-Ayham of the Jafna clan. He fought on the Byzantine side in the battle of the Yarmūk. Afterwards, he requested that the tribe pay *ṣadaqa*, like the rest of the tribes, but 'Umar demanded that the tribe pay the poll-tax. Some say that Jabala converted to Islam, but afterwards returned to Christianity and went with 30,000 of his tribesmen to join the Byzantines in Cappadocia, and there his descendants were known of for some generations. According to one version, Jabala went over to the Byzantines because Abū 'Ubayda refused to have a man executed or to have his hand cut off, for having slapped Jabala in the market-place of Damascus after Jabala's horse had injured him.[53]

[141–144] The first cadi of Palestine was Abū'l-Walīd 'Ubāda b. al-Ṣāmit. He was one of the first to turn to Islam in Medina, and took part in the two meetings in 'Aqaba and also in the battle at Badr. He belonged to the very respected clan of Banū Ghanm b. 'Awf, of the Khazraj tribe. In 'Aqaba, the Prophet made him *naqīb*, or one of the Twelve. According to Ibn Sa'd and many others, he died in Ramla in the year AH 34, or AD 654/5, at the age of seventy-two (once again we are faced with the Ramla problem, as it had not yet been built). During his stay in Palestine, he quarrelled with Mu'āwiya (who was then commander of the army on behalf of 'Umar), for he thought that Mu'āwiya was not behaving

[51] Ṭabarī, *Ta'rīkh*, III, 46.

[52] Ṭabarī, *ibid.*, 47; Ibn 'Asākir, IV, 393.

[53] Ibn al-Kalbī (Caskel), 193, and see *ibid.*, II, 248; Ya'qūbī, *Ta'rīkh*, II, 161, 168; Ibn Qutayba, *Ma'ārif*, 107, 644; Ibn Ḥazm, *Jamhara*, 372.

honestly as the man in charge of al-Shām. He complained to 'Umar, who after listening to his complaints ordered him to return to al-Shām. At first he resided in Ḥimṣ and afterwards moved to Palestine. It was said that 'Umar sent him to al-Shām to teach the Muslims the Koran. It is noted that he was very tall, ten spans in height (*ca.*2.40 metres).[54] His son-in-law, Abū Muḥammad (there are some who say he was Abū Nu'aym Muḥammad b. al-Rabī' b. Surāqa al-Madanī), who was also of the Banū Khazraj and had settled in Jerusalem, died there in 718 at the age of 93.[55] Another Jerusalemite was 'Ubayda's step-son, Abū Ubayy 'Abdallah b. 'Amr (who is perhaps the 'Abdallah b. 'Umar, of the inscription in Khirbat Mafjar). His offspring were also known in Jerusalem for some generations.[56] 'Ubayda's brother, Aws b. al-Ṣāmit, who was also one of the veterans of Islam and participated in the battles alongside the Prophet, also settled in Jerusalem. It is said that he died in Ramla (!) in 652.[57]

[145–149] After 'Ubāda, the name of his successor to the rank of being in charge of legal affairs in jund Filasṭīn, the chief cadi, is known to us as 'Abd al-Wahhāb b. 'Abdallah. He was a man of Quraysh, of a branch of the Banū Jumaḥ, from the family of Mas'ūd b. Umayya. He lived in Palestine (it is not known where) and died there.[58] Following him, the chief cadi in jund Filasṭīn was 'Abdallah b. Mawhib, from the tribes of Yaman; some say from the Hamadān and others say from Khawlān. He served in this position during the days of 'Umar ibn 'Abd al-'Azīz. Khazrajī calls him *amīr Filasṭīn*.[59] From Mu'āwiya's time, the name of al-Mukhāriq b. al-Ḥārith al-Zubaydī is mentioned; he was one of Mu'āwiya's most loyal followers. The clan of Zubayd was affiliated to the Banū Madhḥij, a large tribe which was actually an alliance of tribes, who hailed from Yaman. One of its important branches settled in Trans-Jordan after the conquest.

54 Ibn Sa'd, I(1), 147; VII(2), 113f; Balādhurī, *Ansāb*, I, 239, 251f (he also claims he died in Ramla); Ṭabarī, *Ta'rikh*, I, 2960; Muqaddasī, *Muthīr*, 25f; Ibn Hishām, 311: 'Ubāda participated in all the battles of the Prophet. He was an ally of the Jews of Banū Qaynuqā', and after the hijra, he announced that the alliance was annulled and invalid. Because of him and 'Abdallah b. Ubayy, the order was 'handed down' in the Koran forbidding the Muslims to make pacts with the Jews or the Christians (*sūrat al-nisā'*, iv:143). Ibn Qudāma, 190: his grave is in Jerusalem and its site is known. Some say he died in Ramla, and others Jerusalem. Ibn Ḥabīb, *Muḥabbar*, 270; Ibn Qutayba, *Ma'ārif*, 255; Ibn 'Asākir, VII, 208ff; Mawṣilī, *Wasā'il*, 244; Ibn Kathīr, *Bidāya* IV, 4; Dhahabī, *Siyar*, II, 1; *idem*, *Ta'rīkh*, II, 118; Bustī, 51 (No. 334); Ibn al-Athīr, *Usd*, III, 106f; Ibn Taghrī Bardī, I, 93; Khazrajī, 159: a hundred and eighty-one ḥadīths are told in his name which he heard from the Prophet, and he was one of those who already knew the Koran by heart in the Prophet's day. Ibn Ḥajar, *Tahdhīb*, V, 111f; 'Ulaymī, 253.

55 Bustī, 28 (No. 137); Khazrajī, 317; Dhahabī, *Ta'rīkh*, IV, 52; Ibn Ḥajar, *Tahdhīb*, X, 63.

56 Ibn Sa'd, III(2), 57; VII(2), 123.

57 Nawawī, *Tahdhīb*, I, 129f; Ibn al-Athīr, *Usd*, I, 146: he lived in Jerusalem together with Shaddād b. Aws.

58 Ibn Ḥazm, *Jamhara*, 160.

59 Khazrajī, 183; Dhahabī, *Ta'rīkh*, IV, 139; Ibn Ḥajar, *Tahdhīb*, VI, 47.

Mu'āwiya appointed Mukhāriq head of the tribesmen in jund Urdunn.[60] At the same time he placed Shurayk (or Shurayṭ) at the head of the tribesmen in jund Filasṭīn. To the Banū Ghassān, whose leader Jabala b. al-Ayham deserted to the Byzantines, as we have already seen, a new leader was appointed, Yazīd (or Zayd) b. al-Ḥārith. This tribe afterwards settled in Urdunn.[61] As I have already mentioned, the commander of the army which Yazīd sent in 682 to suppress the insurrection against his reign in Medina was one of the heads of the tribes in jund Filasṭīn, Muslim b. 'Uqba. He came from the Banū Murra, of the Ghaṭafān tribe, and he had 5,000 tribesmen from jund Filasṭīn under his command headed by Rawḥ b. Zinbā', and 1,000 from Urdunn, headed by Ḥubaysh b. Dulja.[62]

[150–152] In the days of 'Abd al-Malik's sons, we know the name of a client (*mawlā*) of Sulaymān, who is Abū 'Ubayd al-Ḥājib. He was a sort of privy councillor (probably similar to the Byzantine cubicular) evidently of Jewish or Christian origin. Sulaymān brought him from Palestine to Damascus when he became caliph. When 'Umar ibn 'Abd al-'Azīz took over as caliph, he sent him back to Palestine, and there he died in *ca.* 740. According to some sources, he was known as al-Madhḥijī, that is, he was evidently a client of the Banū Madhḥij, who lived in Palestine. The reason for his dismissal was that he was arrogant to the tribesmen (*al-'āmma*, the plebs, and certainly the tribes are meant).[63] Another client of 'Abd al-Malik's clan was Nu'aym b. Salama, who acted as a sort of chief secretary (responsible for the *dīwān al-khātim* – 'the office of the seal') of Maslama b. 'Abd al-Malik, the commander of the Umayyad army in the first quarter of the eighth century AD; he also fulfilled this position under Caliph 'Umar ibn 'Abd al-'Azīz. It was said of him that he was a Palestinian by origin, a client of the Yaman tribes there.[64] We also know the identity of the man responsible for taxes (*kharāj*) in jund Filasṭīn under 'Umar ibn 'Abd al-'Azīz; he was Abū'l-Qāsim 'Abdallah b. 'Awf, of the Banū Kināna. He died around 730.[65]

60 Ibn al-Kalbī (Caskel), 270; Naṣr b. Muzāḥim, 206; Khalīfa ibn Khayyāṭ, I, 222; according to Dīnawarī, 172, he was the leader of the Banū Quḍā'a, which is incorrect.

61 Naṣr b. Muzāḥim, 207; Khalīfa ibn Khayyāṭ, 222: Shurayṭ; Dīnawarī, 172: Zayd b. Ḥārith.

62 Ibn al-Kalbī, 127, and see *ibid.*, II, 437; Ya'qūbī, *Ta'rīkh*, II, 298f; Ibn Ḥabīb, *Muḥabbar*, 303; Ibn al-Athīr, *Kāmil*, III, 294, points out that in the year AH 37, which was AD 657/8, that is twenty-five years earlier, Muslim b. 'Uqba was appointed head of the infantry corps in Damascus. See the subject of the governor Meslem mentioned in the papyri of Nessana, above.

63 Khalīfa ibn Khayyāṭ, I. 432. and *ibid.* the editor's note: on the margin of the manuscript it is written that he was called Ḥay, and some say: Ḥuyay, and some say: Ḥamīd; Abū Zur'a, 92 (MS); Ibn Ḥabīb, *Muḥabbar*, 259; Khazrajī, 383; Dhahabī, *Ta'rīkh*, V, 24; Ibn Ḥajar, *Tahdhīb*, XI, 158.

64 Ṭabarī, *Ta'rīkh*, II, 838; Khalīfa ibn Khayyāṭ, II, 468.

65 Dhahabī, *Ta'rīkh*, IV, 138.

[153] A central figure during the reign of 'Abd al-Malik and also during the reigns of other caliphs who succeeded him was Abū'l-Miqdam (some say: Abū Naṣr) Rajā' ibn Ḥayawa. He first resided in Tiberias (some say: in Bet Shean) and from there seems to have moved to Jerusalem and then to Damascus, where he had considerable influence in the court of the Umayyads. In the days of 'Abd al-Malik he was responsible for the treasury. He earned quite a reputation for his knowledge of Muslim law. Rajā' was of the Banū Kinda and claimed descent from the clan of the heads of the tribe, Banū 'Amr, from which the famous Imrā'l-Qays also stemmed. He filled a central and decisive role in the appointment of 'Umar ibn 'Abd al-'Azīz as caliph, since he was the chief adviser to 'Umar's predecessor, Sulaymān, and persuaded him to proclaim his cousin 'Umar as his heir. In the days of Hishām b. 'Abd al-Malik he was known by the title of 'head of the tribes in jund Filasṭīn'. I have already mentioned the role he played in the building of the Dome of the Rock. He also had considerable sway over 'Umar ibn 'Abd al-'Azīz, and it is possible that under his influence, 'Umar introduced his innovations in the matter of taxes. Rajā' b. Ḥayawa earned unusual praise in the Muslim sources, and it appears that the reason for this is that the appointment of 'Umar ibn 'Abd al-'Azīz as caliph (who was considered the only righteous one of the Damascene caliphs) is attributed to him. Rajā' died in the year AH 112, or AD 730/1.[66]

[154–157] In the year AH 119 (AD 737), the tribes of jund Filasṭīn are recalled as having participated in the campaign under Asad ibn 'Abdallah against the Turks in central Asia. At the head of the Palestinian tribes stood Muṣ'ab ibn 'Amr of the Banū Khuzā'a.[67] During the same period, we find another outstanding personality from the Banū Kinda, in a position simi-

[66] Ibn al-Kalbī (Caskel), 238 and see *ibid.* II, 484; Ibn Sa'd, VII(2), 161f; Ibn Ḥazm, *Jamhara*, 429; Khalīfa ibn Khayyāṭ, II, 504; Ṭabarī, *Ta'rīkh*, II, 1341–1345; Khazrajī, 99; Ibn Qutayba, *Ma'ārif*, 472; Ibn 'Asākir, V, 312ff; Ibn al-Athīr, *Kāmil*, V, 39ff, 172; Bustī, 117 (No. 901); Ibn Kathīr, *Bidāya*, IX, 304; Abū Zur'a, 42 (MS); Nawawī, *Tahdhīb*, I, 190; Ibn Khallikān, II, 301ff; Ibn al-Jawzī, *Ṣifa*, IV, 186f; Dhahabī, *Ta'rīkh*, IV, 261f; Ibn Khaldūn, *'Ibar*, III, 161; Ibn Ḥajar, *Tahdhīb*, III, 266f: as to the name of his grandfather (the father of Ḥayawa) it is said that he was called Jarwal, and some say: Ḥandal, but Ibn Ḥajar saw an exact writing of his name: Khanzal. See also: Caskel, *Felsendom*, 23 and see also the article dedicated to him by Bosworth, *IQ*, 16:36, 1972; and *ibid.*, the information from a manuscript that the origin of his family was from Mayshān in Iraq, which according to Bosworth may indicate that his origin was from the Nabaṭīs who spoke Syriac, or perhaps Persian, and that actually he was a client of the Kinda tribe. This is not even hinted at in the Arab sources. In the original seen by Bosworth, Mayshān is probably a distortion of Baysān (Bet Shean). Cf. also above, note 41. Bosworth also attributes to Rajā' decisive influence on the decision of Sulaymān b. 'Abd al-Malik to build Ramla, following the quarrel with the church about the parcel of land in Lod (see above). See also Shaban, *The 'Abbāsid Revolution*, 76f. The son of Rajā', 'Āṣim, is also mentioned. 'Āṣim died around 770, see Dhahabī, *Ta'rīkh*, VI, 86.

[67] Ṭabarī, *Ta'rīkh*, II, 1609.

lar to that of Rajā' b. Ḥayawa, namely Abū 'Amr 'Ubāda b. Nussay; but whereas the former was active mainly in jund Filasṭīn (before transferring to Damascus), the latter was appointed by 'Abd al-Malik chief cadi in jund Urdunn, and in the days of 'Umar ibn 'Abd al-'Azīz he became governor of the region. He resided in Tiberias and was designated 'head of the tribes of Urdunn' (similar to the status of Rajā' b. Ḥayawa in jund Filasṭīn). 'Ubāda died in AH 118 (AD 736).[68]

There were also quite a number of well-known Muslim figures living in Jerusalem immediately after the conquest, or who came to settle there in succeeding generations, in the days of the Damascene caliphate. Among those whom the Muslim tradition links with Jerusalem we find Abū Yūsuf 'Abdallah b. Salām, a Jew of the Banū Qaynuqā', who turned to Islam with the arrival of Muḥammad in Medina. According to Wāqidī, he took part in the conquest of Jerusalem with 'Umar ibn al-Khaṭṭāb, and died in Medina in the year AH 43 (AD 663).[69] Another Jew, *Sham'ūn* (Simon), from the Banū Naḍīr, who is Zayd (or b. Zayd) the father of Rayḥāna (a captive from among the Jews whom Muḥammad took as a concubine after he killed her husband, who was from the Banū Qurayẓa), settled in Jerusalem according to the Muslim tradition and preached sermons on the Temple Mount.[70]

[158–161] Abū Ya'lā Shaddād b. Aws also settled in Jerusalem; he was the nephew of the poet Ḥassān b. Thābit, who had been one of the retainers of the Prophet. His father, Aws b. Thābit, was a notable figure among the Anṣār, the first Muslims in Medina. They were of the clan of the Banū al-Najjār, the closest to Muḥammad, which belonged to the Banū Khazraj. Shaddād died at the age of ninety-five in Jerusalem in the year AH 58 (AD 678), towards the end of Mu'āwiya's reign (but some say that he died in the year AH 64 (AD 683/4). Of his offspring are mentioned Ya'lā, who passed on ancient traditions in the name of his father; and also a daughter whose name was Khazraj, married to a man of the Banū Azd, with three sons, Muḥammad, 'Abd al-Wahhāb and Mundhir. I have already mentioned that Shaddād's house, which he built for himself in Jerusalem, collapsed in the earthquake of 748. It is said that the building's collapse buried many Muslims, including Shaddād's sons, with the exception of Muḥammad, who survived but lost a leg. One should remember, however, that seventy years passed between Shaddād's death and the

68 Ibn Sa'd, VII(2), 162; Khalīfa ibn Khayyāṭ, II, 363f; Khazrajī, 159; Ibn al-Athīr, *Kāmil*, V, 199; Bustī, 180 (No. 1428); Dhahabī, *Ta'rīkh*, IV, 261f; Ibn 'Asākir, VII, 214f; Ibn Ḥajar, *Tahdhīb*, V, 113.

69 Muqaddasī, *Muthīr*, 22; Ibn 'Asākir, VII, 443; Nawawī, *Tahdhīb*, I, 270; Dhahabī, *Siyar*, II, 296.

70 Ibn Ḥabīb, *Muḥabbar*, 93f (his full name: Sham'ūn b. Zayd b. Khunāfa); Balādhurī, *Ansāb*, I, 453f; Ibn al-Athīr, *Usd*, III, 4; cf. Goitein, *Yerushalayim*, 1953/4, 87f.

earthquake; and one must therefore conclude that it is probably his grandsons or great-grandsons that are being spoken of rather than his sons.[71]

Among the Muslims who lived in Jerusalem during 'Umar's time we find Uways b. 'Āmir al-Qaranī, of the Banū Madhḥij, a Yamanī tribe, who is described as one of the first righteous souls of Islam.[72] Another Jerusalemite was the adopted son of Ka'b al-Aḥbār (the son of his wife), Tubay' b. 'Āmir al-Ḥimyarī, that is to say that he stemmed from Ḥimyar in Yemen. He died in 720 in Alexandria.[73] Another Yemenite who lived in Jerusalem was Abū 'Abdallah Thawbān b. Yamrud, who was one of Muḥammad's freedmen. It is said that he settled in Jerusalem by the Prophet's own decree, in order that he beget heirs (however he did not succeed). He died in 674.[74] Among the founding fathers of Islam who settled in Palestine, mention should be made of Murra b. Ka'b al-Sulamī al-Bahzī, who belonged to the Ṣaḥāba, of whom it is said that he settled first in Baṣra, moved afterwards to Palestine, and died in Urdunn in the year 677. He was said to have taken part in a convention of Muslim preachers which took place (evidently in Palestine) after the assassination of Caliph 'Uthmān and that he quoted praise of the murdered caliph, ascribed to the Prophet.[75]

[162–168] One who was considered as having laid the cornerstone of Arab historiography, Abū Bakr Muḥammad b. Muslim b. Shihāb al-Zuhrī (of the Banū Zuhra, a clan of Quraysh) lived in Palestine, and it is said that he had an estate in a place called Shi'b Zubdā (as in Ibn Kathīr; according to Ibn Khallikān: 'Adāmā or Adamī, a place situated behind Shighb and Badā, which are two valleys or two villages between Ḥijāz and

71 Ibn Sa'd, III(2), 63, notes the fact that the offspring of Aws b. Thābit live in Jerusalem; and see *ibid.*, VII(2), 124. See: Ibn al-Kalbī (Caskel), I, 186; II, 522; Balādhurī, *Ansāb*, I, 243f: he was aged seventy-five when he died. Ibn Qutayba, *Ma'ārif*, 312; Ibn Qudāma, 54; Khazrajī, 139; Ibn al-Athīr, *Kāmil*, IV, 174; Ibn Kathīr, *Bidāya*, VIII, 87f; Ibn Ḥajar, *Iṣāba*, III, 196; some say he died in AH 41 or 42 (AD 661, 662); *idem*, *Tahdhīb*, IV, 315f: his grave is in Jerusalem; Ibn al-'Imād, I, 64; Dhahabī, *Ta'rīkh*, V, 39; *idem*, *Siyar*, II, 328–333; Nawawī, *Tahdhīb*, I, 242 noted that one can see his grave until today (around 1250) before Bāb al-Raḥma.

72 Ibn Sa'd, VI, 111–115; on his stay in Jerusalem see 'Ulaymī, 253; see about him further: Ibn al-Athīr, *Usd*, I, 151f. He was one of the followers of 'Alī and was killed in Ṣiffīn. Abū'l-Ḥātim al-Rāzī wrote about him in his book (in manuscript) *Zuhd al-thamāniya min al-tābi'īn*, see Sezgin, I, 179 (No. 7: about eight people whose sayings form the basis of Muslim mysticism. Cf. Sezgin, *ibid.*, 632). See also Ibn al-Kalbī (Caskel), I, 271, II, 580.

73 Dhahabī, *Ta'rīkh*, IV, 95.

74 Ibn Sa'd, VII(2), 140; Ibn Qutayba, *Ma'ārif*, 147, claims that Thawbān settled in Ḥimṣ, and similarly Balādhurī, *Ansāb*, I, 480; Ṭabarī, *Ta'rīkh*, I, 1778: some say he lived in Ḥimṣ and others in Ramla; Ibn 'Asākir, III, 378ff: he lived in Ramla and had a house there, but died in Egypt; some say he lived in Ḥimṣ. Dhahabī, *Siyar*, III, 11; Ibn al-Athīr, *Usd*, I, 249: he had houses in Ramla, Ḥimṣ and in Fustat; see also Ibn Kathīr, *Bidāya*, V, 314, and there different opinions on his origin.

75 On Murra b. Ka'b, see: Ibn al-Athīr, *Usd*, IV, 351. Goldziher, *ZDMG*, 50(1896), 493.

al-Shām; some say: Nu'f, in the same neighbourhood'). He was one of the retainers of 'Abd al-Malik and of his successors, especially of al-Walīd. He died in AH 125 (AD 742) (but there are other versions).[76]

'Abdallah b. Muḥayrīz, of the Banū Jumaḥ, of Quraysh, was one of the important settlers in Jerusalem. He earned much praise for his piety and his knowledge of the Koran. He participated in the battle against the Byzantines in 707, under the command of Maslama b. 'Abd al-Malik, and died in AH 99 or AD 718.[77] Two of his contemporaries were brothers who settled in Jerusalem: Abū Naṣr Ziyād and 'Uthmān, the sons of Abū Sawda. They were originally Palestinians and it is said that their father was a *mawlā*, a client of 'Abdallah ibn 'Umar ('Umar the caliph), but some say, of 'Abdallah ibn 'Amr ibn al-'Āṣ. Their mother was a *mawlāh* of 'Ubāda b. al-Ṣāmit.[78] 'Aṭā' b. Abū Muslim (who is 'Abdallah, and some say Maysara), was a man of Khurāsān who settled in Jerusalem. His father was a *mawlā* of al-Muhallab. According to al-Khaṭīb al-Baghdādī, he was from Jurjān (to the southeast of the Caspian Sea). He died at the age of eighty in AH 135 (AD 752/3), in Jericho, and was brought to Jerusalem to be buried. He was a learned man and many traditions ascribed to the Prophet are quoted in his name, taken from contemporaries of the Prophet.[79] Ibrāhīm b. Abū 'Abla (who is Shamir b. Yaqẓān al-'Uqaylī, evidently from the clan of 'Uqayl b. Ka'b of the Banū Kilāb, of the tribal federation of 'Āmir b. Ṣa'ṣa'a) was a poet. He lived in Jerusalem during the Abbasid revolution and died in AH 151 (AD 768).[80]

The governor of Ramla during the days of 'Umar ibn 'Abd al-'Azīz was Abū'l-Yaman Bashīr b. 'Aqraba al-Juhanī, that is of the clan of Juhayna, of the Banū Quḍā'a.[81] In the middle of the eighth century, Abū Zur'a Yaḥyā b. Abū 'Amr al-Saybānī, of the clan of Saybān (who originated from Ḥimyar in Yemen) lived in Ramla. He was a cousin of the cadi al-Awzā'ī;

76 Ibn Kathīr, *Bidāya*, IX, 340–348; Ibn Khallikān, IV, 177ff. See further: Ibn Sa'd, II(2), 135f; Ibn al-Kalbī (Caskel), 20, and see *ibid.*, II, 424; Ibn Ḥazm, *Jamhara*, 130: he died in Shaghba near Badā; Yāqūt, *Buldān*, III, 302: Shaghb; Abū Nu'aym, *Ḥilya*, III, 360–381; Ibn Ḥajar, *Tahdhīb*, IX, 445f; and cf. the article al-Zuhrī (by J. Horovitz), in *EI*[1]; Sezgin, I, 280ff, and more references in these two places. See also Duri, *BSOAS*, 19:1, 1957.

77 Ṭabarī, *Ta'rīkh*, II, 1192; Ibn Ḥazm, *Jamhara*, 162; Ibn al-'Imād, I, 116; Khazrajī, 181; Ibn al-Athīr, *Kāmil*, IV, 531; Dhahabī, *'Ibar*, I, 117; Ibn Ḥajar, *Tahdhīb*, VI, 22f.

78 Dhahabī, *Ta'rīkh*, IV, 251; Bustī, 117 (No. 903); Khazrajī, 106; Ibn Ḥajar, *Tahdhīb*, III, 373f; 'Ulaymī, 254f.

79 Dhahabī, *Ta'rīkh*, V, 279; Khazrajī, 126; al-Khaṭīb al-Baghdādī, *Mūḍiḥ*, I, 156; Nawawī, *Tahdhīb*, I, 334f; Sulamī, *Targhīb*, 9; Abu Zur'a, 44 (MS); Ibn al-'Imād, I, 192f; Ibn Ḥajar, *Tahdhīb*, VII, 212ff: from Balkh in Khurāsān; Ibn al-Athīr, *Lubāb*, I, 351.

80 Ibn Ḥajar, *Tahdhīb*, I, 142f; 'Ulaymī, 257; he is possibly the author of *Kitāb al-Nawādir* attributed to Abū Shanbal al-'Uqaylī, mentioned by Sezgin, II, 86, No. 9. Ibn Ḥajar calls him: al-Ramlī while 'Ulaymi: al-Maqdisī (the Jerusalemite); Ibn 'Asākir, II, 215–227: Ibrāhīm b. Shamir al-Filasṭīnī al-Ramlī.

81 Ibn Sa'd, VII(2), 144; Ibn 'Asākir, III, 266f.

some say that he participated in the campaign against the Byzantines under the command of Maslama b. 'Abd al-Malik. He died in AH 148 (AD 765), in the days of the Abbasids.[82]

[169–174] Of those Muslims who lived in Tiberias, a number have been mentioned: Ka'b ibn Murra al-Bahzī, of the Banū Sulaym. He lived at first in Baṣra and from there moved to Palestine. He died in AH 57 (AD 677).[83] 'Abdallah b. Ḥawāla, of the Banū Azd, died in AH 58 (AD 678). A number of ḥadīth traditions ascribed to the Prophet in praise of living in al-Shām are transmitted in his name.[84] Two generations later, the name of another man living in Tiberias is recalled: Abū Muḥammad Ṣāliḥ b. Jubayr al-Ṣudā'ī al-Ṭabarānī, of the Banū Azd, who was responsible for the lists (*dīwān*) of taxes (*kharāj*) and the allowances to the tribes (the army – *al-jund*) in the days of 'Umar II, ibn 'Abd al-'Azīz. He died around 740.[85] A number of people who settled in Ascalon are recorded in the sources: Khālid b. Durayk, who died in around 740.[86] His contemporary in Ascalon was Abū Bakr Abān ibn Ṣāliḥ ibn 'Umayr ibn 'Ubayd, of the Banū Khuzā'a.[87] In the following generation in Ascalon, we find the son of the great-grandson of Caliph 'Umar ibn al-Khaṭṭāb, 'Umar ibn Muḥammad ibn Zayd ibn 'Abdallah ibn 'Umar ibn al-Khaṭṭāb. He carried 'Umar's shield, flaunting it in public all the time. He had four brothers living in Ascalon: Abū Bakr, 'Āṣim, Zayd and Wāqid. He was among the transmitters of the traditions of Mālik b. Anas. 'Umar ibn Muḥammad was one of the army commanders in Ascalon, and his offspring continued to live in that city. He made a journey to Baghdad and afterwards to Kūfa as well, and everywhere masses of people came to meet him. He died in about 760, under the rule of the Abbasids.[88]

[175–178] Some Muslim personalities who lived in Eilat are mentioned in the sources of the period. Eilat was particularly connected with the Umayyads, from the days of the caliph 'Uthmān (who also came of the Umayya clan), for at that time in the town there were a group of *mawālī*, or clients. One can assume that they were either Christians or Jews who had

82 Ṭabarī, *Ta'rīkh*, I, 1864; Ibn al-Athīr, *Kāmil*, V, 589; Ibn Ḥajar, *Tahdhīb*, XI, 260.

83 Ibn Sa'd, VII(2), 133; Ibn 'Abd al-Barr, *Istī'āb*, III, 1326; Ibn al-Athīr, *Usd*, IV, 248f; Ibn Ḥajar, *Tahdhīb*, VIII, 441.

84 Ibn Sa'd, *ibid.*; Dhahabī, *'Ibar*, I, 62; Ibn 'Abd al-Barr, *Istī'āb*, III, 894; Ibn 'Asākir, I, 52; Ibn al-Athīr, *Usd*, III, 148; Ibn Ḥajar, *Tahdhīb*, V, 194.

85 Dhahabī, *Ta'rikh*, IV, 258; Ibn 'Asākir, VI, 366; Khazrajī, 144; Ibn Ḥajar, *Tahdhīb*, IV, 383f. Ṣudā, a clan from Madhḥij. Otherwise called al-Azdī. See Ibn al-Kalbī (Caskel), I, 265; II, 539.

86 Dhahabī, *Ta'rīkh*, IV, 246: al-'Asqalānī. Some say he was called al-Dimashqī, and others say al-Ramlī. Khazrajī, 85; Ibn Ḥajar, *Tahdhīb*, III, 86f.

87 Ibn Sa'd, VI, 234; Ibn Ḥajar, *Tahdhīb*, I, 94f, he was a *mawlā* of Quraysh.

88 Dhahabī, *Ta'rīkh*, VI, 104; *idem*, *'Ibar*, I, 215; Khazrajī, 242; Ibn al-'Imād, I, 229: one of the most honourable of his generation; al-Khaṭīb al-Baghdādī, *Ta'rīkh*, XI, 180f; Ibn Ḥajar, *Tahdhīb*, VII, 495f.

accepted Islam and became clients of the caliph. They were given the task of caring for pilgrims, in particular supplying them with drinking water, for Eilat was an important way-station on the road to Mecca. This position rendered Eilat a certain importance and it developed economically; commerce flourished and there were many markets. Those converted clients were known for their erudition in everything concerning the traditions and Eilat became a centre of knowledge of the beginnings of Islam as well as in matters of law. The guide and the living spirit of this group was Ibn Shihāb al-Zuhrī, who lived in that region, as we have seen. Also mentioned as having settled in Eilat was a kinsman of the Caliph 'Uthmān, Abān b. Sa'īd b. al-'Āṣ; he settled in Eilat, because he desired 'solitude and relaxation'. He evidently died in the year AH 29 (AD 650; some say it was earlier, during the conquest of Palestine; however it seems that these other sources may be speaking of his grandfather, also called Abān b. Sa'īd). Some say that he was the person who dictated to Zayd b. Thābit the final version of the Koran, as it was set down in the days of 'Uthmān.[89] Two or three generations later, we find the offspring of those *mawālī* of the Umayyads. Abū Khālid 'Uqayl ibn Khālid ibn 'Uqayl died in about 760. From him, Abū Yazīd Yūnus b. Yazīd b. Abū'l-Najjād heard and learned traditions; he died some fifteen years after his teacher. It is said of 'Uqayl that he was a favourite of al-Zuhrī and his friend.[90] Abū Yazīd Yūnus b. Yazīd was a pupil of 'Uqayl ibn Khālid and of al-Zuhrī. His brother, Abū 'Alī (Khālid?) is also mentioned, as is his nephew, 'Anbasa b. Khālid b. Yazīd. Ibn Ḥajar notes that Yūnus had a weak memory; he therefore had to write everything down and kept a notebook.[91] Another personality in this group was 'Abd al-Ḥakam ibn A'yūn ibn al-Layth, who lived at the same time as the aforementioned. It is said that he and his father emigrated from Eilat and settled in Alexandria. If we consider this together with the fact that the aforementioned Yūnus is said to have died in Egypt, we may assume that the whole group was persecuted under Abbasid rule because of their close connections to the Umayyads, and it is possible that because of this some of them fled to Egypt, where perhaps they felt more secure than in their native city.[92]

[179–186] Apart from these personalities, there are some thirty other

89 Maqrīzī, *Khiṭaṭ*, I, 325; Iṣbahānī, *Aghānī*, X, 62; Ibn al-Athīr, *Usd*, I, 35ff.

90 Ibn Sa'd, VII(2), 206f, mentions several people who lived in Eilat, among them this 'Uqayl; Sam'ānī, I, 410; Ibn al-Athīr, *Kāmil*, V, 528; 'Uqayl died in AH 144, that is AD 761/2; but see *idem*, *Lubāb*. I, 79: in AH 141 or 142, that is, AD 758 or 759; Bustī, 183, No. 1454.

91 Ibn Sa'd, *ibid.*; Sam'ānī, *ibid.*; Ibn al-Athīr, *Kāmil*, V, 608; Bustī, 183, No. 1452; Yūnus b. Yazīd b. Abī'l-Mukhāriq; Khazrajī, 380; Khafājī, 267; Ibn Ḥajar, *Tahdhīb*, XI, 450ff; XII, 174; according to him this family were *mawālī* of the caliph Mu'āwiya.

92 'Iyāḍ, I, 313.

figures recorded in the sources who were active during the Umayyad rule in Palestine, or who had some connection with Palestine. Abū Yaḥyā 'Abdallah b. Sa'īd, ibn Abī Sarḥ, of the Banū 'Āmir, of Quraysh, who was governor of Egypt after 'Amr ibn al-'Āṣ, lived in Palestine and died there around 657. It was said of him that he was the scribe of the Prophet and that he would change what was dictated to him. When this was discovered, he abandoned Islam and fled to Mecca. 'Uthmān managed to obtain the Prophet's pardon for him and when 'Uthmān became caliph, he appointed him governor of Egypt. He played an important role in the conquest of Africa. He built himself a house in Egypt, probably in 646. After the murder of 'Uthmān, however, he moved to jund Filasṭīn, and died in Ascalon or in Ramla.[93]

The poet al-Rabī' ibn Maṭar ibn Balkh, of the Banū Tamīm, was involved in Palestinian affairs, took part in the conquest, and wrote poems about Tiberias and Bet Shean.[94] Abū Muslim 'Abdallah b. Thawb, of the Banū Khawlān, accepted Islam in the days of Mu'āwiya. He lived at first in Baṣra and from there went to Palestine (*al-arḍ al-muqaddasa*), where he died during the time of Caliph Yazīd.[95] Abū Muḥammad 'Abdallah b. al-Sa'dī, of the clan of 'Āmir b. Lu'ayy of the Quraysh, lived in Urdunn. It was said that he was one of the Prophet's retainers. He died in AH 57 (AD 677).[96] Jubayr b. Nufayr (or Nuṣayr) lived at first in Ḥimṣ and afterwards in Palestine. He stemmed from Ḥaḍramawt (of the Kinda?) and converted to Islam at the time of Abū Bakr. He died in AH 75 (AD 694/5; later dates are also mentioned).[97] 'Abd al-Raḥmān b. Ghanm, who was considered outstanding in his generation for his knowledge of traditions, came of the Yemenite tribe of Ash'ar, and settled in jund Filasṭīn. He died in AH 78, or AD 696/7. He was close to Marwān b. al-Ḥakam and visited Egypt with him.[98] Among those who settled in Jerusalem, we find Abū Qirḍāfa Wāthila b. al-Asqa' of the Banū Kināna. He died at the age of ninety-eight in Jerusalem in AH 85 (AD 704); other sources say that he died at the age of 105 in AH 83 (AD 702/3). In Ibn al-Athīr and in Ibn Ḥajar, he is entered under a different name (and it is not certain which

93 Balādhurī, *Ansāb*, I, 358 (points out that some say he died in Ifriqiyā – in the region of Tunis – but he denies this); Ibn Qutayba, *Ma'ārif*, 300ff (ascribes him to Madhḥij); Ibn Ṭūlūn, *Umarā'*, 10; Ibn 'Asākir, VII, 432; Nawawī, *Tahdhīb*, I, 269; Ibn al-Athīr, *Kāmil*, III, 351: he died suddenly in Ascalon during his prayers; Bustī, 53 (No. 358); Ibn Taghrī Bardī, I, 82 (on p. 94 he says that he was murdered in Palestine, and some say in Ramla). See the article 'Abd Allah b. Sa'd in *EI*² (by C. H. Becker).

94 Ibn 'Asākir, V, 306f.

95 Ibn Sa'd, VII(2), 157; Abū Nu'aym, *Ḥilya*, 124f; cf. Goitein, *BJPES*, XII(1945/6), 123.

96 Balādhurī, *Ansāb*, I, 219; Ibn al-Athīr, *Usd*, III, 175; Ibn Ḥajar, *Tahdhīb*, V, 235.

97 Ibn Ḥajar, *Tahdhīb*, II, 64; 'Ulaymī, 257.

98 Dhahabī, *Ta'rīkh*, III, 188f; Nawawī, *Tahdhīb*, I, 302; Ibn al-Athīr, *Kāmil*, IV, 449; Khazrajī, 197; Bustī, 112 (No. 851); Ibn Ḥajar, *Tahdhīb*, VI, 250f; 'Ulaymī, 257.

version of the name is distorted): Jandara b. Khayshana; it is said of him that he was of the *ṣaḥāba*, the circle of the Prophet, and some say he lived in Sinājiya, a village in the neighbourhood of Ascalon. Ibn Ḥajar notes in the name of Ibn Ḥibān that he is buried in Ascalon.[99] Another settler in Jerusalem was Abū Bishr, or Abū Bisr 'Abdallah ibn Fayrūz, a Persian by birth, who died in the year AH 90 (AD 708).[100]

[187–193] In the following generation, we find Abū Sinān Ḥumayd b. 'Uqba of Quraysh, who lived in jund Filasṭīn after Damascus and Ḥimṣ. It is said that he achieved great success in the days of Mu'āwiya.[101] Sharīk b. Judayr, a man of the Banū Taghlib (who were Christians in the time of the conquest) who was close to 'Alī ibn Abī Ṭālib, fought alongside him and was injured in one eye. After Mu'āwiya became caliph, he settled in Jerusalem and also participated in the rebellion of Mukhtār.[102] Farwa b. Mujāhid was a man of Palestine, a *mawlā* of the Banū Lakhm. He lived in Kafr 'Anā in Palestine and died in about 720.[103] Hānī b. Kulthūm b. 'Abdallah b. Sharīk, was also of the Banū Kināna (though some say Kinda) and lived in jund Filasṭīn. 'Umar ibn 'Abd al-'Azīz proposed that he become governor of the jund, but he refused. He died in around 720, in Sāfariyya, a village mentioned by Yāqūt as being 'near Ramla'. He is also known by the name Ibn Ḥibbān.[104] Al-Qāsim b. 'Abd al-Raḥmān b. 'Abdallah b. Mas'ūd, of the Banū Hudhayl, who lived in the region of Mecca, was cadi in Kūfa, appointed by 'Umar ibn 'Abd al-'Azīz and moved afterwards to Jerusalem, where he was noted for three qualities: praying at great length, frequently keeping silent, and giving to charity. He died in AH 120 (AD 728).[105] Abū Salām Mamṭūr al-Dimashqī al-A'raj (the lame) al-Aswad (the black) al-Ḥabashī, was called al-Ḥabashī because he belonged to a clan in Ḥimyar (Yaman), who were so-called, and not because he was an Ethiopian. He lived in Palestine and was one of the

[99] Ibn Sa'd, VII(2), 129; Ibn 'Asākir II(1), 14: while in Damascus he met Ka'b al-Aḥbār who showed him a place in the city where one prays as if praying in Jerusalem; cf. on this matter: Gruber, 68, and see there further references; Ibn al-Athīr, *Usd*, I, 307; V, 276; Ibn Ḥajar, *Tahdhīb*, II, 119, Yāqūt, *Buldān*, III, 154f.

[100] Dhahabī, *Ta'rīkh*, III, 269; Khazrajī, 177; Ibn Ḥajar, *Tahdhīb*, V, 358; 'Ulaymī, 254.

[101] Dhahabī, *Ta'rīkh*, IV, 109; Ibn 'Asākir, IV, 461f; Ibn al-Athīr, *Lubāb*, II, 221.

[102] Ṭabarī, *Ta'rīkh*, II, 714; Ibn al-Athīr, *Kāmil*, IV, 264.

[103] Dhahabī, *Ta'rīkh*, IV, 44; Khazrajī, 262; Ibn Ḥajar, *Tahdhīb*, VIII, 264, quotes Bukhārī with regard to Kafr 'Anā. Bukhārī, *Ta'rīkh*, VII, 127 (No. 572) has: Farwa b. Mujālid(!), and in the printed version, Kafr Ghamā; there is no way of knowing the place with certainty.

[104] Dhahabī, *Ta'rīkh*, IV, 94; in Bukhārī, *Ta'rīkh*, IX, 230 (No. 2823): Hānī b. Kulthūm b. Sharīk; Khazrajī, 350; Busti, 118 (No. 917: sets the time of his death in the days of 'Umar ibn al-Khaṭṭāb, which is certainly an error); Yāqūt, *Buldān*, III, 12; Ibn Ḥajar, *Tahdhīb*, XI, 22; 'Ulaymī, 254.

[105] Ibn al-Athīr, *Kāmil*, V, 105, 228; Dhahabī, IV, 293; Khazrajī, 266; Bustī, 106 (No. 803); Ibn Khaldūn, *'Ibar*, III, 297; Ibn Ḥajar, *Tahdhīb*, VIII, 321f.

pupils of 'Ubāda b. Ṣāmit. He died around 730.[106] Sulaymān b. Sa'd was a Palestinian from jund Urdunn (Tiberias?) who converted to Islam and became a *mawlā* of the Banū Khushayn, a clan of the Quḍā'a. He was the scribe of 'Abd al-Malik and afterwards also of al-Walīd, of Sulaymān and of 'Umar ibn 'Abd al-'Azīz. He was the first to transcribe the lists of the *dīwān* (the collection of taxes and the distribution of allowances to the tribes) from Greek into Arabic, and was the first Muslim to manage the affairs of the *dīwān*s.[107]

[194–200] In the generation which experienced the Abbasid revolution, we find Abū'l-Walīd Rudayḥ b. 'Aṭiyya, of Quraysh, who lived in Palestine and died there in about 765. He served as *mu'adhdhin* in Jerusalem.[108] Abū Umayya 'Abd al-Raḥmān al-Sindī lived in Nābulus, was one of the Palestinians who accepted Islam, was a *mawlā* of Sulaymān b. 'Abd al-Malik and afterwards served as secretary to 'Umar ibn 'Abd al-'Azīz. He died in 760.[109] Masarra b. Ma'bad, of the Banū Lakhm, who was learned in the traditions, lived in Palestine in Bet Guvrin and died in around 760.[110] Abū Sinān 'Īsā b. Sinān was a Palestinian, one of 'Umar ibn 'Abd al-'Azīz's retainers, who stayed as a guest in 'Īsā's house in Jerusalem whenever he visited there. He emigrated from Palestine to Baṣra at some unknown date, perhaps after the Abbasid revolution, settled there with the al-Qasāmil clan of the Banū Azd and was thus known by the name al-Qasmalī; he was also called al-Ḥanafī, as he evidently belonged to the clan of the Banū Ḥanīfa of the Banū Bakr b. Wā'il. He died around 760.[111] 'Abbād b. Kathīr was an inhabitant of Ramla, who died in around 770.[112] His contemporaries were Sawwār b. 'Ammāra, who lived in Ramla and was a pupil of 'Abd al-Raḥmān al-Sindī,[113] and al-Walīd b. Jamīl, apparently of the Banū Kināna.[114]

[201] Special note should be taken of Abū Ruqiyya Tamīm al-Dārī. He was an Arab of the Banū Lakhm, who lived on the Palestinian border before the advent of Islam. According to the Muslim traditions, he joined the Prophet and became his follower during the latter's stay in Medina. He is credited with an astonishing knowledge of the Christian (or perhaps the Manichaean) sources and as a result had influence over the Prophet. It was he who introduced the great innovation in the Prophet's mosque by proposing the use of oil for lighting instead of the palm tree branches

106 Dhahabī, *Ta'rīkh*, IV, 205; Ibn Ḥajar, *Tahdhīb*, X, 296.
107 Ibn 'Asākir, VI, 276.
108 Bustī, 184 (No. 1467); Ibn Ḥajar, *Tahdhīb*, III, 271.
109 Dhahabī, *Ta'rīkh*, VI, 94.
110 Bustī, 181 (No. 1436); Ibn Ḥajar, *Tahdhīb*, X, 109.
111 Ibn Sa'd, V, 280; Dhahabī, *Ta'rīkh*, VI, 112; Ibn al-Athīr, *Lubāb*, II, 263; Ibn Ḥajar, *Tahdhīb*, VIII, 211.
112 Dhahabī, *Ta'rīkh*, VI, 207; Ibn Ḥajar, *Tahdhīb*, V, 102f.
113 Bukhārī, *Ta'rīkh*, IV, 169 (No. 2362); Dhahabī, *Ta'rīkh*, VI, 94.
114 Dhahabī, *Ta'rīkh*, VI, 314; Bukhārī, *Ta'rīkh*, VIII, 142 (No. 2490).

which were set alight there previously. He was promised by the Prophet that after conquering Palestine, he would receive Hebron and Bayt ʿAynūn (some sources mention also Bethlehem). In Ibn Saʿd a version has been preserved of the bill of rights given by the Prophet to Tamīm, which was copied by ʿAlī ibn Abī Ṭālib. When Palestine was conquered, so it is told, ʿUmar fulfilled the Prophet's promise and gave that region to Tamīm al-Dārī. Actually it appears that he was collector of land taxes (*kharāj*) there. It is said that ʿUmar warned him against enslaving the local population or selling their property, and to be content solely with collecting taxes. The chroniclers and other writers of the Middle Ages maintain that those areas are occupied by the descendants of Tamīm al-Dārī 'until this very day'. Among the traditions Tamīm al-Dārī related to the Prophet is the *ḥadīth al-jasāsa* (an apocalyptic creature), who asked its companion details about the dates of Bet Shean, about the Sea of Galilee and the spring of Zoar.[115]

The tribes

[202–221] From the above description of Muslim personalities, one learns that during this period most of them were tribesmen, apart from a comparatively small number of clients, the *mawālī*. The latter evidently served in administrative positions which undoubtedly involved writing

[115] Ibn Saʿd, I(2), 75, tells of the delegation of the Tamīm clan, al-Dārīyīn, who came to the Prophet at the time of the Tabūk campaign, bearing gifts, and the Prophet immediately sold these gifts to a Jew for the sum of 8,000 dirhams. Tamīm al-Dārī had rights of possession (or so it appears) given him by the Byzantines on those two places (*qaryatayn*, two villages: *Ḥibrā wa-bayt ʿaynūn*). Abū Bakr renewed the letter of rights after the death of the Prophet; see further *ibid.*, VII(2), 129f. Ṭabarānī, *Muʿjam*, I, 14, describes him as the prototype of a Bedouin fighter, who knew how to take good care of his horse, and quotes a ḥadīth in the name of the Prophet on the virtue of feeding one's horse during the holy war. Bakrī, 289; Ibn Ḥazm, *Jamhara*, 422; Ṭayālisī, 229. Ibn ʿAsākir, III, 344–357, notes that he himself saw the document of the Dārīs ascribed to the Abbasid caliph al-Mustanjid bi'llāh (1160–1170), and quotes the version in which *Bayt ʿaynūn* and *Bayt Ibrāhīm* are spoken of, and points out that they are in Hebron 'until this very day' (around 1170), and they are a large group, called al-Dāriyya. (One must remember that he is writing at a time when Hebron was in the hands of the Crusaders.) *Ibid.*, p. 345, he mentions that in 1092, in the days of Ghazālī (that is, when he stayed in Jerusalem), the cadi of Jerusalem Abū Ḥātim al-Harawī al-Ḥanafī, refused to recognise the validity of the Dārīs' document, and then Ghazālī said that the cadi was a heretic. See also: Suyūṭī, *Khaṣāʾiṣ*, II, 177f; III, 289; Dhahabī, *Taʾrīkh*, II, 188ff; Suhaylī, *Taʿrīf*, 11b; Samarqandī, *Bustān*, 100; Bustī, 52 (No. 353); Khafājī, III, 301: the al-Dār clan came from Yaman; Nawawī, I, 138f: some say his name was al-Dayrī, from the word *dayr* (monastery), because before Islam, he was in a monastery; Qalqashandī, *Ṣubḥ*, XIII, 120ff has the version of the letter of rights given to Tamīm by the Prophet and which ʿUmar renewed; Maqrīzī, his treatise on Tamīm al-Dārī, in Matthews, *JPOS*, 19:150, 1939/40; and its Cairo edition, 1972; Ibn al-Athīr, *Usd*, II, 243; Mawṣilī, *Wasāʾil*, 23b–24a (according to *kitāb al-madīna* of ʿAskarī); Ibn al-Jawzī, *Wafāʾ*, I, 156; Ḥalabī, II, 88; ʿUlaymī, 428f; Shiblī, 42b; Ibn Ḥajar, *Tahdhīb*, I, 511f; *idem*, *Iṣāba*, I, 183f.

and keeping accounts, drafting official documents, and so on. Some of these converted Muslims, like many similarly placed people in other regions of the Muslim world, were among those who laid the foundations of the new Arabic culture, especially in the sphere of historical writing and legal literature. The fact that there were a large number of tribesmen among the Muslim notables who settled in Palestine should not surprise us, for the Muslim conquest was in its essence the conquest of cultured countries by the Arab tribes. The number of clans and tribes from which these personalities stemmed was about thirty. It should be remembered that the ancient Arab sources preserved only the memory of those people who played active roles in the political and military life of the period. Many were forgotten, which was intentional, because in later generations, during Abbasid rule, a hostile attitude was adopted towards people of the Umayyad administration, apart from the fact that many of the chroniclers identified with the ʻAlids and were filled with antagonism towards Muʻāwiya and his heirs and circle of followers, regarded as the usurpers of the Prophet's family. The possibility of being included in biographical compilations was mainly the lot of those personalities in the Umayyad era who provided information on the days of the Prophet or who taught others ḥadīth traditions attributed to the Prophet. Many of these traditions were not authentic at all and reflected attitudes prevalent during the lifetime of the conveyors or the desires and interests of various groups. In the light of these facts, there is little to glean from the rather archival list of names I have recorded above, with regard to the status of the tribes and their comparative influence, for not every tribe had talented individuals who could fill central political roles or take on military commands. Furthermore, not every tribe had sufficient connections with the Damascene court to enable people of their rank to merit major governing positions, nor did every tribe have enough people who devoted themselves to collecting or inventing traditions. One can undoubtedly assume that in addition to those clans and tribes whose few members merited renown, there were many others in Palestine about whom we know nothing at all, and the tribes' relative numerical strength and the extent of their authority cannot be surmised from biographical lists of Islamic personalities.

We have already encountered the inter-tribal wars and witnessed something of the split between the north and the south, as conveyed in tribal traditions from generation to generation. We are sufficiently aware of the fact that this so-called geographical division did not comply with the reality as it existed at the time of the appearance of Islam, when a whole series of tribes which the traditions describe as having stemmed from the south, that is from the region of Yaman, were actually to be found in the area of Mecca and Medina or even farther north, along the Palestinian border. A marked example of this is the Anṣār tribes in Medina, the Aws and the Khazraj (the Qayla tribes or Banū Ḥāritha), who according to their tradition (and there is no reason to doubt it), emigrated in the distant past from Yaman northward.

The following are the 'southern' tribes whose offspring we find among the inhabitants of Palestine during this period: Khath'am;[116] Judhām (I have already elaborated on this tribe); 'Āmila;[117] Ghassān;[118] Khawlān;[119] Madhḥij, and the clan within it, Zubayd;[120] Ḥimyar (also Yaman in general) and the Saybān clan;[121] Kinda, and the clan of Banū 'Amr.[122] Khuzā'a;[123] Azd;[124] Quḍā'a and the clan of Juhayna within it;[125] Ash'ar; according to Ya'qūbī, writing in 892, this southern tribe were the majority (evidently among the Bedouin) in Tiberias (probably meaning the Tiberias region);[126] Lakhm, as the Judhām, was to be found on the Palestinian border before the advent of Islam.[127]

Among the 'northern' tribes, we find the following represented: Kināna and its clan, Murra;[128] the Sulaym clan of Qays 'Aylān, which apparently lived in jund Urdunn;[129] Thaqīf, whose centre was Ṭā'if in the Ḥijāz, was certainly represented in the administration of Palestine during the time when Ḥajjāj ibn Yūsuf, who was a member of their tribe, ruled the state; but we know that members of this tribe also lived in Trans-Jordan, in the Balqā';[130] Banū Ghaṭafān and the clan of Murra within it;[131] Kilāb, and

116 See Ibn al-Kalbī (Caskel), 45f.

117 *Ibid.*, 53ff; it seems they were located mostly in jund Urdunn.

118 See Watt, 112ff; Ibn al-Kalbī (Caskel), 35ff. They, too, seem to have lived mainly in jund Urdunn.

119 Ibn al-Kalbī (Caskel), 56f.

120 *Ibid.*, 61ff.

121 *Ibid.*, 66ff.

122 *Ibid.*, 47ff.

123 Watt, 83ff; Ibn al-Kalbī (Caskel), 39ff.

124 Ibn al-Kalbī (Caskel), 41ff.

125 Watt, 110f; Ibn al-Kalbī (Caskel), 73ff.

126 Ya'qūbī, *Buldān*, 327; Ibn al-Kalbī (Caskel), 66.

127 Watt, 111; Ibn al-Kalbī (Caskel), 53ff. After some two-hundred years, we still find one of the important Muslim personalities in Palestine, of Tiberias, the writer Sulaymān ibn Aḥmad al-Ṭabarānī (see below), claiming descent from the Banū Lakhm; see Ibn al-Jawzī, *Muntaẓam*, VII, 54 (sec. 73), who mentions that Lakhm is a tribe that lived in Yaman and in al-Shām, and its name is linked with that of Bethlehem (*Bayt lakhm*), the birthplace of Jesus. Similarly in Ibn Taghrī Bardī, IV, 59, the name of the place is not *Bayt laḥm* but *Bayt lakhm*, lest doubts should arise about the connection between Bethlehem and the Lakhm tribe.

128 Watt, 83ff; Ibn al-Kalbī (Caskel), 6.

129 Ibn al-Kalbī (Caskel), 11ff.

130 Ibn Khallikān, VII, 110, in the article on Yūsuf b. 'Umar al-Thaqafī, the son of a cousin of Ḥajjāj; when Yazīd ibn al-Walīd became caliph, after al-Walīd b. Yazīd was murdered, this Yūsuf fled to the Balqā', where his tribe were living; see about this tribe Watt, 101ff; Ibn al-Kalbī (Caskel), 16f; see also Kister, *JSAI*, 1:1, 1979.

131 Watt, 91ff; Ibn al-Kalbī (Caskel), 19ff.

Banū 'Uqayl within it, from the federation of tribes 'Āmir b. Ṣa'ṣa'a;[132] Tamīm;[133] Taghlib, the tribe that was Christian during the time of the conquest and lived on the border of Palestine;[134] Hudhayl.[135]

[222–223] At first glance, it seems as if Palestine was equally divided between northern and southern tribes. But according to the evidence in Ṭabarī it appears that at least by the end of the Damascene caliphate the Yamanī tribesmen had the upper hand. According to the same source, most of the Umayyad army in al-Shām (and one should bear in mind that army meant tribes) were the *Yamaniyya*, the southerners.[136] In the foregoing lists, two important elements are not included and these are the Banū Quraysh on the one hand and the descendants of the Anṣār of Medina (Aws and Khazraj) on the other. In theory, the first were 'northerners' and the others 'southerners'. Banū Quraysh were naturally involved in administration, and when we find them (particularly the clan of Jumaḥ) in Palestine, they are generally there more as individuals who have been given ruling positions, or who have come there for religious reasons. One should note the small number of the Anṣār; they are almost unmentioned among the eminent figures in Palestine.

Ya'qūbī, who as has been mentioned, wrote his book in 892, notes that in jund Filasṭīn there was a mixture of tribes – Lakhm, Judhām, 'Āmila, Kinda, Qays and Kināna – one can imagine that this is copied from an old version, which was correct at the time of the Umayyads. At any rate, this list conforms to the one (a much more extensive list) presented above, which was the result of a study of the names of personalities. That Ya'qūbī's list can be considered limited and does not entirely reflect the real situation, not even in the days of the Umayyads, is proven by the papyri of Nessana from the second half of the seventh century, in which no less than 59 (!) clans, as well as two tribes, the Judhām (Goudam), and Qays, are mentioned. The tribes evidently found Palestine very profitable, preferring to settle there rather than in Iraq. This may have been enhanced by the benefits enjoyed by the people of al-Shām, which was borderland country subject to Byzantine raids and which also served as a base for raids into the latter's territory. Thus we find in Ṭabarī that

[132] Ibn al-Kalbī (Caskel), 13ff. In the tenth and eleventh centuries, we find information about their political and military rise.

[133] Watt, 137ff; Ibn al-Kalbī (Caskel), 7ff; and see Kister, *JESHO*, 3:113, 1965.

[134] Ibn al-Kalbī (Caskel), 27f.

[135] Watt, 90; Ibn al-Kalbī (Caskel), 7.

[136] Ṭabarī, *Ta'rīkh*, II, 1775; and see also two unidentified manuscripts printed by Hinds in *Abḥāth*, 3:24, 1971, containing lists (partial; speaking of participants in the battle of Ṣiffīn on Mu'āwiya's side) of tribes in Palestine. To the list of 'northern' tribes who lived in Palestine the Taym (al-Ribāb) must also be evidently added, who claimed descent from the ancient federation of tribes of Khuzayma-Asad. Ibn Ḥazm, *Jamhara*, 175, 180, mentions two clans who belonged to the Banū Khuzayma (Asad): Ja'wana b. Shayṭān b.

pressure was put on Caliph Marwān b. al-Ḥakam to fulfil his promise to the Banū Kinda in al-Shām to allow them to settle in Trans-Jordan (in the Balqā'), and that this area should be the source of their livelihood.[137]

[224] The period of the Umayyads was undoubtedly the golden age of the Arab tribes who penetrated into Palestine with the Muslim conquest. The leaders of Islam tried to protect the tribes from assimilating to the local populations and to maintain their traditional way of life, with the addition of the new Islamic element. These Arab tribes, both those who had formerly lived on the borders of Palestine and those who came to it within the framework of the Muslim army, were a separate entity of the population of the country. One must remember that the term *'arab* during the Middle Ages meant Bedouin, people of the tribes. These tribes had a common homeland, the Arabian peninsula, even if their ancestors had emigrated from there many generations earlier. On the other hand, there was also a non-Arab population living in the Arabian peninsula, who were neither nomads nor lived in tribes, and who were not of tribal origins. They were farmers, merchants, craftsmen; Jews, Christians, Persians and members of various sects. Religion was not a sign of being non-Arab, for there were Arab tribes who had taken on Christianity, such as the Banū Taghlib, but under Islamic rule they were not considered *ahl al-kitāb* (people of the book). It is well known that for generations prior to Islam, a process of Arab settlement and abandonment of the nomadic way of life began and an urban Arab population grew up, such as that in Mecca and Medina. They were considered Arabs, however, because of their nomadic past. Another identifying factor, naturally, was their common language, Arabic, which despite the differences between various dialects was quite uniform and understandable to the members of all the tribes and spoken by them. But their chief characteristic was nomadism – the culture of the camel. Under Islam, nomadism was considered the most natural and common state of the Arabs, and as I have said, the word *'arab* meant Bedouin. Thus we find in the first century of Islamic rule almost complete synonymity between the terms Muslim, Arab, nomad, tribesman and horseman in the service of Islam; although there are exceptions to this rule, it applies in most cases. To be an Arab at that time meant to belong to the ruling class, enjoying privileges that were bequeathed to successive generations. Alongside the prerogatives, however, there was also the obligation

Wahb, and 'Amr ibn Kināna, who lived in jund Filasṭīn. About the latter, he notes that they are very few. See on Khuzayma: Watt, 87ff.

[137] Ya'qūbī, *Buldān*, 329; he also mentions Judhām, who according to him lived in the region of Bet Guvrin, in the neighbourhood of the Dead Sea. *Nessana*, 340f. On the question of the Greek transliteration of Arabic names see: Isserlin, *Annual*, Leeds Univ. Oriental Society, 7:17, 1975; on the preference of al-Shām, see: Shaban, *Islamic History*, 74, 125. Ṭabarī, *Ta'rīkh*, II, 487 (Ḥuṣayn b. Nimr's request); according to Balādhurī, *Ansāb*, V,

to serve the creed that brought all this about and to fight for it, for it was this belief that gave the Arabs the dominion of an enormous empire.[138]

[225] Therefore it is possible to conceive of a tolerant attitude towards non-believers who were not Arabs, such as the Persians, even if there was some doubt as to their being 'people of the book' and even if they could actually be considered almost idolaters. For the Arabs, however, Islam was absolutely mandatory. If these Arabs were from among the 'people of the book' (speaking mainly of the Christians), it would be possible to compromise, and they would be given time to accept Islam, if not in this generation then in the next. The Arabs who were idol-worshippers, on the other hand, were given only one choice – Islam or death – 'a choice dictated only to the Arab idolaters', in Abū Yūsuf's words. Alongside the constraint to accept Islam, the leaders of Islam also launched an educational campaign among the tribes, evidence of which is found in the account of the offspring of the b. Qurayẓa, the Jews of Medina, Muḥammad b. Ka'b al-Quraẓī:

Five men of the Anṣār already knew the Koran by heart in the days of the Prophet: Mu'ādh b. Jabal, 'Ubāda b. al-Ṣāmit, Ubayy b. Ka'b, Abū Ayyūb and Abū'l-Dardā'. In the days of 'Umar, Yazīd b. Abū Sufyān [Mu'āwiya's brother, who was the commander of the Muslim army in Palestine and Syria until he died of an illness] wrote: in al-Shām there are many tribes and they need someone to teach them the Koran and the laws. So 'Umar requested three people to help him in this matter . . . and Mu'ādh, 'Ubāda and Abū'l-Dardā' volunteered. And 'Umar commanded them: Start in Ḥimṣ, and if you are satisfied, one of you shall go to Damascus and one to [jund] Filasṭīn. 'Ubāda remained in Ḥimṣ while Abū'l-Dardā' went off to Damascus, and Mu'ādh to Filasṭīn; but Mu'ādh died in the year of the 'Imwās plague; and so 'Ubāda went afterwards to Filasṭīn [and remained there] until he died.[139]

[226–229] The Arabs were the military, the horsemen, and they had no responsibilities towards any other sectors of the population. They were not farmers, which they considered a demeaning profession only taken up by the Nabaṭ (a collective term for Aramaic-speaking villagers, and this does not refer to the Nabateans, who lived in southern Palestine in

128, the episode regarding the Balqā' referred to the clan of Sakūn, of Kinda, their spokesman being Mālik Ibn Hubayra.

138 See on the matter of the Banū Taghlib: Abū Yūsuf, 144: the Banū Taghlib, who were Christians, had a tax imposed on them, unlike on the *ahl al-kitāb* but like on the Muslims, that is *ṣadaqa*, but double the sum which the Muslims paid. Mazyād b. Ḥudayr, the first whom 'Umar sent to collect the *ṣadaqa* (*an yu'ashshira*) from the Banū Taghlib, reported: 'he ordered me to put pressure on the Christians, the Banū Taghlib, saying: they are an Arab tribe, not of the people of the book, and should accept Islam'. According to him, 'Umar imposed on the Christian Taghlib tribe the condition that they would not be permitted to raise their children as Christians; and see also Ibn Abī Shayba, III, 197ff; and see the comprehensive discussion in the excellent article by Poliak, *REI*, 12:35, 1938, which has served as the basis for the discussion here.

139 Abū Yūsuf, 81; Ibn 'Asākir, VII, 210f.

previous generations). Their approach to farming is expressed in a ḥadīth attributed to the Prophet, brought in the name of Thawbān, one of Muḥammad's freedmen, who settled in Palestine: 'do not settle in the villages, for he who abides in villages it is as if he abides in graves'.[140] There is no doubt that at the outset, the leaders of Islam, starting with 'Umar ibn al-Khaṭṭāb, did not approve of imitating the urban and village customs of the subdued populations, whether in the economic or in the religious-cultural spheres. There was a tendency to avoid anything which would involve real settlement. In Kūfa, for instance, at the military and urban base set up by the Muslims in Iraq, tribesmen were not permitted to build themselves proper houses; only reed (*qaṣab*) huts were allowed. Only after an enormous fire broke out and destroyed everything were they allowed to build houses of bricks – on condition however that they did not build more than three rooms per person (that is, per family).[141] In Jerusalem, the Arabs were forbidden to enter churches, particularly those in the Kidron valley; it is said that 'Umar prayed at first in the Church of St Mary but regretted it afterwards.[142] Particularly strict was the rule that Muslims should not take on the praying customs of the infidels. It is told that 'Ubāda b. Ṣāmit, when he was in Jerusalem, saw a man praying in the mosque and putting his shoe on the right side (or perhaps the left side), and he castigated him for behaving like *ahl al-kitāb*, people of the book (?).[143]

[230–232] Nevertheless, we hear of considerable interest on the part of the Umayyad caliphs and their retainers on estates in Palestine. Of 'Amr b. al-'Āṣ, one of the commanders of the invasion of Palestine and Egypt, we read that he had an estate (*ḍay'a*) in jund Filasṭīn, in Sab', that is in the region of Beersheba, where he stayed when the war between 'Alī and Mu'āwiya began, in his palace in a place called al-'Ajlān.[144]

Mu'āwiya also had estates in Palestine. It is told that when 'Abd al-Malik became caliph, he bought the al-Khaḍrā (the green palace), from Mu'āwiya's grandson, Khālid b. Yazīd, a building which housed the

140 See the saying in Bukhārī, *Adab*, 85; Suyūṭī, *La'ālī*, I, 478; 'Ajlūnī, *Kashf*, I, 262; II, 355 (and see there: the people of the villages are people of catastrophe); 'Azīzī, III, 461.

141 Burāqī, 103.

142 See Musharraf, 90b; Wāsiṭī, 21; however this ban can be interpreted in two ways; forbidding the Arabs to mix with the local population and preventing damage to the protected peoples' holy places. A ḥadīth in the name of the Prophet forbids entry to the dhimmīs' homes or houses of prayer without their permission, or to offend their wives, as long as they pay the taxes as due – see 'Azīzī, II, 124.

143 'Ulaymī, 253f; see a ḥadīth which forbids *ikhtiṣār*, i.e., placing hands on the hips during prayer in the manner of the Jews (?), in 'Azīzī, II, 128; and censure of people who pray alone loudly and lift up their hands in the manner of the Jews, a custom called *taqlīf*, in Ṭurṭūshī, 59, in the name of Abū 'Alī 'Abd al-Raḥmān b. al-Qāsim al-'Utaqī (who died in Egypt in 191/807, see *GAL* S I, 299), cited according to Abū Salma b. 'Abd al-Raḥmān b. 'Awn (who died in 94/713 in Medina – see Ibn Sa'd, V, 115ff).

144 Ṭabarī, *Ta'rīkh*, I, 2967, 2972; Dīnawarī, 157. In the Middle Ages, the region of Beer-

administration, and for which he paid forty thousand dinars. Apart from this, he bought four other estates in the four junds of al-Shām; in jund Filasṭīn, he chose ʿImwās and in jund Urdunn he chose 'Qaṣr Khālid' (evidently a palace which had belonged to that Khālid). ʿAbd al-Malik also pursued a policy of confining units of tribal horsemen to the cities, particularly the coastal towns, and it seems that this involved the grant of rights to these tribes to a part of the income dervied from taxes.[145] This type of right was called *ma'kala*, and was evidently expressed in the authority to collect taxes due from the inhabitants (non-Muslims) of that place. These arrangements were evidently introduced shortly after the conquest by ʿUmar ibn al-Khaṭṭāb, when he regulated the relationship between the Muslims and the local populations. He initiated the lists of taxes and subsidies to be paid and determined how much each clan or tribe would receive.[146]

[233–235] One can surmise, when speaking of estates that were 'bought' by the Umayyad rulers, that the possession right on these estates was passed on with the change in leadership, and that just as the Abbasids had taken over what had formerly been held by the Umayyads, they also took possession of their estates. We find that in the tenth century AD, 'estates of the Ikhshīdids' in Palestine are mentioned, as well as their manager Ibn al-Ḥārith; also Abū ʿAlī al-Ḥusayn b. Aḥmad b. Rustum al-Mādharā'ī, who was responsible for the taxes (*kharāj*) in Egypt on behalf of al-Muqtadir (from 8 April 919) had a *ḍay'a* named Munyat Hishām, near Tiberias. One can assume that these, and others which are not mentioned, were some sort of permanent 'government property'.[147]

We have seen that the Muslim chroniclers have left us important information concerning the involvement of the Palestinian tribes in the internal

sheba was known by the name of *wādī'l-sab'* – see Tadmurī, 61a (quoting Musharraf), and in the edition of Matthews, *JPOS*, 17 (1937), 136.

145 Ibn ʿAsākir, II(1), 133; VI, 185. Muʿāwiya acquired two estates for himself, al-Baṭnān, in the Ascalon area, which he said was a place of moderate rains, and not arid like al-Dārūm nor wet like Caesarea, see Jahshiyārī, 26; cf. Kister, *Wiet Memorial Volume*, 43f, n. 51.

146 Ṭabarī, *Ta'rīkh*, II, 487: the Banū Kinda (the Sakūn clan) request for themselves as *ma'kala* southern Trans-Jordan (the Balqā'), see above. Abū'l-Fidā', *Mukhtaṣar*, I, 160: ʿUmar introduced the lists: *dawāwīn*. It appears that when the sources speak of 'acquiring' estates they are actually referring to buying the possession rights. It is possible that these rights were also linked with living in the place, and one can surmise that the purchaser would then proceed to build himself a house, or a palace, according to his rank and social status. On the other hand, it is told that Ṭalḥa ibn ʿUbaydallah bought land in Bet Shean in the days of the Prophet – see Ḥassān b. Thābit, II, 279; Ibn ʿAbd al-Barr, *Istīʿāb*, II, 764: therefore the Prophet called him *al-fayyāḍ*, the spendthrift, a word which does not indicate very strong objections.

147 Ibn Khallikān, III, 136; the estate of al-Mādharā'i: Thaʿālibī, *Laṭā'if*, 231f: there was a famous spring on this estate which habitually gushed forth for seven consecutive years, then stopping for seven consecutive years. This same story is found in Qazwīnī, *ʿAjā'ib*, 270.

strife within the caliphate. Less is known of the participation in external struggles. But there is no doubt that the tribes did take a part in the wars which were conducted in distant lands, such as in Central Asia. From the little that is known to us about this, I would reiterate the fact mentioned above, that of the participation of the tribes from jund Filasṭīn, under the command of Muṣ'ab b. 'Amr of the Banū Khuzā'a, in the war against the Turks in Central Asia in AH 119 (AD 737).[148] One can imagine that the tribes took an active part in the campaigns against the Byzantines as well. Concerning the active participation of the tribes of al-Shām in the North African wars we learn from Ibn 'Abd al-Ḥakam, speaking of the days of the last Umayyads (al-Walīd b. Yazīd, Yazīd b. al-Walīd, and Marwān b. Muḥammad). At that time, tribes of the two junds, Filasṭīn and Urdunn, also settled in Spain. Tribesmen of Urdunn settled in Riyya (Reiyo), which was then named after them, as Urdunn, while the tribes from jund Filasṭīn settled in Shadhūna (Sidonia) and this too was named after them, as Filasṭīn.[149]

[148] Ṭabarī, *Ta'rīkh*, II, 1609.
[149] Ibn 'Abd al-Ḥakam, 223f; Ibn al-Athīr, *Kāmil*, V, 491 (under the year AH 139/AD 743), cf. Lévi-Provençal, *Histoire*, I, 44f; Shaban, *Islamic History*, I, 152.

3

THE LOCAL POPULATION AND THE MUSLIMS

[236] Until now, we have followed the course of the conquest and the events of the first century of Muslim rule in Palestine. These have been described in chronological order, with the exception of a few issues, such as the question of the religious status of Jerusalem, or the administrative division of the country. These same questions, though they extend beyond the chronological framework ending with the year 750, warrant discussion in the context of the first hundred years, when the principal foundations were established, to remain valid until the end of the period we are dealing with. Therefore at this point, before discussing the political and military events that occurred in Palestine after 750, it is appropriate that we pause to discuss in general terms the question of the relationship between Muslims and non-Muslims, that is, between the rulers and the ruled, in Palestine.

We shall try to make our way through the sources, which are at times very sparse, dealing with the composition of the population and the status of the cities of Palestine. Although most of the facts in this sphere were also determined in the first hundred years, during the Damascene caliphate, we shall have to go beyond the confines of this period and study these matters as they appear over the course of our entire chronological framework. An important incentive in choosing this path lies in the fact that the information available to us gradually increases the further we approach the eleventh century AD. Due to the conservative character of the social and administrative pattern of those times, the facts and findings of the eleventh century can shed light on the entire period, beginning with the conquest. In choosing this path, I also bear in mind the example of distinguished Muslim historians of the early Middle Ages, who did not hesitate to interrupt the continuity of the chronological account in order to devote space and effort to the writing of a separate discourse on a subject they considered important.

The protected people

We have seen above how the attitude of Islam towards the subjugated population was first expressed, particularly towards the Jews and the Christians, according to precedents established by Muḥammad during the Tabūk expedition. We have seen a further expression of this in ʿUmar ibn al-Khaṭṭāb's treaty with the inhabitants of Jerusalem. With regard to the status of the Jews of Palestine, no significant change took place. Within the context of the Byzantine Christian empire, they were considered inferior to the Christian inhabitants. From now on, they would be inferior to the Muslims. The new element naturally was the changed status of the Christians, who were in this respect now equal to the Jews. The whole population of Palestine now became the protected people of the Muslims; in other words, the Arab tribes who made up the Muslim army were the rulers of the urban and rural populations of Palestine. This was the situation until the Abbasid revolution, when the role of the tribes was taken over by the battalions of the Caliphate, in which the Arab element would gradually give way to the Turks, the Persians and other Muslims who were not Arabs. The governing body and its administration would gradually pass into the hands of those elements as well, and religious personnel, men learned in law and judges would no longer be exclusively Arabs, as was generally the case during the period of the Umayyads.

In theory, the Muslims did not discriminate between Jews and Christians. If in the events described below we find that at times there existed collaboration and affiliation of Muslims with Jews against the Christians, or vice versa, this would not be the outcome of principle but the result of politico-historical circumstances which we shall discuss separately.

The Muslim traditions are mixed in their attitudes towards protected people. There are those which praise justice and tolerance towards protected people and others which are steeped in contempt – particularly towards the Jews. For example, there is the story of the governor who exiled the protected people of Mount Lebanon because they did not pay their taxes, and even killed some of them. The cadi al-Awzāʿī criticised these deeds harshly in writing and promised the perpetrator that he would suffer severe punishment on the Day of Judgment, in accordance with the words of the Prophet who warned against using a heavy hand against 'the people of the agreement'. On the other hand, there is a tradition in Dhahabī which relates that the angel Gabriel refused to shake Muḥammad's hand before he washed it, because he had touched the hand of a Jew. There are sayings attributed to Muḥammad, or to ʻAlī, to the effect that the Jews and the Christians do not deserve to be greeted.[1]

[237] However, the general approach in Muslim religious literature is that the rights of the protected people should be respected as determined by the precedents and sayings of the Prophet and the early caliphs, which religious law recognises as legal and sanctified by God. Compared with what was happening at the same time in the Christian world, we find here a climate of decency and legality. In the early period we are dealing with, the caliphs were well aware of the fact that protecting the rights of the dhimmīs was of importance to the Muslims, first and foremost from the economic point of view. As stated by ʻUmar ibn ʻAbd al-ʻAzīz to one of his governors:

> do not destroy a synagogue or church (*kanīsa, bīʻa*) nor a house of Zoroastrians whose existence has been ensured by the peace treaty; but also no synagogue [or church] or house of Zoroastrians shall be built anew. The sheep should not be dragged to the slaughterer and one must not sharpen the slaughtering knife on the head of the cattle that is being slaughtered.[2]

[238] At a comparatively later stage the traditional rules relating to the dhimmīs were collected into one document called 'the conditions of ʻUmar'. There is no doubt that the intention here is to the caliph ʻUmar ibn al-Khaaṭṭāb (and not ʻUmar ibn ʻAbd al-ʻAzīz, as claimed by some scholars whose opinions are today accepted by many). The basic principles of these traditional rules were decided upon according to precedents from the days of ʻUmar ibn al-Khaṭṭāb, and we find them in treaties of surrender which were preserved in Arab historical writings. I have already mentioned above the treaties that were signed in Tabūk and Jerusalem. It is worth noting some other documents that are characteristic of the early Muslim period and are stamped with the mark of authenticity: the surren-

1 See comprehensive discussions with references to sources on the state of the protected people in Islam: Goitein, *Jews and Arabs*, 62. Strauss (Ashtor), *Hirschler Memorial Volume*: 73; Goldziher, *REJ*, 28(1894): 75. Abel, *RIDA*, 2:1, 1949. See Balādhurī, *Futūḥ*, 162; Dhahabī, *Mīzān*, II, 232; Naysābūrī, *Rawḍa*, 458 (ʻAlī said that it was not worth while greeting a Jew). See the tradition which recommends that a portion of *ṣadaqa* and *khums* go to the poor of the dhimmīs: Ibn Abī Shayba, III, 178; ʻAzīzī, I, 127: 'if you wish to bless a Jew or a Christian, bless him: may God multiply your money, because his money is useful to us through the *jizya*, or after he dies without heirs'. *Ibid.*, I, 384, in the name of the Prophet: 'clean your courtyards, and be not like the Jews who are dirty and their courtyards are dirty'. And counter this, the story of the cadi, ʻAbdallah b. ʻAbd al-Raḥmān b. Hujayra al-Khawlānī, who was cadi in Egypt from 709 until August 717, with intervals: after ʻUmar ibn ʻAbd al-ʻAzīz dismissed him from his post, the Jews made a claim against him of money he had borrowed from them, and ʻUmar forced him to pay because he had no written confirmation of clearance of the debt. Fortunately for him, he succeeded in bringing witnesses that he had paid the debt. See Kindī, 332f; Ibn Ḥajar, *Rafʻ*, 284. One can cite further instances in both directions, the good and the bad.

2 Ṭabarī, *Ta'rīkh*, II, 1372.

der agreement of Najrān (of the Prophet's time), the surrender agreement of Damascus, and 'Umar's pact with the people of al-Shām and the surrender agreement of Lod.[3]

[239–240] The underlying concept of Islam regarding the Jews and the Christians is that they are 'people of the Book', *ahl al-kitāb*. The meaning is not simply that they are peoples with a book. The intention of this by-name was that each of the two religions is an *umma*, that is, a group of people to whom, in earlier generations, God 'handed down' through the medium of messengers (the prophets) the Book, a book which is in its essence one and the same, and identical with the Koran. To these people the Koran promised that the Muslims would no longer fight them, on condition that they submit and pay their taxes, as we have seen above.[4] Non-belligerence, or the right to survive, was bound up, according to this ideology, with foregoing all means of self-defence and the acceptance of protection from or under the aegis (*dhimma*) of the Muslims. This was the condition under which they would receive protection, *amān*. Security was given to men who paid the tax, to their dependants and property. In addition, they would have to be submissive, that is to consider themselves inferior to Muslims and to act accordingly. They would have to differ from the Muslims in their outward appearance and some other aspects which I shall explain in detail below. They would be permitted to fulfil the

3 See doubts as to the attribution of the conditions of the dhimmīs to 'Umar ibn al-Khaṭṭāb (and even to someone from the Muslim army command in his time): Tritton, *Caliphs*, 10, 12. See the articles Dhimma (by C. Cahen) and Amān (by J. Schacht) in *EI*² and the references in these two articles. Finkel, *JQR*, NS 23(1932/3), 271 is of the opinion that 'Umar ibn 'Abd al-'Azīz wished to act on the example of 'Umar I and hence he was the first of the Umayyad caliphs who renewed the decrees of the latter, particularly with regard to dress. The treaty of Najrān: Balādhurī, *Futūḥ*, 63–65. The treaty of surrender of Damascus (in the name of Abū 'Ubayda): Ibn 'Asākir, 504f. 'Umar's treaty with the people of al-Shām: *ibid.*, 563f. The treaty of Lod: Ṭabarī, *Ta'rīkh*, I, 2407. The document called 'The conditions of 'Umar', a compendium of laws relating to the legal status of the dhimmīs, is certainly comparatively late, and its earliest version is evidently that in Shāfi'ī (died in 820), *Umm*, IV, 118ff (see the English translation: Tritton, *Caliphs*, 12ff); see the version of Qalqashandī, *Ṣubḥ*, XIII, 378; see also Shayzarī, *Nihāya*, 106f and the supplement *ibid.*, 120; a Hebrew version of 38 'conditions of 'Umar', as translated by Jacob Skandarī, the Rabbi of Alexandria, from an unidentified Arabic source, is included in Joseph Sambarī's chronicle (the second half of the seventeenth century), see in Fischel, *Zion*, 5(1940) 209ff. As to 'Umar ibn 'Abd al-'Azīz, it seems that the major innovation he introduced was equality between the Arab and the non-Arab Muslims; nevertheless the non-Arabs still had to pay land taxes on their estates, because their land was *fay'* (a *gift* from God to the Muslims) and the owner of property, that is the Muslim state, was entitled to compensation; see: Gibb, *Arabica*, 2(1955), 3. '*Fay'* means what they [the Muslims] obtain by peace treaties, namely the *jizya* and *kharāj*', see Yaḥyā b. Ādam, 23.

4 The expression *'an yadin*, in that verse was explained by Kister, *Arabica*, 11:272, 1964, as being: according to their ability, or their profits. This explanation is preferable to others, because it suits the accepted policy afterwards (though it was not always enacted), which introduced three categories for the payment of the poll-tax: three to four dinars per annum for the rich, two for middle-range incomes, and one dinar for the poor (or their equivalent

obligations of their religion, under certain restricted conditions; they would have no military or political duties, nor serve in public or governmental posts. Subsequently, inheritance regulations would also develop.[5]

The taxes

[241] Taxation policy had not yet been formulated in the days of the Prophet, not even during the great conquests. At the time, the Muslims would impose a global sum in one place, and in another collect a certain portion of the income in agricultural produce or textiles. Each place had its arrangements, as we have seen in the Prophet's covenants and have learned from the treaty with Jerusalem. The terms *jizya* and *kharāj* still indicated a tax in general, and only in the following generations would the former mean a head-tax and the latter a land-tax.[6]

in dirhams). See for instance Ibn ʿAbd al-Ḥakam, 152ff, who mentions these sums in the name of Aslam, ʿUmar's freedman; cf. Stern, *Byzantion*, 20(1950), 239.

5 We have already come across the demand to hand over arms and horses in the discussion of the Prophet's treaties. Certainly the two are tied together in an inseverable knot: the acceptance of the Muslims' protection and the right to survive in exchange for the payment of a tax on the one hand, and the relinquishing of any means of self defence on the other. See also the treaty of Najrān in Balādhurī, *Futūḥ*, 64; there it says that the people of Najrān will submit their arms, horses and all riding beasts; and see the treaty of Damascus (al-Shām), in Ibn ʿAsākir, I, 505: 'we shall not ride on saddles and we shall not keep any arms or make any in our houses, and shall not wear swords'. See also another version ('for the Christians in the land of al-Shām'), 'we shall not keep arms nor swords and will not bear them at home nor on journeys in the land of the Muslims'.

6 It appears that the earliest stage in the development of tax laws in Islam after Muḥammad's death is reflected in the events of the tribes' first raid beyond the Euphrates, when a surrender treaty (*ṣulḥ*) was signed between Khālid ibn al-Walīd and the Jewish population of Babylonia. According to Ibn Saʿd, VII(2), 121, this *ṣulḥ* was signed with 'Ṣalūbā ibn Buṣbahrā, who lived on the banks of the Euphrates, in exchange for the payment of one thousand dirhams'. The time: Ṣafar, of the year AD 12, or May AD 633. According to Ṭabarī, the tax was ten thousand dinars, and this in addition to *kharza* of the Persian king (Kisrā); this sum would have to be collected chiefly by the imposition of a poll-tax of four dirhams; see Ṭabarī, *Ta'rīkh*, I, 2018f, 2049f, 2165f, 2182f; Balādhurī, *Futūḥ*, 242f, 253, 457; Jāḥiẓ, *ʿUthmānīya*, 212; Yaʿqūbī, *Ta'rīkh*, II, 176; Yaḥyā b. Ādam, 34f; Dhahabī, *Ta'rīkh*, II, 5; Ibn Kathīr, *Bidāya*, VI, 343; Ibn al-Athīr, *Kāmil*, II, 384, 392; Yāqūt, *Buldān*, I, 484, Burāqī, 140. Cf. Caetani, *Annali*, II(2), 971, n. 4, who compares the *kharza* and the *kharāj kisrā* in the chronicle of the ninth century of Ibn Khurdādhbih, and see also Caetani, *ibid.*, 173. See the detailed discussion on the identity of Ṣalūbā (= Ṣālōvā, a Syriac-Aramaic word meaning crucifier) in Gil, *Tarbiz*, 48(1978/9), 52f. One can assume that the Arabic *kharāj* is none other than the Persian-Aramaic *kargā*, and not *khorēgia* as is explained in *EI*², IV, 1030, and as was also believed by Henning, *Orientalia*, NS 4:291, 1935. It is interesting that in the neighbourhood of the eleventh century, an Iraqi source is still using the term *ṭasq* (*ṭasqā* in the Talmud) as meaning a land tax, and not the term *kharāj*; see: *al-kitāb al-ḥāwī lil-aʿmāl al-sulṭāniyya* (MS Paris, Ar. 2462), in Cahen, *AIEO*, 10(1952), 333. As to *jizya*, which meant in later generations specifically poll-tax, I believe that this too is Aramaic in its origins, from the root *gzy*, which is found also in the Talmudic sources and its meaning is income, payment, and not from the Arabic root *jzw* (to recompense) as is commonly believed. The payments made by the Byzantines to the Muslims according to peace settlements (or armistice) between them were also called *jizya*. This was money paid by the

[242–243] In those areas that were under Byzantine rule (Palestine, Syria, Egypt) we find a clause relating to taxes in all the letters of protection and surrender agreements which have been preserved in the sources; but we generally do not find any specific details as to how the payments would be made, and one can discern the tendency to collect a global sum from each town. In this connection it is worth noting the tradition preserved in Ibn ʿAbd al-Ḥakam: if a man died in a village on which a global tax has been imposed, rather than a tax on each individual (*jizya musammāh ʿalāʾl-qarya*), the dead man's land would be given to the village. If, however, the *jizya* was a certain sum imposed on each head, the land would be given to the Muslims. In the continuation, it says that ʿUmar ibn ʿAbd al-ʿAzīz introduced a law that the *jizya* would be imposed on every head and not on the land. Here the chronicler comments that the intention was to the *ahl al-dhimma* (that is to the protected people, Jews and Christians); and he continues by saying that essentially the method of collecting taxes from the Egyptian population (al-Qibṭ, the Copts) remained as it was under Byzantine dominion – they would collect taxes according to the size of the population in every village. The elders (*ʿurafāʾ*, *mārūt* [read: *māzūt*, from the Greek *meizōnes*], *ruʾasāʾ*) would be called together to estimate the area of land cultivated by the inhabitants of the village. Afterwards a general assembly of the district (*kūra* = *khōra*) would be held; at this stage they would deduct the donations to the churches and other public institutions and the expenses for housing units of the Muslim army. Then they would decide on the extent of the tax to be imposed on the craftsmen and the hired people who lived in those villages, according to their ability to pay (*iḥtimāl*) and the tax to be imposed on the *jāliya* (literally: the exiles; the expression is undoubtedly parallel to *xenoi*, aliens), the mature and the married living in these villages, according to their ability to pay. The remainder of the *kharāj* would be imposed on the villagers themselves, corresponding to their sowing plans and their ability to pay (*ʿalā qadri ṭāqatihim*).[7] This tradition clearly implies that in the main they would impose a general tax on the town, and the organisation of the distribution of this sum would have to be carried out by the dhimmīs themselves.

emperor when he felt too weak to fight; cf. what happened in the days of the Fatimid caliph al-Muʿizz: Stern, *Byzantion*, 20 (1950), 239.

[7] Ibn ʿAbd al-Ḥakam, 152f. The term *jāliya*, intended to be applied to people living in a village who are not locally born, has in the course of generations become a synonym of *jizya*, in its later meaning, that of poll-tax; see what is said in the version of the conditions in Sambarī, Fischel, *Zion*, 5(1940), 212: 'and whoever dies of them in the same year a portion of his inheritance shall be taken as the part which has passed of this year' (that is, they would pay for the months during which he was still alive); strangers who came to a town 'may stay there four months without having to pay any tax'. This version evidently also reflects

The Byzantine tradition in the matter of taxation, as preserved in the first generations of Muslim rule in Palestine, can be seen in the papyri of Nessana. The poll-tax is called there *epikephalion*, and the land tax is called the *dēmosia*, which is the *dīmūsya* in Talmudic literature. On the other hand, in one place there is mention of a payment of six *solidi*, the equivalent of the Muslim dinar which appeared later (some 4.2 grams of gold). I am inclined to believe that it was a payment on account of the general sum imposed on the town.

As to the roots of this system of lump payments, one can indeed be impressed by its continuity from Byzantine times onward, as described by Ibn ʿAbd al-Ḥakam and as is perhaps discernible in the papyri of Nessana. But we have seen this system also in the treaties of the Prophet himself, and one can add what was said of the agreement with the Christians in the city of Najrān in the southern part of the Arabian peninsula: 'The master of the town and the judge (?) in it (*al-sayyid wa'l-ʿāqib*) came to Muḥammad, both on behalf of the people of Najrān, and made peace for 2,000 *ḥulla*s, 1,000 in Ṣafar and 1,000 in Rajab, each *ḥulla* weighing one ounce.[8]

[244–245] Direct evidence of the collection of land taxes in Palestine is supplied by a document from Nessana, which is a receipt for the land tax, dating from about the end of the seventh century. Apparently the Muslims carried out a new measurement of the land in order to calculate the taxes, and in that document it was said that the tax was imposed according to the measurement of the land carried out by the Arabs. There are also eight orders regarding supplies for the Muslim army from the people of Nessana in the years 672–677.

Palestine was, during the entire period we are dealing with, a sort of gold mine for the central government, whether headquartered in Damascus, Baghdad or Cairo. On the basis of data preserved by Muslim chroniclers and geographers it is possible to reconstruct the sums collected in the treasury at various times from the two junds, Filasṭīn and Urdunn. Naturally, the security situation had a noticeable influence on the amounts, but one can easily deduce that in all the periods it was a matter of hundreds of thousands of dinars. If we take into account that the average monthly wage then was some two dinars, we can say that it was a matter of hundreds of thousands of monthly wages, as Table 1 indicates.

Contrary to what we are inclined to believe today, the question of taxes did not have only a secular and financial character. Indeed, we know that the money from the poll-tax was considered as a kind of sacred money. In

an ancient Egyptian tradition, as bequeathed by the Byzantines.

8 See *Nessana*, 33, and document No. 55, *ibid.*, 172f. The editor, Kraemer, assumes that the payment of six solidi was a tax imposed on the individual. The treaty of Najrān: Balādhurī, *Futūḥ*, 63. It is noted there that they are speaking of an ounce of forty dirhams, and thus the 2,000 *ḥullas* were some 250 kilograms of gold. Cf. Hinz, 35.

Income from non-Muslim taxes, in dinars

Time (rounded)	Filasṭīn	Urdunn	Total	Source
670	450,000	180,000	630,000	Ya'qūbī
780	310,000	97,000	407,000	Ibn Khallikān
800	310,000	96,000	406,000	Jahshiyārī
820	195,000	109,000	304,000	Qudāma
840 (?)	175,000	175,000	350,000	Iṣfahānī (in Ibn Khurdādhbih)
860	500,000	350,000	850,000	Ibn Khurdādhbih
890	300,000	100,000	400,000	Ya'qūbī
895	259,000	170,000	429,000	Muqaddasī[9]

general, a cadi was in charge of collecting this tax and he was obliged to keep it separate from the rest of the treasury's income. As Maqrīzī once said, this was 'the good and pure money', and it would be indecent to mix the money from the *jāliya* (=*jizya*, poll-tax) with the income from port taxes. Among the documents in the Cairo Geniza, a payment order has been preserved written by Abraham Maimuni to the effect that a sum of 81 dirhams had to be paid urgently to the cadi Shams al-Din, for this was the remainder of what is owed for the *jāliya* for the year 614 of the hijra (AD 1217/8).[10]

[246–247] The collection of the *jizya* was generally called *istikhrāj*, which means collection or income. In an inscription discovered in Jerusalem, near the Church of the Holy Sepulchre, evidently dating from the thirties of the eleventh century (i.e. from the Fatimid period), it is written that no dhimmī may come into the mosque, even if he comes in matters of the *istikhrāj*. It is reasonable to assume that the dhimmī would usually come to the mosque to pay the cadi the poll-tax, and this is what the founder of the Jerusalem mosque wished to prevent (and we have no details concerning him or the mosque).[11]

9 See the document from Nessana in Bell, *Proceedings of the American Philosophical Society*, 89:531, 1945; another document tells of a delegation of twenty people appearing before the governor of Gaza in order to request a decrease in taxes. Cf. Lewis, *PEQ*, 80(1948), 114. Table 1 follows that of Le Strange, *Palestine*, 45ff; see the detailed references therein. The figures relating to 670 (Mu'āwiya's time) are according to: Ya'qūbī, *Ta'rīkh*, II, 288. To the taxes of 780, one must add: 300,000 *raṭls* (= pounds) of olive oil per annum, from jund Filasṭīn.

10 See Maqrīzī, *Khiṭaṭ*, I, 187; Gil, *Documents*, 107f and see *ibid.*, 416, the payment order of Abraham Maimuni (no. 114, TS Box K 25, No. 240 [11]). To the Shiites, the poll-tax, the *jizya*, was considered a direct debt of the unbelievers to the *imām* (that is, the legitimate ruler) of the Muslims, like the payment owed by the slave to his master, for the dhimmīs are slaves (*mamālīk*) of the *imām*. See Ibn Bābawayah, *'Ilal*, 541.

11 See the term *istikhrāj* clearly meaning the collecting of the poll-tax in Yaḥyā Ibn Sa'īd, 239; Maqrīzī, *Itti'āẓ*, I, 146: Ya'qūb Ibn Killis and 'Aslūj forbade the use of dinars which were

The question of taxes in Jerusalem is a very special one. We have seen above the clause in 'Umar's treaty with the people of Jerusalem, who were Christians, according to which they had to pay the *jizya* just as did the inhabitants of other cities; but there are no details in that treaty about the conditions of other cities' payment of the *jizya* (there are some details relating to Tiberias, as we shall see). Here the Cairo Geniza comes to our assistance; although it dates relatively late – the eleventh century, it evidently reflects customs that had continued from the time of the conquest, for some four hundred years. The circular letter coming from the yeshiva of Jerusalem, evidently in 1057, appeals to the Egyptian communities for help, pointing to 'the tax and the regular payments imposed on us, whether we are many or few; every year we have to borrow with interest in order to fulfil it'. From this we can assume that the Jews of Jerusalem had to pay a regular lump sum annually; and it is very likely that this continued from the days of the caliph 'Umar. It seems that in the course of generations a form of internal distribution of this sum among the Jews of Jerusalem evolved. The Gaon Solomon b. Judah, writing from Jerusalem in *ca.* 1034 on the subject of Faraḥ b. Dūnash, a man of Sijilmāssa, notes that this man settled in Jerusalem, married a woman of Jerusalem, begat sons, became a Jerusalemite and paid 'the tax as the great do, which is a dinar (*zāhūv*) and a quarter'. We learn that the 'great', undoubtedly the well-to-do, paid a dinar and a quarter in Jerusalem (and this was not much compared with the four dinars that was asked of the rich in other places).[12]

[248] Although the information in the Cairo Geniza documents is not explicit, one can nevertheless learn from them what was the regular annual sum that had to be paid. The Gaon Solomon ha-Kohen b. Joseph mentions in his letter that he wrote from Jerusalem in the spring of 1025 to Ephraim

not the coinage of al-Mu'izz for the purpose of the *istikhrāj*; and see further examples on the same page and on the following page. The Jerusalem inscription, see: Björkman, *Der Islam*, 15(1926), 97; *Répertoire chronologique*, No. 2149 (vol. VII, 80f); Clermont-Ganneau, *Recueil*, II, 308; Hirschberg, *BJPES*, 13(1946/7), 163, and a drawing of the inscription *ibid.*, 162. Hirschberg assumed that *istikhrāj* meant the clearing of refuse and related this to the information on the Jews engaged in cleaning work on the Temple Mount in the period after the conquest. The question of whether it is permissible altogether for dhimmīs to enter the mosque is discussed in Muslim legal literature and sometimes the answer is positive, such as the opinion of Mujāhid in Ibn Abī Shayba, II, 526; cf. Tritton, *JRAS*, 1942, 37: (generally) it was forbidden to dhimmīs to enter mosques, but they entered nevertheless, for a person could not be asked what his creed was on entering a mosque (according to Ghazālī); see also Lazarus-Yafeh, *Tarbiz*, 51(1981/2), 219.

12 The clause in 'Umar's treaty with Jerusalem promising people from the towns and villages (who evidently found a haven in Jerusalem) is also worth noting, that if they would return to their homes, they would only be asked to pay taxes after the harvest. The circular letter: **420**, d, lines 15–17. The letter of Solomon b. Judah: **118**, a, lines 9ff. Solomon b. Judah asks Abraham that he save the aforementioned 'from the hands of the Egyptian oppressors' for he is going there (Goitein, *Mediterranean Society*, I, 49, writes that it was a matter of marriage to a woman of Tiberias, but this is not what is written in the letter; see l. 10).

b. Shemaria, leader of the Jerusalemites in Fustat, that the Jews of Jerusalem had to pay 100 dinars. In about 1030, his successor to the seat of Gaon, Solomon b. Judah, in a letter to the same, confirms the receipt of twenty-nine and one eighth dinars, sent by *diyōqnē* (in Arabic: *suftaja*) with an Egyptian Jew who came on a pilgrimage to Jerusalem. He continues: 'and we obliged ourselves to take from this *diyōqnē* 20 dinars (*zehūvīm*) for the debt we have to pay each year', that is they had to use most of that amount to pay the regular global annual tax.

Further details regarding this annual sum are gathered from a letter written in about 1060 by 'Eli ha-Kohen b. Ezekiel, who was the *parnās* of the community, that is the man in charge of money matters, in Jerusalem. In this letter, he mentioned that the community was asked to pay 150 dinars every year as a regular tax (*rātib*), of which 70 were the *kharāj*, 40 for the armed guards (*aḥdāth*), and a further 40 for municipal expenses there. We may assume that out of the 100 dinars mentioned, 70 were considered *kharāj*, the tax of the Muslim authorities, and the last 30 were evidently intended for the local security people and the city's needs. These are specified in detail in a letter of the yeshiva of Jerusalem from the year 1057 which I have already mentioned above: '. . . the needs of the city: to clear its refuse, clean its drains, repair its walls and pay its watchmen, please its governors, etc.', in contemporary terms: to collect the refuse, maintain the sewage system, maintain the walls and pay the watchmen who guard the walls, and bribe those in official positions.[13]

[249–252] We have learned that the regular annual amount which the Jews in Jerusalem had to pay on the basis of a custom that began immediately after the conquest, was 70 dinars. With this payment, the right to enter Jerusalem as a pilgrim was 'acquired'. Entrance to the city was evidently linked to the payment of a tax, if the person who came to the city was a *dhimmī*. We know of a similar tax in Alexandria from a letter from the Geniza written in 1026 by Joseph ha-Kohen, the judge (*dayyān*) of Alexandria, to Ephraim b. Shemaria. This was a tax of two and a half dinars per head: 'We gave the master of the gate two and a half gold coins'.[14] We also know that Christian pilgrims were asked to pay one dinar (*aureus*) on their arrival in Jerusalem for the right to enter the city.[15] In the

13 Solomon ha-Kohen b. Joseph: **49**, line 16f; Solomon b. Judah: **112**, lines 12–13; TS 20.115, a very faded fragment that remained from another letter of Solomon b. Judah, signed also by Joseph ha-Kohen b. Solomon Gaon and Tobiah 'the third', in which the 'fixed tax' to be paid to the governor and to the 'boys' is mentioned: 'and to the boys a fixed payment' (l.15); 'and to satisfy the governor and the boys' (l.8). The letter of 'Eli ha-Kohen: **443**, a, lines 8–10. Expenses of the city of Jerusalem: **420**, c, lines 34–35.

14 TS 24.29, ll. 29f, edited by Mann, *Texts*, I, 367ff; cf. Goitein, *Mediterranean Society*, I, 62f; *sha'ar shel-ha-yam* as against the Arabic *thaghr*, which means both gate and port.

15 William of Tyre, 30; *De prima inst.*, *RHC*, Occ., V, 402.

above letter, Solomon b. Judah explicitly mentions that the regular lump sum which the Jews of Jerusalem paid was also intended to ensure that the Muslims would not harass the pilgrims; that the Jews of Jerusalem would have permission to encircle the gates of the Temple Mount together with the pilgrims, to pray alongside them, and to pray – even out loud! – on the Mount of Olives.[16]

The subject of taxes is frequently mentioned in letters of the yeshiva, generally urging the addressee to try to aid or organise aid for the people of Jerusalem; the impression is clear that they were unable to bear the heavy financial burden. Some letters of Solomon b. Judah mention the receipt of the *dīyoqnē* sent from Fustat in order to help pay the tax. Appeals of this nature were more frequently repeated during times when additional special taxes were imposed on the Jewish population. Frequently the tax is called *'onesh* (punishment), or in Arabic, *gharāma*, which means both a debt and a fine. Thus for instance, in a letter of Solomon ha-Kohen b. Joseph, written in the spring of 1025: 'the living had to be guarantors for the dead and those who remained were guarantors for those who fled, until they paid the *'onesh* and then they were obliged to pay a further tax. If you would have seen who paid all these sums, you would have been amazed and deplored them, and said: how did such poor people pay such a big *'onesh*?' And in another of his letters: 'since *'onāshīm* were imposed on us, which exhaust the body . . . which we would not have thought that we would be able to bear even partly; (the more so) as such an *'onesh* as that which was imposed on the city'.

The preoccupation of the people of the Jerusalem yeshiva with taxes can be seen in a fragment of a letter in the handwriting of Abraham b. Solomon b. Judah in which the main subject is the tax burden, and in which there is mention of a 'Christian (*'ārēl*) secretary'. This perhaps hints at collaboration between the Bedouin rebels headed by the Banū Jarrāḥ and the Christian tax officials, as the description of the rebellion may suggest (see pp. 384f below). In this passage 'people who do not pay tax' are mentioned and there was something about the *kenēsīyōt* (synagogues), apparently in connection with the destruction of the synagogues in the days of al-Ḥākim; the addressee (perhaps Ephraim b. Shemaria, the *ḥāvēr*), is warned about revealing things to 'the Christian secretary'.[17]

[253] Letters written by Joshiah b. Aaron, Head of the Jerusalem yesh-

[16] **105**, lines 13ff. A similar version: **109**, lines 9–10, his letter to Ephraim b. Shemaria, torn on the right side: 'for there remained there but few of the many [and they had to pay the dues] fixed, to the rulers of the city and its boys so that they should not harm the people of Israel . . . in their going up to (Jerusalem) and coming and going about on the gates of [the temple], saying *qādōsh*, and *bārūkh*, and going up to the Mount [of Olives]'.

[17] See for example **147**, lines 5–22, written in *ca.* 1045; **165**, the remnant of a letter written by Abraham, the son of Solomon b. Judah, and one can still read there 'they are eating us alive

iva, in the first quarter of the eleventh century, speak of *'anīshā*, that is the heavy taxes imposed by the authorities of the day, mentioning a special tax of 2,500 dinars. One of the letters also describes the bargaining with the authorities. The representative of the Gaon, Abū Naṣr b. 'Abdūn, warns the governor of Jerusalem that if they will demand such sums, 'half the population will flee and the city will be destroyed in front of your eyes; and you yourself will have no security against a change of governors'. In this same letter, 'an enormous *gharāma*', an especially large tax is mentioned. Also in another letter, written by a number of people from Jerusalem, evidently in 1024, there is a hint of extraordinary taxes; and one of the *parnāsīm* of Jerusalem went on an urgent mission to Fustat in order to get special help to pay the tax.[18]

[254] At approximately the same time, we are informed about an *'onesh* imposed on the entire city of Jerusalem, to the extent of 15,000 dinars, certainly an enormous sum. This apparently occurred during the war against the Bedouin tribes, and it appears that it was the Fatimid army, then fighting on Palestinian soil, which imposed the tax. To that amount, another sum of 6,000 dinars was added, to be paid by the Jews; half by the

. . . on which the dues are inscribed . . . and the *'ōnesh* to be paid . . . (to the governor) of the city and all his servants . . . since to satisfy them one needs pieces of silver'; pieces of silver, *raṣṣē kesef*, is a play of words on Ps., lxviii:30 (31); and one should read instead of *raṣṣē*: *riḍā* in Arabic, satisfaction by silver, i.e. bribes. See a similar text in **420**, d, lines 1–3, on the Muslim authorities: 'The Children of Kedar [i.e., the Bedouin] oppress us very much, they are a company of spear-men who submit themselves with pieces of silver [Ps., *ibid.*, the Hebrew version may be interpreted differently from the King James version], their throat is an open sepulchre' (Ps., v:9[10]). Similar things were written by the Karaite Salmon b. Yeruḥim (in the middle of the tenth century): 'Submit himself with pieces of silver, means to say that Israel who are among these gentiles are tread underfoot, bring the poll-tax and special tax at any time. Some say: with pieces of silver, broken (*reṣūṣīm*, same root as *raṣṣē*) by silver, by depriving them of their money' (*kesef*, both silver and money). See his commentary to Ps. (Marwick), xcvi. See also: **45**, a letter from Sicily written in around 1020, in which *'onāshīm*, meaning taxes, is used: 'the 'onāshīm . . . since several years . . . they have to pay a fixed tax on every head, being 4½ *ṭarīs*, being a total of more than 17 *ṭarīs*, a big debt . . .'; the *ṭarī* was ¼ of a dinar, which was legal tender in Sicily, see: TS 16.133, lines 13, 20, 23, 27, ed. Assaf, *Meqorot*, 140ff; TS 13 J 16, f. 11, line 12, ed. Goitein, *Finkel Jubilee Volume*, 122; *idem*, *Mediterranean Society* I, Index. The letters of the Gaon Solomon ha-Kohen b. Joseph: **49**, lines 18–19; **50**, lines 10–12; **89**, lines 10, 11, a letter from Solomon b. Judah to Ephraim b. Shemaria: 'what they collected was not enough to pay the *'ōnesh* we owe annually, so we were forced to borrow the rest'. **383**, line 10, written around 1060 by the scribe of the yeshiva: 'and the regular dues and the *'onāshīm*'. The fragment of Solomon b. Judah's letter: **165a**.

18 See **36**, line 13: 'For two years, prior to the heavy tax imposed on our brethren, we were no longer able to request aid from the kingdom'; in other words, the subvention given by the Fatimid rulers to the yeshiva was interrupted for two years (he mentions the subvention in this letter); now even more heavy taxes are imposed, **37**, b, line 18 (*gharāma kabīra*) and see the story of the bargaining in lines 11ff. The letter of the Jerusalemites: **33**, lines 8ff 'the officials of the tax [demanded] the remaining 120 dinars . . . and this year we still owe 30 dinars . . . and we were forced to borrow these dinars with interest . . . and as our emissary came back empty-handed . . . the lenders came and demanded we sell the sacred objects'.

Rabbanites and half by the Karaites. The Jews succeeded in collecting 5,000 dinars and the two communities had to borrow money at exorbitant rates of interest from rich Muslims, on promissory notes for double the sums they had actually borrowed. Afterwards we learn of some Jews who were imprisoned because they were unable to defray the heavy debts. Some were forced to sell or mortgage their houses or whatever other property they possessed. Many died from the terrible torment of being required to pay the tax and in some cases, of subjection to physical torture.

Fifteen thousand gold coins and add to that some six thousand fell on the Jews . . . three thousand on us, and against that, the same on our brethren (that is, the Karaites); and we gave two thousand and five hundred gold coins until we went out of everything we had empty, naked, sad, poor, and nothing remained to a man in his house, even a dress for himself or houseware; some of us mortgaged their houses with interest in order to pay and some sold them completely. Many died of this suffering; for there were those who put blame on them, and struck them without pity, but nothing was found on them; some hid in pits because of the strength of the blows and the force of the afflictions and with all that (we did not arrive at) more than two thousand and five hundred, with the tax twice doubled, and we were forced to take the rest, five hundred for nearly a thousand (that is, obliged to return almost one thousand for five hundred dinars) from the rulers of the city, and likewise the inhabitants of the *ṣela'* (that is, the Karaites), also took . . .[19]

[255] A very typical document, which is so important for an understanding of the question of the tax, is a draft of a petition from the Jews of

[19] See **49**, lines 20–30. See also Solomon b. Judah's letters, for instance **88**, lines 12–16: 'our burden is heavy and everyone eats us with all his mouth and the dues added upon us . . . and we were forced to take on interest the dues imposed on us'. In **84**, a, lines 3–14, Solomon b. Judah mentions the prisoners held in jail because of the same debt and insists on the urgent need to get the money from the rich of Egypt, the Tustari brothers, 'for the debt is more than nine hundred dinars, how can we possibly defray it? Out of the barnfloor or out of the winepress?' (2 Ki., vi:27). The Karaites, though they receive considerable support from Zoan (= Fustat), they, too, still owe 800 dinars and hope that their *nesī'īm* (that is, people from the exilarchic families among the leaders of the Karaites, see below) would get them the money. The Rabbanites in Jerusalem expect that Solomon b. Judah will act in this matter as the *nesī'īm* of the Karaites do, and claim that he must show more initiative in this matter because he was not included as one of those responsible for the debt, as happened to one of the Karaites' *nesī'īm* (from which one can deduce that the same Karaite leader was also imprisoned because of the debt). See also **89**, lines 9–15; and also **405**, a letter written by Joseph ha-Kohen b. Solomon Gaon, almost at the same time, in which he states 'for of forty dinars we borrowed nine at the time of the tax, in addition to the special debt [*neshe*] which is known to you, our mighty one'; by 'our mighty one' he evidently meant Ephraim b. Shemaria, and the intention of the writer was apparently that out of forty dinars sent (to help the poor of Jerusalem?) they were forced to take nine for paying the tax, apart from the debt incurred by the special tax (this is evidently how one should understand the word *neshe*, from the root *nshh*). See also **210**, lines 40f: Zadok ha-Levi b. Levi explains (in about 1029) why he went down from Jerusalem to Ramla, because Jerusalem is 'torturous and breaks every body . . . and the burden is too heavy to bear . . . the *neshes* and the *midda* (the tax of the Babylonian king, Neh. 5:4) of captivity, and the compulsion of the ledgers, which is worse than anything'.

Tiberias concerning their taxes. From this we can deduce that in Tiberias as well, it was customary, apparently from very early times – perhaps since the Muslim conquest, to impose a lump sum as tax on the Jews of the city. One should bear in mind that Tiberias was the capital of jund Urdunn. It seems that the division of the sum between the Jews of the city was determined by their ability to pay. A new governor who was appointed to the city demanded from the leaders of the community that they should put pressure on the rich to increase their share, in order that the global sum should also be larger. The representative of the Tiberian Jews was Sibāʿ b. Faraj. If he is the same as Hillel *he-ḥāvēr* b. Joshua, it doubles the importance of a letter written by this Hillel, evidently to Ephraim b. Shemaria in Fustat, in which he also refers to the heavy pressure placed on the Jews of Tiberias with regard to taxes: 'they have imposed on them an *'onesh*, and now this elder, the *gizbār* (treasurer) is in the hands of wicked cruel people, who wish to end his life'. The reference here is to Abraham the treasurer, a man known for his charity and certainly a rich man. His son, Joseph, came especially from Aleppo where he was staying, to Tiberias, to look after the affairs of his father, and went to Fustat for the same reason.

The matter of the people of Khaybar mentioned in that draft of the petition is also of considerable interest. Some Jews claimed that they were of Khaybar stock and thus exempt from paying taxes. According to what is said in the Muslim traditions, the Jews of Khaybar were ousted from their place in the days of 'Umar, after the Muslims had overrun their villages during the time of the Prophet and made them into tenants. The offspring of the Jews of Khaybar (or whoever claimed to be their offspring) used to claim that they were exempt from paying tax by virtue of a special letter of rights granted them by the Prophet, and they would also display this document. Certain collectors of Muslim traditions have provided evidence of the fraudulent nature of the claim and have accused them of forgery. Several versions of the letter of rights (which is indeed forged) have been preserved in Hebrew writing. It is worth noting that according to Yaḥyā ibn Saʿīd, even the Fatimid caliph al-Ḥākim, known for his destruction of churches and synagogues and for issuing other restrictive laws against the dhimmīs, exempted the people of Khaybar from the restrictions placed on the Christians and the Jews. Here we see that in Tiberias there were also Jews who claimed to have originated in Khaybar and as a result were exempt from paying tax.[20]

[256] As I have said above, 'Umar's treaty with the Christians in

20 See **249** and **251**: it seems that they were both in the hands of Ephraim b. Shemaria, the ḥāvēr from Fustat; this is proven by the fact that on the back of the sheet on which **249** is written, there is a draft of a deed of attorney, written by Ephraim. This apparently takes

Jerusalem did not include any details of the *jizya* which they had to pay, except for the general statement that it would be the same as in the other cities. We already have more exact information about Tiberias and we have seen that at the time of the conquest (January 635) its inhabitants (and one can assume that the majority were Jews) were obliged to pay one dinar per person annually. It is stated there that similar conditions were imposed on the inhabitants of Damascus as well. That the original sum was one dinar per person in Jerusalem is suggested by the tax on Christian pilgrims entering Jerusalem, which, as noted above, was also one dinar. How did this payment of one dinar per head become a global tax? It is likely that both sides, Jews and Muslims, were interested in it being so, in order to avoid modifications; and on the part of the Muslims, to ease the collecting process. If indeed the tax in Jerusalem was one dinar per adult head of a family, then the sum of 70 dinars that the Jews of Jerusalem were asked to pay annually is also understandable, considering the fact that seventy was the number of families at first permitted to settle in Jerusalem after the conquest. Here it is worth noting the information found in the list of Christian holy places *De casis Dei*, according to which the Jerusalem Patriarch pays the Arabs (*ad Sarracenos*) 580 dinars annually. This was apparently the global sum imposed on the Christians in Jerusalem, and was possibly statutory since the time of the conquest. One can deduce from this that at the time of the conquest there were 580 Christian families living in Jerusalem.[21]

[257] This special tax regime that existed in Jerusalem, as well as in other

place in 1048, after the killing of Abraham the Tustari (see **251**: 'due to our many sins, the helping hand of the old man was done away with') when the imposing of oppressive decrees against the Jews became frequent; see Gil, *ha-Tustarīm*, 41ff. As to the Khaybarīs, their banishment is recalled in many sources, see for instance: Ibn Sa'd, II(1), 203; Samhūdī, I, 229; II, 388f. On al-Ḥākim: Yaḥyā ibn Sa'īd, *Ta'rīkh* (*PO*), 508; the matter is also mentioned in Ibn Khallikān, V, 293. De Slane in the English translation of the aforementioned evidently read *ḥayābira* instead of *khayābira* and translated: their doctors (that is: of the Jews; meaning that the Jewish scholars were exempt from the decrees, an unheard-of possibility); and see also Maqrīzī, *Itti'āẓ*, II, 93 (the editor read *ḥabābira* instead of *khayābira*). Braslavi and others were inclined to believe all sorts of late sources with various stories about the Khaybarīs; while Goitein adopted a more critical approach, and brought up the conjecture that those Khaybarīs were Jews who came from Iraq. See Braslavi, *Le-ḥeqer*, 1–52; Goitein, *Mediterranean Society*, II, 386f; Muslim complaints with regard to the fraudulent letters of the Khaybarīs, see for instance: Ibn al-Jawzī, *Muntaẓam*, VIII, 265; Subkī, *Ṭabaqāt* IV, 35; Ṣafadī, *al-Wāfī*, I, 44f; Ibn Kathīr, *Bidāya*, IV, 219; cf. also Mez, 326, n. 4, and more references therein; see the copy of the letter-of-rights in Hebrew script from the Geniza printed and interpreted by Goitein, *Kiryat Sefer*, 9:507, 1932/3. For the sake of comparison, see the discussion on a similar forged document, an alleged agreement between the Prophet and the Christian Bedouin Banū Taghlib: Abel, *SI*, 32(1970), 8f.

21 We have seen above that the Jews who served in the cleaning and maintenance on the Temple Mount in the seventh century were exempt (as were their descendants) from paying poll-tax; that is, the Jewish community in Jerusalem evidently did not impose on

cities in Palestine, created circumstances that could be thought advantageous in comparison with those of cities in other countries in the Muslim world. In the Geniza documents, there is information on matters of the poll-tax in Egypt which could be compared with the tax regime of Jerusalem. We find Israel b. Nathan (= Ibn Sahlūn), a Maghribi merchant who was the cousin of the better-known Nehorai b. Nissim, writing to Nehorai from Jerusalem ten years after leaving Fustat. He had married a woman in Byzantium and remained there for a few years. We have no precise details about his life at that time, but his letters reveal that his marriage was a failure. He had also sat in a Byzantine prison, maybe because he was an alien. While in prison, he pledged that he would live in Jerusalem for a long time if he succeeded in being released. Upon his release he stayed in Jerusalem for a year and then decided to remain there, explaining the reasons for this to Nehorai. In Fustat, he was registered with the tax office (*fī'l-kharāj*) – as a *qāṭin*, that is, a permanent resident, after having previously been registered as *ṭārī*, i.e. new or temporary (certainly after he arrived there from the Maghrib). From what he writes, it appears that if he returned to Fustat after an absence of ten years or more, he would have to pay all that he owed the tax office for the years he was absent. We can learn from this that as long as he remained in Jerusalem, he was not required to pay any personal tax at all, owing to the special conditions that existed in Jerusalem.[22]

[258] The documents from Palestine and its surroundings contained in the Geniza provide us with information about additional kinds of taxes, especially those imposed on imports. Taxes of this kind were levied chiefly on foreigners. A quite clear picture of this state of affairs evolves from a deed of partnership written in Fustat. The death of one of the partners brought to light the matter coming before the court of the yeshiva of Palestine under the Gaon Daniel b. Azariah. Concerning the matter we are discussing here, one detail of the transaction is important, namely that a large shipload of various goods sent to Sicily was registered in its entirety in the name of a certain Moses b. Judah, who was not the owner of the shipment, but who as an inhabitant of the island was exempt from import tax, that is the *maks*, called in this document *al-'issūr min isshmā'ēl* (the tithe of the Ishmaelites).

In around 1055, Nissim b. Ḥalfon, one of the agents of the great international merchant Nehorai b. Nissim, writes from Tyre about flax sent from Egypt. The letter is full of complaints about the port authorities in Tyre and the clerks of the *kharāj* (here meaning taxes in general). The

them participation in the annual sum it had to pay. De casis Dei, see: Tobler et Molinier, I, 305.

22 See **469**, b, lines 7–10 (evidently written in 1059), and see the discussion on the poll-tax in

letter written by the Maghribi merchant Avon b. Ṣedaqa on 11 November 1064 in Jerusalem is similar; apart from all kinds of grievances about the hazards of maritime commerce, and especially commerce with Sicily, he too had complaints about the *maks*. He also mentions the head of the office of the *maks*, the *ṣāḥib al-maks*. A letter from Abraham, son of the Gaon Solomon b. Judah, also mentions the *maks al-kharāj*.[23]

[259] One should note that according to Muslim law *maks* meant a tax of which there is no hint in the sources recognised by the *sharīʿa*, the religious law. The Muslim sources repeatedly mention precedents of rulers who cancelled the *maks*, and this alone goes to prove that these cancellations did not last long. However, it appears that with regard to the dhimmīs, there was no intention whatsoever to cancel the *maks*, as we have seen in the instance of Sicily, and certainly not with regard to those dhimmīs who were not permanent residents of the port city in which it was imposed.[24]

[260] Three letters written in about 1060 by ʿEli ha-Kohen b. Ezekiel, one of the leaders of the Jews in Jerusalem, contain evidence of a special tax on shops. The writer asks his relative in Fustat to try to get him a reduction in the tax he pays on his shop in Jerusalem, which amounts to seven dinars. The year prior to that, he succeeded in getting a reduction of not more than half a dinar, and for this, he had to bribe the 'Samaritan', evidently the tax official, with a quarter of a dinar. He asks that the tax be reduced by two dinars, at least. Approximately two hundred years earlier, the monk Bernard testifies that every merchant who owns a stand in the market-place alongside the Latins' hostel in Jerusalem is obliged to pay two *aurei* (dinars) annually to the overseer.[25]

[261] We have seen that one of the advantages promised to the Jews of Jerusalem in exchange for the global tax payment was an exemption for pilgrims of the payment of an entrance tax. The Gaon Solomon b. Judah

the light of the Geniza documents: Goitein, *JESHO*, 6:278, 1963; *idem*, *Mediterranean Society*, II, 380–394.

23 The question posed to Daniel b. Azariah: **395**, line 19, and see also **394** and **396**, dealing with the same matter. The letter from Tyre: **489**; Avon b. Ṣedaqa: **500**, a, lines 30–31; Abraham son of the Gaon: **170**. There are more instances of *maks* mentioned in this region; see for instance **487** in the right-hand margin, line 2, a letter from Jacob b. Joseph b. Ismāʿīl al-Iṭrābulusī, written in Ascalon, in which there is a detailed description of import and export matters; **495**, line 11, written at approximately the same time in Tyre, by Jacob b. Ismāʿīl al-Andalusī, dealing with sundry wares exported to Egypt.

24 See editor's note in Maqrīzī, *Dhahab*, 88; Maqrīzī, *Khiṭaṭ*, I, 184f; Qalqashandī, *Ṣubḥ*, III, 470f; and see the article Maks (by W. Björkman) in *EI*[1]. According to ʿAzīzī, II, 41, the *ʿushr* (meaning here *maks*) is only legitimate when imposed on Jews and Christians but not on Muslims; *maks* on Muslims is *ḥarām*. See the discussion on *ʿushr* in the days of the Prophet in Kister, *JSAI*, 1(1979), 10f and more references *ibid.*, n. 38.

25 See **446**, from line 24f; **447**, from line 5f; **449**, from line 18. Bribery was self-understood, particularly in the ports; see for instance **494**, a, line 13: Jacob b. Ismāʿīl, writing from Tyre, mentions that he spent all his money on bribes (in around 1060). Bernard, see Tobler et Molinier, I, 314.

distinctly mentions that the people of Jerusalem made extraordinary efforts in order that the authorities should not affect another right of the pilgrims, namely that they should not be asked to show the *barā'a*. A traveller was obliged to carry the *barā'a*, namely the confirmation that he had paid the poll-tax, for if it was found that he did not have this confirmation, he would be in for a great deal of trouble. The Jews of Jerusalem endeavoured to be punctual in paying the global tax imposed on them: 'We are few, we cannot stand up to a small part of it; and the remainder every year is taken in interest: in order that the pilgrims to the holy city should not be caught and required to show the tax-notes'.[26]

[262] From other evidence, we learn to what extent the obligation of settling the tax affairs affected the traveller. Nathan ha-Kohen b. Mevorakh, leader of the Jews of Ascalon, in his letter of 26 October 1093, recommends to the parnās 'Eli ha-Kohen b. Ḥayyim in Fustat, a respected Jewish scholar, Abū Sa'd b. Pinḥās of Damascus, who is travelling to Egypt on business on his first trip there; therefore he asks the parnās of Fustat to help him find his way in this alien situation. His particular worry is tax matters, despite the fact that he is carrying with him the *barā'a dīwāniyya*, the receipt from the tax authorities confirming that he had paid the poll-tax (in his language: *dayn* [= debt of] *al-jizya*). A similar request we find in a letter written in around 1065 by Judah b. Abraham, a Maghribi living in Jerusalem, to the head of the congregation of Jerusalemites in Fustat, 'Eli he-ḥāvēr b. 'Amram. He asks him to help a certain Saadia, a teacher travelling to Fustat, who needs nothing besides assistance with the tax arrangements of the 'masters of the jāliya'.[27]

[263] At times, we find the Jerusalem Gaon expressing anxiety about tax matters in Egypt. In a letter he wrote on 29 November 1042, Solomon b. Judah mentions a census that was taken in Fustat with the intention of inscribing all the poor and demanding of them taxes, and he expresses fear lest similar decrees are imposed in Palestine as well: '. . . [the letter from Fustat] saddened us, as it mentioned the matter of our poverty-stricken brethren, who were counted in order to collect taxes from them just as from the rich . . . and we fear . . . lest it extends from there to this country'.[28]

[26] **105**, lines 18–20, written around 1035. We see that the term *pītāq* (from Greek: *pittakion*) is used to mean *barā'a*. Cf. Goitein, *Mediterranean Society*, II, 384ff; 612, n. 46; he also mentions another Arabic synonym, *ruq'a* (pl. *riqā'*).

[27] See **586**, lines 19ff; **456**, b, line 6 (this part is written in Arabic script, unlike the beginning of the letter: one can still read *aṣḥāb* and apparently it is to be completed: *al-jāliya*).

[28] **133**, lines 2–4. It is interesting to compare this with what Sahl b. Maṣlīaḥ wrote some eighty years earlier to Jacob b. Samuel about the Rabbanites, that they 'boast and subject them (the Karaites) to bans and excommunications and with the help of the rulers of the aliens, and *'onāshīm* (which as we already know meant special taxes, fines) forcing them to borrow on interest and give it to them'; see in Pinsker, *Liqqūṭē qadmōniyōt*, II, 31f.

[264] It is not surprising that the Gaon praises Ephraim b. Shemaria, the ḥāvēr from Fustat. In one of his letters he writes that he is 'concerned about all public affairs, to save those caught for taxes', while another leader whom he does not mention by name, is 'impatient, and has no time to go into the law, and he does not know how to deal with the police and the governor and scribe [official clerk] and tax official'. Solomon b. Judah's heir to the seat of Gaon, Daniel b. Azariah, also had a trustworthy helping hand in tax matters in the person of Abraham ha-Kohen b. Isaac b. Furāt, a physician with considerable influence. In a letter to the latter written in Arabic in around 1055, the Gaon writes that 'our people, may God help them, bless His name, are *in great trouble* [Hebrew in the original: *be-ṣa'ar gādōl*] about their tax in each and every city, especially in Damascus. Therefore perhaps, Sir, you would find it possible to 'champion their rights; act, and God will double your reward . . .' At about the same time, the Jews of Damascus themselves write to the yeshiva and mention among their other difficulties, the fact that they are being asked to pay the tax before payment is due. They demand the possibility of paying the tax once a year, on Muḥarram. On the other hand, there were Jews who co-operated with the authorities with regard to the tax, as one of the Gaon Solomon b. Judah's circle describes a Jew 'who sat many years serving the clerks of the tax and inheritance'; he would serve as a sort of mediator between the Muslim tax officials and the Jews and determine the extent of the tax.[29]

[265] We have seen that the principle of submission and inferiority of 'the people of the book' towards the Muslims is already to be found in the Koran. We find it again in a new version in the treaties of surrender. The following is the version as it appears in the Damascus treaty: the Muslims are permitted to enter churches by day or night; the Christians may not raise pigs in the neighbourhood of Muslims and shall not sell wine to Muslims; they shall not try to convert Muslims to their belief and may not prevent members of their own religion from turning to Islam; they shall treat the Muslims with respect wherever they are located (or in their councils – *fi majālisihim*); they must stand aside and make way for them; they must stand up before them and give up their seats for them; they may not enter Muslims' houses but are obliged to host and feed a Muslim in a reasonable manner for a period of three days; they may not curse a Muslim and whoever hits a Muslim, his blood be on his own head (*fa-qad khuli'a 'ahduhu*, literally: the treaty of his [defence] became invalid).[30]

[29] **95**, lines 15–18; **355**, b, in the margin. The letter from Damascus: **285**, lines 10–12; the Jew mediator: **84**, b, II, lines 19f.

[30] Ibn 'Asākir, I, 505, 563f Cf. Avon b. Ṣedaqa's letter, writing from Jerusalem on 28 August, 1065, to Nehorai b. Nissim, which mentions that Faraḥ ibn Sahlān, the latter's uncle, lives in Muslims' houses, and no one comes or goes there (*lā dākhil wa-lā khārij*

The responsibility for the life of the dhimmī

[266] Muslim religious law did not reach a unanimous conclusion concerning the extent of its responsibility for the lives of the dhimmīs, that is, whether a Muslim who kills a dhimmī is endangering his own life or not (or will pay the same ransom as for the killing of a Muslim). There are ḥadīth traditions ascribed to the Prophet in which there is condemnation of the killing of a dhimmī, but at the same time, 'Alī was credited with the opinion that a Muslim who had killed an unbeliever should not be put to death. The genuine belief of Muḥammad was in fact expressed in 'the constitution of Medina' which was drawn up a short time after the hijra, where it is clearly stated that a Muslim is not to be killed for the murder of an unbeliever, and this is clearly and specifically echoed in the Muslim corpus of traditions. Actually it was accepted that ransom payment for a dhimmī was half that of a Muslim. As to the custom in this matter during Mu'āwiya's time (evidently also during the entire period of Umayyad rule) we can learn from the instance of Ziyād, Mu'āwiya's step-brother, who was governor of Iraq. He refused to allow the execution of an Arab of the Banū Asad who had murdered a dhimmī (a *Nabaṭī*, that is a villager who spoke Aramaic) and imposed on the murderer a ransom to the family of the murdered man, but they refused to accept it and claimed that according to the existing law on this matter, there was equality not only between Muslims amongst themselves but also between Arabs and non-Arabs. Ḥujr b. 'Adī, one of the main followers of 'Alī and afterwards leader of the opposition to Mu'āwiya in Kūfa, then killed that Arab murderer, an act which Ziyād and Mu'āwiya considered to be a guilty one, and on this basis had him arrested.[31]

Dress regulations

[267] The truest indications of the inferiority of the dhimmīs were the prohibitions regarding dress and the rest of the regulations differentiating them in appearance from the Muslims. The principal motive behind these regulations was the desire to prevent social contact between Arabs and the local populations. Perhaps at first there may also have been some security considerations, but there is no evidence of this. At any rate, the Muslims

'alayhi); apparently he wants to say that no one dares to break the custom which bans entering there: **501**, b, lines 8–12.

31 'The constitution of Medina', see Ibn Hishām, 342; Ibn Sa'd, I(2), 172; cf. Gil, *IOS*, 4(1974), 52f, and *ibid*. in n. 62 further references. See the discussion on ransom money for a dhimmī and the responsibility for his murder: Tritton, *Caliphs*, 178ff. See the story of Ziyād in Balādhurī, *Ansāb*, IV(A), 220.

saw in these regulations a symbol of the superiority of Islam and its adherents. The dhimmīs on the other hand saw it as evidence of their humiliation and it is not surprising that they tried to avoid those distinguishing marks whenever possible. The prohibitions regarding dress are generally ascribed to the Abbasid caliphs, especially to Hārūn al-Rashīd (786–809) and al-Mutawakkil (847–861), who imposed the wearing of yellow dress on the Christians and Jews (later, there was a differentiation between Christians and Jews, the colour of the Christians being blue). Additional marks were added, such as the interdiction on women with regard to silken girdles, as only cotton was allowed; distinctive marks while entering a public bath-house; and so on. These restrictions were imposed by the rulers in Palestine as well, but to the best of my knowledge there is nothing in the sources indicating their particular application in Palestine. However there is no doubt that they were theoretically imposed in Palestine. Except that here, as elsewhere in the caliphate they were not rigorously observed; which is the only explanation for the fact that they had to be renewed from time to time.[32]

[268] An even more important question is whether these decrees really began only in the Abbasid era, that is in the days of Hārūn al-Rashīd. A more careful examination of the earliest pacts, from the time of the conquest, will reveal that the embryo of these decrees exists in the early agreements with local populations. According to Ibn ʿAsākir's versions of the pacts with the local people of Damascus and al-Shām, they were obliged to shorten their forelocks in the front and leave the hair loose; to wear girdles (*zanānīr*); they must not resemble Muslims in their outward appearance, nor in their dress or their saddles. In addition, they had to differ from the Muslims in matters of culture and language; they could not insert Arabic in the inscriptions on their seals (there are some distorted versions on this matter which say the contrary), nor be called by Arab by-names, and they must not study the Koran nor teach it to their children.[33]

[32] See the recommendations of Abū Yūsuf, 76, to Hārūn al-Rashīd: lest they resemble the Muslims in their dress, in their riding, and their outward appearance; the girdle (*zunnār*) shall be made of rough threads; they shall wear tall headgear (*qalānis*) with holes; they shall place on their saddles a piece of wood resembling a pomegranate; they shall make a double knot in the laces of their shoes, and more. On the decrees regarding dress of al-Mutawakkil (in 850) see Ṭabarī, *Ta'rīkh*, III, 1389; Mawṣilī, *Wasā'il*, 36b, quotes from al-Ṣūlī details of Mutawakkil's decrees: the obligation to wear clothes the colour of honey (*ʿasalī*), to ride in a special way, to attach coloured patches to the hats and the dress, to attach painted distinguishing signs on the entrances of the houses, and more; because of this, he says, many turned to Islam (and he mentions names). Cf. Sibṭ ibn al-Jawzī, *Mir'āh* (BM Or 4618), 93b; the drawings over the doors had to be of images of devils (*shayāṭīn*); on similar decrees in 907/8 (the days of al-Muqtadir), see Ibn al-Jawzī, *Muntaẓam*, VI, 82.

[33] Ibn ʿAsākir, I, 505, 563f; see also Ibn ʿAbd al-Ḥakam, 151.

Freedom of worship and its limitations

[269] The formulae of the principle of freedom of worship, with various restrictions, also date from the very earliest times. As early as in the treaty of Najrān it is stated: 'there shall be no disturbance to their religion and their way of life'. All the treaties I have surveyed above contain a clause enabling the protected people to maintain their houses of prayer, but not to build new ones, and according to certain versions, even to renew the old ones which had fallen into disrepair. The Christians had to take it upon themselves to practise their religious customs modestly, for example, not to intone the *nāqūs* in public but only within the churches; not to conduct noisy processions holding the cross on high; also to be quiet and modest at funerals, which must not be accompanied by torches when passing through Muslim quarters. It appears that at the time of the conquest many churches and synagogues were destroyed by the invading tribes. Apparently the time of the destruction of the synagogues and Byzantine churches, whose remnants were and are still being discovered in various parts of Palestine, was that of the Muslim conquest or shortly afterward. Clear evidence of this has been preserved regarding the region of Damascus and the Ghawṭa (the valley surrounding the city), in a source saying that in the days of 'Umar ibn 'Abd al-'Azīz, not a single undamaged church was found in the entire area. It seems that the fate of the synagogues, in the large cities at any rate, was a better one, for the Muslim rage to destroy churches was fed to a large extent by their hatred of the Byzantines, against whom they waged perpetual war.

There is evidence of widespread destruction of the dhimmīs' houses of prayer in the ninth century. In 807, Hārūn al-Rashīd decided to demolish all the houses of prayer of the unbelievers, but it is not clear to what extent this decree was carried out. It is quite possible that the intention was to destroy only those places of worship that were built after the Muslim conquests (in which case, in Baghdad for instance, all the houses of prayer would have been destined for destruction, as would those of Jerusalem and Ramla). In 850, we are again told, a decree was issued by al-Mutawakkil to destroy all the new places of worship of the unbelievers (and also to take over a tenth of their homes for the Muslims); old churches and synagogues which were still functional would become mosques, or at any rate, had to be evacuated. We have no knowledge of whether, or to what extent, these decrees were carried out in Palestine.

With regard to the Christians, it appears that similar acts of destruction took place, also in the succeeding generations. As to the outcome of al-Ḥākim's decrees to that effect at the outset of the eleventh century, the synagogues in Palestine were also destroyed. There was certainly a gap between the laws and what actually took place. A notable fact is the existence of the synagogue in Jerusalem, confirmed by the Geniza documents from the eleventh century, although there is no doubt that no synagogue existed there at the time of the Muslim conquest in 638. There were also synagogues in Ramla which were built after the conquest. In the middle of the eleventh century, we find an episode in connection with the Christians, in some unidentified place (but it seems to refer to a city in Palestine) who did not take into consideration the existing prohibitions at all and built their church even higher than the mosque, and so the church was demolished. (In addition, the noise of the knocking on the *nāqūs* was disturbing and a nuisance to the Muslims.)[34]

Professions and offices

[270] The religious autonomy given to the Jews and the Christians is an issue on its own, and which was expressed in the relationship between the Muslim authorities and the institutions of leadership of the two communi-

[34] Ibn ʿAsākir, I, 504f, 563f; Balādhurī, *Futūḥ*, 64 (Najrān). See on the destruction of the churches in Damascus and the whole area: ʿImād al-Dīn, *Tadhkira*, 21ff; see *ibid.* also a story of negotiations between the Christians and ʿUmar ibn ʿAbd al-ʿAzīz, regarding compensation for their church in Damascus (which was destroyed by the Jews according to Caliph al-Walīd's decision); Badrī, 34f. Ṭabarī, *Ta'rīkh*, II, 1372, cites ʿUmar ibn ʿAbd al-ʿAzīz's order, which says: 'do not destroy any Jewish or Christian house of prayer or any temple of the Zoroastrians, if the peace treaty permits them to maintain it, but do not allow them to build new ones'. One should note that the Byzantines had a similar view, as can be seen by a regulation found in the code of Justinian (it is found in: Starr, *Jews*, 145[no. 83]): it is permitted to repair synagogues but not to build new ones; cf. Krauss, *Melila*, 3–4: 77, 1949/50. See on the decrees of Hārūn al-Rashīd: Ṭabarī, *Ta'rīkh*, III, 713; Ibn al-Athīr, *Kāmil*, VI, 206. al-Mutawakkil: Ṭabarī, *Ta'rīkh*, III, 1390; Ibn al-Athīr, *Kāmil*, VII, 52. On the order of destruction of Hārūn al-Rashīd it is said that houses of worship in the ports (*al-thugūr*) were intended; as to al-Mutawakkil, included in his decrees is the destruction of cemeteries of the unbelievers (*taswiyat qubūrihim maʿa'l-arḍ*, whose correct interpretation seems to be destruction, although Ṭabarī adds: so that they should not be like the Muslim graves, that is, allegedly the intention was that the graves should not rise above the ground). See further Abū Yūsuf, 141: ʿUmar ordered Abū ʿUbayda not to disturb the Christians when they are taking the crosses out on the holidays, if this is done outside the town, but without displaying their banners, and only on one day in the year; but they are not allowed to take out the crosses inside the city, among the Muslims and their mosques. The law prohibiting the dhimmīs to put up buildings (and certainly houses of worship) which were taller than the Muslim buildings was apparently introduced in later generations; see Mez, 47 – in his opinion, this idea was taken by the west from the Muslims (one need not necessarily believe him), such as the complaint of Pope Innocent III, that the Jews of Sens built a synagogue taller than the church in its neighbourhood. See his remarks in his letter, in: Grayzel, *The Church*, 106. Such a law prohibiting the building of synagogues is first mentioned (as far as we know) in 423, see the Theodosian Code, xvi–8, 25; it appears that Zeno the bishop of Verona (362–380) hinted at such a law, earlier than the aforementioned by nearly two generations; see: *MPL*, 11, 354ff. Cf. Juster, *Juifs*, I, 469, n. 2; Baron, *Jewish Community*, III, 20f; the affair of the church which was much too tall, see: **404**, letter to Abraham ha-Kohen b. Isaac b. Furāt, lines 14–19, according to the version in Gil, *Teʿuda*, 7(1991), 332.

ties in Palestine. A basic fact was the uninterrupted existence of these institutions for almost the entire period, with a varying degree of intervention on the part of the authorities in their affairs.

Although the Muslim law did not impose any restrictions on the economic affairs of the dhimmīs – on the contrary, the Muslims were interested, as soon as their reign was established, that the dhimmīs should continue to pursue their occupations, as we have seen – there was a distinct opposition to the dhimmīs holding any public posts, as outlined in Muslim law. True, this is not formulated in any of the early sources in which legal principles with regard to the dhimmīs are to be found, and dealing with other areas, from the Koran onwards, but one can rely on the approach of the caliph 'Umar ibn al-Khaṭṭāb in this matter.

It was natural that at the beginning of the conquest, the Muslims had to continue to employ officials who served in the former administration, for they had no people of their own who could fill administrative posts, particularly with regard to finance. It is said that 'Umar ibn al-Khaṭṭāb himself appointed a number of the captives of Caesarea as administrative officials. One can also assume that Jewish and Christian physicians were called upon to serve at the courts of the caliphs in their professional capacities. On the other hand, it is told that 'Umar one day requested from Abū Mūsā al-Ash'arī to bring his secretary to him to read him some letters from al-Shām, and that Abū Mūsā replied that he could not bring the secretary into the mosque. When 'Umar asked him the reason for this, he disclosed that the secretary was a Christian. This roused 'Umar's wrath and he read him the words from the Koran (*sūrat al-mā'ida*, v:56) 'Oh, ye believers, do not take Jews or Christians as your aides, for they aid one another'. It is known from the Egyptian papyri, however, and even from Muslim sources, that the Umayyads employed dhimmīs, particularly Christians (from families that had formerly been Byzantine officials) in administrative posts. We have already seen a few such instances above, particularly the family of Sarjūn b. Manṣūr of Damascus. Some of them converted to Islam, and certainly since they were *mawālī*, their advance would have been much more rapid than if they had maintained their former religion. In the Abbasid period as well, we find Christians serving in administrative positions despite the fact that, from time to time, the caliphs issued orders prohibiting their employment, such as al-Muqtadir's order in 908/9. The participation of both Christian and Jewish dhimmīs in various administrative roles was particularly marked in the days of the Fatimids. In this sphere, we have considerable information from both Arab sources and from the Geniza documents, and below we shall encounter central figures in the Fatimid political scene who were Jews (some of whom converted to Islam), and who were involved in the affairs of

Palestine, such as Manasseh ibn Abraham al-Qazzāz, Jacob ibn Killis, the Tustari brothers and others. There was even a governor in Jerusalem who was a Karaite (Ibn 'Allūn) and a government official in Jerusalem who was a Samaritan, for example.[35]

Matters of inheritance; Muslim courts

[271] Another sphere in which Muslim law influenced the life of the dhimmīs was that of the property of the family, and I refer here to the laws of inheritance. In general, the law recognised the right of Jews and Christians to deal with matters of inheritance according to their own laws as the leaders and judges of the community interpreted them. There was, however, an inclination to confiscate dhimmīs' property when they died without male heirs, although they first allotted to the widows and daughters what was their due in Muslim law (according to which the women and daughters have a share in the inheritance). According to a ḥadīth, the Prophet said that a Muslim does not inherit from the unbeliever nor does the unbeliever inherit from the Muslim, a rule which is in keeping with the basic Muslim approach which places considerable weight on the religious partnership in human relationships – an emphasis which gives them priority over family relationships. This approach is very objective on the surface, for accordingly a Jew who converts to Christianity loses his rights of inheritance as well, as does one who converts to Islam. However, at variance with this is another ḥadīth of the Prophet which says that Islam only brings about profit and not loss (*al-islām yazīd wa-lā yanquṣ*).[36]

[272] In the Muslim law of inheritance there was a loophole, which

35 Caesarea: Balādhurī, *Futūḥ*, 142, the case of Abū Mūsā: Ibn Qutayba, *'Uyūn*, I, 43; Ghāzī ibn al-Wāsiṭī, 387ff; cf. Belin, *JA*, 4e sér., 18(1851), 428; see also Tritton, *Caliphs*, 18, and see there on pp. 19ff many additional details on the employment of Christians in administrative posts in various places of the Muslim world during the period under discussion. See Nuwayrī, VIII, 198f; according to him Greek was no longer being used in financial management in the days of 'Abd al-Malik, since the year AH 81, that is AD 700, after a Greek official urinated into the ink. The caliph then ordered Sulaymān b. Sa'd to introduce Arabic script; it was first used in matters of taxes in jund Urdunn. Afterwards he transferred him to Damascus, where he was put in the place of the Christian Sarjūn. The employing of local administrative officials is shown by the Egyptian papyri; for instance, the case of a Christian who still bore the title *dux*, while the Arabs call him 'the honourable *amīr*', see: Lewis, *PEQ*, 80(1948), 112. Al-Muqtadir's order: Ibn al-Jawzī, *Muntaẓam*, VI, 81. See also the survey in Goitein, *Mediterranean Society*, II, 374ff on this subject: 'Non-Muslim government officials' (and see *ibid.* the corresponding notes), based on Geniza documents.

36 See a comprehensive discussion of this subject: Schreiner, *REJ*, 29(1894), 208, and the supplement *ibid.*, 212. The ḥadīths are cited in many places; see, for instance, Mālik, 255 (No. 728); Ṭayālisī, 77, 87; Ibn al-Athīr, *Jāmi'*, X, 366ff. There were legists who accepted the first ḥadīth as it stands and rejected the authenticity of the other, that is, they claimed that the Muslim cannot inherit from the unbeliever; see Ibn al-Jawzī, *Mawḍū'āt*, III, 230; Tritton, *Caliphs*, 136.

allowed for appeal to the Muslim court, in the hope that the cadi would grant the claimant advantages he could not have obtained at the hands of the Jewish court, particularly when speaking of women. Also with regard to divorce, we know that when the husband refused to grant a divorce, there were some women who applied to the Muslim court. Of this, we have the evidence of Sherira Gaon, who points out in one of his responsa, that a short time after the conquest of Babylonia by the Muslims, when Rabbā was the head of the yeshiva in Pumbedita, and Hūnā in Sura (about 650), an amendment (*taqqānā*) was decided upon, named after the daughter-in-law of Rav Zavīd; this amendment prescribed that the husband must give the wife a divorce immediately, on condition that she renounce what is written in the marriage deed (*ketubbā*), because 'the daughters of Israel were relying on the gentiles to get their divorce by force'. Naturally, at such an early date, there was still no clear-cut Muslim law with regard to divorce, and one can only view this information as incidental evidence of the Muslim authorities' intervention in instances in which the woman succeeded in convincing them that she had been mistreated and that the Jewish decision had been contrary to their sense of natural justice.[37]

[273] This tendency to apply to the cadi can be seen in Jewish sources of the period. One can assume that similar processes occurred among the Christians, but we have no specific knowledge of this. The Jewish public, for whom the authority of their court was the very nerve centre of religious-national uniqueness, opposed this tendency by emphasising again and again the ancient prohibition on appealing to the gentile law courts. The common attitude was that one could apply to them in commercial and financial matters but not with regard to property ('. . . we only admit deeds of purchase and the like; but we do not admit deeds of gift and the like'). It was accepted that one needed a special authorisation from the Jewish court in order to give evidence in the gentile courts; they would also find a way to permit this when speaking of 'robbery' (*gezel*, like non-payment of a debt), on condition that it was 'a gentile court which does not accept bribes and is non-biased'. A verdict or deeds acquired by the coercion of the Muslim court, or the Muslim authorities, were usually considered absolutely invalid. There is mention of a conflict concerning estates belonging to a woman who had converted; the husband considered her as good as dead and that he was her heir, while her paternal family

[37] See the letter of Sherira (Lewin), 101 and *ibid.* in the note the text of his responsum to the scholars of Qayrawān and more references of the editor. Nevertheless in certain instances Muslim law was prepared to acknowledge the right of the women to receive a divorce even without the agreement of the husband; and see the article Ṭalāḳ (by J. Schacht) in *EI*[1] (who mentions this possibility, but does not go into detail); and see also Schacht, *Introduction*, 165f.

demanded her property for themselves and the Babylonian Gaon decided in favour of her family. The opinion of the Palestinian Geonim was also that the marriage deed of the woman who had converted belonged to her family. The Geonim permitted the decision to rest with the Muslim court and with its help, invalidated the right of inheritance of a Jew who had converted, for 'the Muslims, according to the law of Ishmael, do not allow a convert to inherit the properties of his father; thereupon our Sages relied so as to deprive such a man of his father's inheritance...'[38]

[274] The reality that emerges from the Geniza documents in the eleventh century AD is of a strong Jewish legal autonomy, and the Palestinian Gaon is ready to assert his authority vigorously in those cases in which one party appeals for help from the Muslim court; this party can expect excommunication. On the other hand, the habit of registering deals of estates with the Muslim court as well as with the Jewish court became widespread, evidently because of demands from the tax authorities and also, perhaps, because of the need to feel more secure in the face of pressure and expropriation. A document written in Arabic and signed by the cadi certainly made the required impression on the authorities.

As to Palestine, apart from the information mentioned above concerning the attitude of its Geonim in the matter of the marriage deed of the woman who had converted, all our knowledge of this matter is derived from the Geniza, that is, from the eleventh century. The first source is from the days of Josiah Gaon b. Aaron, in around 1020. This is a letter from the Gaon to the community of Rafiaḥ (Rafaḥ): 'Ā'isha (a distinctly Arab name), daughter of Joseph b. Ṣudayq (a pet name for Ṣadaqa), had died. Her cousins on her father's side, Moses and Abraham, the sons of Manṣūr, son of Ṣudayq, applied to the local dayyān, who was Solomon b. Saadia, and he decided that they were the heirs of their cousin. 'Amram b. Fuḍayl (a pet name from Faḍl) and his sister and her son Khalaf b. Mukarram claimed that the legacy was theirs (it is not clear what degree of family relationship there was between them and the deceased; perhaps they were the brother and sister and nephew of her husband, who undoubtedly died before she did). It seems that we have here an instance of difference between the paternal family and that of the husband, though this is merely an assumption. They applied to the Muslim court, to the cadi, and he made the same decision as the dayyān. Then they applied to

[38] See Harkavy, *Teshūvōt*, 51 (No. 82); *Ge'onē mizrāḥ ū-ma'arāv*, 53a–53b (No. 199); A special permit: *Ōṣar ha-ge'ōnīm*, BQ, 99(No. 290, Hayy Gaon). Acts of coercion: the responsum of Saadia Gaon, *Ge'one mizrāḥ ū-ma'arāv*, 8a–8b (No. 22). The woman who had converted (evidently to Christianity): *Ge'one mizrāḥ ū-ma'arāv*, 20b (No. 87): the view of the Palestinians ('the westerners'): *Sha'arē ṣedeq*, 63b; depriving a convert from inheritance: *Ge'one mizrāḥ ū-ma'arāv*, 4b (No. 11); *Ōṣar ha-ge'ōnīm*, Qidd., 30f (Nos. 78–90); see the

the *qā'id*, the government authority (apparently a Turkish or Berber commander, in charge of affairs on behalf of the Fatimids) and they managed to get part of the legacy with his help. The Gaon pronounced them excommunicated; Sahl, the aforementioned 'Amram b. Fuḍayl's brother (it is not clear why 'Amram himself was not indicated) was obliged to appear together with his sister before the great court (that is, the yeshiva in Jerusalem) and hand over what they had taken. If he refused, he too would be excommunicated.

At about the same time there occurred the affair of Mubāraka, in which a memorandum of the court complained that she had evaded the verdict of the court and applied to the Muslim court, to the 'Judge of Judges' (*qādī'l-quḍāh*). She demanded her share of her father's legacy through the medium of the 'gentile laws' (for, as mentioned above, Muslim law grants a share of a legacy to daughters as well). Because of her, the infantry (probably the *rijāla*, soldiers in the service of the Execution Office) arrested her brother, who escaped, however. Clearly the appellants rely on the Gaon's opposition to applications to the gentile court. Solomon b. Judah writes, probably in 1028, to Ephraim b. Shemaria in Fustat, mentioning a man of Jerusalem who was reduced to poverty and went to Egypt. In spite of the very poor state of the manuscript, it can still be understood that this person fell victim to someone who did not hesitate to apply to a Muslim court, and caused him to lose all his property, including 'his house and that of his son-in-law, and land inherited from his forefathers'.

In August 1030, Abraham, son of the Gaon Solomon b. Judah, is in Fustat, when the court there examines the complaints of a certain Sulaymān, a smith of Jerusalem, against Salmān b. Shabīb al-Ashqar (the redhead), who owes Sulaymān four dinars. Salmān lives in Fustat and the claim against him is brought by Yefet ha-Levi b. Tobiah, who holds 'a deed of attorney validated by the signature of his honour, the great and holy Lord and Master, Solomon, head of the yeshiva Ge'on Ya'aqov'. When the court found in favour of Sulaymān the Jerusalemite, Salmān began 'to complain and curse and storm against the laws of Israel and its judges; and this Salmān swore that he would not accept but the gentile laws . . .'; the judge in Fustat, Ephraim b. Shemaria immediately decreed a ban on him 'until he agreed to accept the verdict'.

In around 1030 Solomon b. Judah writes to Abraham ha-Kohen b. Isaac b. Furāt about a deposit demanded by Samuel b. 'Ezrūn, the fiancé of the Gaon's granddaughter, from a man called Nissī (the deposit was left with Nissī by Samuel's mother). Nissī demanded to be judged by the cadi, but

discussion on these questions: Mann, *JQR*, NS 10(1919/20), 140f; 11(1920/21), 457; see also Hirschberg, *Herzog Memorial Volume*: 493.

his wife sharply objected to this. Although Solomon b. Judah refused to sit in judgment on this dispute, as he was Samuel's relative, the family of Shuway', that is the family of Joshua b. Simḥūn, rivals of the Gaon, accused him of siding with one of the contestants, and the Gaon requests Abraham ha-Kohen, a respectable physician who lives in Ramla, to get the support of the *amīr* (the governor of Ramla) who should write to his colleague (the governor of Jerusalem) not to pay attention to these accusations. Some time afterwards, perhaps from 1035, we find another letter from Solomon b. Judah to Ramla, to the same Abraham ha-Kohen, also dealing with the Shuway' family. This time the Gaon writes in their favour, although they are people who 'oppose anything done by someone else'. He asks Abraham to try to intervene with the cadi in Ramla, Abū'l-Ma'ālī (evidently he is al-Musharraf b. al-Murajjā b. Ibrāhīm al-Maqdisī, author of the *faḍā'il*, a work mentioned occasionally in this book) concerning the house of the Shuway' family. The house was confiscated on the basis of false evidence in favour of an old Muslim named al-Shāmī, a malicious person who was co-owner of the house. The Gaon and all the other Jews of Jerusalem know the truth, that the house is in fact the property of the Shuway' family.

In Jerusalem, one would proclaim a ban on the seventh day of the Feast of Tabernacles, at the gathering on the Mount of Olives, on people who applied to a Muslim court. We have evidence of this in a letter of complaint written by the orphan daughters of a certain Dōsā. The eldest daughter turns to the public on her own behalf and that of her younger sister, complaining that they were deprived of their share of their father's legacy by their two married sisters, and her remarks include the following phrase: 'you use to proclaim a ban, on the Mount of Olives, against anyone who obtains an inheritance in a Muslim court'.

Solomon b. Judah reveals in one of his letters that the influence of this act of excommunication did not have much effect; expressing his opposition to the annual excommunication of the Karaites, as was the accepted custom of the Rabbanites in Jerusalem, he states (in a letter written apparently in 1035, whose addressee we do not know):

> . . . (you say) let us excommunicate who desecrates the Sabbath of God! but the majority do desecrate it; is there anyone keeping the Sabbath as is prescribed? And anyone who desecrates the holidays of God; but they [the Karaites] say that it is we who desecrate them; and anyone who applies to the laws of the gentiles and whoever obtains an inheritance by their laws; nevertheless, many whom our laws do not favour, apply to the laws of the gentiles . . .

Indeed, in the Geniza documents there is clear evidence that in Palestine Jews did not hesitate to turn to the cadi when it seemed useful or necessary. A deed of attorney written in Tyre at the end of 1036 or the beginning of

1037, validated in Fustat, of which only a fragment is preserved, includes a power of attorney given by his mother and two sisters to Joseph ha-Levi b. Saadia to collect money owing to the deceased father of the family. It says there that he was also provided with a letter 'to the elders of the Ishmaelites, so that no one would hinder him and that no one would express doubts in the matter'. Apparently it refers to a confirmation intended for the Muslim courts. In a draft of evidence regarding the sale of a shop in Tiberias, a transaction carried out in 1023, it is noted that the draft is a copy according to *al-maḥḍar al-'arabī*, that is according to the document of the court which was in Arabic script, and such a document could only have been written in the Muslim court. In a draft of a deed of attorney written in Tyre, apparently in 1041, we find an accounting between partners after the death of one of them, Manasseh b. Isaac. It mentions that he received goods according to a list 'in *hagari* [Arabic] writing', and that they used 'documents of the gentile courts' drawn up by 'the judge who lives in the city of Tyre'. Avon b. Ṣedaqa, the Maghribi merchant (of the circle of Nehorai b. Nissim), who lived in Jerusalem, writes from there on 17 March 1055, to Ḥayyim b. 'Ammār in Alexandria. His letter is filled with complaints about conspiracies and judgments against himself, without clarifying the matter – accusing Ḥayyim, for instance, of 'gobbling up the money of the Maghribi gentleman'. His opponents pour abuse on him in the Muslim legal institutions, 'and things have come to such a pass that if a governor ['*āmil*] or supervisor of bequests [*ṣāḥib mawārīth*] were to be appointed every week, they would approach him [every week] in this matter'.[39]

[39] See the discussion on applications to Muslim courts and the relationship between the two legal systems, in Goitein, *Mediterranean Society*, II, 395–402, and the corresponding notes. The Rafiaḥ episode: **43**; Mubāraka: **44**; it seems that the applicants are members of the Karaite community (or one of the Karaite communities) in Fustat, and among the witnesses we find the signature of Joseph b. Israel al-Dustarī, that is of the family of the Tustaris, who were Karaites. Here there is proof apparently that the Gaon of Palestine was considered by the authorities as being responsible for all Jewish matters, including those of the Karaites in the Fatimid caliphate; cf. Gil, *ha-Tustarīm*, 45, 49ff; Solomon b. Judah's letter: **75**, b, lines 20ff; the episode of Sulaymān the Jerusalemite: **102**; the debtor Salmān b. Shabīb, is mentioned in the deed TS 13 J 9, f. 5, dated Thursday, 19th of Tammuz, AM 4807, or 16 July AD 1047, drafted in Mahdiyya and validated in Fustat by Ephraim b. Shemaria and others. The episode of Samuel b. 'Ezrūn: **101**; the house of the Shuway' family: **117**; on Abū'l-Ma'ālī al-Musharraf b. al-Murajjā, see below; the orphans' complaint, apparently from the beginning of the eleventh century: **217**; Solomon b. Judah on the ban: **121**, lines 5ff; one should note that his comments on the gentile courts have no direct connection with the matter of the Karaites, he says this only to exemplify the lack of logic in the proclamations of excommunication. It is worth noting that the Karaites also emphasised the ban on having recourse to Muslim courts; see the marriage deed of the Karaite woman wedded to a Rabbanite, Bodl MS Heb a 3, f. 42 (partly edited by Mann, *Jews*, II, 212, and in full: *Texts*, II, 177ff) from 1428 Sel. (AD 1117; there is an error in Mann on this matter and see Goitein's corrections *ibid.* in the preface), and *ibid.* the passage 'and they shall not apply to judgments of the gentiles in exchange for the judgments of the

The population and localities

[275] Undoubtedly, one of the most obscure subjects concerning this period is that of the population and localities. The basic fact that should serve as a starting point in this discussion is that at the time of the conquest, Palestine was inhabited by Jews and Christians. The Arab tribes were to be found in the border areas, in keeping with arrangements made with the Byzantine rulers. There is no doubt that many of the small towns and villages were destroyed during the conquest, and one can imagine that the war and the slaughter of the population considerably decreased its numbers. It appears that the map of localities was no longer what it had been even after 'Umar ibn al-Khaṭṭāb introduced order in the relations between the Muslim tribes and the local population. We now know that out of ninety-three towns in the Sharon of which a geographical survey provides evidence during the Roman-Byzantine eras, only fifty-two remained at the end of the Crusader period. Towns in the western strip and the central strip (the region of the red sand hills and the swamps) in the Sharon, decreased from fifty-eight to seventeen! It is estimated that the erosion of the soil from the western slopes of the Judaean mountains reached – as a result of the agricultural uprooting during the Muslim period – the gigantic extent of 2,000 to 4,000 cubic metres. In a survey made by Guy in 1938 on the region of Rehovot-Ramla-Lod-Ramallah, he found that out of 293 towns, 193 were abandoned, apparently mainly because of soil erosion. We find direct evidence of the destruction of agriculture and the desertion of the villages in the fact that the papyri of Nessana are completely discontinued after the year 700. One can assume that at that time the inhabitants abandoned the place, evidently because of the inter-tribal warfare among the Arabs which completely undermined the internal security of the area.[40]

Torah'; see the same saying also in the Karaite marriage deed which precedes this by some hundred years, from January 1028: **305**, lines 32–33. See also Benjamin al-Nihāwandī, 3a: 'and it is not permitted to apply to a court of the idolaters in a difference with someone of Israel, even when they judge according to the laws of the Torah, as it is said: these are the judgments which thou shalt set before them (Ex., xxi:1); Israel may judge Israel'. See a slightly different version in Mann, *Jews*, II, 156, n. 3; the power-of-attorney from Tyre: **274**, line 8; the shop in Tiberias: **245**, line 14; power-of-attorney deed: **276**, a, lines 6, 10–13; Avon b. Ṣedaqa: **497**, lines 12–17. See also **84**, b, II, lines 20ff, about the Jew who mediated with the Muslim authorities with regard to taxes and legacies, until 'anyone whose relative died had to go to him to write a petition for him to the government officials in charge of inheritances [this is certainly what is meant here by *aṣḥāb al-mawāwrīth*] certifying that the deceased had heirs'.

[40] Guy, *IEJ*, 4:77, 1954; Karmon, *BJPES*, 23: 111, 1959 (and especially the table on p. 130); cf. Ashtor, *Social and Economic History*, 52ff; see also Kochavi (ed.), *Yehūdā*, 24, data on the state of the towns in Judaea (in the mountains and in the *Shefēlā*) in the Byzantine period, when the density of the population reached its peak. On Nessana see: *Nessana*, 35; the assumption of the editor that the destruction was caused by the Abbasid revolution has no

[276] There is no reason to assume that the proportions in the structure of the population varied drastically in the period in question, although it is very likely that the population diminished. In other words, one should not assume that the Muslims were the majority during this period. Al-Iṣṭakhrī mentions in 951 that in all of jund Filasṭīn there were approximately twenty mosques, as against some sixty Christian houses of worship at the beginning of the ninth century.

During the days of the Umayyads, the Muslim element consisted, as we have seen, mainly of tribes who derived their livelihood from taxes from the subdued population. It seems probable that in this early period the Muslims did not implant real roots in the towns of Palestine, and certainly not in agriculture. We have already seen above that at the time of the conquest, the inhabitants of Tiberias had to give up part of their dwellings in order to house the Muslim tribesmen. One can assume that the same conditions were imposed in other cities in Palestine as well, and that from then on, the tribes constituted a certain part of the population; but we have no way of knowing the size of that part. During the Abbasid and successive periods, when Palestine was ruled from Egypt, there was certainly a marked decrease in the importance of the tribes and their place was largely taken by the prominent element of non-Arab Muslim military personnel and government officials, as well as religious personnel. This latter element certainly did not reach impressive demographic proportions and its numerical weight was very marginal, although naturally it is this element on which details are preserved in the Muslim sources. I have summarised above what is known of Muslim personalities in Palestine, and of men of religion and officialdom, during the period of the Damascene caliphate. Below, I shall deal with personalities who were active subsequently, until the Crusaders' conquest. One should remember that in this field of the demographic portrait of the population, we are almost entirely dependant on Arab sources, while the attention which these sources paid to the dhimmīs was negligible. This fact lends singular significance to those scraps of information which have somehow reached us through the medium of these sources. Thus, for instance, we find in Ibn 'Asākir the

foundation, for the documents stop two generations earlier. Cf. also Lewis, *PEQ*, 80(1948), 115f, who also points out that the distress of the inhabitants became acute after the year 700 and conditions became unbearable, partly due to the general political situation and partly because of the worsening attitude to the dhimmīs, and the Negev became a wasteland. The Karaite commentator Yefet b. 'Alī expresses awareness of the fact that there was great destruction in Palestine and that there were places which remained uninhabited while there were other places to which people returned and settled. See his interpretation of Is., 61:4 (And they shall build the old wastes, etc.), Ms. Paris 287, fol. 2a: 'the places which were completely destroyed so that no memory of them remains, like Samaria . . . and the second pair are the places which have been destroyed and ruined, but despite this there are guards and people living there, such as Hebron and others').

information about the Jew Yaḥyā b. Irmiyā (that is, 'the son of Jeremiah') who in the days of Hārūn al-Rashīd (when Ibrāhīm b. Muḥammad al-Mahdī was governor of Damascus, in about 800) joined two of the partisans of the Umayyads and together they practised highway robbery. From the account of their adventures and capture, it would appear as if this was a kind of resistance movement against the Abbasids, and I shall describe the matter in greater detail below. Of particular interest is the passage which states that Yaḥyā was 'from the Jews living in the Balqā'' (*min yahūd al-balqā'*) and so we learn that at that time, there was still a Jewish population in southern Trans-Jordan. With even greater justification, we can assume that there were relatively large Jewish communities in places less distant from the centres of government, in the cities of Ramla, Tiberias, Tyre, Acre, Haifa, Ascalon, Gaza, Hebron, Rafiaḥ and Eilat; the Jewish community of Jerusalem is a subject on its own. As to the rural population, in the main it was still Christian on the eve of the Crusaders' conquest, and here we have the explicit evidence of the distinguished Andalusian writer Ibn al-'Arabī, who is Abū Bakr Muḥammad b. 'Abdallah al-Ma'āfirī al-Ishbīlī (man of Seville), who stayed in Jerusalem in the years 1093–1095, and who states very clearly that: '. . . the country is theirs [the Christians'] because it is they who work its soil, nurture its monasteries and maintain its churches'.[41]

[277–279] Jerusalem was certainly inhabited mainly by Christians during the entire period. We have the specific evidence of the Jerusalemite Shams al-Dīn al-Muqaddasī, writing at the end of the tenth century, the outset of Fatimid rule in Palestine, that there were few learned Muslim religious personalities (*'ulamā'*) in Jerusalem. According to him, most of the inhabitants of the city were Christians and Jews.[42] The strength of the Christians in Jerusalem is also borne out by the events occurring during the first two generations of the Fatimid reign, when the Christians (mostly but not only the Jerusalemites) collaborated with the Bedouin in their struggle against the Fatimids and indirectly against the Jews as well, as Karaite sources indicate. At the beginning of the eleventh century Samuel b. Isaac ha-Sefaradi (the Spaniard) writes from Jerusalem, apparently, to Shemaria b. Elḥanan, leader of the 'Babylonians' in Fustat (the letter was

[41] The number of mosques: Iṣṭakhrī, 58; cf. Mez, 388; Yaḥyā b. Irmiyā: Ibn 'Asākir, II, 267, see Ibn al-'Arabī, *Riḥla*, 81: *al-bilād lahum ya'kurūna ḍiyā'ahum wa-yaltazimūna adyārahā wa-yu'ammirūna kanā'isahā*. According to Prawer, *Ha-ṣalvānīm*, I, 129, most of the inhabitants of Palestine on the eve of the Crusaders' conquest were Muslims; but he does not indicate his sources. The information concerning the extent of the Muslim population in Palestine during the Crusaders' period is not unequivocal, and at any rate one cannot learn from it about the period under discussion. See on this question the article by Cahen, *Syria*, 15:351, 1934, and especially pp. 356f.

[42] Muqaddasī, *Āqālīm*, 167; copied from him by Yāqūt, *Buldān*, IV, 596.

written before 1011, the year of Shemaria's death). In the letter he describes the affairs of a proselyte who abandoned Christianity and fled from his home in Damascus in order to be among Jews. He came from a notable family and influential Christians were trying to persuade him to return to his former faith, but even an offer of money did not entice him to return to Christianity. Samuel b. Isaac found this proselyte in Jerusalem together with Jewish pilgrims from Damascus, and was told by him that he wished to leave Jerusalem and go to Fustat, for in Jerusalem the Christians were persecuting him: 'the *'arēlīm* [the uncircumcised] curse him again and again all the time'. Their influence is considerable, because they have 'most of the secretaries governing the lands' (that is: many government officials].[43] Studying the sources of the period, one is inevitably impressed by the considerable proportion of Christians in the population. Cahen notes that at the end of the eleventh century there was evidently numeric equality between Christians and Muslims in Palestine and Syria. One must bear in mind that this eminent scholar was not familiar with Jewish sources, particularly the Geniza documents, for he would then have been impressed by the number of Jews as well.[44]

[280] As to the Muslims in Jerusalem, from the little we know, these were mostly religious personalities or people who came to gather in the shadow of the Ṣakhra in the belief that the place had a holy character; it appears that most of them were immigrants from distant lands. Shams al-Dīn al-Muqaddasī himself states that his mother's family (his *akhwāl*) came from Biyār in the region of Qūmis, and he points out that quite a number of the Muslims from Qūmis living in Jerusalem came from Biyār. (It is interesting that at about the same time, the beginning of the tenth century, a central figure from among the Karaites arrived in Jerusalem from Qūmis, Daniel al-Qūmisī.) Further on, we shall encounter many Muslim personalities who lived in Jerusalem who were immigrants from various parts of the Muslim world.[45]

[281] Nāṣir Khusraw points out that many Muslims came to Jerusalem because they could not reach Mecca. According to him, more than 20,000 men assembled (that is, in Dhū'l-ḥijja) in Jerusalem, but one cannot ascertain whether he meant the number of pilgrims or all the Muslims then

[43] See ULC Or 1080 J 115, printed by Golb, *Sefunot*, 8 (1963/4), 88ff.

[44] Cahen, *Past and Present*, 6(1954), 6f.

[45] Muqaddasī, *Āqālīm*, 357; on Biyār, which is Biyār Jumand, see Le Strange, *Lands*, 366; Muqaddasī himself, *ibid.* 356f, describes the place: a small town, which has no major mosque (*jāmi'*) and its people make their living from plantations and raising sheep and camels; the place is to the south-east of the Caspian Sea, on the edge of the great desert (see Maps V and VIII in Le Strange, *ibid.*, opposite pp. 185, 335). Also the old Muslim who deprived the Shuway' family of their house in Jerusalem (see above), was an immigrant, as can be seen from his name – al-Shāmī – probably from Syria.

found in the city (Nāṣir Khusraw stayed in Jerusalem in the spring of 1046).[46]

[282] We have some information on the population of Ramla, which was founded by the Muslims, as mentioned above, and incorporated the inhabitants of Lod. Authentic written evidence of the Muslim part of the population of Ramla is the dedicatory inscription (*waqf*) of an inn (*funduq*), from the year 913. We can presume that there were also Christian inhabitants in Ramla, the outcome of the transfer of Christians from Lod to the new city. The only remaining written evidence (as far as we know) of the existence of Christians in Ramla is a funerary inscription of a certain Jabūr, dated 14 April 943. According to Ya'qūbī (writing in around 890) tribesmen and non-Arabs were living in Ramla side by side (*akhlāṭ min al-nās min al-'arab wa'l-'ajam*), and he adds that the dhimmīs there were Samaritans (*wa-dhimmatuhā sāmira*). This addition is undoubtedly distorted, for we are well aware that many Jews lived in Ramla and there were certainly also Christians there, but it seems that Ya'qūbī, after the opening sentence, had a list of what he calls *'ajam*, and from this list, only the word Samaritans remains, and this was at the end of the list.[47]

[283] Later on we shall see that Ramla is frequently mentioned in the Geniza documents. For the time being, it will suffice to point to the fact that as it was on the highway to Jerusalem it served as an assembly point for pilgrims. Apparently the Jewish population of Ramla was greater than that of Jerusalem, and some of the heads of the Jerusalem yeshiva built themselves houses in Ramla, and visited the city frequently. Solomon b. Judah stayed there at the beginning of the winter of 1040, and as he had no house of his own in Ramla, he stayed with a Jew of Ramla, whose daughter was an abandoned wife (*'agūnā*). He states that he could no longer bear her weeping and complaints and therefore decided to cut short

46 Nāṣir Khusraw, 20 (text), 66 (translation).

47 See the *waqf* inscription in Ramla: Sharon, *Arabica*, 13:77, 1966. The funerary inscription: Sharon, *Shalem*, 1:1, 1974, and a comprehensive discussion therein, in which he explains that *al-sabt al-kabīr*, the great sabbath, was among the Eastern Christians the sabbath before Easter; this fact and the fact that the inscription is in Arabic script exclude the possibility of its being a Jewish inscription. See an extended version of his discussion: Sharon, *Arabic and Islamic Studies* (Bar Ilan), 2:31, 1978; Ya'qūbī, *Buldān*, 328; cf. Ashtor, *AESC*, 27(1972), 188; contrary to his opinion, the meaning of *'ajam* here is not Persians, though it frequently does mean this, but the initial meaning of this root is: non-Arab, see for instance: Ibn al-Athīr, *Jāmi'*, III, 354; Ibn 'Asākir, VI, 185; Ṭabarī, *Ta'rīkh*, I, 2374f; Muqaddasī, *Bad'*, V, 33. Apart from this, one should note that Ya'qūbī himself, when he wishes to speak of Persians in Palestine, uses the word Persians (*al-furs*). See for instance what he writes about Iṭrābulus and Jubayl, *ibid.*, 327; see what he writes about Nābulus, *ibid.*, 328f; 'wa-bihā akhlāt min al-'arab wa'l-'ajam wa'l-sāmira' ('they live there side by side – the tribesmen, the non-Arabs and the Samaritans'); also here, as in reference to Ramla, words have been deleted from the list after the expression *'ajam*. On the other hand, see what he says on Egypt, *ibid.*, 340: *wa-'ajam miṣr jamī'uhā al-qibṭ*, all the *'ajam* of Egypt are Copts, which shows that here he is using the word to mean Christians.

his visit to the city. In another letter, Solomon b. Judah mentions Solomon b. Ṣemaḥ al-ʻAṭṭār ('the perfume dealer') who would render services to every learned man who came to Ramla. In the middle of the eleventh century, the influential Jewish physician Abraham ha-Kohen b. Isaac b. Furāt lived in Ramla. He was a man of considerable influence with the authorities, who shall be spoken of further. In about 1035, Abraham b. Samuel 'the third', asks Abraham ha-Kohen to use his influence to rid the area around the synagogue of Abū ʻAlī b. Ayyūb (perhaps a Muslim, if one is to judge by the name Ayyūb, which was very rare among Jews), who built himself a little house near the *miqwē*, the ritual bath-house, and an upper story opposite the entrance hall of the synagogue, and was growing vegetables on the plot of a ruined house which belonged to the synagogue. Abraham is asked to try to persuade him at first in a gentle manner, and to get him to demolish the buildings that were set up illegally. There were three Jewish communities in Ramla: the Jerusalemites, the Babylonians and the Karaites. From the expression *al-kanīsa al-wusṭā*, the synagogue in the middle, one learns that in the eleventh century there were three synagogues. As one can deduce from the documents, it was customary to state in a deed: 'Ramla, the city near Lod', a reminder of the days when Lod was the major centre and Ramla insignificant. In a letter written in February 1039 by Nathan b. Abraham, Solomon b. Judah's rival, it is mentioned that some 400 people gathered in the main hall in Ramla on Purim – more than that in the *qāʻa* (entrance hall) – among them some 200 Karaites. From this we may learn that there were approximately a thousand Jewish families, that is about 5,000 souls, of whom 20 per cent were Karaites.[48]

[284] Tiberias was the capital of jund Urdunn, as we have seen, and it appears that in the eleventh century it was still the centre of northern

[48] Letters of Solomon b. Judah see: **130**, lines 7–11; **159**, lines 20–21; from this letter as well it appears that the Gaon used to stay in Ramla for a long time. The letter of Abraham b. Samuel: **228**; it is possible that the ruined house he mentions was the result of the earthquake in 1033; see Goitein, *Mediterranean Society*, II, 155; 552, n. 31 – he emphasises that one cannot learn from this letter that the ritual bath (*miqwē*) was actually attached to the building of the synagogue, and points out that in Egypt there is no hint of a *miqwē* before 1200; but see document No. 11 (TS Ar, Box 44, f. 223), a, line 19, from the year 1139, in Gil, *Documents*, in which the *mīḍah*, *mikwē*, is referred to. The synagogue in the middle: **306**, lines 25–26. Ramla near Lod: apart from the documents in my collection, see: TS AS 151.47, a very faded fragment of a deed, dated 'the first year of the week (i.e. of the sabbatical cycle of seven years) in the year four thousand and seven hundred and seventy and five years of the creation of the world (1014/5) . . . in Ramla the city near Lod'. One can discern the signature of Solomon ha-Kohen b. Joseph (?). The letter of Nathan b. Abraham: **183**, lines 15ff. See Dropsie 364 II, a fragment of a marriage deed from Ramla printed in: Friedman, *Marriage*, II, 359; Abraham b. Ṣedaqa (his name is found in **425**, line 19; 1065), marries the daughter of Pinḥas b. Levi (the name of the bride has not been preserved) in the sixth year of the sabbatical cycle and this can be 1062 or 1069. TS 12.480 (Friedman, *ibid.*, 362), also a fragment of a marriage deed; the name of the groom: Menaḥem ha-Kohen b. Isaiah; here too Abraham b. Ṣedaqa signed, and others: Mevorakh

Palestine and the northern coastal cities of Acre and Tyre (and evidently also Sidon, and Tripoli – Iṭrābulus) were subordinate to it. With regard to its Jewish population, we know that Tiberias was the major Jewish city and site of the Sanhedrin. The yeshiva of Palestine, which was the direct outgrowth of the Sanhedrin, still remained in Tiberias after the Muslim conquest for many generations. Despite many political and military vicissitudes, it seems that Tiberias remained a Jewish city to a large extent, even as late as the eleventh century AD, when we find some references to the city in the Geniza documents. Bishop Willibald, who visited Tiberias in 723, found 'many churches and a Jewish synagogue' there. Michael the Syrian, on the other hand, speaks of thirty synagogues which were destroyed in the earthquake in Tiberias (in 748). Some eighty years later, in about 810, we find details in a Christian source: the city is the seat of the bishop (Theodoros at the time), and has a monastery for virgins as well as five churches. As to the Muslims, we have seen above that Tiberias became a centre for the Urdunn tribes and that Ya'qūbī mentioned particularly the Banū Ash'ar. Muqaddasī mentions favourably its *jāmi'*, the principal mosque, which unlike mosques in other cities has its courtyard covered in gravel. Nāṣir Khusraw (1047) mentions another mosque in the western part of Tiberias, the 'Jasmin mosque', because of the jasmin growing there. Brief evidence in Mas'ūdī mentions the fact that the descendants of converts to Islam, *mawālī* of the Umayyads from the days of the caliph 'Uthmān, lived in Tiberias. When he visited Tiberias in AH 324, or AD 936, he saw a book they kept, containing the annals of the Umayyads as well as their *faḍā'il* (praises). One can surmise that these *mawālī* were descendants of Christians.[49]

[285] As to the Jews of Tiberias, there seem to have been two communities, one of Jerusalemites and the other of Babylonians, and this can be deduced from the flowery language of entreaty in one of the letters in the Geniza: 'to the holy communities who sit in Hammath and Rakkath' (the

ha-Kohen b. Joseph; 'Eli ha-Levi b. Aaron; Azhar ha-Levi (b.) Shabbāt; Manṣūr ha-Levi b. Solomon; Khalaf b. Manṣūr; Moses b. 'Amram.

49 Willibald, see: Tobler, *Descriptiones*; the translation in *Sefer ha-yishuv*, II, 10, is not correct; and see *De Casis Dei*, in Tobler et Molinier, I, 304; the *jāmi'*: Muqaddasī, *Āqālīm*, 161, 182. Muqaddasī mentions there the unbearable heat in the city; they say of the people of Tiberias, he writes, that 'for two months they dance, for two months they nibble, for two months they bang, for two months they go about naked, for two months they blow on canes, for two months they sink; that is, they dance because of the fleas, nibble on the fruit of the jujube, they bang on pans to chase away the wasps from the meat and the fruit, they go naked because of the burning heat, suck on sugar cane, and sink in mud'. Michael the Syrian, see above, sec. 103, n. 15. See further fragments from Muslim writers describing Tiberias: Le Strange, *Palestine*, 341ff; Nāṣir Khusraw, 17 (text), 56 (translation). Mez, 324, finds in these jasmin bushes remnants of the worship of Baal, which seems an exaggeration. The fact that Tiberias was a centre of non-Muslim population is reflected in a ḥadīth according to which it is one of the four cities of hell (*madā'in al-nār*) together with

latter according to Joshua, xix:35, undoubtedly a by-name for Tiberias), and also from the language of a letter from Nathan ha-Kohen he-ḥāvēr b. Isaiah, of Tiberias: (receive . . .) 'much peace . . . from the two parties living in Tiberias'. However we also find the singular: 'To the great holy community in Tiberias' (using the ancient form, Ṭiberiā, Ṭiberia, which was common at that time), in a responsum of a gaon which was sent to Tiberias, perhaps the Palestinian Gaon addressed 'his' community, that is the Jerusalemites, in the singular. A relatively ancient document (probably from the end of the tenth century AD) being a deed of attorney concerning property in Tiberias, from the son of a deceased to the father's partner, Moses b. Samuel b. Sahl – contains among the signatures of the witnesses a number of uncommon names which are of typical Palestinian heritage, such as: Ḥashmanai, Pashshāṭ, Makhīr. Some deeds deal with transactions in estates in Tiberias. A very old and important document is the copy of a deed drawn up in Tiberias in the year AH 328 (AD 939/40). According to the fragment which has been preserved, one can see that the copy was made from a deed of the sale of estates and fields, etc., drawn up in the presence of a cadi. The copy was requested by R. Elḥanan, apparently Elḥanan b. Shemaria, and if this is the case, it should be dated about 1020. The seller is Hillel b. Nissim and the purchaser is Benjamin. In the original deed (written in Arabic script) there were the signatures of six Muslim witnesses. The copy was brought to Fustat by 'Joshua ha-Kohen *ha-mumḥē* (specialist in law) b. Ya'īr he-ḥāvēr', and from this we learn that the judge, the local *ḥavēr*, in Tiberias in around the year 1000, was called Ya'īr ha-Kohen. Another signature was that of Abraham b. Salmān, the scribe, evidently. In 1023 Musāfir b. Yish'ī b. Isrā'īl bought a shop in the western row of the Jewish market (*al-ṣaff al-gharbī min sūq al-yahūd*) in Tiberias for the orphan (*al-ṭifl al-yahūdī*) Mūsā b. Hiba (Moses b. Nathan) b. Salmūn. In another document, a deathbed will of Khalaf b. Yeshū'ā of 30 August 1034, it appears that the testator was the owner of a large compound (*ḥaṣēr*) in Tiberias, in the market called *suwayqat* (little market of) *al-. . .ḍa* (perhaps *al-rawḍa*, the garden).[50]

[286] Tiberias was also a centre of Jewish spiritual life during the period

Constantinople, Antioch and Ṣan'ā, see Suyūṭī, *La'ālī*, I, 459; 'Ajlūnī, I, 450; on the *mawālī* see Mas'ūdī, *Tanbīh*, 336.

50 Hammath and Rakkath are vocalised with upper punctuation, see: ENA 223, f. 1, lines 18–19, printed by Mann, *Jews*, II, 60f. The letter of Nathan ha-Kohen, **263**, lines 6–7. The responsum: Mosseri VIII 421 (R19), printed by Assaf, *Mi-sifrut ha-ge'ōnim*, 92ff; the query, dated approximately 1000, whose main content is brought at the end of the responsum, dealt with matters of the inheritance of Nu'mān ha-melammēd (the teacher) b. Abū Naṣr; mentioned are Maymūn b. Ḥasan, who was the uncle of the deceased, the brother of his father Abū Naṣr; Ḥassān b. Manasseh, a relative of the deceased on his mother's side (son of her sister) and another man named Yaḥyā, who brought with him a letter, apparently from the head of the community, the local ḥāvēr; the Gaon recognises the father's side of

under discussion. Mas'ūdī mentions that he personally knew Abū Kathīr Yaḥyā b. Zakariyyā', 'the Tiberian scribe' (*al-kātib al-ṭabarānī*); scribe in the sense of a book copyist. According to him, the latter was one of the Jews who translated the Bible into Arabic, and Sa'īd b. Ya'qūb al-Fayyūmī (should be b. Yūsuf that is, Saadia Gaon) learned from him. Hence we find that Saadia Gaon stayed in Tiberias on his way from Egypt to Babylonia, and possibly that his stay there lasted ten years (evidently from *ca.* 910). Yaḥyā b. Zakariyyā' died according to Mas'ūdī in the twenties of the fourth century of the hijra, that is, after 932. Pinsker, and after him Steinschneider, tried to identify Yaḥyā ibn Zakariyyā', the sage of Tiberias mentioned by Mas'ūdī, with Judah b. 'Allān of Tiberias mentioned by Judah Hadāsī in *Eshkōl ha-kofer*: 'We also found in Judah b. 'Allān of Tiberias, my learned man', and so on, and elsewhere he mentions: 'the grammarian of Tiberias, in his book *Me'ōr 'eynayim*' ('light of the eyes'). On the basis of his use of the phrase 'my learned man', which is one of the favourite expressions of Judah Hadāsī, one can see that he considered him a Karaite, though this is not proven in any way. Levi b. Yefet ha-Levi mentioned 'the *pitrōn* [commentary] of our Lord and Master Judah b. 'Allān the Tiberian, head of the Jerusalem yeshiva, may God have mercy on him'. Pinsker points out in his *Liqqūṭē qadm.* that he found in an ancient Karaite prayer-book (written in around 1300), a dirge by Judah b. 'Allān. Undoubtedly similar, though not identical, are the words of David Qimḥī, who mentions the quire of 'Alī b. Judah [that is, not Judah b. 'Alī-'Allān] the ascetic (*ha-nāzīr*), in which he says the people of Maaziah, which is Tiberias, pronounced the *r* and the double *r* differently from one another. One can see that we are dealing here with very obscure sources and it is difficult to decide either way. We have no information about a

the family's right to inherit and negates the mother's side. Assaf read the names of the people involved a little differently; on p. 93, line 24, one should read: *ke-daḥwān* (like a table, cf. Abramson, *Ba-merkazim*, 162). The form Ṭīberia can be found on deeds, see, for example, the marriage deed of Nā'ima daughter of Moses the cantor b. Ḥusayn al-Dulūkī, of Thursday, 12 Nisan AM 4795, 22 May AD 1035, wedding Isaac b. Abraham: 'in the city of Ṭīberia Colonia' (written *qlwny*), **246**, line 3. Of the existence of Babylonians in Tiberias one can perhaps learn from a deed of attorney written in Malīj in Egypt in 1047, concerning a deposit belonging to the Tiberian woman Rayyisa, daughter of Manṣūr, and bearing the signature of the central figure of the Babylonian community in Fustat, Sahlān b. Abraham; see TS 24.73, printed by Assaf, *Yerushalayim*, 1952/3, 115f: Rayyisa gives her brother, Asad b. Manṣūr, a power-of-attorney to go to Fustat and there receive her dowry which was deposited by her uncle, Joseph b. Asad al-Ṭabarānī, with Ḥesed al-Tustarī. Cf. Gil, *ha-Tustarīm*, 35. The deed of attorney: **12**, probably written in Fustat, see Friedman, *Ribbūy nāshīm*, 195f. The fragment of the copy of the deed: **244**. The shop in the Jewish market: **245**. Muqaddasī, *Āqālīm*, 161, notes that the market in Tiberias covered the area between two streets (*wa-sūquhā min al-darb ilā'l-darb*). If we combine the two shreds of information, we can imagine that the market (perhaps the 'Jewish market') continued parallel to the Sea of Galilee between two parallel streets, and the shop which Musāfir purchased was on the side of the street farther from the sea. The testament of Khalaf: **253**.

head of the Jerusalem yeshiva by this name, nor have we information about a Karaite community in Tiberias. Allony returns to the subject again and proves that the *Me'ōr 'eynayim* of the 'Tiberian grammarian' cannot be the same as the *Ōr 'eynayim* mentioned by Abraham ibn Ezra in the introduction to his commentary on the Pentateuch. Allony , like his predecessors, did not stress the fact that actually no ancient source referred to either of the two books as being the work of Judah b. 'Allān. He quoted additional sources in which the names Judah *ha-nāzīr* b. 'Alī and Judah b. 'Allān are mentioned. Also, he printed a page from a treatise on the foundations of Hebrew, found in the Geniza, which he ascribed to 'Alī b. Judah *ha-nāzīr*,[51] and appended a detailed study on the linguistic issues included there. At any rate, it seems that that treatise was written by a man of Tiberias, for a passage refers to his sitting in the squares of Tiberias and listening to the speech of its inhabitants. As to the identity of Mas'ūdī's Yaḥyā ibn Zakariyyā', however, we are still in the dark. It should be added that Mas'ūdī's remarks were made in the context of a short survey on translations of the Bible, in which he praised the translation by Ḥunayn ibn Isḥāq.[52]

[287] Among the group of ancient Palestinian poets: Yose b. Yose, Yannai, Eleazar ha-Kallir, Yehōshū'ā, and Pinḥās, the latter (from Kifrā near Tiberias) was a man of Tiberias living in the Muslim period, in the eighth century. This we learn from his acrostic, and from the poem he wrote about the fast of the earthquake of the sabbatical year, meaning, as we have seen above, the earthquake of the year 748. His full name was Pinḥās ha-Kohen b. Jacob, and he is not to be confused with Pinḥās, head

51 TS Arabic Box 32, f.17.

52 Mas'ūdī, *Tanbīh*, 112f. He defines Yaḥyā ibn Zakariyyā' and Sa'īd (Saadia) – as *Ashma'athīs*, of course meaning: Rabbanites (the expression is also used in other Arab sources). The origin of the expression is evidently Babylonian-Aramaic, *ashma'ta* – 'on a tradition', that is, in the sense of oral law. See: Vajda, *BIRHT*, 15(1969), 144. Abu Kathīr al-Ṭabarānī is mentioned (apparently following Mas'ūdī) also in Ibn Ḥazm, *Milal*, III, 171, who places him among the Jewish *mutakallimūn*; cf. Friedländer, *JQR*, NS 1(1910/1), 187; see Hadāsī, *Eshkol*, 98c (No. 257); 69b (No. 173). He mentions the book *Me'īrat 'eynayim* also on fol. 63b.; Levi b. Yefet, in Pinsker, *Liqqūṭē qadmōniyōt*, II, 64; the prayer-book, *ibid.*, 139. The idea of the identity with Abū Kathīr Yaḥyā ibn Zakariyyā', *ibid.*, I, 5. And see David Qimḥi, *Sefer Mikhlōl* (Lyck 5602/1842), 81b; on the matter of 'Alī b. Judah ha-nāzīr see: Dukes, *Quntrēs*, 1f, n. 1; Geiger, *Qevūṣat ma'amārīm*, 232f, suggested identifying him with Judah b. 'Allān, and assumed that the book ascribed to him, *Me'ōr 'eynayim*, is identical with *Ōr 'eynayim* mentioned by Abraham ibn Ezra. See the editor's note (Poznanski) *ibid.*, 233 (n. 2), who denies this and points out that the book *Ōr 'eynayim* was written by Meir of Kastoria, a pupil of Tobias b. Eleazar (author of *Leqaḥ ṭōv*), and that the whole matter of the book *Me'ōr 'eynayim* is a sort of puzzle, if it actually existed, and if it did, whether its author was a Karaite as Judah Hadāsī claims. See Steinschneider, *JQR*, 13(1900/1), 315. Harkavy, *Zikkārōn*, V, 115, denies that Judah b. 'Allān was a Karaite. See Allony, *Leshonenu*, 34(1969/70), 175f, and see also Alder, *Alei Sefer*, 12(1986), 59ff, who denies the assumption of Allony concerning the Geniza fragment which he edited.

of the yeshiva mentioned in *Seder 'ōlām zūṭā*, for the latter was not a kohen.[53]

[288] Tiberias was also the centre of the masoretes and vocalisers and it was here that the masorah and vocalisation were finally formulated. There is a list of ancient masoretes and vocalisers whose centre was Tiberias, which is to be found in the manuscripts of the *diqdūqē ha-ṭe'āmīm* by Aaron b. Moses b. Asher – manuscripts that were kept by the Karaites in Crimea (Tshufutkaleh) and whose parallels were found in the Geniza. On the basis of these sources, Mann reconstructed the following list of masoretes from Tiberias: (1) Rīqāṭ and Ṣemaḥ b. Abī Shayba, who lived at the end of the eighth century; (2) Abraham b. Rīqāṭ, Abraham b. Furāt, Pinḥās the head of the yeshiva, and Aḥiyahū ha-Kohen ('the *ḥavēr* from the city of Maaziah' that is, Tiberias, who is perhaps the same as Abū'l-'Ūmayṭar in a parallel version); Ḥavīv b. Pīpīm (the Greek name Pippinos); Asher b. Nehemiah; Moses Mūḥā; Moses of Gaza; Ṣemaḥ ibn al-Ṣiyāra (who is Ṣemaḥ Abū Slūṭūm), who lived in approximately the first quarter of the ninth century; (3) Nehemiah b. Asher (*ca.* 825–850); (4) Asher b. Nehemiah *ca.* 850–875); (5) Moses b. Asher (*ca.* 875–900); (6) Aaron b. Moses (*ca.* 900–925).[54]

[289–290] Another source of names of masoretes is the dedicatory colophon in the famous *keter aram-ṣōvā* (the Bible codex of Aleppo). This colophon was first copied by Jacob Zeev for Jacob Saphir, who printed this copy in his book *Even Saphir*. It is noted there that this book of the Bible is dedicated to the congregation of the Rabbanites in Jerusalem; and further that it was ransomed from the spoils of Jerusalem (that is, from the Crusaders) and given to the synagogue 'of the Jerusalemites' in Fustat. Another note mentions that the copyist was Solomon b. Būyā'ā, and that

[53] See: Saadia Gaon in the introduction to the *Agron*, ed. Allony, text, 154, translation, 69f: *al-shu'arā' al-awwalīn* (the ancient poets): Yose b. Yose, Yannai, Eleazar, Yehōshū'a, and Pinḥas; and see the editor's introduction, 79, and n. 315; Qirqisānī, 609, mentions three of them, Yannai, Eleazar, and Pinḥas. See also: Zulay, *Yerushalayim*, 1952/3, 51; cf. Fleischer, *Sinai*, 61(1966/7), 31ff, who finds support for the opinion of the relatively late date of Pinḥas (the Muslim period) in the expressions: 'Qēdār and Edom'; 'Ishmaelites and Edomites'; *idem*, *Sefer Ṭevērya*, 368ff.

[54] See Mann, *Jews*, II, 43ff, and there details also on earlier studies. See: Bodl MS Heb, Cat. 2862, e 74, f. 59, in Mann *ibid.* on p. 43; it is to be noted that the MS. has Abraham Rīqāṭ (and not b. Rīqāṭ) and further: 'and Rīqāṭ his father before him' (in Mann's version the words 'his father' are omitted). BM Or 5554A, f. 29v. Here one has to correct the reading of Mann, *ibid.*, 44, line 4 – *w'ḥyyhw*, read: *w'ḥyhw*; line 12 – *'khtyfw*, read: *'khtlfw* (and n. 1 in Mann, *ibid.*, is superfluous); line 13 – *wthlthyn*, read *wthlthh*; lines 15–16 – the word *alladhī* at the beginning should be deleted and the meaning will be: 'as to this rule which I am discussing, what I say about them is that they read', etc.; also there is no need to read *qur'ān* instead of *qānūn* as suggested by Mann. As to Abū'l-'Umyṭar, see Ibn al-Athīr, *Kāmil*, VI, 249; this was the by-name of the 'Sufyānī' 'Alī b. 'Abdallah, leader of the revolt in 811 in Damascus; it may have been written in the original text that this Aḥiyahū ha-Kohen lived at the time of the revolt.

its vocaliser and masorete was Aaron b. Asher, and that the book was dedicated to Jerusalem by a man of Baṣra, Israel b. Simḥa b. Saadia b. Ephraim, and deposited with the (Karaite) *nesī'īm* Josiah and Hezekiah, the sons of David b. Boaz (here there was an error in copying and Jacob Saphir noticed it). It was to be taken out for the meetings (*majālis* of the Karaites, their houses of prayer, which Jacob Saphir did not understand, and this shall be discussed below) and the Karaite communities on Passover, Shavuoth and Succoth in Jerusalem, and the Rabbanites should also be permitted to read it. Jacob Saphir mentions that he was assisted by Abraham Firkovitch, who examined the colophons for him when he visited Aleppo, but in general he did not accept his corrections, for he wrote 'b. Yeruḥam' instead of 'b. Būyā'ā'. Saphir believed that this was done because he wanted to get closer to Salmon b. Yeruḥim, the Karaite writer. Harkavy, who visited Aleppo in 1886, examined the colophon, reprinted it, and arrived at the conclusion that what was said there about Aaron b. Asher was a forgery and a later addition of the Karaites. Kahle mentions another dedicatory colophon in the same Bible: '*qodesh* before God; for Israel, the Rabbanites who dwell in the Holy City. Not to be sold nor redeemed for ever and eternity'. This colophon had also been copied by Joseph Saphir (although Kahle brings it from another source). In Kahle's opinion, the inscription indicates that this Bible was firstly in the hands of the Rabbanites in Jerusalem and only afterwards, somewhat before the middle of the eleventh century, did they sell it to Israel b. Simḥa of Baṣra, who dedicated it to the Karaites. The permission given to the Rabbanites to examine it was apparently one of the conditions on which it was sold. A leaf with a copy of the colophon from Aleppo was found by Gottheil in a manuscript of the Bible in the Karaite synagogue in Jerusalem. He recognised that this was a copy in modern script, but he could not make out what that copy was. Undoubtedly what Gottheil found was a page of the copy which Firkowitch prepared for Jacob Saphir, in which b. Yeruḥam is written instead of b. Būyā'ā (as noted by Jacob Saphir), that is, it is the correction made by Firkowitch. Gottheil believed that that Bible had been dedicated to the Karaite synagogue in Fustat, when in fact it was first dedicated, as we have seen, to the Karaites in Jerusalem, and from there, after it was in the hands of the Crusaders, it reached the synagogue 'of the Jerusalemites' (Rabbanites) in Fustat.[55] As to Solomon ha-Levi b. Būyā'ā,

[55] See *Even Saphir*, I, 12aff (read *iftikāk* instead of *iftikāq*); *kanīsat Yerūshālayim* is the synagogue 'of the Palestinians' in Fustat (to be discussed below), the synagogue in which the Geniza was kept; see especially notes 2 on fol. 12b and 5, on fol. 13a. See Harkavy, *Ḥadāshīm* (reprint) 104ff; Kahle, *Masoreten des Westens*, I, 9. What Baron writes (*SRHJ*, VI, 447, n. 16) that the Rabbanites (in Jerusalem) on no account called themselves *Israel ha-rabbānīm* except when they wished to make a distinction between the Karaites and themselves, is erroneous; as can be proven from many Geniza documents, they commonly

he is also mentioned in other manuscripts of the Bible which were in the hands of the Karaites in Tshufutkaleh. He was a pupil of Sa'īd b. Farjaway, nicknamed Balqūq (= Abū'l-Qūq), and evidently both were Tiberians and lived at the end of the ninth century and the beginning of the tenth. Ephraim b. Būyā'ā is also mentioned, and was apparently the brother of Solomon.[56]

[291] As we know, the Palestinian Tiberias school differed from that of the Babylonians, both in their versions of the Bible and in their pronunciation, and evidence of this can be found in the account of Qirqisānī, who cites examples of these differences. The Karaites saw in this a proof of weakness on the part of the Rabbanites, as the latter were also divided amongst themselves concerning vocalisation, which they did not view as having been ancient but rather as something decided by the scribes, whereas the Karaites believed that the Bible had been vocalised from the outset.[57]

[292–293] Nevertheless, we find an anonymous Karaite writer, evidently a Palestinian, speaking in praise of the learned men of Tiberias who had determined the correct manner of reading, which is the Palestinian ('the reading of al-Shām'). He writes this in a commentary to Genesis, xlix:21 (Naphtali is a hind let loose: he giveth goodly words), and he mentions Ben Asher and Ben Naphtali, who formulated this manner of reading, and notes that this is the good Tiberian trait. It is not clear whether he wished to imply that the creators of this correct reading were Karaites. If he thought so, it is likely that he would have said so.[58] The good accent of Tiberias is mentioned in a number of places in the Middle Ages. Jonah ibn Janāḥ's *S. ha-riqmā*, for example, states that the people of Tiberias are the most distinct (*afṣaḥ*) in their Hebrew, while the account attributed to Dūnash b. Tamīm, who quoted Isaac b. Solomon, who is Isaac Isrā'īlī, also speaks of the Tiberias accent: '... for there is in the language of the Hebrews of Tiberias the *ṭā'* (should be: the *ẓā'*) and the *ṣād*

referred to themselves as Rabbanites, and it suffices to see, for instance, what is written in **420**, b, line 30: 'we, the congregation of Rabbanites'. See: Gottheil, *JQR*, 17(1904/5), 650f. Gottheil was indeed led astray by Firkovitch's correction, and on p. 651 he notes that the manuscript was written by Salmon b. Yeruḥim! He also did not understand what synagogue in Fustat was being referred to (see *ibid.*, 651, and n. 3). See also: Ben-Zvi, *Sinai*, 43(1957/8), 11f, and there a new copy of the dedicatory inscriptions and also comments on Firkovitch's forgery (he does not mention Gottheil); the same in English: Ben-Zvi, *Textus*, 6(1960), 12ff.

56 On Sa'īd b. Farjaway and his pupil Solomon b. Būyā'ā and his brother Ephraim, see: Allony, *Textus*, 6:106, 1968, who discusses the Geniza fragment TS Arabic Box 35, f. 394, in which the name (fragmented) of Sa'īd b. Farjaway is found; see also in Allony, *ibid.* all the references to the sources.

57 Qirqisānī, I, 31, 135ff. Cf. Klar, *Meḥqārīm*, 294f, 320ff; see Hadāsī, *Eshkol*, 60b (written in 1148).

58 See MS Firkovitch, II, No. 4633, in Mann, *Texts*, II, 104f, and see *ibid.* the discussion on p. 69. See the scroll of Abiathar: **559**, c, lines 2–3.

(should be: *ḍād*) . . . and he would read *afṭānō* (instead of: *afdānō*. Dan., xi:45) . . .'[59]

[294] At this point, one must bring up the question discussed at length in research concerning the Ben Asher family, which is whether they belong to the Rabbanites or to the Karaites. The view that they were Karaites is based on the fact that the Karaites possessed most of the manuscripts of the Bible which have been preserved until the present day; manuscripts which have colophons whose masorah and vocalisation are attributed to Moses b. Asher and his son Aaron. There are instances in which Aaron is called 'Aaron *ha-melammēd*' (the teacher), particularly in the colophon in the Book of Prophets in Leningrad, in which 'the teacher Aaron b. Moses b. Meir b. Asher' is mentioned. Some saw in the by-name 'the teacher' something characteristic of the Karaites, as is the case in the use of the adjective *maskīl*. Another proof of his being a Karaite was seen in the heading on the title page of Saadia Gaon's *Essā Meshālī*: *al-radd 'alā ben Ashar 'ibrānī* ('the response to Ben Asher, in Hebrew'); as *Essā Meshālī* was written against the Karaites, it was assumed that Ben Asher was a Karaite. Further evidence of this can be seen in the poem of Moses ben Asher on 'Israel who are likened to a vine'. The most outstanding of the scholars who claimed that the Ben Asher family were Karaites were Graetz and Klar. More recently, A. Dotan concluded the discussion with evidence of Ben Asher belonging to the Rabbanites and that Saadia Gaon's opponent was not Aaron b. Asher but Abū'l-Ṭayyib Samuel b. Asher al-Jabalī, one of the leaders of the Karaites in Saadia Gaon's generation.

Another important fact is that we know nothing of the existence of a Karaite community in Tiberias at any time. The immigration of Karaites that evidently began in the second half of the ninth century was directed towards Jerusalem, as we shall see below. Also, it does not seem reasonable to assume that at a time when they were just beginning to arrive in Palestine, one would find an old and established school of Karaite learned linguists, grammarians and Masoretes in Tiberias.[60]

59 Jonah ibn Janāḥ, *Sefer ha-riqmā* (Derenbourg ed.), 29; cf. ed. Wilensky-Tenne, I, 39; see Dukes, *Qunṭrēs*, 73; in the list of books TS 10 K 20, f. 9, fol. 1b, lines 11–20, the *kitāb al-ẓā' wa'l-ḍād* is mentioned; see: Mann, *REJ*, 72(1921), 170; Vajda, *REJ*, 107(1946/7), 109f; and see also *Pitrōn Tōrā*, 343: 'Tiberias uses a clear language in the Torah more than anyone in the world, since they have a graceful speech, as blessed by Jacob their father', etc. See notes 91–93 of the editor and his introduction, p. 20. As to *afṭānō*, this is difficult to understand; he might have understood it as being similar to the word *faḍā'*, courtyard, empty space, and would read *afẓān* (because they did not differentiate between *ḍ* and *ẓ*). It is worth noting that the documents in my collection, **243–284** (Tiberias, Tyre, Tripoli), are almost all written in Hebrew.

60 See: Kahle, *Cairo Geniza*, 110, n. 2. An important colophon was copied by Jacob Saphir: 'I Moses b. Asher wrote this *maḥzōr* of the Bible according to the good hand of God on me, well explained, in the city of Maaziah, which is Tiberias, the renowned city . . . written at

[295] To this question of the Masoretes, one should add the subject of 'the book of Jericho', recalled by the Masoretes and which I have seen mentioned in some places as belonging to the Muslim era. It appears that the Masoretes knew this manuscript of the Bible which was brought from Jericho, but this cannot serve as evidence concerning its date, which cannot be known precisely, especially as we have no information on the Jewish population in Jericho during the period we are dealing with (apart from the Muslim tradition according to which some of the exiled Jews of Medina went to Palestine, namely to Jericho).[61]

[296] A sad affair revealed to us by the Geniza documents is that of the Jewish lepers living in Tiberias. There are seventeen documents dealing directly with this subject, apart from others which mention these lepers incidentally. Six out of the seventeen documents are in the hand-writing of the *ḥāvēr* Hillel b. Yeshūʿā the cantor al-Jūbarī, who was the judge and leader of the Jews of Tiberias in the thirties and forties of the eleventh century.

We find at first a letter of recommendation for the lepers' emissaries written by Hillel b. Yeshūʿā, leaving empty spaces for the names of the emissaries, which were still unknown to him. One can deduce from this that there may have been prepared forms for this purpose in the community of Tiberias, and that they would frequently send emissaries to obtain help for these ill-fated beings. From the *ʿalāma*: *yeshaʿ yuḥāsh*, one can deduce that the date of the letter is 1025, when Solomon ha-Kohen b. Joseph, whose *ʿalāma* it was, was head of the yeshiva. The lepers call themselves 'the tormented' (*ha-meyussārīm*) and add rhyming descriptions about their condition, such as: 'from boils there's no release, with eczema they decrease . . . some are deaf, some are blind, some lack a limb, and some are lame . . .' and the like. An unsigned letter (apart from the phrase 'your tormented brethren in the city of Tiberias') addressed to Samuel b. Ezra contains not only a description of the writer's personal distress caused by the illness but also details of the general suffering, particularly the gnawing pain of hunger: 'from great expense and terrible hunger and a pittance to live on'. These were more painful than the disease itself. In

the end of eight hundred and twenty seven years after the destruction of the second temple' (895) – this gives us clear evidence of the time of Moses b. Aaron. See *Even Saphir*, 14b, a version copied after him in many places. Read and printed anew by Gottheil, *JQR*, 17(1904/5), 639; *Essā meshālī* was edited by Lewin, *Saadia Memorial Volume*, 481 (MS Westminster College, Liturgica, vol. 3, fol. 40). The correct reading of the Arabic title was suggested by Klar, *Meḥqārīm*, 276ff; 'the poem of the grapevine', *ibid.* 310f; see the discussion there in the continuation. See: Dotan, *Ben Asher*, who has full details on the history of the argument and references; see his previous publications: *Sinai*, 41(1956/7): 280, 350; see also Zucker, *Tarbiz*, 28(1957/8): 61.

61 See: Ginsburg, *Introduction*, 433, 718; *idem, Massorah*, III, 135; Margoliouth, *Catalogue*, no. 179 (= Or 2696). See about the emigration of the Jews from Medina to Jericho: M. J. and

another letter, it is said that among the diseased there were 'heads of cities' (that is, people who had been community leaders in their home-towns) as well as 'family heads'. A building had been placed at their disposal in Tiberias, but it was demolished, evidently as a result of the Bedouin wars fought in that area in 1028–1029. The wars also led to the discontinuance of letters and the help they had formerly received from Egypt. With the victory of the Fatimids over the Bedouin, tranquillity was restored and requests for aid were renewed. It seems that it was customary to announce the arrival of an emissary in the synagogues so that the public could come to their aid. From some letters, it appears that two emissaries were sometimes sent, one a leper and the other a healthy person. Money would be deposited with the 'merchants' representative' in Tiberias, Saadia ha-Levi b. Moses, and he would distribute it to the sick.

Indirectly we learn from these letters that in Tiberias there were two *ḥavērīm*, people of the Palestinian yeshiva, who undoubtedly acted there as judges and community leaders, for apart from Hillel b. Yeshūʿā, Nathan ha-Kohen he-ḥāvēr b. Isaiah is also mentioned. Interesting information as to the manner in which the money was transferred is found in the letter of Samuel he-ḥāvēr b. Moses, of Tyre, to the leader of the community in Fustat, 'Eli b. 'Amram, written in about 1050. He confirms having received a *diyōqnē* from Fustat for 14 dinars less 2 qīrāṭs, which Solomon b. Saadia b. Ṣaghīr brought with him from Egypt to Tyre. The *diyōqnē* had to be collected from Samuel ha-Levi b. Shemaria b. Raʿbūb. This was done and the money given to a merchant travelling 'to Ṭībēryā', to be distributed to 'our tormented brethren', 'in the presence of the ḥavērīm and elders'; that is to say that the distribution was carried out publicly and in the presence of the community leaders. From the text of the letter, it also appears that the money was collected in Fustat by means of a special campaign ('may the Almighty double the reward of the ḥāvēr, [that is 'Eli b. 'Amram] . . . also of everyone who gave something'). Hence, the money would first reach Tyre from Egypt by sea, and then be sent to Tiberias (as Tyre was part of jund Urdunn, of which Tiberias was the capital).[62]

M. Kister, *Tarbiz*, 48(1978/9), 235, and their suggestion that in fact these Jews returned to Jericho, because that is where they came from originally.

[62] See letters relating to the lepers: **252**ff, and also the supplementary: **262a**, **265a**, **266** (revised). Al-Jūbarī, see the signature of Hillel b. Yeshūʿā on **254** and the note there. Letter of recommendation: **252**, and see the ʿalāma (the concluding formula) on p. b; **254**, **255**, in which there is mention of the death of one of the envoys of the lepers, a man of Aleppo (Ṣōvā) whose name was Khalaf (*ha-melammēd*, the teacher) ha-Ṣōvī b. Yeshūʿā, who was himself ill of leprosy (from which we learn that people with this disease were not prevented from travelling and being in contact with the public; see on the subject of lepers in Islam: Lazarus-Yafeh, *Tarbiz*, 51[1981/2], 215); the death-bed will of this Khalaf has been preserved, and it appears from this will that he was a man of means who dealt in

[297] The lepers' purpose in coming to Tiberias was to 'get healed by the water and the air'. As early as the late sixth century, Antoninus of Piacenza (Placentinus) tells us of the springs of Ḥammat-Gādēr, called 'the baths of Elijah (the prophet)' which cured the lepers. There was also an inn there (*xenodochium*) supported by public funds. In the evening, the baths were filled; towards the front of the pool there was a basin which was filled, and then the doors were locked. The sick entered through a small door carrying lamps and incense and sat there the entire night, falling asleep. A sign of healing was a certain dream which the sick person would describe. Afterwards he would not come to the bathhouse any longer and in the course of seven days (so one should understand) he would be healed. This tradition has evidently been preserved for generations and the place to which the lepers of Tiberias went to be healed in the springs was indeed Ḥammat-Gādēr. Actually, the text of one of the letters confirms this: 'Your tormented brothers, who live outside Rakkath'. That is – in plain terms – the lepers lived outside of Tiberias. Around 1045, Samuel he-ḥāvēr b. Moses of Tyre wrote to Ephraim b. Shemaria in Fustat, asking him to clarify the matter of certain money deposits in Egypt, among them those of 'Moses b. Ṣemaḥ, known as al-Azraq ('the blue-eyed') the magician, who died some years ago', which concern Nā'ima b. Moses al-Dulūkī (from Dulūk in northern Syria), 'who sold wares in front of the Jadariyya baths'. Jadariyya is undoubtedly Ḥammat-Gādēr. However, one can also assume that these lepers would go to get healed in the springs of Tiberias proper. Muqaddasī mentions that there were eight unheated baths in the city as well as ritual pools (*miyāḍ*) of hot water. The baths received their water through canals from the hot springs. He also describes the springs of Ḥammat-Gādēr (*al-Ḥamma*) which apparently could heal various diseases within three days.[63]

textiles and perfumes, and even bought himself a *ḥāṣēr*, that is a compound, in Tiberias (evidently after coming there from Aleppo because of his illness). See **253**. The name of the healthy envoy was Obadiah, see **262**, line 9. Samuel b. Ezra, who is addressed in this letter, **262**, is evidently Samuel b. 'Ezrūn the Jerusalemite, and from this we learn that appeals for help were also made to Jerusalem. 'Heads of cities': **265**. That there were women among the lepers one can learn from **266**: 'and we fell, limb by limb, men and women'. Letter of Samuel the ḥāvēr b. Moses: **283**. Mann, *Jews*, I, 168, assumed that this Samuel b. Shemaria b. Ra'bub was a man of Tiberias, but actually he was from Tyre. The letter from Solomon b. Judah, **72**, written in about 1026, includes an appeal to help 'the tormented . . . the exiles from their homes' etc.; it is clear that this refers to the lepers of Tiberias, and not refugees from the earthquake of 1033 as assumed by Mann, *Jews*, I, 133. **262a** has an additional detail, and that is that the sick were obliged to pay to the people who laundered their clothes. **265a** is a fragment of a letter carried by two of the lepers' envoys, one named David ha-Kohen *ha-me'ullē ba-ḥavūrā* (the excellent one of the yeshiva, an honorific title), and the other whose name was not preserved, only the name of his father, Abraham.

63 The purpose of their arrival: **263**, a, lines 11–12. Antoninus: Tobler et Molinier, I, 94f; cf. Couret, *la Palestine*, 236, and more references there; Avi-Yonah, *Ge'ōgrāfya hīsṭōrīt*, 159f and references in n. 1. 'Outside Rakkath': **265**, line 18. Moses al-Dulūkī: **278**, lines 31–32;

[298] The port of jund Urdunn, and actually the most important port in all of Palestine and Syria was Tyre. According to Ya'qūbī, people of different origin lived there alongside one another. Nāṣir Khusraw, who visited Tyre in February 1047, writes that most of the Muslims there were Shiites while the cadi, Ibn Abī 'Aqīl was a Sunni. We have no further details about the Muslims in the city nor about the Christians (if there were any). About the Jewish community living there, we have a good deal of information from the Cairo Geniza. From the Geniza documents, it appears that Tyre had a relatively large Jewish population, which lived on local industries and maritime trade. The special ties with Tiberias and Acre can be seen in a fragment from a court deed written in Tyre in around 1015 which deals with the legacy of a woman who died in Tiberias, and one of the heirs, who lived in Acre. In around 1020 we find the marriage deed of Ḥaẓiyya (the root of the name means: luck) b. Nathan, written in Tyre. The groom, Manṣūr, was a man of Acre and the young couple were to move to Acre after a year of marriage, where they would be given a house by the father of the bride, Nathan. The bride's parents and their children had the right to stay in the house when they came to Acre, either as guests or else permanently. Tyre was the home of the Baradānī family, an important and well-known Babylonian family who had apparently immigrated from Iraq at the end of the tenth century. In approximately 1060 we find Joseph and Nahum, sons of Sahl al-Baradānī, in Tyre, with their trading ventures covering the entire area: Gūsh (which is Gūsh Ḥālāv), Tiberias, Tripoli and Aleppo.[64]

on Dulūk, the ancient Dolikhē, see: Dussaud, *Topographie*, Index, and see also the article Dulūk (by D. Sourdel) in *EI*[2]. It is now a village which belongs to Turkey near the Syrian border. Muqaddasī, *Aqālīm*, 161, 185; see the subject of the hot baths in Tiberias also in Ya'qūbī, *Buldān*, 115. Sam'ānī (ed. Margoliouth), 366a, tells of visiting Tiberias (in around 1130); he stayed there for one night and visited the bath-house; see further: Idrīsī (Cerulli), 364; Ibn al-Shaddād, *Barq*, 106a, who notes the springs outside the city of Tiberias (certainly Ḥammat-Gādēr) to which all kinds of sick people come to be healed; see more sources: Le Strange, *Palest.*, 334f.

64 On the close ties between Palestine and Tyre in the consciousness of people living at that time one can learn from **212**, lines 29–30 (Zadok ha-Levi b. Levi, around 1030): 'For there are no people in all of Palestine as helpful as the people of Tyre alone'. Ya'qūbī, *Buldān*, 115; Nāṣir Khusraw, 14 (text), 47 (translation); see below, sec. 360. The matter of the legacy: **270**; Manṣūr: **279**; Assaf, *Eretz Israel*, 1(1950/51), 140, n. 8, interpreted the matter of the house incorrectly. The Baradānīs: **492**, the letter of Joseph and Nahum, sons of Sahl (who is Yannai) al-Baradānī, from Tyre, to Nehorai b. Nissim in Fustat; Israel b. Nathan (Sahlūn), who writes to Nehorai b. Nissim on 29 November 1061, mentions that 'the Baradānīs are living in Tyre (see **479**, b, line 3). The father was Joseph the cantor, al-Baradānī; Joseph's son, Nahum the cantor, ha-Baradānī, is mentioned in a poem in honour of Abraham 'rabbēnū' (our master), TS 8 J 1, see in Schechter, *Saadyana*, 66; see on him: Mann, *JQR*, NS 9(1918/9), 154f, and *ibid.*, also a comprehensive discussion on the Baradānīs, 150ff; the sons of Nahum were: Baruch, Yannai, Solomon; and see about the Baradānīs also in: Scheiber *Acta Orientalia* (Hung.), 30(1976), 342. A letter from Nahum al-Baradānī to Samuel b. Ḥofnī, head of the yeshiva of Sura, written in Qayrawān on 22

[299] Tyre is mentioned frequently in merchants' letters printed in my corpus of Geniza documents. Moreover, we have no less than sixteen Geniza documents written in Tyre during the first half of the eleventh century and another four from the end of the century and the beginning of the twelfth century. It was at this time that the Palestine yeshiva moved to Tyre, as we shall see below. At an earlier period, it is Joseph ha-Kohen b. Jacob *ha-sōfēr* who was head of the Jews in Tyre. In a deed of attorney written in Tyre on 25 January 1011, he is still not called *ḥāvēr*; similarly in another deed of attorney from 1012, nor in a clearance deed (receipt) from 24 November 1019 (in his handwriting). Evidently he became *ḥāvēr* in about 1025, as can be deduced from a power-of-attorney written at that time; in his handwriting, there is also a record of evidence relating to a house in Aleppo from 18 October 1028. In a power-of-attorney written in Tyre by Solomon b. Ṣemaḥ, the scribe of the yeshiva of Palestine, evidently at the end of 1036 or the beginning of 1037, Joseph ha-Kohen of

Av 1310 Sel., 7 August AD 999, was among the documents of the Geniza and was edited by: Goldziher, *REJ*, 50(1905), 183ff (Goldziher received the manuscript, written on vellum, from Schechter, but it was lost later on; see Shaked, 49). Nahum writes there that he is delaying his departure from the Maghrib because of some matters of business in Spain; he mentions a letter he had written a year earlier, which shows that he was already in the Maghrib for more than a year; see this letter in Mann, *Texts*, I, 151f. See further: TS 20.100, lines 31–32, the letter of Hayy Gaon, in Mann, *ibid.*, I, 122, in which he mentions 'our treasured beloved friend, our Lord and Master Nahum the cantor . . . son of our Lord and Master Joseph, the great cantor'; the Gaon requests the addressee (evidently in Qayrawān) to inform him as to the well-being of the same Nahum. This shows that from 1006 (when this letter was written), the family was already in the Maghrib. See the fragment of the letter together with another fragment, in Abramson, *Ba-merkazim*, 95ff; see *ibid.*, 91, the comments on Nahum al-Baradānī and his poems, and more references. The Nahum who settled in Tyre was the grandson of this Nahum; the generation order: Joseph (Baghdad) – Nahum (Qayrawān) – Yannai (Sahl) and his sons: Nahum and Joseph (Tyre); three generations of Baradānīs are mentioned in **426**, which is a court document issued in about 1065: Nahum the cantor al-Baradānī (who settled in Qayrawān); his son Yannai (Sahl) and the sons of Yannai: Joseph and Nahum. It says there that Nahum came from the Maghrib and brought books with him, the Talmud and other books, and also *kuḥl*; Mann, *JQR*, NS 9(1918/9), 151, assumed that the court document stemmed from Baghdad and was sent to Egypt, but he was mistaken: the document was from Jerusalem and the defendant was from Ramla (Mann repeats the above-mentioned opinion in *Texts*, I, 153, as well). It seems that Yannai and his sons moved from Qayrawān to Tyre when the sons were already grown, as is shown by the request of the Jerusalemite Abraham B. 'Amram from Nehorai b. Nissim in Fustat that he urgently obtain the evidence of the youngest son, Joseph, in the matter of the rights of a Jerusalemite woman to a legacy in Qayrawān (see **513**). See also on the Baradānīs: Goitein, *Mediterranean Society*, III, 300f; 493, n. 107, with a list of Geniza documents in which they are mentioned. ENA NS 70, f. 19 includes three fragments, written – it seems – by the 'Rav', who is Judah ha-Kohen b. Joseph, leader of the Maghribīs. At the beginning of one of the fragments, the Baradānīs are mentioned, as an example of people 'of decent ways'. The name Baradān is evidently Bihrādhān (Bē-Rādhān), as I have shown in *JESHO*, 71(1974), 320, n. 106; this was a province which stretched east of Baghdad along the Tigris, also called Rādhān (in Arab sources and also in Jewish sources: Jūkhā), homeland of the Rādhānī merchants.

Tyre signs: 'the fourth in the *ḥavūrā*', which shows that he became one of the central figures in the Palestinian yeshiva.[65]

[300] Together with Joseph b. Jacob *ha-sōfēr*, we find another leader of the Jews of Tyre, Samuel *he-ḥāvēr* b. Moses *he-ḥāvēr* b. R. Elḥānān. Six documents written in his handwriting are included in my corpus of Geniza documents. He survived Joseph ha-Kohen and is mentioned as a witness in a power-of-attorney on 12 December 1050. We know the name of his grandfather by the small letters surrounding his signature, in cryptography (*atbash*) meaning: b. R. Elḥānān. His Arabic name was Mawhūb, as he indicates in his letter to 'Eli b. 'Amram, the ḥāvēr of Fustat in the middle of the eleventh century. It appears that he had friendly relations with the ḥāvēr of Aleppo, Jacob b. Joseph. From his letter to the latter, we learn that he visited Buzā'a (some 40 kilometres east of Aleppo), and the people of that community were very interested that he remain with them. We are also informed of an impending visit from this Jacob in Tyre. Some of these letters concern personal matters in which the letter-writers were in need of assistance from the people of Fustat, and indeed Samuel writes for them to Ephraim b. Shemaria and to his heir to the leadership of the Fustat Jews, 'Eli b. 'Amram. It is also evident that he served as a scribe for his community, as there are two marriage deeds from Tyre from the Geniza written in his characteristic handwriting. It seems that in the days of Samuel b. Moses, Tyre was a lively centre of social intercourse and regional communal activities for the Jewish communities in northern Syria, Aleppo and other cities.[66]

65 Documents from Tyre from the first half of the eleventh century: **268–283**; later documents: **600–603**; deeds of attorney: **268**, **269**; deed of compensation: **271**; first appointment as ḥāvēr: **272**; record of evidence: **273**. See also JNUL, 4°577.4 No. 98, in his handwriting, of 28 November 1023, Tyre, edited by: Friedman, *Marriage*, II, 38ff; see also the Geniza letter, MS Reinach (which was in the possession of Theodore Reinach) edited by Schwab, *REJ*, 70(1920), 59ff, which is a copy of a letter sent to Joseph ha-Kohen the ḥāvēr b. Jacob in Tyre, evidently by Ephraim b. Shemaria in Fustat, concerning the money orders (*diyōqnēs*, *suftaja*s) signed by b. Rabī' (Solomon b. Rabī', an important figure in Tyre; mentioned in the years 1010–1015) the deceased, which Ḥasan (Yefet) b. Isaac was supposed to have cashed in Fustat; cf. Mann, *Jews*, II, 355. Joseph ha-Kohen is called in the florid introduction to the above-mentioned letter (line 18), 'whose title is ḥāvēr, like the scholars of Jabneh'. It is worth noting the signatures of Joseph ha-Kohen, surrounded by tiny letters, evidently a code which I have not managed to decipher as yet.

66 The letters of Samuel b. Moses: **278–283**. Witness to the power of attorney: see **307** (a Karaite marriage deed), line 18. See the letters surrounding his signature: **273**, **278**. Mawhūb, see **283**, lines 24–25. His letter to Jacob, the ḥāvēr: **281**; Buzā'a, see the article by this name (by J. Sourdel Thomine) in *EI*², and references there; add Ibn Khallikān, I, 145, who says that it is 'a large village, in the middle of the road between Aleppo and Manbij'. Marriage deeds in the handwriting of Samuel b. Moses: **279**, **280**. As to Aleppo, some information on it from this early period has been preserved in the Geniza. The aforementioned Jacob, the ḥāvēr, was on friendly terms with Solomon b. Judah, the Jerusalem Gaon, even before he became Gaon. See **54**, Solomon b. Judah's letter to him, and then he was still not titled ḥāvēr, but 'Jacob the candidate (*ha-me'uttād*) b. Joseph he-Ḥāsīd'; see **55**,

[301] Acre, another port in jund Urdunn, was apparently neglected during the first part of our period, until the last quarter of the ninth century, when Ibn Ṭūlūn decided to reactivate its port. We have some slight knowledge of the Jewish community in Acre. The oldest piece of information exists in a colophon from a commentary on Isaiah by Saadia Gaon, in which it is written that the book had formerly belonged to Jacob *he-ḥāvēr* b. Ayyūb and was purchased from him by Josiah *he-ḥāvēr* b. Aaron *ha-me'ullē* b. Josiah, *av* of the court in Acre in the year AM 4791 (AD 1031). In that year, Josiah was granted the title of ḥāvēr. It was at about the same time that he visited Fustat, and in a letter written by Solomon b. Nethanel 'the banker', we find expressions of regret at his having to leave Fustat. Afterwards, Josiah became *av* of the court of the Palestinian yeshiva. His son, Zadok, also lived in Acre, evidently until the seventies of the eleventh century. We come across him in Tyre, in the retinue of Abiathar Gaon, and he is then 'the third' in the yeshiva. The grandfather of this Josiah was not Josiah Gaon, of whom we shall hear more below, but Josiah the *av* of the court, b. Abraham Gaon. His brother, Isaac b. Abraham, was 'third' of the yeshiva, and apparently they flourished at the end of the tenth century. The descendants of this Abraham Gaon, it seems, settled in Acre where we also find the nephew of Josiah *he-ḥāvēr*, Elijah b. Aaron b. Josiah, who signs his name and notes the year AM 4800 (AD 1040), on the last page of the book *alfāẓ al-miqrā*, a Biblical dictionary which he copied for his own use. It appears that this family were descendants of Palestinian Geonim of the tenth century, that is, those who preceded the aforementioned Abraham Gaon, Meir Gaon and his son Aaron. There is a hint of truth in this (apart from memorial lists, which are not clear on this point), as can be seen from a letter written by Elijah b. Aaron to Ephraim b. Shemaria in Fustat, in which he confirms the receipt of a money order (*suftaja*) for Isaac *he-ḥāvēr*. This Isaac *he-ḥāvēr* (who is Isaac *he-ḥāvēr* b. Solomon *he-ḥāvēr*, of the descendants of Meir Gaon) also lived in Acre. Isaac *he-ḥāvēr*, it states in the same letter, requested Elijah, who is evidently a young relative, to cash the money order, but Abū'l-Faḍl Meshullam (the banker) claimed that the gold (the dinars) has not yet arrived from Tiberias and that it will arrive shortly; but

also from Solomon to Jacob, and here he is already called ḥāvēr. At the same time, there was another leader in Aleppo, namely Tamīm, the ḥāvēr, b. Tobias, see: ULC Or 1080 J 96, a power-of-attorney from 1037 written 'in the city of Ṣōvā, situated on the river Qūqiyōn' (Qūqiyōn = Quwayq). The importance of the Jewish population in Aleppo is borne out by the fact that one of its gates, the northern gate, was called *Bāb al-Yahūd*: see Muqaddasī, *Āqālīm*, 155; Ibn al-'Adīm, *Zubda*, I, 135, 188; Ibn al-Shiḥna (copied from Ibn Shaddād), 44 (text), 36 (translation). Towards the end of the 11th century, the leader of the Jews of Aleppo was Baruch b. Isaac, some of whose letters have been preserved in the Geniza; it is also known that he wrote a commentary to the Talmud. See on him and the Aleppo community: Mann, *Hatequfa*, 24 (1926/7), 352ff; Assaf, *Tarbiz*, 19:105, 1947/8.

merely a week after the writing of this letter, at the end of Adar, Isaac *he-ḥāvēr* informed him that he has received the money. This matter connects up with the appeal of Moses *ha-sōfēr*, the son of the same Isaac *he-ḥāvēr*, to Abraham al-Tustarī, to help him travel (to Palestine) to visit his sick father. Hence it seems that Isaac *he-ḥāvēr*, who was Meir Gaon's grandson, was receiving financial help for himself and his family from the people of Fustat, both from the 'Palestinians' (Ephraim b. Shemaria) and the Tustaris.

In Acre, a power-of-attorney was written in the name of Rāḍiya, the widow of Abraham b. Nathan (not the son of Nathan the *av* of the court, who will be dealt with below) and given to Mevorakh b. Ezekiel, to handle the property left her by her deceased husband in Ascalon with people who came from Acre, who were all from one family: Wahbān, Ṣedaqa and Ḥulda, the mother of the two. The signature of Joseph *he-ḥāvēr* b. Eleazar appears there, and he was evidently another ḥāvēr who lived in Acre, apart from the above-mentioned Josiah and Isaac.

Another personality among the Jews of Acre was Saadia b. Israel the cantor, who was granted the title of ḥāvēr on behalf of the Palestinian yeshiva on *rōsh ha-shānā*, *ca.* 1045, which Abraham, son of Solomon Gaon b. Judah, mentions in a letter to Sahlān b. Abraham. Preserved in the Geniza is a letter written by Saadia *ha-talmīd we-ha-sōfēr* (student and scribe; that is, prior to his appointment as ḥāvēr) to Samuel b. Shelah in which he asks him to 'come down on the sabbath to his synagogue to hear the words of the Torah'. One may assume that this is probably an invitation to come to the synagogue in Acre. Some thirty years later, Saadia 'the ḥaver of the great Sanhedrin' writes a responsum to a certain *sayyidī al-ḥazān* concerning the calendar of the year AM 4838 (AD 1077/8).

There appears to have been a centre of learning in Acre, as can be inferred from the letter from a refugee from Acre writing to Alexandria (in about 1115), apparently a man close to one of the families of the geonim of Palestine, to judge by the *'alāma yesha' yeqārēv* which used to be that of Nathan *av* b. Abraham. In this letter, it tells that there was a sort of colony of people from Tiberias in Acre. The family of the correspondent was also originally from Tiberias, for his father, Jacob *ha-mumḥē*, came from there. He says that he prays for the well-being of the addressee with a group of the elite, that is, made up of refugees from Palestine, not of Alexandria, whose praying is not heard (and with whom he evidently is on very bad terms). In about 1060, the parnās of the Jerusalem Jews, 'Eli ha-Kohen b. Ezekiel, stayed in Acre. He mentions in his letter to 'Eli ha-Kohen b. Ḥayyim in Fustat that he prayed there (as he also did in Tyre) for the health of the Nagid in Egypt, Judah b. Saadia, and his brother Mevorakh. During the latter half of the eleventh century, the Spanish commentator Moses b. Joseph ibn Kashkīl settled in Acre after wandering from Spain to Sicily, on to Egypt, and from there to Mahdiyya. He appears to have lived there together with his brother and they stayed in Jerusalem for a certain time, as one learns from a letter of Isma'īl b. Isaac al-Andalusī from Jerusalem to Yeshū'ā b. Samuel in Fustat, written in around 1065. The latter wanted some information about the Ibn Kashkīl family, and he mentions that he sees them very infrequently because there are certain reservations about them on the part of 'the head', evidently the Gaon Elijah ha-Kohen b. Solomon. These reservations may be connected with Moses b. Joseph's method of interpreting the Bible.

On 28 November 1099, slightly more than four months after the fall of Jerusalem, we come across a record of evidence, written in Fustat, concerning the legacy of a certain Isma'īl al-'Azāzī al-Ḥalabī, who died in Acre. As the name indicates, he came from 'Azāz, a fortified town which was the capital of a district north of Aleppo, a day's travel from there. We have here a family from northern Syria who came to Acre in Palestine at first, where the father of the family died, while the rest of the family escaped to Egypt, apparently in the wake of the Crusaders' invasion. Two of the heirs still remained in Aleppo with their families, whereas three witnesses, also of Aleppo, appeared before the court in Fustat. It should be noted that Acre was still under the control of the Muslims at the time, for it was only conquered in 1104. We have already seen above the letter of another refugee from Acre, who settled in Alexandria (written to Joseph b. Yaḥyā in Fustat, himself a refugee from Acre), in which he speaks of the strained relations between the refugees and the people of Alexandria. Nathan ha-Kohen b. Solomon, who is himself one of the refugees from Bāniyās and who became a judge in Fustat, writes to his father-in-law Tobiah ha-Kohen b. 'Eli, also from Bāniyās, who has become a leader of the community in Bilbays. He speaks highly to him of another refugee from Acre, a modest man of noble extraction, who at first settled in one of the towns in the Delta, hiding from the tax collectors. After he and his family reached Fustat, they were in great distress and their arrival became known to the authorities. It appears that the family wished to move to Bilbays, perhaps because the refugees had greater chances of coming to some arrangements concerning taxes in the provincial cities. Bilbays seems to have been such a haven, not only for the people of Acre but also for people from other cities in Palestine.[67]

[67] The colophon: **221**. Letter of Solomon b. Nethanel: **215**. See in 'the Scroll of Abiathar', **559**, b. line 18: Zadok b. Rabbi Isaiah Av was appointed 'third' by Elijah Gaon, on the Feast of Tabernacles in 1081, in Tyre (he was 'fourth' before that), see his sermon *ibid.*; see also **574**,b, lines 2–3: Zadok b. Rabbi Isaiah, *av-bēt-dīn*, 'of saintly blessed memory' (perhaps he was murdered, as *zekher qādōsh*, 'saintly memory', may indicate). The refugee from Acre who lived in Alexandria (in the days of the Crusaders) mentions Zadok 'the third' who lived in Acre, see **599** (not as in Braslavi, *Le-ḥeqer*, 86); this is a letter to another

[302] Another coastal city in jund Urdunn was *Haifa*. Nāṣir Khusraw, who visited Haifa in 1047, noted the existence of a shipyard there, where ships of the *jūdī* type were constructed. Ibn Ḥawqal notices the fortresses in its area and Yāqūt also speaks of the Haifa citadel. Here it becomes clear both from Geniza letters and from the history of the Crusaders' conquest, that the fortress of Haifa (that is, that part of the town surrounded by a wall) was inhabited by Jews. A fragment of a deed survived in the Geniza in which 'the people of the citadel of Haifa' are mentioned; it is also mentioned in the description of the earthquake of the year 1033 in a letter written by Solomon b. Ṣemaḥ. Elijah Gaon held an assembly in Haifa in 1082, when the Palestinian yeshiva was already in Tyre, and there he inaugurated the year, reassumed the leadership as Gaon and renewed the appointments to the 'meeting house' (*bēt ha-wa'ad*, a euphemism for the yeshiva). Naturally Haifa was chosen for this purpose because it was within the boundaries of Palestine according to the *halakha*, unlike Tyre where the yeshiva was then located. This was explicitly stated in the

refugee, a man from Acre who lived in Fustat, Joseph b. Yaḥyā; and he also has the other details, memories of Acre. The lineage of Josiah, *av-bēt-dīn*, Bodl MS Heb (Cat. 2443) b 11, f. 24, edited by Poznanski, *REJ*, 66(1913), 62; MS Firkovitch II, 157A, fols. 9–10, edited by Harkavy, *Hamagid*, 21(1877), 134; this is a list at the end of a midrash, see film no. 10280 at the Institute of Micro-filmed Hebrew Manuscripts in the National Library, Jerusalem; cf. Mann, *Jews*, II, 53; see also ENA 2592, f. 118*v*, ed. Marmorstein, *JQR*, NS 18(1917/8), 3 (a very torn and faded fragment) in which on line 11 can be found Josiah b. Abraham Gaon. The colophon of Elijah b. Aaron: **223**. Confirmation of the money order: **222**; this has regards to Joseph ha-sōfēr (the scribe), Ephraim's son-in-law. Joseph died in 1035, hence the letter was written before that year. The letter of Moses ha-sōfēr: **224**. Rāḍiya's deed: **225**. Saadia b. Israel (Sa'īd b. Isrā'īl): **141**, line 5; this is a letter of Abraham, the Gaon's son, and see: Goitein, *Baron Jubilee Volume*, 512f, who assumes that he is the same person as the Saadia b. Israel praised in **64** by the Gaon Solomon b. Judah on the fact that his house in Jerusalem is wide-open to the needy; but that Saadia is evidently Saadia b. Israel al-Tustarī; see Gil, *Tustaris*, in the Index. Saadia's letter: **226**. Samuel b. Shelah is perhaps Samuel b. Sahl, of Khurāsān, whose arrival in Jerusalem is announced by Solomon b. Judah (in a letter written by his son Abraham) to Ephraim b. Shemaria in about 1040, see **138**, lines 19–20. The responsum: HUC 1007, edited by Assis, *HUCA*, 49(1978), Hebrew section, 1–4; see the photostat *ibid.*, pp. 2f. The handwriting is the same as in **226**. The letter of 'Eli ha-Kohen b. Ezekiel: **446**, lines 3, 19–20. On Moses b. Joseph ibn Kashkīl see: Mann, *Texts*, I, 386ff; see there a fragment of his commentary to I Sam., ch. xxviii (in which he criticises Samuel b. Ḥofnī), pp. 389f; this fragment is included in the commentary of Isaac b. Samuel the Spaniard, who says he obtained it when he was in Acre, where Moses b. Joseph died; he mentions that Ibn Kashkīl was a man of considerable knowledge of philosophy and an accomplished linguist. See also Ashtor, *Shazar Jubilee Volume*, 492 and n. 9. The letter of Ismā'īl b. Isaac: **511**, in the upper margin. Khalaf b. Isaac of Acre ('Akkā) is mentioned in a copy of the protocol of the court in Fustat dated Monday, 15 Shevat AM 4788, 15 January AD 1028, dealing with matters of his inheritance. The name of his heiress: Nijwa: Bodl MS Heb d 66, f. 121, edited by Assaf, *Tarbiz*, 9(1937/8), 213, cf. Goitein, *Mediterranean Society* III, 196f. Minutes of witnesses from the year 1099: **598**. 'Azāz, see: Yāqūt, *Buldān*, III, 667; Dussaud, *Topographie*, 195: it is Azetas in Plinius, *Hist. nat.*, V:23. Refugees from Acre: **599**. The letter of Nathan ha-Kohen b. Solomon: TS 12.789. See also the letter **609**, to be discussed below. The deed of partnership: TS 6 J 2, f. 13.

surviving draft of a letter from Shelah 'the sixth' b. Nahum, who apparently writes from Tyre, and is naturally one of the supporters of Abiathar ha-Kohen and the Palestinian yeshiva in their sharp conflict with David b. Daniel: 'and we went to Haifa and at the time of the prayer I was proclaimed 'the sixth'; there was unanimity that Haifa belongs to Palestine . . .' The Jewish character of Haifa is most marked in the account of Albert of Aachen of the Crusaders' conquest, in which it emerges that apart from regular Muslim units (of the Fatimid army), it was the Jews who defended the city, as we shall see.[68]

[303] There is a relatively large amount of information preserved on *Ascalon*, especially in the Cairo Geniza. This can be explained not only by the accidental nature of the survival of the Geniza documents, but also by the fact that the city was the chief connecting link between Palestine and Egypt, owing to the relative proximity of Egypt and to its fortified port, which made it a transit point for goods and travellers, though Muqaddasī held that the port was not among the best. The period we are dealing with ends in Ascalon more than two generations after its conclusion in the rest of Palestine, for the Crusaders conquered it only in 1153. It appears that the most ancient information we have of Ascalon after the period of the Umayyads is the building inscription of the mosque and the *mu'adhdhin*'s tower, which attributes it to al-Mahdī, who became caliph at the death of his father al-Manṣūr in AD 775, but who ordered the mosque to be built in Muḥarram in the year AH 155, that is, at the beginning of AD 772. Al-Mufaḍḍal b. Salām al-Namarī and Jawhar b. Hishām al-Qurashī were in charge of its construction. The next information on Ascalon is in the year AH 237 (AD 851/2), when a great conflagration consumed the houses of Ascalon as well as the plantations surrounding it. There was also a Christian population there and I shall discuss this and the subject of its church, which was burnt down in 939/40, in the chapter on the Ikhshīdids below.[69]

[304] A very unusual episode connected with Ascalon is the matter of

[68] Nāṣir Khusraw, 17 (text), 58 (translation); Ibn Ḥawqal, 166: (*al-quṣūr al-muḍāfa ilā ḥayfa*); Yāqūt, *Buldān*, II, 381. The fragment of a deed: **220**, line 1. The letter of Solomon b. Ṣemaḥ: **209**, line 13. The assembly in Haifa: the Scroll of Abiathar: **559**, b, lines 19ff. The *bēt ha-wa'ad*, 'meeting house' is perhaps the synagogue in Haifa and the author of the scroll uses here an image from Talmudic language, and one should not take it literally, as does Assaf, *Meqōrōt*, 11; one can easily see that the poet does not apply *ziqnē 'agūlā*, that is the people of the Palestinian yeshiva, to Haifa in particular (see in the dirge he edited *ibid.*, 14, line 38 [TS Loan 51]). The letter of Shelah; **550**. See on the subject of Haifa and the borders of Palestine: Braslavi, *Eretz-Israel*, 5(1958/9), 220 and notes 8 and 9 for more references. See on the subject of Haifa during the period under discussion also the article of El'ad, *Meḥqārīm* (Haifa Univ.), 5:191, 1979/80.

[69] Muqaddasī, *Āqālīm*, 174; evidently biased in favour of the port of Acre, which he claims was built by his grandfather (see *ibid.*, 162f). The marriage deed: *Répertoire chronologique*, I, 312f. (No. 42); the fire: Ibn Taghrī Bardī, II, 290.

the mosque where Ḥusayn's head was preserved. Muslim writers, evidently beginning with Harawī (*ca.* 1200), mention that there was a memorial (*mashhad*) in Ascalon in which the head of Ḥusayn was kept. Ibn Muyassar, writing some two generations later, notes that in 1098, when the army of al-Afḍal conquered Jerusalem and Ascalon from the Saljūqs, al-Afḍal moved the head of Ḥusayn from the modest place in which it was formerly kept, to the most impressive building in Ascalon and built a mosque above it. However, according to him some claimed that it was al-Afḍal's father, Badr al-Jamālī, who actually built the mosque and that al-Afḍal only finished it. Afterwards, at the time of the Crusaders' conquest of Ascalon, the head was transferred to Fustat, on Sunday, the 9th of Jumādā II in the year AH 548, that is 31 August AD 1153. The Spanish traveller al-'Abdarī mentions the building of the *mashhad* in Ascalon when describing the tomb of the head of Ḥusayn in Fustat. He depicts it as the most magnificent building in Ascalon. Mujīr al-Dīn al-'Ulaymī, writing towards the end of the fifteenth century, discusses this when he describes the *minbar* situated near the *miḥrāb* in Hebron, in the Cave of Machpelah. He tells that the *minbar* had been made of superb and beautiful wood during the rule of the Fatimid caliph al-Mustanṣir, on the order of Badr al-Jamālī, for the *mashhad* Ḥusayn in Ascalon. According to its inscription, it was made in AH 484 (AD 1091). He imagines that Saladin, when he conquered Palestine, moved this *minbar* to Hebron, since Ascalon was in ruins and because he wanted to add splendour to Hebron. He mentions that the *minbar* was still there 'until this very day'. Indeed, it remains there today. Van Berchem published the inscription in 1915 and it is indeed as al-'Ulaymī described it four hundred years earlier. He was perhaps right in assuming that there was a Shiite sanctuary there many generations before the building of this mosque. It seems that during the struggle over Palestine, the Fatimid rulers wanted to enhance the religious significance of Ascalon, and particularly its Shiite aspect, and therefore built this magnificent building.[70]

[305] Letters in the Geniza from the eleventh century, especially letters of merchants, mention Ascalon frequently. A letter from Ascalon in mid-century contains a reproach against a group of the city's inhabitants for conducting a campaign of slander against the letter-writer and his

[70] On the mosque of Ḥusayn's head, see: Harawī, 32; Ibn Muyassar, 38; Ibn Khallikān, II, 450; al-'Abdarī, 149, 232; Ibn Kathīr, *Bidāya*, VIII, 204, writing in the middle of the fourteenth century and claiming that Ḥusayn's head is in Damascus; Maqrīzī, *Khiṭaṭ*, II, 283; *Itti'āẓ*, III, 22; 'Ulaymī, 56f; see Van Berchem, *Festschr. Sachau*: 298; Vincent *et al.*, *Hebron*, 219–250. The inscription on the *minbar* can be read also in *Répertoire chronologique*, VII, 259f (No. 2790; see also the inscription after that, No. 2791, a similar matter). 'Arif al-'Ārif, *Mu'jaz*, 26, has no doubt about the fact that the head of Ḥusayn was indeed brought to Ascalon after he was killed.

household. The letter is written to a Jerusalemite, Abū'l-Faraj Shemaiah *he-ḥāvēr* b. Yeshū'ā, the great-grandson of Shemaiah Gaon. The writer is evidently one of the community leaders in Ascalon, and he points out that aspersions are cast not only against him, but also against Shemaiah's cousin, Mevorakh. Earlier complaints did not help and no one, neither their relatives nor even the physician b. al-Azhar (b. Meir?) reprimanded the slanderers. The only way to put an end to the slander was that the yeshiva should pronounce the slanderers excommunicated, particularly as they were seeking help from Muslims and Christians ('the uncircumcised', 'gentiles', 'worshippers of the cross', *mu'ahddhins*). A colophon to a commentary of Saadia Gaon on the prayer of *Shemōnē 'esrē*, copied in Ascalon in 1061 by Azariah b. David, has been preserved. There is a fragment of a letter from one of the family of the priestly geonim of Jerusalem, addressed to Ascalon, evidently written in around 1070, in which the writer expresses satisfaction at the fact that Ḥalfon ha-Kohen b. Eleazar reached Ascalon safely. Another letter has been preserved from 'the community of Ascalon' to 'the two holy communities living in Miṣrayim' (that is in Fustat) warmly commending the governor of Ascalon appointed by the Fatimids, Abū Ḥarī', and also the 'elder of the city', perhaps the local cadi, Abū Ḥurayz, on the score of their good treatment of the Jews of the city. The Ascalon correspondents ask the leaders of the Fustat communities to recommend these two Muslim personalities to 'our elders', i.e. the Karaite elders, meaning of course the Tustaris. To judge by the *'alāma*: *yesha' yūḥāsh* ('a swift salvation') one can surmise that the letter was written in 1025, the period of the Gaon Solomon ha-Kohen b. Joseph. Mann wanted to deduce from this letter the existence of a Karaite community in Ascalon and even assumed that it had been written by Karaites. However, he was mistaken in this, and we have no information as to whether there was in fact a Karaite community in Ascalon at that time.[71]

[306] During the period of Turkoman dominion over Palestine, Ascalon remained under Fatimid control, and it underwent difficult times because of the lack of security that existed in Palestine. At that time, the Ascalon community was involved to a large extent in the conflict between Abiathar ha-Kohen and David b. Daniel. We find hints of the difficult

[71] The letter to Shemaiah, the ḥāvēr: **526**; he is frequently mentioned in letters in my collection, in which there is a letter of his and letters addressed to him; see the Hebrew Index (his brother Solomon is also occasionally mentioned). His son, Abraham b. Shemaiah, was one of the judges in Fustat and his name appears on many of the court's documents, beginning from the end of the eleventh century. See on him: Goitein, *Mediterranean Society*, II, 512. The colophon: **528**. The letter from Jerusalem: **529**. The letter from 1025: **314**. See Mann, *Jews*, I, 159; cf. Baron, *SRHJ*, V, 413, n. 75; 415, n. 82: Baron finds here evidence of the absence of any sharp struggle between the Rabbanites and the Karaites in Palestine in the eleventh century, but it is impossible to speak of evidence from something whose very existence is in doubt.

situation in a letter from Nathan ha-Kohen ha-Mumḥē b. Mevorakh to 'Eli ha-Kohen ha-parnās b. Ḥayyim in Fustat: '. . . we remain at this time empty from every side'. From this letter, one can also learn about a Jew of Ascalon who preferred to go down to Egypt, Yefet b. Kālēv, and who took with him books which belonged to Mevorakh ha-Kohen, father of Nathan, the writer of the letter. It seems that the same Yefet b. Kālēv (who is Yefet b. Ḥalfon, or Ḥasan b. Kulayb) is mentioned in the deathbed will of Maymūn b. Khalfa al-Maghribī, dated 17 Tammuz 1383 Sel. (5 July AD 1072) in Fustat. It says there that in a sack that belonged to the testator, there were also three books (*maṣāhif*) of the Bible and Prophets of Ḥasan b. Kulayb al-'Asqalānī, which were evidently the same as the books of Mevorakh ha-Kohen mentioned above. Mevorakh, the father of Nathan ha-Kohen, was still alive when this letter was written, for the writer signs: Nathan ha-Kohen ha-mumḥē b. R. Mevorakh s. ṭ. (*sāfēh ṭāv*, 'may he have a good end'). A vivid portrayal of the conditions in Ascalon in the eighties of that century, can be found in a letter full of the personal problems of Joseph b. Manasseh (apparently a Maghribi) from Ascalon to Abraham b. Isaac *ha-talmīd* in Fustat, a letter I shall refer to below, in the discussion on the Saljūq period.[72]

[307] After the conquest of Jerusalem and the rest of Palestine by the Crusaders, Ascalon remained under Fatimid control until 1153. During this time, it served as a haven for refugees from Palestine who fled from the Crusaders and as a way-station for captives redeemed from the Crusaders. A moving letter written by Hillel b. 'Eli to 'the holy community living in the city of Ascalon' describes the first reactions of the Egyptian Jews after the news reached them of the fall of Jerusalem to the Crusaders. In Ascalon itself, relatively normal conditions of community life prevailed until it, too, fell to the Crusaders, fifty-four years after the taking of Jerusalem. It is amazing to see how the Jewish community in Ascalon carried on a relatively orderly way of life while under the shadow of the constant threat from the Crusaders, its sworn enemies. A court document of Fustat contains a copy of a marriage deed written in Ascalon on 23 January 1100, some six months after the fall of Jerusalem. This is the marriage deed of Sitt al-Dallāl b. 'Ullā, nicknamed Thiqa al-Dawla, who married a certain Shelah (perhaps Shelah b. Ḥalfon). Towards the end of the eleventh century and the beginning of the twelfth, the descendants of the aforementioned Nathan ha-Kohen b. Mevorakh were the leaders of the Ascalon community: his son, Mevorakh, his grandson Nathan and his great-grandson, Mevorakh. The grandson, Nathan ha-Kohen, writes, evidently in the eighties, a letter of recommendation for Solomon b.

72 The letter of Nathan ha-Kohen ha-mumḥē b. Mevorakh: **581**, lines 8 ff. The testament of Maymūn b. Khalfa: TS 18 J 1, f. 10; ed. by Golb, *JJS*, 20(1958), 41. The letter of Joseph b.

Benjamin, who was 'of good stock, one of the respected men of rank, whose table was ready and whose door always open, but on the decline and impoverished due to many misfortunes, and forced to ask for aid from his fellow men; and finally after he escaped death by the sword, he intends to go on a pilgrimage to Jerusalem ...' The letter was addressed to Nathan's relative, the parnās of Fustat, 'Eli ha-Kohen b. Ḥayyim, and its aim was to get financial aid for this Solomon b. Benjamin, who apparently wished to accumulate some money before settling in Jerusalem. On the other hand, 'Eli ha-Kohen would on occasion also ask his Ascalon relative to look after people from Fustat who came to Ascalon, as we see in the instance of Ṣedaqa ha-Levi ha-ḥazān b. Solomon who had to reach *thaghr 'Asqalān* (the fortified port of Ascalon) but according to Nathan ha-Kohen, had not arrived yet. It appears that the Ascalon community was considerably helped by the Jews of Fustat in matters of welfare, and the extent of the grants to the needy was determined in Fustat. This we learn from a letter from the same Nathan ha-Kohen to Abraham b. Eleazar in Fustat, written in 1130, with the request that he intervene on behalf of a blind man from Ḥamāh in Syria, whose monthly allowance has been decreased. His case had already been brought before *al-majlis al-'āl*, apparently the court of the yeshiva, which was already in Fustat. Another letter from Nathan ha-Kohen, to one of the important figures in Fustat, contains a request that he use his influence with Abū'l-Ḥasan ha-Kohen, who is undoubtedly the same 'Eli ha-Kohen b. Ḥayyim (it is interesting that this time he does not write to him directly) to help the son of al-Mufawwakh al-Zajjāj, the son-in-law of Sa'd b. Manṣūr, the husband of Thumāma b. Sa'd, who had fled to Fustat because he owed ten dinars. If help could not be obtained in this manner, the Nagid must be approached and he would undoubtedly know how to deal with someone in such a situation, just as he had helped Abū'l-Ṭayyib (who is evidently Khalaf b. 'Eli ha-Kohen b. Ezekiel). The remark he makes is interesting, that at the time the letter was written none of the Jews of the town remained in Ascalon, save some poor wretches (*fuqarā' shaḥḥādhīn*). In around 1135, a woman of Ascalon staying in Fustat writes a letter to the Fustat judge, Yaḥyā, who is Ḥiyyā b. Isaac b. Samuel the Spaniard, introducing herself as the daughter of Hilāl, who is Hillel, who had been 'the elder of the Jews in Ascalon'. In the letter she asks the judge to use his influence to help her two brothers in Ascalon, one of whom, Sa'd, is *khādim al-yahūd*, i.e. beadle in the synagogue, and he was evidently dismissed and thus their livelihood was gone. She was also in need, for they had supported her and her children, and twice she stresses that she is a refugee. The backbone of the welfare activities in Ascalon was

Manasseh: **593**. Abraham b. Isaac ha-talmīd, a personality in Fustat, a Maghribī, who had a special connection with Ascalon; see on him below.

the community *heqdēsh*. We do not know the extent of its assets; we only know about a flat leased at a quarter of a dinar annually to Solomon ha-Zārīz b. Ḥalfon. In addition to a fragment of the deed of lease, receipts for the rent, from the twenties of the twelfth century through October 1146, written on the *verso* of the deed, have been preserved. Each of these receipts is signed by two judges; receipts with the signature of Nathan ha-Kohen b. Mevorakh – from the years 1132, 1134, 1135, 1139, 1142 and 1143 have been preserved; and with the signature of his son Mevorakh – from the years 1140, 1145 and 1146. It appears that Nathan ha-Kohen died in 1144, as in 1145 his son's signature appears (on the 8th of Shevat: or Thursday, 4 January): 'Mevorakh ha-Kohen b. R. Nathan ha-Kohen ha-me'ullē ha-dayyān ha-muflā, may the memory of a righteous and holy man be blessed, may he rest in paradise'; from the word 'holy' we can assume that Nathan his father had been murdered.

Nevertheless there were also wealthy people among the Jews of Ascalon at that time. Abraham b. Ṣedaqa al-'Aṭṭār (the scent dealer) who was called 'friend of the yeshiva' (that is, he was one of the donors) writes a money order, written in the form of a letter, for the sum of five dinars for his relative Abū'l-Ḥasan Rajā' of Ascalon, who was travelling to Fustat in August–September 1116. Rajā' would collect the money from Nethanel ha-talmīd b. Ṣedaqa Sar Menūḥā al-'Aṭṭār. One is speaking here of relatives, cousins (the father of the writer was the brother of the addressee's mother). This was a family of scent dealers, and we learn from this that there was still commerce in scents going on through the port of Ascalon.

The concerns of the *heqdēsh* was the thrust of an argument which broke out within the Ascalon community at the beginning of the twelfth century. Most of the community wished to use the money of the *heqdēsh* to repair the synagogue, while the cantor wanted to buy mats to sit on. The community protested that mats should be bought from community funds. The cantor and his brother organised their own coterie, with the aid of the local parnās and the *khalīlīyīn*, or people of Hebron, sixteen in number, who were clearly Jews who had fled from Hebron and found refuge in Ascalon after the Crusaders' conquest. The community called a sort of strike and did not appear in the synagogue for several weeks. The letter describes the parnās as an overbearing person and describes how matters almost came to blows; the judge, an emissary of the Nagid (from which we understand that there was no permanent judge in Ascalon at the time), succeeded in becalming the atmosphere while the people of the community managed to extort some concessions concerning the prayer routine in which the son of the parnās had formerly enjoyed priority over others of the same age (in saying the *nishmat kol ḥay*, for instance). The writers continue to complain (evidently to the Nagid in Egypt) that the parnās does not stand by what was agreed upon. From the letter it emerges that there were about one hundred Jewish families in Ascalon.[73]

[308] At the time of the Crusaders' conquest in 1153, the Jews of Ascalon escaped to Egypt. A fragment of a deed of sale written by Ḥalfon

[73] Hillel b. 'Elī's letter: **573**. Copy of the marriage deed: **594**; Shelah b. Ḥalfon b. Solomon is mentioned in **421**, letter of Elijah ha-Kohen b. Solomon (when he was still av-bēt-dīn, see note 72) to his father Ḥalfon in Ascalon. ENA NS 38, f. 11 is a fragment of an illegible letter in the handwriting of Nathan ha-Kohen b. Mevorakh (the grandson), written in his name and that of Yeshūʿā b. Yefet; his son Mevorakh is a signatory thereto as well; their *ʿalāma: yeshaʿ rav* ('a great salvation' like that of the Gaon Solomon b. Judah). Yeshūʿā 'the excellent (ḥāvēr), the judge' b. Yefet was also one of the scholars in Ascalon at the beginning of the twelfth century, and it seems that he was a partner of the Nathan ha-Kohen family in managing the affairs of the Ascalon community (see: **588**, upper margin, line 7; **589**, upper margin, line 6). His son Yefet was also involved in community affairs in Ascalon (see: **592**, where his signature appears a number of times). The letter of recommendation to Solomon b. Benjamin: **582**; written perhaps in 1098, after the Fatimid conquest of Jerusalem, and perhaps during a relatively peaceful period during the Turkomans' rule. In **583**, Nathan ha-Kohen signs his letter to 'Eli ha-Kohen, the parnās of Fustat: 'Your ḥamūd [endeared, i.e. son] Nathan ha-Kohen b. Mevorakh, may he have a good end.' This seems to have misled Braslavi, *Le-ḥeqer*, 45, into thinking that he was addressing his father; but see **586**, where it says in the upper margin, lines 5ff, that Nathan ha-Kohen b. Mevorakh's sister was married to 'Eli ha-Kohen's son, that is, he was the brother of 'Eli's daughter-in-law and hence addressed him as a father. Braslavi was also mistaken in thinking that 'Eli ha-Kohen was apparently a new figure in the Geniza findings; actually he is often mentioned in documents edited by Mann, *Jews* – see in the Index, 'Alī b. Yaḥyā Hakkohen and also 'Alī b. Yaʿīsh Hakkohen, which are merely the names of the same 'Eli ha-Kohen b. Ḥayyim. TS 8 J 4, f. 4, which bears his signature, is mentioned in Mann, *Jews*, II, 240 (see a correction of an error on p. 385, *ibid.*, in the left column); see the Hebrew Index. 'Eli ha-Kohen is mentioned in Geniza documents from 1057 to 1107. Cf. Goitein, *Mediterranean Society*, II, 78, 83, 129, who has details of his functions in the Fustat welfare system; Chapira, *REJ*, 82(1926), 329, n. 1, tried to identify him with 'Allūn, mentioned in a letter of Hayy Gaon to Sahlān b. Abraham, but they are not identical, cf. Mann, *Jews*, II, 254, in the MS; Nathan ha-Kohen (the first) is the writer of **581**. From **582**, line 12, it appears that the permanent addressee of the family in Fustat, the aforementioned 'Eli ha-Kohen, was the grandfather's brother (on the mother's side) of Nathan (the second) b. Mevorakh (grandson of the first). The genealogy would be as follows:

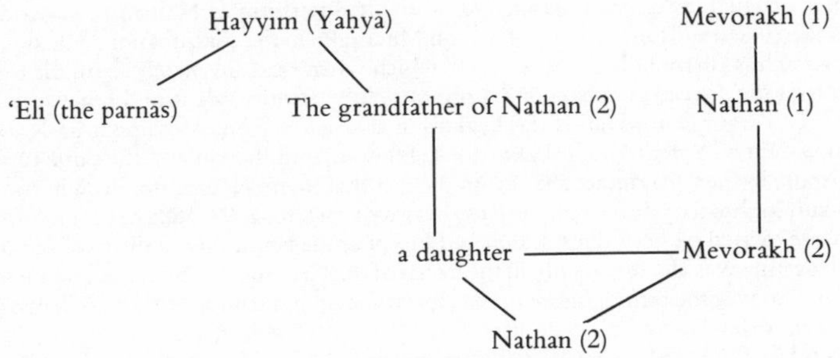

The matter of Ṣedaqa ha-Levi b. Solomon: **583**, a, lines 9–11. The matter of the blind man: **590**, see especially line 16; cf. Mann, *Jews*, II, 339. Abraham b. Eleazar is mentioned in BM

b. Manasseh shows that people from Ascalon had lived in Bilbays even before the Crusaders conquered their city (for Ḥalfon b. Manasseh, the scribe of the community in Fustat, died before that). It mentions 'the Ascalonians who now live in Bilbays'. Some fifteen years after the Crusaders' conquest, Benjamin of Tudela visited Ascalon and he found there 'some two hundred Rabbanite Jews headed by R. Ṣemaḥ and R. Aaron and R. Solomon, some forty Karaites and some three hundred *Kūtīm* [= Samaritans]'.[74]

[309] On Gaza there is little information in the works of the Muslim geographers apart from short and insignificant descriptions. The Frankish monk Bernard, who visited it in 867, notes its tremendous wealth, by which he certainly means the lush plantations in the neighbourhood. In the Geniza documents there is some information about the Jews of the city. During the Byzantine era, Gaza was a way-station for pilgrims coming from Egypt. From about 800 we hear about Moses the Gazan (*ha-'azātī*) grammarian and hence one can assume that there was some sort of centre for study and learning there. In the eleventh century there was still a community in Gaza despite the constant wars raging in the area, but it seems that the Jews began to leave the city during the last quarter of the tenth century. Ephraim b. Shemaria, the leader of the Jews of Fustat during the first half of the eleventh century, generally signed his name as 'ben Shemaria *ha-melammēd* (*ben Yaḥyā*) *ha-'Azātī* (and in Arabic: ibn Maḥfūẓ al-Ghazzī). It seems therefore that his father arrived in Egypt after he left Gaza. The family dealt in perfumes, and apparently laid the foundations for this enterprise while still in Gaza, through which he transacted business. A letter from 'the community of Gaza and the displaced' contains an appeal to the court in Fustat in which there was severe criticism of

Or 5856, a letter containing a request for aid directed to him by Joseph ha-Kohen b. Eleazar. The matter of b. al-Mufawwakh: **591**. Abraham b. Ṣedaqa al-'Aṭṭār, see: **596**. The daughter of Hilāl: **597**. The *heqdēsh*: **592**, in the handwriting of Nathan b. ha-Kohen b. Mevorakh (the grandson) and that of his son Mevorakh in the continuation. The signature of Mevorakh is surrounded by tiny letters which when read alternately from the top and the bottom say; 'great-grandson of Aaron; my Holy, for thy salvation I hope'; see ENA 4011, f. 8, a fragment which is the beginning of a letter from Mevorakh ha-Kohen b. Nathan to 'Eli b. Yefet (Abū'l-Ḥasan 'Alī b. Ḥusayn) and therein also the same formula. The dispute in the synagogue: **595**. From the fact that many Hebronites lived in Ascalon, one can undoubtedly assume that the letter was written after 1099. **588a** has evidence of the commerce carried on between Ascalon and Egypt at the beginning of the twelfth century while Palestine was already mainly in the hands of the Crusaders. This letter also mentions the man who was the central figure in Ascalon at the time, the judge ('the excellent ḥāvēr') Yeshū'ā b. Yefet.

74 See TS 6 J 2, f. 13: 154 (?) dinars is being spoken of as owing to the people of Ascalon residing in Bilbays; also mentioned there is Yaḥyā b. Najm (evidently Ḥayyim b. Hillel) al-'Akkawī, that is a man of Acre who also found refuge in Bilbays; Benjamin of Tudela (Adler), 28f.

the decision taken by Ephraim b. Shemaria concerning the claim of Mevorakh b. Nathan, of Gaza, who asked for the legacy of his brother ‘Amram, who died ‘in the land of Pithom’, that is, evidently in the region of the Fayyūm in Egypt. The date of the letter is apparently about 1030 and it seems likely that Jews from the villages and hamlets in southern Palestine sought refuge in Gaza, and are ‘the displaced’ mentioned in the letter. No less than fifteen people signed the letter, the most important signing last: Yeshū‘ā *he-ḥāvēr be-s.g.* (in the Great Sanhedrin) b. R. Nathan (surrounding his name in tiny letters which when read upwards and downwards alternately made up the words: great-grandson of Gur Arie [lion’s cub]). Yeshū‘ā b. Nathan is the author of a piyyūṭ (*qedūshtā*) on the death of his son Josiah; it seems that Yeshū‘ā was the leader of the Jews of Gaza at that time. One can assume that the entire Jewish community in Gaza was uprooted at the time of the Crusaders’ conquest, and it seems that part of it moved to Ascalon. This emerges from the letter from the Gazan Eleazer ha-Kohen ha-mumḥē, the judge, b. Zechariah, apparently from Ascalon, to ‘Eli ha-Kohen b. Ḥayyim in Fustat, perhaps a relative of the writer. Eleazar asks ‘Eli to help him out with obtaining a prayer shawl, or the money to buy one. It seems that this Eleazar was the son of Zechariah ha-Kohen b. Kulayb (a diminutive from Kālēv = Khalaf = Aaron; hence his entire Hebrew name: Zechariah b. Aaron) signed in the aforementioned letter of the Gazans. In the letter, ‘the community of our people of Gaza’, that is, the Gazans who found refuge in Ascalon are mentioned. The people of Gaza who live in Ascalon are also mentioned in a letter from Nathan ha-Kohen b. Mevorakh, the Ascalonite, who also wrote to ‘Eli ha-Kohen b. Ḥayyim in Fustat – they are suspected of having spoken derogatively of some of the public figures in Ascalon to the *nāsī*, David b. Daniel.[75]

[75] Geographers: see for instance Muqaddasī, *Āqālīm*, 174, who mentions the beautiful mosque and the *mashhad* of ‘Umar ibn al-Khaṭṭāb; they also mention that Gaza is the location of the grave of Hāshim ibn ‘Abd Manāf (one of the forefathers of Muḥammad); see: Le Strange, *Palestine*, 442. Bernard, in Tobler et Molinier, I, 314, (= *MPL* 121, 571); Moses ha-naqdān: Harkavy, *Ḥadashim* (reprint), 20 (= No. 2, p. 8); Mann, *Jews*, II, 47; Assaf, *Meqorot*, 30. Ephraim b. Shemaria, see for instance: **35**, b; **413**, lines 3–4; *bōsmān* (‘spice merchant’) in **46**, line 16; see on the origin of Ephraim b. Shemaria and his signatures: Assaf, *Yerushalayim*, 1952/3, 104. n. 9; Gil, *Documents*, 154, n. 9. The letter from the Gazans: **219**. Fragments from the *qedūshtā* of Yeshū‘ā b. Nathan were edited by Zulay, *Yedī‘ōt*, 3 (1936/7), 176; his signature on one of the colophons: Yeshū‘ā the ḥāvēr b. R. Nathan, great-grandson of Gur Arie, and similarly in **219**, line 64; Zulay (*ibid.*) assumed that this perhaps hints at his being a descendant of the head of the exilarchic family; see also his note in *Yedi‘ōt*, 5(1938/9), 170, that the handwriting of these fragments and that of the Gazans’ letter are identical; see also Assaf, *ibid.*, 34; Fleischer, *Halkin Jubilee Volume*, 185ff, edited additional fragments from the aforementioned *qedūshtā*; his signature in the *qedūshtā*: Yeshū‘a the Judge b. R. Nathan, and as he was as yet not called ḥāvēr, one can assume that it was written relatively early; his son Josiah died at the age of six (see in Fleischer *ibid.*, p. 184, nn. 5, 7); see on Yeshū‘ā the ḥāvēr b. Nathan also in: Goitein,

[310] In the month of March, AD 1052, a group of Karaites, consisting of both Jerusalemites and Gazans, visited the fields in the Gaza area in order to test the *āvīv*, that is, the degree of ripeness of the growing grain, and to decide whether they could declare that year a leap year. From this account we know that there were also Karaites in Gaza. The visit took place in a field on the land of *sūq māzin* (*'alā ḥaql bi-arḍ sūq māzin min kūra ghazza*); 376 years earlier, in February 676, a similar expression is recorded in the papyri of Nessana: *Klēma Sykomazōn khōras Gazēs*; and in the Targum of Jerusalem (to Num., xxxiv:15) we find: '. . . it fell in their lot [the area] to Rafiaḥ and *Shūqmazāyē*, until one reaches the border of the salty sea' [*yāmā de-milḥā*'; it is possible that by *yāmā de-milḥā* the Mediterranean is intended, like in Arab sources of the Middle Ages]. During the Byzantine period Sykomazōn was an important town and the seat of a bishop.[76]

[311] The Muslim geographers have little to say about Jericho as well. It seems that the city was on the decline and nothing is known of its Jewish population; at least there is no mention of it in the Geniza, apart from one man whose name was al-Rīḥānī, who lived *ca.* 1040 in a dwelling of the Jewish *waqf* (*qodesh*) in Fustat, and as his name indicates, he came from Jericho. The Muslim sources dealing with the Dead Sea region particularly mention the date palms which grow in this area in abundance, and also the indigo. The most important city in the region of the Dead Sea was Ṣō'ar (Zoar), in Arabic Zughar, or Ṣughar, near the southern part of the Dead Sea. Frequently in Arab sources, the Dead Sea is called 'the sea of Zughar'.

Mediterranean Society, III, 234; 476, n. 76. The letter of Eleazar ha-Kohen: **619**; it is possible that Ḥalfon ha-Kohen b. Eleazar, about whom it is said in **529**, line 15, that he went to Ascalon 'as ordered', was the son of this Eleazar, the judge from Gaza, and this emigration from Gaza to Ascalon is apparently being hinted at here. The letter from Nathan ha-Kohen b. Mevorakh: **587** (autumn 1093), lines 6–7: 'people from among the Gazans who are not inhabitants of the city [that is, Ascalon] and do not know the real situation of the community . . .'

76 The visit of the Karaites: **302**. See: *Nessana*, 189 (No. 64, line 8); the Targum, see in the *Miqrā'ōt gedōlōt*; also *Neophyti* (ed. Diez Macho, Madrid, 1974), IV, 323: 'it fell in their lot [the area] to *Rfywn* and *Shūqmazāyē* and to the cave of 'Eyn Gedi until one reaches the salty sea' (thus in the photocopy, the *Neophyti*, Jerusalem, 1971, fol. 351), and we can see that the scribe distorted the names and mixed up the order. On the Byzantine period: Hierocles, *Synecdemus*, 44; Georgius Cyprius, *Descriptio*, 52 (where Eukōmazōn is printed); according to Musil, *Edom*, 222, who visited the ruins of Sūq Māzin on 29 March 1898, the Bedouin of Banū Sheyla built a village for themselves out of these ruins; he points out that *Sykōmazōn* is also marked on the Madaba map. In 1906 the land of Sūq Māzin (as the Bedouin called it) was in the hands of the Banū Sheyla and Banū'l-Nājira, who were constantly fighting one another over them, see: Jaussen, *RB*, 3(1906), 607; cf. Klein, *ZDPV*, 33(1910), 33; Abel, *JPOS*, 4(1924), 117. Sūq Māzin, five kilometres southeast of Dayr al-Balaḥ; cf. further: Alt, *Palästinajahrbuch*, 29(1933), 76; see also Clermont-Ganneau, *Recueil*, V, 120, nn. 3, 4; Avi-Yonah, *Ge'ōgrāfya hīsṭōrīt*, 74 and n. 10; 118 and n. 13, and more references there; see Bar Deroma, *Gevul*, 512, 636f and n. 740, who has details that need correcting in the light of what was said above.

In a letter from the Geniza from *ca.* 1065, written by Avon b. Ṣedaqa, it is mentioned that indigo and *wasma* seeds (also a kind of indigo) were brought from Zughar, but the road from there was dangerous and one of the Maghribi merchants, Joseph b. 'Alī Kohen Fāsī, who considered going there from Hebron, changed his mind and forwent the journey. On the other hand, it seems that in the middle of the tenth century there were still Jews living in Ṣō'ar, as is proven by a copy of a court document, whose original is said to be preserved in Granada (Gharnaṭa), and which deals with the legacy of a man of Alisana (Lucena), Abraham b. Meir (whose nickname was b. Qālūs). The court document was made at the request of the son of the deceased, Samuel. The father had left property, merchandise and money in Egypt and Palestine. Joshua b. Nathan (who is Abū'l-Surūr Yamanī al-Andalusī) was appointed trustee in charge of the property; in a list of the details, property with so-and-so living in Ṣō'ar in Palestine is also mentioned (the man's name has not been preserved). In a letter from Jerusalem written by Ḥayyim the ḥaver b. Solomon to Isaac b. Jacob the ḥāvēr in Fustat, dealing with the collection of a debt owing to this Isaac, it says that the debtor lived in Ṣō'ar (spelled Zughrar; evidently this error in spelling was caused by the difficulty of pronouncing the *ghayin* together with the *rā'*). To sum up, it seems that the region of Ṣō'ar, and the region of the Dead Sea in general, was more active during the period under discussion than later on. It is likely that Jews lived in Ṣō'ar, though we have no knowledge of a Jewish community there. However, Jewish merchants were particularly interested in this region because of the indigo plant, which was used for extracting dyes for textiles.[77]

[77] Jericho: see Muqaddasī, *Āqālīm*, 175. Al-Rīḥānī: Gil, *Documents*, 195, n. 9 (see documents No. 22 [TS 20.168], line 33; No. 24 [TS Box K 25, f. 84], b, line 5). Muslim traditions on Ṣō'ar (connecting it with Lot and his daughters) see: Le Strange, *Palestine*, 287ff. Arculf calls the place Zoaroi Arabiae, see in Tobler et Molinier I, 179; 'the sea of Zughar': see Iṣṭakhrī, 13; according to Muqaddasī, *Āqālīm*, 185, youth (*aḥdāth*) and sick people gather at the sea of Zughar, that is, the Dead Sea (apparently at its southern end), during the month of Ab (August); Idrīsī (Cerulli), 354f, describes the region, mentions Sodom and Gomorrah and 'the people of Lot' (these details are also found in other Muslim geographers), and he mentions that there are small sailing ships moving about on the Dead Sea, carrying passengers and goods, mainly dates; see Daniel the Russian, 47: Sigor, where the grave of Lot and his two daughters is situated. The sources also mention the region in connection with the cultivation of indigo; Salmon b. Yeruḥim mentions Zughar in his Arabic commentary on Ecclesiastes, BM Or 2517, fol. 92b (The labour of the foolish wearieth every one of them, because he knoweth not how to go to the city; x:15) 'like a man who leaves Ramla for Jerusalem (Bayt al-Maqdis), which is quite a famous road; if he wants to make a short-cut, he will pass through 'Imwās and Qaryat al-'anab; but he [the fool] will not go this way but will go towards Gaza and turn towards Bayt Jibrīn and from there to Zughar and afterwards return to 'Eyn Gedi and from there to Jericho and from there to Jerusalem . . .' Indirectly we have learned that Ṣō'ar was situated to the south of the Dead Sea, a fact which was disputed for some time (see: Le Strange, *Palestine*, 286f). The letter of Avon; **503**, lines 15ff. The copy of the court document: BM Or 5561A, f. 1, upper part, vellum. The deceased, Abraham b. Meir al-Andalusī, is mentioned in **159**, a letter of

[312] We have detailed evidence of the Jewish community in *Rafiaḥ* (Rafaḥ in Arabic), about which the Muslim sources tell us practically nothing, merely that it had a prosperous population and a market, a mosque and also inns. The city was considered the frontier of Palestine, that is, the last city before entering Egypt. In about 1020, the Gaon Josiah writes to the Rafiaḥ community concerning the division of a legacy, which caused one of the parties to apply to the Muslim courts. In 1044, Karaites went there to examine the state of the fields with regard to the *āvīv*.[78]

[313] During the Muslim period Eilat became an important station on the way to Mecca for pilgrim caravans. We have already seen the treaty between the Prophet and the population of Eilat, as well as the matter of people converting to Islam, the *mawālī* (clients) of the Umayyads (still in the days of 'Uthmān), who lived in Eilat, including a number of important figures in the development of ancient Muslim literature. It is not known whether these *mawālī* were former Jews or Christians. Lammens claimed that Eilat was a Christian city, basing his argument particularly on the fact that the inhabitants' representative in their negotiations with Muḥammad during the Tabūk campaign, Yuḥannā, is said in some sources to have been the bishop of Eilat. Further proof he found in a tradition according to which Marwān ibn al-Ḥakam was aided by 200 Christians(!) of Eilat to organise a police force in Medina when he was still governor of Medina before he became caliph, but the source he mentions does not refer to Christians at all, merely to *ahl ayla*, a term which undoubtedly means

Solomon b. Judah to Abraham ha-Kohen b. Haggai in Fustat; speaking there of a large debt left by the deceased, mentioning also Joshua b. Nathan (his name is found in my Geniza collection, see the Hebrew Index), who was the trustee for the legacy together with Abraham ha-Kohen b. Haggai; cf. Goitein, *Eretz Israel*, 12(1974/5), 200, and n. 7 (= *ha-Yishuv*, 201); however, TS 13J 14, f. 24, a court document dated 7 Teveth 1344 Sel., 12 December AD 1032, which Goitein edited there, is not from Ṣō'ar but from Ḥanēs (as is written in line 14), which is Tinnīs; in the original: 'Ḥanēs the island near the Salty Sea' (lines 14–15); cf. Golb, *JNES*, 33(1974), 143; the city of the island of Ḥanēs is Tinnīs; 'the Salty Sea' meant, in the Arabic of the Middle Ages the Mediterranean – cf. Goitein, *Mediterranean Society*, I, 296; 474, n. 15; *ibid.* he cites ENA 1822, f. 7, line 21: *al-baḥr al-māliḥ*, the Mediterranean. See for instance Idrīsī (Cerulli), 370: *al-baḥr al-milḥ* (the Mediterranean). See also the *qerōvā* for the eighth day of the Feast of the Tabernacles edited by Zulay, *Yerushalayim*, 1952/3, lines 42–43, where the salty water of 'the Great Sea' is put in opposition to the malodorous one of the 'Sea of Sodom'. See also: Friedman, *Marriage*, II, 316f for an opinion similar to mine. (The court document from Ḥanēs confirms the receipt of money from Ḥasana, daughter of Nahum, through Sar Shalom b. Joseph, and signatories there are: Mevasser ha-Kohen b. 'Eli; A[aron(?)] the scribe b. Nahum; Abraham b. Mevasser; Aaron the ḥāvēr b. R. Yaḥyā.) The region of Ṣō'ar (Zughar) is mentioned in **301**, line 31: The Karaites examine the state of the *avīv* (the first crops) there in 1044. The Jerusalem letter: **463**, a, line 22.

78 See Yāqūt, II, 796, who cites al-Muhallabī (end of the tenth century); he mentions that the place is inhabited by tribesmen from Lakhm and Judhām, and that security there is at its lowest (it is difficult to know what period he is talking about). The letter of Josiah Gaon: 43. The Karaites: **301**, line 30.

tribesmen from Eilat. On the other hand, the Muslim tradition found in the commentaries to the Koran states that Eilat was a Jewish city in the period before Islam and identifies it with the city mentioned in the Koran, vii:163–169 (*sūrat al-aʿrāf*) 'ask them about the city near the sea, whose [inhabitants] desecrated the sabbath when the fish [in the sea] there came to them . . . for since they had the nerve to do this evil which was forbidden for them to do, We [i.e. God] told them: be outcast monkeys'; this is evidently the metamorphosis of a Jewish legend about Jewish fishermen who became monkeys on God's orders because they desecrated the sabbath. The commentators generally claim that Eilat (Ayla) is intended, although there are ḥadīth traditions which point to other places. The truth in this case is evidently somewhere in the middle, namely that Eilat in the Prophet's day was a city with a mixed population of Jews and Christians. In the period we are discussing here, however, we have no information regarding Christians in Eilat; and altogether there is very little information about the city. Maqrīzī mentions that in the days of Khumārawayh b. Aḥmad ibn Ṭūlūn, works were carried out in the mountain-pass of Eilat, the *ʿaqaba* (*ʿaqabat ayla* – hence its name for later generations), in order to widen it; the work was supervised by his *mawlā*, Fā'iq, for it was formerly impossible to pass through the road mounted (in *ca.* 860). A house belonging to a Jewish woman in Eilat is mentioned at about the same time.[79]

[314] Hebron is almost never mentioned in Muslim literature before the tenth century, which indicates that it was not rated highly. This is also suggested by the fact that its name is not mentioned in the Muslim traditions of the conquest. In the tenth century, the Muslim geographers Iṣṭakhrī, Ibn Ḥawqal and Muqaddasī, mention Hebron and we find in their writings descriptions of the patriarchs' graves. This is especially true in the account of Muqaddasī, who also quotes praises of the area for its excellent fruits. He furthermore mentions the inn (*funduq*) in Hebron, open to strangers, which boasts a cook, a baker and servants, who serve a meal of lentils (*ʿadas*) with olive oil to the poor and to pilgrims, and even to the rich, should they want it. This inn, together with its services, was supported by revenue from the *waqf*s, which were founded by Tamīm al-Dārī and others, among them rulers of distant countries who left property in their wills for this purpose – all this to maintain Abraham's traditional hospitality to strangers. Nāṣir Khusraw, who visited Hebron in 1047, describes the graves of the patriarchs, especially the *mashhad* of Abraham (al-Khalīl). He also describes the hospitality according to

[79] Lammens, *Moʿāwia*, 433f, who quotes from Iṣbahānī, *Aghānī*, IV, 156; see what is said there. Commentary: see for instance Ṭabarī, *Tafsīr*, XIII, 180ff: some say the intention is to Maqnā or Madyan; cf. Ibn al-Jawzī, *Tafsīr*, fol. 30; Ibn Ḥayyān, IV, 410; in Mawṣilī, *Nihāya*, 57b, Ayla became Īliyā, that is Jerusalem; see Maqrīzī, *Khiṭaṭ*, I, 325. The house of the Jewish woman: Ibn Saʿd, VII(2), 206; Ibn al-Jawzī, *Ṣifa*, IV, 305.

Abraham's tradition: the strangers are given bread, olives, lentils in olive oil and raisins. He also mentions the gifts given to the *mashhad* by the Fatimid rulers of Egypt. Apart from these literary sources, the inscription on the grave of a man named Ḥusayn al-Aḥwal should also be noted, in which it says that he fell in battle, in Ṣafar in AH 390, or January/February AD 1000. There is evidently an indication here that the Muslims (like the Jews) saw some advantage to being buried in Hebron.[80]

[315] It is interesting to note that in the Geniza documents pertaining to this book, the name 'Hebron' is not mentioned, only 'the graves of the patriarchs'. The documents show that there was an organised community in Hebron with a *ḥāvēr* at its head, and that they were largely occupied with the pilgrims who came to the 'graves of the patriarchs'. On visits to Hebron for religious purposes, we find some detailed evidence. Around 1060 'Eli ha-Kohen b. Ezekiel, the parnās of Jerusalem, writes to Abū'l-Ḥasan 'Allūn b. Ya'īsh, who is 'Eli ha-Kohen b. Ḥayyim, the parnās in Fustat, informing him in the opening sentences of the letter that he went to the 'graves of the patriarchs', together with some other people, and said a special prayer there for the ḥāvēr Abū Zikrī and his son (Abū Zikrī is Judah b. Saadia, the Egyptian Nagid), for 'the prince [*sar*] of the congregation' (it is difficult to know who he is referring to, perhaps Abraham ha-Kohen b. Isaac b. Furāt), and for the addressee. He swears by Jerusalem that he did so, and all this before the approaching Days of Awe. He points out that he prayed for them while the Torah was open, proof indeed that there was a synagogue in the place – the synagogue near the graves of the patriarchs. The Maghribi merchant Barhūn b. Mūsā (Abraham b. Moses) al-Tāhirtī writes from Jerusalem to his relative and partner Nehorai b. Nissim and mentions that he intends to visit the 'graves of the patriarchs' together with his father. Another Maghribi merchant, Avon b. Ṣedaqa, writes on 28 August 1065, complaining that his partner went to the 'graves of the patriarchs' and made an unsuccessful deal there in buying wheat. From this we learn that Hebron was also a meeting-place for Jewish merchants. In another letter, Avon complains that the same partner made this deal with money which he had loaned to him, in order to go to Ṣō'ar (Zughar), but he was afraid to go there and remained stuck at the 'graves of the patriarchs'. Some of the letters from Hebron are from the Saljūq period and it can be seen from them that the Jewish community there continued to exist. At the head of the community stood Saadia the ḥāvēr b. Abraham b. Nathan, who calls himself 'the ḥāvēr of the graves of the patriarchs, of blessed memory'. In a letter written in *ca.* 1080 to Yeshū'ā b. Yakhīn in

80 Iṣṭakhrī, 57; Ibn Ḥawqal, 113; Muqaddasī, *Āqālīm*, 172; Nāṣir Khusraw, 33f (text), 99–105 (translation). Ibn al-'Arabī (about 1095) tells of Muslims performing the *ziyāra* in Hebron, see: *Riḥla*, 82; also al-Ghazālī testifies to having performed a *ziyāra* in Hebron himself

Fustat, he mentions that his son Abraham carries Hebron cheese to Egypt. From the letter, it sounds as if this Hebronite is a relative of the Egyptian Nagid Mevorakh, and he sends his regards to him and to the widow of Mevorakh's brother, Judah b. Saadia, and to Saadia, the son of Judah. In another letter he wrote to Abiathar ha-Kohen Gaon b. Elijah at the beginning of the year 1082 (the date emerges from the contents), Saadia the ḥāvēr expresses his joy and congratulations on the appointment of Abiathar ha-Kohen as Gaon (which is described in the 'Scroll of Abiathar'). He mentions that the Hebronites pray for him 'at the graves of the patriarchs' every day, as they did on the last Day of Atonement. From the letter, it appears that Abiathar sends the people of Hebron financial support and mentions that he sent a dinar through a certain Samuel. Their situation is difficult, Saadia himself has been ill for the past two months, they lost an ass worth fifteen dinars on the way from Hebron to Ascalon, and they have nothing to wear nor bread to eat.

A Catholic monk also wrote about the synagogue close to the graves of the patriarchs in 1119. After describing how the Jews helped the Muslims take Hebron (by showing them where it was possible to break into the town), on condition that they are permitted to build a synagogue at the entrance to the graves of the patriarchs, he adds that 'it is impossible to describe in what reverence that people of unbelievers held the place; no one would enter it without taking off his shoes and washing his feet; that prayer-house was splendidly decorated, with gold and silver and silken fabrics. After many years the Almighty Creator and Saviour of the Universe took that whole region from these unbelievers and gave it to the Latin Christians'. As in his story he speaks of both Muslims (the Saracens) and Jews, it is not very clear to which of them the prayer-house refers, but in view of the claims of the Muslim sources that the ritual at the graves of the patriarchs only began after the Crusaders, as we have already seen, and in view of the explicit evidence of the letters from Hebron in the Geniza, we may assume that that Christian source was also speaking of the synagogue. It seems that the community in Hebron was liquidated not long after the above-mentioned letters and it is not clear whether it existed during the whole period between 1082 (the letter of Saadia the ḥāvēr) and the Crusaders' conquest of Jerusalem (when Hebron was also taken). We have found above that there was a large group of Jews from Hebron in Ascalon, but it seems that most of the Hebron community fled to Egypt, particularly to Bilbays, and we have letters from the Hebronite Abraham b. Saadia the ḥāvēr, who became the head of the community in Bilbays, but who still maintained contact with the people of Hebron. He

(after 1090), see: *al-Munqidh*, 75 (I am grateful to Prof. H. Lazarus-Yafeh for bringing this to my attention). Grave inscription: *Répertoire chronologique*, VI, no. 2078 (p. 37).

occasionally speaks of 'the graves of the patriarchs'. We also have a letter from one of his relatives, Joseph b. Jacob b. Joseph ha-mumḥē (specialist in law) ha-Ḥebrōnī b. Saadia 'the ḥāvēr in the Great Sanhedrin, the servant of the eternal fathers'. It seems that the Hebronites did not see eye to eye or live in complete harmony with other people. Tobiah ha-Kohen b. 'Eli, of Bāniyās, and also a refugee from Palestine, writes in around 1115, evidently from Bilbays, of the troubles inflicted on him by the people of Hebron – 'wicked *qawm yahūd khalīlīyīn*' (Jewish people from Hebron).[81]

[81] 'Eli b. Ezekiel: **452**, a, lines 3–6. Al-Tāhirtī: **458**, b, line 10. Avon: **501**, a, lines 15f; **503**, a, lines 28f. The letters of Saadia, the ḥāvēr of Hebron: **613**; Yeshū'ā b. Yakhīn (Thābit), perhaps the son of Yakhīn b. Nethanel 'Head of the Communities' (see some details on him: Gil, *Documents*, 214, n. 7); the story of the unclear scheming in this letter is perhaps connected with the Abiathar ha-Kohen – David b. Daniel conflict; it is obvious that Saadia was among the supporters of Abiathar and of the Nagid Mevorakh and it seems that the letter was written before the deposal of the Nagid (1082); see on this conflict below. Saadia was evidently appointed ḥāvēr by Abiathar, for in the following letter, **614**, b, lines 6–7, 17, he calls himself 'a plant of your hand'; see *ibid.*, a, line 10, the matter of the prayers at the graves of the patriarchs; they also prayed for Abraham b. Ḥalfon (b. Nahum), of Ascalon, who conducted business in Tyre and was in Abiathar's circle; they prayed during 'the Day of Atonement in the Holy Cave' (b, lines 12–13); it seems that part of the family had already left Hebron at that time, for on p. b, line 14, he mentions the 'rumours about his mother and his sister's daughter' (evidently meaning that they had died in Egypt); in the letter there is also mention of the death of Abiathar's brother, Eleazar. The story of the monk, see: *RHC* (Occ.), V, 309, 315; cf. Dinaburg (Dinur), *Zion* (ha-me'assēf), 2(1926/7), 55; Assaf, *Meqōrōt*, 43. Prawer, *Zion*, 11(1945/6), 52f, tried to prove that the reference is to Muslims and not to Jews, for from the text of the Latin monk one learns only that in the seventh century (mistakenly printed: the sixth) a Jewish community settled there, with a synagogue in the vicinity of the Cave of Machpelah. He learns from **617** that there was no longer a synagogue in the place at the end of the tenth century; but the letter **617** deals with matters concerning Bilbays and not Hebron, and its date is the beginning of the twelfth century, as will become clear below. The Hebronites in Ascalon: **595**, a, line 9. There are four letters written by Abraham, son of the aforementioned Saadia the ḥāvēr, of Bilbays: **615–618**; evidently he did not return to Hebron from his journey to Egypt mentioned above; he had relatives in Egypt, one of whom was his son-in-law (or brother-in-law? *ṣihr*) Abū'l-Surūr Peraḥia b. Bunaym, and the other: Moses ha-Kohen b. Ghālib (Ghulayb); it seems that the first lived in al-Qāhira and the other in Fustat. In the first letter, of which only a small fragment has been preserved (**615**), the address of Moses ha-Kohen remains in the body of the letter he addresses Peraḥia; in the second letter (**616**), written before Passover to Moses ha-Kohen, the three sons of the latter are mentioned, Josiah, Saadia and Yeshū'ā, and members of the family of Abraham b. Saadia himself: Abū'l-Ḥusayn (probably 'Alī), Abū Sa'īd, Umm Abī'l-Bayān (evidently Abraham's mother), Bayān, Sittāt (evidently Abraham's daughter); the letter contains details on an epidemic of chicken-pox in Bilbays and some instances of the deaths of Hebronites there. Abraham b. Saadia evidently suffers from an eye disease and he asks for *kuḥl* (antimony) to be sent him; an important personage (*ḥaḍratuhu al-sāmiya*, probably the Nagid, who was a relative) visited Bilbays and had already left. The third letter, **617**, is to Isaac b. Samuel the Spaniard, one of the leaders of the community in Fustat; we learn that the writer, Abraham b. Saadia the Hebronite ḥāvēr, achieved the status of a kind of leader, *muqaddam* (appointee) over the Bilbays community. In the meantime, apparently Moses ha-Kohen b. Ghulayb moved to Bilbays and bought a parcel of land from the local cadi, Hārūn. On that land, they intended to build a new synagogue and the letter contains a description of the

[316–317] Another town in the south of Palestine mentioned in our sources is 'Aqīr, which is Akron, or 'Āqir according to Muqaddasī. He describes it as a large village with a main mosque (*jāmi'*), and he praises its

demolition of the old one and the building of the new, and particularly the difficulties they had with the Muslim authorities, after the cadi explained to them that one cannot build a (new) synagogue in the days of 'our Lord al-Afḍal' (the wazīr of Egypt). Nevertheless the community collected the money needed and continued to build despite the disturbances (from Jewish neighbours as well); the letter also contains complaints about the writer's situation and financial distress. The community does not treat him as they should and do not give him any *pesīqā* (regular allocation). Assaf, *Meqōrōt*, 45f, considered the letter as having been written in Hebron, and in *Sefer ha-yishuv*, 7, explained that the letter dates from the end of the tenth century, and his view was accepted by others as well; but it can be seen that Abraham b. Saadia the ḥāvēr, who was a Hebronite, now lives in a new place; nor does it stand to reason that this whole affair would take place in the year between the re-conquest of Palestine by the Fatimids (July 1098; for al-Afḍal, the Fatimid wazīr is mentioned) and the Crusaders' conquest; Isaac, 'the great Rabbi, *rēsh bē rabbānān 'ēzer ha-nesī'ūt* ('head of the house of learning', 'aide of the exilarchate') can only be Isaac b. Samuel the Spaniard, contrary to Assaf's opinion, *ibid.* Also in **553**, a, line 20, Abiathar ha-Kohen Gaon calls him the 'great Rabbi'; see on him: Mann, *Tarbiz*, 6(1934/5), 75f; *idem*, *Texts*, I, 388; Goitein, *Mediterranean Society*, II, 567, n. 29; his name is mentioned in the Geniza documents from 1088–1127. In this letter of Abraham b. Saadia (**617**) his two sons are mentioned (line 7). The fact that the writer is in Bilbays is also proved in the fragment of a letter **618**, in which Abraham b. Saadia, the Hebronite ḥāvēr, writes in the name of the Bilbays community, to Solomon b. Shelah (who is in Fustat, it seems); it is quite clear there that after he left Hebron, Saadia was given the status of leader in the community of Bilbays. As to Moses ha-Kohen b. Ghulayb, it appears that he too was a refugee from Hebron. One could not say with certainty that there was a family connection between him and Moses ha-Kohen b. Ghulayb, of Fustat, who died in 1026, and whose legacy matters are dealt with in **61** and **76**, b, line 3. It is clear that Assaf's explanations in *Meqōrōt*, 44; *Yerushalayim*, 1952/3, 113, are mistaken. The idiom of the oath 'by the graves of the patriarchs' which we find in **616**, b, line 1, is interesting – *wa-turbat al-ha-avōt*(!). The letter of Joseph b. Jacob, the great-grandson of Saadia the ḥāvēr of Hebron: TS 10 J 10, f. 20 (cited in Mann, *Jews*, II, 203); he writes to Shelah the cantor, *ha-mumḥē* (see above: Solomon b. Shelah, to whom Abraham b. Saadia writes) apparently in Fustat. The letter was evidently written in the latter half of the twelfth century. It deals with the burial of his brother, David, about whom there are rumours that he was not buried in a Jewish grave. The following is the geneaology of this Hebronite family:

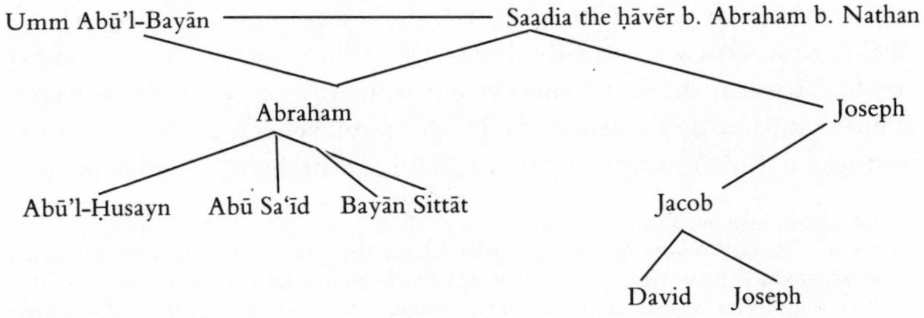

The letter of Tobiah ha-Kohen: TS 12.113.

bread.[82] Of the cities of Samaria, Shechem is mentioned, a city of the Samaritans. According to Ya'qūbī, writing in 892, it is an ancient city with 'two holy mountains', and underneath the city there is a city hewn out of the rock. In his words, its inhabitants are mixed, including Arabs (= tribesman) and non-Muslims (*'ajam*), namely Samaritans. Muqaddasī writes that Shechem excels in its olive groves. It is situated between two mountains which close in on it; its market stretches from gate to gate and there is another market in the centre of the town. It has a *jāmi'* in the town's centre and is a clean city with paved roads. The Andalusian scholar Abū Bakr Ibn al-'Arabī, who, as we have seen, stayed in Palestine in the nineties of the eleventh century, admires the modesty of the women in Shechem; one does not see them in the streets except on Friday when they go to and from the mosque. Shechem is mentioned occasionally in the Geniza documents pertaining to this book. It is told that Elijah ha-Kohen b. Solomon Gaon travelled there in *ca.* 1030, perhaps in order to evade the authorities, evidently at the time of the disturbances connected with the dispute with the Karaites. It was a junction for travellers to Jerusalem from Damascus. Daniel b. Azariah passed through Shechem on coming from Damascus, and thus did not have to go through Ramla. A merchant's letter mentions that its writer stayed *fī Baysān wa-Nābulus*, that is in Bet Shean and Shechem.[83]

[318] Of the towns in Trans-Jordan, Muslim sources mention 'Ammān. Muqaddasī says that it lies on the edge of the desert and is the capital of al-Balqā', and that the region is rich in grain. He notes that its *jāmi'* is situated alongside the market and that its courtyard is paved with mosaic. The fortress of Goliath (*qaṣr jālūt*) looks down on it from the mountain and there is also the tomb of Uriah, over which a mosque has been erected. It also boasts of the theatre (*mal'ab*) of Sulaymān (King Solomon). Muqaddasī notes that the prices are low and the fruit plentiful, but he is disappointed by its inhabitants, who he says are people with no culture (*juhhāl*). He also complains that the roads leading to the city are in a bad state. Abū Zakariyyā' Yuḥannā (or Yaḥyā) ibn Māsawayh al-Jundī Shabūrī, a Nestorian writer of the latter half of the ninth century, mentions that in 'Ammān there is a market day annually on the 10th of August. There is apparently evidence of a Jewish population there in a letter from Solomon b. Judah, written in about 1020, to Abraham b. Sahlān in Fustat,

[82] Muqaddasī, *Āqālīm*, 176.

[83] Iṣṭakhrī, 58: city of the Samaritans 'who claim that the temple is Nābulus, and the Samaritans have no other city on earth except that' (undoubtedly a distortion of a tradition which said that it was the holy city of the Samaritans). Ibn Ḥawqal, 172: 'the people of Bayt al-Maqdis [the intention is apparently Palestine] claim that all Samaritans come from there originally; [but] in Ramla there are some 500 of them who pay jizya'. Muqaddasī, *Āqālīm*, 174. Ibn al-'Arabī, *Aḥkām*, 1523. Elijah ha-Kohen travelled there: **433**, a, line 6 (*ilā*

in which he deals with the affairs of Isaac of Wādī'l-Qurā (northern Ḥijāz) who was living in Fustat after having left his wife 'as a living widow in 'Ammān some four years ago'; this Isaac was a merchant and it appears from the letter that the mainstay of his trade was in 'Ammān. He deserved to be excommunicated 'for his behaviour towards his household in 'Ammān' (*Rabbat benē 'ammōn*). Solomon b. Judah mentions 'Ammān again in a letter he wrote on 19 December 1029 to someone in Fustat. It seems that he deals with the purchase of grain and the source of supply is 'Ammān. In the middle of the eleventh century, a Geniza letter mentions a Maghribi merchant, Abū Sa'īd Khalfa, who was travelling to 'Ammān on business, evidently, or perhaps on family matters, for it is stated that he was the son-in-law of a man from 'Ammān: Yaḥyā al-'Ammānī.[84]

[319–320] 'Amtā, which is east of the Jordan valley, is mentioned only by Yāqūt, a relatively late writer, who says that the grave of Abū 'Ubayda ibn al-Jarrāḥ, one of the commanders of the Muslim conquest, is situated there. He cites Muhallabī in praise of the spices grown in that region. In two documents, in my Geniza collection, the Jerusalemite Mevassēr ha-sōfēr (the scribe) son of Shelah 'the teacher of the orphans', al-'Amtānī, is mentioned, and one can discern from this that indeed there was a Jewish community in 'Amtā. In about 1030 the same Mevassēr signs a letter from the people of Jerusalem to Fustat concerning assistance for the Jewish population of Jerusalem. In the year AM 4805, which is AD 1045, we find a deed of receipt from Jerusalem, signed by the Gaon Solomon b. Judah and Elijah ha-Kohen b. Solomon Gaon; the receipt is given by the same Mevassēr b. Shelah al-'Amtānī and his wife Ghāliya, daughter of Ashlīmūn al-Dalātī (= from Daltūn), who is also called al-Bāniyāsiyya.[85]

Of the regions of Trans-Jordan, Ya'qūbī mentions especially the areas of Fiḥl and Jarash and notes that Arabs, meaning tribesmen, and non-Arabs (*'ajam*) live there side-by-side.[86]

[321–327] On Bet-Shean, apart from being mentioned in the traditions

nābulus). Daniel b. Azariah: **468**, b, line 1. The merchant: **527**, line 14 (but see the introduction to this document, it may be of a much later period).

84 Muqaddasī, *Āqālīm*, 175; Ibn Māsawayh (Sbath), 255. The matter of Isaac: **58**, a, lines 20–24. The wheat: **83**, b, lines 7–8. Abū Sa'īd Khalfa: **525**, a, lines 18–19, and in the margin, line 6. A Fatimid commander is also mentioned; he was from 'Ammān, al-amīr al-'Ammānī – see **381**, line 11 (a fragment from Daniel b. Azariah's letter); it seems that the expression 'may God pay him similarly to what he did' which the Gaon adds after he mentions that same *amīr*, is not necessarily in his favour; possibly the intention is to the governor of 'Ammān.

85 Yāqūt, *Buldān*, III, 722; cf. Braslavi, *Le-ḥeqer*, 100f, who points out that 'Amtā is 'Amtū, which is Ḥamatān in the Talmudic sources. The Jerusalemites' letter: **405**, see lines 24–25; The deed: **564**, see lines 1–2, 13–14.

86 Ya'qūbī, *Buldān*, 327f; he mentions the region of the *sawād* as well, but there seems to be some sort of distortion here, for *sawād* means (in Ya'qūbī's time) district, and the name of the district is missing.

of the conquest, as we have already seen, we have very little further knowledge. Ya'qūbī includes it among the regions with mixed populations, tribesmen and non-Muslims. Muqaddasī mentions its abundant dates and the growing of rice, which is supplied to the two junds, Filasṭīn and Urdunn. Its *jāmi'* is in the market place, and its people are righteous. In what has been said of Shechem above, we found that Bet-Shean was mentioned in a Geniza document, in a merchant's letter.[87]

Kafr Kana is mentioned by Nāṣir Khusraw, who visited there in 1047; he recalls the beautiful monastery situated to the south of the village as well as its strong gate. Willibald, who visited it in *ca.* 725, points out the large church in the village, where one of the six jugs wherein Jesus turned the water into wine, is preserved.[88]

Arbel is also mentioned by Nāṣir Khusraw, who passed through it on his way from Acre to Tiberias. He says that he was shown there the graves of Joseph's four brothers and the grave of 'Moses' mother'.[89]

Gūsh Ḥālāv (Jashsh) was at the time still a comparatively large town. Muqaddasī says that the place looked almost like a *qaṣaba*, that is, the capital of a jund. In the Geniza sources, the town is mentioned in a letter written from there (from *Gūsh*) by Israel b. Nathan (Sahlūn) in about 1060; the addressee is Nehorai b. Nissim, and from the contents of the letter it emerges that the writer stayed in the place and was busy copying books. Hence it appears that there was a Jewish population there. Joseph b. Sahl al-Baradānī, who writes at about the same time to Nehorai b. Nissim from Tyre, mentions that he passed through Gūsh on his way from Tiberias to Tyre and there he met Israel b. Sahlūn, and it seems from his remarks that he found him in great distress. We know from other letters of Israel b. Sahlūn that he moved from Gūsh Ḥālāv to Tyre and Damascus and from there returned to Jerusalem.[90]

[87] Ya'qūbī, *ibid.*; Muqaddasī, *Āqālīm* 162, see another version there under note f.

[88] Nāṣir Khusraw, 18 (text), 59 (translation). Willibald, in Tobler et Molinier, I, 260.

[89] Nāṣir Khusraw, 16 (text), 53 (translation). TS 10 K 16, f. 20c, contains fragments from Josippon, and has, on the last line, the name of the writer: Shemaria b. Abraham, of blessed memory, from the city of Sepphoris; judging by the handwriting it appears to be from the eleventh century. (I am grateful to Dr Simon Hopkins, who brought this manuscript to my attention.) As to Sepphoris, one should also mention the colophon in Mann, *Jews*, II, 357: '[it has matters concerning] the cemetery, *the ṣiddūq ha-dīn* [theodicy], and the funeral oration. Written by me, Yefet, the cantor, b. 'Amram ha-mumḥē, b. Moses, cantor and *mumḥē* [may they rest in Eden, the garden of God], known as b. al-Jazfīnī, from the city of Tirṣa, called Ṣafūriyya, the town of our holy Rabbi' (that is R. Judah *ha-nāsī*). The shelf-mark in Mann: TS 8 K 13, f. 14, was evidently mistaken. In the copy of Mann's book in Cambridge, this is crossed out but no other shelf-mark was inserted; in other words, that particular colophon is still missing, and we have only Mann's version.

[90] Muqaddasī, *Āqālīm*, 163. The letter from Gūsh; **474**. Joseph b. Sahl's letter: **492**. See also: al-ḥazān al-Jūshī, in a list of names, apparently from the last quarter of the eleventh century, from Fustat: Bodl MS Heb c 28, f. 6, line 8, in Mann, *Jews*, II, 246. Braslavi's

The town Daltūn or Dalāta, which I still have not found mentioned in any Arab source from the early Middle Ages, is mentioned in the 'Scroll of Abiathar'. It says that it is the place where the father of Abiather, the Gaon Elijah ha-Kohen, is buried on top of the mountain, together 'with R. Yosē ha-Gelīlī, and around him Jonathan b. 'Uziel, and Hillel, and Shammai, and Eleazar b. 'Arākh, and Eleazar b. Azariah, his ancestor, and all the righteous'. In *ca.* 1030 Solomon ha-Kohen b. Joseph of Daltūn writes a letter to Hillel the ḥāvēr b. Yeshū'ā the cantor, in Tiberias, dealing with the copying of books, which is his source of income. I have already mentioned above Ghāliya, daughter of Ashlīmūn al-Dalātī. The Karaite commentator Sahl b. Maṣlīaḥ mentions disparagingly (about the middle of the tenth century) the custom of the Rabbanites to visit the graves of the righteous; in Palestine they go to Dalāta and to 'Arāba (and there they lay out their requests at the foot of the grave of R. Yose and R. so-and-so').[91]

At the end of the ninth century, Ya'qūbī mentions the *kūra*, that is the district, of Qadas, or Qedesh-Naphtali, which according to him is a very important one. Writing some hundred years later Muqaddasī notes that Qadas is a little town. He mentions the bathhouse there, the *jāmi'* situated in the market-place and the manufacture of mats and ropes from which the inhabitants derived their income. He points out that many of them are dhimmīs, and it is clear that he is referring to Jews. Qedesh is mentioned once in a letter written by Solomon ha-Kohen b. Joseph, of Daltūn, who mentions that he sent there a quarter of a dinar.[92]

Fārōd (Faradhīya) is another Galilean town which gains Muqaddasī's attention. According to him, it is a large village with a mosque (literally: seat of the preacher, *minbar*). Safed is not explicitly mentioned in the sources of the period. However, Mūsā b. Hiba (= Moses b. Nathan) b. Salmūn al-Ṣefātī is mentioned in a draft of evidence written in September 1034, relating to a transaction which took place in 1023 before a Muslim court. About this Mūsā, it says there that he is *al-ṭifl al-yahūdī*, that is, a Jewish boy. On Thursday, the twelfth of Kislev, AM 4784 or 28 November AD 1023, the marriage deed of Nathan ha-Kohen ha-Ṣefātī b. Solomon's wife was written, evidently in Tyre. There is no doubt, therefore,

doubts, *Le-ḥeqer*, 63f as to the time of the list, do not seem to be founded. The letters of Israel b. Sahlūn, see from **475** onwards.

91 See Braslavi, *Le-ḥeqer*, 66ff; 274f (on the synagogue in Daltūn, in Byzantine times); 313–318; the scroll of Abiathar: **559**, b, lines 24–25; cf. Benjamin of Tudela (Asher) I, 45f: 'Meron . . . and there are the graves of Hillel and Shammai . . . ; Qedesh Naphtali . . . and there is the grave of R. Eliezer b. 'Arākh and R. Eleazar b. Azariah . . . and R. Yose ha-Gelili'; cf. the Adler ed. 29f: ''Alma . . . and there is the grave of R. Eleazar b. 'Arakh'; see also in Heilprin, *Seder Had.* (Warsaw 1877), 54, 62. The letter from Daltūn: **250**, and see the discussion in Assaf, *Meqōrōt*, 38ff. See a fragment of the commentary of Sahl b. Maṣlīaḥ to Exodus: MS. Firkovitch, II, No. 4129, in Mann, *Texts*, II, 87f.

92 Ya'qūbī, *Buldān*, 327; Muqaddasī, *Aqālīm*, 161. See mention of Qedesh in **250**, a, line 12.

that there was a Jewish community in Safed, but we have no further information on the subject.[93]

[328] Bāniyās was considered the capital of the Golan and was also called *madīnat al-asbāṭ* (city of the tribes). According to Ya'qūbī, writing at the end of the ninth century, the majority of its inhabitants were of the Banū Murra (a tribe considered northern), but there was also a small number of 'southerners' whose names he does not specify. It is quite possible that he copied this information from an older source, from the time of the Umayyads. According to Muqaddasī, Bāniyās was a town lying between the Ḥūla and the mountains and was the source of supplies for Damascus. It served as a haven for refugees from the coastal cities 'when Ṭarsūs was captured', by which he undoubtedly meant the Byzantine conquest in the summer of 965, which I shall discuss below. These refugees were, in his words, a large part of the population of Bāniyās, which was growing constantly. We may assume that these refugees were Jews and Muslims who fled from the Byzantine conqueror. The Geniza has preserved some details about Bāniyās. We have already encountered Ghāliya, the daughter of Ashlīmūn, al-Bāniyāsīya; this certainly is evidence of a Jewish population there in the first half of the eleventh century. Naturally we cannot expect to find earlier evidence in the Geniza documents, for generally there was no special connection between Bāniyās and Fustat as Bāniyās was nearer to Damascus. Nevertheless, we find a letter dated 8 May 1041, written by Joseph b. Kulayb in Ramla to Nathan b. Abraham, who was then in Tyre apparently. Joseph b. Kulayb mentions 'the son of the *ḥāvēr* who is in Bāniyās', who reached Ramla and asked the followers of Nathan b. Abraham to grant him a title, even stating the title he desired – *rōsh ha-seder*. It appears that Nathan b. Abraham visited Bāniyās himself, or so 'the son of the ḥāvēr' seems to have claimed. We also have a power-of-attorney written in Bāniyās, on the 6th of Tammuz, AM 4816 (11 July AD 1056). Ḥusayn b. Hillel, known by the name Qiṭōs, gives Joseph b. Maḥfūẓ (Maḥfūẓ: evidently his Hebrew name was Shemaria) the right to act on his behalf and receive the dinar and three-quarters of a dinar owing to him from Jacob b. al-Jabbān (the maker of cheese). The deed was made out in *medīnat dan ha-qerūyā pāmīs* (the city of Dan named Pāmīs) like the name of this town in Talmudic literature. Pāmīs is defined there as being *di-shāme'ā le-damesseq*, meaning 'which is subordinate to Damascus'. On the deed and its validation (in a court of three) there are the signatures

Cf. Braslavi, *Le-ḥeqer*, 69f; Braslavi did not heed the important sentence in Muqaddasī, that Qadas has many dhimmīs.

[93] Muqaddasī, *ibid.*, 162. The intention is to Talmudic Fārōd, see Avi-Yonah, *Ge'ōgrāfya hīsṭōrīt*, 143, and n. 5. At a later date, the grave of Nahum of Gamzu is mentioned; see Braslavi, *Le-ḥeqer*, 216. Mūsā b. Hiba: **245**, lines 5–6, 10; Nathan ha-Kohen: JNUL 4°577.4, No. 98, ed. Friedman, *Marriage*, II, 38ff; see what he writes there, 34f, on Safed.

of seven local people. The last, Boaz the cantor b. David, we encounter three months later in Ramla, where he is one of the signatories (the signature is identical with that appearing in the aforementioned deed) in a power-of-attorney in the court of Daniel b. Azariah.

From here onwards, we do not hear anything of Bāniyās until the days of the Crusaders. In a letter sent (perhaps from Damascus) by Eleazer ha-Levi b. Joseph to Bāniyās, to 'Eli ha-Kohen the ḥavēr ha-me'ullē b. Abraham (the father of Tobiah, whom we shall encounter below), he tells him about two brothers (one named Jacob) who succeeded in freeing themselves from captivity 'in the hands of Ashkenaz', that is from the Crusaders. The crux of the letter deals with a matter of divorce and mentions the acquiring of an unspecified object for the synagogue, evidently in Bāniyās. The date of the letter is shortly after 1100, apparently.

In the same period, we find two personalities from Bāniyās in the Geniza, they are Tobiah ha-Kohen b. 'Eli and his son-in-law, Nathan ha-Kohen b. Solomon. The latter was in Tyre in 1102, and there he signed a deed of alimony – an agreement made between Sitt al-Bayt and Ḥasan, her father-in-law, while her husband was not in the city. When some years later, the family emigrated to Egypt, the first of them was Tobiah. A letter has been preserved which he wrote to his father, 'Eli ha-Kohen the *ḥavēr*, on 28 May 1112, about half a year after he arrived in Egypt, after travelling there by sea from Tyre on an exceedingly unpleasant voyage (which was understandable, considering that it was wintery weather, being November or December). In the letter, he mentions 'the two communities living in the fortress of Dan' (that is, Bāniyās), including the names of some Jewish personalities in Bāniyās. Afterwards, Tobiah settled in Bilbays, where he stood at the head of the community, while Nathan, his son-in-law, settled in Fustat and became a judge there. We note then that the emigration from Bāniyās took place in the second decade of the twelfth century and was perhaps linked with the attack and siege imposed by the Crusaders on Damascus in 1111, which ended unsuccessfully for the Crusaders but undoubtedly caused great panic among the Jews of Bāniyās and probably their flight as well. In 'the scroll of Obadiah the Proselyte' there is information concerning a Karaite messianic movement, led by a 'messiah' named Solomon ha-Kohen, whose disciples congregated in Bāniyās in about 1120. Apparently Bāniyās at that time was already untenanted by a permanent Jewish community. That same group of Karaites was possibly liquidated when Bāniyās was taken by the Ismā'īlīs – the *ḥashīshiyya* (the Assassins) – in 1126, led by Bahrām. In September 1129, Bāniyās fell to the Crusaders.[94]

[94] Ya'qūbī, *Buldān*, 326; Muqaddasī, *Āqālīm*, 160; Ibn al-Jawzī, *Muntaẓam*, IX, 69, mentions Bāniyās, which in his words is a town in the Ghawr (the Jordan valley) where in 398

[329] From the descriptions above, with the limited information preserved on the towns in the Galilee, one gets an impression, though somewhat faded and fragmentary, of urban centres and villages which still retained their ancient character. The Jewish Galilean population still existed in towns and villages, and it is certainly possible to draw a parallel with what we found in such places as Daltūn, Qedesh, Dan (Bāniyās), and other Galilean towns, records of which have not been preserved in the Geniza. In the period we are dealing with, the Muslim element, that is the tribesmen, was added to the Jewish population, and they are mentioned here and there. And then there were the Christians, of course, about whom we hear very little. To such questions as what the relative numbers of the three elements were, how they lived alongside one another, and

(1007/8) Mālik b. Aḥmad al-Bāniyāsī, a collector of traditions, was born. (See 'Alī ibn al-'Imād, III, 376); he died in the great fire in Baghdad in 485 (1092); Ibn al-Athīr, *Lubāb*, I, 93, quotes Sam'ānī and stresses that Bāniyās does not belong to jund Filasṭīn, nor to jund Urdunn, but to jund Dimashq. The term 'city of the tribes', see in Sam'ānī, *ibid.* Son of the ḥāvēr of Bāniyās: **195**, b, lines 11–16. The Deed: **609**. Bāniyās is Paneas (after the Greek god Pan), called Caesarea Paneas in the days of Herod and afterwards Caesarea Philippi after Herod's son Philip. See Avi-Yonah, *Ge'ōgrāfyā hīsṭōrīt*, 150. The name Qiṭōs, obviously of Greek origin (**608**, line 4), perhaps confirms Muqaddasī's remarks about the origins of the inhabitants of Bāniyās from the coastal towns of Syria, where the tradition from Byzantine times was perhaps stronger, particularly in the sphere of terms and names. The deed from the court of Daniel b. Azariah: **391**, see lines 21, 27 (Boaz ha-ḥazān b. David). The two deeds **608** and **391** follow one another in the volume of Geniza documents in the Taylor-Shechter collection (TS 13 J 1, fols. 13, 15) and possibly this is not entirely coincidental and they may have been at one time part of the archives of this Boaz ha-ḥazan. The letter to Bāniyās: **609**; Goitein, *Eretz-Israel*, 4(1955/6), 149, assumed that the Eleazar ha-Levi, writer of the letter, is the same as Eleazar ha-Levi b. Joseph to whom Manasseh b. R. Judah, 'great-grandson of the Geonim' (the great-grandson of Shemaiah Gaon) dedicated a piyyūṭ. See Mann, *Jews*, II, 336, n. 2; one can recognise that this letter was sent to Bāniyās by the names of the people mentioned there and also in the letter discussed below, **610**; see notes to **609**. The deed of Tyre: **606**; Tobiah's letter: **610**; there are about a dozen of Tobiah's letters in the Geniza, written when he was in Bilbays, generally to his son-in-law, Nathan. Nathan signed some thirty court documents in Fustat, some of them written in his own hand, until about the year 1150, see Goitein, *Mediterranean Society*, II, 513 (No. 17); see: BM Or 5536 IV, Nathan's letter to Tobiah, from Fustat to Bilbays, from which it clearly emerges that Tobiah is Nathan's father-in-law. ENA 4020, f. 28 is a letter from Tobiah to Nathan before he settled in Bilbays, while he was visiting communities in the Delta region; Bodl MS Heb d 74, f. 45 is also a letter from Tobiah, in which he mentions Shū'a, i.e. Yeshū'ā (the Bāniyāsī); the letter was written from Malīj and not from Palestine, as assumed by Braslavi, *Le-ḥeqer*, 73, and Caesarea is not mentioned there, but in using the word *qaysāriyya*, the reference is to the flax market; also the reading 'Akkō is not certain, and it seems that a certain al-'Akkāwī, i.e. a man of Acre, is being spoken of, and the writer mentions the refugees from Palestine, from Bāniyās and Acre, living in Egypt. On the Crusaders' offensive in the year 1111, see Prawer, *Ha-ṣalvānīm*, I, 188. The scroll of Obadiah: ENA 3098, in Mann, *Hatequfa*, 24(1927/8), 336, and see the discussion in the continuation; and in Golb, *Goitein Jubilee Volume*, 102f, and the discussion, *ibid.*, 89f; Braslavi, *Le-ḥeqer*, 73, mentions documents from the Geniza in which he believes Bāniyās is mentioned, but the correct reading in these is Bunyām, as for instance *Bunyām walad* (= son of) *Abū Naṣr* in TS 8 J 21, f. 15; Bunyām is none other than Benjamin (cf. Goitein, *Letters*, 235, n. 14), a name found in many other

what was their source of livelihood, we have no unambivalent answers. The Jewish communities in these localities were evidently gradually wiped out during the Fatimid wars in Palestine, and the final blows inflicted by the Turcomans who invaded Palestine and their successors, the Crusaders. One becomes aware of the branching out of the Galilean Jewish population also from the locative by-names of the Palestinian refugees and their descendants mentioned in various lists preserved in the Cairo Geniza. An instance of such a by-name we find in 1065: Abraham b. David al-Kafrmandī, recorded in a deed of attorney drawn up in Ramla by the Gaon Elijah ha-Kohen b. Solomon; the intention is to Kafr Manda in the Lower Galilee. This man became an inhabitant of Ramla, as one can assume from the formulation of the deed. Evidently, we have here some evidence of the exodus from the towns and villages to the urban centres. People from Gūsh Ḥālāv are mentioned a number of times in the lists from Fustat, such as Da'ūd b. Ḥasan al-Jashshī al-Kohen, and others; and there are also al-Dalātī, 'the man from Daltūn', the by-name of Abū'l-Ḥasan al-Naḥḥāl (the beekeeper); al-I'billānī, 'the man of I'billīn; al-Ṭabarānī, people of Tiberias; al-'Amqawī, of 'Amūqa, near Safed; and also people of Acre and Haifa.[95]

[330] I should also mention certain localities in the coastal area. Caesarea declined in the period we are discussing. Muqaddasī describes only general aspects and he mentions the citadel which encompasses the over-populated residential areas, as well as its beautiful *jāmi'*. Nāṣir Khusraw visited Caesarea some two generations after Muqaddasī, in 1047. He adds little to the description of his predecessor, apart from information on a lovely marble vessel preserved in the *jāmi'*, which looks as if it was made of Chinese porcelain and can hold 100 *manns* (approximately 90 litres). In the Geniza documents, Caesarea is sometimes called Ḥaṣōr (also Ḥaṣerīya, in poetry). There is a letter in the Geniza from the yeshiva to the community of Ḥaṣōr dealing with a dispute over the prayer routine in the synagogue,

Geniza documents. Bāniyās in the hands of the Assassins and Crusaders, see Lewis, in *A History of the Crusades* (ed. Setton), 116f; cf. also Prawer, *Ha-ṣalvānīm*, I, 218f.

95 Abraham b. David al-Kafrmandī: **425**; cf. Braslavi, *Le-ḥeqer*, 169. Gūsh Ḥālāv: Goitein, *Mediterranean Society*, II, 440 (Nos. 4–5), Ashtor, *Shazar Jubilee Volume*, 495. Al-Dalātī: *ibid.*, 496; see also Goitein, *Mediterranean Society*, II, 467 (No. 108); al-I'billānī, see: Manṣūr b. Joseph al-I'billānī, in **280**, lines 3–4, 14; see also in Ashtor, *ibid.*, 497. See on I'billīn: Le Strange, *Palestine*, 382, following Nāṣir Khusraw: it is close to Dāmūn and the prophets Hūd and 'Uzayr are buried there. See further mention of I'billīn (people called al-I'billānī) in Friedman, *Marriage*, II, 284. Tiberias: Ashtor, *ibid.*, 499. And see the lists printed by him in the supplement, *ibid.*, 501–509. There is some doubt as to the identification of 'Anānī as the man from Kfar Ḥananya as in Braslavi, *ibid.*, 78. It is more likely that he was a follower of 'Anan, i.e. he was a Karaite; al-'Amqawī: Bodl MS Heb c 28, f. 6 (from the latter half of the eleventh century), line 14, in Mann, *Jews*, II, 246. See the proposed correction (al-'Amqawī and not al-'Asqawī as in Mann's reading) in Braslavi, *ibid.*, 71. See also the locative ha-Gelīlī, the letter written by Yeshū'ā ha-Kohen b. Abraham ha-Gelīlī, **201** (*ca.* 1010).

apparently dated 1025. The letter is addressed to 'the entire holy community living in the fortress of Ḥaṣōr' and several personalities are mentioned there, among them a certain son of Ḥalfōn of Ramla, and also the 'head of the community' and the cantor, and a man named Joseph, entitled 'beloved of the yeshiva'. The term 'fortress of Ḥaṣōr' reminds us of what Muqaddasī and Nāṣir Khusraw had to say on the fortress and walls. In June 1053 one of the Maghribi merchants, Moses b. Jacob, makes mention in a letter sent from Jerusalem to Nehorai b. Nisim, of Ṣedaqa al-Qayṣarānī (of Caesarea), who lived in Jerusalem. The synagogue of Caesarea is mentioned in a letter from another Maghribi, Jacob b. Salmān al-Ḥarīrī ('silk merchant') who writes from Ramla, also to Nehorai b. Nissim, in about 1060. The ship in which Jacob sailed, and whose destination was Jaffa, was almost wrecked near the coast of Caesarea and he was obliged to remain in Caesarea. As he did not find a place to stay there, he remained in the synagogue for five days, and only afterwards reached Ramla. Caesarea (Qaysarīn) is mentioned in the 'Scroll of Abiathar', as one of the cities that was dominated by David b. Daniel, during the early nineties of the eleventh century. In around 1099 the *ḥāvēr* of Caesarea, Joshua b. 'Eli, the great-grandson of Samuel 'the third' b. Hosha'na, wrote to the Nagid of Egypt, Mevorakh b. Saadia, stating that the Jews of the city are 'drowning in sorrows' due to 'poverty and constant fear'; 'our souls are in fear and trembling from too many rumours', he says. He asks the Nagid to send a letter of recommendation to the local cadi to help him to move to Ascalon, 'for it is better fortified and maintained than Ḥaṣōr', and the intention is that the cadi should speak 'to the governing *peḥā* (governor) there (in Ḥaṣōr) that he should not force nor detain me'. In addition to the constant dread, he also suffers from the local population, who 'are not good for anything and they do not bring me [any income] but anguish'.[96]

[96] Muqaddasī, *Āqālīm*, 174; Nāṣir Khusraw, 18 (text), 61f (translation); he also stresses the strength of the city walls and mentions its iron gate; on the *mann*, see Hinz, 16. A. Reifenberg, Caesarea, *IEJ*, 1(1950/1), 23, interprets Muqaddasī inaccurately, as if it were a matter of a densely-populated suburb situated outside the town; but *rabaḍ* in Muqaddasī means the unfortified part of the city. On p. 29, Reifenberg points out that while Muqaddasī only refers to wells and reservoirs, Nāṣir Khusraw mentions that the city's water also came via watercourses, and from this he assumes that during the intervening period between the lives of the two, the more ancient lower conduit may have been repaired. The letter to the community of Ḥaṣōr: **48**. Moses b. Jacob, see **460**, a, line 7. Jacob b. Salmān: **507**, a, lines 3–8. The scroll of Abiathar: **559**, c, line 18. Joshua he-ḥāvēr's letter: **569**, his signature: Joshua he-ḥāvēr b. R. 'Eli he-ḥāvēr, great-grandson of Hosha'na: this Joshua signs a marriage deed in 1051, in Ramla: Joshua ha-ḥazān b. R. 'Eli he-ḥāvēr, see **566**, line 20; in 1076 he signed a deed contracted in Ramla: Joshua he-ḥāvēr b. R. 'Eli he-ḥāvēr, see **568**, line 11; it is clear that he is the son of 'Eli b. Abraham b. Samuel ('the third') b. Hosha'na. ENA NS 16, f. 6, a small fragment remaining from a marriage deed, contains the version: 'Ḥaṣōr, which is situated on the coast of the Salty Sea', see in Friedman, *Marriage*, II, 317f. Here too, Ḥaṣōr is Caesarea, on the coast of the 'Salty Sea',

[331] Jaffa (which is Yāfā or Yāfa) was not very developed in our period. Ya'qūbī notes only that it was a transit stop of Ramla, in other words, the port of jund Filasṭīn. Muqaddasī only mentions that it was a small town, but a place for conveying goods abroad and the port of Ramla and jund Filasṭīn. He mentions its strong fortress, its iron-clad gates, its sea-gate wholly wrought of iron, and its convenient port. He also mentions the *jāmi'*, which overlooks the sea. Evidently in 1064, the port of Jaffa is mentioned by Ingulph, prior of the Croyland monastery in England. A fleet of ships from Genoa arrived there in the spring; he sailed back to Europe in one of them. In the Geniza documents, Jaffa is mentioned much less frequently than Ascalon or Tyre, although the Maghribi merchants, from whom most of the information on the ports of Palestine is derived, would visit Jaffa as well. Abraham b. David b. Sughmār, writing evidently in 1038, from Fustat to Jerusalem, mentions that Jaffa was one of the cities to which letters dealing with the conflict of Nathan b. Abraham were dispatched, and from this it is clear that there was a Jewish community there. The Karaite Maḥbūb b. Nissim depicts a journey in Palestine on his way to Lādhiqiyya (Laodicea). At the end of the month of Tishri, he decided to stop in Jaffa and therefore he bribed the captain of the ship to drop anchor there: '. . . and I went down in Jaffa' (*wa-nazalt al-yāfa*). In a letter written by 'Eli ha-Kohen b. Ezekiel in Jerusalem in April 1071, he warns his son-in-law not to import flax via Jaffa but rather via Ascalon, for in Jaffa the authorities seize the goods being imported for the Fatimid army's benefit. In about 1060 Jacob b. Samuel ha-Andalusī of Jerusalem writes to Nehorai b. Nissim that he carried a cargo of oil to Jaffa (*ilā yāfa*), evidently for export to Egypt. Jacob b. Salmān al-Ḥarīrī, as well, wrote at approximately the same time to Nehorai; he wrote from Ramla, and I have

which is the Mediterranean. While Mann, *Jews*, II, 200, wrote that he could not identify the site of Ḥaṣōr, the idea that Ḥaṣōr is Rafiaḥ has become accepted (see, for instance *Sefer ha-yishuv*, 9); but we have the evidence of Tanḥūm ha-Yerūshalmī that Ḥaṣōr was Caesarea; see his commentary on the book of Joshua, 27; 'Ḥaṣōr, which is Caesarea'; see also al-Ḥarīzī, *Taḥk.*, ch. xx, p. 206 'and from Tyre to Ḥaṣōr'; and also ch. xxxvii, p. 299: 'I went from Tyre until Ḥaṣōr with a group', the intention here undoubtedly being: from Tyre to Caesarea (cited in Mann, *ibid.*). Benjamin of Tudela (Adler ed.), 32, says: 'and from there (that is, from Ḥamma, which is Ḥammāh) there is half a day to Shayza, which is Ḥaṣōr'. Clearly he is speaking of Shayzar, which is Larisa, which was also referred to as Caesarea. See William of Tyre, 481: *(urbs) quae vulgo appellatur Caesarea*, and *ibid.*, p. 849, it is called Caesara and not Caesarea; and on p. 1013: *Caesar, quae vulgo dicitur Caesarea magna*; it is clear that the Arabic Shayzar is but a distortion of the ancient name. See doubts about this in Dussaud, *Topographie*, 199f. Dussaud dismissed the opinion of William of Tyre and quoted what Stephen of Byzantium said, that the ancient name of Shayzar was Sizara, as a counter-argument; and in his wake, Ben Horin as well, *Kiryat Sefer*, 24(1947/8), 112; but it is quite obvious that Sizara is also a distortion of Caesarea; Benjamin of Tudela confirms the version of William of Tyre, on the one hand. While on the other hand there is confirmation here that it was common among the Jews to refer to Caesarea as Ḥaṣōr (and as is known, there were a number of cities called Caesarea); cf. Vilnay, *Zion*, 5 (1940), 84,

already described the venture when he was forced to stop in Caesarea, when his intention was to reach Jaffa and thence to Ramla. Clear evidence of the existence of a Jewish community in Jaffa even in the troubled days of the Turcoman rule in Palestine is to be found in a deed of divorce written in Jaffa on the 18th of Sivan AM 4837 (12 June AD 1077): Yefet b. Abraham divorces Sitt al-Ḥusn daughter of Abraham, and it has two witness' signatories, Yefet the cantor b. Abraham (in whose handwriting the document is written) and Aaron b. Mevorakh. The deed was written 'in the city of Jaffa, which is situated on the Great Sea, in the portion of the tribe of Dan'.[97]

[332] Muqaddasī also mentions Arsūf (Apollonia), which according to him is smaller than Jaffa, but well fortified and densely populated. In its mosque there is a handsome *minbar* which was originally intended for Ramla but was afterwards thought too small and was moved to Arsūf. He also mentions Kafrsābā and notes the *jāmi'* there; and also Kafrsalām in the neighbourhood of Caesarea, which also had a *jāmi'*.[98]

[333] The Islamisation of the population is a question which is rather obscure. As I have already said, the impression gained from the sources is

who has further evidence based on a map of Palestine attached to the MS of Moses Basola (1552).

97 Ya'qūbī, *Buldān*, 329; Muqaddasī, *Āqālīm*, 174. See Ingulph, 149; quoted also in Ashtor, *Shazar Jubilee Volume*, 490f, copied from Schaube. As to the chronicle of Ingulph, which I also mention in connection with the Jerusalem patriarch, Sophronius II (*infra* sec. 699) and the pilgrimage of the Gunther group (*infra* sec. 726), one cannot say it is a fake, though one can perhaps call it 'pseudo-Ingulph'. Although, according to students of British history, this is a compilation from the middle of the fourteenth century evidently, they still do not hesitate to call it the chronicle of Ingulph. Essential claims of forgery were directed towards the texts of charters which are included there, but these do not affect our subject. Searle, who studied the chronicle thoroughly, remarked that it contained 'some curious points of accuracy'. Ingulph, himself, is not an invented character and he was actually the prior of a monastery, and also made a pilgrimage to Jerusalem. It seems, then, that in precisely those matters related to his biography, which I have mentioned, the information is genuine, and one can assume that it was copied from an earlier chronicle, truly written by Ingulph, and included in that compilation. At any rate, by whatever name we call it, the use of this source is certainly legitimate. See Liebermann, 25, 33; Searle, 11, 137; 192f, 195; 206ff, 208. Ashtor also relied on this chronicle in what he wrote on the coastal towns of Syria and Palestine and he calls it: a Latin treatise written in about the year 1085, and mentions naturally, Ingulph's pilgrimage (*Shazar Jubilee Volume*, pp. 490f). True, there are sometimes contradictions in biographical data, such as that Ingulph met the emperor Alexius (Comnenus), who reigned from 1080–1118 in Constantinople. The Jerusalem patriarch Sophronius II, however, was in office when Ingulph was in Palestine (contrary to Searle's assumption, p. 137). The letter of Abraham b. David b. Sughmār: **190**, a, line 10. Maḥbūb, **292**, line 12, 'Eli ha-Kohen: **455**, lines 26–28. Jacob b. Samuel: **493**, line 9. Jacob b. Salmān: **507**, a, line 3. The divorce: see MS Mosseri, VIII.482, edited by Ṣemaḥ, *Mizraḥ u-ma'arav*, 1(1920), 358, and copied from there in *Sefer ha-yishuv*, 15, and in Margaliot, *Hilekhōt ereṣ isrā'ēl*, 122. It seems that Jaffa was then in Fatimid hands.

98 Arsūf: Muqaddasī, *Āqālīm*, 174, cf. Avi-Yonah *Ge'ōgrāfya hisṭōrit* 128. Kafrsābā, Kafrsalām: Muqaddasī, *ibid.*, 176f; cf. Nāṣir Khusraw, 18 (text), 62 (translation) according to whom these are two names of the same place. To the survey of the localities one

that during the period under discussion the Muslims were in a minority. The Muslim element was made up of tribesmen, and in the course of time, immigrants and settlers who came from abroad, even from distant lands, such as the family of the mother of Muqaddasī, author of the *Āqālīm*, who came from the region of Qūmis in Central Asia. Below we shall encounter other famous Muslim personalities who lived in Palestine, and whose origins were in other countries (and we have already seen, there were such personalities even during the rule of the Umayyads, such as 'Aṭā' al-Khurāsānī). However, one can assume that there was also a degree of Islamisation, especially among that segment of the population whose communal organisation was weak and in which the individual could not withstand the pressure and enticements of the Muslim world. This is probably true particularly with regard to the Christian population, especially in the small rural localities. At the time of al-Ḥākim there was forced conversion among the Christians, and although these decrees were later abolished, one may assume that a part of those forced converts were lost to Christianity.

The Christian population in Palestine was in the main Monophysitic. To a large extent due to the fanatical religious policy of the emperors, the Christians became submissive and came to terms with their fate, as it were, to live under the rule of the Muslim tribes. As will be evident below, the rulers did not conduct a policy of religious coercion, and their principal demand from the population was the payment of taxes. Only at a later stage did the animosity between the Christians and the Muslims become acute. Christian sources in the first century of Islam reflect a liberal attitude towards the Muslims. An anonymous Spanish chronicle which covers the period until 741, has no expressions of animosity to Islam when it is mentioned there. Ishū'yhab III, the Nestorian catholicus, writes in about 660 that there is no point in converting to Islam, for the Muslims themselves revere the church. An anonymous Nestorian chronicle also reflects the positive attitude to the Arabs and Muḥammad, the 'Messenger of God'. Among the Christians, especially the sects which branched out from the main church, there was the belief that the appearance of additional prophets during the Christian era was still a possibility – prophets who would be sent to nations who had not risen to the heights of Christianity, which is how they viewed Muḥammad. The nature of Islam, which absolutely negates certain basic Christian views, was not clear even to the learned among the Christians at first, and they were inclined to see

must also add Ono, mentioned in a fragment of a deed written on vellum: TS NS 320.99, edited by Friedman, *Yarqōn*, 81. See its facsimile *ibid.*, p. 80. Judging by the script, it seems to be one of the most ancient Geniza documents, perhaps from the tenth century.

Islam as another defecting Christian sect, as was the view of John of Damascus, for instance. Naturally in the course of time, not a few heated situations arose, as we shall see, and pressure was put on the Christians. Nevertheless, apart from the days of al-Ḥākim, we have no explicit evidence of mass conversion of Christians to Islam.[99]

[334] Similarly, we have no evidence of Jews converting to Islam, except for a passage in Dhahabī, who claims that in the days of Mu'āwiya, under the influence of Ka'b al-Aḥbār, forty-two Jewish scholars (*aḥbār*) turned to Islam, and Mu'āwiya gave them grants and subsidies. This information, which is not found elsewhere, has a fictional character and seems to have derived from a distortion of the traditions on the Jewish services on the Temple Mount. Even if it has a grain of truth, it is still no proof of mass conversion among the Jews of Palestine. The validity of the opinion common here and there concerning the Jewish origin of the Arabs of Palestine is dependent on just such a conversion. At the beginning of the twentieth century, Ben Gurion and Ben Zvi tried to provide some foundation for this idea by claiming that because of the pressing tax burden, the population of Palestine, which was to a large extent Christian, had converted to Islam. They cited as evidence the fact that at the time of the Arab conquest, the population of Palestine was mainly Christian, and that during the Crusaders' conquest some four hundred years later, it was mainly Muslim. As neither the Byzantines nor the Muslims carried out any large-scale population resettlement projects, the Christians were the offspring of the Jewish and Samaritan farmers who converted to Christianity in the Byzantine period; while the Muslim fellaheen in Palestine in modern times are descendants of those Christians who were the descendants of Jews, and had turned to Islam before the Crusaders' conquest. The scholar A. N. Poliak attempted to find evidence of such a mass conversion of the Jews of Palestine in the commentary of Saadia Gaon to the book of Daniel, xi:30–31 ('and have intelligence with them that forsake the holy covenant, etc.'): 'these are the Ishmaelites in Jerusalem, and thereafter they desecrated the sanctuary of strength'; and further on, verse xi:36 ('. . . and shall speak . . . things against the God of gods . . .'): 'words which would anger the King of the Worlds, until His rage against Israel will cease; and then the Creator will completely destroy the wicked of Israel'; and further: xii:2 ('and many of them that sleep in the dust of the earth shall awake'): 'this is the resurrection of the dead of Israel, whose fate is to live forever, and those who will not be resurrected are those who deserted God; they

[99] The Spanish chronicle: Dubeer, *Andalus*, 11(1946), 300f; cf. Cahen, *RHR*, 166(1964), 54; see Yeshū'yhav's letter to Simon, bishop of Rewardashīr: in *CSCO*, ser. II, t. 64, 251 (see its Latin translation, *ibid.*, 181); cf. Cahen, *ibid.*, 55. The Nestorian chronicle: *CSCO*, t. 4, 31. Michael the Syrian also finds it advantageous to be free of Byzantine tyranny; see the Chabot ed., II, 413, cf. Cahen, *ibid.*, 56f.

will descend to the bottom of Hell and every living creature will curse them'. And further: ii:43 (. . . they shall mingle themselves with the seed of men' . . .) 'since people of the seed of Israel intermingle with them (i.e. with the Muslims) and stay with them, just like the Persians and Zoroastrians and pagans of several types; but they do not stick to each other, just as iron and smith do not mix so as to become one and the same tool'.

Such quotations cannot serve as sources for the history of Palestine, with which they have nothing to do. They bear absolutely no proof of the Islamisation of Jews in Palestine. From the last passage one may deduce, if anything, quite the contrary.[100]

[100] See Dhahabī, *Ta'rīkh*, III, 101; D. Ben-Gurion and I. Ben-Zvi, *Eretz Israel in Fergangenhait* . . ., NY 1907/8. 43; Poliak, *Molad*, 24:297, 1966/68. See the convincing counter-arguments of Brawer, *ibid.*, 424; but he also has a statement that is insufficiently based: 'when the Muslims conquered Palestine in 636, the Jews carried no political or demographical weight there'; see further comments by Poliak, *ibid.*, 427ff.

4
THE ECONOMY

[335] In the Arab sources and in the sources in general, information about the economy of Palestine during the centuries from the conquest until the eleventh century AD is very sparse. The little that is known is mainly derived from the Muslim geographers, first and foremost among them being Muqaddasī, who was himself a Palestinian from Jerusalem. However, there are dozens of letters from the Cairo Geniza, mostly from Maghribi merchants, which contain a wealth of detail concerning the economy and trade in the eleventh century AD. Within the context of the historical sources of the period, the details contained in these letters are unique and also extremely valuable for the study of the economic life of the Middle Ages.

Despite the close connections between Palestine and the neighbouring countries and its political dependence upon them – firstly on Syria and later on Egypt – Palestine was a relatively self-contained economic unit at the time. Palestine's wealth came from its natural resources, especially its excellent crop of fruits and also, as we shall see, from the various types of craftsmanship that developed there, from its network of ports and not a little, from its influx of pilgrims.

Land and agriculture

We have little knowledge concerning the ownership of land during this period. I have already reviewed the available information about estates belonging to the Umayyad rulers and their immediate circle. We have seen that the tribes, when the Muslim conquest opened up Palestine to them, lived off the local populations by collecting taxes directly from whatever area they occupied, naturally allotting a certain portion to the central authority. These areas were called *ma'kala*. This did not imply, as a matter of course, that the tribe was given the rights of ownership to the land. Those estates (*ḍay'a*, pl. *ḍiyā'*), which according to the sources were held by different rulers at different times, were apparently the property of the state or of the rulers, even prior to the Muslim era, or were the property of public institutions, such as the Church.

After the Abbasid revolution, it was the army commanders, generally Turks, who enjoyed the privileges formerly held by the tribes during the Umayyad period. Discernible changes occurred in the use of terms; we find instead of *ma'kala* the *iqṭā'*. Essentially we are still speaking of the right to collect land taxes that were intended to maintain the military unit under the command of the holder of the *iqṭā'*. With regard to Palestine, these rights are mentioned in the sources, especially during the period of the Fatimid wars, and they were a contested issue among the Banū Jarrāḥ and the Arab leaders in Palestine, as well as others, during that period. We shall also encounter in this chapter the episode of the seven villages or estates (*ḍiyā'*) which the Fatimid caliph al-Ḥākim gave to the rulers of Aleppo in *arḍ Filasṭīn*, and there is little doubt that this meant the right to collect taxes from the inhabitants. Tobiah b. Moses states with a touch of pride, in one of his letters, that he is in charge of the estates of the Fatimid rulers (*wakīl li-ḍiyā' al-sulṭān*) in Palestine. One cannot know in this instance whether he is speaking of the estates of the central government or of the (Turkish) army commander, but at any rate it seems that here too, the collection of taxes is intended.

Although things are not explicitly stated, as I have already mentioned, we can understand the situation in Palestine from what we know in general about the *iqṭā'* system. As Cahen has shown in his studies on this subject, it was basically a method of allocating the income from the taxes. Only at a later stage, under the Ayyubids, does one hear of the rulers dispossessing farmers of their property rights and turning them gradually into tenants.

Through the Geniza documents, we know that the non-Muslim population maintained the right to own land during all the generations from the time of the conquest until the eleventh century. We also have evidence of houses which were the property of local inhabitants, and one can assume that the inhabitants owned the land on which the houses stood as well. In a deed from the Geniza, we find a certain Mu'ammala giving her husband Mevassēr b. Sahlān b. Shelah al-'Amtānī 'all my lands in the city of Ramla which is near Lod' (*ca.* 1030). In one of his letters written about the same time, the Gaon Solomon b. Judah mentions the case of a man who 'sold a field inherited from his parents'. Also about the same time, mention is made in a fragment of a letter from the court in Tiberias to the court in Fustat, of evidence about a legacy due to the daughters of Hillēl b. Nissīn, and the witnesses were questioned 'about the fields'. In a fragment of a marriage deed from Tyre, from the end of the eleventh century, a bride is mentioned who owns property and is part-owner of a third of a new house in western Tyre, evidently in the vicinity of the port.[1]

[336] Palestine seems to have been self-sufficient in grains and bread – at any rate, there is no evidence in the sources of any import of wheat. The Gaon Solomon b. Judah, at the end of 1029, enquires about buying wheat from 'Ammān in Trans-Jordan. We find wheat-trading in Palestine mentioned in a letter from Avon b. Ṣedaqa to Nehorai b. Nissim in around 1065. In another letter, he tells of the purchase of wheat in the Hebron area and in Jerusalem itself; wheat which is 'real gold', as he puts it. Jacob b. Salmān al-Ḥarīrī, preparing to sail from Tripoli to Tyre, transports wheat (but his voyage is disastrous and he ends up in Caesarea minus his entire cargo), and he also shipped wheat to Fustat.[2]

[337] Al-Muqaddasī enumerates in great detail those fruits for which Palestine was noted. He particularly stresses the etrog, almonds, dates (*ratab*, fresh dates), nuts, figs and bananas. Elsewhere he lists olive oil, dried figs, the raisins of 'Aynūn and Dūr, apples, cherries, indigo plants from Jericho and Bet Shean, the dates of Zoar and Bet Shean, the almonds of Moab and the rice from Bet Shean. In Trans-Jordan, they excelled in the cultivation of wheat, sheep-farming and the production of honey. Further on, he points to thirty-six products grown in the Filasṭīn district (*kūra*) which are not to be found growing together elsewhere, seven of which are rare in any other area and twenty-two of which are not found together in any other area (these are his comments and it is difficult to understand him completely, though perhaps there is an error in the text); he further recounts the various types of nuts, apples, raisins, plums, figs, sycamore fruit, carobs, olives, dates, shaddock (*utrujj*, *etrōg*), indigo, sugar-cane, jujube fruit, mandrake, sumach, lupin, and so on.

Bakrī, in the latter half of the eleventh century, praises Bet Shean in particular on its good wine and its dates. Idrīsī, writing in 1154, compliments the dates of al-Dārūm (his form: al-Dāra), Zoar, Jericho and the entire Jordan Valley. Grapes are mentioned in a letter from Avon b. Ṣedaqa, from Jerusalem to Nehorai b. Nissim; he and his partners had prepared grapes for the pilgrims (evidently to sell them) and each one

[1] See Cahen, *AESC*, 8:25, 1953; *JESHO*, 15:163, 1972, and his articles in *EI*²: Ḍay'a; Iqṭā'; see also Duri, *Abḥāth*, 3:22, 1969, an article which deals with the early development of the *iqṭā'*. See below (section 585) the matter of the tax officials of al-Dizbirī, the Fatimid army commander, who wanted to collect taxes in the *iqṭā'* of Ḥassān the Jarrāḥid; and the matter of the *iqṭā'āt*, which the head of the Banū Kalb, Rāfi' b. Abī'l-Layl b. 'Ulayyān, wanted to keep for himself (sec. 592). Mu'ammala: **216**; Solomon b. Judah: **75**, b, line 30; the letter from Tiberias: **244**; the Tyre marriage deeds: **601**.

[2] Solomon b. Judah: **83**. Avon: **501**, a, lines 15–16, 20; **503**. Jacob b. Salmān: **506**, a, lines 8, 9; **507**, b. lines 1, 7. It appears that the supply of wheat in Egypt was much more problematic than it was in Palestine; Israel b. Nathan in his letters to Nehorai b. Nissim, enquires about the price of wheat in Fustat, see **469**, a, line 21; **478**, b, line 4; Nissim b. Ḥalfon, also writing

invested five dinars. A shipment of figs to Alexandria is mentioned by Jacob b. Salmān al-Ḥarīrī, writing to Nehorai from Tripoli in Syria. Nāṣir Khusraw also mentions at the very same time the excellent figs of Ramla (he means jund Filasṭīn), which were being exported far and wide. From another letter, it appears that one of the reasons for the same Jacob b. Salmān's going to Palestine was to purchase fruits for exporting to Egypt. A fruit product mentioned in the Geniza documents is rose-petal preserves – mentioned by Mūsā b. Ya'qūb in some of his letters written in 1057–1058. A shipment of these preserves was apparently sent via Tyre and the writer is anxious as it had not yet reached Fustat – and when it finally arrives, he is again concerned as to how well it would sell. He also speaks of a shipment of plums (or peaches? *khawkh*) of which five camel-loads were loaded aboard a boat in Acre, and he is enquiring whether there is a demand for them in Fustat and whether it would not be preferable to transport this sort of merchandise by land. In a letter from Ascalon written by Nathan ha-Kohen b. Mevorakh shortly after the Crusaders' conquest of Jerusalem, they are still dealing with the essence of acacia (three Shāmī [Palestinian] *raṭl*s, apparently 2.5 kilograms each, that is approximately 8 kilograms in all). Consignments of honey sent from Palestine to Egypt are also mentioned. The apples of al-Shām (Palestine and Syria) were praised, as were their olives, according to Tha'ālibī at the outset of the tenth century. As to sugar cane, we have seen above that it is mentioned in Muqaddasī; both Iṣṭakhrī and Ibn Ḥawqal also refer to its being grown in the area of Tripoli and Beirut in Syria, as does also Nāṣir Khusraw, who observed the production of sugar syrup while visiting the area. Jacob b. Joseph b. Ismā'īl writes to Nehorai b. Nissim from Ascalon in around 1060, saying that he intends buying sugar (evidently meaning syrup); he had already bought a certain quantity but it was of an inferior quality as it was reddish in colour. He sold it at a dinar per five *raṭl*s and lost money on the sale. There is an interesting detail here, namely that it was sugar from *Zīb*, that is Akhzīv, and thus one may assume that there was a sugar refinery there. Joseph b. Sahl al-Baradānī, writing from Tripoli in *ca.* AD 1060, also seems to have been involved in the purchase of sugar, and he mentions the price of 19.5 *nizārī* dinars the *qinṭār*, while Jacob b. Ismā'īl, writing *ca.* 1060 from Tyre, points out that he has sold sugar in the same region (for Nehorai). It is not likely that this was sugar imported from Egypt; rather one can assume that it came from local stock stored in Tyre by the writer of the letter. Nehorai b. Nissim himself, writing from Fustat to Joseph ha-Kohen b. 'Alī al-Fāsī, who was purchasing commodities in

to Nehorai, reminds him that he must buy wheat in good time (he writes from Tyre): **489**, b, line 3.

Palestine, mentions the price of sugar at 6½ dinars, without specifying the unit of weight, in a list of market prices in Fustat.[3]

[338] Wheat and bread and their prices are frequently mentioned in Geniza letters. A woman who emigrated to Palestine and decided to settle in Tiberias writes to her brother in Fustat, who is also contemplating the possibility of settling in Palestine. She speaks of life in Tiberias as being cheaper than in Ramla, the price of bread there being one dirham per *raṭl* (a rather high price for those times – apparently this was a period of scarcity). Nathan b. Abraham points out that the price of wheat (in Egypt) is three dinars per *tillīs* (at about the same time), four times as much, being four dirhams the *raṭl*. It is not surprising, then, that Israel b. Nathan, living in Jerusalem, is anxiously concerned with the price of wheat in Egypt, which was sky-high, especially in those years of drought which were constantly recurring whenever the waters of the Nile did not rise sufficiently. At such times, the prices in Palestine would soar as well, for there were very close

[3] Muqaddasī, *Āqālīm*, 166, 180f; he lists some other plants and their meaning is not clear; cf. Le Strange, *Palestine*, 16f, who has an English translation and some comments. Cherries: *qaḍm quraysh*; apparently this is the correct interpretation. Cf. *qarashiyya*, in **394**, b, line 7; **395**, line 9; in the dictionaries: *qarāsiyā*, which is borrowed from the Greek. Cf. also the editor's notes in: Maimonides, *'Uqqār*, 165 (No. 330); see below note 12. See also the definitions in De Goeje, *Glossarium, BGA* IV; and see Bakrī, 292; the wines of Palestine acquired a reputation and Mas'ūdī even quotes a verse (from the time of the Umayyads) in praise of 'the wine golden like saffron, which the sea brings us from Ascalon'; see *Murūj*, VI, 7, and cf. many references to the wine of Gaza and Ascalon in pre-Islamic times in: Grégoire et Kugener (eds.), Marc le Diacre. *Vie de Porphyre*, 124ff; see Idrīsī (Cerulli), 354 f. Avon: **503**, a, lines 5–7; figs: **506**. Nāṣir Khusraw, 19 (text), 65 (translation). The other letter of Jacob b. Salmān: **507**, in the upper margin, lines 14–15: 21 'pieces' (*qiṭ'a* and it is difficult to know what packaging is being hinted at by this term), of figs; b, line 2, two baskets of raisins (*zabīb*) and there the figs are again mentioned. Rose-petal preserves: **515**, line 12; **516**, lines 5f. **517**, b, lines 10f., 17; in **514**, margin, he requests that the rose-petal preserves should be sold in the order in which they are received, so that they should not turn black. Plums: **517**, b, lines 18–21; cf. Goitein, *Letters*, 95, n. 16, on the meaning of *khawkh*. See also the *Mishna Commentary* ascribed to Nathan, *av* of the yeshiva, *Zera'īm*, 30 (to Kil'ayim ch. i): *khawkh* means *hafarseqīm* – peaches); essence of acacia: **588**, margin; *raṭl shāmī*, see Hinz, 29f. Tha'ālibī, *Thimār*, 531f; Iṣṭakhrī, 61 (line 4); Ibn Ḥawqal, 176; Nāṣir Khusraw, 12 (text), 40 (translation). Jacob b. Joseph b. Ismā'il: **487** b, lines 2–4, 10. Zīb, see sources on it (beginning from the twelfth century): Le Strange, *Palestine*, 555f. Joseph b. Sahl: **491**, line 10; Nizārī dinars, cf. also **517**, b, lines 16–17: Mūsā b. Jacob wants to know the rate of the Nizārī dinars minted in Damascus (*al-kesāfīm*); it is difficult to know whether he means coins in general, or specifically silver coins. Goitein, *Letters*, 94, p. 15, quotes the student of Muslim coins, G. C. Miles, that in the days of Nizār, the Fatimid caliph al-'Azīz, only gold coins were minted in Damascus; cf. **503**, a, lines 6–7: the Nizārī dinars were at that time, in the greatest demand, and a grape-seller would only sell his wares for Nizārī dinars. As to the *qinṭār*, we can assume that the Egyptian qinṭār is being spoken of, as he is writing to Egypt, that is one of 100 *raṭl*s of 144 dirhams each, i.e. about 45 kilograms. See Hinz, 25 (*qinṭār filfilī* is the Egyptian *qinṭār*; as explained also by Abraham Maimuni, *Commentary*, 493); from this we learn that the price of sugar was in this deal approximately eight dirhams of the *waraq* type (40 in a dinar) per *raṭl*. Jacob b. Ismā'īl: **494**, a, line 7. Letter of Nehorai: **508**, a, line 8; cf. on the raising of sugar cane in Palestine: Ashtor, *JAH*, 4(1970), 5.

links with Egypt in trading relations. Israel b. Nathan notes in one of his letters that one bought a *qafīz* of wheat in Jerusalem for 3–3½ dinars, whereas Avon b. Ṣedaqa boasts of having acquired 2 *qafīz*s of excellent wheat for 3¼ dinars, that is, at the cost of 14 dirham per *raṭl*. As these were the prices demanded during a period of drought (Israel b. Nathan specifically mentions that hunger is rampant in Jerusalem), it appears that they are speaking of a small *qafīz* (the *qafīz* can indicate anything from 4 to 201 litres). It is interesting to note the composition of a month's food supply with which a woman stocks her larder at the time, when her husband is away on a long journey (Tyre, 1102): three *wayba*s (some 35 kilograms) wheat and the cost of milling it into flour; a *raṭl* of Shāmī oil (Palestinian olive oil); wood for heating, and apart from these, a bit more than three-quarters of a dinar in cash.[4]

Occupations

[339] We have but a trickle of information on this subject. Muqaddasī, writing at the end of the tenth century, attempts to provide us with a general picture of the occupations of the Jewish and Christian inhabitants (to distinguish them from the Muslims, who were tribesmen, or military, religious or administrative personnel). According to him, the Jews were the majority among the money-changers (*jahābidha*), the dyers (meaning textile-dyers), the bankers (*ṣayārifa*) and the tanners; while the Christians

[4] The letter from Tiberias: **247**, lines 16–17. Nathan b. Abraham: **176**, a, line 18. The *tillīs*, a large sack, see Sobhy, 6; Abraham Maimuni, *Commentary*, 169; but according to Muqaddasī, *Āqālīm*, 204, it had a specific capacity and in wheat it was 15 *manns*, i.e. 30 *raṭls*. Both Nathan b. Abraham and the Tiberian woman undoubtedly refer to the *waraq* dirham, which was 40 to a dinar, common at that time, in Egypt at any rate. Israel b. Nathan: **469**, a, line 21; **478**, b, line 4. The price of wheat: **480**, b, line 5; on the *qafīz*, see Hinz, 48ff; cf. Isaac b. David b. Sughmār's letter from Fustat, from *ca*. 1045, mentioning the price of wheat in the Maghrib: 4 *athmān* per dinar, i.e. ½ a dinar which was 20 dirhams per *raṭl*, a price that was only likely during a period of severe drought, as the writer points out in his letter, see **485**, b, line 11. Avon: **501**, a, line 20. Alimonies in Tyre: **606**, lines 4–6; on the *wayba*, see Hinz, 52f; cf. Suyūṭi, *Muḥāḍara*, I, 145; Jonah ibn Janāḥ, *S. ha-shorashim*, 40, 116f: it is the *eyfā*, i.e. 4,800 dirhams when dry. These wheat prices which we find in the Geniza documents apply, as noted, during periods of unusual dearth, and are many times the normal prices, which were about a ¼ of a dirham (*waraq*) per *raṭl*; see Hinz, *Die Welt des Orients*, 2(1954), 53, 61, 50; Ashtor, *JAH*, 4(1970), 9; Ashtor, *Histoire des prix*, 50; cf. Sāwīrūs, 456: when al-Jarawī put Alexandria under siege (*ca*. 825), the price of a wayba of wheat there reached two dinars and a dirham, i.e. one and a third dirham (*waraq*) per *raṭl*; but there were even much greater increases in prices. See Bianquis, *JESHO*, 23(1980), 74ff; he gathered data on the prices of wheat and bread in Egypt between September 1023 and February 1025, according to Musabbiḥī; a *raṭl* of bread cost from 0.06 dirham in times of abundance, and as much as one dirham during a drought. A *tillīs* of wheat, which cost 0.80 dinar in times of abundance, reached 4.33 during shortages. It seems that it was not clear to Bianquis that they were speaking of dirhams of the *waraq* type.

constituted most of the physicians and the scribes (i.e. the clerks, *kataba*). In my collection of Geniza documents, we do not come across Jewish tanners at all, nor dyers (but see: *dār al-ṣabbāghīn*, the aforementioned house of the dyers in Ramla). Dealing in currency matters and banking activities, however, is often mentioned there, particularly in reference to the Maghribis. Many of the Jews and the Christians were evidently engaged in agriculture, especially in the smaller localities. Information on other occupations we find mainly in the Geniza documents; it is not extensive. There is evidence of the production of pottery in the remains of a workshop from the eighth century discovered during excavations in Ramla in 1965 in the south-western part of the present-day city, in an area covering *ca.* 250 square metres, 2 metres deep. In Haifa, Nāṣir Khusraw found ship-yards building the so-called *jūdī* ships, during his visit in 1047. The same writer-traveller also speaks of the many craftsmen and artisans in Jerusalem.

Another branch which was certainly developed in Palestine was that of the production of building materials, although we have no information apart from what we have been told by Muqaddasī about the marble-producing quarries in Bet Guvrin (Bayt Jibrīl) and the white-stone quarries in jund Filasṭīn.

Tiberias was known for the floor-mats produced there, among them also the *sajāda*s (the prayer-mats used by the Muslims, called also *sāmāniyya*-mats). Evidently occupations involving textiles were mostly the domain of the Jews. A Jerusalemite who fled to Fustat contracted a partnership with a financier from Fustat; the Jerusalemite was Nethanel (his Arabic name was Hibat Allah) b. Yeshū'ā al-Maqdisī and the man of Fustat was Ṣedaqa he-ḥāvēr b. Muvḥār. This Nethanel was a qualified weaver; he invests 15 dinars in the partnership and Ṣedaqa invested 50. The products supplied by Nethanel are to be sold to the *bazzāzīn*, the textile merchants in the *qaysāriyya*s (markets) and the profits or losses are to be divided equally. Ṣedaqa can decide at any moment to dissolve the partnership. Among the craftsmen in Jerusalem, there were also skilled spinners. Jacob b. Samuel the Spaniard (al-Andalusī), when buying in Jerusalem, writes to Joseph b. Naḥum (evidently of the Baradānī family) in Fustat, and mentions that he has bought spun yarn. From the letters of Manasseh b. Joshua (in the middle of the eleventh century) we learn that it was customary to buy spun yarn in Jerusalem and send it to Tyre for finishing before the weaving process. In one of his letters, Manasseh confirms that the *qhazl* (threads, spun yarn), has arrived and that he has handed it over to a reliable Jewish craftsman, after going into the various professional aspects with other craftsmen. This is also an opportunity to familiarise ourselves with the names of the various types of threads. *Qaqālī*, apparently a sort of elaborate dress in demand among the Christian pilgrims, are also supplied together with the threads. Payment was by 'the needle', the meaning of which is not clear, at three-quarters of a dinar per unit. Additional payment was asked for *ṭarz*, i.e., the embroidery along the hem. There was also a charge for *qaṣāra* (a term also found in Talmudic texts, which means the laundering and bleaching of the flax) and for *daqq* (pre-shrinking). The bleaching process could only be performed after Passover, for the summer bleaching was more effective than that of the winter. If the spun yarn had been sent a month or two before the holidays (i.e. before Tishri), it would have been possible to start on time, he writes.

Evidence of the extensive Jewish occupation with textiles, both in their production and merchandising, can be found in a clause in an ancient formulary of a deed of sale in Palestine, still preserved in a receipt from the year AD 1026, in the handwriting of Abraham b. Solomon b. Judah: Turayq, daughter of Abraham, confirms that Muḥassin b. Ḥusayn ('the representative of the merchants'), is no longer indebted to her; 'not even *'sṭm* nor *pū'ā*', i.e. 'neither for fabric nor for dye'.[5]

[340] Evidence of the existence of a flour mill in Jerusalem is apparent in a letter from Joseph ha-Kohen b. Solomon Gaon from Jerusalem to Ephraim b. Shemaria in Fustat (*ca.* 1050). In the margin is a note asking that his correspondence be sent to the following address: The mill of so-and-so (the name has not been preserved), the miller. Soap was manu-

5 Muqaddasī, *Āqālīm* 183; speaking of Syrian and Palestinian areas. The potter's workshop: Rosen-Ayalon and Eitan, *IEJ*, 16:148, 1966. Nāṣir Khusraw, 18 (text), 60 (translation); craftsmen in Jerusalem: 20 (text), 68 (translation). Quarries: Muqaddasī, *ibid.*, 184. Despite the silence in the sources, the Jews evidently also engaged in tanning: in **460**, Moses b. Jacob, writing from Jerusalem, wishes to know the prices of untanned leather and whether it is possible to ship it from Fustat to Jerusalem without damage. It seems that the sumach and gall-nuts mentioned in some letters in my corpus, were used in tanning. And despite the silence in those letters, Jews also seem to have been engaged in textile dying as well. According to Jāḥiẓ, the Jews were the sole possessors of the secret of the crimson worm (the *qirmiz*); see Serjeant, *AI*, 15–16 (1951), 35. Mats of Tiberias: Nāṣir Khusraw, 17 (text), 58 (translation); *sāmāniyya*, called after a quarter of Iṣfahān known for its weavers; see Ibn Taghrī Bardī, II, 95; see on a Tiberian mat preserved in the Athens Museum: Combe, *Mél. Dussaud*: 841; the deed of partnership between Ṣedaqa and Nethanel: **541**, from the year 1086. Ṣedaqa the ḥāvēr is apparently 'Yesōd [foundation of] ha-yeshiva'; see TS 13J 15, f. 4 in Mann, *Jews*, II, 254; see also Gil, *Documents*, No. 43 (TS NS J 342v), line 6: 'rabbēnū yesōd ha-yeshiva' (our Master, the foundation of the yeshiva), in the accounts of the income of the heqdēsh from the beginning of the twelfth century. Spun yarn: **493**, a, line 10. Manasseh b. Yeshū'ā: **522**, a, lines 6f. See *ibid.* the note on the *qaqālī*. In **523**, there is information on the same subject; the fabrics were already in the market for a month or so, and it seems that he intends to send them to Jerusalem when someone reliable turns up; left-overs of the yarn remained in hand and he earned a quarter of a dinar on these, and awaits instructions as to what to do with the money; *'sṭm pū'ā*: **62**, line 26, see the note there. During the Geonic period, they no longer knew the meaning of *'sṭm*, as implied in MS Antonin 891, 2a, lines 19–20: '*Esṭemā* is a kind of jewel' etc.; see Assaf, *Teshūvōt* (1928/9), 159; see the commentary of R. Ḥananel to *BT*, Shabbat, 57b: *kippā* (headgear); Goitein, *Tarbiz*, 36(1966/7) 370, assumed that *'sṭm* meant indigo.

factured in Ramla and there is mention of Ramla's soap storages. Avon b. Ṣedaqa, writing from Jerusalem to Nehorai b. Nissim in Fustat (*ca.* 1065) speaks of a journey to Ramla to purchase soap. In around 1040, Palestinian soap was sold in the markets of Fustat at four dinars per *qinṭār* evidently, while in the 1060s, it seems that the price went down to $2^2/_3$ dinars. Nehorai stresses in his letter, which contains this detail, that this is the price of Palestinian soap (*ṣābūn shāmī*) whereas for the soap from the Maghrib (*ṣābūn maghribī*) there is no demand at all.[6]

[341] In one document, we come across a certain Sulaymān 'who was skilled at forging iron' – a claim for payment due to him came before the Jerusalemites' court in Fustat in the presence of Abraham b. Solomon b. Judah, in August 1030. It is likely that this Jewish blacksmith was a Palestinian. In Tyre, *ca.* 1040, a man is mentioned named Solomon b. al-*Ghallāq*, meaning son of the locksmith. In a letter from Tyre, there is mention of a man from Ḥammat-Gādēr (Jadariyya) called Moses b. Ṣemaḥ, better known by the name al-Azraq the Magician; *al-azraq* – the blue-eyed; by magician (*qōsēm*) they undoubtedly meant an astrologer, which is the *munajjim*, one of the occupations the Jews excelled in.[7]

Book production

[342] Book production evidently provided many of the Palestinians with a livelihood. A large number of letters in my collection contain details concerning scribes or book copyists. The grandson of Josiah Gaon, Josiah b. Aaron, was one of those engaged in this craft and some of his letters have been preserved from his stay in Ṣahrajt in Egypt. He writes that he expects the arrival of a shipment of quires (*karārīs*), evidently empty ones, and asks to be sent ink (*ḥibr*) – even sending an ink-well to Fustat for this purpose. It seems that he was assisted in his work by another scribe, a *Rūmī,* meaning a Byzantine. At about the same time, we find Solomon ha-Kohen b. Joseph in Daltūn in the Upper Galilee occupied in the same profession. Israel b. Nathan (Sahlūn), Nehorai's Maghribi cousin, who had formerly been involved in commerce (and evidently still had a hand in this pursuit), was busy copying books during his stay in Palestine. On the score of this craft, he succeeded in saving the cost of

[6] Joseph ha-Kohen's letter: **409**; this request evidently stemmed from the wish that the contents of this correspondence remain known only to themselves, and it seems that the same miller was a confidant of the writer. Avon: **503**, a, lines 31–32. The price of soap: **176**, right margin; one cannot be certain that the *qinṭār* is being referred to. Nehorai: **508**, b, line 5; cf. Ashtor (Strauss), *Zion*, 7(1942), 152f; see also **494**, a, line 7, Jacob b. Ismāʿīl (apparently in Tyre) also deals with various types of soap (*al-asābūn*).

[7] Sulaymān: **102**, lines 9–10. The locksmith: **276**, b, line 17; at that time, locks were made of wood; see on this: Goitein, *Mediterranean Society*, I, 109; Gil, *Documents*, 179 n. 9; the magician: **278**, lines 32–33, cf. Gil, *ibid.*, No. 16, n. 3 (p. 185).

travelling from Byzantium to Palestine even before starting on the work, by receiving an advance amounting to one dinar. Avon b. Ṣedaqa also speaks of Israel b. Nathan, a copyist living in Jerusalem, and he also mentions another Jerusalem scribe, Yeshuʿā (b. Samuel?). At approximately the same time, Joshua he-ḥāvēr b. ʿEli of Ramla writes to Judah b. Saadia (who was later granted the title 'Nagid' in Egypt) asking him to find some copying work for him among the people of Fustat, for 'the scholars of this city [probably Ramla] are few'. A colophon in the manuscript of the introduction to the Talmud by Samuel b. Ḥofni indicates that this copy was finished in Jerusalem on 10 Marheshwan AM 4796 (Wednesday, 15 October AD 1035). Israel b. Nathan, in 1059, copies the Mishnā orders *Nashim* and *Neziqin* and is prepared to copy anything for Nehorai, such as commentaries (*tafāsīr*), in order not to be idle and to earn something 'until the Lord looks upon him and sees him from heaven'. In September 1060 he has finished copying the abovementioned Mishnā orders and wants to know whether anyone in Fustat is interested in a copy of *tafāsīr* or Mishnā, or *halākhōt* (evidently Sefer Halākhōt Gedōlōt), or Talmud. When in Gūsh Ḥālāv, he promises that during his stay in Damascus, he will copy the order *Qodāshīm* (for he seems to think that he would find a good copy there to work from), from the 'Iraqi Talmud'; he is prepared to copy one of the notebooks (*daftar*) of the head of the yeshiva (evidently he is referring to a collection of responsa). In another letter, he again mentions copying the following treatises (from the Babylonian Talmud): *Qodāshīm, Mōʿēd, Berākhōt*. In a letter dated November 1061, he acknowledges receiving the copyists' ruler (*qiyās*) used for the length of the sheets, and he also requests a 'width ruler', without which he will be unable to finish the chapter he is copying. Also he asks the addressee to find out whether someone is interested in having him copy the treatise Nāzīr, and if so, he must be sent quires for this purpose. After Passover, he intends to copy only the books of the Pentateuch, for the demand is mainly for volumes (*maṣāḥif*) of the Bible. Reliable manuscripts which are worth copying can be found in al-Mahdiyya, he writes (evidently brought there from Iraq in the tenth century) and Labrāṭ (judge of al-Mahdiyya, of the Sughmār family) and Abū Saʿīd, who live there, should be urged to acquire a leather-bound Bible (*mujallad*) for him. Even if it is expensive, they should send him the volumes of the Talmud (*maṣāḥif al-talmūd*). In another letter written on 14 March 1062, he promises that after Passover, he will start work on copying the Midrash Tehillīm (*agādat tehillīm*).

Books are also mentioned in letters from Ascalon at the end of the eleventh century. Nathan ha-Kohen b. Mevorakh requests that eight books of the Prophets, unproofed, that had been left behind in Fustat, be sent to his father. It seems that the family was involved in producing books, or perhaps they used to buy unproofed books, which were cheaper, which they would then correct themselves. In another letter, Nathan mentions that he holds as deposit quires belonging to a certain Sibā' b. Mufarrij, known as Ibn al-Kāzirūnī, which contain an old copy (*nuskha qadīma*) of *Halākhōt Gedōlōt* in a small, reddish script, somewhat faded. Mention is made of selling some of the quires in Ascalon, and the writer is prepared to pay one and a half to two dinars for the *Halākhōt Gedōlōt*. In another letter, he says that there are no longer any books of the Talmud left in Ascalon (meaning that the books which the refugees had brought with them when fleeing from the Crusaders had disappeared). Most of the Bibles have been sold but he found four complete Bibles at the home of a widow, daughter of b. Ṣaghīr (b. Ṣaghīr – undoubtedly Solomon b. Saadia), in good condition, except for the bindings, which were damaged; one volume (*muṣḥaf*) of the Pentateuch had its title pages somewhat obliterated; the volume which contains the four books of the first Prophets has some of its first and final pages piled, but the volume containing the four books of the last Prophets and the scrolls is in a good state, apart from the binding. Some people are prepared to pay her 12 dinars for them and he awaits instructions as to how to proceed. It seems that this was the usual price for a complete Bible, as we can deduce from Joseph b. Sahl al-Baradānī's letter to Nehorai b. Nissim in which the sale of a new Bible for the price of 13 dinars is mentioned, evidently the work of Israel b. Nathan. We find interesting details concerning payment for book-making in a letter from Solomon ha-Kohen b. Joseph of Daltūn, mentioning the fee for copying per quire; for one type, they paid $^{2}/_{3}$ qīrāṭ per quire, whereas for another type, $1^{1}/_{6}$ of a qīrāṭ, apart from the cost of the paper. According to the writer, it appears that in fixing the price, the number of letters per page in the original manuscript (from which the copy was being made) was taken into consideration.[8]

[343] From book-copying we move on to the subject of paper and its

[8] Josiah b. Aaron: **202** (*ca.* 1030). Solomon ha-Kohen: **250**. Israel b. Nathan copies books: **465** (lines 10ff.); advance payment: **466**; the Maghribi Israel b. Nathan can be seen as a pursuer of the tradition of the scribes of the Maghrib (and in a more distant past: of Babylonia) in Palestine; on Labrāṭ b. Moses ibn Sughmār (and on his brother Judah) see below, n. 42. In the colophon written in the MS of the first Prophets, Joseph b. Jacob ha-Ma'arāvī ('the Maghribī') says that he wrote, he vocalised and inserted the *masorah*, 'according to the proofed books vocalised and provided with the masorah by Aaron b. Moses b. Asher'; and this he did in 'Jerusalem the holy city . . . in the year 1300' (Sel.; = 989); see the complete version: Kahle, *Masoreten des Westens*, I, 65, cf. Hirschberg, *Eretz-Israel*, 5(1959), 216. Avon: **498**, a, lines 14f; b, lines 2f; Joshua b. 'Eli: **567**, lines 21ff. Introduction to the Talmud: TS Loan 108. The works of Israel b. Nathan: **469**, b, lines 10f; **470**, a, margin; **474**; **475**, a, lines 12ff; **479**, a, lines 5f, 16f, in the margin and the continuation in b, lines 6f, 11. Ascalon: **581**, a, lines 12–17; **583**, lines 12f; **588**, lines 7f. Joseph b. Sahl al- Baradānī's letter: **492**, a, lines 6–12. Cf. Beit-Arie. *Te'uda*, 1(1980), 197; on the Bible in Ascalon, the property of the widow, daughter of Ṣaghīr, it is interesting to note TS 10 J 5, f. 15, written in the

supply. Parchment (*riqq* and in the plural *ruqūq*, in Arabic; cf. *rōq, rōqīn*, in the Talmudic sources) was still very much in use. Israel b. Nathan sends Nehorai instructions regarding the purchase and manner of shipping *ruqūq*. Due to the lack of parchment, he has wasted the summer. Abiathar, writing on 14 November 1070, from Jerusalem, mentions letters written by his father, head of the yeshiva; one on a long roll of parchment (*riqq kabīr*) and others on red paper. The Karaite Maḥbūb b. Nissim gives the captain of a ship a package of parchment leaves (*shakāra ruqūq*) as a bribe to persuade him to deviate from his usual route.[9]

[344] In the eleventh century, however, most of the writing was already being done on paper, and this can easily be seen from the Geniza, in which the various kinds of parchment are rather rare. Paper is mentioned in a number of documents in my collection. The scribe from Daltūn, Solomon ha-Kohen, writes about a book copied on excellent paper (*waraq jayyid*) in *ca.* 1030. Maghribi merchants also traded in paper and its transport. Israel b. Nathan, who copied books when in Gūsh Ḥālāv, awaits money for purchasing paper. Daniel b. Azariah writes to ʻEli b. ʻAmram and asks to have notebooks copied in Fustat containing geonic queries and responsa (he mentions the Gaon Samuel, apparently referring to Samuel b. Ḥofnī). He would like to have them copied by an expert scribe and on good paper – not on Egyptian paper but on Andalusī or Iṭrābulusī (from Spain or Tripoli), and on a large galley. Each quire should be carefully examined and proofed upon completion. From this we learn that the Gaon may not have relied upon the work of the Palestinian scribes (or perhaps they had too much work), and that paper from Spain and Tripoli, was preferable to Egyptian paper. Indeed, Nāṣir Khusraw points out that the paper manufactured in Tripoli is similar to that made in Samarqand and is of an even finer quality.

Mūsā b. Jacob, who was based in Tyre, dealt in paper on a rather large scale and there are four of his letters included in my collection which were written between August 1057 and January 1058 from Damascus and Tyre. They speak of buying paper in Damascus in hundreds of dinars – mentioning 15 loads of paper (at least two tons). He shipped more than twenty

middle of Shaʻbān 412, i.e. 24 November 1021: Samuel b. Jacob receives twenty-five dinars for copying eight books of the Prophets for Abū Naṣr Salāma (who is Solomon) b. Saʻīd (Saadia) b. Ṣaghīr, according to the *namūdaj* (Persian: model) owned by Abū Isḥāq Ibrahīm b. Ḥujayj (Abraham b. Haggai); for this Solomon b. Saʻīd is the father of the above-mentioned widow, and perhaps they are also referring to the same book; cf. Goitein, *Mediterranean Society*, II, 239; 574, n. 53

[9] See **469**, b, line 3; **472** a, in the upper margin; b, line 1. Abiathar: **547**, a, lines 40–41. Maḥbūb b. Nissim: **292**, a, line 11. On the use of parchment, see the quotation in Pirqoy b. Bāboy, from the opinion of R. Yehudai Gaon concerning the discussion on what is banned and permitted in using *riqq* (see Mann, *REJ*, 70 [1920], 118f, and see the version on p. 137 where the main contention of the Gaon is that it is permitted to use *riqq* only if it has been

parcels (evidently rolls are intended here) of paper to Ramla and they arrived safely. We gather from his letters that paper was sold in Fustat either by wholesale weight or by retail sheets. When the paper arrived at its destination, it had then to be sold quickly, before it darkened. The paper is brought from Damascus (or perhaps also from Tripoli) to Tyre, by land on camels. Special identification marks (*'alāma*) impressed on the paper by the manufacturer are mentioned, these probably being water-marks; the paper he purchased had the *'alāma* of Ibn Imām, evidently a Damascene paper-maker. It seems therefore that there was no local paper manufacturer in Palestine in the eleventh century and paper was imported from Damascus or Tripoli, although Muqaddasī mentions paper (*kāghid*) being made in Tiberias. A possible explanation may be that its manufacture gradually came to an end in the course of the generations from Muqaddasī's time at the turn of the tenth century to that of the Geniza letters in the mid-eleventh century.[10]

Exports

[345] In this section, we must give pride of place to oil, that is olive oil, an important Palestinian export in antiquity. At the start of the ninth century, a certain *mawlā* (client) of the Umayyads, a Jew or Christian who became a Muslim, by the name of al-Ḥakam b. Maymūn, is mentioned. He dealt in the export of oil from Palestine, and would transport it by camel caravan to Medina. Nāṣir Khusraw speaks of the production of olive oil; he notes trees which rendered 5,000 *mann* (some 3,500 litres!) each. The oil was kept in containers in hollows in the earth and was exported all over the world. He adds that owing to its bread and oil, al-Shām (Palestine and Syria) never suffered from starvation. In the Geniza documents from the mid-eleventh century, there are also references

treated with gall-nuts); see also Goitein, *Mediterranean Society*, I, 422, nn. 83, 84; and see *ibid.*, II, App. B. (No. 32, p. 447), the name al-Ruqūqī, maker of (or dealer in) parchment.

10 Solomon ha-Kohen: **250**, b, lines 3–4. On the matter of the Maghribis, see the affair of the partnership which came up before the court of Daniel b. Azariah: **394**, line 12. Egyptian paper was called Manṣūrī paper. It was made in vats (*maṭābīkh*: literally boiling places) in Fustat (not in al-Qāhira), see *al-Mughrib*, V, 29, quoting *al-Kamā'im* of al-Bayhaqī (who is apparently Ismā'īl b. Ḥusayn al-Bayhaqī, who wrote in *ca.* 1010, see Sezgin, I, 451, not as in Brockelmann, *GAL*, S I, 558); Maqrīzī, *Khiṭaṭ*, II, 183–186, quotes a long fragment from the *Mughrib*, also referring to Manṣūrī paper (p. 185). Israel b. Nathan: **474**, a, line 10; in **480**, a, lines 7–8, he confirms that he has sent eleven sheets of paper from his stock in Jerusalem to Nehorai in Fustat, with a certain R. Isaac. Daniel b. Azariah: **371**. Nāṣir Khusraw, 12 (text), 41 (translation). Mūsā b. Jacob: **514–517**. Paper in Tiberias: Muqaddasī, *Aqālīm*, 180, cf. Le Strange, *Palestine*, 19, according to whom paper was made of cotton there; see also Mez, 440; Goitein, *Mediterranean Society*, I, 81; 410 and n. 2; Ashtor, *CCM*, 18(1975), 119.

to the oil trade of Palestine. Israel b. Nathan dealt in oil via Ascalon, and it seems that he met with losses in this sphere. Jacob b. Samuel informs Nehorai from Jerusalem that he has acquired a quantity of two *qirāba*s of oil (some 66 litres) for him, undoubtedly for export, and delivered it to Ibn al-Tuffāḥī (apparently a ship-owner) in Jaffa.[11]

[346] I have already mentioned commerce in fruit and rose-petal preserves. Dried rose-petals and rose-hips were another export item and mention is made of a shipment of this kind in 1037 from Tyre. Fruit syrups (*sharāb*) and sumach (*sumāq*) were goods which Joseph b. Sahl al-Baradānī supplied from Palestine through Tyre. Jacob b. Ismā'īl also sends Nehorai cinnamon via Tyre which evidently first reached Palestine from the Far East and Nehorai is to sell it in Egypt and buy other merchandise there from the proceeds. There were 47 units of cinnamon in all and they were shipped on board b. Shiblūn's vessel. Joseph b. Yeshū'ā al-Ṭarābulusī, a sort of partner or agent of Barhūn b. Mūsā al-Tāhirtī, writes of a shipment of 17 units of myrobalan (*halīlaj*) and a shipment of *ṣabir* (aloe, frankincense) *suquṭrī*.[12]

[347] Another item of Palestinian export was salt produced from the

11 Al-Ḥakam: Iṣbahānī, *Aghānī*, VI, 64. Nāṣir Khusraw, 20 (text), 67 (translation); on the excellent olives and olive oil of Palestine, see also Ibn al-Faqīh, 117; Tha'ālibī, *Thimār*, 532. Israel b. Nathan: **482**, *a* lines 12f. Jacob b. Samuel: **493**, a, lines 8–9; the capacity of the *qirāba* is assumed, see Gil, *JNES*, 34(1975), 68, n. 43. The oil occupied a prominent place in Maghribi merchants' trading, as can be seen from the table, *ibid.*, 68ff. See the matter of marketing indigo in Qayrawān and the purchase of 60 *ziqq*s (evidently = *qirba*, see Gil, *ibid.*) of oil, i.e. approx. two tons: **493**, a, lines 15f; the oil was sent to Sicily.

12 Roses: **275** (the payment for the shipment was deposited in Tyre with Moses b. Isaac 'the Spaniard', perhaps a Karaite, whom we later find in Jerusalem). Joseph b. Sahl: **491**, lines 8–9. Cinnamon: **495**, b, lines 2f. Joseph b. Yeshū'ā: **496**, b; the *halīlaj* (myrobalan) is the *Phyllantus emblica* fruit (see Zohary, 293); the Maghribi merchants dealt in this product extensively, see the Hebrew Index. There were different varieties: black, yellow and kābilī (from Kābil, today the capital of Afghanistan), see Shazarī, *Nihāya*, 45 and there, the editor's note 8; a ḥadīth ascribed to the Prophet recommends the use of black *halīlaj*, see 'Azīzī, II, 454; al-Ghāfiqī, 552: the yellow *halīlaj* is the best remedy for diarrhoea, see also *ibid.*, p. 549; Ibn Mammātī, 362, points out that the kābilī halīlaj is weighed by *mann*s, like saffron; see al-Mu'izz b. Bādīs, 94: how ink is made from *halīlaj*; see further: Ducros, 8, see also *ibid.*, 80, on the *ṣabir suquṭrī* (*Aloe Succotrina*) from which a concentrated syrup is prepared which energises, warms and dries; this is the *levōnā* (*Boswellia*), see the Hebrew Index; see also Maimonides, *'Uqqār*, 157f (No. 318); this ṣabir was brought from the island of Socotra in the Indian Ocean, on the eastern side of the Bay of Aden. See the article Soḳoṭra (by J. Tkatsch) in *EI*[1]. Related to this is the *balīlaj* which is the Indian myrobalan mentioned in **394**, line 6, and in **395**, line 8, and this is the *Belleria myrobalan* or the *Terminalia bellerica*, see Ghāfiqī, 262ff; this myrobalan was used as a medicine for diseases of the intestines, but was also considered helpful for ailing sight, headaches and the vapours. We find in **394** that considerable trading was carried on by the Maghribi merchants in perfumes and essences which they exported to Sicily and here there is mention of (1) bamboo crystals (*ṭabāshīr*), a product also called 'snake ashes'; it was made from the lower parts of the bamboo stalks and contained silicon, calcium and organic material; they would produce an imitation by using ivory or bone meal; this was used as a medicine for inflammations, intestinal diseases and other illnesses; see Maimonides,

Dead Sea. Wax also figured among the products which were concentrated in Tyre for export. Yefet b. Meshullam, a Karaite from Jerusalem living in the Karaite quarter, the Samareitikē, ships 30 *raṭl*s of 'cheese made on the Mount of Olives' including 339 *ṭefūsīm* (moulds).[13]

[348] Tyre was famous for its glass and evidently so was Acre. The Jews of Palestine and Syria were expert at making glass which contained lead and would export it to various countries, including those of Europe, where it became known as 'Jewish glass'. Specific evidence of this can be found in a power-of-attorney deed made out in Tyre on 25 January 1011, in which Khalaf (Ḥalfon) b. Moses b. Aaron, whose nickmane was Ibn Abī Qīda, the 'representative of the merchants' in Tyre, authorises his father-in-law Solomon b. Rabīʻ, who stayed in Fustat, to collect from the 'representative of the merchants' in Fustat, Caleb b. Aaron, what is due him for 37 *mishpālōt* (baskets, parcels) of glass, which were partly his property and partly in partnership with Abraham b. Ḥabashī and Aaron b. Jacob, who is Ibn Abī Rujayf.[14]

'Uqqār, 171 (No. 84); Ducros, 84; (2) aloe (*'ūd*); see Maimonides, *ibid.*, 145f (No. 296): kinds of *Aquilonia*; (3) sweet resin, (*quṣṭ* or *qusṭ*, *ḥulw*; see Maimonides, *ibid.*, 169 (No. 338); which is the *kostos* of the Greeks; and in Persian: *bustaj* or *bustag*; in Aramaic: *kūshṭā*; produced from *Inula Helenium* L. = *Aucklandia Costus* Falc.; made mainly in Kashmir, where at the beginning of this century, its production was still a state monopoly; it is the *Saussurea hypoleuca* Spr.; a remedy for coughing and asthma; see Maimonides, *ibid.*, 169 (No. 338); Ducros, 106; 'Azīzī, II, 159, 442; there are two kinds of *qusṭ*, the Indian, which is black and the marine, which is white, the Indian being the stronger of the two; see Jonah ibn Janāḥ, *S. ha-shorashim*, 642: this is Biblical *qeṣī'ōt*, according to Saadia Gaon's interpretation; (4) *balīlaj*, (5) saffron; (6) cinnamon (*qirfa*). In **470**, b, lines 3–4, Israel b. Nathan asks Nehorai b. Nissim to send him, apart from half a *qīrāṭ* of aniseed, a *qīrāṭ* and a half of good quality cinnamon, ground finely, red and sharp. Nehorai himself asks on behalf of another Maghribi, Abraham b. Isaac ha-Talmid, of Joseph ha-Kohen b. 'Eli al-Fāsī, who is in Tyre, to sell the cinnamon for him *bi'l-qism wa'l-rizq* (see on this below); see Solomon b. ha-Yātōm's commentary on Mashqīn, 65: 'cinnamon in the language of Ishmael is *qirfa*'; (7) myrrh (*murr*), was used for stimulation, as an astringent, for coughs etc., see Ducros, 123; (8) yellow myrobalan (*halīlaj aṣfar*); cardamom (*hāl*) is the *Elettaria Cardamomum*, see Maimonides, *ibid.*, 58 (No. 116). Cf. Zohary, 441; (9) aloe juice (*ṣabir*); (10) water of camphor (*kāfūr*). Apart from these, mention is also made there of *qarashiyya*, cherries perhaps, see Maimonides, *ibid.*, 165 (No. 330). The value of the entire shipment, including packing and storage, was close to 169 dinars, undoubtedly a very large sum.

13 Salt: Baumstarck, *Palästinapilger*, 73; the export of salt is not mentioned in my corpus of Geniza documents and the purchase of salt is only referred to once, for household use, in Jerusalem: **501**, a, line 22. Wax: **276**, b, line 11. Cheese: **309**. Possibly the Jerusalem *raṭl*, i.e. 2.5 kilograms is meant (Hinz, 29) and then it is a shipment of 75 kilograms and each mould of cheese weighs *ca.* 220 grams; at this juncture, we should perhaps refer to what appeared to be evidence of the export of butter from Palestine: the responsum of an anonymous Gaon quoted by the Maharam, who notes that in Africa they would permit the use of butter from 'the pagans', 'but since they began to bring them the butter of Hammāt and Gūsh Ḥālāv, and adulterate it with *ḥelev*, (animal fat), we ban', etc.; see Poznanski, *Harkavy Jubilee Volume* 218; Ginzberg, *Geonica*, I, 31ff, 218; but this is not a source on export from Palestine, as Abramson has proven, *'Inyānōt*, 236f, and it seems that the use of Palestinian names here is merely symbolic.

14 Praise of al-Shām glass: Tha'ālibī, *Thimār*, 532; Idrīsī (Cerulli), 365; cf. Ashtor, *CCM*,

[349] Indigo, which also grew in Palestine, was in demand on the world markets at the time. It grew mainly in the region of the Dead Sea and the Jordan Valley. In one of his letters, Avon b. Ṣedaqa mentions purchasing indigo and grains of *wasma*, another variety of indigo. A record written in Nathan b. Abraham's court in Fustat in 1040, contains details of a litigation between indigo merchants concerning large shipments of indigo to Sicily and Mahdiyya, apparently referring to shipments of indigo from Palestine. Daniel b. Azariah, in one of his letters written from Tyre before he became the Palestine Gaon and was still engaged in trade, notes the going price of indigo in Tyre: 'the prices are rising, approximately nine ...' (no details of the currency or unit of weight remain). A deed of partnership relating to export to Sicily from 1058, mentions large quantities of indigo as well. Nehorai b. Nissim speaks of the rising price of indigo (in *ca.* 1067) because it was in great demand in Palestine itself; and the merchants (evidently Maghribis) preferred to put their money into indigo rather than flax, which was scarce and expensive. There was also considerable demand for this product in the Maghrib. A certain R. Maymūn, located in Fustat, is worried about the fate of a shipment of indigo belonging to him which was to have arrived by ship from Palestine.[15]

[350] Various types of weaving and textiles made in Palestine were also in demand on foreign markets. Fine linen, *shīsh* is mentioned, as having been produced mainly in Palestine – *shīsh shāmī* – (also in Cyprus: *shīsh qubrusī*, and it seems that it was exported from there via Palestine). I have already mentioned the linen yarn sent from Jerusalem to Tyre for finishing. Joseph b. Samuel al-Andalusī, writing from Jerusalem to Joseph b. Nathan al-Baradānī in Tyre, also mentions having bought his spun yarn in Jerusalem, and hence we assume that there was a demand for Jerusalem yarns and that they were exported. Jacob b. Ismā'īl al-Andalusī writes from Tyre to Abū'l-Walīd Yūnus (Jonah) b. Da'ūd, in Egypt or perhaps in Spain, stating that he bought 40 pieces of *qazz* fabric in Tyre. *Qazz* was a kind of silk, evidently mixed with rabbit-wool. In another letter to Nehorai b. Nissim, he also mentions a cargo of *qazz* which he is loading on board a ship. A load of *qazz* sent to Egypt through Tripoli in Lebanon is

18(1975), 119; Lamm, *Gläser*, 15; Heyd, *Hist.*, I, 179f; Power-of-attorney: **268**; Ḥalfon b. Moses is mentioned in a number of documents in my corpus; his wife Dara b. Solomon and his brother-in-law 'Eli b. Solomon are also mentioned; see the Hebrew Index; see also Consistoire israélite VII D 78, a fragment of a marriage deed from Tyre, in which apart from the aforementioned Khalaf b. Moses b. Aaron, several other inhabitants of Tyre are mentioned. Printed by Friedman, in *Marriage*, II, 384 and see details about Khalaf b. Moses *ibid.*, 387.

[15] See on indigo: Muqaddasī, *Āqālīm*, 7, who mentions the indigo of Jericho; cf. Mez, 440; Serjeant, *AI*, 11–12 (1946), 143. Avon: **503**, a, line 15; the court record: **193**. Daniel b. Azariah: **347**, b, line 2; the deed of partnership: **394**, line 1; **395**, line 7. The matter was brought before the court of Daniel b. Azariah. Nehorai's letter, **508**, a, lines 6–7, b, line 10.

also mentioned in Jacob b. Salmān al-Ḥarīrī's letters, speaking of red *qazz* fabric. Idrīsī, writing in the mid-twelfth century, refers to the costly white fabrics made in Tyre which are exported everywhere.

Other goods being sent via Tyre to Egypt by Jacob b. Ismāʿīl were the fabrics of Tustar (*thiyāb Tustar*), but we do not know whether textiles of the Tustar variety were actually manufactured in Palestine or whether fabrics were exported which came from elsewhere, or perhaps from Tustar itself. Abraham b. Isaac al-Andalusī, writing in Jerusalem to Nehorai b. Nissim in Fustat, mentions the possibility of exporting coloured fabrics, apparently through Ascalon, and asks him to take stock of the market conditions in Fustat. Ascalon was itself a centre for the manufacture of textiles and the Ascaloni fabric, *thawb ʿasqalānī*, is spoken of. We find a long list of exports from Ascalon in Jacob b. Joseph b. Ismāʿīl al-Iṭrābulusī's letter to Nehorai b. Nissim. He purchased sumach (*sumāq*), gall-nuts (probably for tanning), cedar resin, sugar from Zīb (see above), cotton (*quṭn*) which was sold in Ascalon at four *raṭl*s and ten ounces per dinar, which he had intended to sell on the spot but for which he could not find customers. We find a similar list of commodities bought in Jerusalem by Avon b. Ṣedaqa: plums (*sabastān*), glue, almonds and soap.[16]

[16] *Shīsh shāmī, qubrusī*, see **507**, a, lines 9–10, the letter from Jacob b. Salmān al-Ḥarīrī to Nehorai b. Nissim from *ca.* 1060; he is staying in Ramla and has with him *shīsh* made in Cyprus, which sells at two dinars per small *raṭl*, and the writer wishes to know whether he should sell it in Ramla or bring it to Fustat, if the selling price there is higher; see *ibid.*, also lines 13, 15; margin, right; b, line 3; also in another of his letters, written from Syrian Tripoli, he mentions the trading in *shīsh*, see **506**, a, margin, right. It is customary to interpret the word *shīsh* (more common in Arabic: *shāsh*) – Mosul weave (English: muslin), which is a fine cotton fabric; but it seems that in the period under discussion, it meant fine linen cloth, for cotton was not commonly used at the time; see also Jonah ibn Janāḥ, *Sefer ha-shorashim*, 692: *Shēsh*, linen. See also Nissim b. Ḥalfon's letter to Nehorai b. Nissim: BM Or 5566 B, f. 20, lines 10–11, containing a request from Nehorai to inform him of the price of *al-shīsh al-shāmī al-khāliṣ wa'l-manqūḍ* (evidently he means two kinds, according to the quality, the pure as against the inferior). Jacob b. Salmān: **493**, a, line 10. Jacob b. Ismāʿīl: **494**, line 8; **495**, a, lines 15–16; Jacob b. Salmān: **506**, a, line 10; **507**, b, lines 1–2; A coat of *khazz* is also mentioned in the dowry list in the Karaite marriage deed from Jerusalem, **305**, line 23 (1028), and it seems that the meaning there is: rabbit-wool. See on *khazz*: Gil, *JESHO*, 17(1974), 312; see Idrīsī (Cerulli), 365. Tustari fabric: **495**, a, lines 14–15; on *tustarī* (or *dustarī*; also *dībāj*, silk, *tustarī*) fabric, see Gil, *ha-Tustarīm*, 21, and *ibid.* further references. Coloured weavers: **505**, line 12. *Thawb ʿasqalānī*, see TS NS J 127, a, line 5, cf. Goitein, *Letters*, 288, n. 7. Jacob b. Joseph: **487**, lines 18f: he loads three shipments of sumach and notes that one shipment remained with him because he did not have a container for it; cedar-resin – see in the upper margin: *kathīrā'*: in Aramaic: *keshartā*, see BT, Berakhot, 43a: R. Ada b. Ahava said: on the *keshartā* one has to say the blessing: . . . who created trees of scents. On the matter of the *kathīrā'-keshartā*, Geonic sources say it is *qusṭ* (resin). In the name of Hayy Gaon it is said: *keshartā* is *ghāliya* which is several scents mixed in oil. Till, 98, according to the Coptic medicinal tradition, defines *kathīrā'*: a resin from various kinds of tragacanth, used to cure skin diseases, rheumatism, spitting blood and more, while *ghāliya* (see above), is defined by Kazimirski, s.v., as a perfume, which is blade, being a blend of musk, ambergris, and other scents. See Epstein, *Commentary*, 144, n. 17; Hayy: *Ōṣar ha-ge'ōnīm Ber.*, Comment., 61; *ʿArūkh*, *qsṭ*, *kshr* (in the supplementary

[351] In the eleventh century, most of Palestine's exports went to Egypt, as is clearly indicated in the Geniza documents and especially in the letters of the Maghribi merchants. This was understandable, partially because of Palestine's political dependence on Egypt and also because Egypt was the major commercial centre in the Mediterranean basin at the time. However, exports from Palestine reached other countries as well. There is the somewhat doubtful evidence of export to Europe in the story of the Jewish merchant who used to visit Palestine and bring precious objects from there, the likes of which had never been seen before. Charlemagne ordered him to fool the Archbishop Richulf of Mainz in order to humiliate him, so the Jew sold him a mouse. In view of the widespread connections maintained throughout the Mediterranean area by the Maghribi merchants – Sicily, Spain, North Africa, Byzantium – apparently such Palestinian items as the glass mentioned above, did reach all these countries by virtue of their mediation.[17]

Internal trade

[352] Not much has been preserved in the sources on the subject of internal trade. The existence of 'Jewish markets' in Jerusalem, Ramla, and Tiberias is evidence of the central role of the Jews in commerce. I have already mentioned 'Eli ha-Kohen b. Ezekiel's shop in Jerusalem and below I shall refer to shops in Ramla which were dedicated to the Jewish *waqf* in Jerusalem. Jews were also engaged in commercial activities in smaller localities, such as the aforementioned trading of goods in Ḥammat Gādēr. There is the episode of the Jerusalem Karaite of Spanish origin who was persecuted by his fellow-sectarians. He went over to the Rabbanites, who set up a shop for him in a village near Jerusalem. Much of the internal trade was conducted on market days, at the large fairs in places throughout Palestine. According to the *Book of the Times* by Ibn Māsawayh, the Nestorian author of the first half of the ninth century, a market day in jund Filasṭīn (undoubtedly referring to Ramla) was held on the 23rd of April. He also mentions other market days in Idhra'āt on the 13th of October, in Buṣrā in the Ḥawrān on the 14th of July, and in 'Ammān on the 10th of August. On the 14th of September, there was a fair which he refers to as 'the Feast of the Church of the Resurrection' in Jerusalem, a holiday more commonly known as the 'Feast of the Cross' (*'īd al-ṣalīb*). Bīrūnī lists it among the Nestorian holidays, occurring on the 13th of September, but he

vol.). Cotton: **487**, b, lines 7f (one *raṭl* = 12 ounces). Avon b. Ṣedaqa: **501**, a, line 38, cf. Hirschberg, *Eretz-Israel*, 5 (1958/9), 219.

[17] See the story of the Jewish merchant, in Aronius, No. 75.

refers to it as being the day Helena, mother of Constantine, discovered the cross (on which Jesus was crucified, of course); and on the morrow, it was displayed before the people. The Christians were divided on this issue: some celebrated the day it was found (the 13th) and others celebrated it on the day it was displayed (the 14th). Arculf tells of a grand fair taking place in Jerusalem precisely on the 15th of September, when countless people of various nations come to Jerusalem in order to trade. Israel b. Nathan mentions the *'īd al-ṣalīb* in a letter he wrote in Jerusalem on 14 March 1062. The text is not very clear but it seems that he wants to say that trading in silk and oil is not successful after the *'īd al-ṣalīb*, that is after the Jerusalem fair, a fact which some of the Ascalon merchants experienced in person.[18]

Imports

[353] We have seen that Palestine was self-sufficient with regard to food and that there was even some exporting of surplus food commodities. Similarly, certain products known for the quality of their workmanship were also exported. On the other hand, it seems that there was also a thriving import trade, at least during relatively peaceful times. The import trade was apparently directed to a large extent towards the pilgrims of all creeds who filled Jerusalem and wanted to buy such items as perfumes, jewellery, clothes and various textiles. It seems that there was considerable consistency in the list of imported items dating from pre-Islamic times, about which we have not a little knowledge. Expensive goods, such as perfumes and spices, a variety of fabrics and weaves, especially silks, jewellery and precious stones, and so on, would reach the country.

Lively trading in imports also continued throughout the Islamic period in such wares as perfumes and medicaments. We have seen above that Palestine also served as a way-station for trading certain goods, such as the *halīlaj* (myrobalan) and others. One should also add here the *kuḥl* (antimony, *pūkh* in Hebrew). Abraham the Fourth b. Samuel the Third (b. Hosha'na) writes from Ramla to Solomon b. Judah in Jerusalem and asks him to send him 'a bit of *kuḥl* to remove the white film in his small daughter's eye'; from which we understand that in Ramla the *kuḥl* had been sold out. It was imported from the Maghrib; Nehorai b. Nissim tried

[18] The Jewish market in Jerusalem: **1**, b, line 12; **92**, a, line 36. Ramla: **213**, line 30. Tiberias, **245**, lines 6–7; **247**, line 23; see the episode of Ibrahīm ibn Fadānj: **457**, b, lines 8–9. On market days see: Ibn Māsawayh, 253ff; cf. Graf, *Geschicte*, II, 113f (erroneously there: the market day of jund Filasṭīn was on the 13th of April; should be on the 23rd); Bīrūnī, 310. Arculf, in Tobler et Molinier, I, 144: 'diversarum gentium undique prope innumera multitudo . . . ad commercia'; Israel b. Nathan: **482**, a, lines 13–14.

to market it in Jerusalem but was sorely disappointed to find the selling price so low.

Another item mentioned in the Geniza documents is the *baqam*, brazil-wood, referred to in a letter from Ascalon. It appears that the writer is interested in importing some, if the price is reasonable. The *baqam* is the *dalbergia*, brought from India and used for red colouring and also as a remedy for diarrhoea, apart from being used in carpentry. Traders were also interested in purchasing *sult 'anzarūt*, which is sarcocolla, from which a medicament for healing wounds and eye-infections was derived. A shipment of dried clove bark – *qirfa qaranful* – was requested from Palestine, and the supplier in Fustat warns the interested merchant that it is a very expensive item. In Ramla, a box of *khiyār shanbar*, 'senna pods' i.e. cassia, a remedy for constipation imported from Egypt, is offered for sale. The Jerusalemite 'Eli ha-Kohen b. Ezekiel, whom we know as the owner of a shop, asks Abiathar ha-Kohen (on 15 April 1071) to bring him two *manns* (slightly more than 1½ kilos) of *tinkār* (Persian, borax) from Fustat. Zadok ha-Kohen b. Elijah, writing in 1056 from Jerusalem to Fustat, evidently to his brother Abiathar, asks him to make every possible effort to sort out with the 'representative known as b. Sha'ya', that is, with the person who was apparently the 'representative of the merchants' in Fustat, the matter of the *shemen mefuṭṭām* which was oil combined with perfume essences, evidently awaited in Jerusalem. *Qafār*, sea-tar, though found in abundance on the shores of the Dead Sea, is requested by Israel b. Nathan from Egypt, particularly the kind produced in Alexandria, for his sickly eyes. It was apparently the accepted practice to call it *qafr al-Yahūd*, i.e. the Jews' tar. Another import in the category of scents was the *'ūd*, the aloe, which I have already referred to above. Isaac b. David b. Sughmār writes about this item (*ca.* 1045) to his partner Abū Sa'īd Makhlūf b. Azariah in Jerusalem, after selling part of their stock of aloe, while retaining part of it in Fustat; it appears from the letter that it is not worth exporting from there, as there is an enormous demand for it among the Byzantines, who even purchase its saw-dust.[19]

[354] Various jewels are mentioned in the Geniza letters from Palestine.

[19] See Couret: *La Palestine*, 219ff on imports to Palestine before the Muslim period, and references therein. Abraham 'the fourth': **230**, line 12; in the continuation, lines 19–20, he recalls something else: '. . . and if you, our Gaon, will remember to send a bit of *halīlaj*, for it cannot be found here'. *Kuḥl* from the Maghrib: **426**, lines 22, 4, 9 ('*pūkh*, known as *kuḥl*'), Nehorai: **500**, a, lines 25f; see on *kuḥl*: Goitein, *Pareja Jubilee Volume*, I, 349 n. 1. The letter from Ascalon: **487**, upper margin; see on *baqam*: Zohary, 264: the genus of the Dalbergieae; Ducros, 55, *Hematoxylon Campechianum* L.; Goitein, *Mediterranean Society*, I, 45. In the Mishna Commentary ascribed to Nathan, *av* of the yeshiva, to Sukka, 4, it is said of the *eshkerō'a* that it is *baqam*; *sult 'anzarūt*: **485**, a, line 17, and see *ibid.* in the footnote. *Qirfa qaranful*, *ibid.*, b, lines 1–2, 8, and also the footnote. *Khiyār shanbar*: **445**, lines 15f; see Maimonides, *'Uqqār*, No. 387, and p. 194: *Cassia fistula* (senna). The term in the letter is

Israel b. Nathan indicates in his letter to Nehorai b. Nissim that the demand for *mirjān*, little pearls, is limited but nevertheless he advises him to bring some to Jerusalem with him (from which we may assume that Nehorai intended to make a pilgrimage to Jerusalem), where he might come across some *'ajam* who would buy it – undoubtedly with the pilgrims in mind. The pearls were apparently imported from the Maghrib, as one can surmise from another of Israel b. Nathan's letters, in which he blames Labrāṭ (of the Sughmār family) for the marred colour of the pearls he supplied. It is implied that he was returning them to Fustat and he asks that they be sold there and in exchange, to buy *'aqīq*, carnelians, on his behalf. According to al-Jāḥiẓ, and also Suyūṭī, who cites al-Kalbī, the meaning of *mirjān* is little pearls, and the Yemen excelled in them. The carnelians were usually set in rings. Elijah ha-Kohen b. Solomon, while still *av-bēt-dīn*, wishes to invest money in carnelians and he asks Avon b. Ṣedaqa, who lives in Jerusalem, to write to Nehorai b. Nissim and ask him to buy carnelians for him in Fustat. In the year 1057, we have an order from Fustat for sixty lined boxes made of fine gold, to be sent to Tyre as soon as possible. We also find evidence of trading in zinc (*tūtiyā*), which was imported from Fustat.[20]

[355] Whereas olive oil (*zayt ṭayyib*), as we have seen, was among the products exported from Palestine, lighting oil was imported from Egypt, where it was extracted from the seeds of radiciflorous plants, particularly from the Cruciferae; indeed it was actually called *zayt bizr* – 'seed oil'. Mūsā b. Ya'qūb in 1057 orders a jar of this oil from Fustat. In a letter written by Moses b. Jacob in Jerusalem in June 1053, we come across an order for Egyptian products. He asks for a quarter of a *mithqāl* (a little more than a gram) of myrobalan (*halīlaj kābilī*) to be used as a medicine, rush mats (*samār*) which should be bought in Alexandria and are intended for the *maghāra*, the synagogue in Jerusalem. In Fustat, one should buy five *raṭl*s of *qirmiz shadūnī*, which is the crimson produced in Shadhūna in Spain. He also orders seven *raṭl*s of fine coloured silk made in Constantinople (*ḥarīr quṣṭanṭīnī maṣbūgh*). In addition, he enquires after the price of raw hides in Fustat and whether it is possible to ship them from Egypt to

Persian: *khiyar* = cucumber; *shanbar* = *čanbar*, round; cf. Loew, II, 408; Ducros 57f; Zohary, **244**; Ibn Mammātī, 250, mentions it is frequently to be found in markets in Adar and Nisan (March and April). *Tinkār*: **455**, line 25. *Shemen mefuṭṭām* (as in the Talmudic sources): **432**, lines 14f; see *Sefer ḥasidim*, 152: *mefaṭṭēm besāmīm*, in the same meaning, of mixing scents in oil. Ben Sha'ya is apparently Joshua b. Sha'ya, the father of Abū'l-Faḍl Sahl b. Joshua b. Sha'ya, mentioned in **577**, a, lines 26–27, cf. on this family: Goitein, *Mediterranean Society*, III, 9f. *Qafār*: see the Hebrew Index and especially **482**, b, line 13; *qafr al-Yahūd*: Khālidī, 56; *'ūd*: **485**, a, lines 7f.

20 Pearls: **477**, lines 3–5; **481**, a, line 7; b, lines 1–2. *'Aqīq*: *ibid.*, a, line 9. Jāḥiẓ, *Tabaṣṣur*, 329; Suyūṭī, *Itkān*, I, 134. The use of carnelians: Ibn Bābawayh, *Thawāb*, 168f: Avon b. Ṣedaqa: **498**, a, lines 12–14. Boxes of gold: **514**, lines 10f. Zinc: **496**, b, line 6.

Palestine without incurring damage. In one of his letters, Avon b. Ṣedaqa mentions wooden and copper *objets d'arts* imported from Tyre (undoubtedly after being shipped by sea) to Jerusalem. The Karaite Maḥbūb b. Nissim had wares which he had bought in Alexandria and shipped by sea in order to sell them in Lādhiqiyya, but when he altered his plans and debarked in Palestine, he managed to sell them in Ramla. Barhūn b. Mūsā al-Tāhirtī, while staying in Jerusalem, orders 50 pieces of *sūsī* silk *muthallath* (triple-layered), embroidered with letters (*munammaq*) and also clothing for a merchant in Ramla, and what he does not succeed in selling there, will be sent to Tyre. The goods would have to arrive during Tishri, for in Marheshwan he intended to travel from Jerusalem to Damascus. Israel b. Nathan also refers to the matter of importing textiles; he notes that in Jerusalem there is a call for light fabrics in black and blue, as well as most other colours, with the exception of purple, which the Jerusalemites do not take to, although in Ramla or Ascalon, perhaps, there may be some demand for it. Mention is also made of imports of clothing and fabrics from Sicily. Abraham b. Isaac al-Andalusī, writing in *ca.* 1052 from Jerusalem to his partner Joseph b. 'Alī ha-Kohen Fāsī, warns him not to send shipments of clothes to be sold in Palestine, because the country is full of armed troops (*aḥdāth*) and no one dares to open a shop.[21]

[356] Flax and flax products were among the notable imports into Palestine. 'Eli ha-Kohen b. Ezekiel bought a bale of flax (*ruzma kattān*) in Tyre with the intention of bringing it to Ramla. The package was delayed *en route* and part of it went astray. His brother-in-law (or son-in-law) Hiba b. Isrā'īl was also importing linen and this seems to have been the major commodity in 'Eli ha-Kohen's shop in Jerusalem. The extensive import of flax from Egypt is reflected in a number of letters in my collection, such as those of Nissim b. Ḥalfon of Tyre, in which figure details concerning packaging and the various chores involved in the shipping and releasing of goods from the port. Similarly, the letter of Solomon b. Moses al-Safāquṣī, from Jerusalem, regarding three loads of flax which Nehorai promised to send him; or Abraham b. Isaac al-Andalusī's letter, also from Jerusalem. The latter came to Jerusalem via Tinnīs, Ascalon (that is, by sea) and Ramla, and notes that on leaving Ascalon (i.e. some days prior to

21 Lighting oil: **514**, line 18; cf. Gil, *JNES*, 34(1975), 65f; Moses b. Jacob: **460**, b, lines 7f. *Qirmiz*: Goitein, *Mediterranean Society*, I, 417, n. 21: Spanish crimson; cf. al-Jāḥiẓ, *Tabaṣṣur*, 339: it is said that *qirmiz* is a grass in which there is a red worm, and it is found in Andalus, apart from Persia; no one knows where those grasses are to be found except for a group of Jews; see also Maqqarī, I, 187: the *qirmiz* is a gift from heaven bestowed on Andalus and is found on oak trees; cf. Serjeant, *AI*, 15–16(1951), 35, 70, who mentions *qirmiz* from Shadhūna. In Byzantium, silk production and trade were in Jewish hands. See Starr, *Jews*, No. 173. Lopez, *Speculum*, 20(1945), 23f; Avon: **503**, a, lines 12-13, Maḥbūb: **292**. Barhūn b. Mūsā: **458**, a, lines 17ff. Israel b. Nathan: **472**, a, **477**. Sicily: **492**, a, lines 14f, and also in the continuation. Abraham b. Isaac: **504**, a, lines 17ff.

writing the letter), all the ships had already set off for Tinnīs and other places in order to load flax. The demand for flax was particularly great in Ascalon, more so than anywhere else in Palestine, and there was interest even in the scraps of the flax. The import of flax from Egypt was undoubtedly one of the major sources of the Jewish, Maghribi and other merchants' incomes, as well as that of their clerks and agents who handled the goods in the ports of Palestine and Syria. This can also be understood from documents of the yeshiva, such as a fragment of a letter from Solomon b. Judah, in which he mentions the legacy of a certain Jacob, who was a partner in some flax transactions.[22]

[357] As is known, the country growing flax on the widest scale was Egypt, and evidently a rather large portion of its import into Palestine was in the form of raw material. Manufactories and workshops in Palestine were engaged in all the stages of producing the various linen fabrics, in spinning, weaving and dyeing. We have seen above the matter of shipping threads to Tyre for finishing. This took place in spite of the fact that during Fatimid times, a textile industry had developed in Egypt as well, especially in the days of al-'Azīz (975–996). Also, the production of the fabric known as *ṭabarī* (after Ṭabaristān) was started in Ramla. We have no detailed account describing the treatment of the raw flax imported from Egypt or of its varieties, but it seems that one of the major requirements was that it should be properly combed. Meir ha-Kohen b. 'Eli asks his brother Tobiah, who lives in Fustat, to see to it that the flax he is about to ship to him has been combed.[23]

[22] 'Eli ha-Kohen: **446**, lines 7–8. Hiba: **455**, line 26. Nissim b. Ḥalfon: **489**, a, line 6f. Solomon b. Moses: **490**, a, lines 15f. Abraham b. Isaac: **505**, lines 7f (*ca.* 1065); Goitein, *Letters*, 288, n. 7; Solomon b. Judah: **156**, a, line 14; see also the query addressed to Daniel b. Azariah (in January 1059), where the matter of exporting flax to Sicily figures, four loads that were to have been against *'amālā*, that is, a share in the revenue; part of the flax was seized in Tripoli of Libya (see: **396**); on *'amālā*, see Goitein, *Mediterranean Society* I, 184; 445, n. 4.

[23] See: Ibn Ẓāfir, 35: in al-'Azīz' times, they began to produce fabrics with signs on them (*muthaqqal*) in Egypt, coloured turbans, ornate (*mu'allam*) and gilded *dabīqī* cloth, *siqlātūn* and *'attābī* weaves, and also dealt in all kinds of shrinkings (*qaṣāra*): the editor's note on p. 189, *ibid.* is misleading for Ṭabarī does not mean 'from Tiberias', but rather from Ṭabaristān; on *siqlātūn* see: Gil, *ha-Tustarīm*, 31f, and *ibid.* references; cf. Ibn al-Jawzī, *Akhbār*, 79: a white *ṭabarī* clothing was bought for 400 dirhams, but it turned out to be *qūhī* (from Qūhistān, the 'land of the mountains', west of the Great Desert, see Le Strange, *Lands*, 352f; *dabīqī*, the name comes from Dabīq in Egypt, near Tinnīs, which was a centre for the manufacture of superior quality linen fabrics, see: Tha'ālibī, *Laṭā'if*, 227; Mez, 432; see also Hilāl al-Ṣābī, 327, on a cadi who appeared before the wazīr 'Alī ibn 'Īsā, dressed in a robe of superior quality *dabīqī* that cost him 100 dinars, he said; Tanūkhī, *Nishwār*, I, 29: the same story; it cost him 200 dinars; and it was *dabīqi shustarī*, that is, they made an imitation of the Egyptian *dabīqī* in Tustar, Persia; see also Canard, *AIEO*, 10(1952), 372, n. 31; who states that the dabīqī was linen embroidered with silk and golden thread; *'attābī*, after the 'Attābiyūn quarter in west Baghdad, named for 'Attāb b. Usayd, the great-

[358] Another important branch in the area of imports was the silk trade. It is mentioned repeatedly in letters in my collection. Daniel b. Azariah dealt in silk before he became Gaon of Palestine and it is quite possible that he did not set this activity aside afterwards. In one letter, he refers to thirty small *raṭl*s (*ruṭayla*s) of unravelled silk from the Ghawṭa (*ḥarīr manqūḍ ghawṭī*), meaning the Ghawṭa in the Damascus region. We have already encountered Barhūn b. Mūsā al-Tāhirtī, on the verge of importing fifty pieces of *sūsī* silk. Ismā'īl b. Isaac al-Andalusī, writing in around 1065, mentions *ibrīsam khurāsānī*, that is, silk from Khurāsān brought from the Maghrib to Tyre, which remained there with the cadi, and which he intends to send to Egypt. Isaac b. David b. Sughmār also refers to the silk trade, when writing from Fustat to his partner Makhlūf b. Azariah in Jerusalem (*ca.* 1045). His brother Joseph, who appears to be staying in Jerusalem as well, informed him that he received two bolts of silk and that he had differences with the purchaser; they seem to be speaking of silk from the Maghrib. Nathan ha-Kohen b. Mevorakh worked hard preparing ceremonial attire for the Nāsī, David b. Daniel, and stresses in his letter from Ascalon (*ca.* 1090) that he had requested superior quality silk threads (*ghazl rafī'*) but did not get them and therefore could not order *thawb mulḥam*, that is, fabric whose warp is of silk, and that he must make do with *thawb muqarran*, a fabric which is a mixture of silk and cotton, as we surmise from his remarks. The expensive silks, such as the *khurāsānī*, would arrive mainly from the Orient, in caravans from regions of Persia, via Aleppo (they would travel in caravans in cultivated and well-inhabited regions - not only in desert areas – for greater security, naturally). Joseph b. Sahl al-Baradānī complains in a letter that it is two months since the last arrival of caravans from Aleppo and hence the price of Persian fabric has risen to three or more dinars the parcel. He also mentions Arjīshī weaves (or clothing?) in his letter (Arjīsh was an Armenian city north of Lake Wan, also called Lake Arjīsh).[24]

grandson of Umayya – there they made a linen mixed with silk, see: Qārī, 202; Canard, *Jaudhar*, 45, n. 11; combed linen: **612**, a, lines 20, 22, 23.

24 Daniel b. Azariah: **354**, line 3, cf. Goitein, *Mediterranean Society*, I, 104; as to Damascus, at that time it evidently was a centre for the manufacture of all kinds of silks and elegant clothes and official robes (*khal'a*) intended for the use of the rulers and their appointees; evidence of the existence of state workshops based on the enforced stationing of artisan-weavers in Damascus can be seen in **291**, a letter from a Karaite who was compelled to adhere to the weaving craft (he mentions that the artisans were all Jews); this was undoubtedly the type of workshop called *ṭirāz*, a word meaning firstly embroidery, and it was so called because of the embroidery along the edges of the fabric; cf. Idrīsī (Cerulli), 369, on the manufacture of silk in Damascus. on the *khazz* and the *dībāj*, which imitate the beauty of Byzantine silk and are equal to the fabrics of Tustar and Iṣfahān and the *ṭirāz* of Naysābūr; see Goitein, *JQR*, NS 45(1954/5), 34f, who quotes from the Babylonian Talmud, Ber. 56a: *ṭārāzāyē de-malkā*, 'the royal embroiderers'; see also on *ṭirāz*: Gil, *ha-Tustarīm*, 21f, 32; we have evidence from the tenth century of the existence of such a workshop in Tiberias, 'of the elite' or 'the aristocrats' (*ṭirāz al-khāṣṣa*), from an inscription

The representative of the merchants

[359] In letters dealing with imports and exports, we come across a special type of official, 'the merchants' representative' (*wakīl al-tujjār*). We have few facts on the nature of the office but it is evident that the merchants' representative was appointed by the Muslim authorities and that in every important urban centre, there was an official of this kind. In my collection, we encounter them in Ramla, Tiberias, Tyre and quite frequently, in Fustat. We find in Nissim b. Ḥalfon's letters from Tyre some revealing hints as to the characteristics of this office. The writer is in Tyre on commercial business and he is dealing with the release of goods from the port as well as purchasing others. It seems that the merchants' representative is holding the income from the sales, freeing the money only on instructions from the merchants themselves, so the writer is asking Nehorai b. Nissim and Abū Naṣr Solomon b. Saadia b. Ṣaghīr to send an instruction of release. In a letter from Joseph b. Sahl al-Baradānī, we read of the death of Abū 'Alī Ḥusayn b. Yūnus. He also mentions 'that it was decided to send a representative (*wakīl*) to Palestine'; apparently he is speaking here of the merchants' representative in Ramla, who is evidently Abū 'Alī *al-wakīl*, better known by the nickname Ibn al-Ṣūfī, and who is mentioned in a letter of 'Eli ha-Kohen b. Ezekiel, dealing with some obscure affair related to the appointment of a *wakīl* and perhaps also speaking of the merchants' representative. Sibā', the representative mentioned in a court record from the time of Josiah Gaon, is the merchants' representative in Ramla at the time (*ca.* 1010). His successor in Ramla is Abū'l-Barakāt Khalaf b. Joseph al-Ḥulaybī (or Ṣōvī; Ḥulayb is the diminutive – or perhaps also a term of ridicule – of Ḥalab, Aleppo, which is Ṣōvā; i.e. his father hailed from Aleppo). In a letter from Hillel he-ḥāvēr b. Yeshū'a ha-ḥazān, the merchants' representative in Tiberias, Saadia ha-Levi b. Moses, is mentioned. Sums of money have been deposited with him and a money order (*diyōqnē*) has to be sent from Fustat in order to receive them. We have already met with the merchants' representative in Tyre, Ḥalfon (Khalaf) b. Moses b. Aaron, who was also called Ibn Abī

marking its foundation, which is now in the Benaki Museum, Athens, see: *Répertoire chronologique*, IV, No. 1542 (pp. 173f). Khurāsānī silk: **510**, b, lines 6f; cf. Goitein, *ibid.*, 60. Isaac b. David: **485**, a, lines 22-23, and margin. Nathan ha-Kohen: **585**, lines 11f; they called fine silk *rafī'* and it seems that the threads cost more than a dinar-and-a-half per *raṭl*: see TS 8.60, lines 2–3: the price of ten *raṭls* of *rafī'* silk was seventeen dinars. See editor's note 4 in Tha'ālibī, *Laṭā'if*, 227. *Thawb mulḥam*, see: Dozy, *Supplément*, II, 530, cf. Serjeant, *AI*, 9(1942), 71, n. 19. Joseph b. Sahl: **491**, in the beginning; on the caravans, cf. Goitein, *Mediterranean Society*, I, 276. Arjīsh, see: Le Strange, *Lands*, 183. Nissim b. Ḥalfon also mentions Persian cloth, as well as Arjīshī and others he intends to buy, in his letter from Tyre, **489**, a, lines 19f; b, lines 5f; see also **494**, lines 5, 7, on a shipment of *qaṭārsh* that reached Tyre; these were crude silk threads (in Italian: *catarzo*). Cf. Goitein, *Mediterranean Society*, I, 104; 418, n. 27.

Qīda. The merchants' representative in Fustat, who was in close contact with the Palestinians, was Abū Naṣr Mevorakh (Muḥassin) b. Ḥusayn, known by a nickname relating to his mother's brother, Sham'ān: 'Ibn ukht (son of the sister of) Sham'ān', who was among the leaders of the 'Palestinian' community in Fustat. One can assume that one of this official's duties would have been to collect the taxes due on imports (the *'ushr*), and this was apparently the reason why the rulers were involved in their appointment.[25]

Seafaring

[360] A very large part of Palestine's external trade was carried out via the sea, and the major port for this purpose was evidently Tyre. From the Geniza documents, it appears that the cadi of Tyre, who together with his offspring came to be the independent ruler of the town from 1063 until 1089, was a ship-owner whose ships sailed the Mediterranean. He maintained close business contacts with the Jewish Maghribi merchants who engaged in exporting and importing from Palestine. The cadi's house in Tyre served as a mercantile centre and a meeting-place for shippers. Daniel b. Azariah, the Jerusalem Gaon, was also in touch with him, and in one of his letters to his close friend Abraham ha-Kohen b. Isaac b. Furāt, he writes '... you are well aware ... of what I explained in my letter from Tyre ... that the one who turned the honourable cadi Abū Muḥammad ... against me, and in his presence, said things I have no knowledge of...' Jewish partners would come to the Tyre cadi to validate their business agreements. In another document, the ship of the cadi ibn Abī 'Aqīl is mentioned as having arrived in Tyre after sailing from Alexandria. Israel b. Nathan writes to Nehorai from Jerusalem, informing him that there is talk in the city that ibn Abī 'Aqīl's ships have already sailed from Egypt – this may be hinting at the delay in their departure owing to differences with the Egyptian authorities. In one letter, we find the cadi making a claim against one of the merchants for the sum of five dinars, but it is not

25 Nissim b. Ḥalfon: **489**, b, lines 4–5. Joseph b. Sahl: **491**, lines 10f. 'Eli ha-Kohen: **453**. Sibā': **30**, line 8. Abū'l-Barakāt Khalaf: **329**, III, lines 6–7; **507**, b, line 6; **445**, line 12. Tiberias: **255**, margin. Ḥalfon b. Moses: see the Hebrew Index. Mevorakh b. Ḥusayn: see the Hebrew Index, and him as one of the leaders of the community in **319**, line 5; see in **62**, lines 9–11, details concerning his family; cf. Goitein, *Baron Jubilee Volume*, 518f; in TS NS 264.5v (in the hand of Yefet b. David b. Shekhania), line 5, he is mentioned together with Ephraim b. Shemaria (= b. al-Ghazzī), Nathan al-Andalusī, Salāma *ra's al-kull* (= Solomon *rōsh kallā*), and others: it is possible that this Mevorakh (Muḥassin) was the son of Abū 'Alī Ḥusayn b. Yūnus, and one can therefore assume that he held an office similar to that of his father, but in Fustat. See the exhaustive discussion on the office of representative of the merchants: Goitein, *Mediterranean Society*, I, 186–192; cf. Cahen, *JESHO*, 12(1969), 217, claiming that *wakīl al-tujjār* was not the merchants' representative, or head of their guild, but the representative of the authorities, supervising imports on their behalf.

clear whether this is for the transport of goods or for port taxes. Both Jews and Muslims helped this merchant and stood as his guarantors for fifteen days, until a statement arrived from Abū Naṣr (evidently Mevorakh [Muḥassin] b. Ḥusayn, Ibn ukht Sham'ān, the merchants' representative in Fustat) that the goods should be released, or until he would manage to sell the goods and acquire cash. The merchants would sometimes store their merchandise at the cadi's house, such as the *ibrīsam* (silk) which Ismā'īl b. Isaac speaks of. Nāṣir Khusraw, who visited Tyre some fifteen years before the aforementioned Maghribi merchants' letters were written, notes that the cadi of Tyre, Ibn Abī 'Aqīl, was a rich man of good character. He also points out that he was a Sunni.[26]

[361] We get some idea of realities in the port of Tyre from Nissim b. Ḥalfon, Nehorai b. Nissim's agent. He describes in a letter the troubles caused him by a certain Ibn al-Wāsiṭī, with whom he apparently brought goods to Tyre. They quarrelled about the packing charges as well as bundles of flax which were missing in the shipment, for there seems to have been an epidemic of thefts in the port. In addition, he complains bitterly of the government clerks and customs (*kharāj*) officials. From the

[26] Daniel b. Azariah: **357**, b, lines 10f; the mention of Tyre in this passage indicates that the cadi of Tyre is being referred to and not the Fatimid wazīr, the cadi al-Yāzūrī (see on him below), whose nickname was also Abū Muḥammad. Confirmation of partnership by the Tyre cadi: **276**, a, line 12: 'the judge who resides in the city of Tyre'; the cadi's ship: **506**, b, lines 1f; Ismā'īl b. Faraḥ writes from Alexandria to Nehorai b. Nissim expressing his delight that the cadi 'Ayn al-Dawla's ship arrived in Tyre safely, see TS 13 J 16, f. 19, a, lines 7f. Israel b. Nathan: **471**, a, line 14. Nehorai b. Nissim writes from Fustat to Joseph ha-Kohen b. 'Alī al-Fāsī, who stays in Tyre but who had previously written to him from Ramla; Nehorai confirms the receipt of the letter which contains the same information as above: the cadi's ship is returning to Tyre and the aforementioned Joseph is on his way there, apparently to await it; see: **508**, a, lines 4–5. Mūsā b. Ya'qūb, writing from Damascus on 17 December 1057, asks Abū'l-'Alā Joseph b. Da'ūd b. Sha'yā in Fustat to write to the cadi (that is, to Ibn Abī 'Aqīl) regarding a shipment of their goods in Tyre, see: TS NS J 463. The claim for money: **518**; Eliash, *Sefunot*, 2(1957/8), 10, did not locate the letter or its circumstances correctly and there is no foundation for his assumption that Ḥesed (Abū Naṣr) the Tustari is being referred to. Isma'īl b. Isaac: **510**, b, lines 9f. Also in TS 12.666, a letter to Fustat to Ephraim b. Shemaria, apparently from Qayrawān, the cadi Ibn Abī 'Aqīl is mentioned, see a, lines 17, 19; the writer is a man who has business relations with Ephraim (medicaments, perfumes and spices); in that same letter, he asks Ephraim to send him the tractate Sukka from the Palestinian Talmud. Nāṣir Khusraw, 14 (text), 46–47 (translation). The cadi was a contemporary of al-Khaṭīb al-Baghdādī; they met and the cadi communicated to him (*akhbaranā*, perhaps wrote to him) a ḥadīth praising Abū Bakr and 'Umar, the righteous veterans of Paradise, another proof of his being a Sunni; see al-Khaṭīb, *Ta'rīkh*, XIV, 216. Cf. also on the cadi Ibn Abī 'Aqīl: Ashtor, *CCM*, 18(1975), 125. Benjamin of Tudela (Adler), 20f, who visited Tyre under the Crusaders, still admires its port, the only one of its kind in the world; and it is interesting that according to him, there were Jewish ship-owners there; cf. Prawer, *ha-ṣalvānīm*, 321. In the documents of my corpus there is no mention of Jewish ship-owners, apart from Ezra b. Joseph b. Ibrahīm *al-Nākhūda*, i.e. the captain or owner of the ship. This Ezra was one of the Karaites whose signatures are found on **302**, lines 21f, and we learn from this that his grandfather was a captain or ship-owner.

letter of a contemporary, Jacob b. Ismā'īl, we learn that bribery in the port was an accepted practice; of course the bribe was then deducted from the profits by the agents or the partner. In this letter, we also find an itemised list of his expenses while unloading the flax from the ship: the charge for releasing the goods (*tafrīgh*), porters, arranging in stacks, repair (?) and customs and an advance (apparently to one of the partners to enable him to purchase other goods in the interim).

A letter written by Barhūn b. Mūsā al-Tāhirtī also contains instructions on the loading of a shipment of wool; it should be placed on stones, not directly on the deck of the ship, in order that the air can also flow beneath it, and it should be covered with cloth. Jacob b. Joseph b. Isma'īl al-Iṭrābulusī also mentions that he did not manage to get packing sheets for the shipment of sumach he was asked to send from Ascalon and this is what prevented him from purchasing a large amount.

Evidence of the hazards of shipping by sea we find in a letter of Jacob b. Salmān al-Ḥarīrī mentioned earlier, who was aboard a ship when a storm swept across the Mediterranean. This is not surprising considering that this journey took place on the eve of winter (Jacob writes from Ramla on the 8th of Tevet after this sea-going adventure). Some of the goods on board had to be thrown into the sea, the ship lost its sails and its helm, and the *'ushārī* (Nile boat) on which they were sailing, turned into a sort of *ma'diyya* (rowboat). Everything was soaked and the cargo destroyed. Apart from all this, there was the danger of Byzantine warships, described in Nehorai b. Nissim's account of ships seized by the Byzantines, in his letter from Fustat to Jerusalem. He becalms his correspondent by telling him that he did not have goods aboard one of the ships. Ismā'īl b. Isaac al-Andalusī writing from Tyre, speaks of his misadventures during the voyage and the losses it occasioned, though he takes it all in good part (and with theodicy), mentioning that in comparison with 'most people's mishaps at sea, my own was slight'. He also states that he is about to go on a pilgrimage to Jerusalem. In a letter of Avon b. Ṣedaqa written on the 11 November 1064, we came across a passage which seemingly hints at the destruction of the entire trade. He gave a letter to the head of the yeshiva from Nehorai b. Nissim wherein he writes 'on the business, generally, that is, the state of the ships and the people arriving on them, and the news from Sicily and the burning of ships and the impoverishment of our people . . .'[27]

[362] Muqaddasī connects the subject of seafaring with the story of

27 Nissim b. Ḥalfon: **489**, a, lines 3–18. Jacob b. Ismā'īl, **494**, a, line 13; **495**, a, lines 10f. Barhūn b. Mūsā: **458**, a, lines 15f. Jacob b. Joseph, **487**, a, lines 21f. Jacob b. Salmān: **507**, a, lines 3f; *'ushārī*, in line 5 and see the note there. Nehorai: **509**, line 9. Ismā'īl b. Isaac: **510**, a, lines 12f; cf. Goitein, *Mediterranean Society*, I, 332. Avon: **500**, a, lines 20f.

the building of the port of Acre. According to him the port was not fortified at all until Ibn Ṭūlūn's times (end of the ninth century). This is actually evidence that during the Abbasid period, the port was completely neglected and ships would not come there because of the lack of security. Only when Egypt became a semi-independent body, as it were, and extended its authority over Palestine, did the development of shipping begin to take shape. In Muqaddasī's words, the difference between the port of Tyre and that of Acre was marked. When Ibn Ṭūlūn decided to recreate the latter, there were considerable problems in trying to find craftsmen who knew how to build a port, which is work carried out in the water, until the expertise of Abū Bakr al-Bannā' ('the builder') became known. Abū Bakr is none other than Maqaddasī's grandfather. He was approached through the good offices of the governor of Jerusalem (where this expert lived) appointed by Ibn Ṭūlūn. He set up a quay of sycamore beams across the entire width of the fortress on land. The beams were then fastened to each other above the water's surface and an opening was left on the western side. On the beams, a strong structure made of courses of plastered stones was set up, connected by columns at every five layers. The wooden platform gradually sunk to the sea floor as the weight of the structure increased. This structure was then attached to the walls and to the ancient quay that was still standing. The opening was closed by a bridge, and during the night, ships would enter the port and the opening would be closed by a chain, as in Tyre. From then onwards, the enemy (the Byzantines) could not raid the ships any longer.[28]

Commercial methods

[363] Merchants' letters in my collection contain information on the ways in which trade was conducted in Palestine, the financing of business and the use of money. Much trading was done in partnership, and in almost every document we find people engaged in business jointly, either with partners or through agents. Sometimes it is difficult to discern whether it is a partner or an agent from Palestine who is writing to Nehorai b. Nissim or another of the Fustat merchants, giving an account of his actions – on business, goods, transport and prices, etc. – and awaiting information of the same order from Fustat. The trend was to constantly invest money in goods, to make money work, and not to set aside cash reserves. The only explanation for this is the simple desire for

[28] Muqaddasī, *Āqālīm*, 162f; see a French translation of the passage: Nāṣir Khusraw, 49f, and an English one: Le Strange, *Palestine*, 328f; Yāqūt, *Buldān*, III, 707f, copied this story and noted that in his time (the thirteenth century) the inscription was still there, with Abū Bakr al-Bannā''s name. See the description of the port of Acre in Nāṣir Khusraw (March 1046), 15 (text), 49f (translation).

profit – not the fear of a decrease in the value of the money, a process which was almost unknown throughout the entire period under discussion. Jacob b. Ismāʿīl of Tyre writes to Nehorai b. Nissim in this manner: 'lest a single dirham (of the deposit) of the partnership remain with you, buy whatever God inspires you to buy, and send it by the first ship . . .' We have also seen above that the priestly family who headed the Palestine yeshiva wanted to activate the yeshiva's money by investing in carnelians (*ʿaqīq*). Daniel b. Azariah also puts his money to work: a certain Abū'l-ʿAlā al-Mubārak b. Isaac will carry out a transaction on his behalf for the sum of 200 dinars. The addressee (whose name has not been preserved) is requested to pay the aforementioned Abū'l-ʿAlā 50 dinars against a *suftaja*, evidently an advance, or perhaps Daniel b. Azariah's share in the deal. Elijah ha-Kohen b. Solomon Gaon shows an interest in his letter to Ephraim b. Shemaria, in the exact rate of the *nuqra* (a dirham with a large silver content) in Fustat. Later on, when he was already 'Fourth at the yeshiva', he also engages in trade and has a partner in Fustat, who wronged him in some manner. Elijah demands that he be excommunicated in Fustat and that Jerusalem should be informed of this, so that they should have a pretext to put a ban on him there as well, for the behaviour of this partner (we do not know his name) is contrary to the regulations of the Fustat community (which are not known to us).[29]

[364] Keeping money, when there was little opportunity of an immediate business investment, presented a serious problem, both from the security angle and also out of fear of the authorities, who would confiscate hoards of gold (dinars) whenever possible. We have ample evidence of this in the sources. The greatest security was achieved by depositing money with Jews close to the throne. In the period which has provided most of our documentation, these were the Tustari brothers. Maqrīzī explicitly writes that the Tustaris had a good reputation for properly returning deposits secretly left with them by the merchants. I have already mentioned the deposit held for a man of Tiberias, Joseph b. Asad, by Ḥesed al-Tustarī. Another aspect of these deposits can be seen in the handwritten lists of Barhūn b. Mūsā al-Tāhirtī on the reverse sides of two letters sent from Jerusalem to Fustat, to Isaac b. Jacob he-ḥāvēr (Jacob he-ḥāvēr b. Joseph lived in Aleppo), in which enormous sums deposited with various people, among them Abū Saʿd (apparently Abraham al-Tustarī) and more of Barhūn's property is mentioned, as well as 500 dinars held by Ibn Ḥayyim (evidently Sahlawayh, a relative of the Tustaris) since the days of al-Ḥākim (some thirty years earlier). These lists were

[29] Jacob b. Ismāʿīl: **495**, b, lines 4f; cf. Goitein, *Mediterranean Society*, I, 200. Daniel b. Azariah: **346**. Elijah ha-Kohen b. Solomon: **413**, lines 15f; *nuqra*: a dirham of $^2/_3$ silver and $^1/_3$ copper; at that time, 22 *nuqra* dirhams were worth a dinar, see **176**, margin; cf. Gil,

apparently drawn up after the killing of the Tustari brothers. The tendency to be secretive about commercial affairs and particularly to conceal the movement of cash from the eyes of the authorities, can also be seen in the request of Mūsā b. Ya'qūb, writing from Tyre to his partner Joseph b. David in Fustat, that the latter write his letters in Hebrew script, rather than in Arabic.

In the Tyre of that time, one of those engaged in the sphere of finance and banking was Abū Manṣūr David (Da'ūd) b. Solomon (Sulaymān), known as Ibn Shu'ayb, and we find that he was also active in Damascus. Israel b. Nathan asks Nehorai b. Nissim to obtain a letter to this Abū Manṣūr, so that when he arrives in Tyre, he can collect two dinars from him with which to buy paper and to cover other expenses. However the letter was not sent, as we learn from a subsequent letter from Israel, who writes that as a result he was in dire straits in Tyre, until he was helped out by Abū Sa'īd (we do not in fact know to whom he was referring as there were a number of merchants who bore this nickname). Joseph b. Sahl al-Baradānī complains in his letter to Nehorai that the *suftaja* for Israel b. Nathan did not reach this Abū Manṣūr b. Shu'ayb, who was prepared to lend him two or three dinars 'on account' but afterwards changed his mind because he was doubtful as to the outcome. Jacob b. Samuel al-Andalusī, writing from Jerusalem to Joseph b. Naḥum al-Baradānī in Fustat, also hints at the fact that it was difficult to get money from the aforementioned Abū Manṣūr b. Shu'ayb, who seemed to have had his own standards. However, he proposed to Mūsā b. Ya'qūb, who dealt in paper in Tyre and Damascus, 25 dinars and 2 qīrāṭs on his own initiative. This Mūsā b. Ya'qūb payed in two *suftaja*s in Tyre, evidently, the rather large sum of 250 dinars on account, for the paper he was buying there. The money orders are drawn on someone in Fustat, perhaps his partner, Joseph b. Da'ūd b. Sha'yā.

Payment through money orders was very common amongst the merchants whose letters are included in my collection, that is, in the mid-eleventh century AD. Money for the Palestine yeshiva and for the poor of Jerusalem, as well as the sick people of Tiberias, was also generally sent in money orders, with the help of the financiers. Solomon b. Judah mentions money orders (he always calls them *diyōqnē*) in twelve of his letters, and in one he speaks of five or six orders from various individuals he is dealing with simultaneously. An important financier in Fustat, Abū Naṣr Solomon b. Saadia b. Ṣaghīr, was also engaged in transferring money from Fustat, such as passing on sums from the Jerusalemites in Fustat to Jerusalem through Ephraim b. Shemaria. However, alongside the relatively

Documents, 407, n. 10 and further references there. The matter of the partner: Barhūn b. Mūsā al-Tāhirtī's letter, **458**, b, lines 2–4.

common use of money orders, a great deal of cash was also in circulation as well as large amounts in precious metals, in coinage of gold and silver, and pouches (*ṣurra*) of dinars and dirhams were transferred, as we learn from Joseph b. Yeshūʿā al-Ṭarābulusī's letter to Nehorai about a deposit of coins which the latter had, reaching the holder (from Egypt) in such *ṣurras*, containing *waraq* (cheap dirhams; 40 to the dinar), and also dinars.[30]

[365] We also encounter in our documents instances of one time partnerships based on financial investment, in which the receiver of the money undertakes to buy certain merchandise and share the profits (*manfaʿa*) with the investor. At times, such an arrangement would be made without anything put in writing, but merely on the basis of mutual trust. Solomon b. Ṣemaḥ of Ramla (Abū Bishr Solomon – Sulaymān b. Ṣemaḥ al-ʿAṭṭār – a perfume dealer) retained 24 dinars belonging to his nephew 'who gave them to him to buy with' (goods), on condition that they share the profits. Abraham b. Meir al-Andalusī took them from him (apparently to trade with them on the same basis) 'and neither the funds nor the profit was returned to him'. This form of one-time partnership was also commonly termed *bi-qismi Allāhi wa-rizqihi*, 'for whatever price God apportions as livelihood'; such as in the case of the deal contracted by Moses b. Judah ha-ḥazān 'the westerner' (of Sicily) who received various goods purchased with the money provided by Ḥasan ha-Kohen b. Salmān al-Dallāl (= the broker) on condition that Ḥasan would receive the usual *ra's māl*, that is the capital invested plus two-thirds of the profits, while one third would go to Moses. This system evidently differs from the *ʿamāla*, which is based on the seller receiving a fixed percentage of the profits. The Maghribi Salāma ha-Kohen b. Joseph describes how he formed such a partnership with the Maghribi Abū Saʿīd Khalfa, the son-in-law of Yaḥyā al-ʿAmmānī (from ʿAmmān); he met him on the road from Jerusalem to Ramla, on his way to Ascalon, and gave him five dinars to do with 'as God helps' until the end of the year, meaning the Muslim year, which then occurred in April. The

30 Maqrīzī, *Khiṭaṭ*, II, 279; cf. Gil, *ha-Tustarīm*, 34–37, and see there further references, especially additional sources from the Geniza relating to money deposited with the Tustaris; *ibid.*, also more details on Barhūn b. Mūsā al-Tāhirtī's lists; see these lists in **463**, b, and **464**, b. Abraham al-Tustarī was killed on 25 October 1047 and his brother, in the summer of 1049 or 1050 (see Gil, *ibid.*, 41f). Mūsā b. Jacob: **517**, b, line 12, Goitein, *Letters*, 94, n. 13, assumed that the request to write in Hebrew script was intended to prevent lack of clarity stemming from the very cursive nature of the Arabic script and the absence of the diacritical signs. Israel b. Nathan: **474**, a, lines 8–10; **476**, a, Joseph b. Sahl: **492**, a, lines 9–12. Jacob b, Samuel: **493**, b. Mūsā b. Yaʿqūb: **515**, lines 8–9; in TS NS J 463, a letter from Damascus from this Mūsā, he again writes about the money he received from the aforementioned Abū Manṣūr and which has to be returned in Fustat to a certain Abū'l-Faḍl. 250 dinars: **514**, a, lines 4f. Solomon b. Judah: see particularly **76**. Ephraim b. Shemaria: **326**. See on the family of b. Ṣaghīr (= 'the son of the little one'): Goitein, *Mediterranean Society*, III, 11; 428, n. 60; see also in the Hebrew Index: *diyōqnē*, *suftaja*; the term *diyōqnē* is only to be found in Solomon b. Judah's letters and those of his contempor-

agreement was made officially, at 'the head', that is, head of the yeshiva. Khalfa actually went to Ascalon, bought merchandise there and took it to Jerusalem – from there he went on to Ramla, informing Salāma that the profit for the two months which had passed was one dinar but that he did not have the money. He promised to pay him when he returned to Ramla on the day after Passover but still had not paid, and Salāma writing, in May 1054, asks Shemaiah he-ḥāvēr b. Yeshū'ā, who lives in Jerusalem, to collect the debt. Another problematic partnership is also reflected in Abū'l-Riḍā ha-Kohen's letter to his partner (whom he calls 'brother'). Here the matter is the transport of goods from Jerusalem to Tiberias and the intention is that the partner would sell the goods on the way from Bet Shean or Nābulus, but he did not manage to do so, and Abū'l-Riḍā was forced to sell it in Tiberias at a loss, leaving him stranded and impoverished.[31]

[366] In those times, people worked hard at collecting debts due to them. A Jerusalemite whose identity is uncertain deals with collecting sums due to Isaac b. Jacob he-ḥāvēr in Fustat. With some difficulty, he managed to extract five dinars from a certain Thābit, but only two of these were good (i.e., of full weight). This same Isaac (who for some reason had suffered severe losses) is owed other moneys in Jerusalem, and one of his debtors is a man who has left Jerusalem for Zoar. The writer tries to get a money order (*suftaja*) on the five dinars from a certain al-Arrajānī, who had collected them for Isaac, but in vain. It appears that Nehorai b. Nissim

aries who were writing in Hebrew; in later letters, generally written in Arabic, they always use *suftaja*; Joseph b. Yeshū'ā: **496**, a, lines 13f.

31 The matter of Solomon b. Ṣemaḥ: **159**, lines 11f; this is a letter from Solomon b. Judah to Abraham ha-Kohen b. Haggai in Fustat; a colophon on the title page of *Bereshit rabbā* shows that it belonged to Solomon b. R. Ṣemaḥ, of blessed memory, and was bought by Abraham b. Nathan Av, of blessed memory, and afterwards bought by Berakhot ha-Kohen b. Aaron, 'may he have a good end, known as b. al-Ẓāhirī'; see ULC Or 1080, Box 15, f. 33. Solomon b. Ṣemaḥ was one of the retainers of Josiah Gaon and thereafter of Solomon b. Judah; he was an occasional scribe and some documents in my corpus are in his handwriting. BM Or 5561 , f. 1 is a fragment of a court document pertaining to the legacy of that Abraham b. Meir; Abraham's son, Samuel, is mentioned there. Nathan b. Samuel 'the Spaniard' appears in court, showing a deed of attorney written in Granada, in which he is appointed trustee of the legacy of the aforementioned Joshua b. Nathan. From the part of the document which has been preserved, it may be understood that Abraham b. Meir was involved in commerce on a large scale and wished to ensure that after his death, his property would be secure from being 'seized by the ruler who governs Egypt', who, it implied, was in the habit of taking over the properties of 'deceased aliens'. The document also contained details on the deceased's business matters in Palestine. Among others, with someone 'living in Zoar'. Moses b. Judah: **394**, **395**, where the expression *bi'l-qism wa'l-rizq* can be found, that is, as God metes out, that is, the income and provides profit or livelihood. See the same expression also in **508**, b, line 7; **516**, margin. Cf. on *'amāla* and on *qism wa-rizq*, Goitein, *Mediterranean Society*, I, 183ff; and see *'amāla* in **396**, referring to the above-mentioned Moses b. Judah. Salāma ha-Kohen: **525**, a, lines 17f; on the dates, see the note to line 24. Abū'l-Riḍā: **527**.

also owes him money. In about 1065 Ismā'īl b. Issac al-Andalusī writes from Tyre to Nehorai b. Nissim in Fustat and encloses in his letter, among other business matters, a power-of-attorney formulated as a deed of trusteeship, to collect the sum of 350 *zūzīm* (undoubtedly dirhams), due to him from Abū'l-Faḍl Sahl b. Salāma for a shipment of silk. If the matter is to come to court, he asks Nehorai to act as witness to the fact that it is indeed in his handwriting and that the power-of-attorney is valid. He hopes that there will be no need for this however, and that matters will be settled without having to resort to law.[32]

Measures and coins

[367] Palestine had its own traditions as far as weights and measures were concerned and Muqaddasī found it fitting to devote an entire section to this subject. According to him, the people of Ramla used the *qafīz*, which was the equivalent of four *wayba*s; the *wayba* equalled two *makkūk*s; the *makkūk* was the equivalent of three *kaylaja*s and the *kaylaja* equalled one and one-half *ṣā'*. We know that the *ṣā'* contained *ca.* 4.2 litres, from which we deduce that the *kaylaja* was *ca.* 6.3 litres; the *makkūk* some 19 litres; the *wayba* some 38 litres and the *qafīz* some 152 litres. In the Geniza documents in my collection, we come across the *wayba* and the *kaylaja* but not the *ṣā'* or the *makkūk*. Muqaddasī states that the Jerusalemites used the *mudī*, which was two-thirds of a *qafīz*, that is, some hundred litres, and the *qabb*, which is a quarter of a *mudī* (*ca.* 25 litres; neither of these are to be found in the Geniza documents). As to weights, apart from the *raṭl* and the *wiqiyya* (equivalent to an ounce), which are well known, he mentions that the dirham, the usual weight of the coin so named, was 60 grains of barley (*ḥabba*; we know that the common weight of the dirham was approximately 3.1 grams). A sixth of a dirham was called *dāniq* (a Persian word) and was worth ten *ḥabba*s. The dinar weighed some 4.2 grams and was divided into 24 *qīrāṭ*s; and *qīrāṭ* was generally considered the equivalent of 3.5 *ḥabba*s (the *qīrāṭ*, Greek *keration*, is the carob seed).

The Jews of Palestine during this period still used the term *ṭrimis* in their marriage deeds, which meant a third of a dinar, the *trimision* or *tremissis* which Theodosius I introduced in 383. We have already learned something of the coinage of the Umayyads and the renewed minting of coins in Palestine in their times. During the rule of the Abbasids, there seems to have been a complete halt to the local minting of money and this was started again only in the days of the Ṭūlūnids, when the mint in Ramla

32 Debts in Jerusalem: **463** (and see there in a, lines 22, the Zoar matter), **464**. Nehorai himself is very busy collecting debts owed to Joseph ha-Kohen b. 'Alī al-Fāsī, who is travelling in Palestine, see **508**, b, line 4. Ismā'īl b. Isaac: **510**, b, lines 16–21; cf. on the matter of payments and debts: Goitein, *Mediterranean Society*, I, 197–200.

was reactivated and coins began to appear with the inscription *bi-filasṭīn*. The first of these were produced in the days of Khumārawayh and his son, Hārūn, from 890 until 904, and these were gold dinars with the unusual weight of 3.2 grams. These practices continued during the period when the Abbasids reconquered Egypt and Palestine, as we can see from the coins with the same inscription from the years AH 296 (AD 908/9), AH 298 (AD 910/1), AH 310 (AD 922/3), as well as from a gold coin of al-Rāḍī from the year AH 329 (AD 940). The Ikhshīdids continued to mint coins in Ramla, as previously, but unlike the inferior quality of the Palestinian coins produced under the Ṭūlūnids, Muḥammad ibn Ṭughj, the Ikhshīd, ordered the minting of dinars of a finer quality. The Palestinian dinars were formerly known as *al-muṭallasa*, 'the worn-off', and the Egyptian officials would refuse to use them because they contained so much base metal. The Ikhshīdī dinar bore the same imprint as the Aḥmadī (i.e. the Ṭūlūnī, after Aḥmad ibn Ṭūlūn), but its quality was improved from AH 331 (AD 942/3). It is interesting to note that in the same year, the Ḥamdānids (Nāṣir al-Dawla and Sayf al-Dawla) still managed during their wavering reign to produce silver coins in Palestine. The mint in Ramla continued working during Fatimid times as well, as is evidenced by the quarter-dinar coins (*rubāʿī*) from the days of al-Muʿizz, from AH 364 (AD 974/5) and dinars from the days of al-Azīz, from the years AH 369, 373, 376, 383, that is AD 979/80, 983/4, 986/7 and 993, and during the rule of al-Ẓāhir, in AH 423 (AD 1032), al-Mustanṣir, in AH 435 (AD 1043), AH 436 (AD 1044/5), AH 442 (AD 1050/1). The mint in Tiberias was also active, as we see from coins dating from the year AH 395 (AD 1004/5), of al-Ḥākim, Abū ʿAlī ʿAbdallah al-Manṣūr; and the days of al-Mustanṣir: AH 436 (AD 1044/5). During the latter's day, the mint in Acre was also working and coins from the years AH 462 (AD 1069/70), 463 (1070/1), 476 (1083/4), 478 (1085/6), 483 (1090), 484 (1091/2), 490 (1097, al-Mustaʿlī) are witness to the fact. After the conquest of most of Palestine by the Crusaders, the mint in Ascalon was activated and there, coins called after al-Āmir were produced. Such coins from the years AH 503 (AD 1109/10) and AH 507 (AD 1113/4) have been preserved. The mint in Eilat was also at work as we see from coins dated AH 514 (AD 1120/1). The mint in Tyre was active in al-Mustanṣir's times: AH 484 (AD 1091/2) and continued to be so in al-Āmir's day as well (that is, after 1101) as can be seen from the coin bearing his name. Another active mint was that of Eilat in al-Āmir's day, as is evidenced by the coin *bi-ayla*, from AH 524 (AD 1120/1).[33]

[368] In the Geniza letters we have already encountered Nizārī dinars,

[33] Muqaddasī, *Āqālīm*, 181f; see the Hebrew Index: *wayba, kaylaja, qafīz*. Muqaddasī gives different (and curious) capacity measures for ʿAmmān, Tyre and Damascus. See Hinz, 1–4; the qīrāṭ and the ḥabba are mentioned in the Geniza documents, see the Hebrew

and those of Tyre are also mentioned. In a query addressed to the Palestine Gaon from Fustat, 100 *shābūrī* dinars are mentioned; these are *sābūrī* in the Arab sources, which are dinars minted in Naysābūr (Nīshāpūr in Persian) and their use is mentioned in these sources in the thirties of the eleventh century. In the Geniza documents in my collection, especially in Karaite documents, the dinars are called *darkemōnīm* (which only figures once in Rabbanite documents, in a letter of Josiah Gaon). *Zāhūv* was the name commonly used in Hebrew.[34]

[369] A very popular coin was that of the quarter-dinar, the *rubā'ī* (pl. *rubā'īyāt* and also *rubā'iyya*, which is shortened from *danānīr rubā'iyya*). For instance, ancient Sicilian quarter-dinars are mentioned in letters of Israel b. Nathan to Nehorai. These coins make Nehorai and Avon b. Ṣedaqa uneasy, for Nehorai asked Avon to get rid of them at any price, and in

Index. Tobiah b. Moses, the Karaite, says: I was not given even a *se'ōrā* (a grain of barley; he means *ḥabba*): **295**, line 26. As to the qīrāṭ, see Qirqisānī, 667: in Ramla, in all of Filasṭīn and in Egypt and Baṣra and the other places, the *mithqāl* (= dinar) is 24 qīrāṭs (in the discussion on Ex., xxx:13: 'a shekel is twenty gerahs'). Ṭrimis is 1/3 of the aureus; see Jastrow, s.v. *ṭrīmīsyā*; see Kyrillos Skythopolitanus, 117, 187; in Festugière, III(2), 42 and n. 58; cf. *PW*, VII, 105 (s.v. Triens); related to this is the matter of the *tūrmūs*, mentioned in the *Sefer ha-ma'asīm*, Bodl Cat. 2680, f. 30a (Lewin, *Tarbiz*, 1[1,1929/30], 89, 95): '*asīmōn* is a kind of uninscribed *tūrmūs*'; Lewin assumed that it meant *lupinus*, the well-known plant of the leguminosae; see J. N. Epstein, *ibid.*, note 2, who derives it from *thermos*, two qīrāṭs; but I think that it is the *trimission*; see also Sukenik, *JPOS*, 15(1935), 138, inscription II: 'Tanḥūm ha-Levi bar Ḥalīfa dehav ḥad trīmīsīn' (donated one trimission in gold); cf. *ibid.*, 140, and also p. 143, inscription III, line 4; 146, inscription IV, line 2. On the coins of the Ṭūlūnids, see: Shamma, *Abḥāth*, 24:43, 1971, and see also *ibid.* the bibliography; see also a Ṭūlūnid coin from the year 285 (898): Lane-Poole, *Cat.*, II, 67 (No. 228). On Abbasid coinage, *ibid.*, 142f. (Nos. 412–415); see also p. 153, No. 456 (al-Rāḍī coin); IX, 76, No. 413g, 213h, from the years 305, 306, (917/8, 918/9); see on the improvement in minting under the Ikhshīd: *al-'uyūn wa'l-ḥadā'iq*, IV, 393 (= MS Berlin, fol. 208b); cf. Bacharach, *Speculum*, 50(1975), 605. See a Ḥamdānid coin in Lane-Poole, *ibid.*, III, 5 (No. 6). Ikhshīdid coins: *ibid.*, II, 68–71 (Nos. 231–235; 237, 239); IX, 174 (Nos. 230t, 232k). Fatimid coinage: *ibid.*, IV, 12 (No. 42); 15 (Nos. 54, 60, 65); 30 (No. 119); 34 (No. 133); 218 (No. 135a); 37 (no. 146); Tiberias: *ibid.*, 35 (No. 135); Acre: *ibid.*, 43 (No. 173); Ascalon; *ibid.*, 51 (No. 51). See also Lavoix, *Catalogue*, 70 (al-Ḥākim), 129 (Tiberias, al-Mustanṣir), 130 (*idem*; 1/4 gold dinar, weighing 0.98 grams), 133 (Acre), 157 (Ascalon, al-Āmir), 161f (Ayla, misprinted); Bucknill, *Monnaies*, 76 (dinar, al-Āmir, Tyre); Karabacek, *ZDMG*, 21(1867), 622ff (coins of Tyre and Acre); Blau und Stickel, *ZDMG*, 11(1857), 451 (on the dirhams from Tiberias in the name of al-Muttaqī and his son). See *ibid.*, 452, a coin from al-'Aziz' day, the year 373, i.e. 983/4, from Ramla. See more matters relating to coins in connection with the events in the tenth and eleventh centuries, in note 101, chapter 5, and notes 6, 11 and 20, chapter 6; in the latter, proof that the mint was still active in Tiberias in 985/6.

34 Tyre dinars: **345**, line 7; cf. TS 12.117, a, line 12: . . . *dinar ṣūriyya*. Shābūrī dinars: **337**, a, lines 6, 11: see Ibn al-Jawzī, *Muntaẓam*, VIII, 60, 65: cf. Busse, *Chalif und Grossk.*, 354; *darkemōnīm*, see the Karaite documents: **303**(1), b, line 9; c, lines 2, 10; **304**, I, lines 12, 13, 19; II, line 9; **305**, lines 10–27; **307**, lines 21–23; in Tobiah b. Moses' letter: **295**, line 25; Josiah Gaon: **31**, lines 11–13; according to Jonah ibn Janaḥ, *S. ha-shorashim*, 166 and Maimonides in his Mishna Commentary, to Shek., ii:i, the dinars are called *darkōnīm* or *darkōnōt*, see in the Mishna, *ibid.*; cf. Salmon b. Yeruḥim, *Commentary on Lamentations*, 14, and the editor's note, *ibid.* Zāhūv, see the Hebrew Index.

Jerusalem, of all places. Avon b. Ṣedaqa speaks of Byzantine quarter-dinars in a letter written on 31 March 1059, and one may conclude that these *rubāʿiyya* which they wished to rid themselves of, were the Sicilian dinars dating from the Byzantine period (that is, they were minted before the island was completely overtaken by the Muslims in 965, or perhaps during the Byzantine occupation from 1038 to 1042). The coins were very old and in Egypt they were painted red, turned green, and were finally sold in Jerusalem at half their value.[35]

The Maghribis

[370] In the mid-eleventh century, according to the Geniza documents which I have surveyed, the Maghribis were a central factor in the import and export trade in Palestine. These Maghribis were the descendants of Babylonian Jews who emigrated to the Maghrib mainly during the first half of the tenth century, when the internal situation in Baghdad and other central areas of the Abbasid caliphate was on the decline while in the Maghrib the Fatimid caliphate was founded. The Fatimid rulers were wise enough to make use of the talents and know-how of those Jewish merchants, and they evidently encouraged them by their tolerance and also by the relatively organised regime and efficient internal order they had succeeded in establishing within their domain. It was due to these Jewish merchants, who had an international trading tradition that went back centuries, and the financial wherewithal and the disposition to work together, that Ifrīqiyā, the region of present-day Tunisia, and especially Qayrawān, its capital, became a major commercial centre in the Mediterranean area. Towards the end of the century, with the conquest of Egypt

[35] See the Hebrew Index: *rubāʿī*. Sicilian dinars: **463**, a, lines 13f; **467**, a, lines 22–24; **469**, a, line 11; **473**, b, lines 1f. from which one can understand that Israel is writing about his cousin Nehorai who is worried about the quarter-dinars. The letters of Avon: **498**, a, line 18: he informs Salāma b. Joseph in Sicily that the *rūmī* quarter dinars have arrived; b, lines 1–2: he asks Nehorai to send them on to him in Jerusalem; **499**, a, line 4: the dinars were brought to Jerusalem by Isaac al-Andalausī; *ibid.*, lines 16f: he sorely complains of the difficulty of selling them, and similarly in **500**, a, line 28; **501**, a, lines 31–37: he sold 39 quarter-dinars weighing altogether eight dinars (some 34 grams, much less than the proper weight, some 41 grams) for 20 dirhams per dinar, while a good dinar was priced at 36½ dirhams (undoubtedly speaking of *waraq* dirhams); **502**, line 5, includes the news of the completion of the sale of these quarter-dinars; it seems that these coins were minted with the sign of a star, and this is perhaps what Avon is hinting at when he writes in anger about the problem of selling them: 'praise to Him who made their star fall down!' (that is, to God, who liquidated the Byzantine rule in Sicily?). Perhaps the *darkemōnīm kokhbāyē* (with stars) which Josiah Gaon mentions in his letter **31**, line 12 were of that type of coins as well, minted during the rule of Constantine XI (Monomachus; 1042–1055), called in the sources *stellati*, because they were minted with a star. See: Morrisson, *Catalogue*, 633. Another possible explanation: Under al-Ḥākim's rule coins were minted whose inscriptions were arranged in a circle (*mudawwara*), or in the form of a star. See Balog, in *Gli Arabi in Italia*, 615, and see the plates Nos. 25, 51, 58 after p. 621 *ibid.*

and the gradual Fatimid domination of Palestine and Syria, the centre moved eastward to Egypt, and the Jewish merchants followed in the wake of this move.[36]

[371] During the period from which most of the Geniza documents relating to Palestine derive, the circle of Maghribi merchants gathered round the figure of Nehorai b. Nissim. We find him living in Fustat and from there, directing the activities of his partners and agents in Palestine. One would be inclined to think that his personality was well known because it so happened that his well-stocked archives were preserved in the Geniza, putting others in the shade. However, he is also frequently mentioned in letters not directly concerned with him, and there is no doubt that he occupied a central position among the Maghribi merchants, both because of his status in trade and because of his activities and social standing in the Babylonian congregation in Fustat. The Palestinian base of the Maghribis of Nehorai's circle was in Ramla, and naturally we also find them in Jerusalem, either for a lengthy stay (as in the case of Israel b. Nathan and Avon b. Ṣedaqa, or some of the Tāhirtī family) or as pilgrims, or for a short visit. Their shipments by sea generally arrived via Tyre, and sometimes Ascalon, and from these ports, goods were shipped abroad. Part of their trade consisted of the transfer of goods: mainly silk, perfumes and various scents and spices, such as pepper.[37]

[372] The pronunciation Nehorai is extant in the Talmudic texts and confirmed by the address of a letter sent to him by Shelah b. Mevassēr, *Ḥaḍra* (the honourable) *Rabbēnū* Nehōrai, etc., but it may be that the usual spelling, Nhr'y, goes to prove that it was pronounced 'Nahray', and this is how it is spelled in the works of my late teacher and guide, Prof. Goitein.

36 For the roots of the activities of the Jewish merchants, known for their understanding of international finance and trade, one should probably look back to a very ancient period, during Persian times. Their base was Māḥōzē, capital of the Persian kingdom and the nearby communities in the region of the Tigris, called Gūkhā in the Talmudic period and that of the early Geonim, and Rādhān among the Aramaic-speaking Christians and afterwards also by the Arabs, who still used the name Jūkhā as well. It is these Jewish merchants, their trading customs and the merchandise they carried, that were described in an ancient source (apparently Syriac) from which Ibn Khurdādhbih, the ninth century Arabic writer, copied; and they are known in research literature by their by-name, the Rādhānites. See on this matter, Gil, *JESHO*, 117:299, 1974, and also: *ha-Tustarīm*, 13ff; see the discussion on the historical background to the economic development in the Fatimid period, in Goitein, *Mediterranean Society*, I, 29–35.

37 Letters to Nehorai: **458–462**; **465–472**; **474–483**; **486**; **487**; **489–492**; **495**; **496**; **498–503**; **505–507**; **510**; **512**; **513**; **519**; **555**; **557**; **560**; and another two letters written by him: **508**, **509**. Altogether 49 letters from his archives. For additional mentions of him, see the Hebrew Index. See details on Nehorai in Goitein, *Mediterranean Society*, I, 153ff; II, 325; *idem, Letters*, 145f; see M. Michaeli's Dissertation on Nehorai b. Nissim, Hebrew Univ., 1968; Udovitch, in: *Individualism*, etc., 65; a characteristic portrayal of how Nehorai conducted his various enterprises can be seen in **508**, his letter from Fustat to his chief partner in Palestine, Joseph ha-Kohen b. 'Alī al-Fāsī, then in Tyre.

We know that Nehorai settled in Fustat in 1045 or somewhat earlier. The base of his trade, and evidently his living quarters as well, were with Abraham b. Isaac al-Tāhirtī and the rest of this family, in *dār al-ṣarf* (house of the money-changers) in Fustat, near *jisr al-ma'ārij* (bridge of the steps). The Tāhirtī family were relatives of Nehorai's mother. The status of *al-kabīra* (the old lady), who is occasionally mentioned in Nehorai's letters, is rather obscure. Her name was Sitt Muruwwa, and her *kunya* Umm Abī 'Imrān.

Nehorai's wife (his second) came from the 'ha-Kohen' family. Israel b. Nathan congratulates him on his marriage in 1052 and points out that there is not a better family in all of Fustat. His son, Nissim, was born much later and it seems that his first children were all girls. In 1064, Avon b. Ṣedaqa writes hoping he will shortly be blessed by a son – which may partly account for Nehorai's own pilgrimage to Jerusalem and the prolonged stay there of his wife and *al-kabīra*. Despite the fact that the purpose of praying for the birth of a son is not mentioned in the letters, it seems very likely that this is what occurred.[38]

[373] Below we shall see that Nehorai and his circle of relatives and associates were involved in matters concerning the Palestinian yeshiva and the struggle between it and David b. Daniel, who wanted to be exilarch in Egypt. From one of Israel b. Nathan's letters, it appears that he addressed certain queries to the Jerusalem yeshiva. The connection between this

38 Shelah he-ḥāvēr, the judge, b. Mevasser: ENA 2805, f. 2, b; see on him: Goitein, *Mediterranean Society*, III, 247, 481, n. 171. He was a judge in Alexandria; see **548**, line 14. *Dār al-ṣarf:* **507**, in the address and in other letters, see the Hebrew Index. Goitein, *Mediterranean Society*, III, 37, assumed that the Tāhirtīs were members of Nehorai's wife's family (his brothers-in-law); see biographical and family details in Michaeli's Dissertation, I, 13f. *Jisr al-ma'ārij*, see the Hebrew Index. Nehorai's marriages: **467**, a, line 7; the letter is from January 1052, but it is possible that this marriage was contracted a few years earlier, when Israel was still living in Byzantium; Avon: **499**, a, line 4. His pilgrimage, see Salāma b. Nissim b. Isaac's letter to him: TS 12.793, a, lines 5f. On Nehorai's wife and *al-kabīra*'s stay in Jerusalem, we learn from some of Avon b. Ṣedaqa's letters, especially **501**. There he tells how he managed to get them supplies: wheat, wood, oil, onions, salt, etc., and he also gave them three dinars in cash. At first they lived in Jerusalem together with Umm Abī Yūsuf, the mother of Ya'qūb b. Ismā'īl al-Andalusī and with *al-shaykh* al-Sharābī, whose son married the daugher of al-Ballūṭī. Afterward they intended to rent an apartment with a Muslim, but he asked too much for it, and finally they found a small lodging with a Jewish woman, in the Jewish quarter, near the synagogue, the bathhouse, and 'our people' (*aṣḥabnā*, i.e. Maghribis); see on this below in the discussion on the quarters of Jerusalem. Avon b. Ṣedaqa shows respect for *al-kabīra*, Umm Abī 'Imrān; see *al-kabīra* in the Hebrew Index, and especially in **482**, b; **500**, b, line 9; **503**, b, lines 10f; her name was Sitt Muruwwa: **498**, b, line 5. The fact of Nehorai's wife and *al-kabīra*'s stay in Jerusalem is confirmed also in Israel b. Nathan's letters, such as **480**, b, see there the note (Umm Shā'ūl, mentioned *ibid.*, a, line 12, is not Nehorai's wife, contrary to Michaeli's opinion, Dissert., I, 15); **483**, a, line 4; it seems that Nehorai was married to someone else, his cousin, in his youth, and he also had a third wife, mentioned some ten years after his death, in a deed of sale of a slave girl: TS 18 J 1, f 17, the 5th of Kislev 1420 Sel. (10 November, AD 1108): a Nubian slave-girl named Na'īm is being sold to Sitt al-Munā b. Nathan, the widow

circle of Maghribi merchants and the Jerusalem yeshiva was very strong, due to the almost constant presence of some of them in Palestine. They were usually called *al-Maghāriba*, the westerners, and in the documents in my collection, twice we find the version 'our people, the travelling western (merchants)' – (*aṣḥābnā al-maghāriba al-musāfirīn*).[39]

[374] From among the Maghribi group which was active in Palestine and which stayed there, I shall mention those who appear most important in the documents in my collection. First among these are the Tāhirtī family, who came from Tāhirt in North Africa (present-day Algeria) and moved from Qayrawān to Fustat. Barhūn (Abraham) al-Tāhirtī, who settled in Fustat, had four sons and a daughter (as far as we know, there may have been others). His daughter was Nehorai's mother.

When I say that Nehorai b. Nissim lived in the house of the Tāhirtīs, I mean that he lived in his grandfather's (on his mother's side) house. Abū'l-Khayr Moses b. Abraham al-Tāhirtī settled in Jerusalem. As can be seen, he was Nehorai's uncle, that is, his mother's brother. Moses' son Abraham (Barhūn), Nehorai's cousin on his mother's side, was active commercially and travelled back and forth between Palestine and Egypt. Moses b. Abraham Tāhirtī was close to the Jerusalem yeshiva and he was even granted the honour of being appointed *ḥāvēr* in *ca.* 1045. Even earlier, the family was busy collecting money for the yeshiva and transferring it to Jerusalem. One member of the family was a woman named Esther, mentioned in a letter from Abraham b. 'Amram in Jerusalem to Nehorai b. Nissim and to Barhūn (Abraham) b. Ṣāliḥ (Nehorai's cousin), apparently written in about 1060, in which he writes of the death of Moses b. Abraham Tāhirtī (and also mentions that he had managed to be proclaimed *ḥāvēr*). His son (undoubtedly Abraham) was at his bedside when he died but the death of Esther seemed to him an even greater tragedy. She had lived with the Tāhirtīs, Moses and his son Abraham, in the house which belonged to Moses he-ḥāvēr, who is perhaps Moses b. Jacob, Nehorai's brother-in-law. Taking into consideration the extreme expressions of mourning on her death and the extravagant eulogies, it would probably not be far from the truth if we say that Esther (an unusual name in the Geniza documents at the time) was the Hebrew name for Sitt al-Muruwwa, that is, *al-kabīra*, who evidently remained in Jerusalem until she died. Another son of the family is also mentioned, Abū Sa'īd Joseph, whom Nehorai calls by the nickname Abū Sa'īd in his letters. We find him in Tyre handing over money to Israel b. Nathan. Finally, there is direct

of Nehorai . . . of blessed memory; printed in Assaf, *Zion*, 5(1940), 276; see on the wives of Nehorai: Goitein, *Mediterranean Society*, III, 161, 273; 487, n. 140.

39 Queries addressed to the Jerusalem yeshiva: **460**, a, lines 22f; **480**, a, line 7, 'The western travellers': **398**, a, line 9; **497**, line 39. See the Hebrew Index, Maghrib.

evidence of the Tāhirtīs stay in Jerusalem in a letter from Abraham (Barhūn) b. Moses to Nehorai, written *ca.* 1045, when the two were fairly recent arrivals in their respective towns – Nehorai in Fustat and Abraham, his cousin, together with his father, in Jerusalem. Apart from many commercial matters, we find mention there of 'a letter to the Sultan', apparently meaning a letter of recommendation for the family, written by one of the Fatimid appointees in Qayrawān. There are also greetings from 'my Lord and Master, my father' and the news that they are preparing to travel to Hebron, to pray for the entire family.[40]

[375] Nehorai's brother-in-law, Moses b. Jacob (who married Nehorai's sister), lived in Jerusalem and four of his letters to Nehorai from Jerusalem have been preserved. In one he mentions his living quarters in Jerusalem, where as we have already seen, the Tāhirtīs also dwelled. He is occupied with the purchase of mats for the 'cave', the synagogue in Jerusalem. In another letter, he expresses his happiness at being in Jerusalem and seeing the holy place, for which he is prepared to forego worldly pleasures and live austerely. It seems that during the gaonate of Elijah ha-Kohen b. Solomon, Moses b. Jacob was given the title *ḥāvēr*, which his father Jacob had held before him. He speaks of other Maghribis connected with the Jerusalem yeshiva in his letters and especially Shemaiah he-ḥāvēr (b. Yeshū'ā) and Abraham he-ḥāvēr b. 'Amram, while Shemaiah he-ḥāvēr mentions Moses b. Jacob's arrival in Jerusalem in his letter to Nehorai.[41]

[376] Israel b. Nathan (Sahlūn), whom I have already mentioned more than once, was Nehorai's cousin, for his father Nathan and Nehorai's father Nissim were brothers, sons of Nehorai the elder. Israel also lived in Qayrawān at first. A letter sent to Nehorai from there, dealing with various commercial matters, is preserved in the Geniza, evidently written before he set out on his travels which took him firstly to Fustat and afterwards to Byzantium and from there to Palestine. In Fustat, he traded

[40] See on the family of the Tāhirtīs: Goitein, *Mediterranean Society*, I, 181; *Baron Jubilee Volume*, 512, and see there on raising funds for the Jerusalem yeshiva. Moses al-Tāhirtī becomes a ḥāvēr: **141**, lines 2, 4f; Abraham b. 'Amram: **513**, a, lines 7–14. The name Esther, cf. Goitein, *Mediterranean Society*, III, 178. Joseph b. Moses, see the Hebrew Index; cf. Goitein, *Tarbiz*, 45(1975/6), 71: in the letters from Nehorai's archive, whenever mention is made of Abū Sa'īd, this Joseph is meant. Abraham b. Moses al-Tāhirtī's letter: **458**; the recommendation: b, line 5, and see also lines 10f.

[41] Moses b. Jacob's letters: **459–462**; the apartment in Jerusalem: **460**, a, lines 2-17; see also: **461**, lines 18f; mats: **460**, b. lines 9–11; in line 11, he mentions Nissim al-Mu'allim, undoubtedly his brother, referred to in **513**, a, line 10, the letter of the aforementioned Jerusalemite, Abraham b. 'Amram; the satisfaction of being in Jerusalem: **462**, lines 22–29. The letter of Shemaiah he-ḥāvēr: **519**, line 24, in which he speaks of his father, Jacob, the ḥāvēr in the Great Sanhedrin. The granting of the title ḥāvēr to Moses, we find in **513**, a, lines 9f. Another relative of Nehorai's, was his uncle Faraḥ (Surūr) b. Sahlān, mentioned in a number of letters: Nehorai's, Israel b. Nathan's, and Avon b. Ṣedaqa's. The latter writes about him in 1065 that he arrived in Jerusalem ill and in financial straits; people do not visit him, nor do they resepct him. He lives in neighbourhood of Muslim houses, and this is

in precious stones and flax on a large scale, as we can see from the letters he wrote to Abraham b. Isaac ha-Talmīd (Barhūn b. Isḥaq, of blessed memory) in Qayrawān. In my collection, there are twenty letters and fragments of letters he wrote from Palestine, of these eighteen are to Nehorai b. Nissim. Apparently he left Egypt in the forties and settled in Byzantium with his wife, who apparently was a local woman. His family life was unhappy and he divorced his wife. He had a son who died and a baby daughter (*ṭufayla*) who remained with his divorcée. From Byzantium he came to Palestine after much suffering, including imprisonment in Constantinople. On his way to Jerusalem, he was forced to sell some of his own clothing in Tyre in order to stay alive.

In his letters, he emerges as a wise and honest man as well as an extremely generous one. When he arrived in Jerusalem, though still in considerable need and after enduring so much suffering, his main concern was to see that a letter of a blind woman living in Jerusalem was sent to Alexandria, where she had formerly lived, and to ask that the sum of half a dinar be collected in Fustat for a poor Jerusalem girl who needed some cotton cloth to protect her from the cold. After Jerusalem, Israel went northward, apparently intending to reach Tyre and Damascus, and passed through the Galilee. We know that he stopped in Gūsh Ḥālāv for a comparatively lengthy stay, during which he was occupied in copying books for Nehorai and others. While in Gūsh Ḥālāv, he was visited by Joseph b. Naḥum al-Baradānī, who was on his way to Tyre from Tiberias. It seems that Israel's life was a sea of troubles, not all of them revealed in his letter. Indeed, as the writer himself puts it, 'not everything can be said in a letter'. Al-Baradānī subsequently sent him small sums of money to help him out. He lived in straitened circumstances and he enlarges on this in some of his letters, especially the earlier ones. He seems to have had a share in a family inheritance, evidently from his grandfather, and he writes to Nehorai about it, sometimes directly, and more suggestively to others. From Gūsh Ḥālāv, Israel went to Damascus. Prior to his departure he asks for a recommendation from *sayyidnā al-rayyis* (our Lord the head); either Daniel b. Azariah, the Gaon, or perhaps Elijah ha-Kohen b. Solomon, who was then *av-bēt-dīn*, to the people of Damascus to deal with him kindly. Apparently, as we have already seen above, his main occupation during his stay in Palestine, where he evidently remained for the rest of his life, was that of copyist. Perhaps this craft affected his eyesight or caused an eye disease, for in a number of letters he asks to be sent sea-tar (*qafār*) from Alexandria, a proven remedy for the eyes, indeed the best of remedies (*akbar 'uqqār*). In Jerusalem, Israel lived in a compound belonging to

probably why they do not visit him; see: **501**, b, lines 8–12; read: Faraḥ, joy in Arabic, and its synonym: *surūr*, whence the bogus Biblical name Peraḥyā: see Goitein, *Letters* 327, n. 1.

b. al-Buhūrī, who is Abū'l-A'lā 'Amram b. Levi (called Rabbēnū 'Amram by Solomon b. Judah), who was Avon b. Ṣedaqa's brother-in-law and lived in the same house, as did R. Isaac, who was Abū Ya'qūb Isaac b. 'Eli, it seems, whom Israel mentions in his letters. But apparently the proximity did not work out very satisfactorily as can be seen from Avon b. Ṣedaqa's letter to Nehorai containing serious complaints against Israel. He tells of an incident involving Abū'l-Surrī Barhūn (Abraham), the brother-in-law (or son-in-law) of the late Daniel b. Azariah, acting on the request of Abū Sa'd – Josiah ha-Kohen b. Azariah, who was Abū'l-Surrī's brother-in-law. Abū'l-Surrī was to have inherited Daniel b. Azariah's books, and Avon b. Ṣedaqa sent them to him in Damascus. Abū'l-Surrī complained that he could not find the treatise *Bava qamma* among the books and claimed that Israel had it. Indeed, the book figured in Daniel's lists as being with Israel but the latter refused to hand it over unless the 'elders' ordered him to do so. Avon asked Nehorai to intervene in the matter and continued to praise his own good behaviour towards Israel, who was a strange and lonely man, but who did not treat Avon properly; he hints at Israel's misbehaviour, though he does not elaborate on it in the letter. Israel, it seems, expresses heretical ideas on the 'resurrection of the dead, the stars, and other such matters'. Daniel b. Azariah used to defend him against such accusations and rebuff those who accused him, but the situation became much worse after Daniel's death, adds Avon. From Avon's remarks, it appears that Israel, together with his brothers-in-law, the Baradānīs, caused the divorce of R. Ḥayyim he-ḥāvēr b. Solomon's daughter. Further, he adds something intended to arouse Nehorai's wrath: that Israel slanders Nehorai as well, and claims that all his time is dedicated to the affairs of the 'Rav' and collecting money for him among the Maghāriba, the Maghribi merchants. Although we are unable to understand these remarks for lack of data, one can grasp that Avon is busy slandering and conniving and it is unlikely that he was taken seriously by Nehorai. Israel, for his part, does not display any affection for Avon either but limits himself to the laconic remark that Avon is well (he has apparently recuperated from some illness). On the other hand, Avon's mother-in-law treats him well and he asks Nehorai to write and thank him and his mother-in-law for their attitude towards him. Information on Israel b. Nathan from another angle can be found in a letter from Abraham b. Isaac al-Andalusī, who arrived in Jerusalem during a trading journey through Palestine, noting that he 'stays with R. Israel, may God the Almighty grant him a livelihood in His mercy', hinting at his neediness. He mentions that Israel has already managed to copy eighty-five quires for Nehorai. The last available information on Israel b. Nathan is his signature on a deed of sale made out in Jerusalem on Wednesday, the 8th of Adar II, AM 4826, or 8 March AD 1066.[42]

[377] As to Avon b. Ṣedaqa himself, we have only the information

[42] It is possible that Israel b. Nathan was also a relative of another central figure from among the Maghribis, the 'Rav', whom we shall speak of below; in **470**, b, line 8 and margin, he asks Nehorai to give his regards to the 'Rav' and also to *al-karīma*, a term which means the sister (see in the notes to **470**). Further on, he mentions that he received a letter from her; it is thus possible that he was the brother-in-law of the 'Rav' (his wife's brother). The letter from Qayrawān: Bodl MS Heb a 2, f. 18, printed by Starr, *Zion*, 1(1936), 439ff. Poznanski knew this letter and used it as the basis for including Israel b. Nathan among the people of Qayrawān, see: *Harkavy Jubilee Volume*, 209. The letter from Fustat (it may not have been sent): TS 12.362; printed by Gil, *Michael*, 7(1982), 250ff; some corrections should be entered in the translation there: on p. 252, a, line 5, should be: apart from a little sack. On p. b, lines 3–4, evidently one should use the past tense: that is, Abū'l-Faḍl came from Alexandria and received the money . On p. a, line 8, it is possible that *akhlaqak* should be translated: 'abused you' and then the guilt does not lie with the addresssee, Abraham b. Isaac ha-Talmid, but with b. al-Abār, and then one has to read in the margin, line 3: *min lisānhi*, that is, that Abraham should free himself of b. al-Abār's tongue (in the sense of flattery, temptation, in the root *khlq*, see Dozy s.v.). I am grateful to Profs. Blau and Somekh for their comments on the foregoing. There he also mentions the arrival of someone (the name is not preserved) in Qayrawān, accompanied by people from the Christian countries (*ma'a aqwām 'ajam*), who invested 300 dinars with that man. His letters from Palestine: **465–484**; **473** was written to a relative in Egypt and **484** to Ismā'īl b. Isaac al-Andalusī, in Fustat. The family details: **467** a, lines 225f. His troubles:**465** a, lines 3f; **467** a, line 26, he asks of God that he should never see Byzantium again; in **465** a, line 3, he curses Byzantium (*balad al-rūm*): may the God of Israel make it a desert: a possible explanation of his troubles in Constantinople is to be found in Ibn al-Athīr, *Kāmil*, IX, 515 – under the year 435 (which began on the 10th of August 1043), where there are details of disturbances in Constantinople during Constantine IX Monomachus' rule (1042–1055); the blame for the disturbances was placed on the aliens and the emperor then issued an order that anyone living in the city for less than thirty years would be evicted; and more than a hundred-thousand people were ousted from the city. Bar Hebraeus (Budge), I, 203, has similar details; cf. Starr, *Jews*, 195f (No. 140 where there is a misprint, vol. X of Ibn al-Athīr instead of IX); cf. also: Sharf, *Byzantine Jewry*, 116f; Starr, *ibid.*, 117, and following him Sharf, *ibid.*, 126, date Israel b. Nathan's letters between 1060–1075, which is apparently the reason why they did not notice the connection between what is said in Ibn al-Athīr (and Bar Hebraeus) and Israel's ordeals. His requests for others: **466**, b, lines 2f. Al-Baradānī's letter: **492**; he was apparently the husband of Israel's sister, see **500**, b, lines 16–17. Matters of inheritance: **470**, a, lines 9f, Abū'l-Ḥasan Labrāṭ (b. Moses b. Sughmār, the brother of Judah) is the one who deals with the matter. He is also mentioned in other letters of his (see the Hebrew Index, Labrāṭ b. Moses); in **479**, a, in the right-hand margin, he mentions that he wrote a letter to Labrāṭ, which is attached to his letter to Nehorai, for the latter to send it to the Maghrib; he is particularly interested in Labrāṭ getting him a leather-bound Bible, to be sent him via al-Mahdiyya and Alexandria. He mentions that letter also in **480**, a, line 6; he also continues to conduct business with Labrāṭ through Nehorai. There is a hint of this also in a letter from Labrāṭ himself, who was the *dayyān* of the city of al-Mahdiyya, to Nehorai b. Nissim, written in August 1061. These above-mentioned letters of Israel, in which Labrāṭ is mentioned, were written between October 1059 and December 1061. From Labrāṭ's letter, it emerges that there were differences between Israel b. Nathan and his older brother, Abū Yaḥyā Nehorai, who still lived in the Maghrib, about an inheritance. Nevertheless, Labrāṭ managed to get ten dinars from Israel, see: INA D55, f. 13, lines 24–27, in Goitein, *Tarbiz*, 36(1966/7), 64–67, and see *ibid.*, 70, n. 36. See on Abū Zikrī Judah, Labrāṭ's brother: Goitein, *Mediterranean Society*, I, 158. The recommendation to the Damascenes: **474**, margin. Until now, I have encountered no

contained in his own letters. There are seven in my collection; with only one exception (a letter addressed to Ḥayyim b. 'Ammār in Alexandria), all are addressed to Nehorai b. Nissim. Avon's full name was Abū'l-Faraj Avon b. Ṣedaqa al-Maghribī al-Qābisī, which indicates that his family originated in Qābis, North Africa. From the very first letter, written in 1055, in which he tells that he is living in Jerusalem, he describes the period as being one of hardship, evidently referring both to the severe drought endured in Egypt and the disturbing events in the Maghrib. He is himself in dire circumstances; at any rate, he is frequently complaining of others, of their attitude towards him and of his own illnesses. In the first letter, he tells that he was being unjustly accused of dishonesty towards one of the Maghribis, from which we learn indirectly how severely the Maghribis dealt with members of their circle who did not behave properly. On the other hand, if we are to judge from the letter or its style, it is hard to believe that the suspicions against him were indeed unjustified, as he claimed. In his letters to Nehorai b. Nissim, he speaks of business matters and he is overly concerned with the aforementioned quarter-dinars in particular. It seems that Nehorai did not fully trust him and considered him an intriguer, and perhaps this accounted for the fact that he did not convey Avon's aforementioned letter to Ḥayyim b. 'Ammār in Alexandria, attached to a letter addressed to Nehorai, with the very specific request that he send it to its destination, and this is apparently the reason why the letter eventually ended up in the Geniza in Fustat.

It is obvious from Avon b. Ṣedaqa's letters that he behaves like a man whose conscience is troubling him, and he tries to win Nehorai's admiration and understanding, going into great detail about his efforts on behalf of Nehorai's wife and *al-kabīra*, when they came to Jerusalem. He stresses the fact that he is weak and ill and has difficulty supporting himself. It emerges from his letters that he dealt in *kuḥl*, silk, fruit, glue, soap and also wheat. He claims to be constantly making an effort to be independent and

literary manuscripts in Israel b. Nathan's handwriting, except (perhaps) for some fragments of halakha and a number of formularies found in the volume Bodl MS Heb f 24 (= Cat. 2642). *Qafār*, see the Hebrew Index. Solomon b. Judah: **75**, b, line 3; **76**, line 39; see Ephraim b. Shemaria's letter: **326**, line 2: "Amram b. Levi known as b. Buhūrī'. See Avon's letter: **497**, a, line 41, calling him: Abū'l-A'lā, our brother-in-law (*ṣihrnā* – perhaps identifiable with Mevassēr, Avon's brother-in-law). The matter of the Bava qamma: **500** a, line 38 and margin; see in the continuation, b, lines 6f. Israel on Avon: **480**, b, lines 1f. Abraham b. Isaac al-Andalusī: **505**, margin. Deed of sale: **544**, line 34. **468a**, is a letter from Israel b. Nathan to Nehorai b. Nissim, written evidently some months before **469**, which was written in Tishri, whereas this was written in Tammuz. In this letter, too, the matter of the queries about problems of halakha, which Nehorai sent to Daniel b. Azariah, is mentioned. Another fragment in the Geniza, TS AS 203.108, of which very little remains, is also in Israel's handwriting, and was part of a letter written in Jerusalem; it is still possible to read the name Khalfon b. Benāyā, a merchant known to us from other Geniza documents; and also Abū Ṣīr, which is Būṣīr, which was a centre of the flax trade.

does not want to enter into partnership with anyone; nevertheless he became involved in a partnership with Ibn 'Allūsh al-Jazzār, who is evidently Joseph ha-Kohen b. 'Alī Fāsī. This partnership ended in a tremendous squabble, because Joseph had used the money to buy goods in Hebron and Zoar and intended to go to Egypt without first returning the money invested by Avon. The quarrel came before the court of the yeshiva, with the *av-bēt-dīn* presiding. Thus we learn that Avon b. Ṣedaqa was a somewhat quarrelsome individual and inclined to get embroiled in arguments with others, and also with himself, it seems. His attitude towards Nehorai is a very special one; markedly his efforts to be liked by Nehorai and to please him. Similarly, he frequently reiterates his feelings of affection for and loyalty to the 'Rav', the spiritual leader of the Maghribis, who lived in Fustat.[43]

[378] The 'Rav' is Judah ha-Kohen b. Joseph b. Eleazer. To the Maghribis, who frequently mentioned him in letters, sending greetings and expressions of admiration, he was *al-rav*; '*rabbēnū* who should live forever'; 'our Lord and Master, the genuine *rav*'; 'the genuine *rav*, distinguished in wisdom'. Israel b. Nathan calls him '*rabbēnū* Judah'. In a colophon over a piyyūṭ in the *rav*'s handwriting, we find . . . Judah ha-Kohen b. Joseph b. Eleazer of a holy family, proclaimed *rōsh ha-seder* by the Great Court of our Lord Hezekiah b. David, exilarch of all Israel'.

The owner of the quire, Tamīm ha-Kohen b. Jacob b. Ya'īsh, notes that the piyyūṭ is in the handwriting of 'our Lord and Master Judah ha-Kohen', etc. At first, Mann was of the opinion that the son of Joseph ha-Kohen b. Solomon Gaon (who shall be discussed below) was being referred to, that is, that he was of the priestly family of the Palestinian geonim, but changed his mind when he found the aforementioned colophon. According to a fragment of a letter, which only contains the address, one can assume that he may have stemmed from Sijilmāssa in North Africa, for the letter addresses 'our Lord and Master Joseph ha-Kohen . . . son of his Honourable Sanctity, our Lord and Master Joseph ha-Kohen Sijilmāssī'. Indeed, in later generations, perhaps in the twelfth century, there lived a man called 'Abū Zikrī Judah ha-Kohen b. Joseph ha-Kohen, great-grandson of Joseph ha-Kohen, *av-bēt-dīn*, the righteous Kohen', who wrote a com-

[43] Avon b. Ṣedaqa's letters: **497–503**, the first of which is to Ḥayyim b. 'Ammār, who is Ḥayyim b. 'Ammār al-Madīnī, named for *madīnat Siqilliyya*, the city of Sicily, that is, Palermo; see on him: Goitein, *Mediterranean Society*, I, 374 (in the Appendix, No. 22) and see the description of his letter there, TS 20.122; 455, n. 56; III, 340; *idem, Letters*, 131, n. 12. See his name vocalised: Āvōn, in **454**, b, line 3. The suspicions: **497**, most of the letter. The delay in his letter to Ḥayyim b. 'Ammār, see the request in **498**, a, margin, right; but the letter was evidently not sent to its destination, and therefore reached the Geniza in Fustat together with the rest of the letters from Nehorai's archives. His illness and difficulties: **499**, lines 14-16. His business: **500**, a, lines 25–28; b, lines 26–27; **501**, a, lines 37–38; the trade in wheat and the quarrel: **503**.

mentary to the Book of Creation, but he had no connection to the aforementioned 'Rav'. The latter was in the habit of encircling his signature with tiny letters, which when read alternately from above and below, became: 'find in me something good' or 'will find in him everything good'. I have already mentioned the possibility that the 'Rav' was the brother-in-law of Israel b. Nathan. From the text of one of the letters of Avon b. Ṣedaqa to Nehorai b. Nissim, it seems likely that he was the cousin of the prominent Maghribi merchant, Abū Yūsuf Ya'qūb b. Ismā'īl al-Andalusī (the Spaniard), who lived in Jerusalem for a long time. Avon b. Ṣedaqa, also writing from Jerusalem, notes that Ya'qūb's mother wrote two letters (from Jerusalem, in Arabic script) to her nephew and her son in Fustat. Avon asks Nehorai to collect them in person from the place to which they were sent (*zuqāq al-qanādīl* – 'the lane of the lanterns') and deliver them personally, because Avon wants him to convey greetings on his behalf to 'our Master, may he live forever'. Apparently the nephew who was addressed was none other than the Rav and Avon even mentions him first, before the son. After 1050, the Rav was involved in some internal quarrel within the Fustat community, having to do with finding a successor to Ephraim b. Shemaria, head of the 'Palestinians'. The Maghribis evidently wished to grant this status to the Rav but they did not succeed, because the latter had some strong opponents. Thus the position went to 'Eli b. 'Amram. In order to oust the Rav, his opponents did not hesitate to slander him and provoke quarrels between him and the other Maghribis, such as Abraham b. Isaac ha-Talmīd. The Rav was one of the supporters and loyal followers of Daniel b. Azariah (as were most of the Maghribis, it seems) and he afterwards also stood by Daniel's son, David b. Daniel. Evidently it was to these struggles that Avon b. Ṣedaqa is hinting at in his letter to Nehorai b. Nissim, and at the same time, he suggests that Israel b. Nathan has reservations about Nehorai's enthusiastic backing of the Rav. Evidence of the latter's Maghribi background can also be seen in a fragment of a deed in his handwriting, written in Mahdiyya.[44]

[379] Ya'qūb b. Ismā'īl married in Fustat while his mother was still

[44] His nickname in the Maghribis' letters, see the Hebrew Index, Judah ha-Kohen b. Joseph; his full name and his descent and the title *rōsh ha-seder*: TS 8 K 22, f. 8; cf. in Mann, *Jews*, II, 346; Allony, *Kiryat Sefer*, 38(1962/3) 548f; rōsh ha-seder also: **432**, margin; **556**, b; see further on the importance of the 'Rav' to the Maghribis: Goitein, *Tarbiz*, 45(1975/6), 64; see Mann, *Jews*, , 101, n. 2, and the Supplement in that volume, p. 346; Goitein, *ibid.*, 66, did not notice Mann's correction nor the colophon, from which we know the name of the Rav's grandfather, Eleazer; **486**, which he prints there, contains no proof that the 'Rav' was a scion of the family of the priestly heads of the yeshiva and the way 'the daughter of the head of the yeshiva' addresses Nehorai b. Nissim can be explained (see the introduction to that letter, in my corpus); and there is also no proof that the writer was the wife of the 'Rav', as Goitein says there, 71. The fragment of the letter: TS 6 J 1. f. 5. The author of the

living in Jerusalem. Israel b. Sahlūn, writing about this in November 1061, adds that the mother is sad and mournful; she is also poor and old, and he asks that she be sent a quarter-dinar. Ya'qūb's brother, Abū Zikrī Judah b. Ismā'īl, also deals in trade and Ya'qūb refers to him in his letters, for it seems that they work together. In my collection, there are two letters from Ya'qūb b. Ismā'īl written in Tyre, one to Abū'l-Walīd Jonah (Yūnus) b. David (Da'ūd), and the other to Nehorai b. Nissim. Ya'qūb is engaged in shipping various types of merchandise: textiles, arsenic, sugar, soap, myrobalan, rhubarb, and gall-nuts. However, one must distinguish between him and Jacob b. Samuel al-Andalusī, whose letter from Jerusalem to Joseph b. Naḥum al-Baradānī in Tyre has been preserved. Despite the fact that Ismā'īl is the Arabic name generally given to people called Samuel and although they both hailed from Spain (Andalus), their handwriting is not similar and they apparently dealt in different merchandise as well.[45]

[380] One of Nehorai's partners, and possibly also a family member, was Jacob b. Joseph b. Ismā'īl al-Iṭrābulusī, who lived in Ascalon and engaged in imports and exports on a large scale. He dealt in tin, yellow myrobalan, brazilwood, gall-nuts, sumach, flax, cotton, cedar resin and sugar. Nissim b. Ḥalfon, also one of Nehorai b. Nissim's partners or agents, generally conducted his commercial affairs in Egypt although we find him on a business mission in Tyre, whence he wrote to Nehorai. In his letter, he gives an account of difficulties in the port regarding a shipment of flax which arrived from Egypt. In addition, he gives details of the items he bought for Nehorai in Tyre, especially textiles. Solomon (Salāma) b. Moses b. Isaac Safāquṣī, another member of Nehorai's circle, writes at the end of December 1059 from Jerusalem, describing the vicissitudes endured by him during the winter; he is not willing to forego fowl in

commentary to the Book of Creation: see manuscripts from the Firkovitch collection and the Mosseri collection, in Mann, *Texts*, I, 456f, where he also quotes from **556**: 'Judah ha-Kohen, the Rav and rōsh ha-seder ... b. R. Joseph he-ḥāsīd, of blessed memory'; Mann there confuses the two. In the letters he quotes, it is said of the father, Joseph ha-Kohen: *s.ṭ.* = *sāfēh ṭāv*, may he have a good end; that is, he is still living; it appears therefore that Judah was a descendant of the priestly Geonim who lived in Fustat (at a later period) and used to mention his illustrious lineage. See the title *rōsh ha-seder* also in TS 10 J 15, f. 8, which is a fragment of a letter from Shelah b. Mevassēr to the 'Rav' (Judah ha-Kohen, the Great Rav, *rōsh ha-seder* ... b. Joseph ha-Kohen, of righteous blessed memory), in Mann, *Jews*, 101, n. 2. The small letters: see TS Box G 1, fs. 5, 6, and see a slightly different version in Goitein, *Tarbiz*, 45(1975/6), 65, n. 5. The letters from Jerusalem: **499**, a, margin. The quarrel in Fustat, see: **399**, b; Avon: **500**, cf. Goitein, *ibid.*, 69. The fragment of the deed from Mahdiyya: ENA 4009, f. 9. On the writings of the 'Rav' see Allony (in this note above), 548–549; see Allony and Scheiber, *Kiryat Sefer*, 48:152, 1972/3. In Goitein, *ibid.*, 65, n. 5, some documents in his handwriting are mentioned. See also: **530**, a letter from the 'Rav' to his Jerusalem relative, in which he strongly objects to the relative's son travelling to Christian countries.

45 Ya'qūb and his mother: **479**, a, lines 21f; his letters: **494**, **495** and see what he writes about his brother in the latter, b, lines 2–3. *Rāwand* is rhubarb: *Rheum palmatum* L., thought to

Jerusalem and intends going down to Ramla to purchase some there. In this letter to Nehorai he also discusses matters concerning the flax market. He, too, has in mind a visit with Abraham b. Isaac ha-Talmīd in Ascalon.

Abraham b. Isaac ha-Talmīd is one of the most important and outstanding individuals among the Maghribis. Israel b. Nathan mentions him frequently and it is obvious that they were partners and perhaps also relatives. Israel emigrated from the Maghrib before Abraham and as mentioned, a letter has been preserved from Israel in Fustat to Abraham in Qayrawān. It seems that Abraham was the younger or perhaps a junior partner, for there is a note of reprimand towards Abraham for promising (or so it claims) to sell the same clothing to two different people, which aroused the anger of Ḥesed al-Tustarī. In another letter, Israel says of Abraham that he is 'cool-brained' (*bārid al-damāgh*), meaning he is none too clever, which is certainly intended as disparaging. Further on, we find Abraham involved in the serious dispute between Abiathar Gaon and David b. Daniel, as one of the latter's supporters, and also serving him as judge and scribe. Joseph b. Manasseh, writing to him from Ascalon, calls him Abū Isḥaq b. al-Talmīd al-Dayyān (indeed, it was his father, Isaac, who was the judge; at any rate, Abraham was David's scribe). In my collection there is a letter of Elijah ha-Kohen b. Solomon Gaon, dating from *ca.* 1060, during the period when Daniel b. Azariah was Gaon and Elijah *av-bēt-dīn* of the yeshiva court, to Ḥalfon b. Solomon in Ascalon, concerning the affairs of Abraham b. ha-Talmīd. Abraham complains that he is suspected of having married a woman in Ascalon in addition to his first wife. Elijah cautions him against rumours of this kind and says that 'Heaven forbid there should arise or be such a thing in Israel, for our elder, may God preserve him is a notable among Jews and liked by most of his brethren'; however, if there is any truth in the matter, he may expect short shrift from the law. We do not know what really happened, since in the Geniza we only find the marriage deed of his wife Sitt al-Dār b. Hanania. Hanania, Abraham b. ha-Talmīd's father-in-law, is evidently Abū'l-Ṭayyib Hanania ha-Levi the parnās, who is mentioned by 'Eli ha-Kohen b. Ezekiel in his letters, and he is also apparently the Ḥunayn (a diminutive) cited in a letter to Daniel b. Azariah in connection with a dispute over the leadership in Fustat. Abraham b. ha-Talmid was a merchant and financier, who lived in the house of the Tāhiritīs (and of Nehorai b. Nissim) in Fustat, *Dār al-Ṣarf* ('house of the money-changers') but it seems that he spent a good deal of his time in Ascalon, perhaps for family reasons, as we have seen.[46]

have strengthening qualities, and a laxative; see: Ducros, 61. The letter of Jacob b. Samuel: **493**.

46 Jacob b. Joseph, see his letter: **487**; he was evidently from Ṭarābulus al-Shām (not from the

[381] Joseph b. Yeshūʿā al-Iṭrābulusī, another Maghribi merchant, whose family evidently settled in Ṭarābulus al-Shām, writes to Nehorai from there. He was apparently especially close to Abraham b. Moses al-Tāhirtī, who dealt mainly in the import of scents and spices. Abraham b. Isaac al-Andalusī was another Maghribi merchant who stayed in Jerusalem for a considerable length of time and we have two of his letters from Jerusalem: one to his partner Joseph b. ʿAlī ha-Kohen Fāsī and the other to Nehorai b. Nissim. His partner Joseph was in Fustat at the time, after returning from a journey to the Maghrib. Their joint activities were trading in textiles; Abraham deals with communal matters of Qayrawān and he asks for a Torah cover for the synagogue there. It also emerges from his letters that he has a shop in Fustat and wants Joseph to replace him there during his absence. While in Ramla and Jerusalem, Abraham contracted a severe illness and had to stay in bed for over a month. He would sometimes travel to Ramla and Ascalon; in Ascalon he was evidently supervising the loading of goods aboard the ships. Another merchant of this group, Jacob b. Salmān al-Ḥarīrī, writes to Nehorai from Ṭarābulus al-Shām, mentioning shipments of textiles, dates and wheat to Alexandria. He arrived in Palestine from Ṭarābulus after a storm at sea and I have already described the misadventures on board. Joseph b. ʿAlī Kohen Fāsī was one of the most active of Nehorai's partners. We find him in Tyre in *ca.* 1067 and Nehorai writes to him there. His base is Ramla but sea-going shipments arrive and are exported through Tyre on board the cadi of Tyre's ships and Joseph goes to Tyre for this purpose in particular. Nehorai sends him a detailed list of prices and merchandise in Fustat and information on the marketing progress of their goods. There is also an echo of political events in the letter: 'the city (Fustat) has already calmed down after what happened'.[47]

[382] In Tyre, we also find Ismāʿīl b. Isaac al-Baṭalyūsī (Baṭalyūs in Spain, Badajoz today) al-Andalusī, in *ca.* 1065, and from there he moved to Jerusalem. He was a friend of Israel b. Nathan, who writes to him from

Libyan), and it was he who evidently signed in **604**, the power-of-attorney written there on the 13th of May 1079. In one of his letters, written from Ascalon to someone in the group of Maghribi merchants, he enquired after Nehorai's well-being, and asked about sums of money owed to him (to the writer); a fragment remaining from this letter: **487**, a. Nissim b. Ḥalfon: **489**. Solomon b. Moses: **490**, and see on his other letters preserved in the Geniza: Goitein, *Letters*, 138f; see also: Udovitch, in *Individualism*, 68, n. 18, Israel's letter to Abraham: TS 12.362; 'cool-brained': **479**, a, lines 10–12. Joseph b. Manasseh: **593**. Elijah ha-Kohen's letter: **421**. The marriage deed of Abraham b. ha-Talmid's wife: TS 20.7, cf. Mann, *Jews*, II, 245, Scheiber, *Tarbiz*, 32(1962/3), 274. Ḥanania, see the Hebrew Index, under Ḥunayn: **399**, lines 31, 33, 35. Cf. more of Abraham b. ha-Talmid: Goitein, *Mediterranean Society*, I, 238f; II, 512.

47 Joseph b. Yeshūʿā: **496**. The letters of Abraham al-Andalusī: **504**, **505**. Jacob b. Salmān: **506**, **507**. Nehorai to Joseph: **508**.

Jerusalem while Ismāʻīl is in Fustat on a business trip, apparently, that his daughter and her children are well. The rest of Ismāʻīl's family evidently remained in Spain and he writes to Abūʻl-Faraj Yeshūʻā b. Samuel in Fustat asking him to try to get news of them. They are living in Majrīṭ (which is Madrid) and Yeshūʻā is in the position to get information about them from people who happen to come from Ṭulayṭula (Toledo) or Majrīṭ. The latter are still in close contact with their old home in Andalus and it seems that they also have commercial dealings with the places they had formerly lived in, for they were well acquainted with the prevailing conditions and also had friends and acquaintances there. In his letters to Nehorai as well, Ismāʻīl writes of family matters in Spain, and apart from this, also cites various details concerning their mutual affairs. Another of Nehorai's partners (or agents) is Abū Ibrāhīm (also: Abū'l-Faḍl) ʻAyyāsh b. Ṣedaqa b. Barūkh al-Maghribī, who lives mainly in Alexandria, and we find him visiting Jerusalem in the mid-sixties. Israel b. Nathan informed Nehorai of the safe arrival of ʻAyyāsh in Jerusalem and Nehorai writes to him there, mentioning ships that were captured by the Byzantines and enclosing letters that have arrived from the Maghrib for him. The price of wheat in Fustat is also referred to, for this was a question which weighed heavily on those Maghribis who travelled and whose families lived in Egypt, because of the severe drought suffered by the country during those years. ʻAyyāsh b. Ṣedaqa was evidently of the family of Ṣedaqa b. ʻAyyāsh, one of the prominent merchants in Qayrawān at the beginning of the century.[48]

[383] Abū ʻImrān Moses (Mūsā) b. Abī'l-Ḥayy Khalīla, who lived in Alexandria, was also a partner of Nehorai b. Nissim and is mentioned occasionally in the letters in my collection. He, too, was one of the important Maghribi merchants living in Egypt. Apart from his widespread commercial activities, he had a special relationship to the Palestinian yeshiva and bore the title *segullat-ha-yeshiva* (worthy of the yeshiva). In 1094, he thought it proper to congratulate Abiathar ha-Kohen Gaon on his victory over his rival, David b. Daniel. This is but one instance, of a belated nature, of the involvement of the Maghribis in the concerns of the Palestinian yeshiva. Apparently, the Maghribis were first considered 'Babylonians', stemming from their ancient origins in Persian or Iraqi regions, and were considered part of the Babylonian congregation in Fusṭat. But it seems that there were also some Maghribis who joined the

[48] Israel to Ismāʻīl: **484**. Ismāʻīl's letters: **510–512**; cf. Goitein, *Mediterranean Society*, I, 69. The letter to ʻAyyāsh: **509**; see on Ṣedaqa b. ʻAyyāsh and on his father ʻAyyāsh (the grandfather of our ʻAyyāsh): Goitein, *Letters*, 307. In **471**, a, lines 9–10, and b, line 2, we find that Israel b. Nathan is very worried about ʻAyyāsh, because he received a letter from Abraham b. Isaac ha-Talmid in which there is information concerning the terrible trouble that has befallen ʻAyyāsh; Israel urges Nehorai to deal with this matter and to inform him of what is happening; we do not know what sort of trouble this was.

'Palestinians' in Fustat. As the Palestinian yeshiva was the accepted leadership of all the Jews under Fatimid rule, including the 'Babylonians' and even the Karaites, the Maghribis were intensely interested in whatever related to this yeshiva. One should also remember that Solomon b. Judah, head of the Palestinian yeshiva during the second quarter of the eleventh century, was a Maghribi, his family stemming from Fās (Fez). In the mid-century and later on, we also find some Maghribi scholars living in Jerusalem who are connected socially and economically with the groups of Maghribi merchants. I have already mentioned Moses he-ḥāvēr b. Jacob he-ḥāvēr, Nehorai's brother-in-law (his sister's husband), and his brother Nissim b. Jacob. Abū'l-Faraj Shemaiah he-ḥāvēr b. Yeshū'ā (Faraj) also has links with the Maghribis. We find him in Jerusalem, apparently a descendant of Shemaiah Gaon, head of the Palestinian yeshiva at the outset of the eleventh century, as one can surmise from the signature of the man who had been a judge in Fustat at the beginning of the twelfth century – Abraham he-ḥāvēr b. Shemaiah he-ḥāvēr, great-grandson of Shemaiah Gaon. Hence it appears that our Shemaiah b. Yeshū'ā was the father of this Abraham. Abraham was born in *ca.* 1050, if indeed he is the infant of whose birth Joseph ha-Kohen b. Solomon Gaon writes to Ephraim b. Shemaria when he mentions that R. Shemaiah had a son (later on, another son was born). Below we find Shemaiah in the company of Moses he-ḥāvēr b. Jacob he-ḥāvēr, the aforementioned brother-in-law of Nehorai. Moses mentions Shemaiah in his letters; we find him managing flax transactions in which the flax is spun in Jerusalem and sent to Tyre for finishing, where his partner, Manasseh b. Joshua he-ḥāvēr, deals with it. One of the notables of the Ascalon community writes to him, asking him to take action – even to the point of declaring a ban – against anyone who slanders the writer and against a certain Mevorakh, Shemaiah's cousin. Also mentioned is Shemaiah's brother Solomon b. Yeshū'ā, who is also living in Jerusalem. A letter of Shemaiah he-ḥāvēr to Nehorai b. Nissim has been preserved, written in Hebrew, which was not customary among the Maghribis, most of whose correspondence is conducted in Arabic. In addition to good wishes and grandiose expressions, he mentions Nehorai's Jerusalemite brother-in-law, the aforementioned Moses b. Jacob, and Abraham he-ḥāvēr b. 'Amram. The *'alāma* at the end of the letter is interesting: *yesha' rav yeqārēv*, a sort of combination of Solomon b. Judah's formula and that of his rival, Nathan b. Abraham. In this letter, there is also further confirmation of the connection between the trio of Jerusalem scholars (Moses b. Jacob, Shemaiah b. Yeshū'ā, and Abraham b. 'Amram) and Nehorai b. Nissim and his circle of Maghribis. The third member of the triad, Abraham he-ḥāvēr b. 'Amram, turns up in a number of letters in which Shemaiah he-ḥāvēr is also mentioned. Abraham b. David b. Sughmār, who played an important role in the split over the gaonate in 1038–1042, sends him greetings in a letter written at the outset of the dispute. According to a list drafted by Ephraim b. Shemaria, he transferred money from Fustat to the people of Jerusalem through Abraham b. ʻAmram – nineteen dinars, in a *diyōqnē*. We also have a letter from Abraham b. ʻAmram himself, written in Jerusalem and addressed to a Spanish merchant staying in Ramla. From this letter it emerges that Abraham had a special link with people from Qalʻat Banī Ḥammād in North Africa and he asks his correspondent to pass on his letter to them.[49]

[384] From the letters of the Jerusalem Maghribis, it is obvious that those who were lucky enough to see Palestine and live there felt they had achieved a treasured aim, and they do not refrain from expressing their enthusiasm and happiness. On the other hand, their hearts remained in the west and they are constantly asking after and interesting themselves in news from there, for they have left behind relatives and friends. These Maghribis, who undoubtedly contributed largely to the prosperity and the renewed flourishing economy in Palestine from 1030 onwards, were later the victims of the political and military events by which the Maghrib was destroyed, and which also affected Sicily, while Palestine was caught up in the whirlpool as well. In one of his letters, Avon b. Ṣedaqa mentions bad news from Sicily – the burning of ships and the Maghribis reduced to ruin. The Jerusalem parnās ʻAlī ha-Kohen b. Ezekiel complains in *ca*. 1060 that the situation in Jerusalem is very bad and that the merchants have stopped coming there. As to Qayrawān in the thirties of the eleventh century, we already find signs of its economic decline, which was undoubtedly the result of the transfer of the Fatimids' centre to Egypt. As early as July 1035, in a letter sent from there to Ephraim b. Shemaria in Fustat, mention is made of merchandise sent by Ephraim to the Maghrib with a certain Abū Saʻīd (undoubtedly a shipment of scents and spices – Ephraim's trade), which was not sold for lack of customers ('all goods are

[49] See on Mūsā b. Abī'l-Ḥayy: Goitein, *Mediterranean Society*, II, 445 (No. 27); Mann, *Jews*, II, 220, quotes from BM Or 5545, f. 7 (a court document from the court of David b. Daniel), line 8: *al-shaykh* Abū 'Imrān, our Lord and Master Moses *segullat ha-yeshiva* (the worthy of the yeshiva), b. our Master Abū'l-Ḥayy, of blessed memory' (1089). See also Udovitch, in *Individualism*, 66, and there in n. 11, a list of his letters written to Nehorai b. Nissim from Alexandria. The letter to Abiathar: **551**. On Abraham b. Shemaiah see Mann, *Jews*, II, 231ff, 342; Goitein, *Mediterranean Society*, II, 512 (No. 13); Schapira, *Yerushalayim*, 1952/3, 118. Joseph ha-Kohen: **409**, line 19. Moses b. Jacob's letters: **460–462**. Two sons: **521**, a, line 3. Manasseh b. Joshua's letters: **521–523**. From Ascalon: **526**. Solomon b. Yeshūʻā: see the Hebrew Index. Shemaiah's letter: **519**. Abraham b. David b. Sughmār: **190**, b, line 4. The list of Ephraim b. Shemaria: **326**, line 11. Abraham's letter: **524**. There is also a letter in his handwriting preserved in the Geniza, on the order of reading the Torah, TS 12.726, printed by Assaf, *Responsa* (1942), 109ff. His signature is surrounded by small letters which I am unable to explain. Assaf read Jacob (instead of Abraham) b. ʻAmram by mistake.

cheap and unfortunately he that earneth wages earneth wages to put it into a bag with holes', quoting Hag., i:6). Nehorai's brother-in-law Moses b. Jacob, writing from Jerusalem in March 1053, expresses his despair at the absence of news from his family in the Maghrib; everyone knows of the economic hardship and the calamities occurring there. Israel b. Nathan also mentions the heavy hearts and notes 'how much harm has been done to people's property and their persons'. Abraham he-ḥāvēr b. 'Amram speaks of profound alarm among the Maghribis in Jerusalem and tells of a letter that arrived from Abraham b. David b. Sughmār, from which one can understand that there is 'a change in the world and a turning over of the heavens' and that they are awaiting more specific news. They are speaking, of course, of the raids of the Banū Hilāl and Banū Sulaym, which eventually led to the destruction of the region. The pressure of these tribes increased, especially since Dhū'l-Ḥijja AH 443 (19 April 1052), and after a short time the regime's institutions were hastily transferred from Qayrawān to Mahdiyya. Qayrawān was completely destroyed in November 1057 after a siege which the Bedouin began in 1054.[50]

The economy of Jerusalem

[385] Against the background of this general survey of economic life in Palestine, Jerusalem's special situation is conspicuous. Actually it should have been a prosperous and flourishing city, being the focus of pilgrims of every religious persuasion, but as a matter of fact, we hear mainly of distress and want. This was an unusual situation, naturally, which was the product of the special conditions reigning in the eleventh century, the period of the Geniza letters. We do, indeed, find echoes of the connection between the economic activities and the arrival of masses of people in Jerusalem. Nehorai b. Nissim intends to send merchandise for sale on the Muslim feast although the likelihood of getting decent prices for them is remote. From Avon b. Ṣedaqa's letters, we have already learned that towards the pilgrimage season, one should stock up on grapes and that

50 Among those who emigrated from the Maghrib to Palestine, one must include Zadok b. Yaḥyā, at whose request and for whom Rabbēnū Nissim b. Jacob wrote his commentary to the first mishna in the tractate *Rōsh ha-shana*. See: MS Mosseri R 12, in Assaf *Mi-sifrut ha-ge'ōnīm*, 122, cf. Abramson. *Nissim Gaon*, 94 (these sources are from about the mid-eleventh century; this Zadok is not mentioned in the letters in my corpus). Avon: **500**, a, lines 20f. 'Eli ha-Kohen: **443**, a, lines 6f. The letter to Ephraim: **330**, lines 23–24. Moses b. Jacob: **459**, lines 11f. Israel: **473**, a, lines 9–10. Abraham he-ḥāvēr: **513**, b, lines 9f. The destruction of Qayrawān: Ibn al-Athīr, *Kāmil*, IX, 569; Idris, *La Berbérie*, 210–229; see BM Or 5542, f. 9, the letter of Ismā'īl b. Faraḥ to Nehorai b. Nissim with a description of some of the horrors experienced by the Jews of Qayrawān, see its translation in Goitein, *Letters*, 154–158.

their sale is profitable. Israel b. Nathan notes, as aforementioned, that only if merchants from the Christian countries (*'ajam*) come to Jerusalem will it be possible to sell pearls, for the town itself is poor (*li-annahu balad ḍa'īf*). Another fact emerges from the letters in the Geniza and that is that most of the trading goes on in Ramla and not in Jerusalem; that is, the pilgrims come to Jerusalem, and when their spiritual needs are fulfilled, the pilgrims, and chiefly the tradesmen among them, turn to Ramla to transact business. This was the case, for instance with Khallūf b. Aaron and Khalaf b. Abraham b. Khalīl al-Iṭrābulusī, who invested 350 dinars in a partnership to buy merchandise, which they purchased in Ramla in order to sell in Damascus. From Ramla, an important and successful commercial centre, Jerusalem received its principal direct support, as the Gaon Solomon ha-Kohen b. Joseph puts it (in the spring of 1025): 'and most of our livelihood was from the clerks [merchants' agents] of Ramla and its merchants; we would buy on credit and sell and cover our debts, and still profit'. There were shops in Ramla which were foundations (*heqdēsh*) for the welfare of Jerusalem and their income would pay most of the tax imposed on its Jews. But assistance came to Jerusalem from all the Jewish communities, and not only from Ramla. Nevertheless it is obvious that life in Jerusalem was hard and there was the danger of being reduced to poverty, as stated in the letter of the Jerusalem yeshiva (evidently in 1057): '... life in big cities is hard, even more so in Jerusalem, where a curse prevails, its nourishments come from afar and livelihood is scarce; many who came to the city were impoverished and demeaned'. In the same fifties, the Maghribi Abraham b. Isaac al-Andalusī, writes from Jerusalem to Fustat to his partner Joseph b. 'Alī Kohen Fāsī. 'The land has died, its inhabitants are poor and die, and especially in Jerusalem; there are no cattle to be slaughtered, neither on a week-day nor on the sabbath, and there is no fowl to be had'. This was written in reply to Joseph's question as to whether he intended to remain in Jerusalem. One can imagine that this scarcity was to a large extent due to the unstable state of security as described in this letter and others. The situation became even worse during those years in which Egypt suffered from drought, and the effect on Jerusalem was two-fold: on the one hand there was the interruption of pilgrimages, and on the other hand, the absconding of the grains from Palestine to Egypt and the soaring prices in general. The situation is described by Israel b. Nathan in 1061 in this manner: 'In Jerusalem there is starvation. A *qafīz* of wheat costs three dinars, reaching three and a half, when it has sand and should be sifted; may God save us and the poor'.[51]

[51] Nehorai: **508**, b, line 3; cf. Goitein, *Mediterranean Society*, I, 195. Grapes: **503**, a, lines 5f. Israel: **477**, line 4. The partnership: **30**. Solomon ha-Kohen: **50**, lines 14–15. The shops of Ramla: **49**, a, lines 16–17. The letter of the yeshiva (1057): **420**, c, lines 28–30. Abraham b. Isaac: **504**, a, lines 21–22. Israel b. Nathan: **480**, b, lines 5–6.

5

Palestine from the beginning of Abbasid rule to the Fatimids

From the revolution to al-Ma'mūn

[386] The Abbasid revolution brought about drastic changes in Palestine's status and its internal events. The ruling centre was considerably removed geographically. The most drastic and basic change effected by this revolution throughout the caliphate – the decline of the Arab tribes' glory – was strongly felt in Palestine. From that time onwards, after the initial shocks were over, one hears no longer of the tribes participating in its political affairs, but only of their rebellions, and in the literary sources of the period there is hardly an allusion to those numerous tribes. The chief rulers, the caliphs, were no longer at home in Palestine, and when one of them paid a visit to Jerusalem, the fact was recorded in the chronicles as an event, and the visit itself bore a special religious-political significance. Baghdad, the new capital of the caliphate established in 762, was also a source of resentment on the part of the former centre of al-Shām, the seat of the Umayyads, whom the new rulers tried to depict as genuine heretics. In a poem in praise of Baghdad written shortly after its foundation, we find the lines (in a free translation): 'A visitor coming to Baghdad can close his eyes quietly and sleep to his heart's content, whereas in al-Shām he would not dare to do so, for Baghdad was almost destroyed by the favours and bounty it regaled them [the people of al-Shām] with; but they respond with enmity and slander, unjustly and undeservedly.' The first officials in ruling positions and local administration were members of the caliph's family, who bore feelings of profound malice towards anyone who had collaborated with the Umayyads. In the course of time, a system of political centralisation developed in Baghdad, which worked through the medium of offices (*dīwāns*), similar to present-day ministries and

evidently modelled along the lines of Sasanid Persia. The central pillar of this system comprised the *kuttāb* (sing.: *kātib*), or the clerks, who were familiar with the techniques of recording and administration and were generally of either Persian (Zoroastrian) or Christian origin, and even some Christians who had not converted to Islam. These were a sort of secular arm of the reign, guided not by Muslim law but by the will and policies of the ruler. They were headed by the *wazīr*, an office created by the Abbasid regime. At first, his role was to direct the central *dīwān*, but he quickly became the actual ruler, the deputy of the caliph. The army, too, saw changes; units from Khurāsān, Persians and afterwards also Turks, replaced the Arab tribes.[1]

1. *Uprisings in Palestine*

[387] During the first years after the revolution, rebellions erupted throughout the caliphate which were crushed by considerable bloodshed and violence. Theophanes tells of a great many murderous acts carried out by the local inhabitants (certainly meaning Bedouin tribes) among the 'wearers of the black' (*maurophoroi*; black was the colour of the Abbasids) in Palestine in 754. Ṣāliḥ b. 'Alī, uncle of the caliph al-Manṣūr (his father's brother), was forced to send an army from Egypt (to which he had been appointed governor by the new rulers) to Palestine in order to fight the rebels, the *khawārij*, and he personally went to Palestine afterwards to command the army, alongside Abū 'Awn 'Abd al-Malik b. Yazīd. The insurgents suffered a crushing defeat and many of them were killed; the severed heads of 3,000 of their men were sent from Palestine to Fustat. Apparently after this collapse, the situation in Palestine was subdued. In 764, Arab tribes still took part in a raid into Byzantine territory, headed by Mālik b. 'Abdallah al-Khath'amī, known as *mālik al-ṣawā'if* (meaning approximately: the summer-raider, from *ṣā'ifa*), and taking considerable spoils in the process.[2]

[388] The first governors were members of the caliph's family, as I have

1 See the verses (there is a difference of opinion as to the author's identity) in al-Khaṭīb al-Baghdādī, *Ta'rīkh*, I, 68.

2 Theophanes, I, 429 (cf. Breyer, 72). The *khawārij* (sing. *khārijī*) were the sworn enemies of the Umayyads, and now of the Abbasids; sometimes this term is used for any rebels and one does not know exactly to whom it refers; see Ibn Taghrī Bardī, I, 331f; cf. Wüstenfeld, *Statthalter*, II, 4. According to Ṭabarī, *Ta'rīkh*, III, 84, Abū 'Awn was then governor of Egypt while Ṣāliḥ b. 'Alī was governor of Trans-Jordan (al-Balqā') and jund Filasṭīn. The uprising in Palestine during al-Manṣūr's time is mentioned in Ṭabarī, *ibid.*, also on p. 436; according to him the leader of the rebels was caught and sent to al-Manṣūr, but he was forgiven, thanks to one of the caliph's advisers, al-Rabī'; cf. Ibn Khallikān, II, 295. The raid: Ibn al-Athīr, *Kāmil*, V, 576.

mentioned; Ṣāliḥ b. 'Alī was appointed commander in jund Filasṭīn in Sha'bān AH 133 (4 March AD 751). Two and a half years later the area of his command was extended to southern Trans-Jordan (al-Balqā'), Egypt and the west (on 8 October 753). 'Abdallah ibn 'Alī, another of the caliph's uncles, was appointed to Urdunn at the same time. During al-Manṣūr's day the governors were 'Abd al-Wahhāb b. Ibrahīm, the caliph's nephew, in jund Filasṭīn, and Muḥammad b. Ibrahīm, 'Abd al-Wahhāb's brother, in jund Urdunn. 'Abd al-Wahhāb was also in charge of the summer raids against the Byzantines, but he was not very successful in this role and was therefore transferred to other districts. In order to demonstrate how his nephew behaved in jund Filasṭīn, the caliph was shown a plucked chicken; this is apparently what brought about his ousting from there. During al-Mahdī's time (775–785) the governor of jund Filasṭīn was Naṣr b. Muḥammad b. al-Ash'ath; he is credited with catching two of the few Umayyads who were still alive in the area, Bakr b. Mu'āwiya al-Bāhilī and 'Abdallah b. Marwān b. Muḥammad. At about the same time, Bishr b. Rawḥ al-Muhallabī is mentioned; he was commander (*amīr*) of the city of Ascalon. At that time, there was an important Muslim scholar living there, Abū 'Umar Ḥafṣ b. Maysara, who collected ḥadīths and hailed from Ṣan'ā in Yemen.[3]

2. *Thawr b. Yazīd and his contemporaries*

[389] At that time, Abū Khālid Thawr b. Yazīd b. Ziyād al-Kulā'ī al-Raḥbī al-Ḥimṣī, evidently one of the pupils of Rajā' b. Ḥayawa, was living in Jerusalem. His grandfather Ziyād had fought alongside Mu'āwiya at Ṣiffin against 'Alī, and it seems that the grandson hated the Shiites as a result. Thawr was in conflict with Mālik b. Anas, the famous scholar of Medina, and it seems that he remained inwardly loyal to the Umayyads and was therefore accused of being a Qadarī (one who believed in the freedom of will), an accusation made against a number of the Damascene caliphs as well. A contemporary who also lived in Jerusalem was

[3] Ṭabarī, *Ta'rīkh*, III, 75, 81, 84; Ya'qūbī, *Ta'rīkh*, II, 461; Ibn al-Athīr, *Kāmil*, V, 454; Ibn Taghrī Bardī, I, 328; II, 30; Wüstenfeld, *Statthalter*, II, 2f; al-Khaṭīb al-Baghdādī, *Ta'rīkh*, XI, 17f, adds that 'Abd al-Wahhāb died in AH 158, i.e. AD 775; Ibn 'Asākir, VI, 376f has a biography of Ṣāliḥ b. 'Alī, especially his wars against Constantine V Copronymus (741–775, the son of Leo: in Ibn 'Asākir, the son of al-Nūn). The story of the chicken: Jahshiyārī, 137; in 764, we find 'Abd al-Wahhāb at the head of the *ḥajj*, the pilgrimage to Mecca, see: Ibn Ḥabīb, *Muḥabbar*, 35. Naṣr b. Muḥammad: Ṭabarī, *Ta'rīkh*, III, 46; Abū'l-Fidā', *Mukhtaṣar*, I, 212. Bishr b. Rawḥ: Ibn 'Asākir, IV, 386. Ḥafṣ b. Maysara (died in AH 181/AD 797): al-Khaṭīb al-Baghdādī, *Mūḍiḥ*, II, 48f; Khazrajī, 75 (who says that he belonged to the Banū 'Uqayl); Ibn al-'Imād, I, 295; Dhahabī, *'Ibar*, I, 279; Ibn 'Asākir, IV, 385f; Ibn Ḥajar, *Tahdhīb*, II, 419.

'Abdallah b. Shawdhib (who came from Balkh in Khurāsān, and only came to Jerusalem after a stay in Baṣra). Abū Isḥaq Ibrahīm b. Adham was also born in Balkh, to a family whose origin was in Kūfa, of the Banū Bakr b. Wā'il. He was involved in government matters at first but afterwards left them and went to Jerusalem where he settled and there lived the life of an ascetic. He fell in battle against the Byzantines in AH 161 (AD 778). Ibrahīm b. Adham is considered one of the founders of Ṣūfism; he was suspected of heresy and arrested, but the people of Jerusalem hastened to the deputy governor of Tiberias (he seems to have had some authority in Jerusalem), and he released him. A collection of ḥadīths thought to have been taught by Ibrahīm b. Adham was assembled by Ibn Manda (who died in 1005). Other contemporaries who lived in Palestine, these in Ramla, were Khālid b. Yazīd and Sawwār b. 'Ammāra, the pupils of 'Abd al-Raḥmān al-Sindī. Abū Miqdām Rajā' b. Mihrān (who is Abū Salama) al-Filasṭīnī, Rajā' b. Ḥayawa's pupil, came to Palestine from Baṣra and lived in Ramla.[4]

[390] A central figure of the Abbasid government during the time of al-Manṣūr was a man who originally came from Palestine, Abū'l-Faḍl al-Rabī' b. Yūnus. He was a *mawlā* of a *mawlā*, of al-Ḥārith al-Ḥaffār, *mawlā* of the Caliph 'Uthmān b. 'Affān. Al-Rabī' served as *ḥājib*, head of the caliph's court, and was later his wazīr and confidant, and also served his heir, al-Mahdī, in the same fashion. When al-Manṣūr favoured someone who approached him, he would send him to al-Rabī'. His family came from the Galilee, where his grandfather was taken captive during the conquest of Palestine; evidently he was from a Christian family. The governor of jund Filasṭīn during al-Manṣūr's day was Abū Muḥammad 'Abd al-Ṣamad b. 'Alī b. 'Abdallah b. 'Abbās, the caliph's uncle.[5]

3. *A Jewish uprising (?)*

[391–392] A short time after Hārūn al-Rashīd ascended the caliph's throne, the insurrection of Yaḥyā b. Irmiyā (Jeremiah) the Jew broke out

[4] Thawr b. Yazīd (died AH 153/AD 770): Ibn Sa'd, VII(2), 170; Ibn Qutayba, *Ma'ārif*, 505; al-Bustī, 181 (No. 1438); Ibn al-Athīr, *Kāmil*, V, 611; Ibn 'Asākir, I, 310; according to whom he was thrown out of Ḥimṣ because of his opinions and he then moved to Jerusalem; Ibn Ḥajar, *Tahdhīb*, II, 33; 'Ulaymī, 255. Cf. the list of sources on him: Van Ess, *SI*, 31(1970), 273. 'Abdallah b. Shawdhib (died in AH 156/AD 773): Dhahabī, *'Ibar*, I, 225; Ibn Ḥajar, *Tahdhīb*, V, 255f. Ibrahīm b. Adham: *Sam'ānī*, II, 304f; Ibn Kathīr, *Bidāya*, X, 135–145; 'Ulaymī, 259, adds that his grave can be seen in Tripoli (of Syria; at the end of the fifteenth century); Sulamī, *Ṭabaqāt*, 13–22; cf. Goitein, *BJPES*, 12 (1945/6), 124; the article Ibrahīm b. Adham (by Russell Jones) in *EI²*. The collection of ḥadīths: Sezgin, I, 215 (No. 12). Khālid b. Yazīd and Sawwār b. 'Amāra: Dhahabī, *Ta'rīkh*, VI, 94; Rajā b. Mihrān (died in AH 161/AD 778): Ibn 'Asākir, V, 315; Ibn Ḥajar, *Tahdhīb*, III, 267.

[5] Al-Rabī' b. Yūnus, see: Ibn Khallikān, II, 294–299; he was called son of the ewe (Ibn Shāh) for his mother died when he was a baby and he was raised on lamb's milk; see also: Ṭabarī,

in Palestine, as I have already mentioned. According to Ibn 'Asākir (who describes him as a highwayman), Yaḥyā b. Irmiyā was a Jew from Trans-Jordan who had two collaborators from among the followers of the Umayyads. From this fact alone one can surmise that they were certainly not highway robbers but that it was an uprising. The two confederates surrendered to the governor of Damascus at the time, Hārūn al Rashīd's brother Ibrahīm, son of the Caliph al-Mahdī, and were pardoned, while the Jew remained intractable. He would not agree to convert to Islam, to pay the *jizya* or to surrender, even if the governor were to pay him 2,000 dinars annually. Finally, the forces sent by Ibrahīm under the command of al-Nu'mān, a *mawlā* of the Umayyads who had formerly been one of Yaḥyā's supporters in the uprising, overcame the rebels and Yaḥyā fell in battle. The source describes his proud bearing, for example that he refused to mount a horse which had been watered while negotiating with the governor, saying that he would not take anything from the Muslims, not even water for his horse.[6]

Information about this uprising, which can be found only in Ibn 'Asākir in a somewhat detailed account, seems to have reverberated in a Christian source describing the considerable destruction in Palestine as a result of the civil war in 788, in the days of the patriarch Elias (II), telling of the utter devastation of Bet Guvrin (Eleutheropolis), Ascalon, Gaza and Sariphaea. The St Chariton monastery was robbed and the Mar Saba monastery was attacked.[7]

4. *The war of the tribes*

[393] In 792–793, an unmitigated war was waged in Palestine by the Arab tribes; this was the war of the North (Muḍar or Nizār or Qays) against the South (Yaman). We know that at the head of the 'northerners'

Ta'rīkh, III, 457; cf. Khālidī, 101 (who has: *jabal al-khalīl* instead of *jabal al-jalīl*). 'Abd al-Ṣamad b. 'Alī: Ibn Qutayba, *Ma'ārif*, 374.

6 Ibn 'Asākir, II, 267f; Ibn Kathīr, *Bidāya*, X, 165, mentions only that in 174 (790) there was insurrection and troubles in al-Shām.

7 See the treatise of Stephen, a monk from Mar-Saba, in: *AA SS*, March, III, 167f. Archaeological evidence of the destruction of Bet Guvrin, see: Constantelos, *Byzantion*, 42(1972), 343f. Sariphea: perhaps Ṣarafa in southern Trans-Jordan, cf. Le Strange, *Palestine*, 531; but it seems more likely that it is Sarafand, Ṣerīfīn in Talmudic sources. See: Guérin, *Description*, I, 33f. It seems that in the wake of the rebellion the Abbasid rulers applied themselves to building projects in Palestine, as can be seen from the inscription in the pool in Ramla, which is dated Dhū'l-Ḥijja AH 172, May AD 789; the building was erected on the orders of the '*amīr* Dinār (?), *mawlā* of the Commander of the Believers', apparently referring by *amīr* to the governor of Ramla, i.e. jund Filasṭīn, and carried out by 'Abdān (?); see *Répertoire chronologique*, V, n. 53 (p. 189), cf. Van Berchem, *MIE*, 3(1900), 422 (I doubt whether the above readings are correct).

stood 'Āmir b. 'Umāra b. Khuraym al-Nā'im Abū'l-Haydhām al-Murrī. The war began because of a quarrel between a man of the Banū'l-Qayn who came to grind his wheat somewhere in southern Trans-Jordan (al-Balqā'), and stole watermelons and marrows from one of the 'southern' tribesmen (Lakhm or Judhām). Ibrahīm b. Ṣāliḥ, one of the caliph's relatives, who was in charge of affairs in al-Shām, especially in jund Filasṭīn, and his son and aide Isḥaq, were inclined in favour of the Yamanis. There was considerable bloodshed, for the tribes of jund Urdunn and the Golan also joined the struggle on the Yamanis' side. It was only after decisive intervention by the caliph and his brothers, that the strife was brought to an end and matters calmed down on 29 December 793.[8]

[394] In AH 180 (AD 796) however, the battles between the tribes broke out anew. Although nothing has been explicitly said on the matter, it seems that the northern tribes were the instigators of this war and that the spearhead of their attacks was directed not only against the Yamanis, but also against the Abbasid regime itself, and hence the rulers saw them as rebels in every respect. Hārūn al-Rashīd sent against them Ja'far b. Yaḥyā b. Khālid al-Barmakī, son of his all-powerful wazīr, at the head of a large and magnificent army. Ja'far put down the rebels with an iron hand and much blood was spilled. He appointed two men as his representatives: Ṣālih b. Sulaymān was to be in charge of southern Trans-Jordan (al-Balqā'), and 'Īsā b. al-'Akkī was to be in charge of al-Shām. The fact that he left a separate person in charge of the remainder of Trans-Jordan points to the probability that this area was the focus of the rebellion.

Hārūn al-Rashīd's strong man in Palestine until then had been Harthama b. A'yun of Khurāsān, who was governor of jund Filasṭīn, and who carried out difficult missions on his behalf, such as putting down the insurrection among the tribes in Egypt. He was also involved in political and military matters after he was transferred from his post in Palestine in 796, until his death on 1 August 816.[9]

[8] Ṭabarī, *Ta'rīkh*, III, 624f; Ibn al-Athīr, *Kāmil*, VI, 127–133; Ibn 'Asākir, VII, 176–193; Abū'l-Fidā', *Mukhtaṣar*, II, 13; Ibn Kathīr, *Bidāya*, X, 168; Ibn Khaldūn, *'Ibar*, III, 465. Ibrahīm b. Ṣāliḥ was the cousin of the caliph al-Mahdī, and also his son-in-law: he married al-'Abbāsa, the caliph's daughter after she had been married to another relative, Muḥammad b. Sulaymān; Ibrahīm had seniority as governor of jund Filasṭīn; al-Mahdī dismissed him in 780, but through the intervention of al-Mahdī's cousin on his mother's side, Yazīd b. al-Manṣūr, Ibrahīm was returned to his post; see: Ṭabarī, *Ta'rīkh*, III, 500; Ibn al-Athīr, *Kāmil*, VI, 61; Ibn Taghrī Bardī, II, 83; Ibn Ḥabīb, *Muḥabb.*, 61; Ibn al-Qifṭī, 217; Ibn Khaldūn, *'Ibar*, 450, 464. According to Ibn al-Athīr, *ibid.*, 113, the governor of Filasṭīn during Ibrahīm's absence, until 787, was Rawḥ b. Ḥātim, one of the central governing figures of the caliphate; this information is missing in Ṭabarī, and it seems that Ibn al-Athīr had another source for this. According to Ṭabarī, *ibid.*, Rawḥ died in AH 174, or AD 780, two years after he was deposed from his position.

[9] Ṭabarī, *Ta'rīkh*, III, 639ff; Ibn al-Athīr, *Kāmil*, VI, 151f; Ibn Kathīr, *Bidāya*, X, 175. Apparently the disturbances in Palestine were part of what was also happening elsewhere in

5. *The episode of Charlemagne*

[395] A chapter to which western scholars have given much attention is that of the relations between the Abbasid caliphate and the Frankish kingdom. This relationship is not mentioned in eastern sources at all and one is tempted to ask to what extent the western sources are faithful to events or whether they were not inclined to exaggerate. According to an anonymous chronicle which continued that of Fredegarius, this relationship had already begun in 762, in the days of al-Manṣūr and Pépin (Pippinus), Charlemagne's grandfather, who had sent a mission to Baghdad, which returned after a stay of three years together with a Muslim (*Sarracenorum*) mission bearing gifts from the caliph (*Amīr al-mu'minīn: Amormuni*). Pépin himself escorted the caliph's mission as far as the port of Marseilles, on their return journey, laden with his gifts for the caliph. Bréhier tried to explain this rapport against the background of increasingly hostile relations with Constantinople and a tightening of the link between the Franks and the Pope, which would have enabled the Muslims to see the Frankish kings as the representatives of the Christian world.[10]

[396] The sources contain greater details of a similar connection between Charlemagne and Hārūn al-Rashīd. The origins of these traditions can be found in the accounts of contemporaries or near-contemporaries. The monk Bernard, who visited Jerusalem shortly after the middle of the ninth century, mentions the hostel which Charlemagne built there, where any western pilgrim ('the Latins') is welcomed; the Church of St Mary, with its library established with Charlemagne's help as well; and the pious foundation with twelve dwellings, fields, vineyards and groves, in the Valley of Jehoshaphat (the Kidron Valley). It emerges (though it is not stated explicitly) that not only the hostel and the library but the church and its property also were the fruit of Charlemagne's generosity. The Byzantine emperor, Constantine VII (Porphyrogenitus), in his book on the administration of the empire, also tells of the considerable sums of money sent by Charlemagne to Palestine and the many monasteries he built there. The account of Bernard, who was an eye-witness, is supported by that of

the caliphate, particularly in the Mosul area and in Egypt; the rebellion of the al-Ḥawfiyya tribes (that is, the tribes of the eastern Delta and northern Sinai), who were mainly 'northerners'; Ṭabari, *ibid.*, 629, mentions Qays (which is a collective name for the 'northern' tribes) and Quḍā'a (a 'southern' tribe); see also: Ibn Kathīr, *ibid.*, 171. Harthama, see Ṭabarī, *ibid.*, 629f, 645 (governor of Ifrīqiyā); 667 (commander of al-Rashīd's personal guard, in 802); 712 (heading the annual raid into Byzantine territories, in 807); 713 (governor of Khurāsān); Khalīfa ibn Khayyāṭ, II, 495, 499, 503ff (on the side of al-Ma'mūn in his war against al-Amīn); 506ff (fought against Shiite insurgents in 815); Ibn al-Athīr, *Kāmil*, VI, 141; Ibn Taghrī Bardī, II, 88; Ibn Kathīr, *Bidāya*, 171; Ibn Khaldūn, '*Ibar*, III, 467; cf. the article Harthama b. A'yan (by C. Pellat) in *EI*².

10 See: Fredegarius, 192; cf. Riant, *MAIBL*, 31(2:1884), 153: *idem, AOL*, 1(1881), 11f, n. 8; Bréhier, *L'église*, 23.

another of Charlemagne's contemporaries, Eginhard (Einhard). In 797, Charlemagne sent a delegation of three men, the Jew Isaac (Isaac Judaeus), Lantfrid and Sigimund, to Aaron, 'king of the Persians'; i.e. to Hārūn al-Rashīd. Four years later, a delegation from al-Rashīd arrived at the port of Pisa, consisting of two men, one 'a Persian from the East' and the other on behalf of 'the Amir Abraham', most probably the governor representing al-Rashīd in North Africa, Ibrahīm ibn al-Aghlab, as it was said that he was the governor in the land of Africa – in Fossato, that is, Fās. Charlemagne invited them to appear before him, as he was then travelling in Italy. He learned from them that the only member of Charlemagne's mission who was still alive was Isaac the Jew and that he was about to return, bearing many gifts. From the year 807 we have more information on delegations going back and forth: Rodbertus, Charlemagne's envoy, died on his return journey from the East; 'Abdallah, sent by the 'king of the Persians' reached Charlemagne together with George and Felix, Jerusalem monks, envoys of the patriarch Thomas. George was a German and his real name was Egilbaldus, and he was prior of the monastery on the Mount of Olives. This delegation brought Charlemagne many valuable gifts which are described in detail in the chronicles, among them a clock (*horologium*). They remained with him in Aachen for some time and afterwards made their way back through Italy.

The pattern of these relationships is interwoven with that of Charlemagne and the Christians in Jerusalem. In 799, a Jerusalem monk sent by the patriarch came to Charlemagne with blessings and relics from the Holy Sepulchre. Charlemagne sent him back with Zachariah, one of the priests of his court, and the two were laden with gifts for the holy places. Zachariah returned from Jerusalem together with two monks, one from the monastery on the Mount of Olives and the other from Mar Saba, and they brought with them the blessings of the patriarch, the keys of the Holy Sepulchre, and keys of the city and the mount (?) as well as a flag. Alcuinus, the learned contemporary of Charlemagne, mentions in a letter he wrote in 801 to Gisla, Charlemagne's sister, his joy on the arrival of the delegation of monks from Jerusalem for the coronation of Charlemagne (a famous occasion, being his coronation by Pope Leo III as emperor of the Holy Roman Empire).

This information regarding the exchange of delegations is considered generally acceptable. The visits of the Jerusalem monks, envoys of the patriarch, and the journey of Zachariah to Jerusalem, are certainly reliable evidence of Charlemagne's connections with Jerusalem and confirmation of the account of the traveller Bernard which I have quoted above, concerning the buildings of the 'Latins' put up in Jerusalem on Charlemagne's initiative. However, in the following generation, we find the monk from St Gallen, Notker the Stammerer, who not only describes the connections but adds that 'the Persian king' that is, Hārūn al-Rashīd, called Charlemagne 'my brother' and that he would have been prepared to give him Palestine as patrimony, but feared that Charlemagne could not defend it from the barbarians, because of the distance. Nevertheless, he granted him the rights of possession (. . . *in eius potestatem*), and he, al-Rashīd, saw himself merely as Charlemagne's representative (. . . *advocatus eius ero super eam*). These are naturally fantasies of the writer. According to Notker, the links with Jerusalem continued into the day of his son and successor, Louis the Pious. He mentions that during the reign of both these rulers, a tax of one *denarius* (a coin introduced by Charlemagne, with *ca.* 1.7 grams of silver content) was levied on every household in the empire for the benefit of the Christians in Jerusalem, whose poverty cried out for help from the West. Indeed, mention of the order given by Charlemagne in 810 arranging the matter of donations to Jerusalem to be used for the restoration of 'God's churches', has been preserved.[11]

[397] The reports on the connections between Charlemagne and Hārūn al-Rashīd gradually assumed the proportions of a myth, at the heart of which stood Charlemagne's status *vis-à-vis* Jerusalem and its holy places. Towards the end of the eleventh century, the monk Benedictus recorded a story according to which Charlemagne went on a pilgrimage to Jerusalem and visited the Holy Sepulchre together with Hārūn al-Rashīd. He adorned everything in gold and Hārūn al-Rashīd then decided that all the places would be inscribed in Charlemagne's name and that he would have the rights of possession (*potestas eius*). The two returned together to Alexandria, and the brotherhood between the Arabs and the Franks rose sky-high, as if they were each other's flesh and blood.[12]

11 Bernard, in Tobler et Molinier, I, 314. See on the church of St Mary also below, in the chapter on the Christians. Constantinus Porphyrogenitus, *De administrando imperio* (Moravcsik), 108 (ch. xxvi) = ed. Bonn *(CSHB)* 1840, 115; *MPG*, 113, 228f; Eginhard: Einhardi *annales*, 186–189, 190, 194. See on Eginhard: Manitius, *Geschichte*, I, 639, 646f; Alcuinus' letter: Alcuini *epistolae*, 358 (No. 214). See: Monachi Sangallensis (= Notker Balbulus), *De gestis Karoli*, 752f; see on Notker: Manitius, *ibid.*, 354f; cf. on Notker's evidence also: Von Grunebaum, *Classical Islam*, 97f. See further: *Annales Iuvavenses maiores*, 87: Charlemagne arrives in *Iuvavum* (Salzburg) in 803 together with envoys from Jerusalem. Charlemagne's order on donations to Jerusalem: Caroli Magni *codex diplomaticus*, 328, *capitularia anni 810: ad Hierusalem propter ecclesias Dei restaurandas*.

12 Benedictus Monachus, *Chronicon*, *MGH* (SS), III, 710f (= *MPL* 139, 34f); see on the author of the chronicle: Baix et Jadin, in *DHGE*, VIII, 241; they note that Benedictus was the first to quote this story, and decide ('without a doubt') that he took it from a source that has been lost in the meantime (about which I am very doubtful). Benedictus' story was the nucleus from which the journey of Charlemagne to Jerusalem grew into folklore; see an English version of the story in Schlauch, *Medieval Narrative*, 77–101. The traditions from the chronicles of Eginhard and Notker were copied in later sources, such as William of Tyre, 14f (ch. iii); Enhardi Fuldensis *annales*, 352; Chronicon Moissiacense (which is

[398] In historical research, an element of scepticism began to emerge at a fairly early stage towards some of the sources in which the descriptions of the links between Charlemagne and the Christians of Jerusalem were viewed as highly exaggerated. Riant, for instance, in 1881, already voices the opinion that many of these sources are part of the myth of an alleged military campaign by Charlemagne to Palestine. This myth developed a long time after the Crusaders' campaigns, in the fifteenth and sixteenth centuries, and grew out of an inclination to view Charlemagne as the first of the Crusaders. Riant points to the apocryphal character of letters ascribed to John, patriarch of Jerusalem, and the Emperor Constantine V (Copronymus) and his son Leo IV (the Khazar), written to Charlemagne in the years 768–775, which contain an invitation to join in the liberation of the holy places. Below we shall find that there was no patriarch named John at the time. On the other hand, in 1926, Kleinclausz came out against the exaggerated criticism of the sources dealing with Charlemagne. He also touched on the problem of the absolute silence on the subject in Arab sources; in his opinion, this was not surprising because these sources scarcely dealt with the Christian world at all, not even with the eastern part, which was within their own vicinity. In his view, the connections between Charlemagne and the Caliphate are well accounted for by their mutual interests, and brought about mainly by the necessity to defend themselves from their common enemies: the Umayyad caliphs in Cordova and the Byzantines. The symbolic rights granted to Charlemagne by Hārūn al-Rashīd should not be seen as ceding the latter's sovereignty but principally as a guarantee of the security of the Christians in Palestine after the waves of persecution they had endured. In contrast to the reliable historic core in Eginhard, this scholar points to the extravagances in Notker and those who followed in his wake. In an article in 1928, Bréhier also tried to attack the extreme doubts regarding the sources on the episode, after his own views on Charlemagne's so-called 'protectorate' of the holy places in Jerusalem were criticised by Kleinclausz and Joranson. In this article, he defined the three factual contexts of the episode: (1) the persecution of the Christians that preceded these connections; (2) the exchange of missions (he enumerates them as being nine) between the Franks and the Caliphate for twenty years; and (3) the Frankish ('Latin') institutions which were established in Jerusalem at the beginning of the ninth century. In order to substantiate the validity of his comments, he made a detailed survey of the persecution of the Christians in the pre-Charlemagne period. I shall deal with this matter in the chapter on the Christians; but at this point another aspect of this relationship should be

Meissen-on-the-Oder), 305; in these three places, some of Eginhard's tale is repeated, and there are many similar instances.

mentioned, which has been ignored by those who saw in Charlemagne a kind of defender and protector of the Christians in Jerusalem in general. The truth is that the inner circles of the Church in the west, with the Pope at its core, whose views were represented by Charlemagne, were imbued with hatred towards those Christians with whom they differed on vital theological issues of historic significance, and constantly tied up with the secular political struggle between the Franks and the Byzantines. Hence there certainly could have been anti-Christian persecution in Jerusalem, while the Muslims gave preference to the Latins, who were also the enemies of the Byzantines as they were themselves. A third factor in the antagonism toward Byzantium and its ecclesiastic representatives in Palestine was the Jews, for whom Byzantium was Edom the Wicked. It is not unlikely, then, that Isaac the Jew took part in Charlemagne's delegation to Hārūn al-Rashīd not only because he could (possibly) act as interpreter, as some have believed, but perhaps also because the Jews were allied to the views and hopes of the two major parties in these contacts.[13]

6. *Muslim personalities in Palestine in the days of al-Mahdī, al-Hādī and Hārūn al-Rashīd*

[399] The central figure in the administration of al-Mahdī's day was the son of a converted Jew, a client of the Banū Ash'ar from Tiberias, Abū 'Abdallah Mu'āwiya b. Yāshār (in the Arabic source: Yashār; and there are versions of his father's name: Yasār, and: 'Ubaydallah; it seems that his father, Yāshār, received the name 'Ubaydallah when he converted to Islam), who was born in 718. He was evidently the first to instil new contents and significance in the office of wazīr, by personally taking on the management of most of the kingdom's affairs, especially its taxes, and he is also believed to have introduced reforms in the system of taxation. Due to his honesty, he evidently made many enemies, a fact which led to his son Muḥammad (another version: 'Abdallah) being accused of heresy (the claim that he was a *zindīq*; i.e. a Manichaean, and perhaps this was the truth). Al-Mahdī ordered Mu'āwiya to kill his son by his own hand, and as

13 Among the first researchers who dealt with the connection between Charlemagne and the Caliphate, and the matter of Jerusalem, see: Tobler, *Golgatha*, 111; Riant, *AOL*, I(1881), 9–13; see further Berlière, *Revue benedictine*, 5(1888), 440ff. Riant, *MAIBL*, 31(2, 1884), 155f; Vincent et Abel, *Jérusalem* II(2), 938; Baumstark *Palästinapilger*, 29f assumed that Charlemagne had to put up buildings for the use of pilgrims from the West (the Latins) because the Nea, which had all the services needed by the pilgrims, had been taken by the Muslims (which is evidently incorrect, see below the discussion on the Nea); Kleinclausz, *Syria*, 7(1926), 212–233; see the bibliography and comprehensive discussion in Joranson, *AHR*, 32:241, 1927; interpretation of the sources: Bréhier, *L'église*, 25ff; he stresses the fact that the initiative to establish connections came from the Franks and not from the caliph. See his article in *RH*, 157:277, 1928; see an additional summary of the sources and the discussions in research: Runciman, *EHR*, 50:606, 1935; see also Musca, *Carlo Magno*, 43f.

he was incapable of doing so, he ordered the son to be killed in his father's presence and even forced the father to engage in writing for the caliph with his son's corpse lying nearby. According to al-Jahshiyārī, the son Muḥammad was found to be a *zindīq* when al-Mahdī commanded him to quote something from the Koran, and he said: 'You are blessed, as are Your worlds, thanks to the magnificence of what you have created'. According to Ṭabarī, Mu'awiya included a passage from the Koran in his testament, iii:19, which says that knowledge is the cause of divisions between the Peoples of the Book. Mu'āwiya was very learned in matters of tradition and literature, and he is attributed with having produced a book on taxes entitled *kitāb al-kharāj*, which was the first of its kind. According to Ṭabarī, he was ousted from his position by al-Mahdī in AH 167 (AD 783/4). He died in AH 169 or 170 (AD 785/6 or 786/7).[14]

[400] During the same period in Ascalon, there lived another descendant of Jews who had converted to Islam, Abū Ghassān Muḥammad b. Muṭarrif b. Da'ūd al-Laythī, who came from Medina and settled in Palestine. He corresponded with a famous Muslim scholar, Mālik b. Anas. Some say that he was one of the descendants of those who converted and were taken under the aegis of Caliph 'Umar ibn al-Khaṭṭāb's family. It is also said that he hailed from Wādī'l-Qurā, the well-known Jewish region in northern Ḥijāz, on the Palestinian border. It is known that during al-Mahdī's time, he lived in Baghdad. He died in AH 170, that is, AD 786/7.[15]

[401–402] In the neighbourhood of Nābulus, in the village of 'Aqraba, there lived one of the retainers of al-Shāfi'ī (founder of the famous legal school called after him), Shihāb al-Dīn Aḥmad al-'Aqrabānī, of Egypt; he died in 'Aqraba in AH 180 (AD 796/7). Al-Walīd b. Muḥammad al-Muwaqqarī al-Balqāwī, of the stronghold of al-Muwaqqar in southern Trans-Jordan (al-Balqā') was a pupil of al-Zuhrī; he died in AH 182 (AD 798).[16] Abū 'Alī (or Abū 'Abdallah) 'Abd al-Raḥmān b. al-Qāsim al-'Utaqī was the pupil of Mālik b. Anas for twenty years; he was one of the

[14] Mas'ūdī, *Tanbīh*, 343; Ṭabarī, *Ta'rīkh*, III, 487: he was hated by the non-Muslims (the *mawālī*) and did everything he could to keep them away from al-Mahdī. On his Jewishness: *ibid.*, 490, which also contains the story of the killing of his son Muḥammad, on al-Mahdī's order, on the accusation of heresy. See further: Ibn Ṭiqṭaqā, *al-Fakhrī*, 246–250; *al-'uyūn wa'l-ḥadā'iq*, 281; Ibn al-Athīr, *Kāmil*, VI, 75, 79; al-Khaṭīb al-Baghdādī, *Ta'rīkh*, XIII, 196f. Jahshiyārī, 102–118, and see the saying on p. 113, *tabārak wa-'ālamūka bi-'uẓmi'l-khalqi*, sounds like a metamorphosis of a version of a Jewish prayer. Vajda, *RSO*, 17(1937/8), 187ff, did not notice that Mu'āwiya was of Jewish extraction; see there additional sources; his tentative translation: *sois béni (ou tu es béni) ainsi que tes mondes par la grandeur de la création*. The testament: Ṭabarī, *ibid.*, III, 532; see also: Ibn Khallikān, VI, 21, 26. Ya'qūbi, *Ta'rīkh*, II, 482f; *Aghānī*, III, 153f; cf. Moscati, *Orientalia*, NS 15(1946), 162ff; the article Abū 'Ubayd Allah (by S. Moscati), in *EI*²; Sezgin, 519.

[15] Khazrajī, 307; *'Iyāḍ*, I, 298; Ṣafadī, al-*Wāfī*, V, 34; Bustī, 181 (No. 1431); Ibn Ḥajar, *Tahdhīb*, IX, 461f.

[16] Khālidī, 169,

descendants of the slaves in Ṭā'if who were freed by the Prophet. He lived in Ramla and afterwards in Egypt and died in Ṣafar, AH 191 (December AD 806).[17]

[403–408] Abū Mas'ūd Ayyūb b. Suwayd al-Shaybānī al-Ḥimyarī, who came from southern Arabia, lived in Ramla. He was the pupil of the scholar of Eilat, the aforementioned Yūnus b. Yazīd. The orthodox Islamic scholars of later generations accused him of inventing ḥadīths and of attributing to himself ḥadīths taught by others. He drowned off the coast of Palestine after returning from a pilgrimage to Mecca, in AH 193 (AD 809).[18] Abū 'Uthmān 'Anbasa b. Khālid b. Yazīd b. Abī'l-Najjād was a man of Eilat, nephew of the above mentioned Yūnus b. Yazīd, who was also a *mawlā* of the Umayyads, and he died in Jumādā I, AH 198 (January AD 814).[19] Abū Sufyān Wakī' b. al-Jarrāḥ b. Malīḥ al-Rawāsī was a native of the Naysābūr region; some say that he was born in Sughd (the Sogdiana in central Asia). He was one of the important scholars in Kūfa and it was noted that he never held a book during his lessons thanks to his excellent memory. He was a money-changer (*jahbadh*) by profession, and out of sheer modesty, refused to accept the post of cadi when it was offered to him. Towards the end of his life, he lived in Jerusalem and died in '*Āshūrā* (10th of Muḥarram) in the year AH 197 (20 September AD 812), after returning from a pilgrimage to Mecca. He wrote several books, among them a *muṣannaf*, a collection of ḥadīths, which has been lost.[20] Al-Kindī mentions three people from Ḥaḍramawt in the southern part of the Arabian peninsula who were appointed cadis in jund Filasṭīn during the period we are dealing with: Ḍamḍam b. 'Uqba, 'Abd al-Salām ibn 'Abdallah and al-Nu'mān b. Mundhir.[21] Abū Zakarīyā' Yaḥyā b. 'Īsā b. 'Abd al-Raḥmān al-Nahshalī, of Ramla, was born in Kūfa and kept up his contacts with the area, dealing in the export of oil from Palestine to Kūfa and elsewhere (the Nahshal being a large clan of the Banū Tamīm). He died in AH 201 (AD 817).[22] Abū 'Abdallah Ḍamra b. Rabī'a al-Qurashī was also from Ramla, son of a family of Damascene converts to Islam. He

17 Ibn Khallikān, III, 129; '*Iyāḍ*, I, 433; Ibn al-Athīr, *Lubāb*, II, 120; Suyūṭī, *Muḥāḍara*, I, 303; Ibn Ḥajar, *Tahdhīb*, VI, 252f. Cf. Brockelmann, *GAL*, S I, 299.

18 Sam'ānī, *Ansāb*, VI, 170; Ibn Ḥajar, *Tahdhīb*, 405f.

19 Sam'ānī, *ibid.*, I, 410; Ibn Ḥajar, *ibid.*, VII, 154.

20 Ibn Sa'd, VI, 275; al-Khaṭīb al-Baghdādī, *Ta'rīkh*, XIII, 466–481 (on p. 475: he was a *jahbadh*); Ibn Ḥajar, *Tahdhīb*, XI, 123–131; 'Ulaymī, 260; cf. Sezgin, I, 96f, and additional references there.

21 Kindī, 425. 'Abd al-Salām b. 'Abdallah is the unidentified 'Ábd al-Salām mentioned by El'ad, *Cathedra*, 24(1981/2), 37, in connection with the sources on the markets of Jerusalem. It is he who was ordered by the caliph al-Mahdī to erect a bench in the pavilion of the Dome of the Rock.

22 Sam'ānī, VI, 170; Dhahabī, '*Ibar*, I, 337; Ibn al-'Imād, II, 3; Khazrajī, 366f; Ibn Ḥajar, *Tahdhīb*, XI, 262f.

was a known expert in legal affairs and died in Ramaḍān AH 201 (March AD 817).[23]

[409] I have yet to mention one of the greatest Muslim scholars of all times, namely Abū 'Abdallah Muḥammad b. Idrīs al-Shāfi'ī. He was a Palestinian, born in Gaza (though information on his place of birth is conflicting; some say Ascalon, while others say Yaman, for example). When he was but a child, he moved with his mother to Mecca. He visited Jerusalem as an adult, and died on the last day of Ṣafar AH 204, that is the 25th of August AD 819.[24]

7. *The uprisings of the years 807–810*

[410] In 807, rebellion broke out in Eilat, in southern Palestine, led by a man named Abū'l-Nidā'. Hārūn al-Rashīd sent an army against him under the command of Yaḥyā b. Mu'ādh. In the following year, Abū'l-Nidā' was caught and brought to Raqqa in northern Syria, where the caliph was encamped at the time, and was executed on the caliph's orders. According to Ibn Taghrī Bardī, the uprising was caused by matters connected with the *kharāj*, that is, land taxes. Perhaps this fact should indicate that this was a non-Muslim rebellion as it was on non-Muslims that such taxes were imposed. The centre of the uprising was in Eilat. The rebels closed off the roads and took possession of the 'Arāvā area (Madyan) and also invaded the rural areas farther north. The Banū Judhām then joined the rebels and the situation became serious. Abū'l-Nidā' is described in this source as a highway robber and it was said that he accumulated considerable wealth from the spoils. The army sent against him from Iraq was joined by units from Egypt, under the command of its governor al-Ḥusayn b. Jamīl. We are told by the Samaritan chronicler Abū'l-Fatḥ ibn Abī'l-Ḥasan that at about the same time, after the year 5239 of the Samaritan calendar, which is AD 807, the Samaritans were persecuted and their synagogues burned in Zaytā, Sālim and Arsūf; however it seems that this maltreatment of the Samaritans occurred after the death of Hārūn al-Rashīd, in the days of al-Amīn, and its background is not clear. Very severe disturbances took place in Palestine in 809. This time it was the people of Ramla (it seems that the source wanted to say the Bedouin tribes in jund Filasṭīn, of which Ramla was the capital) who attacked the caravan which carried the collection of the *kharāj* from Egypt to Iraq and absconded with all the money. The roads were again blocked to such an extent, that the governor of Egypt, who was called to appear in Baghdad, was forced to make his way

[23] Ibn 'Asākir, VII, 36f; Dhahabī, '*Ibar*, I, 337; Ibn Ḥajar, *Tahdhīb*, IV, 460f.

[24] See al-Khaṭīb al-Baghdādī, *Ta'rīkh*, II, 56; Dhahabī, '*Ibar*, I, 343; Ibn al-Athīr, *Lubāb*, II, 5; Ibn Khallikān, IV, 165; Ibn al-'Imād, II, 9; Ibn Ḥajar, *Tahdhīb*, IX, 25ff; 'Ulaymī, 260f; cf. Sezgin, I, 484–490.

through the Ḥijāz. To judge by Theophanes' description, this was a real civil war which lasted for five years. Indeed, one should remember that these rebellions in Palestine took place near the end of Hārūn al-Rashīd's life and continued during the caliphate of Muḥammad al-Amīn, which was actually a period of fratricidal war between al-Amīn and his brother al-Ma'mūn. The account of *al-'uyūn wa'l-ḥadā'iq*, says that local leaders sprung up who turned against the central government. Ramla was ruled by a certain Ibn Sarḥ (or Ibn Sharḥ). The insurrections were accompanied by abuse and aggression towards the Christians, which I shall discuss below in the chapter on the Christians; and as already stated, towards the Samaritans as well. According to Bar Hebraeus, the rebels were led by a man called 'Umar (and he is possibly the same aforementioned Abū'l-Nidā'), who in 1121 Sel., which is AD 810, gathered together a band of robbers and began to attack, kill and rob wayfarers on the roads in Palestine. In all, it is difficult to define the exact nature of these events, which lasted, as we have seen, for at least three years. It seems that the rebellion of the non-Muslim rural population was interwoven with the uprising of the tribes, whereas during the final stages there may have been some link between what was happening in Palestine and the war waged between the brothers al-Amīn and al-Ma'mūn for the throne. Within this framework, the non-Muslim inhabitants suffered from severe acts of persecution and abuse, and particularly the destruction of their houses of prayer. (The sources mention churches and Samaritan synagogues, but one can assume that the Jews were also affected.)

It is also possible that at that final stage, there was a connection between the events in Palestine and the Sufyānī (named after Abū Sufyān, head of the Umayyad clan who lived in the Prophet's time) anti-Abbasid uprising, with its (Muslim) Messianic colouring. The centre of the uprising was Damascus and it was headed by 'Alī b. 'Abdallah b. Khālid b. Yazīd b. Mu'āwiya. It began in Dhū'l-Ḥijja AH 195, that is, September AD 811. The rebels expelled the Abbasid governor Sulaymān b. Abū Ja'far (the son of the caliph al-Manṣūr) from Damascus. Abbasid reinforcements sent to Damascus did not arrive because of the war between al-Amīn and al-Ma'mūn. Apparently the major supporters of that rebellion were the Banū Quḍā'a, which one can assume from a remark attributed to al-Ma'mūn. The mother of 'Alī b. 'Abdallah was Nafīsa b. 'Ubaydallah, a descendant of 'Alī b. Abī Ṭālib, and he pretended to be the representative of both houses, that of the Umayyads and that of the 'Alids. He was known as Abū'l-'Umayṭar. He had supporters in Sidon, led by Khaṭṭāb, son of the converted client (*mawlā*) of the Umayyads, Wajh al-Fuls, and they took control of the city. It was said that the leader, Abū 'Umayṭar, was aged 90 at the time of the rebellion. He was supported by the 'southern' tribes

(Kalb, and I have already mentioned Quḍā'a) and he endeavoured to attract the 'northerners' (Qays) as well, but did not succeed, and battles ensued between the two camps. The 'southerners' suffered severe losses and despite the desperate efforts of al-Qāsim, son of the rebellion's leader, they were beaten. Al-Qāsim fell in battle and his head was sent to al-Amīn. In Muḥarram AH 198 (September AD 813), the 'northerners' achieved their final victory and the 'Sufyānī' was forced to flee from Damascus in the guise of a woman. Shortly afterwards, the army of the victorious caliph, al-Ma'mūn, entered the city.[25]

The days of al-Ma'mūn and his successors

[411] The uprisings of the 'northerners' continued during the days of al-Ma'mūn and this time they were headed by Naṣr b. Shabath (or Naṣr b. Sayyār b. Shabath) of the Banū 'Uqayl, based in Kaysūm in northern Syria (to the north of Aleppo). He succeeded in maintaining his stand against the caliph's army for eleven years, from AH 198 until AH 209, that is, from AD 813 to 825/6. According to the Samaritan chronicler Abū'l-Fatḥ, the rebels caused the Samaritans much suffering, and it would appear that this was due to their loyalty to al-Ma'mūn. While the rebels were abusing the Samaritans and trying to convert them to Islam (leading the rebels in this pursuit was a certain Abū Firāsa), the army, under the command of 'Abdallah ibn Ṭāhir, was defending them. Abū'l-Fatḥ also states that the insurgents murdered the governor of Jericho and, in his words, the caliph himself came to Palestine with an armed force to subdue them (which is naturally not true). Ibrāhīm, the caliph's brother, took Bet Guvrin from the rebels and captured their leaders. The chronicler adds that after putting down the rebellion, there followed a period during which the severest of taxes were imposed on the Samaritans by the governor, Abū'l-Jārūd, (which is not known from any other source). During the period of al-Mu'taṣim's rule (833–842) the Samaritans' situation again deteriorated and there were riots against them in Nābulus and the synagogues of 'the Samaritans and the Dositheans' were burnt down.[26]

[25] Ṭabarī, *Ta'rīkh*, III, 711, 732; Ibn al-Athīr, *Kāmil*, VI, 205, 208. *Al-'uyūn wa'l-ḥadā'iq*, 363. Ibn Taghrī Bardī, II, 135, 141. Abū'l-Fatḥ, LXXX; Theophanes, I, 484 (cf. Breyer, 148); Bar Hebraeus (Bedjan), 135; cf. the translation (Budge), 124; cf. Wüstenfeld, *Statthalter*, II, 26. On the events of 811, see: Ṭabarī, *Ta'rīkh*, III, 830; Ibn al-Athīr, *Kāmil*, VI, 249f; 432 (the saying of al-Ma'mūn); see also a short account in Ya'qūbī, *Ta'rīkh*, II, 532. 'Alī b. 'Abdallah's nickname was given to him since he asked his council, what was the *kunya* of the lizard; he was the only one who knew the answer: Abū 'Umayṭar, and since then he was given this nickname.

[26] See Ṭabarī, *Ta'rīkh*, III, 845, 1067–1073; Ibn al-Athīr, *Kāmil*, VI, 297, 388–391; Abū'l-Fatḥ, LXXXf. In fact, heavy taxes were evidently imposed on the Samaritans even before this; according to Balādhurī, *Futūḥ*, 158, the caliph Yazīd (Mu'āwiya's son) levied *kharāj* on the lands belonging to the Samaritans in jund Urdunn and jund Filasṭīn and every man

[412–413] Apparently during Hārūn al-Rashīd's day and subsequently as well, the Baghdad rulers governed Palestine with an iron hand (and this applied also to other regions) in all matters relating to taxation. This leads one to understand al-Ma'mūn's interest in measurements. In his time, the degree of longitude (*dawr al-arḍ*, the circumference of the earth) was calculated and maps were drawn up. Perhaps this is what the midrash written in the Middle Ages was speaking of, when it says of the kingdom of Ishmael, that as it has come, 'they will measure the land with ropes, for it is said: and shall divide the land for gain (Dan., xi:39). And they turn graveyards into pasture for sheep and places for refuse'.[27]

In the days of al-Ma'mūn, evidently in 814, Palestine suffered from a period of severe hunger due to a plague of locusts. According to Sa'īd ibn Biṭrīq, this brought about a very serious decline in the number of Muslims in Palestine, 'so that only a few of them remained'.[28]

[414] The information at our disposal about what went on in Palestine during the days of al-Ma'mūn and his successor, al-Mu'taṣim, is rather scanty. At the outset of the caliphate of al-Wāthiq (842–847), a widespread rebellion broke out in Palestine; this was the rebellion of Abū Ḥarb Tamīm, called al-Mubarqa' (the veiled). Arab tribes and farmers from the south of Palestine took part in this uprising and their leader was said to be a 'Yamānī', that is, belonging to one of 'the tribes of the south', which was the Banū Lakhm in this case. The initial cause of the rebellion was said to have been a personal quarrel between Abū Ḥarb and one of the soldiers of the caliphate who wanted to enter Abū Ḥarb's house in his absence. Abū Ḥarb's wife (some say his sister) tried to prevent him from entering and the soldier then beat her with his whip. When Abū Ḥarb returned home, saw the whip-lash on his wife's arm, and heard an account of what had occurred, he went out to seek the assailant. When he found him, he slashed him with his sword. Afterwards he fled to 'one of the mountains of Urdunn', covering his face with a veil lest he be recognised. Then a number of farmers and villagers from the neighbourhood joined him and

was obliged to pay two dinars in Urdunn, while in Filasṭīn – five; cf.: Lammens, *Yazīd*, 391. In al-Mutawakkil's time, the tax in jund Filasṭīn was decreased to three dinars. It is difficult to understand what was behind this attitude of discriminating against the Samaritans; according to Balādhurī, *ibid.* (he notes that there are two types of Samaritans: *Dastān* and *Kūshān*), Hārūn al-Rashīd turned the Samaritan-owned land, after a terrible plague that devastated their country, into state-owned land. Balādhurī is referring to the Nābulus area. As to Ibrahīm, he evidently means Ibrahīm b. Muḥammad al-Mahdī, Hārūn al-Rashīd's brother.

27 The measurement, see: Abū'l-Fidā', *Taqwīm al-buldān*, 14. Maps: Mas'ūdī, *Tanbīh*, 33. The midrash, see the 'Mysteries of R. Shimon Bar Yoḥai', in Jellinek, *Beit ha-midrash*, III, 78f; Wertheimer, *Battē Midrāshōt*, II, 507; see a similar version in the Pirqē R. Eliezer, ch. xxx, cf. Chwolsohn, *Ssabier*, I, 98, n. 4, who was the first to notice this parallel.

28 Sa'īd ibn Biṭrīq, II, 55; Papadopoulos-Kerameos, *Analekta*, III, 4; Abū'l-Fatḥ, LXXX (and here the year is: 198 of the hijra, AD 813/4).

he preached to them the doctrine of doing good and refraining from evil, out of which the rumour spread that he was the Sufyānī, that is, the Messiah awaited by the followers of the Umayyads. Afterwards, a number of notables of the tribes, especially from the 'southern' tribes, together with their leader Ibn Bayhas and two important Damascenes, linked up with him. The caliph al-Mu'taṣim sent some thousand men under the command of Rajā' b. Ayyūb against him, but Abū Ḥarb's forces were infinitely superior and Rajā' preferred to wait. Indeed, when ploughing time came around, each of the farmers returned to his land and few remained behind with Abū Ḥarb. At that point, the Abbasid army prepared for battle. Abū Ḥarb attacked and the army retreated. He attacked again and again the army withdrew, but according to a pre-arranged plan, they succeeded in separating Abū Ḥarb from his men. He was caught and brought to the caliph, as were the other leaders of the rebellion. The Samaritan chronicler Abū'l-Fatḥ has additional details: Abū Ḥarb conquered Nābulus and caused its inhabitants to flee; the Samaritan high priest was injured while escaping to Hebron and died of his wounds. According to the Syriac sources, Abū Ḥarb overtook Jerusalem and there, too, brought about the evacuation of all the inhabitants – Muslims, Christians and Jews. He robbed the mosques and the churches and was about to set fire to the Church of the Holy Sepulchre, but was dissuaded from doing so in exchange for a large payment of gold sent him by the patriarch.[29]

[415] In al-Mutawakkil's day (847–861) an event occurred, which though geographically removed from Palestine, was certainly felt there and undoubtedly made an impression on its inhabitants; this was the uprising of the Christians in Ḥimṣ. This rebellion broke out in Jumādā AH 241 (October AD 855). All the indications suggest that taxation was the immediate cause of the uprising, which according to Ṭabarī, was directed against the man in charge of supplies. He was a Persian, as can be seen from his name, Muḥammad b. 'Abdawayh. The caliph ordered the rebellion to

[29] Ya'qūbī, *Ta'rīkh*, II, 586; Ṭabarī, *Ta'rīkh*, III, 1319–1322; there may have been some confusion between this rebellion and the rebellion during the days of al-Ma'mūn (above), see in Ṭabarī, *ibid.*, 1908, in note i, a version saying that 'Abdallah b. Ṭāhir brought Ibn Bayhas (other versions: Ibn Abī'l-Ṣaqar; Ibn Abī Asqar; Ibn Abī Ashqar 'the redhead') as captive to al-Ma'mūn in AH 211, i.e. AD 826; Ibn al-Athīr, *Kāmil*, VI, 522f; Ibn Taghrī Bardī, II, 248f; Ibn Kathīr, *Bidāya*, X, 295; Sibṭ Ibn al-Jawzī (BM Or 4618), under the year AH 227; Tha'ālibī, *Laṭā'if*, 142 (includes Abū Ḥarb among the four who killed more than a hundred thousand men, together with: al-Ḥajjāj b. Yūsuf, Abū Muslim, Bābak); Ibn Khaldūn, '*Ibar*, III, 572; Abū'l-Fatḥ, LXXXII: according to him the rebellion put an end to a period of peace and prosperity among the Samaritans, when Pinḥas b. Nethanel and Dartha repaired the synagogue in Nābulus, and this was a time when the division between the Samaritans and the Dositheans became much deeper. See on the rebellion in Syriac sources as well: Michael the Syrian, III, 103; Bar Hebraeus (Bedjan), 152; (Budge), 139. Despite the addendum on Jerusalem, it seems that the Syriac, as well as the Muslim writers, took their information from Ṭabarī; cf. Goitein, *Yerushalayim*, 1952/3, 93.

be suppressed in the cruellest manner, to burn all the churches, to expel all the Christians from the city and to execute the leaders by whipping and crucifying. The subduing of the rebellion was carried out by an army sent from Damascus and led by the Turk Ṣāliḥ, and by additional forces sent from Ramla. The major source, Ṭabarī, inclines one to believe that many Christians resided in Ḥimṣ at the time and that this population was completely wiped out.[30]

[416] We hear about earthquakes throughout the caliphate in the years AH 242 (AD 856/7) and AH 245 (AD 859/60). According to Ṭabarī, the first province to be affected was principally Khurāsān, and this was in Sha'bān, that is, December 856 or January 857. The number of dead reached 45,096 souls and the afflicted were mainly in the Qūmis region and its major city, Dāmghān. (The geographer Muqaddasī's grandfather on his mother's side as well as the Karaite leader Daniel al-Qūmisī were natives of this place. We may perhaps find in this event a possible explanation for their leaving the place and settling in Jerusalem, apart from Daniel's clear ideological motivation, which will be discussed.) Ibn Kathīr says that the earthquake also reached al-Shām (Syria and Palestine), but we have no further details on this occurrence. Another earthquake hit the Maghrib, according to Ṭabarī, but there were also earthquakes in Baghdad, in Syria (Antioch, Lādhiqiyya, Ṭarsūs and elsewhere), and in Egypt, especially in Bilbays.[31]

The Abbasid caliphs and Jerusalem

[417] A ḥadīth attributed to the Prophet by his retainer Abū Hurayra says: 'Black flags will go out of Khurāsān and nothing shall thwart them until they are firmly hoisted in Iliyā' (Jerusalem). Naturally, this saying was devised at the outset of Abbasid rule, as black was the Abbasid colour. There is certainly some special symbolic significance in the choice of Jerusalem as the goal of their war, perhaps because it was considered the most sacred place in al-Shām, the power-base of Umayyad rule.

Al-Manṣūr, as soon as he had established his sovereignty, found it imperative to visit Jerusalem and pray in the mosque there, on his return from his pilgrimage to Mecca in 141, that is (September) 758. Thirteen years later, in AH 154 (AD 771), he made a special visit to Jerusalem while passing through al-Shām. According to Wāsiṭī, on his first visit, he had

30 Ṭabarī, *Ta'rīkh*, III, 1422f; Ibn al-Athīr, *Kāmil*, VII, 76; Sibṭ Ibn al-Jawzī (BM Or 4618), under the year 241 (fol. 112a).

31 Ṭabarī, *Ta'rīkh*, III, 1433, 1439; Ibn al-Athīr, *Kāmil*, VII, 81, 87; Ibn Kathīr, *Bidāya*, X, 343; cf. Wüstenfeld, *Statthalter*, II, 56.

ordered the renovation of the Dome of the Rock, which had collapsed during the earthquake in the year AH 130.[32]

[418] Al-Mahdī also visited Jerusalem, in AH 163, that is AD 780, with a large family party: 'Abbās b. Muḥammad, Faḍl b. Ṣāliḥ, 'Alī b. Sulaymān and Yazīd b. al-Manṣūr (Al-Mahdī's brother). This visit was made at the height of fierce and constant warring with the Byzantines, in which the Muslims were at first having the worse of it but which ended with a decided victory on their part. At the time of al-Mahdī's visit to Jerusalem, the caliphal army, under the command of his son Hārūn, were pressing westward through Aleppo to attack the Byzantines, and this was the first move in the Muslims' favour. Poliak's view was that al-Mahdī's visit to Jerusalem had a definitely symbolic-religious meaning – that of the Messiah visiting Jerusalem – just as the names of this caliph had a genuinely theological significance: Muḥammad b. 'Abdallah (like that of the Prophet and his father) al-Mahdī ('the Messiah').[33]

[419] Nothing is said in any source of al-Ma'mūn having visited Jerusalem. As we know, his name was entered in an inscription in the Dome of the Rock in place of that of 'Abd al-Malik, in Rabī' II AH 216, that is May/June AD 831. The alteration in the inscription was made by Ṣāliḥ b. Yaḥyā, who called himself a *mawlā* of the caliph (*amīr al-mu'minīn*), at the time when Abū Isḥaq, that is Muḥammad the brother of al-Ma'mūn, was governor of Egypt and al-Shām. It is known that al-Ma'mūn left Baghdad

[32] See the ḥadīth in Tirmidhī, *Sunan, abwāb al-fitan*, end (in the Medina edition: III, 362, No. 2371); Ibn Kathīr, *Shamā'il*, 477 (attributing it to Aḥmad Ibn Ḥanbal); Suyūṭī, *Khaṣā'iṣ*, II, 431; *idem, Ta'rīkh*, 216 (attributing it to a converted Jew named Joseph). Al-Manṣūr in Jerusalem: Ṭabarī, *Ta'rīkh*, III, 128f, 372; Ibn al-Athīr, *Kāmil*, V, 500, 612; Ibn Taghrī Bardī, I, 336f; II, 21; Dhahabī, *Ta'rīkh*, V, 222; VI, 160; Yāfi'ī, 323; Ibn Kathīr, *Bidāya*, X, 75, 111; Wāsiṭī, 84; Ibn Khallikān, VI, 322; Elias of Nisibis, under the years 141, 153.

[33] 'Alī b. Sulaymān and Faḍl b. Ṣāliḥ were afterwards governors in Egypt; 'Abbās b. Muḥammad was later on governor in Mecca. See on the visit: Ṭabarī, *Ta'rīkh*, III, 500; Ibn al-Athīr, *Kāmil*, IV, 61; Ibn Taghrī Bardī, II, 45; Iṣbahānī, *Aghānī*, VI, 67; Wāsiṭī, 84 – who says that al-Mahdī, like al-Manṣūr, ordered the Dome of the Rock to be renovated, when he was in Jerusalem, for it was destroyed again during an earthquake; but we do not know of any earthquake that occurred between these two visits, and it seems to be Wāsiṭī's invention. According to him, the *kanīsa* was also destroyed then and it seems that he is referring to the Church of the Holy Sepulchre; Azdī, *Ta'rīkh Mawṣil*, 243f; cf. Muir, 470f; Vasiliev, *History*, 238; see Theophanes, 452, and cf. Breyer, 105; see Poliak, *Dinaburg Jubilee Volume*, 177; Elias of Nisibis, under the year AH 163, notes that Hārūn, the son of the caliph (who afterwards became caliph, al-Rashīd) visited Jerusalem then. See also: 'Ulaymī, 250. Additional references on this matter are included in the editor's note in Wāsiṭī, p. 84; see Muqaddasī, *Āqālīm*, 168; Le Strange, *Palestine*, 92; Le Strange attributes the tradition on the renovation work to the al-Aqṣā mosque, while Wāsiṭī speaks specifically of the Dome of the Rock. In favour of Le Strange's claims is the fact that al-Mahdī is said to have ordered the cutting of the length of the mosque and to add to its width, which is more suited to al-Aqṣā. Moreover, Muqaddasī points out that it was the al-Aqṣā that was damaged by the earthquake during the Abbasid period. Therefore it is reasonable to assume that it was in need of renovation. In my opinion, it is most likely that the traditions refer to both mosques.

at the beginning of AH 215, that is, in the early spring of AD 830, with the intention of leading the campaign against the Byzantines. He then made a pilgrimage to Mecca, and in the middle of Jumādā I, that is, June AD 830, launched an offensive against the Byzantines in Asia Minor. While his army was to the fore in battle, al-Ma'mūn made his way to Damascus. In June 831, he again attacked the Byzantines and remained with the army until the middle of Sha'bān AH 216, that is, until October AD 831, and then returned to Damascus. Hence the fabrication of the inscription apparently occurred between these two campaigns, while al-Ma'mūn was staying in Damascus, and it is reasonable to assume that he personally visited Jerusalem at this time.[34]

The sixties of the ninth century

[420–421] In July 850, Caliph al-Mutawakkil divided the caliphate rule between his three sons. Palestine was one of the countries that fell to the share of Ibrahīm, known as al-Mu'ayyad; we have no particulars as to what occurred in Palestine during his reign.[35]

In al-Musta'īn's day (862–866) there were tribal uprisings in Palestine. According to Ya'qūbī, rebellions broke out in jund Urdunn and the rebels were from the Banū Lakhm, at first led by an unidentified man and later on by a certain al-Qitāmī. He collected the *kharāj* and defeated the armies sent against the insurgents by the governor of jund Filasṭīn one after the other, but finally the Turk Muzāḥim b. Khāqān defeated him.[36]

[422] At the end of 866, when al-Mu'tazz became caliph (866–869), he appointed 'Īsā b. al-Shaykh b. al-Sulayl of the Banū Shaybān (of the federation of the Rabī'a tribes) to be governor of Ramla (that is, of jund Filasṭīn). It was said that he obtained this appointment by bribing the Turk who had considerable influence at court, Bughā al-Sharābī (the drunkard), known also by the nickname 'the little one' (*al-ṣaghīr*; to distinguish him from 'the big Bughā') with 40,000 dinars. 'Īsā ibn Shaykh did not go at once to Ramla but sent a deputy in his place, Abū'l-Mughrā. According to Ya'qūbī, the Turk Nūshrī b. Ṭajīl, governor of Damascus, attacked 'Īsā ibn Shaykh afterwards. They fought one another in jund Urdunn and the son of Nūshrī was killed, but Nūshrī defeated 'Īsā's forces, who fled from

34 See Ṭabarī, *Ta'rīkh*, III, 1102ff; Ibn al-Athīr, *Kāmil*, VI, 418, 433; cf. Van Berchem, *MIE*, 3 (1900), 425; *Répertoire chronologique*, I, No. 209 (pp. 165f); Caskel, *Felsendom*, 13; see also: Le Strange, *Palestine*, 119f. Muḥammad, al-Ma'mūn's brother, was the one who succeeded him as caliph, al-Mu'taṣim.

35 Ṭabarī, *Ta'rīkh*, III, 1395f; Ibn al-Athīr, *Kāmil*, VII, 50; Ibn Taghrī Bardī, II, 280; Bar Hebraeus (Bedjan), 155; (Budge), 142.

36 Ya'qūbī, *Ta'rīkh*, II, 605.

the battlefield to jund Filasṭīn. ʿĪsā himself took money wherever he could, and escaped to Egypt, and Ramla was taken by Nūshrī. When these events became known to al-Muʿtazz, he sent the Turk Muḥammad b. al-Muwallad from Baghdad to set things in order and then Nūshrī retreated from Filasṭīn and ʿĪsā b. Shaykh returned from Egypt and settled there. He fortified himself in a citadel which he built between Ramla and Lod and called it al-Ḥasāmī, and when Ibn al-Muwallad tried to subdue him he was unable to do so. According to some sources, ʿĪsā seized the caravan carrying tax-monies from Egypt to Baghdad. Yaʿqūbī tells further that ʿĪsā used the considerable wealth he brought with him from Egypt in order to bribe the Arab tribes of Rabīʿa ('the northerners'), while he married into the Banū Kalb ('the southerners'). From this very fragmentary account, one can understand that during those years (*ca.* 866–868), ʿĪsā established a sort of Bedouin rule in Palestine, to the displeasure of the Turks, who fought him to no avail. This war continued during the rule of al-Muhtadī (869–870), who wrote to ʿĪsā b. Shaykh, promising to pardon him but demanding that he return all the money; however ʿĪsā refused. The caliph then ordered the governor of Egypt, Aḥmad ibn Ṭūlūn, to set out and attack him, and indeed he arrived at al-ʿArīsh at the head of an army. At that juncture however, the caliph's orders to return to Egypt reached him. ʿĪsā persisted in refusing to accept al-Mahdī's authority, and afterwards also that of the new caliph, al-Muʿtamid (870–892), and then the governor of Damascus, the Turk Amājūr (or Anājūr) was sent against him with 700 Turkish soldiers. ʿĪsā at first fortified himself in Tyre but afterwards fought back and Amājūr was forced to retreat to Damascus while ʿĪsā besieged the city. Subsequently, the Turks attacked and Manṣūr, ʿĪsā's son, and his principal aide, Abū'l-Ṣahbā Ẓafar b. al-Yamān, fell in battle. ʿĪsā withdrew from the Damascus area southward to Palestinian territory, as far as Ramla. Ṭabarī stresses the sizeable difference between the two forces: while ʿĪsā had at his disposal some 20,000 men, Amājūr, he writes, had only 200 to 400. Al-Muʿtamid sent a delegation to ʿĪsā afterwards (evidently in 870), consisting of Abū Naṣr Ismāʿīl b. ʿAbdallah al-Marwazī, the cadi Muḥammad b. ʿUbaydalla al-Kurayzī and one of his courtiers (*khādim*) Ḥusayn, known by the nickname ʿAraq al-Mawt ('the sweat of death'). They managed to reach an agreement with ʿĪsā, whereby he would leave Palestine in exchange for the promise to be governor of Armenia; he left in Jumādā II AH 257 (May AD 871). Palestine was left to be governed by Amājūr the Turk. In the same year, fierce battles took place between the Arab tribes (Ya'qūbī: between Lakhm and Judhām, but this information is evidently not reliable).[37]

[37] Ṭabarī, *Ta'rīkh*, III, 1685, 1840f; Yaʿqūbī, *Ta'rīkh*, II, 601ff, 613f (the second fragment is not the continuation of the first but appears to be rather a repetition of the major points,

More about Muslim personalities during the Abbasid period

[423–424] During this period, three outstanding Muslim scholars lived in Jerusalem: Idrīs b. Abī Khawla al-Antākī (i.e. from Antioch), who was a physician, a miracle-worker and a noted man; 'Abd al-'Azīz al-Maqdisī and Aḥmad b. Mas'ūd al-Khayyāṭ (the tailor).[38]

Abū 'Ubaydallah Muḥammad ibn Karrām, known as an ascetic, founded a sect, afterwards named after him. He was a Sijistānī by birth. Most of his views are not clearly known. Some say he favoured anthropomorphism (*tashbīh*), and he was therefore thought to lean towards Christianity. He died in Jerusalem in Ṣafar AH 255 (January AD 870); some say he died in Zoar and was brought to be buried in Jerusalem. A century after his death, al-Muqaddasī reports that there was a sect of his followers in Jerusalem where they had hospices (*khawāniq*) and meeting places (*majālis*), and he also had followers in some Persian regions, such as Naysābūr and Jurjān. They would distribute a ḥadīth in the name of the Prophet: 'at the End of the Days, there will come a man named Muḥammad b. Karrām, and he will cause the Muslim law and community (*al-sunna wa'l-jamā'a*) to rise again; he will have a hijra similar to my hijra from Mecca to Medina'. Ṣafadi tells that the *amīr* of Ramla and Jerusalem, Yānis, supported Ibn Karrām's views. Mujīr al-Dīn al-'Ulaymī notes that he lived in Jerusalem for twenty years (that is, he stayed in Jerusalem from about 850 until 870).[39]

and Ya'qūbī seems to have copied from two different sources. See *ibid.*, further, 618, 620f. Here too it is noticeable that he repeats everything twice, according to different sources). 'Īsā ibn Shaykh evidently had special connections with Tyre, which he used as the base of his activities in the days of al-Musta'īn; see Ṭabarī, *ibid.*, 1585 (the year AH 251, i.e. AD 865), where it says that he fought against a rebel named al-Muwaffaq. The inter-tribal war: Ya'qūbī, *ibid.*, 623. See further accounts of 'Īsā ibn Shaykh: Kindī, 214; Ibn al-Athīr, *Kāmil*, VII, 163, 176; Abū'l-Fidā', *Mukhtaṣar*, II, 44; Ibn Khaldūn, '*Ibar*, III, 712; IV, 639; on Bughā see the article Bughā al-Sharābī (by D. Sourdel), in *EI*². In Maqrīzī, *Khiṭaṭ*, II, 93f, there is a distortion and he speaks about Aḥmad, son of 'Īsā ibn Shaykh, instead of about 'Īsā; and in his footsteps, Ḥasan also erred in his *Ta'rīkh*, III, 10f.

38 Ibn al-Jawzī, *Ṣifa*, IV, 218f; Aḥmad b. Mas'ūd: see Ibn 'Asākir, II, 89 (he died in 274, 887/8).

39 See a comprehensive article on him in Subkī, *Ṭabaqāt*, II, 304f; see Muqaddasī, *Āqālīm*, 179, 182, 323, 365; Ibn al-Athīr, *Kāmil*, VII, 217; Maqdisī, *Bad'*, V, 141; Ibn Ḥazm, *Milal*, IV, 204; Ibn Kathīr, *Bidāya*, XI, 20: he opposed the '*amal*, that is, the practical part of the ritual, for which he was expelled by the governor of Jerusalem to the Zoar valley, where he died; he was then brought back to Jerusalem to be secretly buried at night. He was buried near the Jericho gate close to the graves of the prophets; according to Ibn Kathīr's anonymous source, he had some 20,000 followers in Jerusalem, which Ibn Kathīr finds doubtful (*Allāhu a'lamu*). He says that Ibn Karrām only lived in Jerusalem for four years. Abū'l-Fidā', *Mukhtaṣar*, II, 47. The ḥadīth is quoted by Ibn al-Jawzī (and he points out that it is not genuine, of course), *Mawḍū'āt*, II, 50, and he explains that it is from Isḥāq b. Muḥamshādh's book, the *faḍā'il* of Muḥammad b. Karrām; he also gives the names of Muḥammad b. Karrām's teachers: al-Jūbyārī and Muḥammad ibn Ghunaym al-Sa'dī; Ṣafadī, *al-Wāfī*, IV, 375; 'Ulaymī, 262; cf. Mez, 273; Ashtor, *AESC*, 27(1972), 187, n. 14

[425–431] At that time, there lived in Ramla al-Ḥasan b. Wāqi', of the Banū Rabī'a, who immigrated to Palestine from the city of Sarakhs in Khurāsān, and was engaged in the study of ḥadīths. He died in Ramla in AH 220, that is AD 835.[40] There was also Abū Khālid Yazīd b. Khālid b. Yazīd al-Hamadānī, who was the teacher of two other scholars: Abū'l-'Abbās Muḥammad b. al-Ḥasan ibn Qutayba (he should not be confused with the famous 'Abdallah b. Muslim ibn Qutayba), and Abū Zur'a al-Rāzī. Yazīd was known for his ascetic behaviour; he died in AH 232, that is AD 847 (others say in AH 233 or 237).[41] Muḥammad b. Simā'a Abū'l-Aṣbagh al-Qurashī was of a *mawālī* family who were clients of Caliph Sulaymān b. 'Abd al-Malik, who converted to Islam. He died in AH 238, that is AD 852/3. (He should not be confused with Muḥammad b. Simā'a who was cadi in Baghdad in the days of al-Ma'mūn.)[42] Abū 'Abd al-Raḥman Mu'ammal b. Ihāb b. 'Abd al-'Azīz, of the Banū Rabī'a, was born in Kirmān and went from there to Kūfa, afterwards settling in Ramla, where he died on Thursday, the 7th of Rajab AH 254, that is, the 1st of July, AD 868.[43] Abū 'Umayr 'Īsā b. Muḥammad b. Isḥāq was the son of a copper-smith (he was called 'Ibn al-Naḥḥās') from Bayt Māmīn, 'one of the villages in the Ramla area'. He was both pious and an ascetic and died in Ramla, where he was buried on the 8th of Muḥarram AH 256 (the 16th of December AD 869).[44] Abū 'Imrān Mūsā b. Sahl b. Qādim was born in Nasā in Khurāsān and settled in Ramla. He was the teacher of Abū Da'ūd 'Abdallah b. Sulaymān al-Sijistānī, one of the great scholars of the law in Islam, and of Ibn Abī Ḥātim al-Rāzī, one of the outstanding writers and interpreters of the Koran. One of his teachers was Muḥammad b. Rudayḥ b. 'Aṭiyya al-Maqdisī (the Jerusalemite). He died in Ramla on Jumādā I AH 262, that is February AD 876. He wrote a treatise on the people of the Prophet's circle (the *ṣaḥāba*) who settled in Palestine, which has been lost.[45] Abū Sa'īd Ismā'īl b. Ḥamdawayh, of Bīkand in the region of Bukhara, lived in Ramla. One of his pupils was the Jerusalemite Aḥmad b. Zakarīyā' b. Yaḥyā. He died in Ramla in AH 273, that is AD 887.[46]

[432–435] One can also include the following among the spiritual and

(the reference to Yāqūt, *Buldān*, requires correction: vol. II, instead of III); and the article Karrāmiyya (by C. E. Bosworth), in *EI*².

40 Ibn Sa'd, VII(2), 174; Ibn Ḥajar, *Tahdhīb*, II, 324.

41 Sam'ānī, VI, 169; Ibn al-Athīr, *Lubāb*, I, 476; Yāqūt, *Buldān*, II, 819; Ibn Ḥajar, *Tahdhīb*, XI, 322f.

42 Ibn Ḥajar, *Tahdhīb*, IX, 203f.

43 Al-Khaṭīb al-Baghdādī, *Ta'rīkh*, XIII, 181; Dhahabī, *'Ibar*, II, 7; Khazrajī, 337; Ibn al-'Imād, II, 129; Ibn Ḥajar, *Tahdhīb*, X, 381f; Ibn Sa'd, VII(2), 206, mentions Abū 'Abd al-Raḥmān al-Aylī, and evidently he is referring to Mu'ammal.

44 Yāqūt, *Buldān*, I, 781; Ibn Ḥajar, *Tahdhīb*, VIII, 228f.

45 Yāqūut, *Buldān*, II, 819; Ibn Ḥajar, *Tahdhīb*, X, 347; cf. Sezgin, I, 347.

46 Ibn 'Asākir, III, 17; Yāqūt, *Buldān*, I, 797,

intellectual Muslim personalities in Ramla at that time: Abū ʿAbdallah Muḥammad b. ʿAbd al-ʿAzīz b. Muḥammad al-ʿUmarī; whose family hailed from Wāsiṭ in Iraq and settled in Ramla. He was also known by the nickname Ibn al-Wāsiṭī.[47] Abū Sulaymān Ayyūb b. Isḥāq b. Ibrāhīm b. Sāfarī (or Musāfir), came from Baghdad and settled in Ramla. He died on Sunday, the 18th of Rabīʿ II AH 260, that is the 7th of February AD 874; he was one of the devotees of Aḥmad ibn Ḥanbal.[48] In Ramla there lived, for at least two periods, in AH 211 and in 214, that is AD 826/7 and 829, Abū Zurʿa ʿAbd al-Raḥmān b. ʿUmar b. ʿAbdallah b. Ṣafwān al-Naṣrī (or al-Naḍrī; and this was sometimes distorted to al-Baṣrī), one of the great anthologists of the Muslim traditions. He hailed from Damascus and died on Jumādā II AH 281, or August AD 894. He was a follower of the Ṭūlūnids and was arrested in Damascus together with two others of the same view after the battle of Ṭawāḥīn, in which Khumārawayh was defeated.[49] Another contemporary, Abū Mūsā Hārūn b. Zayd b. Abī'l-Zarqā al-Taghlibī, came from Mosul and settled in Ramla, where he was the pupil of Yaḥyā ibn ʿĪsā. Two pupils of this Hārūn are also mentioned: Aḥmad b. Ismāʿīl al-Ṣaffār (the copper-smith) of Ramla, and the Jerusalemite, ʿAbdallah b. Muḥammad b. Muslim. Mūsā b. ʿĪsā al-Baghdādī, a Baghdadi, stayed in Ramla in the year AH 250, that is AD 864 (and there he quoted a ḥadīth in the name of the Prophet which says that the tears of an orphan fall on God's palm, who consoles and becalms the orphan, and he is promised a place in Paradise).[50]

[436–438] Some of the personalities of Tiberias are also mentioned. Ibrāhīm b. al-Walīd b. Salma was the teacher of another Tiberian, Ṭāhir b. ʿAlī.[51] Abū' l-Faḍl Ṣāliḥ b. Bishr b. Salima was the teacher of the Tiberian Ḥāmid b. al-Ḥasan al-Bazzār al Muʿaddal ('seed trader', 'reliable witness', i.e. a notary); he was evidently a *mawlā*, for it was said of him that he was both a Qurashī and an Azdī (that is, belonging to the tribe of Quraysh as well as that of Azd).[52] Abū Saʿīd Hāshim b. Marthad (or Mazyad), was also one of the scholars of Tiberias, and was the pupil of Ādam b. Abī Iyās of Ascalon.[53]

[439–442] Abū' l-Ḥasan Ādam b. Abī Iyās came from Khurāsān, a *mawlā* of Arabs of the Banū Tamīm who settled in Marw. From there he

47 Al-Razzāz, 211f; Ibn Ḥajar, *Tahdhīb*, IX, 313.
48 Al-Khaṭīb al-Baghdādī, *Ta'rīkh*, VII, 9; Ibn ʿAsākir, III, 200f; Ibn Abī Yaʿlā, I, 117f; Ibn Taghrī Bardī, III, 31f (according to whom his manners were bad).
49 Dhahabī, *ʿIbar*, II, 65f; cf. Sezgin, I, 302 and there more references and details on manuscripts of his books that were preserved; see also Rotter, *Welt des Orients*, 6(1970/1), 38f.
50 Ibn Ḥajar, *Tahdhīb*, XI, 5; al-Khaṭīb al-Baghdādī, *Ta'rīkh*, XIII, 45f.
51 Ṭabarānī, *Muʿjam*, I, 184.
52 Ṭabarānī, *Muʿjam*, I, 155; Ibn ʿAsākir, VI, 365.
53 Ṭabarānī, *Muʿjam*, II, 126.

emigrated to Baghdad, and from there to Kūfa and afterwards to Baṣra, and finally to Ascalon, where he remained until his death in Jumādā II AH 220 (June AD 835), at the age of eighty-eight. He was occupied in collecting traditions, and was a scribe by profession (writing deeds and petitions). Bukhārī, the greatest anthologist of ḥadīths, quoted him, as did Ibn Abī'l-Ḥātim al-Rāzī. Two of his books are known; they are *kitāb al-ḥadīth*, of which ten leaves of a thirteenth century manuscript have been preserved in Damascus, and *thawāb al-a'māl* ('reward for pious deeds'), which has been lost.[54] Abū Ibrāhīm Rawḥ b. Yazīd al-Sanājī (from Sanājiya, or Sinājiya, a village near Ascalon) seems to have stayed in Ramla where he met Ibn Abī Ḥātim al-Rāzī in AH 217 (AD 832). His pupil, Abū Zayyān, Ṭayyib b. Zayyān al-Qāsiṭī, who also came from Sanājiya is also mentioned.[55] Muḥammad b. al-Mutawakkil b. Abī'l-Surrī was a descendant of converts to Islam, *mawlā* of the Hāshimids (evidently of the house of 'Abbās). He was a scholar and also an astrologer, and he dealt in pearls. One night, on leaving the *jāmi'* in Ascalon, he looked up at the stars, and announced that he would die that very night. He then returned to his house seemingly healthy, wrote his will and bid his family farewell, and he died the same night (according to Ibn Ḥajar). His death was in Sha'bān AH 238 (January AD 853).[56] Another inhabitant of Ascalon was Muḥammad b. Ḥammād al-Rāzī al-Ṭabarānī (of Rayy near Tehran). He died on Friday the 21st of Rabī' II AH 271 (16 October AD 884). Some of the important scholars in Islam, such as Ibn Māja, copied from him.[57]

[443–452] Above, we have dealt with the notable group of Muslim theologians who descended from local converts to Islam in Eilat during the Umayyad period. In following the lives of the Muslim theologians in Palestine, it appears that there was a continuity in the existence of a spiritual centre in Eilat. Towards the end of the eighth century, it was the home of one of the most important writers of that time (apparently for a lengthy stay), Abū 'Abd al-Raḥmān 'Abdallah b. al-Mubārak b. Wāḍiḥ al-Ḥanẓalī al-Tamīmī, of Marw in Khurāsān, also a descendant of converts. It was said that his father was a Turk and his mother came from Khawārizm. He was a successful merchant but also a writer and a fighter.

54 Ibn Sa'd, VII(2), 186; Ibn al-Athīr, *Kāmil*, VI, 460; Ibn al-Athīr, *Lubāb*, II, 136; Ibn al-Jawzī, *Ṣifa*, IV, 280f; Ibn Qutayba, *Ma'ārif*, 524; Khazrajī, 12; Dhahabī, *'Ibar*, I, 379; Yāfi'ī, II, 80 (in Dhahabī and Yāfi'ī erroneously: he died in 120); Ibn Ḥajar, *Tahdhīb*, I, 196; Ṣafadī, *al-Wāfī*, V, 297; al-Khaṭīb al-Baghdādī, *Mūḍiḥ*, I, 463ff; cf. Sezgin, I, 67, 102 (No. 32).

55 Yāqūt, *Buldān*, III, 154; Khālidī, 152; Ibn al-Athīr, *Lubāb*, I, 567.

56 Wāsiṭī, 3, see editor's note 2; Ibn al-Athīr, *Lubāb*, II, 136; Ibn Ḥajar, *Tahdhīb*, IX, 424f; Ṣafadī, *al-Wāfī*, IV, 384.

57 Al-Khaṭīb al-Baghdādī, *Ta'rīkh*, II, 271f; Ibn al-Athīr, *Lubāb*, II, 94f; Khazrajī, 284; Ṣafadī, *al-Wāfī*, III, 24; Ibn Ḥajar, *Tahdhīb*, IX, 124f.

He died in Hīt (on the Euphrates, north of al-Anbār, which is Neharde'ā), on Ramaḍān AH 181 (November AD 797).[58]

Additional Muslim figures in Eilat are mentioned: Abū Kharbaq Salāma b. Rawḥ, from a family of converts to Islam, *mawālī* of the Umayyads. He was the nephew of 'Aqīl b. Khālid and he copied the book of al-Zuhrī from him; he died in Sha'ban AH 197 (April AD 813).[59] One of his relatives was Abū 'Abdallah Muḥammad b. 'Azīz b. 'Abdallah b. Ziyād b. Khālid b. 'Aqīl b. Khālid, also of Eilat, where he died in AH 267 (AD 880/1).[60] Mention must also be made of Ruzayq b. Ḥakam, one of the collectors of traditions in Eilat, of whom Ibn Ḥajar says that he was also governor of the city in that time. Also the following personalities: Ḥusayn b. Rustum;[61] Abū Ya'qūb Isḥaq b. Ismā'īl b. 'Abd al-A'lā b. 'Abd al-Ḥamīd; who died in Dhū'l-Ḥijja AH 208 (April AD 824).[62] Ṭalḥa b. 'Abd al-Malik, from whom, according to Ibn Ḥajar, some of the most important collectors of Muslim traditions copied;[63] Abū Ḍaḥr Yazīd b. Abī Sumayd (or Sumayya), who behaved in a very pious manner and prayed and wept frequently (Ibn Sa'd has a story of a Jewish woman who empathised with his piety and wept with him).[64] Three men of Eilat are mentioned among the pupils and followers of al-Shāfi'ī, one of the greatest Islamic scholars of those generations: Khālid b. Nizār b. al-Mughīra b. Salīm, a descendant of *mawālī* of Ghassān, who moved to Samarra in Iraq, capital of the Abbasids, towards the end of his life and died there in AH 222, that is AD 837.[65] A pupil of Khālid, Hārūn b. Sa'īd b. al-Haytham, also a descendant of a family of converts, from the *mawālī* of Qays, died on the 6th of Rabī' I AH 253, the 16th of March, AD 867. Hārūn b. Muḥammad.[66] Abū 'Amr 'Abd

[58] His stay in Eilat is mentioned by Ibn Sa'd, VII(2), 206; cf. also 104f; see further Dhahabī, *'Ibar*, 280f; Ibn Ḥajar, *Tahdhīb*, V, 382–387; cf. Sezgin, I, 95, who has more references and also a list of manuscripts of his books that were preserved. His friend and assistant, 'Alī b. Isḥāq b. Yaḥyā b. Mu'ādh al-Dārikānī also stayed in Eilat with him; this 'Alī was afterwards put in charge of supplies to the army in jund Damascus and jund Urdunn on behalf of the caliph al-Wāthiq; in AH 226, or AD 841, he rebelled against the governor of both these junds, Rajā' b. Abī'l-Ḍaḥḥāk and murdered him, see Ṭabarī, *Ta'rīkh*, III, 1313f; Ibn 'Asākir, V, 316. On 'Alī being one of the assistants (perhaps a pupil) of 'Abdallah b. al-Mubārak see Ibn Sa'd, VII(2), 107. Rajā' was evidently one of al-Ma'mūn's retainers, see Ṭabarī, *ibid.*, 994, 1000.

[59] Ibn Ḥajar, *Tahdhīb*, IV, 289f.

[60] Dhahabī, *'Ibar*, II, 36; Ibn Ḥajar, *Tahdhīb*, IX, 344.

[61] Ibn Sa'd, VII(2), 206; Ibn Ḥajar, *Tahdhīb*, III, 273. (Ḥusayn b. Rustum is mentioned only in Ibn Sa'd.)

[62] Ibn Mākūlā, I, 128ff; Khazrajī, 22; Ibn Ḥajar, *Tahdhīb*, I, 225f.

[63] Ibn Sa'd, VII(2), 206; Ibn Ḥajar, *Tahdhīb*, V, 19f.

[64] Ibn Sa'd, VII(2), 206; Ibn al-Jawzī, *Ṣifa*, IV, 305; Khazrajī, 371; Ibn Ḥajar, *Tahdhīb*, XI, 334.

[65] Sam'ānī, 410; according to him, he died in Sha'bān 263, April 876, evidently an error; see Ibn Ḥajar, *Tahdhīb*, III, 123.

[66] Ibn 'Abd al-Barr, *Intiqā*, 114; Ibn Ḥajar, *ibid.*

al-Jabbār b. 'Umar (known also by the nickname: Abū'l-Ṣabāḥ), was also from a family of converts from Eilat, *mawālī* of the Umayyads. He died in AH 260 or 270, that is *ca.* AD 880.[67]

[453–454] Abū Bakr Muḥammad b. al-Ḥārith b. al-Nu'mān al-Iyādī, served as cadi in Palestine; he hailed from Khurāsān and acted as cadi at different times both in Fustat and Baghdad. He died in AH 250, that is AD 864.[68] Abū Sa'īd 'Abd al-Raḥmān b. Ibrāhīm b. 'Amr b. Maymūn al-Qurashī was from a family of converts who were *mawālī* of the Banū Quraysh, evidently of the caliph 'Uthmān and afterwards of the Umayyads. He was known also by the name Duḥaym b. al-Yatīm, and was cadi in two junds, Filasṭīn and Urdunn, and lived in Ramla. He died in Ramla in AH 245, in Ramaḍān (December AD 859). It was said of him that he was a pupil of Aḥmad ibn Ḥanbal. Mūsā b. 'Abdallah b. Mūsā, who is Abū 'Imrān al-Qarāṭīsī, a pupil of Ādam b. Abī Īyās of Ascalon, was a Baghdadi and lived in Acre during the first half of the ninth century.[69]

The period of the Ṭūlūnids

[455] During the last quarter of the ninth century, a political process of great importance to the history of Palestine took place – the seizure of power in Egypt by the Turkish commander Aḥmad ibn Ṭūlūn, and its severance from the central rule in Baghdad. Not many years passed before Ibn Ṭūlūn also ruled over Palestine and Syria. From then onwards, Palestine became subordinate to Egypt. This fact has a two-fold significance. On the one hand, the central government came closer to Palestine and was more interested in what occurred there in every area. In the economic sphere, at least, this fact had definite consequences, such as an improvement in the ports and the development of trade relations, as we shall see below. On the other hand, the creation of an independent political centre in Egypt led to a renewed polarisation of the forces in the Muslim world. During the generations which passed since the Muslim conquest, Palestine experienced wars of a mainly internal nature, that is, inter-tribal conflicts between Arab tribes or between various rebels or insurgents and the central government. Now the country became much as it had been in ancient times, the arena of war between armies from Egypt and armies from the north. These forces were not of a uniform character; not only the army of the Abbasid caliphate was involved but there were many other

[67] Ibn Sa'd, VII(2), 207; Ibn Ḥajar, *Tahdhīb*, VI, 104.

[68] Kindī, 449; al-Khaṭīb al-Baghdādī, *Ta'rīkh*, II, 292f. Al-Iyādī, after Iyād b. Nizār, considered the father of the 'northern' tribes, see Sam'ānī, I, 283f.

[69] Al-Khaṭīb al-Baghdādī, *Ta'rīkh*, X, 265f; XIII, 42. Khazrajī, 189; Dhahabī, *'Ibar*, I, 445; Ibn al-'Imād, II, 108; Ibn Ḥajar, *Tahdhīb*, VI, 131f. Ādam b. Abī Īyās: see p. 303 above.

factors taking part as well. The common element in all these wars was that Palestine appeared to be a vital defensive position to each of the sides as well as a springboard from which to attack.[70]

[456] Aḥmad ibn Ṭūlūn was the son of a Turkish freedman of Caliph al-Ma'mūn. Aḥmad came to Egypt in September 868 as representative of his step-father, the *amīr* Bāqbāq, appointed governor of the country on behalf of Caliph al-Mu'tazz. It was not long before he was dominating Egyptian affairs. On his arrival in Egypt, he found that the person to be reckoned with there was Aḥmad ibn al-Mudabbir, who was in charge of tax matters in Egypt and the three junds of Filasṭīn, Urdunn and Damascus. Evidently, when he first occupied this post Aḥmad ibn al-Mudabbir was only responsible for jund Filasṭīn and treated the inhabitants of the country quite harshly. He stayed in Palestine from about 850 until 855. When Ibn Ṭūlūn arrived in Egypt, 'Īsā ibn Shaykh seized the dispatches of taxes to Baghdad. After a certain period of tension, Ibn Ṭūlūn and Ibn al-Mudabbir found a common language, and the son of the former, Khumārawayh, married the latter's daughter. Aḥmad ibn Ṭūlūn showed considerable resourcefulness in his dealing with taxes, which rose steeply as a result of his anxiety to improve the conditions of the farmers by giving them rights of tenure on their plots and by a policy of credit to improve the agricultural conditions. Apparently he pursued the same policy in Palestine and Syria after he took over these countries in 878, after the death of Amājūr, governor of Damascus. The result was that whereas the income from land taxes in those areas governed by al-Mudabbir diminished to 800,000 dinars, Ibn Ṭūlūn succeeded in raising them to 4,300,000.[71]

70 The Byzantines were also now more inclined to direct attacks into Palestine and the surrounding areas, not a little because the new centre which arose in Egypt displayed aggressive initiative also against the areas under Byzantine rule, and it gradually became a worthwhile target for the imperial army's attacks, particularly at sea. Not all Byzantine campaigns and raids left traces in the records. Hārūn ibn Yaḥyā immortalised in writing the sending of a cargo of Muslim captives from Ascalon to Anṭālia (which is Attalia) in Asia Minor; see in Ibn Rusta, 119; cf. Izeddin, *REI*, 1941–46, 41–62; the article Hārūn b. Yaḥyā (by the aforementioned) in *EI*²; Miquel, *Géographie humaine*, 165, n. 65. (It is not known when this occurred exactly; some believe it happened in 880 and some in 912.)

71 See a general survey on the beginning of Aḥmad ibn Ṭūlūn's rule in Lane-Poole, *History*, 59ff; see Z. M. Hassan, *Les Tulunides*, and the article Aḥmad b. Ṭūlūn (by the aforementioned), in *EI*²; see: Ibn al-Athīr, *Kāmil*, VII, 316f; Ibn Taghrī Bardī, III, 43; Sāwīrūs (1943), 24; Ibn Khaldūn, *'Ibar*, IV, 639, 643; Ibn al-Jawzī, *Muntaẓam*, V, 59f; Wüstenfeld, *Statthalter*, III, 12, 16; Canard's translation of al-Ṣūlī, 221, n. 1 (cf. al-Ṣūlī, 138) wherein he notes that Ibn al-Mudabbir bore the title *ustādh* (though he was not a eunuch); B. Lewis, *Cambridge History of Islam*, I, 183; Goitein, *Yerushalayim* (1952/3), 93. Ibn Ṭūlūn's first military expedition to Palestine took place at the end of Sha'bān 264, May 878. Muḥammad b. (Abī) Rāfi', governor on behalf of Amājūr, received him in Ramla. From there, Ibn Ṭūlūn continued his expedition northward, to Syria. See: Kindī, 219f. Evidently Ibn Ṭūlūn's complete control of tax matters in Palestine (and implicitly all its administrative matters) only began after 267, that is 880, the year in which Ibn al-Mudabbir was imprisoned (see Ibn al-Jawzī). It is interesting to note that although these

[457–459] During this period, Ramla became the administrative centre of Ibn Ṭūlūn's governing policies in Palestine and Syria. There he met the son of Amājūr, who agreed to accept his authority and was appointed governor in Ramla, evidently after the former governor, Muḥammad b. Abī Rāfi', as well as his aide Aḥmad, were dismissed.[72]

If we can believe the letter of the patriarch of Jerusalem, Elias the Third, Ibn Ṭūlūn appointed a Christian governor in Ramla, or perhaps only in Jerusalem, and this put an end to the persecution of the Christians and prompted the renovation of the churches in Jerusalem, on the initiative of that same Christian governor.[73] I have already described the renovation of the port of Acre ordered by Ibn Ṭūlūn. It is said that he also built the citadel (*qal'a*) of Jaffa.[74]

[460] Aḥmad ibn Ṭūlūn died in May 884 and was replaced by his son, Abū'l-Jaysh Khumārawayh. He soon found himself in the midst of a war with Turkish commanders who collaborated with Abū'l-'Abbās ibn al-Muwaffaq, the nephew of Caliph al-Mu'tamid (Ibn al-Muwaffaq afterwards inherited the caliphate and he became Caliph al-Mu'taḍid). This struggle went on in Syria, at first, and in February 885 Ibn al-Muwaffaq entered Damascus. Some two months later, on Tuesday the 15th of Shawwāl (the 5th of April AD 885), the armies met at al-Ṭawāḥīn ('the mills'), the place on the Yarqōn known in later times as the 'Seven Mills'. According to a few of the sources, the forces were uneven; Khumārawayh had at his disposal an army of 70,000 men whereas Ibn al-Muwaffaq had only some 4,000. Nevertheless he had the upper hand. Khumārawayh believed that the battle was lost and he fled with part of his army to Egypt. Part of the Egyptian army, however, under the command of Sa'd (or Sa'īd) al-A'sar (or al-Aysar, or Abū'l-Ma'āshir), attacked the Abbasid army from an ambush and repelled it, causing heavy losses, including the loss of many of the commanders. Ibn al-Muwaffaq was forced to withdraw from all the areas he had conquered. The people of Damascus refused to permit him to enter the city owing to the unquestioned victory of the Ṭūlūnids. The cadi of Damascus, Abū Zur'a Muḥammad b. 'Uthmān,

were unquiet times, the monk Bernard, on visiting Palestine in *ca.* 868, was impressed with the high degree of security in the streets of its cities: a man whose horse happened to stumble and die, could confidently leave all his trappings in the street until he found another; differing considerably from the insecurity he found in Italy. See his account in Tobler et Molinier, I, 319f.

72 See Ibn al-Athīr, *Kāmil*, VII, 316; Ibn Khaldūn, '*Ibar*, IV, 643, 668.

73 See the letter in *RHGF*, IX, 294f. Ibn Ṭūlūn's favourable attitude to the dhimmīs can perhaps be seen from the fact that he had a Jewish physician, see Mas'ūdī, *Murūj*, II, 391, and see there the summary of the argument between the Christian (the Copt) and the Jewish physician. When Ibn Ṭūlūn became fatally ill, both the Jews and the Christians prayed for him: see Lane-Poole, *History*, I, 79.

74 Ibn Khaldūn, '*Ibar*, IV, 652.

participated in Damascus in the deposal ceremony of al-Muwaffaq (brother of caliph al-Mu'tamid, who was considered governor of the region), and said '... behold you are witnesses to the fact that I have dismissed Abū Aḥmad (al-Muwaffaq) as one discards a sealing ring from one's finger; accursed may he be'. Later, when the Abbasid army passed through Damascus in the course of its retreat, Abū Zur'a was captured with a number of other people. They were about to be executed, but Abū Zur'a, with his quick wits, managed to convince Ibn al-Muwaffaq's secretary (*kātib*), al-Wāsiṭī, to release them. The Abbasids had finally to acknowledge the Ṭūlūnids' conquests and the agreement between the two sides was strengthened by the marriage of Khumārawayh's daughter, Qaṭr al-Nadā', to the new caliph, who was Ibn al-Muwaffaq, al-Mu'taḍid.[75]

[461] Of the events which occurred during that period, mention must be made of Khumārawayh's visit to Ramla in AH 275 (AD 888/9), apparently at its outset (June 888), when he organised a large military expedition into Syria to fight the Turkish commander Ibn Abī Sāj, who had invaded the area. The battle took place in the Bashan region and ended with an overwhelming victory for the Egyptians. When in Ramla, Khumārawayh invited Sa'd al-A'sar, the victor of the battle of al-Ṭawāḥīn who later

[75] See general information on Khumārawayh in the article on him (by U. Haarmann) in *EI*²; where the date of the battle of al-Ṭawāḥīn is not exact. See Ṭabarī, *Ta'rīkh*, III, 2106f; Mas'ūdī, *Murūj*, VIII, 64f; Iṣbahānī, *Maqātil*, 686 (who points out that in that battle, 'Ubaydallah b. 'Alī, a descendant of 'Alī ibn Abī Ṭālib, fell); Ibn al-Athīr, *Kāmil*, VII, 410; Sibṭ Ibn al-Jawzī (BM Or 4619 II), fol. 20b; *al-'uyūn wa'l-ḥadā'iq* (MS Berlin), fol. 30a; Ibn al-'Adīm, *Zubda*, I, 81 (here the year is mistakenly: 281); Ibn Shaddād (MS Leiden), fol. 105a (Muḥammad b. [Abī] Rāfi', who was governor of Damascus, does not accept Khumārawayh's authority and invites Ibn al-Muwaffaq to enter Damascus; at the head of Khumārawayh's army stood Muḥammad b. Aḥmad al-Wāsiṭī and Sa'd b. al-Aysar [above-mentioned al-A'sar]); Abū'l-Fidā', *Mukhtaṣar*, II, 54; Dhahabī, *'Ibar*, II, 47; Ibn Kathīr, *Bidāya*, XI, 49 (according to him, the name of the victorious Ṭūlūnid commander was Abū'l-Ma'āshir, and he was Khumārawayh's brother); Ibn Khaldūn, *'Ibar*, 653f, 697; Subkī, *Ṭabaqāt*, III, 196 (he has the story of Abū Zur'a but the names are distorted); Yāfi'ī, II, 186; Maqrīzī, *Khiṭaṭ*, II, 104 (who follows al-Quḍā'ī's account and gives the date of the battle of al-Ṭawāḥīn as the 10th of Ṣafar AH 271, i.e. the 7th of August AD 884); Ibn Taghrī Bardī, III, 50, has the same date as Maqrīzī; cf. Wüstenfeld, *Statthalter*, III, 27f who claims that the date cannot be so early; cf. also Lane-Poole, *History*, 72ff (who evades the issue of the date). On the matter of Abū Zur'a (below, sec. 489) see also Ṣafadī, *al-Wāfī*, IV, 82f: he was arrested together with 'Abdallah ibn 'Amr and Yazīd ibn Muḥammad ibn 'Abd al-Ṣamad. The three were taken to Antioch in chains; there they were interrogated by Ibn al-Muwaffaq, who wanted to know who called his father Abū'l-Aḥmaq (instead of Abū Aḥmad: *aḥmaq* meaning stupid). Abū Zur'a swore that if one of them used this expression, he would divorce his own wives, free his slaves and donate his property to the *waqf*, upon which he was released. Some nine years after the battle of al-Ṭawāḥīn, Aḥmad ibn al-Muwaffaq, who in the meantime had become caliph, al-Mu'taḍid, and Khumārawayh, reached complete agreement. Khumārawayh was given control of all the areas between Barqa in the west and the Euphrates and had to pay the caliph an annual tax of 500,000 dinars. See Kindī, 239f.

became governor of Damascus (and according to one version, he was Khumārawayh's brother) and killed him with his own hands, which aroused the wrath of the people of Damascus.[76]

The Ismā'īlīs: Qarmaṭīs and Fatimids

[462] During the last quarter of the ninth century, an extremist Shiite movement, known as Ismā'īlīs, crystallised. Its name derived from the elder son of the sixth *imām*, Ja'far al-Ṣādiq. (In Shiite terms, the imām was the direct descendant of 'Alī ibn Abī Ṭālib and Fāṭima, the Prophet's daughter; the *imām* was considered the worthy and true leader of the Islam world in his time but had been dispossessed by those who usurped the rights of the Prophet's family, that is, the dynasties of the caliphs.) This Ismā'īl died before his father, whom he was to have succeeded. The Ismā'īlīs claimed that Ismā'īl was the last *imām*, 'lord of the time' (*qā'im al-zamān*). They developed quite a unique religious philosophy influenced by Hellenistic and Neo-Platonic ideas which happened to find their way into the Islamic train of throughts. They aspired to build a new world and a new Muslim society. Their secret societies sprung up throughout the Muslim world and their emissaries were very busy spreading their teachings. An earlier branch of the Ismā'īlī movement were the Qarmaṭīs. According to Muslim sources, in fact, they completely rejected Islam and represented Persian aspirations in opposition to the Arabs, saying that God no longer supported the Arabs because they had killed Ḥusayn. Now He was on the side of the descendants of Khusraw, king of the Persians.[77]

[463] This large stream among the Ismā'īlīs, the Qarmaṭīs, became a political movement fighting for control of the caliphate in *ca.* 890, when Ḥamdān Qarmaṭ gathered his devotees together at a base in the Kūfa region, which he called *Dār al-hijra*, that is 'the house (region, land) of the hijra', as a reminder of the hijra of Muḥammad to Medina, which was the beginning of the Prophet's armed struggle. He had the support of the farmers of the area and also of the Bedouin tribes. The Qarmaṭīs introduced common ownership of the herds, of various property and jewelry, and they also had a common fund into which the individual earnings of the members were placed. In 899 the pupil of Ḥamdān Qarmaṭ, Abū Sa'īd

[76] Ibn al-Athīr, *Kāmil*, VII, 428f; apparently Ibn al-Athīr speaks of the battle twice, and the second time he says that it took place in Thinyat al-'Uqqāb near Damascus. On the killing of Sa'd see: Ibn Taghrī Bardī, III, 72f.

[77] Goldziher, *Muhammedanische Studien*, I, 175. The first preachers and organisers of the Isma'īlīs were Maymūn al-Qaddāḥ ('the arrow maker') and his son 'Abdallah. They came from the region of Ahwāz. Some sources say that 'Abdallah lived in Jerusalem for a time and began his propaganda from there. See on 'Abdallah: Lewis, *Origins*, 54–69; and the article 'Abd Allah b. Maymūn (by S. M. Stern) in *EI*[2]; and see there also the article Isma'īliyya (by W. Madelung).

al-Jannābī, set up a sort of Qarmaṭī state in Baḥrayn, from which he also dominated the neighbouring regions in the Arabian peninsula. There were other Qarmaṭī centres in Iraq, in Ahwāz and Baṣra, and in Salamiyya in Syria. In about 900, the Syrian part of the sect came under the leadership of an opponent of Ḥamdān Qarmaṭ (and of his brother-in-law 'Abdān), Zikrawayh b. Mihrawayh and his two sons, al-Ḥusayn (or al-Ḥasan) and Yaḥyā. Until 903, they established their rule over all of northern Syria. Below we shall see that the Qarmaṭīs were involved in a very substantive way in the events in Palestine. Among the principles of their religion, the sources mention that in their prayer they faced Jerusalem and not Mecca (their *qibla* was Jerusalem).[78]

[464] Another stream which developed from the Ismā'īlīs were the Fatimids (named after Fāṭima, the daughter of the Prophet). In 893, one of their secret emissaries, Abū 'Abdallah, reached North Africa in the company of some pilgrims whom he had met in Mecca before that. He soon found supporters among the Kitāma tribesmen, and succeeded in rousing them and other Berber tribes as well, to fight for the *mahdī*, the descendant of 'Alī and Fāṭima. The region which is today Tunisia was then governed by semi-independent rulers, the Aghlabids; while in the region of Morocco, another dynasty, the Idrīsids, were in control. Abū 'Abdallah succeeded in collecting an army of 200,000 tribesmen, defeated the Aghlabid ruler in 908 and proclaimed as caliph the *imām* 'Ubaydallah, who, he claimed, was a seventh generation descendant of Ja'far al-Ṣādiq and therefore a legitimate *imām*. Sixty years later, in 969, the Fatimids conquered Egypt, and a year later, Palestine as well.[79]

[78] See the article Ḳarmaṭī (by W. Madelung) in *EI*[2]: on the *qibla* see: Ṭabarī, *Ta'rīkh*, III, 2128 (and also in others mentioned below). Another interesting principle of theirs: they honour Monday and not Friday; Malaṭī, 20f: the Qarmaṭīs and the Daylamīs (the Daylamīs were a Persian tribe and it is interesting that he brackets them together) claim that God is the supreme light without any mixture of darkness; they belittle the practical precepts, which in their opinion are merely traditions and not the sayings of God, for He does not need his creatures to thank him; some of them believe in *tanāsukh* (the transmigration of souls, and this evidently applies principally to the soul of the *imām* migrating into that of another person); they deny the existence of Paradise and Hell; they see in their fellow-men *mushrikūn* (idol-worshippers) and are permitted to spill their blood and take their possessions; they share the women and the children and have no limitations on family life; Abū'l-Fidā', *Mukhtaṣar*, II, 55: they see in Jesus, who is the word of God, the messenger of God, and the same applies also to Muḥammad b. al-Ḥanafiyya (see above); they fast on the Persian holidays: the *mihrjān* and the *nayrūz*; Ibn Khaldūn, *'Ibar*, III, 705; Maqrīzī, *Itti'āẓ*, I, 155.

[79] See: Vatikiotis, *IC*, 28 (1954), 491; he lists four factors which made the Maghrib an ideal scene of action for the Fatimids: (a) the distance from the Abbasid centre which enabled their predecessors, the Aghlabids, to set up *de facto* independent rule, (b) the isolationist tendencies of the Berber tribes, (c) the puritanical, conservative character of the population who were at the same time cut off from Islamic thinking, and (d) the existence of many religious sects there, prior to the arrival of the Fatimid emissaries. See the article Fāṭimids, by M. Canard, in *EI*[2]. It is worth noting that the deposed ruler of the Maghrib, Abū Naṣr

[465] One should point out that during those generations, Shiite tendencies were very strong in Palestine. Ibn al-Faqīh wrote in *ca.* 900, that the people of Tiberias, Nābulus and Jerusalem, as well as the majority of the people in 'Ammān (referring to the Muslims, that is the tribes) were Shiites. 'Abd al-Jabbār, writing in 995, also explicitly noted the considerable influence of the Shiites in many places, including Ramla, Tyre, Acre and Ascalon.[80]

[466] The congenial atmosphere for Shiism was the background to the stay of the Fatimid *mahdī*, 'Ubaydallah, in Palestine. After he managed to escape from Salamiyya in Syria, he at first went to Tiberias, where a Fatimid missionary (*dā'ī*) lived. He welcomed him and his entourage and warned them not to go into the city lest they be recognised by the authorities. They continued on to Ramla, where the governor was a follower of the Fatimids, one of 'Ubaydallah's devotees. He looked after them and supplied them with all their needs for two years. When a letter arrived from the governor of Damascus probing into the matter of the *mahdī* and requesting that if he were seen, he should be caught, the governor of Ramla replied that no one of that description had arrived in Ramla. The latter also swore allegiance to the *mahdī*, who lived in his house.[81]

The invasion of Tiberias by the Qarmaṭīs and the return of the Abbasids

[467] These were the last days of Ṭūlūnid rule in Egypt. In about 900, their control of Palestine and Syria disintegrated owing to the rise of the

Ziyādat Allah b. 'Abdallah, found refuge in Ramla, and spent the end of his life in Jerusalem; see: Abū'l-Fidā', *Mukhtaṣar*, II, 63; Dhahabī, *'Ibar*, II, 127; Sibṭ Ibn al-Jawzī (BM Or 4619), 64a: some say he died *bḥfā* (perhaps: in Haifa; but in Dhahabī, in Raqqa), but evidently Ramla would be correct. The enemies of the Fatimids accused them of having falsified their genealogy and that they were not at all the descendants of 'Alī and Fāṭima, and even attributed to them Jewish ancestry. See the summary of these polemics in the (biased) book of an Ismā'īlī of modern times: P. H. Mamour, *Polemics on the Origin of the Fatimid Caliphs*, London 1934.

80 Ibn al-Faqīh, 179. 'Abd al-Jabbār, *Tathbīt*, II, 594f. It is possible that the profusion of Shiite influences in Palestine derived from the fact that the rulers used to remove people with Shiite inclinations from the important centres of the caliphate to distant and less important places; see for instance the case of Aḥmad b. Shu'ayb b. 'Alī al-Nasā'ī, a celebrated writer, one of the scholars of law in Damascus, who showed sympathy for 'Alī, and was therefore expelled from his city and moved to Ramla. See: Subkī, *Ṭabaqāt*, III, 14ff.

81 See: Ivanow, *Ismaili Tradition*, 79, 87, 165, 167, 172, 181, 191f, 194, n. 1: on a night in Rajab AH 289, that is June-July AD 902, the *mahdī*, his son al-Qā'im and many others, went up to the roof of the governor's house in Ramla to watch for falling stars, which it is said were plentiful on that night. It is not possible to establish the exact date on the basis of this natural phenomenon, which was typical of that time of the year, particularly July, and especially from the 15th to the 25th of the month, as emerges from the letter kindly sent me by Professor U. Dall' Olmo of the Observatory of the University of Bologna on this matter. In his opinion, these were the Perseids; he also pointed out to me parallels from

Qarmaṭīs and their raids, under the command of their leader, ʿAlī b. ʿAbdallah. Tiberias at the time was controlled by Abū'l-Ṭayyib Laḥḥā Muḥammad b. Ḥamza b. ʿAbdallah b. al-ʿAbbās (Ibn al-Kilābiyya) b. ʿAlī Ibn Abī Ṭālib – that is, a descendant of ʿAlī but not of Fāṭima, who was of one mind with the Qarmaṭīs. He amassed a great deal of money and took over estates in jund Urdunn but was finally caught by Ṭughj (the father of the Ikhshīdid dynasty, who was then governor of Damascus and Palestine on behalf of Hārūn b. Khumārawayh, the Ṭūlūnid) who had him executed. The Ṭūlūnid Hārūn b. Khumārawayh then set out on a campaign against the Qarmaṭīs and succeeded in recapturing the two junds (Filasṭīn and Urdunn). He appointed his client Ṣawārtakīn to govern over them but then the caliph al-Muktafī sent an army to al-Shām, under Muḥammad b. Sulaymān al-Wāthiqī. He took Damascus and the two junds from Ṣawārtakīn and appointed Aḥmad b. Kayghalagh as governor of the entire area, who in turn appointed as his deputy in Urdunn and Filasṭīn, Yūsuf b. Ibrahīm b. Bughāmardī.[82]

[468] In AH 293, which is AD 906, the Qarmaṭīs again raided Palestine. At their head stood Zikrawayh b. Mihrawayh's envoy, Abū Ghānim Naṣr (ʿAbdallah) b. Saʿīd. They captured Tiberias, which was a major army base at the time, and killed its *amīr*, Jaʿfar b. Nāʿim. The people of Tiberias offered resistance to the Qarmaṭīs and as a result, the city was plundered, many women taken captive and many people killed. Arabs from among the 'southerners' (of the Banū Kalb) participated in this campaign. The governor of Damascus and Urdunn at that time was Aḥmad ibn Kayghalagh and he sent an army against the Qarmaṭīs under the command of Yūsuf b. Ibrahīm b. Bughāmardī, who was defeated and eventually killed by the Qarmaṭīs, although they had promised him an *amān*. When another army was sent against them, under al-Ḥusayn b. Ḥamdān b. Ḥamdūn, the Qarmaṭīs retreated from Palestinian territory to the Euphrates and raided the city of Hīt, on 20 Shaʿbān AH 293 (16 June AD 906). The conquest of Tiberias by the Qarmaṭīs therefore must have occurred in about April or May of the same year.[83]

[469] In the meantime, the Ṭūlūnid dynasty in Egypt began to decline.

Romoaldi *annales*, *MGH* (SS), 19, 938, and from a Japanese source, Keimatsu Mitsuo, A Chronology of Aurorae and Sunspots Observed in China, Korea and Japan, in: *Ann. Sci. Kanazawa Univ.*, part. 5: AD 801–1000. Vol. 11(1974), 18; and from the catalogue: Susumu Imoto and Ichiro Hasegowa, *Smithsonian Contributions to Astrophysics*, II, No. 6 (Washington DC 1958). I am also grateful to Dr A. Segalovitch, of the Dept. of Physics and Astronomy of Tel Aviv University, for his help in this matter.

82 Abū'l-Ṭayyib: Ibn Ḥazm, *Jamhara*, 67. On the other wars of the Qarmaṭīs, see: Ṭabarī, *Ta'rīkh*, III, 2217ff; 2221, 2222, 2224ff; Ibn Shaddād (MS Leiden), 105a.

83 According to Saʿīd ibn Biṭrīq, II, 75, a fierce battle took place between the Qarmaṭis and the Ṭūlūnid army in Rajab of the year AH 289 (June AD 902), near Damascus. Ismāʿīl, the leader of the Qarmaṭis, was killed in that battle and the army returned to its camps in

Hārūn b. Khumārawayh was killed by his uncle Shaybān at the end of December, 904; and some say it was the work of one of his soldiers. Shaybān attempted to take control of the reins of power but he was soon removed by the army and was subsequently killed. Then power in Egypt was seized by the aforementioned Muḥammad b. Sulaymān al-Wāthiqī, who was formerly commander of the Ṭūlūnid army but betrayed the Ṭūlūnids and became a devotee of the Abbasid caliph, al-Muktafī. He led an expedition through Palestine into Egypt and succeedeed in taking it over. Thus, in the year 905, Egypt and also Palestine returned to Baghdadi rule. In the same year, one of the army commanders by the name of Muḥammad b. ʻAlī al-Khalanjī (or al-Khalījī), rebelled against Muḥammad b. Sulaymān al-Wāthiqī. (Some sources have instead of Muḥammad b. ʻAlī al-Khalanjī, Ibrahīm al-Khalanjī, and he is possibly the person mentioned earlier in connection with events in Hebron.) Al-Khalanjī was young and energetic and a sworn enemy of the Abbasids. He wanted (at any rate, so he declared) to reinstate the Ṭūlūnids to power. At first, he reached Ramla in Shaʻbān 292, or June 905, and encamped with his troops near the 'Gate of Olives' (*bāb al-zaytūn*). He easily overcame the governor of Ramla, Waṣīf b. Ṣawārtakīn, and his aide, Muḥammad b. Yazdād, and when he had seized the city, he ordered the people to pray in its mosques for the well-being of the Ṭūlūnid Ibrahīm b. Khumārawayh and for himself too. The commander of Fustat, ʻĪsā al-Nūshrī, could not withstand the strong forces concentrated round al-Khalanjī, and withdrew to Alexandria. The rebels then conquered Fustat. The caliph organised a large expeditionary force. In the interim, in Ṣafar AH 293 (December AD 905), al-Khalanjī defeated Aḥmad b. Kayghalagh, governor of al-Shām on behalf of the Abbasids, in the region of al-ʻArīsh. But in May 906, al-Khalanjī suffered a defeat at the hands of the Abbasid expeditionary force and fled to Fustat, but was eventually caught and brought to Baghdad, where he was imprisoned on the caliph's orders.[84]

Damascus and Tiberias. See on the conquest of Tiberias in 906: Masʻūdī, *Tanbīh*, 373; Ṭabarī, *Ta'rīkh*, III, 2255–2258; information on the expedition reached Baghdad in Rabīʻ I AH 293, i.e. January AD 906; in Jumādā I, that is March, the Qarmaṭis attacked Damascus and the inhabitants defended themselves. It seems that Damascus was not conquered then and the Qarmaṭis turned to the Ḥawrān and the Bashan, and from there continued to Tiberias; ʻArīb, 9; *al-ʻuyūn wa'l-ḥadā'iq*, IV, 117 (there the year is AH 290, that is, AD 903; cf. the same chronicle in MS Berlin, fol. 54, where the year is AH 291/AD 904); Thābit ibn Sinān, 26f (there the year is AH 193, an error which the editor should have noticed); Ibn al-Athīr, *Kāmil*, VII, 541f; he adds that Ibn Kayghalagh, the governor, was in Egypt at the time, engaged in a war against al-Khalanjī (see on this further); Ibn Kathīr, *Bidāya*, XI, 100; Ibn Shaddād (MS Leiden), fol. 105b; Ibn al-Jawzī, *Muntaẓam*, VII, 19; Ibn al-Dawādārī, 80. The leader of the Qarmaṭis, Zikrawayh, died a short time after these events, after being wounded and taken captive near Qādisiyya, on the 10th of January 907, see Canard, translation of al-Ṣūlī, 124, translator's note 7, where his sources are mentioned.

84 Ibn al-Athīr, *Kāmil*, VII, 535f; Lane-Poole, *History*, 67; Ṭabarī, *Ta'rīkh*, III, 2253, 2254f,

[470] From this point onward and for the following thirty years (906–935) Palestine remained under Abbasid rule. We have very little information as to what occurred there during that generation. Three inscriptions found on the Temple Mount belong to that period. One is on a house named *al-turba* (probably intended as 'the grave' but this word has other meanings as well), which was dedicated by a woman whose name has not been preserved, a client (*mawlāh*) of al-Muktafī, for some unknown purpose, though perhaps as *waqf* (*muḥabbasa*). One can assume that the inscription dates from between 906 to 908, that is, between the return of the Abbasids to power and the death of Caliph al-Muktafī. The two other inscriptions also record the dedication of a building, this time on behalf of Caliph al-Muqtadir's mother, in the year AH 301 (AD 913/4). Of the governors appointed by the Abbasid caliphs, apart from Aḥmad ibn Kayghalagh mentioned earlier, we know of Abū'l-Hawā' Nasīm b. 'Abdallah al-Sharābī, who was governor of Jerusalem, evidently at the end of al-Muqtadir's day (that is, *ca.* 930), and of al-Qāhir. The latter came from a family of converts to Islam, *mawālī* of al-Muqtadir. According to al-Ṣūlī, he was replaced by Mufliḥ the Black, a black eunuch who was one of the chief aides of Caliph al-Muqtadir. He was appointed governor of Jerusalem and arrived there in July 935 to stand in for Nasīm. According to al-Khaṭīb al-Baghdādī, Nasīm only lived in Jerusalem and was a sort of supervisor of the proper procedures at the al-Aqṣā mosque; 'Umar b. Aḥmad ibn Muḥammad al-Wāsiṭī (which should be: Muḥammad b. Aḥmad) was one of his pupils, and studied with him in AH 367, that is, AD 977/8. One should rely on al-Ṣūlī, apparently, as he was closer to the times in which these people lived, but perhaps there is no contradiction here, as Nasīm could have returned to Jerusalem in his old age.[85]

2267f (printed: al-Khalījī); Ibn al-Athīr, *Kāmil*, VII, 536, 540f; Ibn Taghrī Bardī, under the year 292, and especially: III, 147f; Maqrīzī, *Khiṭaṭ*, II, 112f (printed: Ibn al-Khalījī); cf. Wüstenfeld, *Statthalter* IV, 6. On the campaign of Muḥammad b. Sulaymān al-Wāthiqī see: Sa'īd ibn Biṭrīq, II, 76.

85 See *Répertoire chronologique*, III, nos. 840, 961, 962. See the discussion on the inscriptions immortalising the works of al-Muqtadir's mother in Kessler, *JRAS*, 1964, 88–93; see details on her there: she had been a slave-girl belonging to al-Mu'taḍid, of Byzantine origin, and her name was Shaghab; after her son became caliph (al-Muqtadir), she was called, in the accepted manner, *al-sayyida* (the lady). The work that was done on the Dome of the Rock on her orders was supervised by her client, a certain Rabīb. Nasīm and Mufliḥ: al-Ṣūlī, 67; see Canard's translation, 118, nn. 2, 5; Hilāl al-Ṣābī, 141: Abū'l-Hawā' Nasīm was one of the most important and respected of al-Muqtadir's aides; both Nasīm and Mufliḥ were regular retainers of al-Muqtadir, see *ibid.*, 336; al-Khaṭīb al-Baghdādī, XIII, 437f. On 'Umar b. Aḥmad ibn Muḥammad al-Wāsiṭī, al-Khaṭīb al-Baghdādī (VII, 325), says he was a preacher in the al-Aqṣā mosque; the connection between him and Muḥammad b. Aḥmad al-Wāsiṭī (*supra*), who occupied the same post at the beginning of the century, is not clear. If there is no mistake in al-Khaṭīb al-Baghdādī, they were perhaps different people. From the account of Ibn Shaddād, fol. 105b, it seems that Abbasid rule in Palestine and Syria was only re-established in AH 301 (AD 913/4), when al-Muqtadir

[471–472] One should note that this was the period in which Saadia b. Joseph al-Fayyūmī, who later became Gaon of Sura, passed through Palestine on his way from Egypt to Iraq. He stayed in Tiberias until the dispute over the calendar, which I shall discuss below. It is difficult to discern any definite connection between the political events I have described and his moving from Egypt to Babylonia, although there have been attempts to do so.[86]

In AH 306 or 307 (that is, AD 918 or 919) the caliphate armies passed through Palestine, under the command of Mu'nis, al-Muqtadir's aide, on their way to assist Egypt, which was being attacked by the Fatimids from the Maghrib, and who had already managed to capture al-Jīza. The advance post of the caliphate's forces was then in Ascalon and it seems that it was from there that they sailed to Egypt.[87]

The Ikhshīdids

[473–474] The thirty years of renewed Abbasid rule in Egypt was in fact under the helm of the Mādharā'ī family, who were called after the place they hailed from, which was a town near Baṣra in Iraq. The members of this family held the treasury of the state in their hands and this was the source of their power, until the Ikhshīd, Muḥammad ibn Ṭughj, seized power in Egypt. He came from a family of nobles from Farghāna in Central Asia, and Ikhshīd was the ancient royal title employed in that area. His grandfather Juff was brought to Baghdad by Caliph al-Mu'taṣim, while his father, Ṭughj, was one of the commanders in Khumārawayh b. Aḥmad b. Ṭūlūn's army. At first, Khumārawayh appointed Ṭughj governor of Damascus, but he dismissed him afterwards. He was arrested and died in jail in Damascus. But according to Ibn Sa'īd, he was only deposed when the Abbasids regained their power in Egypt, and then he was imprisoned together with his sons Muḥammad and 'Abdallah, and he remained in jail until his death in AH 294, that is AD 906/7. Ṭughj's son Muḥammad succeeded in returning to official posts. He became one of the

appointed his son Abū'l-'Abbās, at the age of four, governor of al-Shām, and Mūsā al-Muẓaffar ruled on his behalf, but this is evidently a distortion, for in Ibn al-Athīr, *Kāmil*, VIII, 76, 85, and in Ibn Taghrī Bardī, III, 182, the name of Mu'nis (and not Mūsā) is brought up in the events of the year AH 301 as commander of the Abbasid army, and there is no mention of al-Shām, but of Egypt and the Maghrib; cf. Lane-Poole, *History*, 81.

86 See Malter, 54. Of special significance is the fact that Saadia stayed in Tiberias quite close to the period of the Qarmaṭī wars and their conquest of Tiberias described above; it seems that the Jewish population of Tiberias, with its scholars, preserved in the main, its status and strength, despite the war.

87 Ibn al-Athīr, *Kāmil*, VIII, 113f (the year AH 306); *al-'uyūn wa'l-ḥadā'iq*, IV, 203 (the year AH 307; printed *al-jazīra* instead of *al-jīza*).

assistants to the governor of Egypt, Takīn, and on his behalf fulfilled the role of governor (within the framework of the Abbasid administration) in 'Ammān firstly, and then in the whole of Trans-Jordan, until approximately AH 325 (AD 927). Subsequently he quarrelled with his patron and managed to get an appointment as governor of jund Filasṭīn. He then stayed in Ramla from AH 316, that is AD 928, and in Jumādā II AH 319, that is July AD 931, he became governor of Damascus. Al-Rāshidī, who was formerly governor of Damascus, came to Ramla in his stead.[88] When the Ikhshīd became ruler of Egypt, he took as his major aide, Abū Shujā' Fātik 'the great', also known by the nickname 'the mad' (*al-majnūn*). He had been taken captive as a child in a Byzantine land together with his brother and sister and was educated in Ramla, where he was taught the craft of script-writing and became a *kātib*, that is a scribe in an office. The Ikhshīd took him on for his own use, without paying his price to his owners (for he had the status of a slave). Fātik was employed in many capacities in the Ikhshīdid administration and was later on one of the retainers of Kāfūr.[89]

[475] An affair connected with Palestinian matters is that of the relationship of the Ikhshīd with Abū'l-Fatḥ Faḍl b. Ja'far b. Muḥammad ibn al-Furāt. He was the nephew of the Abbasid wazīr 'Alī b. Muḥammad ibn al-Furāt, who was executed in Baghdad in AH 312, that is AD 924. Faḍl himself acted as wazīr during the last days of al-Muqtadir, from 29 Rabī' II AH 320, that is 7 May AD 932, and continued to serve his successor al-Qāhir for some time, until he was arrested. During al-Rāḍī's rule, he was released by the wazīr ibn Muqla, and appointed governor over a wide area, from the Jazīra, which is northern Iraq, to Egypt. His title was *mukshif* or *wazīr al-kashf*. After the Ikhshīd's daughter married Faḍl's son (Ja'far, who is Ibn Ḥinzāba), the relationship was strengthened, and it was Faḍl who recommended that the Ikhshīd become governor of Egypt in 935, and he helped him dominate the country and dismiss Muḥammad b. 'Ali al-Mādharā'ī from his post. The latter's possessions were confiscated, but the Ikhshīd treated him mercifully and placed him in Faḍl b. Ja'far's hands, who took him to Ramla, where al-Mādharā'ī lived out the last years of his life in Faḍl's house. In AH 326, that is AD 938, Faḍl was again called to Baghdad to take on the role of wazīr, but he died before he could set out on the way, on 8 Jumādā I AH 327, that is 4 March, AD 939, and

88 'Arīb, 159; cf. Lane Poole, *History*, 81f; Abū'l-Fidā', *Mukhtaṣar*, II, 82; Ibn Sa'īd, *Mughrib*, 6; Ibn Khallikān, V, 58; Kindī, 269 (on the Mādharā'īs); 285ff (on the rivalry between Abū Bakr Muḥammad b. 'Alī al-Mādharā'ī and Ibn Ṭughj); cf. Bacharach, *Speculum*, 50(1975), 589f.

89 Ibn Khallikān, IV, 21f, who also knows something of the strong links between Fātik and the famous poet al-Mutanabbī, who dedicated poems to him as well as composing a dirge

was buried in Ramla. Then the Ikhshīd made peace with al-Mādharā'ī, who was even appointed wazīr in Egypt and became the central political figure there, particularly later on, during Kāfūr's rule.[90]

[476] Once again, as in the days of the Ṭūlūnids, Palestine under the Ikhshīdids became the battlefield for foreign armies. Ibn Rā'iq, who in 936 was the supreme commander of the Abbasid army (*amīr al-umarā'*), was appointed governor of the region of the Upper Euphrates. He wanted to prove his trustworthiness and ability by recapturing Egypt from the Ikhshīd. Towards the end of 939, the Egyptians suffered a crushing defeat in a battle in the neighbourhood of al-'Arīsh, but they recovered and succeeded in pushing Ibn Rā'iq as far as Lajjūn, where an indecisive battle took place in the middle of Ramaḍān, AH 328, that is the 24th of June AD 940. In that battle, one of the brothers of the Ikhshīd, Abū Naṣr Ḥusayn, who headed the Egyptian army, was killed. Ibn Rā'iq discovered the body himself and expressed his sorrow in the most unusual manner: he sent his own son, Abū'l-Fatḥ Muzāḥim, aged seventeen, to the Ikhshīd, to do with him whatever he saw fit. The Ikhshīd behaved nobly as well, showered Muzāḥim with presents and splendid robes, and even married him off to his daughter Fāṭima. When peace was made in this fashion, the parties made an agreement that the Ikhshīd would hold southern Palestine, including Ramla, while Ibn Rā'iq would rule over the area north of this and would receive 140,000 dinars from the Ikhshīd annually. It was said that when he took Ramla during his advance to al-'Arīsh, Ibn Rā'iq destroyed and vandalised the grave of Faḍl b. Ja'far out of bitter enmity towards the family of Ibn Furāt. He also executed two men who were in charge of Ramla on behalf of the Ikhshīd and had them crucified, and this is how the

after his death (on 11 Shawwāl AH 350, 23 September AD 961); Abū'l-Fidā', *Mukhtaṣar*, II, 103; Yāfi'ī, II, 344; cf. Wüstenfeld, *Statthalter*, IV, 44f.

90 Ibn Sa'īd, *Mughrib*, 7, 12, 24, 48; *al-'uyūn wa'l-ḥadā'iq* (MS Berlin), 175b; Ibn al-Athīr, *Kāmil*, VIII, 354; Dhahabī, *'Ibar*, II, 208; Hamadhānī, *Takmila*, 113; Ibn Khaldūn, *'Ibar*, III, 840: Faḍl was in charge of the *kharāj* in Egypt and al-Shām before he became al-Muqtadir's wazīr; he was also in the service of Ibn Rā'iq when the latter was supreme commander of the Abbasid army (*amīr al-umarā'*); cf. Sourdel, *Vizirat*, II, 467ff; the article Ibn al-Furāt (No. 4; by D. Sourdel) in *EI*²; Canard, translation of al-Ṣūlī, 154f, n. 11; see further: Ibn Taghrī Bardī, III, 264; cf. also Bacharach, *Speculum*, 50(1975), 593; in Maqrīzī, *Khiṭaṭ*, III, 51ff, we find the following details about al-Mādharā'ī (printed: al-Mārdānī): Muḥammad b. 'Alī al-Mādharā'ī was born in Nisibis, on 13 Rabī' I AH 258, 26 February AD 871; he came to Egypt with his father when he was fourteen, and succeeded to his father's office in the days of Khumārawayh, when he was fifteen. He served as the caliph's scribe, though his handwriting was not beautiful. He became wazīr under Hārūn b. Khumārawayh, amassed riches and estates, until the Ikhshīd took over Egypt. His property was then confiscated and he was handed over to Faḍl b. Ja'far ibn Furāt, in Ramla. Ibn Sa'īd, *Mughrib*, 25, notes that in Rajab AH 328, April AD 940, the son of Muḥammad al-Mādharā'ī, Ḥusayn, was appointed wazīr in Egypt (on the orders of Anūjūr, the son of the Ikhshīd) on 3 Muḥarram AH 335, the 4th of August AD 946; see also *ibid.*, 269, 285ff, on the history of this family in Egypt.

Ikhshīd found them on his return to Ramla. Ibn Rā'iq died two years after the pact was made and it is not known whether it was ever implemented.[91]

[477] At this point, another element appeared on the scene in Palestine, and this was the Ḥamdānids. They were a family of the Banū Taghlib who had gained a reputation at the beginning of the latter half of the ninth century as courageous fighters, when they set up a sort of independent local rule in the region of the northern Tigris. At the start of the tenth century, they were involved in court intrigues and internal squabbles in Baghdad. They were also known for their pro-Shiite leanings. At that time, they gradually established themselves in two centres, Mosul and Aleppo, and the source of their power lay in the Arab tribes in the area. The master of Aleppo during the period we are dealing with was Abū'l-Ḥasan 'Alī ibn Ḥamdān, called Sayf al-dawla, and he set up his base there, relying on the support of the Banū Kilāb. His ambition was to conquer Damascus and also to advance southward into Palestine. At first he met with success, and in a battle on the Rastan, a river which flows southward towards Ḥamāh, he was victorious. He took a thousand men captive and afterwards gained control of Damascus. The Ikhshīd then set up his army's camp in Tiberias and from there started to move northward. As many of Sayf al-dawla's men went over to his side, the Ikhshīd concluded that campaign with a resounding victory over his enemy in a battle near Qinnasrīn, in 945. After the death of the Ikhshīd however, in July 946, Sayf al-dawla considered the time favourable for realising his aspirations. His army thrust southward and took over all of Palestine. On Tuesday, the 24th of Jumādā I AH 335, that is the 22nd of December AD 946, the battle was fought between the army of the Ikhshīdids who had come up from Egypt and Sayf al-dawla's army, at Iksāl in the Galilee, and Sayf

[91] Al-Ṣūlī, 135, and see Canard's translation, 202, n. 10; Kindī, 288f; Ibn Miskawayh, 414: in Dhū'l-Ḥijja, AH 328, or October AD 940, news reached Baghdad of the victory of Ibn Rā'iq in al-'Arīsh; Ibn al-Athīr, *Kāmil*, VIII, 363f; the battle of Lajjūn was on the 4th of Dhū'l-Ḥijja AH 328, the 22nd of September AD 940; Ibn Shaddād, fol. 105b; Hamadhānī, *Takmila*, 116f; Ibn Sa'īd, *Mughrib*, 25: Ibn Rā'iq conquered Ramla on the last day of Dhū'l-Ḥijja AH 327, 17 October AD 939, hence the war lasted for about one year; Ibn Sa'īd returns to the account on Ibn Rā'iq on pp. 28f, as if there were two wars between the parties; he adds that in return for Muzāḥim, Ibn Rā'iq's son, being with the Ikhshīd, the latter's brother 'Abdallah, was obliged to be Ibn Rā'iq's hostage; when Muzāḥim was on his way to the Ikhshīd, he met the Ikhshīd's messengers and they told him, on his behalf, that his brother 'Abdallah's slaves were weeping and would not let him go, and therefore they proposed that Muzāḥim return to his father until the son of the Ikhshīd, Anūjūr, is sent to him. See further: Ibn Kathīr, *Bidāya*, XI, 192; Ibn Khallikān, V, 118 (a short article on Ibn Rā'iq); Ibn Khaldūn, *'Ibar*, III, 853; IV, 669; Ibn 'Adīm, *Zubda*, I, 100, 102; Ibn Taghrī Bardī, III, 253; Maqrīzī, *Khiṭaṭ*, II, 116; Ṣafadī, *al-Wāfī*, III, 69; Baybars, 140a; cf. Wüstenfeld, *Statthalter* IV, 27f; Lane-Poole, *History*, 83. On Ibn Rā'iq (who was a Khazar by origin) see also: Canard's translation of al-Ṣūlī, 82, n. 2; the article Ibn Rā'iq (by D. Sourdel) in *EI*²; cf. Bacharach. *Speculum*, 50(1975), 599f. It is important to note that at the time Ibn Rā'iq was controlling southern Palestine, the mint in Tiberias produced coins

al-dawla suffered a crushing defeat which forced him to retreat to Aleppo in the north while the army of the Ikhshīdids advanced and entered Damascus. At the head of the latter army stood the Ikhshīd's brother, Ḥasan ibn Ṭughj, Abū'l-Qāsim Ūnūjūr (or Anūjūr), the Ikhshīd's son, and the regent of Egypt, the black Kāfūr. This was not the end of the Ḥamdānid involvement in the politics of the area. They continued to be set upon spreading southward, and we shall meet up with them again fighting on Palestinian soil.[92]

[478–479] The court of the Ḥamdānids in Aleppo became a meeting place for writers and thinkers, among them the celebrated poet al-Mutanabbī and the philosopher (Turkish by origin) Abū Naṣr Muḥammad b. Muḥammad al-Fārābī. Al-Fārābī died en route when he was travelling from Damascus to Ascalon, when he was attacked by an armed band. He offered them his pack-animals and arms and everything he possessed, but they refused and as he had no alternative but to defend himself, he fought them until his death, together with that of his party. The Ḥamdānids would not abandon the search until they caught the attackers and crucified them near al-Fārābī's grave. These events, which as far as I know are only reported by al-Bayhaqī, evidently indicate the decline of internal security after the defeat of Sayf al-dawla. One can assume that armed units of this kind (the source refers to them as 'a band of robbers' commonly called *al-fityān*, that is, men of the *futuwwa*) were acting under the aegis of the Ikhshīdids, and thus al-Fārābī and the others paid with their lives for belonging to the Ḥamdānid circles.[93] The internal contradictions and daily rivalry between the two focal points of power and influence, one dependent on the tribes with its centre in Aleppo and the other headed by the Turkish establishment, the Ikhshīdids, is also to be seen in the story of the poet al-Mutanabbī, who was, as I have mentioned, of the Ḥamdānid circle. The governor of Damascus at that time (that is, its governor on behalf of the Ikhshīdids) was a Jew who hailed from Tadmur called Ibn Mālik. He demanded that al-Mutanabbī write a poem in his honour, but

imprinted with the names of the caliph al-Muttaqī and his son Abū Manṣūr. See dirhams of this kind: Blau und Stickel, *ZDMG*, 11(1857), 451 (No. 17).

92 See the entries: Ḥamdānids (by M. Canard) in *EI*², and Saif al-Dawla (by B. Carra de Vaux) in *EI*¹; Kindī, 295; Yaḥyā ibn Sa'īd (*PO*), 67; *al-'uyūn wa'l-ḥadā'iq*, IV, 395f; Dhahabī, *'Ibar*, II, 232; Ibn 'Adīm, *Zubda*, I, 114, 117; Yāfi'ī, II, 312; Ibn Taghrī Bardī, III, 291f: according to whom the battle did not take place in Iksāl but in Lajjūn (he quotes from al-Musabbiḥī, who cited Mas'ūdī, who was actually a contemporary of these events; it is interesting that he does not mention Anūjūr at all, evidently because he was very young at the time); Baybars, 106a; cf. Canard, *Hamdanides*, 581f, 586; Bacharach, *Speculum*, 50(1975), 610f, 609.

93 See the articles al-Fārābī (by R. Walzer) and Futuwwa (by C. Cahen), in *EI*²; see Bayhaqī, *Ta'rīkh*, 33f; he calls those who pursued the assassins, *umarā' al-shām*; this is an expression that is difficult to interpret precisely, but it seems that he wanted to say 'the northern commanders' or the 'Syrians', and he seems to have meant the Ḥamdānids. Bayhaqī

the poet refused and fled to Ramla, where the governor of the city, al-Ḥasan ibn ʿUbaydallah ibn Ṭughj (the nephew of the Ikhshīd), received him with honours.[94]

[480] In the year 962, a rebellion took place in Trans-Jordan which was led by Muḥammad b. Aḥmad al-Sulamī (of the Sulaym tribe). According to the brief description by Yaḥyā ibn Saʿīd, it seems that this was an uprising of the Arab tribes. Kāfūr sent an army from Egypt to fight against them, and the Banū ʿUqayl whose centre was in Syria, came to assist the army under their leader, Thimāl al-Khaffājī. They managed to entrap the leader of the uprising, brought him to Egypt and showed him to the masses riding on an elephant on Saturday, the 5th of Dhū'l-Qaʿda AH 351, that is, 5 December AD 962. Al-Sulamī was kept in jail for some time and eventually released.[95]

[481] Two generations after having controlled the Galilee and the city of Tiberias, the Qarmaṭīs again turned up within Palestinian borders. In Jumādā I AH 353 (May AD 964), they raided Tiberias. They then demanded that Sayf al-dawla, the Ḥamdānid master of Aleppo, supply them with iron. Sayf al-dawla ordered the gates of the city of Raqqa to be dismantled, and that even the scales of the merchants be confiscated, and supplied the Qarmaṭīs with an abundance of iron. This strange story apparently is evidence of the extent of the collaboration between the Qarmaṭīs and the Arab tribes in the north. In continuation to their invasion of Tiberias, the Qarmaṭīs managed actually to dominate all of Palestine, and after a number of raids on Ramla, the Ikhshīdid governor of Palestine, al-Ḥasan ibn ʿUbaydallah, was forced to pay them an annual tax. The Qarmaṭī leader, Abū ʿAlī al-Ḥasan al-Aʿṣam b. Aḥmad b. Bahrām, was in Ramla in AH 356 (AD 967). On 2 Dhū'l-Ḥijja AH 357, that is the 28th of October AD 968, a great battle was fought between the Qarmaṭīs and the Ikhshīdids (evidently in Ramla or nearby). A man related to the ʿAlids, Akhū Muslim known also as Abū Muḥammad or ʿAbdallah ibn ʿUbaydallah, was also active against the Ikhshīdids. Kāfūr,

mentions these things in the name of his teacher, Yaḥyā b. ʿAbd al-Malik (see the Introduction, *ibid.*, 4).

94 See a fragment of MS Paris Asselin No. 705, quoted in Ibn Khallikān, translated by De Slane, I, 183, in the note. It is taken from the treatise of Yūsuf al-Badīʿī al-Dimashqī (the seventeenth century); see: Vajda, *Index*, No. 3107; Brockelmann, *GAL*, I, 88; see also: Goldziher, *Hebraeische Bibliographie*, 10(1870), 59f, who quotes al-Badīʿī from MS Refaia No. 357; Palestine, at the time, was evidently a haven for rebels and people of the opposition, perhaps owing to Ḥasan ibn ʿAbdallah, the Ikhshīdid, who was governor of Ramla. There Muḥammad b. Yaḥyā, nicknamed al-Sirāj ('the candle'), found refuge. He was a Maghribi who was an active opponent of the Ikhshīd's sons after the latter's death and led a rebellion against them, on 18 Rabīʿ AH 335, the 21st of November AD 946; see Kindī, 295, and cf. also Sāwīrūs, II(2), 86, who calls that rebel Ḥanāniyā and says the contrary (which is not credible), that it was the Ikhshīd's sons who fled to Palestine then.

95 Yaḥyā ibn Saʿīd (*PO*), 92.

the Ikhshīdid regent, appointed him governor of Palestine and Syria in April 968. We do not know if the intention was to oust the Ikhshīdid Ḥasan from his office, for he was governor of Ramla at that time. This same Akhū Muslim had far-reaching ambitions and saw himself as the legitimate heir of the 'Alids, worthy of being considered the *mahdī* and of ruling the Muslim world. Thimāl al-Khaffājī, one of the leaders of the Arab tribe of Syria, the Banū 'Uqayl, supported him. When these two headed an attack against Ḥasan, they were defeated in a battle fought near Ramla. But afterwards they attacked again, in an alliance with the Qarmaṭīs. The allies won and the Ikhshīdid was forced to retreat from Ramla to Jerusalem. For two days the Qarmaṭīs plundered Ramla, until the inhabitants undertook to pay ransom to the extent of 125,000 Egyptian dinars. Many of the local inhabitants were taken captive by the Qarmaṭīs. The Ikhshīdid then came to an agreement with the Qarmaṭīs, according to which he had to pay them an annual tax of 300,000 dinars. He then left for Egypt and it seems that his journey was connected with the internal power struggles going on within Egypt at the time and also with the need to raise this money.[96]

[482] Concurrent with these events, the power of Byzantium was on the rise in its unending struggle with the Muslim world. This was a drawn-out process which must be seen against the background of the internal divisions and contentions within Islam. Firstly, one is referring, naturally, to the increasing power of the extremist Shiites, the Qarmaṭīs and the Fatimids, and the gradual separation of Egypt from the body of the caliphate, a process which weakened the Muslim world. This was well understood by a Muslim thinker of the tenth century who wrote:

When the kings of Islam followed the wicked path and began to debase it [Islam], and they began to be attacked by people like 'Alī b. Ḥamdān, or the enemies of the Muslims in Egypt, people who expropriate the property of the *waqf* in the ports,

96 Ibn al-Jawzī, *Muntaẓam*, VII, 19; Ibn Kathīr, *Bidāya*, XI, 254; Ibn Miskawayh, II, 203, describes the year 353 (964) as calamitous, in which there was drought and starvation; some 50,000 people fled, he writes, from the densely populated centres of Iraq to Damascus and Ramla; see further: Baybars, fol. 196; on the arrival in Ramla of Ḥasan the Qarmaṭī and on the battle, see Yaḥyā ibn Sa'īd, 119; Ibn 'Asākir, IV, 148ff; 'Iyāḍ, 301ff; see also Ibn Taghrī Bardī, III, 336; and cf. Madelung, *Der Islam*, 34(1959), 54f; Bianquis, *Annales islamologiques*, 11(1972), 53–57; Mez, 63f; on Ḥasan the Ikhshīdid and his expedition to Egypt: Ibn Khallikān, V, 59ff: he stayed in Egypt until 1 Rabī' II, AH 385, 22 February AD 969, and then returned to Ramla; cf. Ibn Taghrī Bardī, IV, 21 (quoting from Ibn Khallikān). The Jerusalem Karaite, Yefet b. 'Alī, a contemporary, is perhaps hinting at that period of scarcity and heavy taxes in his commentary on Nahum i:13 (For now will I break his yoke from off thee, and will burst thy bonds in sunder): 'that was the end of their enslaving Israel and collecting the *kharāj* from them. Then the *kharāj* will be abolished, as well as those who collect it from Israel, the *jahābidha*' (plural of *jahbadh*, the money-changers who were usually entrusted with the collection of taxes in exchange for the credit they offered the ruler). See the Hirschfeld ed., 20.

the Muslims lost their worth in the eyes of the Byzantines, who say: it is now eighty years that Islam is losing its rule. As these lines are being written we are in *ca.* 385 [AH, that is AD 995].

In other words, in the opinion of the writer (who attributes his view to the Byzantines), the waning process started at the beginning of the tenth century.

The Byzantine armies chalked up a number of important achievements to their credit. In the days of the emperor Romanus II (959–963), the island of Crete was taken, having formerly served as a naval base for the Muslims. At the head of the Cretan campaign stood the commander Niceophorus Phocas, who afterwards became emperor (963–969). During his reign, Cilicia, Tarsus, and Cyprus were conquered and the way to Syria was opened. The Byzantines' first hold over Aleppo was in 351, that is 962. They then seized the city, but did not take the citadel, and after much despoiling and killing, withdrew. In 969, the year the Fatimids conquered Egypt, the Byzantines subjugated Antioch and in fact took possession of the whole area of Aleppo. Abū'l-Ma'ālī Sharīf, known as Sa'd al-dawla, became their vassal. It was the assassination of the emperor Nicephorus which brought a halt to the campaign. Obviously, the purpose of the Byzantine expedition was the fulfilment of their dream to conquer Jerusalem after more than 300 years of Muslim occupation. A Muslim tradition has it that after the taking of Ṭarsūs in AH 357 (AD 968), Nicephorus ascended the *minbar* of the chief mosque there and asked: 'Where am I?' The reply was: 'on the *minbar* of Ṭarsūs'. Whereupon he said: 'not so, I am on the *minbar* of Jerusalem; it is this city which stood between you and it'. Bar Hebraeus points out that it was indeed Nicephorus' intention to proceed to Jerusalem after conquering Antioch and Aleppo, but the army was exhausted and laden down with spoils. According to Hamadhānī, the Byzantine emperor reached as far as Tripoli. He set fire to the city and took captive 100,000 youths and maidens from the coastal towns. He meant to turn to Jerusalem but was afraid of the Qarmaṭīs, who were encamped in Palestine after having attacked (Ḥasan) ibn 'Abdallah ibn Ṭughj (the Ikhshīdid governor of Palestine). According to the treaty between the *amīr* of Aleppo and the Byzantines, the Syrian districts ruled by the Ḥamdānids fell under the suzerainty of the Byzantine emperor and took upon themselves the responsibility for defending the Byzantine merchants' convoys. Byzantine sources see the northern Arab tribes, particularly the Banū 'Uqayl, as a form of vassals of Byzantium, and they appear in this guise in the account of the war against the Fatimids, which I shall deal with below.[97]

97 See what 'Abd al-Jabbār says on the decline of Islam, in *Tathbīt*, I, 168. On the disturbances: Ibn al-Athīr, *Kāmil*, VIII, 541f, 603f; Ibn al-'Adīm, *Zubda*, I, 157–169 (the years AH

[483–484] The period of the Ikhshīdids was marked by a series of acts of persecution of the Christians. In AH 325, that is AD 937, the Muslims assailed the Church of the Resurrection, set fire to it and robbed it of its treasures; three years later, the church of St Mary 'the green' in Ascalon was destroyed and plundered, with the help of the local Jews. The church was burnt down and the local bishop was forced to flee to Ramla and never again returned to Ascalon.[98] There is evidently some connection between these acts and the animosity towards Byzantium, which became more acute during the period of the Ikhshīdids. Into the pattern of this relationship between the two worlds, the Muslim and the Christian, are woven the relations between the two communities of dhimmīs in Palestine – Jews and Christians – between one another and the attitude of the Muslim authorities to each of them. The tension between Jews and Christians is not only evident in the incident in Ascalon but also in echoes that reached the distant west. This is a rather legendary story about a letter sent by the patriarch of Jerusalem to Constantinople and to Rome, whose main points were presented before the Church Council in Erfurt (932). It tells there of a quarrel between Jews and Christians in Jerusalem, in which the Muslims

357–359); Hamadhānī, *Takmila*, 201; Qalqashandī, *Ma'āthir*, 305f; Ibn al-Dawādārī, 130f; Matthew of Edessa, 15–22; Bar Hebraeus (Bedjan), 191; (Budge), 172; see sec. 550 on the description of the continuation of the Byzantine campaign, at the time of the Fatimids, and further references there. The blatant religious background to the Byzantine campaign is borne out by Nicephorus' request that the Church consider those who had fallen in battle against the Muslims as saints. As he was quarrelling with the Church over finances, his request was rejected; see Mez, 286; Krumbacher, *Geschichte*, II, 985; the Byzantine wars against the Muslims in the tenth century are also discussed in: Honigmann, *Ostgrenze*, 93–103. He has many details relating to the historical geography of these campaigns, but the events in Palestine and its region are insufficiently clear, probably due to an unfamiliarity with the Arabic sources. He lacks a proper description of the conquests and the suppressive acts of the Byzantines during their first campaign, while the description of the second campaign is superficial and faulty. He also did not notice the parallel between the emperor's letter to the king of Armenia and the Arab sources, and claims that the so-called great victories of the emperor in 974 are not mentioned in either the Greek or Arab sources – which is incorrect. On the campaign of 959–969, it is also worth noting the account preserved in Dhahabī, al-'Ayn, MS Bodl Digby Or 15, fol. 122b ff; he stresses in particular its cruel character and considerable spilling of blood and the many prisoners captured by the invaders. According to him, Damascus was also taken then (his dates are generally confused; this occurred in AH 353, i.e. AD 968, he writes).

[98] Yaḥyā ibn Sa'īd (*PO*), 21; Maqrīzī, *Khiṭaṭ*, III, 399; cf. Vincent et Abel, *Jérusalem*, II(2), 939; apparently this church became a mosque afterwards, but it reverted to a church in the name of St John or St Paul under the Crusaders. A document from the Crusaders' era, somewhere between 1163–1168, mentions the church of St John and points out that it was formerly known by the name *Mahumeria* (i.e. mosque); and it is evidently the *Mahumeria cathara* or *viridis* (that is, the pure or green mosque), mentioned in 1160 in a collection of documents of the Holy Sepulchre; see the document: Kohler, *ROC*, 7(1899), 143; see also: Vincent, *Hebron*, 241, who quotes the *Cartulaire du St Sépulchre*, edited by de Rozière, pp. 115ff (No. 58): Amalric, Count of Ascalon, confirms the donation of an estate to the Holy Sepulchre in exchange for that *Mahumeria viridis*. It is worth noting the opinion of Albright, *AJSLL*, 41(1925), 91, who still found the veneration, in the region of Ascalon,

(*Sarracenoi*) supported the Jews, as a result of bribery. After the Jews and the Christians locked up their houses of prayer (*templum Domini*, that is, the Church of the Holy Sepulchre and the *sacellum* of the Jews), and each of the sides fasted for three days, the Christian shrine opened like a miracle and revealed the crucified Jesus in all his glory, in the glow of self-lighting incandescence. This caused the Jews of Jerusalem to hasten and convert to Christianity. The only germ of truth in the entire story seems to be that there was inter-faith tension in Jerusalem and that Muslims and Jews joined together against the Christians, as in Ascalon.

The Ikhshīdids did not hesitate to use the Palestinian Christians as a tool to put pressure on the Byzantines when they thought the moment was right. Such was the case in 940, when they found out that the Byzantines were abusing the Muslim captives. The Ikhshīdids put pressure on them through the patriarch of Jerusalem. This is also reflected in the Ikhshīd's letter to the emperor Romanus, a version of which has been preserved in Ibn Sa'īd. The Ikhshīd prides himself on being the ruler of 'Filasṭīn, the sacred land, in which there are the al-Aqṣā mosque and the Christian patriarch . . . and to which Christians and Jews make pilgrimages . . . and where the Messiah and his mother were born, and is the place where the sepulchres of the two are to be found . . .'[99]

[485] Towards the end of May 966, severe anti-Christian riots occurred in Jerusalem, and one can assume that these were also a reverberation of the Byzantine campaign which I have described earlier. The church of St Constantine and the church of the Resurrection were ransacked and the latter's dome collapsed as the result of setting the building on fire, and the patriarch of Jerusalem, John VII, died in that same conflagration. 'The Jews have overtaken the Muslims in their acts of destruction and ruination', remarks Yaḥyā ibn Sa'īd. He attributes the responsibility for these disturbances to the governor of Jerusalem on behalf of the Ikhshīdids, Muḥammad b. Ismā'īl al-Ṣinājī, who was taking his revenge on the

of *al-sitt al-khaḍrā*, or *sittnā al-khaḍrā* ('the green Lady') by Arab women (in 1925) which he assumed to be a remnant of the worship of Ashtoret.

99 See the sources on the letter of the patriarch of Jerusalem: *MGH*, Legum sectio IV, Constitutiones et acta publica (ed. L. Weiland, Hann. 1893), 4f, 7.; *Quellen zur bayrischen und deutschen Geschichte*, I, 410f; Riant, *MAIBL*, 31(1884), 166. Cf. Starr, *Jews*, 151 (No. 90). Sharf (*Byzantine Jewry*, 95) quotes from a secondary source, in an incorrect manner; he evades the fact that a letter from the patriarch of Jerusalem is being referred to, and his discussion there of the degree of truth in the story of the conversion is based on what is said by the Karaite commentator Salmon b. Yeruḥim in his commentary to Psalms, ch. xxx, a generation or more after the Council of Erfurt, the significance of which will be clarified below, in the discussion of the events of 966–975. Pressure by the patriarch (the *jāthalīq*, catholicus): Ibn al-Jawzī, *Muntaẓam*, VI, 353; the Ikhshīd's letter: ibn Sa'īd, *Mughrib*, 18ff, cf.: Canard, *AIEO*, 2(1936), 189–209, and his translation, commentary and discussion. The time of the letter: 325, i.e. 937.

Christians because they would not submit to his demands for gratuities.

Yaḥyā ibn Sa'īd describes the events as follows: this happened in the days of the patriarch Yuḥannā b. Jamī'. The governor of Jerusalem, Muḥammad b. Ismā'īl al-Ṣinājī would wrong him at every opportunity and requested bribes beyond the legal norms of taxation. The patriarch's repeated complaints to Kāfūr were of no avail, despite the fact that Kāfūr asked the governor of Ramla, Ḥasan b. 'Ubaydallah ibn Ṭughj, to intervene and put a halt to these abuses. The efforts of the Christian officials in Egypt also did not help. On the feast of Pentecost (*al-'anṣara*) al-Ṣinājī again tried to extort more than he was due. Whereupon, the patriarch went down to Ramla and complained to Ḥasan ibn 'Ubaydallah, and the latter sent one of the commanders of the army named Takīn, to accompany him and to warn al-Ṣinājī. However, the latter had gathered a large group of his followers together and demanded that the patriarch come to him. When the patriarch learned of this gathering, he hid in the church of the Resurrection. Al-Ṣinājī rode there with his men, while placing Takīn, Ḥasan's messenger, in jail. The patriarch refused to go out to him, though he was promised an *amān*. Then al-Ṣinājī's crew set fire to the gates of St Constantine's church and afterwards also to the gates of the church of the Resurrection. The dome of the church of the Holy Sepulchre collapsed and the church was looted. The church of Zion was also robbed and burnt down. On the following day, Tuesday, the patriarch was found hiding in one of the oil basins of the church of the Resurrection. He was killed, dragged to the church of St Constantine, and there his body was tied to a pillar and set on fire.[100]

[486] In April 968, Kāfūr, the regent of Egypt, died. From this juncture onwards, anarchy reigned in Egypt. The son of 'Alī, the Ikhshīd's son, Abū'l-Fawāris Aḥmad, who was to have succeeded as ruler of Egypt, was eleven years old, and the central political figure was Ibn Ḥinzāba, that is, Ja'far, son of Faḍl b. Ja'far ibn Furāt. The army wanted Ḥasan ibn 'Ubaydallah, governor of Ramla, who was the cousin of the child-ruler's father, to be regent of Egypt. Ḥasan, however, became involved in the struggle going on in Palestine at the time. Out of despair, Ḥasan b. 'Ubaydallah,

[100] Yaḥyā ibn Sa'īd (*PO*), 94f, 101–104; Cedrenus (Bonn), II, 374; Le Quien, III, 466; Baumstark, *Bauten*, 16f; Riant, *MAIBL*, 31 (1884), 164; Dositheos, in Papadopoulos I, 243; see *ibid.*, III, 129. Another version of the governor of Jerusalem's name: al-Ṣabāḥī, and this is understandably the result of the Arabic script. See the fragment from Dhahabī's Ta'rikh al-Islām, quoted in Ibn Miskawayh, II, 220f; the patriarch complained to Kāfūr about the burning of the church, and Kāfūr wrote to the governor of Jerusalem, but in the interim, the attack on the church and the murder of the patriarch took place. Kāfūr informed the Byzantine emperor that he would renovate the church and that it would be even lovelier than it had been before, but the emperor replied: 'No, I shall build it, with the sword.'

the Ikhshīdid, appealed to the Fatimid caliph al-Mu'izz and invited him to come and establish order in Egypt.[101]

[487] It appears that the Ikhshīdids showed special interest in Palestine and Jerusalem, although explicit evidence of this fact is rather meagre. An inscription on the Temple Mount testifies that a wall was built (or renovated?) there on the order of 'Alī, the Ikhshīd's son, and Kāfūr, in AH 350, that is, AD 961/2. As to Ramla, the major city of Palestine, apparently a number of government officials, Turkish leaders and others, preferred it to Egypt. Some of the leaders of the 'Alids, heads of the Shiites, also lived in Palestine at that time. The family of the descendants of 'Abbās b. 'Alī Ibn Abī Ṭālib lived in Tiberias and they seem to have had contacts with the Qarmaṭīs. A member of this family, of the eighth generation since 'Alī, Laḥḥā Abū'l-Ṭayyib Muḥammad b. Ḥamza, who has been mentioned above, succeeded in accumulating a great deal of property and possessed enormous wealth and estates. As mentioned, he was killed by Ṭughj, the Ikhshīd's father, because of his connections with the Qarmaṭīs. In Ramla, there lived the family of the aforementioned Akhū Muslim: the two brothers al-Ḥasan and 'Ubaydallah (the father of this Akhū Muslim), the sons of Ṭāhir b. Yaḥyā and their families. 'Ubaydallah had two other sons apart from Akhū Muslim: Abū Ja'far Muslim and Abū'l-Ḥusayn 'Īsā. Abū Ja'far Muslim was the oldest and considered the leader of the 'Alids in his time. Ibn Sa'īd mentions another family of the 'Alids in Ramla and the *majlis* of Ṭāhir b. Ḥusayn. Of his son, al-Ḥasan, it is told that he received very large grants amounting to 15,000 dinars, from Ibn Rā'iq after the latter reached the agreement with the Ikhshīd and withdrew from Ramla.[102]

[488] I have already mentioned the estates of the Ikhshīdids in Palestine and the coins they minted there. It is obvious that close links existed between Egypt and Palestine in their day. The variety of dinars and their improved quality are witness to economic development and flourishing commerce. The Jews were undoubtedly involved in this process. Accord-

101 See Ibn al-Dawādārī, 120ff; Ibn Khallikān, I, 346 (with an interpretation of the name Ibn Ḥinzāba: Ḥinzāba was his grandmother, his father's mother). Cf. Lane-Poole, *History*, 89f; Bianquis, *Annales islamologiques*, 11(1972), 63f; see coins minted in Palestine (evidently in Ramla) found in Ramla, from the period of the end of the Ikhsīdid's rule, imprinted with the names of the sons of the Ikhshīd: Abū'l-Qāsim (Anūjūr, AH 335–346, i.e. AD 948–958); 'Alī (AH 353, i.e. AD 964); Kāfūr (AH 355, i.e. AD 966); Abū'l-Fawāris Aḥmad b. 'Alī, together with al-Ḥasan ibn 'Ubaydallah (AH 357/8, i.e. AD 968), in: Mitchell and Levy, *INJ*, 3(1965/6), 48ff; see a coin from Ramla (*bi-filasṭīn*) with the name of Abū'l-Qāsim, son of the Ikhshīd, from the year AH 345 (AD 956/7), in Blau and Stickel, *ZDMG*, 11(1857), 458.

102 The inscription: *Répertoire chronologique*, IV, No. 1541 (pp. 172f). Tiberias: Ibn Ḥazm, *Jamhara*, 67; see Ibn Sa'īd, *Mughrib*, 5, 38f (with a story of a woman of Ramla whose son was arrested and how he was returned to her), 51; cf. Bianquis, *ibid.*, 56f (who did not notice Ramla's special status in these matters).

ing to Arab sources, the Jew 'Alī b. Khalaf (Aaron), a Babylonian politician and financier, was in the service of the Ikhshīd, and also stood by him in his war with Ibn Rā'iq. On the other hand, this 'Alī had connections with Nāṣir al-Dawla, the Ḥamdānid ruler of northern Syria. Eventually the Ikhshīd had him jailed, and he was only released after the Ikhshīd's death in the summer of 946, on the orders of Muḥammad b. 'Alī al-Mādharā'ī. Elsewhere I have shown that this 'Alī was evidently the son of Aaron (Khalaf) ha-Kohen Gaon b. Joseph ibn Sarjāda, the adversary of Saadia Gaon and head of the yeshiva of Pumbedita. Another Jew serving the Ikhshīdids was the aforementioned Ibn Mālik, governor of Damascus on their behalf. It appears that the westward migration of the Jewish merchants from Iraq during that period, engendered by the harsh internal conditions in the Abbasid caliphate, contributed greatly to the economic prosperity in Palestine and Egypt.[103]

Muslim personalities in Palestine during the period of the Ṭūlūnids and Ikhshīdids

[489] One of the most pre-eminent and celebrated figures in Palestine during this period was Muḥammad b. 'Uthmān, who is Abū Zur'a al-Dimashqī, and was the chief cadi of Damascus, later appointed to Egypt and the junds Filasṭīn and Urdunn as well. He was given this further appointment by the Ṭūlūnid ruler, Hārūn ibn Khumārawayh, in AH 284, that is AD 897, and he established himself in Egypt. Ṣafadī tells of his home in Damascus, which was near *bāb al-barīd*, and also notes that his grandfather was a Jew who converted to Islam and that his family were clients (*mawālī*) of the Umayyads (or of the Banū Thaqīf). He was the man who prevailed over the Shāfi'ī *madhhab* (school of law) in Egypt, and from then onwards, until AH 664, that is AD 1266, the chief cadis there were of this school. He died in Damascus in AH 302, that is AD 914/5.[104]

[490] Of the scholars of Muslim law who flourished in Palestine, one should also mention Aḥmad ibn 'Alī ibn Shu'ayb al-Nasā'ī, who wrote one of the six compilations of law recognised in Islam. Because of his Shiite convictions he was forced to leave Damascus for Ramla, where he died in AH 302, that is AD 914/5, some say he was murdered.[105]

[103] See Mas'ūdī, *Murūj*, VIII, 65; IX, 31; Ibn al-Athīr, *Kāmil*, VIII, 310, 385; Ibn Sa'īd, *Mughrib*, 45 (see the translation on p. 70, and n. 7; p. 71, n. 2); on the westward migration, see: al-Ṣūlī, 251; Ibn al-Jawzī, *Muntaẓam*, VI, 331; Dhahabī, *Ta'rīkh* (MS Paris 1581), fol. 197a; cf. Gil, *Sefunot*, NS 1(1979/80), 22f.

[104] See Kindī, 480; Subkī, *Ṭabaqāt*, III, 196ff; Ṣafadī, *al-Wāfī*, IV, 82.

[105] Ibn Khallikān, I, 78; Ibn al-Jawzī, *Muntaẓam*, VI, 131f; Subkī, *Ṭabaqāt*, III, 14ff, see also the editor's note, which has more references. Cf. the article al-Nasā'ī in *EI*[1] (by A. J. Wensinck, and there he is called Ibn Shu'ayb, as in Ibn al-Jawzī and in Subkī, whereas

[491–501] One of the most important Arab grammarians, Abū'l-Qāsim 'Abd al-Raḥmān ibn Isḥaq al-Zajjājī al-Nihāwandī, lived in Tiberias for some time. As his name indicates, he came from Nihāwand and was brought up and educated in Baghdad. According to one report, he was a friend of the person in charge of the Ikhshīdids' estates in Syria and Palestine, Ibn al-Ḥārith, and when the latter left Damascus, he moved with him to Tiberias, where he died in Ramaḍān AH 340, that is February AD 952. His great treatise, *al-jumal fi'l-naḥw* (or *al-jumal al-kubrā*) has been preserved in manuscript.[106]

A slightly younger contemporary who also lived in Tiberias was Sulaymān b. Aḥmad b. Ayyūb, Abū'l-Qāsim al-Lakhmī al-Ṭabarānī. He was born in Acre in AH 260 (AD 874), whence he moved to Tiberias. Later on, he spent a year in Jerusalem and after that, in Caesarea. In his old age, he moved to Ḥimṣ in Syria, and wandered as far as Iṣfahān, Persia, where he died on the 18th of Dhū'l-Qa'da AH 360 (12 October AD 971). He wrote many books and he became renowned mainly for his collections of ḥadīths arranged in the order of personalities' names, one of which was printed: *al-mu'jam al-ṣaghīr*.[107]

Tiberias during that century was a thriving centre of Muslim scholarship and apart from those already mentioned, we know of a number of Muslim intellectuals and spiritual leaders who settled there and are mentioned in al-Ṭabarānī's anthology. To mention but a few, there was 'Abd al-Waḥīd ibn Isḥaq, who died *ca.* 900;[108] Ṭāhir b. 'Alī b. 'Abdūs Abū'l-Ṭayyib, a contemporary of 'Abd al-Waḥīd, who was the cadi of Tiberias and a descendant of a family of converts, *mawālī* of the Banū Hāshim, that is, of the Abbasids;[109] and Ḥāmid b. al-Ḥasan al-Bazzār (a seed or grain merchant), who was a notary (*mu'addal*) at the same time and who was a pupil of another Tiberian, Ṣāliḥ b. Bishr.[110]

Another figure who settled in Tiberias was a man from Baṣra, Abū Bakr Yamūt b. al-Muzarra', who died in Tiberias in AH 303 (AD 915/6). It was said that his real name was Muḥammad, and that he was the nephew of the

Shu'ayb was apparently his grandfather's name); Sezgin, I, 167. With regard to his death there is conflicting information; according to one version he died in Mecca.

106 Ibn al-Athīr, *Kāmil*, VIII, 491; Subkī, *Ṭabaqāt*, III, 136; Dhahabī, *'Ibar*, II, 254; Ibn al-Athīr, *Lubāb*, I, 497; Ibn Taghrī Bardī, III, 302f; Ibn Khallikān, III, 136; cf. Brockelmann, *GAL*, G I, 110; S I, 170f.

107 Ibn Abī Ya'lā, II, 49f; Jazarī, I, 311, Ibn al-'Imād, III, 30; Ibn 'Asākir, VI, 240ff; Abū Nu'aym, *Akhbār Iṣbahān*, I, 335; Ibn al-Jawzī, *Muntaẓam*, VII, 54; Ibn al-Athīr, *Lubāb*, II, 80; Ibn Taghrī Bardī, IV, 59; Dhahabī, *'Ibar*, II, 315f (*ibid.* details with dates on his campaigns); *idem, 'Ulūw*, 165; Yāqūt, *Buldān*, III, 510; Ibn Khallikān, II, 407; cf. Sezgin, I, 195ff, who has a list of his books, to which a collection (*musnad*) of ḥadīths in the name of al-Awzā'ī should be added, see Ishbīlī, II, 149.

108 Ṭabarānī, *Mu'jam*, II, 161.

109 *Ibid.*, I, 184; Ibn 'Asākir, VII, 48f.

110 Ṭabarānī, *Mu'jam*, I, 155.

greatest Arab writer of the time, al-Jāḥiẓ.[111] Another émigré who settled in Tiberias was Abū 'Abdallah al-Tawazī, from Tawaz in Persia (in the province of Fāris, near the Persian Gulf). He came to Tiberias via Baghdad, and died there in AH 308 (AD 920).[112] One generation later we find another man of Baghdad living in Tiberias – Abū'l-Faraj Muḥammad ibn Sa'īd, who used to travel to Damascus and even to Egypt in order to expound his teachings. He died in about AH 355 (AD 965).[113] Living in Tiberias at the same time was Sa'īd ibn Hāshim ibn Marthad al-Ṭabarānī, whose father Hāshim I have mentioned above.[114] We also know the name of the governor of Tiberias in the days of the Ikhshīdids; he was Muḥammad b. Takīn. As one can see from his name, he was a Turk.[115] One of the Islamic scholars who moved from Tiberias to Antioch was al-Ḥasan b. Ḥajjāj b. Ghālib, Abū 'Alī ibn Ḥaydara, also called al-Zayyāt, that is to say, he was an oil merchant. He died in AH 347 (AD 958/9).[116]

[502–508] The following were teaching in Jerusalem during the same period: 'Abdallah ibn Muḥammad ibn Muslim al-Faryābī, hailed from Faryāb in Khurāsān, in the Juzjān district (some 150 kilometres west of Balkh).[117] One of the teachers of the Tiberias grammarian Abū'l-Qāsim ibn Isḥaq al-Zajjājī, Salāma ibn Nāhiḍ al-Tiryāqī, also lived in Jerusalem.[118] A man from 'Aynūn (the Hebron area) who lived in Jerusalem was 'Abd al-Ṣamad b. Muḥammad b. Abī 'Imrān, Abū Muḥammad al-Hamadānī, that is, he hailed originally from Hamadān in Jibāl, or Media (ancient Ecbatana). He died in 'Aynūn in AH 294 (AD 906/7).[119] Two figures, perhaps father and son, whose death in Rabī' II 305 (October 917) is commemorated in a grave-inscription on the Temple Mount, were Hiba b. Sulaymān and Salāma b. Hiba, and they may also have been scholars of some stature in Muslim law.[120] A man from Baghdad who settled in Jerusalem was Aḥmad ibn Maḥmūd, Abū'l-Ḥusayn al-Shama'ī (the

[111] Al-Khaṭīb al-Baghdādī, *Ta'rīkh*, XIV, 358; Jazarī, II, 392; Ibn al-Athīr, *Kāmil*, VIII, 96, 106 (in the first place he lists him among the dead in AH 303, and in the other, in AH 304); Ibn Taghrī Bardī, III, 191; Ibn Khallikān, VII, 53; Ibn al-Jawzī, *Muntaẓam*, VI, 143 (who tells that he did not answer when asked what his name was, lest it be implied that he wishes to die: *Yamūt* means: will die, in Arabic).

[112] Ibn Taghrī Bardī, III, 199. Tawwaz (or: Tawwaj), see: Yāqūt, *Buldān*, I, 890f, 894; Le Strange, *Lands*, 259 (according to whom – writing about a century ago – the site of this city, an important industrial town in the Middle Ages, was still unidentified).

[113] Al-Khaṭīb al-Baghdādī, *Ta'rikh*, V, 312.

[114] Ṭabarānī, *Mu'jam*, I, 171.

[115] Ibn Sa'īd, *Mughrib*, IV, 33.

[116] Ibn 'Asākir, IV, 159f; Yāqūt, *Buldān*, III, 513.

[117] Ṭabarānī, *Mu'jam*, I, 215; Faryāb: cf. Le Strange, *Lands*, 425.

[118] Ṭabarāni, *Mu'jam*, I, 174; Ibn al-Athīr, *Lubāb*, I, 175; called al-Tiryāqī because he was good at preparing the *tiryāq*, a medicine for stomach illnesses.

[119] Ṭabarānī, *Mu'jam*, I, 247; Yāqūt, *Buldān*, III, 765; Jazarī, I, 391; Ibn al-Athīr, *Lubāb*, II, 123.

[120] *Répertoire chronologique*, III, 108 (No. 988).

candle-maker), who died in Egypt in AH 352 (AD 963).[121] A contemporary from the same city, who also settled in Jerusalem and taught there, was Muḥammad ibn Ibrāhīm Abū 'Abdallah, a descendant of a family of converts, evidently Persians (the name of one of his ancestors was Mihrān, a genuine Persian name), *mawālī* of the Banū Thaqīf. His father's brother was one of the most famous Muslim teachers of the time, a man from Naysābūr, Abū'l-'Abbās Muḥammad b. Isḥaq al-Sirāj (the candle) al-Naysābūrī, who died in AH 313, that is AD 925.[122] In AH 340 (AD 951/2), a certain Aḥmad b. Abī Karāsa, who constructed a building for religious purposes (*maqām*) on the Temple Mount, is named in an inscription there.[123]

[509–515] In Ramla, the ascetic Ṣāliḥ ibn Yūsuf, Abū Shu'ayb al-Muqanna' (the veiled), became known for his teaching and his wisdom during the Ṭūlūnid period. He originated from Wāsiṭ in Iraq. Aḥmad b. Muḥammad al-Maqdisī, writing about the middle of the fourteenth century, mentions that people would come to his grave to pray for rain. Ṣāliḥ died in Ramla in AH 282, that is, AD 895.[124] Abū 'Abd al-Mu'min Aḥmad ibn Shaybān and his pupil Abū Bakr ibn al-Murajjā, who was a *ḥāfiẓ* (a title given to a very learned man, a prodigy), were both of Ramla.[125] For a time, during the same period, one of the outstanding Egyptian scholars, Bakr b. Sahl b. Ismā'īl b. Nāfi', Abū Muḥammad al-Dumyāṭī lived in Ramla. He was of a family of converts, *mawālī* of the Banū 'Abbās. He remained in Ramla after making a pilgrimage to Mecca and died there in 289, that is 902. It was said of him that when he stayed in Jerusalem, 1000 dinars were collected in order to convince him to remain there and teach *tafsīr*, interpretation of the Koran.[126] Abū'l-Ṭayyib Aḥmad b. Rīḥān b. 'Abdallah, of Baghdad, settled in Ramla and taught ḥadīth there and in Sidon as well.[127] Abū Bakr al-'Atakī, who is Aḥmad b. 'Amr b. 'Abd al-Khāliq, al-Bazzār, was one of the scholars of Islām of Baṣra who settled in Ramla. He died in Rabī' I, 291, February 904 (some say, the following year). The name al-'Atakī is derived from 'Atīk, a clan of the Banū Azd (it seems that one of his ancestors was a client of that clan). He is said to have composed a collection of ḥadīths, *al-musnad al-kabīr*.[128] At the same time, there lived in

121 Al-Khaṭīb al-Baghdādī, *Ta'rīkh*, V, 157.

122 *Ibid.*, I, 411; the time of his uncle's death: *ibid.*, 252; Subkī, *Ṭabaqāt*, III, 109.

123 *Répertoire chronologique*, IV, 125f (No. 1458).

124 Maqdisī, *Muthīr* (Khālidī), 56; 'Ulaymī, 262.

125 Ṭabarāni, *Mu'jam*, II, 150; Dhahabī, *Mīzān*, I, 103; Ibn Ḥajar, *Tahdhīb*, I, 39; who also knows the name of Aḥmad's grandfather: al-Walīd b. Ḥassān.

126 Dhahabī, *'Ibar*, II, 82f; *idem, Mīzān*, I, 245; Sam'ānī, V, 277ff; Ibn 'Asākir, III, 285f; Yāqūt, *Buldān*, II, 606.

127 Al-Khaṭīb al-Baghdādī, *Ta'rīkh*, IV, 160.

128 Al-Khaṭīb al-Baghdādī, *Ta'rīkh*, IV, 334. 'Atīk: Ibn al-Athīr, *Lubāb*, II, 120; Ishbīlī, II, 137f; Khafājī, II, 271: al-Bazzār, because he dealt in producing oil from flax-seed;

Ramla one of the greatest of Shāfi'ī scholars, Abū'l-Ḥasan Manṣūr b. Ismā'īl al-Ḍarīr ('the blind'), who had the reputation of a *faqīh*, that is, an expert on matters of Muslim law. He died in Fustat, in Jumādā I 306, October 918.[129] Concurrently, one of the central figures in early Muslim mysticism (Ṣūfism), also lived in Ramla. He was Aḥmad b. Yaḥyā, Abū 'Abdallah, who used to be called Ibn al-Jallā', and who came from Baghdad. He had been a pupil of one of the first outstanding Ṣūfī figures, the Egyptian Dhū'l-Nūn (who died in 861). It was told that when he was young, he asked his parents 'to give him to God' and they agreed. He then left his home for a considerable time and when he wished to return, they would not let him enter the house despite the fact that it was raining heavily that night, for 'we gave our son to God and we are Arabs, we do not take back what we have given'. He died in Rajab AH 306, that is December AD 918.[130]

[516–525] At the beginning of the tenth century, the cadi of Ramla was Abū'l-Qāsim 'Abdallah b. Muḥammad b. Ja'far al-Qazwīnī; that is, he hailed from Qazwīn in Persia. He spent his last years in Egypt, and died in AH 315, that is AD 927. It was said that towards the end of his life, he deviated from the right path and inclined to Shiism.[131] Following him in this role, we find as cadi of Ramla, Muḥammad b. Muḥammad, Abū'l-Ṭayyib al-Ḥanẓalī, who died in Ramla in AH 337, that is, AD 948.[132] 'Uthmān b. Muḥammad b. Shādhān was cadi in Ramla after that, and died during Kāfūr's rule, in *ca.* 965.[133] Abū'l-Qāsim Muḥammad b. al-Ḥasan al-Nakha'ī, known as Ibn Ka's, also stayed in Ramla. He was a scholar from Kūfa, held various offices in Palestine and Syria, then returned to Baghdad, and from there he was sent to Ramla on a mission. He drowned on 'Āshūrā' in the year AH 324, that is, December AD 935. He was considered an expert in Abū Ḥanīfa's system of law.[134]

Another scholar who lived in Ramla at the same time was a man of Dājūn (Beit Dagan), Muḥammad b. Aḥmad b. 'Umar Abū Bakr al-Ḍarīr

Dhahabī, *Duwal*, I, 139: he was the most famous scholar of his day; *idem, 'Ibar*, II, 92; *idem, Mīzān*, I, 124 (Dhahabī has a different time for his death from that of the others: 192 [i.e. 808], which is evidently an error); Abū Nu'aym, *Akhbār Iṣbahān*, I, 104f (according to whom he visited Iṣfahān twice, the second time in AH 286, i.e. AD 899).

129 Ibn Khallikān, V, 289ff; Subkī, *Ṭabaqāt*, III, 478–483.

130 Al-Khaṭīb al-Baghdādī, *Ta'rīkh*, V, 213ff; Ibn al-Jawzī, *Muntaẓam*, VI, 148f (containing the story of his parents); Ibn 'Asākir, II, 111ff; Sulamī, *Ṭabaqāt*, 166–169.

131 Ibn al-Jawzī, *Muntaẓam*, VII, 152 (according to him, he wrote chiefly summaries based on the books of al-Shāfi'ī; his deviations were noticeable in his poetry, in which there was an inclination towards the Shiites); Subkī, *Ṭabaqāt*, III, 320; Dhahabī, *'Ibar*, II, 162; Ibn al-Athīr, *Lubāb*, II, 261.

132 Al-Khaṭīb al-Baghdādī, *Ta'rīkh*, III, 215f; see *ibid.*, n. 1 on p. 216.

133 Kindī, 583; Tadmurī (BM Or 1284), 63b (who calls him: 'Uthmān b. Ja'far).

134 Al-Khaṭīb al-Baghdādī, *Ta'rīkh*, XII, 70f; cf. Canard, translation of al-Ṣūlī, 128, n. 7.

(the blind). He died in Rajab AH 324, that is February AD 936.[135] Ismā'īl b. 'Abd al-Wāḥid al-Raba'ī (after the Banū Rabī'a) al-Maqdisī, Abū Hāshim, was a contemporary of the aforementioned and lived in Ramla. In AH 321, that is, AD 933, he was head of the cadis in Egypt for two months, but after a paralytic stroke, he returned to Ramla and died there in AH 325, that is, AD 937. He was one of the confidants of the strong man of Egypt at that time, Abū Bakr Muḥammad b. 'Alī al-Mādharā'ī, and according to al-Kindī, the reason for his leaving Egypt was the uprising of the army against al-Mādharā'ī. Ismā'īl was even forced to remain in hiding for some time.[136] Muḥammad b. Ja'far, who is Abū Nu'aym al-Ḥāfiẓ al-Kharā'iṭī al-Sāmirī, that is, a man of Samarrā in Iraq, settled in Ramla. A few of the books he wrote have been preserved in manuscript, among these are *i'tilāl al-qulūb* ('hearts' weakness'), about love and lovers; *makārim al-akhlāq* ('the noble manners') and *masāwī al-akhlāq* ('the bad manners'). It is said that he lived and died in Ramla, though some say Ascalon and others Jaffa. He died in Rabī' I AH 327, January AD 939.[137] 'Abdallah b. Muḥammad b. Ṭuwayt, a man of Ramla mentioned in Ṭabarānī was one of the scholars of the city at that time.[138] Abū Bakr Aḥmad b. 'Amr b. Jābir was a famous *ḥāfiẓ* who settled in Ramla. His livelihood came from milling and he was hence called al-Ṭaḥḥān. He died in AH 333, that is AD 945.[139] Learned men of Baghdad who had settled in Ramla in about AH 350 (AD 961) and taught there were Muḥammad b. Aḥmad b. 'Absūn and Aḥmad b. Ṣāliḥ b. 'Umar b. Isḥaq, known as Abū Bakr al-Baghdādī.[140]

[526–530]. In Ascalon, Ḥamdān b. Ghārim b. Yanār (or: Nayār), Abū Ḥāmid, was famous; he came there from Bukhārā, from a village named Zandanā (and was therefore also called al-Zandī). He died in Ramaḍān AH 280, that is November AD 893.[141]

During this period, the following were also active in Ascalon: Muḥammad b. 'Ubayd b. Ādam, the grandson of the Ādam b. Abī Iyās

135 Jazarī, II, 77; Sam'ānī, V, 268; Ibn al-Athīr, *Lubāb*, I, 402; Yāqūt, *Buldān*, II, 515; cf. Khālidī, 124f; Musharraf, fol. 53a, mentions a scholar called Abū Bakr Muḥammad b. Aḥmad al-Nābulusī, who is possibly the same person.

136 Subkī, *Ṭabaqāt*, III, 222; Kindī, 484.

137 Al-Khaṭīb al-Baghdādī, *Ta'rīkh*, II, 140f; Ibn al-Athīr, *Kāmil*, V, 308; Ibn al-Jawzī, *Muntaẓam*, VI, 298f; Sam'ānī, V, 75f; Ibn al-Athīr, *Lubāb*, I, 352; Dhahabī, *'Ibar*, II, 209; Abū'l-Fidā', *Mukhtaṣar*, II, 86; cf. Brockelmann, *GAL*, S I, 250.

138 Ṭabarānī, *Mu'jam*, I, 220.

139 Dhahabī, *'Ibar*, II, 229; Ṣafadī, *al-Wāfī*, VII, 270.

140 Al-Khaṭīb al-Baghdādī, *Ta'rīkh*, I, 328f; Ṣāliḥ b. 'Umar, see *ibid.*, IV, 205; Jazarī, I, 62 (No. 266).

141 Ibn 'Asākir, IV, 432; Ibn al-Athīr, *Lubāb*, I, 511, with a discussion on the by-name Zandī. Zandanā, a village still existing today, some twenty-five kilometres north of Bukhara. See Le Strange, *Lands*, 462; see Yāqūt, *Buldān*, II, 952, where the by-name derived from the name of this village is Zandanī, or Zandajī (the famous weaves produced there were called by this name).

mentioned above, who emigrated from Khurāsān and settled in Ascalon;[142] 'Abdallah b. Muḥammad b. Abī'l-Sarī;[143] and Abū'l-'Abbās Muḥammad b. Ḥasan b. Qutayba – his father's brother was Bakkār b. Qutayba, who had been chief cadi in Egypt.[144] 'Abd al-Jabbār b. Abī 'Āmir al-Siḥillīnī (in some sources: al-Sijillīnī), from the village of Siḥillīn (according to Yāqūt) in the district (*kūra*) of Ascalon.[145]

[531–542] Of the Islamic scholars in Acre during that period, I shall mention Nafīs al-Rūmī;[146] Muḥammad b. Ibrāhīm b. Sāriya;[147] Abū Bakr al-Khiḍr b. Muḥammad b. Ghawth al-Tanūkhī, who died in AH 325, that is AD 937;[148] Sa'dūn b. Suhayl;[149] and Aḥmad b. 'Abdallah al-Liḥyānī, who was said to have taught in Acre in AH 275, that is AD 888/9.[150]

Living in Gaza during that time were 'Abdallah b. Wuhayb;[151] al-Ḥusayn b. 'Alī al-Naysābūrī, who evidently came from Naysābūr in Persia to study the teachings of Mālik b. Anas with another Gazan, al-Ḥasan b. al-Faraj.[152]

In Caesarea, we find Ibrāhīm b. Mu'āwiya, Abū Sufyān; he is mentioned in the year AH 275, that is AD 888/9.[153] In 'Aqīr (Akron) there lived Abū Ja'far Muḥammad b. Aḥmad b. Ibrahīm; he evidently moved to Ramla afterwards, for he is called al-'Aqarī al-Ramlī.[154]

'Abd al-Raḥmān (Abū Muḥammad) the son of Hārūn b. Sa'īd b. al-Haytham, who has been mentioned above, was still living in Eilat and he died in Shawwāl AH 278, that is January/February AD 892.[155] In connection with Hebron, Tadmurī mentions Muḥammad b. Aḥmad al-Najdī.[156] Muḥammad b. 'Abdallah b. 'Umayr al-Yāfūnī, is mentioned as living in Jaffa, in 900 or thereabout.[157]

142 Ṭabarānī, *Mu'jam*, II, 83; Dhahabī, *Mīzān*, III, 679.
143 Ṭabarānī, *Mu'jam*, I, 214.
144 Ṭabarānī, *Mu'jam*, I, 44; Dhahabī, *'Ibar*, II, 147; on his father's brother, see Kindī, 477ff.
145 Ṭabarānī, *Mu'jam*, I, 249; Ibn al-Athīr, *Lubāb*, I, 533f; Yāqūt, *Buldān*, III, 46. Cf. Le Strange, *Palestine*, 538, who cites Yāqūt, Sijillīn, but did not notice Yāqūt's claim that the correct name is Siḥillīn.
146 Ṭabarānī, *Mu'jam*, II, 161.
147 *Ibid.*, 44.
148 Ibn 'Asākir, V, 165.
149 Ṭabarānī, *Mu'jam*, I, 168; Ṭabarānī met him in Acre and knew him personally.
150 *Ibid.*, 38.
151 *Ibid.*, 215.
152 Subkī, *Ṭabaqāt*, III, 277.
153 Al-Khaṭīb al-Baghdādī, *Mūḍiḥ*, I, 394.
154 Ibn al-Athīr, *Lubāb*, II, 145; Yāqūt, *Buldān*, III, 697; cf. Khālidī, 169.
155 Sam'ānī, 411.
156 Al-Tadmurī (BM Or 1284), 63a.
157 Ṭabarānī, *Mu'jam*, II, 91; Ibn al-Athīr, *Lubāb*, II, 303; Yāqūt, *Buldān*, IV, 1003.

6

The Fatimid Conquest: The War of Sixty Years and Other Events During the Eleventh Century

Fatimid advance northwards (a)

[543] It took the Fatimids more than two generations of rule in North Africa before they could succeed in taking the giant step towards Baghdad, which was still quite a distance. In 969, they managed to conquer Egypt. They had already tried unsuccessfully to do so a number of times, in 913–914, and again in 919–920, but they were unable to get a foothold in the land of the Nile and after each attempt they were forced to retreat after much blood was shed. This time they prepared the invasion of Egypt meticulously, under the command of Caliph al-Mu'izz on the basis of the advice and plans drawn up by Ya'qūb ibn Killis, a Jew of Baghdad, who had become the chief adviser to the Fatimid caliph.

In April 968, as I have mentioned, the black Kāfūr, regent of Egypt, died and Abū'l-Fawāris Aḥmad b. 'Alī the Ikhshīdid was declared ruler of Egypt at the age of eleven. The year before, the Nile had failed to rise sufficiently and there was starvation in the land, accompanied by terrible epidemics. It was said that more than 600,000 souls died in Fustat and its environs and that many of its inhabitants left the area.[1]

[544] The central figure in Egypt at that time was Abū'l-Faḍl Ja'far b. Faḍl ibn Furāt, or Ibn Ḥinzāba, as I mentioned earlier. We have seen that he was married to the daughter of the Ikhshīd and was the strongest supporter of this dynasty. At that time, the army wished to place at the helm

[1] See Lane-Poole, *Hist.*, 89, 100ff; see further details in the article Fāṭimids in *EI*[2] (by M. Canard). Cf. the article by Lev, *Asian and African Studies* (Haifa), 14:165, 1980. On the matter of the Nile and the drought, see Qalqashandī, *Ma'āthir*, 305; wheat sold for a dinar and a half per *wayba*, a *raṭl* of bread for two dirhams, an egg for a dirham and a third.

of government, Ḥasan b. ʿUbaydallah, the Ikhshīdid, governor of Ramla (the cousin of Abū'l-Fawāris Aḥmad). In view of the threat to Abū'l-Fawāris' status and to his own situation as well, Ibn Ḥinzāba began a struggle against Ḥasan which resulted in complete anarchy amongst the ruling circles. Ḥasan the Ikhshīdid arrived from Ramla, placed Ibn Ḥinzāba in custody, confiscated his property and tortured him, but eventually released him and returned to Ramla, apparently because of the dangerous situation that was developing in Palestine. The Qarmaṭīs were pressing there, while on the horizon there were also indications of threats from the Byzantines. He left for Ramla on the 22nd (or 24th) of February 969. However, it seems that prior to this, he managed to send a letter to the Fatimid caliph, al-Muʿizz, to invite him to come to Egypt to restore order. On 5 August 969, the Fatimid army entered Fustat after overcoming some very slight resistance.[2]

[545] Less than a year later, at the beginning of summer of 970, the Fatimid army under Jaʿfar ibn al-Fallāḥ, turned towards Palestine. On Rajab AH 359 (24 May AD 970), it took Ramla. Theoretically, this was the outset of about a century of Fatimid rule in Palestine. In fact, the Fatimids were compelled to join battle with not a few of the enemies who stood in their way: the Arabs, led by the Banū Ṭayy', who in turn were headed by the Banū'l-Jarrāḥ family; the Qarmaṭīs; a Turkish army under the command of Alptakīn, who was based in Damascus; Arab tribes in Syria with the Banū Ḥamdān at their head; and in the background, the Byzantines were lurking, and about to continue their attempts to spearhead southward to Jerusalem. This war was waged in several stages and the enemies changed, but all in all, it was an almost unceasing war which destroyed Palestine, and especially its Jewish population, even before the Crusaders' eventuality.

The Fatimid army invaded Palestine some half a year after Ramla underwent a siege of thirty days imposed by the Qarmaṭīs, in Dhū'l-Ḥijja AH 358 (October/November 969 AD). The might of the Ikhshīdids was weakened and the Fatimids knew how to take advantage of this fact. The cries for help of Ḥasan, the Ikhshīdid governor of Ramla, were cries in the wilderness and no one came to his assistance – neither the people of Damascus nor al-Ṣināji, governor of Jerusalem. As to the fate of Ḥasan the Ikhshīdid, there are conflicting versions. According to Ibn al-Dawādārī, he and many of his men were killed during the conquest. Other sources have it that the Fatimid commander sent him to Egypt, together with other members of his family who were in Ramla at the time. In Egypt, they were kept in jail for some time and afterwards taken to the Maghrib to

[2] See n. 96 above; Ibn al-Dawādārī, 120; Ibn Khallikān, I, 346; cf. Bianquis, *Ann. isl.*, 62ff; Lane Poole, *Hist.*, 102ff.

Caliph al-Mu'izz, who had them released. Ja'far ibn al-Fallāḥ continued his expedition and turned towards Tiberias, where Fātik was then governing in the service of the Ikhshīdids. The control of the Bashan and Ḥawrān regions was in the hands of Arabs of the Banū 'Uqayl, based on an agreement they had had with Kāfūr. Two other tribes, the Banū Murra and the Banū Fazāra, agreed to collaborate with the Fatimid army and help in the conquest of Tiberias. A unit of Fatimid soldiers (Berbers, for the Fatimid army was made up of these tribesmen then), 'the westerners' (*maghāriba*, as they are called in the sources) caught Fātik and he was executed while imagining that they were about to release him. The Berbers plundered Tiberias. Ja'far ibn Fallāḥ ordered that a citadel be built there for him, on the bridge over the Sea of Galilee (?). The Fatimid army could then advance northward without hindrance, and the Banū 'Uqayl, faithful to the Ḥamdānids, fled from the army as far as Ḥimṣ.[3]

[546] There is no doubt that this first expedition of the Fatimids into Palestinian and Syrian territory was for them the first step in the realisation of a dream: that of the conquest of the entire Muslim world. There is no need to display petty pedantry and look for short-term considerations in their decision to drive northward immediately after the conquest of Egypt. Although starvation in Egypt was extreme at the time of the Fatimid conquest and during the following year as well, nevertheless there is no foundation to Bianquis' assumption that the major motive for sending the army northwards was essentially materialistic – the need to relieve the difficult problem of feeding an army whose numbers were myriad and which placed a heavy burden on the treasury.[4]

Fatimid retreat (a)

[547] The Fatimids behaved with a great deal of self-confidence. The

[3] See Yaḥyā ibn Sa'īd (*PO*), 141; Ibn al-Athīr, *Kāmil*, VII, 591, with details on the fate of Ramla after the conquest and on the conquest of Damascus; Ibn Taghrī Bardī, IV, 26; Ibn Khaldūn, *'Ibar*, IV, 100; Ibn Khallikān, I, 361; Ibn Kathīr, *Bidāya*, XI, 267; Abū'l-Fidā', *Mukhtaṣar*, II, 109; Ibn al-Dawādārī, from p. 120; on p. 125 he mentions the citadel, which according to him was near the *jisr* (bridge of) *al-ṣīra*, and it seems that this last word is a scribe's error for *buḥayra*, the lake that is *buḥayrat Ṭabariyya*, the Sea of Galilee; contrary to some other sources Maqrīzī, *Itti'āẓ*, I. 120, and Ibn al-Athīr, *Kāmil*, I, 120, give the date of Ramla's conquest as 18 Muḥarram 359, 1 December 969; Maqrīzī links it to a battle with the Qarmaṭīs, see also what he says on pp. 122f; but it seems that this date should refer to the Qarmaṭīs' siege on Ramla, and one should prefer the later date, contrary to the opinion of Madelung, *Der Islam*, 34(1959), 56f, who relies also on '*uyūn al-akhbār* of Idrīs b. al-Ḥasan, which was available to him in manuscript. As to Tiberias, apart from al-Dawādārī, all the sources insist that there was no battle there but that it surrendered willingly. See also the article Djawhar al Ṣiḳillī in *EI*² (by H. Monés).

[4] Bianquis, *Ann. isl.*, 11(1972), 79f; he mentions two additional motives; the news about the Qarmaṭīs' victorious attack on Ramla and its ruler, al-Ḥasan b. 'Ubaydallah; the internal conditions in Egypt, where the followers of the Ikhshīdids began to renew their activities.

Berber units which formed the major part of the army at the time were remarkably courageous, but their behaviour was uncontrolled and cruel. Not only the civilian population but even the Arab tribes in the north were fearful of the hard hand of the *maghāriba*, and preferred the Qarmaṭīs, the greatest enemies of the Fatimids. If the Qarmaṭīs were wise enough to establish a stable alliance with the Arab tribes, they would have undoubtedly succeeded in preventing the Fatimid domination of Palestine and Syria and in that way, endanger their rule in Egypt as well. But as we shall see later on, this alliance lasted but a short spell.

As mentioned, the Banū 'Uqayl fled from the Fatimid army. At first, they intended to come to terms with the Fatimids. A delegation of their dignitaries even came from Damascus to Tiberias in order to meet the Fatimid commander, Ja'far ibn al-Fallāḥ, but after some Fatimid soldiers attacked and robbed them of everything they bore with them, they became angry and returned to Damascus, whence they had soon to flee again. Damascus was the scene of three days of severe battles and much bloodshed, and the city fell in mid-October, 970. Ja'far ibn al-Fallāḥ energetically began to fortify his position there, reorganised his lines of defence, stationed his troops in the city and even built himself a citadel within the city. Shortly after taking Damascus, the Fatimids continued to overrun all of Syria and even tried to take Antioch from the Byzantines. They placed the city under siege, but were forced to withdraw, either as a result of the Byzantines' strength or because of the dangers threatening them from other quarters.[5]

[548] At this stage, the Fatimids' chief enemies were the Qarmaṭīs, led

[5] Ibn al-Dawādārī, 126f: the battle for Damascus occurred on 8–10 Dhū'l-Ḥijja (the 10th of Dhū'l-Ḥijja is *'īd al-aḍḥā*), i.e. 14–16 October AD 970. The expedition to Antioch, see Cedrenus (Bonn), II, 383f; Maqrīzī, *Itti'āẓ*, I, 126; Ibn al-Dawādārī, 132f; cf. Walker, *Byzantion*, 42(1972), 431ff; the tradition he cites there from *'uyūn al-akhbār* of Idrīs ibn al-Ḥasan 'Imad al-Dīn (a Yemenite who died in AH 872, or AD 1468), according to which Akhū Muslim headed the expedition to Antioch, is not credible, for Akhū Muslim was then an ally of the Qarmaṭīs and the enemy of the Fatimids for a number of years, and did not leave the latter *after* this campaign, as Walker contends. One should add that Antioch had a special significance for the Fatimids, and their ambition to conquer it evidently contributed to the diffusion of Ismā'īlī traditions about it. These traditions are ascribed to the Palestinian retainer of the Prophet, Tamīm al-Dārī, and to some of the first 'Alid *imāms*. According to these traditions, it is in Antioch where the relics of the broken tablets of the ten commandments, Moses' rod, King Solomon's table and chair (the *minbar*) are all to be found; it is fated to be conquered by someone of the Prophet's lineage (that is, a Fatimid), and there Jews, Christians and Muslims will gather around him and everyone will worship God in his own way. See Ivanow, *Ismaili Tradition*, 120ff. Tamīm al-Dārī had to say on Antioch: 'I have not seen in Byzantium a city like the one called Anṭākiya, nor a city in which there is more rain.' To which the Prophet replies: 'for therein is the *tawrah* and Moses' rod, and pieces of the broken tablets, and the table of Solomon, the son of David, in one of its caves; every cloud that somehow passes over it must release the blessing it bears within the valley; and not many days or nights shall pass and a man of my blood will settle there, his name as my name and the name of his father as my father, his image as my image,

by Abū 'Alī al-Ḥasan al-A'ṣam b. Aḥmad b. Bahrām. It was he who radically changed the policy of the sect, which was that of collaboration with the Fatimids as long as the latter were only governing in the west. But now that the Fatimids had conquered Egypt and invaded Palestine and Syria, they were opposed by the Qarmaṭīs, who formed an alliance with the Banū 'Uqayl. These allies achieved their first victory in the month of Dhū 'l-Qa'da AH 360, beginning on the 25th of August AD 971, when they managed to take Damascus from the Fatimids. The Qarmaṭīs wrought havoc in the city. Ja'far ibn al-Fallāḥ, the Fatimid commander, was killed in battle during the conquest. The anti-Fatimid alliance was given much help by the *de facto* ruler of Baghdad, Bakhtiyār, as well as by the Ḥamdānid ruler, Abū Taghlib. They also had at their side elements who were faithful supporters of the Ikhshīdids (mainly Turks).

After taking Damascus, the Qarmaṭīs turned southwards with the intention of conquering Ramla. Their justification was that the Fatimids had not paid them the annual tax of 300,000 dinars promised them by the former Ikhshīdid governor of Ramla. The Qarmaṭīs then took all of Palestine until they reached Ramla, while the Fatimid army withdrew to Jaffa and dug themselves in there. But in the midst of the raging war, the supreme Fatimid commander, Jawhar, sent a new governor to Ramla, namely Sa'āda b. Ḥiyān, in Shawwāl of the year AH 360, that is August AD 971 (according to Maqrīzī). Shortly afterwards, on Tuesday, the 11th of Dhū'l-Qa'da AH 360, the 5th of September 971, Ramla fell to the Qarmaṭīs. They ravaged the city. Afterwards the Qarmaṭīs placed Jaffa under siege, while the major part of their army turned towards Egypt and conquered large stretches of land there until the Fatimid commander Jawhar warded off their invasion near Fustat, at the end of December 971.

From that point onward, the Qarmaṭīs established Ramla as their chief base and established their winter quarters there. In the meantime, there were battles between the navies of the Qarmaṭīs and the Fatimids. The Qarmaṭīs took thirteen of the fifteen ships laden with men and supplies sent by Jawhar in aid of his besieged men in Jaffa, but Jawhar succeeded in lifting the siege on the port by hurling flasks of oil onto the Qarmaṭīs' ships and setting them on fire.

Fatimid advance northwards (b)

The governor of Ramla on behalf of the Arab-Qarmaṭī alliance was a man of the Banū 'Uqayl, Ẓālim ibn Mawhūb (in some sources, ibn

his nature as my nature, he will fill the world with truth and justice instead of oppression and tyranny'. The date of the conception of this tradition, which belonged to Fatimid propaganda, was perhaps the first half of the tenth century, the period of the second Fatimid caliph, al-Qā'im, that is Muḥammad b. 'Abdallah ('Ubaydallah). See al-Khaṭīb

Marhūb, which is evidently a distortion). He stood at the head of the forces which the tribal alliance placed at the disposal of the war against the Fatimids. The major Qarmaṭī forces were aligned alongside them, under the command of Abū'l-Munajjā 'Abdallah b. 'Alī. The supreme commander of this anti-Fatimid camp was Akhū Muslim, whom we already know. Opposing them in Jaffa and the south of Palestine, stood the Fatimid army, numbering some 11,000 soldiers, under the command of the former governor of Ramla, Sa'āda ibn Ḥiyān. The lack of accord between the partners to the enemy alliance acted in their favour. Acute differences occurred between the allies over the distribution of the income from taxes (*kharāj*), for the Qarmaṭī, Abū'l-Munajjā, demanded the money for himself. His men took captive the leader of the Banū 'Uqayl, Ẓālim b. Mawhūb, but he managed to escape and fled to the region of the Euphrates, and his men withdrew from the scene. From then on, the anti-Fatimid alliance disintegrated. The Qarmaṭīs naturally understood that they could not hold their stand on their own. They lifted the siege on Jaffa, abandoned Ramla as well, and retreated northward to Damascus. There are no exact details in the sources on this last move but it can be speculated upon in light of the circumstances and from what occurred afterwards. It seems that the Arabs of the north temporarily went over to the opposing side and supported the Fatimids, who returned and seized Palestine and even part of southern Syria, including Damascus, with the help of the Banū 'Uqayl, evidently not before the summer of 973. The reason for assuming this date is that gold dinars (weighing 3.31 grams) were minted by the Qarmaṭīs in Palestine, in the years AH 360–362 (362 ended on the 12th October AD 973). These coins bear the name of al-Ḥasan ibn Aḥmad (who is al-Ḥasan al-A'ṣam), and they were minted on behalf of 'our masters, the heads' (*al-sāda al-ru'asā'*), the Qarmaṭīs' council, with the inscription *bi-filasṭīn*.[6]

Ya'qūb ibn Killis

[549] The Fatimids felt that their hold on Palestine and Syria was on the wane and that a new attack on these territories was imminent, in which

al-Baghdādī, *Ta'rīkh*, IX, 471. As to Futūḥ, who according to the aforementioned Arab sources led the expedition to Antioch, he is not mentioned in any other sources of the period, and the name may be a distortion of Abū'l-Futūḥ, who was the Jew Faḍl b. Ṣāliḥ, and who shall be mentioned below.

6 See Yaḥyā ibn Sa'īd, 143; Ibn 'Asākir, IV, 148ff; Ibn al-'Adīm, *Zubda*, I, 104; Ibn Dawādārī, 132f; Maqrīzī, *Itti'āẓ*, I, 128, 188f; Abū'l-Fidā', *Mukhtaṣar* II, 111f. Ibn Kathīr, *Bidāya*, XI, 269; Ibn Taghrī Bardī, IV, 62; Ibn Khaldūn, *'Ibar*, IV, 104; cf. Madelung, *Der Islam*, 34(1959), 35f; the article al-Ḥasan al-A'ṣam (by M. Canard) in *EI*². On Abū Taghlib, whom we shall encounter below, see details in Canard's article, Ḥamdānids, his full name: Abū Taghlib Faḍlallah b. al-Ḥasan: at that time, he was the leader of the Ḥamdānids based

Egypt would also be threatened. Apparently, it was this realisation that prompted the Fatimid caliph al-Mu'izz to move his seat from Qayrawān in the Maghrib to Egypt, in May 973. Some five months later, in Muḥarram of the year AH 363, that is October AD 973, when the Fatimids had just renewed their dominion of Palestine and Syria, he appointed the converted Jew Abū'l-Faraj Ya'qūb b. Yūsuf b. Ibrahīm ibn Killis to take charge of internal affairs in Egypt and also to deal with the collection of taxes and with various properties. Ibn Killis was the son of a Jewish family from Baghdad, who emigrated to Palestine, evidently in *ca.* 940, when the desertion of a large wave of Iraqi Jews occurred. He was born in Baghdad in AH 318 (AD 930), and it is known that his family lived at the time near the 'Silk Gate' (*bāb al-qazz*). Some of the sources relate him to Aaron b. 'Amram, which in effect means a family of priestly descent. When the family lived in Ramla and Ya'qūb was growing up, he began to engage in trade and became involved in improprieties, the nature of which are not very clear. During Kāfūr's time, when Ya'qūb was in his thirties, he moved to Egypt and achieved considerable success owing to his talents in the field of economics and management, and he was taken into the service of Kāfūr. According to Ibn al-Ṣayrafī, he began his rise with the knowledge that hidden in the house of a certain Ibn al-Baladī in Ramla was a hoard of 30,000 dinars. After the death of the owner of the house, Ibn Killis informed Kāfūr of this but mentioned only 20,000 dinars. When they found 30,000 dinars after digging for the treasure, Ibn Killis told Kāfūr of his finding, and the latter was impressed by his honesty. Afterwards he found another treasure, that of a Jew who died in al-Faramā, hidden in loads of flax which he had left behind. The flax was sold and the treasure handed over to Kāfūr. It was said that Ya'qūb converted to Islam on Monday, 18 Sha 'bān AH 356 (30 July AD 967). He left Egypt because of court intrigues after the death of Kāfūr and went over to the Fatimids. He was accepted to serve al-Mu'izz in Qayrawān and he is credited with both the initiative and the planning and preparation for the campaign which led to the conquest of Egypt. His status in the Fatimid political and administrative system is undoubtedly one of the signs of the strong links between the Fatimid rulers and the circles of Jewish financiers, experts in financial matters and international commerce, who then converged on Qayrawān. Of his many retainers, the sources speak of 'Aslūj b. al-Ḥasan, who was his administrative aide, and the Jewish commander and statesman Abū' l-Futūḥ Faḍl b. Ṣāliḥ. With the transfer of the Fatimid

in Mosul; afterwards, in 978, he was forced to flee from there by Bakhtiyār, the Buwayhid ruler of Baghdad, and we shall find him involved in events in Palestine; see also the article Bakhtiyār (by C. Cahen) in *EI*[2]. On the coins, see: Nassar, *QDAP*, 13(1948), 125f; Scanlon, *BIFAO*, 59(1960), 37–41, 47f; Mitchell, *INJ*, 3(1965/6), 47f.

caliphate's capital from Qayrawān to al-Qāhira, Ya'qūb ibn Killis found himself in the entourage of al-Mu'izz, and from 976, after his death, he continued to serve his son al-'Azīz, from whom he received the rank of wazīr. He lived in al-Qāhira in his own house, in which other wazīrs subsequently lived until the time of Badr al-Jamālī (the seventies of the eleventh century; the house was centrally located, opposite the gate to the Zuwayla quarter, and afterwards became the centre of the silk trade and was known by the name *dār al-dībāj* [house of silk], and in the days of the Ayyūbids became a *madrasa*).

Ibn Killis is credited with having written a Book of Laws, on commission from al-'Azīz, a book which the latter decided was obligatory reading for the Fatimid legal system, but the Muslim scholars of the law resented it. He was also said to have supported scholars and religious officials, and he managed to get regular annuities (*rizq*) for them from al-'Aziz. He also built a special house for them, which at that time housed thirty-seven of these people, close to the al-Azhar mosque. Of Ya'qūb ibn Killis' family, there is mention of his brother Sahl, who is said to have been executed in AH 394 (AD 1004), on al-Ḥākim's orders; his Turkish son-in-law Yārūkhtakīn and his brother-in-law (his wife's brother) Rashīq al-'Azīzī, were both commanders in the Fatimid army.[7]

Fatimid retreat (b)

[550] The Fatimids' renewed hold over Palestine and Syria did not last long. The Qarmaṭīs recovered their strength and organised their forces anew. Most of these were then in Baḥrayn in al-Aḥsā (the fortress of al-Aḥsā, as opposed to al-Aḥsā, or al-Ḥasā, in the nearby eastern coastal region of the Arabian peninsula). Their leader al-Ḥasan al-A'ṣam, was living there. They even renewed their alliance with the Arab tribes and they were soon to find a new ally of immense power, the Turḳish commander Alptakīn. This tri-fold alliance was soon to endanger the Fatimids' position in the area again.

We have no details about the renewed seizure of southern Syria and

[7] Yaḥyā ibn Sa'īd, 225f; Ibn Khallikān, VII, 27–34; Suyūṭī, *Muḥāḍara*, I, 601; al-Quḍā'ī, fol. 108b; Ibn Muyassar, 45; Abū Shujā', 185; Dhahabī, *Duwal*, I, 180; Yāfi'ī, II, 250f; Ibn al-Ṣayrafī, 14–23; Maqrīzī, *Itti'āẓ*, II, 51 (Sahl is mentioned here); *idem, Khiṭaṭ*, II, 178, 327, 341, 347 (on the house of Ibn Killis); Sāwīrūs, II (2), 98f; Qalqashandī, *Ṣubḥ*, III, 353, 363 (on his house and the house for the Muslim scholars); a Syriac source, the history of Abraham the Syrian, contains a story about a religious dispute in the presence of al-Mu'izz, Ya'qūb ibn Killis (in the source, Ibn Khillis) and his good friend, Mūsā, the Jew who became rich in his company, see: Leroy, *ROC*, 4(1909), 392f; see the summary of information on Ya'qūb ibn Killis, according to part of the aforementioned sources: Fischel, *Jews*, 44–68, and in the article of Lev, *Der Islam*, 58:237, 1981.

Palestine by the Qarmaṭīs. In the spring of 973, the Fatimids were still ruling in Syria, as is proven by the fact that in Rajab AH 362 (April AD 973), they dismissed Aḥmad b. Musawwir from his post as governor of Damascus. He moved to Tiberias, where he died. In the spring of AH 363, that is, AD 974, the Qarmaṭīs already attacked Egypt, together with the Bedouin of Palestine, the Ikhshīdid followers who were still prepared to fight, and those who had been loyal followers of Kāfūr (*al-kāfūrīyīn*).

Fatimid advance northwards (c)

Al-Mu'izz was in an inferior position in relation to the invading force. He then resorted to cunning: promising Ḥassān ibn al-Jarrāḥ (the son of al-Mufarrij b. Daghfal, father of the Banū Jarrāḥ family and their leader at that time; the sources refer to him as 'commander of the Bedouin', *amīr al-'arab*) 100,000 dinars to betray his allies and withdraw in the face of the Egyptian army. The deal was made and the Arabs withdrew as promised, which led to the collapse of the Qarmaṭī offensive. This was a successful deception on the part of al-Mu'izz, for the money was sent to Ḥassān packed in pouches, in which the coins at the top were genuine dinars whereas underneath there was base metal. 10,000 Maghribi horsemen under the command of Abū Maḥmūd Ibrāhīm b. Ja'far b. al-Fallāḥ, pursued the Arabs and cut off their supply routes. The Fatimids once again returned and took over Palestine and Syria even before the end of 974.

Fatimid retreat (c)

When they were obliged to retreat, the Qarmaṭīs turned their attention to an alliance with the Turk Alptakīn (his name is frequently distorted, as Aftakīn, Haftakīn). He had been a freedman of the Baghdadi ruler 'Izz al-Dawla Bakhtiyār. The Turks in the latter's army quarrelled with him after he rose to power in Baghdad in 967 and their commander, Alptakīn, then invaded Syria and made Ḥimṣ his base. On becoming an ally of the Qarmaṭīs, his first act was to attack the Palestinian coast, towards the end of the winter of 975. He opened his attack with a siege on Sidon, where a large force of Fatimid soldiers was concentrated under the command of Ibn Shaykh, who had been appointed by al-Mu'izz. Along with the Fatimids in the city, there were Arabs of the Banū 'Uqayl together with their leader Ẓālim b. Mawhūb, who still collaborated with the Fatimids. Alptakīn took Sidon by storm and there was much slaughter, with some 4,000 fatalities. The remnants of the Fatimid army fled to Tyre, but Alptakīn did not attack this city, making a detour and directing part of his army southward, with the intention of taking Acre, and with another part of the army, drove toward Tiberias, which fell after much blood was shed and the city laid open to pillage and plunder. From Tiberias, Alptakīn led his army towards Damascus. The Fatimid commander of Damascus, Riyān, escaped with his life; Alptakīn entered the city and was received enthusiastically by the Sunnī Muslim part of the population, who pledged their allegiance to him. The conquest of Damascus evidently took place in April 975, and it is said that in Sha'bān of the year 364 (beginning on 16 April AD 975), Alptakīn introduced the Abbasid *da'wa* (the prayer for the Abbasid ruler said at the start of the *khuṭba*, the sermon), mentioning the name of the Abbasid caliph al-Ṭā'i' instead of that of the Fatimid caliph. The efforts of the Fatimid caliph al-Mu'izz to come to an agreement with Alptakīn were in vain. The situation in Damascus was extremely difficult at the time of the conquest, for there were Fatimid soldiers there as well as Arabs of the Banū 'Uqayl, and these two factions were at one another's throats all the time; the Arabs collaborated with the people of the city against the Fatimid garrison. Now the Banū 'Uqayl hastily went over to Alptakīn's side. One of the leaders of the tribe, Shibl ibn Ma'rūf, received Tiberias into his charge, with Alptakīn's blessing. The latter's attitude towards the Arabs was one of familiarity and toughness and he succeeded in restraining them and extending his authority over them at the same time. Nevertheless, some of the Fatimid army units managed to reorganise themselves and overrun Tiberias, under Abū Maḥmūd Ibrāhīm b. Ja'far b. al-Fallāḥ. The continuation of this drama and the retreat of the Fatimids (for the third time), is connected with events coming from a completely unexpected direction – the invasion of the Byzantines.

Renewal of the Byzantine offensive

If we are to believe Bar Hebraeus, the renewed Byzantine offensive against the Muslims was at the outset in the direction of Mesopotamia. According to him they conquered the city of Nisibis in the year AH 362, that is, AD 972. An important source of information on the Byzantine moves on the western side of the front is the letter of the emperor John Tzimisces to Ashot, king of the Armenians, which has been preserved in the chronicle of Matthew of Edessa. It was said that John Tzimisces was also an Armenian, and if this is actually the case, we have an additional explanation for the letter, which is long and in great detail. The emperor at first depicts his advance, in 975, from Ḥimṣ southward through Ba'labakk. The description of his arrival in the neighbourhood of Damascus is especially interesting. The city bestowed precious gifts on him so that he should not destroy it and at the bequest of the townspeople in their surrender agreement, he appointed a Turkish commander as its governor, a man of Baghdad who had converted to Christianity (!). With this description in mind, we shall presently see what the Muslim sources say about it. Hand-in-hand with the Byzantine advance towards Damascus, while Alptakīn was preparing to fight, he was pinned down by the Fatimid danger looming from the direction of Tiberias. There, Abū Maḥmūd Ibrāhīm b. Ja'far was establishing his base while his enemies, the Banū 'Uqayl, were dominating the area and raiding the towns. Abū Maḥmūd sent a Fatimid force of some two thousand men from Tiberias to attack Damascus. At their head, he placed his nephew, Jaysh ibn Ṣamṣāma. Near Subayna (a pair of villages some eight kilometres south of Damascus) this Fatimid army encountered the Banū 'Uqayl, with Shibl b. Ma'rūf at their head. The Fatimid force was routed, Jaysh was taken captive and most of his men were killed, and the remainder were taken as prisoners. Shibl handed Jaysh over to Alptakīn. The latter was busy at that moment negotiating with the Byzantine emperor, who was staying in 'Ayn al-Jarr (which is Anjār today, south of the Litani). The emperor demanded an enormous sum of money. Alptakīn paid him the money and also gave him Jaysh the captive (and evidently other Fatimid captives he had with him; 'Africans', as the emperor says in his letter).

It is especially worth noting the report of the Damascene chronicler Ibn al-Qalānisī: John Tzimisces (called in the distorted variation, Ibn al-Shamashqīq) conquered Ḥimṣ and Ba'labakk and turned towards Damascus. Alptakīn and the people of the city decided to forestall the impending danger by agreeing to pay the emperor what he demanded, a total of 100,000 dirhams. The emperor met with Alptakīn, and was impressed with his horsemanship, while Alptakīn and the townsmen showered him with gifts – among them twenty choice steeds. Hence, the two sources are in complete accord, except that Ibn al-Qalānisī does not mention the conversion of the 'Turkish commander', that is Alptakīn, to Christianity, which was certainly the emperor's own invention. Returning to the emperor's letter: he had similar successes, he writes, in Tiberias, in Nazareth, and on Mount Tabor. Messengers came to him from Ramla and Jerusalem, asking him to appoint governors over them and promising to pay him taxes.He also appointed a governor to *Beniata*, which is *Decapolis* (!), Gennesareth and Acre. Caesarea also succumbed. He took captive a thousand 'Africans'. He liberated all of Phoenicia, Palestine and Syria from Muslim tyranny. But it appears that he did not turn towards Jerusalem, for 'the damnable Africans [that is, the Fatimid army] [fortified themselves] in the fortresses along the coast'. While in Ibn Qalānisī: from Damascus, the emperor continued to advance northward along the Phoenician coast: Sidon, Beirut, Jubayl, Tripoli, until he was forced to return north because of internal troubles in Byzantium. Here there is an essential difference bteween the two sources, although there remains a central element in common: that is the fact that collaboration between the Byzantines, Alptakīn and his allies, the Qarmaṭīs and the Arabs, was achieved, and the emperor was evidently eager to participate in a war against the Fatimids, and, as his letter indicates, was even ready to start it. From now on, the emperor considered Alptakīn a kind of tool, as were certainly the Qarmaṭīs and the Arabs in his opinion. It is not surprising therefore that he enumerates in his letters the cities of Palestine, Tiberias and others, as having allegedly fallen into his hands. This was not vain boasting; Alptakīn and his allies had really seized these cities. We know that Shibl the 'Uqaylī seized Ṭiberias again, after ousting the few Fatimids who were left there together with their commander Abū Maḥmūd Ibrāhīm b. Ja'far. They withdrew to Ramla and the Arabs pursued them and attacked and annihilated them near Jerusalem. A group of Fatimids taken captive were sent to Damascus, where they were led through the streets of the city tied to camels and afterwards decapitated. After these humiliating defeats, Abū Maḥmūd arrived in Ramla with the remnants of his army and there they stayed for the time being.[8]

[8] See the article Ḥasā (by F. S. Vidal) in *EI*². The deposal of the governor of Damascus: Ibn 'Asākir, II, 88f; Thābit b. Sinān, 65f; Ibn al-Dawādārī, 176 (according to him these events took place in 365, i.e. 976); Ibn al-Athīr, *Kāmil*, VIII, 656ff; Ibn Kathīr, *Bidāya*, XI, 280f; Ibn Khaldūn, *'Ibar*, IV, 108 (he also places the beginning of Alptakīn's expedition later, after the death of al-Mu'izz, that is in 976). Abū'l-Fidā', *Mukhtaṣar*, II, 115; Maqrīzī, *Muqaffā*, 195; *idem, Khiṭaṭ*, II, 413 (a short and confused survey); *idem, Itti'āẓ*, I, 208ff, where we find a more extended version of what occurred in the north in 975: there seems to have been a kind of intermediary stage between Fatimid rule in Damascus and its conquest by Alptakīn, when the city was actually governed by the Qarmaṭīs and their allies, under the command of the Qarmaṭī Abūl-Hījā b. Munajjā. As the Qarmaṭīs were in financial straits, they did not pay their soldiers their due, so the latter joined forces with the Banū 'Uqayl against the Qarmaṭī leadership and handed over their power in the city to the Fatimid Abū Maḥmūd. At the end of AH 363, or September AD 974, news reached Egypt that Damascus was again in the hands of Abū Maḥmūd. Further, 211–214, Maqrizi has additional information on the internal deterioration in Damascus and the conflict between the Banū 'Uqayl and the Fatimid army, which I have mentioned above. The temporary success of the Qarmaṭīs in 974 led al-Mu'izz to transfer Abū Maḥmūd and appoint in his stead as governor of Damascus, Riyān, the governor of Tripoli. As we have seen, a short while afterwards, Alptakīn ousted Riyān from Damascus. Ibn al-Qalānisī, 12ff (see there on p. 25 on the family ties between Jaysh and Abū Maḥmūd); Ibn al-Dawādārī, 171f; see further: Bar Hebraeus (Bedjan), 192; (Budge) 173; see more references mentioned in connection with the first Byzantine expedition, above n. 97, and the reference therein to Matthew of Edessa (the letter of Tzimisces); this can also be read in *RHC* (Arm.), I, 12–20; see there, pp. 5, 130, on the Armenian origin of John Tzimisces. Only one source, Michael the Syrian, IV, 553 (= III, 123, the translation), claims that the Byzantines did take Jerusalem then: 'and the Greeks became rulers at that time of Antioch, and of Palestine and Jerusalem'; Starr, *Archiv Orientalni*, 8(1936), 91–95 has already proven that this is not to be believed; see the commentary on the letter to Ashot: Schlumberger, *L'épopée byzantine*, II, 282ff; Walker, *Byzantion* 47(1977), 313–324, and additional references in Walker, *ibid.*; he ignores the aforementioned article by Starr, and tries to explain that the details in the letter stem from exaggeration and boasting, either by the emperor himself, or of whoever

[551] Evidently it was the Byzantines' aspiration to rid Jerusalem of the Jews, for in doing so, they would be turning the wheels of time back to the days preceding the Muslim conquest. One can also assume that the Christian leaders in Jerusalem in particular, were very active in this matter. And although the Byzantines did not succeed in reaching Jerusalem, as told, it seems that they were intent on evicting the Jews with the help of their connections with the Arab tribes, Alptakīn's allies. Explicit evidence of this has been preserved in the writings of two Karaite commentators who lived in Jerusalem at the time: Salmon b. Yeruḥim and Yefet b. 'Alī. The former writes in this fashion in his commentary on Psalms, ch. xxx: 'and even now the "uncircumcised" beat us in order to oust us from Jerusalem by force, and separate us from the city'; and in his commentary on the Book of Ecclesiastes, ix:6: 'and after all this, they want to evict us from Jerusalem and place a heavy iron yoke around our necks, and all because of our transgressions and the enormity of our sins', etc. This is even more clearly expressed by his contemporary, Yefet b. 'Alī, in his commentary on the Psalms, xi:1 (... how say ye to my soul, flee as a bird to your mountain?): 'for the Byzantines do not demand that we leave all of Palestine, only Jerusalem' (therefore the Bible says 'your mountain' and not 'your land'); and further on: 'and they demand that we leave Jerusalem, but they shall not succeed in this'. The continuation is even more pronounced, on Psalms, xi:2 (For lo, the wicked bend their bow): 'meaning to say that the Byzantines correspond with the Arabs constantly, demanding that they drive the Jews out of the city, but they will not succeed. It is obvious and known that they have been doing this for many years now ...'; and again, to Psalms, xi:4 (The Lord is in his holy temple): 'he wished to show the honour of the mountain from which they intended that Israel be ousted ... for how can He dwell with you when you are unclean and uncircumcised ...'

The natural inclination of the Christians in Palestine to side with the Byzantines and their allies (the Qarmaṭīs, Alptakīn and the Arab tribes) is also manifest in the episode of Abū'l-Yumn Quzmān ibn Mīnā, a Christian appointed by the Fatimid caliph (apparently al-Mu'izz, before 976) as a sort of administrator in charge of 'the districts of Filasṭīn', on the recommendation of Ya'qūb ibn Killis, who considered him a reliable man; and evidently his main concern was the collection of taxes. He managed to collect 200,000 dinars, deposited them with the abbé of the monastery on

discovered his letter, after some 150 years, and translated it into Armenian. Michaud, *Histoire*, I, 19–47, described the events in Palestine from the middle of the tenth century onwards, and saw in the Byzantine offensive, a step in the psychological preparation for the Crusades. Subayna: see Dussaud, *Topographie*, 312, and the map after p. 76 (No. IV).

Mount Tabor, and then betrayed the Fatimids and went over to their enemies (in the source: to the Qarmaṭīs).[9]

Fatimid advance northwards (d)

[552] On the 17th Rabīʿ II AH 365 (24 December AD 975), Caliph al-Muʿizz died and was succeeded by his son, Abū Manṣūr Nizār, known as al-ʿAzīz. One of the first moves of the new caliph was to appoint new governors in Palestine, people who were formerly loyal to the Ikhshīdids: Wafī (or Ruqī) al-Ṣaqlabī ('the Slav') in Acre; Bishāra in Tiberias; Rabāḥ in Gaza. On the advice of Yaʿqūb ibn Killis, who was made wazīr, and under his direction, a large army was organised under the command of Jawhar and it was sent to Damascus in Ramaḍān AH 365 (May AD 976). The army again took hold of all of Palestine easily and reached Damascus some two months after the outset of the offensive, on the last day of Shawwāl (1 July). Jawhar wrote to Alptakīn from Ramla and promised him *amān* (personal security) and a letter of forgiveness for all his sins and also a *khalʿa* (ceremonial attire) on behalf of the state, and also money. Alptakīn replied rudely. The siege of Damascus lasted seven months. While it was still going on, the Qarmaṭīs again joined the war against the Fatimids. According to some sources, it was Alptakīn who approached them and asked for their help. But there is no doubt that the Qarmaṭīs saw the Fatimids as their most dangerous enemies, perhaps just because they were closer to them in their views and religio-political philosophy. The Fatimids did everything they could to come to terms with them, but to no avail. Al-Muʿizz even wrote them a message of chastisement and conciliation, but al-Ḥasan al-Aʿṣam's answer was: 'I received your letter full of words but devoid of wisdom; I shall bring you my answer'.[10]

9 See what Salmon writes in his commentary on Psalms, in Mann, *Texts*, II, 18f; Neubauer, who first published the fragment, read *ḥyl* instead of *ḥāl* and assumed that it meant *ḥayil*, that is the Byzantine army. See: Neubauer, *Aus der Petersburger Bibliothek*, 12, 109; *fī ḥāl* is an idiom meaning: now. Cf. also Mann, *Jews*, I, 46, and n. 1; this passage of Salmon b. Yeruḥim was generally seen as evidence of a dispute between Jews and Christians in Jerusalem and nothing more; see for instance Linder, in *Perāqīm* (1979), 23; while the general historical background, and particularly the more explicit statements of Yefet b. ʿAlī, clarify for us the true significance. See his commentary to Ecclesiastes, in Vajda, *Deux commentaires*, 42, n. 4 (from BM Or 2517, fol. 83). See also: MS Paris 286, fol. 70; here, too, one must remember that at that time *ʿArab*, Arabs, meant Bedouin, Arab tribesmen, hence those passages refer to letters written by the Byzantines to the tribes. The episode of Quzmān: Sāwīrūs, II (2), 98f; who also adds an impossible story, according to which al-Muʿizz had Yaʿqūb ibn Killis executed after Quzmān repented and returned the money to the caliph.

10 The appointments: Ibn Taghrī Bardī, IV, 117; see Thābit ibn Sinān, 66; Ibn al-Dawādārī, 176; Yaḥyā ibn Saʿīd (*PO*), 181; Hamadānī, *Takmila*, 226; Ibn al-Athīr, *Kāmil*, VIII, 657f, 663; Ibn Kathīr, *Bidāya*, XI, 281; Maqrīzī, *Ittiʿāẓ*, I, 189–202 (with a version of al-Muʿizz' very long letter and al-Ḥasan al-Aʿṣam's short reply); *idem*, *Khiṭaṭ*, II, 203, 414; *idem*,

Fatimid retreat (d)

[553] In view of the enemy's numerical superiority (Alptakīn, the Qarmaṭīs, the Banū 'Uqayl) Jawhar decided to lift the siege on Damascus and withdraw. According to Yaḥyā ibn Sa'īd, the Fatimids retreated from Damascus in Jumādā I, AH 366 (January AD 977), that is, half a year after the beginning of the siege. According to Thābit ibn Sinān, Jawhar withdrew on 1 Dhūl'-Qa'da AH 365 (2 July AD 976). Considering that most of the sources are in agreement on the fact that the siege of Damascus began on the 1st of July, as mentioned above, and that it lasted for a number of months, Yaḥyā ibn Sa'īd's version is the preferable one. Jawhar retreated southward, in the direction of Ramla, with his enemies advancing in his wake, and while he was entrenching his forces in Ramla, they were encamped on the Yarqōn, in al-Ṭawāḥīn.

The Fatimid army was now entirely surounded by enemies. And these adversaries were soon joined by 50,000 'people of al-Shām', meaning the Arabs of Palestine, of the Banū Ṭayy', under the leadership of the Banū Jarrāḥ. In a fierce battle on the Yarqōn, the Fatimid army suffered a crushing defeat. It was now under siege in Ramla, cut off from water supplies (evidently Ra's al-'ayn and the Yarqōn) and both the soldiers and population were forced to drink rain-water from ditches, and even this rapidly disappeared. At long last, Jawhar decided to abandon Ramla and the Qarmaṭīs entered the city on 18 Rajab AH 366 (12 March AD 977). Jawhar withdrew to Ascalon. In the meantime, Alptakīn's army reached Ramla from Damascus and the allies turned with their combined forces towards Ascalon, which was placed under a siege which lasted for no less than a year and three months. Most of Jawhar's men died of starvation. Out of desperation, he began to negotiate with his enemies, mostly with the Turks evidently, for the Qarmaṭīs objected to any agreement with the Fatimids and demanded that they be left to die of hunger. Finally, Alptakīn agreed to an arrangement whereby he would be given the dominion of all of Palestine, including Ascalon, while the 'Maghribis', that is, the Fatimids, would govern from Gaza southward. Alptakīn would recognise al-'Azīz as caliph but he would collect the taxes in the area under his control. Jawhar was even obliged to endure a humiliating ceremony on his withdrawal from Ascalon together with the remnants of his army; Alptakīn hung a sword over the gateway to the fortress and Jawhar and his men had to pass under it. This evidently occurred in Sha'bān AH 366, that is the beginning of April AD 978.

Muqaffā, 195; Ibn Ẓāfir, 49a (printed: p. 26); Baybars, fol. 487; Ibn Khaldūn, IV, 108; Abū'l-Fidā', II, 115.

Fatimid advance northwards (e)

Jawhar and what remained of his army then returned to Egypt. Al-'Azīz, on Ya'qūb b. Killis' advice, ordered that a large army be prepared for another campaign in Palestine. The caliph himself stood at the head of the army, in Dhū'l-Qa'da, June 978. From this point onward, the anti-Fatimid alliance began to disintegrate. From now on, we do not hear much about the Qarmaṭīs, evidently because of the death of their leader, al-Ḥasan al-A'ṣam, in Ramla, a few days after they entered the city (according to Ibn al-'Adīm: on 23 Rajab, the 17th of March, AD 977). On the basis of coins minted by the Qarmaṭīs in Palestine, we know that during the last five years of his life, al-Ḥasan became their sole ruler; for beginning with AH 362 (AD 972/3) we find the term 'the head' (*al-ra'īs*) and not 'the heads' (*al-ru'asā'*, referring to the Qarmaṭī council of six elders), inscribed on their coins. His cousin, Ja'far b. Abī Sa'īd, inherited his role. According to Hamadhānī, the Qarmaṭīs withdrew to Tiberias, on the order of their leader al-Ḥasan al-A'ṣam, after al-'Azīz reached an agreement with them whereby they would receive an annuity of 70,000 dinars, until 'Jawhar and the cadi of Ramla' chased them away. How this happened, we do not know. The report is apparently fundamentally correct, except for the name of the leader, for most of the sources agree that al-Ḥasan died in Ramla, that is, much before al-'Azīz' expedition. Another version claims that the agreement was made between al-'Azīz and the Qarmaṭīs in Ramla, in the presence of Jawhar and the aforementioned cadi, and that the sum was only 30,000 dinars per year (Ibn Khaldūn: only 20,000). From this time onward, we hear nothing more about the Qarmaṭīs in Palestine.

As to Alptakīn, he left Ramla and withdrew to Damascus (according to Ibn al-Dawādārī, to Tiberias). At the same time, an internal struggle was going on in Iraq among the armies of the Būyids. Bakhtiyār (who had been Alptakīn's master), fought with his cousin 'Aḍud al-Dawla, while Abū Taghlib the Ḥamdānid took part in the war alongside Bakhtiyār, as did Bakhtiyār's brother and son, Abū Isḥaq and Marzubān. Bakhtiyār was taken captive and the Ḥamdānid fled. Abū Isḥaq and Marzubān also escaped to Damascus, and with them the Daylamī army (the Daylamīs were a Persian tribe to which the Būyids belonged). When they reached Damascus, Alptakīn was in Tiberias. These were unexpected reinforcements and Alptakīn was elated by their arrival. He made his wazīr, Ibn al-Ḥimāra, take care of them, and Ibn al-Ḥimāra duly spent a great deal of money on them, saw to their supplies, and escorted them to Alptakīn in Tiberias. Now Alptakīn had a force of 12,000 men at his disposal, all concentrated in Tiberias, and from here they set forth southward for Ramla.

Al-'Azīz at first tried the strategy of negotiating. He sent emissaries to Alptakīn and promised him *amān* and large sums of money if he would accept his authority; he would even appoint him supreme commander of the army (*isfahsallār*) and let him rule over Palestine (perhaps the intention was Palestine and Syria together, that is, al-Shām) but the Turk did not respond and continued his preparations for war. Al-'Azīz was encamped with his army behind Ramla, in Qaṣr Ibn al-Sarḥ, while Alptakīn and his confederates fortified themselves in Birkat al-Khayzurān ('the reed pool'). The battle took place on the Yarqōn, at al-Ṭawāḥīn, on 7 Muḥarram AH 368, the 15th of August AD 978. Alptakīn attacked the left wing of the Fatimids, forced them to retreat, and left many dead among the Maghribis. Then al-'Azīz charged against the centre and right wings, killing some 20,000 of his enemies, and was triumphant. Ibn al-Dawādārī describes the role of the Daylamīs in the battle. In view of the numerical superiority of the Fatimid army, who were overpowering them, they started to shout: *zinhār*! (according to Maqrīzī's version in *'Itti'āẓ*; in other sources it is distorted to *biḥār*), the Persian translation of *amān*. The *amān* was given them, and many were taken captive. The defeated Turks dispersed in every direction, with Alptakīn among them. Arabs of the Banu Ṭayy', the tribe of the Jarrāḥids, pursued him in order to win the award offered by al-'Azīz for his capture. They caught him 'between Qalansawa and Kafr Sābā', according to Yaḥyā ibn Sa'īd and according to al-Hamadhānī, in *Lbny*, by which perhaps Yavne is meant, or perhaps Lobana, which is Tall al-Ṣāfī (eight kilometres north of Bet Guvrin, which in the days of the Crusaders was called the Blanche garde citadel, destroyed by Saladin in 1191). They brought Alptakīn, who was on the verge of death from the blows he had received, before the caliph, who took pity on him and behaved generously. Ibn al-Athīr describes the affair in the following manner: Alptakīn flees from the battle-field and his thirst troubles him. He meets the leader of the Ṭayy', al-Mufarrij b. Daghfal, his old friend and ally, and asks him for water. Al-Mufarrij gives him water, takes him to his home, entertains him with much honour but goes off to al-'Azīz and informs him that he his holding Alptakīn and that he is prepared to hand him over for the reward that has been promised. According to Ibn al-Dawādārī, Alptakīn fled 'in the direction of the Jerusalem mountains'. A simple Bedouin named Rāhib (*rāhib* means monk, it is interesting to note), entrapped him and brought him to al-Mufarrij, on the 23rd of Muḥarram AH 368 (the 31st of August, AD 978).

As I have mentioned, al-'Azīz was generous towards Alptakīn. He gave him the gift of a ring, and when he noticed that the Turk was hesitating to drink the beverage offered him lest it be poisoned, al-'Azīz drank of it first in order to becalm him. A tent was placed at his sole disposal and he was even brought an escort from among his own men in captivity. Al-ʿAzīz took him to Egypt with him, arriving there on the 22nd of Rabīʿ I AH 368 (the 28th of October AD 978). Alptakīn remained at the caliph's court until he was poisoned on Yaʿqūb b. Killis' orders.[11]

The attitude of the Muslims in Palestine towards the Fatimids

[554] We have seen that in this campaign, which began in 974, Palestinian Bedouin are mentioned for the first time, mainly of the Banū Ṭayy'. This tribe stemmed from the southern part of the Arabian peninsula, settled west of the Euphrates and left its mark in talmudic literature as well as in Syriac Christian literature, where it is called *Ṭāʿīyīm*. We do not find them listed among the tribes of Palestine and its surroundings before the period under discussion. It is possible that they wandered to this region in the wake of the internal wars in the Abbasid caliphate during the first half of the tenth century. Canard has pointed out that the Banū Jarrāḥ, the leaders of the tribe,

> maintained a wavering policy, at times on the side of the Fatimids and at others, in favour of the Byzantines. And sometimes they supported both sides at one and the same time. They had no reservations about using flattery towards one camp, in the most contemptible way, when they thought that danger was imminent, or even to betray . . . to use every opportunity to rob in the cities and the villages and the pilgrims' caravans. Basically, they remained Bedouin, with the virtues and faults of the desert Arabs. Their actions were not worthy of any praise.

Although one cannot deny the truth of this statement, one must also see the other side of the coin, which is that the other factors which participated in this continuous political and military whirlpool did not differ in essence or character from the Arab Banū Jarrāḥ. Canard's apt description is applicable to all of them, including the Byzantines.[12]

11 Yaḥyā ibn Saʿīd (*PO*), 181–184; Thābit ibn Sinān, 66f; Ibn al-ʿAdīm, *Zubda*, 108; Ibn ʿAsākir, III, 416; Ibn al-Qalānisī, 15–21; Ibn al-Athīr, *Kāmil*, VIII, 638f, 656–661; Ibn Kathīr, *Bidāya*, XI, 276, 281f; Abū'l-Fidā', *Mukhtaṣar*, II, 115; Yāfiʿī, II, 385, mentions the year of al-Ḥasan al-Aʿṣam's death; in Ibn Taghrī Bardī, IV, 75, the date of his death is Rajab AH 362, i.e. AD 973, which is undoubtedly a mistake; also Dhahabī, *ʿIbar*, II, 341, notes that he died in AH 366, i.e. AD 977. On al-Ḥasan's absolute rule according to the coins, see: Scanlon, *BIFAO*, 59(1960), 394ff; see also the list of publications on Qarmaṭī coins in the Appendix, *ibid.*, 47ff; Maqrīzī, *Ittiʿāẓ*, I, 238–243; *idem, Muqaffā*, 195; *Khiṭaṭ*, II, 414f; in *Ittiʿāẓ*, I, 205, he attributes the story of the treason of the Jarrāḥid to 'eastern writers'; Bianquis, *Annales islamologiques*, 11(1972), 100, concludes from this that Maqrīzī had doubts as to the verity of the story, but this is quite unlikely; see further: Ibn Khallikān, IV, 54. *Isfahsallār* is a Persian word – *sipāh sālār*, see: Canard, *AIEO*, 10(1952), 732; on Lobana see: Avi-Yonah, *Ge'ōgrāfya hisṭōrīt*, 112; Prawer, *Ha-ṣalvānīm*, I, 240, 374; cf. on the events: Wüstenfeld, *Geschichte der Fatimiden-Chalifen*, 137–140; Walker, *Byzantion*, 47(1977), 306, 316; in his opinion the participation of the Qarmaṭīs ended with the hostilities in the summer of 974 and this is certainly an error.

12 See the article: Djarrāḥids (by M. Canard), in *EI²*.

[555] One should remember that the Fatimids were not really accepted by the Muslim population of Palestine. Muslim tradition has preserved the memory of one of the Fatimids' main opponents in Palestine, and one can assume that there were many others like him: Abū Bakr al-Ramlī, who is Muḥammad b. Aḥmad al-Nābulusī, or in brief, Ibn al-Nābulusī. He called for war against 'the Banū 'Ubayd', as the Fatimids were called by their adversaries. According to descriptions in the chronicles, he was a sort of leader of Ramla. In AH 357, that is AD 968, he permitted the Qarmaṭīs to enter Ramla with the consent of the townspeople. It is also very probable that he was more closely connected with the Qarmaṭīs , and that he was executed together with his group of followers as a result of the failure of the Qarmaṭī expedition against Egypt. After he fled from Ramla and the Fatimids, the Fatimid army caught him in Damascus, when it took the city from the Qarmaṭīs at the end of the summer of AH 363, that is, AD 974. They brought him, together with his son and another 300 men, to Egypt. There they were beheaded, but they reserved for Ibn al-Nābulusī a particularly horrible end; he was flayed, and his skin was filled with straw and his body crucified. This was done despite the fact that he offered to ransom himself for the sum of 500 dinars. He is attributed with the saying: 'If I had ten arrows, I would shoot one at the Christians and nine at the Banū 'Ubayd (the Fatimids)'. He continued to pour abuse on the Fatimids until the moment he died.[13]

[556] Notwithstanding, the Fatimids also had supporters in Palestine. First among them were the Jews. As we have seen, however, they had followers among the Muslims as well, who helped the founder of the dynasty to escape his Abbasid pursuers. An outstanding figure among the Fatimids' collaborators during this period was the Jerusalem physician Abū 'Abdallah Muḥammad b. Aḥmad b. Sa'īd al-Tamīmī, who lived during the last half of the tenth century. At first, he was one of the intimates of the Ikhshīdid who ruled in Ramla, al-Ḥasan b. Ubaydallah b. Ṭughj, and afterwards one of the circle close to the new rulers, the Fatimids. He had a special connection to Ya'qūb ibn Killis, and composed a book for him, consisting of several volumes dealing with medicine. It was said that he was the pupil of another Jerusalem physician, Abū 'Alī

[13] Thābit b. Sinān, 62; Ibn al-Athīr, *Kāmil*, VIII, 640; Dhahabī, *Duwal*, I, 175; Ibn Kathīr, *Bidāya*, XI, 277; Ṣafadī, II, 44; 'Iyāḍ, II, 301ff; Ibn al-'Imād, III, 46; Ibn al-Dawādārī, 161 (he adds that Ibn al-Nābulusī was in Egypt when it was taken by the Fatimids, and fled from there; his capture and handing over to the Fatimids was carried out by Ẓālim ibn Mawhūb al-'Uqaylī; Abū Maḥmūd Ibrahīm b. Ja'far, the Fatimid commander, received him and put him in a wooden cage and sent him to Egypt); Maqrīzī, *Itti'āẓ*, I, 210f; cf. the article by Bianquis, *Annales islamologiques*, 12:45, 1974, and the references he mentions there, 45, n. 1. On p. 46, he errs when he writes that he was an inhabitant of Nābulus; it was his father who came from there (as can be seen from his name), but he himself lived in Ramla.

al-Ḥasan ibn Muḥammad ibn Abī Nu'aym. He also derived much of his knowledge from a Jerusalem monk with whom he had become friendly, by the name of Anbāz Kharmā (as Ibn Abī Uṣaybi'a has it), or Asār Ḥarmā (as Ṣafadī has it) b. Thawāba; it seems that the correct name was Anbā (that is, the father) Zakariyyā'.[14]

Events of the year 979

[557] After ridding the political and military arena of Alptakīn and the Qarmaṭīs, it was the Ḥamdānids who remained the most important force still standing in the way of the Fatimids. Merely a few months had passed since the Fatimids' victory and Caliph al-'Azīz was again facing a growing alliance between the Ḥamdānids, the leaders of the Banū 'Uqayl in Syria, and the Ṭayy' in Palestine. Further on, we shall see with what ease this alliance disintegrated. This time, the Fatimids evidently concentrated a sizeable force, headed by the Jew Faḍl, son of Ṣāliḥ the physician. Faḍl was an intimate friend and aide (*ghulām*) of Ya'qūb ibn Killis. Throughout the winter 978–9 Faḍl tried to negotiate with the leader of the Ḥamdānids, Abū Taghlib, who is Faḍlallah b. al-Ḥasan. Faḍl even went to Tiberias for this purpose, but Abū Taghlib refused to sit together with him because he was a Jew. Abū Taghlib's arrogance actually had no real backing, however. A short while earlier, he had quarrelled with 'Aḍud al-Dawla, the Būyid ruler of Baghdad, and was forced to escape from Mosul and transfer the forces still loyal to him through the Ḥawrān, to the region of the Golan and the Sea of Galilee. His new base was the village of 'Āqib. At the time, Damascus was ruled by al-Qassām, of whom I shall speak further. Abū Taghlib tried to negotiate with Caliph al-'Azīz directly by means of letters and even sent him his secretary (*kātib*) 'Alī b. 'Amr. But in the meantime, his situation became increasingly difficult, for the Damascenes were attacking him, and members of his own family began to abandon him one after the other. He was forced to withdraw from the area of the Sea of Galilee and make his base in the Ḥawrān, in Nwy (read: Nawā; which is Nawē in talmudic literature). On *'īd al-fiṭr* AH 368 (3 May AD 979), he received a letter from his secretary with the news that the ruler of the west (*ṣāhib al-maghrib*, that is, the Fatimid caliph) promised to grant all his demands and invited him to come to him in Egypt. Abū Taghlib was too cautious to accept the invitation and continued his contacts with the Fatimids via letters and emissaries. But when his situation became

14 Ibn al-Qifṭī, 105f, 169; Ibn Abī Uṣaybi'a, II, 21ff; 87; Ṣafadī, *al-Wāfī*, II, 81; the name of the book by Abū 'Abdallah: 'Prolonging life by correcting the harm done by the plague and caution regarding the damage it causes'. See on him also in Sezgin, I, 317f.

worse, he agreed at long last to meet with Faḍl, on condition that each of them would be seated on a separate seat (*sarīr*). The meeting took place in al-Ṣinnabra. In his desire to create havoc within the Arab camp, Faḍl promised Abū Taghlib the city of Ramla, whence he would oust the Banū Jarrāḥ. But the Jarrāḥids had made Ramla their base at that time, with the explicit permission of Caliph al-ʿAzīz, who even sent them an official document (*sijill*) to this effect, promising them the rule of Ramla and assistance from the caliph. Faḍl, himself, had handed them the document. Indeed this stratagem succeeded and battles soon broke out between the two Arab factions, the ʿUqaylids and the Banū Ṭayy'. Abū Taghlib launched an offensive on Ramla in August 979. With him were the Banū ʿUqayl and their dignitaries, among them also Shibl b. Maʿrūf. Then al-Mufarrij b. Daghfal, the leader of the Jarrāḥids (the masters of the Banū Ṭayy') turned to Faḍl and asked for the assistance that had been promised him. Faḍl at that moment was on an expedition to Damascus, where he hoped to impose his authority. En route along the coastal road, he received al-Mufarrij's request and immediately turned eastward to Ramla and intervened on his behalf. The battle which ensued took place on the 2nd of Ṣafar AH 369 (29 August, AD 979). There were also deserters from the Fatimid army among Abū Taghlib's forces, mostly Turks under the command of Asakhtakīn. But Abū Taghlib's enemies had the superiority of numbers, his fighters took flight, and he was left with only 700 men on his side. The Bedouin of al-Mufarrij managed to catch Abū Taghlib and led him through the streets of Ramla, tied to a camel. Faḍl demanded that Abū Taghlib be handed over in order to send him to Egypt but al-Mufarrij refused and killed him with his own hands, because he imagined that if he would be left with the Fatimids, he would be pardoned and kept by them to stand against him whenever they wished. His head was sent to Egypt together with the captives of the Banū ʿUqayl. This was the end of the Mosul branch of the Ḥamdānids. Their other branch (descendants of Sayf al-Dawla) managed to hold their ground in Aleppo until 1015.

Ramla endured considerable suffering during that year; the Banū Ṭayy' who controlled the city, destroyed it completely. Ibn al-Dawādārī says: 'people were coming to Ramla looking for something to eat, but found nothing; and the farmers roamed about the markets, begging'.[15]

The episode of al-Qassām

[558] As I have already mentioned, it was al-Qassām who ruled in Damascus in that year, that is in 979. He was one of the closest of

15 Evidence of the consolidation of the Fatimids' rule in that year can be seen in the renewal of minting coins (gold dinars) in Palestine, see: Lane Poole, *Catalogue*, IV, 15; on the events,

Alptakīn's followers and among the most active defenders of Damascus during Jawhar's attempt to conquer the city at the beginning of July 976. Al-Qassām, who is described in the sources as a leader devoted to the local population and who rose from the ranks of the masses, was born in the neighbourhood of the Hermon, in a village called Talfīth. He is said to have been of the Banū Ḥārith b. Ka'b, a Yamanī tribe, that is, of Arab origin, a Bedouin. He lived in Damascus and it seems that he was a farmer (or one who cleans up [?] *tarrāb wa-zabbāl*) at first. When he reached the status of leader of the Damascenes, he exercised his authority stringently and even had his own insignia in the form of a jug. In principle, he acknowledged the Fatimids' sovereignty over the city. We have already seen that it was due to him that the Ḥamdānid Abū Taghlib was prevented from entering Damascus in 979. According to Ibn al-Dawādārī, he even approached the Fatimids and asked for help against the Bedouin. He also tells us that al-Qassām was part of an armed extremist heretic sect, headed by a man called Ibn al-Jisṭār. As we have seen, the Fatimid army was on its way to Damascus to get rid of al-Qassām in 979, when it was called to take part in the battle of Ramla. After the victory in Ramla, at the end of August 979, al-'Azīz sent another army to regain the Fatimid dominion of Damascus, led by Salmān b. Ja'far b. al-Fallāḥ. The 4,000 Maghribis who formed this army were stationed, for the time being, in the al-Wazīr grove in the 'Lane of the Pomegranates' (*zuqāq al-rummān*). The Fatimid army took possession of Damascus and its commander, Salmān b. Ja'far, soon pronounced a ban on bearing arms. A sentry belonging to al-Qassām's party, four armed men led by a certain Ḥamīd, were arrested, and this aroused a violent reaction of al-Qassām and the city's elders. They wrote a complaint to Caliph al-'Azīz, and in their letter promised to defend the city from the ruler of Baghdad ('Aḍud al-Dawla, of the Būyids). The caliph took their letter into account and sent Salmān written instructions that he was to leave the city, which Salmān did, after a stay of only a few months. In his stead, the caliph sent the latter's brother Abū Maḥmūd, who is Ibrahīm b. Ja'far b. al-Fallāḥ, who was staying in Tiberias at the time and was now appointed *walī* (governor) of Damascus. In fact, Damascus became independent and was actually ruled by al-Qassām.

see: Yaḥyā ibn Sa'īd (*PO*), 194ff; Ibn al-Qalānisī, 22; Ibn Miskawayh, II, 401ff (he has many details on the background to the intervention of Abū Taghlib in the affairs of Palestine; he tells that the capturer of Abū Taghlib in the battle of Ramla was the cousin of al-Mufarrij b. Daghfal, called Mushayya'); Ibn al-Athīr, *Kāmil*, VIII, 699; Abū'l-Fidā', *Mukhtaṣar*, II, 120; Ibn Khallikān, II, 116f (who places these events mistakenly in the year AH 367, i.e. AD 977; he notes that he copied it from the book of the wazīr Abū'l-Qāsim, who is al-Ḥusayn ibn al-Maghribī, *Adab al-Khawāṣṣ*. (He is al-Ḥusayn b. 'Alī al-wazīr al-maghribī, who will be mentioned below in connection with the events of 1010; see on him and on his aforementioned book: Brockelmann, *GAL*, S I, 600f.) Ibn al-Dawādārī, 192f, 199, who has details on Faḍl, the Jewish Fatimid commander; and also the credible

Two years later, al-ʿAzīz sent an army under the command of the Turk Subuktakīn (in some of the sources: Yaltakīn, Baltakīn, Baktakīn), and charged him with the capture of Damascus. This put an end to al-Qassām's dominance. The army was stationed near Damascus, in al-Dakka. An indecisive battle was fought with the people of Damascus. In Dhū'l-Ḥijja AH 370 (June AD 981), the city was besieged for several months but it would not surrender. At the same time, differences of opinion sprung up within the Fatimid camp. Manasseh b. Abraham al-Qazzāz, the Jewish *kātib* who was in charge of administrating Fatimid army affairs in al-Shām, favoured al-Qassām, perhaps because the latter had good relations with the Jews of the city, while Jaysh b. Ṣamṣāma, who was appointed governor of Damascus, was determined to oppose al-Qassām to the bitter end. Subuktakīn tried to mediate between the two sides, but then he preferred to act, tightened the siege around the city, and overcame its defenders. This time, Damascus fell to the Fatimids after seven days of siege, on the 20th of Muḥarram AH 373 (5 July AD 983). Al-Qassām was nowhere to be found and only after a large reward was offered for his capture was it learned that he was hiding in the synagogue, among the oil jugs. Then the dayyān was told that the synagogue would be destroyed or burnt down, and he himself helped those who were looking for al-Qassām, but he was not to be found. Only after his wife and children were caught did al-Qassām give himself up to the army. At night he was brought to the tent of Manasseh ibn al-Qazzāz, who handed him over to Subuktakīn, and he was sent to Egypt together with his household. There they were publicly displayed on the backs of mules, in Rabīʿ II AH 373 (September/October AD 983), and remained in jail until the 15th of Dhū'l-Ḥijja, 19 May AD 984. They were then released and al-ʿAzīz treated them kindly.[16]

date of the battle of Ramla, 2 Ṣafar; Maqrīzī, *Ittiʿāẓ*, II, 249–252; cf. Wüstenfeld, *Geschichte der Fatimiden-Chalifen*, 139f and the article Ḥamdānids by M. Canard, in *EI*², and especially pp. 569f.

16 Yaḥyā ibn Saʿīd, 194, 204; Ibn al-Dawādārī, 177, 192, 195, 209; Ibn al-Qalānisī, 26f; Ibn al-Athīr, *Kāmil*, VIII, 697; Ibn ʿAsākir, II, 202f (a brief and confused survey); Maqrīzī, *Ittiʿāẓ*, I, 253–258; *idem, Muqaffā*, 195f; According to him al-ʿAzīz sent a special emissary to Damascus during the battle of Ramla, named Ḥumaydān ibn Ḥirāsh (or Khirāsh), to rid Damascus of al-Qassām; his fate is not known, but we have seen that afterwards the caliph was first inclined to arrive at a reconciliation with al-Qassām and recognise his authority; according to Maqrīzī, Abū Maḥmūd Ibrahīm b. Jaʿfar, who was sent to Damascus at the time of the reconciliation, would have had to be subordinate to al-Qassām's orders. Maqrīzī even notes the date of the death of Abū Maḥmūd as Ṣafar AH 370, or August AD 980, which implies that the worsening of the relationship began later. Ibn Kathīr, *Bidāya*, XI, 292f, notes that the village Talfītā is near Manīn, adding that out of affection, the people called al-Qassām, Qusaym (a diminutive) al-Zabbāl; Abū'l-Fidā', *Mukhtaṣar*, II, 122 (under the year AH 372). On Talfītā, see: Yāqūt, *Buldān*, I, 860; cf. Dussaud, *Topographie*, 283: some 20 kilometres north of Damascus, see there the map after p. 76 (No. IV; see on the same map the aforementioned Manīn). As to Dakka, it is still not identified, see Dussaud, *ibid.*, 298 (Dikka).

Events in Palestine 981–983

[559] After the defeat of Abū Taghlib in Ramla in 979, the Banū Ṭayy', under the leadership of the Jarrāḥids, remained the actual masters of the country. While the Fatimid army was engaged in the campaign against al-Qassām, the Bedouin, in fact, removed the Fatimid yoke and proclaimed a state of rebellion in AH 371 (beginning 7 July AD 981). This uprising, which was taking place at the very rear of the Fatimid army while it was besieging Damascus, was also joined by Bishāra, governor of Tiberias. He had formerly been a supporter of the Ikhshīdids, and afterwards went over to the service of the Ḥamdānids, but he betrayed them when they were on the verge of defeat, and went over to the Fatimids. Ya'qūb ibn Killis received him with open arms and appointed him governor of Tiberias in the same year in which the rebellion of the Jarrāḥids broke out, that is AH 371 (AD 981/2). In the meantime, many men of the Ḥamdānid camp, from Aleppo especially, gathered together and came to him in Tiberias. With the outbreak of the rebellion, they immediately joined the Jarrāḥids and stood constantly alongside al-Mufarrij, the leader of the rebels.

An army under the command of Rashīq al-'Azīzī, brother-in-law (his wife's brother) of the wazīr Ya'qūb ibn Killis, was then sent to Palestine where it quickly routed the Bedouin. Al-Mufarrij and his tribe escaped southward and penetrated into Ḥijāz, where they were busy raiding pilgrims. There, too, the Fatimid army pursued them, under the command of Mufliḥ al-Wahbānī. A battle took place in Eilat, in which the Arabs completely destroyed the Fatimid army together with its commander. The pilgrimage came to a halt and the pilgrims concentrated in Wādī'l-qurā (on the Palestine-Ḥijāz border) and remained there for forty-five days until they decided to forgo the journey and return to Egypt. After his victory, al-Mufarrij went back to Palestine, fought against Rashīq and was defeated. This time, he escaped with his men through the desert to Bakjūr in Ḥimṣ, where the latter governed on behalf of Sa'd al-Dawla, the Ḥamdānid. There he was granted refuge and well-treated. The Banū Ṭayy', however, had a tradition of collaboration with the Byzantines. They moved to Antioch, where they were given protection and assistance on the orders of the emperor, Basil II. In the year AH 373 (in the autumn of AD 983), al-Mufarrij joined forces with the domesticus Bardas Phocas, the Byzantine commander, in his siege on Aleppo against the Ḥamdānid Sa'd al-Dawla, whom al-Mufarrij had to thank for his recent refuge in Ḥimṣ. The aim of the siege was to force Sa'd al-Dawla to pay the tax he owed the Byzantines for two years, a sum of 40,000 dinars. For reasons which we do not know, the caliph al-'Azīz afterwards decided to comply with al-Mufarrij's request and agreed to permit him to return to Palestine on conditions of *amān*.[17]

Jewish personalities in the Fatimid administration: Manasseh b. Abraham al-Qazzāz; Palṭi'ēl

[560] Above I have mentioned the special link that existed between the Fatimids and the Jews, especially the merchants and financiers among them. One of these was the wazīr, Ya'qūb ibn Killis, who converted to Islam. At this juncture we encounter the figure of Abū Sahl Manasseh ibn al-Qazzāz ('the silk-merchant'), the Jewish *kātib* of the Fatimids, in charge of the army's affairs in Syria and Palestine. The Arab sources sometimes call him Ibn al-Farrār, and at other times, Ibn al-Qazzāz. And there are those who call him Mīshā instead of Manashā – and it is obvious that these garbled versions were caused by the misuse of the diacritical dots, while 'the skeleton' of the writing is identical. His correct name is preserved in Bar Hebraeus, in Syriac script, and also in the Cairo Geniza documents, as Manasseh b. Abraham al-Qazzāz. Clearly Manasseh was the most trusted representative of the Fatimids in Syria and Palestine and he had considerable influence on their policy in these areas. It is also obvious from the Arab sources as well as from the Geniza documents that he did much for the Jews of Palestine. In a poem dedicated to 'Adī ('Adāyā) b. Manasseh, the poet says of him that he ruled in Syria and Palestine, Damascus, Ṣōvā (which is Aleppo), Tyre, Sidon, Ramla; that he fought against the Arabs ('the sons of Kedar and Nebaioth') and suppressed them, and he mentions, as I have said, the favours he bestowed on his own people. Contrary to the praise of the Jewish poet, we find abuse in the words of an Arab: a contemporary Damascene writer, al-Wasānī (died in AH 394, that is, AD 1004), whom Manasseh caused to be dismissed from his office (we do not know which office), composed three *qaṣīda*s against him, which have been preserved. Nathan b. Abraham notes in a letter written in1039 that 'one has never seen a Purim like that of the days of b. al-Qazzāz'. Almost all the Arab sources copied a story evidently first recorded by al-Musabbiḥī, according to which the Jew Manasseh and the Christian 'Īsā b. Nestorius, the factors of al-'Azīz, were given to oppressing the Muslims and supporting their own people, until the Muslims contrived a dummy in the form of a woman, placing a letter addressed to al-'Azīz in her hands, in which they ridiculed the fact that al-'Azīz supported the Jews and Christians and

17 Yaḥyā ibn Sa'īd (*PO*), 203ff; Ibn 'Asākir, III, 525f; Ibn al-Qalānisī, 24; Ibn al-Athīr, *Kāmil*, VIII, 562; Ibn al-Dawādārī, 205; Baybars, 252a; cf. the article Ḥamdānids by M. Canard in *EI²*.

oppressed the Muslims. When he read the letter, the story continues, he hastily placed the two under arrest. Manasseh's son 'Adī, evidently filled his father's role, and the Gaon Solomon b. Judah also mentions him in one of his letters as "Adī b. Manasseh known as b. al-Qazzāz'.

According to the aforementioned poem, Adī was a 'ready writer' (Ps., xlv:1), that is a *kātib*. The two sons of 'Adī, Samuel and Ishmael, are also mentioned there. Another of his sons, Solomon, is mentioned in a Karaite marriage deed; in a Damascene marriage deed from the 18th of Kislev, AM 4741 that is, 29 November AD 980 (al-Qassām was then ruler in Damascus), one can still read the name al-Qazzāz, and also: '. . . the Kohen the treasurer b. Samuel b. Moses ha-Kohen . . .'; it is possible that the marriage of 'Adī b. Manasseh is being spoken of, for the poem says of him that 'he succeeded and took the daughter of great ones', and indeed the sum of the bride-money mentioned in the marriage deed is very high – 300 dinars. Manasseh also had a daughter, Ḥusn, and another son, Samuel. A fragment of a deed in the Geniza deals with the division of the inheritance between the daughters of this Samuel, Mu'ammala and Mulayk, and the two sons of Mu'ammala are also mentioned, Ḥayyim and Ḥasan. Most of the family property was situated in a place called *Ṭūr Rūbā* (the big mountain) in the neighbourhood of Tyre. The family tree, as far as its offspring are known to us, would be as shown on the following page.[18]

[561] Palṭī'ēl, one of the figures described in the *Scroll of Aḥīma'aṣ*, also

[18] Suyūṭī, *Muḥāḍara*, I, 601; Ibn al-Athīr, *Kāmil*, IX, 116f; Ibn Taghrī Bardī, IV, 115f; Ibn al-'Adīm, *Zubda*, I, 188; Abū Shujā', 186; Ibn al-Qalānisī, 25, 33. The passage from Ibn al-Qalānisī was copied by Maqrīzī, *Itti'āẓ*, 297 (the editor, the Egyptian scholar Jamal al-Dīn Shayyāl, amends the correct spelling in Maqrīzī: al-Qazzāz, and prefers al-Farrār, as in the printed version of Ibn al-Qalānisi. Shayyāl's edition appeared in 1968! – an example of the total disregard for information on the history of the Jews of the area in the Middle Ages); Abū'l-Fidā', *Mukhtaṣar*, II, 131; Ibn Īyās, *Ta'rīkh*, I, 48; Bar Hebraeus (Bedjan), 196; (Budge), 177; see the *qaṣīda*s of al-Wasānī in Tha'ālibī, *Yatīma*, I, 262–265; see on this poet: Yāqūt, *Udabā'*, IX, 233; cf. further on Manasseh ibn al-Qazzāz: Freytag, *ZMDG*, 11(1857), 248, n. 1, with the explanation that he was in charge of the army's supplies; Mann, *Jews*, see the Index, and especially: I, 19–22; see the poem, TS 32.4, *ibid.*, II, 11ff. Nathan b. Abraham's letter: **183**, a, line 25, right margin; Solomon b. Judah's letter: **90**, line 9; the Karaite marriage document: **307**, see Mann's comments *ibid.*, 431f. The Damascene marriage document: TS 8.129, printed by Friedman, *Marriage*, II, 356, in whose opinion it is from the year AM 4841 (AD 1080); Goitein, *Mediterranean Society*, III, 456, n. 94, relates the name al-Qazzāz with the Kohen mentioned there (whose father's name is Samuel), but what we have here is a torn fragment, and many words are missing between the word ha-Kohen and the word al-Qazzāz. The deed concerning a legacy: **16**; Goitein, *Mediterranean Society*, III, 56, 438f, and n. 33 notes that from that deed it appears that Mulayk, the grand-daughter of Manasseh b. al-Qazzāz, was married to the son of Sahlawayh b. Ḥayyim, a rich Karaite of Fustat, an in-law of the Tustaris (cf. Gil, *ha-Tustarīm*, 60). The Karaite connection can also be seen in **307**. It is not unlikely that Manasseh b. al-Qazzāz and his family were Karaites. Manasseh's end is a mysterious affair, as there are contradictions between the aforementioned sources and the version above. The most far-reaching version is that of Ibn Īyās, according to whom Manasseh and 'Īsā were executed by hanging; according to Ibn al-Athīr, on the other hand, they both

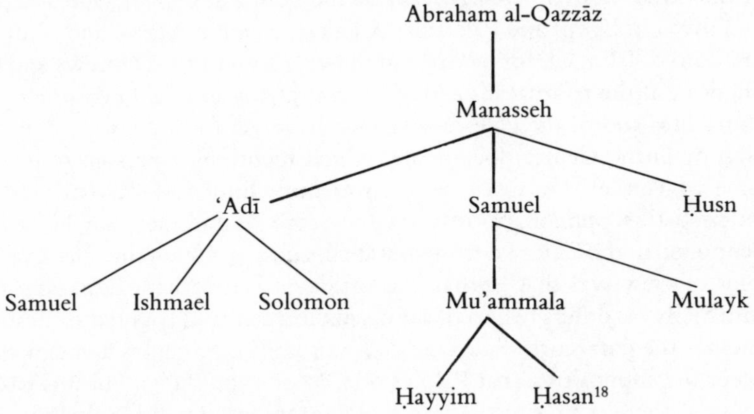

Family tree of Manasseh ibn al-Qazzāz

belongs to this period. Palṭī'ēl b. Shefaṭya, the scion of a wealthy Jewish family in southern Italy, was taken captive and surfaced in North Africa as a result of the vicissitudes of the times. There he earned the esteem of the caliph al-Muʿizz's entourage, joined him during the conquest of Calabria, and won his heart on the strength of his knowledge of astrology and his prediction that al-Muʿizz would conquer Sicily, Africa and Egypt. He eventually became al-Muʿizz's main adviser. When al-Muʿizz was about to die, he placed his son and heir in his charge, 'and the story of the greatness to which the king raised him, over his treasures and how he put him in charge of the kingdom of Egypt and the kingdom of Aramaeans, as far as Mesopotamia and all of Palestine as far as Jerusalem, and his rule and dominion, riches and spendour provided by the king, are recorded in the chronicles of Noph and Anamin' (Biblical names here meaning Egypt). And further on, 'And in the same year, R. Palṭī'el died, the defender

extricated themselves by ransom, ʿĪsā with 300,000 dinars and Manasseh with 'a great sum'; according to Abū'l-Fidā', only ʿĪsā was imprisoned; while Yaḥyā ibn Saʿid (*PO*), 233f, tells us that ʿĪsā was appointed wazīr, over Abū'l-Faḍl b. Jaʿfar b. al-Furāt, in Rabīʿ I, AH 383, May AD 993; one had to address him by the words: 'our honourable Master' (*sayyidnā al-ajall*); and that he was killed in jail, in Ṣafar AH 387 (March AD 997), still in al-Ḥākim's time. It is not clear whether one can learn something about Manasseh's fate from this as well. Mann, *Jews*, I, 21, finds proof in the aforementioned poem dedicated to his son ʿAdī, that Manasseh was not executed, 'for he departed from his people with a good name' (line 28); while Halper, *Hatequfa*, 18 (1922/3), 182, believed that this version indicates the contrary; that he did not die a natural death. It seems that Mann's opinion is the more likely, see further in Mann, *ibid.*, II, 16, another poem, which, to judge by its heading, also deals with Manasseh b. Ibrahīm al-Qazzāz (cf. I, 22); see further on Manasseh's end: Gottheil, *Zeitschrift f. Assyriologie*, 26(1912), 205.

[erroneously written *ha-menaggēn*] of the communities of God's nation who dwell in Egypt and Palestine, in Palermo and in Africa, and in all the kingdom of Ishmael, for he ruled in the kingdom of the Hebrews and the kingdom of the Aramaeans and of the Egyptians and the kingdom of the Ishmaelites and of the Palestinians'. We have yet to find a source, either Arab or in the Geniza documents, which mentions a personage by the name of Palṭī'ēl. De Goeje tried to identify him with Jawhar. Hrbek criticised this opinion, mostly on the score of the fact that he is not mentioned in the Geniza documents at all, and apart from this, because his point of view was that Jawhar was of Slavic-Dalmatian origin (and not from Sicily, as others believed, the discussion centring round the question whether the correct reading was *ṣaqlabī* or *ṣiqillī*). Fischel was inclined to accept the supposition that Palṭī'ēl was Ya'qūb ibn Killis, but it is easily seen that there is no similarity in the biographical details, as Ya'qūb ibn Killis came of a Babylonian family and converted to Islam.

Another attempt to solve the riddle of Palṭī'ēl was made by B. Lewis, on the basis of a brilliant analysis of the sources. On the basis of further Arab sources, including a collection of sources published in 1965 by a Tunisian scholar, he suggests that Palṭī'ēl was Mūsā b. Eliezer, who was the physician to al-Manṣūr, al-Mu'izz and al-'Azīz, and who accompanied al-Mu'izz from the Maghrib to Egypt. He was the author of a number of books on medicine. One of the Arab sources even mentions specifically the raid on the Byzantine regions of southern Italy, including Oria, where, it says, this Mūsā the physician was taken captive. In the biography of Jūdhar, the secretary of the Fatimid court during the period before the conquest of Egypt and immediately afterwards, Mūsā b. Eliezer, physician to the caliph, is also mentioned. His two sons, Isaac and Ishmael, are mentioned, as is Isaac's son, Jacob, and also Mūsā's third son, 'Awn Allah, who became a Muslim. One may still question why the author of the 'Scroll of Aḥīma'aṣ' thought it necessary to camouflage the names of his ancestors to such a degree or why he called Palṭī'ēl a man whose real name was Moses, and members of his family by other apparently invented names such as Shefaṭya, Ḥananel, and the like.

One should bear in mind that the story of Palṭī'ēl's life has three focal points: (1) his captivity, (2) the fact that he was an excellent physician, and (3) that he was one of the most important figures in the state and in charge of political and military enterprises. The Arab sources on Mūsā b. Eliezer only concentrate on (1) and (2), that is to say that there is no mention of his military or political status. Counter to Lewis' conjecture, one can suggest another figure, and that is the Fatimid commander and statesman, the Jew Faḍl b. Ṣāliḥ, whom we have already encountered above at the head of the Fatimid campaign northward in 979. Here we find both (2) and (3): he came from a family of medical men and was also a statesman and commander – these are two factors in common. Here one must mention a third element, the story of the Byzantine envoy who refused to sit down with Palṭī'ēl, which runs parallel with the aforementioned story of Abū Taghlib-Faḍl. At any rate, they seem to have a common nucleus, and perhaps the author of the scroll substituted a Greek villain for an Arab villain. One may also add that there is a phonetic semblance between the names Faḍl and Palṭī'ēl, while no such assonance exists with the name Mūsā. If we return to social status and military and political achievements, we find on the one hand a description of Palṭī'ēl's greatness and actions, while on the other, the Arab sources speak extensively of Faḍl's honourable standing. We have seen how he ran the campaign of 979. In the summer of AH 378, that is AD 988, he suppressed the uprising in the area of the Delta and took its leader captive. In AH 383 (AD 993), he was put in charge of the finances of the Fatimid regime: *al muḥāsaba fī wujūh al-amwāl*. During al-'Aziz' time, he was placed third, in an ironic work which gave pride of place to the converted Jew Ya'qūb ibn Killis, followed by the caliph. These were the rhymes ascribed to a Damascene, al-Ḥasan ibn Bishr: 'Convert ye to Christianity, for Christianity is the true faith, as these times go to prove, for your greatness and glory are three, and all others are nullities when compared to them; for they are: Ya'qūb the wazīr, the father; and that al-'Azīz, the son; and the holy ghost, Faḍl'. And it was said of him further: 'Indeed, al-Faḍl is a brilliant star, beyond all praise, above all others, by his generosity, known far and wide; he is compassion itself, he gives freely to every passerby; everything goes smoothly if ibn Ṣāliḥ is agreed with'. In AH 397, that is, AD 1006, already during al-Ḥākim's rule, he saved the Fatimid regime in a brilliant battle campaign against the rebel Abū Rakwa, in the neighbourhood of Alexandria. The Arab sources point out that Faḍl was one of al-Ḥākim's many victims, for the latter had him executed on the 21st of Dhū'l-Qa'da AH 399 (17 July AD 1009).

There is a certain similarity and parallel also to be found in the description of the family histories of Faḍl and Palṭī'ēl. 'The Scroll of Aḥīma'aṣ' tells that Palṭī'ēl's son, Samuel, was also 'great and honoured in his generation', and died in AM 4768 (AD 1007/8). In the *Sefer ha-ḥasīdīm* however we find a somewhat obscured account of the killing of Palṭī'ēl's brother. The Arab sources tell of Faḍl's brother, Ismā'īl (which is generally the Arabic name of Jews called Samuel), who had had connections with the greatest in the realm, especially with the family of the cadi al-Nu'mān and with the family of Jawhar, the supreme commander of the Fatimid army, and who was executed about a year and a half after his brother Faḍl, on 12 Jumādā II, AH 401 (21 January AD 1011), together with Ḥusayn b. Jawhar and 'Abd al-'Azīz b. al-Nu'mān.

Naturally, none of this offers decisive proof that Palṭī'ēl was indeed Faḍl, and at this stage of research, a conclusive solution does not seem possible. At any rate there is sufficient evidence here to stress the unquestionable fact that a number of Jews held an honourable place in the service of the Fatimids. This certainly found its expression in the attitude of the Fatimid rulers towards the Jews in Palestine, and they in turn responded to this regime with loyalty and support.[19]

The episode of Bakjūr, 983–988

[562] Apparently, the Fatimid regime consciously decided to adopt a policy of appeasement towards the Arab tribes. As part of this policy, as

[19] See the Scroll of Aḥīma'aṣ (Klar), 30–36, and the commentary there, 147–151; Kaufmann, *MGWJ*, 40:462, 496, 529, 1896; *idem*, *ZDMG*, 51:436, 1897; De Goeje, *ZDMG*, 52:75, 1898; Hrbek, *Archiv Orientalni*. 21(1953), 564f. See also Mājid, *Ẓuhūr*, 103f. De Goeje's opinion was also accepted by Marx, *Studies*, 78–85. See: Fischel, *Jews*, 64–68; Lewis, *BSOAS*, 30:177, 1967; attention was already paid to Mūsā b. Eliezer in research (according to Ibn al-Qifṭī's book): Loeb, *MWJ*, 7(1880), 102; Steinschneider, *Arabic Literature*, 96f; Poznanski, *MGWJ*, 49(1905), 48f; cf. Mann, *Jews*, I, 18. Goitein, *Mediterranean Society*, II, 575, n. 9, also had reservations about Lewis' proposal, because of the dissimilarity of the names, and also because we do not find, among the Jewish names of the period, the name Eliezer (since the Biblical Eliezer was a slave!), the name of al-Mu'izz's physician's father according to the Arab sources. The story of the Byzantine envoy: the Scroll of Aḥīma'aṣ (Klar), 31f. In the Scroll of Aḥīma'aṣ there is a story of a kind of prediction of the death of al-Mu'izz. The passage is in the part telling of al-'Azīz, the son, but according to its contents, one can see that it belongs to the life-story of al-Mu'izz, and one can also see this by his nickname in the story, 'king of the Yemenites', as is his nickname elsewhere in the Scroll. The same prophecy applies to the death of 'a Byzantine Greek king' (thus in the manuscript, both in the main text and in the margin, and it clearly refers to the Byzantine emperor), 'the king of Baghdad', 'the Spanish king'; indeed the four of them: al-Mu'izz, John Tzimisces, Bakhtiyār the Būyid ruler, and the Spanish caliph al-Ḥakam, died in the year AM 4737 (AD 976/7). In this matter, too, we find a parallel Muslim story in Suyūṭī, *Muḥāḍara*, I, 601; there it tells of an astrologer who foretold the year of the death of al-'Azīz, the son of al-Mu'izz; the caliph hid in the cellar to avoid his fate while the entire people believed that he went up to heaven, and in the end, died as it was foretold. The suppression of the uprising in the Delta: Ibn al-Qifṭī, 331. The appointment in 993: Ibn al-Ṣayrafī, 25; the rhymes: ibn Khallikān, VII, 35. On the rebellion of Abū Rakwa al-Walīd ibn Hishām see: *al-Mughrib*, V, 57; Ibn al-Athīr, *Kāmil*, IX, 197–203; Ibn Ẓāfir, 57b–58b (printed: 46–48); Abū Ṣāliḥ, 121; the Samaritan chronicle (Adler), in *REJ*, 45(1092), 252 (there he is called al-Faḍl b. 'Abdallah); cf. Lane-Poole, *History*, 128f. The town Munyat al-Qā'id, south of Fustat, was called after Faḍl b. Ṣāliḥ (*qā'id* = the commander), see: Ibn Khallikān, VII, 29; the locality is mentioned in the Geniza documents, cf. Golb, *JNES*, 33(1974), 134; cf. **70**, line 4; see this locality also in the list of Egyptian towns from 1376, in the supplement to 'Abd al-Laṭīf al-Baghdādī, 677; see also Maspéro et Wiet, 49. On the killing of Faḍl see the Arab sources mentioned above, and also Maqrīzī, *Itti'āẓ*, II, 79 (according to Ibn Khallikān, *ibid.*: on the 17th of July). Samuel b. Palṭī'ēl: the Scroll of Aḥīma'aṣ (Klar), 37, 41; Palṭī'ēl's brother: *Sefer ha-ḥasīdīm*, 152; on Ismā'īl, Faḍl's brother, and his circle see: Yaḥyā ibn Sa'īd (Cheikho) II, 199; *al-Mughrib*, V, 63; Ibn 'Idhārī, 259; Ibn Khallikān, V, 423; Ibn Ḥajar, *Raf' al-iṣr*, 364. Al-Ḥusayn b. Jawhar was one of the eminent figures in the kingdom and one of the most prominent Fatimid commanders, see Maqrīzī, *Itti'āẓ*, II, according to the Index at the end of vol. III.

we have seen, Caliph al-ʿAzīz permitted Mufarrij b. Daghfal, the leader of the Banū Ṭayy', to return to Palestine, and this he did evidently in 984. He soon found an ally in Bakjūr, of the Ḥamdānids, who ruled in Ḥimṣ with the help of the tribes and who controlled the supply routes to Damascus. In line with this policy of appeasing the Arabs, for which certain circles in the Fatimid regime were pressing (exactly who they were we do not know, but it seems that they were the Berbers' representatives, of the Kitāma), al-ʿAzīz even agreed to hand over Damascus itself to Bakjūr. This was precisely what the Jews of Damascus and Manasseh b. al-Qazzāz feared most, and this was carried out despite the opposition of Yaʿqūb ibn Killis and the Turkish battalions, who supported Subuktakīn. Those elements in the Fatimid regime who were hostile to Yaʿqūb ibn Killis, tried to have him ousted from his position, and even assassinated. Due to their insistence, the caliph was compelled to issue a written order to the commander of the forces in Damascus, the Turk Subuktakīn, and to the secretary (*kātib al-jaysh*) there, Manasseh ibn al-Qazzāz, to hand over the city to Bakjūr and withdraw. Ibn Killis was obliged to accept this decision and also conveyed orders to Manasseh in this vein. Thus the town was handed over to Bakjūr at the beginning of Rajab AH 373 (December AD 983; Ibn al-Qalānisī gives the date as 7 Rajab 372, but this is not likely, because al-Qassām was still ruling in Damascus then). Hence Bakjūr took over Damascus. He hastily had one of Manasseh's supporters executed – a Jew by the name of Ibn Abī'l-ʿŪd. This aroused the ire of Yaʿqūb ibn Killis, who claimed that this was rebellion and that the instigator of these actions was none other than Mufarrij b. Daghfal, the Fatimids' enemy. At first Yaʿqūb attempted to get rid of Bakjūr with the help of a Christian Damascene perfume merchant (*ʿaṭṭār*) named Ibn Akhī'l-Kuways, in AH 377 (AD 987), but the plot failed and only caused considerable slaughter among those elements hostile to Bakjūr's rule in Damascus. This eventually supplied the Fatimid regime with a pretext for organising an expeditionary force against him. Al-ʿAzīz placed the freedman Munīr at the head of this force. It was a large army and the Arab tribes of the Qays were also called to its side, while the Banū Ṭayy', who were Yamanīs, were their sworn enemies. All the governors of the districts were called upon for every possible assistance. The army started on its campaign at the outset of AH 378, that is May AD 988. Munīr stopped in Ramla first and quickly took control of the town, but Mufarrij b. Daghfal dominated the entire region (Ibn al-Dawādārī: in the entire *sawād* – by which he apparently meant in the entire district of Filasṭīn). With the advance of the Fatimid army, the Jarrāḥids withdrew northward to Damascus, and on their way managed to terrorise Tiberias and bring about governor Bishāra's flight from the town. Munīr then made use of rival tribes to attack the two allies, Mufarrij and Bakjūr. This lasted some two months, with no decisive outcome, until a serious battle took place south-east of Damascus, in Dāriyā. Recognising that he no longer had ground to stand on, Bakjūr appealed to Manasseh b. al Qazzāz the *kātib* and received an *amān* from him, and left the city of his own accord for Raqqa. This occurred on Tuesday, the 15th of Rajab of the same year, that is, the 29th of October AD 988 (in Ibn al-Qalānisī there is some confusion, with conflicting dates on this matter). Manasseh b. al-Qazzāz' tolerance towards Bakjūr caused some tension between him and Ya'qūb ibn Killis, and he was called to Egypt to account for his behaviour. In his defence, Manasseh claimed that he had had no alternative, for Bakjūr had at his disposal a large army and also armoured-clad mounted Bedouin (referring to the Palestinian Banū Ṭayy'). It seems that Ya'qūb ibn Killis dismissed Manasseh from his post temporarily at the time but we again find him in his former position in the days of Ya'qūb ibn Killis' successor, the Christian 'Īsā ibn Nestorius.

At about the same time, there was a marked improvement in Fatimid–Byzantine relations. A Byzantine mission arrived in Egypt to conduct negotiations concerning the renovation of the Church of the Holy Sepulchre, which was damaged in the riots of 966, as we have seen. A peace agreement, valid for seven years, was signed between the two states. The Byzantines were bound to free all the Muslim captives; the Fatimid *da'wa*, rather than the Abbasid, would be introduced in the mosque in Constantinople, and there would be an orderly supply of Byzantine goods according to the caliph's requirements. This agreement evidently had some influence on the subsequent events, as it enabled the energetic military campaign against Bakjūr and Mufarrij and the city of Damascus to take place.[20]

The events of 996–997; internal war in Palestine

[563] The wazīr Ya'qūb ibn Killis died on Monday, 6 Dhū'l-Ḥijja AH 380, 24 February, AD 991, at the age of sixty-two. On his death-bed, he left al-'Azīz a sort of political testament: to live at peace with the Byzantines as long as they kept the peace, to be satisfied with the Ḥamdānids' recognition of his sovereignty, and not to forego any opportunity to destroy Mufarrij b. Daghfal. All this seems quite credible and understandable against the background of considerable harassment and constant

[20] Ibn al-Qalānisī, 28–30, 38; Ibn al-Dawādārī, 220ff; Baybars, 256a; cf. Canard, *Hamdanides*, 686. Bishāra, the governor of Tiberias, as mentioned above, belonged to the Ikhshīdids. His loyalty to the Fatimid regime can be seen in silver coins minted on behalf of the Fatimids in Tiberias in 375 (985/6), see: Mitchell, *INJ*, 3(1965/6), 58. Later on, al-Ḥākim appointed him governor of Damascus first and afterwards of Tiberias, on the 4th of Rabī' I, AH 390, 14 January AD 1000, see Ibn 'Asākir, III, 225f. Dāriyā, see: Dussaud, *Topographie*, 297, and map No. IV (after p. 76). The agreement with the Byzantines: Dölger, *Regesten*, I, 770.

threat posed by the Banū Ṭayy' Arabs to the Fatimid regime in Palestine. They were now the major stumbling block on the way to Damascus and the Fatimids' ultimate goal of Baghdad.

After the death of al-'Azīz on 14 October 996, when his successor al-Ḥākim was still a minor, fierce internal strife blazed up between the Kitāmī battalions, the Maghribi tribesmen who formed the major part of the Fatimid army from the very outset, and the Turks, who had gradually occupied an important role in this army during the rule of al-Mu'izz and al-'Azīz. The leader of the Turks was Manjūtakīn, who had just completed a successful campaign against Aleppo, which was a source of anxiety to the Byzantines. The governor of Antioch rushed to Aleppo's aid and even the emperor Basil II hurried to the battle-field, leaving behind the expedition against the Bulgars. The Byzantines then advanced into northern Syria and reached Tripoli while Manjūtakīn retreated to Damascus. The Turks concentrated their forces in Ramla and were preparing to attack the Kitāmī battalions, who were under the command of al-Ḥasan ibn 'Ammār. The latter complained to al-Ḥākim and requested that he view this as rebellion and indeed, it is quite understandable that al-Ḥākim was not at ease with the fact that the Turks were resorting to internal warfare while the Byzantine enemy was standing at their gates. Possibly it may have been the danger posed by the Byzantines that led to the dismissal and execution of the Christian wazīr, the aforementioned 'Īsā b. Nestorius. Al-Ḥākim then ordered the organisation of a large military force, consisting of Kitāmī battalions, under the command of Abū Tamīm Salmān (or Sālim) ibn Ja'far. The battle between the Berbers and the Turks took place in Ascalon, and ended in the victory of the former. According to Ibn Muyassar, news of the battle (which he says took place in Ramla) and its outcome, reached Egypt by carrier pigeon in the middle of Rabī' II AH 387, the end of April, AD 997. Abū Tamīm offered a prize of 10,000 dinars for the capture of Manjūtakīn. 'Alī ibn al-Mufarrij the Jarrāḥid succeeded in capturing him, but he was pardoned by Abū Tamīm, who wanted to restore the peace and now led his forces to Tiberias. 'Alī ibn Ja'far, Abū Tamīm's brother, overcame Damascus and treated it as an enemy town, although the townsmen had surrendered willingly. The destruction was immense; the city was plundered and its buildings set on fire.[21]

[564] We have already seen that in the events connected with Bakjūr, the Turks sided with Manasseh ibn al-Qazzāz and Ya'qūb ibn Killis against the Arabs; that is, there was apparently a link between the Jewish party and the Turks. But a Geniza letter, evidently from the beginning of 1002,

21 Yaḥyā ibn Sa'īd (Cheikho), 225f; Quḍā'ī, 108b; Dhahabī, *Duwal*, 180; Abū Shujā', 185; Ibn Khallikān, VII, 33ff; Yāfi'ī, II, 251. On the structure of the Fatimid army: Beshir, *Der Islam*, 55:37, 1978; according to him, the status of the Kitāmīs reached its peak during

gives the impression that the Jews later suffered to a great extent at the hands of the Turks as well. The letter is from Samuel b. Hosha'na, one of the central figures in the Palestinian yeshiva, to a certain Abraham of Fustat, perhaps Abraham b. Sahlān, one of the leaders of the 'Babylonian' congregation. The writer mentions 'the submission of the two ill-wishers, one in Egypt and the other here'. Further on, he lists in rhyming verse: 'Edomite *'arēlīm* [uncircumcised, i.e. Christians], ferocious Agags [Agag, king of the Amalekites], ill-wishers of the chosen', one in 'Zoan [which is Fustat, or perhaps he meant Egypt], and the other on the borders of Canaan' [i.e. Palestine]. The one in Egypt 'was finally drowned in deep water'; and the writer adds a note in the margin: 'we were told that he was drowned in the Nile' (i.e. such a rumour reached Palestine). 'The other one', in Palestine, mistreated its communities: '. . . he tormented the people of Zion, incited against the inhabitants of Acre, expelled the people of Tyre . . wounded the people of Gaza, and made the congregation of *Ḥaṣariyya* [Caesarea] wander . . .' The letter is also signed by a man of Gaza, the abovementioned 'Yeshū'ā he-ḥāvēr be-sanhedrīn gedōlā b. R. Nathan, great-grandson of the lion's whelp' (i.e. of Biblical Judah). As noted, a dirge written by Yeshū'ā b. Nathan for his only son Josiah is known; according to what is written there, Josiah died on 19 Adar II AM 4786 (11 March AD 1026), but the date of the letter precedes this considerably, for its writer signs Samuel 'the fourth' in the *ḥavūrā* while in a deed of 10 November 1004, he is already called 'the third'. One can assume that the persecution in Acre was instigated by Wafī (or Ruqī?) al-Ṣaqlabī, and the persecution in Caesarea, by Rabāḥ. These two had been appointed by al-'Azīz as governors of these two cities, as we have seen above, and they were Turks. We do not know what fate lay in store for them under al-Ḥākim. However, we do know that the governor of Tiberias, the Ikhshīdid Bishāra, was transferred by al-Ḥākim to Damascus, and then again moved back to Tiberias on 4 Rabī' I, AH 390 (14 January AD 1000). The governor of Gaza and Ascalon was apparently replaced following these events. We do not know his name but merely that al-Ḥākim appointed a new governor to serve both these towns: Yumn, a *khādim*, probably a freedman. 'The one in Palestine' cited in the aforementioned letter, was evidently Manjūtakīn and we know that al-Ḥākim ordered his execution later on. The 'Edomite *'arēlīm*' are apparently Palestinian Christians, and perhaps supporters of 'Īsā b. Nestorius, encouraged by the presence of the Byzantines in Syria. 'The one in Egypt' who was drowned in the Nile, is evidently the leader of the Turks and their representative at the court, the eunuch Barjawān, who we know was put to death in the

al-Ḥākim's time; but he does not refer to the war between them and the Turks at the beginning of al-Ḥākim's rule at all.

year 999, in the gardens on the banks of the *Khalīj*, a channel of the Nile near Fustat.[22]

[565] In the year AH 386, that is AD 996, there was an uprising in Tyre, led by a mariner named 'Allāqa. The people of Tyre killed the Fatimid representatives in the town. Al-Ḥākim sent naval forces and also land forces against them, under the command of the Ḥamdānid Abū 'Abdallah al-Ḥusayn b. Naṣr al-Dawla and Yāqūt, one of al-Ḥākim's freedmen. (Nāṣir al-Dawla, is al-Ḥasan, son of 'Abdallah, of the Ḥamdānids, who was ruler of Mosul; another of his sons was Abū Taghlib, whom I spoke of earlier. This Ḥusayn was appointed governor of Tyre in 996 by Caliph al-'Azīz shortly before his death.) The Fatimid army established its base of

[22] On Barjawān, who was of Slavic origin, see Maqrīzī, *Khiṭaṭ*, II, 404, 418, cf. Hrbek, *Archiv Orientalni*, 21(1953), 575; the appointment of Yumn in Gaza and Ascalon, see: Maqrīzī, *ibid.*, III, 248. See on the events: Abū Shujā', 222 (he erroneously dates these events and those that followed them, as AH 381, instead of AH 386, AD 996; Ibn Muyassar, 54f; Ibn al-Athīr, *Kāmil*, IX, 119; Ibn al-Qalānisī, 50, under the year AH 387, AD 997, and also Maqrīzī, *Itti'āẓ*, II, 8–11; cf. Lane-Poole, *History*, 124f, 159; on the appointments of al-'Azīz in Palestine see: Ibn al-Qalānisī, 39. On the execution of Barjawān: Ibn al-Athīr, *ibid.*, 122; *Mughrib*, V, 56; Maqrīzī, *Itti'āẓ*, II, 25 (according to him he was executed cunningly, in an orchard called 'the pavilion of the figs and grapes'). Possibly in the following stage of his reign, al-Ḥākim preferred the Berbers to the Turks; we know that in AH 407, that is AD 1016/7, he appointed Mukhtār al-Dawla ibn Nizāl al-Kitāmī governor of Tripoli, see Ibn al-'Adīm, *Zubda*, I, 215. Samuel b. Hosha'na's letter: MS Berlin Community A4 (evidently lost), see quotations from it in Assaf, *Meqōrōt*, 33f; Assaf assumed that it was written before 1011, for he did not know of the fragment of a deed, **17**, with the signature of Samuel 'the Third' b. Hosha'na, from 1004; on *ḥaṣariyya* he assumed that it meant 'its surroundings' (of Gaza). Shirmann, *Yedī'ōt*, 7(1957/8), 159f, printed another version of the same letter from the Geniza, MS Paris, Consist, isr. IV.A 209; one can fill in certain lines by comparing the two versions: '. . . he tormented the people of Zion, incited the inhabitants of Acre against them, expelled the people of Tyre, robbed the dwellings of Ascalon, wounded the people of Gaza, and made the congregation of Ḥaṣariyya wander (MS Paris: Ḥaṣērīm). In MS Paris there is the date on which the *nishtewān*, evidently an order in favour of the Jews, arrived: Wednesday, the last day of Marheshwan; the last day of Marheshwan occurred at that time on a Wednesday in the year AM 4762, 19 November AD 1001. Shirmann, *ibid.*, assumed that the events corresponded to those described in the Scroll of Abiathar (that is, at the end of the eleventh century), but this is an absolutely incredible assumption; Kedar, *Tarbiz*, 42(1972/3), 401f, already noticed the similarity between the two manuscripts, and also found the correct general chronological framework. In my article in *Shalem*, 3 (1980/81), 29, I attributed letter **15** also to this episode; Mann, *Texts*, I, 348f, assumed that it belonged to the Crusaders' period and that the writer was a member of the exilarchic family, because of the mention of the house of (King) David; but this is merely an expression of longing for the coming of the Messiah; see the introduction to **15**; the destruction of the communities in Palestine as described there, and the matter of the ransomed captives, who arrive 'from all the borders of the Land of Edom and its gates', that is to say, from Byzantium and its ports, may perhaps relate this letter to the events described here in which the Byzantines were involved, as we have seen, but perhaps some time between 965–975 is meant, during the Byzantine invasions described above. At any rate, the emphasis upon Byzantium (while there is no hint of the Crusaders) proves that the Crusaders' conquest is not the subject of discussion. See in Assaf, *ibid.*, on the dirge composed by Yeshū'ā b. Nathan and further information about him; see the dirge itself in Zulay, *Yedi'ōt*, 3(1936/7), 176–180.

operations in Tripoli and Sidon. Tyre was placed under siege from the sea and the land. Then ʿAllāqa appealed to the Byzantine emperor for help and he responded by sending a strong navy. In the battle at sea, the Byzantines suffered a serious defeat (Ibn al-Shaddād calls them *al-ifranj*, the Franks, a term afterwards applied to the Crusaders) and most of their vessels were captured. The Fatimid army also assaulted Tyre from the direction of Damascus, under Jaysh ibn Ṣamṣāma, and the city finally fell in Jumādā II, AH 388 (May AD 998). The conquerors despoiled the town and butchered many of its inhabitants. ʿAllāqa and many of his men were taken captive; they were taken to Egypt and there ʿAllāqa was flayed, his skin filled with straw, and he was crucified. The other prisoners were also executed, among them 200 Byzantine soldiers caught on board their ship during the battle. Abū ʿAbdallah al-Ḥusayn, appointed by the Fatimids governor of Tyre, remained from then on the ruler of the city.[23]

The cruelties of al-Ḥakim

[566] For a period of some fourteen years (997–1010), the Banū Jarrāḥ enjoyed almost unlimited power in Palestine, evidently with the consent of Caliph al-Ḥākim. An attempt to get rid of them is recorded in AH 387, that is AD 997, when Jaysh ibn Ṣamsāma, the Fatimid commander and governor of Damascus, attacked the Bedouin during his preparations to take Tyre and suppress the uprising of ʿAllāqa there. The Bedouin fled eastward, to the north of Ḥijāz, but they soon returned and settled again in Palestine, and the relationship between the caliph and their leaders improved. In the summer of AH 396, that is AD 1006, the sons of al-Mufarrij spent some time in Egypt. One of them, ʿAlī, was given a ceremonial dress (*khalʿa*) and other honours by al-Ḥākim, on 17 Shawwāl AH 396, 18 July AD 1006.

A short while after al-Ḥākim ascended to the caliph's throne, negotiations with Byzantium began. A Byzantine mission arrived in Egypt, evidently at the end of 998, in order to conduct negotiations on the signing of a pact of peace and friendship. These were being held concurrently with the ongoing war. Basil II, the Byzantine emperor, was then undergoing a continual series of wars against the Bulgars, which began in 980, when the latter rose up against the emperor. In 989, they advanced southward and Salonika was about to fall into their hands. Until 995, Basil was mainly occupied with this warfaring. From then onward, he was obliged to pay more attention to what was happening in the east, particularly the afore-

[23] Yaḥyā ibn Saʿīd (*PO*), 246f (there is a misprint there: p. 264 instead of 246); Ibn al-Athīr, *Kāmil*, IX, 120; Ibn Shaddād, 115b–116a, and in the printed version: 164f; Ibn Khaldūn, *ʿIbar*, 118; Ibn al-Qalānisī, 51f; Maqrīzī, *Ittiʿāẓ*, II, 18ff; Bar Hebraeus (Bedjan), 201; (Budge), 181.

mentioned hostilities over Aleppo. In the battles against the Byzantines being fought in Syria, the Fatimids were victorious in 999, after the Byzantine commander, the Duke of Antioch, Damianos Dalassenos, was killed on the battlefield (July 998). On 20 September 999, the emperor himself arrived in Antioch and advanced at the head of his army as far as Aleppo, but was unable to conquer it. In the interim, he had to head for Armenia and reinstate Byzantine rule there; when this was done, he again was on his way to Syria, with the intention of renewing his war with the Fatimids. During a short stay in Constantinople, however, it became clear that his negotiating mission to the Fatimids had achieved some progress towards an agreement. According to Yaḥyā ibn Sa'īd, al-Ḥākim sent the brother of his mother (who was a Christian), Orestes, the Jerusalem patriarch, to accompany the Byzantine envoy on his return from the assignment in Egypt. They both received splendid ceremonial outfits and money from the caliph. It was the patriarch of Jerusalem who was responsible for arranging the truce (*hudna*), which lasted ten years. Orestes then remained in Constantinople for another four years and died there. Evidently the agreement between the Byzantines and the Fatimids left a deep impression on their contemporaries. Nāṣir Khusraw, who visited the region some two generations later, tells a somewhat folkloristic story, of the pilgrimage to Jerusalem of the Byzantine emperor himself, in al-Ḥākim's day. He did this in secret and tried to carry it through incognito, but his arrival became known to the caliph, who sent him a message saying that he knew he had arrived in Jerusalem, and that he had nothing to fear, as no harm would come to him. Three years later, however, in 1003, al-Ḥākim launched out on a continuous series of acts of oppression against the Jews and the Christians. According to Ibn al-Dawādārī, the first move in this series of acts was the destruction of the church of St Mark, in the neighbourhood of the great mosque (*jāmi'*) al-Rāshida in Fustat. Al-Musabbiḥī, a contemporary, whose account has been preserved in Maqrīzī, tells that the Christians built this church without a permit (for the building of new churches was not permitted), and that the mosque, al-Rāshida, was built in its place on the caliph's orders. In the course of building, the mosque was extended until it also covered Jewish and Christian cemeteries in the area. According to him, these events occurred in the years AH 393–395, that is AD 1003–1005.[24]

[24] Yaḥyā ibn Sa'īd (Cheikho), 184; (*PO*), 253; Nāṣir Khusraw (text) 35, (translation), 107; see: Bréhier, *Vie et mort de Byzance*, 226ff; see a general survey on the relationship of the Byzantines and the Fatimids in the eleventh century in the (somewhat superficial) article of Hamdani, *Byzantine Studies*, 1:169, 1974; al-Rāshida: Ibn al-Dawādārī, 270; Maqrīzī, *Khiṭaṭ*, III, 243f, 400; see also *idem*, *Itti'āẓ*, II, 44, where the editor quotes a manuscript of al-Nuwayrī, and also information on the obliteration of the cemeteries in Fustat, as well as additional details on the al-Rāshida mosque; Yaḥyā (Cheikho), 186, mentions that a

[567] Apparently al-Ḥākim did not place much confidence in the stability of the pact with the Byzantines and tried to exploit the peaceful interlude by strengthening Egypt's position in the northern regions. Within the context of this policy, it is possible to understand, apparently, his support of the ruler of Aleppo, Lu'lu', and his son Manṣūr, usurpers of the Ḥamdānid dynasty. In the story of the relationship between these two sides, there is also an event which touches on Palestine: Murtaḍā al-Dawla Manṣūr b. Lu'lu' sent his two sons to al-Ḥākim, who gave them large amounts of money and also granted them (*aqṭa'humā*) seven villages (*ḍiyā'*) in 'the land of Filasṭīn'; undoubtedly intending for them to collect the taxes there. This was a year before Lu'lu''s death, that is in 1007.[25]

[568] At the beginning of the eleventh century, there was evidently considerable tension in Palestine. One can find expression of this in the episode of the execution of Abū'l-Ẓāhir al-Naḥwī, who is Maḥmūd b. Muḥammad. The episode is described in the following manner by Ibn al-Qalānisī: Abū Ẓāhir Maḥmūd b. Muḥammad al-Naḥwī originally came from Baghdad and arrived in Egypt in AH 393, which is AD 1003. He was appointed to the office (*dīwān*) dealing with the affairs of the Ḥijāz. Afterwards, he was sent to Palestine, where he instilled fear and terror in the hearts of the population. In Ramla he gathered together all the artisans and merchants and compelled them, by using beating and torture, to pay 200,000 dinars. He afterwards sent his representatives to Damascus and Tiberias and the ports and ordered them to behave exactly as he had in Ramla. Among the multitude of the dispossessed, there was a Christian who had been a retainer of the caliph's sister, Sitt al-Mulk. He wrote to her complaining of the oppression and wickedness of Ibn al-Naḥwī. She promptly used the considerable influence she had on her brother, describing to him the behaviour of Ibn al-Naḥwī and appealing to him to put an end to these acts, which were not in keeping with the traditions of the caliphs, his forefathers. Then al-Ḥākim wrote a secret letter to Wuḥayd, the governor of Ramla, which said: 'Oh, Wuḥayd. May God grant you peace! The moment you read this letter arrest Maḥmūd b. Muḥammad – may God grant him mercy – and send him with someone trustworthy to the High Gate, God be willing.' When al-Ḥākim's sister saw this order, she argued with her brother: 'Oh, commander of the believers! And who is this dog, to whom you would render him such honour as to bring him before your majesty, the bowels of the earth is the place he is worthy of.'

Coptic (Ya'qūbī) church is being referred to, which was in ruins and which the Copts wished to reconstruct; according to Baybars, 283a (I do not know from what source he took this) al-Ḥākim built the *jāmi'* al-Rāshida to fulfil the will of one of his slave-girls who died; the *jāmi'* was called al-Rāshida after that slave-girl.

[25] Ibn-al-'Adīm, *Zubda*, I, 198; cf. the article Hamdanids by M. Canard, *EI*[2], III, 130.

Then al-Ḥākim took the letter and added: 'on the contrary, cut off his head and send it', and sealed the letter with three seals, and called Sa'īd b. Ghayyāth, who was in charge of the mail and gave it to him, and the latter immediately hurried past the hundred parasangs between al-Qāhira and Ramla and gave the letter to Wuḥayd, who was Ibn al-Naḥwī's best friend. When he read the letter, he ordered his assistant Durrī, an Armenian in charge of supplies and a cruel and tough man, to ride to Maḥmūd, who was encamped behind Ramla, ask permission to see him, convey greetings on his behalf, and ask him to ride to him to read a letter which had arrived from 'his majesty, the ruler'. If he says that it is not his (Wuḥayd's) custom, then tell him that this is the order stated in the letter. When Ibn al-Naḥwī was brought to him, Wuḥayd sent one of his courtiers and the man in charge of intelligence (*ṣāḥib al-khabar*) in Ramla, who dismounted Ibn al-Naḥwī and killed him in the textile market (*sūq al-bazz*) in Ramla, and after the local cadi and other witnesses confirmed in writing that this was indeed the head of Ibn al-Naḥwī, sent it via the same man in charge of mail to the caliph. This episode seems to have occurred in *ca.* 1005.[26]

[569] A short time after this, an event of much greater impact occurred, which some view as the height of al-Ḥākim's acts of extreme cruelty, and that is the destruction of the Church of the Holy Sepulchre. According to Yaḥyā ibn Sa'īd's description, al-Ḥākim issued the destruction order to Yārūkh (who is Yārūkhtakīn, Ya'qūb ibn Killis' son-in-law) in Ramla. Yārūkh sent his son Yūsuf and al-Ḥusayn b. Ẓāhir al-Wazzān, and with them also Abū'l-Fawāris al-Ḍayf. They dismantled the Church of the Resurrection to its very foundations, apart from what could not be destroyed or pulled up, and they also destroyed the Golgotha and the Church of St Constantine and all that they contained, as well as all the sacred grave-stones. They even tried to dig up the graves and wipe out all traces of their existence. Indeed they broke and uprooted most of them. They also laid waste to a convent in the neighbourhood; its name is unclear (*dayr al-sry*, perhaps this is garbled). The authorities took all the other property belonging to the Church of the Holy Sepulchre and its pious foundations (*awqāfhā*), and all its furnishings and treasures. According to Yaḥyā ibn Sa'īd, the destruction began on Tuesday, 5 Ṣafar in the year AH 400, that is 28 September AD 1009; but according to the Muslim sources, it was in AH 398, 17 September AD 1007. William of Tyre points out in his chronicle that the renovation of the church was finished during the lifetime of the patriarch Nicephorus, in 1048, after having been in ruins for thirty-seven years, which means that the destruction had taken place in

26 See Ibn al-Qalānisī, 58–61; *Mughrib*, V, 56, where the date of his execution – AH 393 – is incorrect, this is actually the year Ibn al-Naḥwī first arrived in Egypt.

1011. Most of the Muslim sources view the destruction as a reaction to its magnificence and the fact that it was a world centre for Christian pilgrims, among them many Christians from Egypt; to the splendid processions that were held in the streets of Jerusalem, and to the 'Paschal fire' (a matter I shall describe in the chapter on Christians). From Maqrīzī's account, we can read between the lines that at the same time that the churches were being destroyed, the Byzantines were damaging the great mosque (the *jāmi'*) in Constantinople (but it is not clear how), for in speaking of the truce with the Byzantines which took place in AH 418 (AD 1027), he points out that in the mosques in Byzantine cities, prayers for the Fatimid caliph (al-Ḥākim's son, al-Ẓāhir) were reintroduced, the *jāmi'* was again opened in Constantinople', and a *mu'adhdhin* was reinstated. At the same time, al-Ẓāhir gave back the Church of the Resurrection in Jerusalem and cancelled the decree of forced conversion to Islam. Al-Ḥākim's behaviour is even more surprising when one remembers that he (and his sister) had a Christian mother, and that two of his mother's brothers were patriarchs, one in Palestine and the other in Alexandria. His wazīr at the time of his decrees and acts of destruction was a Christian, Manṣūr ibn 'Abdūn. According to Sāwīrūs ibn Muqaffa', even the scribe who wrote the caliph's order ('make its sky equal to its ground and its length to its breadth') was a Nestorian Christian, Ibn Shīrīn (another but less likely version: Ibn Shitrīn). He became ill and died out of sorrow.

We find interesting indirect evidence in the letter which Yefet b. David b. Shekhania wrote from Tyre to his father in Fustat. He asks his father to write to him about the *bāmōt* ('high places', Biblical), that is, the churches (in Fustat); and it is obvious from the letter that they still had not issued decrees to pull down the churches in Tyre, for 'the *'arēlīm* (the uncircumcised) pray here in the *bāmōt*'.[27]

[27] Yaḥyā ibn Sa'īd (*PO*), 283f. Ibn al-Athīr, *Kāmil*, IX, 208f; Ibn al-Jawzī, *Muntaẓam*, VII, 239; Sibṭ ibn al-Jawzī, *Mir'āh* (BM Or 6419), 189b ff; Maqrīzī, *Khiṭaṭ*, II, 162; *idem*, *Itti'āẓ*, II, 176; *idem*, *Khiṭaṭ*, III, 250f, where it appears that the destruction occurred in Rajab AH 398, March AD 1008; see there on the appointment of Ibn 'Abdūn; cf. on the matter of the *jāmi'* in Byzantium: Mājid, *Ẓuhūr*, 140f, who offers the assumption (which is not plausible at all) that the major aim of the destruction of the Church of the Holy Sepulchre was to deprive the Byzantines of any justification for invading Palestine to defend the Holy Sepulchre; Sāwīrūs II (2), 128; cf. Renaudot, 391, who read here: Ebn Chaterin; but in the description of Ibn al-Qalānisī, 67f, the scribe was called Bishr b. Sūr. To the list of executors of the destruction, Ibn al-Qalānisi also added Aḥmad b. Ya'qūb, leader of the Ismā'īlīs in Palestine (the *dā'ī*); and Ibn al-Jawzī (above) copied from him; according to him the intention of the destruction became known to the Christians in Jerusalem in good time and they managed to take all the valuables out of the buildings; Dhahabī, *'Ibar*, 66; Ghāzī ibn al-Wāsiṭī, in: Gottheil, *JAOS*, 14(1921), 395 (who has an impossible date, 17 Sha'bān AH 391, which is 12 July AD 1001); Ibn Kathīr, *Bidāya*, XI, 339; Yāfi'ī, II, 449; 'Ulaymī, 268; see William of Tyre in *RHC* (Occ.), I, 19f; Cedrenus in *MPG*, vol. 122, 189 (= ed. Bonn, II, 456), attributes the action to al-'Azīz, but the date is the same as that of Yaḥyā ibn Sa'īd, AD 1009 (6518 'of the creation'). Yefet b. David: **316**, lines 11, 14. Le Quien, III,

[570] It seems that the destruction of the churches at the Holy Sepulchre marked the beginning of a whole series of acts of oppression against the Christian population, which according to reliable sources, extended to coercion to convert to Islam. In Fustat itself al-Ḥākim ordered the destruction of two other churches standing near the church of St Mark one belonging to the Copts (Ya'qūbīs) and the other to the Nestorians. It seems, however, that this persecution of the Christians began after 1009, or at any rate, not before 1007, for in that year, the Christians in Egypt, according to Yaḥyā ibn Sa'īd were in the midst of a burning division over the date of Easter. They disagreed over whether they should celebrate Easter on the 6th of Nīsān (the Christian Nisan, which is April), which then occurred on the 15th of Rajab, or on the Sunday after that, the 13th of Nīsān, the 22nd of Rajab. The source of the division lay in the uncertainty regarding the date of the Jewish Passover, because Easter should fall on the Sunday after Passover, and if this took place on Sunday, then Easter would fall an entire week later. At the time, however, there were two contradictory computations with regard to Passover, which that year fell on Saturday, 5 April; however according to another computation, its date was Sunday, the 6th of April (perhaps according to the Karaite calendar), and if this was the case, Easter would have to be celebrated on the 13th instead of 6 April. All the Christian sects (Melekites, Nestorians, Jacobites) finally agreed to celebrate Easter on 6 April, apart from the Christians in Jerusalem, who insisted on celebrating it on the 13th. The patriarch of Alexandria, who was, as stated above, substituting for the patriarch of Jerusalem, warned the Jerusalemites not to do so, however. His letter arrived in Jerusalem on 3 April, on the day that Jerusalemites were to refrain from eating meat, in accordance with the custom dating from the time of the emperor Heraclius, who banned the eating of meat for four days before Easter. The Jerusalemites eventually accepted his decision and the only ones who did not bend to his authority were a group of Copts (Ya'qūbīs) in the Delta, who celebrated Easter on 13 April.[28]

476ff, quotes from various sources and notes that during the oppression, the patriarch Orestes was arrested, his eyes were torn out and he was murdered, which is denied by what was written about him by Yaḥyā ibn Sa'īd, as mentioned above; this was already noticed by Schlumberger (*L'épopée byzantine*, II, 443), who assumed that the western sources confused him with the patriarch John, who was murdered in 996; the truth of the matter is that at the same time (1009) there was no patriarch in Jerusalem, and it was Orestes' brother, Arsenius, patriarch of Alexandria, who was taking care of the matters of the Patriarchate of Jerusalem, who was indeed murdered in Alexandria on 4 July 1010; see also: Wiet, *L'Egypte arabe*, 204f; and the article of Canard, *Byzantion*, 35:16, 1965 (on p. 30, n. 2, he quotes from Riant, who wrote according to Papadopoulus-Kerameos that the patriarch at that time was Christodulus of Ascalon, which is not correct); see also 'Inān, *al-Ḥākim*, 68–73.

[28] The matter of the forced conversion to Islam is mentioned in many of the sources I referred to in the preceding footnote. The destruction of the churches in Fustat: Yaḥyā ibn Sa'īd

[571] According to al-Quḍā'ī, who wrote approximately one generation after the decrees, and to Ibn Khallikān, who is generally reliable, the general edicts against the Jews and the Christians only began in 1012 (AH 402, which started on 4 August AD 1011). They were ordered to wear black turbans. The Christians had to wear a cross the length of a cubit and weighing five *raṭl*s around their necks; the Jews were obliged to wear a block of wood of similar weight. They were forbidden to use luxurious carriages or employ Muslims as servants, not even as mule drivers or seamen. In addition, they had to wear some distinguishing mark in the bath-houses, and finally al-Ḥākim decided that there were to be separate bath-houses for their use – all this occurring in AH 408, that is AD 1017/8. Ibn Khallikān and others pointed out that the Jews of Khaybar, the *Khayābira*, were exempt from these decrees. Ibn al-Athīr conveys very briefly, without mentioning the year, that al-Ḥākim ordered (after the destruction of the Church of the Resurrection in Jerusalem, which he claims took place in AH 398, that is AD 1007/8) that all the churches in the realm be destroyed, and this was done, and that the Jews and the Christians were then to accept Islam, or emigrate to Byzantine lands. They were also obliged to wear special distinguishing signs. Many converted. What Ibn al-Athīr has to say about the conversions evidently applies mainly to the Christians, for when speaking of the converts' return to their former beliefs when the decrees were no longer valid, he only mentions the Christians. But there were also many Jews who converted to Islam, as Elḥanan b. Shemaria explicitly wrote. However, the evidence of Yaḥyā ibn Sa'īd is different. He states that the Jews 'generally managed to evade the decree to convert to Islam and only a few of them did convert'.[29]

[572] 'The Egyptian Scroll', a rhymed text preserved in several versions in the Geniza, describes the events which the Jews experienced from Sunday, the 3rd of Shevat, AH 4772, 31 December AD 1011. The Jews of Fustat escorted the funeral cortège of Palṭī'ēl (in the manuscripts - Pūṭī'ēl) the ḥazān to his grave, carrying the bier on their shoulders, when they were attacked and stoned by Muslims, cursed and even subjected to accusations by informers (the nature of which is not clear). Twenty-three of the mourners were arrested, among them a member of the yeshiva in

(Cheikho), 186. The matter of Easter: *idem* (*PO*), 273–277. The chronology of the persecution in the article al-Ḥākim by M. Canard in *EI*² is unfounded.

[29] Al-Quḍā'ī, fols. 110f; Ibn Khallikān, V, 293f; Ibn al-Athīr, *Kāmil*, IX, 209; Maqrīzī, *Khiṭaṭ*, III, 251; Yāfi'ī II, 449; Bar Hebraeus (Bedjan), 204; (Budge), 184, speaks of thousands of churches which were destroyed in the Fatimid kingdom at that time; the decree regarding the wearing of the cross around the neck was also, he says, a means of pressurising the Christians to convert. The wooden block the Jews were obliged to wear, had to be in the shape of a calf, as a reminder of the golden calf. Perhaps the metropolitan of Iconium in Asia Minor, mentioned in 1078 and said to have been a native of Ascalon, was among the descendants of those who fled from Palestine because of the forced conversion

Jerusalem ('a member of the Sanhedrin ... the third of the ḥavūrā'), Samuel b. Hosha'na. The following day they were to be executed, after most of their clothes were taken from them, but they were granted a reprieve when al-Ḥākim responded to the request of the Jews of Fustat who came to ask him to save the lives of the men condemned to death, and he ordered them to be freed and all their possessions returned to them. In the scroll, al-Ḥākim earns many florid praises and even if they are not to be taken literally, it is quite evident that these events must have occurred before the advent of the decrees: '... Our Lord who judges by God's order [his name in Arabic, translated: *al-ḥākim bi-amri'llāhi*] ... who rules the entire realm with generosity and fine wisdom ... since he loves justice and hates evil ...' and so on. The visit by the Jerusalemite Samuel b. Hosha'na is also mentioned in a fragment of a letter in which the writer tells what happened to him when he himself was in Egypt. He mentions that there was a plague raging in the capital at the time and that he lost his three sons and his daughter there. Shemaria *ha-rav* (b. Elḥanan) also died in that plague. During the days of mourning, Samuel 'the third' b. Hosha'na arrived in Egypt. Then Palṭī'ēl the ḥazān (who is also mentioned in the Egyptian Scroll) fell victim to the plague. The blame for which the Jews were denounced was that they had borne the corpse on their hands (perhaps it was forbidden because of the plague?). The 'informers' were 'the pagans', which probably meant the Christians. The writer himself and also Samuel 'the third' were among the twenty-three who were arrested and they were incarcerated in the 'jail of the blood prisoners' where people condemned to die were held. At the end of the fragment, we find the matter of their being released.

Direct evidence of the events in the Egyptian capital is to be found in a letter from Elḥanan b. Shemaria to the community in Jerusalem. When his father Shemaria died, evidently in 1011, Elḥanan was visiting Damascus. Because of the events going on in Syria and Palestine at that time, he tarried a considerable time on his precarious journey. One may assume that he wrote this letter in 1013. He depicts the edicts which had just been imposed on the Jews of Egypt as a payment for their sins ('the guilt has grown and the favours lessened for the many abominations'). He mentions the destruction of the synagogues and the desecration of the Scrolls of the Torah, the black clothing they are obliged to wear and the wooden block that must hang from their necks. He also says that many have converted: 'Many have left behind their creed and dropped their religion'. The destruction of the synagogues in Fustat is also mentioned in a review of the affairs of the *heqdēsh* in Fustat, which was evidently written in 1042.

to Islam, see: Neumann, *Weltstellung*, 40, n. 1. On the limited number of converts to Islam among the Jews see: Yaḥyā ibn Sa'īd (*PO*), 511. Elḥanan's letter: see next section.

It says there that the synagogues were destroyed three years after the passing of Shemaria b. Elḥanan (as far as one can make out, that is, *ca.* 1014 or 1015). Men of the caliph's guards tore out the wooden beams and dismantled the bricks and sold them.[30]

[573] The same decrees were also in effect in Palestine, and there too, churches and synagogues were destroyed. Josiah Gaon wrote in *ca.* 1020 that 'the people of Palestine are still busy with their synagogues', that is, with the renewal of the synagogues that were destroyed. In another letter, he hints at the deterioration of the relations with the Fatimid regime, which formerly helped to support the Jerusalem yeshiva financially: 'We were provided for by the kingdom', but for the past two years, they could no longer ask for any support from 'the kingdom', that is from the caliph. Elijah ha-Kohen b. Solomon Gaon also observes, in a letter of which a draft has been preserved, that 'we have become powerless from the destruction of the synagogues'. It is also worth mentioning the letter from the community of Syrian Tripoli, asking Ḥesed the Tustari to get them a *nishtewān* from the authorities to allow them to transform one of the ruins in which 'the slaves of the king' dwell without paying rent, into a synagogue. The synagogue of Tripoli, they write, was turned into a *marjiz*, that is a mosque, during the persecution. They mention that in all the other places synagogues have been restored, and in Jubayl a new synagogue was built, about which no one complained, and only in Tripoli was there still no synagogue.[31]

[574] Rumours concerning the decrees against the Christians, and especially about the burning of the Church of the Holy Sepulchre, spread

[30] Kaufmann, *ZDMG*, 52(1897), 442ff; Mann, *Jews*, I, 31; II, 31–37, 432–436; the fragment of the letter: **19**, see there the various readings as compared with Mann, and see his discussion *ibid.*, I, 28f, 32. The man referred to is Palṭi'ēl ha-ḥazān b. Ephraim b. Ṭarasūn; Ephraim's father was a *parnās* in Fustat. Elḥanan's letter: **26**, lines 31ff. The *piyyūṭ* written by Elḥanan (Dropsie 312) which Davidson, Poznanski and Mann assumed was referring to these persecutions, was in fact directed against the Karaites, as was proven by Abramson, *Ba-merkazim*, 133ff; see there the references and the *piyyūṭ* itself. The survey on the *heqdēsh*, see: Gil, *Documents*, 138 (document No. 3, consisting of the following fragments: TS Ar. Box 18 [1], f. 35; TS 20.96: ENA 2738, f. 1); on the rebuilding of the synagogue 'of the Jerusalemites' see *ibid.*, 95f, and the documents printed there in the continuation. See also Goitein, *Mediterranean Society*, II, 300, 591, n. 1, and therein proof that community life in Fustat had returned to normal by 1016, that is after some three years. See *Synaxaire arabe jacobite*, 211f, 560f, with the story of the miracle of the monk who was saved from execution in al-Ḥākim's day because the beasts of prey to which he was thrown refused to touch him. Al-Ḥākim tried to win him over by promising that he would be appointed head judge (*qāḍī'l-quḍāh*) if he would become a Muslim. According to this source, the persecution lasted for seven years, and according to another version, in the same source, eight years and a month.

[31] Letters of Josiah Gaon: **32**, a, lines 14–15, to Nethanel b. Aaron, the banker; **36**, a, lines 12–14. Elijah ha-Kohen: **412**, I, lines 12–13. The letter of the Tripoli community: **284**; the use of the root *rjz* in the meaning of Muslim prayer, here as mosque, is typical of the period.

like wildfire throughout Europe and undoubtedly left a deep impression on the Christian world. In the West, the rumours ascribed clear guilt to the Jews. Ademar's chronicle preserved the story that the Messiah's grave was desecrated by the Jews and the Muslims (Saraceni) on 29 September 1010, because Western Jews and the Muslims of Spain despatched letters to the East in which they blamed the Christians and told of Christian armies going out to attack the Muslims in the East. Further details were known to Rudolphus (Raoul) Glaber, who said in his chronicle that the Jews of Orléans bribed Robert, a monk who had fled from the monastery, to bring a letter written to the ruler (*princeps*) of Egypt (Babylon), and that due to this letter, the Church of the Resurrection was destroyed. He mentions that the Church of St George in Ramla was also demolished. As soon as it became known that the Church of the Holy Sepulchre had been destroyed, the Jews of Europe were evicted from their lands and their towns. Some see this as the first growth of the idea of western intervention to protect the holy places in Palestine, a fact which has far greater significance, according to Wiet, than that these accusations aroused rampant anti-Semitism.[32]

[575] The sources do not supply us with clear explanations for the persecution, the coercive decrees, and acts of violence which were instigated by al-Ḥākim. We also know of hideous cruelties which he perpetrated against the Muslims. True, it is obvious that the sources are biased and antagonistic towards the Fatimids in general and towards al-Ḥākim in particular. A present-day scholar, Vatikiotis, looked for an explanation of this persecution and extremist practices in al-Ḥākim's aspiration to realise the concept of the mahdī, that is, the descendant of 'Alī who would lead the world, whereas until his time, this was seen as a vision of the End of Days. One Muslim source even attributes to al-Ḥākim the plot to move the Prophet's bones from Medina to Fustat. Apart from this, the Fatimid caliphate was subjected to the constant pressure of rebellions, such as that of the tribes of Egypt under the leadership of Abū Rakwa mentioned above, and the uprising of the tribes in Palestine which I shall discuss below. Caustic anti-Fatimid propaganda was coming out of Baghdad and in 1011, a strongly-worded manifesto against the Fatimids was

32 See the chronicle of Ademar (Adhémar de Chabannes) in *RHGF*, X, 152f; *MGH* (SS) IV, 43f (the author died in Jerusalem in 1034); cf. Le Quien, III, 478ff. The chronicle of Glaber, see: *RHGF*, X, 34f; Riant, *AOL* I, 38f; see also: Aronius, No. 142. Grossman, *Shalem*, 3(1980/81), 66, assumes that the eviction of the Jews from Mainz (1012) was also the result of the rumours that the Jews were to blame for al-Ḥākim's decrees. Wiet's comments (he indeed wrote this), see *L'Egypte arabe*, 208. A Jerusalem Church source puts a similar blame on the Jews concerning the events of 966 (sec. 485 above): the burning of the Church of the Holy Sepulchre and the death of the patriarch John in the fire occurred because the Jews wrote to the Sultan of Baghdad (!) that the number of Christians was on the increase and that their aim was to rule over Jerusalem; see Papadopoulos-Kerameos, *Analekta*, II, 299 (and the date there is incorrect – 983).

published there, mostly containing slander (perhaps true in the main) as to their true descent.[33]

[576] Exactly when these decrees came to an end is not clear, although it does seem to have been a gradual process. Some Muslim sources mention that al-Ḥākim permitted those who had been forced to convert to return to their original beliefs; those same sources express their disgust at this behaviour, which was unheard of in Islam (but the same sources were not taken aback at the forced conversion or the destruction of houses of prayer, practices which are also forbidden according to the laws of Islam). We have already seen the letter from the Tripoli community, which notes that in many places, the communities restored their synagogues. Yaḥyā ibn Sa'īd mentions that al-Ḥākim was besieged by many requests to permit the return of the churches, in accordance with his new policy, and they even asked to have their foundations returned to the churches. Al-Ḥākim granted all their requests and licensed the rebuilding of all the churches and monasteries in Egypt and the other countries and wrote official orders to each and every one, the only exception being those churches and foundations which had been sold in order to raise money for the regime's empty treasury. As to the Christians who had fled from the forced conversion and gone to Byzantine territory, he points out that they were permitted to return, and they did. However, both these refugees as well as those who returned to Christianity, had to pay the full poll-tax for their entire period of absence. Some two years after al-Ḥākim's death (in 1021), his sister ordered the patriarch of Jerusalem, Nicephorus, to go to the emperor and give him an account of the restoration of the churches and the rebuilding of the Church of the Holy Sepulchre and the other churches in Egypt, Palestine and Syria, and of the return of the foundations. He did actually make the journey and met with the emperor for this purpose. According to Maqrīzī, most of the 'normalisation' was only carried out in AH 418, that is AD 1027, when a new armistice was agreed upon with the Byzantines; the *jāmi'* was then reopened in Constantinople, mats and

[33] See Vatikiotis, *IC*, 29:1, 1955. One of the expressions of belief in the Mahdī which was held by the Fatimids at the time and their views of al-Ḥākim as the redeeming Mahdī who enjoys divine qualities, is the account of the Ismā'īlī-Fatimid writer al-Kirmānī; writing in 1015, he quotes from Dan., xii:12 ('Blessed is he that waiteth, and cometh to the thousand three hundred and five and thirty days') and predicts that in nine years hence, that is in Sel. 1335, which is AD 1023/4, al-Ḥākim will bring salvation (al-Ḥākim died in 1021). See: Krauss, *Der Islam*, 19(1931), 256f; on al-Ḥākim's plotting, see: Samhūdī, I, 470, in the name of some scholars who preceded him; according to him, al-Ḥākim did what he did because he was provoked by a *zindīq* (generally a Manichaean, but evidently the meaning here is merely a heretic). See on the origin of the Fatimids also Lane-Poole, *History*, 95f in the footnote. Mann, *Jews*, I, 72, assumed that the Jews were then ousted from Jerusalem, on the basis of what was said in **412**, II, lines 3–4: 'and they gave him (Samuel b. Ṣemaḥ) a place to settle among us in the city of Ramla'; Mann assumed that the writer was Josiah Gaon; but he is Elijah ha-Kohen b. Solomon Gaon; and the time is evidently 1025.

illumination were installed and a *mu'adhdhin* appointed, while in Jerusalem the Christians were permitted to reopen the Church of the Resurrection, and a stream of donations immediately poured in for this purpose. Also, many who had converted to Islam then returned to Christianity.[34]

The first war of the Jarrāḥids (1011–1014)

[577] A short time after the destruction of the Church of the Holy Sepulchre, a period of tension set in and there was an uprising of the Arabs in Palestine. One can assume that there was not only a chronological contiguity between the two events but that the bitterness of the Christians was at work behind the scenes, and perhaps even Byzantine encouragement. The fact is that the Arab tribes were in contact with the Christians and enjoyed their support.

In AH 401 (AD 1010/1) an incident occurred which affected the relationship between the Jarrāḥids and the caliph. This was the flight of Abū'l-Qāsim al-Ḥusayn, son of 'Alī 'the Maghribi wazīr', to Palestine. 'Alī the father, came to Egypt from Baghdad, where for a time he was in charge of the *dīwān al-maghrib* ('the western office'), the office for affairs of state in the Abbasid regime, and hence his nickname, while his family hailed from Persia. In Egypt, the father suffered the fate of many of those close to the throne when he was executed on al-Ḥākim's orders, together with many members of his family. The son, Abū'l-Qāsim, found refuge in Palestine with al-Ḥassān b. al-Mufarrij, the leader of the Jarrāḥids. Al-Ḥākim then instructed Yārūkhtakīn, governor of Ramla, who was staying in Egypt at the time, to head an army and launch an attack against them in Palestine, and bestowed on him the honourable title of *'alam al-dawla* ('flag of the realm'). At the same time, 'Alī and Maḥmūd, the two other sons of the Jarrāḥid al-Mufarrij, were in Egypt. They rushed to their father in Palestine to tell him of the preparations and advised him to attack the Fatimid army in the Jifār, the northern coast of Sinai, before it reaches Ramla. Abū'l-Qāsim was also of the same opinion, as was al-Ḥassān. Finally al-Mufarrij decided to set up an ambush for the Fatimid army in Gaza. Yārūkhtakīn was informed of this in good time, and consulted his advisers, who suggested two possibilities: either to organise a march during the night as far as Ramla, where a Fatimid garrison was stationed, which would present difficulties for those who planned to attack them, or

[34] Al-Quḍā'ī, 112a; Ibn al-Rāhib, 82f; Ibn al-Jawzī, *Muntaẓam*, VII, 240; Suyūṭī, *Muḥāḍara*, I, 602 (who is upset because al-Ḥākim eventually permitted the rebuilding of the Church of the Resurrection); Yaḥyā ibn Sa'īd (Cheikho), 231, 239, 243; Nicephorus was ordered by the emperor to return to Jerusalem, and exactly at that moment, the news of al-Ḥākim's sister's death became known; Nicephorus sailed from Constantinople and reached Tripoli in Ṣafar 415, April or May 1024; Maqrīzī, *Khiṭaṭ*, II, 162; *idem*, *Itti'āẓ*, II, 176.

to ask that garrison to send him reinforcements of 1,000 mounted troops, who would join him in Ascalon. One of Yārūkhtakīn's trusted retainers. Ibn Sirḥān, left for Ramla to deliver the order to send reinforcements of cavalry, but on his way he was captured by the Bedouin. Yārūkhtakīn was certain that the reinforcements would arrive within three days, and even set out along the coast in the belief that he would meet up with them in Ascalon. The Bedouin under al-Ḥassān attacked him *en route* (perhaps near Rafiaḥ) and took him captive, together with his wives and children, and afterwards returned to Ramla and raided all its districts (*rasātīqhā*). The Fatimid garrison stationed in Ramla went out to meet them when they were about to retreat. Then Abū'l-Qāsim suggested they organise an attack on Ramla and recruit all the tribesmen of jund Filasṭīn (the *sawād*, that is the province, of Ramla) for this purpose. In order to attract the tribes to this action, he suggested that a general licence to despoil and plunder be proclaimed. This was indeed a success and the Bedouin seized Ramla, destroyed and plundered it. According to Yaḥyā ibn Sa'īd, '[al-Mufarrij] allowed the Arabs to pillage the place. Then all the people's goods were taken from them, all the inhabitants arrested and their property confiscated. Many were reduced to poverty there'.

When the news of what had happened to Yārūkhtakīn and the taking of Ramla reached Egypt, al-Ḥākim wrote a letter of rebuke to al-Mufarrij, in which he demanded the release of Yārūkhtakīn and his return to Egypt. He even promised the Jarrāḥids a grant of 50,000 dinars. This became known to Abū'l-Qāsim and he urged al-Ḥassān to quickly decapitate Yārūkhtakīn, before his father al-Mufarrij would be tempted to accept al-Ḥākim's proposal to bring him to Egypt. Al-Ḥassān fell in with his suggestion. This was the height of the Jarrāḥid rebellion, which now became a war of annihilation against the Fatimids. The Banū Jarrāḥ even proposed their own candidate for the office of caliph. On Abū'l-Qāsim's suggestion, they decided to bring Abū'l-Futūḥ al-Ḥasan b. Ja'far from Mecca, a man of the lineage of 'Alī ibn Abī Ṭālib, of the eleventh generation, and proclaim him caliph. Abū'l-Futūḥ at the time held the office of *amīr*, commander of the city of Mecca on behalf of the Fatimids. Abū'l-Qāsim made a special journey to Mecca and convinced him to agree to being proclaimed caliph. He agreed and even called himself by a new name, as was the custom of all caliphs: *al-rāshid bi'llāh* or *al-rāshid li-dīn allāh* ('the righteous with God' or 'in the faith of God'). People of the 'two *ḥarāms*', Mecca and Medina, swore their allegiance to him. A rich man who died in Jidda in that same year, left him an estate, for the purpose of seeing to its division among his heirs, and retaining a portion for himself. On the advice of Abū'l-Qāsim, he took the entire legacy for himself (that is – one may assume – he sold the estate and pocketed the money). Some say that he also took money of the *ka'ba*. In Ramla, which he reached on 23 Ṣafar AH 403, that is 13 September AD 1012, the tribesmen received him with great joy and addressed him as they would a caliph, *amīr al-mu'minīn*. Ibn Nubāta, who was the preacher in Ramla, read in the *khuṭba* (the sermon) from the Koran, *sūra* xxviii, which is the *sūrat al-fatḥ* ('the victory'; its usual name: *al-qaṣaṣ*, 'the story'), verses 1–5, which speak of the wickedness of Pharaoh and of Haman (hinting at the rulers of Egypt) and on the righteousness of Moses. Afterwards everyone turned to *dār al-imāra* (the governor's house). It seems that Abū'l-Futūḥ had excellent chances of earning the affection of the Muslims, as Shiite leanings were held by many of them, and they were inclined to accept a leader whose descent from the family of 'Alī ibn Abī Ṭālib was unquestioned, unlike the doubtful lineage of the Fatimids.

According to Yaḥyā ibn Sa'īd, the Arabs in Palestine then reached the height of their power; 'they were from now on the masters of the country and dominated all its regions, from al-Faramā [which is Pelusion, Balūza] until Tiberias. They even besieged the citadels along the coast for a considerable time, but did not succeed in taking any of them'. He also says that the Jarrāḥids even minted coins stamped with Abū'l-Futūḥ's name. These events occurred, he says, in the course of two years and five months, until 'Alī b. Ja'far's campaign in July 1013. This means that the disturbances began (we do not know which of the events described above Yaḥyā considers to be the beginning) in Shawwāl AH 401, that is February AD 1011, roughly a year and a half after the destruction of the Church of the Holy Sepulchre.

Al-Ḥākim felt that he was in great danger and he now tried cunning. Firstly, he wanted to appease the Jarrāḥids and consequently sent large sums of money to 'Alī and Maḥmūd, the sons of al-Mufarrij. To the eldest son, Al-Ḥassān, he sent a slave-girl who had aroused his interest some years earlier when he was in Egypt. To the father of the family, al-Mufarrij, he sent valuable gifts. Abū'l-Futūḥ evidently felt that his position was not altogether stable and that the Bedouin were but feeble support. They spent the money he had brought with him from Mecca and began to offend him and show him increasingly less respect. He then decided to return to Mecca, which had remained faithful to the Fatimids. Abū'l-Qāsim also took fright and fled to Iraq and later on became wazīr of the ruler of Mayāfāriqīn (which is ancient Martyropolis, in northern Mesopotamia) until his death in AH 418, that is AD 1027, at the age of forty-eight. In Muḥarram AH 404, that is July AD 1013, al-Ḥākim sent a large force, of 24,000 of the best fighters of the Fatimid army, to Palestine, under the command of 'Alī b. Ja'far b. Fallāḥ (the brother of Abū Tamīm), who on this occasion received a new name – *quṭb al-dawla* ('axis of the realm'). The two younger brothers, 'Alī and Maḥmūd, quickly pronounced their loyalty to al-Ḥākim. Ibn al-Mudabbir, the *kātib* (secretary) of the head of the family, al-Mufarrij, poisoned him on al-Ḥākim's counsel, and this happened (according to Maqrīzī) on Dhū'l-Qa'da AH 403 (May AD 1013). Afterwards Ibn al-Mudabbir fled to Egypt, and there he was executed on al-Ḥākim's orders. Al-Ḥassān sent his mother and his slave-girl to beg for mercy and even appealed to al-Ḥākim's sister to intervene on his behalf. At long last, al-Ḥākim gave in to these appeals and even recognised al-Ḥassān's *de facto* authority in Palestine; however the Fatimid army, under Quṭb al-Dawla, entered Ramla.[35]

[578] In the course of their domination of Ramla, the Arabs did not show much consideration for the local population and extracted large amounts of money and property from them, as they did elsewhere. Hence many of the Christians living in Palestine (and in Syria?) made off for Byzantium, most of them settling in Lādhiqiyya and in Antioch. The suffering and these flights were not however caused by the Jarrāḥids' policies, for the latter were generally ready to collaborate with the local Christians and the Byzantines. It would be more accurate to see this as the result of the insecure state of affairs in Palestine, especially because of the savage behaviour of the Bedouin. On the other hand, however, al-Mufarrij urged the Christians to rebuild the Church of the Resurrection and even appointed one of the bishops, Theophilus, as patriarch, apparently in

35 See the description of Abū'l-Qāsim's escape in Ibn al-Qalānisī, 62; see *ibid.*, 64, what is said in praise of his wisdom and learning, and a fragment from *Ta'rīkh al-islām* of Dhahabī on him, quoted by the editor, in which there is also a summary of the events that followed; see also Ibn al-'Imād, III, 210; Maqrīzī, *Khiṭaṭ*, III, 53f; who has further details about the family; Ibn al-Ṣayrafī, 47; Ibn Khallikān, II, 174f; al-Fāsī, *Shifā'*, 207. The battle between Yarūkhtakīn and the Jarrāḥids took place near *fj dārūm*; according to Ibn Ẓāfir, fol. 59: near *rmḥ dārūm*, and originally it evidently was: near *rafaḥ dārūm* (Rafiaḥ); see also the Samaritan chronicle: Adler et Seligsohn, *REJ*, 45(1902), 253 (speaking of the war in al-Ḥākim's day, '... and they destroyed the city of *qāsṭūn* [should be: *filasṭīn*], which is the city of Ramla'. See further on the events: Abū Shujā', 233–239, who has many important details, but he includes them mistakenly in the events of AH 381 (AD 991–992); as does also Ibn al-Jawzī, *Muntaẓam*, VII, 164f; see the article Djarrāḥids (by M. Canard) in *EI*², especially p. 483; Sibṭ ibn al-Jawzī, *Mir'āh*, (MS Munich), fol. 71ff; Yaḥyā ibn Sa'īd (*PO*), 295–298 (according to him Yārūkhtakīn had with him one wife, the daughter of Ya'qūb ibn Killis); see *ibid.*, 312, on Quṭb al-Dawla's campaign; al-Fāsī, *'Iqd*, IV, 69ff; according to its editor, *ibid.*, when Abū'l-Futūḥ arrived there, the preacher in Ramla was Abū Yaḥyā 'Abd al-Raḥīm b. Muḥammad al-Fāriqī, but we know that he died in AH 374 (AD 984; see Ibn Khallikān, I, 283); Wüstenfeld, *Geschichte der Stadt Mekka*, 218f quotes al-Fāsī, and does not notice the chronological contradiction; see also Brockelmann, *GAL*, G I, 92; S I, 149f (following Ibn Khallikān); see also Becker, *Beiträge*, 42f, with a few additional details on the affair of Abū'l-Futūḥ and on Mecca after these events; see further on the Abū'l-Futūḥ affair: Maqrīzī, *Khiṭaṭ*, III, 251 (he has al-Ḥusayn instead of al-Ḥasan); Musabbiḥī, 68, notes that afterwards he fled from Mecca, on 9 Shawwāl AH 415, 14 December AD 1024, because of an internal war which broke out there between the 'Alids and their rivals (the Ṭalḥa clan). On the end of Abū'l-Qāsim see: Ibn al-'Imād, *ibid.*; Mayāfāriqīn: Le Strange, *Lands*, 111f.

Ramaḍān AH 402 (April AD 1012). We learn from Yaḥyā that the patriarch Theophilus died in Ramaḍān AH 410 (January AD 1020), after serving in this office for eight years. We can also see in this appointment evidence of the strong connection between the Jarrāḥids and the Christians in Palestine, a link that would also be expressed in subsequent events. When the Fatimid army under the command of Quṭb al-Dawla was stationed in Palestine, the patriarch Theophilus fled from Jerusalem. He remained in hiding for some time and then returned, and Quṭb al-Dawla welcomed him cordially. It is interesting to note that the Byzantine chronicler Cedrenus also mentions Ibn al-Jarraḥ (Pinzarakh), that is, Mufarrij b. Daghfal, who he says rebelled against the Egyptian regime and was an ally of Byzantium, collaborating with its army.[36]

[579] We can find intimations of the disturbances and anarchy that prevailed in the area in a letter from Elḥanan b. Shemaria to the Jerusalem community, in which he mentions his father's death towards the end of 1011, as I have already mentioned. His father died in Fustat while he was staying in Damascus because of the 'disturbances and disorders in the state and on the roads', and only when 'there was some respite in the world' was it possible for him to go on his way. Apparently, he went from Damascus to one of the ports, Tripoli or Tyre, for he tells in the letter that he travelled to Egypt by sea. *En route*, his party was attacked by 'vicious robbers and vulturous pirates' and it was a miracle that they were not killed but were only soundly thrashed until they were 'sorely bruised'.[37]

Second war of the Jarrāḥids (1024–1029)

[580–581] For roughly eleven years, from 1013 until 1024, peace reigned

[36] Yaḥyā ibn Sa'īd (*PO*), 297f; Cedrenus (Bonn), II, 495f; cf. Schlumberger, *L'épopée byzantine*, II, 446, 448; Wiet, *L'Egypte arabe*, 210f. Wiet sees the need, for some reason, to deny the collaboration between the local Christians, the Byzantines, and the Arabs; Bréhier, *L'église*, 38.

[37] See **26**; Josiah Gaon is evidently also referring to the events of this period in his letter, **31**, when he mentions the difficult situation of the people of Ramla, 'who were at the end of their tether from the hardship and poverty that had overtaken them' while formerly it was they who had helped the poor of Jerusalem; Mann, *Jews*, I, 162, n. 1, assumed that this was a Karaite letter because of the use of the word *darkemōnīm*, but this is not correct. In **58** as well, Solomon b. Judah's letter to Abraham b. Sahlān in Fustat, speaking of these events, it says: 'now our heart is almost at peace and our soul relaxes, after the horrors which spread terror and awe'. It is possible that some of the Jews of Jerusalem tried to escape the Bedouin's swords by undergoing Christian baptism by the patriarch Theophilus, which is perhaps the origin of the story of the converted Jerusalem Jew told by Ekkehard of St Gallen and ascribed to Notker Labeo (who died in 1022); according to that Jew, the patriarch baptised him and many other Jews during Easter, 'after the revelation of the light' (*post luminis adventum*: meaning evidently 'the Paschal fire' which I shall discuss in the chapter on the Christians); see: Dümmler, *Zeitschrift für deutsches Altertum*, 14(1869), 20; see also Aronius, No. 148a.

in Palestine. According to the Arab sources, an earthquake struck in AH 405, the 20th of Rabīʿ I, that is 27 August AD 1016, which toppled the dome of the Dome of the Rock. In a letter from Solomon b. Judah to Jacob *ha-meʿūtād* b. Joseph, however, it is stated that the Dome of the Rock collapsed on Sunday, the 17th of Elul. The 17th of Elul fell on a Sunday in AM 4775, that is 4 September AD 1015. Evidently the information in the Arab chronicles should have appeared among the events of the year AH 406, when 20 Rabīʿ I fell on 7 September, and the difference of three days is of no consequence in this instance. At any rate, the authentic source is naturally Solomon b. Judah's letter, so that we know that the earthquake actually took place on the 4th of September 1015.[38]

Another uprising of the Bedouin, this time with the support of the Christians, broke out in 1024. On 27 Shawwāl AH 411, 13 February AD 1021, al-Ḥākim was murdered by assailants in mysterious circumstances, and his son, Abū'l-Ḥasan ʿAlī, succeeded as caliph and was given the name *al-Ẓāhir li-iʿzāz dīn Allah* ('the victor in endearing God's faith'). He was sixteen when he ascended to the throne. Al-Ḥassān b. al-Mufarrij, sensing the instability of the regime in Egypt, began to cast off the burden of its authority despite the rulers' efforts to gain the Jarrāḥids' affection and influence them by showering them with gifts and honours. One of Ibn Jarrāḥ's sons (we do not know which) was staying in Egypt on the 1st of Jumāda II, AH 414, 21 August AD 1023, and was bestowed the gift of a robe of the *muthaqqal* variety (silk interwoven with gold threads) and a turban embroidered with birds (*muṭāyara*), and he was led through the streets of Fustat 'on two horses with gilded saddles'.[39]

[582–583] In April 1024 the caravan of the *ḥajj* of the Khurāsānīs passed via Palestine on their way from Mecca. They travelled through Eilat and from there to Ramla. They had 60,000 she-camels with them, and according to al-Musabbiḥī, they numbered 200,000 people. The caliph sent official instructions to all the army commanders in Palestine, to receive them cordially and treat them as well as possible. The people of Palestine

[38] Some evidence of the more or less normal circumstances prevailing at the time can be seen in **271**, a deed of receipt written in Tyre on 24 November 1019; Dara b. Solomon, the wife of Ḥalfōn (Khalaf) b. Moses., who is the son of Abū Qīda, the merchants' representative in Tyre, confirms that she has received everything due her from her father's legacy from David b. Ḥayyim of Fustat. The validation of the deed was written by Elḥanan b. Shemaria, who must have come from Fustat to Tyre. Apparently it is proof of normal connections between Tyre and Egypt. See also **42**, a leaf from the notebook of the court of the yeshiva in the days of Josiah Gaon, from August 1023, from which it emerges that business is being conducted as usual, as it contains (on p. b) a list of various commercial deals and a record of a settlement between a man and his wife. On the earthquake see: Ibn al-Jawzī, *Muntaẓam*, VII, 283, who has there the date in full; Ibn al-Athīr, *Kāmil*, IX, 295; Dhahabī, *ʿIbar*, III, 96; Yāfiʿī, III, 20; Ibn Kathīr, *Bidāya*, XII, 5; Ibn Taghrī Bardī, IV, 241; ʿUlaymī, 269; the letter from Solomon b. Judah: **54**, lines 28–30.

[39] Musabbiḥī, 3.

made immense profits from their visits. Naturally they visited Jerusalem (*ziyāra*), and were very favourably impressed by the Fatimid regime.[40] The situation became very tense in September of that year, however, for according to al-Musabbiḥī, al-Hassān the Jarrāḥid raided Ramla. Solomon ha-Kohen Gaon b. Joseph writes in a letter that the Bedouin overran Ramla during the two months of Rabīʿ I and Rabīʿ II, that is from the middle of May until mid-July. At approximately the same time (the news reached Egypt on 4 Rabīʿ II AH 415, 15 June AD 1024) ʿAbdallah b. Idrīs al-Jaʿfarī, and one of the Banū Jarrāḥ, with their men, attacked Eilat. ʿAbdallah b. Idrīs' ambition was to become governor of Wādī'l-Qurā, the region between Palestine and the Ḥijāz, and he demanded of al-Ḥassān b. al-Mufarrij that the latter lay his claims before the caliph. Al-Ḥassān refused. Then ʿAbdallah b. Idrīs poured out his rage on Eilat, indulging in extensive pillaging, extorting 3000 dinars and a great deal of agricultural produce from the city's inhabitants, and taking captive the women and children. A special force was then organised in Egypt under the command of ʿAlī b. Najā and sent out against him. Each of the fighters received five dinars, and the 60 mounted troops of the force received ten dinars and two horses each. On 8 Rabīʿ II, 19 June 1024, ʿAbdallah b. Idrīs overran al-ʿArīsh and plundered considerable property, before setting the city on fire.[41]

[584] The governor of Palestine at that time was the Turk Abū Manṣūr Anūshtakīn b. ʿAbdallah al-Dizbirī. He was the central figure in the events of the next five years in Palestine. According to the sources, he was the most outstanding of the Fatimid governors: courageous and politically astute, a man of integrity and charming manners, with a sense of justice towards his subordinates and his subjects. He was greatly respected and appreciated by the population, they say, mainly because of his devotion to the task of restraining the Bedouin's belligerence. In the course of his career, he earned a number of honourable titles: *al-amīr al-muẓaffar* ('the commander wreathed in victory'); *amīr al-juyūsh* ('commander of the hosts'); *ʿuddat al-imām* ('the treasure of the imām', that is, the caliph); *sayf al-khilāfa* ('sword of the caliphate'); *ʿaḍud al-dawla* ('the support of the realm'); *musṭafā al-mulk* ('the realm's choice'). During his lifetime, al-Dizbirī passed through the usual stages which all Turks of his kind used to pass, from the time he was first taken captive and sold as a slave until he reached the service of al-Ḥākim in AH 403, that is AD 1012/3. In 1016, he

[40] *Ibid.*, 22f; Bianquis, *JESHO*, 23(1980), 78f, mentions the matter of the caravan of Khurāsān in his article dealing with the drought in Egypt at the time and is surprised that in the information on the convoy, there is no mention of the drought; but the convoy did not pass through Egypt at all.

[41] Musabbiḥī, 34ff; Solomon Gaon's letter: **50**, line 28.

arrived in Palestine for the first time with the Fatimid army, and afterwards went to Damascus and Egypt and back on a number of occasions, until he was appointed governor of Baʿlabakk, an office in which he excelled. He was afterwards appointed governor of Caesarea, and there too he excelled, and praise was forthcoming from all sides. At the beginning of the year AH 414, that is in AD 1023, he was made governor of jund Filasṭīn; but in AH 417, AD 1026, he was arrested because of certain accusations made against him, while he was staying in Ascalon. Preserved in the Franciscan monastery in Jerusalem, there should be a bill of protection signed by al-Muẓaffar (none other than al-Dizbirī), dating from 1023, stating that it is forbidden to harm the Franciscan monks.[42]

[585] In August 1024, after restoring order in Ramla, al-Dizbirī sent an army to Bet Guvrin, the estate of Ḥassān b. Jarrāḥ, in order to take over Ḥassān's property. Ḥassān killed al-Dizbirī's messengers and the latter responded by imprisoning al-Ḥassān's closest retainers, Abū'l-Fūl and al-Ḥasan b. Surūr, as well as al-Ḥassān's scribe. Afterwards he sent them enchained to the fortress in Jaffa, and from there to Ascalon. Musabbiḥī apparently repeats the same story in a slightly different version, when he tells of the seizure of two tax officials sent by al-Dizbirī to collect the taxes in the region allotted (*iqṭāʿ*) to al-Ḥassān. Al-Ḥassān had them killed. During the weeks that followed, the rebellion spread like wildfire. Al-Dizbirī attacked al-Ḥassān while he was ill and stationed in the neighbourhood of Nābulus. When he recovered, al-Ḥassān gathered together a force of some 3,000 cavalry, forced al-Dizbirī to retreat to Ramla and pursued him further. Ramla was put under siege and a battle lasting three days was fought at its gates. At the same time, Tiberias was being held by al-Ḥassān and he decimated the population mercilessly, sacking the town, while its governor, Majd al-Dawla Fitāḥ, fled to Acre. At that point, an internal family strife sprung up among the Jarrāḥids, for Thābit, al-Ḥassān's brother, went over to al-Dizbirī's camp. Al-Ḥassān responded by sending out a cavalry unit, which overran and pillaged Thābit's estate. During that month, collaboration between the three federations of tribes became closer: the Banū Ṭayy' under Ḥassān b. al-Jarrāḥ, the Banū Kalb

[42] See especially Ibn al-Qalānisī, 71–74; see on the bill of protection: Boré, *Question des lieux saints*, 5; Berlière, *Revue bénédictine*, 5(1888), 505, sees here a positive attitude to the Latins and concludes from this that it is during this period that the Amalfians built the church of St Mary the Latin, a subject that shall be discussed in the chapter on the Christians. (The people of the Franciscan monastery in Jerusalem – the Monastery of the Saviour – refused to cooperate with me in locating this document.) During his stay in Damascus, al-Dizbirī became friendly with the great poet, Abū'l-ʿAlā' al-Maʿarrī, and it is known that the latter wrote a book called *Sharaf al-sayf* ('The greatness of the sword'), dedicated to al-Dizbirī, who showed much interest in his poetry and displayed generosity towards him; see Yāqūt, *Udabā'*, III, 157; see the biography of al-Dizbirī and all his names and by-names in al-Ṭabbākh, I, 330; cf. the article on him: Wiet, *MUSJ*, 46:385, 1970; he mentions among

under Ṣamṣām al-Dawla Sinān b. ʿUlayyān ibn al-Bannā', and the Banū ʿUqayl under the leadership of Ṣāliḥ b. Mirdās. In addition, Thābit betrayed al-Dizbirī and returned to his family's camp. Al-Dizbirī's requests for help from Egypt were of no avail, as was his request that he be sent 1,000 mounted troops and the same number of infantry. Although al-Ẓāhir ordered the recruitment of men for this purpose, only a few volunteered and no one arrived at al-Dizbirī's side. Finally, he was forced to abandon Ramla, escaping from the town at night with ten Turks and eventually reaching Caesarea. The Arabs then killed many of Ramla's inhabitants, sacked much property and maltreated the women. It was said that al-Ḥassān removed from Ramla 400 heavy loads of property, clothing and jewellery, and all sorts of goods and fabrics, and caused considerable damage and destruction to the markets, until people were practically treading in soap and oil. At the same time, he carried on a propaganda campaign within the Egyptian army, claiming that he was not fighting the caliph but merely al-Dizbirī. He even displayed a faked letter from the caliph, granting him recognition and cancelling al-Dizbirī's appointment. Afterwards, he attacked Ascalon and forced the inhabitants to hand over his two men who were imprisoned there, Abū'l-Fūl and Ḥasan b. Surūr, by threatening that if they were not released he would attack and destroy the city. This was followed by a second pillaging of Ramla by the Arabs, when women and children were taken captive as well. Al-Ḥassān imposed a fine of 40,000 dinars on the Fatimid governor of the city, Naḥrīr al-Waḥīdī, and then appointed his own governor in his place, Naṣr Allah b. Nizāl. On the governor of Jerusalem, Mubārak al-Dawla Fatḥ, he placed a fine of 30,000 dinars and also took all the money and property that al-Dizbirī had accumulated there.[43]

[586] We learn also of an attack of 500 mounted troops on al-ʿArīsh and their advance in the direction of al-Faramā, whose inhabitants fled to Fustat, in Dhū'l Qaʿda AH 415, January AD 1025. Al-Ḥassān charged against al-Faramā at the head of 1,000 horsemen. At the same time, the sides conducted negotiations that had begun in Shaʿbān AH 415, November AD 1024. Al-Ḥassān demanded that the caliph hand over Jerusalem and Nābulus, and also send him ceremonial attire and turbans of fine linen (*shūsh*). He sent him the apparel he requested and promised him Nābulus, but not Jerusalem. Three of al-Ḥassān's brothers who were staying in

others the *dīwān* (collection of poetry) of Ibn Ḥayyūs (ed. Khalīl Mardam, Damascus 1951), which includes a large number of eulogies dedicated to al-Dizbirī.

[43] Musabbiḥī, 47–51, 57f, 98; according to his description, in addition to what one finds in the Geniza letters, one gets the impression that there were two attacks on Ramla, or perhaps three; but perhaps the same event is being referred to; in Musabbiḥī, there are two descriptions of the attack on al-ʿArīsh as well, and it seems that this is the same information recorded twice, which reached Egypt at different times; see further: Maqrīzī, *Khiṭaṭ*, I,

Egypt (evidently for the purpose of negotiating) also received ceremonial robes and other honours from the caliph. In November 1024 al-Ḥassān sent a letter to the caliph declaring his allegiance and informing him that he considered himself responsible for the affairs of jund Filasṭīn, that he would collect the *kharāj* there, which he would use to maintain his soldiers, who would suffice for security purposes; and that there would be no need to send an additional force or a governor from Egypt. Similar conditions were demanded with regard to the positions of Sinān in Damascus and Ṣāliḥ b. Mirdās in Aleppo. From Egypt, the messenger was sent back to al-Ḥassān with no response; in other words, his actions were viewed as a rebellion. On 25 Ramaḍān AH 415, or 26 November AD 1024, the title *amīr al-umarā'* (commander of commanders) was added to al-Dizbirī's titles of honour. In view of the gravity of the situation, al-Ḥassān's two brothers took flight, taking with them all their precious belongings. The third brother, who was ill, remained in Egypt.[44]

[587] From this point onwards, al-Ḥassān also tried to arouse the tribes living in Egypt to rebel, and with this in mind he approached the Banū Qurra, a large tribe living in the Alexandria area (the Buḥayra). The messenger bearing his letter from Ramla was caught by the Fatimids. Al-Ḥassān also had connections to the Byzantine emperor and the Christians in Jerusalem and it was not by accident that one of his demands had been to be given Jerusalem. He also had covert relations with Muḥassin b. Badūs, al-Ẓāhir's keeper of the treasury. Finally, a letter from Muḥassin to al-Ḥassān was intercepted, in which he urged him to go to war, in the knowledge that if he should overpower the Fatimid army, there would be no longer any force in Egypt that could stand in his way. In his letter Muḥassin also requested that in the future, he should be contacted only through monks, because they were the only ones to be relied on. Muḥassin was executed on Sha'bān AH 415, 24 October AD 1024, and it was then discovered that he was actually a Christian, for he was not circumcised.[45]

[588] While the Fatimids continued to maintain control over the ports, the Bedouin controlled the roads. In the early winter of 1025, the Bedouin

326f; II, 160f; *idem, Itti'āẓ*, II, 151–157; Ibn al-Dawādārī, 319f; Becker, *Beiträge*, 44f; Ibn al-'Adīm, *Zubda*, I, 223; Yaḥyā ibn Sa'īd (Cheikho), 244.

44 Musabbiḥī, 82f; the news about al-'Arīsh arrived in Egypt by sea. The negotiations: *ibid.*, 58, 63–66.

45 The connections with the emperor: Musabbiḥī, 49. The affair of Muḥassin b. Badūs: *ibid.*, 59f; Musabbiḥī adds there that some say that it was libel. The matter of the Banū Qurra: *ibid.*, 68. Muḥassin b. Badūs was appointed on the 6th of Rabī I AH 415 (the 18th of May AD 1024) supervisor of income (*zimām*) in Syria and Palestine. This appointment preceded slightly the outbreak of the rebellion of the Jarrāḥids and we may assume that there was a causal connection between these two facts. Musabbiḥī calls him *ṣāḥib bayt al-mal*, that is minister of the treasury (Musabbiḥī, 31f); and see this same information in Maqrīzī, *Itti'āẓ*, II, 141.

were found to have absconded with ten loads of apples from Mount Lebanon, and intended for the caliph. During that same winter of 1024/5, severe starvation was prevalent throughout Egypt because of the low level of the Nile, and in Damascus, a terrible plague caused the death of thousands of inhabitants. Towards the end of 1024, Ṣāliḥ b. Mirdās, the ʻUqaylid ally of the Jarrāḥids, launched an attack on Aleppo, then ruled by Murtaḍā al-Dawla Manṣūr b. Lu'lu', the Fatimid loyalist mentioned earlier. The city fell to Ṣāliḥ b. Mirdās on 13 Dhū'l-Qaʻda AH 415 (16 January AD 1025), although Fatimid soldiers continued to hold the fortress of Aleppo until 10 Muḥarram AH 416, 13 March AD 1025.

The great battle between al-Dizbirī and al-Ḥassān took place this time in November 1024, near the citadel of Ascalon. In al-Dizbirī's army there were 5000 men, and they suffered immensely from the drought in Egypt. According to al-Musabbiḥī, it was decided to allot individual portions of bread to each one. Little is said about the results of the battle but it seems that it was not favourable to the Fatimids. On 21 Dhū'l-Qaʻda AH 415 (24 January AH 1025), the Egyptian pilgrims to Mecca had to return home because they could not pass through Eilat because of tribal attacks. Apparently al-Dizbirī's campaign started shortly afterwards, in February 1025. His men promised they would not take spoils in the Bedouin camps before the Bedouin were finished off. At first, they attacked al-Ḥassān's camp near 'the city of Filasṭīn', undoubtedly meaning Ramla. Alongside al-Dizbirī were also the governors of Jerusalem and Tiberias: Fatḥ – who is Mubārak al-Dawla, and Majd al-Dawla Fitāḥ b. Būye al-Kitāmī. In that camp, thirty Bedouin commanders were killed, as well as all their officials and treasurers, who were in charge of collecting taxes; some also say that thousands of people were slaughtered and the Bedouin women were taken captive. Few managed to escape. Al-Dizbirī wrote to the caliph asking for reinforcements of 1,000 horsemen, and informed him that he had already taken jund Filasṭīn and that during the holiday, he had prayed in Ramla (he is undoubtedly speaking of 10 Dhū'l-Ḥijja AH 415, that is 14 February AD 1025). Nevertheless it seems that there was yet another counter-attack by al-Ḥassān's forces, evidently at the end of February, when al-Ḥassān again seized Ramla while al-Dizbirī withdrew to Ascalon; and it was apparently only in the spring of 1025 that al-Dizbirī succeeded in ridding the south of Palestine of al-Ḥassān's units. According to Maqrīzī, al-Ḥassān then fled to the Byzantines.[46]

[46] See on this drought: Bianquis, *JESHO*, 23(1980), 70f; see on the events: Musabbiḥī, 68, 83f, 89; Yaḥyā ibn Saʻīd (Cheikho), 244–247; Ibn Khallikān, II, 487f (according to him the conquest of Aleppo took place on 13 Dhū'l-Ḥijja 417, 4 February 1027, and this is incorrect). Ibn Taghrī Bardī, IV, 248, 252. Ṣāliḥ also seized Ba'labakk then, see: Sobernheim, *Centenario Michele Amari*, 155; Wiet, *L'Egypte arabe*, 216f; the pursuit of scribes and treasurers is also perhaps reflected in **76**, Solomon b. Judah's letter. The scribe

[589] The position of the Jews of Palestine during this period is obvious from the Geniza documents. (The documents become more frequent at this time, when the synagogue of the 'Palestinians' in Fustat was being rebuilt following its destruction in al-Ḥākim's day, and the receptacle for its Geniza was built there.) The Jews unhesitatingly supported the Fatimids and expected them to restore order in Palestine and to maintain the security of the localities and roads. A letter from Fustat written by the local ḥāvēr, Ephraim b. Shemaria, contains blessings for the caliph's army and wishes for its victory. Owing to the Tustari brothers, who had during this time earned a respected position within the Fatimids' court, the Jewish communities of Palestine had an avenue through which they could exert influence in Egypt. A letter from Ascalon evidently written in 1025 to the two communities in Fustat (the Jerusalemite and the Babylonian), speaks warmly of the governor of Ascalon (which was a Fatimid base during the events), Abū Ḥarī', who had stood by the Jews of the town and did not abuse them in hard times. Solomon ha-Kohen Gaon b. Joseph, who was Gaon in 1025, mentions in his letter (most of which was written by the scribe of the yeshiva) that the community in Ramla had assembled and blessed 'our Master the King, may he live forever . . . and also his deputy (the wazīr) with his large company, whose ways were improved', and they prayed that 'the armies of our Master the King be victorious and nations should bow before him', etc. In another of the Gaon's letters, this one to Yefet b. Tobiah al-Nīlī (the indigo merchant) in Fustat, we read words of blessing and praise for Caliph al-Ẓāhir, 'the king, son of kings', and he also praises 'his dearly beloved forefathers at rest' who 'bestowed favours upon us'. Further on, he asks the people of Fustat to obtain a *nishtewān* from the caliph (that is, a *sijill*), undoubtedly an official letter of appointment, since he had just become the Gaon, after the death of his predecessor, Josiah b. Aaron; similar to the letter of appointment issued to the geonim of Palestine by 'his three forefathers . . . whose *nishtewān*s we keep: the *nishtewān* of his father's grandfather, and of his own grandfather, and the *nishtewān* of his father, which should now be completed by his own *nishtewān*', meaning, naturally, al-Ẓāhir and his predecessors – al-Mu'izz, al-'Azīz, and al-Ḥākim.

The letters of the Gaon Solomon ha-Kohen also contain details of the horrors endured by the Jews of Jerusalem. He is particularly bitter about the *'onāshīm* ('punishments'), the special taxes imposed on the Jews. On Jerusalem, a special tax of 15,000 dinars was levied, and a special additional payment of 6,000 dinars on the Jews apart from that, to be paid equally by the Rabbanites and the Karaites. The Rabbanites collected

Mevorakh received a *diyōqnē*, he writes, but the scribes hide because of the military, that is, the Fatimid army. The flight of al-Ḥassān: Maqrīzī, *Itti'āẓ*, II, 180.

2,500 dinars and were left penniless, for they had to mortgage their property in order to acquire the money. Many were tortured in order to make them pay and there were also denunciations. Both the Rabbanites and the Karaites ('the inhabitants of the *Ṣela'*') were forced to borrow money they did not have from rich Muslims. In Ramla most of the inhabitants had died and the income from the shops dedicated as foundations for Jerusalem which had formerly been the source for the payment of the taxes in Jerusalem, was no longer forthcoming. There was general indigence and luxuries were no longer purchased. These letters in particular contain descriptions of the atrocities and the cruel mistreatment of the Jews of Ramla during the Arab domination of the city. Despite the fact that at first glance, the inclination is to ascribe the imposition of the high taxes on the Jews of Jerusalem to the Jarrāḥids, it appears after further examination that it is the representative of the Fatimid regime who is being referred to. This was the governor of Jerusalem, Mubārak al-Dawla Fatḥ, who collected the 30,000 dinars from the population, which the Bedouin afterwards confiscated. Al-Dizbirī also extracted considerable sums of money.[47]

[590] Correspondence of the succeeding Gaon, Solomon b. Judah, continues to speak about those events and the circumstances that prevailed in their wake. In a letter written when Solomon ha-Kohen was still alive, and Solomon b. Judah himself was head of the yeshiva court, he notes that many Jerusalem Jews died 'in what happened in the city'. (Mann read: *dever*, instead of *dāvār* [thing, event], and understood that it was a plague.) He speaks at length about the debts weighing on the Jews of Jerusalem after they were obliged to borrow money at high rates of interest from rich Muslims. Some of them who signed promissory notes have, he writes, been taken to jail. In a letter to his son Abraham, who was then in Egypt, he mentions that the situation is 'unbearable because of the poverty and distress'; the winter was particularly hard, he has spent all his money and also sold some of his household goods, most of the fields are lying fallow, and the remnants of the community in Ramla are miserably poor. He urges the leaders of the community in Fustat, especially, to use their influence with the Tustaris for those who are imprisoned because of their debts. 'The representative of the mighty elder Abū Naṣr' passed on their letters from prison, referring to one of the agents of Ḥesed b. Sahl al-Tustarī. More than 900 dinars are still needed, and only the Tustaris are

[47] Ephraim b. Shemaria's letter: **323**. Ascalon: **314**, which is not a Karaite letter, as Mann assumed in *Jews*, I, 169. Solomon ha-Kohen's letters: **47**, **49**, **50**, **51**; Frenkel, *Cathedra*, 11 (1778/9), 108, interpreted what is said about the income from the shops in Ramla incorrectly; they were not intended to pay the taxes in Ramla, as he says, but to pay the taxes of the Jews of Jerusalem. Another letter of Solomon Gaon, **52**, contains clear hints, in the elegant phrasing at the beginning, of the distress and poverty prevailing in Jerusalem.

capable of recruiting such a large sum. The Karaites still owe 800 dinars, despite the large amounts that reach them from Fustat; 'when this year arrived, I had to sell everything that remained in the house . . . and would not have thought that the year will pass and we are still alive'. It is possible that sometime during the battles, Solomon b. Judah and his family moved to Aleppo, because in one of the letters he mentions that his son Abraham is staying in Aleppo for a long time, after having gone to the city to fetch some objects he had left there. In some letters, he also mentions the marked decrease in the number of pilgrims because of 'the conflict of the armies and the blockage of the roads'. He talks of the terrible starvation, for 'there is nothing in the whole land of the Philistines' (i.e. jund Filasṭīn). He also speaks of the Muslims' troubles: the Fatimids undoubtedly castigated the rebel Bedouin and those who collaborated with them, especially in collecting the taxes, as we have seen. And here we learn from one of the letters of Solomon b. Judah that the family of one of the people being pursued, Qayn b. 'Abd al-Qādir, have appealed to Solomon b. Judah for urgent help. Solomon b. Judah responds with a letter to the Jewish physician in Ramla who has much influence there, Abraham ha-Kohen b. Isaac b. Furāt, that he should intervene on his behalf with the '*peḥā* (Biblical: governor) whose name is Abū'l-Futūḥ, ruler of the place'. The reference is almost certainly to the govenor of Jerusalem, Mubārak al-Dawla Fatḥ, who intends to punish Qayn for his 'earlier deeds', undoubtedly the aforementioned collaboration with the Bedouin, but he should be pardoned, argues Solomon b. Judah, because 'he has already repented'. Abraham is asked to act on this matter, because of their friendship ('my position with you') and the friendship between Solomon b. Judah and the 'elder', evidently Ḥesed b. Sahl al-Tustarī. Later, the period of the Bedouin uprising would be referred to as 'the days of the son of the wound' (*ḥabūrā*), that is, 'of Ibn Jarrāḥ' (from 'wound' or 'bruise' in Arabic: *jurḥ*).[48]

[591] We come across important information concerning the events

[48] 'What happened in the city', see: **57**, lines 6–7 (cf. Mann, *Jews*, I, 106); see further: **67**, lines 5–10; **75**, b, lines 13ff; it seems that he wrote there about a debt owed to an army commander ('the army', line 15); **78**, lines 5–6 ('the terrible, alarming, irksome rumours'); **80**, a, lines 18–22; b, lines 4ff (the matter of the prisoners); **81**, lines 26f (even the rich were in distress that year, let alone the poor); **83** b, lines 8f (mentioning the disaster that cut down his livelihood); **84**, a (the matter of the prisoners and the appeal to the Tustaris); **86**, a, lines 23–25 (Abraham in Aleppo); **88**, lines 10ff ('we, the people of the Holy City, the congregation that dwindled and bowed down, of which we remained but a few'; and further, the matter of the pilgrims); **89**, lines 6ff (complaints of the same kind: he mentions the starvation). The letter concerning Qayn b. 'Abd al-Qādir: **99**: a certain Murajjā, a good friend of the Gaon, intervenes on Qayn's behalf with Solomon b. Judah. He is possibly the father of Abū'l-Ma'ālī Musharraf b. Murajjā, author of the *faḍā'il*, who shall be mentioned below. **103**, line 12: speaking of someone who 'mortgaged his *ḥāṣēr*', that is, a compound, to pay a debt of (of 100 dinars?); evidently this also relates to the matter of the Jerusalemites' debt (or perhaps to **147**, see below in this note); **107**, a, lines 20–21: mentions the

mentioned in the letters of Zadok ha-Levi b. Levi, who was head of the court of the Palestinian yeshiva at that time. In a letter from Ramla, he mentions those who were murdered as martyrs, when 'the blacks arrived', evidently meaning the Sudanese battalions of the Fatimid army. He explains to Ephraim that he was forced to move from Jerusalem to Ramla because of the 'burden of taxes' (using the term *neshē*); the extent of the *middā* (Biblical: tax, meaning the *jizya*, the poll-tax) and the violence of the *daftars* (the tax account-books). He further asks the Tustari brothers and David ha-Levi b. Isaac, notables of Fustat, to intervene with the rulers, for the harassment of Jews still continues in Ramla and they are assaulted 'whenever they go to the market-place to look for a livelihood'; they are evicted from their houses (evidently to house the military) and their appeals to 'the officer who is prince of the armies' (al-Dizbirī?) are made in vain. In a letter to Ephraim b. Shemaria he asks for help for the Baghdadi cantor Rawḥ ha-Kohen b. Pinḥas, a pilgrim to Jerusalem who, when he wanted to return to his own country, was taken captive by the Bedouin and robbed of all he possessed, but who luckily was left alive. The people of Palestine could not come to his aid because they had all become impoverished 'for in all of Palestine no community remained which could help except the people of Tyre'. And he calls the events 'a bad edict on the land of the Philistines' (that is, jund Filasṭīn). Apparently, one of the results of the uprising was that the Jews who lived in villages or small towns were forced to find refuge in the cities, as is evident from the version: 'from your brethren, the community of Gaza and those who fled to it' found in the signature of a letter from this community to the Fustat court. Similarly, in a letter from Tiberias, written by the leader of the community, Hillēl *ḥe-ḥāvēr* b. Yeshū'ā *ha-ḥazān*, evidently to Sahlān b. Abraham in Fustat, reference is made to 'the disruption of the roads and the change of rulers'. The events led to the destruction 'of the place'

grave events in Ramla; there in lines 12–15 he speaks of changes in the laws of deposits in Ramla, and of the 'quarrel' which occurred there, and it seems that here, too, he is speaking of the extraction of money; **110**, lines 9–11: he mentions their misadventures and confirms the receipt of a donation of ten dinars, intended to be used towards the sum needed to ransom the people imprisoned because of debt (*ibid.*, lines 14ff). 'Days of the son of the wound': **147**, b, line 4; then Solomon b. Judah's son-in-law, Manasseh ha-Kohen b. Abraham, was 'caught', that is, he was jailed because he could not pay the sum imposed on him, and see there in the continuation; cf. also Gil, *ha-Tustarīm*, 50ff. Abraham b. Solomon Gaon b. Judah was visiting Egypt during this period, as appears from the letters reviewed above, in order to get urgent financial aid and deal with the matter of the prisoners. In TS 24.29, a letter of Joseph ha-Kohen, the judge of Alexandria, on behalf of 'the two congregations of Nō' Ammōn', to Ephraim b. Shemaria in Fustat, the writer explains why they could not obtain the money to ransom the prisoners: 'the community was busy with the needs of his honour, the great and holy Lord and Master Abraham *he-ḥāvēr*, son of our Lord the Gaon'.

(house?) of the lepers of Tiberias, and when 'the armies over them decreased', they sent out envoys to recruit help.[49]

[592] In the campaign early in the year 1025, the tribes in Palestine suffered an overwhelming defeat and the Fatimid army returned to govern there. However, it seems that despite the confrontation, links were again renewed between the Bedouin and the Fatimid rulers. As we have already seen, al-Dizbirī fell out of favour due to the Jarrāḥids' accusations against him, and he was imprisoned and brought to Egypt in 1026. The tribes of the north still posed a threat to the Fatimid regime, however, in the person of Ṣāliḥ b. Mirdās and the 'Uqaylids who ruled in Aleppo, and the Banū Kalb, under the leadership of Sinān b. 'Ulayyān, who threatened Damascus. This last concern, however, ceased to exist with the death of Sinān in Jumādā II AH 419 (July AD 1028). The Fatimids' situation was then greatly improved by the new truce agreement reached with the Byzantines in 1027. Immediately afterwards, Sinān's heir and nephew, Rāfi' b. Abī'l-Layl b. 'Ulayyān, appealed to al-Ẓāhir and asked him to confirm his status and promise him control of the areas which his uncle had ruled, that is, those areas in which he had collected the taxes (*iqṭā'āt*). The Fatimid wazīr al-Jarjarā'ī then decided to send a large army to Palestine and Syria and could not find a better man to stand at its head than al-Dizbirī. The army started out towards the end of AH 419, that is AD 1028. According to Ibn al-Qalānisī, it reached Ramla 'in 'īd al-naḥr', that is 10 Dhū'l-Ḥijja, or 20 December. Other sources give the year of the expedition as AH 420, but this is impossible, as is proven by the date of the battle of Uqḥuwāna, which I will discuss shortly. A new alliance now arose between the Fatimids and the Banū Kalb (of 'southern' descent), and with their combined forces they launched out against the Banū 'Uqayl (or the Banū Kilāb) and the Jarrāḥids (the Banū Ṭayy'). The sources say the battle took place on the banks of the River Jordan, not far from Tiberias, at a place called Uqḥuwāna, on 24 Rabī' II AH 420 (12 May AD 1029). There the war was waged against Ṣāliḥ b. Mirdās, but the Jarrāḥids did not participate, for they had suffered a decisive defeat at the beginning of 1025 and they no longer carried any military weight. Ṣāliḥ was killed on the battlefield from the thrust of a spear; this was also the fate of his young son. The leader of the Banū Kalb, Rāfi' b. Abī'l-Layl, identified the bodies of Ṣāliḥ and his son, who were his allies, cut off their heads, and sent them to

[49] Zadok ha-Levi b. Levi's letters: **210**, lines 10–15, 40–43; margin, lines 19 ff; **212**, a, lines 26ff and margin. Frenkel, *Cathedra*, 11(1978/9), 108, in mentioning this letter, defines the writer as 'a student at the Jerusalem yeshiva' as if he were speaking of some school; but he was head of the yeshiva court. See the discussion on the name *Rwḥ*: Poznanski, *REJ*, 67(1914), 289, who believes that it may be *Rywḥ*, which he found in a document from the year 1740; but it seems that it is the Arabic name Rawḥ; although in **407** Joseph ha-Kohen b. Solomon Gaon wrote: *Rywḥ* (Nethanel b. *Rywḥ*), see line 8 (cancelled afterwards but

al-Dizbirī. This gave the latter an opportunity to chastise the Banū Ṭayy' as well as the Jarrāḥids. They fled to Ḥijāz (and with them, al-Ḥassān, who had in the meantime returned from Byzantine territory). The Fatimid army pursued them at close range and killed many of them. In the north, the Banū 'Uqayl retreated from Sidon, from Ba'labakk, Ḥimṣ and other Syrian towns which they had held, while Ṣāliḥ's son, Abū Kāmil Naṣr, who is Shibl al-Dawla, took over Aleppo and continued to rule there.[50]

[593] Al-Dizbirī now ruled in Palestine again and we find him involved in Jewish affairs there. Nāṣir Khusraw, who visited the country some twenty years later, immortalised in his book an inscription he found on the eastern side of the Dome of the Rock, which states that a certain building was built on the orders of al-Dizbirī. In the Cave of the Machpelah, this Persian traveller found a prayer mat which the *amīr al-juyūsh*, again al-Dizbirī, bought in Fustat for thirty Maghribi dinars, and donated to the holy place.[51]

Forty years of Fatimid rule

[594] The Fatimid rulers and their representatives in Palestine were now free to devote themselves to reconstruction. The year 1030 was the first year of peace in the country. As is apparent from the aforementioned inscription, al-Dizbirī initiated works of restoration and renovation. We know of work that was done on the Temple Mount. An inscription in the Dome of the Rock is evidence that the renovation of the building, done on al-Ẓāhir's orders, was finished in the year AH 423, that is AD 1032. Al-Ẓāhir had also shown marked interest in the buildings on the Temple

not because of the orthography). In other places it is written: Nethanel b. *Rwḥ*, see the Hebrew Index. The letter of the Gazans: **219**, line 54. Tiberias: **254**, lines 14–16.

50 See Yaḥyā ibn Sa'īd (Cheikho), 253; Ibn al-Qalānisī, 72ff (see the passages from al-Dhahabī and Hilāl al-Ṣābī the editor quotes there, 73f, in the notes); Ibn al-Dawādārī, 324; Ibn al-'Adīm, *Zubda*, I, 231–234, 259, according to whom 'some say' that the death of Ṣāliḥ b. Mirdās (i.e. the battle of Uqḥuwāna) occurred in 8 Jumādā I, the 25th of May 1029; Ibn Ẓāfir, fol. 64a (printed: 63f); Ibn Taghrī Bardī, IV, 248–253; Ibn al-Athīr, *Kāmil*, IX, 231; Sibṭ ibn al-Jawzī (MS Munich), fol. 98a; Ibn Khallikān, II, 487f; Ibn Kathīr, *Bidāya*, XII, 27 (Ibn Khallikān and Ibn Kathīr say that the battle of Uqḥuwāna took place in AH 419, i.e. AD 1028, but there is no doubt that this is an error); Abū'l-Fidā', *Mukhtaṣar*, II, 141. On the truce with Byzantium, see Maqrīzī, *Khiṭaṭ*, II, 162; *idem, Itti'āẓ*, II, 176. See the article al-Djardjarā'ī (by D. Sourdel), in *EI*²; cf. Becker, *Beiträge*, 38f; Wiet, *MUSJ*, 46(1970), 391. Uqḥuwāna is still not identified (despite a number of attempts which are not convincing); according to a Karaite source, it was the name of the area south of the Sea of Galilee, see the commentary on the book of Gen. MS Firkovitch II, No. 4633, written in 1252.

51 The inscription on the Dome of the Rock: Nāṣir Khusraw (text) 32, (translation) 96; the title of al-Dizbirī there is *layth al-dawla* ('lion of the realm'); the by-name *ghwry* there is undoubtedly a distortion of *dizbirī*. The prayer mat: *ibid.* (text) 33; (translation), 100–101.

Mount some ten years earlier, before the great Bedouin uprising, when he had ordered the construction of a dome on a certain building; the work was executed under the *amīr Thiqat al-a'imma* ('the faithful of the imāms') Sadīd al-Dawla 'Alī b. Aḥmad. We find that in AH 425, that is AD 1034, a number of domes were built on the Temple Mount on al-Ẓāhir's orders. The southern wall was also repaired, as was one of the passages. It seems that this was done after the earthquake in 1033. One dome in particular was finally finished in Dhū'l-Qa'da AH 426 (6 October AD 1035). The wazīr Abū'l-Qāsim 'Alī b. Aḥmad, who is al-Jarjarā'ī, undertook to carry out the construction work. Another building, near al-Aqṣā, was built under the supervision of the Sharīf (that is, a man of the 'Alids) Abū'l-Qāsim (?) b. Abī'l-Ḥasan al-Ḥusaynī.

In Ramla, too, reconstruction was going on immediately after the defeat of the Bedouin. The city's wall was rebuilt. Shortly afterwards, in 1033, al-Ẓāhir gave his attention to Jerusalem's wall and ordered its reconstruction. According to Yaḥyā ibn Sa'īd, the representatives of the Fatimid caliph destroyed many churches in the Jerusalem area in order to use their stones for building the wall. He says that they considered the possibility of demolishing the Church of Zion and others for this purpose.

Evidently, during this entire period al-Dizbirī continued to be the man in charge of affairs in Palestine, until about 1042, when he quarrelled with the wazīr al-Jarjarā'ī. The wazīr ordered him to return to Egypt, but al-Dizbirī escaped to Aleppo, where he died and was buried some two years later. There may have been some connection between his downfall and the division in the Palestinian yeshiva (the affair of Nathan b. Abraham).

Characteristic of the relative political calm that prevailed during this period are the florid opening phrases and eloquent greetings of letters, such as those of Nathan ha-Kohen *he-ḥāvēr* b. Isaiah, writing from Tiberias in a letter of recommendation for the envoys of the lepers of Tiberias, to 'Eli, *he-ḥāvēr ha-me'ullē* in Fustat, 'and know that we are dwelling in quietude and abide in peace . . . blessed be He who grants favours to the guilty'.[52]

[52] See Ibn al-Ṣayrafī, 77, and the editor's n. 1; *Répertoire chronologique*, VI, Nos. 2328, 2329, 2330 (pp. 175–178); VII, No. 2404 (p. 3), where one should probably read *mamarra*; see *ibid.* also 2409, 2410; the amīr *sadīd al-dawla thiqat al-a'imma* 'Alī b. Aḥmad is perhaps also none other than the wazīr al-Jarjarā'ī. In No. 2409 there is the title of the wazīr: *Ṣafī amīr al-mu'minīn wa-khāliṣathu* (something like 'the choicest of the caliph's choice'); see Ibn al-Ṣayrafī, 78; cf. Sharon, *IEJ*, 23(1973), 215; he notes that the wooden beams inserted into the dome during al-Ẓāhir's time still support it to this day, as they are part of the dome's internal framework. The wall: Yaḥyā ibn Sa'īd (Cheikho), 271; cf. Wiet, *L'Egypte arabe*, 223; al-Dizbirī: Sibṭ ibn al-Jawzī (MS Munich), 133b. Nathan ha-Kohen's letter: **263**, a, lines 8–9. Further evidence of normalisation which now began in Palestine is the renewal of minting coins with the inscription *bi-filasṭīn* – see: Lane Poole, *Catalogue*, IV, 30 (the

[595] On the other hand, this was a time of harsh natural disasters. At the beginning of this period a very severe earthquake struck Palestine. The earthquake is most faithfully described in a letter preserved in the Geniza; it is from a man of Ramla, Solomon b. Ṣemaḥ, apparently to Ephraim b. Shemaria in Fustat. We learn from the letter the exact date of the earthquake, which was Thursday, 19 Tevet AM 4794, that is, 5 December AD 1033, and there was another on the morrow, Friday 6 December. According to the letter, even 'fortified buildings' collapsed, meaning perhaps the buildings of the citadel. New buildings also crumbled and many people were lost under the debris. Luckily for the people of Ramla, the earthquake occurred 'before sundown', and therefore many were saved because they were away from their homes. For some days, people refrained from entering their houses out of fear, and even the governor of Ramla and his soldiers ('the king's men') set up tents for themselves. It seems that the earthquake was centred around the area of Ramla, but it was felt throughout the entire 'land of the Philistines', that is, in jund Filasṭīn, in the coastal towns from Gaza to Haifa (from 'the fenced cities to the country villages' [Biblical, 1 Sam., vi:18]'); in the Negev, in the mountains, in Jerusalem and its neighbourhood, in Shechem and Tiberias and their surroundings, in the mountains of the Galilee and in 'all the glorious land' (Biblical, Dan., xi:16, 41). One effect of the earthquake was the rising of water in the wells. Nāṣir Khusraw, who visited Ramla on the 1st of March 1047, some thirteen years after the earthquake, mentions that he found an inscription in the *jāmi'* there noting the earthquake which occurred on 15 Muḥarram AH 425, 10 December AD 1033. Naturally, the Geniza letter in which the earthquake is said to have occurred five days earlier, is more reliable. Nāṣir Khusraw also says that according to that inscription no one was injured in the quake, and there, too, the information seems to be unreliable. In 1038, the community of Ramla leased a ruin near the Jersualemites' synagogue, which may have been a building destroyed in the earthquake. Al-Ẓāhir's building enterprises in Jerusalem were, at least in part, works of restoration of buildings destroyed or damaged by the earthquake. Arab sources state that a third of the city of Ramla was destroyed, which confirms what was said in the Geniza letter, that the people refrained from entering their houses for several days and that many were buried under the ruins. The *jāmi'* was also damaged. A section of the wall of Jerusalem (or perhaps the wall of the Temple Mount: the source says *bayt al-maqdis*) also collapsed. The *miḥrāb da'ūd* and the mosque in Hebron (*masjid ibrāhīm*) were affected, the lighting (*mināra*) above the mosque in Ascalon collapsed, while in Gaza

year AH 423 is AD 1023). From AD 1044/5 (the year AH 436), we also find dinars minted in Tiberias, and from AD 1070/1 (AH 463) dinars minted in Acre (with an inscription of the Fatimid caliph, al-Mustanṣir; see Lane-Poole, *Catalogue*, IV, 35, 43).

too, the upper part of the *mināra* fell down. Half of the buildings in Shechem and Acre were destroyed.[53]

[596] This earthquake and its attendant horrors seem to be the climax of a period beset with afflictions and distress. In contrast to the comparatively tranquil state of security, an endless series of calamities befell the country, most of which stemmed from the scarcity prevalent in Egypt. This was the situation for some twenty years, in the fifties and sixties of the century, until the Turko-Saljūq conquest.

Echoes of this distress resounded in the letters of the people of Jerusalem. Abraham b. Solomon Gaon b. Judah, in the forties, complains of the scarcity of pilgrims. Joseph ha-Kohen b. Solomon Gaon, evidently writing in the autumn of 1053, describes the distress of the people of Jerusalem 'eaten by swallowers ... devoured by the insolent .. the poor, the destitute ... (the congregation) squeezed and mortgaged ...'. At the same time, they have to suffer 'the noise of the Edom masses' that is, the local Christians and the Christian pilgrims, and 'the five-fold mendacious voice, which never stops', that is, the Muslims and their prayers. The

[53] See **209** and the notes there; Mann, *Jews*, I, 156f, bases his discussion on a slightly erroneous reading, and therefore arrived at incorrect conclusions. Nāṣir Khusraw (text), 19; (translation), 64. The lease of the ruin in Ramla, see: **229**. See further: Ibn al-Athīr, *Kāmil*, IX, 438; Ibn al-Jawzī, *Muntaẓam*, VIII, 77; Ibn Kathīr, *Bidāya*, XII, 36; Sibṭ ibn al-Jawzī, *Mir'āh* (MS Munich), 105a; Maqrīzī, *Itti'āẓ*, II, 181 (destroyed: half of Ramla, Jericho, and most of Acre); Ibn Taghrī Bardī, IV, 279; 'Ulaymī, 269; the earthquake is also mentioned in Cedrenus (Bonn), II, 511. The matter of the reconstruction of the walls of Jerusalem in 1033 and the earthquake of that year, is discussed by Prawer in his paper on the topography of Jerusalem on the eve of the Crusaders' conquest; see *Crusade* (ed. Edbury), 2. He assumes that in the year 1033, the walls of Jerusalem began being built according to 'a new line of fortifications', and that new walls were built in Jerusalem as a result of the earthquake of 1033. In Yaḥyā ibn Sa'īd's account, he finds this is 'well attested'. He also finds proof there that the church on Mount Zion was left outside the walls, and also, according to him, that the Jews 'found themselves outside the city walls and moved to the north-eastern part of the city'. Let us see what is really written in Yaḥyā ibn Sa'īd (ed. Cheikho, p. 272):

Al-Ẓāhir began to build in this year [AH 424, which began on 7 December 1032, that is, coincided more or less with 1033] the wall of the noble city of Jerusalem, after having built the wall of Ramla. Therefore those in charge of building [the wall] destroyed many churches in the vicinity of the town and took their stones for the wall; and they also intended to destroy the church of Zion and other churches in order to take their stones for the wall; and a terrible earthquake occurred the likes of which had never been known, at the end of Thursday, 10 Ṣafar of the year 425 [the 4th of January AD 1034; the correct date, according to **209**: 5 December AD 1033, which was 10 Muḥarram AH 425]. The earthquake caused the collapse of half the buildings in Ramla, and some places in its walls, and an enormous number of its people died. The city of Jericho turned upside down with its people, as did Nābulus and nearby villages. Part of the chief mosque (*jāmi'*) of Jerusalem and monasteries and churches in the region collapsed; the buildings fell also in Acre and a number of people died there, and the water of the sea withdrew from its port for some time, but afterwards returned to its place.

Clearly the source does not say anything about a *new* line of walls in Jerusalem; it contains no 'reliable evidence' on the outlines of the wall; and there is no proof that the churches on Mount Zion remained outside the new line of the walls. On the absence of any evidence at all of a Jewish quarter in the north of the city in this period or of a transfer of the Jews of Jerusalem from the south of the city northward, see secs. 838–839.

Spaniard (al-Andalusī) Abraham b. Isaac, writing at that time from Jerusalem, depicts the hard times caused by the *aḥdāth*, the armed Muslim bands. Responding to a question from his partner as to whether it is worth settling in Jerusalem, he answers in the negative and explains to him the difficulties of earning a living: in Jerusalem 'cattle are not slaughtered, not on a week-day nor on the sabbath, fowl is not to be had, and it is cold in the city for a long period of time'. From time to time the conditions would improve, however, as Moses *he-ḥāvēr* b. Jacob writes from Jerusalem on 22 March AD 1053: 'The situation in Palestine has improved these days, for the roads are in a good state and prices have fallen'. Apparently two years later, the hard and continuous years of distress and scarcity were again felt in the land. According to Ibn Muyassar, in AH 447, that is AD 1055, there was 'severe drought and plague and many died in the land of Egypt'. A similar comment is made by Ibn Taghrī Bardī about the following year, 1056. He says that the plague spread all over the world, including al-Shām, and every day some 10,000 people died. Evidently the continuous drought in Egypt necessarily affected the economic situation in Palestine. In a letter from the yeshiva written by Elijah ha-Kohen b. Solomon Gaon, in the autumn of 1057, it says that few have remained in Jerusalem. Indeed, the drought and the plague continued to rage throughout that year, and starvation was felt also in Iraq – and in the following year as well, that is 1058. According to Ibn al-Athīr, 1,000 people were dying in *Miṣr* every day (he is certainly referring to Fustat). The hard time in Palestine and in all of Syria, especially Damascus, is also mentioned in a letter written by Mūsā b. Ya'qūb from Tyre on 14 January 1058. In one of his letters 'Eli ha-Kohen b. Ezekiel mentions the distressing rumours which are reaching Jerusalem about conditions in Iraq, evidently referring to the drought and the plague. In a letter written some six weeks later, he describes the severe conditions in Jerusalem, especially because the merchants no longer come there. The heavy tax imposed on the Rabbanites (150 dinars annually), he writes, weighs heavily on the poor of Jerusalem. The same 'Eli ha-Kohen b. Ezekiel also enquires about the state of the waters of the Nile and the prices in Egypt, and writes further that he sent a Jerusalem cheese, sewn into a little basket, with Marwān b. Suqayr, who is *en route* to Ṣaharajt and who promised to send it on to Fustat from there. This Jerusalem merchandise must certainly have been very precious in those days of starvation. Hunger in Jerusalem itself is also mentioned in a letter from Israel b. Sahlūn, written on 31 December 1061: a *qafīz* of flour sells for three dinars, or three and a half dinars for the added cost of sifting it. From a letter from a contemporary, Avon b. Ṣedaqa, some four years later (October 1065), it appears that Jerusalem was affected by floods due to heavy rains. It is quite likely that the hardship and distress of these years were the major factors contributing to predictions of the imminent end of the world in 1058 ('when 990 years from the destruction of Jerusalem are completed').[54]

[597] A significant political event took place between the years 1036–1038 (the dates in the sources are not unanimous), and this was the truce agreement with Byzantium. Chronologically speaking, the account of Yaḥyā ibn Sa'īd is the closest to the event. According to him, the agreement between al-Ẓāhir and the emperor Romanus was based on three conditions: the rebuilding of the Church of the Resurrection at the emperor's expense; the emperor would appoint a patriarch in Jerusalem; and the Christians would be permitted to rebuild all the churches destroyed during Fatimid rule. On his part, the emperor promised to release all the Muslim captives. In a special request, the emperor asked the caliph to permit Ḥassān b. al-Jarrāḥ to return to his former status (which is further proof of the latter's connections with the Christians and Byzantium), but this was refused. Whereas Yaḥyā ibn Sa'īd ascribes the agreement to the emperor Romanus III (Argyrus; he was killed on 15 April 1034 and he was succeeded by Michael IV, the Paphlagonian), and to the caliph Al-Ẓāhir (died June 1036), Ibn al-Athīr sets the date of the agreement in the time of al-Mustanṣir, in AH 429, which began on 14 October 1037. He mentions only two conditions: that 5,000 Muslim prisoners held by the Byzantines be released and that the Church of the Resurrection be rebuilt. The second condition, he confirms, was indeed carried out; the emperor sent builders for the rebuilding and spent enormous sums on it. Bar Hebraeus was sufficiently knowledgeable to know that the agreement was made be-

[54] Abraham, son of the Gaon: **141**, line 10. Joseph ha-Kohen: **411**, lines 7–19. Abraham b. Isaac: **504**, and especially lines 20ff. Moses b. Jacob: **459**, lines 19ff. Ibn Muyassar, 7; see there also p. 34, where he speaks of the continuous years of drought, AH 457–464 (AD 1065–1072) and compares them with the lean years of Joseph; scarcity also prevailed in al-Shām and the population decreased; in Egypt there was no one to work the land, because of the many armies and the cutting off of the roads and the sea-lanes; Ibn Taghrī Bardī, V, 59; it seems that the drought was caused by the low level of the Nile in 447 (beginning on the 2nd of April 1055); see *ibid.*, 60; see the table of measurements of the Nile according to Ibn Taghrī Bardī: Toussoun, *Mémoire*, 4(1922), 140; correction should be made in Hamdani, *Ankara Univ. Tarih . . . Dergisi*, 6 (1968), 23, who writes that the distress only started in 1057. Elijah ha-Kohen's letter: **420** b, lines 23ff. Ibn al-Athīr, *Kāmil*, IX, 631, 636; Mūsā b. Ya'qūb: **517**, a, lines 6–7; see further: Sibṭ ibn al-Jawzī, *Mir'ah* (BM Or 4619), 238a (the year 1056) and 248b (1062). 'Eli ha-Kohen b. Ezekiel: **440**, lines 24ff; **443**, a; see further on the starvation and plagues of these years: Ibn al-Qalānisī, 86, 97ff. (with horror stories of the starvation in Egypt, such as the eating of corpses, etc); Ibn al-Dawādārī, 369, 371 (every day, 10,000 people died, apart from the innumerable number of poor, who could not be counted, the price of wheat rose to ten dinars per *irdabb*); Suyūṭī, *Muḥāḍara*, II, 286ff (1056–1072); Maqrīzī, *Itti'āẓ*, II, 299f; the additional letter of 'Eli ha-Kohen: **452**, lines 8ff. Israel b. Sahlūn: **480**. Avon b. Ṣedaqa: **502**, margin; see also Ibn Khallikān, V, 230; cf. further: Majd, *Ẓuhūr*, 366. Account of the end of the world: Wertheimer, *Battē midrāshōt* (Jerusalem 1952/3), II, 499 ('the book of Zerubbabel'), cf. Steinschneider, *ZDMG*, 28 (1874), 630f.

tween al-Mustanṣir and the emperor Michael, but he erred as far as the date was concerned, which he states was the year AH 427 (AD 1035). He speaks of the freeing of 50,000 Christian captives held by the caliph, and he also mentions the rebuilding of the Church of the Resurrection, for which the emperor sent envoys from among the aristocracy to Jerusalem bearing huge sums of silver and gold. According to William of Tyre, the renewal of the church was only finished in 1048, that is, after twenty years. Cedrenus and Zonaras both state that the agreement was signed after the death of the Egyptian caliph (in their language: Amer, that is, *amīr*, the *amīr al-mu'minīn*) and that it was his widow and son who sent envoys to the emperor; according to them, the wife of the caliph (al-Ẓāhir) was a Christian.[55]

[598] The comparative calm in the arena of foreign affairs did not lessen the internal discord within the Fatimid regime, most seriously manifested in the antagonism between the various armies. During this period, the quarrel between the Turkish units and the black battalions intensified, developing into a long drawn-out war marked by considerable bloodshed. Al-Ẓāhir's widow, the mother of al-Mustanṣir, acted as the representative of the blacks and defended them, for she herself was formerly a black slave who had been sold by Abū Sa'd b. Sahl al-Tustarī to the caliph. It was mainly owing to her influence that the Tustaris earned their important role in the political life of Egypt, and it was said that Abū Sa'd Abraham was a *wāsiṭa*, a sort of appointee over the treasury on behalf of the caliph's mother, until he was killed on 25 October 1047. Ḥesed b. Sahl, his brother, whom we shall find very active in the affairs of Palestine and its yeshiva and the needs of its communities, acted as scribe to al-Dizbirī around 1040. He was also involved in political matters in Syria, and particularly Aleppo, which led to his assassination, evidently in the summer of 1049.

On 7 Muḥarram 442, 1 June 1050, a Palestinian was made wazīr of the Fatimid regime: he was the cadi Abū Muḥammad al-Ḥasan b. 'Alī b. 'Abd al-Raḥmān al-Yāzūrī. His father was a farmer in Yāzūr who went to live in Ramla when he became wealthy. The father became cadi in Ramla (according to another version, it was his eldest son, brother of al-Ḥasan, who became cadi) and al-Ḥasan inherited the post from him. While still in Ramla, al-Yāzūrī became involved in a quarrel with the *amīr* of Ramla, for al-Yāzūrī's wife wanted her son to marry the daughter of the *amīr*, who

[55] Yaḥyā ibn Sa'īd (Cheikho), 270f; Ibn al-Athīr, *Kāmil*, IX, 460; Bar Hebraeus (Bedjan), 219, (Budge), 196. William of Tyre, 19ff; Cedrenus (Bonn), II, 515; Zonaras, III, 590; cf. Dölger, *Regesten*, No. 843 (evidently he did not know the account of Yaḥyā ibn Sa'īd); Wiet, *L'Egypte arabe*, 223 (he, too, relies only on part of the sources and makes the assumption, which has no foundation, that the Byzantines then relinquished their rights to Aleppo).

was so angered by this that he ordered al-Yāzūrī to be arrested, causing the latter to flee to Egypt. According to an account preserved in Maqrīzī, al-Yāzūrī had close connections with the Tustari brothers and it seems that it was they who brought him to Egypt and promoted him until he became chief cadi and chief preacher to the Fatimids (*qāḍī'l-quḍāh* and *dā'ī'l-du'āh*). One can assume, although it is not stated anywhere, that among his early supporters there were people of the Jerusalem yeshiva who had strong links with the Tustaris (and perhaps also particularly the Karaites of Jerusalem, for the Tustaris were Karaites). This is apparent in al-Yāzūrī's involvement, some years later, in the election of Daniel b. Azariah as head of the Palestinian yeshiva. After some years had passed, however, al-Yāzūrī betrayed his benefactors the Tustaris, left the caliph's mother's faction which they headed, and befriended their enemy, the wazīr Ṣadaqa b. Yūsuf al-Fallāḥī, a Jewish convert to Islam, who had been the confidant and chief administrator of the Berber battalions (the Banū Kitāma) for many years. Although al-Yāzūrī had betrayed the Tustaris, Ḥesed al-Tustarī did not hate him. After the murder of Abraham b. Sahl al-Tustarī, when al-Fallāḥī had fallen out of favour, and when it was proposed that Abū Naṣr, who is Ḥesed al-Tustarī, be appointed wazīr, he pointed to al-Yāzūrī as the man worthy of the post and his suggestion was accepted. Al-Yāzūrī's right-hand-man in money matters was a Jew called Ibn al-'Uṣfūra, who was a faithful retainer of al-Mustanṣir's mother.

At long last, al-Yāzūrī was deposed, evidently because of his connections with Ṭughril Beg, the Saljūq ruler of Baghdad. Correspondence to the latter was seized in which he had expressed his readiness to obey his orders and informed him that in fact all of Egypt was prepared to accept his suzerainty. On the other hand, it was official Fatimid policy to support the brother and rival of Ṭughril Beg, Ibrahīm Yanāl, and through his intermediary, create an alliance with the Arab tribes which would endanger the Abbasid caliphate and finally bring about its end. For this purpose, a special envoy, the preacher (*dā'ī*) al-Mu'ayyad fī' l-Dīn al-Shīrāzī, was sent to conduct negotiations with Ibrahīm Yanāl, and also to convey large sums of money to him. The affair of the sharp quarrel with Ṭughril Beg also caused a disagreement between the Fatimid caliph and Byzantium, because Constantinople had permitted Ṭughril Beg's envoy to pray in the *jāmi'* there and to mention in his prayer the caliph of Baghdad, al-Qā'im. This occurred in AH 447 (AD 1055/6). Al-Mustanṣir's reaction was immediate. He ordered the confiscation of all the property of the Church of the Resurrection in Jerusalem. As to al-Yāzūrī's fate, he was eventually executed in Muḥarram AH 450 (March AD 1058). A short time afterwards, Caliph al-Mustanṣir realised the Fatimid dream. For quite a short time, during some nine months, the Fatimid *da'wa* was imposed in Baghdad, by order of the Turkish rebel who had seized power in Baghdad, al-Basāsīrī.[56]

[599] During this entire period, the Fatimids continued their military activities with the intention of establishing their rule in northern Syria and especially in Aleppo, which was being governed by Thimāl, one of the progeny of Ṣāliḥ b. Mirdās, the ʻUqaylid, with the support of the Byzantines. Palestine and Syria were ruled by Turkish governors and the population suffered from their arbitrariness and from the continuous attacks of the tribes. Typifying this situation is a Geniza letter which was almost certainly written in Damascus, although there is no indication as to where it was written. It mentions the overrunning of Damascus by the Bedouin, the immediate scheming by the Bedouin against the Jews, and the decision of the cadi, 'the nephew of Abū'l-Sayyār', to cut off the Jews' water supply, claiming they had no right to the city's water. The governor despatched by the Fatimids quickly controlled the city; he was a Turk by the name of Ḥaydara, with the title *dhukhayrat al-dawla* (little treasure of the realm). The Jews of the city asked for an order from Egypt, according to which they would be given back their rights to the city's water; they would be promised slaughtering rights in the market; and taxes would be collected from them only once a year, on Muḥarram. Indeed, they succeeded in obtaining a *nishtewān* accepting all three demands, and also letters of recommendation from *khaṭīr al-mulk* (the notable of the reign), who is known to us as the son of the wazīr the cadi al-Yāzūrī. However the condition laid down by Ḥaydara, the governor, to fulfil these claims was the payment of a bribe. The Jews of the city organised a collection and added money from their foundations ('from the poor and orphans and

56 See on the political activities of the Tustaris: Gil, *ha-Tustarīm*, 38ff. Ibn Muyassar, 12, 13f; Maqrīzī, *Ittiʻāẓ*, II, 195ff, 203, 246. On al-Yāzūrī see further: Ibn Ḥajar, *Rafʻ*, 190f; Ibn al-Ṣayrafī, 40–45; his titles according to Maqrīzī: *al-makīn ʻumdat amīr al-mu' minīn*, and also *nāṣir al-dīn* ('the all-powerful, the support of the commander of believers, saviour of the religion'). Ibn Ẓāfir (printed), 78f (MS: 73a-b); cf. Mājid, *Ẓuhūr*, 186 (who quotes from *rafʻ al-iṣr* of Ibn Ḥajar, MS Dār al-kutub, *Ta'rīkh*, 105, p. 85); al-Barghūtī, *Al-wazīr al-yāzūrī*, is a monograph on this personality, with no reference as to his sources; cf. also Lane-Poole, *History*, 142f; Hamdani, *Ankara Univ. Tarih ... Dergisi*, 6 (1968), 23; see Maqrīzī, *Ittiʻāẓ*, II, 141: the Jew Ṣadaqa b. Yūsuf al-Fallāḥī was appointed in charge of the affairs of the Kitāmīs in AH 415, that is 1024. Ibn ʻUṣfūra: Maqrīzī, *Ittiʻāẓ*, II, 245; he is evidently Judah ibn al-ʻUṣfūra whose death (in 1059) is mentioned in a letter of Solomon b. Moses al-Safāquṣī, **490**, b. line 10; in PER H 89, lines 1–2, edited by Goitein, *Sefunot*, 8(1963/4), 119f, Abū'l-Faraj Yeshūʻā b. Judah 'known as b. ʻUṣfūra' is mentioned, in Tishri 1449, which is September–October 1137, evidently the son of the aforementioned; his wife, Sitt al-Ahl b. Zadok b. Mevorakh, 'head of the communities', is also mentioned; and her mother's brother, Nathan ha-Kohen *he-ḥāvēr* of the Great Sanhedrin b. Solomon (judge in Cairo, who hailed from Bāniyās). The Fatimid *daʻwa* was introduced in Baghdad on the 22nd of Shawwāl AH 450, the 12th of December 1058, see: Ibn Muyassar, 10. The disagreement with the Byzantines and the matter of the Church of the Resurrection: Ibn Muyassar, 7; Maqrīzī, *Khiṭaṭ*, II, 127; cf. Lane-Poole, *History*, 143.

widows') to the sum they collected. Ḥaydara then opened up the water mains despite the objections of the city's venerable Muslims. He once again permitted the Jews to slaughter in the market and demanded a document from the cadi confirming this; however the cadi not only refused, but began to harass the Jews even further. The governor exploited this state of affairs and demanded an immediate payment of 250 dinars – and here the letter is cut off. This Ḥaydara is also known to us, he is Ḥaydara b. al-Ḥusayn b. Mufliḥ, known by his nickname Abū'l-Karam al-Mu'ayyad. He was appointed governor of Damascus in AH 440 (AD 1048/9), in place of Ṭāriq.[57]

[600] Shortly afterward, the threat posed by the Saljūq Turks and their associates, who had overtaken Baghdad in 1055, began to be felt. The tension that was built up in Palestine as a result can be seen in the episode of the lighting system of the Dome of the Rock. This lighting system was said to have collapsed in AH 452, that is AD 1060, with its 500 tapers, and everyone saw this as an evil omen. It is interesting that the governor of Jerusalem at the time was a Karaite Jew, Abū Sa'd Isaac b. Aaron b. 'Eli (Isḥaq b. Khalaf b. 'Allūn). He was called *al-kātib al-miṣrī* (the Egyptian secretary). 'Eli ha-Kohen b. Ezekiel notes in a letter from Jerusalem in about 1060, that 'the governor of Jerusalem is in trouble'. In another of his letters, in which he calls him b. 'Allūn, he mentions that the governor has already been dismissed from his post in Jerusalem and that he has been living in Ramla for a long time. In his stead there is a Christian, b.

57 Ibn Muyassar, 4; cf. Zakkār, *Aleppo*, 142ff; at the head of the Fatimid army, which numbered 30,000 men, whose aim was to take over all of Syria, including Aleppo, stood the eunuch Rifq, whom the caliph intended to appoint governor of Damascus and Aleppo. He established his base in Ramla and there negotiated with the Byzantine representative who attempted to mediate between him and the ruler of Aleppo, Thimāl, during the summer of 1049. In August of the same year the Fatimid army started to advance but the attempt to take Aleppo ended in failure. During this campaign northward, news arrived of another uprising of the Arabs of Palestine, when the Banū Ṭayy', who were to have joined the Fatimid forces, were raiding them instead. We have no further details concerning these events in Palestine and we do not know how they ended. The letter from Damascus: **285**. On Ḥaydara, see: Ibn al-Qalānisī, 85; Ibn Taghrī Bardī, V, 300; his titles: *'uddat al-imām* ('treasure of the imām', that is, of the caliph); *muṣṭafā al-mulk* ('choice of the reign'); *mu'īn al-dawla* ('aide of the realm'); *dhū'l-riyāsatayn* ('the man of two leadership roles'); and his father was called *'aḍb al-dawla* ('*aḍb* – a very sharp sword); according to Ibn al-Qalānisī he entered Damascus only in AH 442 (AD 1050/1), and remained there until AH 448 (AD 1056/7). On Khaṭīr al-Mulk, al-Yazūrī's son, see: Ibn Muyassar, 8. Ibn al-Qalānisī, 86, notes that Ḥaydara behaved well both with the army and with the population of Damascus. He probably means the Muslim population; thus this does not refute the mistreatment and blackmailing described in the Geniza letter; on the contrary, this is what explains the appreciation and general gratitude he enjoyed, according to Ibn al-Qalānisī. In Dinur, *Israel ba-gōlā*, I (1), 201f, there are comments concerning **285** that have no foundation whatever, such as that *dhukhayrat al-dawla* means treasurer of the state; or that instead of *khaṭīr al-mulk* one should read *katīb (!) al-mulk*, intended as the royal scribe; *ibid.*, p. 259, n. 5, he assumes that the letter was written in Ramla (in the first edition – in Jerusalem); these comments have been copied by Assaf, in *Sefer ha-yishuv*, 87.

Mu'ammar. The Jerusalemite 'Eli ha-Kohen asks 'Eli ha-Kohen b. Ḥayyim, the parnās of Fustat, to meet with the 'prince of the congregation', who is Abraham ha-Kohen b. Isaac b. Furāt, and with his help to get a letter to Abū'l-Munā *al-'ārēl* ('the uncircumcised'), evidently another Christian notable in Jerusalem, with the aim of drawing some attention to the Jews of Jerusalem with regard to tax and other matters. In Jerusalem, rumours were spreading to the effect that the *amīr* Najāḥ al-Dawla, the former governor, was evidently about to return to Jerusalem, which seems to have aroused the trepidation of the Jews. (This letter mentions the names of three governors of Jerusalem in that period.) There was also tension and disquiet in the north of Palestine. In AH 454, that is AD 1062, al-Mustanṣir sent Makīn al-Dawla al-Ḥasan b. 'Alī b. Mulham to govern Tiberias and Acre and to be in charge of the two Arab tribes in the area, Banū Sulaym and Banū Fazāra.[58]

[601] The same tension that prevailed in Jerusalem during the fifties is also reflected in the letters of the Gaon Daniel b. Azariah. In a letter written in about 1055 to Abraham ha-Kohen b. Isaac b. Furāt he mentions the profound anxiety of the Jews of Jerusalem with regard to the wall, and ends with a prayer: 'May God provide salvation for the sake of His great name.' The source of that anxiety becomes clear from the account in the chronicle of William of Tyre. According to him, the patriarch had authority over a quarter of the city, by which William of Tyre evidently wished to say that there was a Christian quarter in the city (it seems that he had access to an Arabic source which said *rub'*, which means a quarter, but also a quarter in the sense of a neighbourhood; the word is also used as a collective term for immovable property). He adds that the wall of Jerusalem and its turrets were in ruins as a result of the protracted periods of war and siege. The caliph ordered the governor of the city to reconstruct the walls and its turrets (*moenia et turres*). The governor (*procurator*) passed on the burden of this task to the inhabitants and a quarter of the finances needed to execute this mission was imposed on the Christians. The Christian population of the city was destitute and they begged the governor to lessen their share of the burden but he dismissed them out of hand and even made threats against their lives if they should disobey the ruler's orders. Only by stringent intercession did they manage to get the date of

58 The Dome of the Rock: Maqrīzī, *Itti'āẓ*, II, 261; 'Ulaymī, 270. Letters of 'Eli ha-Kohen: **449, 450**; cf.: Goitein, *Mediterranean Society* II, 610, n. 20, who quotes from two additional Geniza documents; TS 20.187 – a deed trusteeship written in al-Mahdiyya, in AM 4823 (AD 1063), in which in line 26, al-Shaykh Abū Sa'd Isḥaq b. Khalaf b. 'Allūn al-kātib al-miṣrī is mentioned; TS 8.14 – a merchant's letter, which mentions in line 2, goods belonging to 'Abū Sa'd b. 'Allūn al-Kātib' the Karaite. Tiberias and Acre: Ibn al-Qalānisī, 91; Maqrīzī, *Itti'āẓ*, II, 264; Ibn Mulham was formerly in charge of Aleppo, see Ibn al-Qalānisī, 86; Ibn al-Athīr, *Kāmil*, IX, 232f.

payment deferred; they then sent a delegation to the Byzantine emperor (Constantine IX, Monomachus) to obtain the necessary sum. The emperor granted their request but made one condition, namely that only Christians would be allowed to live within the perimeter of the wall built with his money. From then on, the taxes from Cyprus would be set aside to cover the expense of rebuilding the Jerusalem wall, and after the caliph agreed, they started to build the wall. Here we have a story of the building of a wall within a wall, that is the enclosure of the Christian quarter. William also explains that formerly, Muslims had lived among the Christians and that there were frequently skirmishes between them. The wall was finished, he says, in 1063.[59]

[602] On 24 Rajab AH 460 (29 May AD 1068), a severe earthquake shook Palestine (some thirty-five years after the previous quake), whose effect this time was centred in Ramla. The city was completely destroyed, with the exception of two streets (another version: apart from two houses). According to the sources, all of which are Muslim, 15,000 people lost their lives. The wall of Ramla was also destroyed. It was said that the sea withdrew a day's distance from the coast and that many were drowned as they were busy collecting the fish that remained on the shore when the sea suddenly surprised them by returning. It was also said that the water in the wells rose and that in Jerusalem, the Dome of the Rock cracked, but settled back in its place of its own accord.[60]

59 See Daniel b. Azariah's letter: **357**, b, lines 9–10. See William of Tyre, 389ff; see on the significance of the term *rub'*, *rab'*: Gil, *Documents*, 146; cf. on the wall also: Guarmani, *Gl'Italiani*, 18; Erse, in: *Peraqīm*, 121, speaks of the destruction of the southern part of the city wall and the shortening of the wall on the orders of Caliph al-'Azīz. This is not said in any source (the aforementioned does not take the trouble to mention any source). The changing of governors in Jerusalem, mentioned above, may have had some connection to this episode of the building of the wall.

60 The first to mention this earthquake was Abū 'Alī al-Ḥasan b. Aḥmad al-Bannā'; see al-Bannā', 239 (and the translation and editor's comment, *ibid.*, 248). He was a contemporary and told this on the basis of merchants' letters which, he says, reached Baghdad on 1 Shawwāl 460, 3 August 1068; *ibid.*, 240, he tells of another earthquake, prior to that of Ramla, which occurred in Ḥijāz (Medina and elsewhere), and destroyed Eilat as well, on 11 Jumādā I of that year, 18 March AD 1068. Starting with Ibn al-Jawzī, this account was copied by many. Apart from Ibn al-Jawzī, who gave the information on the quake in Ḥijāz separately (but erroneously ascribed it to the year 462), all the others combined the accounts and made of them a story of one earthquake, and those who took the trouble to give the date, gave it as Jumādā I. See: Ibn al-Jawzī, *Muntaẓam*, V, 248, 256; the fact that he mistakenly recorded the year as AH 426 is proven by the Christian date he himself gives as parallel to 11 Jumādā I: 18 Ādhār (March), and this was correct only in AH 460. See further: al-'Aẓīmī, in Cahen, *JA*, 230 (1938), 358; Ibn al-Athīr, *Kāmil*, X, 57 (who increased the number of killed to 25,000); Dhahabī, *'Ibar*, III, 246; *idem*, *Duwal*, 208; Ibn Shaddād (MS), 119b; (printed), 182; he is the only one who has the strange addition: 'most of the inhabitants of Ramla afterwards passed to Jerusalem (Īliyā) and built it and fortified it'; it seems that the version is distorted and it was probably written there (approximately) that the inhabitants of Ramla fled to Jerusalem after the earthquake, but that they returned and rebuilt their city afterwards. Ibn Kathīr, *Bidāya*, XII, 96 (who also speaks of two

The invasion of the Turcomans

[603] From the middle of the eleventh century, we witness the rise of the Turkish tribes called the Ghuzz, as it was also customary to call them at the time. We know them also as Turkmāns (or Turcomans), that is, 'noble Turks', because of their supremacy over other Turkish tribes. Since the Saljūq family played an important role in the events related to the conquests and other achievements of these Turks, these tribes are usually called Saljūqs, both in the sources of the Middle Ages and in present day research, although not all the rulers who rose from their midst belonged to the Saljūq family. At first they extended their rule over areas of Persia, and then they proceeded to drive westward from their centre in Iṣfahān. In 1055, their leader Ṭughril Beg entered Baghdad and the Turcomans soon took over northern Syria as well. Their leaders were gifted administrators and also excellent commanders; and their advance was borne on the waves of devotion to Sunni orthodox Islam for which they fought. They also launched a new holy war against the Byzantines and their allies, the Armenians. Under the command of their ruler Alp Arslān they broke through the defence lines of the Byzantines in Manāzjird (or Manāzkird, as it is called in the Arab sources; in the Byzantine sources it is Mantzikierte; and today it is usually written Manzikert), in eastern Asia Minor, within the borders of Armenia, north of Lake Wan. The emperor Romanus was taken captive and his people had to pay ransom to have him returned while Byzantium had to pay an annual tax to the Saljūqs and release all the Turks in captivity.

According to Maqrīzī, the Turks in al-Mustanṣir's army invaded Ramla in Muḥarram AH 460, that is November AD 1067. Naturally, this event has no connection with the invasion of the Turcomans, who were to appear on the scene some four years later. I am referring to the state of anarchy that prevailed among the Turkish battalions in the Fatimid army. We have no details as to what occurred in Ramla at the time nor what happened to the local population; this was about half a year prior to the earthquake just mentioned.

Heading the Turcomans' (the Nāwakī tribe's) invasion into Palestine stood Atsiz b. Uwaq, a man of the Saljūq court of Alp Arslān, who had deserted his master and even served the Fatimids for a time, and it was they who had first sent him to Palestine in order to overcome the Bedouin

earthquakes, like Ibn al-Jawzī, from whom he copied); Ibn Taghrī Bardī, V, 80; 'Ulaymī, 270; Maqrīzī, *Itti'āẓ*, II, 277, who adds: the destruction of Ramla was final, for it was not rebuilt (it seems that what the aforementioned account of Ibn Shaddād intended to contradict is that latter opinion, which does not sound credible at all); Ibn al-Dawādārī, 387; see more references in the editor's note to al-Bannā': Maqdisi, *BSOAS*, 18(1956), 250, n. 5.

tribes. When he was already in Palestine, he betrayed the Fatimids, for it seemed to him that he was insufficiently compensated. This happened in AH 463, evidently in the latter half of the year, that is, in the spring and summer of AD 1071. Ramla fell to the Turcomans and Jerusalem was put under siege. According to Ibn al-Jawzī, Sibṭ ibn al-Jawzī, Ibn al-Athīr, Maqrīzī, Atsiz conquered Jerusalem only in Shawwāl AH 465 (June/July AD 1073), and then introduced the Abbasid *da'wa* in Jerusalem, according to Ibn al-Athīr. Atsiz earned the title *al-malik al-mu'aẓẓam* (the honourable king). We find a detailed description of this invasion in Sibṭ ibn al-Jawzī, according to whom the seceding Turkish tribe, the Nāwakīs, established its domination in AH 464 (beginning on 29 September AD 1071), and it is possible, therefore, that their major achievements in Palestine took place in 1072. Badr al-Jamālī, the wazīr and commander of the Fatimid army, was at that time in Acre, and the Nāwakī envoys who came to him there with demands for money, were sent away with the response that they would have to make do with the spoils they took in the course of their attacks on the Arab tribes and that part of the taxes from Palestine which he had granted them. Then the Nāwakīs began to take control of Palestine and set up their base in Tiberias at first. Badr now tried to come to terms with the Arab tribes and to turn them against the Turcomans. Army units from other Turcoman tribes seized Trans-Jordan at that time and occupied Ḥiṣn Nu'mān (the Nu'mān fortress), the Arab tribes' stronghold there, where they found a considerable quantity of spoils. Afterwards, the Turcomans also took Ramla, which they found in ruins, uninhabited, 'and its market-place without gates'. They then recruited the farmers of the neighbourhood and set to work rebuilding the city. The olive harvest was also gathered under their protection, and it was plentiful that year. The farmers' income was large, and a goodly portion was set aside for the Turcomans (according to Sibṭ ibn al-Jawzī 300,000 dinars, of which the Turcomans received 30,000).

The date of the conquest of Jerusalem as not until the summer of 1073 (contrary to the date accepted in research of 1071) is confirmed by a poem written by Solomon ha-Kohen b. Joseph, head of the court. In this poem, written on 25 Shevat AM 4837 (22 January AD 1077), it says that the oppression has lasted for 'two times two years', that is to say, four years, i.e. from 1073. Afterwards the Turcomans went out to conquer Acre under the command of Shuklī, one of the commanders subordinate to Atsiz who became his rival. Acre was taken in AH 467 (beginning 27 August AD 1074). At the time of the conquest, members of Badr al-Jamālī's family were staying in Acre, among them his two sons. They were well treated but the conquerors killed the governor of the city and other notables. Shuklī pronounced himself *amīr* in Tiberias. A year later,

Atsiz took Damascus from Razīn (or Zayn) al-Dawla, who is Intiṣār ibn Yaḥyā al-Maṣmūdī, the Fatimid governor. The two made an arrangement whereby Atsiz left Bāniyās and Jaffa to Intiṣār in exchange for the surrender of Damascus. After taking Damascus, Atsiz advanced on Egypt but suffered a defeat at the hands of Badr al-Jamālī, and Atsiz' brother Ma'mūn fell in the battle there.[61]

[604] We find indications of the Saljūq invasion in a deed of compensation issued by the great court, that is the Palestine yeshiva in Jerusalem, in a matter of alimony. The deed was written by the Gaon Elijah ha-Kohen b. Solomon, in May or June 1071, and states that the husband, Yeshūʿā b. Moses *ha-qāṣōr* (the fuller), travelled to Egypt two years earlier (that is, in the summer of 1069); in the meantime 'Ramla was despoiled and they became captives, naked and hungry'. Apparently Jerusalem was then still

[61] See a concise summary on the rise of the Turcomans: Von Grunebaum, *Classical Islam*, 153–156. On the name Manzikert and its various versions cf.: Ben Horin, *Kiryat Sefer*, 24(1947/8), 112. On the names Ghuzz, Turcomans, see the article by Kafesoğlu, *Oriens*, 11:146, 1958. Good surveys on the Saljūqs: Prawer, *Ha-ṣalvānīm*, I, 20–34; Cahen, in: *History of the Crusaders*, 139ff; see particularly on the religious factor in their wars: Sivan, *L'Islam et la croisade*, 15–20. The invasion of Ramla by Turkish battalions, see: Maqrīzī, *Ittiʿāẓ*, II, 275; the article Atsiz (by C. Cahen) in EI^2. The Turcoman invasion: Ibn al-Jawzī, *Muntaẓam*, VIII, 284 (the news of the conquest of Jerusalem reached Baghdad on Ṣafar 466, August 1073, and it was said that the city was taken on Shawwāl 465, June-July 1073); Ibn al-Athīr, *Kāmil*, X, 68, 88; Maqrīzī, *Ittiʿāẓ*, II, 310, 314f; Sibṭ ibn al-Jawzī (ed. Suwaym), 169; Jerusalem surrendered without a battle, according to him, because the governor of the city was also a Turk; see *ibid.*, 171–175, with a more detailed story of the capture of Acre and the taking captive of Badr al-Jamālī's family; Shuklī quarrelled with Atsiz because of the large amount of spoils he amassed in Acre; in Ramaḍān AH 467, April-May AD 1075, Atsiz overcame Shuklī and chased him out of Acre; eventually he was caught and executed in Tiberias as he was about to reach an agreement with the Fatimids. Atsiz then presided over the slaughter of the population of Tiberias and the city was pillaged. Due to these internal conflicts, the Fatimids succeeded in taking Acre again and they sent Jawhar al-Madanī as governor there. The poem of Solomon ha-Kohen b. Joseph: TS Loan 174, a, lines 16ff and b, bottom; printed by: Greenstone, *AJSLL*, 22(1905/6), 159–163; Greenstone, *ibid.*, 172, n. 143, assumed that there was a hint in this poem of the two Saljūq attacks on Jerusalem, according to him, in 463 of the hijra (AD 1070/1) – during the conquest, and in AH 469 (AD 1076/7), while suppressing the inhabitants' uprising (see also *ibid.*, 151); the uprising, of which I shall speak below, took place after the writing of the poem, however, and this invalidates his views, inclusive of what he says of the inexactitude in that poem. It is not clear on what Frenkel, *Cathedra*, 21 (1981/2), 59, bases his claim that there were two conquests of Jerusalem, in 1071 and 1073, apart from his assumption that the poem of Solomon ha-Kohen b. Joseph 'says simply that Jerusalem was conquered twice within two years'; but the poem does not say this, and this is only his own interpretation. The poem says 'they were oppressed two years twice' and this is open to a number of interpretations. See also: Dhahabī, *ʿIbar*, III, 252; Ibn Kathīr, *Bidāya*, XII, 113; Ibn ʿAdīm, *Zubda*, II, 31; ʿAẓīmī, 361; Ibn Taghrī Bardī, V, 87, 101; Ibn al-Qalānisī, 108f, and in the editor's note there, the account of the deal in Damascus, according to al-Dhahabī; see also Ibn Khaldūn, *ʿIbar*, III, 981. See further on the conquest of the cities of northern Palestine and Damascus: Ibn ʿAsākir, II, 331; Ibn Muyassar, 23; according to Mājid, *Ẓuhūr*, 191, Atsiz took Jerusalem only in 1076, which is certainly an error. The retiring Turcoman commander is called in the Arab sources Shiklī, while the correct name was evidently Shughlū, or Shuglū; cf. Cahen, *Byzantion*, 18(1948), 35.

under siege and as yet unconquered. At about the same time, on 15 April of the same year, 'Eli ha-Kohen b. Ezekiel, the Jerusalem parnās, wrote to Abiathar ha-Kohen b. Elijah Gaon in Fustat. He expresses his regret that he has had to postpone his own journey to Fustat, and mentions the state of emergency (some half a year before the time noted by Sibṭ ibn al-Jawzī). Rumours reached him daily; 'there is fear and hunger'; 'Tyre is closed, no one can leave Jerusalem for Ramla, and all the roads are endangered'; and as it is written: 'neither was there any peace to him that went out or came in . . .' (Zech., viii:10). He asks that his son-in-law (or perhaps his brother-in-law, *ṣihr*) be warned that if he brings flax, he should bring it via Ascalon and not via Jaffa, for in Jaffa the authorities (*ha-shālīsh*) confiscate the goods arriving at the port for the benefit of the army (the commander of the camps).[62]

[605] The defeat suffered by Atsiz hastened his downfall. The great battle in Egypt took place on 22 Rajab AH 469 (19 February AD 1077), after which Atsiz withdrew to Ramla, and then to Damascus. According to Sibṭ ibn al-Jawzī, Atsiz was forced to flee owing to the uprising of the local Muslim population, which began in Gaza and spread to Ramla and Jerusalem. The families of Atsiz and the other Turcoman leaders remained in Jerusalem. The cadi and the notaries (literally: 'the witnesses', *al-shuhūd*) together with the rest of Jerusalem's inhabitants, then seized the Turcomans' women and property, dividing them among themselves, and took the Turcoman children as slaves. Then Atsiz advanced on Jerusalem from Damascus, placed the city under siege, and promised its inhabitants the *amān*; on this basis, the inhabitants opened the gates of the city to him. Atsiz prevailed over Jerusalem, completely ignoring his promise of *amān*, and went on a rampage. He slaughtered 3,000 people there, among them the cadi and the notaries. He also conducted campaigns of annihilation against Ramla, until all its people had fled, and against Gaza, where he murdered the entire population. He likewise massacred people in al-'Arīsh and elsewhere and wrought endless havoc in Damascus, where only 3,000 of the original 500,000 inhabitants had remained, due to starvation and scarcity. Jaffa, too, was attacked, and its governor, Razīn al-Dawla Intiṣār, fled from the town to Tyre, together with all the city's inhabitants, while the walls of Jaffa were destroyed on Atsiz' orders.[63]

[606] Badr al-Jamālī made strenuous efforts to put an end to Atsiz' control of Palestine and Damascus, and conducted two extensive but

[62] See **428**, lines 2–3. 'Eli ha-Kohen's letter: **455**, a, lines 13ff, 26ff.

[63] Sibṭ ibn al-Jawzī (ed. Suwaym), 179f (on hunger in Damascus), 182–185, and in the editor's note in Ibn al-Qalānisī, 111. The battle in Egypt: Ibn Muyassar, 25; see Sibṭ ibn al-Jawzī (ed. Suwaym), 181: a letter written by Atsiz at the beginning of his campaign through the Jifār (northern Sinai) to Egypt, dated 29 Ṣafar AH 469, 2 October AD 1076. On the rebellion in Jerusalem: Ibn al-Athīr, *Kāmil*, X, 103.

unsuccessful campaigns against him. In order to fortify his position against Fatimid pressure Atsiz solicited the help of Tāj al-Dawla Tutush, the son of the Saljūq ruler, Alp Arslān. Tutush, then a youth of fourteen, reached Damascus with the blessing of his brother Malik-Shāh, who headed the Saljūq hierarchy. His first act was to have Atsiz executed, and from then onward, Tutush remained the only ruler in the city. This occurred in AH 471, that is AD 1078/9. It is difficult to know to what extent Tutush' authority over Palestine was genuine, as during most of his rule, until he fell in battle, on 15 Ṣafar AH 488 (26 February AD 1095), he was engaged in waging war in northern Syria. In Jerusalem the actual ruler was Artuq, one of the Saljūq commanders subordinate to Tutush, and the latter turned Palestine over to him in AH 479, that is 1086. He set up his headquarters on the Temple Mount. Artuq died in 1091, after ruling the city for five years (or eight, according to Sibṭ ibn al-Jawzī). His two sons succeeded him as rulers of the city, first Īlghāzī and afterwards his brother Sukmān. The two brothers were also involved in the struggle for the control of Damascus and Aleppo following the death of Tutush, when Tutush's eldest son Dukāk seized the reins of power, and Artuq's sons supported Riḍwān, one of Tutush's other sons. The sons of Artuq were unsuccessful in their efforts to gain power and Īlghāzī was taken captive and imprisoned for some time. Afterwards Īlghāzī and Sukmān returned and ruled over Jerusalem.[64]

[607] Badr al-Jamālī, the wazīr of al-Mustanṣir, took ill in Rabī' I AH 487 (March AD 1094). He was a man of Armenian extraction, and at the time of his appointment as wazīr in 1073, he was serving as the Fatimid governor of Acre. Prior to that he had been governor of Damascus and had

64 'Aẓīmī, 362; Ibn Taghrī Bardī, V, 155; Ibn 'Asākir, II, 321; Ibn Kathīr, *Bidāya*, xii, 113; cf. the article Tutush (by M. Th. Houtsma) in *EI*[1]; Cahen, *Byzantion*, 18(1948), 37f; Bar Hebraeus (Bedjan), 259, (Budge), 230f (on Artuq). An event recorded only in 'Aẓīmī, 365, is the battle over Ascalon which began in Dhū'l-Ḥijja 477, April 1085; it seems that a Saljūq attempt to take the city from the Fatimids is being referred to. On Artuq and his sons see: Ibn 'Adīm, *Bughiya*, 139; see the articles: Riḍwān (by K. V. Zetterstein) in *EI*[1], Artukids (by C. Cahen) in *EI*[2]. The sources of this period speak of *miḥrāb da'ūd*. Johns, *QDAP*, 14(1905), 162, tried to prove that the citadel west of the city is meant, usually called David's tower; but *miḥrāb* has manifold meanings: the *qibla* in the mosque, the mosque itself, Jews' prayer places (meaning mainly the Temple), a palace. Busse, *JSAI*, 5(1984), 79f summed up the meanings of *miḥrāb da'ūd* as: the rock (the *ṣakhra*) in its entirety; the tower of David; the Church of St Mary on Mt Zion, according to the Christian tradition that identifies Mt Zion with David's city, the ancient city of the Jebusites. I believe one can add: the Dome of the Rock. See *miḥrāb* in *Lisān al-'arab* and *Tāj al-'arūs*. But it seems to me that for the early mediaeval Arab sources *miḥrāb da'ūd* was the Temple Mount; see Idrīsī, IV, 358 (on Jerusalem): at its western end there is the gate of the *miḥrāb*, and this is the gate above which there is the Dome of Da'ūd'. According to Sibṭ ibn al-Jawzī, *Mir'āh* (ed. Suwaym), 213, the appointee of Atsiz, Turmush, still ruled Jerusalem in the year AH 475, that is, AD 1082/3. Only in that year did Artuq, arriving on behalf of Tutush, receive Jerusalem from the aforementioned, peacefully.

fought with considerable distinction against the Turcomans. After overcoming the anarchy that had spread throughout Egypt, by annihilating the commanders of the Turkish battalions in the caliph's service, he was appointed supreme commander of the army, that is *amīr al-juyūsh*. After the state of dreadful economic hardship and the unrestrained havoc wrought by the Turkish battalions, he managed to establish order and improve the economic conditions. Despite all his efforts, however, he could not restore the control of Palestine to the Fatimids, apart from its ports, where Fatimid rule continued in effect. Now that he succumbed to the illness from which he was to die a short while later, his son Abū'l-Qāsim Shāhinshāh, who is al-Afḍal, took over his role. Some years later, on Friday, 25 Ramaḍān AH 491 (26 August AD 1098), al-Afḍal succeeded in taking Jerusalem. Ibn al-Athīr notes that Jerusalem was again under Fatimid control after a siege lasting more than forty days. At last, the Fatimids employed a war machine (*manjanīq*) and managed to destroy part of the wall. The Saljūqs then asked for an *amān* and abandoned the city.

Typical of the times were the fears expressed in the letter I have already mentioned, written from Caesarea by Joshua *he-hāvēr* b. 'Eli, to the Nagid Mevorakh b. Saadia in Fustat. He describes the state of terror in which the people live and expresses his wish to move from Caesarea to Ascalon, which was 'more strongly fortified than Ḥaṣōr' (Caesarea), and for this reason, he needs a letter from Mevorakh to the cadi of Caesarea; this indicates that Caesarea was then under Fatimid control.[65]

The situation in Palestine during Turcoman rule

[608] We have very little knowledge of what happened in Palestine during the period of Turcoman rule. According to Albert of Aachen, the

[65] On Badr al-Jamālī see Lane-Poole, *History*, 150–157. On the appointment of al-Afḍal and the conquest of Jerusalem: Ibn Khallikān, II, 450f; Ibn al-Athīr, *Kāmil*, X, 282f; according to him it occurred in Sha'bān 489, i.e. August 1096, but this is not credible, although Ibn Khallikān, too, I, 179, cites this as 'some say'; see also: Ibn Muyassar, 28; Maqrīzī, *Itti'aāẓ*, III, 22; Ibn Taghrī Bardī, V, 159, also has the same date as Ibn al-Athīr (1096) and notes that the two brothers, Artuq's sons, were released – Sukmān went to Ruhā (which is Edessa, Urfa) and Īlghāzī to Baghdad; 'Aẓīmī, 373 (who is the closest in time) also confirms the year AH 491, but he has the month as: Shawwāl, that is September 1098; the anonymous Syriac chronicle, *CSCO*, vol. 154, p. 39, also records the two dates, 1096 and 1098. The latter date is supported by the account of Albert of Aachen, who describes the taking of Jerusalem from Sukmān the Saljūqid (Socomanus), and says that the Fatimids (he calls them: 'the king of Babylon') placed a siege on Jerusalem at the time the Christians put Antioch under siege; see Albert of Aachen, 484ff (ch. 32, cf. *MPL* 166, 552f); we know that the siege of Antioch began on 21 October 1097 and lasted until 2 June 1098. Also a Maghribi merchant, who waited in Egypt for an oppportunity to go on a pilgrimage to Jerusalem, mentions in a letter that he did not manage, because the Sultan (al-Afḍal) controlled Jerusalem for only a short while before it was conquered by the Crusaders. See: **575**, lines 24–25. The letter from Caesarea: **596**.

Turcomans imposed very heavy taxes on the entire population, including the Muslims, and on the pilgrims as well. As if to emphasise the superiority of the Fatimids, Albert argues that when they reconquered Jerusalem, they displayed respect for the Church and did not try to deflect the Christians from their religion. There is much bewailing over the dire straits in which the people found themselves, especially with regard to the severe drought in the area, evidently in 1075. At that time, a *ghirāra* (some 200 kilograms) of wheat cost more than 20 dinars in Damascus, according to Ibn ʿAsākir. The general impression that emerges from the sources I have quoted until now is that Atsiz' Turcomans were at first welcomed approvingly and that this was an expression of the reservations the Muslim population had about the Fatimids. But this attitude gradually gave way to animosity towards the Turcomans and a yearning for the former rulers, and this feeling was evident in the rebellions of the year 1078, which are described as though they constituted a kind of popular uprising.

We also know little about the Turcomans' attitude to the Christians. According to Sāwīrūs ibn Muqaffaʿ, a Jacobite Christian called Manṣūr al-Blb''ī (?) was appointed governor of Jerusalem, and he saw to the restoration of the Jacobite church and was very helpful to the pilgrims. The Turcomans, however, abolished the rite of the Paschal fire in the Church of the Resurrection.

The endless wars waged by the Turcomans led to endless destruction, and created an atmosphere of the End of Days. Indeed there were rumours that the end of the world would come in AH 485 (AD 1092/3). A commentary on the Book of Daniel written at that time dealt with *al-mamālik wa'l-malāḥim* (the kingdoms and the wars) expected in the year 1386 Sel. (AD 1074/5). The book has not been preserved, but it is clear from its title that it described in prophetic parlance the Turcomans' invasions of the coastal cities of Palestine and Damascus, and it seems that it also contained a prophecy concerning the imminent End of Days. A Russian source of the time notes that the Turcomans destroyed and desolated the cities and the villages from Antioch to Jerusalem. They murdered, took captive, pillaged, set on fire; they destroyed churches and monasteries. In contrast, Cahen tried to paint a picture of a positive attitude towards the Christians, or at any rate, towards the Latins and the Jacobites, distinguishing them from 'the Greeks' (adherents of Byzantium). He ignores the account of Albert quoted above. One of the results of the Turcoman conquest, according to him, was the removal of Byzantine patronage over the Christians in Palestine, and the increasing strength of the Latins. He points out that in 1078, during the suppression of the rebellion in Jerusalem, Atsiz did not harm the Christians, and even the

Greek Patriarch, Simeon, was permitted to remain in the city. On the other hand, al-'Aẓīmī notes that the people of the coastal towns (that is, the ports) prevented pilgrims, both Latins and Byzantines, from coming ashore in AH 485 (AD 1093), and whoever reached his own country safely spread information to this effect; and that it was this which provoked the Christian world to organise a Crusade. As far as we know, the ports were then in the hands of the Fatimids.[66]

[609] According to some of the sources in the Geniza, as we have already seen, the Turcoman occupation denoted terrible calamities, such as the taking captive of the people of Ramla, the cutting off of roads, the obduracy of the commanders, the aura of anxiety and panic, and so on. The poem of Solomon ha-Kohen b. Joseph speaks of destruction and ruin, the burning of harvests, the razing of plantations, the desecration of cemeteries, many acts of violence and slaughter ('they cut off the ears and even the noses are finished off'), and of course, plunder. We do not know what Atsiz' attitude was to the Jewish population in 1078, during the cruel suppression of the uprisings and the destruction of towns, but the fact that from this date onwards, we barely find letters from Palestine (apart from Ascalon and Caesarea) in the Geniza documents, speaks for itself. Before that, the communities still existed and were active, as were their courts; from this time onwards, there was a serious deterioration in their situation. Below we shall see that some of the outstanding Muslim personalities who were active in Jerusalem, such as Abū'l-Fatḥ Naṣr b. Ibrahīm, one of the heads of the Shāfi'ites during that period, were also forced to abandon Jerusalem at that time, and one can assume that they escaped from the city by the skin of their teeth. Apparently it was during that period, i.e. after 1078, that the Jerusalem yeshiva moved to Tyre. A fragment of a letter has been preserved in the handwriting of the Gaon Elijah ha-Kohen b. Solomon, evidently written in Tyre, in which Jerusalem is mentioned, as well as the distress of the community in Ascalon. A fragment of the deed written in Ramla on 10 August 1076 proves that the community still existed and the signatures are those of people well known to us: Abraham b. Nathan, head of the court, and Joshua *he-ḥāvēr* b. 'Eli, the grandson of the poet Samuel 'the third' b. Hosha'na, who was one of

66 Albert of Aachen, see the foregoing footnote: Ibn 'Asākir, II, 331 (*ghirāra*: see Hinz, 37f); Ibn al-Jawzī, *Muntaẓam*, V, 297: the *kāra* (some 100 kilograms; see Hinz, 41) reached more than eighty dinars in Damascus (speaking of the end of AM 468, around July AD 1075); see on this also: Ibn Taghrī Bardī, V, 101; Ibn al-Qalānisī, 108, who tells of instances of the eating of corpses and even of cannibalism. Also Ibn al-Qalānisī and al-'Aẓīmī, 361, mention that it was only Atsiz who brought about an improvement in conditions and was accepted by the people; see also Sāwīrūs, II(3), 229, who also mentions rumours about the End of Days. The commentary on Daniel: TS Loan 149, ed. by Mann, *Texts*, I, 644ff. See fol. 2a (*ibid.*, 645), lines 1ff, and see Mann's remarks, *ibid.*, 663f, and n. 14. See on the Jacobites in Jerusalem during this period also: Cerulli, *Etiopi*, 11; Cahen, *Bull. de la fac. des*

the personalities of the Palestinian yeshiva. Mention should also be made of the divorce deed from Jaffa, dated 12 April 1077, which I have already mentioned. In 1085 a certain Joseph b. Manasseh of Ascalon writes to Abraham b. Issac ha-Talmīd in Fustat, telling him that he dared to travel from Ascalon to Jerusalem, where he went to his (abandoned) house to look for items he had buried there before fleeing. He did not find anything, only quires and books spoiled by the dampness of the walls. Thus we have evidence that at least some of the Jews of Jerusalem fled from the Turcomans, during the rule of Atsiz, or that of Artuq. The subject of retrieving books also figures in a letter from Tripoli (Syria) and this is but further evidence of the difficulties of the times. This is a letter from a refugee from Jerusalem to her brother-in-law in Fustat, written *ca.* 1075. The writer was evidently a member of one of city's notable families, as the wife of Abū'l-Khayr b. Mevorakh ha-Kohen, and who had two brothers, Shemaria ha-Kohen, who is Abū'l-Wafā' Ḥaffāẓ of Ascalon, and Abū'l-A'lā, the merchants' representative in Tyre. She was also a relative of the Egyptian Nagid Judah b. Saadia and his brother Mevorakh (perhaps his wife's sister). She and her children are in great distress in Tripoli. Her husband Abū'l-Khayr has disappeared and one of her children, Muntaṣir, has died. Her brothers-in-law and sisters show no interest in her fate, and have forgotten how she treated them when she still lived in Jerusalem. Her brother-in-law Abū'l-Wafā' was taken captive by the Arabs (who were generally allies of the Saljūqs). At that time, there was still a Jewish community in Hebron, as we see from a letter from Saadia 'the ḥāvēr of the graves of the patriarchs', and particularly from the letter he wrote to Abiathar ha-Kohen. These letters were written at the beginning of 1082, and they contain the interesting information that the writers continued to maintain connections with Ascalon, which was evidently under Fatimid control.

Abū Bakr ibn al-'Arabī, a Spanish writer and scholar (of Seville), who visited Jerusalem in 1093–1095, that is during the rule of Īlghāzī and Sukmān, the sons of Artuq, paints a rather idyllic picture of Jerusalem in the journal of his travels. He stayed mainly in the neighbourhood of the Temple Mount, and speaks of lively spiritual activities in the Shāfi'ite *madrasa*s near *bāb al-asbāṭ* (the gate of the tribes, the Crusaders' gate of Jehoshaphat, on the northern side of the eastern wall), and of the Ḥanafites. He mentions discussions with Christians and Jews on religious subjects, and among the Jews, he particularly singles out the *ḥabr* (scholar) al-Tustarī (he is perhaps Sahl b. Faḍl, the Karaite writer). Religious and learned figures come and go, even from far-off Khurāsān. He stayed more

lettres de Strasbourg, 29(1950), 119–122; *idem, Past and Present*, 6(1954), 12; al-'Aẓīmī, 369. The Russian source: Leib, *Rome, Kiev et Byzance*, 66.

than six months in Ascalon (evidently during the year 1096) and there too found a spiritual centre which aroused his admiration. From Ascalon he sailed to Acre and from there he continued on to Tiberias and Damascus, and on to Baghdad.[67]

Events in Tyre

[610] We have seen how important Tyre was to the economy, being the major port of the entire region of Palestine and Syria. I have also described the role played by the cadi of Tyre, Ibn Abī 'Aqīl, in maritime trade and in connection with its principal factor, the Jewish Maghribi merchants. I shall now review the special political events connected with the city in the latter half of the eleventh century, events which for a time turned it into a sort of city-state. As we shall discover, these events also affected to a great extent the Jewish communities of Palestine. The Palestinian yeshiva moved to Tyre during Turcoman rule in Palestine, perhaps in 1078; from Tyre it conducted the struggle against David b. Daniel, who lived in Egypt and wanted to be exilarch and the sole leader of the Jews in the Diaspora.

The political events, at the core of which was the endeavour to achieve Tyre's independence, centre round the personality of the cadi Ibn Abī 'Aqīl 'Abdallah b. 'Alī b. 'Iyāḍ, who is Abū Muḥammad or 'Ayn al-Dawla. Apparently, he is first mentioned by Nāṣir Khusraw, who visited Tyre in February 1047, and I have already quoted him on the subject. In AH 448, that is AD 1056, he participated in the delegation negotiating with the ruler of Aleppo, Mu'izz al-Dawla Thimāl b. Ṣāliḥ b. Mirdās, on behalf of Caliph al-Mustanṣir. In AH 455, that is AD 1063, Ibn Abī 'Aqīl rebelled against the Fatimids and set up a form of independent city-state. Badr al-Jamālī, commander of the Fatimid army, tried to reconquer Tyre, but to no avail. His principal attack was made in the summer of AH 462 (AD 1070). The cadi then approached the Turcomans in the area who had the *amīr* Qurlū at their head, and asked for their help. Indeed, they came to his aid, concentrating an army of 6,000 cavalry around Sidon, and placing

[67] See: Greenstone, *AJSLL*, 22 (1905/6), 159–163, a, lines 16ff, col. 2. Elijah ha-Kohen's letter: **429**. The fragment of a deed from Ramla: **568**. The deed of divorce from Jaffa: *supra*, n. 331. Joseph b. Manasseh: **593**, b, line 4. The letter from Tripoli: **605**. Goitein, *JQR*, NS 66(1975/6), 70ff, 80–83, interprets the letter somewhat differently, assuming that it is from the Crusaders' period, but see: *ha-Yishuv*, 278–282, where he recognises that it is from the period of the Saljūqs. Saadia's letters: **613**, **614**, and see n. 315 above. See Ibn al-'Arabī, *Riḥla*, 79–85; *idem, Aḥkām*, 1586, describes a battle in Jerusalem between two military factions, and the siege placed on the Temple Mount (*miḥrāb Da'ūd*). All that time, according to him, life in Jerusalem went on as usual, as if nothing had happened. On Sahl b. Faḍl al-Tustarī see Gil, *ha-Tustarīm*, 63f and further in the chapter on the Karaites. Frenkel, *Cathedra*, 21 (1981/2), 57, 71, tries to prove that it is not to Atsiz' Turcomans that the descriptions of destruction and vandalism refer.

it under siege in order to take it from the Fatimid garrison stationed there. Badr was forced to lift the siege on Tyre in order to save his own men who were trapped in Sidon, and although he renewed the siege again afterwards and brought its inhabitants to a sorry state, with a *raṭl* of bread selling at half a dinar, he saw that it was hopeless, for his hold on the entire area was dwindling due to the unceasing flow of Turcoman battalions, and he left Tyre to its fate.[68]

[611] Owing to the Turcomans' help, Tyre remained under the cadi's aegis until his death in AH 465 (AD 1073), and in the hands of his son Nafīs and his brothers until AH 482, that is AD 1089, when the Fatimid army, under Munīr (or Naṣīr) al-Dawla al-Juyūshī, conquered it. Jubayl, Beirut, Sidon and Acre were then taken by the Turcomans. Munīr remained in Tyre and kept the reins of authority in his own hands, hoping to throw off the bonds of Fatimid rule. He stood his ground at the head of his people until 14 Jumādā II AH 486, or 12 July AD 1093, when agents of the central authority brought him to Egypt together with many of his supporters and had them executed. Despite the fact that the population of Tyre demonstrated their backing of the Fatimids, the city was pillaged and fined the sum of 60,000 dinars, and a new governor, by the name of al-Katīla, was appointed by the Fatimid caliph. However, he too rebelled against the Fatimids afterwards and managed to stand up to them until Ramaḍān AH 490 (August/September AD 1097), when a Fatimid army succeeded in suppressing the rebellion with considerable bloodshed. Al-Katīla was caught, brought to Egypt, and executed. The events of 1089–1093 are reflected in two letters from the Geniza: one from 'Amram ha-Kohen b. Aaron, the son-in-law of the Gaon Abiathar ha-Kohen, from which it emerges that Damascus (under Saljūq rule) was cut off from Ascalon

68 Negotiations with Aleppo: Ibn al-'Adīm, *Zubda*, I, 274. On the events of the year AH 462 see: Ibn al-Qalānisī, 98; Ibn Shaddād (MS Leiden 3076), fol. 116a-b, and in print: 165f. See details on the cadi in Ibn Taghrī Bardī, V, 63; according to whom he died in AH 450, i.e. AD 1058, which is not correct because he is still mentioned in letters of the Maghribi Jewish merchants of the sixties as well; he died in Zīb (Akhzīv), 'a village between Acre and Tyre'; Ibn al-Athīr, *Kāmil*, IX, 651; Sibṭ ibn al-Jawzī, in the editor's quotation in Ibn al-Qalānisī, 96f; according to whom the cadi took control of the city only in AH 462 (AD 1070), but he evidently mentions a situation which existed already for seven years, in order to emphasise the state of complete anarchy that prevailed then in Fatimid-controlled areas, when the population also rebelled in Damascus, Tripoli and Ramla, while only Acre and Sidon remained loyal to the Fatimids; 'Aẓīmī, 359; Maqrīzī, *Itti'āẓ*, II, 303 (with another of the cadi's titles: *al-nāṣiḥ* (the adviser); Ibn Muyassar, 20 (where Ṣafad is printed instead of Tyre; and instead of the name Qurlū, we find: Lw'). The siege placed by Badr al-Jamālī on Tyre is reflected in the letter of 'Eli ha-Kohen b. Ezekiel, of 15 April 1071: 'Tyre is closed'; 'the one in Tyre, who contrived, was left without any helper, and it is his (supporting) rock which threw him down', see **455**, a, lines 17, 31–32 (there is a play of words here: Ṣūr, which is Tyre, and also: a rock; and perhaps God is also meant, 'his rock'); it seems to have been written when the cadi was in the worse possible state, while Badr's army had closed off Tyre.

(under Fatimid control), and that in order to reach Ascalon, one had to travel via Egypt. The Jewish community of Damascus was utterly occupied with ransoming captives, undoubtedly captives taken in Tyre at the time of its conquest from the cadi's family. From the other letter, written by the Gaon Abiathar ha-Kohen to the people of Baghdad, it appears that due to the lack of security and the innumerable soldiers stationed throughout the region, the brother of a man who had died in Iraq was unable to leave Tyre in order to go there and perform the *ḥalīṣā* for his brother's widow.

Comparative calm and political and military stability existed in Palestine under Fatimid rule for only some forty years. The invasion of the Turkish tribes put an end to this near-stability at one blow. Palestine was drawn into a whirlpool of anarchy and insecurity, of internal wars among the Turks themselves and between them (generally in collaboration with the Arab tribes) and the Fatimids. Here and there, in one or another area, a delicate state of balance was arrived at for a few years. By and large, however, the Turcoman period, which lasted less than thirty years, was one of slaughter and vandalism, of economic hardship and the uprooting of populations. Terrible suffering, eviction and wandering, was the particular lot of the Jewish population, and chiefly its leadership, the Palestinian yeshiva. Nevertheless, most of the communities evidently remained in their places, and only were finally uprooted during the Crusaders' conquest.

Brief chronological summary

The period I have surveyed until now lasted in all for more than four and a half centuries (or to be precise: 465 years; from AD 634 until AD 1099). It comprised the following stages: (1) one generation of the Muslim conquest and establishment (precisely twenty-seven years, from 634 until 661); (2) some one-hundred years of Umayyad-Damascene rule, from 661 until 750; (3) some one-hundred years of Abbasid-Baghdadian rule, from 750 until 878; (4) some one-hundred years of Turco-Egyptian rule – Ṭūlūnids and Ikhshīdids – lasting from 878 until 970, of which thirty years were again under Abbasid-Baghdadian rule, between 905 and 935; (5) some two generations of war with many participants, the dominant factor among them being the Fatimids, from 970 until 1030; (6) some forty years of Fatimid-Egyptian rule, from 1030 until 1071; and (7) one generation of Turkish rule over most of Palestine, from 1071 until 1099, and towards the end some ten months of renewed Fatimid rule. These facts do not call for much interpretation; together they simply form a picture of almost unceasing insecurity, of endless rebellions and wars, of upheavals and instability.[69]

Muslim personalities during the last generations of the period

[612–613] As far as spiritual activity is concerned, the most famous personality of the period was undoubtedly the geographer Abū ʿAbdallah Muḥammad b. Abū Bakr al-Bannā', Shams al-Dīn al-Maqdisī (in research literature it is customary to call him al-Muqaddasī, and he is known also by the nickname al-Basharī), author of the book on regions of the Muslim world which serves as one of the major sources for present-day scholars on the political and social geography and history of this world in the early Middle Ages. We have little information on his life, apart from what he himself has told us in his book. He was the grandson of an architect-builder who was famous in his day, Abū Bakr al-Bannā' (mentioned earlier in connection with the building of the port of Acre). His mother's family arrived in Jerusalem two generations earlier from Biyār, in the region of Qūmis in Khurāsān. Al-Muqaddasī was born in around 945 – we know that in 966 he went on a pilgrimage to Mecca at about the age of twenty and that he died in around the year 1000. His book was written in or about 985, that is, at the height of the wars waged by the Fatimids in Palestine and Syria.[70] His cousin, also a Jerusalemite, was al-Muṭahhar b. al-Muṭahhar (or: al-Ṭāhir) al-Maqdisī, who emigrated to Bust in Sijistān and there wrote his book *On the Creation and on History* in about 956, in which many facts about the beginnings of Islam have been preserved which are not found in any other source known today.[71]

[614–619] Of the personalities living in Jerusalem in around 1000, there is mention of al-Qāsim b. Muzāḥim b. Ibrahīm al-Jandānīnī, who was the *imām* of Jerusalem.[72] Abū'l-ʿAbbās ʿUbaydallah b. Muḥammad Nāfiʿ b.

[69] ʿAẓīmī, 368f; Ibn al-Athīr, *Kāmil*, X, 176 (according to whom the cadi died during the siege, but this is not confirmed in any other source); Ibn al-Qalānisī, 124; Ibn Taghrī Bardī, V, 128 (he has Naṣīr instead of Munīr; and he is of the opinion that Tyre was taken from the Saljūqs, not from the cadi's sons); Ibn Muyassar, 28 (he too has Naṣīr instead of Munīr); Ibn Kathīr, *Bidāya*, XII, 145; Maqrīzī, *Ittiʿāẓ*, II, 326, 328; III, 20 (he has: Naṣīr al-Dawla instead of Munīr al-Dawla). Sibṭ ibn al-Jawzī (ed. Suwaym), 178, notes that there was a non-aggression pact (*hudna*) between the rulers of Tyre and the Turcomans (al-Ghuzz). The letter of ʿAmram ha-Kohen: **552**, line 18. Abiathar's letter: **553**, c, lines 15–16. Cf. on Tyre in general: Ashtor, *CCM*, 18:117, 1975, where there is also information on the economic life of Tyre and Tripoli in the period under discussion and a survey of events in Tripoli in the decade between 1070–1080; see also his book: *Social and Economic History*, 226f.

[70] See the article al-Muḳaddasī (by J. H. Kramers) in *EI*[1].

[71] See: Sezgin, I, 337.

[72] Wāsiṭī, 41 (I have no explanation for the nickname Jandānīnī).

Mukarram al-Bustī made a pilgrimage to Mecca from Naysābūr in Persia and on his return, stopped in Ramla and Jerusalem. He died in AH 384, that is AD 994.[73] 'Abdallah b. al-Walīd al-Anṣārī, an Egyptian by birth, settled in Jerusalem and died there in around the year AH 410, that is AD 1010.[74] The preacher (*al-khaṭīb*) in the al-Aqṣā mosque, Abū Bakr Muḥammad b. Aḥmad b. Muḥammad al-Wāsiṭī, wrote a treatise in AH 410, that is AD 1019/20, in praise of Jerusalem, the first of its kind, entitled: *Concerning the (religious) status of Jerusalem.*[75] Abū'l-Fatḥ Muḥammad b. Ibrahīm b. Muḥammad b. Yazīd al-Bazzāz (the textile merchant) al-Ṭarsūsī (that is, he stemmed from Ṭarsūs in Syria), known also by the name Ibn al-Baṣrī, settled in Jerusalem and died there in AH 409, that is, AD 1018/9.[76] Another contemporary, Ja'far b. Muḥammad al-Naysābūrī, that is a man of Naysābūr in Persia, also settled in Jerusalem.[77]

[620–625] In the mid-eleventh century, there lived in Jerusalem Abū'l-Ma'ālī al-Musharraf b. al-Murajjā b. Ibrahīm al-Maqdisī, author of a book in praise of Jerusalem. As we have seen, he was a contemporary of the Gaon Solomon b. Judah. His book is called 'the *faḍā'il* (precedence) of Jerusalem and of the Rock; he also wrote a book on the *faḍā'il* of al-Shām, edited by his pupil Abū'l-Qāsim Makkī al-Rumaylī. Al-'Ulaymī complains in his book that he could not find any article about him in any biographical literature.[78] Salāma b. Ismā'īl b. Jamā'a al-Maqdisī al-Ḍarīr ('the blind Jerusalemite') died in Jerusalem in AH 480, that is AD 1087. Al-'Ulaymī praises him for his keen intellect.[79] In the year AH 463, that is AD 1071, on the eve of the Turcoman conquest, we find among those engaged in teaching traditions in Jerusalem, Ṭāhir b. Muḥammad b. Salāma al-Quḍā'ī al-Miṣrī, who was born in Egypt, as his name indicates.[80] In his travel journal, Abū Bakr ibn al-'Arabī, the Andalusian writer who stayed in Jerusalem from 1093 until 1095, as we have seen,

73 Ibn al-Jawzī, *Muntaẓam*, VII, 175.
74 'Ulaymī, 256.
75 Wāsiṭī, 3; cf. Sivan, *IOS*, 1(1971), 263. A critical edition of his book called *Faḍā'il bayt al-maqdis* (Jerusalem 1979), was published by I. Hasson; see in his introduction details on al-Wāsiṭī; see also Ashtor, *Tarbiz*, 30 (1960/61), 210.
76 Ibn al-Jawzī, *Muntaẓam*, VII, 292; al-Khaṭīb, *Ta'rīkh*, I, 415 (according to whom he died in 410); Ibn Taghrī Bardī, IV, 243. Jazarī, II, 48; it is not clear whether he is speaking of the same personality, because he mentions that his *kunya* was Abū Umayya.
77 'Ulaymī, 256.
78 See **117**, lines 21–22; **453**, lines 8, 18; his father Murajjā is also mentioned – see **99**, line 6; 'Ulaymī, 264; cf. Sivan, *IOS*, 1(1971), 264; I have used the treatise of al-Musharraf in this book, on the basis of the photocopy of the MS Tübingen in the National Library, Jerusalem. The dissertation of Dr Livne (Hebrew University 1985) contains the critical edition of this important work.
79 'Ulaymī, 263.
80 Ibn 'Asākir, VII, 49.

mentions 'Aṭā' al-Maqdisī.[81] He seems to have been the pupil of another Jerusalemite, Abū'l-Fatḥ Naṣr b. Ibrahīm b. Naṣr b. Ibrahīm b. Da'ūd, al-Maqdisī al-Nābulusī (i.e., he came from Nābulus). Naṣr evidently lived most of his life in Damascus, and it was there that Abū Bakr ibn al-'Arabī met him, shortly before his death. It was said that he earned his living from land in Nābulus. He studied in Tyre, and from there moved to Jerusalem, then returning again to Tyre, where he taught for some ten years. He died in Damascus, on 9 Muḥarram AH 490, 26 December AD 1096. He was the author of many books on Muslim law and had many pupils, one of the outstanding among them being Idrīs b. Ḥamza, of Ramla. According to Mujīr al-Dīn al-'Ulaymī, Naṣr lived in Jerusalem in a *zāwiya* (a sort of hostel for scholars of religion near the *bāb al-raḥma*), known as al-Nāṣiriyya and afterwards as al-Ghazāliyya, because al-Ghazālī lived there. (Abū Bakr ibn al-'Arabī speaks of the Shāfi'ī *madrasa* near *bāb al-asbāṭ*; perhaps he is referring to the same institution.)[82]

Another important personality in Jerusalem during this period was the *shaykh al-islām* Abū'l-Faraj 'Abd al-Wāḥid b. Aḥmad b. Muḥammad al-Shīrāzī (i.e. of Shīrāz in Persia) al-Anṣārī, who was one of the heads of the Ḥanbalī school. He was the teacher of many of the heads of the Ḥanbalīs of the following generation and wrote many books on *fiqh* (Muslim law). He died in Damascus on 28 Dhū'l-Ḥijja AH 486, 19 January AD 1094.[83]

[626–630] One of the outstanding figures among the Muslim intellectuals of his generation was Abū'l-Qāsim 'Abd al-Jabbār b. Aḥmad b. Yūsuf al-Rāzī (that is, a man of Rayy, today the Tehran neighbourhood) al-Zāhid (the ascete). He lived in Baghdad for many years and from there moved to Jerusalem. He was killed in the slaughter carried out by the

81 Ibn al-'Arabī, *Riḥla*, 81. The editor does not shed any light here but 'Aṭā' is mentioned also in 'Ulaymī, 264: he is Abū'l-Faḍl 'Aṭā', who was head of the Shāfi'ites in Jerusalem, and a contemporary and pupil of another important figure among the Shāfi'ites at the time, Naṣr b. Ibrahīm al-Maqdisī (mentioned next).

82 Ibn al-'Arabī, *Riḥla*, 84; Subkī, *Ṭabaqāt*, V, 351f; Ibn al-Athīr, *Kāmil*, X, 484; Ṣafadī, *al-Wāfī*, IV, 376f: he was a strong opponent of Muḥammad b. Karrām; evidently during this period there were still many disciples of this thinker in Jerusalem, as is confirmed also by Abū Bakr ibn al-'Arabī, *Riḥla*, 81; Dhahabī, *'Ibar*, III, 329: he was a pupil of Muḥammad b. Ja'far al-Mīmāsī (from Mayūmas, the port area of Gaza; see Avi-Yonah, *Ge'ogrāfya hīsṭōrīt*, 117; Muqaddasī, *Āqālīm*, 174) in Gaza; Dhahabī, *'Ulūw*, 187; Yāqūt, *Buldān*, V, 600: he moved to Damascus in AH 471, AD 1078/9; Ibn al-'Imād, III, 395f; Yāfi'ī, III, 152; Ishbīlī, II, 159; 'Ulaymī, 264, cf. Ibn al-'Arabī, *Riḥla*, 80. See further: Brockelmann, *GAL*, S I, 609; Goitein, *Yerushalayim* (1952/3), 102 (= *Ha-yishuv*, 24); *idem*, *Mediterranean Society*, II, 201, 562, n. 14, who expresses the credible assumption that his leaving Jerusalem was connected with the Turcomans' conquest, and the same applies to the transfer of the Palestine yeshiva to Tyre; one can add that the transfer took place in 1078/9 (see in this footnote above), that is after Atsiz' cruel acts of oppression, which I have described above, and that he moved at first to Damascus, and only afterwards to Tyre.

83 'Ulaymī, 263; it seems that he too moved to Damascus in 1078, after Atsiz took Jerusalem

Crusaders during their conquest.[84] We also know the name of the Shāfi'ite cadi in Jerusalem at that time; he was Yaḥyā ibn al-Ṣā'igh (the jeweller).[85] When the Turcomans took control of Jerusalem, they appointed as chief cadi of the city a man of the Ḥanafite school, whose loyalty to the Turks was not in doubt, and a Turk himself – Muḥammad b. Ḥasan b. Mūsā b. 'Abdallah al-Balāshā'ūnī, also known by the name al-Ashqalī. Due to the complaints about him on the part of the other cadis in Jerusalem, he was dismissed and given a similar post in Damascus. He died in Jumādā II AH 506, December AD 1112.[86]

We find the important Spanish scholar Abū Bakr Muḥammad b. al-Walīd b. Maḥmūd (or Muḥammad) al-Ṭurṭūshī (of Tortosa) al-Qurashī al-Fihrī, living in Jerusalem during the 90s of the eleventh century. He was a man of the Malikite school, who spent most of his years in Alexandria and was a retainer of the Fatimid wazīr al-Afḍal. He died in Alexandria in AH 520, that is 1126. Abū Bakr ibn al-'Arabī met him in Jerusalem, and describes with admiration how he listened to his lectures. According to him, al-Ṭurṭūshī lived in a *ghuwayr*, that is, a small cave, between Bāb al-Asbāṭ and Miḥrāb Zakariyyā'. Some of his impressions of Jerusalem are recorded in al-Ṭurṭūshī's book on fake traditions. He is primarily known, however, for his work on political philosophy, *sirāj al-mulūk* (the candle [the light] for kings).[87]

Abū'l-Qāsim Makkī b. 'Abd al-Salām al-Rumaylī al-Maqdisī was a pupil of al-Musharraf ibn al-Murajjā, the collector of the praises of Jerusalem. He was also killed by the Crusaders at the time of the conquest. According to a tradition quoted by Dhahabī in his *Tadhkira*, he was stoned while in captivity, near Beirut, on 12 Shawwāl AH 492, 1 December AD 1099. He also studied with Muḥammad b. 'Alī b. Yaḥyā b. Silwān al-Māzinī, with Abū 'Uthmān b. Waraqā and with 'Abd al-'Azīz b. Aḥmad al-Naṣībīnī. For some time, he studied in Ascalon with Aḥmad b. al-Ḥusayn al-Shammā' (the candle-maker or merchant). It was said that the Crusaders were willing to release Abū'l-Qāsim for the sum of 1,000 *mithqāls* (dinars), but the money could not be raised. It was also said that he had with him a book in which he collected traditions on the history of

a second time; Ibn Abī Ya'lā, II, 248f; Ibn Rajab, I, 85–92; Ibn al-Qalānisī, 125; cf. Goitein, *ha-Yishuv*, 24.

84 Subkī, *Ṭabaqāt*, V, 98; cf. Goitein, *ha-Yishuv*, 23.

85 Ibn al-'Arabī, *Riḥla*, 80 (he met him in Jerusalem, in around 1095); Subkī, *Ṭabaqāt*, IV, 324.

86 'Ulaymī, 265.

87 Ibn al-'Arabī, *Riḥla*, 80. This cave was perhaps *maghārat Ibrahīm*, mentioned by Ibn al-Faqīh, 101, on the northern side of the Temple Mount; cf. below, sec. 842, n. 115. See Ṭurṭūshī's book *al-ḥawādith wa'l-bida'*, 81, 116, 121f, 127, and the introduction on the life of the author, by the editor (Muḥammad al-Ṭālibī), 3f; see also Ibn Khallikān, III, 394; 'Ulaymī, 266f; Dhahabi, *Tadhkira*, 1271; cf. Brockelmann, *GAL*, I, 459; Lévi-Provençal,

Jerusalem, *ta'rīkh bayt al-maqdis*, and a book on the praises of Hebron, but these works have been lost. He had quite a reputation as a scholar on Shāfiite law, and people would come from far and wide to hear him pass judgment.[88]

[631–634] Another pupil of Abū'l-Fatḥ Naṣr b. Ibrahīm was the Jerusalemite Shāfi'ite scholar Abū'l-Fatḥ Sulṭān b. Ibrahīm b. al-Muslim. He wrote a book entitled *al-dhakhā'ir* (the treasures). He was born in Jerusalem in AH 442, that is AD 1050/1. At some unknown date, he moved to Egypt and was the leader of the Shāfi'ites there. He died in AH 518, that is AD 1124.[89]

Among the personalities mentioned by Ibn al-'Arabī in his journal, one should also note Abū'l-Ma'ālī Mujallī b. Jamī' b. Najā al-Makhzūmī, who was one of the outstanding figures among the Shāfi'ites in Jerusalem. He stemmed from Arsūf, and was a pupil of the above-mentioned Abū'l-Fatḥ Sulṭān. Towards the end of his life, in AH 547, that is AD 1152, he became the chief cadi of Egypt for a period of two years. He died in Dhū'l-Qa'da AH 550, January AD 1156.[90]

Among the famous people staying in Jerusalem at this time, one must mention Abū Ḥāmid Muḥammad b. Muḥammad al-Ṭūsī al-Ghazālī. One of Islam's greatest thinkers of all times, he stayed in Jerusalem after leaving his post in Baghdad and decided to devote himself to spiritual matters and writing. He seems to have arrived in Jerusalem not earlier than 1096, for Ibn al-'Arabī, who lived in Jerusalem from 1093–1095, does not mention him.[91]

A native of Jerusalem who earned fame and recognition was the poet and collector of traditions, Abū'l-Faḍl Muḥammad b. Ṭāhir b. 'Alī b. Aḥmad al-Maqdisī al-Shaybānī, who was called Ibn al-Qayṣarānī (son of a man of Caesarea). He was born in Jerusalem on 6 Shawwāl AH 448 (17 December AD 1056). From AH 468, that is AD 1075, he studied in Baghdad and spent many years travelling in the East, looking for traditions. He generally went on his travels by foot and lived an austere and

History, III, 5, n. 1, see *ibid.*, 100f, the translation of a fragment of *sirāj al-mulūk*; a Spanish translation was edited by M. Alarcon (Madrid 1930/1).

88 Ibn al-'Imād, III, 398f; Subkī, *Ṭabaqāt*, V, 332ff; *idem*, Shifā', 110f; Sam'ānī (Ḥaydarabad), VI, 173; Ibn al-Athīr, *Lubāb*, I, 477; Dhahabī, *Tadhkira*, 1229f; Yāqūt, *Buldān*, II, 824; 'Ulaymī, 264f; cf. Rosenthal, *History of Muslim Historiography*², 464, 468; Sivan, *IOS*, 1(1971), 263f.

89 'Ulaymī, 266; Dhahabī, *Tadhkira*, 1270.

90 Ibn al-Arabī, *Riḥla*, 80; Suyūṭī, *Muḥāḍara*, I, 405, where there is a list of his works, among them a book on judges' procedures; Ibn Khallikān, IV, 154.

91 See the article al-Ghazālī (by W. M. Watt) in *EI*², and references therein to many studies written on his life and his works. See the survey of his biography and his achievements: Lazarus-Yafeh, *al-Ghazālī*, in the introduction: pp. 11–17. It is possible that his stay in Jerusalem took place before Ibn al-'Arabī arrived there in 1092, as emerges from Ibn 'Asākir's account (see above, sec. 201, n. 115).

ascetic life, being an adherent of extremist Ṣūfism. He wrote many books, of which four were printed – one of them dealing with identical names of genealogical descent. He died after a visit to Jerusalem, *en route* to Baghdad on his return from a pilgrimage, in Rabīʿ I AH 507, August AD 1113.[92]

[635–642] We also know of a number of personalities who lived in Ramla at this time. Most prominent was Abū Muḥammad Khalaf b. Muḥammad b. ʿAlī b. Ḥamdūn al-Wāsiṭī, from Wāsiṭ in Iraq. It was said that he settled in the region of Ramla and engaged in commerce, and eventually left his studies (*ʿilm*) behind. In his youth, he studied in Baghdad, Damascus, and in Jurjān and Khurāsān. He wrote a book on the traditions in Bukhārī and Muslim. He died in AH 401, that is AD 1010/1.[93]

There seems to have been a centre of Shiite personalities in Ramla during this period. The Shiite writer al-Ṭūsī mentions some of them in his book *Āmālī* (telling of a dream in which ʿAlī ibn Abī Ṭālib appears), among them Muḥammad b. Ibrahīm b. Qarwazī and Abū ʿAlī Maṣbaḥ b. Hilqām al-ʿIjlī. Two Shiites who were active in Eilat are also mentioned in the book: ʿAlī b. Ayman, and Abū Yaʿlā Muḥammad b. Zuhayr, who was the Shiite cadi in Eilat.[94]

We know the name of the chief cadi in Ramla in 1024, he was Abū'l-ʿAssāf al-Kabbāshī. Evidently he was also the superior of the cadi of Jerusalem.[95] Owing to the preservation of a part of Musabbiḥī's book, we also know the name of the man in charge of collecting taxes (*kharāj*) in Ramla (apparently referring to jund Filasṭīn) at that time – Abū Ṭālib al-Gharābilī, who was appointed to the position on 1 Rabīʿ II AH 415 (12 June AD 1024), replacing ʿUbaydallah b. Yūnus.[96] In Ramla there lived one of the offspring of many generations of descendants of ʿUmar ibn al-Khaṭṭāb; he was Abū'l-Qasam ʿĪsā b. ʿAlī al-ʿUmarī. Al-Karājilī notes that he met him in Jumada II AH 412, September AD 1021.[97] Another man of Ramla was Aḥmad b. Muḥammad al-Kattānī (the flax merchant), who settled in Damascus where he taught traditions. He died in Damascus

[92] See the article Ibn al-Ḳaysarānī (by J. Schacht, No. 1) in *EI*² and the references there; to which must be added: Ibn al-Jawzī, *Muntaẓam*, IX, 177f; ʿUlaymī, 265f (who has an error in the year of his death); cf. Goitein, *ha-Yishuv*, 24.

[93] Al-Khaṭīb al-Baghdādī, *Ta'rīkh*, VIII, 334f, Ibn ʿAsākir, V, 170f; Ibn al-Jawzī, *Muntaẓam*, VII, 254; Ibn al-Athīr, *Kāmil*, IX, 226; Dhahabī, *Tadhkira*, 1067f; cf. Brockelmann, *GAL*, S I, 281; Sezgin, I, 220.

[94] Al-Ṭūsī, *Āmālī*, II, 232; he wrote it in AH 457, that is AD 1065, see p. 225 *ibid*.

[95] Musabbiḥī, 17, 30 (in the second place he is called Ibn al-ʿAssāf). He calls him *sharīf*, that is he was related to the ʿAlids.

[96] Musabbiḥī, 34. One cannot know if in fact the appointment was fulfilled, for it seems that Ramla was under the control of the Banū Jarrāḥ at the time.

[97] Al-Karājilī, 247.

in AH 464, that is AD 1071/2.[98] Abū'l-Munajjim Muḥammad b. Makkī b. Muḥammad b. Ibrahīm al-Dārī (related to Tamīm al-Dārī of Hebron) was a poet in Ramla. He was born in AH 417, that is AD 1026.[99] The leader of the Shāfi'ites in Ramla, Abū'l-Ḥasan Idrīs b. Ḥamza b. 'Alī, was a pupil of the above-mentioned Abū'l-Fatḥ Naṣr b. Ibrahīm. After the Turkish conquest, he seems to have moved to Baghdad, and from there to Khurāsān and then to Samarqand, where he died in AH 504, that is, AD 1110/1.[100]

[643–645] For a certain time, Muḥammad b. Muḥammad b. Aḥmad al-Naysābūrī, that is, of Naysābūr in Persia, lived in Tiberias. He wrote many books, but their names have not been preserved, apart from a book about names and nicknames, parts of which are preserved in manuscript. He died in Rabī' I AH 378 (July AD 988).[101] Another Tiberian was Abū Aḥmad 'Abdallah b. Bakr b. Muḥammad, who was an ascete (*zāhid*). He lived in Akwākh near Bāniyās. In his youth, he studied in Syria, Mecca and Baghdad. He died on 13 Rabī' I AH 399 (15 November AD 1008).[102]

Abū Muḥammad Hiyāj b. 'Ubayd b. al-Ḥusayn, also an ascete, lived in Ḥiṭṭīn. He moved to Mecca and died there during a struggle between the Sunnis and the Shiites in AH 472, that is, AD 1080. He died of the blows inflicted by the ruler of Mecca (undoubtedly on behalf of the Fatimids), Muḥammad b. Abī Hāshim.[103]

[646–650] In Ascalon at this time there was an important Muslim spiritual centre. It was said that Abū'l-Ḥasan 'Alī b. Faḍlān al-Jurjānī, of Samarqand, settled for a while in Ascalon and studied with Da'ūd b. Aḥmad.[104] At about the same time, we find Abū'l-Ḥusayn Muḥammad b. Aḥmad b. 'Abd al-Raḥmān al-Malaṭī, one of the Shāfi'ite leaders and a man of considerable knowledge of law, staying in Ascalon. He wrote many treatises in this field, as well as on theology and the teachings of the Koran. He died in AH 377, that is AD 987/8.[105] Of the following generation in Ascalon, Abū Muḥammad Ismā'īl b. Rajā' b. Sa'īd is mentioned, and it was said that he settled for a time in Sidon but returned to Palestine

98 Ibn 'Asākir, I, 449.

99 Ṣafadī, *al-Wāfī*, V, 57; his *kunya* apparently indicates that he had a son who was an astrologer.

100 Ibn Jawzī, *Muntaẓam* IX, 166f; Ibn al-Athīr, *Kāmil*, X, 484.

101 Ṣafadī, *al-Wāfī*, I, 115; Ibn al-Jawzī, *Muntaẓam*, VII, 146; Dhahabī, *Tadhkira*, 976–979; cf. Sezgin, I, 203f; and more references there.

102 Ibn 'Asākir, VII, 311; Yāqūt, *Buldān*, I, 344; al-Khaṭīb al-Baghdādī, *Ta'rīkh*, IX, 423; Ibn Jawzī, *Muntaẓam*, VII, 244f; Akwākh, see Le Strange, *Palestine*, 391.

103 Ibn al-'Imād, III, 342; Ibn Taghrī Bardī, V, 109; Ibn al-Jawzī, *Muntaẓam*, V, 326. The sources note, in mentioning Hiyāj and Ḥiṭṭīn, that the grave of Shu'ayb, father of Ṣippōra, Moses' wife, is found there.

104 Al-Sahmī, 278.

105 Jazarī, II, 67; Subkī, *Ṭabaqāt*, III, 77f; cf. Brockelmann, *GAL*, S I, 348; Sezgin, I, 607, who has more references, and details on his book against schismatics preserved in manuscript.

and died in Ramla in AH 423, that is AD 1032.[106] Abū 'Alī al-Ḥasan b. 'Abd al-Ṣamad b. Abī'l-Shiḥnā of Ascalon was one of the high Fatimid officials (he worked in the *dīwān al-inshā'*, the state secretariat, where official letters were written) and became famous for his letters (*rasā'il*) and his poetry. He was killed in AH 486, that is AD 1093.[107] Abū'l-Qāsim Thābit b. Aḥmad was a Baghdadian who settled in Ascalon and engaged in the collecting of traditions. Ibn 'Asākir confirms that he saw his book written, in his own handwriting, and its *ijāza* (permission to distribute it) at the beginning of Rabī' I AH 477, July AD 1084.[108]

[651–653] Gaza was evidently the centre of the Mālikite school during the period being described. There, Abū Bakr Muḥammad b. al-'Abbās b. Waṣīf was engaged in teaching Mālik's *Muwaṭṭa'*, as he had learned it from another Gazan, al-Ḥasan b. al-Faraj, who was also the teacher of Yaḥyā b. Bukayr. Abū Bakr Muḥammad died in AH 372, that is AD 982/3.[109] Another personality in Gaza many years later was Abū Isḥaq Ibrahīm b. Yaḥyā b. 'Uthmān, who was both a poet and a Shāfi'ī scholar. He was also a pupil of Naṣr b. Ibrahīm, in Damascus, beginning in the year AH 481, that is, AD 1088, when he was forty. It seems that he did not return to Gaza afterwards but moved to Baghdad, where he taught in the *madrasa al-niẓāmiyya* for many years. Towards the end of his life he lived in Khurāsān, and he died there in 1130.[110]

A well-known poet in his day, Abū 'Abdallah Muḥammad b. Naṣr b. Ṣaghīr b. Khālid al-Makhzūmī, who was called Muhadhdhib al-Dīn, or 'Uddat al-Dīn, or Sharaf al-Dīn, and also known by the name Ibn al-Qayṣarānī, was born in Acre in AH 478, that is AD 1085/6, and grew up in Caesarea. He later moved to Damascus and from there to Aleppo, where he was in charge of the local library (*khizānat al-kutub*). He died in AH 548, that is AD 1153/4. He was the most important Syrian poet of his day.[111]

[654–660] During this time, we encounter a number of Muslim spiritual leaders in Tyre. Among them we find Aḥmad b. 'Aṭā' b. Aḥmad b. Muḥammad b. 'Aṭā' al-Rūdhbādī, one of the Ṣūfī leaders. According to Ibn al-Athīr, he came from Baghdad and at first lived in the neighbourhood of Acre. He died in Tyre in Dhū'l-Ḥijja AH 369 (July AD 980).[112] Three generations later, we find another Baghdadian who settled

[106] Ibn 'Asākir, III, 19.
[107] Ibn Muyassar, 29.
[108] Ibn 'Asākir, III, 362.
[109] Ibn al-'Imād, III, 79.
[110] Ibn Khallikān, I, 57–62; Brockelmann, *GAL*, G I, 253.
[111] Ṣafadī, *al-Wāfī*, V, 112; Ibn Khallikān, IV, 458; Dhahabī, *Tadhkira*, 1313; cf. Brockelmann, *GAL*, S I, 455; see the article Ibn al-Ḳaysarānī (by J. Schacht, No. 2) in *EI²*.
[112] Ibn al-Athīr, *Kāmil*, VIII, 710; Dhahabī, *'Ibar*, II, 350; Ibn al-Jawzī, *Muntaẓam*, VII, 101; Ṣafadī, *al-Wāfī*, VII, 184. Cf. Sezgin, I, 663, and further references and details there on some of his books that have been preserved in manuscript.

in Tyre; he was Abū'l-Faraj 'Abd al-Wahhāb b. Ḥusayn b. Burhān al-Ghazzāl (the spinner). He died in Tyre in Shawwāl AH 447 (December AD 1055). Al-Khaṭīb al-Baghdādī, on returning from a pilgrimage to Mecca, met him in Tyre.[113] Muḥammad b. 'Alī al-Karājikī (from Karājik, near Wāsiṭ, in Iraq) was a Shiite leader and a grammarian, a linguist, an astrologer, a physician and a theological scholar (*mutakallim*), who wrote many books. He died in Tyre on Rabī' I AH 449 (May AD 1057).[114] In the latter half of the eleventh century, we find one of the central figures of the Ṣūfī movement, Abū 'Abdallah Muḥammad b. Muḥammad b. Muḥammad al-Ṭāliqānī, a scholar and poet. He died in AH 466, that is AD 1073/4.[115]

Abu Ṭāhir Ibrahīm b. Muḥammad b. 'Abd al-Razzāq, who is described as 'one of the men of the Haifa citadel (*qaṣr*)', lived and worked in Haifa. He studied in Tripoli; in the year AH 486, that is AD 1093, he was teaching in Tyre.[116] Among the collectors of traditions, one must also mention a man of Bāniyās, Abū 'Alī Jamīl b. Yūsuf b. Ismā'īl al-Mārdānī. He came to Damascus in AH 456, that is AD 1064, and studied *ḥadīth* there. He died in AH 484 (AD 1091).[117] Another man from Bāniyās and contemporary, Ṣamdūn b. Ḥusayn, of a family which stemmed from Tyre, also engaged in the study of ḥadīth. He died in Bāniyās in AH 491, that is AD 1098.[118]

113 Dhahabī, *'Ibar*, III, 214; al-Khaṭīb al-Baghdādī, *Ta'rīkh*, XI, 34.
114 Dhahabī, *'Ibar*, 220; *idem, Tadhkira*, 1127; Ṣafadī, *al-Wāfī*, IV, 130.
115 Ṣafadī, *al-Wāfī*, I, 273.
116 Ibn 'Asākir, II, 286; Sam'ānī, IV, 332, see n. 2 of the editor; Yāqūt, *Buldān*, II, 381; Khālidī, 72.
117 Ibn 'Asākir, III, 406.
118 Ibn 'Asākir, VI, 446.

7
THE CHRISTIANS

The Christian leadership after the conquest

[661] When Christianity had triumphed and become the official religion of the Byzantine empire, it gradually lost something of its vitality and its potential for spiritual influence, becoming part of the imperial establishment. At the same time, especially at the outset of the fourth century, a process of schism and fragmentation was emerging and intensifying. In the East, the school of Antioch, in which a rich tradition of commentaries on the Holy Books had developed, predominated. Born out of these exegetical traditions was the excessive stress on Jesus the man, but without a complete discrediting of his divinity. He was seen to possess two separate natures (*physeis*), human and divine. When this concept spread among the masses, its format was narrowed to the claim that Jesus had only the human nature. On the other hand, in the West, the school of Alexandria emerged, with the claim that Jesus had but the divine nature, and that he was the embodiment of God the Father, and in essence, his equal. It was in this school that the term Theōtokos, mother of God, originated (with the emphasis on being the mother of no ordinary mortal) as the definition of Mary. In 428, Nestorius, a monk from the region of Antioch, was appointed patriarch of Constantinople. He and his circle began to conduct energetic propaganda against the idea of 'the mother of God' and in favour of the principles of the school of Antioch. At the council of the Church at Ephesus in 431, Cyril, the bishop of Alexandria, succeeded in uniting round him many of the bishops who objected to Nestorius' views, while the latter and his followers (mainly Syrians) organised themselves into a separate council, and this marked the beginning of the schism and the mutual ostracism. Finally, Cyril gained the ascendancy and Nestorius and his disciples turned eastward to Persia, setting up a separate Church, independent of Constantinople. The majority of Christians within the Persian state followed suit, and even after the Muslim conquest, the Nestorian creed remained the dominant one in the East. The head of the Nestorians, the Catholicos, established his seat in

Baghdad after the Abbasid revolution, and the Abbasid caliphs saw in him the representative of all the Christians in the caliphate. Cyril, on the other hand, continued to be based in Alexandria, until his death in 444. Thereafter, a number of extremist trends emerged in Alexandria around the new doctrine, according to which the two natures of Jesus, the human and the divine, became solely one of divinity at the time of his *incarnatio*. This view, which was called Monophysitism, provoked the opposition of both the patriarch of Constantinople and the pope in Rome, Leo I. In 450, the emperor Theodosius II died and his successor Marcian (who was his brother-in-law, his sister's husband), convoked a Church Council in Chalcedon in 451, where he succeeded in prevailing over the Monophysites, who were declared heretics. In Chalcedon, they formulated the creed of Jesus' two natures, which are whole and cannot be divided, though separate. The Christian masses in Syria, Palestine and Egypt remained loyal to the Monophysite creed in the main, and left the official Byzantine Church. The new heresy became the focal point for all the economic, social and political dissatisfaction with the bureaucratic ways of the empire. In 482 the emperor Zeno ('the Isaurian', that is from the region of Seleucia, the south-eastern corner of Anatolia, who reigned from 474–494) issued a decree known as the *henotikon*, the decree of unity. This was an attempt to resolve the problem and reunite the Church by avoiding any mention of such concepts as 'one nature' or 'double nature'. It soon became obvious that a compromise was impossible and the schism became even deeper. At that time, Jerusalem was the centre of fanatical Monophysitism and the followers of Severus, leader of the opposition to the *henotikon*, during the years 507–511, who was a Palestinian himself, dominated the scene. The Pope in Rome also vehemently opposed the *henotikon* and banned the emperor. The result was that relations between Rome and Constantinople were severed for thirty years. This was the beginning of the split between the 'Latins' and the 'Greeks'. From then on, Christianity was divided into three factions: the Nestorians (who are today known as the 'Assyrians'), the Monophysites and the Diophysites. The latter were the orthodox and at their head stood the emperor and the patriarch of Constantinople. In the East they had comparatively few followers, and they were known as 'people of the king's church', the Melekites. At that time, there was a continuous rift within this mainstream between the centre in Constantinople and the pope in Rome, though they finally separated only in 1054. As to the Monophysites, in Syria and Palestine they organised themselves in a separate Church called the Jacobites, after Ya'qūb bar Ada, the first Monophysite bishop to be recognised by the emperor (Justinian, 542); while in Egypt, where most of the Christian population supported Monophysitism, the Monophysite Coptic Church was established, as opposed to the Melekite-Greek Church.

During the Byzantine era, Jerusalem was a focal point for stormy quarrels over the various religious views. There was a centre of the followers of Origenes, who believed in the pre-existence of souls, including that of Jesus. Here, too, Epiphanius and Hieronymus fought against John, bishop of Jerusalem (389–415) over the fact that he did not denounce the followers of Origenes. At the very same time, another schismatic movement concentrated in Jerusalem, that of Pelagius of Rome, who held the extremist view based on the principle of freedom of will and personal responsibility. Furthermore, there were in Jerusalem the followers of Severus the Monophysite whom I have already mentioned. One should bear in mind that the bishop of Jerusalem always occupied a special status and position of influence within the Church, which was considerably strengthened during bishop Juvenal's day (422–458). At first, Juvenal was one of the supporters of Cyril, the patriarch of Alexandria, and backed him at the Council of Ephesus, but at the Council of Chalcedon, he reneged and joined the emperor in his opposition to the Monophysites. The immediate result of this stand was the further enhancement of his status in the hierarchy of the Church. From then on, he controlled the three chief bishops (metropolitans) of Palestine: of Caesarea, Bet Shean and Petra, and was given the rank of patriarch, on a par with the patriarch of Antioch. The patriarchate in Jerusalem can then be reckoned as starting from 451.

Sophronius, the patriarch of Jerusalem at the time of the Muslim conquest, was the representative of extreme orthodox religiosity, the keen opponent of a new formula of the *henotikon*, the doctrine of Monotheletism, which emperor Heraclius hoped to instil. This creed quietly ignored the problematic subject of Jesus' natures, and spoke of God's unity of will and action (hence its name). Here again the intention was clearly to reunite the church.[1]

[662] It should be noted that at the time of the Muslim conquest, the Christians in Palestine were only one decade away from the terrible distress brought on by the Persian conquest, which caused enormous loss of life and property to the ecclesiastic system. Many captives from among the clergy and the monks were taken to Persia; only a small remnant returned after the final victory over the Persians, bringing with them the Holy Cross. Towards the end of their reign in Palestine, however, the

[1] See: Pargoire, *L'église byzantine*, 34, 222f; Couret, *La Palestine*, 9f, 152ff; Vasiliev, *History*, I, 107ff; Hotzelt, *ZDPV*, 66 (1943), 79; Mas'ūdī, *Murūj*, III, 407, notes that at first there was no patriarch in Jerusalem, only a bishop in charge of Christian affairs in the district of Lydda and in Jerusalem.

Persians modified their attitude to the Christians, and I have already mentioned the part played by Modestus, the patriarch's locum tenens, in the restoration of the Church of the Holy Sepulchre. As we have already seen, Sophronius did not last long after the conquest and his death was followed by days of anarchy and desolation in the Jerusalem patriarchate, and the patriarchal seat remained unoccupied for some sixty years. Nevertheless the churches and monasteries of Jerusalem withstood the times, evidently mainly due to 'Umar's policy to avoid any offence to churches and monasteries in Jerusalem, a policy which was explicitly expressed in the agreement he contracted with the inhabitants of Jerusalem.[2]

[663] Sources on the connections between Byzantium and Jerusalem at that time have not been preserved (and there may have been complete disruption due to the continual warfare between the Muslims and the Byzantines). As against this, sources on the connection between Rome and Jerusalem have been preserved and Catholic scholars emphasise this fact, in which they see evidence of the priority of Rome over Constantinople. These sources are the letters of Pope Martin I (649–653) to John, bishop of 'Ammān (Philadelphia), to Theodore, bishop of Heshbon (Esbonitorum), to Antoninus, bishop of Baq'a [?] (Bacathorum), and to George, the archimandrite of the Monastery of St Theodosius. The latter three are asked to obey John, bishop of Philadelphia. According to a source mentioned by Dositheos (patriarch of Jerusalem, 1669–1707), it was Sergius who became patriarch after Sophronius, but he was not accepted by the monks and they sent Stephen, bishop of Dor, to Rome and the Pope dismissed Sergius. However, as Dositheos points out, this account is false, because the aforementioned Sergius was never patriarch at all, but was the bishop of Jaffa. Indeed, Pope Martin's letter states that it was Stephen, bishop of Dor and his people, that is, the monks of the Monastery of St Theodosius, who recommended the appointment of John, bishop of 'Ammān, as his representative (*vicarius*) in the East, granting him the authority to appoint bishops and other ecclesiastic offices in the regions within the jurisdiction of Jerusalem and Antioch. This appointment of John as bishop of 'Ammān was intended to counteract the appointments of 'the pseudo-bishop', Macedonius, and of Petrus, who were appointed on behalf of 'the heretics of the Church of Alexandria'. In another letter, the Pope even castigates a certain Pantaleon who spread slander about that Stephen, bishop of Dor. It seems that basically what is

[2] See: Le Quien, *Oriens Christianus*, III, 131. Although there are Muslim traditions according to which 'Umar prayed in the church of St Mary and in this fashion, sanctified it for Islam, the church of St Mary definitely maintained its status, as can be seen from the Christian sources. See the Muslim sources collected by Caetani, III (1), 937; cf. the discussion: Dressaire, *EO*, 15(1912), 237.

being dealt with here is still Pope Martin's struggle against Monotheletism; an appeal to him from John, abbot of the monastery Mar Saba and others in the monastery, has been preserved, in which they request that the Lateran Council (649) take action against Monotheletism. With regard to the period after the conquest, when the relationship between Islam and Byzantium and its partisans, people of the Church in Jerusalem, was at its most tense, it is reasonable to assume that the clergy in Palestine could more easily maintain ties with Rome. Apparently, Pope Martin I even tried to establish direct contact with the Muslims and indeed, such accusations were made against him in Constantinople, but he managed to explain away his actions and to free himself of all suspicion, by claiming, so he said, that his only motive was to send donations to Jerusalem.[3]

[664] Arculf, the Christian traveller who visited Jerusalem in around 670, finds little to tell of the life of the Christians and the Church there, and merely describes the holy places and a miracle concerning Jesus' shawl, as told to him by the people of Jerusalem. This shawl, they said, was stolen by a Jew from Jesus' grave and bequeathed to his descendants, who by virtue of this memento, acquired great wealth and property. Until in Caliph Mu'āwiya's day, three years before Arculf's visit, the shawl was discovered with the help of some Jewish 'believers' (that is, Jewish converts to Christianity). Both parties, the Jews and the Christians, appealed to the caliph to judge between them, and he agreed to do so. He ordered that the shawl be thrown into the fire, but the fire naturally did not consume it and it floated in the wind until it finally alighted on the side of the Christians. Some see in this story evidence of the atmosphere prevailing

[3] It is not clear from what they write about the church of St Mary whether the Muslim sources mean the church in the Kidron Valley or the Nea or the Church of the Resurrection. See: Mansi, X, 805–814, 909; Dositheos (see on him: *DTC*, IV, 1788–1800) in Papadopoulos-Kerameos, *Analekta*, I, 240f; he quotes this account from Anastasius Bibliothecarius, but we do not find it in his chronicle (based mainly on Theophanes' chronicle). See the letters of Martin I: Jaffé, *Regesta*, I, 231 (Nos. 2064–2070); cf. Pargoire, *L'église*, 154; Vailhé, *EO*, 3(1899–1900), 20, who tries to straighten the matter out; according to his description, it is Sergius, the bishop of Jaffa, who headed the Church in Palestine at first, and was considered a heretic by Pope Theodore I, who proclaimed Stephen of Dor patriarch, while Martin I, his successor, placed the management of the affairs of the Church in Palestine in the hands of John of 'Ammān and his aides, among them Theodore of Heshbon and Antoninus of Baccatha. In the sources, however, these things are far from being that clear. Another link between Martin I and Palestinian people is mentioned in the year 652, when 'slaves of God' who came from the Holy Land, visited him and asked for donations; see Mansi, X, 240, 395, cf. Riant, *AOL*, I, 28; see further on Stephen of Dor, John bishop of Philadelphia, etc.: Amann, *DTC*, VIII, 1000. On relations with the Muslims, see Martin's letter XIV, in *MPL* 87; the letter begins on p. 197 and the account of the Muslims (*Sarracenoi*) is on p. 199; cf. Runciman, *Pilgrimages* (he has mistakenly, letter XV).

among the Christians of Jerusalem at the time – an atmosphere steeped in superstition, giving credence to miracles and the supernatural.[4]

Christendom in Jerusalem

[665] In 638, at the time of the Muslim conquest, Jerusalem was entirely a city of Christendom, and all its inhabitants were Christians. The city was full of churches and monasteries. Arculf, who as I have mentioned, visited Jerusalem around a generation after the conquest, described its holy places but his description is undoubtedly incomplete. Pride of place is naturally given to the Church of the Holy Sepulchre. According to him, it was in the form of a circle (commonly called the *rotunda*) surrounded by three walls; this is the *Anastasis*, that is, the resurrection. The church was supported by twelve columns. Along the central wall stood three altars. Close by the Church of the Holy Sepulchre, to the south, was the Church of St Mary, which was square in format. We know that this Church of St Mary belonged to the monastery of the Spoudaei (monks of a monastery in Constantinople, the Spoudaion, or perhaps they were so-called because of the literal meaning of the word – 'the alert') which was above the Anastasis (Church of the Resurrection), and Arculf is not very precise in this matter. On the eastern side stood the Church of the Golgotha (Latin: *calvaria*; Greek: *kranion*) where Arculf was particularly impressed by the lighting fixture: a copper wheel with lamps, suspended by ropes, and beneath it a large silver cross indicating the place where the original wooden cross formerly stood.

Moving eastward, past the Church of the Golgotha (the Calvary), stood Constantine's church, the *martyrium*, where (in the days of Helena, Constantine's mother) the holy cross was discovered together with the two crosses 'of the criminals'. Between the two, the Calvary and the Martyrium, stood 'Abraham's Altar' where a large wooden table stood on which charitable donations were placed. Some two generations after Arculf, the place was described by Willibald, who restricts himself, however, to depicting only the Sepulchre on which a large square stone in the form of a pyramid rested, with fifteen vessels containing oil to keep the lighting continuously aglow. The original stone which the angel rolled off the opening of the grave at the time of Jesus' resurrection was also kept there. At the beginning of his account in around 870, the monk Bernard speaks of four churches but he only describes three: the one named for Constantine in the east, the other in the south and one in the west; the

[4] See Tobler et Molinier, I, 155, and see there, 219, the account of Beda, on the same matter; see the Hebrew version in Ish-Shalom, *Masse'ē nōṣerīm*, 221f; Baumstarck, *Palästinapilger*, 47; see *ibid.*, 80, on the considerable spiritual influence of Christian Jerusalem at that time, which can be seen from the Church poetry and ritual.

sepulchre is situated in the western church, and it is surrounded by nine columns which are connected by walls built of excellent stone. In early Arab sources, the Golgotha is called by its Greek name *kranion*, *al-aqrāniyūn*, but also *juljulta* at times. According to al-Muṭahhar al-Maqdisī, the grave of Ādin b. Zechariah was also situated there, and we do not know who is being referred to.[5]

[666] Apart from the buildings around the Holy Sepulchre, we can divide those churches of which we have actual knowledge into the following groups: (1) the Mount of Olives, (2) the Kidron Valley (which is the Valley of Jehoshaphat in the Christian sources, the southern part of which is sometimes called the Valley of St Jacob), (3) east of the Cardo, which was the main artery (north–south) of Jerusalem at that time (although the name is not to be found in the sources of the period under discussion; during the Crusaders' era, it was called the Street of St Stephen), (4) west of the Cardo, (5) south of the city, and (6) outside the walls.

Two churches stood in the area of the Mount of Olives, according to Willibald. One was the church where Jesus spoke to his pupils before his crucifixion, which is the Church of the Sermon, or the Church of the Mount of Olives, the Eleona (from *Elaiōn*, of [the Mount of] Olives). Constantine's mother, Helena, is credited with its construction. This church stood above the cave mentioned by Arculf, where it is said that Jesus met with his pupils. Arculf does not refer to the church, merely to the cave, and it is possible that the church stood in ruins in his day. The place is also mentioned (with no reference to the church) by the monk Bernard. In Milik's opinion, this is the church of which remains were recently discovered near the *Dominus flevit* of our time. The other church mentioned by Willibald is the Church of the Ascension. This church was built in 378, and restored by the monk Modestus after the Perisan conquest in 614. An

[5] From here onward, the description of the churches in Jerusalem is based mainly on the accounts of Arculf, Willibald, Beda, on *De casis Dei* and the monk Bernard, which can all be found in Tobler et Molinier, I, 157–159, 221, 264–268, 301f, 315; on the surveys of Abel in *DACL*, VII, 2318ff, 2351; see the map there, after p. 3336; on the survey of Milik in *RB*, 67(1960), 358–367, 550–556, and in *MUSJ*, 37 (1961), 145–151, and there will be no further detailed references to these sources, which are convenient for the use of the reader. Beda generally repeats what Arculf has said. Pétridès, *EO*, 4(1900–1901), 227f, deals with the question of the Spoudaei and tries to prove that they were Byzantine monks, connected with the monastery in Constantinople, known since the fifth century; they lived near the Church of the Holy Sepulchre. In his opinion, the monastery *Panagia megalē*, which stood to the south-west of the Church of the Holy Sepulchre, belonged to them. *Aqrāniyūn*: see Sa'īd ibn Biṭrīq, I, 135; Maqdisī, *Bad'*, IV, 88. See also the survey of Leclercq in *DTC*, XV, 517–538; see the discussion on Arculf's description: Mommert, *ZDPV*, 20:34, 1897; and in contrast: Clermont-Ganneau, *Receuil*, II, 250f; see the sources and the discussion: Vincent et Abel, *Jérusalem*, II, 218–247, and the survey on the Church of the Holy Sepulchre: Macpherson, *EHR*, 7(1892), 669–671; see on the theological significance of the buildings: Linder, in *Perāqīm*, 13. See the discussion on the matters of architecture in the Church of the Holy Sepulchre and its development in Coüasnon, *The Church of the Holy Sepulchre*.

inscription was found there commemorating the work of restoration. *De casis Dei* refers to a third church on the Mount of Olives, in the name of St Mary, but apparently the reference is to the church in the Kidron Valley. According to the same source, there were also monks' cells on the mount, inhabited by eleven Greek (that is, Byzantine) psalmists, four Georgians, six Syrians (that is, Aramaic speakers), two Armenians, five Latins and one Arab. Near the steps of the Mount of Olives, there were, according to him, two solitary monks, one a Syrian and the other a Greek, and another three living near the Gethsemane (on the northern slope of the Kidron valley): a Greek, a Syrian and a Georgian, and another in the Valley of Jehoshaphat. In the area of the Mount of Olives, there is also mention of the 'Monastery of the Virgins' which was perhaps in the Kidron Valley as well, where twenty-six nuns lived. It seems that the monks on the Mount of Olives became well known. In the chronicle of Eginhard, Dominicus, 'the monk from the Mount of Olives' is mentioned (in the year 826).[6]

[667] In the Kidron Valley, one should mention firstly the ('temporal') grave of St Mary. A round, two-story structure stood on the grave, according to Arculf. On the upper story, there were four altars. Close to this building, to the south, was the Church of the Gethsemane, which Arculf does not mention; he speaks only of the vicinity of the Gethsemane. Indeed, according to the evidence of Sa'īd ibn Biṭrīq, the Church of the Gethsemane was destroyed during the Persian conquest and was never rebuilt. According to sources quoted by Milik, the 'Cave of the Betrayal' was arranged to be used as a place of prayer, and according to present-day archaeological exploration, it was still considered a sacred place in the early Arab period. Willibald mentions the Church of St Mary in the Kidron Valley, as does the monk Bernard, who says that it was 'a church in honour of St Mary, and it had a library (established) with the help of the emperor (Charlemagne), with twelve compounds, fields, vineyards and a plantation – in the Valley of Jehoshaphat'. This has generally been interpreted as meaning that in the Valley of Jehoshaphat there were estates donated by Charlemagne to another church in the name of St Mary, which was allegedly built in the 'Latin' quarter, south of the Church of the Holy Sepulchre, but it is more likely that Bernard is speaking here of that same church in the Kidron Valley.

Other churches stood in the Kidron Valley: the church in the name of St Leontius, which was near St Mary's grave and the church of the Gethsemane, the church of the Forty Saints (the *Quaranta* [the saints of Sebas-

[6] See on the Eleona: Garitte, *Le Muséon*, 73 (1960), 127f; it was also called *tōn mathētōn*, the church of the pupils, and seems to have been the burial place of the patriarchs of Jerusalem. See: Einhardi *annales*, 214. The Russian traveller, the abbot Daniel, who visited Jerusalem in 1106, also describes the Church of the Ascension (see Daniel, 25).

tia]), and nearby, an Armenian monastery (Monophysite) also called after them. Two other buildings stood there, called after St Christopher and St Aquilina. This group of churches in the northern part of the Kidron Valley is mentioned also by the anonymous guide from the Geniza: 'the churches built by Solomon, to study the teachings of the Ammonites and the Moabites'. According to him, this place was in the vicinity of the Valley of Hinnom (Gehinnom); according to what has been preserved of his description, the churches stood on both sides of the road leading up to the Mount of Olives, and it is interesting that Mas'ūdī, writing about a century before this guide, in the first half of the tenth century, also attributes the construction of some of the Christian churches in Jerusalem to King Solomon.[7]

[668] A subject which merits a study of its own is that of the buildings in the southern part of the Kidron Valley. In Antiochus Eustratius' description of the massacre of the Christians in Jerusalem at the time of the Persian conquest, the 'Church of the Samaritan Woman' is mentioned as being nearby the site where 723 Christians were slaughtered. From this description, written originally in Greek, versions have been preserved in Arabic and Georgian. In the Arabic version, we read: *wa-min ḥārat smrtq' sab'ami'a thalātha wa-'ishrīn*, and another version: *min quddām kanīsat al-sāmira* ('opposite the Church of the Samaritan woman'). The Georgian version speaks of 'the church of the Samaritan woman'. Apparently in the original version, it said 'the quarter of the church named after the Samaritan woman' and its above-mentioned name in Arabic is also found in the Geniza documents and in Karaite sources, due to the fact that afterwards it was in that area that the Karaites established their quarter: *smrtq'*, and this is none other than the Greek-Byzantine name *Samareitikē* (the Samaritan woman) and should be vocalised accordingly. Here we must make use of a later source, al-Harawī's book on the holy places, written at the beginning of the thirteenth century. He says: *wa-bi'l-quds kanīsat al-ya'āqiba bihā*

[7] See the 'guide of Palestine': **2**, I, b, lines 3–7; Mas'ūdī, *Murūj*, I, 111, counts among the churches, the *al-Jismāniyya* (in addition to the Church of the Holy Sepulchre and the Church of Zion). Barbier de Meynard, editor and translator of the book, translated *l'Incarnation*, according to the assumed literal meaning of the Arabic word (from *jism*, body); however a church by this name is unknown in Jerusalem; this name (found in other sources as well), *al-Jismāniyya*, is evidently merely a distortion of Gethsemane. According to Mas'ūdī, it contained the grave of King David. As to the church of St Mary, one may assume that it was destroyed at the time of al-Ḥākim's decrees. Riant claims that it was restored before the Crusades; he based this claim on a document preserved by the Benedictines and according to which Hugo, abbot of the Benedictine monastery during the latter half of the eleventh century, sent certain relics to Simon Crispiacensis (who is Simon d'Amiens et Crépy), when he was 'abbot of (the monastery of) the grave of the Holy Virgin Mary in (the Valley) of Jehoshaphat'; White, *Speculum*, 9:404, 1934, has already proven that the document is forged, and was intended to explain (in 1740) the existence of relics in the monastery of St Arnulf in Crépy.

bi'r yuqāl an al-masīḥ ightasal minhā wa-āmanat al-sāmira 'ala yadihi 'indahā wa-yazūrūnhā ('and in Jerusalem there is the church of "the Jacobs" containing a well in which they say the Messiah is supposed to have washed and alongside which the Samaritan woman received her creed [and the Christians] visit it and believe in it'). It is clear here that this is a reference to the Samaritan woman whose meeting with Jesus is described in the Gospel according to John, ch. iv. Although it says there that the meeting took place in Sykhar in Samaria (there are various suggestions as to the identity of the place, but who can say anything definite about it?), the fact is that her memory was immortalised in Jerusalem. Thus, this church was named both after the 'Samaritan woman's well' within its confines and after 'the Jacobs'. It is not the Jacobites who are meant but rather the two Jacobs, one the brother of Jesus (the younger, the son of Alphaeus), and the other, Jacob the Apostle (son of Zebedee). *De casis Dei* mentions a church in the name of St Jacob, in the Jehoshaphat Valley. 'The Guide to Palestine' of the Geniza reinforces our awareness of the fact that this church was indeed situated in the Kidron Valley, for it explicitly states that the church of Jacob, brother of the Messiah (*kanīsat ya'qūb akhū'l-masīḥ*) is situated above one of the monuments in the Kidron Valley. According to its description, the famous structure, the 'Tomb of the Benē Ḥezīr' is meant. John of Würzburg also mentions the building (in around 1165) when speaking of the remains of the grave of Jacob son of Alphaeus, as does another source from the year 1320, Franciscus Pipinus: there Jacob son of Zebedee was executed on Herod's orders and on that place there is a small domed building and an altar. The three buildings in the Kidron Valley are mentioned by Arculf: the tower of Jehoshaphat, which is evidently Absalom's Tomb; the tombs of St Simeon and St Joseph, which are evidently the 'tomb of Benē Ḥezīr'; and the tomb of Zechariah. A Christian source prior to the Muslim conquest, Theodore (or Theodosius), speaks (in around 600) of St Jacob, St Zechariah and St Simeon, who were buried in one grave (*Sanctus Jacobus et sanctus Zacharias et sanctus Simeon in una memoria positi sunt*). Jewish popular tradition was more unequivocal and generally ascribed the building known today by this name to Zechariah (Zechariah the priest, who was stoned by command of King Joash, 2 Chr., xxiv:20–21). However, 'the guide of Palestine' of the Geniza assigns it to Ornan the Jebusite and also mentions the cave to which it is connected. This derives from the proximity of the place to the 'city of David', which was once the city of the Jebusites.[8]

[8] See Antiochus' story, MS Bibliothèque nationale, Paris, No. 262, in the Arabic collection, edited by Couret, *ROC* 2(1897), 153; see the translation *ibid.*, 163 (by J. Broydé). Cf. Clermont-Ganneau, *PEFQ*(1898), 44; see the matter of the Georgian versions: Conybeare, *EHR*, 25:502, 1910; Peeters, *Tréfonds*, 210; see also Vincent et Abel, *Jérusalem* II (2), 928 (they interpret: 'the synagogue [!] of the Samaritans'); as to the Arabic version, I proposed

[669] *De casis Dei* also speaks of the church in the name of Cyriacus, which is also mentioned in the aforementioned tract of Antiochus Eustratius, on the massacre during the Persian conquest. There was evidently also a wadi called after Cyriacus, and this church was situated in the village of Yason and called by its full name after the Saints Cyriacus and Julitta. Milik identifies the place with the Wadi Yaṣūl at the southern corner of the Mount of Olives, approximately one kilometre south of the Kidron Valley. The church of St John is also mentioned, which according to Abel was in this region, although in Milik's opinion, it was situated outside the city wall, at the foot of the Mount of Olives. This is confirmed by what is said in *De casis Dei* and also by the monk Bernard.

East of the Cardo, that is, between the Cardo and the Temple Mount, we find three churches in the period we are dealing with: the Church of St Mary *in probatica*, that is, alongside the Sheep Pool and the Sheep Gate (called *bāb al-asbāṭ* [of the tribes], St Stephen's Gate, today the Lions' Gate) to the north-east of the city (where Mary is said to have been born, and where the house of Anne and Jehoiakim was also shown); the church of Cosmas mentioned in *De casis Dei* (although Milik assumes it to have been outside the city wall); the church of St Sophia, which is said to have stood on the site of the Praetorium, or 'house of Pontius Pilate', between the Holy Sepulchre and the Probatica mentioned above. Apparently it was a ruin during the period under discussion.

West of the Cardo, that is between the Cardo and the western wall (apart from the buildings surrounding the Holy Sepulchre), mention is made of only two churches: the church of St Theodore, which it seems was west of the Holy Sepulchre, although there is some doubt about this, as shown by Milik; and the church of St Sergius, which was contiguous with the north-eastern side of the Church of the Holy Sepulchre.

In the south of the city, there were two famous churches. One, the church of Zion, stood according to Willibald 'in the middle of Jerusalem'. It was said that it was on the site where Jesus' disciples wanted to bury his mother Mary, but the angels came and carried her off to heaven, to

the correct vocalised reading of *smrtq'* (Gil, *Shalem*, 2 [1975/6], 35), without knowing then that Milik, *MUSJ*, 37(1961), 136, had already proposed this reading; see the matter of the distorted readings in the two aforementioned references. However, Milik errs in placing the church 'of the Samaritan woman' in the neighbourhood of today's Armenian quarter; see al-Harawī, 27; see the French translation: Schefer, *AOL*, 1(1881), 604, who translates: l'église des Jacobites. 'The guide of Palestine', see **2**, I, a, lines 18–19; b, line 2. See the account of John of Würzburg: Tobler, *Palestinae Descriptiones*, 167; and the account of Franciscus Pipinus in Tobler, *Dritte Wanderung*, 405; on Zechariah's tomb see: Tobler, *Itinera*, 18, 66, 220f; *idem, Topogr.*, II, 269; Jeremias, *Heiligengräber*, 67ff; Slouschz, *Qoveṣ*, I (1925), 37; Tobler, *Palestinae Descriptiones*, 36, 113; *idem, Dritte Wanderung*, 345; see the detailed descriptions and discussions in Avigad, *Maṣṣēvōt*. The structures in the Kidron Valley are also mentioned in Nāṣir Khusraw, 21 (text), 69 (translation).

Paradise. According to the monk Bernard, the church was called after St Simeon. It was originally an ancient building, and in its attic (*hyperōon*), according to Epiphanius, the early Christians would congregate, and it was therefore also called the Church of the Cenaculum, and thought to be the first church. The other was 'the new church in the name of St Mary', which is the Nea. According to Procopius and Cyril of Scythopolis, it was built on the emperor Justinian's orders and inaugurated on 20 November 543. Procopius describes the unusual building process, as it had very large proportions and the builders wished to achieve the greatest possible height, and they therefore built it partly on the ground and partly on a special subterranean structure put up for this purpose. He especially noted the extremely unusual columns of its façade, made of red stone. Of the Latin Christian sources of this period, only *De casis Dei* mentions it, noting that twelve churchmen resided there. The fact that the writings of Latin travellers of the time say nothing about this church, confirms the evidence of Sa'īd ibn Biṭrīq that the Nea remained a ruin ever since the Persian conquest. At the end of the ninth century, the Karaite Daniel al-Qūmisī mentions the Nea in his commentary on Daniel, xi: 31–32 (and arms shall stand . . . and they shall place the abomination that maketh desolate . . . but the people . . . shall be strong . . .): 'after him strong people from among his nation [of the King of the South, who is the Byzantine emperor] . . . and they will lay . . . the church of the Niyya desolate'. It appears, however, that he intended to say that it was the Ishmaelites who destroyed the Nea ('laid it desolate') and this contradicts what was said above and also what is said by Sa'īd ibn Biṭrīq, that the Persians were responsible for destroying the Nea and the church of the Gethsemane (*al-jismāniyya*), and they are in ruins 'until this very day' (beginning of the tenth century). In around 985, Muqaddasī lists the Nea Gate (*bāb al-niyya*) among the gates of Jerusalem and Yāqūt copied this from him. Views on the exact site of the Nea were undecided, and there was a supposition that it stood on the Temple Mount, on the spot where the Muslims built al-Aqṣā; but in 1869, Couret disproved this opinion. One must also mention in this area the church in the name of St Thaleleus, which was evidently near the Church of Zion, and is mentioned in *De casis Dei*; the church in the name of St George, in the same area apparently; the tomb of St Stephen; and the church of St Peter.[9]

[670] There were other churches outside the city wall: the church of St

[9] See: Epiphanius, De mensuribus et ponderibus, *MPG* 43, 261; Couret, *La Palest.*, 23; Procopius, *De aedificiis*, V, 6 (Loeb VII, 342–348); Kyrillos Scythop. (ed. Schwartz), 175–178, 216; Daniel al-Qūmisī, see TS 10 C 2, ed. Mann, *JQR*, NS 12(1922), 518, misprinted there: TS 10 G 2; Mann did not realise that *al-Niyya* means the Nea, and suggested to correct it as: the church of al-Yūnāniyya (the Greek church), and assumed that the Church of the Holy Sepulchre was being spoken of. Cf. also Ben-Shammai, *Shalem*,

Stephen, in the north; the church of St Mamilla (so it is written in *De casis Dei*), undoubtedly in the neighbourhood of the pool mentioned in the story of Antiochus Eustratius (and also in other church sources and in Sa'īd ibn Biṭrīq) as the place where most of the massacre of Christians took place at the time of the Persian conquest. A church named for Dometius (in *De casis Dei*) about which we have no further information, and in *De casis Dei* as well as Willibald, the church of the Holy Cross, which stood on the spot where the cross was found in the days of Helena, Constantine's mother. In that church, it was said, Jesus' shawl was kept, to which the legend mentioned above referred. It appears that this church (in the Valley of the Cross) was destroyed during al-Ḥākim's decrees, since we have been told of its rebuilding in 1038–1054 on the initiative of the king of Georgia, Bagrat the Fourth.[10]

[671] *De casis Dei* lists some thirty holy Christian buildings in Jerusalem, a very impressive number considering the fact that it reflects the situation after some 150 years of Muslim authority over the city. I have already discussed above the population of Jerusalem and the evidence that the Christians were the majority there. We have almost no information on the ties between the Jewish and the Christian populations in Jerusalem, apart from what has been said in former chapters on the rivalry between the two communities. In the Geniza letters there is almost no mention of the Christians. There are only a few facts about commercial ties with a Christian (*'ārēl*, or in Arabic – *naṣrānī*). The epigraphic finds on Christians in Jerusalem from that time are also very scarce indeed.[11]

Christianity in other Palestinian localities

[672] Whereas in the case of Jerusalem, there are a number of sufficiently detailed and reliable sources, especially those of the Christian travellers, on

3(1981), 303; see also *ibid.*, 305ff, a new revised version of this fragment. Muqaddasī, *Āqālīm*, 167, where in the main text we find: *al-tīh*, which was generally understood as 'the gate of the desert', but see there the version in the editor's note o (according to the MS of Istanbul), and also Yāqūt, *Buldān*, IV, 596, with the correct version; cf. on the reading of *al-niyya* also: Tsafrir, *IEJ*, 27(1977), 152. On the location of the Nea see: Couret, *La Palestine*, 181; but in 1905, Pargoire, *L'église*, 115, is still repeating that the Nea was built partly on the *esplanade* of the Temple. On the Nea in Antiochus Eustratius' list, see (apart from Milik): Clermont-Ganneau, *Receuil*, II, 150f; see further: Creswell, *Early Muslim Architecture*[2], 132; Avigad, *Qadmōniyōt*, x, 80, 1977, on the unearthing of the Nea in excavations a few years back. As to the Church of St George, Milik assumes that it was outside the wall, in the neighbourhood of Sheikh Badr (today the Qiryā). See also Sa'īd ibn Biṭriq, I, 216.

10 On the massacre in Mamilla, see Sa'īd ibn Biṭrīq, I, 216; on the rebuilding of the church of the Holy Cross, see: Richard, *Mél. Brunel*, 424.

11 See the inscription on the tombstone: Sharon, *IEJ*, 23(1973), 217f; dated 8 July 1002; the fact that the buried person was a Christian Sharon determined by the opening phrase: 'in the name of the Living One, who shall not die'.

few other places in Palestine is there much in the way of information concerning the Christian populations and churches. One must bear in mind that the Christian population was mostly rural, while the Jews constituted the majority of the population in the towns. Some facts concerning the Christians have already been brought up in the discussion on the population and localities in Palestine; in what follows, I shall fill in mainly what is known to us with regard to churches and monasteries and a number of Christian personalities whose memory has been preserved.

The most important monastery during this time was undoubtedly the Monastery of Mar Saba. During the seventh and eighth centuries, this monastery was a prominent centre of spiritual activities, with which the personality of John of Damascus was strongly involved. St Saba, after whom the monastery is called, was born in Caesarea of Cappadocia (Asia Minor) in 432. Although the monastery is named after him, he was not the founder, who was the Armenian Euthymius. In the seventh century, the first version of the story of Barlaam and Josaphat was written here by a monk named John (not John of Damascus, who came later), evidently after the story by a monk from India. The essence of the tale is that of the conversion to Christianity of an Indian prince, and it is a sort of paraphrase on the life of the young Buddha. It is possible that its author was John, abbot of the monastery, who was one of the first signatories to the petition to Pope Martin I on the subject of Monotheletism, which would be dealt with at the Council of Lateran. As to John of Damascus, he was a scion of that wealthy and aristocratic Christian Damascene family which collaborated with the Muslims, a son of Sergius b. Manṣūr, and he was in fact called Manṣūr. It seems that John joined the Monastery of Mar Saba in around 732, together with his adopted brother, Cosmas, who afterwards became bishop of Mayūmas, the port of Gaza, in 743. John of Damascus became known mainly as a fighter for the practice of image-worship and as such, aroused the wrath of the emperor Constantine V Copronymus (741–775), who called him *manzeros* (a bastard, on the basis of his Arabic name, Manṣūr). In 754, at the church council organised by the Iconoclasts, a ban was declared against him, and the version is that the Holy Trinity vanquished the three (John, the patriarch Germanus of Constantinople, and a certain Georgius of Cyprus, for the three were the leaders of the struggle against the 'image-breakers'). This may have been an indication that John had died that year. Another famous personality linked to the monastery of Mar Saba was Stephen, the 'miracle maker', the nephew of John of Damascus, who was also a monk of the monastery from the year 735. Theodore Abū Qurra, who afterwards became bishop of Haran, another ecclesiastic writer, was also a monk at the monastery. He lived from 740 to 820, approximately.

In what follows, we shall encounter the Monastery of Mar Saba in connection with persecution and brutality, in the main. In the mid-eleventh century, we hear about the monk Lazaros, of Magnesia in Caria on the river Meander in Asia Minor. He was a monk at the monastery on Mount Gelasion in that region. Afterwards he travelled to Palestine and joined the monastery of Mar Saba, remained there for six years and earned the esteem of the Jerusalem patriarch, who at first appointed him archdeacon and afterwards advanced him to the priesthood. He stayed for a while in Jerusalem but returned to Mar Saba and remained there 'until the city and the churches were pillaged during the rule of Azizes', meaning, of course, the decrees of al-Ḥākim, and he then decided to return to his own country.[12]

[673] Three churches stood on Mount Tabor according to Arculf. Shābushtī, *ca.* 1000, mentions only *dayr al-ṭūr*, the monastery of the Mount (Tabor), describing a small spring nearby, and stating that it stands atop the mountain, surrounded by vineyards. It was also called *dayr al-tajallī*, the monastery of the Revelation, because 'Jesus appeared to his disciples there after ascending to heaven'. In *De casis Dei* (at the beginning of the ninth century) it is said that a bishop named Theophanes stayed on the mountain. It also states that there were four churches there, one in the name of the Saviour, on the site where he spoke with Moses and Elijah;

[12] John, the abbot of the monastery: Mansi, X, 909; cf. Vailhé, *EO*, 3(1899–1900), 20; see the biography of John of Damascus by John, patriarch of Jerusalem, in *MPG* 94, 430–502 and see p. 430 in the footnote: this is not John the patriarch of the time of Leo III, the Isaurian (717–741), who was a contemporary of John of Damascus; see: Jugie, *EO*, 28:35, 1929, on the identity of the author of the biography; some thought that it was John VI, the patriarch of Jerusalem who was killed in 966, and see *ibid.*, 35, the assumption that the author is John VIII, patriarch of Jerusalem during the Crusaders' period (1105), who was a Jerusalemite who had lived in the city before the conquest. Jugie mentions two other biographies of John of Damascus there, one written in Arabic by a monk of Antioch, in 1085, and another whose manuscript is preserved in the church of St Mark in Venice, and was edited in *Oriens Christianus*, VIII, by M. Gordillo. Earlier, Jugie published an article summarising the life of John of Damascus: *EO*, 23:137, 1924. For confirmation that John of Damascus was the grandson of Manṣūr the collaborator: see William of Tripoli's treatise on the Muslims, in Prutz, *Kulturgeschichte*, 575–598 (written in 1273, see p. 579 *ibid.*); see also: Erhard, *Römische Quartalschrift*, 7(1893), 35; Vailhé, *EO*, 3(1888/9), 34–37 (Vailhé has there a list of John's writings); Lammens, *Mo'āwia*, 395, who is very sceptical with regard to the biography of John of Damascus attributed to John the patriarch; in his opinion this is merely a collection of legends; see the article on John of Damascus in Bardenhewer, *Geschichte*, V, 51–65. See on John of Damascus, also Blake, *Le Muséon*, 78(1965), 369ff; his dates differ somewhat from mine. On Stephen 'the miracle maker': Vailhé, *EO*, 3(1899–1900), 22f; *idem*, *ROC*, 6(1901), 316. On Theodore Abū Qurra: Graf, *Die arabischen Schriften. idem, GCAL*, II, 7–21; Brockelmann, *Geschichte der christlichen Litteraturen des Orients*, 68; on the monk Lazaros: Kurtz, *BZ*, 7:474, 1898; cf. Dölger, *Regesten*, No. 855 (letters written by the emperor Constantine IX to a monk, a swindler who pretended to have brought Constantine, before he became emperor, an alleged prophecy in the name of that Lazaros, that he was fated to become emperor); cf. Canard, *Byzantion*, 35(1965), 19, n. 1, on the confusion between al-Ḥākim and his father, al-'Azīz.

another in the name of 'Holy Moses' and the other in the name of the 'Holy Elijah'. The name of the fourth church has not been preserved there. Willibald only mentions the monastery and a church dedicated to the Saviour, Moses and Elijah. At the beginning of the Crusaders' rule, the Russian traveller, the abbot Daniel, mentions three churches, of which one is of the Transfiguration, and the other in the name of the 'Holy prophets Moses and Elijah'. John Phocas (in the eleventh century) notes two monasteries on Mount Tabor and he enthuses on the view overlooking the swamps and the River Jordan.[13]

[674] In Nazareth, Arculf says that he found two very large churches, the one in the centre of the city, on the site of the house where Jesus lived as a boy, and the second on the site where Gabriel appeared to Mary. He is speaking of the church of the *Nutritio*, the site of which is not known, and of the Church of the Annunciation. Some two generations later, Willibald mentions only the Church of the Annunciation. As to Gaza, we have already seen that in the eighth century, Mayūmas, the port area of Gaza, was the seat of a bishop. In the mid-eleventh century, there is still a bishop there called Samonas, who is credited with having written a polemical treatise entitled *The argument with the Arab Ahmad*. In Shechem, Arculf saw a church in the form of a cross, while in *De casis Dei*, it says that there was a large church there, where the 'holy Samaritan woman' is buried, as well as other churches. This city also was the seat of a bishop. A large church in Sebastia is also mentioned in this list, and it says that John the Baptist is buried there. In Sebastia at that time there was also a bishop whose name was Basil. I have already mentioned above the churches in Tiberias; now it is worth adding something from the accounts of Christian travellers in the Middle Ages. These describe Tiberias and the area around the Sea of Galilee, places that were known to be connected with the life of Jesus. Willibald mentions Magdala, Mary Magdalene's village, and Capernaum. *De casis Dei* mentions a monastery called Heptapegon, 'the seven springs', which is Ṭabgha (usually called Ṭabḫa today), which is where the miracle of the loaves and the fishes occurred. Farther along, on the banks of the Sea of Galilee, there was the church called 'the twelve chairs' (*duodecim thronorum*) containing the table around which Jesus sat with his disciples. One should also mention here the Tiberian deacon Theodore, who in 862 copied the Uncial Codex (that is, written in large letters an inch in height and separated from one another), the most ancient to be found in Palestine. This work was commissioned by the local bishop, Noah. Mention is made of Stephen ibn Ḥakam, of Ramla, who copied a Christian-Arab theologi-

[13] See Arculf in Tobler et Molinier, I, 184f; *De casis Dei*, *ibid.*, 304; Willibald, *ibid.*, 260; Shābushtī, 25; Daniel (Khitrowo), 69; John Phocas, see: Dieterich, *Byzantinische Quellen*, I, 65.

cal treatise ascribed to Theodore Abū Qurra, at the behest of a certain *anbā* ('father') Basil. He finished the work in December 877 in the monastery of St Chariton and also copied the four Gospels, according to the pericopes, in AM 6389 (AH 284, AD 896). A copyist by the name of Da'ūd al-'Asqalānī is also mentioned in Ascalon, who copied some of the Epistles of Paul in 902. Of somewhat far-off places, it is worth noting Fīq (which is Afēq), where in the year 1000 there still stood Dayr Fīq, a monastery which according to Shabushtī was claimed by the Christians to be the most ancient of monasteries. In al-Quwaysma near 'Ammān, an inscription from the year 717 was found, referring to the restoration of a church and the paving of its floor with mosaics in the days of the priest Obeos and with the assistance of Makedonios, Abbibos and Iōannos (two of the names are distinctly Arabic: Ubbay, Ḥabīb). Another inscription is to be found in Mā'in, eight kilometres south-west of Madaba, in the ruins of a church, with verses from the Psalms to mark the restoration of the church in 719/20. Here we have proof of the existence of a Christian population in the rural regions of Trans-Jordan, towards the end of the Umayyad period, in the days of 'Umar II ibn 'Abd al-'Azīz. From Adhruḥ, a manuscript copied by *anbā* Mūsā b. Ḥakīm al-Qasīs ('the priest') in AH 288, that is AD 901, has been preserved.[14]

[675] From travellers' accounts, and especially that of *De casis Dei*, it is worth mentioning additional churches and monasteries in Palestine: in Bethlehem, priests and monks are mentioned in the Church of the Nativity; also mentioned is the monastery in the name of St Theodosius with its seventy monks. Willibald notes that the Church of the Nativity is in the form of a cross, while Bernard the Monk, in the ninth century, speaks of the very large church of St Mary and describes the crypt of the birth. According to Saewulf, the pilgrim who wrote in 1102, the Muslims utterly destroyed Bethlehem, apart from the Church of the Nativity (he calls it the church of St Mary). There is also mention of the monasteries of St Chariton and St Euthymius in the neighbourhood of Jerusalem (in Khān al-Aḥmar, in the region of Ma'alē Adummīm). In Koziba there was a monastery in the name of St Mary. On the River Jordan was the monastery of St John, as well as a church, at the site where the pilgrims

[14] Nazareth: Arculf, *ibid.*, 184; Willibald, *ibid.*, 260; the treatise of Samonas: *Dialexis pros Akhmed tou Sarakēnou*, *MPG* 120, 821–834. Shechem, Sebastia: Arculf, *ibid.*, 181f; *De casis Dei, ibid.*, 304. The codex of Tiberias: Ehrhardt, *Römische Quartalschrift*, 5(1891), 257; see Willibald, *ibid.*, 261; *De casis Dei, ibid.*, 304. Stephen (Iṣṭāfna) of Ramla, the theological treatise: BM Or 4950; see Graf, *GCAL*, II, 16f; the Gospels: MS Sinai, No. 72, see: Padwick, *MW*, 29(1939: after p. 135 there is a photograph of the colophon); cf. Blau, *Scripta Hierosolymitana*, 9(1961), 208. Da'ūd al-'Asqalānī: Troupeau, *Catalogue*, II, 107 (No. 6725–3). *Dayr Fīq*: Shābushtī, 14. The inscription of Quwaysma, see: Saller, *JPOS*, 21(1948), 140ff; The inscription of Mā'in: De Vaux, *RB*, 47(1938), 239f; Adhruḥ: MS Strasbourg, see: Oestrup, *ZDMG*, 52(1897), 455.

went down to bathe in the river; and also a monastery in the name of St Stephen; on Mount Paran (near 'Ayn Fāra, in the mountains of Jerusalem) there was a monastery in the name of St Theoctistus. He also mentions the monastery at Kafr Kanna.[15]

Christian sects

[676] Apparently, the singular situation in Jerusalem does not reflect what was happening among the Christians throughout Palestine at that time. One may assume that while Jerusalem was subject to the unqualified influence of the Byzantine Church, the Monophysite Church carried more weight throughout the land, particularly in the villages. We already find evidence of this in the findings at Nessana where two inscriptions bear the term *Theotokos* (mother of God), characteristic of Monophysitism; the term is also found in one of the documents discovered there, dated 16 July 605, and in another document whose exact date is unknown, but which is around the Muslim conquest. One should bear in mind that the Christian population was Syriac (that is, Aramaic) speaking, and that this was the language of its churches, including the Melekite, which was under the authority of Byzantium. Evidence from the pre-Muslim period shows that this population did not speak Greek, and the Church sources indirectly confirm this, as exemplified by the story of the child who spoke of the destruction of a pagan temple, in the biography of Porphyrius written by Mark the Deacon: a child of seven 'said it in the language of the Syrians'. The pilgrim Sylvia (also called Aetheria or Egeria) mentions in the fourth century that the population in Palestine speaks *Syriste*, that is Syriac, unlike the bishop, who speaks only Greek, although he may know Syriac; the priest (*presbyter*) who accompanies him translates the Greek into Syriac, as is also customary for the sermons in the church. The Byzantine writers, when using the word 'Syrians', also meant the retainers of the Orthodox patriarch, whose language of ritual was Syriac; but frequently the Jacobite Monophysites were also meant (not the Maronites, who were rarely to be found outside the region of Lebanon; nor the Nestorians, who were few in number). However, the annals of the Jacobites during the period under discussion are obscure. It is known that they had bishops in Acre and Jerusalem, and that they submitted to the authority of the Jacobite patriarch in Antioch; the Monophysite bishop in Jerusalem was never considered a patriarch, unlike his counterpart in Antioch.[16]

15 See Willibald, *ibid.*, 260; *De casis Dei*, *ibid.*, 304f; the monk Bernard, *ibid.*, 317. See the articles by H. Leclercq: Bethleem, in *DACL*, II, 837; Palestine, *ibid.*, XIII, 857–859; Cana, ibid., II, 1802ff; Kefr-Kenna, *ibid.*, V, 702ff.

16 See *Nessana*, 18; see papyrus No. 46, line 1, *ibid.*, 136; No. 89, line 44, *ibid.*, 257. See the

[677] We encounter an interesting phenomenon in the latter half of the tenth century, during the never-ending warfare going on in Palestine, when Byzantine influence was on the rise. It seems that while subject to threat on the part of the Byzantines, the Monophysite priests hastened to join the official Church, and perhaps this applies to entire rural communities. Something of this state of affairs is revealed to us in the letter sent by Theodore, archbishop of Egypt, and Orestes, patriarch of Jerusalem, to Hugo Capet and his son and fellow-ruler Robert. They mention in this letter that they have sent emissaries to Rome to ask whether the Jacobite infidels (as the official Church spoke of the Jacobite priests) would be permitted to officiate as priests in the official Church if they were to return to the fold.

It is a characteristic fact that the local Christians were called *Suriani* during the Crusaders' rule, and it is more than likely that it is mostly Jacobites, as well as the other Eastern Christians who spoke Aramaic, who are being referred to. Thus, for instance, in Jean d'Ibelin's book it says that 'the Syrian people' came before the king and requested that their litigations be held according to their own customs whenever there is a dispute, and that the head of their court be called *rays* (in Arabic: *ra'īs*) and that this custom, it is implied, be kept throughout the country and not only in Jerusalem. William of Tyre also calls the Christians of Jerusalem (who were, he says, people of the poorest level, wretched and impoverished) *Suriani*.[17]

[678] The Jacobite church in Jerusalem was in the monastery of Mary Magdalene (and Simon the Pharisee). It was also the seat of their patriarch from the Crusaders' time and onward. According to Sāwīrūs' version, the church was built during the time of Ya'qūb, the Monophysite patriarch of Alexandria (819–830). Sāwīrūs tells that its building was financed by an Egyptian, Maqāra (Macarius) al-Nabrāwī (of Nabrūwa) al-Arkhūn (the arkhon, that is from among the notable Copts) who was a wealthy and generous man. His newborn son died a few days after birth, and the patriarch restored him to life through his prayers, a fact which became known in Jerusalem. As a token of his gratitude, Maqāra built the church

treatise of Mark the Deacon: Grégoire et Kugener (eds.), Marc le diacre, *Vie de Porphyre*, 52–55, see there n. 1 on p. 52; see, *ibid.*, 128f, additional literary proofs quoted by Grégoire, the editor, that Syriac was the major spoken language at the end of the fourth century and the outset of the fifth. See the account of Sylvia in the Heraeus ed., 51; cf: Peeters, *Tréfonds*, 61; Rey, *ROL*, 8(1900,1901), 150; Every, *ECQ*, 6(1946), 363ff, 367; on the bishop of Antioch, who was considered the patriarch by the Monophysites, see: Nau, *ROC*, 4(1899), 323 (speaking of the year 659).

17 See the letter to Hugo and Robert: *MGH*(SS), III, 686–690; by the way, it refers to another interesting fact, namely that out of fear of the Muslims, they can only have small altars in their churches; the time: about 990. See: Livre de Jean d'Ibelin, ch. iv, *RHC* (Lois), I, 26. William of Tyre, 285; cf. also Prawer, *ha-Ṣalvānīm*, Index: Syrians.

of the Orthodox ('those who held the correct creed', by which Sāwīrūs means Monophysites like himself) in Jerusalem, known by the name al-Majdalāniyya (that is, the church of Mary Magdalene). This account was written towards the end of the tenth century, describing something which happened around 820. According to information found in the account of Michael the Syrian, however, the church existed before then; it had been destroyed by order of Hārūn al-Rashīd in the year 1118 'of the Greeks', that is AD 807, and rebuilt during the rule of al-Ma'mūn in the years 820–830 (what Sāwīrūs describes as essentially the building of a new church). In 1092, when the Saljūqid sons of Artuq were in control of Jerusalem, and the governor of the city was the Jacobite Christian Manṣūr, the latter restored the church, with the help of the patriarch of Antioch, Cyril II, who even sent a bishop to take part in its inauguration. At that time, the Jacobite bishop of Jerusalem was Anastas of Caesarea. Two of his works are known; one on the fast of the *Deipara* ('the mother of God', the Latin equivalent of *Theotokos*), and the other a polemical work against the Armenians on religious matters.[18]

[679] The Nestorians, who were almost entirely concentrated in the eastern part of the Muslim world, and whose centre was Baghdad, were few and far between in Palestine and little is known about them. A version of a letter from the Nestorians in Jerusalem to Isaac of Nisibis has been preserved, which deals with refugees who fled from Iraq with the intention of reaching Jerusalem, but who then returned to Ḥīra, on the Euphrates. A letter has also been preserved from the Catholicus Yishō'-yhav to the Jerusalemites 'Master Elia, Priest and Synkellos [aide of the

18 See: Martin, *JA*, VIII–12 (1888), 477. Sāwīrūs (*PO*, X[5]), 460f; Michael the Syrian, III, 21; cf. Vincent et Abel, *Jérusalem*, II, 938f; Meinardus, *Copts*, 11 (who had no knowledge of the account of Michael the Syrian); Michael the Syrian visited Jerusalem himself, in 1179 (see his *Chronicle*, III, 379), where he mentions a Syriac book of Masorah belonging to the church 'of the holy Mary Magdalene', cf. Nau, *ROC*, 19(1914), 379f; also Bar Hebraeus mentions this church, in his church chronicle (ed. Abbeloos), I, 653f; the Jacobite Patriarch of Antioch, Ignatius II and his retainers, stay in the church of Mary Magdalene, during their visit to Jerusalem, on Easter 1168, and then again in 1179. After the conquest of Jerusalem by Saladin, the building became a *madrasa*: *al-Maymūniyya* (in 1197); but in 1229, according to the treaty of Jaffa, under Frederick II, the monks returned there; see Vogüé, *Eglises*, 292; he studied its ruins in 1854; see Chabot, *AIBL*, *Comptes rendus*, 1938, 452; Kawerau, *Jakob. Kirche*², 111, 116. Cf. Cerulli, *Etiopi in Palestina*, 10–16; Sāwīrūs, II(3), 229. On Anastas see: Rey, *ROL*, 8(1901), 150; Every, *ECQ*, 6(1946), 367. The treatise on the Deipara was printed, see in *MPG* 127, pp. 516ff, see the biographical details there, 517. On the *madrasa al-Maymūniyya* see: 'Ulaymī, 339. Its site, which was also the site of the Jacobite quarter, was near the Flower Gate (Herod's Gate), that is, in the north-eastern corner of the city, and in the Middle Ages: between Jehoshaphat street and the wall. During the Crusaders' times, this quarter was called 'la Guiverie' (other versions: Juderie, Juerie, Iueria, Judairia), that is, the Jews' quarter; see: Tobler, *Palestinae Descriptiones*, 219; Vogüé, *Eglises*, 443; it is difficult to know the reason for this; perhaps because the place was assigned as the dwelling place for the handful of Jews living in Jerusalem in Crusaders' times; see the discussion below, in sec. 839.

Head of the Church], Master Paul, Beadle and Archdeacon [evidently: chief of the church beadles], and Master Theodore, Beadle and Churchman, and to all Churchmen'; all these were people 'of the Holy Congregation of Jerusalem'. In this letter, emissaries are mentioned who came to Yishō'yhav, who was 'the Catholicus of the East', namely 'Masters Procopius and Cosmas', and gratitude is expressed for the gifts sent him. He thanks everyone and especially the scribes who wrote the letter, Melchizedek and Qayōmā, and the 'slave-girl of God, Lady Pelagia' (perhaps a nun). This letter was written in the middle of the seventh century. The appointment of a Nestorian bishop in Jerusalem is mentioned in 835; in 893 the Nestorian bishop of Jerusalem, Elia Jawharī, was raised in rank and became Metropolitan of Damascus. A treatise is known which he wrote on the religious consensus among the Syrians. In around 1040, in a commentary on the book of Genesis, the Baghdadian Nestorian priest Ibn al-Ṭayyib stressed the importance of Jerusalem, being the centre of the world, as the head is to the body (to Gen., xii:4; 'So Abram departed . . .'). From 1065, the head of the Nestorians in Jerusalem held the rank of Metropolitan.[19]

[680] The Georgians and the Armenians should be considered separately. Those who came to Jerusalem from their homelands generally collaborated with each other and we find them in the main all together in their monasteries and churches. The Georgians (who were then called Iberians and Lazians) are already mentioned by Procopius in the sixth century. He states that there was a monastery of the Iberians built by the emperor Justinian in Jerusalem; in the Jerusalem desert, he built a monastery of the Lazians. Anastas of Armenia, writing in the seventh century, lists no less than seventy monasteries of the Armenians in Jerusalem, such as the monastery of Peter near the Siloam, outside the city (undoubtedly referring to the spring of Siloam and not the pool); the monastery of Panda (who is Pantaleon) on the Mount of Olives; the monastery of the forty martyrs, which was seized by the Muslims; the monastery of St John; and he mentions others there, in the Jehoshaphat Valley and elsewhere, which were taken or destroyed by the Muslims, or abandoned because the monks could not pay the taxes. According to him, they also had a monastery near David's Gate, which was the Yeretz monastery, and he also notes the monastery of the Gogarenes, near the gate of the Church of the Resurrection. The Muslims also confiscated, according to him, three monasteries

[19] See: Išō'yahb, *Epistulae*, *CSCO* (Syri), 64, 215ff; 245f; cf. Hage, 81. The appointment of the bishop in 835: Atiya, 266. Elia, bishop of Jerusalem: Every, *ECQ*, 6(1946), 363, and see his treatise in al-Sam'ānī, *Bibliotheca Orientalis*, III, 513–516: *Tractatus de concordia fidei inter Syros*; cf. the article Syriens; église, by I. Ziadé, in *DTC*, XIV, 3084. The commentary of Ibn al-Ṭayyib: *CSCO* (Arabici) 24, 62; see also: Graf, *GCAL*, I, 69; Spuler, *Kirchen*, 142, 159; the metropolitan of Jerusalem: Atiya, 266.

of the Albanians. These monasteries were established, he says, during the reign of Tiridates and the priesthood of Gregorius. From the seventh century, Michael and Eustachius, the Georgian monks who lived in Sinai, are also mentioned. From the eighth century, or perhaps even earlier, there was a centre for translating and copying books in Georgian at the Mar Saba monastery. Similar centres existed in the monastery attached to the church of the Calvary and the one in Gabbatha, named after the queen Mary (the name Gabbatha: in the Gospel according to St John, xix:13). We know the names of two of the Georgian translators, 'the translating fathers' who lived in Jerusalem at the time; they were David and Stephen. They translated Greek and Arabic books into Georgian. Towards the end of the ninth century, John the Physician, of Jerusalem, translated Georgian books into Armenian. A group of copyists of Georgian books were active in Mar Saba in the latter half of the tenth century as well. Many splendid illuminated manuscripts remained in these monasteries. *De casis Dei* also mentions Georgian monks on the Mount of Olives and in the Gethsemane church in around the year 808. Two central figures of the Georgian Church visited Palestine in the ninth century, the Saints Hilarion and Constantine. The former, who belonged to the Georgian nobility, visited Mount Tabor, Jerusalem, Bethlehem and the River Jordan, and afterwards settled down at the monastery of Mar Saba and remained there for seven years. Constantine, a wealthy and highly respected figure in his country, who had been governor of Upper Georgia during the reign of the empress Theodora and that of her son Michael III ('the drunkard', 842–867) visited Palestine in the first half of the ninth century, bringing with him substantial donations to its monasteries. He was seized by the Muslims and died of torture in Baghdad, in mid-century. Towards the end of the tenth century (according to one source, in 992) Prochore came to Palestine and joined the monastery of Mar Saba. He restored the church of the Cross near Jerusalem, in the Valley of the Cross, as ordered by 'the holy man' Euthymius, of Mount Athos in Greece, and with his assistance. The text of his thanksgiving to God on this accomplishment, from the year 1038, has been preserved; but his work of restoration of the church was then still unfinished, for when one of the saints of Georgia, Georgius Mtzamindeli, visited Palestine for a second time in 1056, coming from Antioch (his first visit took place in 1044), he found Prochore still busy with the restoration. During the same period, the monastery of St James (son of Zebedee) on Mount Zion was founded; king Bagrat, the *curopalat* of Georgia on behalf of the Byzantine emperor, is credited with its foundation. This monastery was sold to the Armenians some 400 years later. The (Georgian) abbot of the monastery of the Holy Cross in the Valley of the Cross also served as abbot of the monastery of the Calvary and was the intermediary between the Georgian king and the patriarch of Jerusalem. According to another version, King Bagrat received half of the church of the Calvary from the Byzantine emperor, and appointed a Georgian bishop as its head. A Georgian monastic order was established at the Church of the Holy Sepulchre in 1049. The fact that the patriarch of Antioch, John III (993–1020) proffered the income from one hundred Georgian estates to the Church of Jerusalem is a further indication of Georgia's close ties with Jerusalem.[20]

[681] The first offshoots of the rivalry between Rome and Constantinople over the souls of the Christians in Palestine during the period under discussion could already be seen in the mid-ninth century, in the days of Pope Martin I, as I have already noted. I have already discussed extensively the matter of the relations between the Frankish kings, especially Charlemagne, and the caliph of Baghdad, which involved considerable activity on the part of the Latin Church's institutions in Jerusalem. Catholic scholars of the end of the last and the beginning of this century, especially the French scholars, have somewhat over-stressed this matter, and as we have seen, developed a theory concerning Charlemagne's genuine protectorate of the holy places. Some were of the opinion that this situation continued even after his time. These ties between Rome and Jerusalem, which were essentially political, naturally had religious consequences, and in particular, one can point to the direct contacts that were apparently created as a result, between personalities of the Western Church and the Jerusalem patriarchs, such as Alcuin's letter to George, patriarch of Jerusalem, in around 800. In 809, Thomas, patriarch of Jerusalem, wrote a letter of recommendation to Pope Leo IX, for two monks, Agamus and Roculphus, emissaries of the Pope and of Charlemagne. These two emissaries carried a letter concerning the serious dispute which had broken out on Easter of that year between the local Church and the Latins – the *filioque*

[20] Procopius, *De aedificiis*, V, 9 (ed. Loeb, VII, 358). See Anastas' treatise, in Alishan, *AOL*, 2(1884), 395–399, and see: Couret, *La Palestine*, 184f, on the monastery of the Iberians, that according to him was 'to the right' of Jerusalem and the Tower of David (it should be, evidently: to the west) and still existed in the twelfth century; cf. on the matter of the monasteries: Macler, *Congrès français de la Syrie*, II, 153; Peradze, *Georgica*, 4–5(1937), 184. The translation centres: Peeters, *Tréfonds*, 203, 206, 210. Benoit, *RB*, 59(1950), 545–550, tries to prove that the Gabbatha monastery stood in the vicinity of Herod's palace. The 'translating fathers' in Jerusalem: Peeters, *ibid.*, 210. John the Physician: *ibid.*, 212; *De casis Dei*, in Tobler et Molinier, I, 302; cf. Janin, *EO*, 16(1913), 33; Peradze, *ibid.* (above in this note); see especially: Zagarelli, *ZDPV*, 12(1889), 41–45. According to Peeters (above in this note), 207, the monastery of the Holy Cross was only founded in 1038; see further on this monastery: Tobler, *Topographie*, II, 727, 737. On the matter of the monastery of St James and the Church of the Calvary, see also Dowling, *PEFQ*, 1911, 185. (In view of what was said above on the churches in the Kidron Valley, it appears that the monastery of St James stood there, not on Mount Zion.) See also Janin, *EO*, 16(1913), 32–47, 213–218; Richard, *Mél. Brunel*, 424.

dispute – over the origin of the Holy Ghost. This was an argument of theological principle, which focused on the formula which says that the Holy Ghost, the third factor in the Holy Trinity, derives from both the Father and the Son; hence the term *filioque*. This principle was first formulated at the Church Council in Saragossa, Spain, in 380. For the following generations, this formula was repeatedly expressed, with slight variations, by several ecclesiastic figures in the West, and also at the first Church Council in Toledo, in 400, and again some generations later by the fourth Council there, in 633. This formula was not accepted by the heads of the Church in Constantinople, however. Unlike the Church in Spain, the Popes did not hasten to identify with it, in order not to cause a further rift within the Church. In 796, this formula was officially confirmed at the Council called by Paulinus, patriarch of Aquilaea (today the region of Friuli, near Venice). It seems that due to the considerable influence exercised by the Latins over the Muslim authorities in Jerusalem as a result of Charlemagne's policies, the Latins in Jerusalem dared to flaunt their support of the *filioque*. Two monks from the Mount of Olives, Egilbald (or Egilbard) and Felix, set off for Europe in 807 and spent some time at the court of Charlemagne, who was an enthusiastic supporter of the *filioque*. When they returned to Jerusalem, they introduced this supplement to the credo (the *symbolum*), thereby causing much anger among the monks of Mar Saba. One of them in particular, John, accused the Latins of heresy. Much rage was aroused, particularly against a group of Latin monks who prayed on Christmas eve near the Cave of the Nativity in Bethlehem. A fight broke out and a public quarrel ensued, with the crowd openly expressing its anger with the Latins. The monk Leo then wrote to Pope Leo III, on behalf of all the Latin monks on the Mount of Olives, and described the attacks on them. Six monks signed the letter. The Pope passed on the letter to Charlemagne, attaching also the aforementioned letter from Thomas, patriarch of Jerusalem. The emperor called a Council of the Church in Aachen, in November 809, where the matter of the *filioque* was widely discussed and the doctrine on which it was based confirmed. In January 810, the Pope expressed his approval of the conclusions reached at Aachen; nevertheless he avoided validating the inclusion of the *filioque* formula in the *symbolum* when it is being intoned (generally sung) during the ceremonies of the Church.[21]

[682] The influence of Charlemagne's enterprises was felt for gener-

21 On Latin influence in Palestine after Charlemagne, see: Riant, *AOL*, 1(1881), 13, n. 16, with lists of sources, and some quotations. Alcuin's letter, see *ibid.*, 29, and also on Thomas' letter. On the *filioque* see: the article by this name (by A. Palmieri) in *DTC*, V, 2309–2315; see also in the chronicle of Eginhard (Enhardus) of Fulda, 354, and in that of Ado, 320, on the Council of Aachen; cf. Hefele, *Conciliengesch.*, III, 749f; Berlière, *Revue bénédictine*, 5(1888), 442ff; Vailhé, *ROC*, 6(1901), 322f; Pargoire, *L'église*, 289.

ations in the comparative strengthening of the Latins in Jerusalem, and we have an indication of this in Bernard the Monk's descriptions of his travels in 867, mentioned above. Twelve years later, we have evidence of the connections between Rome and Jerusalem in a letter from Pope John VIII to Elias III, the patriarch of Jerusalem, written in May 879. The Pope confirms the arrival of the patriarch's emissaries, Theodosius, David and Saba. They were obliged to wait for some time because the Pope had been travelling in the country of the Franks. He apologises for the modesty of the gifts he is sending with the emissaries, for out of 'fear of the Muslims', it is impossible to send things of greater value. Musset, in his book on the history of Christianity in the East, saw in these connections *un touchant témoignage de l'union fraternelle qui existait alors entre Rome et Jérusalem*. Two years later, in 881, Theodosius' successor, the patriarch Elias III, writes to the kings, the bishops, abbots and monks, and the believers in the country of the Franks, noting the existence of the Latin monks in Jerusalem. The letter is borne by emissaries of the patriarch, the monks Rainard and Gispert, whose mission is to collect money to free the Jerusalem Church of the debts incurred during the restoration of so many of its churches.

Our attention is again drawn to the relationship between Rome and Jerusalem in around the year 1000, by a letter from Jerusalem requesting aid from Pope Sylvester II. (Sylvester II is Gerbert, one of the greatest Western scholars of his time; he was involved in educational endeavours, but also in politics and the intrigues of the period, beginning when he was archbishop of Rheims and afterwards in Ravenna. He held the office of pope from 2 April 999 until 12 May 1003, and made a pilgrimage to Palestine.) These are the major facts at our disposal concerning the institutions of the Latins and their status in Jerusalem. Apart from these, the remaining information is mostly about pilgrimages from western Europe, that is, of members of the Latin Church. Here and there, the institutions of the Latins are also mentioned in connection with the persecution of Christians, and with the dedication of property and various kinds of aid for Jerusalem initiated by the Latins in Europe.[22]

The patriarchs and other personalities in the Church of Jerusalem

[683] Information on the patriarchs of Jerusalem in this period derives from various sources. First are the sources of the Greek Church of Jerusa-

[22] John's letter: Mansi, XVII, 116; cf. Riant, *AOL*, 1(1881), 29. John's letter is also printed in *MPL* 126, 829f, where the correct year is cited, and not in Mansi – 872 (for John was not yet pope in May 872); the editor of the letter assumed, mistakenly, through misunderstanding the text of the letter (*Monachi vestri Theodosius videlicet, David et Saba venientes Romam*), that Theodosius was the name of the patriarch and entitled the letter accordingly; but the patriarch in 879 was Elias III (see below); see also: Musset, *Histoire*, 256f. The letter of Elias

lem itself. In addition to these, there are the chronicles, particularly those of Sa'īd ibn Biṭrīq and Yaḥyā ibn Sa'īd, and letters that were preserved in compilations of the Catholic Church. We possess several lists of the Jerusalem patriarchs which contradict one another at times. These lists are not complete, as a rule, and we have to determine the times of these patriarchs' lives according to the events in which they were involved. In general, I must stress that many of the dates are estimates; with the discovery of additional sources, they may have to be amended.

The Jerusalem patriarchs, 634–1099

1. Sophronius I, 634–638
2. Anastasius, 691–706
3. John V, 706–735
4. Theodore I, 745–770
5. Elias II, 770–797
6. George, 797–807
7. Thomas I, 807–820
8. Basil, 820–838
9. John VI, 838–842
10. Sergius I, 842–855
11. Solomon, 855–860
12. Theodosius, 860–878
13. Elias III, ibn Manṣūr, 878–907
14. Sergius II, 908–911
15. Leo I, 912–929
16. Athanasius I, 929–937
17. Christodulus I, 937–950
18. Agathon, 950–964
19. John VII, 964–966
20. Christodulus II, 966–968
21. Thomas II, 969–978
22. Joseph II, 978–983
23. Agapius, 983–984
24. Orestes, 984–1005
25. Theophilus I, 1012–1020
26. Nicephorus I, 1020–1036
27. Ioannicos, 1036–1058
28. Menas, 1058 (eight months)
29. Sophronius II, 1059–1070
30. Mark II, 1070–1084
31. Simeon II, 1084–1096
32. Euthymius, 1096–15 July 1099.[23]

and his emissaries: *RHGF*, IX, 294f; cf. Berlière, *Revue bénédictine*, 5(1888), 445; Bréhier, *L'église*, 29; Riant, *AOL*, 1(1881), 26f. The letter to Pope Sylvester, see: Guarmani, *Gl'Italiani*, 10: see the article on Pope Sylvester: E. Amann, in *DTC*, XIV, 2075–2083.

[23] Sa'īd ibn Biṭrīq and Yaḥyā ibn Sa'īd include data on the Jerusalem patriarchs in the text of their chronicles, in chronological order, and they are the oldest sources on this subject. Apart from this, lists of patriarchs are to be found in the collection of the archbishop of Athens, Chrisostomos Papadopoulos (= A. Kerameos), *Analekta Ierosolymitikēs*

[684] The patriarchal seat was vacant for a period of two generations, as we have already seen, following the death of Sophronius, patriarch of Jerusalem at the time of the Muslim conquest. Some are of the opinion that Theodore, bishop of Heshbon, whom I have mentioned above, served in his stead during that period. His representative, Andreas of Crete, who was a monk in one of Jerusalem's monasteries, participated in the sixth Church Council in Constantinople, 680–681 (the Trullanum Council). According to Dositheos Notara, Theodore was not actually a patriarch; Theophanes calls him *proedros*, president, and perhaps he meant to say bishop, rather than patriarch. According to a source written in 1660, the Muslims banished Theodore in 680 to a location 2,000 miles from Jerusalem. Another deputy for Theodore is mentioned, an old monk named George, who was also present at the Council in Constantinople. In fact, most of the sources agree that it is Anastasius who was the first real patriarch after Sophronius, and it is interesting that he is not mentioned in the rhyming obituary lists.[24]

[685] John (706–735), the next patriarch, was according to Theophanes an opponent of the emperor Leo the Isaurian (717–741), who introduced the reform of breaking the images. According to Theophanes, he objected to the reform 'together with all the bishops of the East'. He adds that John already became patriarch in 704. There are differing opinions as to the

Stakhyologias, edited at the end of the nineteenth century (1st edition: St Petersburg 1891–1898); in the rhymed ecclesiastic obituary lists (*diptykha*), in vol. I, 125; in the essay on the history of the patriarchs of Jerusalem written by Maximos Simaios, *ibid.*, III, 1ff; in the annals of the Jerusalem saints written by the monk Procopius of Nazianzos (which is Diocaesarea in Cappadocia) according to Sa'īd ibn Biṭrīq and evidently (in the continuation) also to Yaḥyā ibn Sa'īd (with many inaccuracies), *ibid.*, III, 123; in the history of the Jerusalem patriarchs written by Dositheos Notara in 1705, based mainly on sources collected by the metropolitan of Gaza, Paisios Ligarides (who died in 1678) – see *ibid.*, I, 231–307, and see the list *ibid.*, 237ff (see on the author: *DTC*, IV, 1788–1800); see the list compiled by Papadopoulos himself in the index to his book: *Historia tēs ekklēsias Hierosolymōn* (1910), 796. A survey of the Jerusalem patriarchs was also written by Michel Le Quien in *Oriens Christianus*, first printed in Paris in 1740; see vol. III, 280–500. The chronology of my list is mainly based on that of the aforementioned Papadopoulos, with certain deviations where it was justified. It is also worth noting the lists of Dowling, *PEFQ*, 1913, 171ff (who based his data on Sa'īd ibn Biṭrīq and Yaḥyā ibn Sa'īd), and of Grumel, *Chronologie*, 451f (who followed in the wake of the aforementioned, taking very much into consideration some of the Greek sources). The former diverges from my list with regard to Sergius I (he has: 842–844), and to the patriarchs of the eleventh century, beginning with Nicephorus. The other, diverges more frequently, evidently due to his limited use of the two above-mentioned Christian-Arabic sources.

[24] Andreas: see the article by E. Marin, in *DTC*, I, 1182f. Dositheos, in Papadopoulos-Kerameos, *Analekta*, I, 239f. The banishment of Theodore: *ibid.*, II, 299. Cf. Pargoire, *L'église*, 155. George, see: Procopius in Papadopoulos-Kerameos, *Analekta* III, 128. On Anastasius, see the *diptykha*, *ibid.*, I, 125. According to Procopius, *ibid.*, 128, Anastasius held office for twenty-five years; but see Papadopoulos-Kerameos, *Historia*, 796; and Dositheos in Papadopoulos-Kerameos, *Analekta*, I, 239,

duration of his office as well. Dositheos claims that he was patriarch only for four years.[25]

[686] The next patriarch in our list is Theodore (745–770); it seems that there was an interval of ten years between the two (735–745) and it is difficult to know precisely what occurred. Possibly, internal warfare and persecution prevented the Christians from choosing a patriarch. Sa'īd ibn Biṭrīq mentions here another patriarch, Elias, who is not recorded anywhere else. According to him, Elias became patriarch in the year AH 17 of Hishām, that is AD 740, and served in this office for thirty-four years, until his death, that is until 774. But this information is contrary to all other Christian sources, according to which there was a patriarch by the name of Elias (the second) only from 770. In his account of the year 753, Theophanes mentions the Jerusalem patriarch, that is Theodore, sitting idly by (together with Rome, Alexandria and Antioch), and displaying no opposition to the decision against icon-worship made by the Council of 338 bishops who convened at the palace of Hiereia. Theophanes adds that in the twenty-third year of Constantine (the fifth, namely Copronymus, 741–775), that is in AD 764, Theodore, patriarch of Jerusalem, proclaimed a ban on the iconoclast Cosmas, bishop of Epiphania (which is Ḥama, some 30 kilometres north of Ḥimṣ), together with Theodore, patriarch of Antioch, and Cosmas, patriarch of Alexandria, and all the other bishops. This was done on the feast of Pentecost, after the reading of the Gospels. In a biography of Stephen the Young (written in 808), there is mention of a joint appeal to the emperor Constantine on the part of the patriarchs of Antioch, Jerusalem and Alexandria. According to Procopius, Theodore was patriarch for only nineteen years, and he was preceded by George II for four years. Dositheos, however, quotes a source which says that Theodore became patriarch in 749.[26]

[687] Elias II (770–797) sent representatives to the seventh Church

[25] See Theophanes (De Boor), 375, 382, and the contradictory data. The veracious ones are evidently those on p. 382: the first year of the reign of emperor Philippicus Bardanes (711–713) is the same here as John's seventh year, that is, according to him he became patriarch in 704. On his opposition to the iconoclasts, see *ibid.*, 408; see Dositheos in Papadopoulos-Kerameos, *Analekta*, I, 241; see also: Procopius, *ibid.*, III, 128; Maximos Simaios, *ibid.*, III, 1ff; Papadopoulos-Kerameos, *Historia*, 278. The year of John's death, AD 735, see: Le Quien in *MPG* 95, 306; during the period of the patriarchs of the eighth century – John V and his successors – see Amann, in *DTC*, VIII, 1000, Jerusalem undergoes a process of increasing independence towards Constantinople, especially felt in the years of struggle against the iconoclasts, for both Rome and Jerusalem opposed the image-breakers.

[26] Sa'īd ibn Biṭrīq, II, 46; the matter of Hiereia: Theophanes, 427f; cf. Breyer, 70; the matter of Epiphania: Theophanes, 434, cf. Breyer, 79, see Dussaud, *Topographie*, 181, and map XIV, after p. 472; the life of Stephen, see *MPG* 100, 1117f. Procopius, in Papadopoulos-Kerameos, *Analekta*, III, 128; Dositheos, *ibid.*, I, 241; Le Quien, see the previous note; cf. Musset, *Histoire*, 255; Bréhier, *L'église*, 22f.

Council, in Nicaea, in 787 (in which Peter, the abbot of the monastery of Mar Saba also participated; he was accredited by Pope Hadrian, according to one source). Apparently it was this Elias who wrote the letter to Tarasius, patriarch of Constantinople, 'the reply of the Patriarchates in the East', in 787, complaining bitterly of the Christians' plight:

After the most holy letters from Your Holiness were read out to us [in public] . . . we, the wretched, the last of those dwelling in the wilderness, were taken by trembling, but also by joy. Trembling, on the one hand, for fear of those creatures who have been chosen to enslave us for our sins, the wicked all around us, as is written: the ungodly walk on every side [Ps., xii:9]. Every day, in fact, they invent pretexts to kill and destroy us. Joy, on the other hand, for the truth of our genuine faith glows from those letters like sunshine, and because of such rich interpretation of the teachings of the apostles and the fathers [in your letters]. Indeed your words reminded us of the prophet Zechariah [who is Zechariah, father of John the Baptist], who created the saying, also read aloud by us: whereby the day-spring from on high hath visited us [Luke, i:78] to give light, by God's mercy, to them that sit in darkness and in the shadow of death, among Arabs who have no reverence of the Lord.[27]

[688] Of George (797–807) Sa'īd ibn Biṭrīq tells us that he became patriarch in the twentieth year of the reign of Caliph al-Manṣūr (that is, 773) and remained in office for thirty-six years, until his death, that is, according to him, until 809. He was the patriarch at the time of Charlemagne's reign and the relationship between the Frankish kingdom and the caliph of Baghdad. He is mentioned in sources which speak of the ties

27 See the chronicle of the monk Georgios Hamartolos (ed. De Boor), 769 (cf. *MPG* 110, 961). Pétridès, *EO*, 4(1900–1901), 226, quotes a story about Elias, found in *AA SS*, July, III, 537, 549–554 (he mistakenly has 522–527), according to which a certain Theodosius dislodged Elias from his office, with the help of his brother and a group of friends, and he was exiled and died in Persia (and according to another version, was brought back from exile to his post). The same source also mentions Basil, a monk of the Spoudaioi in the Church of the Resurrection, who became abbot of the monastery in Jericho and afterwards bishop of Tiberias. However, the story of the ousting of Elias belongs to the pre-Islamic period. See Theophanes, 107, where the monk Theodosius, who wanted to be patriarch, is mentioned; thus the story in *AA SS* has no historical validity (it is cited in the biographical framework of the monk Stephen the miracle-worker of Mar Saba). The same mistake is made by Pargoire, *L'église*, 277, who evidently did not examine the sources and attributes this information to Theophanes; also following in his wake (evidently) are Musset, *Histoire*, 255; and Constantelos, *Byzantion*, 42(1972), 346. As to the representation at the Council of Nicaea (789), the information is contradictory; according to Theophanes, Jerusalem was not represented at all; while other sources say that Thomas (who afterwards became patriarch) was Elias' representative at that Council. See Theophanes, 461; cf. Dobschütz, *BZ*, 18(1909), 85f. An outstanding Jerusalem personality at the Council was John, who had been formerly synkellos (see below on this office) of the Jerusalem patriarch, and author of a tract against the iconoclasts. It was said that at the Council he represented the three patriarchs of the East; see Kurtz, *BZ*, 11(1902), 542; see the article on him (by L. Petit) in *DTC*, VIII, 766 (No. 47). See the letter in Mansi, XII, 1127; 300 years later, Abiathar, Gaon of Palestine, would use the same passage from the Psalms in order to say that he is surrounded by the wicked, see: **559**, a, line 8. Cf. also: Procopius in Papadopoulos-Kerameos, *Analekta*, III, 129.

between Charlemagne and Jerusalem. A letter ascribed to Alcuin written to this George has been preserved, containing mainly courtesies, and the request to pray for him and those with him, just as he prays for the patriarch and his people.[28]

[689] Thomas I (807–820) was the patriarch in whose lifetime the aforementioned dispute over the *filioque* took place in Palestine. At almost the same time, another schism began to take shape, connected with icon-worship. We have seen that in this dispute, which lasted for many generations (717–867), the Jerusalem patriarchs sided with the icon-worshippers, that is, with the traditional conservative trend, in opposition to the iconoclasts. This derived, not a little, from the fact that it was the monks who were the spinal cord of the official Church of Palestine, and they persisted in their fanatical support of the worship of icons and crosses. The specific affair I am speaking of here is that of the *Graptoi* brothers, that is, 'the marked'. This refers to two Jerusalemites, whose father Jonas, became a monk at the Mar Saba monastery. The two brothers, Theodore and Theophanes, were the pupils of Michael, the *synkellos* of the patriarch Thomas. (*Synkellos*, literally 'cell-mate', which shows something of the monasterial background of the holders of the ecclesiastic offices; the *synkellos* was the permanent escort of the patriarch, the chief official of his palace.) Michael was a close friend of Theodore, head of the monastery of the Studites, or Spoudaioi, near the Holy Sepulchre. When Theodore asked the Jerusalem patriarch to send people to help him in his struggle, these two brothers were sent to him, for they had in fact been engaged in spreading propaganda for iconolatry. They were finally arrested on emperor Theophilus' orders, evidently in around 830 (the patriarch of Jerusalem being Basil at the time). They were severely tortured and at the emperor's request, their faces were engraved with humiliating rhymes which he himself had devised; hence their reputation and nickname – the Graptoi. According to Sa'īd ibn Biṭrīq, Thomas served from 809 until 819. He credits Thomas with the restoration of the dome of the Holy Sepulchre, during the reign of Caliph al-Ma'mūn. He also tells us Thomas' nickname, which was Tamrīq.[29]

[28] Sa'īd ibn Biṭrīq, II, 49. Alcuin's letter: *MPL* 100, 359; Procopius (see the previous note) ignores George and places Thomas after Elias; Maximos Simaios, in Papadopoulos-Kerameos, *Analekta*, III, 4, gives him thirty-seven years on the patriarchal throne; cf. Musset, *Histoire*, 255.

[29] On the Graptoi, see: Zonaras (Bonn), III, 365f; Cedrenus (Bonn), II, 114ff; cf. Ehrhardt, *Römische Quartalschrift*, 7(1893), 40, 50f; Vailhé *EO*, 2(1898/9), 41f; 3(1899–1900), 27; *idem*, *ROC*, 6(1901), 319f; Dobschütz, *BZ*, 18(1909), 84; Musset, *Histoire*, 255. On the office of *synkellos* see: Pargoire, *L'église*, 62; on p. 64 he mentions another important ecclesiastic office that existed in Jerusalem, 'the guardian of the cross' (the *staurophylakos*), who was in charge of guarding the holy cross; Sa'īd ibn Biṭrīq, II, 54f (there is confirmation here of the data on the time Thomas held office, but according to him, he served for only ten years,

[690] Basil (820–838) was patriarch in 845, according to Sa'īd ibn Biṭrīq, and was the pupil of his predecessor, Thomas. It was during his time that the iconoclast emperor Theophilus organised the Church Council, specifically in 835/6, and that the aforementioned episode of the Graptoi occurred. In 836, Basil convened a Council in Jerusalem, with the participation of Christopher, patriarch of Alexandria and Ayyūb, the patriarch of Antioch, together with a number of bishops, who all protested against the iconoclastic policy of the emperor. That Council also produced an epistle signed by its participants in favour of iconolatry.[30]

[691] John VI (838–842) became patriarch, according to Sa'īd ibn Biṭrīq, in the seventh year of al-Mu'taṣim's rule, and this is more or less in accordance with the date noted here. He also adds that very disturbing rumours were heard about him and that he finally fled from the people of his Church and abandoned his office.[31]

[692) Sergius I (842–855) became patriarch of Jerusalem in the second year of al-Wāthiq, according to Sa'īd ibn Biṭrīq, and this is as listed here. He was also called Ibn Manṣūr, as he was one of the descendants of the Manṣūr who helped the Muslims capture Damascus. Sa'īd ibn Biṭrīq says that he remained in office until he died, after serving for sixteen years.[32]

[693] Solomon (855–860) was called Salmūn ibn Zarqūn by Sa'īd ibn Biṭrīq. He took office in the tenth year of al-Mutawakkil, and remained there until his death five years later.[33]

[694] Theodosius, or Theodore (860–878), was also called al-Miqlātī (evidently: 'the bereaved'), according to Sa'īd ibn Biṭrīq, who says that he rose to the patriarchal seat in the first year of al-Musta'īn (that is, a year or two after the date noted here). He is mentioned in connection with the eighth Church Council in Constantinople, in 869, which was directed against the patriarch of Constantinople, Photius. The legates of Theodosius, Elias, who was then a priest and *synkellos*, and Thomas, the metro-

until the seventh year of al-Ma'mūn, that is 819, and therefore he should have started his service in office in 809.

30 Sa'īd ibn Biṭrīq, II, 57. On the Council of Theophilus there is no further information; see on this: Dositheos, in Papadopoulos-Kerameos, *Analekta*, I, 241; see more on Basil: Procopius, *ibid.*, III, 129; Maximos Simaios, *ibid.*, III, 4. See the epistle of the participants in the Jerusalem Council (wrongly ascribed to John of Damascus) in *MPG* 95, 346–385; see on the Council: Constantinus Porphyrogenitus, *Narratio de imagine Edessena, MPG* 113, 442; and cf. R. Janin in *DHGE*, VI, 1411 (where there is an error in the reference to the aforementioned Constantine Porphyrogenitus: 412 instead of 442); see also: Musset, *Histoire*, 256.

31 See Sa'īd ibn Biṭrīq, II, 60; cf. Procopius (as in the previous note); Maximos Simaios (as in the previous note): he fled from the Arabs, to Eutychius, patriarch of Alexandria. In the *diptykha* (Papadopoulos-Kerameos, *Analekta*, I, 125) he is not mentioned.

32 See Sa'īd ibn Biṭrīq, II, 61f; and see the Greek sources noted in the previous note.

33 Sa'īd ibn Biṭrīq, II, 64. See the Greek sources in the previous notes. He was also called Salmonas.

politan of Tyre, participated in the Council. They were given permission to leave the country by the *hamera*, that is, the *amīr*, apparently meaning the caliph. A letter from Theodosius to the patriarch of Constantinople, Ignatius, has been preserved, in which he at first apologises for the infrequency of his letters; the reason being that the Christians in Jerusalem do not wish to arouse the suspicions of the authorities. He praises the good will of the Muslim rulers, who permit the Christians to build their churches and carry on their religious customs, treating them fairly and justly and avoiding any offence or iniquity. The letter, he explains, is being written at the behest of the *amēr*, that is the *amīr*. He asks Ignatius to influence the emperor to show greater readiness to concede to the Muslims, which would, as a result, redound to the benefit of the Christians living under their rule. He also mentions that his emissaries are bearing gifts from Jerusalem. Theodosius-Theodore is also mentioned by the monk Bernard, who visited Jerusalem at the time he was serving as patriarch there. As I have already noted, Theodosius intervened in the dispute around the patriarch Photius. Towards the end of his life he also sent a letter to Photius with Elias, his emissary, blaming the Council of 869; this he did when Photius returned to the patriarchal throne in Constantinople after Ignatius was deposed, in 878.[34]

[695] Elias III ibn Manṣūr served from 878 to 907. The date of his death is mentioned in a manuscript kept in the Monastery of St Catherine in Sinai (a Georgian calendar) as 4 October 906, but this date is questionable. According to Sa'īd ibn Biṭrīq, he became patriarch in the tenth year of al-Mu'tamid, that is, in AD 878, and stayed in office until his death twenty-nine years later. It is accepted that he died in 907. He was a descendant of the Damascene Manṣūr, of the same family that collaborated with the Muslims mentioned above, that is, he was the brother of the patriarch Sergius. I have already referred to the letter Pope John VIII wrote to him in 879, and Elias' letter to the notables of the Franks, in 881. In around 880, he was the host of Elia da Castrogiovanni of Sicily, who had come on a pilgrimage to Jerusalem and stayed there for three years. Elias, the patriarch, received him courteously, unlike the welcome he received in Alexandria prior to this visit. According to Sa'īd ibn Biṭrīq, it was Elias who annointed Christodulus of Aleppo, patriarch of Alexandria, 'on the

[34] Sa'īd ibn Biṭrīq, II, 66. The Council and the letter to Ignatius: Mansi, XVI, 25ff, 314; cf. Riant, *AOL*, 1(1881), 13, n. 16, who takes seriously the flattery paid the rulers for their decent attitude while ignoring the fact that exactly the contrary is implied in the letter; see that same naive seriousness in: Bréhier, *L'église*, 31; see further: Dositheos, in Papadopoulos-Kerameos, *Analekta*, I, 242; see Bernard the monk in Tobler et Molinier, I, 315; see also the Greek sources mentioned in the previous notes. The letter to Photius, see: Papadopoulos-Kerameos, *Historia*, 336f; cf. Musset, *Histoire*, 256, n. 3.

great sabbath, 4 Nīsān [April], that is, 19 Jumādā II, in the fifth year of al-Muktafī', that is AD 906 (at the height of al-Khalanjī's rebellion).[35]

[696] Sergius II (908–911) is mentioned in the writings of Sa'īd ibn Biṭrīq, who states that Jurjus (perhaps an error of the copyist) ibn Di'jān (perhaps Diogenes), became patriarch in the sixth year of al-Muktafī, that is, in AD 907, which corresponds roughly to what is said in the Greek sources. According to him, he held office for four years and eight months, that is, until 910. After him, in the third year of al-Muqtadir, that is in the same year, 910, he says that Leo I was crowned. One should bear in mind that the last days of Elias and the years in which his successors Sergius, Leo and Athanasius held office, fell at the time of the return of Baghdadian rule in Palestine, between the rules of the Ṭūlūnids and the Ikhshīdids. As to Athanasius (929–937), he is only mentioned in the Greek sources. In his day, his synkellos John, who lived in the monastery (evidently of the *Spoudaioi*) near the Church of the Resurrection, was the better known of the two. He was engaged in translating from Arabic into Greek; among other things, he translated in 934 an epistle of Theodore Abū Qurra.[36]

[697] Christodulus ibn Bahrām (937–950) was patriarch, according to Yaḥyā ibn Sa'īd, for a period of fourteen years. He died in the fifth year of al-Muṭī', that is, in 950, and took office in 936 or 937. In some instances, he is called Christodoros or Christophoros. He was said to originate from Ascalon. The period of his patriarchate was one of dreadful persecution of the Christians, as we shall see, and he was eventually forced to flee from Jerusalem. He died in Ramla and was buried there. A letter written in the year 947 by an official of the Byzantine court, Nicetas, to emperor Constantine VII (Porphyrogenitos) has been preserved; in it he describes the events connected with the Paschal fire during his stay in Jerusalem; and mentions Christodulus' presence there. Agathon succeeded Christodulus (950–964), and was followed in turn by John VII (964–966), whose name

35 On the date of his death, see: R. Janin in *DHGE*, XV, 191; Sa'īd ibn Biṭrīq, II, 56, 69; see also Dositheos (see previous note), 242. Elia of Sicily: Amari, *Storia*², I, 657; see the Greek sources mentioned in the previous notes. On the annointing of Christodulus in Alexandria, see Sa'īd ibn Biṭrīq, II, 75; it is unlikely that Sa'īd was mistaken about the personality of the Jerusalem patriarch, for he was so close to these times; cf. Gutschmid, *Kleine Schriften*, II, 486: Christodulus was Sa'īd ibn Biṭrīq's predecessor in the office of the patriarch of Alexandria. However, 19 Jumādā II fell in 906 (that is: 293 of the hijra) on 17 April. Nearer to these dates is the year after that, 907, when 19 Jumādā fell on 6 April; and in that year 4 April actually fell on a Saturday. Thus it is possible that the date recorded in that manuscript in the Sinai is not correct and that Elias died then in 907 and not 906.

36 Sa'īd ibn Biṭrīq, II, 75, 79; see the Greek sources mentioned in the previous notes. See on John the Synkellos: Bios et al., *Izvestiya* (Constantinople), 11:227, 260, 1906, with two of his biographies. See also: Peeters, *Tréfonds*, 186; according to Procopius (Papadopoulos-Kerameos, *Analekta*, III, 129), Athanasius remained in office only two years and left it because of his illness, and in his stead came Nicholas, who was patriarch for a period of

was Yuḥannā ibn Jamī', according to Yaḥyā ibn Sa'īd, and we have already seen above that he was killed during the persecution of the Christians in 966.[37]

[698] Christodulus II (966–968) was a man of Caesarea. His Arabic name was Ḥabīb, and his nickname was Abū Sahl; his other Greek name was Agapios. He died in Egypt on Wednesday, 28 Ṣafar AH 358 (23 December AD 968), after serving for two and a half years. He was buried in Alexandria, in the church of St Theodore. His successor was Thomas II (969–978), patriarch during the early days of the Fatimid wars in Palestine. It was said that he was considerably aided by a Jacobite Christian official by the name of 'Alī b. Sawwār, nicknamed Ibn al-Ḥammār, a man who was one of Alptakīn's retainers and who reached Iraq with him and was very helpful to the Christians when Alptakīn ruled Palestine. With Alptakīn's downfall, this Christian official was killed. Thomas' successor was Joseph II (978–983), who became patriarch in the fifth year of al-'Azīz – according to Yaḥyā – that is, in 979. He was a physician, or *iatrosophistēs* (in Procopius: *iatrophilosophos*, undoubtedly a distortion). He remained in office for three years and eight months. He died in Egypt and was also buried in the Church of St Theodore, near Christodulus' tomb. The next patriarch, Agapius (983–984) is only mentioned in Greek sources.[38]

[699] Orestes, serving from 984 to 1005, is also known in Greek sources as Ariston. According to Yaḥyā ibn Sa'īd, he was crowned in Ramaḍān AH 375 (January/February AD 986). He was an uncle of Caliph al-'Azīz' daughter on her mother's side (in other words, the caliph's wife's brother). He served for twenty years, according to Yaḥyā, and we have seen above that he was sent as an emissary of the caliph to Constantinople, where he died. His brother Arsenius was the patriarch of Alexandria. During his patriarchate, his synkellos, Ṣadaqa b. Bishr became known for his role in the restoration of the church of the Resurrection. In 995, Orestes sent emissaries to Pope John XV, to clarify ecclesiastic ritual and customs. We have already encountered his successor, Theophilus (1012–1020) in the discussion on the Arab rebellions of the same period, and have seen that he was appointed on behalf of the Banū Jarrāḥ. He died in Ramaḍān AH 410 (January AD 1020). Nicephorus (1020–1036) was appointed in his stead. He was a carpenter by trade, 'a descendant of the Byzantine slaves' and had worked as a carpenter in the palace of Caliph al-Ḥākim, who responded to

fifteen years, that is, one assumes, from 931 to 946; but this contradicts the data in the other sources, especially Yaḥyā ibn Sa'īd, as we shall see below. According to Maximos Simaois (*ibid.*, III, 4), Nicholas is none other than Agathon, who was patriarch from 950 onward.

37 Yaḥyā ibn Sa'īd (*PO*), 71, 94f; see the Greek sources noted above. Nicetas' letter, see: Riant, *AOL*, 1(1881), 377–382 (text, and French translation), cf. Canard, *Byzantion*, 35(1965), 30ff.

38 Yaḥyā ibn Sa'īd (*PO*), 104, 120, 200; and see the Greek sources noted above.

his request and appointed him patriarch of Jerusalem. He took office on Sunday, 10 Tammuz AH 411, that is July AD 1020. Yaḥyā adds that Nicephorus asked the caliph for 'a *sijill* (an official order) of defence, protection and guardianship of the churches left in Jerusalem and the monasteries outside the city, the church of St George in Lydda, and consent to restore their foundations to them'. And indeed, the caliph gave him the *sijill*, and Yaḥyā quotes its version, which says it was written in Jumādā II AH 411, that is November/December AD 1020. With regard to the following patriarchs – Ioannicos (1036–1058), Menas (1058), Sophronius II (1058–1070), Mark II (1070–1084), Simeon II (1084–1096) and Euthymius (1096–1099), we are almost entirely dependent on comparatively late Greek Church sources. Sophronius II is mentioned by Ingulph, the English abbot, who reports that he visited him and praises his virtues, piety and honesty. The Latin sources describe Simeon II as the patriarch of Jerusalem who held office until close to the Crusaders' conquest, and then escaped from Jerusalem to Cyprus during the Crusaders' advance, where he later died. The Greek sources, on the other hand, speak of Euthymius. According to Maximos Simaios, he became patriarch in the 17th year of Alexius Comnenus, that is, in AD 1096, and remained on the patriarchal throne for thirteen years, that is, until 1109.[39]

Ritual and customs

[700] This is not the place for a detailed analysis of the Christian ritual practices, prayers, holidays, customs and so forth. Here I shall merely try to assemble the information dealing with these matters contained in the sources of the period, some of which are Arab sources. I have already mentioned the custom peculiar to the Christians of the East, the use of the *nāqūs*, or pieces of wood, instead of a bell. To the Karaite Daniel al-Qūmisī

[39] Yaḥyā ibn Sa'īd (*PO*), 105, 207, 253. Arsenius, who evidently replaced his brother Orestes in his absence, is ascribed with having written the encyclical letter to the believers in the East and the West, in which he recommends (Saint) Simeon the Armenian, see Riant, *AOL*, 1(1881), 29 and more references there, in n. 17. From the same period, a letter is quoted, ascribed to the Jerusalem Church, written to the Latin Church and copied by Pope Sylvester II (Gerbert) in which there is an appeal to the Latin world calling for military action against the Muslims; see Riant, *ibid.*, 31–38, who proves that this is a forgery; see his references. The emissaries of the Pope: Riant, *ibid.*, 35, n. 19. Orestes is credited with a treatise in praise of Saints Saba and Macarius, edited by Cozza-Luzi in 1893, and see in the introduction there some remarks about Orestes. On Orestes and Arsenius see also: Gay, *L'Italie méridionale*, 262. On Theophilus: Yaḥyā ibn Sa'īd (Cheikho), 228, 230, 231; and he is also mentioned in the Greek sources noted above; see Ingulph's chronicle, 148f; on Simeon II, see: Grumel, *EO*, 38(1939), 115f; he is credited with having written a letter in 1094, allegedly, to Pope Urban II, with complaints about the Muslims' mistreatment of the holy places; see Riant, *ibid.*, 92–100, proving that it is a forgery. On the fact that this Simeon was patriarch until close to the conquest, see for instance Amann in *DTC*, VIII, 1001f.

(writing in ca. 900), the *nāqūs* seemed to be characteristic of the Jerusalem Christians. Muqaddasī, the Jerusalemite, writing in 985, knew the principal dates of the Christian calendar and the Christian holidays. He gives pride of place to Easter, which, according to him fell during the *nayrūz* (the Persian new year); he then mentions the feast of Pentecost, *'anṣara*, 'during the heat'; Christmas, 'when it is cold'; the *Barbāra* holiday, 'during the rains' (apparently on 4 December); the *Qalandas*, that is, 1 January; *'īd al-ṣalīb* ('Feast of the Cross') 'during the wine harvest'; *'īd Ludd* ('holiday of Lod') 'in sowing time' (if this is the holiday of St George, it was always celebrated on 23 April, and one cannot understand how it fits in with 'the sowing time').

An important holiday in Palestine was that of *'īd al-ṣalīb* (Feast of the Cross), the holiday of the Church of the Holy Sepulchre. Al-Bīrūnī, who lived during the first half of the eleventh century, says that it was celebrated on 14 September (*īlūl*), and that it was the day on which the emperor Constantine and his mother Helena found the cross (on which Jesus was crucified) and took it from the Jews, who had kept it with them buried in Jerusalem. He also notes that the Nestorians had their own rules in this matter, celebrating the Feast of the Cross on 13 September, because in their opinion this was the day the cross was found, while on the 14th, Helena showed it to the people. The holiday is mentioned in Geniza documents, for it was an indication that the time had arrived for the ships to put into their home ports, with the approach of the winter's stormy seas. A ship named *ṣalībiyya* is mentioned, and I assume that the reference is to a particularly strong vessel, whose crew would dare to sail even after the holiday. There is also mention of *'īd al-sha'ānīn*, which is Palm Sunday (a week before Easter Sunday); this was a holiday which originated in Jerusalem and spread from there to other places. According to Yaḥyā ibn Sa'īd, the Christians in Jerusalem would carry a huge olive tree from the church of *al-'Āzariyya* to the Church of the Resurrection, despite the great distance between the two; the streets of the city were crowded with people bearing crosses, intoning and praying in open procession, while the governor of the city, with his entire retinue, would ride along and clear the way for them. A similar ceremony spread to Egypt until al-Ḥākim, in the year 328 (1007/8), absolutely forbade these ceremonies and particularly any kind of Muslim involvement in Christian feasts. In general, one may conclude that Palestine had immense influence on the formation of ritual customs and the order of prayers and ceremonies. In the monastery of Mar Saba, its famous *typikon* was produced; this was a book of prayers which contained lists and the principal versions of the prayers for the entire year. There was a special Jerusalem ritual of intoning the Psalms, which at the end of the ninth century consisted of 4,882 verses instead of the accepted

2,542. *Antiphones* (outer verses) were inserted and sung by the choir in between the Reader's rendering of the Psalms. An unusual Jerusalem custom was the use of the Eucharist (the symbolic 'Lord's Supper' given to believers) of wafers and not of leavened bread; from Jerusalem, this custom evidently spread to the Latins, while the Byzantine Church calls for the use of leavened bread.[40]

[701] The theme of the Paschal fire, which took on such comparatively large proportions in the Arab chronicles of the period, also falls within the context of rites and ceremonies. Easter was undoubtedly the central holiday of the Jerusalem Church, and pilgrims would come from all over the Christian world to celebrate it there. In the Church of the Resurrection, there was a device whereby all the oil-lamps in the church could be lit at the moment when the Resurrection was to be proclaimed, and if one is to believe the Arab writers, starting from al-Jāḥiẓ, the Christians claimed that this was a miracle and that the candles were lit from heaven. About a century after al-Jāḥiẓ, Mas'ūdī described the lighting of the candles in the Church of the Resurrection: fire descends from the sky and lights the candles, he writes, with the help of a trick which he described in another book (which has not been preserved). Al-Bīrūnī, writing in the first half of the eleventh century, has preserved the story of the fire from a version recorded in the previous century, according to which the episode occurs in the presence of representatives of the Muslims, among them the governor of Jerusalem. They place lamps and torches on the covered tomb of Jesus. The Christians extinguish the candles and torches which they are holding, until 'a clean, white fire' descends; from this, they light the lamps 'in the

40 See the text of Daniel al-Qūmisī in TS 10 C 2, fol. 1b (in his commentary to Dan., xi:32) in Mann, *JQR*, NS 12(1921/2), 518 (where it was read *nāqūm* instead of *nāqūs*); see Muqaddasī, *Āqālīm*, 182f; he lists further the months of the Christian year, starting from October. Bīrūnī, 301, 310. *'Īd al-ṣalīb*, see **482**, a, line 14 (the letter of Israel b. Nathan); see also **491**, line 8: *ṣalībiyya*; cf. Goitein, *Mediterranean Society*, I, 317, 482, n. 32; Ibn Māsawayh, a Nestorian writer from the first half of the ninth century, notes that in Jerusalem they would celebrate the 'Feast of the Church of the Resurrection' on 14 September (see the Sbath ed., 256). The *Qalandas* is also mentioned in Mas'ūdī, *Murūj*, III, 406: 'in al-Shām (Palestine and Syria) the population celebrates it by lighting fires'. *'Īd al-sha'ānīn*, see: Yaḥyā ibn Sa'īd (*PO*), 279f; it seems to me that the word *sha'ānīn* is a Hebrew loan-word, from *hosha'nōt*. In the year AH 244 the Muslim chroniclers recorded an event the likes of which they say had never before occurred in Islam, namely the Feast of Immolation (10 Dhū'l-Ḥijja), the Passover (*fiṭr, faṭīr*) of the Jews and *al-sha'ānīn* all three fell on the same day; see Ibn al-Athīr, *Kāmil*, VII, 85; Sibṭ ibn al-Jawzī, *Mir'āh* (BM Or 4618), 128a; Ibn Taghrī Bardī, II, 318; an examination of the date shows, however, that the Feast of Immolation fell that year (859) on 19 March, while the first day of Passover AM 4619 fell on 23 March, on a Thursday. The *typikon* of Mar Saba: Krumbacher, *Geschichte der byzantinischen Litteratur*², I, 314. See Linder, in: *Perāqīm* (1979), 12f, on elements of the hatred of Jews in the Jerusalem Christian ritual, especially during the Passion Week, as it was observed in the tenth century, following a Greek manuscript copied in Jerusalem in 1122; see his references in n. 13. The intoning of the Psalms: Pargoire, *L'église*, 64; the matter of the bread: Every, *ECQ*, 6(1946), 367; cf.: A. Michel, *Humbert and Kerullarios*, II,

mosque [!] and the churches'. Afterwards an official account of the descent of the fire is written and sent to the caliph. If the fire came down swiftly and near noon-time, it was a sign that it would be a fruitful year, but if the fire came in the evening or even later, then a year of drought would follow. According to another version, it was the Muslim governor himself who entered the Holy Sepulchre and was the first to light the candle he was holding. Al-Bayhaqī, a contemporary of al-Bīrūnī, has still another source, attributed to Abū Sahl 'Īsa b. Yaḥyā al-Masīḥī, a Christian of Jurjān, who described the episode of the fire in the first half of the tenth century. According to him, the fire descends from the air (*athīr*, a Greek loan-word, *aithēr*) in front of all the people, and although there is no aperture or window in the ceiling of the building, it penetrates through the roof without burning its wooden beams, the lamps and candles are then lit, and the fire disappears with the dawn. Ibn al-Qalānisī, in the mid-twelfth century, connects the story of the fire with al-Ḥākim's decrees, which have been discussed above. He attributes the descent of the fire to a trick and the use of a special oil, balsam oil (*duhn al-balasān*), which together with jasmin oil (*duhn al-zanbaq*) gives a bright white light. They draw a fine iron wire smeared with balsam oil, keeping the wire unseen, then they open the door of the altar above the Holy Sepulchre and light the fire from there, at which time all the lamps light up simultaneously, while the crowd assembled there assume that the fire has come down from heaven. Sibṭ ibn al-Jawzī, writing in the thirteenth century, claims that he himself lived in Jerusalem for ten years and that on Easter, he would go to the Church of the Resurrection to look into the matter. He describes the fire as coming from lamps that were lit in the dome above the Holy Sepulchre, after sundown on the eve of Easter Sunday, while the worshippers believed that the fire had descended from heaven.

Alongside the Muslim sources, we also find Christian descriptions. The *typikon* of the Church of the Resurrection, from the ninth or tenth century, tells us that the starting point of the fire was in the Martyrion (that is, St Constantine's church). The ceremony begins in the evening, with everyone dressed in white, and none of the lights aglow. It opens with the evening prayer intoned behind the Holy Sepulchre. After reading from the Book of Daniel, the patriarch goes up to the altar, distributes incense, and they begin to swing the incense burners while walking around the Sepulchre three times. After this, the patriarch lights the holy fire (*hagion phos*), passes on the fire to the head deacon, who in turn passes it on to the worshippers, and from there they walk in procession to the Church of St Constantine. A fragment from an anonymous Syriac writer, evidently

116ff. On the immense influence Jerusalem had on the matter of ritual and church ceremonies see: Baumstarck, *Palästinapilger*, 80.

from the Muslim period, mentions explicitly that the fire is lit simultaneously by the patriarch and all the people. Arethas of Caesarea of Cappadocia, writing to the governor of Damascus at the outset of the tenth century, uses the example of the fire descending from heaven as proof of the superiority of Christianity. He also mentions the presence of Muslim officials at the ceremony when the fire suddenly appears. The Byzantine courtier Nicetas writes in 947 to emperor Constantine VII, Porphyrogenitus, describing the Easter ceremony in Jerusalem. The *amīr* of the area (undoubtedly Ramla), was present at the ritual, as was an *amīr* from Baghdad, who had with him an order forbidding the ritual, giving as the reason for the ban, the tremendous impression it made on the entire Syrian population, who were easily influenced by acts of magic and thereby attracted towards Christianity. The patriarch Christodulus I defended the ceremony and stated that it was a miracle and not a magical act. Finally, after the Christians paid 7,000 dinars (including 2,000 in cash), they were permitted to carry on the ceremony and the miraculous appearance of the fire, with the sudden simultaneous lighting of all the candles, actually took place. In around 870, Bernard the monk also provides evidence of the belief that after the prayers of the eve of Easter Sunday, an angel descends who lights the fire in the lamps hanging above the Holy Sepulchre, and it is from this fire that the patriarch passes on fire to the bishops and to all the people. The story of Bar Hebraeus should also be mentioned; it notes in the description of the destruction of the Church of the Resurrection in al-Ḥākim's time that the decree was imposed on the Christians when one of the Christian-haters told al-Ḥākim of the trick whereby the masses were made to believe that the fire actually descended from heaven. Bar Hebraeus naturally does not ascribe any truth to this story. However, it seems that according to the Christian sources, the belief that the fire came down from heaven was indeed common among the Christian masses, and that what the Muslims writers had to say about the stunt was founded on fact.[41]

41 Among the Muslim writers, it appears that the first to mention the matter of the lighting in the Church of the Resurrection was al-Jāḥiẓ in the first half of the ninth century; see *Ḥayawān*, 201f; Mas'ūdī, *Murūj*, III, 405, where he writes (apparently by mistake) that the event occurs on 5 *tishrīn al-awwal*, that is, in September. In his other book that has been preserved, *Tanbīh*, 143, he notes however that 'the appearance of the fire' occurs on 'the great sabbath' on the eve of Easter Sunday. See the fragment from Bīrūnī: Fück, *Documenta islamica inedita*, 94; cf. Canard, *Byzantion*, 35(1955), 35f, who has references to other publications of the same source. See al-Bayhaqī, 96; Ibn al-Qalānisī, 66; from whom Ibn al-Jawzī copied, *Muntaẓam*, VII, 239 (with a few omissions), and after him, his grandson, Sibṭ ibn al-Jawzī, *Mir'āh* (BM Or 4619), 189b. Canard, *ibid.*, 20, assumed that Ibn al-Qalānisī and Sibṭ ibn al-Jawzī used a common source, Hilāl al-Ṣābī – a Baghdadi writer of the first half of the eleventh century; see *ibid.*, 39f, the translation of a further fragment from Sibṭ ibn al-Jawzī, a Paris manuscript, and see the editor's supplement in Ibn al-Qalānisī, 68. Ibn Kathīr, *Bidāya*, XI, 339, explains this stunt as follows: silk threads and

The authorities and the Christians

[702] We have seen that in theory the Muslim authorities were obliged, according to the rules and precedents laid down in the days of the Prophet and the first caliphs, to respect the rights of the Christians. The Christians became 'protected people', deprived of political rights and sovereign status, forbidden to carry arms and obliged to pay taxes. On the other hand, they were given the freedom to practice their own rituals and the assurance of having their lives, property and their various holy places defended. One cannot say that these rules were not observed at all, but a picture of maltreatment and varying degrees of persecution emerges from the sources. The endless state of war with the Byzantines naturally contributed to this to a large extent. Despite the fact that they were politically isolated for many generations, and that the cultural and linguistic differences between the Aramaic and Arabic-speaking Eastern Christians and the Byzantine Greeks grew and intensified, the Byzantine emperor still saw himself as the defender and patron of the Christians and the holy places in Palestine during this entire period. On the other hand, the Muslim rulers saw the Christians and their holy places as Byzantine hostages to a certain degree. On more than one occasion they reacted to hostile acts or mistreatment on the part of the Byzantines, by applying pressure and carrying out reprisals on the Christians in Islamic countries, especially in Palestine, and primarily in Jerusalem.

I have already mentioned the letter written by the Ikhshīd (937) to the emperor Romanus I in which he boastfully describes in detail the size of the Christian population and the importance of the Christian holy places which he controls. We have also seen how the patriarch Theodosius was

rags dipped in sulphur and similar materials; the Christian fragments: *Le Codex*, 84–100, see the Syriac fragment on p. 91. The letter of Arethas to the *amīr* of Damascus describes the Easter ceremony, held in the presence of the *amīr*, governor of Jerusalem, who closes and seals the Holy Sepulchre, while the Christians hold a single candle. That candle lights itself and is used to light the candles of all those present (while Muḥammad's tomb, adds this polemical treatise, remains completely in the dark). See Abel, *Byzantion*, 24(1954), 365; Karlin-Hayter, *ibid.*, 29/30:281, 1959/60; Canard, *ibid.*, 29, who has further references; and in the continuation, *ibid.*, 30–34, Nicetas' letter; see it in its entirety, with an introduction and French translation: Riant, *AOL*, I(1881), 375–382, with references to earlier publications. Bernard: Tobler et Molinier, I, 315. See Bar Hebraeus (Bedjan), 204; (Budge), 184. From the research literature, I would point out the aforementioned comprehensive article of Canard, with a detailed discussion of almost all the sources I have mentioned and a few more sources, and with references to earlier scholars. I shall note further: Baumstarck, *Palästinapilger*, 6f; Cheikho, al-*Mashriq*, 1913, 188:16 (from a manuscript of the twelfth century writer, al-Jūbarī, he also quotes the story of the Ayyūbid ruler al-Malik al-ʿĀdil who wished to enquire into the matter of the fire, but a monk explained to him that if he wished to know the secret, he would not receive the money, and the Sultan understood the hint); Vincent et Abel, *Jérusalem* II(1), 229. A description of the Easter fire is also to be found in the treatise on the calendar by the Copt al-Asʿad ibn al-ʿAssāl, of the mid-thirteenth century (see: Graf, *GCAL*, II, 403, 405f).

duty-bound to write in praise of the Muslim rulers' behaviour, while making the point that he writes on the basis of 'a proposal which cannot be refused' and requesting concessions for the Muslims so that they should not mistreat the Christians. We are also aware of how in around 940, when information regarding brutality towards the Muslim captives became known, the Muslims put pressure on the patriarchs of Antioch and Jerusalem in this matter. One of the excellent Arab writers of the latter part of the tenth century, the Baghdadian al-Tanūkhī, innocently tells of two Christian leaders, the patriarch of Antioch and the patriarch of Jerusalem (whom he calls, for some reason, the catholicus – *al-qāṭalīq*), whose authority is accepted by the Byzantine emperor to such an extent that these two can even put a ban on him or remove a ban. It is accepted among the Byzantines, he writes, that anyone whose opinion differs from that of these two is an unbeliever and that an emperor cannot sit on the throne in Byzantium unless these two consent to it, and he owes them allegiance and they have to justify his deeds. All this, 'despite the fact that we are the rulers in these lands and these two are our clients'. On occasion we find one of the close retainers of the Byzantine emperor being sent on a special mission to Palestine; it appears that there was even a kind of resident emissary, permanently staying in Palestine, as Maqrīzī implies, mentioning 'the envoy of the Byzantine emperor in Palestine' (or literally, in jund Filasṭīn, for in that period the terms Filasṭīn and Palestine were not identical, the former meaning the southern part of the country, as I have already explained). Maqrīzi is referring here to Kāfūr, the ruler of Egypt, who, it was said, took this emissary to Egypt with him in Dhū'l-Ḥijja AH 334 (August AD 946).

Despite the persecution and maltreatment, one should bear in mind that the Christians had immense influence and positions of power, chiefly because of the gifted administrators among them who occupied government posts despite the ban in Muslim law against employing Christians, or who were part of the intelligentsia of the period owing to the fact that they were outstanding scientists, mathematicians, physicians and so on. In the mid-ninth century, for instance, Būlus (Paulus) b. Ḥanūn 'the physician to the people of Filasṭīn', is mentioned, as is his conversation with Salawayh b. Banān, Caliph al-Mu'taṣim's physician, carried on in Aramaic (*bi'l-suryāniyya*). 'Abd al-Jabbār, writing in 995, notes that 'kings in Egypt, al-Shām, Iraq, Jazīra, Fāris, and in all their surroundings, rely upon the Christians in matters of officialdom, the central administration and the handling of funds. It is the Christians who manage the Muslims' affairs, collect money from them, imposing taxes on them for everything, which is contrary to law, being a deed which God has not permitted according to the Koran, and by doing so, they impoverish Islam and spend the money on contemptible things.' On the other hand, the learned Muslim intellectuals were inclined to console themselves with the hope that eventually all the Christians would accept Islam and even ascribed to the Prophet the following tradition on the subject: 'in the future, Jesus himself – when he descends from the heavens a second time, onto the eastern white lighthouse in Damascus – will break the cross, kill the pigs, and cancel the *jizya*; he will refuse to receive the *jizya* from anyone, and will not agree to anything else but that they, and all the rest, should accept Islam'.[42]

[703] Almost generation after generation, the Christian writers recorded acts of persecution and harassment, to the point of slaughter and destruction, suffered by the Christians at the hands of the Muslim rulers. Foremost among these is the account of sixty Byzantine soldiers who were taken captive by the Muslims after the capture of Gaza and executed because of their refusal to accept Islam. The conquest of Palestine by the Muslims was naturally an act of war accompanied by a great deal of bloodshed, but this story in itself has no historical truth and was merely invented along the lines of the pattern of the later relationship between the two worlds – Christianity and Islam.[43]

[704] As to the eighties of the seventh century, we have the story of the ousting of the alleged patriarch Theodore (sec. 684); but this is of no historical value. A more credible description, though of a general nature, is to be found in the annals of the patriarchs by Sāwīrūs ibn Muqaffa', who notes that the Christians were persecuted in 'Abd al-Malik's day (685–705). They were considered allies of the Byzantines and were treated accordingly, with their lives unprotected. The collection of the *jizya* was carried out relentlessly; for instance, a corpse could not be buried before the *jizya* was paid, even if the deceased had been a poor man who did not have enough for bread. One can also include here the legendary story of the death of a monk from Mar Saba called Michael, who sold baskets and mats in Jerusalem. The wife of Caliph Adramelek (!) tried to seduce him and when he rejected her, she accused him of assault, and he was eventually executed outside the walls of Jerusalem. Theophanes tells a more credible story about 'Abd al-Malik, who wanted to remove the pillars of

42 See Ibn al-Jawzī, *Muntaẓam*, VI, 353; Tanūkhī, *Nishwār*, I, 30. The Byzantine emissary: Maqrīzī, *Khiṭaṭ*, III, 108. Kāfūr may have tried to win the hearts of the Christians through the emissary and thus prevent them from supporting the Ḥamdānids, who invaded Palestine at that time. Paulus the physician: see Ibn Abī Uṣaybi'a, I, 168, according to a 'history of the physicians', written by Yūsuf ibn Ibrahīm ibn al-Dāya, who died in AH 265, that is AD 878; cf. Sezgin, III, 231; 'Abd al-Jabbār, *Tathbīt*, I, 191. The tradition on Jesus is to be found in many places in different versions; see for instance Ibn Kathīr, *Bidāya*, VII, 256; he will cancel the *jizya*: meaning that he will take away the protection given in exchange for the *jizya*, and whoever wishes to live, will accept Islam.

43 See the story of the sixty martyrs: Delahaye, *Analecta Bollandiana*, 23:289, 1904; see on this matter the article of Pargoire, *EO*, 8:40, 1905, who even discusses the names of those

the church of Gethsemane in order to build the temple in Mecca. However, he yielded to pleas of Sergius b. Manṣūr, who was the *logothetēs* (a Byzantine office, a sort of prime minister) and a friend of 'Abd al-Malik; of a certain Patrikios, also one of the caliph's friends, and of the man who was the leader (*proukhōn*) of the Christians in Palestine (*tōn kata tēn Palaistinēn Khristianōn*), Klausus. These three convinced him to ask Justinian II (Rhinotmetus) for other pillars in their stead. One can give more credence to this story, as even in Muslim sources similar episodes have been recorded. An example is that of the destruction of the church of St John in Damascus during the rule of Caliph al-Walīd b. 'Abd al-Malik (705–715), because of its proximity to the mosque and the Muslims' desire to extend the mosque. Al-Walīd was not taken aback by the warnings of the Christians that if he did this, he would turn into a *jinn*. He turned over the actual destruction to the Jews, who came and razed the church to the ground. Afterwards when al-Walīd wanted to start on the construction of the mosque, he asked the emperor to send him a master builder (*ṣāni'*) from Byzantium, or else he would destroy all the churches in the land and also that of Jerusalem (undoubtedly referring to the Church of the Resurrection), as well as the church in Ruhā (that is, Edessa) and the rest of 'the holy buildings (*āthār*) of the Byzantines' (he probably means the Christians).[44]

[705] A Georgian source tells a story of a saint named Petrus, who was executed by the Arabs on 13 January 713, and how he cursed the Muslim religion when he was about to die. This occurred in Capitolias, that is Bayt Ra's in Trans-Jordan (north of Irbid). Here, too, the Jews are involved, demonstrating their hatred of the Christians, and especially the Kubaris (Khaybarīs?). Theophanes tells a parallel story, similar in all its details, except that it takes place in Mayūmas (the Gaza port).[45]

Byzantine soldiers and discovers proof of the presence of two cohorts there, one of Scythians and one *cohors voluntariorum*.

44 The banishing of the patriarch (to a distance of 2,000 miles), see: Papadopoulos-Kerameos, *Analekta*, II, 299. Sāwīrūs, I (Seybold), 136. The story of Michael: in a Russian source, *The Life of Theodore of Edessa*, see: Vailhé, *EO*, 3(1899–1900), 25; he places this story in the first half of the ninth century, but the name of the caliph should apparently be 'Abd al-Malik. Theophanes, 365. The church of St John: Ibn 'Asākir, II(1) (new edition), 23, 26.

45 The story of Petrus, see: Peeters, *Analecta Bollandiana*, 57:299, 1939; Theophanes, 416f. Peeters tried to prove that the *dayr* (monastery) of Mīmās in Syria is meant, which is mentioned in Yāqūt, *Buldān*, II, 702. According to Yāqūt, a Christian saint was buried there who had healed the sick; the poet Buṭayn came there to be healed, but in his illness he could not restrain himself and urinated on the grave and the saint killed him; the people of Egypt were angered by this, and they came there and demanded that the bones of the saint be burned, but the Christians bribed the governor of Ḥimṣ and through him, managed to get rid of them. It seems that there is an error in Yāqūt and the story is in fact referring to Mayūmas of Gaza (also mentioning 'the people of Egypt' makes this likely), as in Theophanes. Naturally, one cannot conclude anything definitely in such a matter, as it is a source of a legendary nature; but it seems that an element of historical truth is found in

[706] Another story concerns seventy young Christians from Iconium, in Asia Minor, who wanted to go on a pilgrimage to Jerusalem in the days of Leo III the Isaurian (717–741). They were not given permission to do so (apparently the intention of the story is that the refusal was due to the fact that the emperor was an iconoclast) but nevertheless set out on their way. The Arab governor of Caesarea caught them and accused them of espionage; he then had them executed, barring seven who agreed to accept Islam. A similar incident is related, as having occurred during the rule of Sulaymān b. 'Abd al-Malik (715–717) or of 'Umar b. 'Abd al-'Azīz (717–720): sixty pilgrims from Amorion, also in Asia Minor, were apparently crucified in Jerusalem, according to a Syriac source translated into Greek. What Willibald witnessed during his own pilgrimage, when the Muslims threatened to destroy the 'Church of the Christians' (that is, again, the Church of the Resurrection) if they were not paid enormous sums of money, also applies to the same period. Willibald further notes that in Nazareth, the Christians had repeatedly to pay ransom to the Muslims for the return of the Church of the Annunciation.[46]

[707] We also have information on the persecution of Christians during the early part of Abbasid rule. A Greek Church source speaks of the ban which 'Abdallah, 'head of the Arabs', put on placing a cross in Jerusalem. According to this source, he evicted the monks from their monasteries. He made the Jews destroy the Holy Sepulchre and the other places of worship. As the writer attributes these acts to the time of Constantine V Copronymus (741–775), one can assume that perhaps Abū'l-'Abbās 'Abdallah al-Saffāḥ, the first Abbasid caliph, is being referred to; or perhaps the reference is to his uncle, 'Abdallah b. 'Alī, who was governor of jund Urdunn and whose rule may also have extended to jund Filasṭīn.

In 755, so Theophanes tells us, 'Abdallah (evidently the same governor) increased the tax (*phorologia*) imposed on the Christians. He also ordered that a tax be imposed on the Christian priests and monks (certainly contrary to what had been the custom until then). He confiscated (literally: put his seal on) the valuable sacred articles and compelled the Jews to buy them, and these 'protected people' actually put these sacred articles up for auction. Theophanes also mentions that the ruler also ordered the crosses over their churches to be removed and forbade the Christians to hold midnight services or even teach their scriptures. In 772, when 'Abdallah

Theophanes, who is referring to persecution during the days of al-Walīd, in the Gaza region, and perhaps also in Trans-Jordan.

[46] Iconium and Amorion – perhaps speaking of the same episode. See: *AA SS*, October, IX, 359f; Papodopoulos-Kerameos, *Historia*, 278; Peeters, *Tréfonds*, 180; Constantelos, *Byzantion*, 42 (1972), 340f. Willibald, in Tobler et Molinier, I, 260, cf. Baumstarck, *Palästinapilger*, 70; Bréhier, *RH*, 157(1928), 279; Vincent et Abel, *Jérusalem*, II, 938. See more on the persecution of the Christians during the rule of 'Umar ibn 'Abd al-'Azīz, according to the

(Caliph al-Manṣūr, this time) visited Jerusalem, he ordered that a special mark should be stamped on the hands of the Christians and the Jews. Many Christians then fled to Byzantium.[47]

[708] Persecution persisted throughout the following decade as well. One source tells of a Muslim who converted to Christianity and became a monk, and renamed Christophoros. He was beheaded on 14 April 789. At around the same time, evidently, there was an Arab attack on the monastery of St Theodosius, near Bethlehem. The monastery was pillaged, many of the monks were slaughtered and some escaped. The attackers also destroyed two churches near that monastery. A Church source tells about the suffering endured by the monasteries in the Judaean mountains during the inter-tribal war which broke out in 796, which I have already described. While Bet Guvrin was being abandoned by its inhabitants, who were falling captive to the Arabs, assaults were being made on Ascalon, Gaza and other localities. Everywhere there was pillage and destruction. The Bedouin came from the direction of Jerusalem and attacked the monastery in Wadi Chariton; sixty Bedouin invaded the monastery of Mar Saba, abusing sixty of the monks, some of whom were killed and some wounded. This happened on the Wednesday before Easter, 13 March 796. The attack was renewed on 20 March, and 20 men died in the flames.[48]

[709] Again, Theophanes tells us of the events of 809 – and as he was a contemporary, his evidence with regard to these years is both interesting and quite credible – when Hārūn al-Rashīd died and a fratricidal war broke out between the brothers al-Amīn and al-Ma'mūn. According to him these events caused the Christians an enormous amount of suffering. Many churches and monasteries in Jerusalem and its environs were aban-

Armenian writer Ghévond (Leontius); Jeffery, *HTR*, 37(1944), 269, and see references there, n. 3.

47 The decrees of 'Abdallah al-Saffāḥ: Papadopoulos-Kerameos, *Analekta*, II, 299; cf. Musset, *Histoire*, 255; see Theophanes, 430, 439, 443f; cf. Breyer, 97; 'Abdallah b.'Alī is mentioned above, see Ṭabarī, *Ta'rīkh*, III, 84. The assumption that it is he who Theophanes is speaking of is supported by the fact that Theophanes notes that he (that is, 'Abdallah ibn 'Alī, Ibnalim – as Theophanes has it) died in AM 6258, that is AD 764/5, which is not the year of the caliph's death. Theophanes uses the term *apeleutheroi*; Anastasius translated it as: *liberti*; that is, apparently meaning freedmen, but this is not so, since he is using the term to correspond to the Arabic dhimmī (protected people); that is, after having mentioned the Jews (*Hebraioi*) he continues: 'and [these] dhimmīs put them up for auction', etc. Cf. Bréhier, *RH*, 157(1928), 279 (he is wholly mistaken in his reckoning of the dates and speaks of 749 and 758; nor does he even try to clarify the identity of that *amīr* named 'Abdallah).

48 The monk Christophoros: Vailhé, *ROC*, 6(1901), 315. The monastery of St Theodosius: *De casis Dei* in Tobler et Molinier, I, 303. See on the events of 796: Vailhé, *EO*, 3(1899–1900), 23; the date is evidently an error, because Easter had to fall on 17 March according to this, but Passover fell on 29 March in that year (AM 4556) and Easter never comes before Passover; see also: Vailhé, *ROC*, 6(1901), 316; the story is also found in *AA*

doned, such as those of Sts Cyriac, Theodosius, Chariton, Euthymius, and Mar Saba. Four years later, in 813, the disturbances broke out anew and many Christians, both monks and laity, fled from Palestine to Cyprus and Constantinople, where they found a refuge from the Arabs' terrible persecution in those days of anarchy and civil war. Palestine was the scene of violence, rape and murder. Here Theophanes repeats his account of the abandonment of churches; according to him, this applied to the Church of the Resurrection and other churches in the vicinity as well. The emperor Michael I (Rangabē) and the patriarch of Constantinople, Nicephorus, did everything in their power to help the refugees. In Constantinople, an important monastery was placed at their disposal and they were also given considerable financial aid. Apparently, the disturbances and the flight of the Christians are also reflected in Maqrīzī's account, that when the Coptic patriarch of Alexandria, Ya'qūb, held office (after the year AH 211, which is AD 826/7), the church in Jerusalem was rebuilt for the Christians who had returned from Egypt, from which we learn that they had also fled to Egypt – not only to Cyprus and Constantinople.[49]

[710] It seems that after al-Ma'mūn established his rule on firm foundations, a certain stability began to be felt throughout the caliphate, and although it would be impossible to define this period which began and continued almost until the days of the Ikhshīdids as one of internal peace and tranquillity, it seems that the situation of the Christians became more secure. In fact, we no longer hear of acts of persecution during the ninth century, nor in the first quarter of the tenth century.

Waves of persecution broke out anew in Jumādā II AH 311 (October–November AD 923). According to Sa'īd ibn Biṭrīq, the Muslims attacked two churches of the Melekites (the central sect connected with the Byzantines); namely the church of St Cosmas and the church of St Cyriac in Ramla. There were also atrocities in Ascalon and Caesarea, where, too, churches were destroyed. The Christians complained to Caliph al-Muqtadir, and his response was to order the rebuilding of what had been destroyed (despite the Muslim law which forbade the dhimmīs to build houses of worship). After a peaceful interlude, disturbances recurred during the rule of Muḥammad ibn Ṭughj, the Ikhshīd, in AH 325, which covers *ca.* AD 937. According to Sa'īd ibn Biṭrīq, the Muslims attacked the

SS, March, III, 20, pp. 166–179; cf. Constantelos, *Byzantion*, 42(1972), 343 (he has the year 786 instead of 796); cf. further: Musset, *Histoire*, 255.

49 Theophanes, 484, 499; an echo of these disturbances can be found in the Saxon chronicler, see Annalista Saxo, *MGH* (SS), VI, 570 who speaks of the destruction of Jerusalem 'by the Persians' and the great persecution of the Christians in the East in 814; cf. Papadopoulos-Kerameos, *Analekta*, II, 299; III, 4; Vailhé, *EO*, 3(1899–1900), 24; *idem*, *ROC*, 6(1901), 325f, Tobler, *Golgatha*, 112; Berlière, *Revue bénédictine*, 5(1888), 444; Bréhier, *RH*, 157 (1928), 279, see Maqrīzī, *Khiṭaṭ*, III, 397.

church in Jerusalem on Palm Sunday (*al-sha'ānīn*; 26 March 937) and set fire to the southern gates of Constantine's church and to half of the exedra, whereupon the Church of the Calvary and the Church of the Resurrection collapsed. This occurred in the year Christodulus the first ascended the patriarchal seat. According to al-Makīn and Maqrīzī, the Church of the Resurrection and the Church of the Calvary were also robbed of their treasures.[50]

[711] It seems that at the same time, the Muslims attacked in Ascalon again. According to Yaḥyā ibn Sa'īd, the assault was made on the 'great church there, known by the name of Mary the Green. They destroyed it and robbed it of all its contents and then set fire to it'. He stresses that it was the Jews who demolished it, with the Muslims' support. The Jews gutted its timber beams with fire, firstly on the roofs, so that their lead would melt and the supporting pillars would collapse. The bishop of Ascalon then left for Baghdad to get permission to rebuild the church, but he did not succeed. The church was left in ruins, for the Muslims who lived in Ascalon agreed amongst themselves that they would not allow it to be built again. As to the bishop, he never returned to Ascalon and remained in Ramla until his death.[51]

50 Cahen, *Bulletin de la faculté des lettres de Strasbourg*, 29(1950), 122; idem, *Past and Present*, 6(1954), 6f, claims again that Muslim rule, in general, saw a period of peace and security, and that the sole persecution of the Christians recorded under Islam occurred during al-Ḥākim's rule. This is an apologetic and incomprehensible approach which ignores the facts. The period of some hundred years, beginning in around 815 and ending in 923 is the only period from which we have no information on the persecution of Christians in Palestine. The riots in 923: Sa'īd ibn Biṭrīq, II, 82; evidently his source when speaking of Ramla actually meant jund Filasṭīn, for the churches in the name of Cosmas and Cyriac were in Jerusalem, not in Ramla. At the same time, there were also atrocities against the Christians in Tinnīs in Egypt and in Damascus, see *ibid.*, in the continuation; the riots continued for a whole year, until the middle of Rajab AH 312, mid-October AD 924. The disturbances in Jerusalem: Sa'īd ibn Biṭrīq, II, 87; al-Makīn, 208; Maqrīzī, *Khiṭaṭ*, III, 396; cf. Clermont-Ganneau, *Receuil*, II, 308 (the inscription relating to the mosque supposedly built near the Church of the Holy Sepulchre, according to him, spoke of the ban on dhimmīs entering a mosque [unidentified] in order to pay taxes and was dealt with above); Baumstarck, *Bauten*, 17f, tries to understand the intention of what is said about the southern doors of the Church of Constantine and suggests two possibilities: either it is referring to the southern façade of the church (according to Heisenberg), or the southern side entrance of the eastern wing.

51 The Jerusalem patriarch mentions in his letter, *RHGF*, IX, 294f, that in *ca.* 880, the governor of the region (Ramla?) was a Christian. See on the church in Ascalon: Yaḥyā ibn Sa'īd (*PO*), 21; we have seen above that in Damascus as well it was the Jews who destroyed the church; which may naturally be considered slander and calumny on the part of the Christians, but on further consideration, there is apparently no real reason to question the authenticity of this information. The situation is understandable against the background of hatred between the Jews and the Christians and in view of the fact that the Muslims were the minority in this urban population and it was the Jewish masses who executed the work, with the consent and support of the authorities. See above later evidence with regard to the 'green mosque' in Ascalon, that is, the church was turned into a mosque some time afterwards.

[712] The riots and the ravaging of the churches in the year 966 have already been described, and we have seen how this formed part of the pattern of general tension and warfare carried on by the Byzantines in their attempt to regain control of the region, particularly Jerusalem, and it is difficult to distinguish between the motive and the results. On the one hand, there is no doubt that the Byzantine offensives aroused antagonism towards the Christians; while on the other hand, the mistreatment of the Christian population, and especially the churches of Jerusalem, was what drove the Byzantines to recruit forces for a struggle of a decidedly religious nature – namely, to free Jerusalem of the Muslims in a sort of tenth-century crusade. The hostile acts and the religious assaults reached their peak during al-Ḥākim's rule, as we have seen, when openly and brazenly, in a wholesale manner, he ignored the basic principles of Muslim law with regard to the dhimmīs, compelled the Christians to accept Islam and destroyed the Christians' and Jews' houses of worship. These acts of destruction were widespread and exhaustive, as can be concluded from the facts I have given above, and the demolition orders were executed even in far-off localities, relatively distant from the reigning centre, such as Jubayl and Tripoli in Syria. One exception was evidently the Church of St Mary (the Nativity) in Bethlehem. According to Adhémar de Chabannes, who was a contemporary (he died in 1034 in Jerusalem), the 'pagans' did not succeed in reducing it to ruins, for the appearance of a heavenly light caused the death of those who came to destroy it and no one has since dared to touch 'the church of the mother of God'. In the days of al-Ẓāhir, as we have seen, the destruction of the churches continued and their building stones were used to restore the walls of the city. We have also seen the matter of the confiscation of valuable sacred articles of the Church of the Resurrection in al-Mustanṣir's time, a reprisal for the fact that in Constantinople orders were given to pray for the well-being of the caliph in Baghdad. Rumours of the confiscation spread to the West and accumulated substance on the way, until there was talk of the repeated destruction of the Church of the Holy Sepulchre.

The building of a wall around the Christian quarter in Jerusalem in the sixties of the eleventh century is also linked to the question of the rulers' attitude towards the Christians. The source from which we derive most of our information on this affair, the chronicle of William of Tyre, is somewhat ambivalent on the subject. What at the beginning of the description seems to be concern for the fortification of Jerusalem, a kind of overall interest in the city, gradually becomes a matter of the maltreatment of the Christians. At first, he describes the pressure put on the Christians to supply money, despite their poverty and distress. Afterwards, and this is the main point, comes their enclosure in a kind of ghetto. For if we look into the description of the borders of the quarter allotted to them, we see that they have been crowded into the northern part of the city. This is how William of Tyre depicts the outlines of its wall: from the western gate called David (today, the Jaffa Gate) via the square tower known by the name of Tancred (in the neighbourhood of today's New Gate), until the northern gate named for Stephen (that is, today's Lions Gate), and the outer wall being its boundary; while within the city, the boundary was 'the public way' (*via publica*) which stretches from that gate until the 'moneychangers' tables' and from there, to the western gate. That is to say, they crowded the Christians into the area surrounding the Church of the Holy Sepulchre. I have not surveyed this matter to the full, and we shall learn of additional details concerning the rulers' attitude to the Christians in the discussions below, especially in the discussion on the subject of Christian pilgrims.[52]

[713] After the Turcomans' conquest, it seems that most of the pressure was directed towards the central Greek Church, which was linked with Byzantium. In Cahen's view, this conquest caused the abolition of Byzantine patronage of the Christians, which had existed under the Fatimids and was generally accepted by them. Conversely, the status of the Latins rose, and particularly the activities of the Amalfians. The Latins dominated the churches and interfered with the rituals of the Greeks.[53]

Aid and reconstruction

[714] Against the background of waves of persecution and destructive acts, the efforts at reconstruction stand out and projects to raise money to help Jerusalem are repeated again and again – projects in which Church organisations throughout the Christian world and rulers of Christian countries focus on Jerusalem. In the sources I have surveyed above, the special connection with Byzantium is noted: the role of the Byzantine emperor and his intervention on behalf of the Christians in the Holy Land, the involvement of the Byzantine Church and its monks in the events in Palestine, the aid to refugees from Palestine, and similar matters.

We have information on the restoration of the Church of the Holy Sepulchre in around 820, after the devastation carried out in 813, as we have seen above. Sa'īd ibn Biṭrīq makes a point of the fact that this was a time of internal warfare among the Muslims; Jerusalem was undergoing severe hardship and scarcity, and the Muslims almost completely abandoned the city. The patriarch Thomas I managed to obtain fifty cedar and

52 See Adhémar in *RHGF*, X, 152, cf. De Vogüé, *Eglises*, 62. The rumour about the destruction of the Church of the Holy Sepulchre in 1056: *Annales Augustani*, *MGH* (SS), III, 127. The wall: see William of Tyre, 392 (Book IX, ch. xviii). See above, sec. 601.

53 Cahen, *Bulletin de la faculté des lettres de Strasbourg*, 29(1950), 120ff and references there.

pine beams to restore the dome of the Church of the Holy Sepulchre. The money came from a wealthy Egyptian Christian by the name of Bakām, who hailed from a place called Bayt Būrah. He insisted that they should not take donations for this purpose from anyone other than himself. When the Abbasid commander ʿAbdallah ibn Ṭāhir came to Jerusalem *en route* to Baghdad from Egypt (827), the Muslims came to Jerusalem to complain to him that the Christians had disobeyed Muslim law by building a larger dome than the former one, as big as the Dome of the Rock. ʿAbdallah ordered that the matter be investigated and warned the patriarch Thomas that he would have him whipped had he found the accusation to be true. Then a certain Muslim suggested to the patriarch how he could fool the ruler, and received a bribe of 1,000 dinars for his suggestion as well as a promise that he and his heirs would receive an allowance similar to those received by the sextons of the church. As the Muslim had suggested, the patriarch was to claim that he had not enlarged the dome but merely repaired it; anyone who claimed the contrary would have to prove that the former dome had indeed been smaller. The scheme was a success and that Muslim's heirs continued to receive an allowance until there were no heirs left, apart from one daughter, and then patriarch Elias ibn Manṣūr (878–907) stopped the allowance.[54]

[715] We have considerable evidence from the Latin world. This evidence has been preserved in western archives, while the Byzantine archives have been lost. In 881, Elias, patriarch of Jerusalem, sent a letter to all the bishops, princes and nobility of the Frankish kingdom, informing them that a Christian has become governor of the region and that he has ordered the rebuilding of the churches. In order to raise the funds needed for this project, the Christians have mortgaged all the lands and property of the Church, even the vineyards and the olive groves. This was obviously written with the intention of getting financial support from the Franks. There are also sources which speak of Rome's increasing support for the Christians in Palestine in this period (the end of the ninth century) and large donations even arrived from far-off England.[55]

[716] We have seen that after the fire which consumed the Church of the

[54] Saʿīd ibn Biṭrīq, II, 55f; what he writes about the Muslims abandoning Jerusalem is definitely credible and to a certain extent, this is evidence of how far the Muslims in Jerusalem at that time were still a minority without roots; cf. Papadopoulous-Kerameos, *Analekta*, III, 4; Tobler, *Golgatha*, 112. One should note the chronological contradiction in the sources, which is that the patriarch Thomas died in 820, while Saʿīd ibn Biṭrīq claims that the meeting with ʿAbdallah ibn Ṭāhir took place at the end of his campaign in Egypt, which fell in 827.

[55] Elias' letter: *RHGF*, IX, 294f; the matter of the Christian governor has already been mentioned in the description of the events of that period, as well as Aḥmad ibn Ṭūlūn's positive attitude towards the dhimmīs. Assistance from Rome and from England: Riant, *AOL*, 1(1881), 28.

Resurrection in 966, Kāfūr, the ruler of Egypt, was prepared to restore it, but the Byzantine emperor rejected his proposal and threatened that he would achieve this end by warfare. As we have seen, this war indeed took place. Hence, it seems that the first reconstruction of the Church of the Resurrection was executed only in the year 1011, after the total destruction carried out on al-Ḥākim's orders, when Palestine was ruled by Arab tribes under the leadership of the Jarrāḥids. As we have seen, they appointed a new patriarch, Theophilus, and initiated the reconstruction of the Church of the Resurrection and even demanded that the Christians come forward in this matter, while in the meantime the buildings surrounding the Holy Sepulchre suffered additional ruination in the days of al-Ḥākim. It seems, however, that the basic restoration of the churches after al-Ḥākim's decrees and extensive destruction only began during al-Ẓāhir's rule, although we have seen that even in his day there was some destruction of churches. The work of restoration was made possible by the notable assistance coming from Constantinople. The work was finished during al-Mustanṣir's day, in 1048, some forty years after the destruction. The patriarch of Jerusalem, Nicephorus, sent a special mission to Constantinople, headed by John of Caria (a district in Asia Minor), a native of Constantinople who had become a monk in Jerusalem. Al-Ẓāhir expressed his consent to the rebuilding of the church. Actually, it seems obvious that these facts are related to the negotiations with the Byzantines which al-Ẓāhir conducted towards the end of his life and which reached their conclusion after his death. It appears that most of the assistance came during the reign of Constantine IX Monomachus (who ascended the throne in 1042).[56]

[717] The assistance from the West referred to above began to assume greater proportions in the eleventh century. Towards the end of the ninth century, we already find the instance of the dedication of agricultural property in the village of Arisa, donated by Hugo of Tuscany and his wife Julitta (her real name was probably Juditha) to the Church of the Holy Sepulchre. The date of the dedication was 29 October 993. The property included twenty-four houses as well as lands and various dependencies. When Hungary became a Catholic country, another Latin factor was added to the donors to the Holy Land. In 1002, Stephen, king of Hungary, established a monastery in Jerusalem, which was to be devoted to the care

[56] See Dhahabī, *Ta'rīkh*, on margin of Ibn Miskawayh, II, 221; Baumstarck, *Bauten*, 16f (he notes that in the restoration work, they refrained from repairing the roof of the church of Constantine, as it was too large). On the restoration of the Church of the Resurrection, the major source is William of Tyre, 19f. See also: Yaḥyā ibn Sa'īd (Cheikho), 228, 270f. The matter of the considerable assistance from Byzantium is also confirmed by Bar Hebraeus (Bedjan), 219, (Budge), 196; according to whom the 'king of the Romans' sent the noblest of the kingdom with an enormous amount of silver and gold, and they restored the church

of the Latin pilgrims. He granted this monastery a foundation consisting of farm lands and vineyards. Another Latin endowment is dated 1053: Odilus, son of Rudolph, *de comitatu Rudense* (Rouergue) 'was inspired by God' when he went on pilgrimage, to dedicate a tenth of his property to the Church of the Holy Sepulchre, for the exaltation of his soul after his death and the exaltation of the soul of his wife Cecilia, of his father Rudolph, and others. According to the document, the patriarch of Jerusalem, Sophronius, was the person who received the donation. A short time before the Crusades, in 1083–1085, people of the Albigeois in southern France (Tarn), set up trusts for 'the hostel in Jerusalem and the paupers in the hostel' (*ad honorem et pauperibus hospitalis Ierosolimitani*); these trusts were established through the mediation of Anselinus; the man in charge of the Jerusalem hostel, Aldegarius; and the bishop of Albi.[57]

[718] The story of the people of Amalfi forms a special chapter in the saga of assistance from the West. The merchants of this southern Italian city maintained excellent relations with the Fatimid authorities, as they played an important part in maritime trade with Egypt. In the latter half of the eleventh century, they received licence from Caliph al-Mustanṣir to put up a monastery, a church, a hospital and two hostels, one for men and the other for women, in front of the Church of the Resurrection. They carried out this project and the monastery was called Sancta Maria de Latina. They also built hostels for pilgrims and an *oratorium* which they dedicated to the memory of John 'the generous' (Eleymon), a man of Cyprus who became patriarch of Alexandria (and who died on 23 January 616). Heyd doubts the tradition that ascribes the establishment of the monastery in the name of 'the Latin Mary' to the people of Amalfi, for this monastery is already mentioned in the deed of dedication of Hugo of Tuscany from the year 993. Riley-Smith tried to prove that the monastery was built above the hostel built by Pope Gregorius I, in 603; and furthermore, that the original guardian saint of the hostel and the prayer-hut attached to it was John the Baptist, and that it was the Hospitallers who changed it to John the Generous, and that the monastery and the adjacent hostel were afterwards the birthplace of their order, the Knights of St John, though it is possible that the order stemmed from a military

as it had been beforehand; this occurred, he says, in 427 of the hijra, AD 1036; see further: Riant, *AOL*, 1(1881), 52, n. 9, containing a list of sources.

57 Martène, *amplissima collectio*, I, 347ff; Riant, *MAIBL*, 31(1884), 158–162 (*ibid.*, 168f, he doubts the authenticity of the document – but not the information on the dedication – and assumes that it is a copy and not the original, containing alterations from the original version); see also Berlière, *Revue bénédictine*, 5(1888), 446; Bréhier, *L'église*, 30f. who has further details on dedications for the Church of the Holy Sepulchre; Heyd, *Histoire*, I, 104; the Hungarians: *Vita Stephani*, *MGH* (SS), XI, 227–235; Riant (above, in this note), 165; Odilus: Martène, *Thesaurus*, I, 176f. (cf. Riant, *ibid.*, 157). The people of Tarn: Saige, *Bibliothèque*, 25 (1864), 554ff.

organisation. Evidently, the Maurus family (de Comite Maurone) were at the centre of the activities of these Amalfians in Jerusalem. Maurus and his sons, especially Pantaleone, were extremely rich merchants who had accumulated their wealth from trading in the Mediterranean.[58]

Christian pilgrimage

[719] Throughout the generations, Jerusalem has attracted Christian pilgrims. At first, it is true, Christianity spoke of the heavenly Jerusalem and berated the importance of the earthly Jerusalem, in which it saw the erroneous ways and digression of the Jews. However, after the Roman-Byzantine empire became a Christian one, interest in the holy places in Jerusalem and elsewhere in Palestine gradually increased, particularly with regard to those places connected with the life of Jesus and the early Christian saints. When Jerusalem fell to the Muslims, an element of adventure and danger was added to the act of pilgrimage and a sort of romanticism developed, based on the desire to see the holy places and to pray within their range, despite the hardships and hazards involved. There was also the wish to be pardoned for one's sins, particularly for the act of murder, and the Holy Sepulchre and the other sites where Christian saints had met their fate, or in which holy relics were kept, were thought to be particularly suitable for this purpose.[59]

[58] William of Tyre, *RHC* (Occ.), I, 30ff; Marinus Sanctus, *Liber secretorum*, 178; *De prima institutione, RHC* (Occ.), V, 401f; Aimé, *L'ystoire*, 231 (= *Storia*, 341f); De Funes, *Coronica*, I, 1f (all these and their like copied from William of Tyre); Strehlke, *Zeitschrift für christliche Archaeologie und Kunst*, 2(1858), 118f; Guarmani, *Gl'Italiani*, 17, 20 (who mistakenly assumes that the building projects of the Amalfians belong to the first quarter of the century); Saige (see the previous note), 552f; Berlière (see the previous note), 505; Riant, *MAIBL*, 31(1884), 157f; Citarella, *Speculum*, 42(1967), 311, n. 85; Riley-Smith, *Knights*, 35; on the remains of buildings of the Amalfians in Jerusalem (in the Mūristān), see: Schick, *PEFQ*, 1902:42; on the Maurus family, see, apart from the aforementioned article of Strehlke also: Schwarz, *Amalfi*, 56f. On John the Generous see: Sa'īd ibn Biṭrīq, I, 217f; see also: Schönborn, *Sophrone*, 71, n. 67; according to him this John died on 11 November 620; the patriarch Sophronius (known from the time of the Muslim conquest) wrote his biography.

[59] See Runciman, in the *History of the Crusades* (Setton), I, 68, who finds that to a certain extent the desire to see the holy places in Palestine derived from Jewish influence; a rather strange view. In the continuation, *ibid.*, he speaks of the interruption of transport and maritime trade for a few centuries after the Muslim conquest, and as a result, also of pilgrimages – which is not proven and has no foundation; for we have the evidence of Arculf, Willibald and others, whom he mentions himself. Labande, *CCM*, 1(1958), 164, tries to stress the difference between two types of pilgrims: the one who comes to Jerusalem out of piety and the other to earn fame and respect for daring to venture on such a difficult journey. See the general description and discussions on the subject: Grabois, in *Ha-yam ha-tīkhōn*: 68; see what he writes on the drive forward given to the pilgrimage movement from the West by Charlemagne's idea of the empire, which was based on the revival of Biblical statehood and accompanied by a widespread cultural-religious awakening. See the general survey on the Christian pilgrimages: Leclercq, *DACL*, XIV, 150ff.

[720] One may assume – and what has been said on Christian pilgrimage in the Muslim sources which have been preserved supports this – that most of the pilgrims did not come from the West. However, the Byzantine documents have been lost in the main while in the West, much has remained on this subject in the chronicles of the Middle Ages. One should keep this in mind and understand that for this very reason, the scene as portrayed in the sources and in the work of modern scholars as well, is unavoidably distorted. Pilgrims from the West were but a tiny stream added to the continuous flow of pilgrims to Jerusalem from the East, including Byzantium; we have seen something of this in the traditions on the visits of the emperors and nobility of Byzantium to the Holy City. Indeed, here and there some details on certain pilgrims from the East have been preserved. Jibrīl ibn ʿUbaydallah b. Bukhtīshūʿ, a Christian physician from Baghdad, was said to have made a pilgrimage to 'the land of the temple (*arḍ al-maqdis*), he fasted one fast there, and from there proceeded to Damascus'. The mother superior of a Jerusalem nunnery writes to a woman in Egypt, who had visited Palestine and passed through Ramla, saying 'I ask Christ's mercy that I should see your face in this holy place, facing the Temple Mount'.[60]

[721] I shall now survey the sources which mention Latin pilgrims. As I have already stated, we have a relatively large number of details about them. We shall see that the descriptions of journeys have preserved merely short accounts, a dry summary of chiefly names and dates, and a few details concerning the routes of the journey. Some pilgrims travelled eastward to Constantinople (mostly through Hungary, especially from the beginning of the eleventh century, after the Christianisation of the country) and from there overland; and there were those pilgrims who sailed from one of the ports (generally from Italy) and reached Alexandria or Tyre or Jaffa. The journey by land was preferably made riding on a mule, or in the language of the time – a *bourdon* (compare this with the Arabic: *birdhawn*). Another aspect worth stressing here is the attitude of the Muslims towards the pilgrims. Here and there, we hear of harassment and of their arrest, which would generally end with the extraction of large

It is also worth mentioning the work of Röhricht, *Die Deutschen im Heiligen Lande*, on the German pilgrims. According to him, there were six pilgrimages from Germany in the ninth century; eleven in the tenth, and thirty-nine in the eleventh.

60 The Baghdad physician: Ibn al-Qifṭī, 150; Ibn Abī Uṣaybiʿa, I, 146f. The abbess of the monastery: Anawati et Jomier, *Mélanges islamologiques*, 2(1954), 92; the editors read *dayr hinda* but this reading does not seem correct; perhaps *dayr al-samiyya* was written there, which is a monastery mentioned in the 'guide of Palestine' (see: **2**, b, p. 1, line 10); the writer did not return to Egypt, contrary to the opinion of the editors. As the letter is written on papyrus, it appears to be a comparatively early document, but it is impossible to establish the exact date.

bribes, which is particularly marked in a story quoted below, of the pilgrimage of the monk Bernard. As noted, the matter of payment to enter a city and especially Jerusalem is also mentioned, and we find mention of this in the Geniza documents as well (see sections 249–251).

In *ca*. 750, bishop Madelveus, of Verdun in France, made a pilgrimage to Jerusalem. He made his way through Greece, and from there went by sea to Jaffa and then on to Jerusalem. It was said that he returned home with many relics of the saints which he received from the patriarch and with a hand-wrought crystal urn. In around 850, St Elia of Castrogiovanni in Sicily, a man with a stormy past, stayed in Jerusalem for three years. His parents had fled from Castrogiovanni to the citadel of St Mary on the island, out of fear of the Arabs, but the citadel was also captured by the Arabs after some years. He was taken captive, but some Christians who were with the victors' forces (who came from North Africa) ransomed him. In mid-sea, he encountered a Byzantine ship which returned him to his family. He fell captive again and became the slave of a Christian from Africa, and afterwards the slave of a rich landowner, with whom his status grew until he became well known as a saint and healer, and then, as stated, he went on a pilgrimage to Jerusalem. From the ninth century, we also know of the journey of Frotmund, a French aristocrat, who is said to have left Rome on 29 September 855, and reached Egypt by sea, finally arriving in Jerusalem after three years, in 858. Bernard the monk was more or less his contemporary. He left via Bari, which was then under Muslim control, equipped with letters from the sultan (*suldanum*) of the place, permitting him to sail (with a description of his appearance for purposes of identification) to Taranto in Apulia, and to sail further on from there. On board the ships anchored in the port at that time, there were thousands of Christian captives taken by the Muslims in southern Italy who were to be taken to North Africa, according to him. After thirty days on board ship, they arrived in Alexandria, and there he was only allowed to disembark after paying six gold coins (dinars) to the controller of the port. The sultan of Alexandria demanded an additional thirteen dinars for a letter of recommendation to the authorities in Fustat, where he appeared before an official named 'Abd al-Ḥakam, sitting there in jail for six days despite the letters of recommendation he carried with him. After paying thirteen dinars there too, he received a travel document stating that no one could demand of him further sums. Nevertheless, he still had to pay a dinar or two at the gates of every city he entered. In Fustat, he sailed northward on the Nile to the Delta region, to Maḥalla, Damietta, Tinnīs, and from there to Faramā (which is Pelusion) through northern Sinai and al-'Arīsh to

Gaza. In Jerusalem, he stayed in a hostel established on Charlemagne's orders.[61]

[722] From around 900, there is an account of the pilgrimage of Countess Adelinda of Swabia, made after her three sons were killed. On her return from Jerusalem, she devoted the rest of her days to spiritual matters. In 970, Judith, the grandmother of the emperor Henry II (Saint), together with a large party of ladies of the court, made a pilgrimage to Jerusalem – just when the Fatimid wars in Palestine were at their fiercest. At the same time, Hidda, the mother of Gero, the bishop of Cologne, and sister of Siegfrid and Vito, was also in Jerusalem. In 988, Gontier, the abbot of the St Aubin monastery in Angers, also went on a pilgrimage, and in 990, Adalpert, the bishop of the Slavs, was given hospitality in the monastery of Monte Cassino when he came on pilgrimage to Jerusalem. In 992, Adso, the abbot of the Benedictine monastery in Lotharingia, also came as a pilgrim to Jerusalem. He died on board a ship on his way to Egypt. One must also mention the chief monastery in Cluny, established by William (Guillaume) I, Count of Aquitaine, which was for some decades the organising centre for pilgrims.[62]

[723] In 1002 or 1003, the Count of Anjou, Foulque Nerra, went on a pilgrimage; he repeated it in 1008. In the same period, we learn of a great pilgrimage of Normans – some forty Norman pilgrims are mentioned on their return from Jerusalem. In around 1016, Simon of Syracuse (in Sicily), one of the most famous Christian personalities of his time, made a pilgrimage. For some time afterwards, he was a monk in the Sinai before returning to Europe. He was one of the outstanding representatives of the Norman Church during that period, when the relations between Byzantium and the Normans were at their worst. The Byzantines began to

[61] On the *bourdon* see: Labande, *CCM*, 1(1958), 339. The bishop of Verdun: *Gesta episcoporum Virdunensium*, *MGH*(SS), IV, 43f; Elia, see: Gay, *L'Italie méridronale*, 255f. Frotmund: *AA SS*, October, X, 24th of the month, 847f; cf. Runciman, in *History of the Crusades* (Setton), I, 73 (contrary to his view, one cannot learn from this how long the journey usually took; the man certainly stopped on the way of his own accord, before reaching Jerusalem). Bernard: in Tobler et Molinier, I, 310–314. Cf. Bréhier, *L'église*, 31ff, with additional details on famous pilgrims in the tenth century and the beginning of the eleventh century.

[62] Adelinda, see *Quellen* (1856), 629 (from the chronicle of Herimannus Augiensis, Hermann of Reichenau). Judith: Riant, *MAIBL*, 31 (1884), 166; she was duchess of Bavaria, sister-in-law of Otto I. Hidda: Thietmari *Chronicon*, *MGH*(SS), III, 751; Annalista Saxo, *ibid.*, VI, 619 (Gero was archbishop of Cologne from 969, and died on 28 June 976). Gontier, see: Halphen, *Anjou*, 245; Adalpert: Chronicon Mon. Casinensis, *MGH*(SS), VII, 640; Adso, see: Widrici *vita Sancti Gerardi*, *ibid.*, IV, 488. See more details on pilgrims to Jerusalem in the tenth century: Riant, *MAIBL*, 31(1884), 166f, and in his wake, Runciman (see previous note), 73f: Hilda, Countess of Swabia, in 969. Counts from Vienna and from the following: Ardèche, Arcy, Anhalt, Verdun, Gorizia and Church dignitaries: the bishop of Olivola (in Piedmont) in 920; abbots of the monasteries of Aurillac, St Cybar, Flavigny; St Conrad, bishop of Konstanz, went on a pilgrimage to Jerusalem three times and St John, bishop of Parma, six times.

harass the pilgrims from the West (who came via Italy and through Byzantine lands) and they would intercept them and imprison them in Constantinople. The Norman count Richard II (the great-grandfather of William the Conqueror of England, 996–1026) fled to Jerusalem to escape the anger of Canute, king of Denmark and England (because of family affairs), together with 700 pilgrims, according to one of the sources.[63]

[724] In around 1025, Werinharius (who is Werner) preferred to go on a pilgrimage to Jerusalem when the emperor Conrad II wanted to send him as his envoy to Constantinople, but he did not succeed in fulfilling his ambition and died on the way on 14 April 1028. William Engolismensis (that is, man of Angoulême) passed through Bavaria on his way to the Holy Sepulchre, in 1026, together with a large group of Church dignitaries and noblemen. Stephen, the king of Hungary, received him with great pomp. They set out on 1 October 1026 and reached Jerusalem in the first week of March 1027, staying there until the third week of June, that is, more than three months. Adhémar de Chabannes, author of the famous chronicle on the history of the Franks, came on a pilgrimage in 1034 when he was forty-six, and died in Jerusalem. At the start of the forties of that same century, it was recorded that the bishops Benno II of Osnabrück and William of Strasbourg went on a pilgrimage. In *ca.* 1045, the *praepositus* Edo went on a pilgrimage to Jerusalem after the archbishop of Hamburg dismissed him from his post. Hildegarde, the second wife of the aforementioned Count of Anjou, Foulque Nerra, also went on a pilgrimage to Jerusalem, for which she set out on 1 April 1046 with the intention of remaining in Jerusalem for the remainder of her life.[64]

[63] On Foulque see: Halphen, *Anjou*, 31ff; see there also supplement II, pp. 213ff on the same subject, and doc. No. 20, on p. 249 (the year 1002/3). The Normans: *Chronicon Mon. Casinensis*, *MGH*(SS), VII, 651f. Simon (sometimes called Simon of Treviri, that is Trier): Sigeberti, *Chronica*, *ibid.*, VI, 355; Annalista Saxo, *ibid.*, VI, 570. He died in 1031 (and not in 1035, as some believe), that is, more than fifty years before the Normans captured Syracuse; Simon, of course, has no connection with this conquest; he was indeed born in Syracuse, of an aristocratic Christian family but when he was seven, his parents took him to Constantinople and from then on, he did not return to his home town in Sicily but worked among the Benedictines in Europe (he was one of the founders of the Order of Hospitallers), and spent the last seven years of his life in Trier. Clearly he was called 'of Syracuse' not because he lived there but because he hailed from there. See further: Octavius Caietanus (= Gaietani), *Vitae*, II, 101ff; Fleury, *Histoire*, IV(59), 95ff, who has details on Simon's relations with Richard II, Duke of Normandy. The interruption of pilgrimages: Adhémar, *Histoire*, *MGH*(SS), IV, 140; cf. Gay, *L'Italie méridionale*, 404f. Richard the Norman: *Adami Gesta*, *MGH*(SS), VII, 325; *idem*, in *Quellen* (1961), 292; Annalista Saxo, *MGH*(SS), VI, 689; Hugo Flaviniacensis (Flavigny), *ibid.*, VIII, 394, Hugo Floriacensis (Fleury), *Regum Francorum actus*, *ibid.*, IX, 387 (the editor, *ibid.*: n. 28: the information on Richard is false, as it is not found elsewhere, but this is not correct). Cf. Douglas, *EHR*, 61(1946), 129.

[64] Werner, see: Wipo, *Gesta Chuonradi II*, *Quellen* (1961), 578 f and the editor's note there. William: Adhémar, *Histoire*, *MGH*(SS), IV, 145f. On Adhémar himself see the introduction to his chronicle, *ibid.*, 108, and in the note; see the article Adémar de Chabannes

[725] People who managed to stay in Jerusalem for some time were enveloped by a special sort of aura on their return to Europe, and frequently acquired titles and important posts as a result. One of the permanent confidants of Bishop Adalbert of Bremen was a certain Bovo, a man whose origins and past were something of a mystery. He would tell of going on a pilgrimage to Jerusalem on three occasions, and that the Muslims caught him and brought him to 'Babel' (that is, al-Qāhira). When he was eventually released, he went on a number of journeys and visited many countries. A man by the name of Aristo who arrived from Jerusalem was appointed to take charge of the church in Ratzeburg on behalf of that bishop. He stayed in this post for eleven years, until he was ousted from there.[65]

[726] An unusual pilgrimage, both because of its extent and because of the turn of events in which it was involved, was that of the group of Gunther, bishop of Bamberg, in 1065. According to the sources, 7,000 men participated in the journey, which included noblemen and bishops from southern Germany, among them also Siegfried, bishop of Mainz. When they were at a point which was a day's journey from Ramla, on 15 March, they were attacked by Arabs. The attack lasted for several days, until Easter. At first the members of the convoy did not put up any resistance and their situation was desperate. Only when they began to defend themselves and even took captives did there seem to be some prospect of extricating themselves from this situation, though many of them were wounded. They were saved by the *amīr* of Ramla, that is, the Fatimid governor, who when he heard of the assault, quickly came to their aid. His attitude towards the Bedouin was one of intense hatred, as he saw them as rebels against the Fatimid rule, and immediately gave orders for them to be arrested and sent to Egypt. Evidently the attack was prompted by a desire for plunder, for the bishops did not refrain from displaying their wealth. Less than 2,000 of these pilgrims managed to return home safely. The chronicle of the English abbot Ingulph may possibly be evidence of one of the participants of this pilgrimage, for Ingulph explicitly mentions that he went on a pilgrimage together with 7,000 men, among them thirty horsemen, under the leadership of the bishop of Mainz. On their way from Lycia (Lydda?), he says, they were attacked by Arab robbers, who robbed them of large sums of money and killed many of them. On the return journey they were again attacked, until they managed to reach Jaffa. He mentions the patriarch Sophronius (1059–

(by J. de la Martinière), in *DHGE*. The two bishops: Norberti Abbatis, *Vita Bennonis II*, 378; Edo, see: Adami, *Gesta*, *MGH*(SS), VII, 334; Hildegarde, see: Halphen, *Anjou*, 11, n. 1.

[65] Bovo, see: Adam the aforementioned of Bremen, in *Quellen* (1961), 431. Aristo: *ibid.*, 354.

1070) in his story, and these events took place before the death of King Edward (about whom he speaks in the continuation; he died in 1066) and from all the indications, he appears to have been speaking of the same pilgrimage. Perhaps the affair of Count Theodoricus, who was exiled by the emperor Henry IV because of the murder of the archbishop of Trier, St Kuno, was also linked to this pilgrimage, but the dates of this affair are not clear. It was said that Theodoricus died during a pilgrimage to Jerusalem.

There have been scholars who have tried to see this great pilgrimage (and there have evidently been more pilgrimages of this kind) as part of a large pilgrims' movement which could be considered a sort of prelude to the Crusades. Actually, there is no resemblance between the pilgrimages, regardless of how populous they were, and the Crusades. The pilgrimages were naturally undertaken by unarmed people, were of a peaceful nature, and were expected to be met with tolerance on the part of the Muslim rulers. As a matter of fact, Christians continued to go on pilgrimages to Jerusalem throughout the centuries following the Muslim conquest. Information concerning harassment, atrocities and the mistreatment of pilgrims had undoubtedly been going the rounds for generations. It is therefore difficult to see any causal connection or even any chain of continuity between Gunther's pilgrimage and the Crusades.[66]

[727] We do not know of many sources on Latin pilgrimages after that of Gunther. In 1087/8, we hear of the pilgrimage of Urso, archbishop of Bari. Apparently, the latest information (before the Crusades) on Christian pilgrimages is to be found in al-ʿAẓīmī, who speaks of the year AH 486, which is AD 1093 (when he was three years old). In that year, according to him, the people living in the coastal areas of Palestine prevented the Latin (literally: the Franks – *al-firanj*) and Byzantine pilgrims from going to Jerusalem. Those who survived (clearly implying that there had been a massacre) spread the news of what had happened, in their own

[66] Ingulph, 148f. According to the heading on these pages, it seems that the translator-editor attributes these events to 1051, but this is not correct; the events are described also in some other sources, which are very close to the time of the events: Lambert (or Lampert) of Hersenfeld, who wrote in *ca.* 1075; Lamberti *Annales*, *MGH*(SS), V, 168ff (= Lamperti Monachi Hersfeldensis *Annales*, 94ff); Mariani Scotti, *Chronicon* (a contemporary of the aforementioned), *ibid.*, V, 599; *Ann. Augustani* (Augsburg, an anonymous chronicler and a contemporary of the aforementioned), *ibid.*, III, 128; *Annales Altahenses* (Oefele; written at about the same time, in Niederaltaich in Bavaria), 67; one source says that the mass pilgrimage was led by Siegfried, bishop of Mainz (Sigefridus Moguntinus) who in fact participated in Gunther's convoy, see *Annales Ottenburani*, *MGH*(SS), V, 6 (Ottobeuren, Bavaria). The matter of Theodoricus, see: *Annales Wirziburgenses*, *MGH*(SS), II, 224; Bernoldi *Chronicon*, *ibid.*, V, 429; *Annales Hildesheimenses*, *ibid.*, III, 105; Sigeberti *Chronicon*, *ibid.*, VI, 362. Cf. on Gunther's journey: Michaud, *Histoire*, I, 34; Riant, *AOL*, 1(1881), 55; see the comprehensive research work on the journey: Joranson, *D. C. Munroe Presentation Volume*: 3; see further: Bréhier, *L'église*, 45ff; Vasiliev, *History*, 398f; Ross and McLaughlin, *Medieval Reader*, 430–437 (English translation of Lambert's account).

countries, and he claims that this was the reason why the Christians started on their preparations for the campaign which was to become the first Crusade.[67]

[67] Leib, *Rome* etc. 80, claims there was a strong wave of pilgrimages during the Saljūq period. Urso, see: Prawer, *Tarbiz*, 45 (1975/6), 281, with references to the sources. See al-ʿAẓīmī, 369, and see *ibid.*, 368, the matter of the year of his birth; see *ibid.*, 430, the editor C. Cahen's comments on the significance of this information, for this is the only instance (known to us) of a Muslim source speaking of the connection between the distress of the Christian pilgrims and the Crusades.

8

THE JEWISH POPULATION AND ITS LEADERSHIP

The problematics of Jewish leadership in the Middle Ages

[728] The question often heard today, generally from elements unfriendly to the Jews, as to whether the Jews are a nation or only a religious community, did not trouble the Jews of the mediaeval period. They called themselves a nation as a matter of course. In recent times, the study of society has tried to fit this term into a tight matrix of precise definitions. As a matter of fact, however, it is obvious and known to intelligent people that the Jews were not for many generations, and are not even today, a nation like other nations, owing to a lack of territorial concentration. Nevertheless, they were always more of a nation than all those nations settled on their own land, due to an awareness of their common fate, their internal solidarity, their shared past and their deep cultural roots. All these features were characteristic of the Jews for generations, more so than of other nations. The strong communal organisation and central institutions of leadership preserved the unity of the nation no less than territory may have done, and perhaps even more so.

The unifying spiritual factor was naturally the Torah, which meant a common and shared belief in a supreme omnipotent force bearing a special relationship to the Jewish people. Apart from this, there was a body of customs and laws encompassing every aspect of life, from ritual and the routine of daily life to the laws regulating family affairs, inheritance, civil litigation, and all the other laws which today pertain to civil law. To the ancients, the meaning of *dāt* (generally translated as religion) was primarily the law, as the term is understood in the Bible, a meaning making it more or less synonymous with the term Torah. The separate judicial system, a network of Jewish courts of judgment, was viewed as the buttress and principal focus of the life of the nation.

Included within the same framework of strong communal organisation were also the developed institutions of mutual aid: the *heqdēsh*, the concern for the poor, for the stranger and for the ransom of captives. The Jewish population was utterly dependent on its surroundings, subject to the need to maintain its physical existence and livelihood within a regime in which a ruler could within seconds arbitrarily confer life or death. The Jews were a part of the general economic system and were in daily contact with their non-Jewish surroundings, but they were nevertheless self-centred. Though they took on the outward signs of Muslim culture by way of language, manners and even dress, an enormous chasm lay between the two worlds in everything concerning their *Weltanschauung* and daily customs. A marked indication of this isolation was the severity with which they observed the principle of not applying to Muslim courts in civil matters, such as inheritances, and the like. We have already seen some instances of excommunication of people who applied to a Muslim judge in order to achieve different conditions from those which could be expected from the Jewish courts.

It should be clear that in speaking of the Jews in the diaspora during the early Middle Ages, I am referring first of all to Jews of the Muslim world, for it was in this world that the greater part of the Jewish people lived – in countries where they had lived in ancient and crowded localities for centuries before the Muslim conquest: Palestine, Persia, Babylonia, Syria, Egypt, North Africa and Spain. The Jews outside the borders of Islam were to be found mainly in Byzantium, that is, in Asia Minor, in Constantinople, Greece, Rome and southern Italy. The Jewish communities of Western Europe, at that time the barbarian and most backward part of the continent, were small and insignificant. Hence it is not incidental that the historical sources of that period called the 'period of the geonim', all stem from the Orient – from Babylonia, Palestine, Egypt or North Africa.

How were those hundreds of communities, spread throughout that part of the world, organised? From what did they derive their inner strength and to whom did they look for guidance in times of perplexity and distress? Who did they turn to when they needed someone to pass judgment on those difficult problems that arise between fellow-men or between man and his social context, and were unable to find a solution? From the sources of that period, we learn that the Jewish people maintained no less than four central authorities within their midst: the exilarch in Babylonia, two yeshivot in Babylonia – in Sura and Pumbedita – and the Palestinian yeshiva. How were their powers divided and who had the supreme authority? Under the influence of ideas created in more recent periods, there is a tendency to view the exilarch as having been the supreme authority, bearing some of the attributes of a secular authority and whose major concerns were of a socio-political nature, as distinguished from the yeshivot, which were mainly occupied with religious matters. This seemed to students of Jewish history to be the case in Talmudic times (during the era of Rome and Persia) and during the Middle Ages. However, this was not quite so. From the story of Nathan the Babylonian it emerges that the division of power was not at all vertical, but rather horizontal – or one may say, geographic.

The exilarch and his court exercised their authority over the communities east of the Tigris, that is, the communities of Persia: 'Nahrwān and all its surroundings ... Ḥulwān'; the son of the exilarch David b. Zakkai 'went out to the land of Persia which is under the authority of his father'; and also: '... from Persia which is his father's domain and from all its surroundings'. Indeed, we are familiar with the exilarchs from the Talmud, and with their lineage from King David. According to their genealogical lists, Jehoiachin, the king whom Nebuchadnezzar banished, was the first exilarch. The Babylonian Talmud expounds on them on the basis of Genesis (xlix) in the blessing of Jacob: '[The sceptre shall not depart from Judah] which means the exilarchs of Babylonia, who tyrannise Israel with (their) sceptre' (BT, Sanhedrin, 5a). Reliable information credits the exilarch with having acquired a very high and revered status from the Persian rulers before Islam. At the time of the Muslim conquest, the exilarch Bustanai stood at the head of the Jewish population in the Persian kingdom and actively participated in the war against the Muslims, alongside the Persian king and army. The Muslim era brought about a sharp decline in the status of the exilarchs. This process stemmed chiefly from internal developments and quarrels within the exilarchic family. It seems that one of the early manifestations of this process was the secession of 'Anan, a member of the family, who cut off his relationship with the yeshivot and started a faction of his own. There also seems to have been a fierce controversy between two branches of the descendants of Bustanai, who was exilarch at the time of the conquest. The Muslim conquerors gave him a present of one of the daughters of the Persian king they had taken captive. She gave birth to three sons apart from those he had had by his Jewish wife. In later generations, there were claims that the offspring of the Persian wife were not legally qualified – so they claimed – for Bustanai had not converted her to Judaism and hence her offspring were not Jewish at all. A serious rift continued for generations on the score of these claims. Internal schisms, reservations, and rivalry on the part of the scholars of the yeshivot, and not necessarily the intervention of the authorities, were the cause of the decline of the exilarchate, for the Muslims actually treated the exilarchic house with respect, knowing that the Jews viewed the exilarchs as descendants of King David, who had his honourable place in Islamic tradition as a prophet.

The Jewish masses naturally felt a great deal of affection for the exilarch, seeing in him, as we have seen, a scion of the House of David. They truly believed in this ancestry and would customarily call a member of the exilarchic family: *al-Da'ūdī* – 'the Davidian'. Nevertheless, this fact did not keep the yeshivot from fighting with the exilarch, at times bitterly. We know of enormous rifts of this kind, particularly in the tenth century, but there is no reason to believe that there were not similar quarrels at other times as well, and there is more than a hint of this in the famous letter of Sherira Gaon. Division from without and within thus caused the eventual loss of status suffered by the exilarchs, as Sherira Gaon puts it in his letter: 'at the outset of the days of the Ishmaelites the exilarchs possessed harsh authority and much power', but 'in the middle of the Ishmaelites' days, at the time of David b. Zakkai the *nāsī*, they were abased through the king's authority'. And in another source, Samuel b. 'Alī's letter (of the twelfth century): 'they were dismissed from serving the rulers'. In the course of time, there were instances of descendants of the exilarchic house emigrating westward; some of them reaching Palestine, Egypt and even the Maghrib. Below I shall discuss those sources in the Geniza documents that refer to their involvement in public affairs in Palestine, especially in the eleventh century.

The Babylonian yeshivot, like the exilarch, had their roots in ancient times, as we know. Nathan the Babylonian, whose object seems to have been to tell his listeners – evidently in Qayrawān – about Babylonian affairs, spoke only of the Babylonian yeshivot, Sura and Pumbedita. A mediaeval source expounds on them (according to Micah, iv:10): 'for now shalt thou go forth out of the city, and thou shalt dwell in the field, and thou shalt go even to Babylon; there shalt thou be delivered', as follows: 'for oral law is given to the sages of the Babylonian yeshiva, and the details of the commandments are kept by those sages, which are not teachings [invented] by their hearts or by their wisdom . . .' (that is, the origin of the teachings is divine).

Sura lay in southern Iraq while Pumbedita was further to the north, close to the Euphrates. Nathan the Babylonian describes their disposition: seventy elders sat in the yeshiva, among them the head of the yeshiva and second to him the *av-bēt-dīn* (head of the court). They would sit in rows of ten, and at the head of each row sat a *rōsh kallā*, which meant head of the row; each of these seven dignitaries of the yeshiva was also called *alūf*. The head of the yeshiva was called *gaon*. Nathan the Babylonian claims that at first only the head of Sura bore the title Gaon, but he may have been biassed in favour of this yeshiva. The yeshivot usually called themselves *yeshivat ge'ōn ya'aqōv*, both in Babylonia and in Palestine. Apparently this by-name had its origins in Ps., xlvii:4: 'He shall choose our inheritance for us, the excellency of Jacob [*ge'ōn ya'aqōv*] whom He loved.' Evidently the title Gaon (excellency in English) was an abbreviation of 'Head of the *yeshīvat ge'ōn ya'aqōv*'. The seven row masters went by the name of *dārā qammā*, or *dārā rabbā* (the first, or great row); in Pumbedita, it was the row of the Neharde'ē (people of Neharde'ā), evidently named after the place where the yeshiva had been located before it moved to Pumbedita. The geonim heading the Babylonian yeshivot behaved like royalty; before their sermons the reader would proclaim in a ceremonial manner: 'hearken ye to what the head of the yeshiva has in mind to say!'

The yeshivot of Sura and Pumbedita directed the affairs of the many Jewish communities in the diaspora, also outside the confines of Persia and Babylonia, especially among those 'Babylonian' communities which had sprung up in the West as a result of the mass migration of Jews westward from Iraq. This also applied to the ancient local communities in North Africa and Spain, which evidently recognised the superior quality of the learning and wisdom of the Babylonian yeshivot. Sura, the older of the two, enjoyed greater prestige than the yeshiva of Pumbedita for many generations but this seems to have changed in the tenth century, particularly after the death of Saadia Gaon, head of the Sura yeshiva in 942. The Babylonian yeshivot were maintained by regular taxes paid them by the Jews of Babylonia; the exilarch too was paid. In addition, a stream of donations would reach them from the diaspora, together with queries on matters of law issued both from study and from matters of practical decisions, in which local courts would apply to the Babylonian yeshivot.

Before embarking on a discussion of the fourth authority, that is, the Palestinian yeshiva, I should note that the leadership of the diaspora was a pluralistic one – that is, the four authorities existed alongside one another, without reaching a schismatic situation, although there were many differences on various issues and competition between one another, which were at times expressed with intense bitterness. There were periods when the reputation of one would override that of the other, but there was always at least one central authoritative body by which the communities in the diaspora abided. These institutions were active for many generations – for more than a thousand years – and not a little of that inner strength of the

Jewish communities and their capacity to withstand waves of enmity and the temptation to assimilate lay inherent in their existence.[1]

The Palestinian yeshiva in ancient sources

[729] Owing to the Geniza documents, we now know that the Palestinian yeshiva (the Sanhedrin) continued to exist, evidently uninterruptedly, from the days of the Second Temple until the period under discussion here, and that during this period, it still assumed the leadership of the Jews of Palestine and also of some of the Jewish communities outside Palestine.

Brief information on the Palestinian yeshiva is to be found in *Seder 'olām zūṭā* ('the small order of the world'): 'Mar Zūṭrā b. Mar Zūṭrā the exilarch went up to Palestine and was admitted as *rōsh pereq*. It is in the year 452 from the destruction of the Temple, which is the year 4280 of the creation [that is: AD 520] that he went up to Palestine, and became [there] head of the Sanhedrin.' In the various versions of this chronicle, another eight to thirteen names of Mar Zūṭrā's successors are mentioned, the last being that of Rav Ḥāṣūv, the son of Rav Pinḥas or his grandson. One may evidently assume that Mar Zūṭrā was at first *rōsh pereq* and afterwards, head of the Palestinian yeshiva. In other words, one of the descendants of the exilarch in Babylonia became head of the Sanhedrin of Palestine. Below we shall see that it is not an isolated occurrence and that we know of three other descendants of exilarchs who became geonim in Palestine: Jehoshaphat and Ṣemah, sons of Josiah, and Daniel b. Azariah.[2]

[1] See the account of Nathan the Babylonian on the division of the Babylonian authorities and their organisation and activities, in Neubauer, *Med. J. Chron. II*, 85ff. Sherira Gaon on the exilarchs: *ibid.*, I, 33. The letter of Samuel b. 'Alī: Assaf, *Tarbiz*, 1(2) (1929/30), 67 (fol. 30b). See the midrash on Micah ch. iv (from Pirkoy b. Bāboy) in Lewin, *Tarbiz*, 2(1930/31), 402f. Cf. Mann, *Tarbiz*, 6(1933/4), 78f. On the name *yeshīvat ge'ōn ya'aqōv*, see Harkavy's note (19) in Graetz (Hebrew), III, 128; see further: Zunz, *Die gottesdienstlichen Vorträge*, 178, n. a; Sh. Rapoport, *Kerem ḥemed*, 4(1838/9), 225, in the note; Poznanski, Review of Ginzberg's *Geonica*, *JQR*, NS 3(1912/3), 408; see on the use of this name in the Pumbedita yeshiva: Harkavy, *Teshūvōt*, Nos. 198, 200 (pp. 88, 90). Salmon b. Yeruḥim, the Karaite commentator of the tenth century, claims that ge'ōn ya'aqōv means Jerusalem, while interpreting Ps., xlvii:5: 'when He says ge'ōn ya'aqōv He means Jerusalem in particular, since this is how He called it when He said: I will profane my sanctuary (i.e. the Temple, Jerusalem), the excellency (ge'ōn) of your strength' (Ezek., xxiv:21); see the Marwick ed., 20. A detailed discussion on the matters of Babylonia will be published by me elsewhere, hence I have limited myself to only a few references here.

[2] Indeed, in the Codex Theodosianus (xvi– 8–22, 29) orders are recorded of the years 415 and 429, abolishing the office of the Nāsī (Gamaliel III) and the yeshivot of Palestine: *in urtriusque Palestinae synedriis* (evidently meaning the Jewish courts); but the Sanhedrin was alive and well in the sixth century, as we shall see below, and it is completely inconceivable that the Jewish population in Palestine in fact submitted to these orders. See the account of *Seder 'olam zūṭā* in: Neubauer, *Mediaeval Jewish Chronicles*, II, 69–73, and the Hebrew version *ibid.*, 76ff. There is also a version saying that the exilarch went up to Jerusalem

[730] Syriac sources which describe the events in the southern part of the Arabian peninsula, when the Jewish king Joseph (his real name according to inscriptions was Yūsuf Asār; Dhū Nu'ās in the Arab chronicles, Masrūq in the Syriac sources) started persecuting the Christians and the Monophysites in his realm, Ḥimyar, particularly in Najrān, mention the 'Jewish priests of Tiberias'. They were the driving force behind the king's persecution of the Christians. This occurred at about the same time as the aforementioned arrival of Mar Zūṭrā in Palestine, that is, around AD 520.[3]

[731] The Targum (homiletic translation, Aramaic) of the Song of Solomon, made during the Byzantine era, tells us (The Song of Solomon, vii:[2]3: 'Thy navel is like a round goblet [of the moon] . . .') 'the head of your yeshiva, from whose grace [with God] all the people are at a gain, just as a fetus gains from his navel in the belly of his mother. He shines in [his knowledge of the] Torah just like the goblet of the moon . . . and seventy sages surround him like a round barn. Their treasuries become full from the holy tithes and the vows and donations allotted to them by Ezra the priest and by Zerubbabel . . . and by the people of the Great Assembly'. This is an obvious reference to the Palestinian yeshiva as well as an explicit statement on the Jews' obligation to support it.

Immediately after the Muslim conquest, in the Jewish-Christian polemical tract which I have already mentioned above, 'the Didaskalia of Jacob the recently baptised', the Jewish participants in the argument mention 'our priest in Tiberias'.[4]

[732] Sherira Gaon mentions in his letter a serious struggle over the office of exilarch in around the year 825, which he calls the 'controversy of Daniel and David' but the letter contains no details concerning the controversy. A Syriac Christian source, however, has more information. It attributes the rift to the people of Tiberias on the one hand and the Babylonians on the other; the former supported David, while the latter supported Daniel, who was of the 'Ananite sect, 'those who profane the

(*ibid.*, 76, n. 14), but one cannot rely on this as the seat of the Sanhedrin was then in Tiberias. See on the manuscripts of this chronicle and on its first printed editions (Mantua 1514, Basle 1527, Venice 1545, Basle 1580, etc.) in Lazarus, *Jahrbücher* (Brüll), 10(1890), 157ff (in the appendix). The Hebrew translation, by Abraham Zacuto, was written *ca.* 1505, and included in his *Sefer yuḥasīn*, printed in 1566 by Samuel Shulam; see the Filipowski edition (London 1857) according to the Bodleian MS 2202, the only MS to have been preserved, pp. 91ff. There are also versions which give the date of Mar Zūṭrā's immigration to Palestine as 522; cf: Marx, *JQR*, NS 1(1910/1), 68; Mann, *Jews*, I, 58f, in the note. On the title *rōsh ha-pereq* see below, sec. 742.

3 See the letter of Simon of Bet Arsham: Schröter, *ZDMG*, 31(1877), 361ff; cf. Hirschberg, *Israel ba-'arāv*, 88ff, and the matter of the 'leaders of the priests of Tiberias', *ibid*, 90; *Ketāvā de-ḥimyarē* (Moberg), in the MS fol. 7a, line 2; cf. Hirschberg, *ibid.*, 84; see also *idem* in *Sefer Zikkaron* (Vienna), 113.

4 See a slightly different version in the Sperber edition of the Targum. Cf. Landauer, *Nöldeke Jubilee Volume*, 506 (who tries to prove that the Targum was written in the Muslim period,

sabbath and keep Wednesday [instead]'. It is difficult to see any connection between that controversy and that barely unknown sect which consecrates Wednesday instead of the sabbath, and there must have been some misunderstanding there. The information concerning the involvement of the people of the Palestinian yeshiva ('the people of Tiberias') in the controversy over the office of exilarch is certainly credible, however.[5]

[733] In an early version of the *yeqūm purqān* prayer, the opening blessing has been preserved for 'our Lords and Masters, the holy assemblies [ḥavūrōt] that are in Palestine and in Babylonia, the *rāshē kallā*, and the exilarchs, and heads of the yeshivot and the judges of the courts'. This version was first found in the *maḥzōr* of Vitry (in the early twelfth century); it was certainly accepted for generations beforehand but was not preserved in a more ancient source.[6]

[734] In the Scroll of Aḥīma'aṣ, where it speaks of the time around 800 of the destruction of the Temple, that is 868, 'a man who came from Palestine' to Venosa, is described as having 'stayed there days and weeks and would preach a sermon every sabbath'. Silano, the local scholar, who explained, or rather translated the sermons, inserted into the translation a

but he is not convincing); see also: Marx, *JQR*, NS 1(1910/1), 66. The *Didaskalia*, see Bonwetsch, 77, lines 5–6; Krauss, *Zion* (ha-me'assēf), 2(1927), 28.

[5] See Sherira's letter in Neubauer, *Mediaeval Jewish Chronicles*, I, 38; the Syriac source was usually quoted from Bar Hebraeus' chronicle. Bar Hebraeus copied from Michael the Syrian, who copied from the chronicle (which is lost) of Dionysius of Tel Maḥrē, who lived during these events. See Michael the Syrian, 517 (text); III, 65 (translation); Bar Hebraeus (Abbeloos), 366; cf. Graetz (Hebrew) III, 421; Lazarus, *MGWJ*, 78(1934), 279, and there are Latin translations in both places. Graetz tried to prove that Bar Hebraeus' version is garbled and should read: *anbārāyē* (al-Anbār, which is Pumbedita) instead of *ṭiberāyē*, but this has no foundation; while if there was the same clear evidence in Graetz' day as there is today, of the existence of the Palestinian yeshiva (then in Tiberias) he would not have suggested this.

[6] The term *rōsh kallā* is explained above, and will be discussed in the continuation below. *Maḥzōr Vitry* (of Simḥa b. Samuel of Vitry, a pupil of Rashi – 1040–1105), see the Hurwitz ed., 172; also Nathan the Babylonian hints at this blessing (see in Neubauer, *Mediaeval Jewish Chronicles*, II, 84); cf. Duschinsky's article in *Poznanski Jubilee Volume*: 182. From here and also from some other sources, we learn that the term *ḥavūrā* found in the Talmuds, is used as a synonym for yeshiva, just as the term *ḥāvēr* had the special meaning of scholar, man of the yeshiva, as we shall see; the term *ḥavūrat ha-ṣedeq* is to be found in the piyyūṭ of 'the ancient questions', which will be discussed below, and is a florid nickname for the yeshiva in the writer's day, the 11th century. It can also be found in *essā meshālī* of Saadia Gaon, and meant there the sages of Jabneh and Usha, as shown by Abramson, *Tarbiz*, 32(1962/3), 160f. Many years later, this term, *ḥavūrat ha-ṣedeq* is still included in a *reshūt* for a bridegroom, whose author was Menaḥem b. Makhīr of Regensburg (see on him: Fleischer, *Shīrat ha-qodesh*, 431; the second half of the twelfth century): 'the scholars [of the Torah], who know how to open and how to close it; . . . heads of the yeshivot and heads of the dispersed exiled ones; with the authority of the *ḥavūrat ṣedeq*, the happy congregation'. See also Stern, *Berliner Jubilee Volume*, 115. It seems that a similar version was also included in the *qaddīsh* during the Middle Ages, which contained blessings for the leaders, also those of the community. ENA 2742, f. 6, has the demand of a *muqaddam* (in charge of the community, see below) that he be included among those blessed in the qaddīsh; cf. Goitein,

rhyme which hinted at a controversy which had arisen among the public in Venosa, for which he was banished, until Aḥīma'aṣ went up 'there' (that is to Palestine) 'with the *nedārīm*' (the vows). He went up to Jerusalem during the 'ten penitentiary days' and 'he was reconciled to the *ḥavērīm* and the head of the yeshiva and he [was asked] to be the reader'; during the prayers, he praised Silano, until the latter was released from the ban. It is further stated that Aḥīma'aṣ went up to Jerusalem with the *nedārīm* three times, and on each occasion brought 100 gold coins with him, 'to bestow upon the students of the Torah, and those who mourn [the destruction] of the palace of His splendour'. On his third visit, 'they would sit down and dine with the head of the yeshiva and students of the *reḥāvā*' (*reḥāvā*, the comprehensive one, meaning Torah).[7]

[735] The yeshiva is also mentioned at the end of a letter from Joseph b. Aaron, 'the king of Togarmah' (the Khazars) to Ḥasdai ibn Shaprūṭ: 'and our eyes look toward the Lord our God and to the sages of Israel, the yeshiva in Jerusalem and the yeshiva in Babylonia, although we are far from Zion', etc. Yefet b. 'Alī, the Karaite commentator of the tenth century, also does not refrain from mentioning the Palestinian yeshiva in his commentary on Zechariah, v:9 ('. . . and looked, and behold, there came out two women, and the wind was in their wings', etc.) 'as to the two women, they are the two yeshivot, the one in Palestine and the other in Iraq'.[8]

[736] Information on a query from the year 960 has been preserved, in which 'the people of the Rhine ask . . . the communities of Palestine' about the time of the coming of the Messiah and about a matter of ritual slaughter. On the Messiah, an evasive answer is given; as to the other matter, the Palestinians quote the responsum of Rav Jacob b. Mordecai, head of the Sura yeshiva in the late eighth-early ninth century, and conclude with: 'know ye for true that we do not omit prayers for you on the Mount of Olives on all the holidays; and it would befit you to draw from the depths of [the tractates] Yevamot and 'Eruvin'. These last comments contain an element of rebuke or ridicule; it seems that this responsum too may stem from the Palestinian yeshiva.[9]

Mediterranean Society, III, 245; 480, n. 145; Friedman, *Gratz College Annual*, 1(1972), 57, n. 5.

7 See *Megillat Aḥīma'aṣ*, 14, 16f; cf. Klar, *Tarbiz*, 15(1943/4) 48f.

8 Mention of the yeshiva in the letter of Joseph, king of the Khazars, see *Oṣar ha-ge'ōnīm to 'Eruvin*, 28, and n. 1; cf. Marx, *JQR*, NS 1(1910/1), 68, n. 15; his opinion that the mention of the Palestinian yeshiva there is the result of the decline of the Sura yeshiva in the tenth century does not seem to be correct. Yefet b. 'Alī: Poznanski, *JQR*, 18(1906), 245f; cf. Marx, *ibid.*, 68f.

9 Perles, *H. Graetz Jubelschrift*, 31, copied what is quoted above (ascribed to Isaac b. Dorbelo) from the MS of 'the small 'Arūkh' kept in Bern, from the last page of the MS; see Büchler, *REJ*, 44(1902), 237–243; Marx, *JQR*, NS 1 (1910/1), 75; Marx has there parallels from the

[737] Until now, we have examined cursorily some of the information on the Palestinian yeshiva, the Sanhedrin, which continued to be active from the days of the Second Temple onwards. It is obvious that the Palestinian yeshiva, as was also the case with the Babylonian yeshivot, had little resemblance to the yeshivot of times nearer our own, which were actually schools. During the period under discussion, the three yeshivot (the two Babylonian and the one Palestinian; and no one conceived of the idea of creating another yeshiva, as we shall see) were centres of leadership, housing councils of scholars, some of whom resided where the yeshiva was located and directed it and some of whom were judges and communal leaders in various localities, appointed on behalf of the yeshiva, its *semūkhīm* (the ordained). The sources I have quoted until now are early, up to the eleventh century. From now on, we can resort to the Geniza documents, which shed so much light on the Palestinian yeshiva, its struggles and personalities. The Geniza has also preserved copies of earlier sources from the tenth century, writings dealing with the dispute over the calendar, between Babylonia and Palestine, containing important data on the yeshiva.[10]

[738] At the time of the Muslim conquest, the Palestinian yeshiva was situated in Tiberias. As we have seen above, the Jews of Tiberias, meaning the people of the yeshiva evidently, were those who organised the first settlement of Jews in Jerusalem – those seventy families who moved from Tiberias and re-established the Jerusalem Jewish community. We have no explicit information as to the date of the transfer of the yeshiva from Tiberias to Jerusalem. As we have seen, according to the Syriac Christian sources (Dionysius, Michael the Syrian, Bar Hebraeus), the yeshiva was apparently still located in Tiberias during the first half of the ninth century. Evidently it was still in Tiberias during the first two decades of the tenth century, at the time of the dispute over the calendar. This we can assume, it seems, from a fragment of Saadia Gaon's *Sefer ha-Mo'adim*, in which it says (about the Palestinian Gaon, evidently Meir Gaon, as we shall see): 'and he sent his son in the seventh month of the year two [hundred and thirty] three and he came to Jerusalem', that is, in July AD 922 (1233 Sel.,

hēkhālōt literature according to which there was an expectation of the arrival of the Messiah at that time, and he concludes that no such computations of 'the end of the days' were known in Palestine then. 'Responsa of the people of Palestine' are also mentioned in a Bodleian MS, in a fragment dealing with ritual slaughter (see in Lewin, *Ginzē qedem*, 4 [1930], 50). See Epstein, *Hagoren*, 6:65(1905/6), a discussion on the responsum in the *Sefer ha-pardes* ascribed to Rashi, on the law concerning a widow whose child has died; judging by linguistic elements in the text of the responsum, Epstein assumed that it was from Palestine; see the end of the responsum (which is TS Misc 35, f. 98): Ginzberg, *JQR*, 17(1905), 277; cf. idem, *Geonica*, I, 33.

[10] See earlier studies in which sources on the Palestinian yeshiva are collected, prior to the Geniza documents: Poznanski, *REJ*, 48(1904), 147ff; Marx, *JQR*, NS 1(1910/1), 62–85;

AM 4682, in which Tammuz started on 30 June) the Palestinian Gaon sent his son from Tiberias to Jerusalem, it appears, to inform the people there of the fact that the months of Marheshwan and Kislev would be 'short ones' (of twenty-nine days). However, the letter from Joseph, king of the Khazars (*ca.* 960) speaks of the 'yeshiva in Jerusalem' and according to this, if the information is reliable, one can assume that the yeshiva moved to Jerusalem towards the middle of the tenth century. During the eleventh century, the Palestinian Gaon was still called *al-Ṭabarānī* (the Tiberian) in a letter from Fustat (apparently from Ephraim b. Shemaria) to the Gaon in Jerusalem, mentioning the fact that half of the income from ritual slaughtering in Fustat is taken by 'the Tiberian', that is, the Gaon. In a poem written by 'Eli b. 'Amram, leader of the Jerusalemites in Fustat in the latter half of the eleventh century, in honour of the *berīt* of a child, the writer mentions, apart from the authority of the Almighty, 'with the authority of the Nāsī and Gaon of Tiberias and Head of the yeshiva of Israel, which is in Jerusalem, House of God, our Lord Daniel' (Daniel b. Azariah).

At the beginning of the eleventh century, Geniza letters definitely disclose that Tiberias is no longer the seat of the yeshiva. The *av-bēt-dīn* of the yeshiva, Ḥanania ha-Kohen b. Joseph, mentions in his letter the serious differences within the Tiberias community and the yeshiva's intervention. It appears that Ḥanania's brother served as judge in Tiberias, and when he died, the people of Tiberias asked the yeshiva to send them someone to take his place. Someone was indeed sent, after a group of Tiberian notables promised they would treat him well, but that person apparently tried to discard the authority of Jerusalem, and even took the liberty of proclaiming leap years (!), whereupon the Gaon and the yeshiva excommunicated him. Nevertheless, he continued to do as he saw fit and even organised a faction of supporters, and it seems that they also took for themselves the revenue from the ritual slaughtering that was intended for Jerusalem. It does appear, then, that there was some sort of rebellion in Tiberias which tried to re-establish the old order.

I have already mentioned the responsum which has been preserved, to 'the holy community in Tiberias'. The questioner is a certain R. Yaḥyā, who brought with him a letter from someone who 'intercedes for Israel with their Heavenly Father'. It concerns the matter of an inheritance left by a certain Na'amān the teacher, over which two heirs are quarrelling. The responsum decides in favour of one party, according to the Babylonian Talmud, and claims that the Palestinian geonim would have taken such a stand from the days of Ben Meir and onwards. At the same time, someone who claimed that he stemmed from the exilarchic family, tried to establish

see the article of Assaf on the geonim of Babylonia's responsa as a source on Palestinian matters: *Zion* (ha-me'assēf), 1:21, 1926/7; see also: Goitein, *Baron Jubilee Volume*, 503ff.

a foothold and control the Tiberian community. Joshua ha-Kohen *ha-mumḥē* b. Ya'īr wrote about the affair from Tiberias to the community in Aleppo. That alleged *nāsī* also wished to dominate Syria, Tiberias, Jerusalem, and all of Palestine, and even Egypt, or as he says 'from Egypt until Kalnē' (which is Raqqa). Finally, it was revealed that he was not a *nāsī* (that is, a scion of the exilarchs) at all, and they banished him from Tiberias.[11]

Palestinian customs

[739] Palestine was characterised by a number of customs with regard to law and ritual that it did not share with Babylonia. On examining the nature of these customs, it can be observed, however, that generally speaking, the matters at stake were not fundamental and therefore it is not surprising that these differences never caused schisms or even severe quarrels, although they evidently stemmed from very ancient roots. A treatise written at some undetermined date in the Middle Ages enumerates these differences, although it is doubtful whether it includes all the differences. This treatise was published in two critical editions by modern scholars within a period of a few years; the one by M. Margaliot and the other by B. M. Lewin.

One of the most ancient of these variances, already recognised in Talmudic times, was that of keeping two days of holiday outside of Palestine as against one day within the country. This custom received legal validity because of the uncertainty of obtaining reliable information as to the precise calendar order, as determined in Palestine. A responsum of a

[11] See a fragment from the Adler collection first printed by Adler et Broydé, *REJ*, 41(1900), 225ff and published again by Bornstein, *Sokolow Jubilee Volume*, 74ff; see *ibid.*, 74 n. 2; Bornstein assumes that the Gaon's seat was perhaps in Tiberias; not so Mann, *Jews*, I, 63, n. 1 who assumes that the reference is to Ramla, which is less convincing, for it is not likely that a journey from Ramla to Jerusalem would merit such special mention. Here one must note that in the letter of the Palestinian Gaon during the dispute, we find the passage: 'the glory of Israel is but Jerusalem the holy city, and the great Sanhedrin there, as our sages, of blessed memory, taught: he who has never seen the joy of the Bēt ha-Shō'ēvā' (the house of the woman who draws water) has never in his life seen joy' (*Mishnā*, Sukka, v:1). This is merely recalling ancient times in order to stress the superiority of the Palestinian yeshiva over the Babylonian yeshivas; see the letter in Bornstein, *ibid.*, 62. See below, p. 563, in the note, on the source published by Fleischer. The letter of Joseph king of the Khazars: above, n. 735. Al-Ṭabarānī, MS. Reinach, line 4, and see the comments of Mann, *Jews*, II, 351. The poem of 'Eli b. 'Amram: TS 12.358, a, lines 4–5, quoted also by Mann, *Jews*, I, 55, n. 1; cf. Goitein, *Shalem*, 2(1975/6), 92f; Ḥanania's letter: **23**. The responsum: Mosseri, VIII, 421; cf. Assaf, *Mi-sifrūt ha-ge'ōnīm*, 91 (its shelf-mark there: R 19) and the letter there, 92–96; cf. the opinion of Mann, *Tarbiz*, 5(1933/4), 300f, n. 189, that the responsum is not from the Palestinian Gaon but from one of the scholars of Fustat and that its time is the end of the eleventh century; which is not likely; see above, pp. 176f, n. 50. The alleged nāsī: **24**, lines 42ff; it appears that Josiah Gaon is referring to the same person in his letter, **29**, and see on the entire affair below, in the discussion on the exilarchs.

Gaon attempts to regulate the keeping of the custom of outside Palestine by someone who 'went up' to Palestine, saying that after twelve months, he has to accept the Palestinian custom, even if he has not decided to remain in Palestine permanently. This applies to the entire diaspora, including Ifrīqiyā, but with the exception of Babylonia, whose Jews must observe the custom adopted outside Palestine for many years, and only when they have decided to settle in Palestine for good, they have to observe the local custom. Another variation in this sphere was that the Babylonian would read the *shema'* while sitting down, on the basis of 'when thou sittest' (Deut., vi:7), whereas the Palestinian would stand. Another somewhat important difference was that of the marriage deed (*ketubbā*), which according to the Babylonians was imposed 'by the sages' (i.e. the Talmud), while the tradition of the Palestinians was that it was imposed by the Torah; therefore *mi-de-oraytā* was written in the Palestinian marriage deeds while *mi-de-rabbānān* was written in the Babylonian marriage deeds. There was also a variation regarding divorce deeds; in Babylonia, it was written by one and signed by an additional signatory, while the Palestinian deed was written by one and there were two additional signatories.

From the deeds included in my corpus of Geniza documents, one can discern certain characteristics typical of the Palestinian deed in general: the deed is generally dated 'from the creation'; frequently they note the year 'by the week', that is by the sabbatical cycle. There is always a clause mentioning 'free will' and sometimes also 'of sane mind'. They use such terms as *epitropos*, and *anṭīlār*, and do not call a deed of attorney *sheṭar ūrkhetā* as the Babylonians do.

Another departure was in the matter of the priests: among the Babylonians, 'a kohen does not bless the people unless he is married, whereas the Palestinians bless only before they are married'. Another Palestinian custom relates to the priest who has married a divorcée: 'the tips of his fingers are severed', so that he cannot make the blessing.[12]

12 The matter of the holidays: *Ge'onē Mizrāḥ ū-ma'arāv*, 12 a (No. 39); Margaliot, *Ḥillūqīm*, 161–164; Lewin, *Ōṣar ḥillūf*, 81f. The matter of *shema'*, *Ōṣar ha-ge'ōnīm*, to Berakhot, responsa, 25ff (from *Seder Rav 'Amram* and other parallel versions); another rift is mentioned in Ibn Ghayyāth, *Sha'arē simḥā Hilekhōt lūlāv* (see the Fuerth edition [1860/61], I, 117): '. . . this is what Rav Hayy said: we have heard that some people read: For this commandment (Deut., xxx:11) which is still the custom of Palestine and Jerusalem . . .' (i.e., in the blessing over the lūlāv.) cf. Assaf, *Zion* (ha-me'assēf), 1(1925/6), 28; the matter of the Palestinian marriage deed has now merited comprehensive treatment in Friedman, *Jewish Marriage*, I, 246ff; the comparison between the Palestinian and Babylonian marriage deeds is discussed in many places in the first volume of his book, see particularly the introduction, *ibid.*, 1–47; one should note that in the texts of the marriage deeds he quotes, there is no formula *min oraytā* (from the Torah), but it says: 'as Moses decreed to give the virgin daughters of Israel'; there is no reason to disqualify the evidence of Sherira Gaon, however, that *min oraytā* was indeed being written despite the lack of evidence from the

[740] The Karaite writer al-Qirqisānī, has some details on differences in the versions of the Bible which have been preserved, and he ridicules Jacob b. Ephraim the Palestinian (al-Shāmī) who says that both ways of reading are legitimate. For instance, the people of Palestine read in 2 Kings, xix:31: 'the zeal of the Lord of *hosts* [*ṣevā'ōt*] shall do this'; the word *ṣevā'ōt* is absent in the Babylonian reading (in our present Bible, *ṣevā'ōt* is read but not written). Or in Zechariah, xiv:4: 'And his feet shall stand in that day'. The words 'in that day' are lacking in the Babylonian reading (but are found in our present Bible), and other such instances. According to him, the Babylonian reading prevailed from the borders of Raqqa to those of China, and was common to most people of al-Jazīra (northern Iraq), Khurāsān, Fāris, Kirmān, Iṣfahān; Yamāma, Baḥrayn, Yaman (the latter three in the Arabian peninsula) and elsewhere.[13]

[741] The Babylonians, in belittling the values of the Palestinian customs, claimed that these were the outcome of the terrible conditions and persecutions the Palestinians had undergone, because of which they were unable to know things properly or to carry out the precepts as prescribed by the correct law, that is, the Babylonian. We find these claims repeated in a number of places; in the treatise known by the name of Pirqoy b. Baboy, for instance, we encounter statements on the ban on the use of *rīq* (vellum, which is *riqq* in Arabic, and I have already mentioned it in the

Geniza. We do not have enough material on this subject in the collection of documents he presents, for we need evidence from Sherira Gaon's time and preceding that, that is from the tenth century, and there are none. It is reasonable to assume that towards the eleventh century, Babylonian influence increased and the opposition to the Palestinian version to which the Gaon opposed, spread. See *ibid.*, I, 248f; II, 62; and his quotation of Sherira's opinion, from *Sefer ha-makhrī'a*, on p. 246f. See the differences on the subject of divorce in the above-mentioned books by Margaliot and Lewin, according to the indexes. On the matter of the Palestinian deed, cf. Assaf, *Mi-sifrut ha-ge'ōnīm*, 204f; the Palestinians are credited with the custom of 'defloration with the finger' and cf. Pirqē R. Eliezer, xvi (Friedlander evaded this in his English translation). On the blessings of the priests, see Margaliot, *Ḥillūqīm*, 88, cf. *ibid.*, 174f; Lewin, *Ōṣar ḥillūf*, 103f. In a deathbed will from Fustat, from the middle of the twelfth century, there is mention of *al-kohen alladhī yifrōś*, ('who separates the fingers' while putting hands together for the blessing), referring evidently to a bachelor, for this was the congregation of the 'Palestinians' and they evidently behaved in this matter according to Palestinian custom; see: Gil, *Documents*, 270, 273, n. 6 (Document No. 55 [TS 13 J 22, f. 2], a, line 8). A kohen who married a divorcée: Assaf, *Zion* (*ha-me'assēf*, 1(1925/6), 26: the responsum of Ṣemaḥ Gaon, and see Assaf's doubts on this matter, for the parallel version he quotes there refers to Babylonia, not to Palestine.

[13] Qirqisānī, I, 135–141; see: *ibid.*, 49ff on further differences between Babylonia and Palestine, some of which are mentioned in the aforementioned treatise on the differences between Babylonia and Palestine, particularly with regard to marriage. On Jacob b. Ephraim we do not know much. Qirqisānī mentions him frequently and he seems to have been his contemporary. From Salmon b. Yeruḥim's commentary to Ps., cxl (see in Pinsker, *Liqqūṭē qadmōniyōt*, II, 14) it appears that he wrote a commentary on the Palestinian Talmud. Qirqisānī, 52, tells that he questioned him on the positive attitude of the Rabbanites to the followers of Abū 'Īsā, and Jacob b. Ephraim told him that it was because

chapter on the economy) made of hides that were not tanned with gall-nuts for writing a Torah scroll. The writer of the treatise stresses that: 'and such is the law in the two yeshivas . . . they only wrote on such *rīq* for a few years because of the apostasy decreed by Edom the Evil on Palestine, forbidding them to read in the Torah; so they hid all the Torah scrolls because [the Byzantines] would burn them and when the Ishmaelites came, they had no Torah scrolls nor scribes who knew the proper way of tanning the hides . . . and they would take *rīq* from the gentiles', etc. These explanations should naturally be taken with a pinch of salt. At any rate, the difficult times under the Byzantines led to a spiritual decline among the Jews of Palestine and there is no doubt that in the development of the law, Palestine could not compete with Babylonia and its yeshiva could not reach the prestigious stature in learning and wisdom achieved by the Babylonian yeshivot. The same situation prevailed during Islamic domination, because of the constant wars and frequent catastrophes that beset Palestine, as we have seen. There is therefore a grain of truth in the opinion accepted by many scholars, that the law developed mainly in Babylonia, while in Palestine, more emphasis was laid on the *piyyūṭ* (which included elements of prayers which had been banned during the persecution), on mystical literature, on midrash, and also on the *merkāvā* literature whose major ingredients were Gnostic influences and a belief in miracles. It is also possible that this state of mind was also characteristic of the sphere of influence of the Palestinian yeshiva abroad, that is, in those areas which belonged to Byzantium before the Muslim conquest, as well as those which remained under Byzantine rule, such as southern Italy. Evidence of this can be found in the Scroll of Aḥīma'aṣ, with its story of the boy who was kept alive, though he had actually died, by virtue of the Divine Name being etched into his forearm. As Klar has shown in his discussion of the Scroll of Aḥīma'aṣ, we have the evidence-cum-criticism of Hayy Gaon, in his responsum to Joseph b. Berekhia and Jacob *rōsh kallā* b. Nissim and others of Qayrawān, on the use of 'names' to perform wonders, which he considered vain talk, saying: 'We were amazed to find that some scholars of Palestine and scholars of Edom, wise and learned men, good and faithful *ḥavērīm*, claim they have seen these things manifestly . . . and altogether, the simple believeth every word (Prov., xiv:15), and we pity you for believing in such things.' He continues and notes there that 'people from Rome and Palestine' had all sorts of 'formulae and books' such as *sefer ha-yāshār*, the great and small *hēkhālōt*, in which 'some of the names and angels' names and forms of emblems are written'. And the Gaon does not hesitate to take the yeshiva in Sura to task, adding that there too, they

the latter accepted the Rabbanite calendar. See the article by Poznanski, *Gedenkbuch Kaufmann*: 169; see also Mann, *Tarbiz*, 5(1933/4), 291f.

occupy themselves with such matters, 'for they are close to the city of Babylon and the House of Nebuchadnezzar'. Indeed, the characters who figure in the Aḥīma'aṣ Scroll are 'people who understand mysteries' and the 'knowers of secrets', 'keepers of the name' 'who teach the *sefer ha-yāshār* and watch the mystery of the *merkāvā*'. The Karaite Sahl b. Maṣlīaḥ also ridicules the customs of the idolaters 'among some of the Jews; sitting in graves . . . and applying to the dead and saying: oh, R. Yosē ha-gelīlī, heal me, make me pregnant', etc. The Palestinian Gaon Solomon b. Judah, was also not at ease with these customs and beliefs, and it is implied from what he wrote that actually a ban should be placed 'on all those who make magic' but this did not seem feasible, 'for many people, men and women, do these things'.[14]

The organisation of the yeshiva and its titles

[742] The yeshiva was headed by the *rōsh ha-yeshīvā*, also called *gā'ōn*, and we have already discussed the origin of the title Gaon, which was evidently only used during the Muslim period. The *av-bēt-dīn* was second in rank and there were five other yeshiva people, usually designated according to the order of their importance, such as 'the third', 'the fourth', etc. They were styled, for instance, 'the third in the yeshiva' or 'in the Great Sanhedrin'. Apparently there was actually a sort of 'leadership triumvirate' which consisted of the Gaon, the *av-bēt-dīn*, and 'the third'. The Gaon Solomon b. Judah notes in one of his letters that all his decisions are made together 'with the *av* and the third'. Scholars who were recognised as such and ordained by the yeshiva to serve as *dayyānīm* (judges) in

14 See Mann, *REJ*, 70(1920), 137f, and see his explanations *ibid.*, 118f (Mann assumed that a ban on a certain thin vellum was meant; but as mentioned above, they were referring to the vellum which had not been tanned with gall-nuts). With regard to the inferiority of Palestine in matters of religious law, Mann seems to have tried in *Tarbiz*, 5(1933/4), 288, n. 167 to qualify the severity of the comments by attempting to explain the scarcity of responsa of the Palestinian geonim in the Geniza documents. He assumed that the people of the Palestinian yeshiva would usually send the responsa directly by sea, not like the Babylonians, who sent them via Fustat and they were therefore preserved. See on the spiritual state of Palestine: Klar, *Megillat Aḥīma'aṣ*, 118ff; the episode of the boy, and books of superstitions: *ibid.*, 12, 14f, 30, 47. The responsum of Hayy Gaon, see: *Ṭa'am zeq.*, 16ff; similar to the complaint of Hayy Gaon about the people of Sura is also the story of Nissim ha-Nahrwānī, who would open locks by the use of the Divine Name, in Nathan the Babylonian's story, Neubauer, *Mediaeval Jewish Chronicles*, II, 78. On Joseph b. Berekhia and Jacob b. Nissim: Poznanski, *Harkavy Jubilee Volume*, 203–207 (Jacob b. Nissim b. Josiah ibn Shāhīn), where he quotes the responsum of Hayy Gaon I have mentioned here. The statement of Sahl b. Maṣlīaḥ: Pinsker, *Liqqūṭē qadmōniyōt* II, 32. Solomon b. Judah: **121**, line 9. See the strange episode of Solomon the cantor, nicknamed Sābiq, who was excommunicated in Ramla 'for his magic' and who reached Fustat with a recommendation from Solomon b. Judah: Ephraim b. Shemaria's letter, **334**, a, line 24. Hayy Gaon also criticised the Palestinian custom to collect bones and transfer them for a second burial; see Assaf, *Zion* (ha-me'assēf), 1(1925/6), 29 and references there.

their communities and localities were called *ḥavērīm*, a term also to be found in Talmudic literature, where it is used as a synonym for a learned man, and the opposite of an ignoramus. *Ḥāvēr* was the cognomen generally applied to the dayyān who headed the community (and not *rav*, rabbi), as we can observe in the mere fact that the term *ḥāvēr* became a loan-word in pre-Islamic Arabic (*ḥabr*) meaning a Jewish scholar, or a leader of the Jews. The title, *ḥāvēr*, was more or less the equivalent of the *rōsh kallā*, the Babylonian title for scholars who were ordained and acted as judges or trustees of the yeshivas (and in their Arabic were termed *ra's al-kull*), which was also a synonym for *alūf*. We learn from the sources in the Geniza pertaining to Fustat, that the rivalry between the yeshivot of Babylonia and the Palestinian yeshiva was sometimes expressed by getting an important public figure to accept the title of the yeshiva: the Palestinian *ḥāvēr* as opposed to the Babylonian *alūf* or *rōsh kallā*, and we shall see an example of this below. The ancient title *rōsh ha-pereq* (which became part of Byzantine legal terminology – the *arkhipherekitai*), was no longer in use during this period and in my corpus, it is found only once: *Peraḥia rōsh ha-pereq b. Mu'ammal* (see the Hebrew Index).

We get the impression that the principal qualities which were thought to merit an appointment were indeed knowledge of the Torah, wisdom, erudition, and being well-versed in the law, but it seems that one's distinguished relatives and ancestry were also significant in this matter to a certain extent, as for example we found to be the case in the Babylonian yeshivot, as borne out by the description of Nathan the Babylonian. In this matter, we have the case of Abū Yūsuf *ra's al-kull* who received the title *ḥāvēr* from the Gaon Solomon ha-Kohen b. Joseph, but who was not content with this and asked for more (apparently something like 'seventh in the yeshiva' or perhaps only *he-ḥāvēr ha-me'ullē*). The Gaon Solomon b. Judah explains in his letter that it is presumptuous on the part of Abū Yūsuf to make such a request; he should know that he lacks the qualities to be more than a *ḥāvēr*, for 'some eyes would watch him'.[15]

[743] Similar to the order of importance was the order of signatories on a deed or in letters, from the less to the more important, with the most important signing last. This is emphasised by Solomon b. Judah in the

15 Solomon b. Judah: **152**, line 29; see also **79**, line 11, where he mentions that he consulted with 'my brother the third'. See Nathan the Babylonian in Neubauer, *Mediaeval Jewish Chronicles*, II, 87: 'And this was their custom, if a *rōsh kallā* died and he had a son, he would inherit his father's seat and sit there even if he was young in years', etc. The letter of Solomon b. Judah about Abū Yūsuf: **83**, b, lines 13ff. That Abū Yūsuf he-ḥāvēr seems to have been Jacob he-ḥāvēr b. Joseph, and perhaps he may be identified with Jacob *ha-me'uttād* (that is, a candidate to become ḥāvēr), to whom Solomon b. Judah wrote the letters **54**, **55**, and who later became a judge in Aleppo (see the Hebrew Index); cf. Goitein, *Shalem*, 1(1973/4), 27, who notes that he was a dayyān first in Fustat and quotes there the matter of his signatures from the year 1018; it should be noted that he also had the title of

letter mentioned earlier. As to the *av-bēt-dīn*, he was a sort of deputy of the Gaon, and as such headed the religious-legalistic activities of the yeshiva, as his name indicates. From the sixties (*ca.* 1065) there is the case of two contestants going to court – Avon b. Ṣedaqa and Joseph b. 'Alī Kohen Fāsī, both Maghribi merchants. They presented their case before the *av-bēt-dīn*; from the spirit of Avon's letter, one senses the considerable extent of the *av-bēt-dīn*'s prestige.[16]

[744] A letter in the handwriting of Josiah Gaon's scribe speaks of regulations written by the communities (in Ramla?) in Hebrew and Arabic 'on maintaining the *netīvōt* (pathways)', and a letter is mentioned there to 'the ḥavērīm and the elders, concerning the maintaining of our *netīvōt* and the perpetual prayers'. This expression, maintaining the *netīvōt*, belongs perhaps to the hierarchal order and appointments in the yeshiva, or according to Goitein, to the order of advances in official status. We are aware that they were pedantic about the order of advancement, as we shall see. If the *av-bēt-dīn* died, for instance, 'the third' would take his place. On the other hand, we find the expression *nesī' ha-netīvā, rōsh ha-yeshīvā*, which sounds as if there was a parallel between *netīvā* and yeshiva. If this was the case, why the use of *netīvōt* in the plural, as above, when there was only one yeshiva in Palestine? A quandary indeed.[17]

[745] As to the order of the rows in the Palestinian yeshiva, it seems that they observed the ancient Palestinian tradition of the three rows of the Sanhedrin, arranged according to the degree of erudition. This custom was evidently also observed in the Pumbedita yeshiva, as can be seen from the statement of Sherira Gaon about Shemaria b. Elḥanan: 'And if this were not so (if we did not know of his qualities), we would not have appointed him as our deputy nor would we have him appointed as head of the Great Row of the three rows of the yeshiva'. As against this, as mentioned, Nathan the Babylonian, while evidently referring to the Sura yeshiva, speaks of seven rows of ten. In a letter from the yeshiva written by Elijah ha-Kohen b. Solomon Gaon in 1057 (the writer and the date

rōsh kallā of the Babylonian yeshiva. His son Isaac is also mentioned in the documents in my corpus.

16 The matter of the signatures: **83**, b, lines 35–36 and margin. The litigation of the two Maghribis: **503**, a, lines 39ff. Cf. on the matter of the order of importance: Bodl MS Heb 100, f. 55, a fragment of a letter from the yeshiva to a community, from which it mentions *al-ḥakīm al-jalīl* (the honourable physician) Mr. Faraj b. 'Alī, Badal and Abū Naṣr, sons of Tobiah; the letter is written in the name of the [*rōsh ha-yeshīva*], deputy of the yeshiva and some of the scholars, ḥavērīm and *talmīdīm* [pupils, by which are meant also scholars] . . . and all those associated with the yeshiva'; in which that community is informed that the representative of the yeshiva is due to arrive there at any minute; but it is impossible to make out what yeshiva they are speaking of and there is also no certainty regarding the date of the letter.

17 The *netīvōt*, see **38**, c, lines 6–7; d, lines 4–5; the *nāsī of the netīvā*: **8**, line 7; cf. Goitein, *Mediterranean Society*, II, 522, n. 36.

being assumed), he speaks of seventy-one *berūrīm* (elects), in three rows and in a semi-circle. There is also a description of the arrangements in the Palestinian yeshiva in a poem from the Geniza, first edited by Schechter in 1901 ('The Oldest Collection of Bible Difficulties'). This poem presents a subject for discussion on its nature and the identity of its author. The poet speaks of the tents of Ben Barōqā, on the round barn, the holy *ḥavūrā* of justice, the Gaon of Ya'aqōv, the stone (put under) the head of Jacob, the seven ḥavērīm, the *av-bēt-dīn* on the right side of the Gaon and 'the third' on his left side.[18]

The status of the yeshiva and its prerogatives

[746] From a document first identified and edited by Goitein, it emerges, without any doubt, that the Gaon who headed the Palestinian yeshiva was the recognised leader of the Jewish communities within the framework of Fatimid rule and was accepted as such by the authorities. I have already stated that the Gaon's authority and prestige extended over all those communities in regions which were at one time under Byzantine dominion. This document is the draft of a letter, or a memoir, written in Arabic and in Arabic script; a singularly important document, not only

[18] The three rows, see in the *Mishnā*, Sanh. iv:3–4 ('like half of a round barn . . . and three rows of scholars sit before them'); see on the letter of Sherira Gaon: Epstein, *JQR*, NS 12(1921/2), 371 according to Bodl MS Heb e 44, f. 81 and see there further references to Talmudic sources; the letter of Sherira Gaon was first published by Neubauer, *JQR*, 6(1894), 223; and cf. the notes of Mann, *JQR*, NS 8(1917/8), 349ff; the letter of the yeshiva: **420**, b, lines 16–18. Nathan the Babylonian, in Neubauer, *Mediaeval Jewish Chronicles*, II, 87. The poem, see Schechter, *JQR*, 13(1901), 364f; see also: Porges, *JQR*, 20(1908), 187; Mann, *AJSLL*, 46(1930), 268f. Mann, *Jews*, I, 277; Klar, *Tarbiz*, 14(1943/4) 167ff; *ibid.*, 15(1943/4), 46ff, where he expresses the view that the poem was written before *essā meshālī* of Saadia Gaon; and he has an interesting comparison between the two; Rosenthal, *HUCA*, 21(1948), 52, lines 10ff (with the verses dealing with the yeshiva, in an improved second printing); an additional fragment from that poem, from the Kaufmann collection, was edited by Scheiber, *HUCA*, 27(1956), 292ff, where there are remnants of an acrostic with the name of the author; it seems to me to be possible to complete it: [Isaac b. Mxxx b.[Dan]ie[l], who is perhaps Isaac the cantor, of Fās, who wrote **241**, with a rhymed introduction which fits the style of the author of our poem; the writer says of himself (in Rosenthal, *ibid.*, lines 21ff) that when he was a youth of eighteen he left 'the land of Tubal' and went west. The writer of **242** is named Daniel b. Isaac, who is perhaps the son of the aforementioned and named after his great-grandfather. And that same Isaac is perhaps Abū Daniel al-Fāsī who is mentioned in 1018 by Hayy Gaon in his letter to Elḥanan b. Shemaria: TS 10 J 27, f. 10, line 3, see in Mann, *Texts*, I, 135f; and see his comments there, 117. Nevertheless, this identification is naturally only an assumption; Fleischer, *HUCA*, 38(1967), 17, thought the author was an early Spanish commentator: Isaac called *ha-mahavīl* (or in another version: *ha-mavhīl*), or ha-Yiṣḥaqī, whom Abraham ibn Ezra mentions frequently; Fleischer has shown that the copyist (not the author!) of the poem as it is found in the Geniza was the Karaite Tobiah b. Moses (who will be referred to below), see: *Kiryat Sefer*, 55:183, 1979/80.

with regard to the status of the Palestinian Gaon but applicable, in general, to the standing of Jewish institutions of leadership under Islamic rule. This is the only document which has been preserved from the early Middle Ages which speaks of the appointment of a Jewish leader, his recognition and prerogatives. The document includes the following points: (a) his appointment is based on the community's approval; (b) the Gaon is the supreme judicial authority; (c) he has the power to decide on matters relating to matrimony, marriage and divorce; (d) he superintends the observance of the religious precepts; (e) he guides his community towards the good rather than the evil (which means in the jargon of Muslim law: to observe the regulations pertaining to the status of the dhimmīs, particularly the payment of taxes); (f) he has the prerogative to excommunicate or reverse excommunication; (g); he has the prerogative to appoint cantors, ritual slaughterers, *ḥavērīm* and judges, or to dismiss them from their posts; (h) he oversees the *parnāsīm* and the public trustees (the intention here is the management of community property, particularly the *heqdēsh*); and (i) he has the right to appoint a representative in every locality or region. In conclusion, the document stresses the fact that everyone is obliged to obey the Gaon, unqualifiedly.

It is worth comparing this with two other similar documents; one, the letter of appointment of the Nestorian catholicus of Baghdad, dating from 1138, and the other, the letter of appointment of the head of the Jews in Egypt (*ra'īs al-yahūd*) at the time of the Mamlūks. In the former, we also find the point with regard to the community's approval of the appointment. The prerogatives are not spelled out in detail, apart from a general statement that he has the authority of a leader, and a sentence concerning the management of the foundations (inclusive of the management of the Church foundations: *tadbīr wuqūfihim*). His legal prerogative is hinted at in a saying that he would protect the weak against the strong; there is emphasis on the special dress he is to wear, the exclusiveness of the title, and the obedience due to him from all Christians of all sects (for the Nestorians were the largest Christian sect). The Mamlūk document resembles the document of the Gaon's appointment to a greater extent. It speaks explicitly of the prerogative to direct the legal system; to be responsible for matters of marriage and divorce; to excommunicate; to supervise the observance of the religious precepts; to be concerned with the behaviour of his flock in accordance with the regulations relating to the dhimmīs (cited in detail); to appoint *ḥavērīm* and their subordinates; to superintend all matters concerning all the synagogues.

We can see then that this memoir, which has preserved for us a record of the status of the Palestinian Gaon under the Fatimids, is in keeping with what was customary and accepted Islamic rule in general. The Muslim authorities recognised the dhimmīs' right to choose their own leaders, and this is undoubtedly a notable indication of their freedom to associate and communal autonomy. At the same time, the rulers strictly observed the principle that it was they who appointed the leader of the community, in accordance with recommendations from its heads and notables, however. It appears that during the first years of Islamic rule, it was the exilarch who was granted such an official appointment, and from Benjamin of Tudela's account, we understand that in Iraq this was still the custom in the latter half of the twelfth century: 'he has great power over all the communities of Israel' on behalf of the caliph, who grants him 'the seal of power over all the holy communities who live under the authority of his learning'. A solemn expression of the stature of the head of the yeshiva was in the mention of the *rāshūt* (from *rōsh*, head). This was customarily used in the opening phrases of the sermons held in synagogues, and evidently also in the *qaddīsh* prayer, and also in deeds in the following form: 'under the *rāshūt* of so-and-so, the Gaon'.[19]

[19] See **311**; among the ideas on judicial prerogative and the supervision of the implementation of the religious precepts, one must also include what was said there further, that it is he who decides on matters of the law and who preaches sermons. By *ḥavērīm* (*aḥbār*), the judges who head the communities are meant, as explained above. The letter of appointment of the *catholicus* is included in the *tadhkira* of Ibn Ḥamdūn (died 1168), an anthology of political science in twelve volumes, of which only the second volume was published (Cairo 1927). [In Dinur, *Yisrael ba-golah*, I–1, 78, mistakenly: Ibn Zaydūn.] The letter of appointment was evidently granted by al-Muktafī II, to Mar 'Abd Ishū', of Mosul; we know that the coronation of the latter took place on Wednesday, 3 Rabī' I 535, October 1140, in the presence of the wazīr, who came to the ceremony on horseback accompanied by the commander of the police (*ṣāḥib al-shurṭa*) and a group of Turkish soldiers and escorts and he was led in procession to Madā'in, the ancient Persian capital (which is Māḥōzē – Ctesiphon-Seleukeia), the Nestorians' centre. See: Mārī b. Sulaymān, *Akhbār*, 156ff (text), 132 (translation). This letter of appointment was first edited by Amedroz, in *JRAS*, 1804, 468; and again: von Kremer, *ZDMG*, 7(1853), 219ff; Mingana, *BJRL*, 10(1926), 127f. On Ibn Ḥamdūn see: Brockelmann, *GAL*, I, 281; S I, 493, and the article on him in *EI*[2] (by F. Rosenthal). The Mamlūk version: Qalqashandī, *Ṣubḥ*, XI, 390f; cf. Gottheil, *JQR*, 19(1907), 530f; see the Hebrew translation in Poliak, *Zion*, 1(1936), 35ff; cf. also Ashtor, *Toledot*, II, 240. An interesting example of the authorities' involvement in the appointment of the leader of the community and providing backing for his actions, we find also in an official letter (*sijill*) which al-Ḥākim wrote to Nicephorus, the new patriarch of Jerusalem after the death of Theophilus, after al-Ḥākim withdrew his decrees in the summer of 1020. He exploited the opportunity, as it were, of the rise of a new patriarch in order to once again ensure the rights and protection of the Christians and their churches; see Yaḥyā ibn Sa'īd (Cheikho), 230f; Benjamin of Tudela (Adler), 40. See also TS Arabic Box 38, f. 93, the letter of appointment of the leader of the Jews (*ra'īs al-yahūd*) in Damascus; in the right-hand column, lines 14–15, it says that he is given the leadership (*al-riyāsa*) of the two communities, the Rabbanites and the Karaites; cf. the comments of Goitein, *Mediterranean Society*, II, 527, n. 41. At this stage, it is difficult to determine the date of this document, but it emerges from another document that during Fatimid times (and evidently also during previous generations of Muslim rule) it was accepted that a local leader had to receive an official appointment from the ruler: **315**, which is a fragment of a draft of a petition intended to obtain recognition of Joseph ha-Kohen, dayyān of Alexandria, from the ruler. It says there that the aforementioned acted as dayyān in the days of

Peace-making

[747] Settling differences was not one of the roles and prerogatives of the Gaon listed in the aforementioned letter of appointment. It was, however, one of his principal preoccupations, according to the documents at our disposal. Disputes were an everyday affair within the Jewish community. Mostly, one gets the impression that these disputes were mainly motivated by pride – the ambition to occupy a leading position and to be granted titles and honours. Our inclination would be to blame the quarrellers and merely shake our heads over the parties' motives, but we cannot ignore another aspect of this affliction. After all, the inclination to dispute is evidence of the vitality of the social context and the intense involvement of the individual in this framework. For a person to invest all his intellectual energy in the differences which we encounter in the documents preserved from those times, and to strive to dominate the community, indicates that the community was of considerable importance to him. Moreover, the power struggles within the community, if a compromise was not arrived at, generally led to the elimination of one of the parties and the victory of the other. This does not mean that the victor was either wiser or more learned than the man he defeated, but merely that he had more power. This may have been due to certain character traits or to the fact that his supporters in the way of family, relatives or friends – were both stronger and more numerous. In the long run, what happened here in the course of time was a process of social selection, which eventually placed the management of community affairs in the hands of the more capable, the

former geonim, Josiah and Solomon ha-Kohen b. Joseph, and also in the days of al-Fāsī, Solomon b. Judah. He was appointed on behalf of the Gaon to the office of dayyān, to deal with marriages and divorces, to appoint cantors (and here we have an example of the delegation of authority by the Gaon to his representative), to appoint or dismiss the welfare officials (*parnāsīm*); everyone had to obey him whereas he was obliged to obey only the Gaon. The petition seems to have been written on the ascendance of a new caliph (evidently al-Mustanṣir, 1036). The son of the dayyān, Yeshū'ā ha-Kohen he-ḥāvēr b. Joseph, is known to us from a number of Geniza documents, see also the Hebrew Index. Cf. Goitein, *S. W. Baron Jubilee Volume*, 528. On the matter of the *rāshūt*, see: Goitein, *Mediterranean Society*, II, 20f. Yaḥyā ibn Sa'īd (*PO*), 15, tells of the episode of the patriarch Sa'īd ibn Biṭrīq (the author of the chronicle) whose rivals wished to isolate him 'and they stopped mentioning his name in some churches and bishops' seats, such as Tinnīs and al-Faramā'. Cohen, *Self-Government*, 268, wonders whether there is mention of the *rāshūt* in what is said in TS 20.177, about the Nagid Mevorakh b. Saadia; but there it only says (lines 16–18) that the community thanked the Nagid for his concern for them, and that they joyously prayed for the welfare of the Nagid and his son, and one certainly cannot compare this to prayers for the caliph nor to the mention of the *rāshūt* as was the custom towards the Gaon. As to the appointment of a representative in every community (above, clause i), what is said in **331**, a court record from Fustat 1038 (line 8) is a good example of this: 'our Lord and Master Ephraim, the ḥāvēr in the Great Sanhedrin, who is the deputy of our Lord and Master Solomon, head of the yeshiva *ge'ōn ya'aqōv*'; see also **332**, with a complaint against a man of Spain, who did not mention the Gaon in his sermon.

stronger and those of its members with the greatest support. Objectively speaking, both the community and its management were strengthened as a result. Naturally we are not speaking of a democratic framework but of a struggle between individuals and factions who were trying to achieve the greatest backing from the people of the community and its notables, while their major efforts were devoted to securing the support of the yeshiva and its head, the Gaon. The Gaon would try to establish peace, but frequently we find him supporting one of the parties; that party which seemed to him – or so we assume – to be more loyal and more worthy of coming out ahead.

One of the first instances we encounter in a letter in my collection (from *ca.* 1025) is a dispute in Caesarea (Ḥaṣōr) on the honour of saying the prayer *nishmat kol ḥay* in the synagogue, an honour which was apparently generally granted to the younger son of one of the notables, and in this case, given to the son of Ḥalfon al-Ramlī; while the local cantor decided to prepare the son of Eleazar b. Joseph, *ahūv* ('the beloved of') *ha-yeshiva*, for this role as well. The yeshiva's judgment was that they should perform the prayer alternatively. About a century later, the community of Ascalon was enraged by a similar occurrence, at a time when most of Palestine was already under the control of the Crusaders and the Jews of Ascalon were also living under the threat of the capture of their city. Here, too, they were quarrelling over whether the privilege of saying the prayer *nishmat kol ḥay* be given to the son of one of the community's dignitaries. However, the yeshiva was no longer in Jerusalem but (it seems) in Damascus, and therefore the contestants applied to the Nagid in Egypt, after a dayyān who was sent to Ascalon to settle the matter peacefully, was unsuccessful in his mission, and the solution of saying the prayer either alternately or together was rejected.[20]

[748] In the autumn of 1025, Abraham, son of the Gaon Solomon b. Judah, was staying in Damascus, and he mentions in a letter that he succeeded in 'returning peace to peace'; possibly meaning that apart from the general state of peace which prevailed after al-Dizbirī's victory, he also succeeded in appeasing the Damascus community. Not long after this, his father the Gaon is involved in a difficult quarrel which broke out in Fustat, due to which the endeavours to release the Jerusalemites who were imprisoned because of the debt remaining from the war of 1024 were unsuccessful. The Gaon devotes most of a letter to Ephraim b. Shemaria to admonitions blaming the dispute. The quarrel seems to have been between Ephraim b. Shemaria himself and some other dignitary from Fustat who also bore the title *ḥāvēr*, for in another letter, Solomon b. Judah writes

[20] Caesarea: **48**. Ascalon: **595**, a, line 22, and b.

that 'it is worthy of the two *ḥavērīm* to be loved by one another like those who dwell in the garden and hearken' (S. of S., viii:13), hinting at a quarrel. In a brief fragment of another letter from that period, Solomon b. Judah praises someone who avoided a dispute, and did not aspire to an appointment to which the other was more entitled, nor did he ask it of the yeshiva, and he reacts to the information that the dispute in Fustat has ended (so it appears) with satisfaction.[21]

[749] Some ten years later, we again come across echoes of a dispute in Fustat. Solomon b. Judah had evidently reproached Ephraim b. Shemaria for the latter's involvement in that dispute, the details of which are not known. Now he retracts what he said, but advises him to behave in a manner which would prevent disputes. Another decade and more have passed, and in 1048 evidently, another quarrel broke out in Fustat, as we understand from a letter from Solomon b. Judah to Ephraim b. Shemaria, in which he mentions that his son Abraham received a letter about the behaviour of 'the man who was appointed by the *av*'; he meant to say that the *av-bēt-dīn* of the yeshiva (perhaps Nathan b. Abraham) appointed another ḥāvēr in Fustat. The Gaon is amazed at the behaviour of the man: 'not for this was he appointed, but to behave modestly', and so on. Although there are 'good qualities' to this rival of Ephraim b. Shemaria's, and 'if he would have acted as a pious man should, and kept his honesty with courage, he would have been found worthy of being appointed, for he is of a good ancestry'; but further on, Solomon b. Judah suggests to Ephraim that he has nothing to fear, for he will not authorise the granting of the title: 'not everyone who wishes to obtain a title, can obtain it by himself, by gathering people around him in order to arouse disputes'; '... we do not grant support to people eager to quarrel'. The struggles of Ephraim b. Shemaria seem to be typical of the relationships that prevailed in the Jewish communities. Even more characteristic are the remarks made by Ephraim in the draft of a letter to the Gaon: the opposition is referred to as 'the agitators and the complainers'; they are 'difficult' towards him; 'many help the boys to light the fire'; 'the generation has been extremely spoiled and concerning them the saying has become true that, the child shall behave himself proudly against the ancient, and the base against the honourable' (Is., iii:5). He requests the Gaon to write a letter of appeasement to the community, worded wisely and carefully, in his own handwriting, which the community knows and can recognise, and not that of a scribe.[22]

[21] Abraham son of the Gaon: **59**, lines 17–18 (the Gaon was still Solomon ha-Kohen b. Joseph then, and not the father of the writer). Solomon b. Judah criticising the quarrel in Fustat: **66**; the other letter: **68**; the fragment: **69**; the settling of the quarrel: **72**.

[22] The advice to Ephraim: **122**, a, lines 4–5; the matter of the competitor: **147**. Ephraim's letter: **334**, b, lines 4–11.

[750] The quarrels in the Fustat community were resolved, but not for long. In the summer of 1053, the emissary of the yeshiva writes a sort of account to Joseph ha-Kohen b. Solomon Gaon, then *av-bēt-dīn* of the yeshiva, on what is happening in Fustat. The letter contains a gloomy description of the situation. That was at the time when Daniel b. Azariah was Gaon, while 'Eli b. 'Amram stood at the head of the community. The 'Palestinian' congregation in Fustat and its synagogue were very much on the decline. The Maghribis, who joined this congregation (and not that of the 'Babylonians') are most of the time on journeys elsewhere. Their representative, who was to be responsible for the synagogue, Abū'l-Surūr (Joshua) b. Nathan the Spaniard, is in the Ṣa'īd (Upper Egypt), while Abū 'Alī, who is Yefet b. David, is old and weak and cannot settle the quarrel because no one listens to him. The emissary writes that he himself tried to make peace between the adversaries, with the help of 'Eli b. 'Amram and Judah ha-Kohen b. Joseph (who is the *Rav*), and he indeed managed to reconcile the parties. Some years later there was again dissension in Fustat, on which we have no details, between Abū Zikrī, who is Judah he-ḥāvēr b. Saadia (afterwards known by the title Nagid), and Joshua he-ḥāvēr b. Dōsā. The Jerusalem parnās 'Eli ha-Kohen b. Ezekiel writes about it to the Fustat parnās, 'Eli ha-Kohen b. Ḥayyim, in the late fifties. He also describes the joy in Jerusalem when it was learned that 'Eli ha-Kohen b. Ḥayyim (that is, the addressee) succeeded in making peace between the two ḥavērīm (perhaps he writes this to flatter him). In another letter, written a month later, 'Eli ha-Kohen the Jerusalemite again writes to 'Eli ha-Kohen of Fustat, of the joy everyone in Jerusalem felt on learning of the accord arrived at between 'our Lords the ḥavērīm . . . and our Lord the *Māsōs (mesōs ha-yeshīvā)* ('joy of the yeshiva'; evidently meaning Abraham b. David b. Sughmār).[23]

[23] The letter of the emissary: **398**. 'Eli ha-Kohen b. Ezekiel: **440**; Judah b. Saadia shall be mentioned below, in the discussion on the negidim; as to Joshua he-ḥāvēr ha-me'ullē b. Dōsā al-Lādhiqī, from a family originating in Lādhiqiyya in northern Syria, as the name indicates: he is mentioned in the genealogic list: **4**, and in several letters in my corpus, see the Hebrew Index; as is his father as well, Dōsā 'the honourable prince'; TS 13 J 23, f. 5 is a letter to Abū Manṣūr Dōsā, the grandson, son of the aforementioned Joshua, who lives in a *darb* (a courtyard or lane) in *Qaṣr al-Sham'* ('the fortress of the candles'), from Sahl b. Ḥātim, from Raqqa in northern Syria. The additional letter of 'Eli ha-Kohen b. Ezekiel: **443**; *al-māsōs* (the māsōs – an abbreviation of the title *mesōs ha-yeshīvā*) was frequently called Abū Isḥaq, or Abraham, as in the letters of Yefet b. David dealing with matters concerning the income from slaughtering, as in: **313**; **402** is a letter to the Gaon Daniel b. Azariah, which is in the handwriting of Abraham b. David b. Sughmār, and deals precisely with these matters (after the death of Yefet b. David). It is evidently he who was nicknamed *al-māsōs*; Abraham b. David b. Sughmār played an important role in the dispute of Nathan b. Abraham, to be described below, and Solomon b. Judah mentions then the letters of the *māsōs* – see **129**, line 8; and in the continuation, lines 27ff, he notes that 'his grandfather is one of the righteous of Israel . . . and they are the foremost of the city of

[751] We find similar occurrences in Alexandria. The people of this city complain about Yeshūʿā ha-Kohen b. Joseph the dayyān, to the Gaon, and he replies that Joseph the dayyān enjoys the confidence of the local people and also of the yeshiva. He also has some doubts as to the signatories to the letter of complaint, for all the signatures are in the same handwriting. In another of his letters, the Gaon takes Yeshūʿā to account for belittling the title of *ḥāvēr* which he was granted. In the same letter, addressed to the community in Alexandria, he also mentions the matter of the cantor Shelah b. Moses (who evidently headed the opposition to Yeshūʿā ha-Kohen). He explains in elegant terms that he cannot accept the recommendation of Sahlān b. Abraham, leader of the 'Babylonians' in Fustat (we find him, strangely enough, involved in the affairs of the 'Palestinians' in Alexandria) to appoint this cantor *ḥāvēr*, for in such a matter there must be a consensus of opinions. For someone to be appointed *ḥāvēr* ('to be prayed upon as ḥāvēr') he must be of unquestionable suitability for such a degree.

The Alexandrian affairs also troubled the succeeding Gaon, Daniel b. Azariah, who succeeded some twenty or more years later. Yeshūʿā ha-Kohen b. Joseph ha-dayyān, the same ḥāvēr, still has stubborn opponents. The Gaon, writing to Abraham ha-Kohen b. Isaac b. Furāt, claims that he always liked Yeshūʿā as well as his father, Joseph the dayyān, and tried to influence their opponents to leave them in peace because he thought the latter were not behaving properly. He also asked ʿEli he-ḥāvēr b. ʿAmram, leader of the 'Palestinians' in Fustat, not to become involved in the dispute in Alexandria and not to have anything to do with Yeshūʿa's opponents.

Fās' – and it seems that the reference is to this Abraham b. David. One can identify the handwriting of Abraham b. David by TS 13 J 1, f. 12, a court record in the handwriting of Ephraim b. Shemaria, dated Friday, 26 Kislev 1361 Sel., that is, 24 November AD 1049, which includes at the end additional evidence, written in Tevet, that is, December 1049, in the handwriting of Ibrahīm b. Da'ūd b. Sughmār, with his signature: Abraham b. R. David, of blessed memory; cf. Goitein, *Mediterranean Society*, III, 564, n. 118; in 1032, he stayed in Sicily; see TS 8 Ja 2 in: Hirschfeld, *JQR*, 16(1904), 575f., line 10: 'son of Zughmār' (!). Perhaps he is the same as Abraham b. David b. Labrāṭ, in TS 24.6, line 47 (a letter from Sicily to the community of Qayrawān, see: Mann, *JQR*, NS 9[1918/9], 175ff); it also seems that the MS Mosseri II 150 (L151) is in his handwriting; his son Nethanel is mentioned there, and he is mourning another of his sons who died, David; one can also recognise the handwriting of Abraham b. David from **190**, the letter of ʿEli ha-Kohen b. Ezekiel; also from another Geniza fragment, Westm. Coll. Misc., f. 124, which deals with commercial matters, which has his signature: 'Abraham b. R. David', in the right-hand margin. Another fragment in the Geniza, ENA 2808, f. 45, which also seems to be in his hand-writing has the signature: 'Abraham b. David b. Labrāṭ', and this proves that my assumption that the name of his grandfather was Labrāṭ is correct. **402a** is a fragment from a letter also in his handwriting, and can be added to the information on his involvement in the matters of the ritual slaughtering in Fustat. It seems that the letter was directed to ʿEli b. ʿAmram, and the Abū ʿAlī mentioned there is Yefet b. David b. Shekhania, see *infra*, sec. 805. The nickname *al-māsōs* is also to be found in the Adler MS edited by Bacher, *REJ*, 40(1900), 56f, lines 29, 34; the editor assumed that it was an Arabic word: *al-mushawwash*, and translated it *le troublé*.

On the other hand, it appears that Daniel b. Azariah also makes some critical remarks on Yeshūʻā ha-Kohen and reproaches him, particularly for the fact that he does not participate in the meetings convened by Abraham ha-Kohen.[24]

The judicial prerogative

[752] The network of law courts was the main backbone for maintaining the Jewish communal framework. It was not unwarranted that the Jewish leadership, in all its various branches, kept a careful eye on the ban to appeal to the gentile courts, as we have seen in the discussion above. The Palestinian yeshiva was at the top of the judicial hierarchy in the areas under its rule and influence. The Gaon and his court had the final decision in these matters. This is explicitly stated by the head of the 'Babylonian' community in Fustat, Sahlān b. Abraham, writing to an unidentified ḥāvēr with regard to a power-of-attorney given to Abū'l-Ḥasan ʻAllūn, in a matter that cannot be discerned in the remaining fragment. In the letter he repeats again and again that the final decision lies with the Gaon. The court of the yeshiva is 'the grand court' as opposed to a local court, such as 'the court of Miṣrayim' (that is, of Fustat), which is subordinate to it. Of the 'court of Ṭarābulus' (Tripoli in Libya), it was said that it did not accept the dictates of the 'grand court, may it be guarded from Heaven'. Nathan b. Abraham, the *av-bēt-dīn* of the yeshiva, passes on instructions to Fustat to sue a certain person, and the head of the local court, the ḥāvēr, Ephraim b. Shemaria, informs him that the accused has indeed been called to court. One single page remains of the court diary of the Jerusalem yeshiva, from August 1023; the diary was usually called *shimmūsh bēt-dīn*, evidently. From its contents, it emerges that people would come from Ramla to litigations before the court of the yeshiva. A decision concerning an agreement between a man and his wife who are apparently living apart is recorded there, along with the signatures of five witnesses. There is also an arrangement for paying off a debt by instalments and a confirmation on the part of a jeweller of the receipt of a quantity of silver. The status of the yeshiva court can also be seen in a fragment of a letter remaining from the

24 Alexandria, see: **73**, **74**; Joseph the dayyān, the father, was mentioned above, and it seems that the father and son continued to devote themselves to public service for many years, but only the son Yeshūʻā, earned the title ḥāvēr. The first letter speaks of the communities of Alexandria, that is, he evidently represented the two communities, the 'Palestinians' and the 'Babylonians'. In **74**, Alexandria is called Nōʼ Āmōn, taken from Nahum iii:8; the city is called thus in deeds (although frequently also Iskandariyya); cf. Golb, *JNES*, 33(1974), 117; and see also: *Bereshit rabbā* (Theodor and Albeck), 1–2; Eusebius, in Hieronymus, *MPL*, 25, 1260: 'Hebraice No dici Alexandriam, Amon autem mutltitudinem, sive populos' ('in Hebrew, No is Alexandria, while Amon – the masses, the people'); cf. Gil, *Documents*, 478, n. 2. The letter of Daniel b. Azariah, see **355**, a, lines 32ff.

time of the Gaon Daniel b. Azariah, written by the scribe of the yeshiva. It contains instructions to the ḥāvēr in Fustat, ʿEli b. ʿAmram, how to behave in a matter which has to be brought before the court, a litigation between parties living in provincial towns in Egypt. They must be summoned, if the court cannot go out to those places, and the proper legal procedures must be punctiliously observed. It seems that the Maghribis, the great maritime traders, were very insistent that their deeds should bear the validation (*qiyyūm*) of the grand court, that is the court of the Jerusalem yeshiva. Thus, Moses b. Jekuthiel, a physician and merchant of Fustat, a Spaniard by origin (al-Andalusī), who had come especially from Tyre (where he had stayed on business matters), to Jerusalem in order to receive the validation of the grand court on deeds relating to his dealings with some of his partners.[25]

[753] There are a variety of remnants of letters and documents of the court which are evidence of the extent of the court of the yeshiva's activities and its involvement in practical decisions, starting from matters of the synagogue and ending with commerce and deposits. In a letter from Solomon ha-Kohen Gaon b. Joseph, we find a discussion on the affair of Muḥassin (Mevorakh) b. Ḥusayn son of Samʿān's sister, a merchants' representative whom I have mentioned above, who has sworn that he will no longer go to the synagogue for reasons which are not known to us, and the Gaon quotes the law and Talmudic sayings admonishing him on this. Matters of inheritance evidently occupied first place in the yeshiva court's activities, if we can judge by the letters that have been preserved. I have already mentioned the responsum to 'the holy community in Tiberias', dealing with the legacy of Naʿamān the teacher. Solomon b. Judah also deals with an inheritance in his letter to Abū Ghālib David ha-Levi b. Aaron al-Barqī (from Barqa in Libya). The letter concerns a certain Mevassēr, of Ramla, who died and left three sons, Mawhūb, Moses, and Isaac. Mawhūb went to Egypt to collect his father's bequest. The court in Ramla appointed Ṣabgha b. Yeshūʿā he-ḥāvēr, who travelled to Egypt, to represent the two younger brothers – Moses, who was in Egypt, and Isaac, who was in Ramla and was deaf-and-dumb – in order to obtain what

[25] Sahlān b. Abraham: **339**. The grand court, etc.: **396** ('the court of Tripoli, which did not obey the order of the grand court, may it be guarded from Heaven'). Nathan b. Abraham: **333**, b, lines 19–20 (March 1043). The page from the court diary: **42**. The instructions to Fustat: **375**. Moses b. Jekuthiel: **243** (on his deals with partners see **276**); he mentions in his letter (written to one of his friends), the head of the yeshiva, the 'third' Tobiah b. Daniel, the 'fourth' Joseph ha-Kohen, and the 'fifth' Elijah ha-Kohen, but not the *av-bēt-dīn*, that is, Nathan b. Abraham, from which we assume that the letter was written during the dispute, that is in *ca.* 1040; Jekuthiel the father was executed in Spain in 1039, and Moses emigrated to Fustat; he died in the Fayyūm and left a son, Abū Yaʿqūb Jekuthiel, who was the 'merchants' representative', see Goitein, *Mediterranean Society*, III, 207f.

was due to them. 'The court is father to the orphans', writes the Gaon, and he asks David b. Aaron to deal with the matter, in other words, to pay Moses what was due to him against a receipt ('a deed of compensation'). The share of the deaf son should be sent by a *diyōqnē* to the court, and the court (evidently in Ramla) would send him a receipt from the deaf son. Another instance of inheritance is mentioned in a fragment of another letter from Solomon b. Judah, to an unidentified ḥāvēr, evidently in Fustat. The Gaon requests that he deal there with the inheritance of a certain Jacob, a flax merchant, who was in partnership with several people. One of the heirs is said to be unbalanced. Another fragment of a letter, also from Solomon b. Judah to some personality in Fustat, contains reproaches against the trustees who were withholding the property of an orphan. It should be publicly known, he writes, 'that they are not trustworthy'. Not that anyone had complained to him – neither the heir nor anyone on his behalf – but he felt that wrong was being done while looking into a query the trustees put to the yeshiva. He had studied the matter with the 'third' and the responsum on that query was agreed upon by both of them. Even the fact that the heir appealed to the gentile courts, he writes, does not justify the behaviour of those trustees. Their dishonourable behaviour can be seen in their refusal to take the oath, claiming that the father had absolved them of this before his death. According to law, it was their duty to bring the account before the heir in the presence of the court and to swear that the sums remaining to his credit were correct. We also find concern with the affairs of an orphan in a query and responsum copied by Yefet b. David. The responsum comes from the Gaon of Jerusalem, and it deals with a deposit of an orphan lost during the great pillage in Fustat. Apparently, this is also a responsum of Solomon b. Judah. Another instance of an ineritance is discussed in a letter to Abraham ha-Kohen b. Haggai in Fustat, who was appointed executor of the will of Abraham b. Meir al-Andalusī, together with Joshua b. Nathan al-Andalusī. The deceased had owed more than fifty dinars to Abū Bishr Solomon b. Ṣemaḥ al-'Aṭṭār ('the perfume dealer'), of Ramla, which had been given him by this Solomon, who was a generous man helpful to everyone, who happened to be in Ramla and needed help. We also find an orphan's claim in a letter of the Jerusalemite 'Eli ha-Kohen b. Ezekiel, written in the time of Daniel b. Azariah. A power-of-attorney on behalf of the orphans was given to the writer in order to sue a certain b. al-Ḥulaybī (who is Khalaf b. Joseph; Ḥulayb, a diminutive of Ḥalab, Aleppo), and the matter is being clarified in the court of the Gaon. B. al-Ḥulaybī evidently made claims that were incredible, to the effect that he owed practically nothing, and he was given the opportunity to go down to Ramla to re-examine his accounts. In the meantime, the Gaon left Jerusalem for Damascus, and the matter dragged on.[26]

[754] Other family matters also called for the intervention of the Gaon from time to time. In the remnant of a responsum written by Solomon b. Judah we read about a man whose marriage deed was written during *ḥōl ha-mo'ēd*. The Gaon replies that he is inclined to moderation in this matter. It seems that the couple were later divorced, and the Gaon is consulted and replies, with regard to the payments due the woman on the basis of the marriage deed.

In 1015, many years before he became the Gaon, Solomon b. Judah was already dealing with a matter of divorce. He writes to Fustat, to Jacob 'the candidate' b. Joseph *he-ḥāsīd*, who later became dayyān in Aleppo. The letter is concerned with the payment of four dinars to a woman in Fustat, whose husband Solomon b. Khalaf al-Barqī wants to divorce her if she does not join him in Palestine. A number of Maghribis who travel from Palestine on business are involved in this affair, such as Azhar b. Jonah the Spaniard. Nathan (who is Hiba) b. Zechariah is the woman's representative, and he demands two dinars due her, held by Jacob 'the candidate'. The husband, Solomon, asks for those items belonging to him in their house in Fustat, her handiwork executed during the time they were together and whatever he bought her, while whatever remained in the house should be used to maintain his daughter, if she preferred to remain with her mother. The wife's representative, on the other hand, stated that the woman swore she had no property of the kind her husband stipulates. She will be satisfied with four dinars; on receiving two dinars she will hand over the marriage deed and when it is confirmed that it has reached Palestine, Solomon will hand over the two remaining dinars, deposited for the time being with Solomon he-ḥāvēr b. David, and they will be sent to Fustat in a *diyōqnē* together with the deed of divorce, which has already been written and placed with Nathan. In about 1050, when Solomon b.

[26] The matter of Muḥassin b. Ḥusayn: **51**. The responsum to Tiberias: Mosseri VIII 421 (R19). The letter of Solomon b. Judah to David b. Aaron: **125**; he was one of the leaders of the 'Palestinian' congregation in Fustat, see the Hebrew Index; he is mentioned also in TS 10 J 5, f. 11, line 12, a court record from Fustat, in 1021/2; the matter of this inheritance is also mentioned in **230**, the letter of Abraham the 'fourth' b. Samuel the 'third', to the Gaon. That this Mevassēr had lived in Ramla, is recognisable in the fact that one of the sons was still in Ramla, see: **125**, line 6. Jacob the flax merchant: **156**. The matter of the unworthy trustees: **158**. The query and responsum: **337**. The letter to Abraham ha-Kohen b. Haggai: **159**, and the matter of this inheritance is described in a deed from Fustat: BM Or 5561 A, f. 1; see on Joshua b. Nathan: Goitein, *Letters*, 111ff; cf. *idem*, *Shalem*, 1(1973/4), 47; Solomon b. Ṣemaḥ is already mentioned above. 'Eli ha-Kohen: **445**, line 12f; the matter of the inheritance is also dealt with in **329**, fragments from a court record dealing with an inheritance due to three brothers, sons of Mawhūb b. Faraj: Mevorakh, Yefet and Joseph. The latter is seventeen and is 'in the *shefēlā*' (probably Ramla); the Gaon is asked, through deeds written in the court in Fustat, to instruct 'the three elders'

Judah was nearing the end of his life, he writes to Sahlān b. Abraham (evidently) concerning a woman who married a man who seems to have been married already. Apparently the man was excommunicated and they are trying to influence the Gaon, even via pressure on the part of the governor of Jerusalem, to invalidate the ban. The letter is very faded and the matter rather illegible. We would have liked to know, for instance, what was the nature of this excommunication – were they speaking of a regulation against polygyny? Possibly we have here a case connected with the regulation in Fustat against polygyny. It emerges that there was quite an outcry in Fustat over this affair and even a serious rift between the two communities (evidently the 'Palestinians' and the 'Babylonians'; the Karaites do not seem to be involved here). The addressee's brother (if the addressee is Sahlān, the reference is to his brother Nehemiah), is staying in Jerusalem and he is asked to deal with this matter (on his return to Fustat, apparently). Abraham, son of the Gaon, also devotes some of his time to this affair.[27]

[755] The existence of a quarrel between the community and one of its members emerges from a letter addressed to Daniel b. Azariah, apparently in *ca.* 1060. The name of the writer is not preserved. It seems that the community objected to the fact that he had built a *ṭārima*, that is a wooden structure, perhaps building it on the property of the *heqdēsh* in Fustat or on some other site belonging to the synagogue. The writer applies to the Gaon, but out of a sense of fairness, submits his letter firstly to the local dayyān, 'Eli (*he-ḥāvēr ha-me'ullē*) b. 'Amram. 'Eli did not merely read the letter, but kept it for a considerable time, and finally reformulated it as he saw fit, and the writer was not at all pleased by the wording in which it was eventually presented to the Gaon.

We learn of the intervention of the Gaon in commercial differences and appeals to him in such matters, from a letter written by the sons of Benāyā b. Mūsā of Alexandria, to Nehorai b. Nissim. A serious quarrel broke out among the Maghribi merchants and the people of Alexandria. The matter came before the *shōfēṭ*, evidently meaning the cadi, otherwise the word *dayyān* would have been used. The letter concerning this affair from His Excellency *sayyidnā al-rayyis*, that is, the Gaon (evidently condemning the application to the gentile courts), aroused a stormy argument 'in the presence of the judge'. A letter on the matter had already been written to

(evidently the executors of the inheritance) to release the 'inheritance to the sons of Mawhūb out of their hands'.

27 The fragment of the responsum: Mosseri, Ia, 20, at the head of the folio on which **63** is written, see there in the foreword; edited by Assaf, *Mi-sifrūt ha-ge'onīm*, 97, see his comments there, 91f. The matter of the divorce: **54**. The second wife: **148**; this letter was re-edited by Friedman, *Ribbūy nāshīm*, 244f, and see there the readings offered by him and the discussion. On the regulation of Fustat: Friedman, in *Perspectives in Jewish Learning*, IV

the Gaon, and the writer intends to meet with him; apparently the letter is referring to the Gaon Elijah ha-Kohen b. Solomon.[28]

[756] At times the Gaon was directly applied to in order to obtain his intervention in correcting acts of violence and injustice. We find a letter from an anonymous writer, for instance, who was evidently from Jerusalem or Ramla, with the request that the Gaon inquire into the matter of a shop belonging (fully or in part) to the writer. A certain witness (*shāhid*, perhaps used in the meaning of *mu'addal* – an honest or trusty witness, which assumed the significance of a notary) by the name of al-Mu'akkar put it up for sale. He asks that an account be made of the income from the sale and that he should receive his share, after a deduction of expenses.

The yeshiva was also a sort of central institution of trusteeship which helped out merchants in situations where the accounting was complex or when a difference arose which could be settled out of court. In *ca.* 1065, we encounter the instance of a Maghribi merchant whose name has not been preserved, who was a partner of a certain Isaiah al-Fāsī. The authorities demanded that the man pay for this Isaiah – during a time of stress and penury – sixty dinars, which Isaiah evidently owed to the authorities. The man in fact paid, and this was truly the salvation of his partner Isaiah. Three years went by, and Isaiah was asked to hand over the money to the head of the yeshiva in Jerusalem, Elijah ha-Kohen b. Solomon, but he shamelessly denied owing the money and claimed the very contrary, that the money was owed to him. The writer then turned to the court in Fustat, received from them a *ma'asē bēt-dīn* (court document) and sent it accompanied by a letter addressed to the Gaon, together with a letter from a certain Abū Ya'qūb, through whom the payment of the sixty dinars had been made, to the addressee, who was a relative or a friend and evidently staying in Ramla. At this point, he asks of that Palestinian to confirm that the court document and letters have arrived, and that he take the trouble to send them all to Jerusalem, to the yeshiva. Similarly, we have a court document from Fustat, written by the cantor and scribe Yefet b. David, which records the agreement arrived at 'in the synagogue called of the Palestinians' by Mufarrij b. Yefet b. Shu'ayb ha-Darmashqī and Jacob b. Joseph ha-Bavlī – that is to say, by a Damascene and a Baghdadi – 'to accept the order of our Lord the Gaon that an oath be taken from him'. We have no details concerning the quarrel between the two, but it is clear that there was an appeal to the Jerusalem Gaon, and he responded that one of

(1972), 20. It stands to reason that the letter was written to Sahlān b. Abraham, as it includes regards to his uncle, Saadia *alūf*.

[28] The *ṭārima*: **397**; usually it meant an additional room built over the upper storey(*ṭabaqa*), see: Gil, *Documents*, 270, n. 1. The matter of Alexandria: TS 13 J 23, f. 3, a, lines 26–27; b, lines 7, 13–14; the *sar ha-sārīm* ('prince of princes') is also mentioned there, referring to Mevorakh b. Saadia, the Nagid, evidently.

the sides would have to depose an oath, though we do not know which one.[29]

Excommunication

[757] It is self-evident that the court of the yeshiva had no right to deal in criminal law and could not officially impose physical punishment, such as flogging or imprisonment. It did, however, have a very effective means of punishment, in the form of excommunication. One of the greatest Muslim writers, al-Jāḥiẓ (of Baṣra, who died in 867) correctly grasped its significance. When he explains the meaning of a *shōfār* (*shābūr* in his tongue) he describes a kind of trumpet (*būq*) which originated in Persia. The Jews use it, for example, when the exilarch wants to punish a guilty person and forbids the people around him to have anything to do with him. Then they use the shōfār. He says further that the ban on talking (to the banished) is not included among the punishments recorded in their books; but as the catholicus (*jāthalīq*) and the exilarch are not permitted to flog or imprison in Islamic countries, they can merely impose fines and forbid talking. Further on, he notes that the catholicus is frequently prejudiced in such matters and does not punish the bullies or the rulers' favourites. (In the continuation, he quotes the behaviour of the catholicus Timotheus [there is a distortion here in the printed version of the text: Ṭīmān] who considered pronouncing an excommunication on the Nestorian 'Awn, when he learned that he kept concubines, but the latter threatened that he would accept Islam if he was excommunicated.)

From the Geniza letters in my corpus, we learn that excommunication was in comparatively frequent use in those areas under the aegis of the Palestinian Gaon. Generally, it was the Gaon himself who pronounced the ban, and if it were a matter occurring within a community outside of Jerusalem, he would send instructions to pronounce an excommunication, or give his authorisation to do so to the community which wished to declare the excommunication. The lighter form of the excommunication, which was a curse, the *pātīaḥ* or *shamtā* (or *petīḥā* in Babylonian parlance), is also mentioned once in the letter written by the Gaon Solomon b. Judah to his son Abraham, during the dispute with Nathan b. Abraham; and again in the letter of Nathan's son, Abraham, evidently writing from Tyre in *ca.* 1089.[30]

[29] The matter of the shop: **218**, see the notes there. The Maghribi merchant: **520**. The oath: TS 20.117*r*, cf. Goitein, *Mediterranean Society*, II, 158, 553, n. 11.

[30] Jāḥiẓ, *Ḥayawān* (ed. Hārūn), IV, 27f; contrary to what Jāḥiẓ says and contrary to what we are inclined to assume, **370**, b, lines 6–7, mentions the possibility of incarceration by the community, see on this below; cf. Mann, *JQR*, NS 10(1919/20), 342–345 (on the *de facto* existence of physical punishment, flogging, incarceration, according to the responsa of the geonim). The *patīaḥ*: **127**, line 31; **553**, line 19; cf. the version of the Babylonian *petīḥā*:

[758] Apparently, the most common reason for excommunication was the non-payment of debts; though naturally not until the person was found guilty by the court. In a letter, Solomon b. Judah requests Ephraim b. Shemaria to have such a debtor, evidently a Jerusalemite, excommunicated in Fustat. From the draft of a court record written in Daniel b. Azariah's time, on 12 October 1057, it seems that a number of Maghribi merchants who were unwilling to accept the decision of the court regarding a certain money matter, or who perhaps applied to the gentile courts, were excommunicated. Apparently, not everyone observed the ban and special efforts had to be made to have it imposed, as we learn from the fact that Joseph b. Shemaria of Barqa, who was staying in Jerusalem, signs an obligation to treat all the decisions of Daniel b. Azariah and Elijah ha-Kohen (the *av-bēt-dīn*) with respect and obedience, and to not maintain any contact with the excommunicated individuals. 'Eli ha-Kohen b. Ezekiel, the Jerusalem parnās, who deals with the collection of debts due to a certain b. al-Ḥijāziyya, mentions in his letter the pronouncement of a type of excommunication known as the *ḥerem setām* ('anonymous excommunication') on whoever owes this man money ('dinar' or 'dirham'), or goods, or commission. Such a ban was proclaimed in the entire region of the Rīf (the Delta) on *Hosha'na rabba*, and renewed on every holiday. A court document from Fustat, enacted in August 1030, in the presence of Abraham son of the Gaon, included the decision to excommunicate al-Ashqar ('the red-head') Salmān b. Shabīb, who refused to accept the decision of the court to pay four dinars to Sulaymān the smith, through the latter's representative, Yefet ha-Levi b. Tobiah; and what is more, who ran riot in the court and cursed the son of the Gaon and the judges, even announcing that he would appeal to the gentile courts. It is interesting that in this instance, there is no mention at all of receiving an authorisation to pronounce the excommunication from the Gaon in Jerusalem, perhaps because the son of the Gaon was present. The matter of a ban imposed because of an application to the gentile courts is also encountered in a letter of Josiah Gaon to the community of Rafiaḥ, mentioned above; the heirs who took over property with the help of the *qā'id*, the Fatimid commander and governor, are to be excommunicated until they return the property, and the excommunication shall also apply to Sahl, the brother of the major defendant, if he does not appear together with his sister in the grand court and declare there what was taken from the inheritance.[31]

Aptowitzer, *JQR*, NS 4(1913/14), 126: 'I decreed to declare a curse on him at the gate of the yeshiva and this *petīḥā* was written against him, so that he be cursed in all places . . . so you should curse him always every day . . . and any synagogue where this *petīḥā* is shown has to curse him immediately'.

[31] The excommunication of a debtor: **78**. The court record: **393**. 'Eli ha-Kohen: **445**, lines 8f. The court document: **102**. Josiah Gaon: **43**.

[759] Ephraim b. Shemaria turns to the Gaon and asks him what judgment should be passed on a shopkeeper for whom carpenters built shelves in his shop during the holiday, and on the sabbath within the holiday week. In the court in Fustat, opinions were divided as to whether he should be flogged or fined, or both, and also excommunicated. In a letter from Ascalon to Shemaiah he-ḥāvēr the Jerusalemite, which has been mentioned above, the writer, who is being persecuted together with his family, asks that the yeshiva place a ban on those who harass him. According to him this is the only means by which an end can be put to the mischief being done. It seems that officials of the yeshiva also had the power to declare an excommunication apart from the Gaon, and perhaps someone who was merely a ḥāvēr of the yeshiva also had this prerogative. We find this assumption supported by the draft of a letter from Ephraim b. Shemaria to the Gaon Solomon b. Judah, on the matter of the cantor whom Solomon nicknamed Sābiq, and who arrived in Fustat with a recommendation from the Gaon, but whom the community refused to receive, claiming that a ban had been imposed on him by Joseph ha-Kohen the 'fourth' b. Solomon Gaon. There was a great quarrel about it in Fustat, and Ephraim asks the Gaon to send him a letter in which he explicitly states that the ban is now void.[32]

[760] Not infrequently, excommunication was used in some communities as a weapon against the opposition, or creators of rifts, as they were generally defined, and also against factors outside the 'Palestinian' congregation, especially the 'Babylonians', who at times had claims that were not acceptable to the Jerusalem Gaon. This is illustrated in the case of the leader of the 'Babylonians' in Fustat, who wanted to deprive Ephraim b. Shemaria of the right to supervise the markets (meaning the slaughtering, which was done in the markets). He was excommunicated in Jerusalem on Monday, 25 Sivan (evidently: AM 4789, that is, 9 June AD 1029); 'we assembled in the cave, a great multitude, and took out the Torah scrolls and proclaimed a ban on all those that decree unrighteous decrees and on all that write grievousness (Is., x:1) and deceiving statements and who arouse dissent between brethren in order to achieve their ambitions'. At the same time, Nathan he-ḥāvēr proclaimed a similar ban in Fustat.

An occurrence of a figure of the opposition being excommunicated was that of Abraham b. Aaron al-Baṣrī, cantor and preacher, who 'stirred up trouble' against Ephraim b. Shemaria, 'slighted him and those who ordained him, the dead and living geonim of Israel, and spoke obscenely'; hence 'he was excommunicated and banned'. Abraham the son of the

32 The query from Fustat: **336**; the handwriting is that of Ephraim b. Shemaria, but there are eight signatories and he is not one of them. Ascalon: **526**. The episode of Sābiq: **334**, a, line 16f.

Gaon writes about this to the community of Taṭai. The community is required to cut off any contact with him, and the ban also applied to anyone who assisted or maintained any relationship with him. During the succeeding Gaon's day, that is of Daniel b. Azariah, we also find that excommunication is being enacted towards the rivals of the leader of the 'Palestinians' in Fustat. Two fragments of a letter written by the Gaon's scribe to 'Eli b. 'Amram contain a licence granted him by the Gaon to proclaim a ban on anyone who disobeys him or to firstly announce a ban on Yefet b. David b. Shekhania, the cantor and scribe who is known to us from many letters in the Geniza. The writ of excommunication against him had already been prepared at the yeshiva, together with all the other necessary documents, in two identical copies, and these were sent to Abū'l-Ḥasan and Abū'l-Ṭayyib. It was not important which of them received the documents first, the proclamation of the ban had to be done quickly. The letter had to be read in the synagogue, its clauses clearly presented, and it had to be read without errors, for it contained matters of law. The letter also mentions the teacher Abū'l-'Amīrayn al-Sha'rānī al-Maghribī, who has already lost much of his public stature and upon whom there is no need to 'waste' an excommunication. Nevertheless he should be punished and taught a lesson, for if such a thing had occurred in Jerusalem, writes the Gaon (or rather his scribe), the people of Jerusalem would have firstly jailed him and afterwards expelled him from Jerusalem (perhaps meaning that this was actually done to him when he was in Jerusalem). From the same letter, it emerges that the Fustat leader 'Eli b. 'Amram enjoys the backing of two of Fustat's notables, and at the end of the letter, he is asked to thank them and pray for their welfare. Below we shall encounter further matters connected with excommunication and ostracisation in the discussions on the power-struggles for leadership of the yeshiva, and also in the discussion on relations with the Karaites.[33]

Aid for individuals

[761] We have quite a number of documents with evidence of assistance being given to individuals by the geonim through requests for support and

[33] The excommunication relating to Fustat: the letter of Solomon b. Judah, **79**, lines 27f; it is not clear who is this Nathan he-ḥāvēr. Abraham b. Aaron: **93**, lines 8f; Taṭai, a locality in the Delta, some 14 kilometres south-east of Ṭanṭa, see more details on it: Golb, *JNES*, 33(1974), 142f. Daniel b. Azariah: **370**; the person mentioned there is b. Shekhania, with no further details, hence Goitein, *ha-Yishuv*, 182, assumes that he is referring to Manṣūr, Yefet's brother; see in the notes to **370**, details on the assumed identity of the people of Fustat who are mentioned there. See the discussion on the subject of excommunication according to the responsa of the geonim: Mann, *JQR*, NS 10(1919/20), 348ff and see the discussion in Goitein, *Mediterranean Society*, II, 331ff.

recommendations. We find Abraham, for instance, the son of the Gaon, writing as usual on behalf of his father, to David b. Aaron in Fustat, asking him to help Ṣedaqa b. Menaḥem who intends to go down to Egypt with his family. At the same time, the Gaon himself writes to Sahlān b. Abraham, leader of the 'Babylonians' in Fustat, on the same subject. Then again we find Abraham, the Gaon's son, writing – it seems to Alexandria – asking for support for a man who fled to Damascus because of the pressure of taxes, and who while *en route* to Palestine was attacked by robbers and left wounded and penniless. He managed to get to Jerusalem and now wished to go to Egypt and obtain enough help there to enable him to return to his own country. The main request implied in the letter is to organise a campaign to which every member of the community would contribute and thus enough money would be accumulated to make his journey possible. One assumes that someone from a distant land is being referred to, perhaps from somewhere within the Byzantine empire. In another letter of recommendation to Sahlān b. Abraham, Solomon b. Judah writes about the affairs of a man we cannot identify, who is leaving for Fustat. According to the Gaon 'he is one of our cherished . . . his place is with us and he is like a favourite son . . .' Solomon b. Judah is generally given to cultivate and praise those who are active in public matters, and he writes a letter – evidently at the request of Sahlān b. Abraham – to Nethanel ha-Levi b. Ḥalfon in Fustat, full of praise for his great generosity and his abundant gifts. People from the inner circle of the yeshiva, relatives and intimates of the leaders of the yeshiva and its personalities, were also exploiting its prestige and writing to Fustat in order to help individuals. Thus we find the grandson of Samuel the 'third' b. Hosha'na, 'Eli ha-Mumḥē b. Abraham, when writing to Ephraim b. Shemaria, repeatedly asking after Abū'l-Faraj b. 'Eli, a cantor from Mosul whom he recommended to the people of Fustat. No fewer than five of his letters contain queries as to the welfare of that cantor. The Jerusalem cantor Judah b. Abraham ha-Ma'arāvī (the Maghribi) b. Faraj writes in *ca.* 1065 to the Fustat ḥāvēr, 'Eli b. 'Amram, asking him to help Saadia the teacher, who arrived in Fustat to arrange his tax matters with the man in charge of the *jāliya* (he has already been mentioned in the discussion on taxes), for apart from this assistance, he is not in need of any *pesīqā*, that is, a regular allowance from the community. 'Eli ha-Kohen b. Ezekiel, the Jerusalem parnās close to the geonim includes in one of his letters to the Fustat parnās, 'Eli ha-Kohen b. Ḥayyim, some comments on Abū 'Imrān Mūsā *al-ḥazān al-'ajamī* – evidently someone of European origin. It seems that 'Eli b. Ḥayyim was interested in the fate of this man, and the Jerusalemite informs him that he has arrived safely from Tinnīs, and that a letter from him had been received from there. Shortly before the Turcomans' conquest, in November 1070, the son of the Jerusalem Gaon, Abiathar ha-Kohen b. Elijah, writes to the same parnās of Fustat, 'Eli ha-Kohen b. Ḥayyim, and asks for information on a man who came from Europe (*bilād al-ifranj* – 'the country of the Franks'). A letter of recommendation of an unknown date, evidently written from the yeshiva, asks for the help of 'all the communities in the *shafrīr* of the land of Egypt' for a poor woman burdened with little children, who cannot support herself by working. (*Shafrīr*, i.e. Fustat; see Jer., xliii:10, 'royal pavilion' in the King James version. In Jewish traditional interpretation, it is said to mean 'a tent', which was also the original meaning of *Fusṭāṭ*.)[34]

'Palestinians' versus 'Babylonians'

[762] I have already spoken of the division of authority in the diaspora during this period. According to tradition and the historic connections, the communities of Egypt came under the authority of the Palestinian yeshiva, the Sanhedrin. Waves of immigrants coming from Iraq, however, caused the setting up of Babylonian communities even in Palestine, and there were 'Babylonian' communities in Ramla, in Tiberias, and other places as well. The immigrants from Iraq also established 'Babylonian' communities in Egypt and the Maghrib, the largest of these being the 'Babylonian' (in Arabic *al-'irāqiyīn*) community in Fustat. As the Palestinian Gaon was the leader and the recognised representative of all the Jews in the Fatimid caliphate, the Palestinian yeshiva also established ties with the 'Babylonian' community in Fustat, and with the 'Babylonian' communities elsewhere, evidently. The Geniza documents have supplied us with some information on the relations between the 'Babylonians' and the 'Palestinians' in Fustat, and also the extent of the involvement of the yeshivot, both the Palestinian yeshiva and that of Pumbedita, in the affairs of the communities in Fustat. One should bear in mind that in that period there was a deep sense of identity between the congregation and the synagogue; in fact the word *keneset* or *kenēsiyya*, in Hebrew and in Aramaic (*kenishtā*) and Arabic (*kanīsa*), is frequently used in the sense of community, or congregation. For instance, we find Josiah Gaon, at the outset of the eleventh century, addressing the *battē kenēsiyyōt*, 'which sit in

[34] The assistance to Ṣedaqa b. Menaḥem: **59**, **60**. The man who fled because of taxes: **123**. The letter to Sahlān: **144**, see what is said there in the introduction. On Nethanel: **140**. 'Eli b. Abraham: **231–235**. Judah the cantor: **456**; he is mentioned a number of times in my collection, and the beginning of his deathbed will has been preserved; the son of Moses is also mentioned in two letters, see the Hebrew Index; from the name, one can see that this is a Maghribi family which settled in Jerusalem. 'Eli ha-Kohen: **451**. Abiathar: **547**, b, lines 1–2. The poor woman: **570**.

righteousness', referring, of course, to the two congregations, the 'Palestinians' and the 'Babylonians'.

In Solomon b. Judah's day, there was some form of perpetual competition between him and Hayy Gaon, regarding their influence in Fustat. The letters of Solomon b. Judah to Abraham b. Sahlān and to his son Sahlān, heads of the 'Babylonians' in Fustat, seem to be evidence of the fact that there was quite a degree of understanding between the Palestinian yeshiva and the Babylonian yeshiva in the Egyptian capital. The 'Babylonians' even sent money to Jerusalem in their hour of need, and there are letters to this effect, such as that in which the Gaon thanks them for the sum of seven and a quarter dinars. Babylonian and Persian merchants who had settled in Qayrawān during the first half of the tenth century were evidently also in the habit of sending financial aid to the Jerusalem yeshiva, though their principal contact was with the Babylonian yeshivot, which received the larger sums of money. This was still the situation at the beginning of the eleventh century, when we discover Joseph and Nissim, sons of Berekhia, sending instructions to Joseph b. Jacob ibn 'Awkal in Fustat concerning money to be forwarded to the yeshivot. Here the sum mentioned is 200 dinars, of which ten are to go to the *shāmiyīn* (Palestinians) and the remainder to the *'irāqiyīn* (Babylonians), consisting of money orders from various people.

In the case of Solomon b. Judah in particular, it seems that all he wanted was to maintain good relations with both the 'Babylonians' in Fustat, and Hayy Gaon. In one of his early letters, evidently written in around 1015, a decade before he became Gaon, to Isaac ha-Kohen b. Abraham (Ibn Furāt) in Fustat, Solomon b. Judah notes that his son, Yaḥyā, is staying in Baghdad, where he is being taught by Hayy Gaon ('applies himself to the *halakhōt gedōlōt*'). A letter from Yaḥyā, he writes, arrived together with one from Hayy Gaon (to Solomon b. Judah, apparently).[35]

[763] Actually the relations went smoothly for some time. We find a

[35] Josiah Gaon: **41**, line 4. Solomon b. Judah on receiving the moneys: **104**. The letter of the sons of Berekhia: Bodl MS Heb, d 65, f. 9, edited by Assaf, *Tarbiz*, 20(1948/9), 179ff; in Assaf, line 22: read: *'aynan*, that is in gold; of these sums of money it was said that they were from *safaqāt muftaraqa*; *safaqāt* – handshakes, but the meaning here seems to be: money orders. Solomon b. Judah on his son Yaḥyā: **53**, margin, lines 13f; in the same letter, Solomon b. Judah also mentions his two other sons, Abraham and Manṣūr; in later letters, Abraham is mentioned, and one does not know what happened to the other sons. Mann, *JQR*, NS 8(1917/8), 348f, notes this letter, in which there is evidence that Hayy Gaon resided in Baghdad (not in Pumbedita any longer). Connections established between the Pumbedita yeshiva and the Palestinian yeshiva are apparently shown in a fragment of a letter from Sherira Gaon and his son Hayy (then *av-bēt-dīn*), dated 13 Av 1300 Sel. (18 July AD 989); this was sent to the *rōsh ha-yeshiva*, obviously meaning the Palestinian Gaon. In the part that has been preserved, it says among other things, 'and we also demand from you, head of the yeshiva, may you live forever, to please order this letter to be read out publicly, since this was frequently the custom regarding [the letters of] our

letter from Ephraim b. Shemaria to Solomon b. Judah, however, in which Ephraim very emphatically denies the Jerusalem Gaon's claim that he is carrying on a correspondence with the Babylonians – the yeshivot and the exilarch. Ephraim even feels the need to quote from the exilarch's letter to him: 'and here we have begun to write to you in order to make you write to us more frequently', and he quotes this as proof that it was not he who had written. They had written to him in the hope of moving him to establish relations with them, or so he says in justification. As to Hayy Gaon, he writes, it is true that he received a letter from him which was sent to Fustat together with a letter to Samuel ibn al-Tāhirtī, but as it contained a slanderous statement about the Palestinian yeshiva, he thought it sufficient to reply to the letter in order to refute the slander and to avoid a quarrel. He denies having sent Hayy Gaon a query on a matter of law (about eating meat after fasting); someone else must have sent the query and the responsum reached him, that is, Ephraim. Ephraim describes further the beginning of the quarrel, which is essentially between the 'Palestinians' and 'Babylonians' in Fustat. There are some who want to appoint Abraham b. Sahlān as the dayyān in Fustat and to dismiss Ephraim from the post. (Abraham b. Sahlān was one of the leaders of the 'Babylonians'.) Ephraim points out that the relations between Abraham b. Sahlān and himself have always been good, but a letter from Solomon b. Judah mentioning complaints that Ephraim had brought to his notice, landed in Ḥasan's hands. We do not know who this Ḥasan is; he may be Yefet b. David b. Shekhania, the cantor and scribe of the 'Palestinian' congregation, or perhaps Tobiah al-Nīlī, or Yefet *rōsh ha-qāhāl* (head of the community), who are mentioned in some of the letters in my collection. This Ḥasan, together with the son of al-Raqqī – perhaps referring to David b. al-Raqqī – and b. Ṭalyūn (Samuel ha-Kohen b. Avṭalyon) organised a sort of faction against Ephraim b. Shemaria and they are the people trying to remove him from his position. Solomon b. Judah mentions a letter which arrived from the 'head of the yeshiva of Babylonia', undoubtedly meaning Hayy Gaon. It seems that the letter in question reached Fustat and it dealt with the matter of the Jerusalemite prisoners about whom Solomon b. Judah wrote frequently, namely those who were imprisoned because of their debts dating from the events of 1024. Solomon b. Judah hints at the disagreement between them, for Hayy Gaon – it is implied – is rather

forefathers. We explicitly mention that: it should be read under the authority of the head of the yeshiva. Please do so and let us know, without delay, that our request has been fulfilled and the letter read out in public and that the persons whose names were mentioned in it had blessings recited on them, as we specified', etc. This fragment, ENA 4009, f. 15, was edited by Mann, *Texts*, I, 106 (it was previously edited by Marmorstein, see details in Mann, *ibid.*; Mann assumed at first that the letter was written to one of the communities, contrary to Marmorstein's opinion, but changed his mind afterwards).

remote and unaware of the situation as it really is. We also have a letter written to Solomon b. Judah by one of the Babylonian dignitaries, perhaps Hayy Gaon himself, or perhaps the exilarch of that time, Hezekiah b. David, but the handwriting is that of the scribe of that personality. It is mainly a courtesy letter; the Babylonian writer asks Solomon b. Judah to pray 'tomorrow, on the feast of *maṣṣōt* (Passover), also on his behalf and on behalf of the Jews in Palestine, Egypt, Damascus and Ṣōvā (Aleppo), and so on, and also together with 'the elders of Jerusalem and the elders of Ramla who honour us' – a clear allusion to the 'Babylonians' in these places. The writer also mentions the son of the Gaon, Yaḥyā, and hopes he will see him shortly and in good health and that he derives satisfaction – 'from all your sons'.[36]

[764] Hayy Gaon's letter of Tevet Sel. 1349, that is December AD 1037 or January AD 1038 (Tevet in that year began on 13 December) to Sahlān b. Abraham, the leader of the 'Babylonians' in Fustat, bears witness to his

[36] Ephraim b. Shemaria's letter: MS Reinach. As to the identity of David b. al-Raqqī, the editor may have erred, and perhaps David b. Aaron al-Barqī was meant there; or David ha-Levi b. Isaac, who will be discussed below; with regard to the accusations made by Solomon b. Judah that Ephraim b. Shemaria asked for the guidance of Hayy Gaon, we have some evidence that this had some foundation, and this is a letter from al-Mahdiyya written by Samuel b. Abraham to Ephraim. The letter is written on vellum and is in a poor state of preservation. We find here 'and as our Master Hayy Gaon, may God bless him, [wrote] his responsum to this query . . . what I said, and I regretted very much that you were not allowed to read . . . in order to grasp it much better and be convinced that what I wrote was true', etc. From the continuation, it emerges that the writer dealt with a difference in matters of *halākhā*, concerning merchants' negotiations. See MSs. Schechter, at the JTS, NY, No. 13, from line 10; to be included in the collection of documents relating to Babylonia that I am at present preparing for publication. Samuel ha-Kohen b. Avṭalyon had the title *ha-mumḥē*, and afterwards also *ḥāvēr*; he had strong connections with the Jerusalem yeshiva, see the Hebrew Index; his struggle with Ephraim b. Shemaria is also mentioned in **67**; it seems that he stemmed from a family of geonim, for in **107** Solomon b. Judah calls him: the great-grandson of the righteous and geonim; and in some documents he is called *rōsh ha-qāhāl*. Mann has assembled a number of data relating to this discussion (*Jews*, II, 97ff): TS 8 J 32, f. 8 (from 1024), contains the signatures of Abraham b. Sahlān and Samuel ha-Kohen *rōsh ha-qāhāl* b. Avṭalyon; in TS 8 J 4, f. 2 (1027): Samuel ha-Kohen b. Ṭalyūn; TS 8 J 6, f. 18 (part b, the same year) signed by Ephraim b. Shemaria together with Samuel ha-Kohen b. Ṭalyūn; their names are also mentioned together in the court record: TS 13 J 5, f. 1 (1028); and in TS 8 J 4, f. 3 (the same year); Samuel ha-Kohen *rōsh ha-qāhāl* b. R. Ṭalyūn; called so also in TS 8 K 20, f. 1, and in TS 8 J 4, f. 1 (the same time); he was later granted the title ḥāvēr: Samuel ha-Kohen he-ḥāvēr b. R. Avṭalyon: TS 13 J 1, f. 9, Nisan 1352 Sel. (AD 1041). See: ENA NS 7, f. 25, a court record from the synagogue in Fustat, of 5 Tevet 1339 Sel., Thursday, 7 December 1027, signed also by Samuel ha-Kohen *rōsh ha-qāhāl* b. R. Avṭalyon. The letter about the prisoners: **65**, lines 8ff. The Babylonian letter: **174**. Hayy Gaon's true attitude to the Palestinian yeshiva is also reflected in one of his responsa: '. . . but in the days of R. Ashi and Ravina peace reigned in Babylonia whereas in Palestine there was much forced baptism and learning was in great decline there, so the people who were there migrated to Babylonia, such as R. Avin and R. Dimi; among the total of immigrant scholars who came down to Babylonia, the majority were scholars from Palestine . . .' See *Sefer ha-eshkōl*, II, 47ff. (*Hilekhōt sēfer tōrā*), cf. Poznanski, *Hakedem*, 1 (1907/8), 143.

intense involvement in the affairs of that city and the relations between its congregations and its prominent personalities. The letter deals with complaints against Sahlān made by members of the 'Babylonian' congregation. The complainants are Sulaymān b. Mubārak (Solomon b. Mevorakh), Ephraim b. al-'Akkī, Mubārak b. Abraham, while the Gaon is aware of the fact that the majority of 'Babylonians' support Sahlān. He promises to ask Ḥesed al-Tustarī (Abū Naṣr Faḍl b. Sahl) to stand by Sahlān. The Gaon also mentions a letter he has received from Ḥasan al-'Āqūlī (al-'Āqūla, the ancient Aramaic name for Kūfa) undoubtedly one of the emigrants from Iraq to Egypt whom the Gaon knew. The passage in which Hayy Gaon notes that he received a letter from Solomon b. Judah al-Fāsī, and that he was very happy with it, is particularly interesting in this connection. He asks Sahlān to let him know what is the position and status of the Jerusalem Gaon. Naturally, this does not mean that the Palestinian Gaon was unknown to him.[37]

[765] From the two succeeding generations after these letters, we have no information on contact between the Babylonian and Palestinian yeshivot. However, on 4 July 1091, we find Abiathar ha-Kohen Gaon writing from Tyre to the heads of the Jews in Iraq, or more specially, the head of the yeshiva of Baghdad and Hezekiah the exilarch, mentioning 'all the princes and dignitaries and heads of synagogues . . . and cantors, schoolteachers, and *parnāsīm* of the communities . . .'. The subject of the letter is a case of the levirate procedure, being an answer to the letter of Kohen-Ṣedeq b. Joseph ha-Kohen, the *av-bēt-dīn* of the yeshiva of Baghdad.[38]

[37] The letter of Hayy Gaon: Mosseri I a 5, edited by Chapira, *REJ*, 82 (1926), 327f. Hayy Gaon died on the 7th day of Passover that year, 18 April 1038, that is, three to four months after writing this letter; cf. on the letter: Mann, *Texts*, I, 118. Instead of Ephraim b. al-'Anī (a, line 11) read: b. al-'Akkī. Chapira understood, with regard to Solomon b. Judah (p. 330 *ibid.*): 'Je te prie de me renseigner sur sa situation et sur le rang qu'il occupe' (b, lines 3–4). However, Hayy Gaon knew the Jerusalem Gaon well, as his son Yaḥyā studied Torah with him. Chapira, himself, noted this (p. 326 *ibid.*) but assumed that the question stemmed from the uncertain standing of Solomon b. Judah at that time, when the rift with Nathan b. Abraham was taking place. But this quarrel had not broken out as yet at that moment, as we shall see below. On the links between Hayy Gaon and the Tustari brothers see Gil, *ha-Tustarīm*, 46ff. Evidence of the close connections between the 'Babylonians' in Fustat and Hayy Gaon, can also be seen in TS 16.318, a letter to the latter from 'the communities which pray in the synagogue of the Babylonians named after his yeshiva'. A letter is mentioned there written by Hayy Gaon to Abraham b. Sahlān. Cf. Mann, *JQR*, NS 7(1916/7), 477f. Some nine months after Hayy Gaon's aforementioned letter to Sahlān (and about six months after the death of the Gaon), Daniel b. Azariah, who is in al-Mahdiyya in the Maghrib, writes to Sahlān, and among other things, he mentions 'what you have undergone on the part of people whose behaviour is known' and the sorrow he felt because of this, and he expresses his pleasure that the intervention of Abū Naṣr (the Tustari) helped to settle Sahlān's affairs satisfactorily; see **344**, a, lines 9ff.

[38] Abiathar's letter: **553**; possibly *rāshē yeshīvōt*, in the plural, is said there, for in the florid opening sentences, one can still decipher: '*Mātā maḥsiyya u-fumbedītā*'; Hezekiah the exilarch is certainly the grandson of Hezekiah, who was exilarch during Hayy Gaon's

[766] As we have already seen, there was agitation in Fustat and the marshalling of supporters for the appointment of a dayyān, and a faction existed which hoped to appoint Abraham b. Sahlān, the 'Babylonian', in place of the 'Palestinian' Ephraim b. Shemaria, as dayyān of the community. There are comparatively numerous references to this situation in my collection. Solomon b. Judah wishes to make peace, as we have seen, but it seems that he also wants to introduce new arrangements, and as he himself admits, it is these very arrangements which have caused the excitement and the renewed schism. It appears that the differences were about the procedures in court: when the two leaders (the *ḥavērīm*) of the two congregations sat in court together, who was to preside and how were they to address one another. Solomon b. Judah turns to Ephraim b. Shemaria and appeals to him to get along harmoniously with Abraham he-ḥāvēr. It seems that one of the innovations introduced by the Palestinian yeshiva, even before Solomon b. Judah became Gaon, was the granting of the title *ḥāvēr* to the heads of the 'Babylonian' congregation, referring here to a father and son, Abraham b. Sahlān and Sahlān. In this manner, they hoped in fact to have both congregations come under one authority, that of the Palestinian yeshiva. 'For formerly you were under your own authority and now you have entered the authority of God and the authority of Israel'; writes Solomon b. Judah to Ephraim b. Shemaria, who was in any case under the authority of the Palestinian yeshiva beforehand. However, the intention here was to create the impression of a new common framework, which called for a solemn and serious approach.[39]

[767] Of the efforts to establish a common framework for the two congregations in Fustat, one can also learn from three Geniza fragments in the handwriting of Ephraim b. Shemaria, which relate to the discussions being held in Fustat on this matter. The first is a fragment of a record of a discussion held in the 'Palestinians' synagogue, with the participation of the 'Babylonians', headed by Abū Isḥaq Alūf, who is Abraham b. Sahlān.

time, and the son of David, who is mentioned in Solomon b. Judah's day; see below in the discussion on the exilarchs. As to Kohen Ṣedeq b. Joseph ha-Kohen, he is apparently a descendant of the Kohen Ṣedeq who was head of the Pumbedita yeshiva in the first half of the tenth century; at any rate there is no foundation to Mann's assumption in *Jews*, I, 193, that he was a relative of the family of the priestly geonim in Palestine.

39 See the letters of Solomon b. Judah, **75**, **84**; cf. Mann, *Texts*, I, 311, 319, n. 28a. Abraham b. Sahlān and Ephraim b. Shemaria sign together on Friday, an intermediate day of the holiday (Tabernacles or Passover?) 1333 Sel. (1022): TS 10 J 5, f. 11; from this and other documents, it is evident that there was a common court for the two congregations in Fustat before Solomon b. Judah's time as well; this is also clear from the documents signed jointly by Abraham b. Sahlān and Samuel ha-Kohen b. Avṭalyon, who was also of the 'Palestinian' congregation. The aforementioned document is an obligation to Samuel ha-Kohen b. Avṭalyon (Ismāʿīl b. Ṭalyūn) himself, that the signatories (there are six more in addition to the abovementioned two) agree in advance to hand over to him the matter of ransoming two captives, and will recognise the sum paid by him.

From the remaining fragment, it can be understood that there was a consideration of the qualities and failings of each of the yeshivot, the Babylonian (Pumbedita) and the Palestinian. The second fragment also deals with a similar debate, held jointly with the 'Babylonians' and the 'Palestinians', and it belongs to the draft of a letter to Solomon b. Judah, in which Ephraim b. Shemaria asks to be informed of the main points made there. The reason for the discussion was Solomon b. Judah's demand that they continue to maintain a common court of law. Abraham b. Sahlān objected to the idea and claimed that each one should sit in judgment in his own synagogue, he in the 'Babylonian', which was 'his authority', and Ephraim in that of the 'Palestinians'. Ephraim b. Shemaria attacked this view and claimed that it would lead to a rupture. Ephraim ha-Kohen b. Abraham, one of the leaders of the Palestinian congregation, also spoke in the same vein. Nevertheless, Abraham b. Sahlān stood by his opinion and opposed the existence of a joint court of law, pointing to the example of Iraq, where they had four *mathā'ib* (from *mathība*, yeshiva, in plural; by which he evidently meant that there were four courts of law in Baghdad). This discussion continued until late in the afternoon, when Ephraim b. Shemaria decided to end it and demanded that they write a letter in the name of some of the community leaders ('the elders') to *al-rayyis*, that is to the head of the Jerusalem yeshiva, in order to make him aware that it was not Ephraim b. Shemaria who had caused the rift. Indeed, such a letter was written and a fragment of it has been preserved in the Geniza, which is the third fragment. Whereas the former letter was a personal one from Ephraim to the Gaon, this letter was written on behalf of the community, which met on *shabbāt wa-yiggāsh* with 'the two ḥavērīm' (undoubtedly Ephraim b. Shemaria and Abraham b. Sahlān); the chairman of the discussion was Ephraim ha-Kohen b. Abraham. In this fragment, there is also mention of that letter of Solomon b. Judah in which he asks these 'two ḥavērīm' to keep the peace between them ('it is worth being friendly, and be strong with the help of their Rock, and to live as one heart and one man').[40]

[768] Afterwards there was a quarrel between the two communities over a matter of bigamy, which I have mentioned above. Apart from this, we learn of a serious rift over the question of the income from ritual slaughtering. Hayy Gaon was undoubtedly involved in this affair. Solomon b. Judah writes about it in a letter to Ephraim b. Shemaria, evidently in the summer of 1029. According to the letter, he is prepared to go as far as pronouncing the excommunication of the opposing side, in order to prevent the control of the markets and *kashrūt*, that is to say the income

[40] See the fragments **320**, **321**, **322**; cf. Goitein, *Schirmann Jubilee Volume*, 74f; see the introductions to these documents in my collection.

from slaughtering, by the 'Babylonian' leader, evidently Abraham b. Sahlān. The 'Babylonians' are not at all inclined to compromise on this issue, and the Jerusalem Gaon asks bitterly: 'Do they really want to uproot the Palestinian yeshiva from the land of Egypt, so as to make its name disappear?' It seems that the 'Palestinians' proposal was to assign one of the markets only to the 'Babylonians', and in the Gaon's words: 'just as this place is in my name, there will be another in his name, this one in the name of the Babylonians and the other in the name of the Palestinians'. Also in another of his letters, mainly devoted to relations with the Karaites in Jerusalem, Solomon b. Judah considers it necessary to return again to the subject of the 'Babylonians' in Fustat. He mentions the prerogatives requested by the 'Babylonians' in their attempt to withdraw even the 'Palestinians' synagogue from the authority of Palestine, and to transfer it to Babylonia, rendering that authority all the income from Egypt. 'The horn should be in my hands and the udder in his', he writes, referring evidently to Hayy Gaon.[41]

[769] This constant competition was not restricted to the yeshivot, in trying to ensure for themselves the largest degree of influence in Fustat (and certainly in other localities as well), each at the expense of the other, but it also was carried on in the place itself, between the two synagogues. Each synagogue tried to enlarge its membership. Solomon b. Ṣemaḥ writes to Ephraim b. Shemaria (in *ca.* 1030) mentioning that the yeshiva is receiving many letters of complaint against him, among them a letter with more than thirty signatures of witnesses who complain against him and his son-in-law, claiming that they were the reason why many people were going over to the 'Babylonians'' synagogue, and even to the Karaite *majālis* (literally: councils, as the Karaites called their places of congregation or the congregations themselves). Also, whereas the reconstruction of the 'Babylonians'' synagogue was already completed (undoubtedly after it was destroyed at the time of al-Ḥākim's decrees) the condition of the 'Palestinians'' synagogue (*al-shāmiyīn*) was going from bad to worse, with work on it having ceased.

We find echoes of this situation in a letter from Ephraim b. Shemaria, or rather, in a draft of a letter which he prepared for the beadle of the synagogue of the 'Palestinians'. The writer, Ephraim b. Shemaria, can be definitely identified by his handwriting. In this letter, intended for the Jerusalem Gaon, the beadle is supposed to complain of the alienation and undermining of the synagogue. This subversiveness is expressed chiefly in trying to attract people to go over to the 'Babylonians'' synagogue. But the congregation is beginning to come to itself. Ephraim was asked to

[41] The rift over bigamy: **148**; see what is said about this above. The quarrel over the income from slaughtering: **79**. The additional letter: **92**, b, lines 6ff.

appoint *parnāsīm* and he was appointed by Ephraim to be in charge of the synagogue. Now he asks the Gaon to write to the congregation, to urge them to see to their synagogue and show their devotion to it. Their first achievement is a group of Maghribis who went over to the 'Palestinians' from the 'Babylonians', but it is very difficult to compete with the latter, because they attract people by granting them titles of honour.

We find a sort of overall review of the turbid relationship between the 'Palestinians' and the 'Babylonians' in Fustat, in a letter written by Solomon b. Judah to Sahlān b. Abraham. Firstly he defends himself against the claim that he tried to undermine the stature of the Babylonian yeshiva, or that he attempted to influence the 'Babylonians' to accept the authority of the Palestinian yeshiva. Every yeshiva represents God's doctrines. Sahlān's father, Abraham, writes the Gaon, took pleasure in his responsa concerning laws of the markets, and even used arguments which he had quoted (it is not clear to whom, whether to the members of his congregation in Fustat or to the Babylonian yeshiva). And he continues in a somewhat indifferent manner: if it happens that a community should leave his authority and go over to that of the 'Babylonians', he would not regret it, for that would lessen his responsibility for the sins of others. He adds other tokens of modesty, such as that he is aware of his insignificance and would prefer it if someone more worthy would take his place, 'as it was at first'. Further, he thanks Sahlān for the money he took the trouble to collect and send to the Palestinian yeshiva, although contributions of this kind arouse criticism and slander; by which he evidently wished to say that people soon rush off to complain to Hayy Gaon about Sahlān. It emerges that the Jerusalem Gaon read Sahlān's letter about letters from Hayy Gaon which contained accusations against the Palestinian yeshiva. Sahlān decided to hide these letters, but Solomon b. Judah's advice was that he should do quite the contrary, bringing them to the public's notice, and in a very dignified manner. Finally, Solomon b. Judah cannot refrain from complaining about Hayy Gaon, who he claims is trying to increase the influence of his yeshiva wherever it is possible.[42]

[770] It seems that eventually the two congregations reached an agree-

42 Solomon b. Ṣemaḥ's letter: **205**; it seems that Solomon b. Judah refrained from writing himself, because of his special relationship with Ephraim; see the introduction to this document. As to the restoration of the synagogue of the 'Palestinians' (which is the synagogue of the Geniza), we know that the major building work was completed only in 1039 (see Gil, *Documents*, 95f). The letter of the beadle: **328**; Goitein, *Eretz-Israel*, 7(1963/4), 88, assumes that the letter dates from the period of the Nathan b. Abraham dispute, on the basis of the expressions of loyalty to the Jerusalem Gaon found there; but these were intended to express loyalty to Palestine, as against the Babylonian temptations he speaks of in the continuation. Solomon b. Judah to Sahlān: **106**; it is obvious that the letter is intended for Sahlān by its contents, which speaks of the Babylonian congregation in Fustat; see line 10: 'my brother the ḥāvēr your father', who is certainly Abraham b.

ment, and this renewed the possibility of their collaboration. There are letters from Qayrawān at that time to Ephraim b. Shemaria, expressing satisfaction with the version of the agreement 'which the two parties took on themselves; how good and how pleasant [Ps. cxxxiii:1], how great is peace and despised is the rupture'. One of the leaders of the 'Babylonians', the representative of the Babylonian yeshivot, Joseph b. Jacob ibn 'Awkal, participates in the efforts to recruit money to restore the synagogue (*ha-me'ārā*, the cave) in Jerusalem, but at the same time, he has reason to be angry with the Jerusalem Gaon, who did not mention his son (evidently on *hosha'na rabba*, during the assembly on the Mount of Olives) or his title (the Babylonian) *rōsh kallā*. And so he wishes to cut off all contact with the *ḥavūrat ha-ṣevī*, that is, the Palestinian yeshiva. Solomon b. Judah writes to him in order to justify what happened, 'for it is not customary to mention the son in place of the father'. This certainly displayed a desire to keep on good terms with the people of the Babylonian yeshivot and their representatives in Egypt. This was also evident in the Gaon's letter to Abraham b. Sahlān and his brother-in-law (his wife's brother) Saadia b. Ephraim, both leaders of the Babylonian community in Fustat, on the subject of a certain Isaac, a merchant from Wādī'l-Qurā. This man had abandoned his wife and family in 'Ammān four years earlier, and a pronouncement of excommunication had to be issued against him in Fustat. The letter was specifically written to the 'Babylonians', apparently in order to honour the connection between Wādī'l-Qurā and the Babylonian yeshivot. On the other hand, when the people of Jerusalem were being arrested because they had not paid their debts (in light of the fines and high taxes imposed on them), we find Sahlān b. Abraham and all the people of the Babylonian congregation in Fustat endeavouring to help them, using all their influence with the caliph and the wazīr to this end.[43]

[771] The main bone of contention between the Jerusalem Gaon and the Babylonians as far as the *rāshūt* was concerned, was the system of law courts. The Jerusalem Gaon was insistent on the existence of one common court-of-law in Fustat, as we have seen. But this was also the source of trouble from close at hand, from the 'Babylonian' community in Ramla. This can be seen from a version of a letter sent to the caliph, a copy of which, in Hebrew script, has been preserved in the Geniza. The people of the yeshiva, or whoever was writing on their behalf, state their unqualified

Sahlān; Mann, *Jews*, I, 114f, assumed mistakenly that the letter was written to Ephraim b. Shemaria.

[43] The letter from Qayrawān: **330** (23 July 1035). The matter of Ibn 'Awkal (Joseph b. Jacob Alūf; *alūf*, the title from the Babylonian yeshiva, the equivalent of *rōsh kallā*): **120**, a, lines 29ff. The matter of Isaac of Wādī'l-Qurā, see: **56**, a, lines 18ff. See remnants of the responsa to queries sent by the people of Wādī'l-Qurā to Sherira Gaon and to his son Hayy: Ginzberg, *Geonica*, II, 54, 61; Harkavy, *Teshūvōt*, 94. The assistance to the 'Palestinian'

opposition to recognising the authority of a separate Babylonian court-of-law outside the authority of the Jerusalem yeshiva, in Palestine or the neighbouring countries. The call for the permission to establish separate courts came from a certain Joseph ibn al-Sijilmāssī, known as an inhabitant of Ramla, and evidently leader of the 'Babylonians' in that city. The opposition to this demand was a matter of principle and based on a series of arguments which have no equal in any clash amongst Jews, but they were useful in making the matter intelligible to the Muslim ruler. It was inadmissable that there should be two authorities. The caliphs did indeed permit the 'Babylonians' (in view of the approval of the heads of the Palestinian yeshiva, it is implied; evidently a pretension that had no real basis) to maintain separate synagogues, the reason being that the 'Babylonians' celebrated the feasts for two days instead of one. A separate authority, however, had no precedent, for Jerusalem is the very centre of the Jews, which they face in their prayers (their *qibla*) and to which they travel as pilgrims. This demand on the part of Joseph, it was said there, is merely a plot between him (and his supporters) and 'the head of Iraq', that is, head of the Babylonian yeshiva, who promised them as many titles of honour as they wished, if their efforts were crowned with success. The letter ends with a moving appeal to the caliph to continue to retain the good tradition of exclusivity held by the Jerusalem yeshiva. It was the same Joseph ibn al-Sijilmāssī who envisioned the wonderful dream in Jerusalem which led to the pronouncement of a public fast and the mending of the ways of the Rabbanites and the Karaites in Palestine, thus preventing some unspecified act of oppression. Perhaps the relinquishment of the idea of a separate authority was also part of that repentance.[44]

[772] Something of the latent feelings and the inner mood of the Palestinian yeshiva, in view of its inferior status compared with the Babylonian yeshivot, made itself felt in the letters of the yeshiva, and also in the affair in which one of the dignitaries of Fustat (evidently Sahlān b. Abraham) decided to forgo the Palestinian title of *ḥāvēr*, preferring that of *alūf*. In contrast to the current lower status, there was a nostalgia for the splendid past of the ancient Talmudic period. Then, it was the Palestine yeshiva which made the decisions concerning the law and appointments: 'from it [i.e., the Palestinian yeshiva] the makers of decision [in the local communities] would seek advice as to whom they should appoint as heads; since its appointees were elected according to their high rank, not their coins'.

In our own terms, we would say that the appointments were then

captives: **90**, in which Solomon b. Judah thanks Sahlān and 'all the people of his congregation' (lines 1–5).

[44] The matter of the law-court: **312**, see the references noted there in the introduction; see the

decided by the Sanhedrin according to the degree of learning and not according to wealth, which is more than a slight hint at the Babylonian yeshivot in the days of the Geonic period, which combined their judgment of rank and learning with that of wealth. In the continuation, the Gaon complains that the Jewish people have neglected the Palestinian yeshiva and on the other hand, constantly provided the Babylonian yeshiva, which is like a stepmother, with large sums of money: 'and the shares belonging to the mother are being sent to the father's wife, needlessly, where the [mother's] eyes are longing for it, with no hope . . .' Concerning the same man of Fustat who 'rejected the waters of Siloam and went to drink water from the river' (Euphrates), the Gaon writes that his preference for the title of *alūf* over *ḥāver* stems from his contempt for the teachings of Jerusalem and a partiality for that of Babylonia, where God 'left for it '[the Torah] a remnant'. He expresses the hopes that Jerusalem will return to its former greatness: '[the Torah] will return to its former quarters'; that man 'treats his mother with little honour . . . and over-praises his father's wife', once again using the simile of a stepmother. This affair of the preference for a Babylonian title caused Solomon b. Judah a great deal of anguish. He wrote to Fustat 'a long sheet' and asked that it be read aloud 'to all the people of the Jews'. The matter disturbed him deeply, for the man was dear to him and he refrained from reacting violently, even tearing up two letters after writing them. Nevertheless, he does not abstain from stating that in fact the man is not worthy of the title given him by the Babylonians: 'he was given this title for nothing'. Someone specific stands behind the nebulous talk, and that someone is 'the Gaon of the diaspora', that is, most probably, Hayy Gaon. According to what emerges from the letter of the Palestinian Gaon, Hayy Gaon not only granted the title, but also wrote critically of the Palestinian yeshiva. Heartfelt comments on the status of the Palestinian yeshiva were also written by Zadok ha-Levi b. Levi, its *av-bēt-dīn* in around the year 1030, such as: 'learning only declined among the people of Palestine in the past few years, when its scholars were no longer able to find sustenance and were subjected to many calamities and therefore did not find the energy to teach their children, whom they were unable to supply with food'. Another reason was the excessive number of disputes, in which hoodlums were involved. Nevertheless: 'the wisdom of their ancestors is still there among them, as is the heritage of the Mishna, the Tosefta, the Mekhilta, the Midrash, the Baraita, the traditions and the Haggada', and so on.

The rivalry between the two *rāshūyōt* can be seen in the affair of a man who came from Mosul to Ramla on the Friday of the week of Passover,

assumptions regarding the identity of this Joseph also in Hirschberg, *Eretz-Israel*, 5(1958/9), 217. The dream: **313**.

AM 4801, that is 27 March AD 1041, during the peak of the dispute concerning Nathan b. Abraham, which will be discussed below. The man was *rōsh kallā*, that is, one of the dignitaries of the Babylonian yeshiva. Joseph b. Kulayb, one of Nathan b. Abraham's supporters, writes about it to his master, who was staying at the time in Tyre (apparently), after that man of Mosul had been staying in Ramla for a month and a half. The latter asked to preach to the public on the holiday (that is, on the last day of Passover) but he was not permitted to do so unless he would fit in with the general atmosphere of the public and mention the authority of 'Nathan, the head of the yeshiva', so that he should not be considered a supporter of his rival, Solomon b. Judah. The man of Mosul refused, not wanting to be involved in the dispute, and mainly, he claimed, because he belonged to another authority altogether, the 'Baghdādī'. Finally, he actually went over to the 'Babylonian' synagogue, and the 'Babylonians' in Ramla welcomed him gladly and supplied him with all his needs.

As to the law, it seems to me that in the documents emerging from the Palestinian yeshiva itself, one cannot discern any specifically characteristic Palestinian system. A fragment of a letter in the handwriting of Abraham, son of the Gaon, contains a discussion on the wording of a divorce deed, saying something about Iraq, but because of the poor state of the fragment, it is impossible to understand any part of it. A divorce deed written in Ramla at the beginning of 1026, indicates that Manasseh b. Samuel divorces his wife, Ḥusn, b. Joseph, and it is signed by the scribe and one witness, as was the Babylonian custom. One must bear in mind that there was a large 'Babylonian' community in Ramla and it is possible that 'Babylonians' are being referred to here. Some of the personalities of the Palestinian yeshiva and its heads were not natives of Palestine either, such as Solomon b. Judah who came from Fās, or Daniel b. Azariah who came from Babylonia, and there are other similar instances. Indeed, a deed of trusteeship from the court of Daniel b. Azariah, the Palestinian Gaon, written by the scribe of the yeshiva and bearing the validation by the Gaon in his own handwriting, is formulated in the Babylonian version, similar to the one in the *sefer ha-sheṭārōt* (book of documents) of Hayy Gaon.[45]

[45] See the letters of Solomon b. Judah: **71**, **82**, **94**, **95**, **96**. The veiled complaints against Hayy Gaon: **95**, lines 3–7. **96** is a letter to Sahlān's father, Abraham, according to which one can assume who is being spoken of; the Gaon expresses joy that 'the water is again flowing along its course as in the past', and we guess that the intention is that Sahlān returned and adopted the title ḥāvēr. The letter of Zadok ha-Levi b. Levi: **210**, lines 19 ff; this Zadok ha-Levi was *av-bēt-dīn* during Solomon b. Judah's day, *ca.* 1030, and not in Elijah ha-Kohen Gaon's time, as Braslavi assumes in *Tarbiz*, 32(1962/3), 174; as to the elegy there (TS 12.834) one cannot say which Rabbēnū Zadok it is referring to, just as it is impossible to know who is 'the fourth' in the letter included there in the continuation, and which the editor decided was Elijah ha-Kohen. The letter of Joseph b. Kulayb: **195**, III, a, margin right-hand and further. The fragment on the formulae of the deed of divorce: **168**.

The exilarchs

[773] Some of the descendants of the exilarchic house left their mark in our sources. The family of the Babylonian exilarch was already involved in Palestinian affairs in the Persian period, when Mar Zūṭrā went to Palestine. We shall return to this subject in the discussion on the annals of the Palestinian Geonim and their lineage, and at that point, we shall encounter some of the offspring of the exilarchic house: Jehoshaphat and Ṣemaḥ, heads of the Palestinian yeshiva, Daniel b. Azariah, who will play an important role in our discussions below, as will his son, David b. Daniel. In addition, in the discussion on the Karaites, I shall deal with a special branch of the exilarchic house, the Karaite *nesī'īm*. Here we shall concentrate on the descendants of Hezekiah b. Judah b. David b. Zakkai. His grandfather was David b. Zakkai, the famous exilarch, a contemporary of Saadia Gaon. David b. Zakkai's son was too young to succeed him, and therefore Solomon b. Josiah (who is Ḥasan, David b. Zakkai's brother) became the exilarch, and after him, his son Azariah. Josiah's branch of the family was ousted from the exilarchy, for some unknown reason. Daniel b. Azariah, who later became the Palestinian Gaon, belonged to this branch. We do not have any positive information about the circumstances which led to the return of the exilarchy to the descendants of David b. Zakkai, nor the date. Hezekiah (II) b. David was called exilarch when he wrote his letter to Judah, *rōsh ha-seder*, b. Abraham, apparently in February 1021. Evidently he became the central figure among the Babylonian scholars after the death of Hayy Gaon in 1038, and it was due to this fact that he had a special relationship with the 'Babylonians' in Fustat.

While Hayy Gaon was still alive, in Tammuz 1347 Sel. (July AD 1036), we find Hezekiah writing a letter to a certain *sanhedrā rabbā* in Fustat, and it seems that this is none other than Sahlān b. Abraham. The major part of the letter consists of courtesies and the request that the addressee should keep in close touch with him. Apparently, during the year of Hayy Gaon's death, when he was travelling in the Maghrib, Hezekiah b. David also intervened in the lengthy dispute in the 'Babylonian' congregation in Fustat, which was basically a struggle with Sahlān b. Abraham, and we have already seen how Hayy Gaon was involved in this dispute. In the meantime, however, Abū Naṣr Ḥesed al-Tustarī intervened and came down in favour of Sahlān, as the Gaon had requested. Daniel b. Azariah mentions these events, as we have seen, in a letter to Sahlān (12 September 1038). He shall speak of this with 'our *nāsī*, the exilarch', who had already

The deed of divorce from Ramla: **227**; see Assaf, *Meqōrōt*, 25. The deed of trusteeship: **391**; cf. Assaf, *Tarbiz*, 9 (1937/8), 17.

written a letter to the congregation and also a letter of thanks to the Tustari, and a letter in a similar vein was written by Daniel b. Azariah himself. In a letter which Hezekiah wrote a year later in the month of Av, 1351 Sel. (July–August AD 1040), he again requests the 'Babylonian' congregation to obey Sahlān b. Abraham. Although Abraham ibn Da'ūd says in his *Sefer ha-qabbālā* that Hezekiah was placed on the seat of Hayy Gaon, namely that he was made head of the yeshiva, in addition to being exilarch, it seems that this was not quite so, and Abraham ibn Da'ūd interpreted in his own fashion what was written in the version of the *Seder 'olām zūṭā*: 'and after Rav Hayy, no one was appointed head of the yeshiva in Babylonia but there is an exilarch whose name is Rabbēnū Hezekiah who is now [1047, when this chronicle was copied] head, and stems from the family of David'. It does not say that he was made head of the yeshiva, and obviously 'head of the diaspora' was meant. Abraham ibn Da'ūd's other account, which says that terrible calamities befell Hezekiah two years after the death of Hayy Gaon, that is in about 1040, and that his two sons fled to Spain to Joseph b. Samuel the Nagid (Ibn Naghrila), is not confirmed by any other source. Hezekiah and his sons are mentioned in the Geniza documents of my collection. Mann points to the complexity of the story of the flight to Spain; if indeed the reference is to the year 1040, Samuel the Nagid was still alive then, while Abraham ibn Da'ūd refers to him as to a deceased person. Poznanski and Assaf alredy understood that it was not likely that Abraham ibn Da'ūd's account was correct, and suggested that it be amended to read twelve years, or else twenty (instead of two). Perhaps those terrible troubles did indeed occur in about 1050 or 1058. The latter date is more likely, for in 1055, Samuel, the Spanish Nagid, dedicates a poem to Hezekiah b. David and therefore we have proof of contact between the two. We know from documents in the Geniza that David b. Hezekiah stayed for a time in Palestine, and afterwards perhaps also in Egypt, before continuing on his way to Spain – if there is indeed a grain of truth in the writings of Abraham ibn Da'ūd. We can assume that he returned to Iraq, for his son Hezekiah was exilarch in Baghdad towards the end of the eleventh century. One should add that in Solomon b. Judah's day, a *nāsī* is occasionally mentioned, though without actual reference to him by name. *Nāsī*, in that period, generally meant exilarch or someone from the family of the exilarchs, but there is no reason to assume that they were referring to the exilarch Hezekiah b. David himself, and it is more likely that the reference was to one of the Karaite *nesī'īm*, who shall be discussed in the chapter on the Karaites.[46]

[46] See the article of Goode, *JQR*, NS 31:149, 1940/1. The list of generations of descendants of Judah b. David b. Zakkai can be seen in the verso of **27**, the letter to Judah *rōsh ha-seder*; see the introduction to this document; and see also the *Letter* of Sherira Gaon (Lewin), 136; cf.

[774] During the period under discussion, we encounter a number of *nesī'īm*, or descendants of the family of the exilarchs, who wanted to become and sometimes succeeded in being appointed geonim in Palestine. This seems to be a kind of tradition that had been handed down since the sixth century, from Mar Zūṭrā's day. In the time of Josiah Gaon, that is in *ca.* 1020, there was a struggle for the Gaon's seat in Palestine, in which a member of the exilarch's family was involved, a *nāsī*, whose name we do not know. The only source of information on this affair is a letter from Josiah Gaon to the Palestinian congregation in Fustat. Only half the letter is extant. It bears eloquent style and is written in rhyme. That *nāsī* wanted to oust the Gaon from his office and carried on a propaganda campaign in writing to this end. The Gaon calls him 'the king of Sheshach' (Babylonia, in cryptogram, Jer., xxv:26, li:41), and he undoubtedly means a descendant of Bustanai, a veiled reference to the latter's Persian wife, a subject that was constantly exploited as a weapon by the rivals of the *nesī'īm*. The *nāsī* being spoken of is said to be the seventeenth generation to Bustanai. The exilarchic house are the 'progeny of uncircumcised and shameful [relations]'; nevertheless 'out of five generations, two inherited sanctity', and the reference here is evidently to Jehoshaphat and Ṣemaḥ, the sons of Josiah (who were geonim of Palestine in the ninth century). The writer repeats the matter of his rival's guilt, which appears to be the desire to change laws or the calendar order, and he writes this twice: 'to change his

Mann, *Poznanski Jubilee Volume*, 19–23. See the letter from 1036: TS 13 J 9, f. 1, edited by Assaf, *Teqūfat ha-g.*, 286f (= *Tarbiz*, 11 [1939/40], 152–155). See the letter of Daniel b. Azariah, **344**, a, lines 14ff; Goitein, *Shalem*, 2(1975/6), 47 (= *ha-Yishuv*, 136f), assumed that that conversation with the exilarch took place in Mosul and that that exilarch was Zakkai, Daniel's brother. See the letter of Hezekiah to the 'Babylonian' congregation: TS Loan 40, in Mann, *Texts*, I, 181–184; and see the editor's comments *ibid.*, 117, 179. The fragment from *Seder 'olām zūṭā*: in Neubauer, *Mediaeval Jewish Chronicles*, I, 178 (where there are contradictions as to the date it was written, from 1043 to 1047); Abraham ibn Da'ūd, *Sēfer ha-qabbālā* (ed. Cohen), 44f, see the editor's notes to the translation on p. 61, to line 209. It is typical that in his aforementioned letter, Hezekiah does not call himself head of the yeshiva; if he had been, he would not have refrained from doing so; cf. my similar arguments: Gil, *ha-Tustarīm*, 47f. See: Poznanski, *Babylonische Geonim*, 1–3; Assaf, *Teqūfat ha-geonim*, 285, and n. 1. Doubts regarding the information of Abraham ibn Da'ūd concerning the appointment of Hezekiah as head of the yeshiva in Pumbedita, were already expressed by Mann, *Texts*, I, 209, n. 14, who noted that actually he is never mentioned as Gaon, for which he quotes several examples, and concludes that, in view of the proven fact that Abraham ibn Da'ūd is not to be relied on concerning matters of the history of the Gaonate, there is reason to be sceptical here too, as long as we have no further proof. He cites further the example of Daniel b. Azariah, who is so often called '*nāsī* and Gaon', and we would expect something similar in Hezekiah's case if he had actually become the Pumbedita Gaon. A *nāsī*, who is evidently Hezekiah b. Solomon, *nāsī* of the Karaites, is mentioned by Solomon b. Judah, see **64** and other documents, in the discussion on the Karaites; see Solomon b. ha-Yātōm, *Pērūsh massekhet mashqīn*, 46; 'the *nāsī* of the Jews is called *rōsh gālūt*'. The exilarch Hezekiah is also mentioned (together with Hayy Gaon) in the Cambridge manuscript edited by Schechter, *Berliner Festschrift* (the Hebrew section), 110ff, which is a letter from a community (signed: Elijah ha-Kohen bet

laws' and further: 'to change laws established by covenants' phrases based on the quotation, '. . . and think to change times and laws': (Dan., vii:25), an accusation made two generations later against another descendant of the exilarch, David b. Daniel. It was evidently to that very person that Joshua ha-Kohen ha-mumḥē b. Ya'īr, of Tiberias, was referring when he wrote his letter to the congregations of Aleppo. He speaks of great schisms within the communities of Syria, Palestine, and Egypt, created by a man 'called *nāsī*'. He gave himself 'a good name' (that is, he evidently meant to say, he perhaps gave himself titles such as *rōsh gāluyōt kol Israel*, exilarch of all Israel) and he possessed written proof of his lineage, and he appointed courts, and advisers and assistants to manage his affairs. He received enormous honours, from Raqqa (Kalnē) in northern Syria to as far as Egypt. It was later revealed that he was not a *nāsī* at all and that 'he was relegated [from Tiberias] to the land of Edom [Byzantium] and died on the way'.

David b. Hezekiah stayed in Palestine, as I have mentioned. Evidently, he is the *nāsī* who is being referred to by the *av-bēt-dīn* Zadok ha-Levi b. Levi in a letter on behalf of the Rabbanites in Ramla to the Rabbanite congregation in Fustat, written in around 1030. According to him, the *rōsh*, that is Solomon b. Judah, received him warmly and even granted him a title ('prayed on him') on behalf of the yeshiva: *me'uttād* (its meaning: a candidate for being a *ḥāvēr*). It seems that this *nāsī*, who as I have said, may have been David b. Hezekiah, intervened in the internal affairs of the yeshiva, and for some reason acted against the *av-bēt-dīn* in particular (that is, against Zadok, who is writing the letter but who does not sign it in his own name). In the letter it is hinted that it is 'the *rōsh* and his son', that is, Solomon b. Judah and his son Abraham, who were responsible for his leaving for Ramla afterwards in order to undermine the status of Zadok, whose main occupation seems to have been the supervision of the market (that is, the ritual slaughtering) in Ramla. Zadok found something unkosher in the stall of a Maghribi cantor-slaughterer in Ramla. The *nāsī* tried to intervene on behalf of the *shōḥēṭ* but only displayed his own ignorance in these matters. Later on, the *nāsī* took over the affairs of the market, ritual slaughtering was placed in the hands of a man who was professionally a baker, and the *nāsī* promised him not to disqualify any of his slaughtering. He also plotted to get rid Ramla of Zadok altogether. Perhaps a further letter provides us with an answer to the question of whom the Gaon and his son, and also the *nāsī*, actually favoured when they wanted to replace Zadok ha-Levi b. Levi. Indeed, from the letter from Elijah ha-Kohen b. Solomon Gaon to David b. Hezekiah, written in *ca.*

din b. Abraham) to Jacob he-ḥāvēr b. Joseph in Aleppo. Samuel ha-Nagid dedicated a poem to him, No. 143 (see the *Dīwān*, 101ff) written in AM 4815, that is AD 1055.

1046, we learn that David was apparently forced to leave Jerusalem, and the writer deplores this fact, while also bewailing the decline in moral standards but probably regretting in fact that it was not possible for him to take Zadok's place.

Thus David b. Hezekiah left Jerusalem in the forties of the century. That he did indeed go to Spain first is perhaps borne out by the poems of Samuel ibn Naghrila, the Spanish Nagid, dedicated to him (we have seen that a poem was also dedicated to his father Hezekiah), in which Samuel says of him that he is at the head of the returners to Zion, something which Samuel thinks of as happening in his own day, as one can see by the text of the poem: 'please go to Zion, pride of all lands, and be there judge of its *qenāsōt* (meaning criminal matters, a prerogative of the Jewish courts which existed only at the time of Jewish independence); and know ye that you, David, have a lodging in the palace which is there'. The verses of the Nagid sound as if they are intended as an expression of sympathy with David b. Hezekiah for having been forced to leave Palestine.

As stated above, it seems that David afterwards returned to Baghdad and was exilarch there after the death of his father Hezekiah. We encounter his son Hezekiah (III) in the same office towards the end of the century. Abiathar ha-Kohen b. 'Elijah writes on 4 July 1091 to the yeshivas of Baghdad (Mātā *Maḥsiyya*, that is Sura, and Pumbedita, whose scholars were then staying in Baghdad) and to 'the *rāshūt* of Hezekiah the exilarch'.[47]

The lineage of the exilarchic house from Zakkai onwards is outlined as follows:

47 The letter of Josiah Gaon: **29**, lines 18ff; Dinur, *Zion* (ha-me'assef), 3(1928/9), 66, connects this affair with the quarrel between the parnāsīm described in the *Sefer ḥasīdīm*, but this is only guesswork; Mann, *Jews*, II, 68, assumes that the 'five generations' refer to the five sons of Bustanai, only two of whom were from a Jewish wife, and see *ibid.* his debate with Marmorstein, who assumed that the entire attack was directed against someone from the family of the priestly geonim; in *Texts*, II, 134, Mann assumes that the attacked *nāsī* was Solomon b. David b. Boaz, a Karaite *nāsī*, but it is not likely that a Karaite *nāsī* would arouse such affection on the part of the Rabbanites, to the point where the Gaon had to attack him in this manner, without mentioning explicitly that he was a Karaite. On the Bustanai affair, see Gil, *Tarbiz*, 48(1978/9), 36ff, and references there to sources and research literature. The letter of Joshua ha-Kohen b. Ya'īr: **24**; Mann, *Jews*, I, 172f, assumed that the man's name was Shem-Ṭōv and that the letter was written in Raqqa. The letter in Zadok's handwriting: **213**, lines 29ff; Goitein, *Shalem*, 2(1975/6), 51 (= *ha-Yishuv*, 139f), assumes that that *nāsī* was Daniel b. Azariah, but this is not possible, as we know the likely date of the letter on the basis of its sender, and Daniel was not in Palestine at the time; Cohen, *ASJR*, 1(1976), 9, n. 25, even finds here proof that Solomon b. Judah wanted Daniel as his successor. Elijah's letter: **416**; Dinur, *Isrā'ēl ba-gōlā*, 1(3), 99, n. 61, understood that the opposition to David b. Hezekiah (which caused him to leave Jerusalem) came mainly from the family of the priestly geonim, who claimed to be the offspring of the ancient sage Eleazar b. Azariah; but we have seen that the writer of the letter himself (who expresses his loyal friendship to David b. Hezekiah) stemmed from the same family, which cancels out his assumption in any case. Mann, *Jews*, I, 112f, also did not identify the

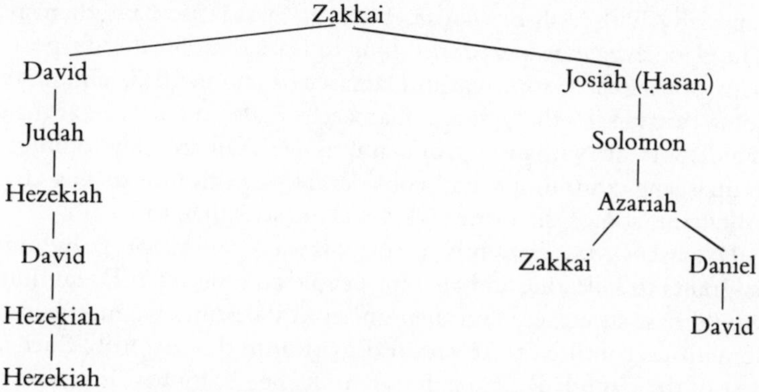

Relations between the Palestinian yeshiva and the communities in Palestine and the diaspora

[775] We have seen the extent to which the yeshiva was an institution whose activities were directed outwards towards the other institutions of leadership and the local communities. Up to this point, we have dealt mainly with the connections with the communities of Fustat and the relationship between Jerusalem and Babylonia, that is, with its yeshivot and exilarchs. From among the communities in Palestine, we have seen the special ties of the yeshiva with Tiberias. We have also seen, and shall see further, the ties with Ascalon and Tyre, the two major ports of the area in the period under discussion. Although evidence of each of the other communities in Palestine has not been preserved, there is no doubt that the yeshiva had contact with them as well, as we have seen, for instance, in the intervention in the matter of the synagogue routines in Ḥaṣōr (Caesarea), or in the letters to Rafiaḥ and others. Evidence exists of links with other countries, apart from Egypt, such as Syria, for example. Abraham, son of the Gaon, writes of his stay in Damascus, evidently in 1025, and his father also mentions this stay there at the height of a serious rift there, in two of his letters. People of the yeshiva were taken to Damascus to be imprisoned, in connection with the excommunication of the Karaites, and the Gaon was making an effort, with the help of public leaders there, and

writer of the letter in his discussion, but afterwards did identify him, see *ibid.*, II, 347. **417** is also a fragment of a letter from the aforementioned Elijah (the 'third') to David ha-Nāsī b. Hezekiah; unfortunately, only the opening part has been preserved. As to the date of the letters, which is the time of David b. Hezekiah's departure from Jerusalem, see in the introductions to these letters. The poems of Samuel ha-Nagid: No. 53 (the *Dīwān*, 36); No. 95(66, *ibid.*); No. 97(69, *ibid.*). In the first, 'Rabbi Sahlān' is also mentioned, perhaps Sahlān b. Abraham. Abiathar's letter: **553**.

especially with 'Adī b. Manasseh ibn al-Qazzāz, to have them released. The Gaon even considered travelling to Damascus for this purpose. Abraham, son of the Gaon, was in Damascus again in 1033, undoubtedly on some mission for the yeshiva. Damascus is also mentioned at the time of the dispute of Nathan b. Abraham, as we shall see. The opinion of the Damascene community had considerable significance in this affair, and Abraham, son of the Gaon, visited Damascus then too.

Damascus was evidently a sort of way-station for Babylonian immigrants to Palestine and also for people coming from Byzantium, who would first stop there and then go on to Palestine, whence some would sometimes continue westward to Egypt or to the Maghrib. Such was the case of the Baghdādī cantor, Rawḥ ha-Kohen b. Pinḥas, in whose interest Zadok ha-Levi writes at least two letters to Ephraim b. Shemaria. That cantor was at first in Damascus, 'prayed there in the congregation but did not want to benefit from them'; that is, he refused to take payment for this. Another cantor too, Isaac al-Fāsī, a Maghribi who was apparently on his way to Egypt from Byzantium, stopped in Damascus and then in Jerusalem. Daniel b. Azariah had a special relationship with the people of Damascus and tried to help them in Fustat with their tax affairs, as I have shown above. When he was already Gaon, he stayed for some time in Damascus, in 1054 or 1055, as was his custom from time to time, before becoming Gaon. From among the priestly geonim we find Elijah b. Solomon Gaon there, writing a deed in his own hand on 5 May 1031, and from the time of his holding the rank of Gaon, a letter is mentioned written to 'the Damascus neighbourhood', some time prior to 1070.

In order to round out the picture, I should add the information we have on the existence of two communities in Damascus during the period under discussion – the 'Palestinian' and the other ('the smaller' – its synagogue was also called thus), the 'Babylonian'. The remnants of a notebook from the year 933, 'from the small synagogue of the Babylonians', found in the Geniza, is witness to the fact.[48]

[48] Abraham, son of the Gaon, in Damascus: **59**, line 17. The letters of Solomon b. Judah: **81**, line 15; **84**, b (II), line 14. The matter of the prisoners in Damascus: **90**, and others; see 'Eli ha-Kohen b. Hezekiah's letters: **433**. The second visit of Abraham to Damascus: **212**, margin. Isaac the cantor: **241**. Daniel b. Azariah in Damascus: **357**, a, line 4; see the letter of 'Eli ha-Kohen b. Ezekiel: **445**. The deed from Damascus: **415**. On the letter of Elijah Gaon to the neighbourhood of Damascus: **547**, a, line 40. The remnants of the note-book of the 'Babylonian' congregation (TS 16.181) were edited by: Assaf, *Meqōrōt*, 64–69; Goitein, *Leshonenu*, 30(1965/6), 200–208; Friedman, *Marriage*, II, 396–435; see also a marriage deed from the year 956, Bodl MS Heb d 65, f. 30, in Assaf, *Tarbiz*, 9(1937/8), 26f; Friedman, *ibid.*, 198–207. We have seen above that the synagogue is mentioned in an Arab source, in connection with the ensnaring of the Damascus ruler, al-Qassām; this was certainly the great synagogue of al-Shāmiyīn, the 'Palestinians', see on this also in Gil, *Documents*, 217, n. 5. *Kanīsat al-'Irāqiyīn* mentioned by Nathan b. Abraham in his letter: **183**, a, line 21, was in Ramla, not in Damascus, contrary to Mann's view in *Jews*, I, 150, and following him,

[776] Apart from contacts with Egypt and Syria, in relation to which the central position of the Palestinian yeshiva is proven and documented in the Geniza, one should also note connections with more distant regions. Unique evidence is found in the letter of Abū'l-Ḥay b. Ḥakīm, on behalf of 'the holy community who live here on the isle of Sicily', to Hanania ha-Kohen *av-bēt-dīn* b. Joseph, head of the yeshiva, dated *ca.* 1020. The letter refers to the difficult situation of the Jews of the island, made so especially by the heavy taxes imposed on them. The letter is dated the first day of Elul, and the writer apologises on behalf of the people of Sicily for not having written for some time and for not writing to the Gaon himself, for it is not fitting to write him without also sending a donation. On the holidays they will write and also send a gift. This letter confirms a fact which we could have assumed, that is that the Jews of Sicily, like in the other areas that had formerly been under Roman and Byzantine rule, continued to maintain constant contact with the Sanhedrin, the Palestinian yeshiva. In one of Solomon b. Judah's letters, there is a hint that some of the contacts with Sicily are carried on through Egypt, undoubtedly owing to the busy maritime trade conducted by the Maghribi merchants in Egypt with the island. In around 1035, Ephraim b. Shemaria mentions in the draft of a letter to the yeshiva, the very respectable sum of 35 dinars which have arrived from Sicily for the Jews of Jerusalem, to somewhat ease their heavy burden of debts. It is characteristic that in order to settle a dispute amongst them, these Maghribi merchants appealed to the court of the head of the yeshiva, as we see from a court record written in the spring of 1040 in the court of Nathan b. Abraham (at that time, Solomon b. Judah's competitior for the office of Gaon), which met in Fustat. In 1058, we encounter matters of partnership and a legacy attached to it, in which the Gaon Daniel b. Azariah is asked to pass judgment. And above, we have seen evidence of more ancient connections between the Palestine yeshiva and Southern Italy, in the Scroll of Aḥīma'aṣ.[49]

Friedman, *ibid.*, 398, n. 6. Apart from Damascus, Aleppo, Tripoli (Iṭrābulus), and Tyre also left their mark in documents preserved in the Geniza; some of these have been mentioned above and I shall return to them in the discussion on matters of the yeshiva at the end of the eleventh century.

49 The letter from Sicily (when speaking of Siqilliyya, or Ṣiqilliyya, they mean Palermo): **45**. There are tens of letters in the Geniza containing evidence on matters relating to the Sicilian Jews, particularly with regard to the economy, but there is also some general information on political events (the eleventh century was rife with awesome events occurring on the Island: the Byzantine invasions, and the Norman domination which began in the fifties of the century) and also information on community life. A central figure there was the dayyān Maṣlīaḥ b. Eliah (Eliah, is Baṣaq, or Abū Sahl), mentioned in **426**, lines 7–8. He is mentioned in the commentary on the Song of Solomon by Joseph b. Judah ibn 'Aqnīn (see the Halkin ed., 494), cited there from the *kitāb al-istighnā'* by 'the Nagid' (i.e. Samuel b. Naghrila) containing mention of Maṣlīaḥ's stay in Baghdad with Hayy Gaon. See my article on matters of the Jews in Sicily during this period

[777] Information on the yeshiva's connections with the rest of Europe is very meagre. The responsum of Elijah ha-Kohen Gaon b. Solomon to Meshullam b. Moses of Mainz is preserved, and is also signed by the son of the Gaon, Abiathar: 'Abiathar ha-Kohen the fourth of the yeshiva'. This information on connections between Meshullam b. Moses and the Palestinian yeshiva, which undoubtedly existed in the sixties of the eleventh century, has been preserved in a number of sources ascribed to people of Mainz.

Another matter relating to this subject is the anxiety of 'Eli ha-Kohen b. Ezekiel, of the Jerusalem yeshiva, for the aforementioned cantor Abū 'Imrān Mūsā al-'Ajamī. I have also mentioned Abiathar ha-Kohen, son of the Gaon, who asks the parnās of Fustat, 'Eli ha-Kohen, in November 1070, for details about someone who came from the land of the Franks and happened to be in Fustat.

It appears that the matter of Reuben b. Isaac 'from the land of Franṣa' belongs to the same period. He wanted to come to Palestine after a tragic event in his family, namely that his only son was killed by assailants and robbed of all his property. As Golb has proven, the man came from Rouen (in the letter: 'from the city of *rdwm*'). The letter of recommendation for

according to Geniza documents in *Italia Judaica* (Bari 1981), 87; see also Goitein, *Archivio storico per la Sicilia Orientale*, 67:9, 1971; Golb, *JNES*, 32:105, 1973. See various information on Sicily and its Jews in Goitein, *Mediterranean Society*, I, according to the Index (Sicily, Palermo). The letter of Solomon b. Judah: **80**, b, line 25. The record from the court of Nathan b. Abraham: **193**. Ephraim b. Shemaria: **326**. Daniel b. Azariah: **394–396**. See also: Mosseri VIII, 410r, the beginning of a deed relating to Simon Siqillī, written 'before our Master, the Honourable, etc., David the Great Nāsī, head of the yeshīvat Ge'ōn Ya'aqōv'. Apart from the Scroll of Aḥīma'aṣ, Mann quotes, *Jews*, I, 73f, as further proof of the connections with Southern Italy, the foreword in the book *hōrayat ha-qōrē* 'which was brought here from Jerusalem *lb'r* (which he interpreted as Bari) in a short way' by Joseph b. Ḥiyya the scribe; the book was written in Arabic and Nethanel b. Meshullam (as in the Bodleian MS, whereas the Vatican MS has: Meshullam b. Nethanel) translated it into Hebrew 'in the city of Magenza' (Mainz; in Mann erroneously: Jacob b. Meshullam, and see Goitein's note in the preface to the second edition of Mann's book). *Hōrayat ha-qōrē* was first mentioned by Porges: *REJ*, 23(1891), 310f; MS Bodl., Opp. 625, see: Neubauer, *Catalogue*, 1465, No. 11, fol. 241b; see film 16384 at the Institute of Microfilmed Hebrew MSs, Jerusalem; however the whole matter is doubtful and it seems that one should read here: *le-vā'ēr*, to interpret, and not to Bari. That same Nethanel b. Meshullam (if that is indeed his name) may have been the son of the Meshullam b. Moses mentioned below. See also Fleischer, *Sefunot*, NS, 1 (1979/80), 43ff, who proves that the holiday Torah readings in Italy in the ninth century were according to the custom of Palestine; Klar, *Megillat Aḥima'aṣ*, 152ff, discusses ancient connections between Southern Italy (which until 1057 was part of Byzantium) and Palestine; one may question his assertion that the famous inscription from Venosa, which mentions elegies said there over the deceased by two emissaries and two rabis (*duo apostoli et duo rebbites*) does actually relate to the matter, for Palestine is not mentioned there. He notes further the benediction for the new month that was customary among Greek Jews: 'Ye the whole people heed to listen to the sanctification of this month, as decreed by our forefathers, the holy *ḥavūrōt* (i.e. the Sanhedrin) who used to convene in Palestine, namely that we have a new month, on such-and-such, on this-and-this day of the week'; cf. Brann, *MGWJ*, 62(1918), 276f; Zunz, *Ritus*[2], 82.

him was written by the people of the community where he stopped on his way, which, in Golb's opinion, was the city of Arles (the first letter of the name of the city has been preserved in the letter, an *alef*).

The people of Europe evidently did not have a good reputation in the eyes of the yeshiva and its circle. This we can discern from the letter of Judah ha-Kohen b. Joseph, the Rav, or spiritual leader of the Maghribis in Fustat, to one of his relatives, called 'the fifth in the yeshiva', in Jerusalem or perhaps Tyre. The writer and the addressee have a relative in common, whose name is R. Judah, and the writer has learned that the addressee's son Nissim wants to leave and go to the city in which R. Judah resides, apparently, somewhere in Europe. The journey will last three years at least; the people (that is, the Jews) there are cruel and mean, they barely greet a strange Jew, and after a month and a half, they will ask him to leave, because of the *ḥerem ha-yishshūv* (the settlement ban), while their knowledge of the Torah is negligible. In short, the Rav is strongly opposed to Nissim's going there and it seems that these words are being written in the hope that they will have some influence on the young man.[50]

The Jewish leadership and the Fatimid authorities

[778] A large number of writings in the Geniza shed light on the question of the relationship between the Jewish population of Palestine

[50] See the responsum of Elijah ha-Kohen and his son Abiathar: Bodl MS Heb c 23, f. 42; a fragment of which was first edited by Epstein, *MGWJ*, 47(1903), 354; similarly, with regard to the saying of the prayer *we-hassī'ēnu* (in the *musaf* prayer) on *Rōsh ha-shānā* and *Yom kippur*, one mentions 'the lions that sit in Jerusalem, the Holy City', 'the yeshiva of Palestine', 'the yeshiva of Jerusalem', and it is said that R. Meshullam addressed a query to them on this matter. See the references in Epstein, *ibid.*, 344; cf. also the *Ma'asē rōqēaḥ* of Eleazar b. Judah b. Kalonymus of Mainz, 27: 'and the geonim of Mainz introduced the custom [to bless] over the *hadas* [myrtle], as did our Master Meshullam of Mainz, who sent [a query] to the Holy City and they answered us that one has to say a blessing over it'; see also: Poznanski, *Babylonische Geonim*, 93f, n. 5, who adds similar references from the *Siddūr* of Rashi, and others. Marmorstein, *REJ*, 73(1921), 88–92, edited the Bodleian manuscript, which indeed deals with the prayer *we-hassī'ēnū*, and also the rules regarding Passover eve which falls on the sabbath, the blessing on the *hadas* on a holiday eve which falls on the sabbath night, on the question of the freeing of a slave by his owner without the knowledge of the latter's wife, and the rules regarding fruit picked by a gentile on a holiday, cf. Marmorstein, *ibid.*, 86. Echoes from the responsum regarding Passover eve can be found in ENA 2941, see *Ōṣar ha-ge'ōnīm*, Pesaḥim, 66f; cf. also Mann, *Jews*, I, 186; II, 223f, 378; Grossman, *Ḥakhmē Ashkenāz*, 283, 391f. In the version of the responsum of Elijah ha-Kohen the following sentence is found: 'since this is the way we are doing it in both yeshivot, of the Land of . . .' (the manuscript is torn here). Mann (*ibid.*, II, 223) suggested to complete it: 'of the Land of Israel and Babylonia'. Dr Yoram Erder indicates (and he is correct) a preference for Marmorstein's completion of that sentence: 'of the Land of Israel and of Neharde'a' (not Babylonia, as in Mann). In the *maḥzōr* of Vitry, the dispute over the prayer *we-hassī'ēnū* is presented as a dispute between the Palestinian custom and the Babylonian. In the *Pardes* of Rashi, it says that *we-hassī'ēnū* is said in Palestine and in Neharde'a: 'since this is the way we are doing it in both yeshivot . . . in Palestine and in

and its leadership, and the Fatimid authorities. Within the Fatimid ruling system and the political ideology on which it was built, there is no sign of deviation from the deep-rooted and hallowed principles of the Muslim law regarding dhimmīs. The Jews and the Christians had the right to enjoy the security and other rights promised them, but also the obligation to pay their taxes and observe the restrictions imposed on them. In everyday reality, however, if we are to generalise, the Fatimid caliphate brought with it an improvement in the life of the Jews, and especially those of Palestine. One should bear in mind certain central facts in the overall situation: (1) the major standing of the Jewish merchants (the Maghribis in particular) in maritime trade in the Mediterranean and the supply of goods to Spain, the Maghrib, Sicily, Egypt, Palestine and Syria, (2) the unprecedented role of the Jews in political and military events, and (3) Jewish support of the Fatimid rulers against their enemies – though according to the information at our disposal, this support was mainly expressed in the form of prayer, but one should also take into consideration that in those times, prayer had a greater significance than it has today.

The principal factor in the Fatimids' policy towards the Jews of Palestine lay in its respect for Jewish autonomy and self-rule. The principle of tolerance towards the independent leadership of the dhimmīs has deep roots in Muslim tradition, going as far back as the Prophet. As we have seen, great importance of a very special nature was attached to the yeshiva, as the leadership of the Jews of Palestine, because it also controlled the

Neharde'a, where one says *we-hassī'ēnū* on Rōsh ha-shānā and Yom kippūr, as it is said in the Palestinian Talmud . . . that Samuel said: one has to say *we-hassī'ēnū'* (see *PT*, Ber. ix, 13d, bottom). See the *maḥzor* of Vitry, 360 (Nos. 321–322); the *Pardes* (ed. Ehrenreich, Budapest 1924), 214; cf. Elbogen, 133f, 146. The matter of the cantor: **451**, lines 13–14. Abiathar's letter: **547**, b, lines 1–2. Reuben b. Isaac, see: BM Or 5544, f. 1; the significant part of the letter was edited by Mann, *Jews*, II, 191, see *ibid.*, I, 165; the letter was edited in full by Golb, *Rouen*, 163–170, see the discussion *ibid.*, 3–12; on the basis of the fact that on the verso of the letter someone, evidently one of the scribes of the yeshiva, wrote versions and formulae, common in letters of the yeshiva – which may be used when needed – he concludes that this Reuben did in fact reach Jerusalem and hand over the letter, and it is at the yeshiva that it was used for writing those versions and formulae. Golb, *ibid.*, 11f, relates to this matter **123** as well, but this is only an assumption, particularly as this letter, written by Abraham b. Solomon b. Judah, refers to a man who fled because of taxes, and passed through Damascus; if one were referring to a man from 'the land of the Franks', the writer would have noted this; and they are speaking of the possibility that the man would return to his home, which does not fit the situation of this Reuben who wanted to die, and because of this, remained in Jerusalem. This letter concerning Reuben undoubtedly landed in the Geniza together with other Jerusalem letters which reached Fustat with the remnants of the archives of the yeshiva, and the fact that it is found in the Geniza is no proof that Reuben himself in fact came to Fustat from Jerusalem; cf. Grossman, *Shalem*, 3(1980/1), 64 (for some reason, he does not mention Golb). The letter of the *Rav*: **530**; *Ḥerem ha-yishshūv* was not known of in Islamic countries (nor apparently in Byzantine lands either) and seems quite indecent in the writer's opinion; see on *ḥerem ha-yishshūv*: Baron, *SRHJ*, IV,

Jewish communities in the other countries under Fatimid rule. The representative of this leadership, the Gaon, had access to the rulers in al-Qāhira through the Jewish notables of Egypt, the Jewish elite, who were the bankers, wealthy merchants, and physicians to the Fatimid court. A large proportion of the information at our disposal are matters dealing with the ceaseless acts of intercession. Whenever there was some injustice towards the Jewish population, or even towards an individual, whether this was harshness in matters of taxes or some maltreatment (*ẓulm*), urgent letters would be sent from Jerusalem to Jewish notables in Fustat and, through them, Jews close to the court, such as the Tustaris, would be made to exert their influence, until the matter was rectified by the caliph's official order (*sijill, manshūr, tawqīʿ*). These orders were addressed to the commanders of the army (the *amīr*s) for it was they who actually ruled Palestine in the state of the endless warfare existing there.

Against the background of a government with whom it was possible to come to terms, one must also view the frequent involvement – evidently more frequent than is reflected in the letters – of the Fatimid authorities in the Jewish schisms and rifts and the continuous quarrelling between the Rabbanites and the Karaites. The Jews themselves invited this official intercession and supplied the authorities with ample occasions for involvement. The classic formula of Fatimid bureaucracy often repeats itself in this reality in approximately the following manner: 'In your hands, our Master (that is, the caliph), may you enjoy God's blessing and his prayers, is the supreme authority to prevent so-and-so [a Jew] from doing such-and-such' (such as the closing of a synagogue). Iniquity and scheming on the part of the local rulers were also included in this state of affairs alongside the inner divisions and quarrels amongst the Jews themselves, while on the other hand, the central authorities manifested greater receptivity than was common in the Muslim world, and were prepared to make amends, generally in the form of written orders.

A fact worth noting is the financial support rendered by the Fatimid rulers, at any rate during the first generation of its dominion (or attempts at dominion) of Palestine. We learn of this from a letter of Josiah Gaon to the community of Damietta. In the course of describing the distress and need, he notes that 'when we were provided for by the kingdom, we would not trouble you'. According to him, this financial sponsorship continued until two years before the imposition of the great tax [or fine] on the Jews. Perhaps he is referring to the special taxes imposed during al-Dizbirī's time, apparently in 1024, which we have already dealt with

71; 274, n. 91, and references therein. A similar attitude towards Jews of Ashkenaz can also be sensed in the responsum of 960 quoted above, in sec. 736.

above, and thus the year in which the support was withdrawn would be 1022 – though this is merely an assumption.[51]

[779] I have already mentioned above that in about 1060 the governor of Jerusalem was a Jew, a Karaite by the name of Abū Sa'd Isaac (Isḥaq) b. Aaron (Khalaf) ibn 'Allūn. We have also seen that the Jews of Jerusalem were required to appoint a *wakīl* over themselves. For this purpose, it states in a letter from Jerusalem to Ramla, the Jerusalem cadi al-Tīzī would travel to Ramla to clarify the affair at the seat (*majlis*) of the cadi of Ramla, Abū'l-Ma'ālī. It seems that one of the pieces of evidence proving that the Jews of Jerusalem did indeed need a *wakīl* was the fact that the matter of the *ḥiṣn*, (the fortress), had been neglected. We do not know which fortress they are referring to; perhaps there is some connection between this matter of the fortress and the building of the wall in Jerusalem, of which I have already spoken. Evidently there was a legal investigation in which the Muslim judges relied on the evidence of two strangers, whereas none of the *'ādiliyya*, the pious Muslims, who were qualified as witnesses and notaries, gave evidence against the Jews. The writer of the letter, 'Eli ha-Kohen b. Ezekiel, prompts the people of Ramla to influence the Ramla cadi, Abū'l-Ma'āli, to go into the matter thoroughly together with the cadi of Jerusalem, especially into the standing of the witnesses. The cadi of Ramla, he writes, would have some influence on the Jerusalem cadi, for they both belong to the same legal school (undoubtedly meaning the *madhhab*) and the former is the more knowledgeable.

A Jewish dignitary who had a special relationship to the rulers was Abraham ha-Kohn b. Isaac ibn Furāt, the physician of Fustat who spent much of his time in Palestine, in Ramla, and apparently served there as physician to the governor. He is frequently mentioned in my collection, from Solomon b. Judah's day onward, and we also have one of the latter's letters to his father, Isaac ha-Kohen b. Furāt. In this letter, he thanks him for supporting Ephraim b. Shemaria (one can assume that he is referring to the aforementioned rupture with his rivals). At that time, it seems that Isaac's son, Abraham, was the one who dealt with community affairs, but he was away attending a funeral elsewhere. Later on, we find Abraham

51 For the general background to the relationship with the authorities, see: Goitein, *Mediterranean Society*, II, 345–380. On the subject of the considerable influence of the notables of Fustat, one should mention that this was the major metropolis of the Muslim world, a status it owed to the Fatimids. The Jerusalemite al-Muqaddasī (*Āqālīm*, 36) writes: 'Fustat of Egypt is like Baghdad in times past; I do not know of another city of greater importance in the entire Muslim world'. The letter of Josiah: **36**, a, lines 12–14. As to the Jews' relatively positive attitude towards the Fatimid rulers in general, this is expressed in somewhat veiled terms in **214**, a letter from Fustat to Zadok ha-Levi *av-bēt-dīn* of the yeshiva in Jerusalem, written *ca.* 1030, which mainly contains complaints against a certain David b. al-Raqqī. It is interesting that this David swore in the 'Palestinians' synagogue (not a ritual oath) 'by the Torah, vowing his entire property, and also by the head of the

ha-Kohen in Ramla, as mentioned, until the beginning of Daniel b. Azariah's office as Gaon, when he returned to his home and family in Fustat. His stay in Ramla may have lasted twenty years, from the outset of the thirties until the beginning of the fifties. In around 1030, the Gaon Solomon b. Judah complained to him of the Shuway' family, who were harassing him, and asked him to obtain a letter from the *amīr* (meaning undoubtedly the governor of Ramla) to his colleague (*ṣāḥib*; obviously the governor of Jerusalem) to defend him against them. This appeal on the part of the Gaon may have been due to some family connection as well, for Solomon b. Judah, as we shall see, was related by marriage to the family of the priestly geonim, who were relatives of Abraham ha-Kohen. Elijah ha-Kohen b. Solomon Gaon, in his letter of condolence on the death of Abraham's father Isaac, calls Abraham 'our cousin', and also signs as 'your cousin'. In a letter of thanks from an old man in Sicily, Eliah ha-Kohen al-Siqillī b. Jacob, the writer adds the closing expression (*'alāma*) *yesha' yuḥāsh* (salvation will soon come), commonly adopted by the family of the priestly geonim. In a note to Abraham ha-Kohen, another Jerusalemite Kohen, 'Eli ha-Kohen b. Ezekiel, who may also have been a family relative, speaks of a sum of money sent by Abraham to 'Eli via the son of his friend, when Abraham was on his way to Egypt. Apparently, Abraham ha-Kohen was generally taken up with sending money to the needy in Jerusalem. For instance, he sends a dinar in the fifties (from al-Qāhira) to the people of Jerusalem, who gratefully confirm its receipt.

In some sources, it emerges that the family of Abraham ha-Kohen was involved in a law suit which an orphan had instituted against them, undoubtedly concerning an inheritance. Evidently the people of the Jerusalem yeshiva favoured Abraham ha-Kohen in this matter, as he was their benefactor, and it is doubtful whether their approach in this instance was unprejudiced. Solomon b. Ṣemaḥ of Ramla, one of the intimates of Solomon b. Judah, writes in this vein to Ephraim b. Shemaria, *ca.* 1030, asking him to help the brother of Abraham, *ibn al-'amm* (the cousin – we have seen already that he was the cousin of the priestly geonim). He claims that just as they have to protect the orphans, they also have to see to it that no one should be illegally deprived by them and that there is a very explicit law about it. All of 'our congregation' (that is, the Palestinians in Fustat) would be grateful for this, and Solomon b. Ṣemaḥ repeats this request in another letter written to Ephraim b. Shemaria. The subject of this controversy will come up again with Daniel b. Azariah. The personality and standing of Abraham ha-Kohen, especially his connection with the authorities, were particularly important when the choice of Daniel b. Azariah

king'. One of the complaints against him was that he belittled the king ('and the king, what will he do to us'), and it is clear that he means the Fatimid caliph.

as Gaon was being considered, a matter which shall be given further consideration. In addition, I shall look into the considerable extent to which the authorities were involved in the struggle between David b. Daniel and Abiathar ha-Kohen.

In one of his letters to Abraham ha-Kohen, Daniel b. Azariah mentions the subject of the *ruq'a* (the note) – meaning here the official document – which the addressee received from 'our Lord, may God grant him long life', etc., and he expresses his satisfaction and gratitude in moving terms. The document was issued by 'his high excellency', (*al-ḥadra al-sāmiya*), evidently the wazīr. The letter also mentions that Abraham has been offered a very high position, and the Gaon tries to convince him not to turn it down by any means. In another letter, Daniel asks for his intercession with the wazīr – evidently al-Yāzūrī – from whom he wants a letter of recommendation to the governor of Jerusalem, for Daniel already has 'the high official document' (*al-manshūr al-mukarram*) which states that the Gaon must be treated with respect, with cordiality and that his needs be fulfilled. We are not absolutely certain regarding Abraham ha-Kohen's handwriting, but there is reason to assume that some of the drafts of petitions to the caliph are in his writing, such as the letter to the caliph against the official recognition of a 'Babylonian' authority in Palestine (in around 1030), or the petition from the supporters of Solomon b. Judah (evidently from the end of 1041). There seem to have been many Jewish personalities at the time who sought the friendship and support of Abraham ha-Kohen, as we see in a letter written to him by Zakkai, the *nāsī*, b. Yedīdyāhū the *nāsī*, addressing him as 'Abraham ha-Kohen the physician called the prince of the congregation . . . b. Isaac ha-Kohen the physician'. Only the opening phrases have been preserved and these are solely grandiloquent expressions of praise.[52]

[52] The Karaite governor: above, section 600: see the matter of the wall, above, sections 601, 712. The letter of 'Eli ha-Kohen: **453**. Goitein, *Mediterranean Society*, II, 243, and also: *ha-Yishuv*, 123, assumed, due to an error in reading the address in **117** (see there in the *variae lectiones*), that Abraham ha-Kohen was director of the department of dysentery; but it says there only that he was a physician. The letter to Isaac ha-Kohen: **100**; he too was a physician (see *ibid.*, lines 4ff); one can assume that the support for Ephraim b. Shemaria implied intercession with the authorities. The fact that Abraham ha-Kohen was the court physician emerges from **439**, in which the Jerusalem parnās 'Eli ha-Kohen b. Ezekiel congratulates him on his marriage, saying: 'and may He [God] make him obtain the goodwill of our Lord the King, may he live forever, and of the Lady (i.e. the caliph's mother), and the grandees of the kingdom'. His stay in Ramla is first explicitly stated in **229**, a court record from 1038, in which he is one of the witnesses. The matter of the Shuway' family: **101**. The letter of condolence: **414**. It seems that Isaac ha-Kohen's death was connected with certain political events, for it says there among other things, 'alas for the generation whose noblemen and great and leaders become fewer and plucked from them and imprisoned', and further on: 'may [the God of Israel] . . . save you from the turmoil and give your life unto you as a prey'. Mann, *Jews*, I, 84, found here proof that Isaac ha-Kohen did not die a natural death. The letter of Eliah ha-Kohen al-Siqillī: **439a**;

[780] Towards the mid-eleventh century, the Tustari brothers, Abū Naṣr Faḍl (Ḥesed) and Abū Sa'd Ibrahīm (Abraham), the sons of Abū'l-Faḍl Sahl (Yāshār) b. Israel, occupied a singular status in the relationship

the letter was sent to Ramla, as it says in the address. The note of 'Eli ha-Kohen: **437**. The letter to the people of Jerusalem: **439**; the time of the letter is confirmed by the title 'Pride of the Elders', which we know that Daniel b. Azariah granted him; at that time, Abraham still had no offspring (certainly no sons), for he is wished that God shall 'provide him with the right seed'. Six people sign the letter, the last (that is, the most important) being 'Eli ha-Kohen b. Ezekiel. The letters of Solomon b. Ṣemaḥ: **205**, **206**. The nickname *ibn al-'Amm* – cf. **76**, lines 11–12. As to the family relationship, if we assume that Furāt is Pōrāt, (see the Hebrew Bible, Gen., xlix:22) it is possible that the name of the family's father in an earlier generation was Joseph; and then one may assume that Isaac ha-Kohen the father of Abraham was the brother of the Gaon Solomon ha-Kohen b. Joseph. When he returned to Egypt, Abraham ha-Kohen evidently played an important role in the community. It is characteristic that he expected that the leader of the congregation, the judge (*he-ḥāvēr ha-me'ullē*) 'Eli b. 'Amram would take the trouble to visit him on some matter and not the contrary. TS 13 J 31, f. 5 (edited in Mann, *Jews*, II, 84f with the Arabic part missing) is a letter from 'Eli b. 'Amram to Abraham ha-Kohen, in which he in fact promises him that: 'you are praised by anybody whenever there is an assembly or a lesson . . . in His (i.e. God's) house, the yeshiva *ge'ōn ya'aqōv*'. At the same time, he apologises for not coming to him, for there is no one to replace him in his shop (Goitein, *Shalem*, 2 [1975/6], 64 = ha-Yishuv, 150, interprets that an office is being spoken of, that is, of the dayyān, not a shop). One should note that 'Eli b. 'Amram ends his letter with the *'alāma – yesha' yuḥāsh* – of the priestly family, the rivals of Daniel b. Azariah, and this is no coincidence. In **354** Daniel b. Azariah indeed wrote to Abraham ha-Kohen that the local ḥāvēr (that is, 'Eli) will be his subordinate. See the matter of the *ruq'a* and the office in **355**, b, lines 3 ff and lines 26–30. Goitein, *Shalem*, 2(1935/6), 81ff (= ha-Yishuv, 163), assumes that the Nagid, Judah b. Saadia, is being referred to. The request for a recommendation: **357**, b, lines 21–27. Drafts in the handwriting of Abraham ha-Kohen: **312**, **197**. Also in his handwriting apparently, is **399**, which contains accusations against 'Eli he-ḥāvēr b. 'Amram, leader of the 'Palestinians' in Fustat during Daniel b. Azariah's time. Zakkai the nāsī: TS 13 J 15, f. 14, was edited by Mann, *Jews*, II, 83f; Halper, *Hatequfa*, 18(1922/3), 191f, claims that this letter is actually a poem (but this is not so, since we only have its beginning); similarly Worman, *JQR*, 19(1907), 734, defines it as 'a poetical epistle'. One cannot identify the lineage of that nāsī, cf. Mann, *ibid.*, I, 85, and see his comments in n. 1 on a Karaite *nāsī* whose name was Yedīdyā, mentioned in a document from 1081, who may have been the son of this Zakkai (despite Mann's reservations regarding this possibility, for how could a Karaite nāsī praise Abraham ha-Kohen for 'the excellent titles' and for the 'ranks' he received from the yeshivot? – referring to his honorary titles). Poznanski, *Babylonische Geonim*, 122, tried to link this Zakkai to the *nesī'īm* of Mosul (who flourished in the second half of the twelfth century) but this does not fit chronologically. Concerning the titles of Abraham ha-Kohen (see in the Hebrew Index), one should note that he is generally called, *sar ha-'ēdā* (prince of the congregation), a title perhaps granted him by Solomon b. Judah. Apart from this, he is also called 'the splendour of the princes', 'the elder of the two parties' (that is: 'Palestinians' and 'Babylonians'), 'glory of the priesthood' or 'glory of the priests'. In **354**, the Gaon Daniel b. Azariah informs him that he has decided to add to his titles 'pride of the elders'. It is worth mentioning that his father, Isaac ha-Kohen, bore the title 'the elder of the communities', see: **101**, lines 1–3; **117**, lines 1–4. In an opening fragment of a deed of attorney written in Ramla, Isaac, the father of Abraham 'the prince counsellor, the physician son of . . . Abraham the elder of the communities in Ramla' gives a power of attorney to Judah (nicknamed Asad) b. Moses. See TS NS 324.67, edited by Friedman, *Tarbiz*, 49(1979/80), 203. Friedman assumes that a son of Abraham is meant there, but it is more likely that it is his father, both because in the relatively numerous letters mentioning Abraham, there is no mention of his having a son,

between the yeshiva and the Fatimid rulers. This was a family of merchants and financiers which had its roots in the Persian city of Tustar, hence their name. They were Karaites, but belonged to a separate faction within the Karaite community, one that was actually called 'the Tustaris'. A branch of this family settled in Egypt, evidently at the beginning of the century. The two aforementioned Tustari brothers, Ḥesed and Abraham, are noted in Arab sources in connection with their financial activities and also with the important political standing they had achieved at the Fatimid court. Abraham in particular occupied a significant place in this sphere, apparently owing to his special connections with the Caliph al-Mustanṣir's mother. She was black and a former slave, the property of Abraham al-Tustarī, who had sold her to Caliph al-Ẓāhir and she was the mother of his successor, al-Mustanṣir. During the subsequent disturbances, she backed the black units of the caliph's army in the continuous conflict between them and the Turks and the Berbers. Abraham's rise to such a high rank thus began in 1036, evidently, with the death of al-Ẓāhir, and in the summer of 1044, he earned the official status of *wāsiṭa*, a form of chief administrator on behalf of the caliph's mother, a status similar to that of wazīr. His involvement in the struggle between the various factions in the Fatimid army eventually led to his assassination by Turkish soldiers, on 25 October 1047. The older brother Ḥesed was also involved in Fatimid politics. In around 1040, he was appointed chief clerk (*kātib*) to Anūshtakīn al-Dizbirī, who then commanded the army in Palestine and consequently ruled the country. After his brother's murder, he was busy negotiating on behalf of the Fatimids with the ruler of Aleppo, Thimāl b. Ṣāliḥ b. Mirdās. However, Thimāl then violated the agreement that had been reached between the two parties and launched out against the Fatimid army in northern Syria. In consequence, Ḥesed al-Tustarī was then accused of spying for Thimāl while playing the role of mediator, in order to avenge the murder of his brother; consequently he was tortured and executed in the summer of the year 1049.

Although they belonged to a Karaite faction, the Tustaris had close contacts with the entire Jewish community in Egypt and other countries under Fatimid rule, and they frequently exploited their connection with the rulers for the benefit of the communities and particularly for the Jews of Jerusalem and its yeshiva. This again goes to prove that the yeshiva was

and also because Abraham left Ramla for Egypt in the early fifties of the eleventh century. One should also consider **404**, in its full text as edited by me in *Te'uda*, 7 (1991), 331ff, where it is clear that an appeal was being made to Abraham ha-Kohen, to intercede with the wazīr against a Christian governor named b. Jurjis, who was wronging the Jews of the city (we do not know which).

the recognised representative of all the Jews, including the Karaites and their various factions. In this context, our sources mostly mention the older brother Ḥesed, but it seems that Abraham was also involved in the affairs of the Jewish communities.

In the draft of a letter, probably dated *ca.* 1043, Ephraim b. Shemaria asks the Gaon Solomon b. Judah to write a letter of thanks to Ḥesed b. Sahl al-Tustarī, 'the great old man . . . to be grateful to him, for he is busy with all our troubles and holds the bridle as tightly as he can, in order to assist us . . . and how much he loves the well-being of our people! May [God] grant him a covenant of well-being, and also to his seed'.

In around 1035, we find 'the elders *al-Dasātira*' heading a list of donors to a special fund organised by the Rabbanites and Karaites in Fustat for the Jews of Jerusalem. The Tustaris' brother-in-law, Sahlawayh b. Ḥayyim, is also mentioned there. The Tustaris are also frequently mentioned in the letters of Solomon b. Judah; we do not find direct appeals to them, but he addresses the leaders of the Fustat community, Ephraim b. Shemaria and Sahlān b. Abraham, and asks them to get the Tustaris' support, particularly that of Ḥesed ('the mighty old man', 'the elder of the house of Israel') in matters required by the yeshiva.

The yeshiva went out of its way to secure the Tustaris' assistance after the terrible events of 1024–1029, when the people of Jerusalem were being pressed to pay the enormous debt imposed on them. The yeshiva tried to have those imprisoned debtors released and asked that the Tustaris try to influence the authorities to this end. Solomon b. Judah then asked his son Abraham, who was staying in Fustat, to urge Abū Kathīr, who is Ephraim b. Shemaria, to act in this matter, and he complains that the letters he wrote to Ḥesed al-Tustarī were of no avail. The Gaon is saddened by this, for Ḥesed is close to the seat of power, and 'there are none among us who have greater wealth or standing'. Another of the Gaon's letters is directed to the attention of the Tustaris, and in it we find details concerning the sufferings of those debtors who are imprisoned in Damascus. They threaten to write leaflets (*pittāqīn*) complaining that the Gaon is doing nothing to save them, and to have these leaflets distributed throughout the city. It mentions that they were visited in prison by the *shālīsh*, by which they probably meant the *kātib*, the chief clerk. After consulting experts in Muslim law, it was decided that a witness should come forward and give evidence that the entire Jewish community of Jerusalem owed this money, and by this means, get the prisoners released (evidently the intention being that it was not the personal responsibility of each debtor but a communal responsibility). In further letters, the Gaon insists that only the Tustaris could help in this matter. As we shall see below, the Tustaris were very involved in the dispute between Solomon b. Judah and Nathan b.

Abraham, in favour of the latter, and did not refrain from using their influence with the rulers for this purpose.[53]

[781] In general, it seems that there was no love lost between the yeshiva and the local rulers in Jerusalem. A letter of the yeshiva, apparently from 1057, notes that seated in Jerusalem are 'the worst of gentiles' 'the sons of Kedar in Jerusalem and Palestine . . . who are very troublesome'; it speaks there of 'the pride of an ungodly nation which took over our temple', and so on. Nevertheless, in everyday life it is possible that things were different, and that when stability reigned, a good relationship developed between the yeshiva and the authorities and also with the local Muslim population. The Jews of Jerusalem were very aware of the change of governors and tried to influence their choice, as we see in a letter of Solomon b. Judah (or his son Abraham), where it is hinted that the change of governors is decided by the exertion of pressure in Egypt, and includes a sort of report on the *mutawallī*, the governor about to arrive in Jerusalem, of whom good reports were heard.

We find instances of the Gaon acting on behalf of a local Muslim, speaking of cases in which lives are at stake; and then the Gaon uses his channels of influence among the central authorities in Fustat. This was the case with Qayn b. 'Abd al-Qādir, undoubtedly a participant in the war of the Arabs against the Fatimids (1024–1029), and evidently a man from Ramla. Now, he is awaiting punishment for 'his first deeds'. Murajjā, 'an elder from among the town's notables', is trying to get help for him from Solomon b. Judah. Qayn himself, along with his family, came to implore the Gaon to try to get his influential friend in Egypt to help. On the other hand, Abraham ha-Kohen b. Isaac b. Furāt asks Murajjā's son, the cadi Abū'l-Ma'ālī (al-Musharraf), to try to get justice done for the Shuway' family, who have been unjustly deprived of their house by a wicked Muslim, a matter I have already mentioned. Some years later, Daniel b.

[53] The sources and research dealing with the Tustaris I have summarised elsewhere, see: Gil, *ha-Tustarīm*, and especially 38–57. As to the murder of the Tustaris, Mann was of the opinion that they were both assassinated on the same day, see Mann, *Jews*, I, 78–83. See in Gil, *ibid.*, 42f, the discussion on this and additional references there. The appointment of Ḥesed al-Tustarī as chief clerk of al-Dizbirī: TS AS 157.231–232r, see Gil, *ibid.*, 95 (supplement 6). See the draft of Ephraim b. Shemaria: **334**. The list of donors: **326**. Solomon b. Judah's letter to his son: **80**, b, lines 8–12. The matter of the *pittāqīn*, etc.: **65**; the letter was written in *ca.* 1025, and cannot relate to the arrest of the two priestly brothers Joseph and Elijah, the sons of Solomon Gaon (contrary to what is said in *Sefer ha-Yishuv*, 24, n. 76), since Elḥanan b. Shemaria is mentioned, who died before Iyar 4386 (1026; cf. Mann, *Jews*, I, 41). The rest of Solomon b. Judah's letters: **84**, a, lines 4–13; **91**; **103**; in **143**, which is an opening fragment of a letter from the Gaon (written by his son) to Ephraim b. Shemaria, one feels the dependence on the Tustaris and the fear that their anger may be aroused. Ephraim is asked to speak appeasingly to 'the mighty elder, the elder of the house of Israel' and 'to mollify his wrath'. This was written, it seems, after the arrival of a letter of complaint from Ḥesed to the Gaon.

Azariah asks the same Abraham ha-Kohen to do what he can for a particular family, one of whose sons is imprisoned and scheduled to be executed on the morrow. It is not clear where or when this is happening, and actually one can only assume that here, too, it is a Muslim who is being referred to.[54]

[782] Some details that have been preserved give us an inkling of the authorities' and the local military's persecution of the Jewish population. There is the case of a Jewish debtor, for instance, the brother of a certain Daniel b. Sahl, whom one of the Berber commanders of the Banū Kitāma wanted to take as his slave. A complaint about it was sent from Fustat to Josiah Gaon in Jerusalem after Elḥanan, *rōsh ha-seder* (that is, Elḥanan b. Shemaria) dealt with the matter unsuccessfully, evidently, and the Gaon is asked to use his influence. To this matter of persecution, one can also add the local friction concerning taxes, which has already been discussed.

A fragment of one of Daniel b. Azariah's letters informs us of a decree or injustice on the part of someone from Ramla (al-Ramlī, perhaps the governor?), and he demands that someone should intervene in this matter with the authorities, requesting particularly the intervention of the Fustat parnās 'Eli ha-Kohen b. Ḥayyim. The names of certain Muslim dignitaries are mentioned: the cadi Thiqa al-Dawla, the *amīr* Munjib al-Dawla, the *amīr* al-'Ammānī. There was also the case of an informer, as we see in the letter of Solomon b. Judah to Ephraim b. Shemaria, in *ca.* 1030, which contains information concerning a man who engaged in 'cheating and conniving' and served 'the clerks of the taxes and inheritance' for many years, and would mediate between them and the Jews who applied to them in matters concerning legacies, and would determine the amount of the tax they had to pay, to the detriment of the Jews. He was like a 'brother and friend' of the Muslim officials. A man whose close relative had died would need a confirmation from him that the deceased actually had heirs (or else the authorities would confiscate his property); he would also mediate between the authorities and people who came from other countries, such as from the Maghrib. It is possible that the same man occupied the Gaon in a letter written some years later, to some unidentified person in Fustat. Wicked Jews are mentioned in the letter, and especially the informer, who squealed to the rulers. He says that he has already asked Ephraim b. Shemaria to assemble the Jewish notables and to go with them to the *amīrs*

[54] The change of governors: **142**, lines 11–12. The letter of the yeshiva: **420**, b, lines 34ff; c, lines 33ff. The case of Qayn: **99**, cf. Goitein, *Mediterranean Society*, II, 243; this Murajjā is evidently the father of the writer, the cadi Abū'l-Ma'ālī al-Musharraf ibn al-Murajjā, as stated above. The house of the Shuway' family: **117**. The appeal of Daniel b. Azariah: **351**. The fleeing of the prisoners mentioned by Solomon b. Judah in **156**, a, line 20, is something of a puzzle.

and try to influence them to act against the informer; he adds that Ephraim b. Shemaria in particular could be helpful here.[55]

[783] At times, when relations between the Rabbanites and the Karaites became tense, the authorities would be summoned to intervene in the internal affairs of the Jews in Jerusalem. A pretext for intervention was the custom of pronouncing a ban on the Karaites during the gathering on Hosha'na Rabba, the last day of the Feast of Tabernacles, on the Mount of Olives, when masses of Jewish pilgrims to Jerusalem gathered there. From the letters of Solomon b. Judah, one can see that he tried to abolish this custom for a number of reasons: firstly, he was evidently a man of peace; secondly, the authorities wanted this custom revoked; and thirdly, he was obliged on behalf of the yeshiva to the Tustari brothers, who were also Karaites, and who had aided the Jews of Jerusalem and the yeshiva to such a great extent. We shall return to this ban in the discussion on the Karaites below. Here I shall describe the intervention of the authorities in the event: after a number of the central figures of the yeshiva were insistent about proclaiming this ban on the Karaites, although they had been warned not to do so, the authorities intervened and those who had proclaimed the excommunication, the priestly brothers, Joseph and Elijah, sons of Solomon Gaon, were jailed. Leading the soldiers of the Fatimid unit who acted against the gathering during the pronouncement of the ban stood Mu'tazz al-Dawla, who was evidently governor of jund Filasṭīn at the time. The Gaon was then forced, as a counter-measure, to activate the Rabbanites in Fustat, and especially a number of prominent people of the 'Babylonian' congregation who had influence and access to the court. This he did through the mediation of Sahlān b. Abrham, leader of the Babylonians. Through the intercession of these personalities, the caliph and the wazīr issued special orders. The authorities presented very tough conditions, among them the demand that the Gaon stop the custom of excommunicating the Karaites on the Mount of Olives; that the Karaites would be permitted to open their own butcher shop in the Jewish market, which would not be under the supervision of the Rabbanites; that the Rabbanite butchers would not slaughter pregnant cows, in order that the Karaites would not have to use their meat (according to their interpretation of Lev., xxii:28 – 'ye shall not kill it and her young both in one day'); and that if Karaite holidays fell on different days from those of the Rabbanites, they would be permitted to open their shops during the Rabbanite holidays.

The caliph then issued two separate orders, one at the request of the Karaites and the other at the request of the Rabbanites, and it is clear that

[55] The matter of the Kitāmī: **28**. Daniel b. Azariah's letter: **381**. The informer: **84**, b, II, lines 18ff. On matters of inheritance of the sort mentioned here, see: Gil, *Documents*, 6f. The additional letter about the informer: **119**, lines 6–15.

this was planned to maintain a balance between the two sides and to display the ruler's impartiality. The order in favour of the Karaites has been preserved in its entirety and in its original. It is dated 11 Jumādā I AH 425, 3 April AD 1034, and is still preserved in the Karaite synagogue in Cairo. The *amīr al-juyūsh* (commander of the armies) to whom the caliph (al-Ẓāhir) addresses this order without mentioning his name, is undoubtedly Anūshtakīn al-Dizbirī, which goes to prove that in 1034 he was still holding his post in Palestine. As to its contents, it determines (1) that every sect will continue to observe its own religious precepts, without affecting or interfering with the other, (2) that tradesmen (or artisans) in each sect will decide for themselves on which holidays they shall work, (3) that no sect shall attack the other, (4) that anyone violating these rules will be severely punished, and (5) that the Karaite synagogue is the sole property of the Karaites and no one else may interfere with it. The caliph placed the responsibility for carrying out the terms of the order on the *amīr al-juyūsh* and the rest of the governors ruling Palestine.

Unlike the order in favour of the Karaites, the order in favour of the Rabbanites has not been preserved in the original, but a version is included in a copy in Hebrew script, which was evidently executed on the basis of a notebook of drafts in the archives of the Fatimid court. At the beginning there is a list of the Rabbanites' major demands from the caliph, according to which they ask that they and their leaders should not be hindered in their observance of the precepts and customs of their religion in Palestine ('in Jerusalem, Ramla, and the other cities'); they also request that those whose actions are not in accordance with accepted custom be restrained, meaning that there should be some authority and coercion over the Karaites. The reference here is undoubtedly to the yeshiva's authority over the Karaites, which was expressed in precisely those matters which the Karaites wished to be free of: kashrūt, holidays and the synagogue order (which may also have included matters of judgment and law). From the text of the caliph's order, it is obvious that these demands were not met. On the contrary, there is a repetition of what was said in the aforementioned order which sided with the Karaites, with the emphasis chiefly on non-disturbance and non-interference by either sect towards the other. At the same time, it says there that the authorities would not comply with the Karaites' request to banish the Rabbanite personalities from Jerusalem and from Filasṭīn (meaning Ramla), and this clearly has some connection with the priestly brothers, Joseph and Elijah, imprisoned in Damascus.[56]

[56] See **92**, a, lines 1–14, with a description of the quarrel and hints on the affair of the prisoners, until salvation arrived with the order of the king (that is, the caliph) and the *mishnē* (the wazīr); the Karaites had more influence on the authorities, because of their many 'princes and scribes and wealthy' (meaning mainly the Tustaris), see there lines 16–22. The intervention of Mu'tazz al-Dawla: **85**, lines 17–22 (which speaks about 'the

Calendrical matters

[784] Deciding the calendrical order was the exclusive prerogative of the Sanhedrin in ancient times, and although the order was undoubtedly recorded at a very early period and was available for study, the Sanhedrin, that is the yeshiva, guarded its symbolic right to pronounce the calendrical order and the holidays. The Targum of the Song of Solomon interprets 'thine eyes like the fishpools in Heshbon' (vii:4) as 'these are the scribes, who proclaim leap years and determine new years and new months at the gate of the Great Sanhedrin'. We find similar statements in Pirkei de-Rabbi Eliezer (ch. viii), dealing mainly with the exclusive right of Palestine to determine matters concerning the calendar, for 'nobody has the right to proclaim a leap year outside Palestine'. In the eleventh century, we still find 'ascending [the Mount of Olives] and proclaiming as was the custom, the order of God's holy days', as written by Solomon b. Judah in one of his

prince who rules the city', and about 'the ruler of the country, called Mu'tazz al-Dawla'). Also in another of his letters, **84**, lines 12–13, Solomon b. Judah notes the Karaites' advantage in money matters, thanks to their *nesī'īm*; evidently speaking of Hezekiah and Josiah, the sons of Solomon, cf. Mann, *Texts*, II, 47. And further: Solomon b. Judah knew well the Karaites' ability to obtain the intervention of the authorities, with the help of the Tustari brothers. He writes to Abraham b. Sahlān about the Tustaris' request that he should receive the Karaite *nāsī*, who is about to arrive in Jerusalem, cordially, and demands in this respect: 'and it is my desire that he should leave with a letter from the Kingdom, may God defend it, to give him strength against those who foment contention'. We do not know what quarrel he is speaking of, but perhaps he is referring to the Jerusalem Karaites, who have to be restrained with the help of the *nāsī* and the letter from the authorities; see **64**. In **90** Solomon b. Judah thanks Sahlān b. Abraham and the people of his congregation for having obtained the letters from the caliph and the wazīr concerning the prisoners in Damascus, that is, the priestly brothers Joseph and Elijah. The condition of their release, as they were informed by 'Adī b. Manasseh b. al-Qazzāz, was that they take upon themselves not to be engaged in appointing ḥavērīm nor hold any other office, and that they would not be permitted to enter Jerusalem or Ramla; and see *ibid.* also their demands from the Gaon. The matter of the shop in the Jewish market and the order of the holidays proves, it seems to me, that most of the Jews in Jerusalem were Rabbanites, and that, at any rate, the standing of the Karaites there was lower. The official order in favour of the Karaites was first edited by Gottheil, *Harkavy Festschrift*, 115–125, and then again by Stern, *Fāṭimid Decrees*, 23ff; Stern did not see the document but made certain amendments, according to his understanding and common sense. The date printed in both editions is not correct; in line 47 it is: *sana khams wa-'ishrūn*, the year 425, and not 415, as copied by Gottheil. This date indeed fell on a Wednesday, as stated in the document. Further, concerning Gottheil's edition and Stern's corrections: The order of lines 1–7 is as Gottheil copied them and not as Stern amended them; in line 32 it is written: *wltnth*; all the other corrections proposed by Stern are correct and substantiated by the excellent photograph at the Institute of Microfilmed Hebrew MSs. at the National Library in Jerusalem. The other order: **310**, and see references in the foreword there. Here and there, some other orders issued by the caliph on Jewish matters are mentioned, and we have already discussed above the matter of the orders of appointment of geonim. In the autumn of 1070, Abiathar ha-Kohen writes to the Fustat parnās 'Eli ha-Kohen b. Ḥayyim and asks him to put pressure on Abū Naṣr b. al-Faraj (we do not know who or what he was) to obtain the *sijill* for the Jerusalemites (*al-maqādisa*), see **547**, b, lines 15–16.

letters (in *ca.* 1030). From this letter, it is clearly indicated that the proclamation was made on Hosha'na Rabba, the seventh day of the Feast of Tabernacles, and not, as was customary according to ancient tradition, in the month of Av, as we find specifically in an early commentary to the Babylonian Talmud, Sanh. 12a: 'and when does one decide on it? In the month of Av, and this has been the custom until now that in the fifth month the leap year is determined'. In the sources on the dispute over the calendar in the tenth century, we encounter the Palestinian Gaon writing on 'the proclamation of the order of holidays by our scholars', and he blames the Babylonians 'and you gave up the proclamation on the Mount of Olives and threw it behind your backs', and Saadia Gaon notes that the Palestinian Gaon 'sent his son in the seventh month . . . and he came to Jerusalem and spread the word', and so on. From a letter of Abraham, Solomon b. Judah's son, written in about 1045, we learn that it was at first customary to announce the calendrical order (*al-'ibbūr*, the intercalation) in the synagogue in Jerusalem on New Year's Day, but for some reason, they could not 'go down to the synagogue' that year (undoubtedly due to some restrictive order). Abraham's house was not suitable for this purpose and therefore they gathered at the house of the *av-bēt-dīn*, who was Joseph ha-Kohen b. Solomon Gaon at that time.[57]

[57] See the matter of 'the handing over of the secret' of the calendrical order to the sages and the Sanhedrin in the Scroll of Abiathar, **559**, ix, lines 5f, and the note to line 6 there. The Targum to the Song of Solomon, see the Sperber edition, 138 (instead of *'wvdy* it should read *'wbry*, as in better MSs); cf. on this matter: Marx, *JQR*, NS 1(1910/1), 6ff. Solomon b. Judah: **85**, lines 17–18. Cf. Mann, *Texts*, I, 316, in the note, who quotes from the commentary to the Talmud, then found in TS Box F 8, but today its shelf-mark is: TS Box G 2, fs. 18–21; cf. also Assaf, *Teshūvōt* (1941/2), 147, 154. See the sources: Bornstein, *Sokolow Jubilee Volume*, 74f, 105; Guillaume, *JQR*, NS 5(1914/5), 546ff; contrary to Bornstein's opinion (based on the version which he had before him, in which it was written: in the fourth month), that one should count from Nisan and say that the fourth month was Tammuz there, was the view of Epstein, *Hagoren*, 5(1905/6), 138f, that one must count from Tishri and thus Tevet was meant, and that the purpose of the proclamation was merely to state the date of Passover; and following it also: Malter, *Saadia*, 81, n. 168. Recently an additional and important fragment from the *Sēfer ha-Mō'adīm* was published, see TS NS 194.92, ed. Fleischer, *Zion*, 49(1984), 379f; and see *ibid.*, p. 385. This fragment solved the riddle about the alleged proclamation of the calendrical order in the fourth month ('sent his son' – that is, Meir Gaon sent Aaron – 'in the fourth month') for we now have a more reliable version of what Saadia Gaon said, namely: in the seventh month, and the intention is to the proclamation on the accepted date, which is the last day of the Feast of Tabernacles, in the gathering on the Mount of Olives. The letter of Abraham son of the Gaon: **141**, line 3. In **27**, a letter from the year 1021 of the exilarch Hezekiah b. David concerning Elḥanan b. Shemaria, there is no trace of calendar matters (line 8), contrary to what was suggested by Kamenetzky, *REJ*, 55(1908), 49ff; and what he again claimed *ibid.*, 56 (the same year), 255, as Poznanski already understood, *ibid.*, 55, p. 248; cf. Abramson, *Ba-merkazim*, 110, n. 29. In the scroll of Abiathar, **559**, b, lines 19–21, it says that Elijah ha-Kohen Gaon 'went to Haifa to sanctify the year'; although it is not definitely stated there, one can assume that the reference is to the last day of the Feast of Tabernacles, 18 September 1082; the yeshiva was then in Tyre and its people came to Haifa in order that the ceremony take place on Palestinian soil.

[785] In view of the survival of the ancient tradition of having the Palestinian yeshiva proclaim the calendrical order, the famous affair of the dispute between this yeshiva and the Babylonian Jewish leadership on this issue seems very strange indeed. This is an interesting and raging chapter in the annals of the period. It was as if the *nesī'īm* of Palestine and the Babylonian exilarchs of Talmudic times had returned to life and were struggling with each other over the hegemony of the diaspora, with the proclamation of a leap year and the order of the holidays serving as significant symbolic expressions of supremacy.

For the most part, the rift centred on the question of when Passover was to be celebrated in AM 4682 – whether on Sunday, as the Palestinian yeshiva demanded, or on Tuesday, as the Babylonians preferred. It had been accepted that the Gaon Aaron b. Meir stood at the head of the Palestinians in the quarrel. As will become apparent, the Palestinian Gaon at that time was his father, Meir, but Aaron (whom the sources generally call Ben Meir) was the head spokesman in this affair. Naturally, the communities in Palestine itself sided with the yeshiva, but evidently the communities in Egypt did as well. It should be noted that this rift took place during the renewal of Abbasid rule in Palestine (905–935), between that of the Ṭūlūnids and the Ikhshīdids. Undoubtedly this also meant a significant improvement in the connections between Palestine and Babylonia, and to a certain extent, a larger degree of Palestinian dependence on Babylonia in all their dealings with the central authorities. In order to understand the background, one should also bear in mind that on the eve of this rift, Babylonia itself was in the midst of an internal quarrel, with the yeshiva of Pumbedita divided between the disciples of Mevassēr and those of Kohen Ṣedeq, the rival Gaon, who was supported by the exilarch David b. Zakkai. In addition, one must remember that Saadia was still a newcomer to Babylonia, after a journey from Egypt of more than six years, most of which he evidently spent in Tiberias. Another detail to bear in mind is that the rupture took place one or two generations after the first settlement of Karaites in Jerusalem. They were then a young sect, eager to win over people, and it is well known that in calendrical matters, they would not accept Rabbanite computation, but continued to determine the beginning of the month according to the actual appearance of the new moon, and to decide on the leap year according to the *āvīv*, the ripening of the grain, in Palestine.[58]

[58] Most of the sources dealing with the dispute were collected and edited by Bornstein in his comprehensive article on the subject, in the *Sokolow Jubilee Volume*, 19–189 (and also published separately). Added to it: Hirschfeld, *JQR*, 16(1903/4), 295ff; Guillaume (see previous note); Adler, *REJ*, 67(1914), 44ff; Bornstein returned to the subject in another article, in *Hatequfa*, 14–15:321: 16:228, 1921/2; and see in Bornstein references to earlier research, and particularly in *Sokolow Jubilee Volume*, 52–58.

[786] In the summer of AM 4681 (AD 921), Saadia learned of the Palestinian Gaon's intention to celebrate the Passover of AM 4682 on Sunday (by announcing that Marheshwan and Kislev of AM 4681 were both months of twenty-nine days). He was then in Aleppo, *en route* to Iraq. He left his native Egypt not later than AD 915, for he mentions in his letter, in which he writes about the seeds of the quarrel which broke out in AD 921 (Kislev 1233 Sel.), that it was six and a half years since he last had news from Egypt. Mann even assumed that the onset of the quarrel was a personal confrontation between Ben Meir and Saadia during the latter's stay in Palestine. A year and a half later Saadia writes from Baghdad (his third letter) and reproaches the people of Fustat who were drawn on by the Palestinian Gaon, that is, they celebrated Passover on Sunday, and he demands that they correct their erroneous way.

Even before the discovery of documents in the Geniza dealing with the rift, the matter was known from the letter of rebuke written by the Karaite Sahl ha-Kohen b. Maṣlīaḥ, a contemporary of Saadia Gaon. In the letter, he hints that the cause of the rift was Saadia Gaon (*ha-Pītōmī* – hinting at the Fayyūm in Egypt, the region where Saadia was born – 'he who enticed people'; there is a pun on the word 'enticed', *pittā*, which in Hebrew sounds close to Pītōm). He adds that just as there were those in Palestine who followed the Babylonians, in Babylonia ('in the land of Shin'ār'), there were those who followed the people of Palestine. Another ancient source which recorded the dispute is the chronicle of the Syrian Elias of Nisibis, who wrote in the first half of the eleventh century. Writing of the year Sel. 1233 (AD 921/2), he reports that 'a division fell between the Jews of the West and the Jews of the East over the computation of their holidays; the Jews of the West celebrated their New Year on Tuesday while those of the East on Thursday'. The surprising fact is that our two major sources of information on Babylonian Jewry of the tenth century – the account of Nathan the Babylonian and the letter of Sherira Gaon – say nothing at all about this quarrel between Babylonia and Palestine.[59]

[787] The fact that the Babylonians prevailed in the long run proves that their authority was greater than that of the Palestinian geonim; and leaves

59 The first letter of Saadia Gaon, see Bornstein, *Sokolow Jubilee Volume*, 81ff, and see the facsimile of part of it, in Halper, *Hatequfa*, 20(1922/3), 279; the address (written in Arabic letters) tells us that the letter was sent to Abū'l-Faraj Salīm, Abū Isḥaq Abraham, Abū Sahl 'Ezra, by Sa'īd b. Yūsuf Ra's al-kull (*rōsh kallā*), to Qaṣr al-Sham' ('the candles fortress') in Fustat, to the shop (*dukkān*) of 'Ali b. Salīm; cf. Goitein, *Mediterranean Society*, I, 444, n. 5; it seems that Salīm is none other than Rabbānā Shelāmā in the third letter of Saadia Gaon, see: Hirschfeld, *JQR*, 16(1904), 295ff at the end, and Bornstein, *Hatequfa*, 16(1921/2), 246f. This letter was written on 11 Tevet 1233 Sel., 3 January AD 923, that is, after the event. See the letter of rebuke in Pinsker, *Liqqūṭē qadmōniyōt*, II, 36; see Elias of Nisibis: Baethgen, 84 and in *CSCO*, 204ff. Adler, *JQR*, 2(1890), 106, called attention to it, but there was no reaction to his remarks at that time for the many sources in the Geniza were

no doubt that this was largely due to the personality of Saadia, even before he was the Gaon of Sura. This can be seen from the offensive remarks in the Palestinian Gaon's letters, aimed mainly at Saadia: 'Sa'īd b. Yūsuf al-Dilāṣī' (he came of a locality called Dilāẓ in the Fayyūm), and also against the two other protagonists in the quarrel, the exilarch David (*Da'ūd*) b. Zakkai, and the head of the Pumbedita yeshiva, Kohen Ṣedeq (the Palestinian Gaon calls him: 'Kohen'). Of Saadia, he writes: 'the son of Fayyūmī of Dilāṣ, of whom it has been clearly revealed to us by reliable witnesses who attested that his father would strike with the hammer as an idolater in the Land of Egypt and eat non-kosher food and was driven from Egypt and died in Jaffa'. He also calls Saadia a Canaanite, among other things. In retaliation, we encounter pejorative names being aimed at the Palestinian Gaon Meir and his son: he is called 'the malignant' (*mam'īr*, a pun on his name, Meir); 'the darkener' (as against Meir, which means 'the one who lightens'); he is said to have tried to divert Israel 'from the way of light to that of darkness', and so on.

There is no point in going into the details of the dispute, that is, to probe into the basis of the Palestinian arguments, at this juncture. Bornstein thought that they were based on an ancient system of computation which differed from that of the Babylonians. Cassuto, who was at variance with him on a number of details and who attempted to define precisely the difference between the two systems, also admitted that basically the Palestinians computed the calendar according to a system of their own. He tried to prove that since a stable method of computing the calendar had been agreed upon by both the Babylonians and the Palestinians, there had never been any difference between the two parties, except in that year, AM 4682.[60]

[788] In order to understand the historical development of the prerogative of fixing the calendar, it is important to study the document

still not known then. See the versions of Sahl b. Maṣlīaḥ and Elias of Nisibis also in Bornstein, *Sokolow Jubilee Volume*, 21; *idem*, *Hatequfa*, 16(1921/2), 237.

[60] See the first letter of the Palestinian Gaon in Bornstein, *Sokolow Jubilee Volume*, 64, according to a Cambridge manuscript (see Shaked, 3*); see ENA 2556, f. 2, edited by Adler, *REJ*, 67(1914), 44f, which contains a more reliable version, which includes in the opening the words *av-bēt-dīn* (of the Palestinian yeshiva), who is Isaac; cf. Bornstein, *Hatequfa*, 16(1921/2), 264f; the word *palhedrīn* which Bornstein had difficulties with, is found in the Palestinian Talmud, see in the dictionaries (see also *parhedrin*); the other letter of the Palestinian Gaon: Bornstein, *Sokolow Jubilee Volume*, 104; Guillaume, *JQR*, NS, 5 (1914/5), 552. The slander and ugly words about Meir Gaon and his son: in the remnants of the *Sēfer ha-mō'adīm* of Saadia Gaon, Bornstein, *ibid.*, 78, and the additional fragment, of an anonymous Babylonian, *ibid.*, 101. The expressions used by the parties in the quarrel are very sharp; but obviously their slander is not to be taken seriously. Bornstein especially expressed his view of the nature of the dispute in the aforementioned article in *Hatequfa* in its two parts; see the view of Cassuto, *Saadya Memorial Volume*, 333ff, based on fragments from the midrash *Sekhel Ṭōv*.

from the Geniza found by Mann, and edited almost simultaneously by him and by Bornstein. It is the exilarch's letter from the year 1147 Sel., that is, AM 4595, or AD 835. In this document, the exilarch attributes the prerogative of the calendar to the *rōsh ha-ḥavūrā* and people of the *ḥavūrā* ('we rely on them forever, so that Israel shall not be divided into sections; I and the heads of the yeshivot and the scholars and all of Israel rely on the proclaiming of the leap year as decided by the *ḥavērīm*'). It is clear that he is speaking of the Palestinian yeshiva. On the other hand, one of the Babylonians writes at the time of the dispute on the calendar, that at first they indeed relied on Palestine, 'but many years ago some scholars went from Babylonia to Palestine and learned the secret of the intercalation from the sages of Palestine . . . and for many years now, the Babylonians decide on the order of the months themselves . . . and behold in the Babylonian yeshivot there are many elders who have reached the age of eighty . . . and none of them remember that the Babylonians ever needed to ask . . . Palestine', and so on.

On the basis of this, Mann has shown that a development took place between two chronological extremes: the year 835, in which the exilarch's letter speaking of complete obedience to the Palestinian yeshiva was written, and the year 921, some eighty-five years later, when the rift over the calendar broke out. As stated in the exilarch's letter, the study and inquiry on the part of the Babylonians into the matter of the calendar, which eventually led to their independence of Palestine, happened long before the dispute, for even men in their eighties no longer remembered that they ever had to resort to the computation of the Palestinians; hence one may assume that this change occurred shortly after 835.[61]

[789] Without going into the very core of the dispute, as I have said, we may assume that the Palestinian Gaon acted with sincerity, according to his own computations, and also with the strong desire to guard the hallowed prerogative of the Palestinian yeshiva to determine the calendrical order and to proclaim it in public on the Mount of Olives to all the communities in Palestine and the diaspora. At the same time, one should note some other facts which are hinted at, rather than stated explicitly, in the sources at our disposal. The Palestinian Gaon's major claim was that the leap year could not be decided on abroad, and he based this on a specific Talmudic law. True, in the continuation, he presented in detail the relevant arguments, and chiefly the matter of the 642 parts (*ḥalāqīm*) that

[61] The exilarch's letter: TS 8 G 7, f. 1, in Mann, *Jews*, II, 41f, see the discussion *ibid.*, I, 53; cf. Bornstein, *Hatequfa*, 14–15(1921/2), 349ff. See the version of the Babylonians: Bornstein, *Sokolow Jubilee Volume*, 88f; Guillaume, *JQR*, NS 5(1914/5), 547. Bornstein describes what happened as if this were a meeting, a sort of convention of Babylonians and Palestinians. Mann assumed that the exilarch who wrote the letter was David b. Judah, whose dispute with his rival Daniel, is mentioned by Sherira Gaon in his letter. I have

constituted the difference between his calculations and those of the Babylonians. However, in principle, the dispute became a distinct struggle over the hegemony of the communities, and this is further verified by the fact that the Babylonians were even considering applying to the authorities and requesting their intervention, but ultimately did not dare to do so ('they did not make up their minds to obtain letters from the king to have him removed'). They also ascribed to the Palestine Gaon hidden intentions which we can hardly understand today. They understood, they write, 'why and wherefore he acted as he did'. They also emphasise that what was done stemmed from malicious intentions ('he behaved maliciously'), and from foolish erring partisanship. On the other hand, we hear the not very relevant comments of the Palestinian Gaon; according to him the Babylonians claimed 'you became a joke ... among the *mīnīm*' (the sectarians). Using a sort of oath, the Palestinian Gaon calls on God 'to take revenge on whoever wants the help of the enemies'. This posture of self-defence is also evident in what he says in the continuation, about the many calamities endured by the family of the geonim in Palestine (it emerges), on 'R. Mūsā [Moses] who was killed in the *'azārā* [the synagogue?] at the hand of 'Anan's progeny'; on his forefathers 'R. Meir and R. Moses, whom the enemies tried to kill a number of times'; and he himself, the writer, who suffered 'many terrible troubles and imprisonment and the torture of manacles and beating to the point of agony ... at the hands of the hateful sons of 'Anan'. In conclusion, there are again comments that seem to be made in his own defence, their meaning termed in a rather curious Hebrew: 'we did not rely on those enemies you mention; we only trusted in God'. It is quite certain that those sons of 'Anan, the enemies, are the *nesī'īm* of the family of 'Anan, who started to collaborate with the Karaites at that time, and the writer is defending himself against the accusation that he acted in accord with them. On this point, however, we are not obliged to believe him. It is possible that the Babylonians had information on the subject and that the accusations were not unfounded. We may assume that the Palestinian Gaon was interested in a compromise with the Karaites and would have wanted to celebrate Passover with them, specifically on Sunday.

One should also bear in mind that there was a strong faction among the Babylonians who supported the Palestinians, as Sahl b. Maṣlīaḥ bears out, and as we have already seen. This can also be seen in the first letter of the Palestinian Gaon, from the remarks he directs at the faction of Mevassēr Gaon, the rival of Kohen Ṣedeq in Pumbedita. Mevassēr, however, did not live up to expectations and went over to the remainder of the Babylo-

described this above (sec. 732) and we have seen the information of Dionysius of Tel Maḥrē that David enjoyed the support of the Palestinians ('the Tiberians').

nians, as one can see from the second letter of the Palestinian Gaon. Nevertheless, this did not restore the unity of the yeshiva of Pumbedita, and Mevassēr Gaon set up a separate yeshiva until his death, in Kislev Sel. 1237 or 1234, that is, AD 925 or 922. Aaron b. ʿAmram, the outstanding representative of the Jewish financiers of Baghdad, remained loyal to the Palestinian stand to the very end, and the Gaon calls him in his letter 'Saviour of the generation, who would not be led to leave the laws of God'. These two points, the possible surreptitious connection with the Karaites and the obvious connection with the Baghdadi bankers, maintained by the Palestinian yeshiva, cannot be ignored when considering the dispute over the calendar which caused a storm among the Jewish communities in the East and the West.[62]

Yeshiva and community

[790] In all the sources at our disposal, there is no hint of rebellion against the central body, the yeshiva. We are aware that competition existed between the aforementioned central bodies, and during the period under discussion, much of the rivalry was apparently between the yeshiva of Pumbedita and that of Palestine. But we cannot find evidence of any community's ambition to achieve independence, just as there is no sign of an attempt to establish another yeshiva; although there are obscure indications that there were two yeshivot in Palestine at one time, this may have been caused by rivalry between personalities of the yeshiva and by no means derived from a desire for independence on the part of any community.

The status of uncontested leadership was notably expressed in the character of the letters from the yeshiva. The opening phrases of a letter usually contained florid expressions and certain established courtesies, as if part of a ceremony. Opening eloquences with which a certain Eleazar ha-Dayyān graced his letters to the congregation in Fustat have been preserved in letters from the end of the tenth century or the beginning of the eleventh. One introductory section included in my collection is directed to: 'all the communities of Israel in Palestine and in its fortresses, its towns and villages . . . which have remained in Palestine and to those in the land of Egypt calling themselves Palestinians' and so on, and after-

62 A leap year cannot be proclaimed abroad: see in Bornstein, *Sokolow Jubilee Volume*, 64. Calculations of the 642 parts: *ibid.*, 65f, 'The king's letters', *ibid.*, 79; and see there also the matter of the hidden motives. Malice: *ibid.*, 102f. Derision among the *mīnīm*: *ibid.*, 105; Guillaume, *JQR*, NS 5(1914/5), 552; the calamities which befell the Gaon's family: Bornstein, *ibid.*, 106f; Guillaume, *ibid.*, 554f. The letters of the Palestinian Gaon: the first, Bornstein, *ibid.*, 59f; the second: 104ff; Guillaume, *ibid.*, 552ff. These matters were amply clarified by Mann, *Tarbiz*, 5(1932/3), 150–156. Mevassēr: Sherira Gaon's Letter (Lewin ed.), 120, and the version there.

wards we find the people of the community addressed according to their rank: (1) their sages and learned (that is, scholars and judges), (2) cantors, (3) parnāsīm, (4) teachers, and (5) the rest of God's people, great and small. We find Josiah Gaon writing to the 'holy communities living under the canopy of Egypt (Fustat). Solomon b. Judah also lists people according to categories: the *ḥavērīm*, the *berūrīm* (elect), the judges, the scribes, the treasurers (parnāsīm). People of the community would write in a similar vein, when writing to a community in another locality; firstly *he-ḥāvēr*, after that the sages and scholars, that is, the learned in the law who participate in the law courts, the parnāsīm and trustees who are engaged in the welfare of the poor, and then the remainder of the population. Abraham b. David ibn Sughmār, however, writes to the Nagid of Qayrawān, on behalf of those 'who pray in the great accomplished synagogue in Fustat and adhere forever to the Great Sanhedrin'.

A letter from the yeshiva was not a trivial matter. It was anxiously anticipated and had considerable influence on the daily life of the community. A typical note was that sent by Sahlān b. Abraham, leader of the Babylonians in Fustat, to Aaron the cantor *ha-mumḥē* b. Ephraim, in which he informs him that a certain physician has arrived from Jerusalem, bearing letters from the Gaon to people in Fustat. He asks him to drop everything and go to the physician in order to deliver the letters to their addresses.

Apart from the yeshiva's official letters, generally written by the Gaon himself or by his son or scribe, but mostly bearing the signature of the Gaon, there were also letters of another nature, in general of a factional character or based on private hidden connections, calling for personal favours, between personalities of the yeshiva and leaders of the local community. A good example of this is a letter of Joseph ha-Kohen b. Solomon Gaon, writing in about 1050, to Ephraim b. Shemaria, summing up the events in the yeshiva. It is evident that this was one of a series of letters and that they were written secretly. Such unofficial letters were sometimes written by the communities as well. For instance, there are two anonymous letters, evidently from Aleppo, containing endless grievances and intrigues. The writer complains that the Gaon only pays attention to those who slander him but takes no notice of him. He describes his own devotion, whether by day or night, to the needs of the community, for which he receives no payment. He has now moved to a new location, and is about to go to Kalnē (Raqqa) in order to pacify people quarrelling over the appointment of a new dayyān.[63]

[63] The remarks of Hirschberg (*History*, 324f), that there were yeshivot in North Africa headed by Jacob b. Nissim, a yeshiva in Qayrawān, or the yeshiva of R. Ḥūshī'ēl (p. 322), lack any foundation. It would not have occurred to anyone to set up another yeshiva apart

[791] To what extent the communal office-holder, even in a large community such as Fustat, was dependent on the Gaon's decisions, one can see by Daniel b. Azariah's resolute and unambivalent statement to his friend and chief supporter, Abraham ha-Kohen b. Isaac ibn Furāt, that the local dayyān, 'Eli he-ḥāvēr ha-me'ullē b. 'Amram, would be Abraham's subordinate, and might not take on the responsibility for any communal matter unless ordered to do so by Abraham. It is very likely, however, that much depended on the Gaon's personal style and the awe in which he was held by the public. In this respect, it seems that the Gaon who succeeded Daniel, Elijah ha-Kohen, differed from him, for we find that the emissary who carried his letters to the Damascus region, among them a long sheet of parchment which was evidently meant to be read to the public, did not deliver them to their addressees, but instead, as Abiathar, the son of the Gaon writes, kept them for one to three years.[64]

[792] As we have seen, making public appointments was the prerogative of the Gaon, and we encounter a number of actual instances of this. The local leader was the man in charge on behalf of the yeshiva. In Arabic, he was called the *muqaddam*, meaning, the appointee. Actually, in the documents of the period under discussion, this term does not have a fixed and established definition, as we find in Christian Spain. A man who is a ḥāvēr and dayyān could also be called simply *muqaddam*, when Arabic was being written or spoken, just as in a Hebrew letter, he would be called

from the three ancient yeshivot. Similarly, the comments of Cohen, *Self-Government*, 84, are rather strange; after he himself elaborated in detail on the political and military causes leading to the decline of security in Palestine, which forced the yeshiva to leave Jerusalem, he still claims that the formation of the office of the Nagid in Egypt was the result of an *internal* (his emphasis) process within the Jewish population in Egypt. The fact is that this community never attempted to free themselves of the authority of any central body, although there were Jews who transferred their loyalty from the Palestinian Gaon to the Babylonian, or to the exilarch. The Nagid himself, as we shall see below, was appointed by the Palestinian Gaon. And finally, that same yeshiva Ge'ōn Ya'aqōv, which wandered from Tyre and Damascus to Egypt, again occupied a central role in the leadership of the Jews in Egypt in the first half of the twelfth century, during Maṣlīaḥ Gaon's day. The eloquence of Eleazar the dayyān: TS 10 J 24, f. 9; see the opening fragment, **571**; see BM Or 5544, f. 1, b; and also BM Or 5542, f. 1. Josiah: **40**. Solomon b. Judah: **71**. See the letter from Tyre to Aleppo: **273**. To the Nagid: **191**, line 6. Sahlān: **340**. Joseph ha-Kohen: **409**. The unknown man from Aleppo: **286**, **287**. On the subject of Raqqa, see: Mann, *Jews*, I, 245, n. 1, who quotes Benjamin of Tudela (Adler ed., 33); cf. Le Strange, *Lands*, 101f; Ashtor, *Tōledōt*, II, 391, finds in **286** proof that many of the ḥavērīm and dayyānīm did not work for payment; the dayyān about to be appointed in Raqqa was a man from Lādhiqiyya, and he may be 'Eli the cantor b. Joshua al-Lādhiqī, who was 'permanently' (*qāvū'a*) in Raqqa, see: **198**.

[64] Daniel b. Azariah, see **354**, margin. The matter of Elijah Gaon's letters: **547**; the matter of dispatching letters was at times a difficult and complex problem; at the beginning of the eleventh century, the yeshiva (then in Tyre) sent its letters to Egypt via Ascalon, and in the opposite direction as well, probably because of the absence of direct sea links between Tyre and Egypt, while the overland connection was naturally cut off due to the Crusaders' domination of the country.

ha-memunnē (the appointee), as indeed Solomon ha-Kohen Gaon called Ephraim b. Shemaria in 1025, in a letter couched in flowery terms, saying that he 'was the *memunnē* to judge in matters of inheritance and testaments, and supporting those in need because of their poverty and humiliation'. It is clear that in a small locality, where there was no learned scholar worthy of being a judge, the yeshiva would appoint someone to be responsible for public affairs, and he was the *memunnē*, that is, *al-muqaddam*. Such a person would consider himself as having been appointed by the nation. The caliph's order which tried to rectify the relationship between the Rabbanites and the Karaites also speaks (in 1034) of *muqaddamī al-rabbāniyīn* that is, the appointees of the Rabbanites, meaning people of the calibre of Joseph and Elijah ha-Kohen, the sons of Solomon Gaon. At about the same time, a letter from Fustat written by Ghālib ha-Kohen b. Moses, the son-in-law of Ephraim b. Shemaria, describes how a certain Abraham (perhaps b. David ibn Sughmār) defends himself in the face of accusations that he slandered those appointed over the Jews (*muqaddamī al-umma*). The Gaon himself (evidently Solomon b. Judah) was described in the caliph's order which defined his prerogatives, as being the person 'appointed over all the Jews'. In 1025 Yefet b. David was declared 'appointee over the community' in matters of ritual slaughtering – *muqaddam lil-jamā'a*. A supporter of Nathan b. Abraham, writing in 1042 to Solomon b. Judah, styles himself as a public servant, 'appointed by the nation' (the *umma*).[65]

[793] There is no doubt that the appointment of the local ḥāvēr was a step of enormous significance and portentious influence within the local community. The ḥāvēr appointed by the Gaon was due to be the focal point for all aspects of communal life for many years. Ephraim b. Shemaria, leader of the Fustat community, was a typical example. We find details relating to his appointment and status in a draft of the record of a meeting of the 'Palestinian' elders of the city, written on 7 July 1028, in which they express their trust in Ephraim and promise him their backing. One also learns from that document that he was first appointed by Shemaiah Gaon,

[65] There are no grounds for the view of Cohen, *Self-Government*, 119, that *muqaddam* is a title that replaced the title ḥāvēr which was held by the local leaders of the communities, just as it is also incorrect that it was first used during David b. Daniel's time, that is, at the end of the eleventh century, as one can see by the Hebrew Index. Solomon ha-Kohen's letter: **49**, lines 7–8. See the caliph's order, **310**, line 23. The letter from Fustat: **177**, line 14. Another of the caliph's orders, **311**, lines 11–12. Yefet: **319**, line 8. The supporter of Nathan: **198**, lines 15–16. See other views of the *muqaddam*: Ashtor, *Zion*, 30 (1964/5), 138–141 ('supervisor of public affairs, especially the religious services'); the opinion of Goitein, *Mediterranean Society*, II, 68–75, is similar to that stated here, but he would emphasise the characteristics and specific duties attached to the bearers of this name, while as far as I understand it, this was merely a neutral term, like 'head' or 'leader'. One can see that they did not have permanent names for local leaders in localities with small communities where there was no local ḥāvēr. We encounter the title 'trustee of the grand court' in a letter from the middle of the eleventh century written by Elijah ha-Kohen b. Solomon Gaon to an

apparently at the beginning of the century, as *bēt-dīn*, that is, not as yet a ḥāvēr. Josiah Gaon, at the outset of 1025, appointed him ḥāvēr, and he was appointed again by his successor Solomon ha-Kohen b. Joseph and his *av-bēt-dīn* Zadok ha-Levi b. Levi (1025). These things were written in the days of Solomon b. Judah, and we know that he vigilantly guarded Ephraim's status. He also strongly objected to the appointment of another ḥāvēr in Fustat, as proposed by the *av-bēt-dīn* (undoubtedly Zadok ha-Levi b. Levi); and we are also aware of the fact that Solomon b. Judah's constant and uncompromising support of Ephraim b. Shemaria aroused considerable resentment among the latter's rivals in Fustat, for he wrote to Ephraim b. Shemaria about it himself. 'Most of the community' in Fustat were about to complain to the authorities about the Gaon for having granted the rights of leadership and judge to Ephraim (*hirshā*, that is, 'granted the *rāshūt*', the authority). There were also those who claimed that his motives in supporting Ephraim were materialistic, because of 'gifts and largesse'.

The appointments of ḥāvērīm were generally made in Tishri, during the congregation of pilgrims in Jerusalem, in order to accord them a festive and public character. Abraham, son of the Gaon, mentions in a letter the proclamation of ḥāvērīm on Rōsh ha-shana. A certain Damascene named Yaḥyā was appointed the 'seventh', and other appointments were also announced there on the sabbath after Rōsh ha-shana.

In addition to the titles of real content, such as ḥāvēr, dayyān, mumḥē, which as we can assume had a direct connection with the local courts of law, the yeshiva also had in store some honorary names which it would confer on those whom they considered worthy of the honour, unrelated to the person's knowledge of the law or his scholarship with regard to the Torah. Thus, for instance, Solomon b. Judah calls the Fustat parnās Abraham b. Mevassēr '*segūl* (the distinguished) of the community of Zoan' (Fustat). This was not a casual or unique instance of applying this name, but rather a title bestowed officially, evidently in a letter from the Gaon, or from the *av-bēt-dīn*, read aloud in the synagogue in Fustat. It was precisely on this matter that Solomon b. Nethanel, the moneychanger of Fustat, wrote to the *av-bēt-dīn* Zadok ha-Levi b. Levi. The additional by-name given to Abraham b. Mevassēr by the *av-bēt-dīn*, he writes, made quite an impression in Fustat, and made both congregations happy (that is, the 'Babylonians' as well), for Abraham and his brother (Jacob b. Mevassēr, who was also a parnās in Fustat) were known and famous for their God-fearing piety.

The yeshiva frequently displayed personal and devoted interest in those

unknown community; he did not even remember the name of that 'trustee', but only that of his father – Sheraia, whom he calls 'the elder of our generation', see **419**.

who supported it abroad and to whom it had granted honourable titles; this is evident in a number of letters written by the yeshiva to various personalities, particularly in Fustat. Just as we encountered Solomon b. Judah stoutly supporting Ephraim b. Shemaria, we find Daniel b. Azariah backing 'Eli b. 'Amram, Ephraim's successor, despite the rancour which at first existed between them. Daniel b. Azariah writes to him, evidently in the early stages of his role as Gaon, that he intends to patiently await the time when opposition to him will subside. He expects the support of 'Eli b. 'Amram, *he-ḥāvēr ha-me'ullē*, and even promises him payment in very picturesque terms: 'your efforts shall not be in vain . . . we have not forgotten nor shall we forget, we have not abandoned nor shall we abandon, Heaven forbid; but will pay with the help of God, if He grants us life, in exchange for every *perūṭā*, a *sheqel*, and in exchange for a *sheqel*, several *mānīm*'. As 'Eli evidently expressed in his letters some fear lest he lose the affection of the public, the Gaon promises him to support him by his letters, 'and whoever dares to be impertinent, shall be the target of sharp arrows'.[66]

[794] Characteristic evidence of the manner of leadership of the local

[66] The draft of the record: **324**, lines 12–14; *bēt-dīn* means here *av-bēt-dīn*. See a somewhat different view of the document: Goitein, *Shalem*, 1(1973/4), 16 (= *ha-Yishuv*, 83f); the handwriting is that of Ephraim b. Shemaria, not of Yefet b. David. Similar in subject to this document is **325**; it is a sort of agreement between the congregation and Ephraim b. Shemaria, certainly written at the same time; see on this below. Solomon b. Judah and the matter of the additional ḥāvēr: **86**; his letter to Abraham ha-Kohen is also related to this matter: **100**, which contains his gratitude for Abraham's support for Ephraim b. Shemaria. See on this matter: Mann, *Jews*, I, 129, who here mistakenly involves the *nāsī*; these events took place between the yeshiva and the local community, with no other factor involved. The resentment in Fustat: **67**; cf. Goitein, *Mediterranean Society*, II, 405. The proclamation of ḥavērīm: **141**; it seems that the title 'the seventh' was mainly a title of honour. The expression *al-ḥavērīm al-qevū'īm* ('the permanent ones') *be-ashqelōn* found in the copy of a marriage deed, **594**, a, line 9, is quite interesting. There were undoubtedly in Ascalon at the time (the beginning of 1100, the winter immediately following the conquest of Jerusalem by the Crusaders) also ḥavērīm who were not local people, but from among the refugees. '*Segūl* (*sāgūl*) of the community of Zoan': **139**. Between Abraham b. Mevassēr and Zadok ha-Levi b. Levi there existed a special relationship, as is shown in Zadok's letter to this Abraham, TS 8 J 3 (edited by Schechter, *Saadyana*, 147f); see what Abraham son of the Gaon writes him in **87**, lines 5–6: 'our Master Abraham, the trustee, to whom the *av* of the yeshiva has conferred the title '*segūl* of the community of Zoan'; that is, the title was apparently granted him by the *av-bēt-dīn*. The letter of Solomon b. Nethanel: **215**. This family of parnāsīm stemmed from Fās and was very active in congregation affairs. Their father Mevassēr (Bishr) was called al-Arjawānī, that is, he traded in purple cloth. Abraham son of the Gaon asks for their help in the aforementioned letter in connection with his anticipated visit to Fustat: apart from the two brothers, Ḥalfon b. Jacob b. Mevassēr is also mentioned. See the Hebrew Index and cf. Gil, *Documents*, 143, n. 28. See a further list of names and titles of the yeshivot, such as 'the beloved of the yeshiva', 'the choice of the yeshiva', 'the cherished pride of the yeshiva', 'the joy of the yeshiva', etc. in Mann, *Jews*, I, 278. At times, they would shorten the titles and call someone *al-māsōs* or *al-ḥemdat*, etc., instances which can be found in my Geniza collection. The letter of Daniel b. Azariah: **368**.

community as it was accepted in those days can be found in a preserved fragment of the regulations (*takkānōt*) laid down by the 'community of Rabbanites living in Fustat' during Ephraim b. Shemaria's time, which form a sort of covenant set down between the forum of leaders and Ephraim b. Shemaria, as follows: (1) they take upon themselves the responsibility to see to all public matters, (2) they will observe the precepts, (3) ten of them will sit with Ephraim b. Shemaria in court and help him to manage public affairs, (4) their special responsibility will be in fulfilling the requirements of the Gaon and the people of his yeshiva, the yeshiva of Jerusalem, (5) Ephraim b. Shemaria promises to consult them on all matters about which there is no definite law, and (6) together with him, they shall deal with the income from the ritual slaughtering. It seems that a section is missing in the continuation, in which decisions were evidently made with regard to the money of the *heqdēsh* in Fustat. We know that this institution of the pious foundations was the chief economic basis for communal activities, which supplied the needs of the synagogue, cared for the sick and the poor, paid for public offices, hosted strangers who happened to arrive in the city, ransomed captives, and so on.

One should also mention the direct contact existing between the communities in an emergency – contact which sometimes touched on people and matters at a great distance from one another, such as the letter of Samuel b. Moses of Tyre to Ephraim b. Shemaria, in which he asks him to proclaim in the synagogues the case of Nā'ima the daughter of Moses the cantor b. Ḥusayn al-Dulūkī. This woman asks for the return of property (debts and deposits) which belonged to her son-in-law Moses b. Ṣemaḥ al-Azraq (*ha-qōsēm*, astrologer) who died some years previously, and to her father Moses b. Ḥusayn. The money should be sent with a certain b. 'Amram Ajīsī, of Āmid ('the Āmidī' – Āmid was the capital of the Diyār Bakr region of northern Mesopotamia) or with David ha-Levi b. Isaac. If the debtors should not come forward of their own accord, they would be excommunicated.[67]

Communal leaders in close contact with the yeshiva

[795] Naturally, the list of people mentioned in letters of the yeshiva or in the documents in my collection is a very long one. Here I shall merely

[67] See the regulations of Fustat: **325**; cf. Goitein, *Mediterranean Society*, II, 58; the subject of the heqdēsh is dealt with extensively in my book (Gil, *Documents*); see in my collection **229** (the renting of a ruined building belonging to 'the people of the great synagogue in the city of Ramla'), **592** (renting of a house of the heqdēsh in Ascalon), **273** (a record of evidence from Tyre concerning the dedication of a house to the synagogue in Aleppo). The claim of Nā'ima, see: **278**; cf. Goitein, *Mediterranean Society*, II, 545, n. 37, and see n. 297 above. Āmid, see Le Strange, *Lands*, 108–111.

tarry over the few most outstanding among them. In chronological order, I shall begin with Shemaria b. Elḥanan. The information about him and his son Elḥanan, available in the Geniza, has been the subject of extensive discussion by some of the most important scholars – Mann, Abramson and Goitein. The father, Shemaria b. Elḥanan, was one of the four in the famous story of the four captives in Abraham ibn Da'ūd's Book of Tradition. He was in contact with the Pumbedita yeshiva and possibly stayed there for some time. There is no doubt that he was the leader of the 'Babylonians' in Fustat and the recipient of honorary titles from the Babylonian yeshiva, such as 'the head rav', 'the head' and 'the great of the yeshiva'. He is mentioned a number of times in the Geniza documents in my collection. In around 1010, Samuel 'the third' b. Hosha'na of Jerusalem writes to him from Jerusalem, recommending Nathan b. Abraham b. Saul, who was to become *av-bēt-dīn* of the yeshiva and Solomon b. Judah's rival. Nathan is travelling to the Maghrib on matters relating to an inheritance from his father and Shemaria is asked to look after him and help him during his stay in Egypt. The opening phrases of the letter are very florid and praise the addressee and his father Elḥanan ('the great rav who was a light and crown to his generation'). Although it seems that Elḥanan was indeed one of the most important figures in Babylonia, perhaps in the Pumbedita yeshiva, Samuel refrains from using his Babylonian titles. Samuel evidently maintained a close friendship with Shemaria, for he afterwards came to Egypt especially to participate in his funeral. The visit of Samuel 'the third' to Egypt is mentioned, as we have seen, in a fragment of an anonymous letter and also in the 'Egyptian Scroll'. The death of his father, Shemaria, is mentioned by Elḥanan in his letter to the community in Jerusalem, in which he notes that he himself was in Damascus at the time. Shemaria b. Elḥanan is apparently also mentioned in a court record of Josiah Gaon's day, which includes a copy of a deed of partnership evidently drawn up before Shemaria b. Elḥanan in his court in Fustat. To this data on the links established between Shemaria b. Elḥanan and the Palestinian yeshia, we can add the explicit evidence of Hayy Gaon, who writes that he sent Shemaria responsa to a number of queries put him by Bahlūl b. Joseph, in two quires. He received confirmation of the receipt (from Shemaria) of only one of these quires and not of the other, for 'after they were sent, his letters ceased, for he had joined the *ḥavūrā* [the yeshiva] of Palestine'.[68]

[68] See Mann, *Jews*, I, 34–39, 110f; *ibid.*, II, 38–41 (where he edited Elḥanan's letters and quotations from his letters); *idem*, *Texts*, I, 199–201; Abramson, *Ba-merkazim*, 105–182; Goitein, *Mediterranean Society*, II, 28f; see his articles: *Tarbiz*, 32: 266, 1962/3; *Finkel Jubilee Volume*: 117. My own student, Dr E. Bareket, wrote a study towards her M.A. degree entitled, 'Elḥanan b. Shemaria and Sahlān b. Abraham', Tel Aviv Univ. 1979/80. See also her article on Sahlān b. Abraham: *Tarbiz*, 52: 17, 1982/3. The letter of Samuel 'the third':

[796] Elḥanan b. Shemaria bore the title *rōsh ha-seder*, which it seems was customarily granted by the exilarch in that day. At times, father and son even called themselves *ha-rōsh*, 'the head', or *al-rayyis* (probably an abbreviation of *rōsh ha-seder*) and apparently, most of the honour attached to this title came from the fact that they were the heads of the 'Babylonian' congregation in Fustat. On one occasion, Elḥanan even signed *Elḥānān bēt dīn bīrrabbī Shemaria*. We know that *bēt-dīn* stood for *av-bēt-dīn*, and from this we understand that he headed the 'Babylonian' court in Fustat. Among the 'Babylonians', it was usual for the local dayyān to call himself thus, as one can see from the Babylonian custom in Ramla, when Joseph ibn al-Sijilmāssī, is called in their particular parlance, *abbēdīn*, or *al-bīdīn*. We have clear evidence of the fact that Elḥanan was the dayyān of the 'Babylonians' in Fustat from a deed of trusteeship drawn up in the court of the 'Palestinians' there, during the stay of Abraham, the son of the Gaon, who wrote the deed himself. It emerges that to this court, a court record was presented written at 'the council of our Lord and Master Elḥanan *rōsh ha-seder*, of blessed memory' (that is, the debate in the 'Palestinian' court occurred after Elḥanan's demise). It is obvious that 'the council' here means court, as has also been acknowledged by Assaf. It seems that the purpose of Elḥanan's letter to the community in Jerusalem, mentioned above, was connected to some legal matter, but unfortunately the latter part of the letter, which undoubtedly dealt with the principal subject, has been lost. The idea that Shemaria the father and Elḥanan his son established a sort of yeshiva in Fustat, which even enjoyed the authorities' support, and that its establishment was linked with the Fatimids' control over Egypt, is rather fanciful. This exaggeration is, to a certain extent, based on the impressive titles that the Babylonians were inclined to use. This is not to say that Shemaria and his son Elḥanan were not learned men; they had indeed achieved the highest status among the 'Babylonian' community of Fustat and were at the very heart of Torah study there,

18. The death of Shemaria: **19** (he is called Shemaria the Rav there). Elḥanan's letter: **26**. The deed: **30**; contrary to Mann's opinion, the record was not written in Shemaria's court but this is a copy made by Tobiah b. Daniel, one of the central figures of the Jerusalem yeshiva; one should note that Shemaria's name has not been preserved in the document, which is torn and faded, but it seems that the reconstruction is correct: Shemaria *ha-rav bīrrabbī* Elḥanan *ha-rav*; to the documentation on Shemaria b. Elḥanan one must now also add TS AS 200.347, 349, two fragments, the first of which mentions his commentary to the Song of Solomon, see: Abramson, *ibid.*, 82, 163. The letter of Hayy Gaon, see the fragment TS 20.100, in Mann, *Texts*, I, 120; see his discussion there, 109f; *idem*, *Tarbiz*, 5(1933/4), 295f n. 181; Abramson, *Ba-merkazim*, 97; both Mann and Abramson ascribed these remarks to Bahlūl, that is, that he left the authority of Pumbedita and went over to the Palestine authority. The fact that this is not so is proven both from the rest of the information on the connections between Shemaria and Elḥanan his son, with the Palestinian yeshiva, and from the letter of Hayy Gaon himself, for in the continuation he is amazed that Bahlūl discontinued his connection with Pumbedita; and if the statement from which stems the information that a *midrāsh*, or a house of learning, was founded by them in Fustat. We have no actual information, however, about this midrāsh – whether it was an independent institution existing in a special building of its own or whether it was merely another nickname for the court of the 'Babylonians', which was located, we assume, in their synagogue.[69]

[797] The letter of the exilarch Hezekiah b. David to Judah '*alūf* of the yeshiva of the diaspora' b. Abraham, written in February 1021, has aroused considerable interest. We are not certain as to the identity of Judah b. Abraham, but it seems likely that he was one of the supporters of the Pumbedita yeshiva in Fustat, perhaps one of the Maghribis who settled in Egypt. The exilarch mentions a letter sent by Elḥanan *rōsh ha-seder*, that is Elḥanan b. Shemaria, to the yeshiva, in which he says that he asked the Jerusalem Gaon (then Josiah b. Aaron) 'not to take any new decision before appointing him *av* (*bēt-dīn*)'. Hezekiah strongly objects to this. He mentions (not very positively) Elḥanan's many activities in Syria (Ṣōvā, that is Aleppo, and Damascus), Fustat (Zoan), and Palestine ('the land of Canaan'), and his characteristic pursuit of power, and the fact that he maintained a court (*qāva' pereq*) in Fustat, at the request of Barhūn, evidently referring to Abraham b. Sahlān. Here Hezekiah swears and claims that people in those places (that is, people of the Palestinian yeshiva) are not worthy of establishing a 'Babylonian' court, for they were not aware of what a yeshiva must do in these matters. All their wisdom is in the writing of deeds (*ha-shimmūsh*). When Elḥanan was visiting Baghdad, he met with Asaf *rōsh ha-seder*, and Elḥanan, for some days, displayed to him his knowledge of the Talmud, but this was very superficial. To sum up, this letter was apparently intended to arouse the opposition of 'Babylonians' in Fustat to Elḥanan's being called *av-bēt-dīn*. Relating to the appointment of Elḥanan as *av-bēt-dīn* of the 'Babylonians' in Fustat are his own comments in a letter, a fragment of which has been preserved in the

above were referring to him, there would be no justification for this amazement. (Hirschberg, *Eretz-Israel*, 5[1958/9], 214f follows Mann in this respect.)

[69] Elḥanan *bēt dīn*: Bodl MS Heb a 2, f. 15, edited by Assaf, *Tarbiz*, 9(1937/8), 217f. Joseph ibn al-Sijilmāssī: **313**, lines 4, 16, 22. The title *rōsh ha-seder*, apart from all the places mentioned in the works pointed out in the previous note, also: TS AS 148.156, a small fragment of a letter to '*rōsh ha-seder* of all Israel'; and the same also on the verso, in the address. 'The council' of Elḥanan: **61**, lines 4–5; cf. Assaf, *Meqōrōt*, 44. The letter to the Jerusalemites: **26**. Exaggeration concerning Elḥanan's status is also felt in Goitein, *Mediterranean Society*, II, 202; there he bases his remarks on **141**, but Elḥanan is not spoken of there, see the notes to this document. A certain lack of clarity can be seen in Abramson, *Ba-merkazim*, 111, n. 40, where it emerges from his remarks that the Palestinian yeshiva also granted the title *alūf*, or *rōsh kallā*, which he bases on Mann, *Jews*, II, 45, 159; as to the first place, he evidently erred as to the page number; in the other one, we find Solomon b. Judah's letter to Sahlān b. Abraham, **136**; although the Gaon calls him *alūf*, Sahlān received this title from the Babylonian yeshiva, as leader of the 'Babylonian' congregation in

Geniza: 'and in this week Ḥasan b. Sa'dān b. Aṣbagh met with the caliph ['the commander of the faithful'], may God guard his peace, who said to him: Ibn 'Imrān has brought a legal decision from Palestine in my matter [i.e. of Elḥanan], in which it is said that they unanimously approved that all judgments and legal decisions be the prerogative of Yaḥyā (Elḥanan) b. Shemaria and of no one else'. From this we can assume that in fact the Gaon and the entire yeshiva eventually agreed and confirmed that Elḥanan should be appointed *av-bēt-dīn*.[70]

[798] One should mention here that Elḥanan's father Shemaria called himself '*av-bēt-dīn* of all Israel' in a court record dealing with a quarrel between Maghribi merchants, and also in a fragment of his letter which

Fustat. Similarly, there are no grounds for referring to the 'yeshiva of Fustat', as Abramson does in the above-mentioned article.

70 Hezekiah's letter: **27**; the complaint that their wisdom consists only in writing deeds resembles the claim of al-Jāḥiẓ, *Ḥayawān*, I, 78 (ed. Haroun²), written 200 years earlier: 'there are those who study the sources and occupy themselves with commentaries of the Koran for fifty years and are still not considered learned in the law (*faqīh*) and this still does not make them cadis; but a man who has looked through the books of Abū Ḥanīfa or others like him, and learned by heart the formularies of deeds (*shurūṭ*) for a year or two, suddenly becomes like one of the governors, and it will not be long before he is a judge in one of the cities'; cf. Goldziher, *Muhammedanische Studien*, II, 233; cf. a similar reproach from Saadia Gaon in his *Sefer ha-gālūy* against Aaron (Khalaf) ha-Kohen b. Joseph ibn Sarjāda that he was not a scholar and that all his wisdom lay in the writing of deeds, like the *warrāq* of the Muslims; whereas among them (the Muslims), such a man would not merit any status in the world of the law and judgment; see in Stern, *Melila*, 5(1954/5), 141–147. Cf. Gil, *Sefunot*, NS, 1(1977/8), 13. Hezekiah's letter was meticulously studied and commented upon, see the references in the introductory note to **27**. Mann (*Texts*, I, 135f) edited TS 10 J 27, f. 10, a letter dated 19 Shevat, 1329 Sel., 7 February AD 1018, from Hayy Gaon to a *rōsh ha-seder* in which he also mentions an exchange of letters between that *rōsh ha-seder* and the exilarch (that is, Hezekiah). Mann assumes (*ibid.*, 117) that the letter was written to Elḥanan. It was indeed written to Elḥanan, since the address, in Arabic script, reads: Abū Zakariyyā' Ibn Shemaria, who was none other than Elḥanan. The fragment in the handwriting of Elḥanan: TS 8 J 7, f. 13. One can think that *'alayhi al-salām*, 'peace be with him', is used in the same sense as it is used in Hebrew, i.e. about someone deceased, and then it sounds like the story of a dream in which the caliph appears to be dead; but this expression is not found in this sense in the Geniza letters from the period under discussion here; whereas in Arabic, this is not its only meaning, especially here, when speaking of the caliph. In 1896, Goldziher already showed, that contrary to the Sunnis, the Shiites used this blessing when mentioning the descendants of the house of 'Alī in the widest sense, either towards the dead or the living, and such was the custom mainly among the Fatimids. Naturally the reference then is not to a dream but to an actual confirmation, both of the Jewish leadership and of the authorities, of the appointment of Elḥanan b. Shemaria as *av-bēt-dīn*. See: Goldziher, *ZDMG*, 50(1896), 121, 124; on the matter of the status of Shemaria b. Elḥanan and his son Elḥanan: the improved version of **38** (Gil, *Te'uda*, 7[1991], 311ff) somewhat clarifies the matter of their claim to the title *av-bēt-dīn*. It appears from this letter that Joseph ha-Kohen b. Menaḥem promised and even granted Shemaria b. Elḥanan the title *av-bēt-dīn me'uttād* in the Palestinian yeshiva, near 990, during the rift with Samuel ha-Kohen Gaon b. Joseph, when Joseph probably declared himself Gaon. Shemaria saw himself as bearing the title justifiably on behalf of the Palestinian yeshiva. And, although we do not have sufficient data, we may assume that his son Elḥanan also claimed this title for himself, after having been 'the candidate for third'. Ben-Sasson, *Zion*, 51(1986), 405ff, first published the improved version of **38**; see *ibid.* his discussion on this subject.

has been preserved, while Elḥanan was called in that court record 'Elḥanan the sixth the candidate for the third', from which we can assume that the two acted in accord and in connection with the Palestinian yeshiva. Otherwise there is no explanation for that title. This also supports the opinion that the title *av-bēt-dīn*, which Elḥanan devised for himself, was intended to be like that of his father. We have seen that both the father and the son used this title when sitting in court, and also in their court records. At any rate, we have a possible answer (though not a certain one) as to why the exilarch Hezekiah was so embittered against Elḥanan and spoke of him as if he were not a serious scholar; for evidently his initial connections were with the exilarch, from whom he had received the title *rōsh ha-seder*, and now he was establishing links with the Jerusalem Gaon.[71]

[799] At the same time, there seems to have been some activity among the Babylonians in Palestine. They wanted to set up, in addition to a separate legal system and independent courts, local appointments on their own. It is possible that Elḥanan b. Shemaria was behind this activity. We have the evidence of Yefet b. David b. Shekhania on this matter, in a letter to his father David, from Tyre in *ca.* 1010. He explicitly writes that he found the people of Acre, which he visited, accepting of the judgment of 'the head R. Elḥanan' and in the continuation, hints that he refrained from getting into an argument with him; that is, that although he witnessed Elḥanan trespassing on the territory of the Palestinian Gaon, to whom Yefet owed his loyalty, he did not take issue with him and even prevented others from doing so. We have seen that at that time, Elḥanan also stayed in Damascus for some time, and it seems that the purpose of these journeys was to be active among the 'Babylonians' in Syria and Palestine and perhaps also to win over people from among the followers of the Palestine Gaon. There is also evidence of the nature of Elḥanan's activities in northern Palestine in the validation, written in his own handwriting, on a deed of compensation drawn up in the court in Tyre, on 24 November

[71] See the court record: TS Loan 18, edited by Assaf, *Teshūvōt* (1941/2), 115f; cf. Mann, *Texts*, I, 200; Goitein, *Finkel Jubilee Volume*, 118f; Goitein already understood the practical significance of the links with the Jerusalem yeshiva; contrary to his opinion *ibid.*, 120 (and also Mann's, *Jews*, II, 40, 41), the letters which end with the *'alāma: berīt tām*, are Sahlān b. Abraham's, and not Elḥanan's; see the fragment of the letter with the signature 'Shemaria *av-bēt-dīn* of all Israel', in Goitein, *Tarbiz*, 32(1962/3), 271; Abramson, *Ba-merkazim*, 170f; see *ibid.*, 111, his assumption that the selection of the *av-bēt-dīn* of the Palestinian yeshiva is being referred to and that Elḥanan then acted in Aleppo or Damascus; hence Abramson also surmised that it was not possible that Barhūn, mentioned in **27**, is Abraham b. Sahlān. The connection between Elḥanan's court records and the Palestinian yeshiva also emerges from **28**, a, margin; this is a letter from Fustat to Josiah Gaon, describing the incident of the mistreatment of the brothers of Daniel b. Sahl the teacher, and 'our Lord and Master Elḥanan *rōsh ha-seder*' is mentioned there; because of the poor state of the letter, it is impossible to understand exactly what is being spoken of, but it seems that Elḥanan tried to intervene in that incident, with little success.

1019. The deed itself is in the handwriting of the local ḥāvēr, Joseph ha-Kohen b. Jacob; in his signature Elḥanan calls himself '*rōsh ha-seder* of all Israel'.

The subject of the letter from Joshua ha-Kohen b. Ya'īr of Tiberias to a community in the North (he mentions Palestine and Syria, but not Egypt) – perhaps Tyre, Tripoli, or Aleppo, is evidently related to those Babylonians' activities as well. He informs them that he has the sole right to appoint public figures in the communities, and that he appoints Moses the cantor b. Khalaf in charge of the court records, as well as an additional sixteen people to sit with him in the court. These appointments, which apparently relate to the 'Babylonians', may have been made after Elḥanan's stay in these areas and indicate a sort of reorganisation of these 'Babylonian' communities. One cannot imagine that Palestinian communities are being referred to, for in that case, it would be the Jerusalem Gaon who would have made the appointments.[72]

[800] Elḥanan b. Shemaria is mentioned by name in a letter written by Solomon b. Judah to someone in Fustat, of which only a fragment has been preserved. Due to the poor state of the letter, it is impossible to draw any substantive information concerning Elḥanan from it; after the mention of his name, a number of words are missing, and this is followed by the words 'he knew the man and his ways', and it is not clear whether Elḥanan is the subject or perhaps the object. However it is characteristic that this is immediately followed by the mention of a letter from the head of the Babylonian yeshiva, 'which arrived not without a purpose'; the Gaon expresses his bitterness about something, and here the text is very obscure. However, there is confirmation here that Elḥanan belonged to the 'Babylonian' community. In another letter, written by Solomon b. Judah, perhaps after the death of Elḥanan in 1026 apparently, it is recalled that he had reproached R. Elḥanan, for his involvement in the severe rift between the 'Palestinians' and the 'Babylonians' in Fustat. Everyone supported the Gaon in this matter, he writes.

72 Yefet b. David's letter; **317**, lines 9–11, 17, cf. Goitein, *Finkel Jubilee Volume*, 133f, who assumed that it referred to a *fisāqa* (Heb. *pesīqā*) with the meaning of vows and collection of money; but it seems that in the light of all the foregoing, it refers to a court decision, as in line 17 in the same letter, it also mentions *fisāqāt*, evidently meaning copies of legal decisions he asked to be sent to him in Fustat. The same letter also mentions (it seems) some commentary written by Elḥanan. The deed drawn up in Tyre: **271**. The letter of Joshua ha-Kohen: **25**. He also wrote **24**, in which he described the affair of the *nāsī* who wanted to control all the communities in those regions. There is also the possibility – which is difficult to prove at this stage – that the man who pretended to be a *nāsī* was none other than Elḥanan, for according to the evidence of Yefet b. David, he indeed moved around the communities in that neighbourhood and called himself dayyān, as we have seen.

It seems that Elḥanan pursued his activities in the course of his continuous journeys back and forth from Fustat to the north. In the abovementioned letter to the Jerusalem community, he describes his exploits on his return to Fustat after his wearisome journey to Damascus: he strengthened his congregation, convened his people ('most of the congregation') on the sabbath and attempted to return them to the right path (it is not clear what he means by this – perhaps to make peace between them and the 'Palestinians'). Elḥanan used the 'Babylonian' congregation in Fustat as a sort of base for his communal activities among the 'Babylonians' in Palestine and Syria. Interesting confirmation of this comes from his letter to the 'Babylonian' congregation in Damascus. This letter is expressed entirely in flowery phraseology and is also utterly ambiguous, so that today we are quite unable to understand its actual purpose. It may have aimed at getting help from the people of Damascus, but it seems more likely that its intention was more modest, namely merely to keep in contact with the community there. He mentions troubles ('we are affected by harsh judgment'), and it is not clear whether he is writing about himself and personal difficulties or possibly about al-Ḥākim's decrees. This latter possibility is sustained by what follows: 'a law is imposed on us not to claim or ask for anything of our Master the King' and there are those who see in this evidence that Elḥanan had formerly been granted a subvention by the Fatimid caliph, though this is highly doubtful. That he was the central figure among the 'Babylonians' in the entire area of Egypt, Palestine and Syria, is proven by the fact that he (like his father Shemaria before him) was the intermediary for queries and responsa and the contact for correspondence (and evidently money as well) between the 'Babylonian' yeshivot and the Maghrib.[73]

[801] For more than a generation, it was Ephraim b. Shemaria who headed the 'Palestinians' in Fustat. His considerable involvement in the affairs of Palestine in general and the yeshiva in particular can be seen in the constant repetition of his name in the sources of the Geniza in my collection, for his name is linked with seventy-one of these documents, eleven of which he wrote himself. In addition, his name is connected with many additional documents in the Geniza which are not included there, which he himself had written or in which he is mentioned, for he was head of the congregation from which the major part of the Geniza documents stem and whose synagogue housed the Geniza. As his full name indicates –

[73] Solomon b. Judah's letters: **65**, lines 8–9; **67**, lines 29ff. The letter to the Damascenes: TS 18 J 4, f.5; edited almost fully in Mann, *Jews*, II, 39f, and fully in Abramson, *Ba-merkazim*, 176–179. Abramson (*ibid.*, 108) discusses the contents of the letter and assumes that Elḥanan indeed received a subvention from the caliph, and also from the people of Damascus. Elḥanan as intermediary between Babylonia and the Maghrib, see Harkavy, *Teshūvōt*, 2; cf. Mann, *JQR*, NS, 8 (1917/8), 354f.

Ephraim b. Shemaria *ha-melammēd ha-'azzātī* – his father was a Gazan who settled in Egypt. We also know that his grandfather's name was Yaḥyā. At times, he calls himself Ephraim z. '., perhaps *ze'īrā 'aniyā*, meaning something along the lines of small and miserable. His Arabic by-name, in frequent use, was Abū Kathīr, perhaps hinting at fruitfulness, on the basis of 'for God hath caused me to be fruitful (*hifranī*, phonetically close to Ephraim) in the land of my affliction' (Gen., xli:52). In a letter to him from Elijah ha-Kohen b. Solomon Gaon, from around 1055 (or at any rate, during Daniel b. Azariah's time, that is, after 1051), he notes 'may God grant you attain the age of eighty', from which we may deduce that Ephraim was born in the seventies of the tenth century, at the height of the first Fatimid wars, which were evidently the cause of the family's move to Egypt. However, part of the family may have stayed behind and continued to live in Palestine, if we interpret correctly what the Gaon Daniel b. Azariah writes to Abraham ha-Kohen b. Isaac ibn Furāt, at about the same time as the letter mentioned earlier. He writes that Ephraim is about to arrive in Palestine in order to transfer his family to Egypt. Ephraim's income came from his trading in perfume, and Josiah Gaon called him '... the Gazan perfumer'. His shop was in Fustat, in the 'square of the perfumers' (*murabba'at al-'aṭṭārīn*) and he seems to have been a man of wealth.[74]

[802] Ephraim completed his studies in Palestine and its yeshiva appointed him dayyān in Fustat, as we can see from Solomon b. Judah's expression, 'graduate of our yeshiva'. We have already seen that he was appointed dayyān in Fustat in about the year 1000, in Shemaiah Gaon's day. In about 1024, during Josiah Gaon's time, the people of the yeshiva address him in letters as 'the *mumḥē* appointed by us, the *bēt dīn*', and it emerges from this that at first he was appointed to sit in court as *mumḥē*, before he had the title ḥāvēr; only at the end of the Gaon's life was he appointed ḥāvēr by Josiah Gaon. In a statute of the 'Palestinian' congregation in Fustat, decided upon in February 1025, he is called *Ephraim ha-shōfēṭ*

[74] His handwriting can be recognised by his signature (unforced) in TS 10 J 5, f. 11 (a court record written by Abraham b. Sahlān, in 1332/3, 1021/2); letters in Ephraim b. Shemaria's handwriting: **131**, **320–329**. His grandfather's name Yaḥyā, see for instance **274**, line 22 and the note on this; the meaning of z. '., as proposed by Friedman, *JAOS*, 274 (1974), 94. One can compare the signature of Ezra, head of the Palestinian yeshiva when the yeshiva moved to Damascus (at the beginning of the twelfth century): Ezra *'aniyā ze'īrā*. See: Assaf, *Qoveṣ*, 4. Abū Kathīr, see: Goitein, *Shalem*, 2(1935/6), 61, n. 47. The letter of Elijah ha-Kohen: **418**, line 14; further on, he says: *we-shimmashtā dōrēnū*, which is a simple expression, that is that Ephraim served all that generation in which Elijah lived, and it is surprising that Mann, *Jews*, I, 100, did not understand this. TS 13 J 10, f. 10 is a piyyūṭ written by Shemaria ha-Melammēd, perhaps Ephraim's father. The letter of Daniel b. Azariah: **355**, b, lines 19ff. The perfumer: **46**, line 16; the square of the perfumers: **292**, a, line 22, TS 12.666 is a letter sent to Ephraim, evidently from Qayrawān, and one can see that the writer had commercial dealings with Ephraim, trade in medicaments and scents; in the same letter, the cadi of Tyre Ibn Abī 'Aqīl is also mentioned (see a, lines 17, 19); apart

ha-mumḥē. During Solomon ha-Kohen b. Joseph Gaon's day, we find the Gaon calling him 'Ephraim he-ḥāvēr, who is in charge of the law of inheritance and wills . . .', and in Solomon b. Judah's time, they also began to call him *he-ḥāvēr ha-me'ullē.*

Ephraim had no male offspring. However we do know the names of his two sons-in-law, one being Abū Ya'qūb Joseph the scribe, mentioned in several letters to Ephraim, particularly those from Solomon b. Judah, who always remembered to send him regards – 'and give my regards to your son-in-law'. This Joseph died in 1035, apparently. In a letter to Ephraim from Qayrawān dated 23 July 1035, mention is made of 'the demise of Mr Joseph . . . who was like a son standing by you in all your needs'. Ephraim's other son-in-law was Abū Naṣr Ghālib ha-Kohen b. Moses b. Ghālib, who was a scribe with a beautiful handwriting. He wrote some of the documents found in my collection. Of his lineage, we know that he was a cousin of Elijah ha-Kohen b. Solomon Gaon, as the latter clearly states in his letter to Ephraim b. Shemaria. A letter of condolence on the death of Ephraim b. Shemaria from Daniel b. Azariah has been preserved, which was sent to his son-in-law Ghālib. It is interesting that Daniel did not know the name of Ghālib's father and left an empty space for it in his letter. The address written on verso, in Arabic script, reads: Abū Naṣr Ghālib, son-in-law of the Ḥāvēr Abū Kathīr. The Gaon notes that Ephraim was meticulous about regularly sending the Gaon what was due to him and that there was a great friendship between them.[75]

[803] There is an interesting description of the man Ephraim b. Shemaria to be found in one of the letters written him by Solomon b. Judah. His forbearance is outstanding. He is a responsible person who faithfully

from commercial matters, the letter contains a request that Ephraim should send the writer the tractate Sukka from the Palestinian Talmud.

[75] 'Graduate of our yeshiva': **82**, line 4. 'The mumḥē appointed by us': **34**, a, line 4; Mann, *Texts*, I, 314, n. 6, sees here proof that Ephraim was made ḥāvēr in the days of Josiah Gaon. The statute: **319**, lines 4, 25; cf. Goitein, *Shalem*, 1(1973/4), 21. In **46**, b, the letter of Josiah Gaon to him, he is still called *ha-talmīd.* The appointment by Josiah Gaon: **324**, lines 15–16, and see there further the re-appointment by Solomon ha-Kohen Gaon b. Joseph and Zadok, *av-bēt-dīn.* Solomon ha-Kohen: **49**, a, line 7; in the continuation he undoubtedly listed other matters the dayyān was in charge of, but the letter is torn. *He-ḥāvēr ha-me'ullē,* see for instance **112**, line 2 (Solomon b. Judah). The letter from Qayrawān: **330**, lines 4–5; see the Hebrew Index, under Joseph the scribe; perhaps he is Joseph b. Obadiah, to whom Solomon b. Judah sends regards, see **58**, margin, line 19; and he also sends regards to his father, see *ibid.*, and also in **120**, lines 15, 20. The handwriting of Ghālib (his Hebrew name was evidently Yōsēf) ha-Kohen, is recognisable by his signature in **331**, line 24. Elijah ha-Kohen b. Solomon Gaon: **418**, a, margin top, line 9. Moses ha-Kohen b. Ghulayb (diminutive from Ghālib), who is mentioned in two of Solomon b. Judah's letters (see the Hebrew Index), is perhaps the father of this Ghālib. The assumption of Mann, *Jews*, I, 100, that it is Abraham ha-Kohen b. Isaac ibn Furāt who was Ephraim's son-in-law, naturally becomes invalid. The letter of condolence: **362** (and what is said here is unlike the opinion of Goitein, *Shalem*, 2[1975/6], 95).

performs his public duties; shows devotion in matters of saving people from the tax collectors and Muslim law; knows how to maintain good relations with the authorities; is talented in making peace and fair judgments. In another letter, the Gaon also says of him that he is 'the cautious alert man at the service of his people'.

On the eve of Thursday, 21 Tevet 1327 Sel., 4 January AD 1016, Ephraim b. Shemaria was involved in an unpleasant personal quarrel. We learn of this from a record of evidence written six days later in the court of the Palestinians in Fustat. It was a rainy night and the roads were muddy, it says in the record. Three slaves of a Jewish Maghribi merchant, from Palermo, Sicily (*mi-medīnat Ṣiqilīya*), brought Ephraim to the Fustat police (the *shurṭa*), as that merchant, 'Amrūn b. Eliah, claimed that Ephraim owed him money. Ephraim argued that as they were Jews, there was no reason to be judged by a cadi; but the governor before whom they were brought ordered them to be held 'imprisoned under guard' for the night, and with 'Amrūn's agreement, ordered them to be tried by the cadi afterwards. Ephraim then presented witnesses who gave evidence that his appearance before a Muslim court was made under duress. Some eight years later, Ephraim was the victim of a plot based on perjured evidence, the nature of which we know little. A letter from the Palestinian yeshiva, sent from Ramla, and partly written in the handwriting of Solomon ha-Kohen Gaon, evidently in 1025, mentions this affair and expresses satisfaction that the plot was uncovered and that the 'king' himself (that is, the caliph al-Ẓāhir) and also the wazīr ('the deputy with the big retinue') intervened in his favour. Among the intermediaries involved in this affair, we encounter Abū Naṣr ha-Levi David b. Isaac, of whom we know (though not with certainty) that he was then in charge of the administration of the income from taxes, a post granted him by Caliph al-Ẓāhir on 21 Jumādā II AH 413, that is 10 February AD 1023. The Tustari brothers of the older generation (Sahl, Saadia and Joseph, the sons of Israel) and other notables who are not named, 'the elders of the two parties', that is, the Rabbanites and the Karaites, are also mentioned. Also the draft of a letter has been preserved from Ephraim b. Shemaria himself, addressed to 'the elder of the generation David b. Isaac', describing how he was rescued from imprisonment: 'they planned to kill me, and set up a trap to catch me . . . and my eyes have seen the dungeon'. The affair produced a furor among the Jews of Fustat ('and the city was in turmoil'); such malice as was meant to be practised against him 'had not been known since the days of Naboth the Jezreelite'.[76]

[804] Various documents have been preserved in the Geniza, among

[76] Ephraim's traits: **95**; 'the cautious alert man': **120**, a, line 3. The record of evidence: Bodl MS Heb b 13, f. 42, edited by Poznanski, *REJ*, 48(1904), 171f; the document is torn on the

them many court records in the handwriting of Ephraim, in connection with his role as dayyān. In these documents, there are also indications of his special relationship with Palestine and its yeshiva, such as in the court record dealing with an inheritance due to three brothers, one of whom lived in Ramla. The Jerusalem Gaon intervened on their behalf, as their money had remained in the hands of the Tustaris. A fragment of the Gaon's letter contains an appeal to Ephraim concerning a man who is prepared to give his wife a divorce only on condition that his wife tear up the marriage deed; the fragment speaks of a Maghribi, but also mentions a certain b. Qiṭōs from Tiberias. There was a constant interchange between the Jerusalem Gaon and Ephraim on questions of law, and this is particularly marked in the letters of the yeshiva. Josiah Gaon uses the most ornate and elevated phraseology in writing to him: 'our dear and beloved, a man who is close to our heart . . . a man of intelligence and much wisdom, right qualities and perfect ideas . . . a good soul . . . a blessed man'; and in another letter: 'who is surrounded by splendour . . . sustains the broken one (i.e. the congregation) . . . pure and learned . . . a man of mercy . . . excellent in wittiness . . . to be trusted in any good deeds'.

And even more than in Josiah's case, we find in Solomon b. Judah's

right side, but one can adequately understand the major part of its contents; the names of four witnesses are preserved there, among them Samuel ha-Kohen b. Ṭalyōn (= Avṭalyon; misread by Poznanski). The letter of the yeshiva: **47**, lines 6ff, 22, 29–32. Ephraim's letter to David b. Isaac: TS 12.273; the *'alāma* is *yesha' yuḥāsh* from which it is understood that it was written in the Gaon Solomon ha-Kohen b. Joseph's day, that is, in 1025. On David ha-Levi b. Isaac (mentioned in a number of documents in my corpus, see the Hebrew Index) see Musabbiḥī, 12: he calls him Da'ūd al-Yahūdī; he was appointed supervisor over the moneys which the new man in charge of the *dīwān al-kharāj*, the caliphate's office of taxes, was responsible for collecting, and who replaced a certain Ibn Salmūn *al-kātib*. Hillel b. Yeshū'ā calls him, in **251**, lines 11–12: 'Our Lord and Master David ha-Levi, pride of the house of Levi'. Dropsie 401 contains a letter in rhyme written by David b. Shekhania (the father of Yefet b. David) to '. . . our Lord, his honour and sanctity, our Lord and Master David b. Isaac, the honourable prince, who resists every attack and is the defender of Israel before the King and the princes and the Lady (i.e. the caliph's mother) and the eunuchs . . . may he have the upper hand over Kaslūḥīm and strike terror in the hearts of the Naftūḥīm (Biblical names, by which the Egyptians are meant), like Joseph under the Pharaohs and Mordecai under Ahasuerus'. That David ha-Levi b. Isaac was a Karaite now seems certain in view of **272** (Gil, *Te'uda*, 7[1991], 324f), with a remnant of a power-of-attorney which he receives from his daughter for her marriage, a distinctly Karaite custom. Here we also have some indication of the social status of the Karaites (*infra*, sec. 935). It emerges that David ha-Levi had a house in Tyre as well, and connections with the Tustaris (Gil, *ha-Tustarīm*, 48, 56). He was also a relative of Manasseh b. Abraham al-Qazzāz; he was the father-in-law of Manasseh's son, 'Adīya. Cf. Mann, *Jews*, II, 446; the wazīr at the time was 'Amīd al-Dawla Abū Muḥammad al-Ḥasan b. Ṣāliḥ al-Rūdhbādī, a veteran in the Fatimid administration, who in al-'Azīz' day was in charge of the taxes in jund Filasṭīn ('Ramla and its neighbourhood'), and afterwards in charge of the army in Palestine and Syria instead of Manasseh b. Abraham al-Qazzāz (in the year AH 381, that is AD 991). He was the wazīr until 418, that is 1027, when as a result of accusations against him, the caliph appointed in his stead al-Jarjarā'ī: see Ibn al-Ṣayrafī, 34f.

letters the most striking manifestation of his very close connections with Ephraim for an entire generation. He calls Ephraim *band al-rabbānīn* (banner of the Rabbanites) in a letter dealing with the recruitment of funds to rescue the Jerusalemites who were imprisoned because of the famous debt. Apparently there was a legal decision forbidding the use of the money of the Fustat heqdēsh for such a purpose, and the Gaon tries to remind Ephraim that there had been a precedent for such an act, when money of the heqdēsh was used (evidently in Fustat itself) to restore the synagogue and buy two buildings. It does seem that the eloquent phraseology and praise were well merited in this instance, but they were generally employed to soften Ephraim's feelings on the matters dealt with in the letters. This close relationship became one of real affinity and preparedness to defend Ephraim b. Shemaria from attacks when his authority was being questioned, as we can see from the Gaon's letter to the Taṭai community – mentioned above – concerning the pronouncement of a ban on Abraham b. Aaron, cantor and preacher, for abusing and quarrelling with Ephraim. And if there was any misunderstanding between the Gaon and Ephraim, it was swept aside, with the statement that 'what was in the heart was quickly erased . . . and no grudge remained, to be insisted upon'. The letters of the yeshiva to Ephraim b. Shemaria reveal an almost continuous drama, in which local legal matters are juxtaposed with disputes within the Palestinian congregation, quarrels with the Babylonians and even echoes of the differences with the Karaites which erupted from time to time in Fustat. Indeed, an instance of the latter emerges in the remnants of a letter from Josiah Gaon, which also mentions, amidst the praise and eloquence complimenting Ephraim b. Shemaria, the 'sect of the *benē 'ōnenā'* (a play on the name 'Anan); and it seems that the text, most of which is missing, spoke of Ephraim's effective opposition to the Karaites.

As to the subject of intercession and requests for assistance, these are also frequently found in the letters to Ephraim. Abraham, the son of the Gaon, asks him to continue aiding someone whose name has not been preserved, evidently someone from the Gaon's family or one of his close friends, who lives in Egypt, even if he has sinned against Ephraim. Solomon b. Ṣemaḥ, who also acted as scribe to the yeshiva, writes to him after explaining that the Gaon is not in the city and therefore not writing himself, and asks him to go quickly to the aid of an orphan, the daughter of Abū 'Alī b. Azhar. The latter had been a rich and generous man, but was reduced to ruin by the catastrophe that befell Ramla (evidently referring to the events of 1024) and died penniless. His daughter was engaged but her prospective husband would not go through with the marriage if she did not receive a dowry (*levūsh*). The deceased had a sister and brother in Fustat and Ephraim is asked to get them to help. In addition, Ephraim is requested to help in the affairs of a certain Abū'l-Najm Hilāl (who is Hillel b. Sahl al-Ṣahrajtī, a parnās of Fustat) but the matter is not clarified. I have already mentioned the repeated requests from 'Eli *ha-mumḥē* b. Abraham, that Ephraim concern himself with Abū' l-Faraj b. 'Eli, the cantor from Mosul, who went to Fustat.[77]

[805] Ephraim's chief associate and the dynamic spirit in matters relating to the synagogue of the 'Palestinians' in Fustat was Yefet (Ḥusayn) b. David b. Shekhania, cantor and scribe of the court. Many of the letters pertaining to the 'Palestinian' congregation in Fustat which are preserved in the Geniza are in his handwriting. I have already mentioned the letters written from Tyre in his youth, at the beginning of the eleventh century. His father, David b. Shekhania, served in the same position; his grandfather, Shekhania (Sakan, in Arabic) was a poet, and some of his piyyūṭīm are in the Geniza. I have mentioned above the rhyming letter written by David, Yefet's father, to David b. Isaac. The family apparently came from Palestine, and from his letters from Tyre, it is evident that he had relatives there, among them a cousin of his father's (that is, the son of Shekhania's brother). Yefet's brother, who also lived in Fustat, was called Manṣūr, and he had sons. His mother was still alive when Yefet was staying in Tyre, and there is also mention of his grandmother and his father's sisters and their children. In Fustat, the family lived in Darb al-Silsila (the lane of the chain) in the Maṣāṣa quarter, in the Tujīb region, near Suwayqat al-Yahūd ('the little market of the Jews'). While in Tyre, he earned his living as a cantor, as can be clearly discerned from his letters from there. Yefet himself had a son and a daughter; his son-in-law Khalaf is also mentioned in his letter from Tyre, and in the letter of Yeshū'ā ha-Kohen b. Abraham the Galilean, there are also regards to Khalaf 'the son-in-law of the cantor'.

We know that Yefet earned his livelihood from supervising the ritual slaughter, and we have already seen how he was appointed to this office, which his father held before him. Ephraim b. Shemaria points out in a letter written at about the same time, that Yefet ('the son of Shekhania' as

[77] The matter of the inheritance: **329**. The divorce: **153**. The letters of Josiah: **35**, **46**. The affair of the heqdēsh money: **80**, b, lines 7ff. The letter to Taṭai: **93**. The words of appeasement: **122**, a, lines 3ff. The sons of 'ōnenā: **34**, a, lines 5–6 ('*ōnenīm*, augurs, much criticised in the Bible). The request for aid from Abraham son of the Gaon: **167**. The letter of Solomon b. Ṣemaḥ: **207**; Hilāl – perhaps Hillel b. Sahl, see: Mann, *Jews*, II, 99, n. 2; Gil, *Documents*, in the index: Hillēl, Hilāl, and see also: **204**, in which Solomon b. Ṣemaḥ asks Ephraim to help a certain Faraj b. 'Eli, who is in danger of having his goods confiscated; **206**, in which the aforementioned asks Ephraim to see to it that the friend of the writer, Barakāt b. Hillel al-Ramlī b. Qartaway, gets help with regard to the tax and is not mistreated when he buys goods. The cantor from Mosul: **231–235**. Any stranger arriving in Fustat would evidently turn to Ephraim b. Shemaria, as we also see in the letter of the man from Constantinople 'Eliah, the poor man, son of R. Solomon, of blessed memory, the scholar from the city of Constantinople', who suffered some calamity (not known to us) in Fustat and lost all his money, including that which others had lent to him. He writes

he is called there) receives one-half the income from the slaughtering, while the other half is taken by al-Ṭabarānī, that is, the Palestinian Gaon; at first the latter only took a third, but later on there was a request for half which could not be refused. At the outset of the forties of the century, Yefet was energetically engaged in the final restoration of the synagogue, which still needed finishing and repairs after it had been destroyed in the days of al-Ḥākim. In the fifties, when Daniel b. Azariah was Gaon, Yefet was among those who were undermining the authority of the dayyān, leader of the Palestinians in Fustat, 'Eli he-ḥāvēr ha-me'ullē b. 'Amram. Daniel b. Azariah stresses in his letter to the latter that 'the son of Shekhania' must first of all be excommunicated. In further letters to Abraham ha-Kohen b. Isaac b. Furāt, he expresses himself sharply on the subject of 'the cantor', demanding that he change his ways. He would have excommunicated him himself a long time before that, were it not for the fact that Abraham was defending him. He provokes quarrels within the congregation, demands special prerogatives in the prayer rote and engages in plots between the 'Palestinians' and the 'Babylonians'. He must set down in writing that he would no longer pursue these aberrant ways. It seems that Yefet was indeed excommunicated, for in another letter to 'Eli b. 'Amram, the Gaon deals with the cancelling of a ban on an unidentified person, on condition that a written obligation is undertaken by that person not to continue to engage in matters concerning the synagogue and the marketplace (that is, the slaughtering). It seems certain that the person was Yefet. After this stormy affair, Yefet evidently decided to leave for Jerusalem, and he stayed for some time at its yeshiva. In a letter to the Gaon, he describes what occurred afterwards. On his return from Jerusalem, he found that terrible calamities had befallen his family. His daughter died in childbirth and shortly afterwards, the son she had borne also died. He returned to public affairs and to those of the synagogue, and he mentions in particular that he had collected ten dinars to buy new mats for the synagogue. The congregation once again restored the handling of 'the market' to him, that is, the slaughtering, but for some eighteen weeks, his income was very slight, at 339 dirhams, half of which was taken by Abraham *ha-māsōs* ('the joy' of the yeshiva, who was evidently Abraham b. David ibn Sughmār) to be sent to the yeshiva in Jerusalem. There remained only 169½ dirhams, which amounts to less than ten dirhams per week. A *pesīqā* was organised for him, but the results were very poor, for the people were poor and miserable and 'the takers are more numerous than the givers', while he had to support both himself and his son. The work of supervision is so exhausting that frequently he cannot sleep on

'and God will repay you your good compensation, if you see to it that I am adequately treated' (that is, if Ephraim tries to raise donations for him): see Dropsie 378.

Thursday nights (the slaughtering was performed on Thursday nights, in order that the meat be fresh for the sabbath). He therefore asks the Gaon to let him have the second half that is due to the yeshiva. Yefet returns to this subject in another letter to the Gaon (from his remarks, it seems that he wrote a number of letters). He complains that he has not received a reply, but in the meantime he is informed that the Gaon's reply is contained in his letter to 'Abū Isḥāq Abraham, the *māsōs*' and that it is apparently in the negative, which is a reason for despair. Once again he makes the account: from the middle of Sivan until Kislev, that is, six and a half months, he sent the Gaon 23 dinars and $5^1/_4$ qīrāṭs. According to the going rate of 40 dirhams per dinar, at the time, it seems that the income increased threefold or more since the previous letter, for from the latter numbers, the weekly average was *ca.* 70 dirhams, as against *ca.* 20. In the interim, the congregation placed a partner alongside him, a man who had been the pupil of Nathan ha-Levi he-ḥāvēr (son of Yeshū'ā), and they decided that each of them would receive half a dinar (that is, 20 dirhams) per week; they also appointed a certain b. Sabra to take charge of the money. We get a glimpse of the other side of the picture, that is, how the Gaon reacted to all this, from the letter he wrote to a certain 'Palestinian' staying in Fustat. He objects to 'the son of Shekhania' taking over the market, because decisions concerning the market and the synagogue must rest with the community. He, himself, Daniel b. Azariah, is not in need of this income. In another letter, however, which he wrote from Damascus to Abraham ha-Kohen b. Isaac ibn Furāt, he takes note of what the latter wrote to him, that the community loves Yefet and wants him to continue in his post, and he even promises to submit to Abraham's request and to send a letter of confirmation to the community on this matter. After Yefet's death, the subject of ritual slaughtering in Fustat is again reappearing in a letter written by Daniel b. Azariah to one of the figures in Fustat. This letter seems to have contained stringent instructions on the safeguarding of the money from slaughtering and the demand that these matters are not left in the hands of one individual, and that anyone appointed supervisor should be tested for his knowledge of slaughtering and inspection, and an explicit court record is to be written and then read aloud in public, in the synagogue. In Fustat, the storm concerning the slaughtering continued to rage, as we learn from Abraham b. David ibn Sughmār's letter to the Gaon from the beginning of June 1056. Here we find that the individual in charge of slaughtering after Yefet's death was Berākhōt he-ḥāvēr. He was joined by Aaron b. Ephraim b. Ṭarasūn, '*mumḥē* and cantor', called in this letter *ḥazān al-kenēsiyā*; but Berākhōt he-ḥāvēr ousted him and began to slaughter and examine the meat himself. 'Eli b. 'Amram intervened and took upon himself the responsibility to instruct Berākhōt on the subject of ritual slaughtering in the two markets, the one near 'the bathhouse of the rat' (*ḥammām al-fa'r*), and the 'great market' (*sūq al-kabīr*); and they also set up a special committee of ten men, which had already convened, but nothing came of this.[78]

[806] In the second quarter of the eleventh century, the Palestinian yeshiva had a special relationship with Abraham (Barhūn) b. Sahlān and his son Abū 'Amr Sahlān (Shelah), leaders of the Babylonian congregation in Fustat. We have a rather considerable number of details concerning this family. Its lineage has been preserved in a colophon at the end of a *piyyūṭ* from the Geniza in which we find the names Abraham and Sahlān alternating, but in the fifth and sixth generation preceding our Abraham, we find Solomon b. Shabbāt Sunbāṭ. Mann suggested reading this last name as Sunbāṭī (that is, coming from Sunbāṭ, a locality in Egypt), but it is merely a deformation of the Jewish name Shabbāt, Shabbetai, as one can easily discern from the coupling of 'Shabbāt Sunbāṭ', that is, the Hebrew name accompanied by the Arabic name. 'Abraham he-ḥāvēr b. Sahlān, known by the name of Ibn Sunbāṭ' is the address on a letter from Solomon b. Judah. Elsewhere, I have suggested that the family hailed from northern Persia (on the basis of the form Sunbāṭ, which seemed to me characteristic of those regions), but in the meantime, I have come across a fragment of a letter to Abraham b. Sunbāṭ (apparently intended for our Abraham b. Sahlān, and 'b. Sunbāṭ' should be considered a kind of family name), with the address there as follows: 'to my son Abū Isḥaq Ibrahīm b. Sunbāṭ al-Siqillī', that is, the Sicilian. Hence it appears that the family came to Egypt from Sicily.

[78] On Sakan see the note of Goitein, *Finkel Jubilee Volume*, 133. Details on the family and where they lived: **316**, **317**; see Ibn Duqmāq, 25f, and cf. details on the places: Gil, *Documents*, Index. Khalaf is mentioned in **317**, line 20. The letter of Yeshū'ā ha-Kohen: **201**. The letter of Ephraim b. Shemaria: MS Reinach. This position of supervisor of the slaughtering was called in Arabic *ḥallāl*, that is, 'the permitter', for it is the supervisor who would permit the sale of the meat if everything was in order. Daniel b. Azariah calls Yefet in one of his letters: b. al-Ḥallāl, see **355**, a, line 21, and this is not 'the man who unfastens coils of silk' as assumed by Goitein, *Shalem*, 2(1975/6), 83, n. 3. On the restoration of the synagogue, see the documents of the forties in Gil, *ibid*. The ban: **342**, **370**. The letters to Abraham ha-Kohen: **355**, **358**. Cancelling the ban: **371**. Nathan ha-Levi he-ḥāvēr b. Yeshū'ā, see: Mann, *Jews*, II, 103, n. 1, 220, who notes his signatures on court documents together with Sahlān b. Abraham and Ephraim b. Shemaria in 1040 (thus it should be read) and before that. The letters of Yefet to the Gaon: **400**, **401**. The Gaon's letter to a Jerusalemite in Fustat: **356**, b, lines 19ff. Confirmation of Yefet's office: **357**, a, lines 31ff. After Yefet's death: **367**. The letter of Abraham b. David b. Sughmār: **402**; Aaron b. Ephraim b. Ṭarasūn, of the family of cantors, is mentioned occasionally in my collection, see the Hebrew Index; TS 13 J 16, f. 1 is a piyyūṭ in his handwriting, in honour of a certain Solomon the elder; Consist. isr. VII A18 is a letter written him by Sahlān b. Abraham, leader of the 'Babylonians' in Fustat; he asks him to raise money for a poor man while Sahlān is ill himself. To the documents mentioning Yefet b. David one must add an unidentified Geniza fragment edited by Toledano, *Mizrāḥ u-ma'arāv*, 1(1919/20), 345; with the signature: Yefet the cantor b. David; Solomon b. Yefet is also a signatory there,

According to a court record from Fustat, dated Thursday, 28 Adar 1339 Sel. (AD 1028), Abraham was a money-changer: '*Barhūn b. Sahlān ṣayrāfā*'; but in some places it explicitly states that they were perfume merchants, as indicated by: 'Barhūn al-'Aṭṭār', as a letter to him from Solomon b. Judah is addressed. There is no need to discount either of these possibilities, and it is very likely that they were engaged in both occupations at the same time. At any rate, in the above version, Sahlān, the father of Abraham, is the one who is called *ṣayrāfā*, a money-changer. As can be seen in the Hebrew Index, Abraham is frequently mentioned in my collection, and I have already stated that he held the title ḥāvēr of the Palestinian yeshiva. In addition to him and his son Sahlān, his other son Nehemiah (or Naḥum) is also mentioned, as well as his brother-in-law, his wife's brother (that is, Sahlān's uncle on his mother's side), Saadia b. Ephraim.

It appears that the relations between Solomon b. Judah and Abraham b. Sahlān were extremely cordial, despite the occasional problems that would arise between the Babylonians and the Palestinians spoken of earlier. After the death of Abraham (evidently in 1028) the Gaon wrote a number of letters of condolence, one of which has been preserved in the Geniza. Since a man of his age has been gathered to his forefathers, writes the Gaon, he is depressed and prays that he shall not die in the same year, 'it should not be said that they both died in one year'; and there are other expressions of friendship and appreciation in the letter.[79]

[807] As to Sahlān b. Abraham, it seems that his relationship with the Gaon was far more complex. We have already seen how he gave up the title ḥāvēr. Like his father, Sahlān was blessed with titles which he had received from the Babylonian yeshiva (evidently Pumbedita), from the Palestinian yeshiva and apparently from the exilarch: *ha-mumḥē, he-ḥāvēr, rōsh ha-seder* (which evidently came from the exilarch), *ha-alūf, rōsh kallā, segān* (deputy) of the yeshiva, *ḥemdat ha-nesī'ūt* ('the cherished one of the

and perhaps he is Yefet b. David's son; the signature of Samuel ha-Kohen *rōsh ha-qāhāl* (he is b. Avṭalyon), Abraham b. Mevassēr, Ephraim b. Shemaria, and another three signatories, are also found there; this is a court record of the year 1339 Sel. (AD 1028).

[79] The colophon: BM Or 5557 A, f. 58; cf. Mann, *Jews*, II, 102; Gil, *Tarbiz*, 48(1978/9), 38. Details concerning Abraham and Sahlān his son, were collected and commented on in the M.A. thesis of E. Bareket; al-Siqillī: TS AS 180.92; although this word lacks the diacritic signs, the reading seems to me to be quite certain. See the letter written by Samuel (*Samā'ual*) b. Ibrahīm to his father, Abū Isḥaq Ibrahīm b. Shabbāt, to Sicily, TS 10 J 11, f. 22. He informs him of the illness of his sister, Turfa ('affluence'). In the address, written in Arabic script, one can read: 'Ibrahīm b. Sunbāṭ, known by the (nickname) al-Nashā'ī', which means, 'the starch-maker'. This Abraham may have been the great-grandfather of Sahlān b. Abraham. Ṣayrāfā: TS 8 K 20, f. 1; Abraham declares that he owes thirty dinars to Manasseh b. Joseph; cf. Mann, *ibid.*, 98. Al-'Aṭṭār, see: **90**, b; cf. Chapira, *REJ*, 82(1926), 319; see the objections of Mann, *Texts*, I, 118, n. 20 to the above-mentioned. Abraham's writing can be recognised by TS 10 J 5, f. 11, a court record concerning a public

exilarchate'). Hillel he-ḥāvēr of Tiberias (son of Yeshū'ā the cantor) calls him 'Shelah, *tannā and amōrā* (scholar of the Mishna and the Talmud), *rōsh kallā* of the yeshiva of the diaspora (Pumbedita) . . . son of Abraham *he-ḥāvēr* of the Great Sanhedrin'. A letter of Sahlān's has been preserved in the Geniza, written to Fustat, perhaps to his father, when Sahlān was away, which deals with a commentary to a piyyūṭ of ha-Kallir and other spiritual matters. He mentions that he is boarding with someone who supplies him with food. Evidently the letter was written during Sahlān's youth, although he already signs it 'Sahlān ha-mumḥē'. The marriage deed of Sahlān's wife has also been preserved in the Geniza. He married Esther, daughter of Joseph b. 'Amram the judge, on 26 Elul, 1348 Sel., that is 9 September AD 1037, and they apparently had a son. His wife is mentioned in the late fifties, after Sahlān's death, in a letter from 'Eli ha-Kohen b. Ezekiel. News concerning the widow of the *ra's al-kull* (=*rosh kalla*) has reached Jerusalem, stating that she is in terrible distress, 'and that is a great shame'. There is almost no doubt that the reference is to Sahlān's widow. One must bear in mind that this was a period of scarcity and plague in Egypt. The writer wishes to know whether Sahlān's brother (Nehemiah) is looking after her.[80]

[808] There are many accounts in the Geniza of Sahlān b. Abraham's public activities, from which it is possible to study the affairs of the Babylonian congregation in general, though this is a separate subject which I shall not deal with in depth here. What should be reiterated, however, is the strong contact he maintained with Solomon b. Judah,

matter, from 1021 or 1022, which is in his handwriting and with his signature. The letter of condolence: **86**.

80 See the titles in document No. 7 (Dropsie 336) in Gil, *Documents*, 152, and the commentary there, n. 8. Sahlān b. Abraham is one of the signatories in TS 8 Ja 2, f. 1: *rōsh ha-seder, ha-alūf, beḥīr* (elect of) *ha-yeshīvā, ḥemdat ha-nesī'ūt* (the titles are abbreviated; the reading of Hirschfeld, *JQR*, 16[1904], 576 in this place is not correct; the date: Thursday, 21 Adar II, 1345 Sel., 14 February AD 1034). As to the title *segan ha-yeshiva*, this is evidently a Babylonian title, given to Sahlān by Hayy Gaon, as assumed by Chapira, *REJ*, 82(1926), 325. The title *rōsh kallā* may have been the origin of the nickname Abū Dawra (Arabic for *kallā* = the curved row of the yeshiva) which we find in **92**, b, lines 26ff. Sahlān's letter to Fustat: ENA 4020, f. 18, edited first by Marmorstein, *Midrash ḥasērōt*, 76–79, edited again by Mann, *Tarbiz*, 6(1934/5), 80–84; it may have been written in Alexandria, to which Sahlān had a special link; he was involved in community affairs there, as one can see from Solomon b. Judah's letter to the community of Alexandria, **74**, lines 17–18, which is an answer to the complaints of people of this community against the local dayyān; Sahlān then proposed that the cantor of Alexandria, Shelah b. Moses, should be the ḥavēr of the city, but the Gaon turned down this proposal in his letter. It seems that the letters from Alexandria: ENA 4020, fs. 44, 45, are in Sahlān's handwriting, see them in Mann, *Jews*, II, 91f. The opinion of Mann, *Jews*, I, 97, that the letter-writer is not our Sahlān but his grandfather, is not correct. The marriage deed of Sahlān's wife: TS 20.6; edited by Assaf, *Tarbiz*, 9(1937/8), 30ff, and partly by Mann, *Jews*, II, 103. According to **105**, lines 3–5, he still did not have a son; but in **137**, b, line 9, Solomon b. Judah mentions his son (evidently at the beginning of 1043). 'Eli ha-Kohen's letter: **444**, lines 7–8.

though this was not always one of understanding or friendship. The Gaon preserves a very friendly tone, generally, and does not hesitate to shower him with praise. He calls Sahlān *ha-yashrān* or *meyashrān*, on the basis of the Arabic meaning of his name, 'for *mīshōr* [plain] in Arabic is *sahla*'. In times of distress, the Gaon turns to him for help for the people of the yeshiva or the Jews of Jerusalem in general. He was evidently in the habit of writing two almost identical letters, one addressed to Ephraim b. Shemaria and the other to Sahlān b. Abraham. The Gaon and his son also used the latter's assistance in mediating with the Tustaris, and also in the transfer of money or fines. A real complication in their relationshsip arose when Solomon b. Judah took a sum of money destined for the yeshiva as a loan for himself for a certain time, a matter which I shall return to. Sahlān was very angry at the time, apparently, and Solomon b. Judah was prepared to sell his own woollen robe, through his son Abraham, who was staying in Egypt, in order to mollify Sahlān. It is possible that this affair, together with the local quarrels between the 'Babylonians' and the 'Palestinians' in Fustat and the episode of preferring the Babylonian title to the Palestinian, as well as other factors about which we know little, may have prepared the ground for Sahlān's support of Nathan b. Abraham against Solomon b. Judah in the dispute over the office of Gaon, from 1038 to 1042. When the differences had been settled, however, the contact between the two was renewed, as one can see from my collection. In around 1045, we even find that Abraham, son of the Gaon, has taken the trouble to write out for Sahlān a detailed account in Arabic script, of the honours and titles and other daily events in Jerusalem between *rōsh ha-shānā* and the last day of the Feast of Tabernacles.

Owing to his widespread activities in public affairs in Fustat and his connections with the local 'Palestinians' and the Palestinian yeshiva, there are quite a few documents in his own handwriting (which is a quite distinctive one) which can be found in the Geniza. Also, Sahlān apparently was frequently occupied copying books, either for his own or general use, and there are in the Geniza responsa of the geonim copied out in his handwriting, as well as remnants of treatises on law, such as fragments from Pirqoy b. Bāboy; a halakhic treatise in Arabic; rules of witnesses, also in Arabic. Sahlān b. Abraham also wrote many piyyūṭīm, some of which have been identified and classified by their acrostics and others which have yet to be noted in research literature.[81]

[81] The *yashrān* and other compliments: **58**, **75**. Identical requests for aid sent to Sahlān and Ephraim, see for instance: **88**, **89**. The woollen robe: **80**, b, lines 16ff. The letter of Abraham son of the Gaon: **141**. Responsa copied by Sahlān: TS Box G 2, f. 146 (the sale of a house); TS 8.2 (lost articles and deposits). Pirqoy b. Bāboy: TS 10 K 9, f. 4, see Ginzberg, *Ginzē Schechter*, II, 638f. The halakhic treatise: ENA 2464, fs. 43–44, cf. Adler's *Catalogue*, 140 (Talmud commentary); witnesses' procedures: ENA 2852, fs. 22–23. Lists of Sahlān's

The *negīdīm*

[809] The question of the *negīdīm* in Egypt, that is, whether there arose among the Jews of Egypt, a leader whose office and title were permanent, and who apart from being called 'head of the Jews' (*ra'īs al-yahūd*) also bore the Hebrew title *nāgīd*, has occupied a serious place in the research literature of our time. At the foundation of the current view on this question in Jewish historiography lie a number of sources which refer to the *negīdīm* in Egypt. The first is related to the problematic figure of Palṭī'ēl, the all-powerful Fatimid courtier, mentioned in the scroll of Aḥīma'aṣ. Twice, he is called *nāgīd* there: 'and to R. Palṭī'ēl the Nagid all their sayings he [the king] was telling', that is, the caliph al-'Azīz would tell Palṭī'ēl everything said against him. 'Representative and Nagid in charge, viceroy in the house of the king' (in a poem in his honour quoted there). Whereas in the latter, it merely says that he was a Nagid in the house of the king, that is, he held an office in the caliph's court, in the former, one may attribute the meaning of a permanent, established, communal post to the term Nagid. But the author of the scroll only employs this word as a hyperbole (like the word *pāqīd*, 'representative'); elsewhere he uses it also, for example, 'princes, *negīdīm*, who understand secrets', speaking of the sons of Shefaṭya; also 'He procured him the sympathy of al-Mu'izz, his *nāgīd*' (that is, God made the caliph cherish Palṭī'ēl), and here it is the caliph who is called Nagid.

The next source which served as a basis for a view of the institution of the Nagid is a responsum of the Radbaz (David ben Solomon ibn abī Zimra), that is, in about the middle of the sixteenth century, according to whom the role of the Nagid was born out of the marriage of the Abbasid caliph's daughter to the son of the caliph of Egypt. She wanted to create in Egypt something along the lines of the exilarch, which she knew from Baghdad, and a man from the lineage of the *nesī'īm* was thus chosen to be Nagid in Egypt. In his chronicle, Sambarī describes the event, adding details taken from Arab sources known to him. He notes that this took place during the days of the Abbasid caliph whom he calls Ṭāyy'ā, who came to power in 363 of the hijra, that is AD 973/4, and it was his daughter

poems: Mann, *Jews*, II, 104f, cf. Halper, *Hatequfa*, 18(1922/3), 193; Marmorstein, *JQR*, NS 8(1918), 26f; Chapira, *REJ*, 82(1926), 320; see the chapter on Sahlān in Schirmann, *Shīrīm ḥadāshīm*, 75–78, where two of his piyyūṭīm are printed, the second being a dirge on the death of Samuel 'the third'; details on Sahlān's other piyyūṭīm are included in the aforementioned E. Bareket's Master's thesis; see further: ENA 2795, 3844, f. 1; also ENA 3785, fs. 5, 6 (with a piyyūṭ 'In the night of the fast of the tenth' [of Tishri, Yom kippūr]). Among Sahlān's poems, one should also mention a poem in honour of Abū Sa'īd al-Da'ūdī, written by 'al-ra'īs al-jalīl', that is, 'a noble leader' for a 'Davidian', a descendant of the exilarchs. The poem is in the handwriting of Sahlān b. Abraham. For the time being,

who married the 'Egyptian king', whom he names 'Aṣar al-Dawla, in AH 366, that is AM 4745 (366 of the hijra corresponds to AD 976/7, while AM 4745 is AD 984/5). According to him, the exilarch in Baghdad at the time was Daniel b. Ḥasdai and he describes his elevated status, his splendour and standing with the caliph of Baghdad. It was from the family of this Daniel that a *nāsī* was chosen and sent to be the Nagid in Egypt. As Ayalon has shown in an article published in 1939, the historical germ of this story is made up of two elements which are completely at odds with Sambarī's story. Firstly, there is the aforementioned marriage of Qaṭr al-Nadā, the daughter of the Ṭūlūnid Khumārawayh, to the Abassid caliph al-Mu'taḍid, that is, the marriage of an Egyptian woman to a Baghdadi, and not the reverse. Secondly, there is the marriage of the daughter of the Būyid 'Aḍud al-Dawla to the caliph al-Ṭā'i' in 369 of the hijra (AD 979/80), which has no connection to Egypt whatsoever. At that time, the Fatimid caliph al-'Azīz sent an emissary with letters to 'Aḍud al-Dawla, which had nothing to do with the marriage; only that the two facts are recorded close to each other in an Arab source (Ibn al-Athīr). As to Daniel b. Ḥasdai, he was exilarch some 200 years after these events, in the latter half of the twelfth century, during the time of Benjamin of Tudela, from whom Sambarī copied the description of this Daniel's grandeur. Sambarī then seems to have wanted to stress the antiquity of the institution of the Nagid (at the outset of Fatimid rule!) and its importance, and composed an imaginative tale out of several sources. On the other hand, one cannot entirely discard the possibility of the existence of a popular tradition which described the arrival of a member of the Babylonian exilarch's family in Egypt as a result of the link established between the rulers of the two countries, but we have no inkling of either details or timing, and such a tradition would certainly have no bearing on the subject of the Nagid, specifically. It is possible that interwoven into Sambarī's story are threads from the affair of Daniel b. Azariah's son David (confusing one Daniel for another), who was crowned exilarch in Egypt in 1092. As Goitein has shown, the institution of the Nagid only began to take shape in conjunction with the decline of the Palestinian yeshiva's status, from the time of the Turcomans' conquest onward, and Jewish leaders, who were descendants of Maimonides, were beginning to be called Nagid in a regular fashion only in the thirteenth century. Goitein has also succeeded in understanding the reason for the appearance of this title and the beginning of its becoming a permanent one. From the outset, it was a title of honour granted by the Babylonian yeshivot, similar to *alūf*, *segān* of the yeshiva, and so forth. In around the year 900, the title was held by the

we do not know who this Abū Sa'īd was. The date there is: Iyar, 1357 Sel. (April or May AD 1046). See TS 10 J 22, No. 3.

father of Kohen Ṣedeq, the Pumbedita Gaon, in addition to another title: 'Joseph the Nagid, *nēzer* [crown] of the yeshiva'. The same yeshiva also granted these titles to the *negīdīm* of Qayrawān, one of whom, Jacob b. 'Amram, we shall encounter below, and more than likely, to the famous Spanish Nagid Samuel ibn Naghrila as well. Naturally, the word *nāgīd* is more honourable than all the other accepted titles of the yeshivot, for it is the precise equivalent of the Arabic *amīr*. However, in the period we are dealing with, the order of things was not that the yeshiva would endow the title of Nagid, and that the bearer of the title would become head of the Jews and hence be recognised by the rulers. The procedure was just the opposite: a man who came close to the authorities, who became the chief intermediary (generally a physician), and who also achieved considerable influence and prestige among the Jews for this reason, being able to perform significant services for the yeshiva (primarily raising funds), was the person granted this title. In the discussion until now, I have been able to portray more or less fully the Jewish communal organisation and the role of the Palestinian yeshiva, with the Gaon at its head, as the central institution and leader of the Jews of Palestine and the neighbouring countries – an institution enjoying the full recognition of the Fatimid regime in the eleventh century. We have also seen the course of communal life in Egypt within the two congregations in Fustat, and how they were closely tied to that yeshiva and how they accepted its authority. Within this structure, there was no room for a Nagid, and this is not merely an *argumentum e silentio*. That is to say that not only the fact that this title is not mentioned during two-thirds of the eleventh century in the Geniza documents, let alone in the Arab sources, is proof of the non-existence of this institution at that time. We have indeed encountered Jewish intercessors and courtiers such as the Tustaris, and Abraham ha-Kohen b. Isaac ibn Furāt, but they did not think of themselves as the leaders of the Jews, and even the authorities did not consider any one of them as *ra'īs al-yahūd*; this rank was reserved for the head of the Palestinian yeshiva. And we have no reason to assume things were otherwise at any time during this period, neither prior to the Fatimids nor in their time.[82]

82 The Scroll of Aḥīma'aṣ (Klar), 35, 38; 12 (the sons of Shefaṭya), 31 (the caliph); cf. Ayalon (Neustadt), *Zion*, 4(1939), 135–143; see *ibid.*, 126–134 the sources from the Radbaz and Sambarī and the discussion on them; see also: Cohen, *Self-Government*, 3–50, with a survey of all the sources and discussions in research to date. On p. 9, he calls the responsum of the Radbaz 'a simplified version' of Sambarī's story; but it would be more correct to say the contrary, that Sambarī, who wrote about 100 years after the Radbaz, elaborated on the story; it is always worth discussing the sources according to their chronological order. See Goitein, *Zion*, 27(1962), 22f., 165; *Mediterranean Society*, II, 23–40, and the references there, 524f, n. 2. Mann's views of the Nagid can be read in his books: *Jews*, I, 251–257; II, 459–462, 477–482; *Texts*, I, 416–434; despite the extensive information included in his Geniza research, Mann did not arrive at a clear and precise view of the negidim, and

[810] This is the general background against which we can understand the rise of the family of Saadia the physician b. Mevorakh. Apparently the family came from the Maghrib. 'Eli ha-Kohen b. Ezekiel notes in a letter from Jerusalem to the Fustat parnās 'Eli ha-Kohen b. Ḥayyim, in about 1060, that owing to 'the mercy of God . . . the ḥāvēr Abū Zikrī [Judah b. Saadia] . . . [came] from the Maghrib, to become a high hill in Egypt for all who come from elsewhere, from Iraq and from Palestine and from the west and from the land of Byzantium'; further on he highly praises his many generosities (but he still does not call him Nagid). This must be proof of the fact that the family hailed from the West, either Spain, north Africa or Sicily. Abū Zikrī Judah was also a physician who had evidently achieved a certain status among the Egyptian authorities, and he held a rank more or less parallel to that of Abraham ha-Kohen b. Isaac ibn Furāt, who died in the fifties of the century. He was called ḥāvēr and also rōsh kallā, that is to say, he was connected to both yeshivot, the Palestinian and the Babylonian. In a letter from the yeshiva to that 'Eli ha-Kohen b. Ḥayyim, dated *ca.* 1065, the two brothers are mentioned: 'Judah, the dear ḥāvēr, the excellent rōsh kallā in the *ḥavūrā* [i.e., in the yeshiva], and his brother, the *alūf ha-bīnōt* [foremost in wisdom], the excellent in the *ḥavūrā* [who is Mevorakh]'. He is still not called Nagid here either. There is

assumed that this institution was created in Egypt because the Fatimids wanted to cut off the Egyptian Jews from Iraqian influence, for their enemies, the Abbasids, were based in Baghdad. Baron, *SRHJ*, V, 308f, n. 45, still holds this view, despite what Ayalon has revealed; Ashtor, *Zion*, 30(1965), 141–147, also claims the validity of that opinion, and is still prepared to consider Palṭī'ēl as the first of the negidim; one should also consider Ashtor's view (*ibid.*, 141, nn. 280, 281) alleging that it is the court of the Nagid which appointed local judges and only 'from time to time' would they turn to the head of the Palestinian yeshiva. This appeal to the Palestinian Gaon, quoted by Ashtor, is mentioned in **73**, dated *ca.* 1025, and written by Solomon b. Judah, who explicitly states that it is the yeshiva which appointed Yeshū'ā ha-Kohen b. Joseph as judge (*ḥāvēr*) in Alexandria (as all judges were appointed in that period); while the appointment by the court of the Nagid Mevorakh, which he mentions, is from the year 1122 (!): TS 20.125, see: Worman, *JQR*, 18(1960), 13. Daniel b. Azariah, before he became Gaon, mentions a Nagid in his letter written from Qayrawān, in 1038, to Sahlān b. Abraham: he writes that the letter from 'our mighty one, the Nagid, may our Rock make him a [real] Nagid' (i.e. a real leader), has still not arrived. Perhaps he means the Nagid of Qayrawān, Jacob b. 'Amram, which is the view of Goitein, *Shalem*, 2(1975/6), 47; but he may also be referring to Samuel, the Spanish Nagid, see: **344**, a, right margin. The accidental and unestablished character of the use of the term Nagid can be seen in a letter from Sicily written by a merchant, evidently in 1063. It says there that a certain Zakkār b. 'Ammār (undoubtedly the brother of Ḥayyim b. 'Ammār, who was the merchants' representative in Sicily) was appointed Nagid of the Jews in Palermo on behalf of Ibn al-Ba'bā', who after he conquered the city, killed all the local commanders (*quwwād*) and even wiped out many local Muslims. We have not heard of a Nagid in Sicily anywhere else, and this is merely the writer's way of saying that the man was appointed as head of the Jews of the city. See: Bodl MS Heb, d 76, f. 59 (the reading Ibn al-Na'nā' in Goitein, *Mediterranean Society*, II, 25, 525, n. 11, should be corrected, as it should in the Hebrew version of the present book as well, p. 490). Ibn al-Ba'bā' is mentioned in several Geniza letters.

almost no doubt that Judah could not have received the title of Nagid from the Babylonian yeshiva nor from Daniel b. Azariah, the Jerusalem Gaon, who died in 1062. He evidently received the title Nagid only towards the end of the sixties, for he is so-called in 'Eli ha-Kohen b. Ezekiel's letter to Abiathar (15 April 1071) and another comparatively early use of the title can be found in a letter from a woman, a refugee from Jerusalem, writing from Tripoli (Syria) in about 1075, apparently Judah b. Saadia's sister-in-law (his wife's sister). It seems that these were the first occasions on which Judah was called Nagid.[83]

[811] It is very likely that Judah received the title of Nagid from the Palestinian Gaon Elijah ha-Kohen b. Solomon. Mann already assumed that he was granted the title during this Gaon's time. Supporting this opinion are first of all the close ties between the family of the priestly

[83] Originating in the West: **451**, a, lines 3–7; Goitein, *Mediterranean Society*, I, 159, attributes this to another Abū Zikrī, Judah b. Moses ibn Sughmār; but 'Eli ha-Kohen certainly writes about Judah b. Saadia, because he mentions this family of the *negīdīm*, in almost all his letters. One can of course split hairs and say that this passage is explicit proof only of the fact that Judah himself came from the West, and not the family, as is argued against my own opinion by Cohen, *Self-Government*, 133, n. 91. 'Eli ha-Kohen b. Ezekiel evidently had some family relationship to the family of Saadia; in **450** he sends them regards and states that he is praying for them all the time, and also for the son of the ḥāvēr, that is, Judah's son; in **455** (1071), as in his other letters, he asks that they should appeal to 'our Lord the Nagid, may God preserve him' and to 'my Master the ḥāvēr, *alūf ha-bīnōt*, 'the wise of the yeshiva, may God preserve him', with the request to sent him aid, for he is in great need. In the same letter, he sends greetings to the Nagid, that is, to Judah, and also to his sons (lines 29ff). 'Eli ha-Kohen b. Ezekiel undoubtedly came of an old Jerusalem family, and was evidently appointed ḥāvēr during Daniel b. Azariah's time. It seems that he was the author of two poems (*piyyūṭīm*) found in Bodl MS Heb f 29, fs. 67, 71, edited by Habermann, *Sinai*, 53 (1962/3), 191f, which seem to be in the handwriting of 'Eli ha-Kohen. Both are dedicated to Solomon b. Judah, and the first has an acrostic: ''Eli b. Ezekiel ḥazaq' ('be strong') and the other: ''Eli'. In the letters in my collection, his sons, Abū'l-Ṭayyib Khalaf and Abū Naṣr Ezekiel are mentioned. The latter served as an emissary of Jerusalem in July 1091, when he travelled from Jerusalem to Tyre and from there to Fustat, see **553**, a, lines 8–13. In **591**, line 20 (*ca.* 1130) it was said that Mevorakh the Nagid brought about the release from jail of a certain Abū'l Ṭayyib, who had been arrested because of his debts. Perhaps he is Khalaf, the son of 'Eli ha-Kohen b. Ezekiel. In 1079 Ezekiel is in Alexandria, where he is a signatory on a deed, TS 28.6: 'Ezekiel ha-Kohen b. 'Eli ha-Kohen he-ḥāvēr in the Great Sanhedrin'. His name is found in TS Box K 6, f. 120, a colophon of 'the book of corrections of the errors in the books of the head of the yeshiva (Saadia Gaon), of blessed memory', where on the verso it is written 'belonging to Ezekiel ha-Kohen b. R. 'Eli ha-Kohen he-ḥavēr of blessed memory'; cf. Abramson, *'Inyānōt*, 67. Judah's titles can also be seen in my collection, according to the Hebrew Index. See Cohen, *ibid.*, 132–156, for details on the family, from the eleventh century until the mid-twelfth century, and the family tree on p. 155. The letter of the yeshiva: **423**; indeed, the important status of the two brothers is already shown by the fact that the Fustat community are asked to inform them in particular of the matter contained in that letter (a warning against a certain Shemaria b. Meshullam). The letter of 'Eli ha-Kohen: **455**, where he is called *sayyidnā al-nāgīd*. The letter of the refugee: **605**, a, line 14: *mawlā'ī al-nāgīd*. See Mann, *Jews*, I, 254.

geonim and that of Saadia. One can even surmise that the two families were connected by marriage, for the son of Elijah ha-Kohen, Zadok, speaks in a letter written on 28 June 1056, to his brother Abiathar, evidently, about 'our Lord and Master Mevorakh, our son-in-law', that is, the son-in-law of the family, perhaps of Elijah ha-Kohen, father of the writer of the letter. This is not certain, since there were many Mevorakhs. It is interesting that Solomon ha-Kohen b. Joseph *av-bēt-dīn*, that is the nephew of the Gaon Elijah, enjoyed the patronage of Judah b. Saadia after he emigrated from Jerusalem to Egypt, as we learn from a letter from 'Eli ha-Kohen b. Ezekiel, who expresses his deep gratitude for this. From another letter, written to the son of the Gaon, Abiathar, when the latter was in Fustat, on 15 April 1071, it seems clear that Abiathar was also in contact with the family of the Nagid when he was in Fustat. Abiathar himself speaks of the Nagid Judah b. Saadia in a letter he wrote on 14 November 1070 from Jerusalem to that same parnās in Fustat, 'Eli ha-Kohen b. Ḥayyim. He writes (about the Nagid): 'may there be salvation for our Nagid and may he be saved from any horror' – perhaps because Judah was having troubles at the time. There are also indications of links between the priestly family and that of Saadia in the letter of Saadia ha-Kohen b. Nathan, from Jerusalem, to Mevorakh b. Saadia. The writer is one of the intimate friends of the Gaon, as he says of himself, that 'most of my days are spent in praying and praise [of God] in the company . . . of the Gaon'. He mentions the devotion of Mevorakh, grandfather of Mevorakh b. Saadia, on his mother's side, to the priestly family and how he would pray for them; Abiathar as well, he says, prays for the family of Saadia.

All the above facts seem to lead us to the conclusion that it was none other than the Gaon Elijah ha-Kohen who first called Judah b. Saadia Nagid. One should note that this occurred when security in Palestine was deteriorating, shortly before the Turcoman conquest. The roads were cut off and the resulting poverty in Jerusalem certainly imposed tremendous pressure on the yeshiva and weakened its direct influence on the communities in Egypt. This may have been the reason for the Jerusalem Gaon's need to enhance Judah b. Saadia's status, for he had always been a faithful and loyal follower. This loyalty towards the priestly geonim on the part of the Saadia family would later on be expressed in the bitter dispute between Abiathar ha-Kohen and David b. Daniel.

Upon the death of Judah in around 1078, his status and title were inherited by his half-brothr Abū'l-Faḍl Mevorakh b. Saadia. He is frequently mentioned in the documents in my collection and his name is accompanied by the most glowing titles and praises. We shall meet up with him again in the discussion on the dispute between Abiathar and David b. Daniel.[84]

Aid for the yeshiva and the Jewish population of Jerusalem

[812] I have already spoken of Jerusalem's economy and the hardship of living there. The existence of its Jewish population and its yeshiva depended upon considerable and continuous aid from the diaspora. Many of the letters in my collection deal with this aid, or contain requests for aid, information concerning transfers of money, matters of donations, and so on. For instance, we have the Gaon Solomon ha-Kohen writing to Ephraim b. Shemaria in 1025 on 'the poor of the Holy City ... the remnants ... the pained, the afflicted, the sad, the robbed, the deprived ... the depressed and the maimed ... the poor and impoverished'. Solomon b. Judah also appeals to the people of Fustat with an urgent request, proposing that they turn to the *Dasātira* (the Tustaris) and show them the Jerusalemites' letters with their pleas for urgent help. The son of the Gaon, Abraham, writes about the taxes – 'they are eating us alive', and the people of Jerusalem are in need of immediate assistance as the governor of the city 'and all his henchmen', 'satisfy themselves with pieces of silver' (this expression is explained in sec. 252).

At times, the appeals for money speak explicitly of the Jerusalem poor. For example Daniel b. Azariah's entreaty states that a large sum of money should be sent in order to enable them to distribute wheat. In another letter, he describes how, with the help of the ḥavērīm in Jerusalem and especially a certain R. Joshua, the parnās, he dealt with money received from Fustat from Abraham ha-Kohen b. Isaac ibn Furāt, which was evidently earmarked for the poor.

The appeals for help, which were the consequence of the war between the Fatimids and the Bedouin in 1024–1029, are especially poignant. As I

[84] The letter of Zadok ha-Kohen: **432**; Abiathar is in Fustat and he is asked to see to the collecting of a sum of money due to Mevorakh from the son of Sha'yā, the merchants' representative, for *shemen mefuṭṭāam* (that is, fragrant oil). 'Eli ha-Kohen: **451**. The letter to Abiathar: **455**, a, lines 14–16. Saadia ha-Kohen b. Nathan: **546**; cf. Cohen, *Self-Government*, 140f, who assumes that it was written in 1064, according to his decision that this was the time when Judah was first called Nagid, whereas he is still not called Nagid here. However, it seems that this letter should be fixed at a later date, to 1070; Cohen here ignores the connection between the two families expressed in that letter, but he also arrives at the conclusion that it is Elijah ha-Kohen who granted Judah the title of Nagid (see *ibid.*, 161f). See the discussion on Mevorakh: Cohen, *ibid.*, 171–177, 213–271. Mevorakh died on Saturday, 30 Kislev 1423 Sel., 2 December AD 1111, as it appears from **610** (see there in the note), and what Goitein wrote in his corrections in the Preface to Mann, *Jews* (to vol. II, 203), should be rectified and also: *Mediterranean Society*, II, 30. In the same letter (from Tobiah ha-Kohen b. 'Eli) it says that he died of the plague. This plague is mentioned in Ibn al-Qalānisī, 181, who says that it caused the death of some 60,000 people in Fustat; see also: Maqrīzī, *Itti'āẓ*, III, 49.

have already mentioned, taxes beyond their means were imposed on the Jews of Jerusalem and they were forced to borrow money at exorbitant rates of interest, which eventually led to the arrest of those Jews of Jerusalem who had signed promissory notes. Enormous efforts were made to raise money for this purpose of paying debts. Many letters from the yeshiva deal with this problem. A draft of a letter from Ephraim b. Shemaria has been preserved, apparently intended for Solomon b. Judah, which speaks of a great money-raising drive with the participation of both the Rabbanites and the Karaites, among the latter the Tustaris. Indeed, we know that the Karaites of Jerusalem were also seriously affected by the authorities' imposition of these special taxes. Also among the participants in this campaign to raise money were David b. Isaac, Abū'l-A'lā 'Amram b. Levi al-Buhūrī, Ḥalfon (Khalaf) b. Tha'lab (of Tyre), Joseph *rōsh kallā* (evidently Joseph b. Jacob ibn 'Awkal), Ephraim ha-Kohen b. Abraham, Ezra b. Samuel b. Azariah, Solomon b. Saadia (b. Ṣaghīr), Sahlawayh b. Ḥayyim, and others. Ephraim b. Shemaria was also among the donors. The aim of the campaign was to: 'give to our elders the Jerusalemites and save them from the money-lenders'.[85]

[813] In such situations it was customary to send special emissaries to the communities in the diaspora to ask for urgent help and to organise money-raising campaigns. Evidence of emissaries of this kind has been preserved in the letters of Solomon b. Judah. In 1015, before he became Gaon, he mentions the emissary Azhar b. Jonah the Spaniard, who may have been related to the family of Jonah b. Judah the Spaniard, who was the emissary of the Jerusalemites during the fifties. When Solomon b. Judah was already the Gaon, we encounter the emissary Joseph the cantor b. Yefet the teacher, whom the Gaon sent to Fustat on behalf of the yeshiva, and of whom he writes that he is 'a modest man' and also that he is carrying with him 'letters of the communities to Egypt [that is, Fustat] and to the entire region and to all the elders'. A short time later, the Gaon sent another emissary, Simḥa b. Dūnash, who also bore letters to the people of Fustat, and the purpose of his journey was also to recruit funds. In a letter of

[85] Solomon ha-Kohen: **52**. Solomon b. Judah: **91**, lines 10–11; Abraham: **165**; Daniel b. Azariah: **353**, margin; **355**, b, lines 39–41; see also: Daniel b. Azariah's scribe: **383**, on behalf of 'the remainder of the Holy City, the sect of the poor Rabbanites', and mentioning 'the payments, both regular and extraordinary'. Aid for the prisoners, see Solomon b. Judah's letters, **75**, b, lines 13–15; **87**. The campaign: **326**. The poem written by the cantor David b. Shekhania in honour of Sahlawayh b. Ḥayyim is perhaps related to this aid: Mosseri II 246 (= P. 46), in which he wishes, among other things, that 'he shall see the return of the released captives'. (My thanks to Prof. E. Fleischer, who drew my attention to this poem.) Ḥalfon b. Tha'lab of Tyre was the father-in-law of Ḥalfon ha-Levi b. Yefet, 'the merchants' representative' in Tyre, see **278**, line 18, undoubtedly one of the wealthy men of the city, who is mentioned a number of times in the documents in my collection (see the Hebrew Index).

recommendation given him by the Gaon, the latter asks the parnās, Abraham b. Mevassēr, to help him. At the end of this mission, the Gaon thanks Ephraim b. Shemaria for all the assistance which was given this emissary. In around 1055, Daniel b. Azariah's scribe writes of the success of yet another emissary – 'Eli ha-Kohen b. Ezekiel, who was then the parnās of the Jews of Jerusalem. 'Eli b. 'Amram, the Fustat ḥāvēr, had been helpful to him: 'and on this day his letter arrived [of 'Eli ha-Kohen] to us and to the elders of the Holy City telling of the good deeds of our honourable *ḥāvēr me'ullē*, for us and the elders of Jerusalem'.[86]

[814] Contributions to Jerusalem bore an aura of holiness, as did the institution of the heqdēsh, or the tithes in the days of the Temple. In this respect, they were considered the equivalent of charity and earned the donors a place in the world to come. In a letter from the yeshiva, we find equation of donations from the communities to Jerusalem with the treasures of the Temple. Indeed, Jerusalem attracted donations, as well as fines and pledges, such as the episode of Ḥayyim ibn Hārūn of Ṣahrajt in Egypt, who pledged five dinars to Jerusalem and five more to the local synagogue, if it was found that he had a wife in Fustat when he wished to marry another woman in Ṣahrajt. Unfortunately for him, it was found that he actually had a wife in Fustat, and the court decided that he was obliged to pay the fine in instalments.

Another significant source of income for the yeshiva was the slaughtering fees in those communities that were subject to its authority, as well as the fees for drawing up deeds. We have already witnessed something of the matter in Fustat, and it seems that the same arrangements that applied there were generally valid, that is that the yeshiva should receive half the income from slaughtering. When Yefet b. David was appointed supervisor of the slaughtering in 1025, he was explicitly asked to send half the income to the Gaon, Josiah. We have also seen how in Solomon b. Judah's day, the 'Palestinians' and the 'Babylonians' fought over the right to benefit from the slaughtering in Fustat, when the latter wanted to deprive

86 Azhar b. Jonah: **54**. Jonah b. Judah: **420**, d, line 26; **466**, b, line 8; Assaf, *Zion* (ha-me'assēf), 2(1926/7), 113, assumed that the former was the son of the latter, because the chronology of the letters was not clear to him. Joseph the cantor: **88**, lines 19–20; **89**, lines 17–21; he returned from his mission safely and continued to live in Jerusalem, for we find him mentioned in court records also in the times of the geonim Elijah ha-Kohen and Daniel b. Azariah, see in my collection, according to the Index. This Joseph has no connection to Yefet b. David b. Shekhania, contrary to Toledano's opinion, *Mizrāḥ u-ma'arāv*, 1(1919/20), 348. Simḥā b. Dūnash: **111**; he is undoubtedly the same as Faraḥ b. Dūnash (Faraḥ in Arabic is joy, like the Hebrew Simḥā), of whom it was said that he originated from Sijilmāssa and settled in Jerusalem where he married. I have already mentioned him above, in the discussion on taxes; see: **118**, in which the Gaon recommends him, during another of his journeys to Egypt in 1034; the letter of thanks to Ephraim b. Shemaria: **109**, where the only part of his name preserved is Faraḥ, but there is no doubt that this is the same man. The scribe of the yeshiva: **376**, lines 9–14.

Ephraim b. Shemaria of his authority over the markets, which led to the pronouncement of their excommunication on the Mount of Olives. In his letters, Solomon b. Judah generally turns down proposals that he should receive part of these earnings, as did former geonim. On the other hand, he realises that local supervisors are entitled to receive half the income from slaughtering ('from the markets') and the deeds drawn up in the courts ('half the fee of the deeds'). In his opinion there is no reason to object to this, for 'a man does not serve but for benefit', on condition that he really labours and that he states explicitly that these payments are due to him for his work. In Daniel b. Azariah's day, we encountered the affair of Yefet b. David and his appeals to the Gaon concerning the income from slaughtering.[87]

[815] The major source of income for financial assistance to Jerusalem came from the institution of the heqdēsh, however, which was established for that purpose from the outset. Apparently, in Muslim law the question arose whether the *waqf* of the dhimmīs should be recognised; with regard to the waqf for the poor there were no reservations and it was accepted as being self-evident in much the same way as the Muslim waqf. There was also a favourable attitude to the dhimmīs' waqf for the benefit of places of worship. We have already witnessed the pact between 'Umar and the Christian population of Jerusalem in which one of the conditions was that no church property would be confiscated. Al-Khaṣṣāf, a scholar in Muslim law in the ninth century (he died in 875), states explicitly in his book on the rules of the waqf: 'if a Christian dedicates his land or house as waqf and says that the income should go to restorations in Jerusalem, or the purchase of oil for the lamps there or any other purpose needed there [it is permitted] . . . similarly, the Jews in this matter have the same rights as the Christians'. I have already mentioned the shops in Ramla which were heqdēsh dedicated to the payment of the taxes of the Jews of Jerusalem.

In Fustat, about which we have the most information, there was an

[87] See the discussion on the religious background to charity, donations and endowments: Gil, *Documents*, 11ff. The letter of the yeshiva: **420**, d, lines 5ff. Ḥayyim ibn Hārūn: **389**. During the consideration of the case, there was someone who claimed that he had donated the entire sum of ten dinars to Jerusalem. See also the two fragments of the deed of gift from Tyre: TS 12.177, together with TS NS J 338, in which it says that in case of violation of the conditions of the deed, 100 dinars of Tyre had to be paid to the Gaon (though the reading of the word Gaon is not certain). Joshua's time: **319**; the document was written in February 1025, shortly before the Gaon's death. The struggle in Fustat: **79**. Solomon b. Judah: **158**. The affair of Yefet b. David: **400–402**; Daniel b. Azariah himself behaved as Solomon b. Judah did, and stated that he was willing to forego the income from slaughtering ('he does not want a market') – **356**; on the other hand, he submits to Yefet b. David's request that the income from slaughtering should be handed over to him, on the recommendation of Abraham ha-Kohen b. Isaac ibn Furāt: **357**, line 31; but see also **374**, in which Daniel b. Azariah asks 'Eli he-ḥāvēr b. 'Amram to deliver to someone whose name has not been preserved, 'everything that has been collected from the market from the

entire compound dedicated to the support of the poor of Jerusalem. In *ca.* 1030, a letter from Jerusalem to Ephraim b. Shemaria asks him to send a list of donors and details on the income from the building donated as heqdēsh for the poor of Jerusalem. They are awaiting Ephraim's letter on the collection of donations 'as to what he arranged to be done and what was done' with information about the collectors and the donors, in order that they may be blessed and prayed for in Jerusalem. They also ask for details on the rent from the building which is heqdēsh for the poor of Jerusalem, for they are in great distress. This may be the same building that Solomon b. Judah mentions in one of his letters to Ephraim b. Shemaria, when he speaks of a man who went up to Jerusalem on a pilgrimage during the holidays and told of a house dedicated in Fustat. The donor was Tobiah, 'prince of the congregation', evidently a Baghdadi, whose clerk, Rajā' b. 'Alī, had misappropriated his master's funds and 'ran off to the land of Meshekh (perhaps Khurāsān), and sat there eating and drinking'. We find a fragment of a letter from about the same time which the people of Jerusalem wrote to Ephraim b. Shemaria, complaining that the income from the *dār* (the compound) has not reached them and that another sum of money, evidently a special contribution from Ḥesed al-Tustarī for the poor of Jerusalem, did not arrive in time for the holiday, contrary to what they had been promised, and that they were in dire straits. The matter of the money from the house in Fustat again comes to the fore in some of 'Eli ha-Kohen b. Ezekiel's letters. A large sum of money was being kept by a certain 'son of Kuraysh' (?); this man died when 80 dinars of this money were still due to the Rabbanites and the Karaites; but the money, from the rent from the houses of the heqdēsh, is not available, despite many letters written on the subject. There still remained a debt of 18 dinars, given to a certain Abū Rāshid, who denies having the money. Daniel b. Azariah himself undertakes to arrange the matter. It emerges that in Fustat, rent was collected for a period of six years and the money has still not reached Jerusalem, while in Jerusalem they have to borrow money at interest in order to be able to distribute wheat to the poor. As the affair continues, it emerges that Abū Rāshid reached Damascus and the cadi there had already received a number of financial claims against him. In Jerusalem, they seem to have had some reservations about presenting their claims, for evidently this Abū Rāshid was a relative of one of the dignitaries.

The money from this *heqdēsh* is again referred to in 1085, that is, after the Turcomans' conquest of Jerusalem, when Solomon b. Ḥayyim 'the seventh' confirms that he received the sum of 20 dinars from the Fustat

beginning of Elul until the end of Kislev', and it appears that the money must be sent to Jerusalem.

parnās, 'Eli ha-Kohen b. Ḥayyim, which he had formerly lent to the Rabbanite community ('the remnants of Israel') in Jerusalem by means of a *ḥawāla*, that is the endorsement of a money order; now he has received them from the income from that compound in Fustat donated for the benefit of the poor of Jerusalem, the *dār al-maqādisa*. After the Crusaders' conquest, at the beginning of 1105, we find the sum of 90 dinars being transferred from Fustat to Abiathar ha-Kohen, head of the Palestinian yeshiva, which was already in Tyre then, of which 75 were from the sale of goods and 15, from the income from *dār al-fa'r* (the house 'of the rat') in Fustat, which was evidently a nickname for that house which had been dedicated for the poor of Jerusalem.[88]

[816] We have information as to how the money was being transferred to Jerusalem. This was generally done through the Jewish merchants who maintained most of the trading in the Mediterranean. A letter of Joseph and Nissim, the sons of Berekhia, to one of the important merchants of the time, Joseph b. Jacob ibn 'Awkal, contains instructions regarding such transfers amidst various other instructions concerning trade and moneys. In *ca.* 1040, Moses b. Jekuthiel, a Spaniard by origin, happened to be in Jerusalem. He had come from Tyre and intended to return there, the reason for his visit being to receive the validation of deeds relating to his business from the Grand Court, that is, the court of the yeshiva. As he happened to be in Jerusalem, he was asked to deal with money matters of the heqdēsh in Fustat. Moses b. Jacob, a Maghribi staying in Jerusalem, writes on 27 May 1054, to Nehorai b. Nissim in Fustat, and also mentions in his letter a *suftaja* (money order) which had arrived from Egypt and which was being dealt with by Abraham he-ḥāvēr b. 'Amram. Here, too, public funds are evidently being referred to. Moses b. Isaac b. Nissim al-'Ābid, a Maghribi merchant, writes to Ismā'īl b. Barhūn al-Tāhirtī about the sale of 22½ *raṭl*s of silk, the income from which being exactly 60 dinars, of which 58 had to be set aside for the Palestinian yeshiva (*mathībat al-shām*).[89]

[817] Generally, the money was sent by *diyōqnē* (in Arabic *suftaja*), that

[88] Al-Khaṣṣāf, 341. The heqdēsh in Ramla: **49**, line 17. On the *dār al-maqādisa*, the house in Fustat dedicated to the welfare of the Jerusalemites, see: Gil, *Documents*, 109. The letter to Ephraim, **405** ('what he brought about to be done' *'issā*, cf. **420**, d, line 36; **89**, line 16; see the note *ibid.*). The letter of Solomon b. Judah: **147**; the matter of 'the land of Meshekh', cf. Mann, *Jews*, I, 130, 275, n. 2. Fragment of the Jerusalemites' letter: **562**. The letters of 'Eli ha-Kohen: **440**, **442–444**, **446**; in this last letter, 'Eli ha-Kohen again mentions letters he sent to the parnāsīm of Fustat about the income from rent from the estate dedicated to the poor of Jerusalem (*al-rab' alladhī bi-rasm al-'aniyīm*). Solomon b. Ḥayyim: **540**. Money to Abiathar: **561**.

[89] The sons of Berekhia: Bodl MS Heb d 65, f. 9, lines 19–22; of 200 dinars only ten were *lil-shāmiyīn* (i.e. the Palestinian yeshiva) and the remainder *lil-'irāqiyīn* (the Babylonian yeshivot). One should remember that these Maghribi merchants were of Babylonian or Persian extraction. Moses b. Jekuthiel: **243**, a, line 13. Moses b. Jacob: **462**. Moses b.

is, a money order. At times, however, it seems that the money arrived in cash, as it did in the day of Josiah, who confirms that he received 30 *darkemōnīm kokhbāyyē*. At other times, the money intended for the yeshiva and collected by smaller communities would be deposited with a larger community, as we see from a letter from Solomon b. Judah to Sahlān b. Abraham, a letter which confirms that 'we wrote on this [that is, on the receipt of the money] to Zoan [Fustat] and we also sent a letter to the communities to congratulate them'. In one of his letters, the Gaon is again speaking of a *diyōqnē* that has evidently gone astray. After he notes that that *diyōqnē*, for the sum of 19½ dinars, has not arrived, and as he wishes to avoid any suspicion of deceit, he says: 'if there is any anxiety over the *diyōqnē*, is it not written on my name? Would I cash it twice?'.

We also have evidence of legacies bequeathed directly to the Jews of Jerusalem. In one of his letters, Solomon b. Judah thanks Sahlān b. Abraham, head of the Babylonian congregation in Fustat, for a *diyōqnē* of ten dinars for the poor of Jerusalem, left them by Abraham b. Naḥum Ṭulayṭulī (of Toledo); he collected the money and gave it to the *parnāsīm* of the poor to distribute it among them. They said prayers in Jerusalem for the deceased and for those people who busied themselves with the despatch of the money. These people are also mentioned by name in the letter: Mevorakh b. David, a money-changer, who received the money before Abraham b. Naḥum's death and handed it over to Ḥesed b. Yāshār, the Tustari, who wrote a money order on the sum to the Jerusalemite Faḍl b. Daniel.[90]

[818] It was common practice to make special donations to the *me'ārā* (the cave), the synagogue in Jerusalem, which was evidently situated beneath the 'Priest's Gate', in the Western Wall, as we shall see below. We know of such donations mainly from the time when the synagogue was damaged as a result of the collapse of the wall, evidently on a higher level

Isaac: ULC Or 1081 J 24, b, lines 1–2 cf. Goitein, *Baron Jubilee Volume*, 512; *idem*, *Mediterranean Society*, I, 223.

[90] Josiah: **31**; where he mentions Sahl b. Aaron and his son Abū'l-Ṭayyib 'Allūn b. Sahl, and as this term *darkemōnīm* is to be found in Karaite marriage deeds (see in the Hebrew Index) Mann assumed, in *Jews*, I, 162, that the senders of the letter were the Karaite congregation in Jerusalem; and in *Texts*, I, 376, he brought up the possibility that these two were of the Tustari family, of which there is no proof, as he stated there himself. Solomon b. Judah to Sahlān: **60**, lines 7–10. The *diyōqnē* that went astray: **82**, lines 14–23; the matter is mentioned also in **118**, lines 5–8, except that there most of the text has been lost; see the matter of the diyōqnē expected in Jerusalem which had still not arrived, also in **75**, a, lines 37ff. Here is a small list of dispatches of money from Fustat to the yeshiva by *diyōqnē*, the details of which have been preserved in the letters: **110**, line 16 – 10 dinars; **112**, a, lines 7–10 – 29⅛ dinars; **116**, a, lines 15–19 – 18⅔ dinars; **120**, a, lines 5–11 – 19½ dinars; **121**, lines 24–25 – 25 dinars; **146**, lines 5–7 – 10 dinars, and the same sum in **147**, a, lines 5–12; and in the last two letters, there is also the matter of the legacy. I have already mentioned the matter of the legacy found in **440**; see another example of a legacy: **154**.

of the Temple Mount, apparently in 1035. In one of his letters to Ephraim b. Shemaria, Solomon b. Judah mentions sums of money which had arrived from Fustat for the restoration work, for 'the stones and the plaster and the workers' wages'; 'the work is great', and hence 'the amount needed for the restoration of the *me'ārā* was great as well'.

In return for collecting money for Jerusalem, the donors and those who raised and collected the contributions were honourably compensated by having their names read out during the assembly on the Mount of Olives on the last day of the Feast of Tabernacles. At that time, Jerusalem was full of Jewish pilgrims who would gather on the mount to hear the Gaon's sermon. The mentioning of a person's name on this solemn occasion was considered the greatest of honours. It was said that in this fashion, for instance, a benediction was said for Ephraim b. Shemaria, who sent a *diyōqnē* for the sum of 29 and $^{1}/_{8}$ dinars 'from our brethren, the people of Egypt': 'and we blessed him on the day of *Hosha'na'*. Letters of thanks were also written, apart from this. Solomon b. Judah expresses his gratitude to the '*māsōs* [joy] of the yeshiva' and to another anonymous contributor, and promises to pray for their healing. Abraham, the son of the Gaon, sends a letter of thanks, full of praise (evidently at Sahlān b. Abraham's request) to Nethanel b. Ḥalfon for his extreme kindness and his abundant gifts. Another letter was sent by the Gaon's son to Abraham, the son of 'Solomon the representative, may he rest in Paradise', to thank him for his donations. The letters of thanks from the yeshiva were usually couched in the most ornate and rhyming phraseology, such as: 'these are the congregations of Zoan [Fustat], who make wormwood sweet, are the support of those who dwell in Canaan, are the ones who erect a tabernacle that shall not be taken down' (Is., xxiii:20).

One should bear in mind that the information available to us from the Geniza letters relates mostly to the *heqdēsh* foundations in Fustat and the contributions from Fustat, which was where the Geniza was situated. But there is no doubt whatsoever that similar arrangements existed in the other communities in the whole diaspora as well as in Palestine itself, as we have seen. Above, we have encountered the episode of the pledges to Palestine brought from southern Italy, as we are told in the scroll of Aḥīma'aṣ. Sums of money sent from Sicily are mentioned and the people of Sicily promise Josiah Gaon that they will try to renew the shipments of money which had come to a halt owing to the heavy taxes imposed on them. A certain b. Manṣūr, who arrived in Fustat from Sicily, brought 35 dinars with him and he added them to the aforementioned fund for the imprisoned debtors. There is also mention of more than 200 dinars sent to this special fund with a caravan of Muslim pilgrims from the Maghrib. Donations from Tyre are also mentioned, in the form of various amounts of money, as are personal gifts, from a dinar to a quarter of a dinar, sent to the head of the yeshiva, to the *av-bēt-dīn*, to the 'third', by Joseph b. Naḥum al-Baradānī with Jacob b. Samuel al-Andalusī (the gifts are listed according to the status of the recipients). Fifteen dinars sent to the yeshiva are also mentioned there, which were handed over to the 'fourth', who confirmed having received them. The major portion of assistance for the aforementioned restoration of the *me'ārā* also came from Tyre (as Solomon b. Judah notes in his letter to Ephraim b. Shemaria). In a letter to his son Abraham, who is staying in Fustat, the Gaon states that 20 dinars arrived from Sicily and ten more are about to arrive, and in the continuation, he mentions sums of money which came from Tyre. The man who brought the money from Tyre demanded too high a fee for this task – half a dinar for four dinars and three-quarters of a dinar. This was apparently a regular monthly sum which Tyre would send to Jerusalem. The Gaon suggests that instead of this expensive arrangement, they should put together the money collected for a number of months and with the accumulated money, they should buy merchandise. In another letter, the Gaon tells of the aid from Syria: 'and if it were not for the *ma'asē* (meaning here: fund-raising) of Syria and other countries abroad, we would be in the earth'.[91]

'Aliyā (immigration to Palestine) and pilgrimage

[819] During the period under discussion, despite the availability of hundreds of preserved letters from the Palestinian yeshiva, we do not find letters or literary sources which call for immigration to Palestine. From these letters and fragments, it is clear that the Jews of the diaspora were not called on to emigrate to Palestine and to settle there; furthermore, the act of leaving Palestine does not appear to have made much of an impression on the Palestinian Jews. In the twenties of the eleventh century, we find the Gaon Solomon b. Judah giving a letter of recommendation to Ṣedaqa b. Menaḥem, whom 'the Great Elder, the Mighty Master [that is, Ḥesed al-Tustarī] promised to write for him to one of his servants to enable him

[91] The restoration of the *me'ārā*: **120**. The benediction for Ephraim: **112**, line 14. 'The *māsōs* of the yeshiva': **130**, lines 30–32. Nethanel b. Ḥalfon: **140**. Abraham b. Solomon the representative: **150**; Solomon 'the representative' is evidently Abū Naṣr Solomon [Salāma] b. Saadia [Sa'īd] b. Ṣaghīr; it seems he was called 'the representative' because he was a trustee of orphans, see **61**, line 22; **76**, b, line 2; he is frequently mentioned in my collection, see the Hebrew Index. The ornate phraseology: ENA 223, f.2v, lines 9ff; there are many similar documents in my collection. The people of Sicily: **45**, a, lines 22f. B. Manṣūr: **326**, and *ibid.*, the matter of the money from the Maghribis as well. Tyre: **493**. Help from Tyre for restoring the *me'ārā*: **120**, a, line 27. Solomon b. Judah: **80**, b, lines 25ff, written on 17 May 1029. The information there on moneys evidently parallels what Ephraim b. Shemaria writes on the aforementioned special appeal, for it speaks of aid to release imprisoned debtors. 'Syria's fund-raising', see **151**, line 11.

to get help . . . in transferring his household to Egypt, in order to obtain a livelihood there. I would wish that you, the *ahūv* (beloved; of the yeshiva), should guide him, as is your custom', and so on. In his letter to Ephraim b. Shemaria, Abraham, the son of the Gaon, recommends someone, with only the name of his father preserved: Moses, a Maghribi who had tried to settle in Jerusalem and was forced to return to the Maghrib because of the distress in Jerusalem. He even asks Ephraim to speak to 'the people to come to give him donations'. The man came from 'the birthplace of our Master the Gaon', that is from Fās, as did Solomon b. Judah. In a similar vein, there is another letter from Abraham, son of the Gaon, about a man who fled to Damascus because of the heavy taxes imposed on him by the governor of the town; from Damascus, he came to Palestine. On the way, he was attacked by highwaymen and robbed of all he possessed. He wishes to go to Egypt where he may be able to obtain the means he needs to return to his own locality. However, we find in another letter from Abraham, son of the Gaon, a blessing for someone who 'went down' to Egypt: 'God [will help him] to return to settle in the Holy City'. Rawḥ ha-Kohen b. Pinḥas, a cantor from Baghdad, writes to Ephraim b. Shemaria, from Tyre evidently, that he considers staying in Acre or Tyre for the winter until 'God changes things for the better' and he intends reaching Egypt. Yeshū'ā he-ḥāvēr b. Ṣabgha arrives in Fustat with his family and requests the townspeople to help him settle there. There is no doubt that this man came from Palestine, as can be seen from the fact that he is mentioned in the letters of Solomon b. Judah and 'Eli ha-Kohen b. Ezekiel. The tiny letters surrounding his signature indicate that Ṣabgha was the son of Ḥedwetā b. Yaḥyā b. Shevnā, names that were still in use in Palestine.

Daniel al-Qūmisī, who wrote his manifesto to the Karaites 'to go up' to Jerusalem in about the year 900, understood exactly the view of the Rabbanites on this subject: 'and know that the villains who are in Israel speak to one another; we must not go to Jerusalem until He [God] will gather us just as He dispersed us'.[92]

[820] True, the people of Jerusalem were well aware of their position and value as viewed by the Jews of the diaspora. In their letters, they did not call for immigration, but stressed their special status and the advantage of being in Jerusalem. This idea was generally expressed in opening phrases requesting financial aid. According to a letter from the Jerusalem yeshiva, they 'are mishandled, plucked . . . broken by oppressors . . . erect a tabernacle that shall not be taken down . . . are the cream of the assembly, keepers of the regulations, poorest among people, the most honourable

92 Ṣedaqa b. Menaḥem: **60**. The Maghribi: **113**. Abraham son of the Gaon: **123**, **166**. Rawḥ b. Pinḥas: **211**. Yeshū'ā b. Ṣabgha: **338**; he is mentioned in **120**(Solomon b. Judah) and in **449** ('Eli ha-Kohen). The comment of Daniel al-Qūmisī (his treatise will be dealt with in the

among paupers'. These florid expressions, to the extent that they express an awareness of the importance of living in Jerusalem, also reflect the hardship. Above, we have already witnessed the straitened circumstances to which the city was reduced. Abraham b. Isaac al-Andalusī's letter, written in about 1050 from Jerusalem to his partner Joseph b. 'Alī ha-Kohen Fāsī, makes interesting reading. He describes the severity of the situation in Palestine due to the *aḥdāth*, the local armed bands, and that he and those members of his family who are living there, suffered from serious illnesses when they stayed in Ramla and also in Jerusalem. He is still very attached to Qayrawān, where he left the remainder of his family. Indeed, he asks his partner to buy two scarves, one green and the other blue, for his cousin, an orphaned girl who remained in Qayrawān, as well as a *mindīl* (a kerchief) for a Torah scroll, and to see to it that they are sent to their destinations in Qayrawān. In the continuation, in answer to the question put him by his partner as to whether he intends to settle in Palestine and whether he believes that he will have sufficient income to live on there, he explains to him how difficult life is in the city, and adds that after 'the little fast' (apparently meaning the 9th of Av) he will set out on his way. Moses b. Jacob, brother of Nehorai b. Nissim's wife, who lives in Jerusalem, writes from there on 27 May 1054 and also complains of the poverty in the city and the meagreness of his income. Even a strong and healthy man with a great deal of money would find it hard to live in Jerusalem; how much more so is this the case with him, an ailing man in reduced circumstances. Yet he does not intend leaving Jerusalem, for just being in the holy place outweighs all else.

We have seen then that while their self-estimation was high, they had to cope with difficult circumstances, including terrible hunger and physical dangers. In the main, however, the Muslim world was open, and whoever wished to come and settle in Palestine was free to do so. At any rate, the Jewish population in Palestine was an established fact. As we have seen, there were many Jewish communities in Palestine, and one can generally assume that they consisted of the descendants of the Jews who had lived in Palestine permanently since Joshua bin Nun's day. They were not faced with the task of renewing the Jewish population and this was evidently the main reason for the absence of sermonising on the need to immigrate. In this respect they differed from the Karaites, as we shall see.

The picture would not be complete if I ignored the basic state of mind that was common at the time, namely the reservations regarding thoughts, and even more so, actions, that could be interpreted as if they were setting a close date for events that were to happen in the future, in the

chapter on the Karaites): Bodl MS Heb d 36, fs. 13, 16, edited by Mann, *JQR*, NS 12(1921/2), 273 ff, see *ibid.*, 283.

days of the Messiah. Messianism and hastening the coming of the Messiah are the refuge of dissenting sects. Saadia Gaon rejected the Karaite interpretation – awakening to immigration – of the verses in Isaiah (lxii:6–7), 'I have set watchmen upon thy walls, O Jerusalem', etc. With this he also repudiated the very idea of hastening the arrival of the Messiah, which was the aim of the Karaites. In his view, the words of the prophet in these verses express abstract ideas, and their purpose is to point to the humiliating circumstances which would exist before salvation; also, in the words of the Bible, there is the demand that Jews mend their ways, but that the act of salvation should be left to Heaven. He also objected to the saying of the benediction: 'You shall kindle a new light over Zion', 'because the sages did not make this benediction on the light of the future during the days of Messiah but on the daylight which shines daily . . . therefore whoever says it would be better silenced'. In the prayers, he also stressed that one should be strict about saying only: (God) 'who redeemed Israel' and not 'who redeems Israel'. In the same manner, he also rejected the version 'the Rock of Israel and its redeemer'. It is also possible, however, to see in all this a basic general attitude against adding benedictions to those decided on by the ancient Sages, as Heinemann presumed. However, someone who would have supported the hastening of the coming of the Messiah and induced salvation, and who had been prepared to expound on immigration to Palestine in his day, would certainly not have formulated his comments in the manner chosen by Saadia Gaon.[93]

[821] Although there was no formal encouragement to immigrate, immigration did occur. This was undoubtedly motivated by the deep love of Zion imbedded in the heart of every Jew, but there were also topical causes. If that were not the case, we certainly would not find Babylonian congregations in Palestine, as we have seen above. In about the mid-eighth century, R. Aḥai of Shabḥa, author of the *She'iltōt*, immigrated ('went up', *selīq*) to Palestine. The Babylonians in Palestine and their customs are mentioned in the early writings of the geonim. They say the Kedushah (benediction) every day 'in Jerusalem and all the cities where there are Babylonians, and they stirred up quarrels and ruptures until (the communities) agreed to say the benediction every day; but in the rest of the cities and towns in Palestine which have no Babylonians, they do not say the benediction except on the sabbath and holidays'. There was a sizeable

[93] The letter from the yeshiva: ENA 223; see similar phrases also in **420**. Abraham b. Isaac: **504**. Moses b. Jacob: **462**. See the *Commentary* of Saadia Gaon to Is., lxii (ed. Derenbourg), III, 140; cf. Wieder, *Judean Scrolls*, 103, n. 3; Baron, *Saadia Anniversary Volume*, 47. On the deletion of the passage 'You shall kindle a new light over Zion' from the benediction on the creation of the luminaries, as enacted by Saadia Gaon and his reasons for this act: see the *Siddūr* of Saadia Gaon in the introduction, 25, and in the text of the Siddūr, 37 and the notes to line 6; see Heinemann, *Sēfer ha-shānā* (Bar Ilan), 1(1963), 221–227.

addition to the Jewish population of Palestine after 943, when there was a large Jewish migration ('the rich among the Jews') due to the internal wars and persecution prevailing in Baghdad. We have the direct evidence of a Babylonian who immigrated to Palestine and lived in Jerusalem, in the form of a divorce from the year AM 4633, that is AD 872/3, given to his wife by 'Ḥanīnā b. Yannai Joseph (?) from a place named Baghdad and living in Jerusalem'; the name of the woman is 'Tamar . . . from Nisibis and living in Jerusalem'.

Waves of immigration also came from the Maghrib, especially during the period of political disintegration and severe persecution of the mid-eleventh century, when nomad tribes took over Qayrawān. We have evidence of these new immigrants, for they generally were in need of aid from the local Jewish leadership or of relatives who had remained in the diaspora, and some of their letters reached the Geniza. At times, there were recriminations and complaints on the part of relatives who had remained in their places. For instance, a certain person from Qayrawān writes and asks of his son who is living in Egypt, to try to obtain the Mishnā bequeathed him by his father, from his son-in-law who has left for Palestine. If the latter does not respond, he proposes to pronounce him excommunicated because in addition to the Mishnā, he also owes him 1000 dirhams. I have already mentioned the affair of a certain b. Moses the Maghribi of Fās. There was a colony of Maghribis in Jerusalem at the time, as we have seen, and I have already spoken of Israel b. Sahlūn, Avon b. Ṣedaqa and others. The episode of a family from Fās which settled in Jerusalem is hinted at in two letters, one written from Damascus by Isaac the cantor, father of the family, and the other from his son Daniel from Jerusalem. The first is a letter of thanks addressed to the parnās of Fustat, Abraham b. Haggai, who together with Sahlān b. Abraham, looked after his brother Mufarrij when he arrived from Byzantium (they evidently also helped him settle the matter of the poll-tax). The writer arrived (from the Maghrib?) in Tyre and from there went to Damascus, where he became the guest of Meshullam b. Yefet, who looks after him as if he were his own son. Another Damascene and one of the heads of the community, 'Eli b. Yefet ha-Levi, also cared for him. He has arranged that prayers should be said in the synagogue in Damascus for the generous people of Fustat. In the meantime, he married the daughter of his uncle on his mother's side in Damascus (evidently his second wife). After Passover, he thinks of leaving for Egypt in order to earn something towards his livelihood, and afterwards to move to Jerusalem. If this Daniel is indeed the son of this Isaac, then the letter which he wrote from Jerusalem to 'Eli b. Ṣedaqa goes to prove that the family did in fact settle in Jerusalem. An interesting letter from a Maghribi who lives in Jerusalem is that of Abraham he-ḥāvēr b.

'Amram, who writes to a certain b. Moses ha-Kohen in Ramla, who is about to leave for the Maghrib. After expressing his regret at not being able to meet with him personally, he asks if he would take two letters for him to Qal'a (which is Qal'at Ayyūb), one to the dayyān and the other to the brothers Maymūn and 'Imrān the cantor, sons of al-Jurāwī ('Imrān is perhaps the father of the writer of the letter). In addition, he asks him to travel to Qal'a and deliver the letters himself, so that no one else could read them. We learn from the letter that the addressee's planned itinerary is: Alexandria, Mahdiyya, Qayrawān, Qal'at Ayyūb. The most important of his requests, he explains, is that if the addressee should meet his brother somewhere along the way, or in Alexandria, he should try to convince him to come to Jerusalem as well. There seems to have been a group of people from Qal'at Ayyūb in Jerusalem, and one of them was evidently Israel b. Sahlūn. It is also worth mentioning the appeal of Nathan ha-Kohen b. Mevorakh of Ascalon to 'Eli ha-Kohen b. Ḥayyim in Fustat, on behalf of Solomon b. Benjamin, a war refugee who intends to immigrate to Jerusalem. Apparently he is referring to a Maghribi. In the meantime, it is said, he has had to look for charity and has gone to Fustat for this purpose.[94]

[822] The Spanish immigrants to Jerusalem are a subject on their own (although Spain, al-Andalus in the letters of the period, was also included in the term Maghrib, and referring to a Maghribi may indicate a Spaniard). A fragment of a letter written in 1049 contains information concerning an important man, whose identity has not been preserved, who evidently came from Spain to Jerusalem and died there. It emerges that a trustee was appointed on behalf of his sister to deal with the matter of the inheritance. After leaving his homeland, this man stayed for two months with 'the western king's slaves', that is, in a region of the Maghrib under

[94] R. Aḥa: the letter of Sherira Gaon (Lewin), 103. The matter of the Kedushah: Ginzberg, *Ginze Schechter*, II, 524; see also: Mann, *REJ*, 70(1920), 139f. in the epistle of Pirqoy b. Bāboy; cf. Grossman, *Cathedra*, 8(1977/8), 137ff. See the opinion of Lewin, *Tarbiz*, 2(1930/31), 389, that Yehudai Gaon wanted to convince the people of Ifrīqiyā (that is, the region of Tunis), who practised according to Palestinian custom, to behave according to Babylonian custom, through Pirqoy b. Bāboy; see also: Spiegel, *Wolfson Jubilee Volume*, 243ff. The exodus from Iraq in AH 331 (which began on 15 September AD 942): al-Ṣūlī, 251; Ibn al-Jawzī, *Muntaẓam*, VI, 331, who adds that some of them went to Egypt, while al-Ṣūlī speaks only of *al-Shām*; Dhahabī, *Ta'rīkh* (MS Paris), 197a. The divorce: TS NS 308.25, see in Margaliot, *Hilekhōt ereṣ isrā'ēl*, 121, and see the photocopy, No. 21. The episode of the son-in-law: TS 13 J 29, f. 7, written on vellum. The family from Fās: **241**, **242**. On Abraham and Isaac, sons of Haggai (Ḥujayj) ha-Kohen, cf. Davidson, *Ginzē Schechter*, III, 243 and the poem TS 8 K 14, f. 1 printed by him there, 248ff, evidently a dirge on the death of the father Haggai, containing high praise of their generosity. The letter of Abraham he-ḥāvēr: **524**. Nathan ha-Kohen: **582**. One should also mention Faraḥ b. Dūnash of Sijilmāssa, whom I have already mentioned above, who immigrated to Jerusalem, married and had children there, and even began to pay the tax as a permanent inhabitant, see: **118**.

Fatimid rule. He had to flee from there (because of tax matters?) to Egypt (evidently Fustat), where he became a cantor and seems to have acquired the reputation of being a learned man, and to have carried on a correspondence with Nathan '*av-bēt-dīn* of all Israel', that is, Nathan b. Abraham. He reached Jerusalem in AM 4806, or AD 1046, three years before the letter was written, from which we have ascertained the time of its composition, which is undoubtedly shortly after the death of that immigrant. He was well-received in Jerusalem and was even given the honour of serving as cantor on Yom kippur. When he fell ill, the entire community prayed for his recuperation. It appears that he came from a family of *negīdīm*, but we cannot be certain. He may have stemmed from Samuel the Spanish Nagid's family, or perhaps the reference is merely to people of standing or public leaders. Elijah ha-Kohen b. Solomon Gaon mentions in a letter to Ephraim b. Shemaria, 'a man of Spain' who arrived in Jerusalem and who was 'crying out for his wife', that is, an immigrant from Spain who shouted and demanded that his wife be brought to him in Jerusalem. They quickly arranged a power-of-attorney deed (*wakāla*) for someone to fetch his wife from Egypt.

In 1057 Simon b. Saul, of Ṭulayṭula (Toledo) writes from Jerusalem to his sister Ballūṭa, who had remained in Ṭulayṭula. This was a large, widespread family, some of whom (among them Saul, father of the family) immigrated to Palestine while part of the family remained in Spain. The writer prays for them 'in that exalted place, Jerusalem the Sanctified'. He has taken a wife in Jerusalem and is pleased with his wife's family. In his letter, he describes a serious illness contracted by her father. In Ṭulayṭula – it appears from the letters he receives from there – there is starvation and plague (which may partly account for their immigration). From what he writes about other Spanish families in Jerusalem, one gets the impression that there was an entire colony of Spaniards there. There was also a family from Majrīṭ (Madrid), he writes, but they all died and no one from Majrīṭ was left in the city. He speaks of the women of Ṭulayṭula as if they were a faction of their own. People from Spain still continue to reach Jerusalem, some coming via Byzantium.

We find an inhabitant of Ramla named Mukhtār b. Solomon (Salāma) al-Dimashqī, that is, his father immigrated from Damascus to Palestine. 'Aṭiyya ha-Levi b. Judah was a man from Aleppo who settled in Palestine from whom a divorce is sent to his wife Jamīla, daughter of Ṣedaqa, who remained in Aleppo.[95]

[823] We also encounter immigrants from Egypt. A number of them are

[95] The fragment from 1049: **565**; Goitein, *Shalem*, 2(1975/6), 56 (= *ha-Yishuv* 143) assumes that perhaps Daniel b. Azariah and his arrival in Jerusalem is being referred to; he undoubtedly assumed this for the reason he notes there – the absence of a photocopy of the

mentioned in the Geniza owing to litigation dealing with their wives. A certain Joshua relinquished 'the many worldly pleasures, with which he became sated, and preferred to avoid the masses, to get rid of devils and [spirits] wandering in the desert, but wanted to increase his faith and dwell in the city of the palace. Therefore it becomes anyone who fears [God] and loves Him, to support and aid him, with no refusal', and so on (all this is expressed in rhyme). The man cannot return to Egypt (perhaps because of his fear of taxes?), and Solomon b. Judah asks that his wife, who refuses to leave her father's house, should be induced to join her husband. It seems that he has left with her a conditional divorce. Hiba al-Baṣrī (that is, his origins were in Baṣra, Iraq) ibn Isrā'īl al-A'raj settled in Ramla, but his wife remained in Fustat. He gives a power-of-attorney to Abraham b. David al-Kafrmandī to bring her from there, 'for I am in Ramla and cannot go down to her in Egypt'. Ṣedaqa al-Bāwardī b. 'Eli al-Dimashqī also immigrated from Fustat and settled in Ramla. His wife, Mudallala, daughter of Wahbān, appoints Joseph b. Manṣūr as trustee, in order to obtain a divorce, alimony for a year and the *me'ūḥār*, that is, the sum due her according to the marriage deed. A similar case is mentioned in Solomon b. Judah's letter to Jacob *ha-me'uttad* b. Joseph: Solomon b. Khalaf al-Barqī, of Barqa in Libya, left his wife in Egypt and immigrated to Palestine. He asks that she join him in Palestine; if she refuses, he is prepared to give her a divorce, though there are still details which need clarification regarding property and the financial support of their daughter, who stays with her mother.

In one of Daniel b. Azariah's letters, from the fifties of the eleventh century, he mentions another immigrant from Egypt, a certain Moses who immigrated to Jerusalem from Fustat and who, on arriving in Jerusalem, poured into the ears of the Gaon his praises of 'Eli b. 'Amram, especially on 'his great love and care and response to our needs'. There were people of Byzantium, who in passing through Palestine on their way to Egypt decided to settle in Jerusalem. This was the case in 1061, when the Maghribi Israel b. Sahlūn mentions in a letter to his cousin Nehorai b. Nissim the brothers Rūya and Levi, Simon, Isaac (the scholar of the group), his son Baruch (perhaps this is the same Baruch b. Isaac who afterwards settled in Aleppo). In another of his letters, he mentions an immigrant from southern France, Yeda'yā of Narbonne.

We also find immigrants from Egypt in Tiberias. Mubārak b. Wahb immigrated from Fustat and settled in Tiberias, and he writes to his brother-in-law who remained in Egypt, Khalfa ibn Ibrahīm: 'and if you

fragment. The matter of bringing the woman: **413**. Simon b. Saul: **457**; al-Dimashqī: **22**, a deed of trusteeship from 29 April 1015 written at the request of his wife, Malka daughter of Rawḥ. 'Aṭiyya ha-Levi: **406**.

have indeed decided to go to Palestine, then go to Tiberias'; 'Tiberias is cheaper than Ramla'; the bread there costs only one dirham per *raṭl*. And to end this chapter concerning immigrants and against a background which lacked any sermonising on immigration and displayed indifference to the incidence of people leaving Palestine, I shall quote the letter of Elijah ha-Kohen b. Solomon Gaon, who was then *av-bēt-dīn* of the yeshiva, to Ephraim b. Shemaria, in about 1055: 'Amram ha-Melammēd ['the teacher'] the Jerusalemite left his wife and children in Jerusalem and is staying in Egypt, and Elijah ha-Kohen writes to Ephraim b. Shemaria that 'Amram is grateful for the benefactions he bestowed on him in Fustat [it seems he wrote to the yeshiva about this] but, the writer adds, 'help him to return to his home, to eat onions in Jerusalem rather than chicken in Egypt'.[96]

[824] Unlike the Rabbanites, who were the major group among the Jewish people, the Karaites conducted vigorous propaganda in favour of immigration to Palestine. Those verses I cited from the book of Isaiah, 'I have set watchmen upon thy walls', etc. (Is., lxii:6), were used as the slogan for this propaganda. Early Karaite literature, especially in the tenth century, is full of calls to their brethren in the east, living mainly in Persian districts, to rise and 'go up' to Jerusalem. 'And if you do not come' says Daniel al-Qūmisī, 'send from every city five people with their upkeep for . . . always to plead to our God on the mountains of Jerusalem as it is written . . . upon thy walls, O Jerusalem, etc.'. In a similar manner,

[96] Joshua: **104**; cf. Friedman, *Sinai*, 74(1973/4), 20, n. 3, on the custom of leaving a conditional divorce with the wife, if the husband does not return by a set date; see TS 10 J 28, f. 9, 1. 23, edited by Friedman, *Tarbiz*, 40(1970/71), 356ff: '(until he will write her a gēṭ) *zemān*'; the reconstruction is by the editor, who explains: *gēṭ zemān* means a conditional divorce; see also *Sha'arē ṣedeq*, ch. ii, No. 11 '. . . and if he does not come by the fixed time (*zemān*) then this becomes a divorce'; see also ULC Or 1080 J 22 and the translation in Goitein, *Letters*, 315–319; cf. *idem, Mediterranean Society*, I, 61. Hiba: **425**; it seems that Hiba al-Baṣrī eventually divorced his wife in Fustat, Ḥasana daughter of Sahlān, and married the daughter of 'Eli ha-Kohen b. Ezekiel, who mentions him in his letter, **455**, lines 19, 26 (15 April 1071); this time he went to Fustat and left his Jerusalemite wife and children with her father, who is having difficulties maintaining them; cf. Goitein, *Mediterranean Society*, III, 198. (In my article: Gil, *Cathedra* 8[1977/8], 128, there is an error: Hiba al-Miṣrī should be al-Baṣrī.) Ṣedaqa: **318**; Bāward was in Khurāsān, that is, we have here a family whose father ('Eli) was a Damascene who migrated to Khurāsān while the son Ṣedaqa came from there to Fustat and thence to Ramla. The letter of Solomon b. Judah: **54**; cf. the matter of a woman who refuses to go after her husband to Palestine: *Tosefta*, Ketubbot, xiii:2 (Zuckerm. 275): '. . . if he wants to come to Palestine and she does not want, one forces her to go'; in the Babylonian Talmud, Ket., 110b this Baraita is quoted somewhat differently; and one can see that they did not enact this rule; later commentaries note that this rule applied only to the times of the Temple. Daniel b. Azariah: **377**. The Byzantine group: **479**. The man of Narbonne: **465**, a, line 21. Tiberias: **247**. Elijah ha-Kohen: **418**; Prof. Goitein, in his letter to me dated 31 January 1979, remarked that Elijah ha-Kohen certainly recalled the saying: eat *bāṣēl* (onions) and sit *ba-ṣēl* (in the shade; BT, Pes. 104a).

Abū'l-Surrī Sahl ha-Kohen b. Maṣlīaḥ says: 'gather ye to the Holy City and gather in your brethren for at present you are a nation which does not long for its Father in Heaven . . . and know brethren that Jerusalem is now a wilderness . . . yearning for its scattered children . . . and let there come one of a city and two of a family . . . elders and youths . . . but you are idle and sleeping on your beds . . . while Jerusalem is crying out for its children'. In his epistle to Jacob b. Samuel, he says in praise of the Karaite propaganda for immigrating to Palestine: blessed be the Karaite leaders 'who because of their good chastisement and letters to their brethren, the righteous and the pious have assembled in Jerusalem, may it be rebuilt and re-established speedily in our own day, and set up watches to pray day and night', etc. And so praised be the Karaite immigrants: 'who left their trades and forgot their families and rejected the lands of their birth . . . set aside their fine clothes and wore sacks, sighing and moaning . . . may God keep his promise to comfort those that mourn in Zion, to give them beauty' (Is., lxi:3). Referring to the Karaite immigrants, Yefet b. 'Alī expounds on the verse 'as the hart panteth after the water brooks, so panteth my soul after thee, O God'. (Ps., xlii:2): 'the *maskīlīm* who came from the diaspora to Jerusalem, for which they panteth' (*maskīlīm*, 'the understanding ones' in the book of Daniel, is an appellation often used by the Karaites for themselves).[97]

[825] Until the days of Daniel al-Qūmisī, Karaites did not settle in Palestine. The call issued by him and again by his successors to come to Palestine bore fruit, and thus the Karaite quarter arose in Jerusalem, newly built outside the wall. According to their own tradition, the Karaites began to immigrate in about the middle of the ninth century, after Benjamin al-Nihāwandī's time. According to Salmon b. Yeruḥim, those who participated in the immigration were 'people from the east and the west . . . who decided to settle in Jerusalem, and so they left their safe havens and lands of their birth . . . and now they sit in Palestine . . . for they are the *shōshānīm*'. In continuation, the Karaite writer identifies them with the mourners of Zion, according to Ps., lxix: 11–12: 'When I wept and chastened my soul with fasting, that was to my reproach. I made sackcloth also of my garment'. We also find in his work a vision of ever-increasing Karaite immigration, and he interprets 'the shaking of an olive tree' (Is., xvii:6): 'I gather that they are people who congregate in Jerusalem to worship [God]; though they are few, they will gradually increase in

97 Daniel al-Qūmisī: Bodl MS Heb d 36, fs. 13, 16; Sahl b. Maṣlīaḥ: in Harkavy, *Me'assēf*, 13, 197f; and in Pinsker, *Liqqūṭe qadmōniyōt*, II, 30f. One should note that the sermonising is directed towards the Karaites and not to all the Jews; as to the remark of Ben Shammai, *Cathedra*, 5(1977/8), 145, that the epistle does not advocate immigration to Palestine, one should point out that the epistle is addressed to the Rabbanites; and at any rate, it does contain praise of the Karaite immigration. Yefet b. 'Alī: MS Paris 287, fol. 2a. See more

number, and afterwards the remnant will appear ... and the division within the nation will cease'. And further (on Is., lxvi:10: 'Rejoice ye with Jerusalem ... all ye that mourn for her'): 'And none mourn over her but those who desire her rebuilding'; 'how much more so should we mourn and eulogise and lament over our souls and the weight of our sins and iniquities and might of our transgressions and the extent of our exile'. And in his commentary on Eccl., v:9 ('Moreover the profit of the earth is for us all: the king himself is served by the field'), he even seems to be advocating going over to a rural life: 'and they shall not be turned away from their worship [of God] by goods, but they shall sow seeds and rely upon the Creator. For whoever buys himself land is insured against any circumstance ... just as our forefathers, Abraham Isaac and Jacob, may they rest in peace, were sowers and herdsmen, they trusted and relied on the merciful one, may He be exalted'. He says similar things in his commentary on Eccl., v:12 ('the sleep of a labouring man is sweet, whether he eat little or much: but the abundance of the rich will not suffer him to sleep').

Shōshānīm (lilies), and mourners of Zion, was what the Karaites called themselves. *Shōshānīm*, according to 'to the chief musician upon *shōshānīm*' in the Psalms (xlv:1). A tradition ascribed to the Rabbanites by Eliah b. Abraham, author of the *ḥillūq ha-qārā'īm we-harabbānīm*, claimed that the Karaites' immigration began in the days of 'Anan, which has no foundation or basis anywhere unless the tradition is referring to 'Anan II.[98]

[826] The designation 'mourners of Zion' derives from the Bible (Is., lxi:2–3): 'to comfort all who mourn. To appoint unto them that mourn in Zion, to give unto them beauty'. Daniel al-Qūmisī uses the designation in speaking of the Karaites, and in the tenth century, in addition to its use by Salmon b. Yeruḥim, it is used by Sahl b. Maṣlīaḥ: 'how long will you stay idle ... whereas your brethren, the mourners, do not stay still either night or day, when they see the coffins of the dead being brought to the site where God's ark was standing'. And Yefet b. 'Alī, in his commentary of 'the voice of the turtle is heard in our land' (Song of Sol., ii:2) 'he meant by this the captains of justice and mourners of Zion who come from the diaspora to Palestine and withdraw to study and pray and plead ceaselessly and do not set this aside until they can see their redemption'. Qirqisānī writes in his book on the Karaites' ceaseless prayer shifts (*mashāmīr*) which

quotations from Karaite commentaries which repeat the homily on the abovementioned verses from Isaiah: Wieder, *Judean Scrolls*, 100ff.

98 See the text of Salmon b. Yeruḥim, in his commentary to Ps., lxix:1, Marwick ed., 98. 'The shaking of an olive tree': his commentary to Lam., MS Paris 295, 48a; see his *Commentary on Lamentations* (Feuerstein), XXXI, XLIII; *shōshānīm*, apart from the commentaries, see: Salmon b. Yeruḥim, *Sefer ha-milḥāmōt*, 57; his commentary to Eccl., v:8–11, BM Or 2517. The *ḥillūq*, see in Pinsker, *Liqqūṭē qadmōniyōt*, II, 104, cf. Poznanski,

continued throughout the day and night, to fulfil the prophet's words 'I have set watchmen upon thy walls, etc.'. But it is interesting that this writer, who has left us the description of the Karaites nearest the assumed historical truth, is alone in not using the expression 'mourners of Zion' at all. In the text of Sahl b. Maṣlīaḥ, we also find the most authentic evidence on the part of a contemporary, of the congregation of Karaite mourners from various countries in the Karaite quarter of Jerusalem: 'and you shall know, brethren, that Jerusalem at this time is the haven of every fugitive and the comfort of every mourner, and within its gates, worshippers of the Almighty are gathered, one from a city and two from a family. And within, there are women who lament and bemoan in Hebrew, in Persian and in the language of Ishmael'.[99]

[827] In the eleventh century too, we find evidence of this characteristic element in Karaite preaching and even of the existence of Karaite 'mourners' (*avēlīm*). *Ha-she'ēlōt ha-'atīqōt* ('the ancient questions'), a rhymed treatise evidently written in the first half of the century, contains a rhyming and mocking description of the endless mourning practices of the Karaites. Some generations earlier, Salmon b. Yeruḥim had already complained that the Rabbanites were ridiculing the Karaite mourners of Zion. At about the same time, Aḥīma'aṣ wrote his scroll and the 'mourners of Zion' are mentioned there. Samuel b. Palṭī'ēl donated money, he says, also

Yerushalayim (Luncz), 10 (1913/4), 85ff. See on Eliah b. Abraham and his treatise: Poznanski, *JQR*, 20(1908), 80f.

99 See Daniel al-Qūmisī 'to the *maskīlīm*, the mourners of Zion', in Marmorstein, *Zion* (ha-me'assēf), 3(1928/9), 39, line 10; see *ibid.*, 27f, explanations of the designation 'mourners of Zion'. See further what Daniel al-Qūmisī says *ibid.*, 28: 'for in the diaspora there are priests who mourn and lament over Jerusalem'; 'to convey tidings to individuals, to the mourners who strictly observe the message of God'; *ibid.*, 37, line 19: '. . . the *maskīlīm* of Israel, who are outstanding among them and mourn permanently, mourning for Jerusalem, by fasting and putting on sackcloth and ashes, and become ascetics', etc.; see his interpretation of Lev., xxiii:27 ('on the tenth day of this seventh month there shall be a day of atonement'), in Ginzberg, *Ginzē Schechter*, II, 485f: '. . . to torment oneself for the sake of God . . . to refrain from eating and drinking . . . to change clothes for sackcloth and ashes, and to weep aloud until one faints'. Yefet b. 'Ali: his commentary to the Song of Solomon, BM Or 2520, 56b. See Qirqisānī, 919, on the shifts; cf. Wieder, *Judean Scrolls*, 99. Sahl b. Maṣlīaḥ: Harkavy, *Me'assēf*, No. 13, 198f, 203. See the article by Gartner, who deals with the possible influence of the Karaite 'mourners of Zion' on the severity of the 9th of Av among the Babylonian geonim, in *Sēfer ha-shānā* (Bar-Ilan), 20(1983), 128ff. It is also worth noting the remarks of the student of Eastern Christianity, Vööbus, *History*, II, 34: in the Syriac translation of Eusebius' Ecclesiastic Chronicle the term 'mourners' means 'monks'. In his opinion, this translation was already written before the first half of the fourth century. He mentions what is said in the BT, Bava batra, 60b (dealing with customs of mourning the destruction of the Temple, where 'mourners of Zion in Jerusalem' are mentioned, as in Is., lxi:3) and what Benjamin of Tudela says (see the Adler ed., p. 26) and he arrives at conclusions about the Jewish influence on the Christian monastic movement. One can hardly agree with him on this; it seems that perhaps the very opposite is true; that the terminology of the Karaites may have been influenced by the Nestorian ambiance in the East.

to 'the poor mourners of the Temple, those who grieve on Zion and mourn'. Did this Samuel contribute money to the Karaites? There is no reason to believe that this is so, nor can one conclude that the use of the designation 'the mourners of Zion', a Biblical expression, was forbidden among the Rabbanites. It is true that the Karaites turned it into an established formula, as we can see from the description of the miracle that befell the Jews of Ramla: a decree that was to have been imposed on them was cancelled owing to a joint fast of the Rabbanites and the Karaites, after they appealed to one *āvēl* – 'mourner'. It emerges, then, that there were individuals among the Karaites in Palestine who were called *avēlīm*, 'mourners', who evidently belonged to the elite of the sect, and one can assume that they were recognisable from their dress and their daily mourning customs.

From the letters of Karaites in my collection, it is clear that Karaite immigration to Palestine also continued into the eleventh century. Nathan b. Isaac was one of those who reached Jerusalem from Egypt and he writes to his teacher there, Solomon b. David al-'Arīshī (evidently from al-'Arīsh in Palestine). Moses b. Isaac, some of whose letters in his characteristic handwriting have been preserved, was also an immigrant from Fustat. According to the pronouncement he makes in every letter, that he prays day and night (in shifts!) alongside the gates of the Temple Mount, it is obvious that his congregation sent him there and supported him, just as the Karaite scholars of the tenth century prescribed. One of his letters was written to two brothers, Isaac and Benjamin, sons of Joseph of Warjlān. Their brother Moses lived in Jerusalem for many years and died there one year prior to the writing of the letter in 1038. The writer of the letter, Moses b. Isaac, gives the brothers some details about the deceased: his first wife had died and he married again, and he had a son (who is in Egypt) and three daughters, two of whom live in Jerusalem. The elder, Rachel, lives in Ramla and is married and has two daughters, and the writer turned over to her the four dinars sent by the two brothers to their brother in Jerusalem, who has died in the interim. Moses b. Isaac was not a native of Wārjlān, it seems, but apparently lived there and became acquainted with the Karaite sect at the time. The letter also mentions the intention of the two brothers of Warjlān to immigrate to Jerusalem themselves.

Impressive evidence of Karaite immigration from Spain is to be found in a letter (which I have already mentioned) of Simon b. Saul b. Israel al-Ṭulayṭulī, written in 1057 in Jerusalem to his sister Ballūṭa in Ṭulayṭula. It contains an account of Karaites from Toledo, Abraham b. Fadānj and Abraham b. al-Hārūnī (that is, 'the son of the Kohen'), who reached Jerusalem via Byzantium, stayed at first in Ramla and afterwards settled in Jerusalem. (The account itself has some interesting details concerning

Karaite marriage restrictions and their situation in Jerusalem, which I shall discuss later on.)

To sum up, we can state that we find among the Karaites of the tenth and eleventh centuries both the idea of immigration and the process of enacting the idea which became reality. Karaite writers, and particularly the commentators on the Bible, headed this immigration in the tenth century, and as we shall see below, the eleventh century Geniza documents also contain evidence of spiritual leaders of the Karaites, such as Tobiah b. Moses and Yeshū'ā b. Judah, who stayed in Palestine and also settled there.[100]

[828] We have a great deal of evidence on Jewish pilgrimages from various countries. The time for pilgrimages was mainly in Tishri, in anticipation of the Feast of the Tabernacles, as in the days of the Temple. Aḥīma'aṣ, of southern Italy – that is, within the Byzantine framework – 'went up' to Jerusalem three times, and on each occasion, brought 100 *zehūvīm* (dinars) with him. The pilgrims were called *ḥōgegīm*, probably influenced by the Arabic *ḥājj*, which is its etymological parallel. Samuel b. Isaac, the Spaniard, writes to Shemaria b. Elḥanan in Fustat, at the begin-

100 'The ancient questions': Scheiber, *HUCA*, 27(1956), 299f. The complaint of Salmon b. Yeruḥim, cf. Zucker, *Albeck Jubilee Volume*, 384. *Megillat Aḥīma'aṣ* (Klar), 37, where it is vocalised: *we-ha-mishkānīm*, which is not acceptable, but should be *we-ha-miskēnīm* 'and the poor ones'; Mann's assumption in *Jews*, I, 49, n. 2., that *we-ha-maskīlīm* was originally written there, has no foundation, for in the manuscript it explicitly says *we-ha-miskēnīm*, see film No. 7359 in the Institute of Microfilmed Hebrew MSS in Jerusalem (Mann was followed by Zucker, in *Albeck Jubilee Volume*, 385); the general view of Mann, that in *pesiqātā Rabbati* and in *Megillat Aḥīma'aṣ*, a sect, or a movement, are meant by *avēlē ṣiyōn*, is unfounded. Implicitly he seems to have assumed that it first started among the Rabbanites, from whom the Karaites adopted it, which is again void of any proof. See the episode of the *āvēl*: **313**. See the list of references to the term 'mourners of Zion' in *Sefer ha-yishuv*, 115f: in the afternoon prayer for the 9th of Av; in *Pesiqātā Rabbati*; in the book *Halākhōt qeṣūvōt* ascribed to Yehudai Gaon. See the discussion in Zucker, *Albeck Jubilee Volume*, 378ff. What he wrote on the positive attitude of the Rabbanites towards the Karaite 'mourners of Zion' is not proven, and the sources he quotes use this designation without referring to the Karaites at all. Similarly unfounded are the comments of Grossman, *Cathedra*, 8(1977/8), 143, who also attempts to prove that there were also Rabbanite 'mourners of Zion'. Nathan b. Isaac: **297**; the letters of Moses b. Isaac: **298–301**, in the first of which the matter of the brothers from Warjlān figures; see Assaf, *Meqōrōt*, 49, on Warjlān and on the Karaites there (at a later period). The fragment TS AS 167.129 is also in the handwriting of Moses b. Isaac; it is possible to decipher there the expression *devīr mequddāsh* ('the sanctified Temple') and other expressions he was wont to use in his letters, such as: *quddām hādhā'l-bayt al-mubārak* ('in front of this blessed house'); twice *al-nāsī al-jalīl* ('the noble *nāsī*') is mentioned there, by which he undoubtedly means the *nāsī* of the Karaites in Egypt. In **300a**, there are the usual ornate phrases about praying in Jerusalem and on the gates of the Temple, and he complains of his distress which is due to the fact that he does not work to earn a living but prays all the time. **300b**, is also in his handwriting and was written for a certain Abraham b. Jacob, evidently also a Karaite living in Jerusalem, to the latter's son in Fustat. Abraham ibn Ezra's mention of 'the heretics in Warjlān' is interesting: (as it should be read: to Ex., xii:10); cf. also Hirschberg, *Sinai Jubilee Volume*, 344f. Simon b. Saul: **457**, a, lines 29ff. Cf. Ashtor, *Qōrōt*, II, 141,

ning of the eleventh century (before 1010), incidentally describing his meeting with a proselyte in Jerusalem: 'and after coming from Damascus to Egypt, I went to the Holy City, where I found him, for he had gone up to it with our brethren who went from Damascus to carry out the pilgrimage (*lāḥōg*) there'.

The first to 'go up' to Jerusalem in the month of Tishri were naturally the Palestinians themselves. It seems that during one such pilgrimage, a quarrel broke out in the synagogue between people from Tyre and Tiberias, which is described by Ḥasan b. Mu'ammal in a letter written for him by 'Eli ha-Kohen b. Ezekiel, on 27 September 1052. They had to bring the *ṣāḥib al-shurṭa* (the police commander) to the synagogue. People from distant Khurāsān also reached Jerusalem, as can be seen from Abraham b. Solomon b. Judah's letter to Ephraim b. Shemaria, in which he asks for help for a man of Khurāsān, Samuel b. Sahl; the latter having brought with him a letter from Saadia b. Moses, of Seville, whom he evidently met somewhere *en route*. Zadok ha-Levi b. Levi writes about Rawḥ ha-Kohen the cantor b. Pinḥas, who 'was exiled from the exile of Babylonia [! – undoubtedly a distortion: *gālā* (went into exile) instead of *'ālā* (ascended, i.e. immigrated) to Palestine] to prostrate himself in Jerusalem and was lucky to go on a pilgrimage in the previous year'. There were those who came to Palestine in order to make a pilgrimage to Jerusalem and to pray and to conduct business, all at the same time. Ramla was their base for conducting business affairs, and from there they would go up to Jerusalem for the Days of Awe and the Feast of the Tabernacles. This is described in detail by Abraham, son of the Gaon, who refers to the most important of the Maghribis to have come from Ramla to Jerusalem: Abū'l-Khayr b. al-Tāhirtī, who is pronounced ḥāvēr (he is Moses b. Abraham – Mūsā b. Barhūn). Maṣlīaḥ b. Eliah, who is Maṣlīaḥ b. Baṣaq, dayyān of Sicily, is involved with claims of the Baradānī brothers of Tyre and stays in Ramla in this connection, and seems to have been on a pilgrimage at the time, although he may have actually settled in Palestine after the disturbing events in Sicily in the mid-eleventh century. We also encounter Karaite pilgrimages. David b. Ḥayyūn, a Karaite from Tripoli in Libya was such a pilgrim and he writes to the Karaite leader there and thanks him for the aid sent him through the writer's nephew Ismā'īl, and promises to pray for him on the Mount of Olives and on the Gates of Mercy and sends greetings to the entire congregation. Maḥbūb b. Nissim the cantor, a Maghribi Karaite, describes his pilgrimage in a letter to a certain Abū'l-Faraj in Fustat. After portraying the vicissitudes of the journey and his losses, he

referring to the Ibn Fadānj family, which is mentioned in the thirteenth century: documents signed by Solomon b. Fadānq (1205); a matter of property belonging to Isaac b. Fadānq (1254).

announces that he has decided to stay in Palestine when his ship reaches Jaffa. He stayed in Jerusalem from 1 Kislev until the middle of Tevet.[101]

[829] Nāṣir Khusraw notes that many Christians and Jews come on pilgrimages to Palestine from regions of Byzantium and other countries, in order to visit 'the church' (*kalīsā*) and the synagogue (*kunisht*). I have already mentioned the advantage the Jews had over the Christians, in that they did not have to pay a tax in order to enter Jerusalem, for the taxes paid by the Jews of Jerusalem also gave the Jewish pilgrims the right to enter the city. There were undoubtedly Jewish pilgrims from Europe as well, though little has reached us on the subject. Above, I have referred to one such pilgrim, Yeda'yā of Narbonne. What Jonah ibn Janāḥ writes in the first half of the eleventh century in the *Sefer ha-riqmā* about a Jerusalem book which 'Mr Jacob *ha-ḥōgēg hlywny* brought us from *Bet ha-miqdāsh* [Jerusalem] which was in his own handwriting' should actually be read *ha-līwānī*, that is, 'the pilgrim, the Levite', for this is what they used to call the Levites. Hence he was not a man from Leon in Spain or from Lyons in France. There is also a letter of recommendation from the community of Salonika to a man 'from the community of Rūsiyah', evidently Russia, who wanted to make a pilgrimage, probably from the thirteenth century (as opposed to Mann's assumption that it was 'certainly' from the eleventh century).

It was common practice in times of distress to make a vow to make a pilgrimage to Jerusalem and pray there for deliverance. A pilgrim in similar circumstances, evidently from a Christian land, writes to the community in Alexandria after his ship sank near the coast of their city; he was miraculously saved, and was in hiding from the authorities who had imposed a high tax on him: hence 'I have made a vow to go to Jerusalem'.

101 The scroll of Aḥīma'aṣ (Klar), 15. Samuel b. Isaac: ULC Or 1080 J 115. Ḥasan b. Mu'ammal: **436**. Another such Palestinian pilgrim was evidently Boaz the cantor b. David, of Bāniyās, who signed as witness on a deed in Ramla on 17 October 1056, at the court of Daniel b. Azariah; see **391**, lines 21, 27 (his signature in Ramla), and **608**, line 34 (his signature in Bāniyās, on 11 July of the same year); cf. Braslavi, *Le-ḥeqer*, 74, n. 5. Khurāsān: **138**, line 20; Mann read Khayrāwān and assumed that it was Qayrawān, see: *Jews*, I, 102; and following him Hirschberg, *Eretz Israel*, 5(1958/9), 217, n. 35, who finds here an example of the connections between Palestine and the Maghrib. Rawḥ ha-Kohen: **212**, lines 26f. Moses al-Tāhirtī: **141**, lines 2, 4–5. There seems to be some truth in a fragment of *Sefer ḥasīdīm* (169, No. 630) on Hayy Gaon, who would 'go up' to Jerusalem on the Feast of Tabernacles (every year! – which is undoubtedly highly exaggerated), and would participate in going round the Mount of Olives seven times, and preceding him were the *kōhanīm* (of the family of the Gaon Samuel ha-Kohen b. Joseph?); *ibid.* also contains a strange story on a conversation in Jerusalem between Hayy Gaon and a criminal; cf. Epstein, *MGWJ*, 47(1903), 342f. Ben-Sasson, *Zion*, 51(1986), 396–399, finds in this story and in the mention of the *kōhanīm*, echoes of the epistle of Hayy Gaon 'to the unruly *kōhanīm* of Ifrīqiyā' (see: Lewin, *Ginzē qedem*, 4[1929/30], 51–56). He assumes that the source of the story lay in Hayy Gaon's opposition to the family of *kōhanīm* who took over the Palestinian yeshiva in the eleventh century, descendants of Joseph ha-Kohen b.

Above, we have seen the story of Israel b. Nathan, who made a vow to stay in Jerusalem should he be saved from a Byzantine jail. A calamity befell Moses b. Abraham (the aforementioned Mūsā b. Bahūn) al-Tāhirtī, a relative of Nehorai b. Nissim, when the son of the family died. In view of this tragedy, Moses he-ḥāvēr b. Jacob he-ḥāvēr, a Maghribi of Jerusalem, writes to Nehorai b. Nissim that the days of mourning would be the most appropriate time to come on a pilgrimage. In another letter, the same Moses b. Jacob tells of how much of an effort he is making to prepare proper housing for Mūsā b. Barhūn al-Tāhirtī in anticipation of his pilgrimage. He considered renting the same apartment for him in which he had stayed himself when he had come on pilgrimage previously, but in the meantime it had been let to someone else. Hence, he has rented another apartment for Mūsā and keeps it for him even though he is tarrying so long and the apartment stands empty.

Barhūn al-Tāhirtī assures Nehorai, after he arrives in Jerusalem, that he carefully fulfils his promises to him every day – by which he means that he says prayers for him, particularly that a son should be born to him, and for this reason, he also intends to go to the 'graves of the patriarchs', that is to Hebron. Some hundred years earlier, Sahl b. Maṣlīaḥ ridiculed the Rabbanites for a similar practice: 'they are idolaters . . . sitting at the graves . . . pleading with the dead and saying: Oh, Rabbi Yose ha-Gelili! heal me, make me pregnant.'[102]

[830] At times, the pilgrims would describe in their letters something of their experiences and life in Jerusalem. Solomon b. Moses Safāquṣī writes enthusiastically to Nehorai b. Nissim on 26 December 1059 about the view of the Holy City; he also mentions the snowstorm they encountered on the way to Jerusalem. To judge by his description, it seems to have been a particularly hard winter that year, with endless rain and snow. He also says that in order to get chickens, he had to go down to Ramla. It is

Menaḥem; cf. also Bornstein, *Sokolow Jubilee Volume*, 175f. Maṣlīaḥ b. Eliah: **426**. David b. Ḥayyūn: **290**. Maḥbūb: **292**.

[102] Nāṣir Khusraw (text), 20; (translation), 66f; cf. Starr, *Jews*, 197 (No. 142). Jonah ibn Janāḥ, *Sefer ha-riqmā*, I, 338; cf. in the Hebrew Index: 'Eli b. Joseph, al-parnās al-Līwānī; and *Sefer ha-yishuv*, 39, n. 29. The Russian: Bodl (Cat.) 2862 No. 26, fs. 71b–72a, edited by Marmorstein, *REJ*, 73(1921), 94f and by Mann, *Jews*, II, 192, and see the note of Goitein in the Preface, *ibid.*; also 'the placard of a Jerusalem pilgrim' of Abraham b. Judah the Spaniard 'from the city of Jī'ān', TS Box K 21, f. 9, edited by Eliash, *Sefunot*, 2(1957/8), 24, in a handwriting that seems to be from the thirteenth century, and not from the eleventh century, as stated *ibid.*, 10. The vow: **403**; also edited by Assaf, *Meqōrōt*, 59f, see line 3; this pilgrim requests aid from the Alexandria community, and it is not clear why Assaf assumed that it was referring to a locality near Alexandria; see *ibid.*, lines 16–17: 'I wrote this letter to be my mouth, for I do not know your language', from which one may assume that he was from a Christian country (as Assaf also assumed). Moses he-ḥāvēr: **460**, a, lines 22ff; **461**, lines 16ff (July 1053). Barhūn al-Tāhirtī to Nehorai: **458**, a, lines 25ff; b, line 10. Sahl b. Maṣlīaḥ: Pinsker, *Liqqūṭē qadmōniyōt*, II, 32.

interesting to note that some of the pilgrims' letters, such as this latter one, show that pilgrimages were not restricted to the holiday season but that pilgrims went up to Jerusalem at any time the possibility arose, even during the winter. This may also have been due to the fact that the merchants were less occupied with their business during the winter, as there was no possibility of travelling by sea then.

Nehorai b. Nissim also made a pilgrimage to Jerusalem, which we learn of in the letter from Salāma b. Nissim b. Isaac, writing to him from Būṣīr, the flax centre in Egypt: 'and you noted [in your letter] the matter of your return from Jerusalem, may it be rebuilt . . . and your coming to Fustat . . . may the Almighty God gladly accept your pilgrimage and show you and us Jerusalem rebuilt'. In a fragment of a letter whose writer is unknown, addressed to a cousin (on the mother's side: 'daughter of my mother's sister', *bint khālatī*) we read: 'Almighty God may grant that you go up to Jerusalem and see the tomb of Eleazar [?], the gates of mercy and the place of the altar and the Mount of Olives and Rachel's tomb, may she rest in peace, and the graves of our ancestors, may they rest in peace', and so on.[103]

[831] The Mount of Olives was the centre for congregating and praying during pilgrimages in the month of Tishri. Some thought that the reason for this was the gradual exclusion of the Jews from the Temple Mount. However, it seems that the practice of gathering on the Mount of Olives had earlier roots. In Talmudic literature, we already find the description of the passing of the Shekhina (Divine Presence) from the Temple Mount to the Mount of Olives: 'R. Yoḥanan said: for three years and a half the Shekhina stayed continuously on the Mount of Olives, and was crying out three times a day, and proclaiming as follows', and so on. The idea of considering the Divine Presence as residing on the Mount of Olives is anchored in the homilies of Talmudic literature concerning verse xi:23 in the book of Ezekiel: 'And the glory of the Lord went up from the midst of the city, and stood upon the mountain which is on the east side of the city.' In Karaite commentaries as well, we find similar interpretations. This is how Salmon b. Yeruḥim interprets the verse: 'this means that from the eastern gate it moved to the city and from the city to the Mount of Olives and from the Mount of Olives passed to the gates of Paradise, as it is written: I will go and return to my place' (Hos., v:15). During the period under discussion, we find the most ancient evidence of Jews praying on the Mount of Olives in the letter of the Palestinian Gaon to the Babylonians, at the time of the dispute over the calendar: 'and we blessed you on the Mount of Olives opposite God's Temple'; 'we pray for you very often,

103 Solomon b. Moses: **490**. Salāma: TS 12.793, lines 5ff; the formula of the blessing is certainly influenced by what was accepted among the Muslims. The letter to the cousin:

and also for your honoured elders, on the Mount of Olives, opposite God's Temple, the place which served as the foot-stool for our God'. In the same vein, Josiah Gaon writes, to Nathanel b. Aaron, about a hundred years later: 'our prayers and blessings are always for you in Jerusalem and on the Mount of Olives during the holidays among all the congregations of our brethren Israel'. In around 1029, Solomon b. Judah writes that in Jerusalem they would persevere in mentioning the communities in Fustat (*Miṣrayim*), and especially in mentioning the name of Ephraim b. Shemaria 'among the entire congregation and on every holiday and on the Mount of Olives'. In a letter to Sahlān b. Abraham in *ca*. 1035, he mentions going up to the Mount of Olives 'singing', as well as the gathering there during the holidays: 'and their ascent to the Mount of Olives in song, and their stance there facing the Temple of God on the holidays, the place of the Divine Presence, his strength and footstool'. In another letter to Ephraim b. Shemaria, he notes that benedictions were said for Ephraim (on the Mount of Olives) on 'the day of *hosha'na*', and in yet another letter the ascent to the Mount of Olives on *hosha'na rabba* (the seventh day of the Feast of Tabernacles) is described.[104]

[832] In a letter from the yeshiva, evidently written in 1057, we find similar details: the tax which the Jews of Jerusalem pay entitles them 'to encircle the gates and stand on the Mount of Olives praying out loud'; 'also in the lesser temple [undoubtedly the synagogue] also on the Mount of Olives in the congregation of our brethren of the house of Israel in the month of Tishri'; 'this is the place we pray in on the holidays facing God's Temple on the day of *hosha'na* and there benedictions are said for all the House of Israel'; the contributors to the welfare of Jerusalem shall merit being mentioned during the gathering on the Mount of Olives. In the letter it says that at the time of the Muslim conquest ('when they stretched out their hands and took Palestine from the Edomites') the Jews came 'and bought the Mount of Olives, where the Divine Presence stood, as is written: And the glory of the Lord', etc. 'For three years it has been proclaiming as follows: turn, O ye backsliding children (Ez., iii:14), but they turned a cold shoulder and did not hear or listen; and then He said: I will go and return to my place' etc. This matter of 'buying' the Mount of Olives should naturally be understood as acquiring the right, or obtaining an agreement. A few years after this letter, 'Eli ha-Kohen b. Ezekiel writes

TS AS 162.167, lines 8ff. There is no absolute certainty that it is from the eleventh century; on the verso, one can see the name Abū'l-Faḍl, perhaps the name of the writer.

104 Cf. the article of Hirschberg, *BJPES*, 13(1946/7): 156. See the saying of R. Yoḥanan: *Pesiqātā de-R. Kahana* (Buber²), 103a, and see the notes to the text *ibid*., Nos. 103–105; (Mandelbaum), 234; BT, Rosh hash. 31a; cf. Urbach, *Sages*, 54f, and n. 65; see *Avot de-R. Nathan* (Schechter), ch. xxxiv (p. 102) and the editor's notes 33 and 38. Salmon b. Yeruḥim, *Commentary to Lamentations* (Feuerstein), XXI. See the letter of the Palestinian

from Jerusalem to 'Eli ha-Kohen b. Ḥayyim in Fustat, that he prays for him while going around the gates of the Temple Mount and on the Mount of Olives, the place of the Divine Presence. There is no question but that the month of Tishri, the time for pilgrimages and gathering on the Mount of Olives, was the most important time of the year, and a month of considerable activity and bustle for the people of the yeshiva. Evidence of this can be seen in a letter from Israel b. Nathan to his cousin Nehorai b. Nissim, written from Jerusalem in October 1059, in which he apologises for not having been able to get a responsum from the Gaon on a query on a halakhic matter from Nehorai; the Gaon was not free during the month of Tishri, 'because all his activities are in that month'. As one could see from the commentary of Salmon b. Yeruḥim quoted above, the Karaites also maintained the custom of going up to the Mount of Olives and indeed, Sahl b. Maṣlīaḥ also mentions the ascent. I have already mentioned the cheese made by the Karaites 'produced on the Mount of Olives'. In his letter, the Karaite David b. Ḥayyūn speaks of his prayers while going up to the Mount of Olives.

I have already discussed the matter of the proclamation of the calendrical order and the fact that this was done on the Mount of Olives, the first mention of which we find in the literature dealing with the quarrel over the calendar. The custom of the gathering of the Jews on the last day of the Feast of Tabernacles was well known. Al-Bīrūnī, who was a contemporary of Solomon b. Judah, knew that 'the last day of the holiday of Succoth, that is the seventh day of the holiday and the 21st day of the month, is called *'arāfā* (he means, of course, *'arāvā*), on the day the quails were over the heads of the *banū isrā'īl* in the desert and on which the holiday of the congregation falls, because on that day the Jews gather on the *hār harā* in Jerusalem as pilgrims and they walk around the *ūrūn* [the ark] which is in their synagogues, which is like the *minbar* [of the Muslims]'. Mas'ūdī, who lived about a hundred years earlier, during the first half of the tenth century, also notes that the Mount of Olives faces the *qibla* (the direction faced during prayers) of the Jews, exactly in the way it is described in the writings of the Jews, that it is 'opposite the Temple'. Contrary to this, Ibn al-Faqīh (in the latter half of the ninth century) does not mention Jews in connection with the Mount of Olives, but does state that situated on its peak is a mosque built by 'Umar at the time of the conquest (which is not mentioned in any other source) and a church, from which Jesus ascended to heaven. As to Abū Bakr ibn al-'Arabī, the Spaniard who stayed in Jerusalem but a few years before the Crusaders' conquest, the thing which he found interesting there was the 'table', that

Gaon in Bornstein, *Sokolow Jubilee Volume*, 63, 107. Josiah Gaon: **32**. Solomon b. Judah: **89**, lines 23–25; **105**, lines 16–17; **112**, lines 13–14; **122**.

is, the very hard rock on which he usually ate, for it emerges that he lived on the Mount of Olives. This rock was formed, according to the Muslim traditionists, 'when its owners became monkeys and swine' (here there is a clear hint at the Jews, see the Koran: vii: 163–169, the aforementioned story which Muslim tradition relates to Eilat). According to him, people's dwellings on the mount were hewn into the stone and the dust which accumulated, would also turn into stone, and frequently the dust surrounding a door would petrify to the extent that the door could no longer be opened from within and would cause someone's death. He was always careful to leave a stone the size of an eighth of a dirham at the entrance, in order to prevent the door from closing altogether. Mujīr al-Dīn al-'Ulaymī, who wrote close to the year 1500, notes that at the top of the Mount of Olives is the grave of Umm al-Khayr, who was Rābi'a, daughter of Ismā'īl, a woman from Baṣra who converted to Islam and was a client of the 'Aqīl family. She died in 185, that is, 801, and her grave is near the site of Jesus' ascent to heaven, to the south.[105]

[833] A favourite place of prayer in Jerusalem, apart from the Mount of Olives, was the gates of the Temple Mount. Daniel b. Azariah, for instance, notes in one of his letters that he prayed 'at the gates of the Lord's house' and at 'the resting place of my forefathers', that is, alongside the tombs of the house of King David. We are not aware of which such site was indicated at that time. Joseph ha-Kohen b. Solomon Gaon 'prostrates himself before the gates of His sanctuary with supplications, falls down at the gates, caresses the stones [and prays] at the spot where the *shekhīnā* of God stood [that is, the Mount of Olives]'. Avōn b. Ṣedaqa would usually pray near the gates, and it seems that he preferred them to the synagogue. Shemaiah he-ḥāvēr, writing to Nehorai b. Nissim, mentions that he prays for him daily 'at the gates of the Temple . . . and on the Mount of Olives'.

It was the custom to pronounce the excommunication of the Karaites on the Mount of Olives during the gathering there. Concerning this excommunication, Abraham ibn Da'ūd tells us: 'when the Jews used to celebrate the festival of Tabernacles on the Mount of Olives, they would encamp on the mountain in groups and greet one another warmly. The heretics would encamp opposite them, like two little flocks of goats. Then the Rabbanites would take out a scroll of the Torah and excommunicate the heretics by name right to their faces, while the latter remained silent like

[105] **420**, c, lines 8–21; d, lines 3–4, 32–33; cf. also the statement of Salmon b. Yeruḥim above. 'Eli ha-Kohen: **451**, a, line 12. Israel b. Nathan: **469**, a, lines 22–25. More interesting evidence: Mūsā b. Abī'l-Ḥayy Khalīla, of the Maghribi merchants, writes in 1059 to Nehorai b. Nissim and notes that he rode up to the mount (the Mount of Olives); see: Bodl MS Heb d 75, f. 20, a, lines 8–9; cf. Udovitch, in *Individualism* etc., 67, n. 13; Sahl b. Maṣlīaḥ, in Harkavy, *Me'assēf*, No. 13, 204. David b. Ḥayyūn: **290**, line 8; Bīrūnī, 277. Mas'ūdī, *Tanbīh*, 143. Ibn al-Faqīh, 172. Ibn al-'Arabī, *Aḥkām*, 523f. 'Ulaymī, 258.

dumb dogs'. As I have already mentioned, this custom was the source of serious quarrels which even caused a division among the Rabbanites and brought about the intervention of the authorities, and the arrest and exile of some of the people of the yeshiva. The Mount of Olives was also the site of proclaiming the yeshiva's appointments and the titles of honour granted to the devotees of the yeshiva in the communities.

On the Mount of Olives, there was a stone, ten cubits in length and two cubits wide, which was called 'the chair of the cantors'. It was believed that this seat was lying where the Divine Presence had stood for a period of more than three and a half years (according to Ezekiel and the homily I quoted above), and where it would return in the future. This was the site where the head of the yeshiva would preach during the gathering. Solomon b. Judah writes: 'so I stood upon the chair'.[106]

[834] There is no doubt that the pilgrimages were of great significance to the status of the Palestinian yeshiva, its material and spiritual influence and strength. Hence, we naturally find repeated calls from the Palestinian yeshiva to awake and 'come to Jerusalem', that is, to come on a pilgrimage. In the autumn of 1039, at the height of the quarrel between him and Solomon b. Judah, Nathan b. Abraham writes to 'the *yedīd* (friend) of the yeshiva', undoubtedly one of his followers, and he reminds him that the holidays are approaching, that 'all of Israel' would be shortly coming on pilgrimage to Jerusalem. It would be a good thing if many of his true and genuine supporters would be prominent among the pilgrims, and the addressee should make every effort to recruit a large number of his circle in order that 'they should make up the majority and not the lesser part'. He asks that the people of his faction should convene a general assembly to discuss organisational arrangements for this purpose, to compose a list of participants, and to try to make propaganda to attract the largest number of people. Daniel b. Azariah, in one of his letters, expresses satisfaction at the success of the mass pilgrimage at the beginning of his office as Gaon and particularly at the calm and peaceful atmosphere among those taking part. 'Not a bad word was spoken between two Jews. The pilgrims ascended in song and prayer and went to their tents happy and good-tempered.'

106 Daniel b. Azariah: **379**, line 8. Joseph ha-Kohen: **411**, lines 35–36. Avon b. Ṣedaqa: **503**, b, lines 27ff. In the same letter, he says that he also intends visiting 'the graves of the patriarchs', that is, Hebron. Shemaiah he-ḥāvēr: **519**. Abraham b. Da'ūd, *Sefer ha-qabbālā*, 68, see the editor's notes there, 94, 127 (in the English part); see also Mann, *Jews*, I, 135f; on the excommunication see mainly: **85**, **122**, **182**; the latter source contains a lively description of the ascent to the Mount of Olives in Tishri, in order to proclaim the holidays, with the blowing of the *shofar*, when Abraham, son of the Gaon, leads the pilgrims; and also a description of the pronouncing of the excommunication of the Karaites. The 'chair of the cantors': **2**, a verso, lines 8ff. Solomon b. Judah: **85**, line 13; the custom of the head of the yeshiva preaching on the Mount on Hosha'na rabba (standing on

The pilgrimages involved great difficulties and innumerable hardships, partly because the sea-ways were risky, and this was the major means of reaching Palestine. It seems that pilgrims seldom travelled by camel caravan – partly due to the dangers encountered while travelling by land, for the roads were frequently troubled by troops or brigands. Hardships of the kind encountered by the Christian pilgrims, especially the caravan of pilgrims led by Gunther, Bishop of Bamberg, who were attacked near Ramla in March 1065 (see above), were evidently not the fate of the Jewish pilgrims. The latter were generally inhabitants of the Muslim world and were well acquainted with the conditions of the region. Many of them used to travel and visit Palestine regularly for commercial purposes. However, we are aware of the fact that the number of pilgrims decreased in insecure times. Solomon b. Judah writes to Sahlān b. Abraham, leader of the Babylonians in Fustat, saying, 'I will not conceal from you that even those pilgrims who came every year have stopped coming because of the warring troops and the impassable roads.' There is also a complaint about the straitened circumstances of the 'pilgrims [who] this year were mostly takers [and not givers]; this is their way in their folly' – as Solomon b. Judah writes to Ephraim b. Shemaria. In the letters from the eleventh century in my collection, we do not hear of local Christians mistreating the Jewish pilgrims in Jerusalem. However, the Karaite Sahl b. Maṣlīaḥ wrote about this in the tenth century in his Hebrew introduction to his Book of Precepts: 'and when the women go there, the *'arēlīm* [the uncircumcised] come out . . . to damn, offend and curse'.

To sum up, one may say that at the time of the period under discussion, from the Muslim conquest until the Crusaders' conquest, Jewish pilgrimage went on continuously, as long as external circumstances permitted. It was one of the major expressions of the continuity of Jewish life in the transition from antiquity to the Middle Ages. Pilgrimage was also an oft-repeated practical expression of the Jews of the diaspora's deep spiritual ties with Jerusalem.[107]

Burial in Palestine

[835] The Jewish custom of bringing the dead to be buried in Palestine was already common in antiquity, as exemplified by the graves of the

'the chair'): Abraham son of the Gaon, **141**, lines 9–10; an Arab source mentions the *kursī sulaymān*, Solomon's chair, on the Mount of Olives, see al-Musharraf, *Faḍā'il*, 47b.

107 See the call of Solomon b. Judah (*ca*. 1035): **121**, lines 24–28. Nathan b. Abraham: **187**. Daniel b. Azariah: **365**, lines 12ff. Solomon b. Judah: **88**, a, lines 14–15. The majority are poor: **112**, lines 11–12; Mann, *Jews*, I, 164, did not grasp the significance of the letter and saw in it an expression of the division between factions; what seems to be a description of the hardships suffered by a pilgrim, can be found in the letter of 'Eli ha-Kohen b. Ezekiel to Abū'l-Surūr Faraḥ b. Isaac, **447**. See also **403**, the story of the difficulties of a pilgrim –

fathers of the nation and borne out by the cemetery in Bet Shearim. It seems that in those generations, they adhered to a distorted version of the saying of R. Meir, the *tannā* of the second century, who said that whoever *lives* in Palestine 'is certain to be resurrected in the world to come'. The sages of Palestine even treated with contempt those who lived abroad and were brought after their death, to defile the soil of Palestine. However, we know that a very different attitude evolved at the same time, especially in Babylonia, which was that burial in Palestine was akin to being 'buried under the altar'. The Karaite 'Alī b. Sulaymān, in the latter half of the eleventh century, confirms the existence of the custom of burial in Palestine in his time. Muslim writers also bear witness to the fact. Al-Jāḥiẓ attributes this custom to the descendants of Aaron and David (that is, the priests and the exilarchs) specifically, and he goes into detail and says that they are taken out of their graves after one year and brought somewhere in al-Shām for another year and from there, they are taken to the Bayt al-Maqdis (meaning Jerusalem). An inscription on a tomb in Venosa in southern Italy, of a certain R. Abraham, who died in the year 753 from the destruction of the Temple, that is 821, ends with the words: 'and whoever shall carry him to the Temple will be inscribed among those destined to live in Jerusalem'. In a Karaite memorial list of an unidentifiable date, mention is made of 'his great sanctity Aaron the physician, who is buried in the Holy Land, may God have mercy on his soul'. He had been a member of the al-Kāzirūnī family (from Kāzirūn in Persia), well known in Fustat, and was evidently taken to Palestine to be buried there. In 1006, a childless woman in Fustat bequeaths in a death-bed testament, two *qīrāṭs* (that is, one twelfth) of a compound belonging to her, to 'be sold and used to bring my bones to Jerusalem, the Holy City'. In around 1020, the Nagid of the Maghrib, Abraham b. 'Aṭā', thanks the merchant Joseph b. Jacob ibn 'Awkal in Fustat for having dealt with the transfer of his brother's remains from Qayrawān to Jerusalem, and he asks him to compensate Abū Ibrahīm Isḥaq b. al-Sahl, evidently a Jerusalemite, for his efforts and expenses in connection with this burial. A woman of Fustat authorises an emissary to spend up to seventeen dinars to 'uncover the bones' of her husband Nathan (Hiba) ha-Levi and move them to Jerusalem. One can assume that wills requesting the transfer of bones to Jerusalem were generally executed, because this matter was treated with awe, as emerges from a responsum of an anonymous Gaon to a query regarding a certain Jacob, who appointed over his two sons 'trustees . . . and ordered his two sons to take his bones to Palestine'. The Gaon replies that 'this is the law of the Torah, that his sons should carry out his wishes . . . it is imperative to

evidently from a Christian country – who was stuck in Alexandria, as mentioned above. Sahl b. Maṣliaḥ, in Harkavy, *Me'assēf* No. 13, 204.

carry out the wishes of the dead to take his bones to the Temple' (that is, to Palestine, as it was commonly used by the Arabs as well), and so on. A letter from the community in Gaza, written by Josiah he-ḥāvēr b. Nathan, to the court in Fustat, mentions Mevorakh b. Nathan of Gaza, who is travelling to Egypt in connection with the inheritance of his brother 'Amram, who died in the Fayyūm, and also in order to 'carry his coffin'. Apparently there is an indication here that he intends to bury his brother in Palestine.

In the succeeding centuries, Hebron was the city where Jews wished to be buried; but burials in Hebron are not mentioned in the sources of the period under discussion. Thus it says in the commentary of Solomon b. ha-Yātōm to the tractate Mashqīn (apparently in the first half of the twelfth century): 'as is done still today in all the neighbourhood of Hebron . . . sending their dead to Hebron'. This information is questionable as the Crusaders controlled Palestine at the time, and it is possible that an earlier tradition is reflected here. Moses Naḥmanides writes in a letter to his son in 1267, that he now travels to Hebron 'the city of the graves of our forefathers, to prostrate myself before them and to dig a grave for me there'.[108]

[836] Muslim tradition adopted the idea of the preference of being buried in Jerusalem. Nāṣir Khusraw, the Persian traveller who visited

[108] The saying of R. Meir: 'Everyone who lives permanently in Palestine': PT, Shabbat, i, 3c; see *ibid.*, Kil'ayim, ix, 32d, where they speak of the dead of the diaspora who are buried in Palestine (according to Jer. ii:7): 'ye defiled my land, and made mine heritage an abomination'. *Tosefta*, Av. Z., v:3 (Zuckerm. 466); BT, Ket. 110b–111a. See also 'the most Babylonian' version: 'Whoever is buried in any other country is like buried in Babylonia, and whoever is buried in Babylonia is like buried in Palestine', in *Avot de-R. Nathan* (Schechter ed., 82); cf. Urbach, *Sages*, 998, n. 87, and more references *ibid.* 'Alī b. Sulaymān, his *Commentary on Genesis*, 156. Jāḥiẓ, *Rasā'il* II, 411; on the Jewish custom of burying their dead in Palestine see also Tadmurī, MS BM Or 1284, 74b (They do so according to the precedent of the burial of Jacob); Ibn Bābawayh al-Qummī, *'Ilal*, 296f (according to the precedent of the burial of Joseph); he speaks of *ahl al-kitāb*, 'people of the book', but it is clear that he means the Jews and not (also) the Christians, as believed by Mez, 372. The Venosa inscription: *Sefer ha-yishuv*, 40 (according to U. Cassuto's reading). The Karaite memorial list: Mann, *Texts*, II, 281, MS Firkovitch II, No. 1464, fol. 18a, and cf. on Kāzirūn and Kāzirūnīs: Gil, *Documents*, 286, n. 3. The woman from Fustat: Document No. 1, *ibid.* (edited earlier by Assaf, *Tarbiz*, 9[1937/8], 206ff). Abraham b. 'Aṭā': TS 10 J 9, f. 26, lines 10ff., see in Goitein, *Tarbiz*, 34(1964/5), 166f. The wife of Nathan ha-Levi: ULC Or 1080 J 262, quoted by Goitein, *Sefunot*, 8(1963/4), 107, n. 5. The letter of a Maghribi merchant to his son in Fustat, deals among other things, with the burying of the bones of a deceased in Jerusalem. We find there a passage in which he informs him that he intends sending him 'the bones. Go with them to Jerusalem, may it be rebuilt', etc. It was written *ca.* 1050. See TS 8 J 18, f. 16. The responsum of the Gaon: *Ōṣar ha-ge'ōnīm*, Giṭṭin, No. 56 (p. 25) see *ibid.*, quotations in which the Temple (*Bēt ha-miqdāsh*) means Palestine; cf. further on this: Assaf, *Tarbiz, ibid.*, 19; and see also Maimonides, *Responsa* I, 200. Mevorakh b. Nathan the Gazan, **219**, lines 5–6. The *Commentary on Mashqīn* of Solomon b. ha-Yātōm, p. XIII; cf. Hirschberg, *Tarbiz*, 42(1972/3), 385. See the letter of Moses Naḥmanides according to a Munich manuscript, in Kedar, *Tarbiz*, 41(1971/2), 93.

Palestine in 1047, mentions that many (Muslims) come to Jerusalem, because they believe that the resurrection of the dead will start from the 'rock' and that the Muslim cemetery is thus to be found at the edge of the plateau, on the Mount of Olives. According to al-Wāsiṭī, writing in *ca.* 1020, the cemetery is situated in Māmillā (he has: *zaytūn al-milla*, 'the olive trees of the religion', a commonly used distortion of the name Māmillā, as is also another version: *bāb al-milla*). He also goes into detail over the advantages of being buried in Jerusalem. According to al-Zarkashī (writing in the fourteenth century), the person being buried in Jerusalem is not subjected to the purgatorial torments of the tomb (*fitnat al-qabr*), and if he was buried in the *zaytūn al-milla*, it would be as if he was buried in heaven. It is attributed to Ka'b al-Aḥbār that for whoever is buried in Jerusalem, it is as if he has already gone down the straight road, for Jerusalem is the land of the resurrection (*al-maḥshar*, 'the gathering', the by-name for the resurrection of the dead at the End of Days). And for whoever dies in Jerusalem, so said the Prophet, it is as if he died in heaven.

Apart from the many Muslim personalities buried in Jerusalem, whom we have seen in the lists of personalities above, the desire to be buried there was most marked among the Ikhshīdids. Even before their time, Takīn, who had been governor of Damascus and afterwards of Egypt, was buried there. He died in Egypt in AH 321, that is AD 933, and was brought to Jerusalem to be buried. It is told that this Takīn quarrelled with one of the leaders of the Ṣūfīs, the ascetic Abū'l-Ḥasan 'Alī b. Muḥammad b. Sahl al-Dīnawarī, who was a silversmith by profession (he died in AH 331, that is AD 942/3). Takīn ousted him to Jerusalem. Some time later, exactly as foretold by al-Dīnawarī, Takīn's coffin arrived in Jerusalem, and on reaching the city, it fell from the back of the mule, and the animal urinated on it. The Ikhshīd who died in Damascus on Dhū'l-Ḥijja AH 334 (July AD 946), was also brought to Jerusalem and buried there. His brother, al-Ḥasan ibn Ṭughj, was also buried in Jerusalem (he died in Ramla in AH 342, that is AD 953/4), as were the Ikhshīd's sons, Anūjūr, on 7 Dhū'l-Qa'da AH 347 (20 January AD 959), and 'Alī, on 11 Muḥarram AH 355 (8 January AD 966), and the regent of Egypt, Kāfūr, in AH 356, that is AD 967.[109]

109 Nāṣir Khusraw (text), 20, (translation), 68; it seems that his intention is *al-sāhira*, the plateau on the northern part of the Mount of Olives; cf. Le Strange, *Palestine*, 218ff. Wāsiṭī, 46f, and see the editor's note there. Zarkashī, *I'lām*, 294. In Mujīr al-Dīn al-'Ulaymī's time, the cemetery was near *bāb al-raḥma*, that is, east of the Temple Mount, apparently in the Kidron Valley, for he indicates: under the wall of al-Masjid al-Aqṣā (see *ibid.*, 233, 413). Takīn: Dhahabī, *'Ibar*, II, 186. The story of the Ṣūfī: Suyūṭī, *Muḥāḍara*, I, 514; Ashtor, *Annales ESC*, 27(1972), 187, n. 14, sees in this evidence that the Ṣūfīs preferred to live in Jerusalem; but this is not stated there, nor even hinted at; more on Takīn: Ibn Taghrī Bardī, III, 211: Takīn died on 16 Rabī' I, 321, 16 March AD 933. The Ikhshīd: Yāfi'ī, II, 315; Dhahabī, *'Ibar*, II, 186; Ibn Sa'īd, *Mughrib*, 44 (according to him he

[837] The burying of Muslims on the Temple Mount or its environs was undoubtedly very painful to the Jews of that time, as must have been the presence of many Christian graves from pre-Islamic times. This is confirmed in Karaite Bible commentaries of the tenth century. Salmon b. Yeruḥim complains about 'the graves of the uncircumcised and the Kedarites' to be seen in Jerusalem; there are in the city a large number of unclean things, 'and women and men with issues, and menstruating women and lepers and uncircumcised ones, camels and asses and coffins of the dead, and male prostitutes and homosexuality, and blaspheming and cursing, and pronouncements of idolatry and of the false prophet, and the eastern gate, the place of Meshelemiah, the porter [1 Chr., xxvi:1], has become a latrine for the Ishmaelites, and all the monuments of the House of God have become graves of the wicked'. And in the same commentary: 'The House of God. . . lo, it is now an altar for the sons of Hagar instead of the sons of Aaron, its servants; lo, the uncircumcised and the unclean enter there instead of sacrifice and altar . . . and within they proclaim the name of a statue and a false prophet five times a day . . . lo, they bring the coffins of the dead within and pray over them every day . . . and lo, there are in their stead, cemeteries at the gates'. Elsewhere, he speaks of 'the *'arēlīm* and the unclean, and the images, and people with issues, and lepers, and adultery, and man lying with man, and privies, and they pray over the dead in its courtyards, and proclaim in the memory of an idol and a false prophet five times a day'. Sahl b. Maṣlīaḥ, in his introduction to his Book of Precepts, also speaks of the heart-break of 'the mourning brethren' on 'seeing the coffins of the dead being brought into the place where the holy ark stood'. In the same vein, Yefet b. 'Alī also has his say: 'the castrated and the unclean and the coffins of the dead and the sodomites and those who commit abominable acts, are instead of the ark of God'. In the eleventh century we find such complaints only on one occasion, in a letter from the yeshiva written in 1057: 'and the unruly people came and defiled the place, its gatekeepers are alien, its neighbourhood graves'.[110]

The Jewish quarters of Jerusalem

[838] The following discussion focuses on three central issues: (1) Whether there was one Jewish-Rabbanite quarter in Jerusalem; or whether

was buried in Jerusalem after camphor [*kāfūr*] was not found in Damascus for his embalming and rats ate the ends of his fingers and ants his eyes; black slaves bore his corpse on the back of a blind camel); Ibn Kathīr, *Bidāya*, XI, 215; Ṣafadī, *al-Wāfī*, III, 171; Maqrīzī, *Khiṭaṭ*, II, 438. Al-Ḥasan ibn Ṭughj: Ibn 'Asākir, IV, 186; Ibn Taghrī Bardī, III, 310; Anūjūr: Maqrīzī, *Khiṭaṭ*, II, 17; Ibn Taghrī Bardī, III, 293, 326; Kāfūr: Ibn Khallikān, III, 270; Ibn Taghrī Bardī, IV, 10. (The sources are not unanimous on the date of Kāfūr's death.)

110 Salmon: *Commentary to Lamentations* (MS Paris 295), 48a, 54a. (Feuerstein), XXIII–

there were two, one in the southern part of the city and the other in the north; (2) whether one can define the site of the southern quarter precisely; and (3) what was the site of the Karaite quarter?

We have seen above the fragment from the Jewish chronicle containing a description of the meeting of the Jews with the caliph 'Umar ibn al-Khaṭṭāb, and how the Jews requested and received from him permission to settle in the southern part of Jerusalem, near the gates of 'the *qodesh*', that is, of the Temple Mount and the Siloam. According to the chronicle, the region was covered with the ruins of many generations and it is the Jews who undertook to restore that area. It emerges that this was the Jewish market, and it remains so at the time the chronicle was being written. They built their houses in the same neighbourhood, using building materials which they found there among the ruins.

An indication of the responsibilities which the Jews took on themselves when they received permission to settle in Jerusalem can be found in a letter of the yeshiva written in 1057, and we have already seen that it included the obligation to clear away its rubbish, to clean its sewerage, to repair its walls and to take care of the city's guardians. It would be rather far-fetched to assume that these obligations on the part of the Jews to maintain cleanliness and repair and guard the wall applied to the entire city, and they were undoubtedly applicable merely to the section in which they lived. At any rate, we learn from this that their quarter was located within the walls.

We find confirmation of the fact that there was a Jewish quarter in the southern part of the city from Mujīr al-Dīn al-'Ulaymī, writing in 1496. According to him, the Zion Gate was known by the nickname 'the Gate of the Jewish Quarter'. Avon b. Ṣedaqa, in his letter to Nehorai b. Nissim, written on 11 November 1064, states that ever since the funeral of Daniel b. Azariah, the Jews have not been permitted to pass in front of the 'house of the community' (*dār al-jamā'a*) with their dead unless they pay two dinars for every corpse. They are only allowed to pass through the Zion Gate or through the Gate of Siloam (Silwān), that is, the two gates that were in the southern wall of the city. At any rate, we understand from this as well that the quarter was situated in the southern part of the city, within the walls.[111]

[839] The idea that there existed a Jewish quarter in the northern part of

XXIV; *Commentary to Ecclesiates* (To Eccles. ix:6; BM Or 2517), fol. 83, in Vajda, *Deux commentaires*, 92. Sahl b. Maṣlīaḥ, in: Harkavy, *Me'assēf* No. 13, 199. Yefet b. 'Alī: *Commentary to Psalms* (MS Paris 289), 48a. The letter of the yeshiva: **420**, c, lines 1ff.

111 See **1**, the fragment of the chronicle, and see the various readings there: 'the Jews' market', *sūq al-yahūd*, mentioned in the letter of Solomon b. Judah – see **92**, a, line 36; it is not mentioned in some of the Muslim sources which contain details on the markets of Jerusalem; al-Musharraf, 23b, mentions the *sūq Sulaymān* (should perhaps be: Silwān),

the city was first proposed by Le Strange. He suggested that a Jewish quarter existed there at the time of the Crusaders' conquest, a detail he mentions incidentally when quoting the fragment of al-'Ulaymī about the Zion Gate mentioned above. Evidence to sustain the assumption of the presence of a Jewish quarter in the north of the city was put forward by Prawer, namely: (1) the part played by the Jews in defending the city according to a Crusaders' source, and it is known that the latter's major efforts were in the north of the city; (2) the name *Juiverie* or *Judearia* given to the north-eastern quarter of the city during the Crusaders' period; (3) Jewish inscriptions found in the *madrasa al-Sa'rdiyya* in the northern part of the Temple Mount, where some Jewish names were found; and (4) a quotation from a Geniza letter (mentioned earlier), from Avon b. Ṣedaqa to Nehorai b. Nissim.

Let us examine these arguments one by one. We read about the participation of the Jews in the city's defence during the Crusaders' conquest in the rhymed chronicle of Gilo of Paris. He had first been a monk in Cluny, and afterwards became a bishop and then a cardinal, and the pope sent him on a mission to Palestine in about 1130. He says: 'Mox gentilis adest, Judaeus, Turcus Arabsque, missilibus, jaculis obsistitur igne, veneno' ('then, the local people came, the Jew, the Turk and the Arab, they fought with spears and arrows, even with fire and poison'). Prawer concludes from this and from the fact that most of the Crusaders' pressure and breakthrough took place in the northern sector of the city, that the Jewish quarter was in the north. No other source mentions the participation of the Jews in the defence of Jerusalem, though this does not discredit the validity of the chronicle. Indeed, it is known that the greater part of the Crusaders' effort and breakthrough was in the northern part of the city, but what evidence do we have that the Jews were defending this area in particular, or that it was impossible for them to come from the city's southern part to defend the northern sector?

The matter of the *Juiverie* (other versions: *Juderie, Juerie, Iuerie, Judairia, Judearia*) is mentioned in a treatise from the year 1187 (the year Jerusalem fell to Saladin), *La citez de Jerusalem*, which says that this was the name of the street that led from the street of Jehoshaphat to the left, leading to the Jehoshaphat Gate (*bāb al-asbāṭ*). This was where most of the Syrians (that

near Mount Zion; perhaps it is the one called *sūq al-yahūd*; 'Ulaymī, 401, mentions the *sūq al-qaṭṭānīn, al-'aṭṭārīn, al-khaḍrawāt, al-qumāsh* (cotton, perfume, vegetable, and textile-traders), but this is at the end of the fifteenth century. See on the Jerusalem markets: El'ad, *Cathedra*, 24: 31, 1981/2. The letter of the yeshiva: **420**, c, lines 34–35. 'Ulaymī, 406. Avon's letter: **500**; *dār al-jamā'a* is mentioned also in **141**, a letter of Abraham son of the Gaon, line 17: Abū'l-Khayr Ṣāliḥ b. Mu'ammar is given the task of going up to *dār al-jamā'a*; one should note the expression 'to go up to', but we do not know which ascent is being referred to.

is, the local Christians) lived in Jerusalem; the monastery of Mary Magdalene was also situated there – this refers, as I have already explained, to the monastery of the Jacobites and to the Jacobites themselves. As we have seen, one can assume that the name *Juiverie* was used for this place because the small number of Jews who lived in Jerusalem at the time lived there, or perhaps it derived from the habit of Christian sects to call one another 'Jews' in a pejorative sense. One should also bear in mind that this fact pertains to a time which is almost a century later than the period being discussed here.

The Jewish inscriptions to the north of the Temple Mount do not offer evidence of a Jewish quarter in the northern part of Jerusalem. They contain names of Jews, some of which are in fact Arab names, such as Mwsy (Mūsā), Sulaymān and 'Imrān, and others of which are Greek names, such as Theophilactus, Sisina, and Anastasia. The following sentence is also found there: 'May the Lord God of hosts build this house.' As the editor of the inscriptions, L. A. Mayer notes, this only goes to prove that Jews were passing and praying near the gates of the Temple Mount (in this instance: *bāb al-'aṭm*, 'the Gate of Darkness', which in the Middle Ages was called *bāb sharaf al-anbiyā'*, the 'Gate of the Honour of the Prophets').

As to Avon b. Ṣedaqa's letter, he writes from Jerusalem to Nehorai b. Nissim in Fustat, telling him that after considerable efforts, he has rented a small room (or: a small apartment) in the house of a Jewish woman for two dinars for a period of five months. The house stands in 'our people's vicinity' (that is, of Jews from the Maghrib) and has all the conveniences: the bath-house is not far and the house is situated in the Jewish quarter, near the synagogue. In the continuation, the writer adds that he does not have the strength to tell how much trouble he went to with regard to the *rubā'īya*, the quarter dinars; there was not a single person – grocery merchants nor wool traders nor clothing merchants – to whom he did not offer the money. He succeeded in selling 39, weighing 8½ dinars, for 20 dirhams per dinar, when the rate was thirty-six and a half. The first editors of the letter erred in two places: they interpreted *kenēsiyā* as meaning a Christian church instead of a synagogue. This term, *kenēsiyā*, can be found in my collection, and is included in the Hebrew Index. Secondly, as they were not familiar with the term *rubā'īya* (quarter dinars), they assumed that a square was being referred to (in Arabic a square is called *murabba'a*), and Prawer added his interpretation that they were speaking of the *quadrivium*, or *quarefor*, in the French of the Crusaders' time, the crossroads at the street leading from the Nābulus Gate (Solomon street) with the street parallel to the via Dolorosa, which allegedly was the borderline between the Christian quarter to the west and the Jewish quarter to the east.

In addition to the above arguments, which we have seen are generally invalid, Prawer quotes the fragment of the aforementioned Jewish chronicle as the basis for his view, according to an incorrect reading in the first edition, in which it is said that the Jews 'built their quarter [consisting] of buildings, the remnants of which have remained for generations'. In this passage, Prawer finds evidence that the southern quarter ceased existing at some unknown date in the eleventh century and that 'at any rate, the southern quarter no longer existed on the eve of the Crusaders' invasion'; but as we have seen, the meaning of that passage is quite different. The Jews built their quarter (in the south) from material taken from old ruins. As we have already seen from the decree concerning Jewish funerals described by Avon b. Ṣedaqa in his letter, the Jews still lived in the southern part of the city in 1064, that is, nine years before the Turcomans' invasion. There is no reason to believe that they evacuated their quarter and established a new one in the course of nine years, and even less so in the twenty-six years between the Turcomans' conquest and that of the Crusaders.

The matter of the cave of Zedekiah is also relevant at this juncture. In a letter from Ramla to Jerusalem, written by Salāma ha-Kohen b. Joseph to Shema'yā he-ḥāvēr b. Yeshū'ā, in May 1054, the address in Jerusalem was *bāb al-maghāra*, the Gate of the Cave. The first editor of the letter, B. Chapira, says that this is 'without doubt, a street near the cave of Zedekiah within proximity of the Nābulus Gate'. Thus we return to the north. The cave of Zedekiah is not mentioned in any sources of the period, however, nor is it the only underground structure in Jerusalem. And as we shall see further on, the 'cave' was a by-name which the Jews of Jerusalem used for their synagogue.[112]

112 Le Strange, *Palestine*, 215; Prawer, *Zion*, 11(1946), 42, 46f; *ibid.*, 12(1947), 147ff. See: Gilo, 794, lines 159–160, cf. the introduction there, CXLIII. On this point, the defence of Jerusalem, Ben Horin has already commented on Prawer's view, see *Kiryat Sefer*, 24(1947/8), 111; see there doubts as to the possibility of a Jewish quarter existing in the northern part of the city altogether. *La citez de Jerusalem*: Vogüé, *Eglises*, 443; Tobler, *Descriptiones*, 219; see: Kyrillos Skythopolitanus, 128: the Nestorians are called Jews because they would not acknowledge that Mary is the mother of God; in the year 512, Marinos, adviser to the emperor, claims that the inhabitants of the city of Jerusalem are Nestorians, who are like the Jews (so one is given to understand), see *ibid.*, 146; cf.: Festugière, *Moines*, III(2), 53, n. 81, who quotes similar expressions. See also the discussion above, section 678. Dinur, in his article on the Jews in Palestine during the Crusaders' conquest, *Zion (ha-me'assēf)*, 2(1926/7), 53, n. 3, already deals with the possibility that the quarter was called *Judearia* because the Crusaders permitted the Jews to live there, and he denied this possibility, just as he denied the veracity of Benjamin of Tudela's statement that he found 200 Jews in Jerusalem, 'living under David's tower on the edge of the city', and preferred the version: four Jews (the Rome MS). One must add to the sources that mention *Judearia*, a document by which William, who is in charge of the Holy Sepulchre, donated a bakery to the church of St Mary in the Kidron Valley; that bakery was in that part of the city called by the special name *Judearia* (*in illa urbis parte*

[840] Braslavi attempted to locate the site of the Jewish quarter on the Mount of Olives, or at least at its base. He tried to support his assumption by such expressions as 'it (the Rabbanite congregation) is situated opposite the Temple', repeatedly found in the letters of the Palestinian yeshiva from the days of the calendrical dispute in the tenth century and in the above-mentioned letter of the Palestinian yeshiva, but it is clear that such expressions would apply to anywhere in Jerusalem, for one can always draw a direct line ('opposite') between two points, one of which is the Temple Mount. We have also seen that the Jewish quarter was situated within the wall, and therefore the assumption that it was located on the Mount of Olives or on its slopes is out of the question.

Corroborating evidence of the location of the Jewish quarter is the *sha'ar ha-kohen*, the 'Priest's Gate'. The documents of the period mention in a few instances, a gate on the Temple Mount which is so called (see the Hebrew Index), and it emerges that the Jewish quarter was in its vicinity: 'the Rabbanite sect which lives at the Priest's Gate'. In the letters of the Palestinian Gaon at the time of the calendrical dispute, we also find mention of this gate: 'our prayers for you are constant . . . on the Mount of Olives . . . and at the Priest's Gate and at the gates of God's Temple . . .'; 'and we blessed you on the Mount of Olives . . . and at the Priest's Gate'. There were some who assumed that it was self-evident that the Priest's Gate would be to the east of the Temple Mount. Thus, Luncz assumed that the Priest's Gate and the Eastern Gate were one and the same, as did Yehuda, who decisively claimed that the Priest's Gate and the Gate of Mercy were identical; but the two did not elaborate on their arguments. Braslavi also assumed that the Priest's Gate was the eastern gate of the Temple Mount, by comparing the text of the midrash in *Shīr ha-shīrīm rabbā* (to the Song of Sol., ii:9 'Behold, he standeth behind our wall'): 'the Priest's Gate and the Ḥulda Gate were never destroyed', and the text of the *Mishnā* (Middot, i:3): 'the High Priest, who burns the cow, and the cow and all its care-takers, go out to the Mount of Olives'. It is quite easy to understand that there is no real proof in this.[113]

[841] Prawer also establishes a connection between these two sources,

positum que specialiter Judearia nuncupatur). See Delaborde, *Notre Dame*, 43. See Mayer, *Zion (ha-me'assēf)*, 3(1928/9), 24. Avon's letter: **501**; Vilnay, *Zion*, 5(1980), 75f, interprets *kenēsiyā* as the Holy Sepulchre or some other church, and assumes that the *rubā'īya* was perhaps a square courtyard at the edge of the Jewish quarter; see further the discussion on Avon's letter in Goitein, *Mediterranean Society* I, 378 (No. 35), and *ibid.* his remark on the error of the editors; one must take into consideration that the first editors, Gottheil and Worrell, did pioneering work in their publication (in 1927); see the view of Prawer, *Zion*, 12(1947), 147f. The fragment of the chronicle: **1**. The letter from Ramla: **525**, see the introduction to that letter.

113 Braslavi, *BJPES*, 5(1936/8), 28ff, and the sources there; 'the Rabbanite congregation', etc.: **49**, line 11; the letters of the Gaon: Bornstein, *Sokolow Jubilee Volume*, 63, 107.

and adds Christian sources on the everlastingness of the Eastern Gate or the Gates of Mercy, or the Golden Gates, as well as the account of Nāṣir Khusraw (1047), who notes that the Eastern Gate of the Temple Mount was built by King Solomon, and that of Estori ha-Parhi on the Shushan Gate and the Gates of Mercy. He quite rightly claims that the Priest's Gate could not be the same as the Gates of Mercy (as was the opinion of Yehuda, it will be recalled). This he gleaned from a Geniza document *ṣalawāt al-abwāb fi'l-quds* ('prayers at the Gates of Jerusalem'), where the Priest's Gate and the Gates of Mercy are mentioned separately. Hence, he identifies the Priest's Gate with the 'Gate of the Funerals' (*bāb al-janā'iz*) mentioned in al-'Ulaymī, who says that this gate was to the south of the Gates of Mercy. However, one must bear in mind that the accounts of the Christian sources, as well as of the Persian traveller, had mainly a theological meaning and one cannot learn from them about the actual eastern gates, just as one certainly cannot identify the Priest's Gate on the basis of these sources. On the other hand, it is the text of the Midrash about the Gates of Ḥulda and the Priest's Gate, which reflect a real situation even though they deal with the period before the Muslim conquest. We should note that the

Bornstein, who was very careful in his statements, notes *ibid.*, 63, n. 6, in connection with the Priest's Gate: it is not known; Luncz, *Yerushalayim*, 10(1913/4), 9; Yehuda, *Zion* (ha-me'assēf), 3(1928/9), 113, nn. 6, 9; and also in his wake, Hirschberg, *BJPES*, 13(1946/7), 159, and n. 16. Braslavi, *ibid.*, 27; in his article: *Eretz-Israel*, 7(1963/4), 72, he uses his first article as documentation for the renewed decision that during the period under discussion, the Eastern Gate was called by the Jews of Jerusalem, the Priest's Gate. See *Shīr ha-sh. rabbā* (Vilna Press), 37a. Hirschman, *Tarbiz*, 55:217, 1985/6, edited supplements to the Midrash Ecclesiastes rabba which were preserved in manuscript. It says there (p. 220, lines 20ff): 'When we stood on the Mount of Olives on Hosha'na rabba, although people came from all the communities of the world one could see but 200, whereas they were 12,000 from the Ḥulda Gate until the Priest's Gate'. Indeed, this is interesting evidence of the pilgrimages, in addition to what I have already quoted, *supra*, secs. 831 and 832. The intention of the writer (if he indeed wanted to say that those pilgrims were seen by him when actually standing on the Mount of Olives, although he does not say this explicitly; he may have mentioned the congregation on the last day of the Feast of Tabernacles merely to define the time): he who stood on the Mount of Olives merely saw 200 people out of the masses. That is, he saw those who were standing near him, approximately until the Ḥulda Gate to the south, but from there onward, westward to the Priest's Gate (in the Western Wall) there were thousands more whom someone standing on the Mount of Olives could not see, naturally, because they were hidden by the Temple Mount. Strangely, Hirschman turns these simple words around; that whoever stands on the Mount of Olives sees the Ḥulda Gate as well as the Priest's Gate (p. 221). However, the Priest's Gate was situated in the Jewish quarter, which was in the south and not in the east. Similarly, he tries to prove that a certain MS of Shīr ha-shīrīm rabba is earlier than the others, in order to conclude that there is no connection between the Western Wall and the Priest's Gate. There is no basis to his arguments, nor can one learn anything from them about the age of the manuscript. There is also no foundation to his claim that the name 'Priest's Gate' came into use only after the Muslim conquest. His assumption that the Elijah b. Menaḥem mentioned there, was a member of the family of the priestly Geonim (*infra* secs. 853, 858) is also groundless, for in the genealogical tree of this family, we only find Menaḥem ha-Kohen b. Elijah (or: b. Solomon b. Elijah). It was

Midrash mentions the Priest's Gate together with the Western Wall and the Ḥulda Gates; the latter were certainly situated in the south, according to the *Mishnā* (Middot i:3). On the Priest's Gate, it is said in *Shīr ha-shīrīm rabbā* (to the Song of Sol., ii:9, behold, he standeth behind our wall): 'behind the Western Wall of the Temple, why? For the Lord has sworn that it will never be destroyed; indeed, the Priest's Gate and the Ḥulda Gate have never been destroyed'. In *Num. rabbā* (xi:3): it is 'the western wall of the Temple' which has never been destroyed; and also in *Lam. rabbā*. The version in *Shīr ha-shīrīm rabbā* should therefore be viewed as an interpretation, as if it intended to say: the western wall has never been destroyed, the proof being that the Priest's Gate and the Ḥulda Gate were not destroyed. The 'guide of Palestine' in my collection does not mention the Priest's Gate at all in its description (preserved almost in its entirety) of the eastern wall, and we would expect it to be mentioned if it was there. It says that the south-western side existed ever since it was built by Solomon, and here one feels the influence of the aforementioned Midrash ('it has never been destroyed'). The passage preceding the Ḥulda Gates has not been preserved there, and we may surmise that the gates of the western side were mentioned there, including the Priest's Gate. It seems that the writer of the 'Prayers at the Gates' also lists the gates, starting from the southern corner of the western side of the Temple Mount with the Priest's Gate, and ending with *bāb David* and *bāb Shelomo*, that is, the western wall.[114]

not customary to omit the designation ha-Kohen in those times, and apart from this, the names Elijah and Menaḥem were frequently used.

114 Prawer, *Zion*, 12(1947), 139ff; Braslavi was of the same opinion as Prawer, see *Kinnūs* xxv, 135–140. 'The prayers at the gates': TS Box K 27, f. 2a, edited by Mann, *Texts*, I, 459; it is most likely that the mediaeval scribe who copied this document was not very familiar with what he copied; it seems that the *abwāb al-khamsa* in this list, are in fact the *abwāb al-akhmās* in **2**, I, a, lines 6–7, i.e. the gates of the slaves of the *akhmās*, that is the plural of *khums* (fifth part) of the spoils, the property of the Muslim community; these were the slaves who were charged with cleaning the Temple Mount, and this entire matter has been discussed above in relation to the first settlement of Jews in Jerusalem. According to **2**, a, recto, lines 10–14, the two Gates of Mercy (*bābayn al-raḥma*) in the east are identical with the Gates of Nikanor, that is, they are not identified with the Priest's Gate; see in that document the description of the eastern wall in which the Priest's Gate is lacking, whereas the description of the south-western side has been lost in the main. It is worth noting that the name 'Gates of Mercy' (*abwāb* [or *bābayn*] *al-raḥma*) is of Muslim origin. It may have been copied from the Prophet's mosque in Medina. There *bāb al-raḥma* served as the place to pray for rain, and its location was at the western end of the mosque. It was also called *bāb 'Ātika*, after 'Ātika, daughter of 'Abdallah b. Yazīd b. Mu'āwiya, for it was opposite her house. Prior to that, it was called *bāb al-sūq*, for the market-place of Medina was alongside it to the west. See Samhūdī, I, 503; Ibn Jubayr, 172; the name is connected to a verse in the Koran, lvii:13 (sūrat al-ḥadīd, of the Iron): between the believers and those who are undecided a wall will raise, with a gate; inside will be mercy, outside castigation. According to one of the interpretations, the meaning of *raḥma* is rain: al-Jawzī, *Tafsīr* (to the *sūra* of the Heights, vii:56), 28b; Suyūṭī, *Durr*, VI, 174, who quotes traditions according to which the verse in the Koran relates to the gate in the eastern wall of the Temple Mount in Jerusalem; other traditions of commentators, for instance:

[842] One could also try to identify the site of the Priest's Gate by comparing the lists of gates on the Temple Mount as they figure in the works of early Muslim writers, Ibn al-Faqīh, Ibn 'Abd Rabbihi, al-Muqaddasī, Nāṣir Khusraw, and in two Jewish sources. We would note the absence of the western and northern gates in the remaining fragment of the list in the 'guide of Palestine'; on the other hand, the names of the gates of the south and the east are preserved there. Also, it seems that a comparison with the list in the 'Prayers at the Gates' helps to solve the mystery of the Priest's Gate, by showing its proximity to the *bāb ḥiṭṭa* in the Muslim lists.[115]

al-Zajjāj, *Ma'ānī* (MS BM Or 8248), 238b, do not mention geographical details. The Koranic background to the name *bāb al-raḥma* for the gate in Jerusalem has already been noted by Vincent et Abel, *Jérusalem*, II, 840; the Jews of the period were not aware of this fact and used to visit the gate and pray alongside it, and write about it, mentioning its name (in the singular or plural) in letters; see **198**, line 44 (*ca.* 1042); **469**, a, line 17 (7 October 1059); the account of the Karaite in **290**, line 8. See *Lam. rabbā*, the Buber edition, fol. 35a.

115 Ibn al-Faqīh, 101; Ibn 'Abd Rabbihi, VI, 264; Muqaddasī, *Āqālīm*, 170; Nāṣir Khusraw (text, 24–28; (translation), 83–87. The list in Ibn 'Abd Rabbihi was copied by al-'Ulaymī, 248 (he attributes it to al-Qurṭubī, who is Ibn 'Abd Rabbihi, of Cordova). There remain gates, with uncertain locations, which may have had more than one name. Thus in the west: al-Khiḍr (a personality of the early Muslim tradition, who was commonly identified with Elijah); Umm Khālid; al-Saqar ('the fire of hell', the name brings to mind al-Baqar in the 'Prayers at the Gates'); al-Sakīna (the Divine Presence, like the Hebrew *shekhīnā*). In the south, it is possible that *bāb miḥrāb Maryam* was the same as *al-akhmās* in the Jewish sources. In the east, it is likely that *bāb al-wādī* (the Gate of the Kidron Valley) and *bāb al-tawba* are the same. In the north, there is little certainty concerning the Ḥanna, Isaac, al-Baqar and Judah Gates in the list that is found in the 'Prayers at the Gates', nor concerning their identity with the gates in the Muslim sources, nor is there any clarity concerning the comparison of the latter to each other, as there are notable differences in the names that are mentioned. In the story of the miracle that occurred in Ramla: **313**, line 15, it says that they go to pray at *bāb Yehūdā*. Yefet b. 'Alī, in his commentary to Psalms (MS Paris 289), fol. 106 (Ps., cxxii:2) says that the City of God has twelve gates, three on each side. In the north: Reuben's gate, Judah's gate, Levi's gate; in the east: Joseph's gate, etc. At any rate, we have here some confirmation that Judah's gate was in the north; the *ḥillūq ha-qārā'īm we-ha-rabbānīm* in Pinsker, *Liqqūṭē qadmōniyōt*, II, 104, also mentions that the Karaites who emigrated from Babylonia to Jerusalem 'settled there at Judah's Gate'. As to the *al-baqar* Gate in the 'Prayers at the Gates': in Mann, *Texts*, I, 459, and also in Gil, *Shalem*, 2(1975/6), 26f, the reading is incorrect: *Bab Elqānā*; according to Salmon b. Yeruḥim, in his *Commentary to Lamentations*, (Feuerstein), XVII ff, in his explanation of the word *parbār* (1 Chr., xxvi:18), which according to him is derived from *par ben bāqār* ('a young bullock'), this gate 'is known to this day' by the name *bāb al-baqar*, on the western side of the sanctuary (*al-quds*; the *parbār* of the Bible is in the west); through this gate they would bring in the sacrifices. It is not clear whether by *quds* he means the Temple Mount or Jerusalem, and possibly he is speaking of one of the city gates, and not of the Temple Mount. As to *bāb al-Walīd* and *al-Hāshimīn*, see the information in Ibn Khallikān, I, 234ff, on the gates built by 'Abd al-Malik and al-Ḥajjāj ibn Yūsuf, which I have mentioned above. As to *bāb al-Nabī* or *bāb Muḥammad*, Gildemeister, *ZDPV*, 4(1881), 91, n. 20, mistakenly identified it with today's Gate of the Maghribis. It is true that *bāb Burāq*, which is the Barclay's Gate beneath the Gate of the Maghribis (see more on this below), was

Comparison of the names of the gates of the Temple Mount

	Ibn al-Faqīh	Ibn 'Abd Rabbihi	Al-Muqaddasī	Nāṣir Khusraw	'The guide of Palestine'	'The Prayers at the Gates'
	(900)	(930)	(985)	(1047)		
West		al-Khiḍr				
	Umm Khālid	Umm-Khālid				
				al-Saqar		
		al-Sakīna		al-Sakīna		David
	Da'ūd	Da'ūd	Da'ūd	Da'ūd		Solomon
		Sulaymān				al-Kohen
	Ḥiṭṭa	Ḥiṭṭa	Ḥiṭṭa	Ḥiṭṭa		
South	al-Nabī	Muḥammad	al-Nabī	al-Nabī	Ḥulda	
					(=al-Nabī)	
					al-Akhmās	al-Khamsa
			Miḥrāb			
			Maryam			
				al-'Ayn	Water Gate	
					(=Song Gate)	
					(=Womens' Gate)	
East	al-Wādī	al-Tawba		al-Tawba		
	al-Raḥma	al-Raḥma	al-Raḥma	al-Raḥma	al-Raḥma	
					(=Nikanor	al-Raḥma
					=the eastern)	
North	(Maghārat					
	Ibrāhīm)	al-Asbāṭ	al-Asbāṭ	al-Asbāṭ		
	(Miḥrāb			Bāb		
	Ya'qūb)			al-Abwāb		
	(Miḥrāb					
	Zakariyya)	al-Hāshimī	al-Hāshimīn			
		al-Walīd	al-Walīd			
			Ibrāhīm			
						Ḥanna
						Isaac
						al-baqar
						Judah

The order of listing the names is from the northern end of the western side southwards, then the southern side from the west to the east, the eastern side from the south to the north, the northern side from the east to the west.

[843] It should be noted that a special place was accorded to the Ḥiṭṭa Gate in Muslim sources, in conjunction with what was said about it in the Koran in *sūrat al-baqara* (ii:58): 'Since God said: enter this city and eat [of its fruits] in comfort, as much as you like, but enter the gate prostrating yourself, and saying: *ḥiṭṭa* [atonement!]. Then, I shall forgive you for your sins and reward the virtuous [among you]'. Muslim tradition interpreted these words of the Koran (addressed to the Children of Israel) as meaning Jerusalem, and the gate through which the Children of Israel were ordered to enter is none other than *bāb ḥiṭṭa*. The word *ḥiṭṭa* was not a common Arabic word and the commentators tried to explain its meaning as a plea for atonement and forgiveness. The gate was low and whoever wished to enter had to bend down, and the gate would press down on those guilty of wicked deeds. In this way, the criminals were identified. The Children of Israel were ordered to say *ḥiṭṭa* (atonement!) on entering but they tried to outwit the order by saying *hiṭṭa(!) sumqātā* (red wheat), or *ḥabba fī sha'ra* (a grain in a hair) and the like. This gate was thus set apart from all the other gates of the Temple Mount, for Muslim tradition accorded it a special role in the atonement requested by the Children of Israel.[116]

sometimes called *bāb al-Nabī*; see Schick, *Beit al-Makdas*, 119f. Schematically, one can present the assumed locations of the gates as follows:

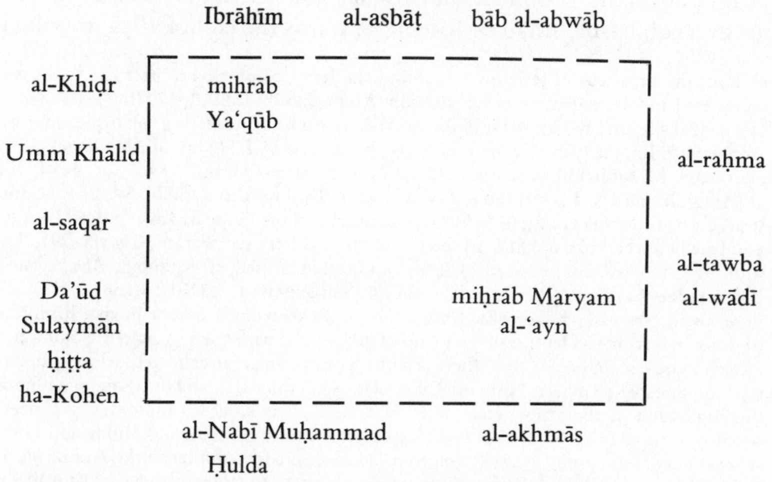

[116] See on *bāb ḥiṭṭa*: Ṭabarī, *Tafsīr*, I, 299; Mawṣilī, *Nihāya*, 53ff; Ibn Qutayba, *Gharīb*, 50; *idem*, *al-Qurṭayn*, I, 43; Abū 'Ubayda, *Majāz*, I, 41; Ṭurṭūshī, *Ḥawādith*, 21ff; Silafī, *Faḍā'il* (MS Cambridge Or Qq 91, part 2), fol. 78; 'Ulaymī, 381ff; Ibn Ḥajar al-'Asqalānī, *Tafsīr*, 71; *idem, Fatḥ*, IX, 374; Ibn Kathīr, *Bidāya*, I, 324; Musharraf, *Faḍā'il*, fol. 23b, (according

[844] It is difficult to answer the question as to whether the Priest's Gate and the *bāb ḥiṭṭa* of Muslim tradition were one and the same, and how the latter stood in relation to the Ḥulda Gate in the south, mentioned in the *Mishnā*. All the indications, however, point to the fact that the Priest's Gate was in the west.

While the Jewish sources viewed the Priest's Gate as the most outstanding and important site in the environs of the Jewish quarter and the favoured place of worship of the Jews of Jerusalem apart from the Mount of Olives, we find that the Western Wall is almost not mentioned at all. The only source that mentions the wall during this period is the Scroll of Aḥīma'aṣ according to which Samuel b. Palṭī'ēl donated money also for the 'oil for the Temple in the Western Wall for the altar within'. In other sources, we find no mention of the Western Wall for the simple reason that the area of the Western Wall was called after the gate in the wall within it, which was the Priest's Gate.

In the above-mentioned quotation from the Scroll of Aḥīma'aṣ, Dinur tried to find a confirmation of his view that there was a synagogue on the Temple Mount. Actually, this quotation seems merely to justify the assumption that the synagogue ('the altar') was indeed close to the Western Wall. As to Dinur's assumption concerning the synagogue on the Temple Mount, it has no real foundation in the sources. There is also no reason to believe that the Muslims would have permitted the Jews to erect a synagogue on the Temple Mount. What was said in Solomon b. Judah's letter to Jacob ha-me'uttād b. Joseph, towards the end of 1015, in which

to him, the gate was in Jericho at first and the Jews transferred it after the town was conquered and destroyed); see *ibid.* also 51b; Abū'l-Su'ūd, *Tafsīr*, I, 179 (the Jews used to say in Nabaṭī, that is, Aramaic: *ḥiṭṭa sumqātā*, red wheat, instead of *ḥiṭṭa*, pleading for atonement); Ibn Ḥayyān, *Tafsīr*, I, 224; al-Khāzin, *Lubāb*, I, 56; Suyūṭī, *Mu'tarak*, II, 76; Hammām b. Munabbih, *Ṣaḥīfa*, 448; al-Naysābūrī al-Qummī, *Tafsīr*, I, 293ff; Ibn al-'Arabī, *Muḥāḍara*, II, 371; Ibn al-Jawzī, *Zād*, I, 86; Ibn 'Abd Rabbihi, VI, 264; a Shiite source attributes this saying to Mūsā al-Kāẓim, one of the Shiite Imams: 'Indeed I am for you [the believers] like *bāb ḥiṭṭa* to the Children of Israel', see Warām, *Tanbīh*, 291. The source of these Muslim traditions has not yet been identified; cf. Rudolph, *Abhängigheit*, 198; scholars have not given it much thought; Gildemeister, *ZDPV*, 4(1881), 91, mentions them; see also; Leszynsky, *Juden*, 32, n. 1, who finds here a Jewish homiletic tradition referring to Deut., viii:8 (A land of wheat, and barley, etc . . .). In the opinion of Hirschfeld, *New Researches*, 107, there is in the Koranic verse, an echo of the description of the high priest entering the Holy of Holies (*Mishnā*, Yoma v:1), and the term *ḥiṭṭa* hints at the confession of the priest (*ibid.*, iii:8, iv:2, vi:2). It is indeed a topic that still needs probing. It is worth noting the etymological proximity of the names Ḥulda and Ḥiṭṭa; from the semantic point of view, the root *ḥld* in Aramaic is similar to the Arabic *ḥṭṭ*. In Aramaic (particularly in Syriac), it also means to creep, to stoop, also *ḥuldat ha-mōlīm* in the PT (Yoma i, 38c, middle; Meg. iv, 75c, bottom) which requires a *mezūzā*, apparently means a sort of low entrance, as meant by *bāb ḥiṭṭa* (speaking of the wicket in the gate, the *mesaulion* which was distorted there to *molim*, see Gil, *Tarbiz*, 44[1976/7], 27, n. 33). Cf. also: 'God *maḥlīd* (i.e. opens a wicket) for them inside the earth and they roll like jars . . . to Palestine' (speaking of the Babylonian scholars after they die); see PT, Kil'ayim, ix, 32c,

Dinur also tried to find proof of his assumption, is to be understood very differently from his interpretation. Solomon b. Judah (who became Gaon only ten years later) states his disappointment that Jacob did not return to Jerusalem from Fustat, not for the *'aṣeret* (Shavuot) nor on the 9th of Av, and also 'the holidays' (of Tishri) passed without his appearance, and he wishes: 'may our Rock . . . hasten my encounter with you in His Temple', by which he was naturally referring to the days of the Messiah. In the continuation, he says 'the splendid building built on it (on His Temple) collapsed'. This occurred, according to him, on Sunday, 17 Elul; as we have seen above (in sec. 580) he is referring to the earthquake which occurred on 4 September 1015, and caused the caving in of the Dome of the Rock, an event that is also recorded in Arab chronicles. Clearly it is the Dome of the Rock to which Solomon b. Judah referred in his letter, and not a synagogue.[117]

[845] On this question, that of the site of the synagogue of the Jews of Jerusalem and its alleged proximity to the Western Wall, as it emerges from the text of the Scroll of Aḥīma'aṣ, it should be noted that the synagogue is mentioned in letters in my collection. Solomon b. Judah writes about a pronouncement of excommunication: 'and he was excommunicated in the synagogue'. He explicitly mentions the synagogue in his description of the collapse of the wall, and says that the people were then in the synagogue ('and children and women were coming and going'), and it was the time for the reading of the Torah. Abraham, son of the Gaon, calls the synagogue *al-kanīs* (or perhaps: *al-kunays*) in Arabic. He, together with the *av-bēt-dīn*, goes down there, and so does the head of the yeshiva. Joseph ha-Kohen b. Solomon Gaon also writes about going down to the *kanīsa*. The Jerusalemite 'Eli ha-Kohen b. Ezekiel writes to a relative in Fustat, 'Eli ha-Kohen b. Ḥayyim, that he prays for everyone on *rōsh ḥōdesh* (the first day of the month) *fi'l-kanīs*, in the synagogue. Avon b. Ṣedaqa writes in two of his letters about *al-knysyā*, and we have already seen that we are to read *kenēsiyā* i.e., the synagogue.

top (the parallel version *ibid.*, Ket., xii, 35b is an 'improved' one). One can also learn from this that there was no connection between Ḥulda the Prophetess and the Ḥulda Gates.

117 One should note that the *Mishnā* (Middot iii:1) speaks of only one gate in the west, the Kiponos Gate, while Josephus, *Antiquities*, XV, 410, says there were four gates in the western part of the Temple Mount. Hence this question remains something of a mystery. It strikes one, though at this stage it cannot be proven, that the Priest's Gate is the same as the Ḥulda Gates and *bāb ḥiṭṭa* in Muslim tradition. It is possible that the *Mishnā* meant that the Ḥulda gates were in the southern part of the western side. As to the Muslim tradition, it may have absorbed some remnants of a Jewish tradition with regard to the Ḥulda gates. (Today *bāb ḥiṭṭa* is shown in the north of the Temple Mount, and the ancient traditions have been forgotten, according to which it was in the south, as one can see from the sources quoted above. 'Ulaymī, 383, claimed that it was close to *miḥrāb Maryam* in the south-eastern corner of the Mount.) See *Megillat Aḥīma'aṣ*, 37; Dinur, *Zion* (ha-me'assēf), 3(1926/7), 62, 67ff. On the use of 'altar' meaning synagogue, cf. Klar, *Megillat Aḥīm'aṣ*,

In that same letter, Joseph ha-Kohen mentions alongside the synagogue (*al-kanīsa*), *al-maghāra*, the cave. Despite the letter's poor condition, it is easy to discern that 'the cave' is used as a synonym for the synagogue. Indeed, 'the cave' is frequently mentioned in the sources as the place where the Jews of Jerusalem congregate, and it is clear that they are referring to the synagogue. Solomon b. Judah writes to Ephraim b. Shemaria that on the morrow after receiving his letter, they hastened to declare his rival excommunicated in Jerusalem: 'On Monday, we and a large public gathered in the cave and we took out the scrolls of the Torah and banned all those 'that decree unrighteous decrees' (Is., x:1). After mentioning the collapse of a wall which caused damage to the synagogue, he writes, following the work of reconstruction, 'the cave was restored'. As to the collapse, it occurred on the first day of Passover, when the synagogue was full of people, but no one was injured. It seems that he is referring to the collapse of part of the Temple Mount wall, that is, the Western Wall. According to the Gaon, the wall collapsed along a stretch of some 15 cubits (about nine metres) and some 20 or more layers. Apparently, this was written in 1034, and from this we understand that the caving in of the wall perhaps occurred on Passover of the same year, 7 April. Two further letters of the Gaon contain details of the reconstruction work, clearing the debris from the road, and the beginning of laying the foundations, with many Jews of Jerusalem lending a helping hand to clear away the remains of the wall along a stretch of 30 cubits (some 18 metres) nearly 20 cubits (12 metres) wide. The thickness of the wall is also mentioned: 1–1$^{1}/_{2}$ cubits. They used 62 beams, 600 planks, and 'mosaics' (stone slabs?). Financial assistance for this work came from Fustat and Tyre. This collapse is explicitly mentioned in Ibn al-Jawzī, who links it with the earthquake which occurred on 5 December 1033 (described above in sec. 595), and notes that part of the wall of *bayt al-maqdis* fell in (it is difficult to know whether he means the wall of the city or the wall of the Temple Mount, though the latter seems most likely) and a large part of *miḥrāb Da'ūd*, meaning the area of the Temple Mount. Apparently what the Gaon describes is correct, that is that some months after the earthquake, the collapse of the wall occurred, as a belated consequence.

The Maghribi merchant Moses b. Jacob, writing in June 1053 to Nehorai b. Nissim, requests that he buy 'dark mats in Alexandria' that he send them to Jerusalem as soon as possible, 'for they are a donation (*muqaddasa*) to the cave'. Abraham b. David b. Sughmār blames his rivals in Fustat for wasting money belonging to 'the cave' (*māl al-maghāra*) and it is obvious

173, who quotes a similar usage in a poem of ha-Kallir, cf. also Yehuda, *Zion* (ha-me'assēf), 3(1928/9), 121, n. 5. Solomon b. Judah's letter: **54**, lines 27–30; cf. Mann, *Texts*, I, 313ff; II, 20, n. 35.

that he is again referring to money donated to the synagogue in Jerusalem. In the will of Wuḥsha, a stout-hearted woman of Fustat, she bequeaths 25 dinars *lil-maghāra*, to the cave, and the intention is the same as above.[118]

[846] One may assume that al-Muqaddasī is referring to the synagogue of the Jews of Jerusalem when, towards the end of the tenth century, he describes 'a cave under the rock' with room for 69 people. A more reliable version, preserved in Yāqūt (who copied from al-Muqaddasī), speaks of 960 people. As in many other similar instances, the Muslim writers, or the scribes who copied the manuscripts, did not take the trouble to mention that they were speaking of Jews, as this description would seem to call for. Apparently, in the late Middle Ages, this underground hall was called *masjid Da'ūd* and evidently this 'cave', used as a synagogue by the Jews of Jerusalem, is the underground hall behind Barclay's Gate, measuring 12 by 6 metres, called by recent generations of Muslims *masjid al-Burāq*.

It is also worth noting what Samuel b. Samson wrote in 1211 about the gate of the Western Wall which had appended to it a large hall in the 'foundation of the Temple'. The priests would go, he writes, via this gate of the Western Wall through a tunnel to 'Eyn 'Eyṭām, where 'the house of immersion' was situated. The name 'Eyn 'Eyṭām in this tradition is puzzling, and Tobler considered it void of any credibility, but this text is evidently influenced by the Babylonian Talmud (Zev. 54b), about the spring 'Eyn Eyṭām which was at a higher altitude than the Temple, and it is implied that this is the source of its water supply. Evidently, Samuel b. Samson's story (a little more than 100 years after the annihilation of the Jewish population of Jerusalem) hints at a tradition which aimed at explaining the designation 'the Priest's Gate'. Possibly that hall 'in the foundations of the Temple' is none other than the 'cave', that is, the synagogue.

Earlier I quoted Avon b. Ṣedaqa concerning the fact that the authorities

[118] The excommunication in the synagogue: **78**, a, line 29. The collapse: **118**, line 14. Abraham son of the Gaon: **141**, lines 3, 6, 8; see also **182**, line 4: Abraham son of the Gaon goes to *al-kanīs*. Joseph ha-Kohen: **409**, lines 10–11. Avon b. Ṣedaqa; **500**, b, line 21; **501**, a, lines 26, 31. We have seen above that the synagogue of Jerusalem is mentioned in the episode of the argument between the Jews and the Christians which came before the church council in Erfurt (932); there they call the synagogue *sacellum*, which in Mediaeval Latin means approximately 'a little prayer-house'; also in the letter of the yeshiva, **420**, c, line 8, it is called 'the little temple'. The letter to Ephraim b. Shemaria: **79**, lines 27–29. The restoration of 'the cave': **120**, a, line 23; the collapse I interpreted somewhat differently elsewhere (mainly the date): Gil, *Shalem*, 2(1975/6), 30, n. 41. The restoration work: **119**, **120**; Ibn al-Jawzī, *Muntaẓam*, VIII, 77, copied from him by Ibn Kathīr, *Bidāya*, 12, 36. Moses b. Jacob: **460**, b. Wuḥsha's will: TS Arabic Box 4, f. 5, a, lines 13–16, edited by Goitein, *JQR Anniversary Volume*, 239ff; he assumed that the cemetery in Fustat was being referred to; see also *idem*, *Mediterranean Society*, III, 349. If my interpretation is correct, the will was written before the Crusaders' conquest, whereas Goitein assumed that it was written after that.

did not permit Jewish funerals to pass in front of *dār al-jamā'a*, demanding instead that they go through the Zion Gate or the Siloam Gate, or pay two dinars for every funeral. Indeed, the writer continues, the Jews feared to pass through these gates because of the danger of being cursed or stoned. So great was their fear that they decided to bury a deceased woman in one of her own houses or shops. Finally, they bribed the guard and took the corpse out at night to the *Samaritiqā*, where the community congregated; through the Samaritiqā, they took the deceased to the graves. I shall try to interpret what emerges from Avon's account. It is implied that the usual funeral route was as follows: it moved northwards, passed in front of the Priest's Gate (that is, the Western Wall) and *dār al-jamā'a*, and in order to reach the graves, which were in the Kidron Valley or on the Mount of Olives, passed through the Christian quarters in the north of the city, thereby circumambulating the Temple Mount and its gates, and perhaps leaving through the Sheep Gate (which is *bāb al-asbāṭ*, the Tribes' Gate, that is St Stephen's Gate, or today's Lions' Gate). One can imagine that the incident during Daniel b. Azariah's funeral, hinted at in the same letter, was connected with passing through the Christian quarter, and it is also possible that the two dinars were intended to provide proper protection when they were passing through, or perhaps this was a toll for passing through the wall built around the Christian quarter, which was completed in 1063, that is one year prior to our letter, and a year or more after the death of Daniel b. Azariah. From then on, the Jews were asked to turn southward, through one of the southern gates. From there, they had to reach the Kidron Valley and turn northward until they came to the burial site.[119]

[847] One should remember that evidently the southern gates of the city, the Zion Gate (the western) and the Siloam Gate (the eastern) were, in the period under discussion, very much to the south of today's wall, for it emerges that Eudocia's wall was still standing at the time. This wall passed through the area of Mount Zion and turned on its slope eastward until the Siloam pool and from there to the south-eastern corner of the Temple Mount. We have seen that according to Theophanes, the caliph Marwān destroyed the walls of Jerusalem in 745; hence we must assume that they were rebuilt after that, but we have no details pertaining to the matter.

Tsafrir has tried to prove that Eudocia's wall no longer existed in the period under discussion here. He based his argument on passages about

[119] Muqaddasī, *Āqālīm*, 171; Yāqūt, *Buldān*, IV, 594, 598; on the underground structure near the Western Wall, see also: Clermont-Ganneau, *Archaeological Researches*, I, 165f. The later Middle Ages: Khafājī, II, 296. See Solomon b. Samson's letter in Yaari, *Iggarot*, 78; cf.: Tobler, *Topographie*, II, 865. The matter of the funerals, see **500**, lines 7ff. The deceased was the sister-in-law of the Gaon, Elijah ha-Kohen b. Solomon (see *ibid.*, lines 4, 14).

the Silwān spring in Muqaddasī, Nāṣir Khusraw and Yāqūt, and claimed that these passages proved that the pool of Siloam was already at that time outside the city. However, these writers do not refer to the pool of Siloam itself. Muqaddasī notes that Silwān is a place in the *rabaḍ* of Jerusalem and that beneath it runs the spring which waters the gardens in the neighbourhood. It is clear that he is not referring to the pool but to the spring. The literal meaning of the word *rabaḍ* is that area beneath the fortress of a town, its open surroundings. Yāqūt also speaks of a spring beyond the city, in *wādī Jahnam*, that is, the Kidron Valley. Nāṣir Khusraw also writes of a spring welling from a rock on the slope of the mountain, half a *farsakh* (some three kilometres) south of the city, called the Silwān spring. It is obvious that these three writers did not mean the pool of Siloam but the *bi'r Ayyūb* ('Eyn Rōgēl). Today, there is no way of determining the point from which 'Eyn Rōgēl was issuing at that time, nor can one know exactly Nāṣir Khusraw's point of departure at the time, whether he estimated the distance from the city wall or from the Temple Mount. At any rate, as these writers were not referring to the Siloam pool, it is difficult on the basis of their accounts to arrive at any conclusion with regard to Eudocia's wall.

We have no idea why the Jews were afraid of going to the burial site through the southern gates. Perhaps there were Bedouin tents there. It is nevertheless clear from the text of the letter that the Jews preferred a third route with less danger (though still at night); this being through the *Samareitikē*, the Karaite quarter discussed above (sec. 668). This means that instead of turning northward or southward, they preferred to turn eastward and pay bribes in order that the gate of the city wall would be open to them at night. We do not know the name of that gate, but one can assume that it was at the southern corner of the eastern wall of the city. Hence we learn that the Jewish quarter evidently stretched from the proximity of the south-western sector of the Temple Mount southward, until the Zion and Siloam Gates of that time, and the southern section of the eastern city wall was the eastern border of the quarter.[120]

[848] As to the Karaite quarter, it emerges that it was outside the wall.

120 See: Crowfoot, *PEFQ*, 77(1945), 67ff, 77. On the enterprise of Eudocia, Theodosius' wife, see: Evagrius, 2483; Nicephorus, 146, 1240. This latter source says that Eudocia widened (and not only restored) the walls of Jerusalem: *eurynasa kai ananeōsasa*. See also Antoninus Placentinus (in Tobler, *Itinera*, I, 105) who says that the Siloam pool was then also within the city (*intra civitatem inclusa est*) and one can learn from this that it was included within the wall. Cf. on the enterprises of Eudocia in Jerusalem and other places in Palestine, and the restoration of the walls of Jerusalem: Couret, *La Palestine*, 119f, and see the sources listed there in nn. 1–3. See Tsafrir, *IEJ*, 27(1977), 157; Muqaddasī, *Āqālīm*, 171; Yāqūt, *Buldān*, IV, 594; Nāṣir Khusraw, 21. The meaning of *rabaḍ* may be understood from many literary sources of the Middle Ages; in Ṭabarānī, *Mu'jam*, II, 16 the term is clearly explained as the opposite of *a'lā* (the upper part). An Arabic commentary

As we have seen above, the Karaites were indeed 'new immigrants' in Jerusalem. They began to arrive in Jerusalem more than 200 years after the return of the Jews to the city commenced, and there was no room for them within the wall. In the sources, it says that the Karaite quarter was in the *ṣela' ha-elef ha-yevūsī*, the Karaites' version of Josh., xviii:28: ('Zelah, Eleph and Jebusi which is in Jerusalem', etc.). (*Ṣela'* means rib, and also the slope of a mountain.) This obviously refers to the area of the 'city of David', south of the Temple Mount. This is also the view of the commentary to *Megillat Ta'anit*, evidently written in the Middle Ages, on the passage in the Megilla: 'on the 23rd (of Nisan), the people of the Ḥaqrā left Jerusalem'; here the commentary says: 'as it is written: David took the strong hold of Zion, the same is the City of David (2 Sam., v:7). This is now the place of the Karaites'. A fragment from the commentary of the Karaite Salmon b. Yeruḥim to Lam., ii:20, where it speaks of the murder of Zechariah b. Jehoiada in the Temple (2 Chr., xxiv:25), points to the shared identity of the Samareitikē, the *ṣela'*, and the *ḥārat al-mashāriqa* (the easterners' quarter): 'and this Zechariah, may he rest in peace, is buried in Noble Jerusalem, in Samaritiqā, which is the *ṣela' ha-elef ha-yevūsī*, known today as the quarter of the easterners, as Mevorakh b. Nathan b. Nisan, of blessed memory, said; for this Mevorakh, may God have mercy on his soul, said in one of his dirges: and I wept opposite the grave of Zechariah son of Jehoiada, whose grave is known, in the *ṣela' ha-elef*, etc. The same verse of Mevorakh b. Nathan was also quoted by another Karaite commentator, Yefet b. 'Alī.

We have a number of supporting arguments which help us define the location of the Karaite quarter: the City of David, Zechariah's grave, and the Samareitikē. The sites of Zechariah's grave and the Samareitikē are known to us from the discussion on the Christians (sec. 668). In the above-mentioned fragment of Avon b. Ṣedaqa's letter, we have seen that the funeral passed into the Karaite quarter at night, apparently through a gate in the eastern wall of the city. It appears, then, that the Karaite quarter was outside the wall, on the eastern slope of the Ophel, at the place commonly called 'the city of David' even today. The wall separated the Rabbanite quarter from that of the Karaites. Against this background, we can more easily understand the verses of the poet who wrote 'the ancient questions': 'indeed I was zealous for the sanctity of my congregation, and

on the Bible could also add to one's understanding of the word *rabaḍ: ha-perāzīm* was interpreted as *al-rabaḍiyīn*, as Moses said: 'all these cities were fenced with high walls, . . ., beside unwalled towns' (*'ārē ha-perāzī*; Deut., iii:5). See DK 207g, line 4 from bottom. Goldziher also wrote on *rabaḍ*, and according to him it means: outside the inhabited part of the city (a not very precise definition) and he quotes an example from the *Aghānī*, concerning a woman who was menstruating and they excluded her to the *rabaḍ*, see *REJ*, 28(1894), 86. On *bi'r Ayyūb* see Hecker, *Sefer Yerushalayim*, I, 198f. *Farsakh*, see Hinz, 62.

my wrath was kindled, against the 'limping one' (*ṣōlēʿā*, from the root *ṣelaʿ*, a pejorative nickname for the Karaites), who sits joining me on the opposite side', etc. Thus we find that the two congregations were adjacent to one another, with the wall of the city dividing them.[121]

The geonim of Palestine

The elder geonim

[849] The most ancient genealogical tree of the Palestine geonim is found in the *Seder ʿolām zūṭa*. Mar Zūṭrā, son of the exilarch Mar Zūṭrā, emigrated to Palestine from Babylonia and became 'head of the Sanhedrin' in the year 520. The Hebrew version of the chronicle lists his descendants, and it is not clear whether all, or only some of them, succeeded to the position of Gaon: Gūriyā, Zūṭrā, Jacob, Shemaiah, Nīnā, Mīgas, Mīsā, Nehemiah, Avdīmī, Jacob (and his brother Pinḥas) and Ḥaṣūv. In

[121] See the *Megillat Taʿanit*: Lichtenstein, *HUCA*, 8–9 (1931/2), 327; cf. Munk, *JA*, 4e sér., t. 15(1850), 310, n. 3; Poznanski, *Yerushalayim* (Luncz), 10(1913/4), 96, 98; Mann, *Jews*, I, 274ff; *idem, Texts*, I, 317, n. 20; Braslavi, *BJPES*, 5(1936/8), 27ff. On Mevorakh b. Nathan cf.: Pinsker, *Liqqūṭē qadmōniyōt*, I, 105; Poznanski, *Yerushalayim* (Luncz), 10(1913/4), 96: Salmon b. Yeruḥim took the passage from the dirge beginning: 'gather ye from everywhere, every woman and every man, to wail with me (at the place) facing the grave of a prophet killed on a day of calamity' (see in Pinsker, *ibid.*, II, 139). Poznanski questions whether this Mevorakh was a Karaite, because in the Karaite prayer book (where there are some of his piyyūṭīm) he is called Mevorakh b. Nathan b. Nisan ha-Levi *he-ḥāvēr*; and one of his poems is based on the *aggādā* from Pesiqātā Rabbati. See the names of his poems in Davidson, *Ōṣar*. One should note that in a letter from the year 1100: **577**, b, lines 11–12, a Karaite named Abū'l-Khayr Mubārak (= Mevorakh) b. Hiba (= Nathan) b. Nisan is mentioned; and Nathan (his father, evidently) b. Nisan ha-Levi *ha-melammēd* is mentioned in a Karaite marriage deed drawn up in Jerusalem: **305**, line 37. For documentation on the Karaite quarter, one should add the formulae of a Karaite marriage deed in florid Hebrew, in the handwriting of the abovementioned Moses b. Isaac, where the place is noted: 'in the *ṣelaʿ ha-elef* in Jerusalem, the Holy City'. See ULC Or Box 13, No. 52. The *al-mashāriqa* quarter still existed in the 13th century and was then inhabited by Christians; see Ibn al-Qifṭī, 379 (the article 'Yaʿqūb b. Ṣiqlān al-Naṣrānī al-Maqdisī al-Mashriqī ['the eastern Christian Jerusalemite'; he died in AH 626, that is AD 1229]): 'The eastern Christians in Jerusalem come from the Balqā' region (southern Trans-Jordan) and from ʿAmmān and they are called easterners because they are in the area which is to the east of Jerusalem, called the quarter of the easterners'. Drori, *Perāqīm*, 172, quotes a passage from ʿUlaymī on the quarter of the easterners in his time (*ca.* 1500), when this name was applied to the north-eastern part of the city, inhabited by people from Persia and Central Asia. His note there: 'M. Gil is of another opinion', etc., is not to the point, for nowhere have I mentioned this source; and one should note the enormous differences in time: the Karaites, in the tenth century; Ibn al-Qifṭī, the 13th; ʿUlaymī, the end of the fifteenth century. See '*the ancient questions*': Schechter, *JQR*, 13(1901), 364. Prawer, *Zion*, 12(1947), 143ff, arrives at the conclusion that the Karaite quarter was on the slope of the Temple Mount. One should also note Simon b. Saul al-Ṭulayṭulī's letter, which says: 'they went up to Samaritiqā' when speaking of Karaites who arrived in Jerusalem, see: **457**, a, margin right, lines 7–8.

addition, three sons of Abāyē (Avdīmī?) are mentioned, Jacob, Pinḥas and Azariah. According to one version, Ḥaṣūv was the son of Jacob, and according to another, he was the son of Pinḥas. This latter Pinḥas was possibly the Pinḥas who was head of the yeshiva, one of the masoretes of Tiberias (mentioned in sec. 288). In all, ten generations are listed after Mar Zūṭrā, and taking an average of twenty-five years per generation, this would add up to some 250 years, which brings us roughly to the year 800.

After this period, of which only names have remained, we can compose an assumed list of the names of geonim only from the mid-ninth century onwards, thanks to a tiny fragment preserved from a treatise or letter, written by Sahlān b. Abraham, leader of the 'Babylonians' in Fustat. The chronological departure point for fixing the times of the geonim mentioned in this list is the affair of the calendrical dispute which I have reviewed above. Today, we know the name of the son of Meir, the rival of Saadia Gaon – he was Aaron. 'Meir and his son Aaron Gaon' mentioned in that fragment are thus undoubtedly the father and son who were the geonim during the dispute. It seems that the father, Meir Gaon b. Aaron, was head of the Palestinian yeshiva and his son Aaron would make the public pronouncements and act as chief spokesman. This emerges from what Saadia Gaon wrote: 'and he sent (the Palestinian Gaon) his son in the seventh month of the year two [hundred and thirty]-three and he came to Jerusalem'. That is to say that Meir Gaon sent his son Aaron (he is Ben Meir in the polemical literature) to Jerusalem (evidently from Tiberias). We find the following quotation in the account of Saadia Gaon, from 'the copy of the letter sent by the scholars (i.e. the Babylonians) to him (to the Palestinian Gaon), from the place of their gathering, that is Babylonia: 'greetings to the head of the *ḥavūrā*, to your son, and brother, and all that are in your retinue: we could hardly believe the rumour which reached us, that your son fixed the holiday not as prescribed by the law; even if you say that your son made a mistake, lift up your eyes to our Holy one, and have mercy on us and on your son', etc. Here too he is referring to Meir Gaon and his son Aaron.

The other letter from Babylonia to Palestine on the same matter, claiming that the scholars of Babylonia had the right to decide on the order of the calendar, also mentions several times the 'head of the yeshiva', referring, one may assume, to Meir Gaon. However, in all the sources on the subject of the calendar dispute, one cannot find Ben Meir being called head of the yeshiva or Gaon and it is now obvious why this was so. Meir Gaon is evidently also the author of the letter to Babylonia in which he mentions the journey of the Palestinian Gaon to Babylonia in order to ask for aid for his yeshiva against the 'progeny of 'Anan, the enemies', and it is possible that it is he who helped the people of the Pumbedita yeshiva of

Mevassēr Gaon's faction in their struggle against David b. Zakkai, the exilarch, and against Kohen Ṣedeq ('against those who plotted against you'). These contacts could have occurred after 917, the year which marked the death of Judah, the Pumbedita Gaon [grandfather of Sherira Gaon]. Meir Gaon is evidently the one who describes the suffering his forefathers endured at the hands of the descendants of 'Anan, and he mentions R. Mūsā, who was killed in the *'azārā* (the synagogue?) and 'our fathers R. Meir and R. Moses'. We shall soon see that these latter three lived during the mid-ninth century.[122]

[850] One should note that Sahlān b. Abraham, the compiler of the list, draws our attention to the fact that two of the geonim mentioned there 'have already been dealt with above': and likewise, refers to 'Aaron b. Moses b. Meir mentioned above'. This refers to the description of the lineage of Joseph ha-Kohen, in which this Aaron is mentioned, and in writing 'Meir and his aforementioned son Aaron Gaon', he refers to that part of the manuscript which is missing. One of course cannot discern why he would have mentioned Aaron b. Meir's name in the missing part of the document; this may have had some connection with the transfer of the yeshiva from Tiberias to Jerusalem. On this matter, it is worth looking into the following genealogical tree based on the list from which we can get some idea of the time of Joseph ha-Kohen Gaon b. Yoḥai, son of the sister of Aaron b. Moses b. Meir, whom he places at the head of the list.

Although one should perhaps place Isaac Gaon between Aaron (I) Gaon and Meir (II) Gaon, the document does not say that there was any family relationship between them. At any rate, we see that Joseph ha-Kohen Gaon b. Yoḥai was more or less a contemporary of Meir (II) and his son Aaron (II) Gaon, that is, the geonim who held office during the calendar

[122] *Seder 'olām zūṭā*, in Neubauer, *Mediaeval Jewish Chronicle*, I, 178; II, 73, 76, and cf. the discussion in Mann, *Jews*, I, 58f., and the references there to some earlier studies. The fragment in the handwriting of Sahlān: **3**. Aaron b. Meir is mentioned in a letter of Sherira Gaon: MS Strasbourg, Cat. Wickersheimer, No. 4038, f. 6*v*, line 4, edited by Mann, *HUCA Jubilee Volume* (1925), 248. See above, sec. 784, and: Bornstein, *Sokolow Jubilee Volume*, 63, 74, 105ff; Mann, *Jews*, I, 63, n. 1, assumed that the son of Ben Meir was being referred to and drew the conclusion that Ben Meir himself stayed in Ramla and sent his son to Jerusalem; but the more credible view is that of Bornstein (*ibid.*, n. 3), that the Palestinian Gaon still stayed in Tiberias at the time. Thus one must attribute the letters from Palestine remaining from the time of the dispute to the period when Meir held office as Gaon, though some of them were written by his son, according to Saadia Gaon, in Bornstein, *ibid.*, 116: 'we therefore ordered a gathering of the heads and *alūfim* . . . and took advice how to overcome this enormous obstacle caused by Ben Meir and thwart his plot. They said: we cannot destroy all the copies written by Ben Meir about this matter to all localities. Moreover, his letter may have been copied amongst the people. However, they recommended writing this epistle to you . . . to inform you of the deed of this Ben Meir . . . as Ben Meir has invented.' As to the contacts with Babylonia which preceded the calendar dispute, see Mann, *Tarbiz*, 5(1933/4), 148–157, and especially 151, 154. See also the sources in Guillaume, *JQR*, NS 5(1914/5), 552–555; cf. also Mann, *Jews*, I, 57, n. 1.

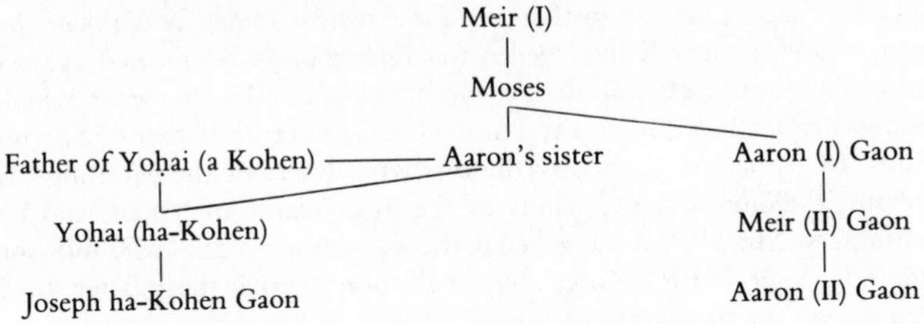

Genealogical tree of the early geonim

dispute. Joseph ha-Kohen's status as Gaon still remains something of a puzzle for the time being. One cannot identify him with Joseph ha-Kohen b. 'Ezrūn, for their fathers' names were different and it does not seem to be chronologically consistent. Perhaps there was a rift in the Palestinian yeshiva at the time of, or due to, the calendar dispute and a rival Gaon appeared on the scene. The major account of the affair was undoubtedly included in the first part of the manuscript, which is not available, and it is in connection with this account that Sahlān went on listing the geonim of Palestine. It is possible that the priestly geonim found in the list beginning with Aaron ha-Kohen, were members of the family of that same Joseph ha-Kohen b. Yoḥai, but as we shall see below, the dynasty of priestly geonim which we find in the eleventh century did not stem from this family.[123]

[851] We know little about Meir Gaon and his son Aaron, apart from their involvement in the calendar dispute. It seems that in the period under discussion, a quire containing queries and responsa was known and attributed to Ben Meir. A number of Geniza documents from the eleventh century mention offspring of the family of Meir Gaon: Solomon he-ḥāvēr b. Meir *rōsh ha-seder*, great-grandson of Meir head of the yeshiva Ge'ōn Ya'aqōv; Solomon, son of Isaac great-grandson of Meir Gaon; Isaac b. Solomon he-ḥāvēr b. Meir Gaon; Moses ha-Sōfēr ('the scribe'), son of Isaac he-ḥāvēr, son of Solomon he-ḥāvēr, son of Meir Gaon. The genealogical tree of the family according to the data in the Geniza is outlined as follows:

123 This discussion is based on the abovementioned fragment, **3**. Abramson, *Ba-merkazim*, 32, proposed identifying Joseph ha-Kohen b. Yoḥai with b. 'Ezrūn. See further (sec. 852) the assumed list of the Palestinian geonim, based on **3**. The fragment TS NS 194.92 also confirms the fact that the Palestinian Gaon during the calendar dispute was Meir, and it has interesting evidence on the division between Meir Gaon and the priestly family who were his rivals over the leadership of the Palestinian yeshiva. Fleischer, in his article in *Zion*, 49(1984), 385, is right in assuming that the family of Joseph ha-Kohen b. Yoḥai is meant.

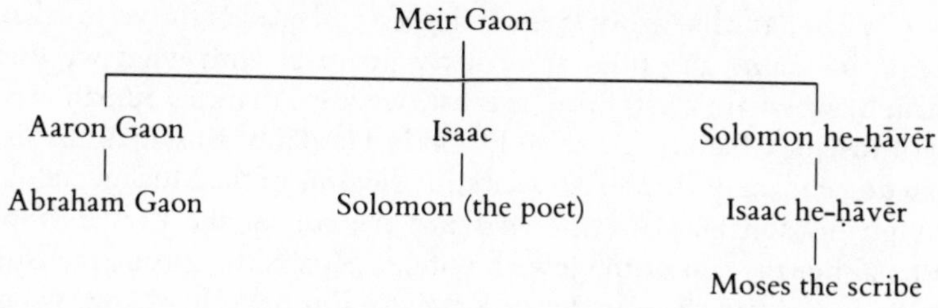

Genealogical tree of Meir Gaon's offspring

We do not know who was the father of Meir *rōsh ha-seder*, father of Solomon he-ḥāvēr, from among those mentioned here. Solomon he-ḥāvēr b. Meir *rōsh ha-seder* was Ephraim b. Shemaria's rival within the 'Palestinian' congregation in Fustat. Solomon b. Judah writes to Ephraim b. Shemaria: 'For Solomon b. Meir has made peace with the band of plotters'. Nathan b. Abraham, Solomon b. Judah's competitor, writes to Berākhā b. Rawḥ and expresses his anger about *al-ṣabī* (the youth) b. Meir, who evidently joined the opposing faction in the struggle for the seat of the Gaon, but then changed his mind and joined him again, as we shall see in the discussion on that dispute.[124]

[852] As to Ṣemaḥ, the *nāsī* and head of the yeshiva, it is clear that he stems from the exilarchic family, as one can see from the title *nāsī*. He and his brother Jehoshaphat are the first whose names are known to us after the dynasty of Mar Zūṭrā, knowledge of which ceased at one point, as we have seen above, and we know of no uninterrupted family connection between

[124] Responsa of Ben Meir: see TS 10 K 20, f. 9, fol. 2a, verso, lines 8–9; Mann understood it as a responsum to the queries of Ben Meir, perhaps answered by Saadia Gaon, but it seems that his interpretation is not correct. Solomon he-ḥavēr b. Meir *rōsh ha-seder*: TS 8 J 14, f. 24 (the beginning of a letter to Abraham ha-Kohen b. Isaac ibn Furāt); **604** (a deed, Solomon b. Isaac great-grandson of Meir Gaon signed its validation); cf. Mann, *Jews*, II, 54f. Solomon b. Isaac he-ḥāvēr signed the piyyūṭ: Bodl 2708/1 fs. 36–37, in Zulay, *Yedī'ōt*, 5(1938/9), 175ff. Isaac he-ḥāvēr b. Solomon he-ḥāvēr: see a colophon from 1001 edited by Assaf, *Mi-sifrut ha-ge'ōnīm*, 206. Mann, *Jews* (MS), II, 52: MS Harkavy R No. 67, two leaves which contain the end of *kitāb al-sharā'i'* (Book of the Laws), in the colophon: 'I Isaac b. Solomon he-ḥāvēr b. Meir Gaon, may he rest in Paradise, wrote this for me' etc.; 'finished Monday in the month of Iyar in the first year of the sabbatical cycle, which is 4761 of the creation' (28 April AD 1001). The Isaac (the father of Moses ha-Sōfēr) evidently lived in Acre, see **222**, lines 8, 10: *al-ḥāvēr R. Isaac*. Moses ha-Sōfēr signs in **224**, which is a letter to Abraham b. Sahl al-Tustarī, whose help he requests in order to be able to travel to his father, Isaac he-ḥāvēr, evidently in Acre; he is mentioned also in TS 8 J 8, f. 6, in Mann, *Jews*, I, 54; see also TS 10 J 26, f. 6 (*ibid.*, II, 55), where the name of 'Iṣḥaq (thus it is written, as Mann assumed, *ibid.*) *he-ḥāvēr* great-grandson of Meir Gaon' has been preserved (what I have written on this matter in *Tarbiz*, 44 [1974/5], 149, n. 31, has to be emended). The letter of Solomon b. Judah: **129**, margin. Nathan b. Abraham: **183**, line 9; 'al-ḥāvēr b. Meir' is also mentioned in a document of the heqdēsh in Fustat, from the end of 1039, see document no. 11, a, line 17, in my book: Gil, *Documents*, 168.

them. We find the lineage of 'Ṣemaḥ the *nāsi* and head of the yeshiva' in the Geniza; his name and titles are exactly identical with what we find in Sahlān b. Abraham's list. From this list, we learn that this Ṣemaḥ was the son of Josiah b. Saul b. 'Anan b. David b. Ḥasdai b. Bustanai, that is, he was a descendant of Bustanai, exilarch at the time of the Muslim conquest, through his son Ḥasdai (who was not the son of the Persian wife of Bustanai but the son of the Jewish wife), and was the great-grandson of 'Anan, considered the founder of Karaism. On the other hand, we have before us Karaite lists of exilarchs, mentioning another son of Josiah father of Ṣemaḥ, Jehoshaphat; and this Jehoshaphat, Ṣemaḥ's brother, is also called there 'the great *nāsī* Jehoshaphat, head of the yeshiva Ge'ōn Ya'aqōv'. We may assume that Jehoshaphat was the elder and preceded his brother Ṣemaḥ. How are we to understand the surprising fact that people of the exilarchic family who were considered Karaites and were descendants of 'Anan, headed the Palestinian yeshiva? Poznanski was of the opinion that the Karaites had a yeshiva, which they called 'yeshivat Ge'ōn Ya'aqōv', despite their hatred for the Rabbanite yeshivot of Babylonia. Mann transferred the events to Jerusalem and assumed that the two brothers, Jehoshaphat and Ṣemaḥ, sons of Josiah, set up a rival yeshiva in Jerusalem, and that this was the background to the quarrel between the 'progeny of 'Anan' and the forefathers of Meir Gaon and his son Aaron, the quarrel described in the aforementioned letters of the Palestinian Gaon at the time of the calendar dispute, that is, the murder of Mūsā and the persecution of Meir and Moses. Owing to the fragment from Sahlān's list, however, it is now clear to us what was not clear to those eminent scholars, namely that indeed these two were heads of the Palestinian yeshiva. The only rational solution to this puzzle is that during the period when these descendants of 'Anan headed the Palestinian yeshiva, the final split between the Rabbanites and the sect of the Karaites had not yet occurred, and at any rate, this branch of the exilarch's family descending from 'Anan had as yet not been drawn into this rift, and still held a strong position among the Jews of the diaspora. Naturally, this conclusion has a special significance with regard to Karaite history, and I shall return to it further in the discussion on the Karaites. Here it will suffice to note the fact that from the mid-ninth century until close to its end, descendants of 'Anan headed the Palestinian yeshiva. The end of the ninth century is also the supposed date for the beginning of Karaite immigration to Jerusalem. Jerusalem became the arena for the struggle between the two camps: the offspring of 'Anan, heads of the Palestinian yeshiva and the newly immigrated Karaites, on the one hand, and the head of the family of Meir Gaon (evidently his grandfather) Aaron b. Moses, on the other. The end of that struggle is clearly accounted for in Sahlān's list, that is, the sons of

Ṣemaḥ dissented and were ousted. The division only began with those sons of Ṣemaḥ (their names are known to us; one being Asa and the other [with no certainty] Yefet. We also know that the name of the son of Ṣemaḥ's brother Jehoshaphat was Boaz). It would not be accurate, then, to describe the sons of Josiah, Jehoshaphat and Ṣemaḥ, as Karaites. In Sahlān's list, it explicitly states with regard to Ṣemaḥ: 'And he was of the *benē rabbānān*, that is, he was one of the loyal and apt scholars of the yeshiva, unlike his sons. It does not say in that list that in that struggle in Jerusalem, Aaron b. Moses, the rival of the sons of Ṣemaḥ (and the Karaites) was helped by any personalities from Baghdad. This help, mentioned in a letter of the Palestinian Gaon at the time of the calendar dispute ('and we came to you [in Baghdad] to be helped', etc.) was rendered two generations later.

Further, it is worth noting that the descent from Bustanai was a recognised fact among the Rabbanite exilarchs, and the fact that Ṣemaḥ stemmed from this family is not to be questioned. However, this lineage was the subject for slandering the exilarchic family in the eleventh century, both in the responsa of the geonim and in a story in Arabic about Bustanai, ascribed to Nathan b. Abraham and copied by Sahlān b. Abraham. It seems that Sahlān wrote his genealogical list of geonim and copied the story of Bustanai not only for their purely historical value. Rather, he seems to have been motivated by a degree of tendentiousness which is not clearly definable as yet. The story of Bustanai went so far as to claim that all the exilarchs in Baghdad stemmed from Bustanai and his Persian wife (who the story claimed was his only wife, and not proselytised), that is, that Ṣemaḥ also belonged to that slandered family. In the continuation of our discussion, we shall find another offspring of the exilarchic family, Daniel b. Azariah, called '*nāsī* and Gaon' because he became head of the Palestinian yeshiva. He was even praised in a piyyūṭ as being 'a spark of Bustanai's', that is, that he too was of Bustanai's progeny.

If we assume, somewhat arbitrarily, that the fourteen years in which Meir Gaon and his son Aaron Gaon held office, began in 912 (if we place in the middle of these years the period of the contacts and the dispute with Babylonia, from 917–921), we arrive at the following chronological table of the Palestinian geonim, in which there may be differences of a few years (up to five), forward or backward:

(1)	Jehoshaphat b. Josiah		before 862
(2)	Ṣemaḥ b. Josiah (31 years)		862–893
(3)	Aaron b. Moses (17 years)		893–910
(4)	Isaac (two years)		910–912
(5)	Meir	(14 years)	912–926
(6)	Aaron b. Meir		

(7) Abraham b. Aaron (7 years) 926–933
(8) Aaron ha-Kohen 933–[?]
(9) Joseph ha-Kohen b. ʿEzrūn (2 years)
(10) ʿEzrūn (b. Joseph?) (30 years)
(11) Samuel (ha-Kohen b. Joseph b. ʿEzrūn [?])[125]

[853] Above we have seen the obscure matter of Joseph ha-Kohen Gaon b. Yoḥai, who was a relative of Meir Gaon, and that his time was somewhere in the first half of the tenth century. Another Kohen in the list of the Palestinian geonim is Aaron ha-Kohen (Number 8 in the list above), whose time was close to the middle of that century. In the continuation of the list, we find Joseph ha-Kohen b. ʿEzrūn (Number 9); another Gaon whose name may also have been ʿEzrūn (Ezra), perhaps son of the former

[125] See: TS 12.138 (Ṣemaḥ the Nāsī and head of the yeshiva b. Josiah b. Saul b. ʿAnan) in Mann, *Texts*, II, 131. See the discussion *ibid.*, 44f. The lists of Karaite exilarchs: see mainly in Lewin, the *Letter of Sherira Gaon*, 136; and in Pinsker, *Liqqūṭē qadmōniyōt*, II, 53, in the footnote; cf. Poznanski, *Babylonische Geonim*, 127f; see also Mann, *Jews*, II, 210f, 453–457; cf. Sahlān's list, **3**. Regarding ʿAnan's descendants who headed the Palestinian yeshiva: Mann, *Yearbook*, 44(1934), 229, wrote that with the Ṭūlūnid regime in Palestine (according to him from 868, but actually from 878) easier conditions were created for the Karaites and that the establishment of the exilarchic family from descendants of ʿAnan (he calls them: the *nesīʾīm* of the Karaites, a designation not yet in use then) was in the interest of the new regime in Egypt. As against this, he stresses the fact that after 905, when the Abbasids returned to rule Palestine, the family of Aaron b. Meir (more precisely: the family of Meir Gaon) were assisted by the rulers of Baghdad and one of the wealthy men of Baghdad (Aaron b. ʿAmram) is called in their letters, the 'saviour of the generation'. However, we know today that the sons of Ṣemaḥ were ousted during the Ṭūlūnid period. Klar, *Meḥqārīm*, 189, n. 20, comments on the sentence 'until the soul would expire because of the ransom money – *ha-kippūrīm*' (thus he reads in Guillaume, *JQR*, NS [1914/5], 555; cf. Schechter, *Saadyana*, 22; Bornstein, *Sokolow Jubilee Volume*, 107, n. 1, suggests the reading: 'until the souls of the unbelievers [ha-kōferīm] would expire') under the enemies (*ha-sōneʾīm*), the progeny of ʿAnan', and expresses the opinion that the word *ha-sōneʾīm* (the enemies) is a pejorative distortion of the word *ha-nesīʾīm*, an interesting idea. Baron, *Saadia Jubilee Volume*, 39, sees the dispute in Jerusalem between 'the progeny of ʿAnan' and the family of Meir as a division between Karaites and Rabbanites, in which the Karaites exploited their considerable influence with the Muslim authorities against Ben Meir, who was saved only by the intervention of the people of Baghdad. Abramson, *Ba-merkazim*, 27ff, presents the matter differently, mainly by differentiating between the status of Jehoshaphat and that of Ṣemaḥ, and on the other hand, he considers them both Karaites and reaches the conclusion that 'a Karaite *nāsī* and head of the yeshiva stood at the head of the Jewish community, evidently in its relationship to the authorities, for thirty-one years (referring to Ṣemaḥ); and the Rabbanite Jews could not but accept the power of its authority'. The sources on Bustanai, see Gil, *Tarbiz*, 48(1978/9), 36–45. See TS 12.358: 'the *nāsī* and Gaon of Tiberias, head of the yeshiva which is in Jerusalem, the House of God, our Lord Daniel'. The piyyūṭ (qaṣīda): BM Or 5557 K, f. 8, line 10, is mentioned in Mann, *Jews*, II, 220; edited by Fleischer, *Shalem*, 1(1973/4), 62–74; as one can clearly see from the acrostic, the author of this piyyūṭ in honour of Daniel b. Azariah was ʿEli (not Eliah, as Mann has it) ha-Kohen; he wrote it on 'Friday, 13 Nisan (the date in Mann and Fleischer should be corrected) i.e. 21 March 1057 (AM 4817). 13 Nisan fell on Friday that year, and then again in 1060 (4820). What I have written here on Jehoshaphat and Ṣemaḥ the sons of Josiah is an addition to what I wrote elsewhere: Gil, *Tarbiz*, 44 (1974/5), 148f. The list of geonim is based mainly on **3**, as mentioned.

(Number 10); Samuel ha-Kohen b. Joseph (Number 11). In the eleventh century, we find the priestly family, some of whose sons served as geonim: Solomon ha-Kohen Gaon b. Joseph and his descendants. Some of the genealogical lists of these kohanim, the progeny of Solomon ha-Kohen b. Joseph, are found in the openings of letters of Maṣlīaḥ ha-Kohen, head of the Palestinian yeshiva Ge'ōn Ya'aqōv when it had already moved to Fustat, in the twelfth century. In these openings, the lineage of earlier generations is:

(a) Aaron ha-Kohen 'the chief priest' (*ha-kohen ha-rōsh*)
Joseph ha-Kohen *av-bēt-dīn*
Solomon ha-Kohen Gaon, etc.

while in Maṣlīaḥ ha-Kohen's memorial list (not the opening of a letter!) the lineage is:

(b) Mordecai (ha-Kohen) Gaon
Elijah (ha-Kohen) Gaon
Menaḥem ha-Kohen
Joseph ha-Kohen *av-bēt-dīn*
Solomon ha-Kohen Gaon, etc.

and in another memorial list of the same:

(c) Elijah (ha-Kohen) head of the yeshiva of the diaspora
Solomon (ha-Kohen) head of the yeshiva of the diaspora
Menaḥem head of the yeshiva of the diaspora
Mordecai ha-Kohen
Joseph ha-Kohen *av-bēt-dīn*
Solomon ha-Kohen Gaon, etc.

Another type of this family's lineage lists are those of Eleazer ha-Kohen b. Solomon, who lived in the twelfth century in Fustat. Here we find:

(d) Aaron ha-Kohen
Elijah ha-Kohen head of the yeshiva of the diaspora
Menaḥem ha-Kohen head of the yeshiva of the diaspora
Mordecai ha-Kohen
Joseph ha-Kohen *av-bēt-dīn*
Solomon ha-Kohen Gaon, etc.

As we can see, there are differences between the lists, both in the names and the titles.

A fragment of a letter from the yeshiva to a community, evidently from the latter half of the tenth century, contains the signatures of Joseph ha-Kohen, head of the yeshiva Ge'ōn Ya'aqōv; of Samuel ha-Kohen 'the third' in the *ḥavūrā* (the yeshiva); and of Aaron ha-Kohen 'the fourth' in the *ḥavūrā*, who calls himself: great-grandson of a Gaon. At the top of this letter, the latter's signature with the words *'avdī beḥīrī*, 'my servant, mine elect' are written. It would not be far from the truth to say that the Joseph ha-Kohen, whose signature is found here, is the abovementioned b. 'Ezrūn (Number 9 in the list; for in no list is there anyone else named Joseph who was the Gaon at that time) and that Samuel (who later became Gaon) and Aaron, who are mentioned here, are his sons. Also, we find no support for those lineage lists in which one of the forefathers of Solomon ha-Kohen Gaon b. Joseph (1025) is said to have served as Gaon before the eleventh century.

There is therefore a distinct contradiction between Sahlān's list and the lineage lists of the priestly geonim of the eleventh and twelfth centuries. Confirmation of the lineage of the latter is only to be found with regard to the names of the father and grandfather of Solomon ha-Kohen, who was Gaon in 1025. His father's name was Joseph and his grandfather's, Menaḥem. This we gather from the fragments of a letter of Josiah Gaon, but nowhere does it state that they were heads of the yeshiva.

The incidence of Elijah ha-Kohen, Solomon ha-Kohen and Menaḥem ha-Kohen being called heads of the 'yeshiva of the diaspora' is strange, their time, according to the lineage lists of the family, being approximately the mid-tenth century. We know that it was the Babylonian yeshivot which were in the habit of calling themselves yeshiva of the diaspora. This puzzle does not seem to have any solution for the time being. An address written on the back of a piyyūṭ (which is faded and illegible) says: 'its waters fail not (Is., lviii:11); receive ye many greetings from the gate of the yeshiva of the Aaronids (i.e. the priestly one), which is aided by the name of the God of Jacob, and also from all our party and our assemblies', etc. Perhaps the appellation 'the yeshiva of the Aaronids' suggests that a separate yeshiva was set up by this priestly family. Another matter worth looking into is the claim of the priestly geonim of the eleventh century, that they were the offspring of the *tannā* Eleazar b. Azariah (around AD 100). Abiathar ha-Kohen writes in his scroll that his father, the Gaon Elijah ha-Kohen, is buried in Daltūn 'close to . . . Eleazar b. Azariah his ancestor'. Another personality who claimed descent from Eleazar b. Azariah was Aaron ha-Kohen Gaon b. Joseph (Gaon of Pumbedita from 943 to 960, the rival of Saadia Gaon. He was also called Khalaf b. Sarjāda).[126]

126 See the lineage lists **4–9**, **11**; in **9** (MS Sasson), line 3, there is the editor's doubtful reconstruction, with an additional name: Solomon ha-Kohen, between Elijah and Menaḥem. Another lineage list of Maṣlīaḥ Gaon: TS Box K 6, f. 139; see also the fragment TS NS J 605, and similar fragments with Maṣlīaḥ ha-Kohen's lineage list, from the David Kaufmann collection in Budapest, edited by Weisz, 7–8. The letter of Josiah Gaon: **38**, b, line 4. In a memorial list: TS Box K 6, f. 118, edited by Mann, *Jews*, II, 58 (cf. *ibid.*, I, 66), Samuel ha-Kohen head of the yeshiva Ge'ōn Ya'aqōv and his son Yōsē ha-Kohen head of the yeshiva Ge'ōn Ya'aqōv are mentioned. We do not know anything about the latter (the list is in the handwriting of Samuel b. Saadia, and not as Mann assumed; and is dated 1452 Sel. (AD 1141)). The Aaronite yeshiva: TS Box K 16, f. 69, edited by Mann, *Jews*, I, 21,

[854] There is no doubt, then, that we have here two priestly families, one mentioned in Sahlān's list, of which there is documentary evidence with regard to the existence of Joseph ha-Kohen (b. 'Ezrūn, apparently) and his son Samuel. The other family is mentioned in the list of priestly geonim of the eleventh century, of which there is evidence of the existence of Joseph (Yehōsēf) ha-Kohen b. Menaḥem, who was *av-bēt-dīn* of the Palestinian yeshiva.

Joseph ha-Kohen of the first family, is mentioned in a letter dealing with a legacy of a freedman named Bundār, of Palermo. He bequeathed a quarter of his property (the sum of some thirty-five dinars) to 'the poor of Jerusalem, may it be rebuilt soon ... to Rabbanites only'. Samuel b. Hosha'na, of the Jerusalem yeshiva, then visited Sicily, and arranged to

n. 1. On the 'yeshiva of the diaspora' in the priestly lineage lists, see Poznanski, *REJ*, 51 (1906), 55f; in his opinion, this appellation proves that those personalities lived in Egypt. The Scroll of Abiathar, see: **559**, b, lines 23–25; cf. also in 'the ancient questions' the matter of the descent of the head of the Palestinian yeshiva from Eleazar b. Azariah, see in Rosenthal, *HUCA*, 21(1948), 45, lines 29–30: 'so he counted me among his flock, the *ḥavūrā* of righteousness (i.e. the Palestinian yeshiva), and his own generation, and Eleazar b. Azariah'. Cf. also Assaf, *Kiryat Sefer*, 5(1927–29), 46, who also noted the matter of the descent from Eleazar b. Azariah; the claim of descent of the abovementioned Aaron ha-Kohen b. Joseph from Eleazar b. Azariah emerges from his responsum, edited by Assaf, *Jeschurun*, 5/6(1925) 45ff, and re-edited in: *Made'ē ha-yahadūt*, II, 72ff. See on the entire matter: Gil, *Sefunot*, NS 1(1979/80), 22f, n. 19, and some assumptions there as to the origins of the Palestinian priestly geonim (Mr Aaron Naḥlon draws my attention to the fact that these mentions of Eleazar b. Azariah were evidently due to his status in the Sanhedrin, where he had the rank of *nāsī*). Apparently, the people of that generation were aware of the fact that a *nāsī* need not necessarily have to stem from the house of David; as Abraham Maimuni says in one of his responsa; 'as was the case with R. Eleazar b. Azariah, who was *nāsī* although he was a Kohen'. (See BT, Ber. 27b: Eleazar b. Azariah was about to be appointed instead of Rabbān Gamliel, 'as he was a scholar, and rich, and a tenth-generation offspring of Ezra'.) See the *Responsa* of Abraham Maimuni, 20. We have seen that at the end of some of the lists 'the grandson of Aaron the priest' is written, or 'the grandson of Aaron, the chief priest' (according to Ezra, vii:5) and also 'the grandson of Aaron the priest, the Saint of the Lord' (see Ps., cvi:16). There are contradictions between the lists, but Elijah ha-Kohen 'head of the yeshiva of the diaspora' is found in all of them, and it is said of him that he was the grandson of Aaron ha-Kohen 'the head'. True, common sense tells us that the reference is to Aaron, the brother of Moses, but it is not impossible that the above-mentioned Aaron ha-Kohen Gaon b. Joseph, the head of the Pumbedita yeshiva, is meant. On the outset of the involvement of Joseph ha-Kohen b. Menaḥem's family (and after him, Solomon ha-Kohen Gaon, his sons Joseph and Elijah, etc.) in the Palestinian yeshiva, we have an important additional detail in **3a**. This is an additional fragment of what Sahlān b. Abraham wrote on the geonim of Palestine and it emerges that that family of geonim stemmed from Sijilmāssa in the Maghrib (Joseph ha-Kohen, father of the family, is called there Sijilmāssī). This fact is linked with the matter of Judah ha-Kohen b. Joseph, 'ha-Rav'. Above I wrote that he was perhaps the person of the same name mentioned in a Geniza document, whose father's designation was: 'his honourable Sanctity, our Lord and Master Joseph ha-Kohen Sijilmāssī (*supra*, sec. 378); if this is the case, one can assume that the 'Rav', leader of the Maghribis in Fustat, was indeed a member of that priestly family who headed the Palestinian yeshiva, and the brother of Solomon ha-Kohen Gaon. However, the fact that the 'Rav' was still active towards the end of the eleventh century, speaks against this assumption, for

transfer the money to Jerusalem through a certain Joshua al-Ḥalabī. Part of the money went to 'Joseph Gaon head of the yeshiva'. Although the letter does not specifically state 'ha-Kohen', there is no doubt that Joseph ha-Kohen, the father of Samuel, is being spoken of. According to Sahlān's list, he was succeeded by 'Ezrūn (Ezra), who was Gaon for thirty years. If this is correct, it means that Joseph ha-Kohen became Gaon at about the onset of the Fatimid period (970). About 'Ezrūn, we have no further information. A list at the end of a midrash manuscript says: 'his honourable Sanctity, our Lord and Master Joseph ha-Kohen, head of the yeshiva Ge'ōn Ya'aqōv, and our Master Josiah *av-bēt-dīn*, and our Master Isaac, his brother, 'the third', and our Master Samuel b. 'Ezrūn, of blessed memory'. It is difficult to determine which Joseph ha-Kohen this refers to; perhaps it is the grandson of the above-mentioned Joseph ha-Kohen and the son of 'Ezrūn, who succeeded him. We have seen that in one of the lists Yōsē ha-Kohen Gaon is mentioned, and Samuel b. 'Ezrūn, in the continuation of the list, was evidently his brother. If indeed there was another Gaon by the name of Joseph ha-Kohen, it sems that the extent of his office was very short.

As to Ṣamuel ha-Kohen b. Joseph, we know that he occupied the Gaon's seat at the end of the tenth century. Joseph b. Isaac ibn Abītūr's letter to him from the year 989 has been preserved, in which Joseph ibn Abītūr requests that he support him in his struggle against Ḥanōkh b. Moses, who had appealed to Shemaria b. Elḥanan for support. In my collection, there is a fragment of a marriage deed of a woman named Sutayt, written during the days of 'our Lord and Master Samuel ha-Kohen Gaon'. We also know that before he became Gaon, Samuel ha-Kohen was *av-bēt-dīn* of the yeshiva, which is explicity stated in the fragment of a letter dealing with the distribution of money to the people of the Palestinian yeshiva. Sherira and Hayy wrote to him on 13 Av 1300 Sel., or 18 July AD 989.

Samuel ha-Kohen's brother, Ḥanania, was *av-bēt-dīn* of the Palestinian yeshiva. He is mentioned in a court record in Fustat, of 16 Elul 1318 Sel., 1 September AD 1007, when before 'the council of the *av-bēt-dīn* Ḥanania b. Joseph Gaon', none other than Ephraim b. Shemaria and his rival Solomon b. Pashshāṭ, came to be judged. A poet from Aleppo dedicated three piyyūṭīm to Ḥanania; in one of them he expresses his joy on Ḥanania's visit to Aleppo (he thanks 'God who brought you to me, to Ṣōvā'), and ends with 'greetings . . . to our Master Ḥanania *av* of the yeshiva'. Elsewhere he writes: 'Our Master Ḥanania who is called the father of all and the excellent'. Apparently, Ḥanania was already *av-bēt-dīn* at the time of his brother Samuel's term of office as Gaon and continued in this role during

Solomon Gaon died in 1025. Then perhaps the 'Rav' was the grandson of that Judah ha-Kohen, the assumed brother of Solomon ha-Kohen Gaon.

the terms of the succeeding geonim, Shemaiah and Josiah. He is mentioned in the draft of a court record in Fustat concerning the dispute over slaughtering, mentioned above, and which is to be found in my collection. It mentions in the past tense, 'Shemaiah Gaon, of blessed memory', as well as Ḥanania: 'Our Master Ḥanania ha-Kohen, may God preserve him, his *av-bēt-dīn*', who was still alive then. On the same subject of slaughtering, Ḥanania wrote a letter which is also to be found in my collection. The letters from the people of Sicily to the yeshiva are also addressed to him.

We also have a letter from the Gaon Samuel ha-Kohen b. Joseph to Shemaria b. Elḥanan, which besides containing explicit confirmation of my conclusions concerning the existence of *two* priestly families who headed the Palestinian yeshiva, reveals considerable hostility between the two families in around 990. The letter is an appeal from the 'veteran' kōhanīm at the head of the yeshiva, to the people of Fustat, asking them to refrain from supporting their rival Joseph ha-Kohen b. Menaḥem. It seems that the latter managed to gain the support of the central figure of the day among the Jews of Fustat, Shemaria b. Elḥanan, and promised to give him the status of *av-bēt-dīn* of the yeshiva. Samuel b. Hosha'na and Josiah b. Aaron, who later on was to become Gaon, were among those who took issue with the Gaon. Ben-Sasson finds in Joseph b. Abītūr's letter to the Gaon Samuel ha-Kohen traces of anxiety and anger towards those who try to undermine the Gaon, while in the remnant of a letter written by Sherira Gaon and his son Hayy to Samuel ha-Kohen, he finds an expression of support for the Palestinian Gaon. (The date of the letter is 18 July 989.) In addition, he assumes that the letter, ascribed to Hayy Gaon, 'to the unruly kōhanīm of Ifrīqiyā', was directed against the 'new' priestly family, who challenged the Palestinian Gaon. His views are supported by the fact that indeed the 'new' priestly family stemmed from the Maghrib (Sijilmāssa). The 'elders of Ramla' supported the 'veteran' family, while the two sides tried to obtain the authorities' assistance. The letter of the Gaon Samuel ha-Kohen mentions 'the ruler of the *bādiya*' (the Bedouin), meaning, it seems, Mufarrij b. Daghfal, the leader of the Bedouin, who ruled at that time in Palestine (see secs. 562, 563).[127]

[127] Bundār: TS 16.133. The list at the end of the midrash: MS Firkovitch II, 157 A, fols. 9–10, cf. Abramson, *Ba-merkazim*, 31. Samuel b. 'Ezrūn, perhaps grandson of Samuel ha-Kohen Gaon, is mentioned in a letter of Solomon b. Judah, **101**, lines 6–7; and it is to him (Samuel b. Ezra) that the lepers of Tiberias are appealing for help: **262**. The letter of Joseph Ibn Abitur: ENA 4009, f. 15, see in Mann, *Tarbiz*, 6(1934/5), 84ff; see on Joseph ibn Abitur and his struggles: Mann, *Tarbiz*, 5(1933/4), 282–286; Ashtor, *Qōrōt*, I, 233–247. The marriage deed of Sutayt: **14**. Samuel ha-Kohen *av-bēt-dīn*: **13**. Sherira and Hayy: Mann, *Tarbiz*, 6(1934/5), 84. Ḥanania ha-Kohen: see Mann, *Jews*, II, 440, with a fragment of the court record, Mosseri I a 9; as to Solomon b. Pashshāṭ: Pashshāṭ b. Samuel is mentioned in **12**, line 19, in a deed from Fustat (dealing with property in Tiberias) from the end of the tenth century; and also TS 12.462, which relates to a deed from the year

[855] In about the year 1000, it appears that the Gaon was Shemaiah; he was evidently a Maghribi by origin. As I have mentioned, Ḥanania ha-Kohen b. Joseph remained *av-bēt-dīn* and continued in this role after Shemaiah, but there were no more geonim of this first dynasty of the priestly geonim. Shemaiah Gaon is mentioned in a court record in Fustat dealing with the above-mentioned slaughtering dispute. A memorandum written in Fustat concerning Ephraim b. Shemaria notes that Ephraim received the first appointment as *bēt-dīn* from Shemaiah Gaon. In fact, the name of Shemaiah is not preserved there, for a part of the document is torn, but one can safely assume that it was included, for the document mentions Josiah Gaon in the continuation. The name of Shemaiah Gaon is mentioned in the lineage of his descendants, who lived in Palestine and Egypt in the eleventh and twelfth centuries. We find his grandson, the above-mentioned Shemaiah he-ḥāvēr b. Yeshū'ā, among the Maghribis in Jerusalem, and this makes it appear likely that Shemaiah Gaon originated from the Maghrib. The great-grandson of Shemaiah Gaon, Abraham b. Shemaiah he-ḥāvēr, was dayyān in Fustat, and his name is to be found in the city's court deeds dating from between 1092 and 1132. Shemaiah he-ḥāvēr had another son, Josiah, and the latter's son (that is, the nephew of Abraham the dayyān b. Shemaiah), Joshua, is mentioned in documents from Fustat in around 1140 and thereafter, and his signature is 'Joshua b. Josiah great-grandson of Shemaiah Gaon'. Below we shall see that evidently Solomon b. Judah was also a descendant of Shemaiah Gaon. Mention should also be made of the son of Shemaiah's sister, Tobiah b. Daniel. In Josiah Gaon's day, he was one of the people of the yeshiva and he held the title of ḥāvēr, like his father Daniel. This was also the case in Solomon ha-Kohen b. Joseph's time, when Solomon b. Judah was already 'third'. The two sons of Tobiah, Aaron and Solomon, are also mentioned in the documents in my collection.[128]

Josiah b. Aaron

[856] Josiah Gaon, who replaced Shemaiah, stemmed from a different family. No lineage list indicates any family connection between the two.

1277 Sel., that is AD 965/6; perhaps he is the father of this Solomon; see Solomon b. Pashshāṭ in **271**, line 40 (Tyre 1019); and in TS 16.191, a deed whose exact time is not known. The piyyūṭīm: TS Loan 9, edited by Davidson, *JQR*, NS 2(1911/2), 227–231; see **20**, line 12; **23**; the letter from Sicily: **45**. See the letter to Shemaria b. Elḥanan: **38** (Gil, *Te'uda*, 7 [1991], 311ff); the fragment of the letter by Sherira and Hayy to Samuel ha-Kohen: ENA 4009, f. 15; Hayy's letter 'to the priests': ed. Lewin, *Ginze qedem*, 4(1930), 51ff; see also **3a**; see Ben-Sasson, *Zion*, 51(1986), 386ff.

128 The memorandum: **324**, line 12; see Mann, *Jews*, II, 342. On Abraham b. Shemaiah see Goitein, *Mediterranean Society*, II, 512. Joshua b. Josiah: see Mann, II, 232; Goitein, *Mediterranean Society*, II, 268, 584, n. 53. Tobiah b. Daniel and his sons: see the Hebrew

The lineage lists which include the lineage of Josiah contradict one another and are not at all trustworthy, for those of the Gaon's forefathers whose names are listed there, such as Josiah and Abraham, did not exist at all, or at any rate, were not geonim. In a few of the lists, the name of Josiah's father, Abraham, is included, but we know for certain that his name was Aaron. We recognise from the lists that the descendants of Josiah wished to be recorded as members of the family of Meir Gaon, but they were not familiar with its lineage. This, however, does not mean that the lineage is not genuine in the main. Josiah's father was Aaron, of which we have proof in the opening phrase of a letter sent to him, in which he is called: 'Josiah head of the yeshiva Ge'ōn Ya'aqōv, son of his great honourable Sanctity, our Lord and Master Aaron, ḥāvēr in the Great Sanhedrin'. From this, we also learn that his father was ḥāvēr, and not more than that, contrary to what was stated in the lineage lists. It seems that the *'alāma*, the formula adopted by Josiah to end his letters, was *yesha' ṭōv* (good deliverance). The time of Josiah's death can be clearly arrived at from letters of Solomon b. Judah. In a fragment of a letter in his handwriting, he notes that the Gaon who preceded him, Solomon ha-Kohen b. Joseph, died six days before Rōsh ha-shānā. As we shall see below, Solomon b. Judah became Gaon in AM 4786; 23 Elul AM 4785 fell on 21 August AD 1025. He complains there that something similar occurred 'during the past holidays'. What he meant by this was that a Gaon also died 'during the past holidays'. He did not mean the holidays of Tishri of the year before, for Josiah Gaon was still alive in the month of Adar 1336 Sel. (AM 4785, that is February AD 1025), as we can clearly see from a regulation adopted by the 'Palestinians' in Fustat during that month. Solomon b. Judah then refers to Passover and Shavuot, that is to say that Josiah Gaon died in the spring of 1025.

There are more than thirty letters in my collection written by Josiah Gaon himself, or by some of his retainers, during the period in which he held office. Some of them deal with disputes in which he was involved. A quarrel involving Ḥanania ha-Kohen b. Joseph, who was *av-bēt-dīn* in Josiah's day, is immortalised in a letter in which Ḥanania tells that he was ill, but has recovered since. His letter was delayed because of his illness. In the continuation, he writes about events in Tiberias, which I have mentioned above, when a man wanted to revolt against the yeshiva, and for this purpose, was in contact with two brothers in Fustat who helped him – it emerges – to have the slaughtering taxes paid to him rather than to the

Index, and see especially **34**, a, line 12 (where is called *ḥāvēr*); **199**; the name of his father: Daniel he-ḥāvēr; see **181**, line 2: Tobiah son of Daniel he-ḥāvēr, son of Shemaiah Gaon's sister. What Mann writes in *Jews*, I, 143; *Texts*, I, 326f., on Tobiah b. Daniel, is not exact. 'The third' mentioned in **147** is Elijah ha-Kohen b. Solomon Gaon, not Tobiah b. Daniel.

yeshiva. I have also mentioned the letter which speaks of the quarrel with someone from the exilarchic family, and another letter in the handwriting of the yeshiva's scribe, from which it appears that there was a dispute within the yeshiva. It seems that Josiah was taking issue with the *av-bēt-dīn* who succeeded Ḥanania, Joseph ha-Kohen b. Menaḥem (father of the priestly dynasty of the eleventh century), and here too, people of Tiberias are involved. Josiah may have risen to the office of Gaon as a result of disputes, and it is not fortuitous that his rise was connected with the ousting of the earlier priestly family from the office of Gaon. There seems to have been a very strong faction which opposed that priestly family, and Josiah hints in one of his letters that he actually tried to elude the office imposed on him. Perhaps his appointment was intended to put an end to that ongoing dispute.

In some of his letters, Josiah deals with aid, particularly as a result of the tax decrees. One should bear in mind that Josiah was Gaon during a very difficult period for the Jews of Palestine, that of the disturbances and battles of 1011–1014 and the great war of the year 1024. In one of his letters written to Ephraim b. Shemaria, he mentions a man, evidently a Palestinian who lived in Egypt, Samuel b. ha-Rōqēaḥ, who helped the Jerusalem population with considerable sums of money 'so that they should not be afflicted'. He compares Ephraim with 'Joseph [of the Bible] for his father's house' and confirms the receipt of 30 *darkemōnīm kōkhbayyē* (dinars with a star, and it is not clear what he means by this) which have been distributed to the Jerusalem poor. He mentions Abū'l-Ṭayyib 'Allūn b. Sahl and his father Sahl b. Aaron favourably. He describes the sad situation of the people of Ramla (undoubtedly as the result of the events of 1011–1014), 'who have been motionless under the weight of calamity and distress', while formerly it was they who supported the poor of Jerusalem. In his letter to the community of Dumyāṭ, he also deals with matters of aid. A tremendous cry for help emerges from another letter, in which he mixes complaints about the external situation with bitter remarks about some among the Jewish leadership. The Palestinian Jews are in great distress, many had died and others were dying of starvation; 'people of the cities were shattered and people of the villages dispersed, and poverty surrounded them'. 'The days of the Turk' are mentioned in the letter, and the suffering then endured by the Jewish population (we do not know who he is referring to). A certain Kohen ('the Aaronite') helps the authorities on matters of taxes; also helping them is a certain Ibn Garmān (perhaps a Christian: b. Germanus?). B. al-'Akkī, the son-in-law of Joseph ha-Kohen (b. Menaḥem) *av-bēt-dīn* was forced to flee the city. Owing to the letter's poor state, it is impossible to fully understand the writer's intention, but the impression given is one of extreme distress and sharp internal quarrels. In another letter to Ephraim b. Shemaria, the people who were imprisoned because of their heavy debts are mentioned; this problem also troubled the geonim who succeeded him.[129]

[857] Josiah had a son called Aaron. Although it states in the lineage lists mentioned above that Aaron was *av-bēt-dīn*, we have no proof of this. On the contrary, the appellation used for Aaron's son – 'the grandson of geonim' – clearly means that his father, Aaron, did not serve in that high office, nor is he mentioned in the documents in my collection except with reference to his son, Josiah. We find Josiah the grandson in about 1030 in Ṣahrajt in Egypt. It seems that he did not reach a high rank in the yeshiva either; it is possible that he merely attained the rank of 'fourth'. His letter

[129] See the lineage lists compiled by Mann, *Jews*, II, 50ff. Poznanski, *REJ*, 66(1913), 71, composed a family tree of Josiah which includes his forefathers and descendants, who lived in Egypt, until the 13th century. The lineage is based on Bodl MS Heb b 11, f. 24, see also ENA 2592, f. 18v; cf. Mann, *JQR*, NS 9(1918/9), 409. See also the lineage of Samuel ha-Nagid b. David (Egypt, the thirteenth century), in MS Merton College, Oxford, in which the early generations are entered on an imaginative basis, undoubtedly from someone's need to boast (the shelf-mark of the MS is Or No. 6, which is a commentary by the abovementioned, to Genesis; cf. Poznanski, *ibid.*, 62; Mann, *Jews*, 50, mentioning this MS according to Neubauer's *Catalogue*, Bodl 2443. This MS is from the year 1821 Sel., 1509). Josiah's father's name: see **39**. *Yesha' ṭōv*: **32**, line 22; **33**, b. The deaths of the geonim: **56**. The regulation of the Fustat community: **319**, see lines 24 ('our Lord and Master Josiah Gaon, may God preserve him'), 37–38 (the date). See also Goitein's discussions on the chronology of the geonim: *Shalem*, 1(1973/4), 16, 21f; in *ibid.*, 2(1975/6), 102, he withdrew the opinions expressed in the first place; see also his: *ha-Yishuv*, 82; what he writes there on David b. Shekhania, that he was still alive in Kislev, 1338 Sel., according to TS 32.2, is based only on the fact that his son Yefet mentioned David, his father's name, without the addition of a blessing for the dead, which is no proof; similarly, there is no foundation to his opinion that there was another Gaon at the same time whose name was Zadok, based on his completion of **324**, see in the notes to the version of this document. The letters of Josiah Gaon and his yeshiva: **16–47**; also **315, 319, 324**. The letter of Ḥanania ha-Kohen: **23**. The matter of the man from the exilarchic family: **29**. The quarrel with Joseph ha-Kohen b. Menaḥem: **38**. Josiah on his unwillingness to be Gaon: **28**, a, line 11. The letter to Ephraim b. Shemaria: **31**. (Samuel b. he-Rōqēaḥ is perhaps Samuel ha-Kohen b. Avṭalyon.) To the community of Dumyāṭ: **36**. The cry for help: **37**. The other letter to Ephraim b. Shemaria: **46**. As regards the situation in Palestine in the days of Josiah Gaon, the complaints contained in the letter of the sons of Berekhia should also be taken into consideration, TS 16.64, ed. Goitein, *Tarbiz* 38(1968/9), 22–26. The writer is the elder brother, Joseph b. Berekhia, who writes from Qayrawān to Joseph b. Jacob ibn 'Awkal in Fustat, evidently in 1015 or somewhat later. A state of *iltiyāth*, a complex situation, is mentioned there, referring either to the tough conditions caused by the Bedouin revolt or to some internal difficulties. He learned about the situation from a letter which was brought by Abū Ibrahīm b. Sahl, apparently from Jerusalem. Due to the letter's poor state of preservation, not all the details are clear. The son of Daniel is mentioned there, probably Tobiah b. Daniel, and the banker Sha'ya. On Tobiah b. Daniel, see *infra*, secs. 855, 872. Abū Ibrahīm (Isaac) b. Sahl is also mentioned in TS 10 J 9, f. 26, the letter of the Nagid Abraham b. 'Aṭā' to Ibn 'Awkal, in which he asks him to repay Isaac b. Sahl's expenses when dealing with the sending of the remains of the Nagid's brother for burial in Jerusalem, see Goitein, *Tarbiz*, 34(1964/5), 166f. See also *supra*, sec. 835.

to Abraham b. Haggai in Fustat has been preserved, as well as a fragment from a letter to Ephraim b. Shemaria.

A notable personality at the Palestinian yeshiva at the beginning of the century and during the period of Josiah Gaon, was the poet Samuel b. Hosha'na. He rose to the rank of 'third' of the yeshiva. His letter to Shemaria b. Elḥanan in Fustat has been preserved, with a warm recommendation for Nathan b. Abraham, when he set out on his way to the Maghrib via Fustat (as mentioned in sec. 795). A letter evidently written at the beginning of 1002 describes, as we have already seen, the distress and calamities suffered by the communities of Palestine at the time. In that letter, he still calls himself 'the fourth of the *ḥavūrā*'. Before that, in *ca.* 990, he is mentioned in a letter dealing with the distribution of money to the people of the yeshiva, without any title attached to his name. In the fragment touching on what occurred during his visit to Egypt to participate in the funeral of Shemaria b. Elḥanan (1011) (which I have mentioned in sec. 572) he is spoken of with a blessing of the dead following his name, and as that fragment was undoubtedly written shortly after the events (also described in the 'Egyptian Scroll'), he apparently died soon after the death of Shemaria b. Elḥanan and those events in Egypt. His status in the yeshiva is also confirmed by a promissory deed drawn up in Jerusalem before the 'Grand Court' on 10 November 1004, in which Samuel 'the third' b. Hosha'na is the last of the signatories, that is, the most important among them. Evidently, he travelled to Fustat frequently, and to other places as well, on behalf of the yeshiva. Letters have been preserved written by Samuel's son, Abraham, who became 'fourth' in the yeshiva and who called himself 'son of the third'; there are also letters from his grandson, 'Eli ha-mumḥē b. Abraham. The latter had gone through many hardships, and had been imprisoned but managed to escape to Egypt, where he hoped to get help from Ḥesed al-Tustarī, but when he arrived, Ḥesed was no longer alive. We also encounter the great-grandson of Samuel 'the third', Joshua he-ḥāvēr b. 'Eli ha-Mumḥē. On 10 August 1076, he writes a deed in Ramla, when this city had already been under the Turcomans' rule for some time, and a fragment of the deed is preserved in the Geniza. Afterwards, he moved to Caesarea, and from there wrote to Mevorakh the Nagid b. Saadia in about 1098, asking him to help him move to Ascalon.[130]

[130] 'Grandson of geonim': **210**, lines 27–28. 'The fourth': **238**, line 9; his letters from Ṣahrajt: **202, 203**. The fragment of a letter of Josiah b. Aaron, grandson of Josiah Gaon: **203a**; from which it emerges that he made his living by copying books. A commentary of *ēlē masse'ē* (Num., xxx–xxxvi) is mentioned (in **202** he mentioned a commentary of *ēlē ha-devārīm*, Deut., i–iii). Samuel b. Hosha'na's letter: **18**; the letter from the beginning of 1002: MS of the Berlin community: 4A; the letter from *ca.* 990: **13**; the Jerusalem deed: **17**. TS 16.14 contains evidence concerning a Damascene promissory deed which Moses b. Shahriyār

[858] As we have seen, Josiah Gaon died in the spring of 1025, and Solomon ha-Kohen b. Joseph b. Menaḥem succeeded him. We have already discussed the family's origins and how we suddenly found the family amidst the Palestinian geonim. This family had widespread connections by marriage, some of them with outstanding personalities. I have already marked their family relationship (cousins) to Abraham ha-Kohen b. Isaac ibn Furāt, the influential physician of Fustat who spent many years in Ramla. They were also related to another priestly family of the wealthy of Fustat, the brothers Ephraim and Manasseh ha-Kohen, sons of Abraham. Manasseh, the younger of the two, was the son-in-law of Solomon b. Judah, and I shall speak of him again. Solomon ha-Kohen was also related by marriage to Solomon b. Judah, and although this is not quite clear, we may assume that Solomon b. Judah married the sister of Solomon ha-Kohen, for it was said of Joseph ha-Kohen b. Solomon that he was the cousin of Abraham b. Solomon b. Judah. Evidently, there was also a marital connection between Solomon ha-Kohen Gaon and Ephraim b. Shemaria, for Ghālib ha-Kohen b. Moses, Ephraim's son-in-law, calls Elijah ha-Kohen b. Solomon Gaon 'our cousin'. One can assume that Joseph ha-Kohen also had a son whose name was Moses:

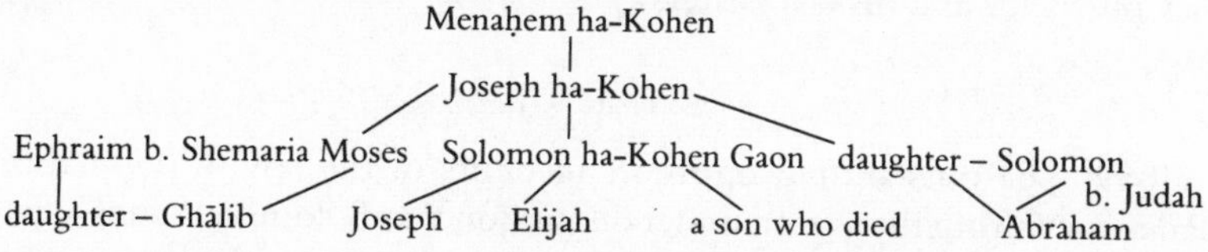

The special connection with Ephraim b. Shemaria is also obvious from a letter of 'Eli ha-Mumḥē, the grandson of Samuel b. Hosha'na, to Ephraim, in which he advises him how to maintain his correspondence with the two priestly brothers, Joseph and Elijah. The connection is also confirmed by the letters of Joseph ha-Kohen b. Solomon Gaon to

made out to the credit of Joseph b. Jacob *rōsh kallā* (evidently Ibn 'Awkal); this Moses remained owing 164 dinars after the death of Jacob, the father of Joseph. The deed was dated Tuesday, 6 Tammuz 4767, 24 June 1007, in the court of Samuel 'the third in the *ḥavūrā*' (the evidence on the deed was given in Fustat, and was written by Yefet b. David). On the piyyūṭīm of Samuel b. Hosha'na see: Halper, *Hatequfa*, 18(1922/3), 187; Schirmann, *Shīrīm ḥadāshīm*, 63–69 (who assumed that Samuel was the author of the 'Egyptian Scroll' but I have not seen any proof of this); see there details on his piyyūṭīm which were published, on research about him, and some additional piyyūṭīm; Fleischer, *Ha-sifrut*, 4(1972/3), 344, and n. 64, and more piyyūṭīm there, 350–353. See in Schirmann, *ibid.*, 77f, a dirge written by Sahlān b. Abraham on the death of Samuel 'the third'; see further: ENA 4007, f. 4*v*: 'a *widdūy* (confession) by R. Samuel the third b. Hosha'na, of righteous blessed memory'. The letters of Abraham: **227–230**. The letters of his son 'Eli: **231–240**. Joshua b. 'Eli: **567–569**.

Ephraim, in which the family relationship is felt. I have already mentioned (in sec. 790) the secret correspondence used by the two brothers to maintain contact with Ephraim, in order to give him information about events in Jerusalem and its yeshiva, which can be clearly discerned from the letter sent him by Elijah ha-Kohen b. Solomon.

Av-bēt-dīn in Solomon ha-Kohen Gaon's time was Zadok ha-Levi b. Levi, clearly stated in the document relating to Ephraim b. Shemaria. The *'alāma* (the formula for greeting and ending in a letter) of Solomon ha-Kohen is known to us as *yesha' yuḥāsh*. Six letters written by Solomon ha-Kohen have been preserved, much of their contents naturally dealing with the distress prevailing in Palestine, and especially in Jerusalem, for the war against the Bedouin was still at its peak, although it had moved to the north of Palestine. A letter written by his son Elijah, of which a draft has been preserved, also belongs to the period of his holding office. This is a recommendation to 'Samuel b. Ṣemaḥ the cantor known as b. al-Lādhiqī' (that is, from Lādhiqiyya in Syria), of whom it was said that he was the 'court scribe' of the yeshiva, and that 'he was given a seat with us in the city of Ramla'. This man seems to have gone to Egypt to secure financial aid for his heavy family burden: his old mother, abandoned by her husband, and his two sisters.[131]

Solomon b. Judah

[859] The outstanding figure in accounts of the Jewish population in Palestine during the period under discussion was Solomon b. Judah, partly due to the long stretch of time during which he held office, and also because it was during his time that the synagogue of the 'Palestinians' in Fustat was rebuilt and its repository of the Geniza was constructed. When the time came for his letters and other documents written during his day to be removed and 'hidden', they were placed in that repository and hence

[131] Manasseh ha-Kohen: **76**, lines 54–56. Joseph ha-Kohen and Abraham son of the Gaon were cousins: **182**, line 5. Ghālib ha-Kohen b. Moses: **418**, in the upper margin, lines 9ff. Solomon ha-Kohen had three sons, and we shall encounter Joseph and Elijah below; the third son must have died at a young age, for we hear no more of him; see **48**, which ends with greetings from the Gaon's three sons. The letters of Joseph ha-Kohen b. Solomon: **407**, **408**. Elijah ha-Kohen: **413**. On Ephraim: **49**, line 7; see also: **324**; it seems that also in TS 13 J 6, f. 23 mention is made of Ephraim b. Shemaria: this is a court record written by Yefet b. David, dealing with a quarrel over a burial plot; there we find the phrase: 'appointed by the authority of the Kohen, our Lord and Master Solomon head of the yeshiva, of blessed memory', see lines 14–15. Zadok ha-Levi *av-bēt-dīn*, see: **324**. *Yesha' yuḥāsh*: see the Hebrew Index. In a small fragment of a letter written by Yefet b. David on behalf of Ephraim b. Shemaria to Qayrawān, the sender's name has been preserved: 'the son of al-Ghazzī (= the Gazan), *yesha' yuḥāsh*'; this letter was undoubtedly written during the year Solomon ha-Kohen held the office of Gaon, 1025: see ENA 2735, f. 4. The letters of Solomon ha-Kohen Gaon: **47–52**. Samuel b. Ṣemaḥ: **412**; he is also mentioned in **22**, line 28, where he is signatory as witness.

have been preserved until this very day. His many letters and others in which he is mentioned, as well as documents of the period, quickly attracted the attention of the first Geniza students. When Schechter published one of Solomon b. Judah's letters to Ephraim b. Shemaria in his *Saadyana*, he still had no idea who the author of the letter was, and assumed that it was Solomon b. Elijah ha-Kohen (the Gaon), the brother of Abiathar. Gottheil and Worrell, who edited a collection of Geniza documents from the Freer Gallery in Washington in 1927, still could not positively identify him. Similarly Assaf, who in that same year wrote a review of their publication, still had doubts as to whether Solomon b. Judah or his predecessor Solomon ha-Kohen b. Joseph was the writer.

The first publication of a Geniza document in which Solomon b. Judah is mentioned was that of a draft of a letter written to him by Ephraim b. Shemaria. This document was published by Müller and Kaufmann in 1892. In 1903, Abraham Epstein noted that this document was related to *Seder 'ōlām zūṭā* and *Seder tannā'īm we-amōrā'īm*, published by Neubauer, in which there is mention of 'our Master Solomon b. Judah head of the Jerusalem yeshiva . . . who is head of the yeshiva now in the year 4807' (and there are other dates which are not consistent with one another; around 1045). A. Epstein was the first to discriminate decisively between Solomon b. Judah and Solomon ha-Kohen b. Joseph. At the very same time, Bacher had still not discriminated between the two, and assumed that Solomon b. Judah was the grandfather of Abiathar ha-Kohen, the main figure of the scroll of Abiathar. Poznanski supported this idea (opposing Epstein), and realised his error only a decade later. Some years afterward, in 1918, Marmorstein attempted to survey the subject in an article devoted to Solomon b. Judah and his generation. However, it was only thirty years after the first scientific publication on this figure that the personality of Solomon b. Judah was described in the round, by Mann, firstly in a sharp article reviewing Marmorstein's article, in 1919, and later in his books. Of the more recent studies, the comprehensive article by Goitein on the history of the geonim in Palestine should be noted in particular, in which many additional letters of the Gaon were edited by him, and accompanied by a comprehensive discussion on the various questions they evoke.[132]

[132] See: Schechter: *Saadyana*, 111ff (**79**); Gottheil and Worrell, No. 5 (**54**); Assaf, *Zion* (ha-me'assēf), 2(1926/7), 114. Ephraim's draft: **334**, see the introduction there. See: Epstein, *MGWJ*, 47(1903), 341f; Neubauer, *Mediaeval Jewish Chronicles*, I, 178; Bacher, *JQR*, 15(1903), 81; Poznanski, *ZfhB*, 7(1903), 180, n. 2; Worman, *JQR*, 19(1907), 725f followed Bacher and connected Solomon b. Judah with the priestly family, assuming that he was the father of Joseph ha-Kohen b. Solomon Gaon. Poznanski, *REJ*, 66(1913), 68, already suggested that there was no such family connection, but only explained his view

[860] The origins of Solomon b. Judah are enshrouded in mist, to a certain extent. In his signature, he generally called himself *bīrrabī*, which means 'son of a scholar'. At times, his signature would be encircled by tiny letters, which when read alternately at the top and at the bottom, stated, 'But I am a worm, and no man' (Ps., xxii:6). In one of his letters, he mentions his appointment as Gaon and says: 'not by virtue of my father was I appointed nor because of my family was I called and not now was I confirmed, but by the will of God and through Him have I reached this name'. Apparently, the stress here is on his modest origins. However, it seems that one should interpret these words somewhat literally, that is, that his appointment did not derive either from his family or lineage, but from the will of God, however this does not mean that he did not have an honourable background. On the contrary, there is evidence that he was apparently one of the descendants of Shemaiah Gaon. Firstly, it is worth noting the letter he evidently wrote before becoming Gaon to someone in Egypt, in which he mentions the Gaon 'our Master', and signs: 'the younger Solomon b. Judah'. Solomon speaks there of letters to a certain 'Awkal, and it seems that he is speaking of an important international merchant who was famous at the time, Joseph b. Jacob ibn 'Awkal. The letter deals with a matter of law, and also mentions a query put by Joshua he-ḥāvēr, who may have been Joshua ha-Kohen he-ḥāvēr b. Joseph, *dayyān* of Alexandria. Attached to this letter was one to Ascalon, which the recipient is asked to send to Ascalon for a *shetūt* (*dāniq*, a sixth of a dirham) which had been paid in advance, and the letter-carrier coming from Jerusalem is to take it to Ascalon on his way back. He is to deliver it to the son-in-law of Solomon b. Judah's brother. Solomon b. Judah asks that a certain Manasseh should carry out this request. Common sense leads us to conclude that Manasseh is the brother of Solomon b. Judah and the father-in-law of the man in Ascalon. Indeed, among the Geniza documents we find a receipt signed by a number of people, among them Sahlān b. Abraham, and also Manasseh *ha-mishnē* (the deputy) *bīrrabī* (as in Solomon b. Judah's signature), and around the name, in tiny letters: 'great-grandson of Shemaiah, of blessed memory'. There is also a letter written by 'Manasseh, the younger [Solomon b. Judah also calls himself 'the younger' in his signatures] *bīrrabī*, great-grandson of Shemaiah, of

in a book published in 1914, see his *Babylonische Geonim*, 87ff. Marmorstein, *JQR*, NS 8:1, 1917/8; in an article published a few years earlier, Marmorstein still assumed that Solomon b. Judah was the grandson of Joseph ha-Kohen (father of the Gaon Solomon ha-Kohen) see *REJ*, 68(1914), 40. See: Mann, *JQR*, NS 9(1918/9), 412ff; *idem, Jews*, I, 75–152, and the corresponding documents in vol. II, and the supplement there, 445ff; see also *idem, Texts*, I, 310–345. See Goitein, *Shalem*, 1: 15, 1973/4 (= *ha-Yishuv*, 82ff). TS AS 147.58, a small fragment, also belongs to the remaining letters of Solomon b. Judah, being part of a leaf in his handwriting, from which it is only possible to discern that a *ḥērem setam* (an anonymous excommunication) intended to obtain the rights of a certain man named Yaḥyā, is being spoken of.

blessed memory'. He asks the addressee, a cantor, brother of Zadok the scribe, to write a letter of recommendation to Alexandria for him, to be signed by Sar Shalom, 'head of the community, *bēt-dīn* and *alūf* of the yeshiva', and the letter was apparently written from Ṣahrajt. Evidently it refers to people of the Babylonian (*alūf* and [*av*]-*bēt-dīn*) communities, although the Shemaiah mentioned there is undoubtedly the abovementioned Palestinian Gaon. This Manasseh composed a piyyūṭ in honour of a certain Eleazar b. Joseph ha-Levi: 'composed by the slave of your honour, Manasseh b. Judah, great-grandson of geonim'. Thus apparently we have here evidence that Solomon b. Judah was of Shemaiah Gaon's lineage. The name of his grandfather, Berekhia, is found in the signature of the Gaon's son, Abraham: '[Abraham he-ḥāvēr in the great Sanhedrin] the son of R. Solomon head of the yeshiva Ge'ōn Ya'aqō[v son of R. Judah]' and tiny letters around the name, read alternately at the top and at the bottom: 'ben Berekhia'. This is also confirmed in a piyyūṭ, in which it states among other things: 'our Master Solomon son of R. Judah great-grandson of Berekhia'.

The family was from the Maghrib, as I assumed with regard to Shemaiah Gaon, the father of Solomon b. Judah's grandfather. Solomon b. Judah's hometown of Fās is still mentioned, as for example when his rival Nathan b. Abraham calls him 'al-Fāsī'. It is likely that the family left Fās towards the end of the tenth century. This city fell to the Fatimids in Sha'bān AH 368, that is March AD 978 (according to another source, it had already fallen in 959). In AH 389, that is AD 999, there was bitter fighting in the town and its vicinity, and it is very likely that these events were what led the family to leave the region and wander eastward until it came to Palestine.[133]

[861] As stated, there was evidently a marital connection between Solomon b. Judah and the priestly family; that is, he married the sister of

133 *Bīrrabī*, probably the singular of *benē rav*, scholars who were not counted with the main rows of the yeshivot in Babylonia; this clearly emerges from the account of Nathan the Babylonian, see in Neubauer, *Mediaeval Jewish Chronicles*, II, 87; see the detailed discussion on this term in the Talmudic sources: Friedman, *Marriage*, II, 411ff; and as noted there, Solomon b. Judah did not use this term in the accepted sense, but wished to say that his father was a scholar. We do not know why he was in the habit of not mentioning the name of his father. In **58**, b, in the address, he calls himself 'Solomon son of Judah the head', and this was a letter he wrote before he became Gaon. Perhaps his father was granted a Babylonian title, *rōsh kallā*, and the son refrained from using it because of the rancor of the Palestinian yeshiva towards the Babylonian yeshivot, particularly after he became Gaon. As to the events in Fās which may have caused the family to emigrate eastward towards the end of the tenth century, it is worth noting the responsum of Sherira Gaon to 'queries asked of Sherira by the transferred community of Fās', while in the responsum it said, 'who now live in Ashīr, after having been moved from Fās', which is explicit evidence of the flight of the Jews from Fās, and their settling in the town of Ashīr. The queries reached the yeshiva 'during the *kallā* (gathering of the Babylonian yeshivot, which took place in Adar and Elul) of Adar in the year 1298', i.e., February AD 987. See Lewin, *Jahrbuch* 7(1909), 254. How he became a Gaon: **128**. The letter to Alexandria: **108**. It is interesting

Solomon ha-Kohen Gaon b. Joseph. It is possible that another link was established, if indeed Abraham son of the Gaon married the daughter of Solomon ha-Kohen (that is, his cousin on his mother's side). The opening of a letter may perhaps provide evidence of this (only the opening has been preserved), in the handwriting of Abraham, son of the Gaon, to Isaac ha-Kohen ibn Furāt, in which the *'alāma* of Solomon ha-Kohen, *yesha' yuḥāsh*, is to be found. We find a similar instance in another of the letters of Abraham son of the Gaon, to Abraham and Jacob, sons of Mevassēr, and to Ḥalfon b. Jacob, all people of Fustat. This letter is headed by the name of the writer: 'Abraham he-ḥāvēr, son of the Gaon', whereas we find in the signature: '*yesha' yuḥāsh*'.

I have already spoken of the dates of the demise of Solomon b. Judah's predecessors, Josiah and Solomon ha-Kohen. There is no doubting the fact that Solomon b. Judah became Gaon after the death of Solomon ha-Kohen, that is in Tishri AM 4786, that is September AD 1025. A short time after he became Gaon, Solomon b. Judah wrote to Ephraim b. Shemaria: 'I am weeping over myself and over such a time that is in need of me. I am not the right man for the people of these times; but what is there to be done, as the title has been called upon me, and to reject what our God has invested me with is out of the question'. In the same letter mention is made of Elḥanan b. Shemaria, who was still alive at the time, for we know that he died in 1026. Further evidence that Solomon b. Judah was already Gaon in 1026 can be found in a court record written by his son Abraham, in Fustat, on 8 December 1026, signing there 'Abraham son of R. Solomon Ge'ōn Ya'aqōv'. Apparently the document closest to the outset of his holding the office of Gaon, was the letter of his son Abraham to David b. Aaron in Fustat, concerning the affair of Ṣedaqa b. Menaḥem, in which we find the *'alāma* of the Gaon Solomon ha-Kohen, *yesha' yuḥāsh*, and also the formula 'our Master the Gaon', undoubtedly referring to his father,

that a letter being sent from Jerusalem to Ascalon had to go via Egypt, which would seem to indicate that the roads were impassable due to internal warfare. The receipt: TS 16.191. The letter of Manasseh: TS 16.267, edited almost in its entirety in Mann, *Jews*, II, 336, see there also: I, 249, where he expresses the (correct) opinion that the letter is from the eleventh century; see *ibid.*, II, 336, n. 2, on the piyyūṭ; cf. Goitein, *Mediterranean Society*, II, 596, n. 30. The letter of Abraham, son of the Gaon: **114**. The piyyūṭ (great-grandson of Berekhia): Bodl MS Heb f 29, f. 71r, cf. Mann, *Jews*, I, 75. One can say that the sources complied with Halper's opinion, who without any documentary basis wrote that Solomon b. Judah 'inherited the seat of Gaon from his forefathers and strongly believed that this office should be handed down from father to son', see *Hatequfa*, 18(1922/3), 194. Poznanski already noted that Solomon's grandfather's name was Berekhia (Poznanski, *Babylonische Geonim*, 87), but did not mention his source. Nathan b. Abraham: **183**, a, line 21; see also the letter of one of Nathan's followers: **198**, line 13. See also the petition to the authorities concerning the confirmation of the appointment of Joseph ha-Kohen as dayyān in Alexandria, **315**, line 4: Sulaymān b. Judah al-Fāsī. The

to Solomon b. Judah, who had written to Sahlān b. Abraham on the matter of Ṣedaqa b. Menaḥem, and signed 'head of the yeshiva'.[134]

[862] Record of Solomon b. Judah's widespread and continuous activity has been preserved in the Geniza in 120 letters and fragments of letters written by him or his son, and additional letters sent to him or in which he is mentioned. Let us not forget that this correspondence was centred almost exclusively in Fustat, but his activities certainly encompassed a large number of communities, large and small, in Palestine and elsewhere. It seems that while he was Gaon, he was not in the habit of visiting communities, and his visit to Egypt, which he mentions in one of his letters, certainly took place before he became Gaon. He even explains in one of his letters that he refrains from travelling because of his age, speaking of a trip to Damascus on behalf of the Jerusalemite prisoners (jailed because of their debts, as we have seen). It is difficult for him to go to the market without a helping hand and even writing is impossible due to the frailty of his hands, and he is consequently dependant on others to write for him. In a letter to Sahlān b. Abraham, he complains of weakness and pains: 'my eyes are dimmed', he writes like a pupil 'learning to write', his lines are not always straight ('sometimes they are crooked'), and he thinks that his end is approaching. An actual example of this can be found in a fragment of a letter of recommendation, evidently written by him in 1048, for a man who asked that the recommendation be written by the Gaon himself, and one can indeed see that it is written by a trembling hand. Abraham, the son of the Gaon, confirms there that this is the handwriting of the Gaon, and a similar confirmation is made by Sahlān b. Abraham. Indeed, some of the letters in my collection are written by his son Abraham, or by Solomon b. Ṣemaḥ, or by Joseph ha-Kohen b. Solomon, and signed by the Gaon. In another letter, he also writes that his strength is ebbing and that his eyes are dimmed 'with the burden of years'.

Apparently, Solomon b. Judah spent a great deal of time in Ramla, and we find him there in 1029, during the terrible times of distress shortly before the end of the war against the Bedouin. In his letter, he describes the state of scarcity and poverty which he himself endures, the very hard winter, and the assistance he requires from Jasūs al-Maghribi during his visits to Jerusalem, though his family do not want that help. If he stayed in Jerusalem throughout the entire period, his situation would be much

events in Fās: Ibn 'Idhārī, 231, 249f; Ibn Ẓāfir (printed), 22: Fās was already taken by al-Mu'izz' army, under the command of Jawhar, on 20 Ramaḍān 348, 24 November 959.

134 The opening of the letter: **162**, cf. Goitein, *Baron Jubilee Volume*, 522, n. 37; *idem, Tarbiz*, 45(1975/6), 75. The letter to Fustat: **87**. The letter to Ephraim b. Shemaria: **67**, and Elḥanan is mentioned there in line 29. The court record **63**. The letters concerning Ṣedaqa b. Menaḥem: **59** (see line 18: 'our Master the Gaon', **60**).

worse, for the people of Jerusalem are not to be relied upon (apparently because of their own destitution). His stay in Ramla was evidently the result of pressure on the part of the 'elders of Ramla', who asked him to remain there, for 'they were like a herd of sheep without a shepherd'. Also there was a serious internal dispute in the city, which 'was corrupted by the betrayal of evil men'. The nature of these evil men is not made clear to us. Finally he had no choice but to declare them excommunicated. In later years, when he had already made his home in Jerusalem, he would continue to stay in Ramla from time to time.

At the outset of his holding office, Zadok ha-Levi b. Levi continued as his *av-bēt-dīn*, and he, too, lived in Ramla and had a house there. Rawḥ ha-Kohen b. Pinḥas, the Baghdadi cantor, writes at the end of 1029 to Ephraim b. Shemaria that he arrived in Tyre at first, after having been attacked and robbed by Bedouin of everything he possessed, and is now in Ramla and living with 'our Master the *av-bēt-dīn*'. From this we may perhaps understand why Zadok ha-Levi wrote to Ephraim b. Shemaria in an effort to help Rawḥ in Fustat, where he was trying to raise the money needed to return to Baghdad.

Despite the sojourns in Ramla, the Gaon spent most of his time in Jerusalem, and there is no doubt that this was the seat of the yeshiva, from which the yeshiva's letters and those of most of its personalities were sent. There is a passage in one of Solomon b. Judah's letters apparently alluding to his move from Ramla and the settling into the new house in Jerusalem. In the letter to Abraham ha-Kohen b. Isaac ibn Furāt concerning help for the Muslim Qayn b. 'Abd al-Qādir, mentioned earlier, he notes that 'the family [Qayn's] came to the place where I am now living'. Elsewhere the Gaon describes the beginning of his settling in Jerusalem, before he became Gaon. This was when he returned from Egypt and the Jerusalemites persuaded him to be their cantor, and he notes that: 'I would pass the time, sometimes full, sometimes empty.' Then he adds that the Jerusalemites have still not paid him anything, although the payment is now due for two years, for they have no money.[135]

[863] Solomon b. Judah was unquestionably a man of considerable moral and spiritual stature. He was imbued with a sense of mission, as if

135 The visit to Egypt: **154**, line 5. The matter of old age and frailty: **90**, lines 17–20, 33–34; **150**, lines 9–10; **86**, lines 22–23. The letter of recommendation: **144**; see the letter in the handwriting of Joseph ha-Kohen: **173**; see also **79**, a, lines 8–12; where it says that Ephraim b. Shemaria's letter was read to him by 'the third' ('he read for me what was written there'); it emerges that he was unable to read it himself because of his weak eyesight. The distress in Ramla: **80**, a, lines 18–31; Jasūs = Jāsūs, see on him in Goitein, *Shalem*, 1(1973/4), 40, n. 37 (= *Ha-yishuv*, 99); it seems that Hillel b. al-Jāsūs, mentioned in **559**, c, line 26 (the scroll of Abiathar) is his son. Pressure from the people of Ramla: **94**, lines 8–15. The sojourn in Ramla: **116**; in **159**, the letter to Abraham ha-Kohen b. Haggai, he mentions that he wrote three letters from Ramla before this, and it seems that he was

the hand of God had placed him on the seat of the Gaon and charged him with standing guard over the Palestinian yeshiva and the Jewish population of Jerusalem. Together with his spiritual and moral qualities, one could also add that he was modest in his needs and ways, honest, restrained and peace-loving. Some years before becoming Gaon, perhaps in 1015, in a letter to Isaac ha-Kohen ibn Furāt, who had suffered a setback in a court case with the heirs of his partner, he consoles him by extolling the eternal values: men must obey the moral order for 'they are only trustees, appointed [by God] over everything they possess'.

Perhaps one can most truly judge Solomon b. Judah, the man, by what he wrote to his son Abraham, for in a personal letter of this kind there is less likelihood that a person would write things that do not reflect his genuine inner feelings. In his letter, we find him rejecting proposals to behave as former geonim did and to accept additional income on the side from the communities – as he hints in the letter, his predecessors did this by way of improper actions on the part of appointees of the communities. He does not intend to be caught perpetrating a transgression, for in the future he would have to make his account with God. In a later letter, however, under the pressure of his dire straits and his heavy family burden, he enquires of Ephraim b. Shemaria about the possibility of receiving from 'the payments that were for our Master Gaon and for the Av, may they rest in Paradise' (he undoubtedly refers to Solomon ha-Kohen, his predecessor, and Zadok ha-Levi b. Levi), on condition that there is no transgression involved, however. In another letter, we hear complaints about his difficult plight – people think that 'one can live on air' and since his appointment as Gaon, 'a peck of troubles from heaven' have fallen upon him, by which he is certainly referring to family troubles, as we shall see.

The forgiving and restrained character of Solomon b. Judah is revealed in a number of letters. He writes a letter of recommendation for a certain Ṣedaqa b. Menaḥem despite the fact that this man did him harm in the past. He stresses his own modesty at every opportunity, as one sees from the use of such terms as 'the young' or 'the humble' in his signatures, or the phrase 'and I am a worm and not a man' which sometimes embellishes them. In one of the signatures he adds: 'the humblest of the Rabbanite sect living in the Holy City'. To Ephraim b. Shemaria, he also preaches restraint and advises him how to behave with his entourage 'and leave them a way to respect you'. He also speaks of himself as peace-loving, despising quarrels, and he does nothing without first consulting with the '*av* and the third'. He is also very critical of those scholars whose letters request benefits for

there for a relatively long stay. The letter of Rawḥ: **211**. Zadok's letter: **212**. Qayn b. 'Abd al-Qādir: **99**, lines 16–17. The letter to Ephraim b. Shemaria: **84**, lines 20ff.

themselves but not for others, unlike the letters of merchants, which seek reciprocity in benefits. Hence he does not write much himself. In the same letter, he speaks in favour of giving; it is the giver who comes closer (*mitqārēv*) to God (here it is worth noting the Muslim term of the same root, *qurba*, which means closeness to God, piety and awe) while the receiver of gifts moves away from Him and lessens his merits. His respect for his fellow-man is shown in Solomon b. Judah's reaction to Joseph ibn al-Sijilmāssī's dream, in which Moses, Aaron and Samuel, came to him and warned him of an imminent and atrocious decree. The Gaon certainly did not believe in miracles or dreams, but he nevertheless thought it proper to tell Joseph that he, too, had had this very dream for three nights.

This characteristic moderation which he cultivated was evident in the stand he adopted in the dispute with the Karaites. He demanded, although unsuccessfully, that the yearly practice of declaring a ban on the Karaites on the Mount of Olives be discontinued. His son Abraham and the latter's cousins, Joseph and Elijah, sons of Solomon ha-Kohen, were stubbornly fanatic and proclaimed the excommunication, with very bad results, and I shall return to the subject in the chapter on the Karaites. His son, Abraham, also showed the same zeal to act against the Karaites in Fustat and the Gaon, who knew his son only too well, seriously warned him not to intervene in the quarrel between the Rabbanites and the Karaites there.[136]

[864] Solomon b. Judah had endless family troubles. In one of his early letters, written before he became Gaon, he mentions three sons: Abraham, Manṣūr and Yaḥyā (the latter was then in Baghdad studying with Hayy Gaon), while later on, we only hear about the one son – Abraham. We know nothing of the fate of the other two. There was also the difficulty with his son-in-law, Abū Sahl Manasseh ha-Kohen b. Abraham. In a letter to Abraham b. Sahlān, written in around 1020, that is before he became Gaon, he notes that Manasseh went to Fustat and that he sent two letters with him. It seems that from that time onward, Manasseh did not return to Jerusalem and the Gaon's daughter remained an abandoned wife (*'agūnā*) in her father's house, maintained by her father. Manasseh was the brother of Ephraim ha-Kohen, who was a man of considerable importance in the Fustat community. There seems to have been double marital connections between them and the family of Solomon ha-Kohen Gaon. Manasseh's

136 The letter of Isaac ibn Furāt: **53**, lines 15–16. The letter to his son: **80**, a, lines 32ff. To Ephraim b. Shemaria: **84**, a, lines 16ff. The additional letter: **158**, a, lines 2ff; he writes that he prays to God that he shall not fail 'in any matter of the law, of permitted and forbidden, kosher and non-kosher; I trust that He who provides for everyone will provide for me'. The recommendation for Ṣedaqa b. Menaḥem: **60**, lines 15ff. 'The humblest': **105**. To Ephraim: **122**, a, lines 6–11. Hatred of disputes: **152**, lines 25ff. On the letters of the scholars: **137**. The episode of the dream: **313**. The excommunication of the

first wife was evidently the sister of Solomon ha-Kohen b. Joseph, Solomon b. Judah's predecessor, whereas the sister of these two brothers was married to Solomon ha-Kohen. Manasseh ha-Kohen married Solomon b. Judah's daughter (who was much younger than her husband) after the death of his first wife. Afterwards, Manasseh began to send money to his wife, the daughter of the Gaon, in Jerusalem; and in his letter to his son, the Gaon mentions a letter that arrived from Manasseh containing a money order. What followed on this is very obscure. Solomon b. Judah writes to Abraham his son (in Tyre) and sends him greetings from Abū Sahl, who is Manasseh. Did he return to his wife? Moreover, the Gaon writes that Abraham's sister, that is, his daughter and Manasseh's wife, gave birth to a son in the seventh month of her pregnancy, but that the child had died. Later on, in one of his letters, he again complains about his son-in-law, who he claims, left his wife 'three years ago'. The Gaon's son discussed the matter with him when he was in Fustat in his brother Ephraim's presence and also separately, for the Gaon could no longer bear his daughter's weeping. Solomon b. Judah mentions here the great difference in age between Manasseh and his daughter. At one time, he submitted to the entreaties of his brother-in-law, the Gaon Solomon ha-Kohen, without worrying, for he was aware of the kind manner in which Manasseh had treated his first wife – that is, 'she was much respected and was not in want'. Now his daughter cries all the time, as stated, and she claims that her father takes the trouble to impose law and justice on strangers but is not concerned with justice for his own daughter. Solomon b. Judah, it emerges from that letter, also sent a personal letter to Manasseh, warning him that if he does not return, it will be necessary to appoint a trustee over him, by which he probably meant that one of the travellers to Fustat would be given a power-of-attorney to sue him there before the court. At long last, peace evidently prevailed – as emerges from a letter the Gaon wrote in about 1048 to Ephraim b. Shemaria, in which he asks him to help his son-in-law Manasseh with regard to a compound which had been 'stolen from him'. He is referring to a house in the name of their mutual brother-in-law, Solomon ha-Kohen b. Joseph, the former Gaon, but which actually belonged to Manasseh ha-Kohen and his sister, the wife of Solomon ha-Kohen. In the days of *ben ḥabūrā*, that is, the period of the Bedouin revolt (the Banū Jarrāḥ, which has been discussed in sec. 590), a large fine was imposed on Manasseh which he was unable to pay, and so he borrowed 100 dinars from a certain Khalaf b. 'Allūn. The latter died, but his widow was not content with the return of the money and claimed that she had a deed of purchase on the house, drawn up before a Muslim, and

Karaites: **85**. The warning about Fustat: **80**, b. The restrained approach to the Karaites is also reflected in **122**, the letter to Ephraim b. Shemaria.

that she had promised the house as her daughter's dowry. It is implied that the case had been discussed in Ramla (evidently before the cadi), but the opposing side had no proof. One can assume that the case was about to come up before a higher instance, in Fustat, and this was the reason why the Gaon asked Ephraim b. Shemaria to help.

Apparently, Solomon b. Judah had other family troubles as well. Five women 'without a man' sit around him, he complains in one of his letters, undoubtedly referring to his abandoned daughter, his two other daughters, and perhaps also to his daughter-in-law (for his son was frequently travelling about), and perhaps to his granddaughters, for he mentions there that one of his daughters is a widow with one son and two daughters. It seems that his daughter, the wife of Manasseh ha-Kohen (who in the meantime has become a widow) calls herself, in a letter to Nehorai b. Nissim from Bilbays: 'your relative, daughter of the head of the yeshiva, of blessed memory'. She was evidently related to Nehorai through his wife, who was a member of the priestly family, the relationship being evidently through Manasseh and Ephraim, sons of Abraham ha-Kohen. Thus, the reference may be to Solomon b. Judah's daughter, who was perhaps Nehorai's sister-in-law.[137]

[865] Apart from personal and family problems, it emerges from Solomon b. Judah's letters that his eminent status attracted considerable dismay. Even before he became Gaon, in about 1020, he complained that Jerusalem did not receive him graciously, and that the city was full of slander and envy. It is a small town and called 'a threshold of poison' (Zech., xii:2). And when he occupied the office of Gaon, his major com-

[137] The sons of Solomon b. Judah: **53**, lines 11ff. Manasseh goes to Fustat: **58**, b, margin; see further on Manasseh: **75**, a, lines 34ff; **80** (the letter to his son Abraham), a, lines 9–10; in **81**, line 26, the Gaon mentions Manasseh, who 'went to Zoan [Fustat] to his brother' (Ephraim ha-Kohen); and indeed he 'looked after her a little', that is, sent her some money; **83**, b, lines 3ff, where there is a strong complaint against him; because of him the Gaon has many hours of anguish (*miḥna*); Manasseh still owed the bridal money; *ibid.*, on recto, lines 14ff, the Gaon rejects the rumours being spread by the brothers Ephraim and Manasseh that it was due to them that his status in the yeshiva rose during the former Gaon's period, until he was made *av-bēt-dīn*; in **94**, line 18, he mentions a personal letter he wrote to Ephraim ha-Kohen, Manasseh's brother, and there too, he seems to have spoken about Manasseh. The matter of the birth: **115**. The story of the marriage and other details: **119**, lines 15ff. The reconciliation and the matter of the house: **147**, a, margin and further. The 'third', whom Solomon b. Judah criticises there for not dealing with this matter properly ('he wants others to make the effort while he sits still'), is evidently Joseph ha-Kohen b. Solomon Gaon, and not as in Mann, *Jews*, I, 131, who writes that it refers to Solomon ha-Kohen's nephew. 'The five women': **81**, line 24. 'The daughter of the head of the yeshiva': **486**; it is difficult to see any other head of the yeshiva who could be the father of this woman; Goitein, *Tarbiz*, 45(1975/6), 71f, assumed that the writer was the daughter of the Gaon Solomon ha-Kohen, and that she was married to her cousin, Judah ha-Kohen b. Joseph, 'ha-rav'; the matter of the *rav* has been explained above (sec. 378), and this possibility seems to be excluded; the purpose of her letter was to obtain the sum of forty dinars owed to her from Nehorai's family, which means, Nehorai himself, and Abū

plaint was that the people did not listen to him. 'I am left without authority and I am merely a name'. Indications of the opposition that was beginning to form only a few years after he became Gaon, can be seen in the letter of the *av-bēt-dīn* Zadok ha-Levi b. Levi, written in 1029. Ideas about opposition already occurred to Zadok, or so it is implied in a letter written by him at the beginning of Solomon b. Judah's office as Gaon 'when the head of the holy yeshiva, may God preserve him, began his rule'. On the basis of the greetings Zadok wishes to convey through the addressee and the personalities he mentions, one can recognise his supporters: Josiah b. Aaron, grandson of Josiah Gaon, who lived in Ṣahrajt; Faraḥ *rōsh ha-pereq* b. Mu'ammal b. Peraḥia the judge; Abū Naṣr Aaron b. Ephraim he-ḥāvēr b. 'Eli b. Ṭarasūn; the Tustari brothers; David ha-Levi b. Isaac; Haggai ha-Kohen b. Joseph (the father of Abraham ha-Kohen b. Haggai). Evidently, some of these formed the nucleus which later became a faction of supporters of Nathan b. Abraham in his struggle against Solomon b. Judah – which we shall deal with in due course.

The feeling that everywhere he was surrounded by censure and even slander undoubtedly accompanied Solomon b. Judah at all times. In one of his letters, he stresses that he does not complain of the criticism directed against him but of those who are angered by his legal decisions, for in matters of law, he prays that the Lord should 'guide him in the way of the law, in what is permitted or forbidden, in what is proper and improper'. One can understand that the major pretext for rivalry was his legal decisions, in which he evidently tried to be consistent and uncompromising. He regrets that God has made him Gaon; 'I wish he would have released me' (of the office), he writes, 'so that there would not have been those who curse me in my lifetime and after my death'. Many envied him, believing he enjoyed many benefits, and some raised false charges against him. Indications of this unpleasant atmosphere can also be found in a secret letter written by Joseph ha-Kohen b. Solomon Gaon to Ephraim b. Shemaria, where it implied that certain individuals are disrespectful to the Gaon. The letter describes a gathering (of people of the yeshiva?) in the *majlis* (apparently meaning the reception hall) of the home of the writer's brother Elijah, to discuss the impending atrocious decree on the Jews of Jerusalem on the part of the 'boys of the city', that is, the authorities. The two communities declared a public fast and they all went to 'the cave', that is the synagogue, where someone (the cantor?) insulted the Gaon. This man was forbidden to enter the synagogue, but the parties were reconciled afterwards. On the sabbath, neither the writer (Joseph ha-Kohen) nor 'the third' (his brother, Elijah) went to the synagogue. Only Abraham, son of

Sa'īd, who is evidently Joseph b. Moses b. Barhūn al-Tāhirtī, Nehorai's cousin and partner.

the Gaon, 'the fourth', went there and pronounced a homily on the pericope 'and it came to pass on the eighth day' (Lev., ix:1; read in Adar II or Nisan). Thus an atmosphere of depression and internal dissension prevailed.

An affair of a special order was that of a sum of money from the yeshiva's funds, nineteen dinars in all, which the Gaon pocketed for his private use. In a letter to Abraham b. Sahlān, Solomon b. Judah explains what happened. He was forced to help himself to the money because of 'the hard times'; his letter was evidently written when the war in Palestine was at its height, towards the end of 1028. In Fustat, they assumed at first that the money went astray during its transfer, and a certain Abraham b. Isaac (evidently: Ibn Furāt) even brought with him a letter from Abraham son of the Gaon, who was staying in Fustat at the time, 'about the loss'; that is, the loss of the money. The Gaon gave that Abraham b. Isaac five dinars and also a *ṭalīt* (prayer shawl) and a suit of clothing to take to his son to sell for five dinars in Fustat – in this way, accounting for ten dinars. He received a confirmation of this from Abraham b. Isaac and also from a certain person called Levi. However, in the meantime, the man who had donated the nineteen dinars began pressing him and the Gaon received letter after letter concerning the matter and he feared that the outcome would be a quarrel. He solemnly promises to repay the remainder to the Jerusalemites and it is not clear whether he means the 'Jerusalemites' in Fustat or the funds for the poor of Jerusalem. In the continuation, the Gaon mentions in detail various sums which were sent to Jerusalem and how they were received and handled. Evidently Ephraim ha-Kohen b. Abraham and his brother Manasseh (the son-in-law of the Gaon) are among the leaders of those agitating against him in the financial affair. Many similar details are to be found in a letter he wrote at the same time to his son Abraham in Fustat, and there too, he writes of the money he took and how he intends to return it. It is likely that the matter of the nineteen dinars grew like a snowball and we find a letter written from Qayrawān to Ephraim b. Shemaria in 1035, that is, six and a half years later, in which the sum had grown to sixty dinars – though perhaps this was just a rumour. That letter mentions letters on the matter being sent to the Nagid (of the Maghrib, Jacob b. 'Amram) in Mahdiyya, stating that sixty dinars were sent by the man in charge of funds 'in order that all the people of the yeshiva should enjoy it but the head of the yeshiva took the money for himself and everyone was left empty-handed'. The writer doubts whether there is any truth in the rumour but he intends to clarify the matter during his impending meeting with the Nagid.[138]

138 The complaints: **58**, b, lines 7ff; they do not listen to him: **86**, line 21. Zadok's letter: **210**, lines 26ff. Criticism of his decisions: **158**. Regret on his being Gaon: **137**, b, line 15. Joseph

[866] Just how marked was the tension between Solomon b. Judah and his rivals, which found its main outlet in the division with Nathan b. Abraham, as we shall see below, can be observed in the episode of 'Eli b. Joshua al-Lādhiqī. The episode is mentioned incidentally in a letter from some anonymous follower of Nathan b. Abraham, who explains his point of view after the dispute. This 'Eli was the uncle of the writer on his mother's side, and was a teacher and permanent cantor in Raqqa, and came to settle in Jerusalem. Here, he apparently offended the Gaon (perhaps he is the cantor mentioned in the previous section, about whom Joseph ha-Kohen wrote to Ephraim b. Shemaria). Solomon b. Judah drove him out of Jerusalem and he was forced to go to live in Ramla. In his testament, he requested that he should not be buried in Jerusalem because Solomon b. Judah lives there. The writer himself, who is an old man and sees himself as learned in the Torah, also cannot live in the same city with Solomon b. Judah.

An unusual accumulation of bitterness and grievance amassed around the Jerusalem family, named in letters 'the children of Shuway'', that is, the children of Yeshū'ā (Shuway' being an Arabic diminutive for Yeshū'ā). We do not have much information about them. These adversaries of Solomon b. Judah were evidently of the family of Ṣemaḥ (called Ṣabgha) b. Yeshū'ā. The elder of the family was Mevorakh b. Yeshū'ā, and he was probably the only member of the family who maintained good relations with the Gaon, who writes in one of his letters that it is thanks to Mevorakh that he refrains from acting against the family. In the same letter, addressed to Abraham ha-Kohen b. Isaac ibn Furāt, the Gaon complains that these people make his life a misery and incite the public in Jerusalem and even in Ramla against him. They vilify him, and especially his son Abraham, in letters. They also try to recruit the Karaites against him and even speak to their *nāsī*, Abū'l-Ḥasan Josiah (Josiah b. Solomon b. David b. Boaz). Apparently, the Gaon fears that they may influence the Tustari brothers against him, and therefore he has already appealed directly to 'the great, mighty and tremendous elder', that is, to Ḥesed al-Tustarī. Solomon b. Judah reaches the height of aspersion in another letter he sent to the same Abraham ha-Kohen, to Ramla. He describes there the matter of a court claim in which both he and the Jerusalem cadi are involved, and accuses the Shuway' family of intervening on behalf of one of the parties. Apart from this, they are mistreating

ha-Kohen's letter: **409**; the matter of the decree and the public fast is perhaps connected with the description of the affair of Joseph b. al-Sijilmāssī and his dream, see **313**. The letter to Abraham b. Sahlān: **76**; *ṭalīt* may also evidently mean some piece of clothing worn on the body, which he calls in Arabic in his letter to his son, *badan*; see the letter to his son Abraham, **80** (*badan* in verso, line 16). The letter from Qayrawān: **330**, lines 18ff.

the Gaon's family, and he asks Abraham ha-Kohen to obtain a letter from the *amīr* (of Ramla) to his colleague (*ṣāḥib*, who is the *amīr* of Jerusalem) with the request that he take action against them and prevent them from behaving in this manner. However, it seems that these adversaries became reconciled afterwards, as can be understood from a letter in the handwriting of Abraham, son of the Gaon, signed by the Gaon, and addressed also to Abraham ha-Kohen. He is asked to get the cadi of Ramla, Abū'l-Ma'ālī, to act in the matter of the house of the Shuway' family, which had been taken from them on the basis of false evidence given at the Muslim court in favour of an old Muslim, an affair which I have already described. True, the Shuway' family deserve this punishment, he writes, for they are forever at odds with what others do, but this is a public matter, and this must be the first consideration in such a case. It seems that the Shuway' family were also active in the dispute with Nathan b. Abraham, naturally siding with the Gaon's opponents.

We have seen that the Gaon expressed fears that people would curse him even after his death, just as they do during his lifetime. It seems indeed that this fear was justified, as there were some who continued to hate him after he died. One such instance is immortalised in a letter written from Jerusalem by Ḥayyim he-ḥāvēr b. Solomon, some years after the passing of the Gaon. He mentions there a certain 'Imrān, who vilifies the memory of Solomon b. Judah, and the writer sharply takes exception to this.[139]

[867] Solomon b. Judah's letters are illuminating evidence of the rich quality of his personality and activities. Generally, it is not difficult to identify his own characteristic handwriting and the elegant handwriting of his son Abraham. The *'alāma*, the distinguishing phrase of his letters, was *yesha' rav* (a 'great deliverance'). His style was also typical, both in letters written in Hebrew and in Arabic, and it is interesting and merits special study.

Apart from letters, there are also a number of piyyūṭīm in the Geniza written by Solomon b. Judah, many of which have been recorded in works of students of Hebrew poetry, and some of which have been edited. As to responsa on matters of law, one has been preserved on the laws concerning inheritance, written in Arabic; this was the case of a father who

139 The episode of 'Eli b. Joshua: **198**. The letter to Abraham ha-Kohen: **142**; cf. Goitein, *Baron Jubilee Volume*, 511f; *idem.*, *Mediterranean Society*, II, 243. In a letter from Qayrawān to Ephraim b. Shemaria, **330**, which contains the matter of the rumours about the Gaon who took for himself sixty dinars intended for the yeshiva, a certain Mawhūb is mentioned, the in-law of b. Isaiah (*ha-mithabbēr*, see line 9, not: who travels together, as translated in Mann, *Jews*, I, 124); perhaps the reference is to an in-law of the Shuway' family; also mentioned there is 'the known representative' b. Sha'ya (see in **432**, lines 15–16), of Fustat, of a well-known family of merchants; perhaps they are also of the Shuway' family. The other letter to Abraham ha-Kohen: **101**. The matter of the house: **117**. Ḥayyim he-ḥāvēr: **463**.

bequeathed his property to one of his two sons and left nothing to the other. In a brief responsum, lucidly phrased, the Gaon decided that the witnesses had to be interrogated with regard to the expressions which had been used by the deceased when he was dictating his will (undoubtedly from the death-bed). We also have a fragment (in poor condition) dealing with the discussion on the food of the gentiles, in which he also includes laws of impurity and purity, and of conversion to Judaism. On the latter, he comments on what is said in the book of Ezra. The end of a responsum has also been preserved which he wrote about a woman's marriage deed which had been drawn up on the intermediate days of a feast, and it seems that the query was whether this was a transgression. The Gaon proves that this is a case for leniency.

In a letter to Sahlān b. Abraham, Solomon b. Judah expresses his reservations about the midrāshīm, the *haggādōt*, as he calls them. These are merely personal opinions, and whoever has some intelligence can invent homilies on the Bible 'different from what is said' (in the midrash). Nevertheless, here and there, he did introduce phrases from midrāshīm into his letters.[140]

[868] The son of the Gaon, Abraham, enjoyed a special status in the yeshiva. He was his father's right-hand man, writing his letters (and also court records) for him and travelling on various missions on behalf of the yeshiva. This was not an unusual phenomenon, and we find similar instances in the Babylonian yeshivot as well. In the Palestinian yeshiva, we have already encountered the pair Meir Gaon and his son Aaron, and below we shall meet Elijah ha-Kohen Gaon and his son Abiathar. There were certainly others but we only have sources on those mentioned here.

Among the missions which the Gaon imposed on his son Abraham, that of the latter's journey to Fustat in 1026 is clearly evident. In Iyar 1337 Sel. that is, April or May 1026, Abraham writes a deed of trusteeship in his handwriting, in which he appoints 'Eli b. Yefet to be trustee over the orphans of Moses ha-Kohen b. Ghulayb, who are Ghulayb, the eldest, a daughter named Mulk and a little boy aged four. One may assume that they were relatives of the priestly family of geonim in Jerusalem. The son (here named Ghulayb, a diminutive) is evidently Ghālib (Joseph?)

140 *Yesha' rav* was also the *'alāma* of Sherira Gaon, see: Bodl MS Heb c 28, f.49, in Mann, *JQR*, NS 8(1917/8), 359. Marx, *PAAJR*, 16(1946/7), 195, wrote on 'more than fifty letters' of Solomon b. Judah, but as one can see in my collection, their number is more than twice that. The poems of Solomon b. Judah, see in Davidson, *Ōṣar*; see also: Zulai, *Sinai*, 25(1948/9), 48–52; Scheiber, *Tarbiz*, 22(1950/51), 171ff; Habermann, *Sinai*, 53(1962/3), 186ff; ENA NS 18, f. 4*v* contains two fragments of a piyyūṭ of Solomon b. Judah in his handwriting. The responsum concerning the legacy: **157**; the fragment of a responsum: **160**; the matter of the marriage deed: Mosseri Ia 20 (formerly L 290); cf. the introduction to **83**. The matter of the *midrāshīm*: **146**, lines 24–25; sayings from the

ha-Kohen b. Moses, who afterwards became the son-in-law of Ephraim b. Shemaria, while Abraham, son of the Gaon, was a relative by marriage, and it is possible that the latter's journey to Fustat was made in order to participate in the funeral of that Moses ha-Kohen. A receipt from the same year written by Abraham the son of the Gaon in Fustat, has been preserved. In it, Turayk, daughter of Abraham ibn Qurdūsī, extends credit to the merchants' representative Muḥassin (Mevorakh) b. Ḥusayn, known by the nickname Ibn ukht Sham'ān, 'the son of Simon's sister'. In the same year, there is another court deed, of 8 December 1026, written by the Gaon's son in Fustat, in which he and Ephraim b. Shemaria are the signatories. This is a receipt crediting the Fustat parnās Jacob b. Mevassēr. Abraham also used his stay in Fustat in order to deal with the problem of the imprisoned Jerusalemite debtors, and the Gaon asks Ephraim b. Shemaria not to detain Abraham in Fustat needlessly and to see to it that he does not enjoy any benefits from his stay. Another mission occurred apparently in the summer of 1029, when the son of the Gaon went to Tyre, and it seems that from there he went to Ṣōvā, which is Aleppo. According to what we find in his father's letter to Sahlān b. Abraham, he went there to 'bring back some objects which had been left there', perhaps from the time the family lived in Aleppo or else he had fled there during the events of 1024–1029. The journey to Aleppo was undoubtedly only possible after the victory of the Fatimid army in Uqḥuwāna (12 May 1029). In around 1030, Abraham, son of the Gaon, again paid a visit to Egypt, and we have information that he also visited such country towns as Munyat al-qā'id and Ṣahrajt. In Fustat, in Elul 1342 Sel. (beginning 23 August AD 1031), he wrote a court record in which Salmān b. Shabīb, known as al-Ashqar ('the red-head') was found to be the losing party. This led to an outburst of temper against Abraham, son of the Gaon, and the judges, on the part of Salmān b. Shabīb. The result was that Ephraim b. Shemaria declared a ban on him until he repented. Apparently, at about the same time as this incident, a huge scandal took place in the synagogue of the 'Palestinians' in Fustat at the hour the two congregations (the 'Babylonians' and the 'Palestinians') assembled to listen to the homily of Abraham, son of the Gaon. Some participants seem to have insulted him, and Abraham wrote a letter to his father, on his own behalf and on behalf of the people of Fustat, asking him to excommunicate the trouble-makers. On the same trip, he apparently visited Alexandria as well. The people of the Alexandrian community wrote to the 'Palestinians' in Fustat and explained that they were unable to deal with collecting ransom money for the prisoners because 'the community was busy supplying the needs of his honourable

midrāshīm in Solomon b. Judah's letters can be located with the help of the marginal notes in my collection, with the help of the Hebrew Index.

great Sanctity, our Lord and Master Abraham he-ḥāvēr, son of our Lord the Gaon, may Heaven preserve him'. That was during the week of Passover, in 1031. In another letter, Abraham evidently informs the people of Fustat that 'we are coming to you on this week; may our Rock . . . bring about our encounter with you with a good outcome' (3 December 1031). On 27 June 1033, he is in Tyre and Solomon b. Judah writes a letter to him from Ramla, from which we understand that Abraham is about to leave there in order to take some merchandise to Damascus. The letters addressed to him were sent to Moses he-ḥavēr of Tyre (the father of Samuel).[141]

[869] Abraham, son of the Gaon, was well-placed in the scale of the yeshiva's titles, and reached the 'fourth'. In the draft of a letter from Ephraim b. Shemaria to Abraham's father, the Gaon, he calls Abraham the

[141] In the Pumbedita yeshiva, Sherira and his son Hayy, were outstanding and there were other fathers and sons who stood out; see for instance the epistle of Samuel ha-Kohen b. Ḥofnī: Bodl MS Heb f 34, fs. 39–46, edited by Cowley, *JQR*, 18 (1906), 401ff, fol. 45, top, where he mentions as a special category among the important figures in the yeshiva, the 'sons of geonim' (who were in the Sura yeshiva with him, such as Dōsā b. Saadia); a leading place is given to his own son, 'Israel, the scribe of the yeshiva, our son'; cf. Mann, *Texts*, I, 150f. The deed of trusteeship: **61**; Consist. isr. VII D, f. 4*v* is a court deed written by Yefet b. David one year later, on 18 Av 1338 Sel., 24 July AD 1027, in which the abovementioned Ghulayb ha-Kohen b. Moses appoints as trustee of his father's inheritance, a certain Joseph b. Yeshū'ā (who is also mentioned in **201**, lines 8–11 and in **331**, line 26). The receipt: **62**. The letter to Jacob b. Mevassēr: **63**. The matter of the prisoners: **66**. The mission to Tyre: **79**, lines 8ff. Aleppo: **86**. The journey in 1030: **70**. The case of Salmān: **102**. The commotion in the synagogue: **164**; see a similar complaint: **332**: a Spaniard went up to the podium to preach on the sabbath without mentioning the *rayyis*, that is, the Gaon. Such instances teach us to what extent the synagogue was the centre of community life, where all its inner quarrels were expressed. The fact that the prayers were interrupted when there were serious grievances, can be seen in the case of Eleazar the teacher b. Samuel, of whom it was said that 'twice, he stopped the reading in the presence of the congregation and of the court', and demanded that justice be accorded him after he was falsely charged (according to him); see **331**. This custom they called *istighātha*. On this matter see also the complaints of Dōsā's orphans, **217**; Assaf, *Battē ha-dīn*, 25f, and also *Teshūvōt* (1942), 105f, quotes on this matter what was said in PT, Pe'a, 15d: the saying of R. Yonathan to a man whose son refused to support him: 'go and close the synagogue before him so that he be ashamed' (different from Assaf's interpretation); we also have a responsum of a Babylonian Gaon, that one does not behave in this way in Babylonia, for carrying out the law is the responsibility of the court and not the public. For the purpose of comparison, it is worth noting the episode of a woman of Spain, who interrupted the prayers in the synagogue for several days 'in order to get her marriage deed'; see document No. 18, from the documents of the Catalonian Jews, edited by Millàs y Vallicrosa, *Institut d'Estudis Catalans, Memòries*, I (3), Barcelona 1927; cf. the review of F. Baer, on Finkelstein's *Jewish Self-Government*, in *MGWJ*, 71(1927), 393; see also on the custom of interrupting the prayers: Baron, *SRHJ*, V, 66f; 321, n. 81, and more references there; see on this custom in Islam: al-Ṣūlī, 66 (cf. Canard's translation, 116): the Hāshimite *sharīfs* (the offspring of 'Ali and 'Abbās) who were in difficulties because their allowances had been delayed, 'painted their faces black and prevented the *imām* of the western bank [in Baghdad] from praying'. Only after great efforts, was the praying resumed, but he shortened the *khuṭba* (the sermon). The letter from Alexandria: TS 24.29, line 35ff. The letter from 1031: **114**. The letter to Tyre: **115**.

'sixth', when Abraham was in Fustat. In a deed of trusteeship which he wrote in 'the city of Ramla near Lod, in the patrimony of the tribe of Judah', he signs 'Abraham, the fourth of the *ḥavūrā*'. In a letter written by Solomon b. Judah to Nethanel ha-Levi b. Ḥalfon, he also calls his son 'our son, the fourth'. Apparently, Abraham became 'the fourth' some time after 1045, in the aftermath of the death of Nathan b. Abraham, when Joseph ha-Kohen became *av-bēt-dīn*, and his brother Elijah became 'the third'.

It seems that unlike his father, Abraham was not characterised by his modesty. In a letter to a friend in Fustat, of which only a fragment is legible, there is a list of objects that he asks to be bought for him, among them precise instructions for a head covering (*ghiṭāra*) and other things. We have also seen that the Gaon himself asked Ephraim to see to it that his son should not benefit from any favours. In one of his letters to Ephraim b. Shemaria he expresses his frank displeasure at his son's mission in Fustat (evidently in 1026), for instead of lamenting the fate of the 'indebted prisoners' of Jerusalem, he spends his time enjoying himself: he 'dresses and covers himself' and gets involved in public disputes by visits and investigations. It is not surprising then, in the words of his father, that he has become the object of slander and plots.

As he was a facile scribe and had an elegant handwriting, Abraham engaged in copying piyyūṭīm and various other writings. He was preoccupied with the matter of the calendar, and it seems that he copied a treatise on the principles of the calendar, in rhyme, or perhaps wrote it himself; it is written there *seder ha-'ibbūr* (the order of intercalation). A fragment of the Passover Haggadah which he copied has been preserved, as have been some fragments of the Babylonian Talmud, a responsum in Arabic concerning the slaughtering laws and something from a Bible commentary (on Saul and David). In my collection there is a fragment of a letter he wrote (to Fustat, evidently) regarding the formulae of the deed of divorce and especially the passage which begins, 'and this shall be the divorce letter from me'. Abraham also wrote what can be considered the oldest version, in Judaeo-Arabic, of the Jewish story of Baḥīrā, the monk who met the prophet of Islam.

Solomon b. Judah died in Iyar 1362 Sel., April AD 1051, or shortly before that. We know this from the *selīḥā* written in his memory by Ephraim b. Shemaria, which is dated the middle of Iyar 1362; but he certainly died earlier than that and the date conforms more or less to the time his death became known in Fustat. As to his son Abraham, from what we can construe from a letter written by Israel b. Sahlūn, it is implied that after his father's death, he lived in Ramla and was involved in quarrels over 'the market', that is, over the slaughtering there. In connection with this, a certain Maymūn al-Dawla is mentioned, perhaps a Muslim official who intervened in that affair, which is utterly obscure. In a letter written later on, in March 1062, Israel b. Sahlūn mentions the *dafātir* (the quires) of 'the fourth, of blessed memory', which, he writes were no longer for sale, since his sister's son had taken them and had no intention of selling them. From this we learn that Abraham died some ten years after his father.[142]

The affair of Nathan b. Abraham

[870] Nathan b. Abraham was the scion of a family of geonim. The colophon in the Arabic story of the exilarch Bustanai attributes the story to him, on the basis of what had been handed down to him from his forefathers, 'the holy [heads of] the yeshivot'. We know the name of his grandfather, Saul, and that Nathan was 'the son of the sister of b. Yoḥai *av*'.

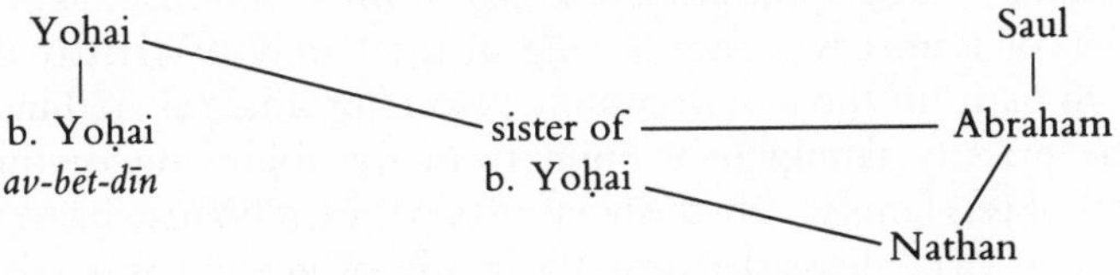

The genealogy of Nathan b. Abraham

It seems that the *av*, that is *av-bēt-dīn*, was the son of Yoḥai and the uncle of Nathan on his mother's side, for it was said that Nathan was appointed to the office of *av-bēt-dīn* in the yeshiva, which had previously been held by his mother's brother ('we gave him the place of his maternal uncle'). We may venture to assume what as yet cannot be proven, namely that the claimed descent from geonim was through the mother, and that the reference is to the earlier priestly dynasty, the descendants of Samuel ha-Kohen Gaon. This is to say that Yoḥai, grandfather of Nathan on his

142 'The sixth': **334**, a, line 12; b, lines 7–8. The deed from Ramla: **169**, line 20. The request for goods: **163**. The complaints of Solomon b. Judah: **66**. The object of slander: **142**, lines 18, 24–25. Writings in his handwriting: ULC Or 1081 J 38*v* (apparently a *qedushta*, a fragment beginning: *nisgelōt qōl 'al ha-mayim*); ENA 3184, f. 3, containing the matter of the calendar, in rhyme; see a *qerōvā* by ha-Kallir copied by him: PER H 8, which is a leaf from an entire quire he evidently copied. The Haggadah of Passover: ULC Add 3366. From the BT: TS Ar. Box 30, f. 171: Yev. 77b. The responsum and the Bible commentary: TS Ar. Box 22, f. 13. The formulary of the divorce: **168**. The story of Baḥīrā: TS AS 161.32, which I shall discuss elsewhere. TS AS 125.74*v* is a fragment in his handwriting, evidently the opening of a letter. Also preserved in the Geniza, written by Abraham b. Solomon Gaon, is a leaf from a quire with part of an enumeration of the precepts, which, I believe, are unlike anything known to us in this area; the precepts preserved are from the fourth (the prayer) to the tenth (the interdiction of robbery, or illegal acquisition); see DK 242 e–f. The *selīḥā* written by Ephraim b. Shemariah: **335**; Israel b. Sahlān's letter: **472**, b; the matter of the quires: **482**, b, line 9.

mother's side, was the descendant of this family. Indeed, we have seen that the name Yoḥai is to be found in the lineage of this family. The fact that the name of his uncle on his mother's side was included in his appellation, speaks in favour of this assumption, which goes to show that the mother's side was considered the more illustrious. If they had traced the descent from geonim on the father's side, we would have come across some sign of this and would have found the appellation 'great-grandson of the Gaon so-and-so', as was the case in other instances.

One can add another detail here, and that is Nathan b. Abraham's *'alāma*, the formula used at the end of letters, which was *yesha' yeqārēv* (may He hasten deliverance, as against Solomon b. Judah's *yesha' rav*, 'a great deliverance'). We find this *'alāma* in Salāma (Solomon) ha-Kohen b. Joseph's letter, written from Ramla to Shemaiah he-ḥaver b. Josiah, the grandson of the Shemaiah Gaon mentioned earlier. Apparently this *'alāma* was commonly used by the priestly family. It also seems that this Solomon ha-Kohen of Ramla was an offspring of the family of priestly geonim known to us from the tenth century. Naturally, this has nothing to do with the priestly family of geonim from the following century, for members of this family were the main adversaries of Nathan b. Abraham. As we have seen, the earlier priestly family of geonim was related by marriage to the family of Meir Gaon, which may be a partial explanation for the stance of one of Meir Gaon's offspring in the dispute to be described below.[143]

[871] The first knowledge we have of Nathan b. Abraham is from a letter of recommendation which Samuel the Third b. Hosha'na wrote on his behalf from Jerusalem to Shemaria b. Elḥanan in Fustat. It states that Abraham b. Saul died and that his son Nathan is setting out on his way 'to see that his inheritance is not lost'. Abraham, the father, evidently died in Egypt and not in Palestine, for it says there: 'we have heard rumours that R. Abraham b. Saul has died'. Evidently the journey in search of his inheritance, undoubtedly in pursuit of people who were still indebted to the deceased, took Nathan to the Maghrib. This we learn from what Solomon b. Judah writes, that Nathan 'went (when he was young) to the west to look for the inheritance of his father'. According to him, Nathan stayed there for 'many years' and studied Torah with 'Ḥushiel ha-Rav'. Nathan must have left Palestine before 1011, for Shemaria b. Elḥanan died

[143] See the fragments of the Bustanai story grouped together in Gil, *Tarbiz*, 48(1978/9), 65ff, and the colophon there (in ENA 4012), 69: 'as he had transmitted from his forefathers, the holy heads of the yeshiva'; see there further references; on the use of the word *yeshīvōt* in the sense of 'heads of the yeshiva' see *ibid.*, 70, n. 74; see also Goitein, *Mediterranean Society*, II, 595, n. 17, with a Muslim parallel. The name of his grandfather, Saul, see: **18**, line 17. The son of b. Yoḥai Av's sister: **127**, line 8. 'The place of his maternal uncle', *ibid.*, line 15. The letter of Salāma (Solomon) ha-Kohen: **525**. The affair of Nathan b. Abraham

in that year. Samuel b. Hosha'na signed the letter as 'the third', and we know that he was 'the third' from at least 1004; hence Nathan's journey could have taken place even seven years before 1011, or perhaps more. If we take a mean time, for example 1007, and say that he was at that time fifteen years old, he would have been born in around 990–995, and during the dispute (1038–1042) he would have been in his mid-forties.

We do not have any details regarding Nathan b. Abraham's stay in the Maghrib, but it seems that he had a faction of friends there. This is implied in his letter, written in Fustat, to Mevorakh b. David, a Babylonian scholar who lived in Qayrawān. In this letter, he praises a certain Abraham the physician b. 'Eli, and another man from Qayrawān, Ḥanania. As we shall see, when he left Qayrawn to go eastward to Egypt, he was given warm letters of recommendation by the Nagid of Qayrawān, Jacob b. 'Amram.

From Nathan's stay in Fustat, on his way to Palestine, we have a letter which he sent to a certain Abū Yūsuf Eleazar b. Samuel (Ismā'īl), to Qūṣ in Upper Egypt. We recognise the fact that the letter was from Fustat by his mention of Ḥesed al-Tustarī (Abū Naṣr al-Dustarī) there. One can see that during his stay in Fustat, in the thirties of the century, Nathan was perhaps engaged in trade for a stretch of a number of years, and one can assume that his connections with that merchant in Qūṣ, which was a junction for goods *en route* to India, point to his participation in this trade. He devotes much of the letter to the affair of Abraham b. David ibn Sughmār, which I shall discuss further. In the second part of the letter, most of which is written in mirror-writing for fear of the evil eye (of his competitors, evidently), there are details about the price of various kinds of merchandise for the addressee's information. It seems that Nathan dealt in supplying tar and gypsum, probably for building construction in Qūṣ. There are also details there of the price of wheat, pepper, brazilwood, almonds, camphor, musk, copper, soap, *nuqra* dirhams (which were worth 22 dirhams per dinar).

We also find echoes of his journey from the Maghrib and his stay in Fustat in the letter which Nathan wrote to Nethanel b. Rawḥ in Fustat. He addresses him as 'our pupil'. Evidently the letter was written in the spring of 1038. He mentions the farewell-taking and notes that he had hoped that in Fustat he would earn some rest, after the 'burden of trading and traversing the desert and sailing the seas', that is, after his journey from the Maghrib. From the letter, it seems that he was reduced to poverty, and was left owing money to various people. His creditors treated him with extreme severity, which was not in accord with the laws of the Jews. Even

was discussed by Mann, *Texts*, I, 323ff; as one can see, the discussion here differs in various details.

his father-in-law seems to have been angry with him, owing to his failures, and did not permit his wife and son to accompany him from then on. A Christian is also mentioned, evidently a business partner of his father-in-law. The latter, Mevorakh b. 'Eli, was to be one of his chief supporters during the dispute. The letter was evidently from Dumyāṭ (Damietta), and he mentions that on Monday, he intends to set out for Ḥanēs (which is Tinnīs). He probably meant to sail to Palestine from there. In the interim, he is occupied with the affairs of the local community, who received him in a friendly manner (probably because of his learning and lineage). He stays with his good friend Ḥusayn b. 'Allān and he asks his pupil, the addressee, to gather together the community, without fearing his father-in-law.[144]

[872] The quarrel in Jerusalem broke out half a year after Nathan reached Palestine. Solomon b. Judah relates in his letters, some of which were written during the dispute and others afterwards, how the dispute began. According to him, the people of the yeshiva received Nathan on his arrival in Jerusalem with considerable courtesy and respect: 'we called him *rōsh le-Israel*'. They assumed that the wisdom and learning which he acquired from Ḥushiel, his Master, would be reflected in his behaviour. However, he began to organise a faction in Ramla ('. . . and began to make himself the more important and his fellow-men insignificant'). *Rōsh-le-Israel*, it appears from a number of places, meant that he was appointed *av-bēt-dīn* in the yeshiva, as his uncle on his mother's side had been. He was given this title because the previous *av-bēt-dīn* had died, and thereafter

[144] The letter of Samuel 'the third': **18**; in this letter, there is no hint that Nathan will go to the Maghrib, and it is implied that his destination is only Fustat: he was certainly very young then, for in the letter it says that he is 'a tender innocent child, grown by us in purity and in exaltation of our Torah, and from day to day his learning increases'; he was then still a bachelor, although he has had matches proposed to him: 'he has not tried what has been proposed to him'. The letter of Solomon b. Judah: **127**. There is no firm basis to the assumption of Mann, *Texts*, I, 323, that the father died in Qayrawān. I do not understand how Abramson, *Ba-merkazim*, 32f, finds in Nathan's journey to the Maghrib proof of the fact (correct in itself) that he stemmed from a family of geonim. As to Ḥushiel of Qayrawān, he is undoubtedly Ḥushiel b. Elḥanan, father of Rabbēnū Ḥananel, see the discussion on him in Poznanski, *Harkavy Jubilee Volume*, 192ff, and in Mann, *Tarbiz*, 5(1933/4), 286ff; Ḥushiel's great learning is confirmed by the words of Hayy Gaon in his letter: 'we were told that there is in your place a man of great learning, a mountain of Torah, our Lord and Master Ḥushiel b. Elḥanan', etc.; see the complete version of the letter in Abramson, *Ba-merkazim*, 95ff. and the abovementioned passage in lines 36–37. On Mevorakh b. David: **178**; see on this Mevorakh: Poznanski, *ibid.*, 209; we do not know who Ḥanania of Qayrawān was. Ḥanania b. Berekhia in Poznanski, *Harkavy Jubilee Volume*, 187, is a misreading. In TS 8 J a 2, f. 1, b, line 7, Nissim (not Ḥanania) b. Berekhia is mentioned. It seems that Mann, *Texts*, I, 329, was correct in writing that the letter evidently was written at the time Nathan was on his way back from the Maghrib to Palestine and stayed in Egypt, for in the address he is still called Nathan b. Abraham, without any title. The letter to Eleazar b. Ismā'īl: **76**, where in line 11 the name of the Tustari is mentioned; on the mirror-writing, cf. Goitein, *Mediterranean Society*, I, 218.

forty of the elders met for the purpose of granting the title. There is no certainty as to the identity of the *av-bēt-dīn*, who died when Nathan arrived in Jerusalem. Solomon b. Judah says: 'the rumour has reached us about [the death] of the *av*, may God have mercy on him', from which we learn that he died in some distant locality. According to what he says – that Nathan received the position of his uncle – one can assume that his mother's brother, b. Yoḥai, about whom we know nothing, is intended. Perhaps what he meant to say was, the position that at some time in the past was held by Nathan's uncle. Hence it is possible that the *av-bēt-dīn*, who died before Nathan's arrival, was someone else and not Nathan's uncle.

Tobiah b. Daniel, who was then 'third' in the yeshiva, relinquished the office of *av-bēt-dīn* to which he was entitled according to the advancement usage of the yeshiva. When he was asked, he immediately agreed after he was told: 'The place [you hold] is yours, stand in your place, and let the man who arrived be called *av*, and there will be peace among [the people of] Israel and quarrelling will stop. So he did as he was told'. Solomon b. Judah was not entirely pleased with this decision, thinking that those who had made it 'destroy the *netīvōt*'; that is, that they had violated the accepted advancement order of the yeshiva by giving the office of *av-bēt-dīn* to Nathan and not to Tobiah b. Daniel. 'And those who forbade me to call him, called him themselves', that is, at first everyone objected to the appointment of Nathan by Solomon b. Judah to an office of such high rank in the yeshiva, but afterwards they appointed him despite his opposition. 'And I was then like a deaf person', that is, he failed and blames himself for it. The Gaon saw Nathan as the source of the dispute: 'the land was quiet from the day his maternal uncles passed away [from which we understand that he was speaking not only of b. Yoḥai]; from the moment he arrived, the quarrel started'. As to the 'third', Tobiah b. Daniel, we have seen that he was the son of Shemaiah Gaon's sister. Apparently, we have here a sort of offensive of followers of the early priestly family, who ruled the Palestinian yeshiva for more than a generation before that, in support of a scion of this family and against the descendants of Shemaiah Gaon, Solomon b. Judah himself and Tobiah b. Daniel, as well as against the other priestly family of Solomon ha-Kohen Gaon b. Joseph. The family relationship was not the only motivation of this quarrel however.[145]

[873] As to the two priestly brothers, they were at first vigorously opposed to Nathan. This can be understood if we take into consideration

The letter to Nethanel b. Rawḥ: **180**; what Mann wrote in *Jews*, I, 147, that during his stay in Fustat Nathan had 'a sort of school' has no foundation.

145 See the letters of Solomon b. Judah: **126**, lines 44ff; **127**, lines 7ff; **133**, lines 8ff; **136**, a, lines 2–32; **137**, b, lines 10ff.

the fact that we have here two priestly families who were continuously at odds with one another, evidently from the days of Shemaiah Gaon onwards. After the death of Solomon b. Judah, when the struggle for succession was at its height, Daniel b. Azariah writes disparagingly about his rival Joseph ha-Kohen b. Solomon Gaon. He notes that many people of Ramla (where Daniel then lived) are hostile to the two priestly brothers, while he himself had made every effort to pour oil on troubled waters. Joseph was not only ungrateful but began to slander him in every possible way. Here Daniel recalls forgotten incidents from the days of the dispute with Nathan b. Abraham and blames the two priestly brothers, Joseph and Elijah, for having been the main instigators of the dispute. On the other hand, he sees evidence of Joseph ha-Kohen's fickleness in the fact that he eventually came to terms with Nathan, after having promised that 'he would go [against him] to the end of the world'. In his opinion (revealed rather late in the day), Nathan was the offended and not the offender, which everyone now knows (that is, in *ca.* 1051, nine years after the dispute), and he suggests that this was also the opinion of Solomon b. Judah.

One of Nathan b. Abraham's supporters, writing in the autumn of 1038 and describing the eruption of the quarrel, also emphasises the part played by Joseph ha-Kohen, but also that of the Shuway' family. Solomon b. Judah, in fact, suggests in one of his letters that it is the priestly brothers who tried to prevent him from dealing with appointments, and thus make him incapable of appointing Nathan b. Abraham as *av-bēt-dīn*. It seems that the matter of the appointments was a major issue in the dispute. We lack clear and precise details but the impression is that a large part of the bitterness that spread among the public and which supplied Nathan b. Abraham with supporters and followers, can be ascribed to the arbitrary fashion in which people were appointed to communal offices. As we shall see, one of Nathan b. Abraham's obvious activities was the appointment of his supporters to such offices. Financial matters were also undoubtedly at the core of the dispute, particularly the struggle over the funds of the *heqdēsh*. One explicit accusation against Solomon b. Judah was that he had sold property of the *heqdēsh*, but it is not clear just what he had sold and for what purpose (we have seen above that he considered the expenses of restoring the synagogue as a legitimate use of the heqdēsh funds). As against this, in a complaint brought before the caliph against Nathan b. Abraham's supporters, Solomon b. Judah's faction claimed that they 'destroyed the foundations'. In addition, his adversaries also claim that Solomon b. Judah is a Maghribi, from which it is to be understood that Nathan b. Abraham was a Palestinian: 'It is unacceptable that a man from the people of the West should be appointed head and it is unacceptable that he who ascends to this seat is any but a man from the people of Palestine'. This claim the supporters of Solomon b. Judah ascribe to Nathan b. Abraham's followers (in a letter to the Maghrib!).

The followers of Nathan b. Abraham then decided to proclaim him Gaon instead of Solomon b. Judah. One can see that this matter was not to be taken lightly, and it is not surprising that it split the Jewish communities in Jerusalem and Ramla, in Fustat and Qayrawān, and undoubtedly in many other places of which we have little knowledge.[146]

[874] A first-hand account of the dispute's eruption can be found in a letter of one of Nathan b. Abraham's followers, of which unfortunately only a fragment, the middle section, has been preserved. It contains a description of the events of Tishri AM 4799, October AD 1038. It appears that with the first signs of dissension and manifestation of rebellion, the son of the Gaon, Abraham, hastened to Damascus, and returned with a *tawqī'*, an official order, confirming the status of Solomon b. Judah. The community gathered in the synagogue in Ramla, where the son of the Gaon pronounced a homily, in the presence of Joseph ha-Kohen b. Solomon Gaon, who was then 'fifth' of the yeshiva. From there, the entire community went up to Jerusalem headed by the two. It seems that they went up to the Mount of Olives, where they blew the *shofar*s in the presence of Solomon b. Judah and Joseph ha-Kohen. Afterwards, they declared a ban on 'all those who profaned the holydays of the Lord', which was a new formula of excommunication never heard of before (presumably a new formula for the excommunication of the Karaites). The family of Shuway' (who were even earlier enemies of the Gaon, as we have seen) opposed this and voiced their claims against the Gaon. At this point, Solomon b. Judah's supporters became violent, they struck the father of the Shuway' family and even gnawed one of his fingers to the bone. These incidents occurred on Hosha'na rabbā (23 October 1038). On the morrow, the eighth day of the Feast of Tabernacles, the excommunication of the Karaites was proclaimed in the usual manner, that is, the ban was placed on those who mixed 'vessels for meat with vessels for milk'. According to the writer, the public opposed this and hence the pilgrims (almost all of whom, it is implied, were on Nathan's side) gathered at the house of the Shuway' family, and proclaimed Nathan b. Abraham Gaon, a record being written to this effect, and signed by all those present. Hence, the date on which Nathan b. Abraham was proclaimed Gaon was 24 October 1038. Afterwards, on the sabbath after the Feast of Tabernacles (28

146 The letter of Daniel b. Azariah: **363**. The supporter of Nathan: **182**. Solomon b. Judah's letter: **136**, lines 26–27. The property of the heqdēsh: **182**, line 16; **197**, c, line 20. The Palestinian origin: **192**, lines 15–16.

October 1038), the pilgrims in Ramla congregated in the *majlis* (it is not clear whether they mean the reception hall or whether he had set up an office in his house) of 'our Master Nathan Gaon' and, at the request of the assembly, Nathan pronounced a homily, and by doing so pleased all those present ('no one remained in the synagogues').

We read the parallel story from the other side in a letter from Solomon b. Judah to Solomon the physician b. 'Eli, sent to Tripoli in Syria. According to the Gaon, he received a warning from his loyal supporters in Ramla ('the elders of Ramla . . . wrote to us') that Nathan b. Abraham was planning to pronounce himself Gaon ('he laid his hands on everything') and therefore hurried to Ramla together with Elijah 'the sixth' (who is ha-Kohen, b. Solomon Gaon), intending to place Elijah in charge of the community of Ramla ('to seat him in Ramla'). In the meantime, he writes, Nathan organised a large faction of supporters ('empty and irresponsible people, whom he bought with money and clothes and food and drink'). And this is how he describes the events of the sabbath *berēshīt* (the first after the Feast of Tabernacles) in Ramla (above we have seen the version of the opposing side). In his words, Nathan gathered his supporters in the synagogue. When he saw that a skirmish was about to take place ('each of them wanting to fight the other'), Solomon b. Judah left the synagogue in order to prevent the intervention of the authorities. Then Nathan proclaimed himself head of the yeshiva to his supporters ('the hired rose up . . . and he prayed on himself head of the *tō'ēvā*'; abomination, instead of *yeshīvā*). Solomon b. Judah and his followers moved over to the other synagogue (it is not clear which one) and there he excommunicated Nathan and his assistants: 'the son of the third and his cousin, and Maṣlīaḥ his pupil, and the Shuway' family, and 'Ammār the physician'. The Gaon asks that a similar ban be proclaimed in Tripoli as well, as he evidently requested from all the communities that were connected with the Palestinian yeshiva.[147]

[147] The fragment of a letter: **182**; 'the fourth' of the yeshiva was then Abraham b. Samuel b. Hosha'na, see **230**, line 26, and 'the third', Tobiah b. Daniel, as we have seen above; Elijah, Joseph's brother, was 'the sixth'. The writer speaks of 'the Shū'a b. Simḥūn family', and there is almost no doubt that he is referring to the Shuway' family. The passage concerning the holidays arouses second thoughts. Did Nathan b. Abraham have in mind making changes in the calendar in order to come closer to the Karaites? We have no proof of this, and perhaps this was part of the counter-defamation of Solomon b. Judah's side, though it may have contained a grain of truth. The letter to Solomon the physician b. 'Eli: **127**. Tripoli is called here 'the fortress of Sinim'. As noted by Mann, *Texts*, I, 337, n. 4, Saadia Gaon translates 'and the Sinite' (Gen., x:17): *al-ṭarābulusīyīn*; and see David Qimḥi, to Is., xlix:12 (from the Land of Sinim): 'Rav Saadia interpreted it: *iṭrābulusīyīn*' (this is the correct reading). It is surprising that Mann himself brought up the assumption that Aswān in Egypt was being referred to. Assaf, *Tarbiz*, 3(1931/3), 345, already objected to it, also quoting scholars of later generations, who say that 'the Sinite' is Tripoli in Syria; and it is worth seeing also Bereshit rabba xxxvii, the Theodor and

[875] The next item of information is dated four months later, when Nathan b. Abraham wrote to Abū'l-Barakāt Berākhā b. Rawḥ of Fustat. The letter was evidently sent with Berākhā's mother, who was perhaps at that time in Palestine. The letter is dated: after the night of the eve of Purim, AM 4799 (12 February AD 1039); and it contains a description of the reading of the *megillā* in Ramla. It was attended by more than 800 people, 400 in the *majlis* and more than that in the *qā'a*. Rabbanites and Karaites took part together and, so did *al-gōyīm*, that is, Muslims. The illumination was very impressive: 30 'daylight' candles, more than 200 ordinary candles, some 30 lamps and chandeliers (and who can tell what was precisely the nature of these forms of lighting). The *megillā* was read from approximately 30 books and the reading was beautiful. No one remained in the Babylonian synagogue, in the Palestinian synagogue there were some 20 souls and with *al-Fāsī* (that is, Solomon b. Judah, evidently in his home) less than ten. Nathan b. Abraham emphasises in particular that the Karaites were also present at his synagogue, perhaps 200 of them, including all their notables. He describes the gay ambiance and adds that such a Purim had not been seen since the days of (Manasseh b. Abraham) Ibn al-Qazzāz.

Apparently, not long after that, towards Passover, Nathan tried to establish contact with Abraham ha-Kohen b. Isaac ibn Furāt, the physician with considerable influence with the authorities in Ramla. From a brief letter he sent to him, it emerges that he had already sent him an emissary, who had not succeeded in finding him, and thus Nathan was unable to carry out his intention to come to him to offer his salutations for the holidays. It is possible that this failure to establish connections with Abraham ha-Kohen was not accidental, considering that the latter was one of Solomon b. Judah's most loyal supporters.

Later on, we find a letter from Tammuz 1350 Sel., June or July AD 1039, with the heading 'Nathan head of the yeshiva Ge'ōn Ya'aqōv'. This was a letter written by Nathan to 'Amram b. Yefet in Fustat. The latter had gone over to Nathan's camp, as Nathan had been informed by Mevorakh 'head of the communities', evidently Mevorakh b. 'Eli,

Albeck ed., 348: (the Sinite) Artūsiyya; see also in the Targums: Artīsa'ē (Neofiti) and various other distorted versions. This is Orthōsia, some 15 kilometres north-east of Tripoli. See also: Hippolytos, *Khronikon*, 72, who interprets 'the Sinite' – Orthōsiastai; see the entry Orthōsia (by E. Honigmann) in *PW*, vol. 36, 1494ff.; cf. Gildemeister, *ZDPV*, 8(1885), 135, line 29: arṭūsiya; the manuscript *ibid.* has *armūsiya*, which is certainly a distortion; this was a citadel, and considered the citadel of Tripoli; the old Tripoli was abandoned and the inhabitants set up a city called Ṭarābulus, four miles from the sea; see Idrīsī (Cerulli), 372f; see Canard, *Hamdanides*, 208: Arethusa is al-Rastan, south of the Orontes; see further: Wild, *Libanesische Ortsnamen*, 343, and further references there (he does not mention the Jewish references). The subject of Nathan b. Abrahams's supporters will be discussed below.

Nathan's father-in-law. The letter merely contains greetings and praise in very ornate language. In that same month, Tammuz 1350 Sel., Nathan wrote another eloquent letter (he probably wrote many letters of this kind, to many communities), to Nethanel b. Rawḥ, also of Fustat. He calls him 'the holy scion, descendant of holy ones ... who sanctifies the name of God [i.e. is endangering his own life] and is undergoing any risk for the study of the Torah'. We are not aware of the reason for all these phrases. He even grants him the title: 'aid of the yeshiva'. (We have seen above that Nathan saw this Nethanel as his own pupil and wrote to him when he was *en route* to Palestine, evidently in the spring of 1038.)[148]

[876] In the summer of 1039, the Jewish world around the Mediterranean was in a ferment. The first evidence, explicit and aroused, concerning the involvement of Fustat and Qayrawān in the dispute, can be found in two drafts of letters intended to be sent from Fustat to the Nagid of Qayrawān, Jacob b. 'Amram – one in Hebrew, written by Abraham b. David ibn Sughmār and the other in Arabic, written by Ghālib ha-Kohen b. Moses, son-in-law of Ephraim b. Shemaria. In the first letter, there is a complaint that it was the people from the Maghrib who were behind Nathan b. Abraham and who encouraged him at the outset of his activities. The Nagid is asked to intervene and write to Nathan to mend his aberrant ways and try to persuade the authorities to intervene and put a stop to the dispute. The people of Fustat, the letter states, suffer immensely from the activities of Nathan's relatives and supporters there. In the other letter as well, the subject of the pressure in Fustat is spoken of and in a careful and polite style, the people of the Maghrib are blamed for backing Nathan's actions. In order to make a greater impression on the Nagid, they quote Nathan b. Abraham's claim, that it is not conceivable that a Maghribi (Solomon b. Judah came from Fās, as we have seen), should stand at the head of the yeshiva of Palestine. There is a repetition of the request that the Nagid intervene to put an end to the dispute, mainly by appealing to the authorities in Fustat, to whom he evidently had special access.

Thus the mood became increasingly overwrought, especially with the

148 The letter to Berākhā b. Rawḥ: **183**; *majlis* and *qā'a* were large halls characteristic of that time, and it seems that the writer is referring to a private house, as was the opinion of Goitein, *Mediterranean Society*, II, 591, n. 39; it is interesting that Nathan mentions four public centres; naturally this could not have happened in Jerusalem, for we do not know of a 'Babylonian' synagogue there. The letter to Abraham ha-Kohen: **185**. To 'Amram b. Yefet: **188**; a year earlier, 1 August 1038, 'Amram b. Yefet was among the signatories to a record, **331**, in favour of Eleazar ha-melammēd b. Samuel, who was accused of cursing Solomon b. Judah; Mann, *Jews*, I, 146 commented on Nathan's custom of writing his name and his title at the head of his letters, as Josiah Gaon and Elḥanan b. Shemaria were also wont to do. To Nethanel b. Rawḥ: **186**; this Nethanel is a signatory to a Karaite marriage deed, see **309**, line 7; in a letter he wrote to Ephraim b. Shemaria in Fustat,

month of Tishri and the time of pilgrimage approaching. In the wake of the pilgrimage to Jerusalem, an unusual atmosphere of expectation prevailed among the Jewish communities. It was clear that the congregation on the Mount of Olives would turn into a demonstration of the power of each of the two camps and that it would be possible to correctly gauge whose force was the stronger of the two. It is therefore not surprising that Nathan b. Abraham was anxious to recruit his followers in view of the imminent pilgrimage, as can be seen in his explicit letter to a certain '*yedīd* [friend] of the yeshiva', whose identity and location is not known to us. This letter contains a request to recruit as many supporters for the pilgrimage as possible, as I have already mentioned. We shall see that we have some indications that the pilgrimage and the congregation on Hosha'na rabbā on the Mount of Olives was a success (however passing) for Nathan b. Abraham. In this letter, there are also further echoes of the flaring of passions. The letters of 'the friend' did not reach him, writes Nathan, and he suspects that Solomon b. Judah's supporters ('a congregation of hypocrites', Job, xv:34) obtain them by deception. Nathan b. Abraham appointed people to hold community offices and distributed titles to his followers. For instance, Mevassēr b. Jesse is mentioned as 'head of the communities' and he is also called 'faithful of the yeshiva'. This Mevassēr visited Ramla and received writings from Nathan for his followers. Nathan also appointed Abraham b. Shelah ḥavēr, and he explains in detail how important it is that there should be 'an ordained man' in every community, meaning of course, someone loyal to Nathan. According to his statements, he enjoyed notable success in Ramla. The authorities were pressed lest they agreed to the demands of Solomon b. Judah's backers: they even warned the local ruler that they would approach the *mishnē*, that is, the wazīr. The 'sixth' (it is not clear who this was at that time) went over to Nathan's side, and even banned one of his rivals. It seems, then, that an optimistic mood prevailed in Nathan b. Abraham's camp in the summer and autumn of 1039 and that he had the upper hand in Ramla. We have no information about the recruiting of supporters for Solomon b. Judah in anticipation of the month of Tishri and the pilgrimage, but it seems that in his camp, too, there were considerable preparations for the impending events.

We find indications of what was happening in Ramla in the fragment of a letter evidently sent from Fustat to Jerusalem mentioning figures involved in the dispute who belonged to the faction of Abū Sahl, that is

Joseph ha-Kohen b. Solomon Gaon intended to propose that Nethanel become trustee to the heirs of a certain Surūr ha-Levi, but he erased his name and wrote that of Nīḥūmā b. Samuel instead, see: **407**, line 8; this erasure may have been connected with the struggle between the factions in the yeshiva which preceded the dispute described here, and in which we find Nethanel in the opposite camp to that of Joseph ha-Kohen.

Nathan b. Abraham. Somewhat more extensive information, though also very obscure, is to be found in a letter from Abraham b. David ibn Sughmār, who wrote from Fustat to 'Eli ha-Kohen b. Ezekiel in Jerusalem. One can see that these two were followers of Solomon b. Judah. The writer mentions a long letter from b. Meir (evidently Solomon he-ḥāvēr b. Meir *rōsh ha-seder*, who was also one of Solomon b. Judah's supporters at first, and I have already mentioned him above). From this letter, which was sent to Nathan b. Abraham (he calls him *al-zānāv*, 'the tail', for Nathan calls himself 'the head'), copies were made and distributed to every country in the east and the west, says Ibn Sughmār; he anticipates that 'Eli ha-Kohen will also copy it and show it to all his friends. He assumes that the copy he sent to 'Eli went astray and regrets the fact. Indirectly, we learn that a letter arrived in Fustat from 'Eli ha-Kohen b. Ezekiel with details of the incidents of the dispute in Ramla, and that also, *aṣḥābnā* (our people, that is the Maghribi merchants) already wrote about it from Ramla to Fustat. From Nathan b. Abraham there are also letters and copies of letters arriving in Jaffa and Tyre, and according to the writer, they are full of lies. Nathan lies to his followers and they in turn, lie to him – apparently about the extent of the support he enjoys. According to Ibn Sughmār, similar things occurred in Fustat. Working there for Nathan's side is a certain 'Allūn, who even proclaimed an excommunication in the synagogue (apparently against the supporters of Solomon b. Judah). The backers of Nathan b. Abraham 'the sons of the Kohen' (we do not know who they are), and b. al-Ṣippōrī (Judah ibn al-'Uṣfūra?) are active against the followers of Solomon b. Judah in Fustat – they bribe people with money and offer them wine (*nabīdh*), and use for this purpose the money set aside for 'the cave', that is, the synagogue in Jerusalem. This refers to a sum of 400 dinars collected by that b. al-Ṣippōrī for 'the cave', and now it was being spent on the dispute. Ibn Sughmār wrote about this to *ha-rōsh av-bēt-dīn* (perhaps he means Nathan b. Abraham, although he was aware that no good would come of it, but we do not know of anyone being appointed to the office of *av-bēt-din* during the course of the dispute). He received a long letter from him in response, and even was given the title 'banner of the Rabbanites', but Ibn Sughmār would have preferred it if he had gone down to Ramla instead and resolved the dispute there.[149]

149 The letters to the Nagid of Qayrawān: **191**, **192**. The letter to the 'friend of the yeshiva': **187**; the 'sixth' mentioned there is according to Mann, *Jews*, 149, Elijah ha-Kohen b. Solomon, also in: *Texts*, I, 330, but this is impossible, for we have seen the extent of the rivalry between Nathan and the priestly brothers. Mann himself (*Jews, ibid.*, in the MS) noted that this should be corrected. The fragment from Fustat: **189**. The letter of Ibn Sughmār: **190**; Moses b. Jekuthiel, physician and merchant of Fustat, originating from Spain, who requests validation of a deed from the Jerusalem yeshiva, at the time he came there from his stay in Tyre, mentions in his letter personalities of the yeshiva: the Gaon,

[877] Evidence of the situation in Ramla is found in a letter from Abraham 'the fourth' b. Samuel 'the third' b. Hosha'na, written from Ramla to Solomon b. Judah in Jerusalem after Passover, apparently in AM 4799, that is AD 1039. In his words 'most of the authorities in the city support our enemy; he deludes the people with his lies, like Absalom son of Maachah'.

In Fustat, the friction between the two camps, and the clashes which undoubtedly accompanied it, led to the closing of the synagogue of the 'Palestinians'. It is possible that the immediate reason for the closing of the synagogue was the fact that the majority of the congregation were loyal to Solomon b. Judah, and as we shall see, the aggressive individuals among Nathan b. Abraham's supporters put pressure on the authorities and convinced them to close the synagogue. We learn from a heqdēsh account written in Fustat in 1041, that the synagogue was closed towards the end of Marḥeshwan 1351 Sel., that is, approximately mid-November AD 1039. Solomon b. Judah mentions the closing of the synagogue in Fustat in a number of letters written during the dispute, and in other letters written when it was over. It seems that the synagogue remained closed almost to the end of the dispute, or perhaps even until the very end, that is, almost three whole years. In research works written on the dispute, there is some confusion between the synagogue in Fustat and that of Ramla. The latter was only closed for a few days, on Purim AM 4801, that is February AD 1041.

We gather further details of what happened in the autumn of 1039 from a draft written in Arabic script on the margin of a court record in the handwriting of Ephraim b. Shemaria. The draft was intended to form a petition to the caliph, and one can assume that it was written by Ephraim b. Shemaria himself, or by one of his assistants. According to this draft, the dispute was a result of the deterioration in the status of the Jewish leadership during the past two years (that is, from about the beginning of 1038). Leading the offenders was a man who came from the west, Nathan b. Abraham, who attempted to oust Solomon b. Judah from his office. It was he who obtained the closing of the synagogue of the 'Palestinians' in Fustat, two months before the writing of this letter. Nathan b. Abraham is now in Fustat for a month, organising his supporters, with the backing of his many influential relatives and the Karaites. It emerges that in December 1039, Nathan b. Abraham was staying in Fustat, and he was still there in Adar I Sel. 1351, that is February–March AD 1040, as is proven by a deed drawn up in his court that met in Fustat.

'the third' Tobiah b. Daniel, and others; but not the *av-bēt-dīn*, Nathan b. Abraham. The reason for this is clear – it was the dispute – but from this we also learn that no one else was appointed in Nathan's stead, see **243**.

We have no precise or dated details on the events of the year 1040 and the beginning of 1041. We find interesting material in a letter from Joseph b. Kulayb (a diminutive from Biblical Kālēv, which is a transformation of Khalaf, which is Ḥalfon, which is usually Aaron), a follower and intimate of Nathan b. Abraham, who writes from Ramla to his Master on 8 May 1041. He notes that the synagogue (of the 'Palestinians') was closed on Purim (20 February) for a few days. A meeting of the two factions was held and there were negotiations concerning the appointment of a certain b. 'Eli to some office (cantor?). At that gathering, it was decided to call a meeting of the entire community regarding Judah the cantor, who was loathed by the followers of Nathan b. Abraham (he was probably Judah 'the western cantor' b. Abraham b. Faraj). It was decided that Judah himself should go to Nathan (who was then somewhere outside of Palestine, apparently Tyre) in order to clarify his situation. From this it emerges that Nathan's followers dominated Ramla; they were the majority and decided on the management of communal affairs. They were also able to dismiss a cantor who evidently was not an ardent supporter of Nathan. Their own man, b. 'Eli, waited to be appointed in his stead, and although he had been waiting since Purim (February 20, that is, for two months), he was persuaded to be patient until the matter of Judah was finally decided. From this letter, we also have information concerning the opposing side, the people of Solomon b. Judah. They apparently abandoned the synagogue, at least in part, and rented a house for themselves. Abraham, son of the Gaon, was in Ramla at the time but was on the verge of leaving after his unsuccessful attempt to persuade people to go over to his father's camp. Nathan continued to appoint ḥavērīm from among his supporters and distribute honorary titles. This is illustrated in the episode of the son of the ḥāvēr from Bāniyās who arrived in Ramla, claiming that he was one of Nathan's supporters and asking to be recognised as a *ḥāvēr* or as a *rōsh seder*; however the community refused to accept his status until he could produce a written confirmation from Nathan. At the time, Nathan behaved in the traditional manner of geonim and was busy writing responsa to queries on matters of the law, and even during his absence from Ramla, such queries were sent to Tyre and their responsa were anticipated.[150]

[878] To a large extent, the letters of Solomon b. Judah reflect the emotional pressure under which he laboured as a result of the success of his

150 The letter of Abraham 'the fourth' b. Samuel 'the third' (identified by his handwriting): **230**; he writes to 'rabbēnū Gaon' about the division of an inheritance between Moses, Mawhūb (Nathan) and Isaac the sons of Mevassēr, a matter dealt with by Solomon b. Judah in **125**, his letter to David b. Aaron, Fustat; even from the comparison of the adversary with Absalom, it is obvious that Abraham writes to Solomon b. Judah and that he is one of those who oppose Nathan. Mann, *Texts*, I, 325, n. 2, assumed that the 'son of

rival and the widespread support which the latter enjoyed in Palestine as well as in the communities outside of Palestine, if we can judge by what occurred in Fustat. He calls Nathan b. Abraham all sorts of disparaging names, such as 'head of Peor', and so on. He calls down curses on his head, such as 'evil shall not depart from his house (Prov., xvii:13), to make him pay', or 'to deprive him of anyone that pisseth against the wall', and others. Nathan is over-ambitious, arrogant, and behaves like his deceased uncle, his mother's brother, recruiting supporters from among those who were formerly his rivals, distributing numerous writings full of lies and being helped by the Karaites ('the other sect'). He has a great deal of money and is assisted by the authorities. His influence has reached as far as the Maghrib, 'for his hand was stretched out towards them'. The Gaon emphasises that he is himself an old man: 'and I am at the end of my days and do not know how long I shall live'. In a letter written after the dispute, on 29 November 1042, he points out that it is already three years that he has been ill, and if we assume that he was being accurate, the onset of his illness (the nature of which is not known – he lived for another nine years) began in the autumn of 1039, when Nathan b. Abraham began to dominate Fustat and evidently succeeded in recruiting a large number of pilgrims to go up to Jerusalem. These facts were especially disturbing to Solomon b. Judah, and he even points out the exact date: 'from the morrow after *Hosha'na rabbā* or the eighth day of the Feast of Tabernacles'. We can assume then that the gathering on the Mount of Olives on Hosha'na rabbā AM 4800 (12 October AD 1039) turned into a successful demonstration of support and victory for Nathan b. Abraham.[151]

the third' mentioned as one of Nathan b. Abraham's supporters was this Abraham, son of Samuel 'the third', but this opinion is invalid in the light of this letter: **230**. The closing of the synagogue: Document No. 12 (Bodl MS Heb b 11, f. 5) in Gil, *Documents*, 175f, see lines 31–32; despite its closure, it appears from that account of heqdēsh expenses, they continued to light the oil lamps there. Solomon b. Judah on the closing of the synagogue in Fustat: **131**, b, lines 5–6 (assumed reading); **130**, lines 21ff: 'in order that one listens to what he says . . . that a house of prayer should be closed . . . and to reduce a congregation to a wilderness'; **133**, line 8 (happy at the reopening of the synagogue); **135**, lines 19–20: much of his anxiety during the dispute was that people would say that he was the cause of the synagogue being closed. The draft of the petition to the caliph: **196**. The deed in Nathan b. Abraham's court: **193**. Joseph b. Kulayb's letter **195**, see the matter of the date in the notes to this document; b. 'Eli is perhaps Mevorakh b. 'Allūn b. Moses, signed on the 'peace agreement': **199**, b, line 5. The closing of the synagogue in Ramla on Purim was evidently the result of a scandal which broke out on the question of Judah the cantor's dismissal, and according to Goitein, *Eretz-Israel*, 10 (1970/71), 106f, there was the problem of mentioning the *rāshūt*, that is, mentioning the name of the Gaon during public prayer. Stern, *REJ*, 128 (1069), 204, and following him Cohen, *AJSR*, 1(1976), 7, n. 18, assumed that this information concerning the extended closure of the synagogue applied to Ramla, but this is not so; it is the synagogue of the 'Palestinians' in Fustat; and the discussion in Cohen, *ibid.*, on the date of the closure of the synagogue is irrelevant in the light of the clear date as we know it, mid-November 1039.

151 The complaints of Solomon b. Judah, see: **126** and also **128**: 'who lurks like a beast', etc.

[879] In order to thoroughly understand the procession of events in the course of the dispute, which I have surveyed in the main, we should direct our attention to the forces and factors which helped each side. They may be divided into two categories, Jews and non-Jews, the latter being the authorities. Most of Nathan b. Abraham's supporters remain an anonymous element, although some of them are mentioned by name in my collection of Geniza documents, only in connection with the dispute. There are possibly two reasons for this: one is that obviously those who were active on Nathan b. Abraham's side were new to public affairs, and their thirst for novelty (for we have no precise information as to their characters), led them to pursue these activities. The other reason was that, working in his favour, as we shall see, were people outside the framework of the 'Palestinian' communities, that is, people of the 'Babylonian' and even the Karaite communities. Again, these people are naturally unknown to us, for most of the documents which reached the Geniza were from the 'Palestinian' congregation in Fustat.

As we have seen, Solomon b. Judah counted among the first supporters of his rival, the son of 'the third' (whose identity we do not know); Maṣlīaḥ, 'his pupil' (it is not clear whose pupil); his cousin (as aforementioned); 'Ammār the physician; and the Shuway' family. We are familiar with the latter and I have already surveyed the available information on them, and we have seen that they were evidently identical with the family of Shū'a b. Simḥūn, who were keen followers of Nathan when the dispute erupted. Abū'l-Ḥasan 'Ammār the physician is mentioned in a number of documents, not only in connection with the dispute, but we have no further details about him.

What is most impressive is the mass support described in Nathan's letters. Although we have seen that his opponents accused him of distributing lies about the extent of that support, the general impression is that they were not correct and that Nathan b. Abraham's spontaneous and enthusiastic description of the reading of the *megillā*, for instance, was certainly true in the main. He had heard from Damascus, he says in that letter, that 400 people there have already signed a court record (*maḥḍar*) recognising his authority. Apparently, Nathan b. Abraham had sway over the masses due to his lineage and his reputation as a scholar, but he also seems to have been knowledgeable and experienced in public relations and in nurturing friendships. A letter he wrote to a certain Ḥalfon, who left the city (Fustat), can serve as an example. Nathan expresses his regrets that he did not manage to take leave of him properly because he was too ill to be

and the matter of the Maghrib there; **130**, with his thoughts on the approaching end of his life, and remarks about the large sums of money at Nathan b. Abraham's disposal and on the fact that he bribes his supporters with money (lines 21ff). His illness: **133**.

able to walk or even to ride to see him. From the letter, it emerges that Ḥalfon was one of his financial backers. Perhaps the reference here is to this Ḥalfon (his Hebrew name was Aaron) b. Ephraim b. Ṭarasūn, a veteran and central public figure in Fustat. Also, we already know of a number of people of Fustat with whom Nathan had friendly relations and was in the habit of writing to: Nethanel ha-Levi b. Rawḥ and Berākhā b. Rawḥ (perhaps the brother of the former), both evidently Karaites; Abū'l-Surūr Peraḥia (Faraḥ) *rōsh ha-pereq* b. Mu'ammal b. Peraḥia the judge, who may also have been a Karaite, for he had a special relationship with Tobiah b. Moses, one of the Karaite leaders; 'Amram b. Yefet, to whom Nathan b. Abraham wrote in Tammuz 1350 Sel., July AD 1038; Solomon b. Nathan, to whom there is a fragment of the opening of a letter from Nathan b. Abraham in my collection, and who may have been identical with Solomon b. Nethanel, the money changer, whose letter to the *av-bēt-dīn* Zadok ha-Levi b. Levi has been preserved.

To this subject of Nathan b. Abraham's supporters in Fustat, we must also add the deed dated Adar I 1351 Sel., February–March AD 1040, already mentioned above. The deed was drawn up in Fustat, before 'the Grand Court of our Master Nathan head of the yeshiva Ge'on Ya'aqōv'. It deals with a quarrel between indigo traders. This court met at the home of Nethanel he-ḥāvēr b. Yeshū'ā. Nethanel apparently received the title *ḥāvēr* from Nathan b. Abraham, for he is not mentioned anywhere else as having this title. Another signatory to the deed was Eleazar b. Samuel, that is, Eleazar b. Ismā'īl, who was involved some year and a half earlier in a scandal and was accused of cursing Solomon b. Judah, as we have seen. He was the man who had conducted business with Nathan b. Abraham from Qūṣ in southern Egypt, when the latter was in Fustat, before coming to Palestine. Strangely, the handwriting on the deed resembles that of Ghālib ha-Kohen b. Moses, Ephraim b. Shemaria's son-in-law, and these two were the most loyal supporters of Solomon b. Judah.

A letter from an anonymous supporter of Nathan b. Abraham arouses particular interest, and it is difficult to discern whether it was written shortly before the dispute or after it ended. He praises Nathan in the letter, for according to the writer, he acquired a reputation for piety, learning, and knowledge of people and also because of his distinguished lineage (*jalālat al-bayta*). His devotion to Nathan b. Abraham can be seen from the fact that he concludes his letter with the latter's *'alāma, yesha' yeqārēv*. We learn of other followers of Nathan b. Abraham in Jerusalem from this letter: the Shū'a family (which is the Shuway' family), Abū'l-Surūr Joshua (Yūsha') b. Nathan al-Andalusī, one of the Maghribis who lived in Jerusalem and who is mentioned in their letters. On the Shū'a family and the aforementioned Joshua he says that they support him (the writer), from which we understand that they share his attitude towards Nathan b. Abraham. Their support is especially meaningful, he writes, for Solomon b. Judah's people are persecuting him and they demand that he swears not to pray for Nathan b. Abraham, from which we understand that the man was a cantor, and that he was referring to the mention of the *rāshūt* of Nathan b. Abraham during public prayers. He went to visit Solomon b. Judah to resolve the differences, but the visit, which he describes in the letter, did not help him at all, and he has some hard things to say about the Gaon. It is interesting to note that despite all this, the writer still thinks he merits the appointment of *dayyān* or *ḥāvēr*.

One of the most distinguished of Nathan b. Abraham's supporters was his father-in-law, Abū'l-Faḍl Mevorakh (ha-Kohen?) b. 'Eli b. Ezra (Zur'a). He was one of the wealthy men of Fustat and belonged to the 'Babylonian' community. Solomon b. Judah mentions him in two of his letters to Sahlān b. Abraham, leader of the 'Babylonian' community in Fustat: 'Mevorakh *ha-sār* ['the prince'] b. 'Eli; *ha-sār*, our Master Mevorakh b. 'Eli *ha-sār* b. Ezra'. It was he who pressed for the appointment of his son-in-law Nathan b. Abraham as *av-bēt-dīn*, as we have seen. The title 'head of the communities' was evidently granted him by his son-in-law. In a receipt drawn up in Fustat on a Monday, 26 Iyar 1381 Sel., 10 May AD 1070, it states that Ṣedaqa (Zadok) b. Mevorakh *rōsh ha-qāhāl* (b. 'Eli) collected money for his sister's son, Abraham b. Nathan (b. Abraham), that was owed to him by a certain Hillel b. Manasseh. Hence we have clear evidence of the family connection.

In the month of Av AM 4800, July AD 1040, the exilarch Hezekiah b. David wrote to the 'Babylonian' community in Fustat. This was at the height of the dispute, but there is no direct reference to it in the letter. He asks the entire community to accept the authority of Sahlān b. Abraham, 'for his words are our words and he is not to be disobeyed', and threatens the excommunication of those that oppose him. The letter also contains special greetings for Abū Naṣr, who is Ḥesed al-Tustarī. In the first part of the letter, he speaks in praise of someone's virtues. This part of the letter has been preserved only in shreds and it is difficult to make out the name of the man to whom he is referring, although it is not unlikely that it is Nathan b. Abraham. The latter notes, we have seen, that on the first Purim of the dispute, all the 'Babylonians' in Ramla came to participate with him in the reading of the *megillā* (according to him, no one remained in the synagogue of the 'Babylonians'). Apparently, Sahlān b. Abraham, leader of the Babylonians in Fustat, was also on Nathan's side. This can be discerned from the colophon of the story of Bustanai, mentioned earlier. The story was copied by Sahlān himself, whose handwriting could hardly be mistaken. He notes there that it is the work of 'our Lord and Master

Nathan Gaon, as he received it from his forefathers the holy [heads of the] yeshivot and from his teacher Ḥushiel, *rēsh bē rabbānān* [head of the learning house of scholars], of blessed memory, copied in Fustat in the year 1352 Sel.' This means, that in AD 1041, when the dispute was still raging, Sahlān distributed a lampoon written by Nathan against the exilarchs of the Bustanai house. This was undoubtedly one of the results of Nathan's stay in Fustat for a few months during the previous year. Naturally, it may be argued that by doing so, Sahlān was trying to besmirch Nathan's reputation among the 'Babylonians' and other devotees of the exilarchic family; that is to say, it could have been interpreted as an act in favour of Solomon b. Judah. Or perhaps Nathan had written this story quite some time before the dispute and probably regretted it when trying to get the support of the 'Babylonians' and the Karaites. The truth is that we have no explanation for this action and can arrive at a number of assumptions, such as that the story was directed against Daniel b. Azariah, who also stemmed from the family of the exilarchs, that is the descendants of Bustanai. Daniel was staying in Fustat at the time and was one of Solomon b. Judah's supporters. On the face of it, it seems possible to assume that Sahlān was indeed one of Nathan b. Abraham's supporters, since he took the trouble to copy the story, while calling Nathan Gaon, and the latter's forefathers: heads of the yeshivot.[152]

152 'Ammār the physician: see: **127**; Chapira, *Yerushalayim*, 1952/3, 119, states – though I do not know on what basis – that he was a Karaite. The *Megillā*, and the support in Damascus: **183**; the letter itself is from Ramla, not from Damascus. The letter to Ḥalfon: **179**; possibly from the time of Nathan b. Abraham's stay in Fustat in December 1039; I have already discussed Aaron b. Ephraim b. Ṭarasūn above. **183a**, is a fragment of a letter to Abū'l-Barakāt b. Rawḥ; it seems that the letter contained details on the dispute; someone is compared to *a zāqēn mamrē* ('a rebellious elder', who disregards the decision of the Sanhedrin), perhaps referring to Solomon b. Judah; in line 14, one can read: *al-maḥlōqet* (the dispute); the writer notes that he visited 'the graves of the eternal fathers', that is, Hebron. Faraḥ b. Mu'ammal signs a letter of complaint (to Josiah Gaon), **44**, about Mubāraka who applied to a Muslim court; Zadok ha-Levi b. Levi, *av-bēt-dīn* of the Palestinian yeshiva, calls him in his letter, **210**: Peraḥia *ha-rōsh* (1029); he is a signatory to a deed from the year AM 1329, or AD 1018, in Fustat: TS 28.3. The letter to 'Amram b. Yefet: **188**. To Solomon b. Nathan: **194**, and see the letter of Solomon b. Nethanel: **215**. The deed in Nathan's court: **193**. The anonymous letter: **198**. Mevorakh b. 'Eli in the letter to Sahlān: **90**, line 16; **136**, lines 11–12; 'head of the communities': **188**, line 15. The receipt: Antonin 349 (Prof. Goitein was kind enough to send me a photograph of a copy of the deed made when he was in Leningrad); cf. Goitein, *Tarbiz*, 36(1966/7), 62, n. 16. In **196**, line 6, there is explicit mention of *aṣhār lahu min al-'irāqiyīn*, that is, relatives on his wife's side, from among the 'Babylonians', who helped Nathan b. Abraham; also in **192**, the letter to the Nagid of Qayrawān, Jacob b. 'Amram, relatives of the family are mentioned (line 6), Nathan b. Abraham's father-in-law and brothers-in-law (lines 48–49), who support him and approach the authorities on his behalf; cf. Mann, *Texts*, I, 326, n. 4, mentioning a marriage deed from the Bodleian collection, in which there is the signature of Mevorakh b. 'Eli b. Ezra (Zur'a) ha-Kohen. The letter of Hezekiah b. David: TS Loan 40. The 'Babylonians' in Ramla: **183**, line 21. The colophon, see the text (ENA 4012) in Gil, *Tarbiz*, 48 (1978/9), 69, and the translation *ibid.*, 73; cf. Mann, *Texts* I,

[880] The Karaites were unmistakable supporters of Nathan b. Abraham; this was especially true of the Tustari family (who probably represented a sect of their own called by this name among the Karaites). The Karaites took part *en masse* in that aforementioned reading of the *megillā* in Ramla. In the anonymous draft of an appeal to the caliph, which I have also mentioned, it was stated explicitly that they were supporters of Nathan. Solomon b. Judah also wrote explicitly of 'people of the other sect' who side with his rival; 'many of them assist him secretly, while pretending that they are with me'. And we have seen that some of those with whom Nathan carried on a correspondence were evidently Karaites. As to the Tustaris, to whom Solomon b. Judah would appeal for support for the Jewish population in Jerusalem and the yeshiva in its struggles, he hoped that they would stand by him on this occasion as well. From what he wrote to Ephraim b. Shemaria, it appears that he indeed expected Ḥesed al-Tustarī to back him. The fact that the Tustaris decided to support his rival disheartened him immensely, and he accuses Nathan of making overtures at 'the doors of the great'. From one of his letters, it emerges that someone was even attempting to bribe the people of the yeshiva with 200 dinars in order to get them to go over to his rival's camp, perhaps referring here to the Tustaris. In the drafts of the petition to the caliph, written by Solomon b. Judah's followers in *ca.* 1041, there is a clear reference to the Tustaris' support of Nathan. In the petition, they ask the caliph to make amends and to see to it that a person who does not belong to their religion should not be permitted to intervene in the dispute, and they specifically mention 'Faḍl b. Sahl al-Dustarī', who intervened in the dispute and opened the synagogue (in Fustat) for the followers of Nathan.[153]

[881] One can assume that the Jews in the entire disapora, and not only in Fustat, were involved in the dispute, and the rift probably split and divided many communities. We have some information on Qayrawān. According to Solomon b. Judah, the Maghribi Nagid, Jacob b. 'Amram, did his best to curb the followers of Nathan in Qayrawān; he was 'of some help.' In another of Solomon b. Judah's letters, it is again implied that the Nagid of the Maghrib supports him, and even sent a warning from the Maghrib to Nathan b. Abraham 'not to touch me'. This fact deserves special attention considering that we know of Nathan b. Abraham's prolonged stay in the Maghrib, and also that he had close friends there.

333–336, whose translation of the colophon should be corrected; the explanation for the story which belittles the exilarchic house written by Nathan, is sought by Mann in the tradition of the Palestinian yeshiva and its rivalry with the Karaite *nesīʾīm*, see *ibid.*, further thoughts on the possible aim of the story; also see on this matter: Gil, *ibid.*, 40f.

153 The episode of the reading of the *Megillā*: **183**. Mention of the Karaites: **196**; 'the other sect': **126**, lines 24–25. Solomon b. Judah on the Tustari: **128**, lines 15–20; **130**, lines 25ff. The bribery: **131**, b, lines 9–10. The Tustaris in the drafts: **197**, b, lines 11–12, 19, 23–25.

The two letters written from Fustat by Abraham b. David ibn Sughmār and Ghālib ha-Kohen b. Moses, to the Nagid of Qayrawān, indicate that they expected him to exert greater efforts on behalf of the old Gaon. We find there the information that Nathan b. Abraham's supporters claimed that the Nagid was on their side, the writer anticipating a very staunch denial of this claim. It also says that from the outset, Nathan b. Abraham left the Maghrib with two letters of recommendation from the Nagid to the wazīr in Fustat, in order to help him get closer to the Fatimid court. They also ask the Nagid to write to Fustat and to Palestine and state their support for the excommunication which the Gaon pronounced against Nathan b. Abraham. In addition, they sent to the Nagid letters written to him by Solomon b. Judah, in two copies, one by camel caravan and the other by sea.

One of Solomon b. Judah's major followers was Daniel b. Azariah. Most of the available information about him shall be discussed in the continuation, as he later became the Palestinian Gaon. As I have already mentioned, he wrote a number of letters some years after the dispute about his backing of Solomon b. Judah and the priestly brothers (which he regretted). This is also clearly implied in the above-mentioned letter to the Nagid written by Abraham b. David ibn Sughmār, in which he precedes his comments on the dispute with expressions of joy and enthusiasm on the arrival of Daniel b. Azariah in Fustat, which in fact have no connection with the affair of the dispute, but for all that, confirm the closeness between Daniel and Solomon b. Judah's supporters, the 'Palestinian' congregation in Fustat. This congregation, led by Ephraim b. Shemaria and his son-in-law Ghālib ha-Kohen b. Moses, was the major bastion behind the old Gaon, and the arrival of Daniel b. Azariah, the scion of the exilarchic family, certainly added both weight and prestige. On the other hand, there were some members of this congregation as well who went over to Nathan b. Abraham's side, such as Solomon he-ḥāvēr b. Meir *rōsh ha-seder*, who at first was loyal to Solomon b. Judah and afterwards moved over to the opposition.

Abraham b. David ibn Sughmār, whose letters I have discussed and about whom I have described whatever information we have at our disposal (see sec. 750), was undoubtedly one of the most active of the old Gaon's followers in Fustat. Solomon b. Judah insisted that the letter he was sending to Ephraim b. Shemaria should also be sent to the *māsōs* so that he could send them on to the Maghrib. There is no question then that the '*māsōs* [joy] of the yeshiva', Abraham b. David ibn Sughmār, who was a sort of intermediary between the Maghrib and the Palestinian yeshiva,

Here there is clear proof that the Tustaris were Karaites, cf. Stern, *REJ*, 128 (1969), 211; Gil, *ha-Tustarīm*, 59–63.

was active on behalf of the Gaon. In another fragment of a letter of Solomon b. Judah which has been preserved from the days of the dispute, the *māsōs* and his correspondence with him are mentioned, and he may have been referring to him when he writes there that 'his grandfather was one of the righteous of Israel', 'and they belong to the great of the city of Fās'. It seems that the antagonism between Abraham ibn Sughmār and Nathan began when the latter was staying in Fustat. In his letter from there, Nathan describes how Ibn Sughmār became implicated in an affair with 'a gentile prostitute', that is, a Muslim. He depicts the affair in his letter to the above-mentioned Abū Yūsuf Eleazar b. Samuel (Ismā'īl). There may have been a certain amount of exaggeration and slander in this description. From another letter, written (or copied) by Ghālib ha-Kohen b. Moses, it appears that the congregation sided with Ibn Sughmār, and decided that the Gaon (Solomon b. Judah) should be asked to cancel the excommunication on him (an excommunication declared by Nathan b. Abraham, as is implied from the above-mentioned letter). We have an additional document connected with this subject, which consists of two parts. The first is a fragment of a letter from the Jerusalem parnās 'Eli b. Ezekiel. It contains accusations against Nathan b. Abraham's camp for persuading the Karaites in Fustat to support him; those supporters vilify Ephraim b. Shemaria and the Karaite personalities who, it seems, stand behind Solomon b. Judah. Evidently this letter was written in Ramla, and it says that attached to it are letters from one of the personalities of Ramla, Ḥayyim he-ḥāvēr b. Solomon he-ḥāvēr, written to Abū Isḥaq Abraham al-Andalusī, whose identity is not clear to me at the moment, but who was certainly one of the leaders of the Maghribīs. Abraham b. David ibn Sughmār, who can be recognised by his handwriting, affixed another leaf with a copy of a letter, also from Palestine, to 'Eli b. Ezekiel's letter. The anonymous writer, probably one of the loyal supporters of the Jerusalem Gaon and perhaps one of the priestly brothers (Joseph and Elijah, sons of Solomon Gaon), turns to one of Fustat's notables and asks him to use his influence with the caliph to obtain an official order in favour of Solomon b. Judah (he calls him: Abū Da'ūd Sulaymān b. Judah al-Fāsī). The spirit of the letter is similar to what we find in letters to the caliph and also in the memorandum on the prerogatives of the head of the yeshiva. Here too, the role played by Abraham b. David b. Sughmār in the dispute is stressed, as well as that of the mediator with the authorities, Abū'l-Qasam ('Alī ibn 'Abd al-'Azīz), Ibn al-Ukhuwwa.

In Palestine itself, there were certainly many followers loyal to the old Gaon, despite the fact that the scales were at first inclined to come down in favour of his rival. Their names have not been preserved, with the exception of a man whose Arabic name was Rawḥ. Nathan b. Abraham mentions him in his letter to the anonymous 'friend of the yeshiva': 'why should Rawḥ and his relatives force us to have a man appointed over us, whom we do not want'. This Rawḥ was apparently one of the wealthy men of Ramla. Solomon b. Judah mentions him in connection with the transfer of money in money orders from Fustat to Jerusalem, but we cannot identify him more precisely. Perhaps, he is *sar menūḥā*, whom the Gaon praises in a letter written after the dispute, alluding perhaps to the Arabic word Rawḥ, which corresponds to the Hebrew *menūḥā*, rest, relaxation.[154]

[882] As to appeals to the authorities, this was a central and obvious fact in the course of the dispute. At first, the authorities in Palestine favoured the old Gaon and supported him against the young rival who had appeared on the scene. We have already witnessed Abraham, son of the Gaon, hastening to Damascus when the dispute broke out, whence he brought a *tawqīʿ* (order), probably from the Fatimid army commander in al-Shām, which confirmed the status of Solomon b. Judah. Nathan b. Abraham and

[154] 'Some help': **128**; Hirschberg, *History*, I, 214, mistakenly assumed that the reference was to some trouble experienced by the Jews in the Maghrib. The warning: **131**, a, line 19; b, line 2. The complaint that the Nagid supported Nathan, and what they asked of him: **191**, lines 33ff; **192**, lines 19ff; the Gaon's letters to the Nagid, *ibid.*, lines 41ff. See on Jacob b. 'Amram: Mann, *JQR*, NS 9(1918/9), 162f; *idem, Jews*, I, 144; see TS Loan 40, Part II, the opening of a letter to him from the exilarch Hezekiah b. David, cf. Goitein, *Mediterranean Society*, II, 24f; 525, nn. 6–10. The connection between Abraham b. David ibn Sughmār and the Nagid is also shown in Mosseri II 150 (formerly L 151), in the handwriting of Ibn Sughmār (see above, in the note to section 750). The additional document: **192a**; the letters to the caliph: **196**, **197**; the memorandum on the head of the yeshiva: **311**. Another interesting item: on the reverse side of these attached letters, **192a**, Abraham b. David ibn Sughmār affixed a fragment from the *Letter* of Sherira Gaon (written by the Gaon some sixty years earlier). This fragment is a parallel to what is printed in the Lewin edition, p. 109, line 13, to p. 114, line 12, and on the whole, the version resembles what Lewin calls 'the French version'. It seems that the copyist was especially interested in that passage of Sherira Gaon's *Letter*, because it describes the disputes and divisions that occurred in the Pumbedita yeshiva, when there were two geonim, and how Rav Joseph withdrew and was satisfied with the rank of *av-bēt-dīn*. Also further (what was preserved): the split between Rav Menaḥem and Rav Matityahu. See ENA 1490, f. 7*v*; in comparison with the edited version of Sherira Gaon's *Letter*, there are some omissions. An interesting reading (Lewin, p. 110, line 3: line 6 in the MS): *mi-seṭar 'arīshā*, i.e., one has to leave place (for the prophet Elijah) on the right side of the sitting place. Mann, who did not know the letters **191** and **192** in their entirety, was undecided about the identity of the Nagid, to whom the fragments he knew were written, and assumed at first that the reference was to Joseph b. Samuel, the Spanish Nagid; see his *Jews*, II, 352; and also in *Texts*, I, 328, he could not identify him. The joy at the coming of Daniel b. Azariah to Fustat, see the beginning of **191**. Solomon b. Judah on the *māsōs*: **126**, line 27; the other fragment: **129**, lines 8, 27–28; Mann, *Jews*, I, 132f, was mistaken in thinking that the fragment dealt with a dispute in Fustat, for in the margin it says there: 'it was said indeed that Solomon b. Meir made peace with the band of plotters', referring to Solomon he-ḥāvēr b. Meir *rōsh ha-seder*, whose support for Solomon b. Judah I have mentioned above; and he seems to have changed his mind. Nathan on Abraham b. David ibn Sughmār: **176**. The Fustat congregation on Ibn Sughmār's side: **177**. Rawḥ and his relatives: **187**, lines 19–20. The transfer of money: **116**, line 13. *Sar menūḥā*: **132**, line 14; Mann, *Jews*, I, 146, n. 1, assumed that he was David ha-Levi b. Isaac.

his faction then started to put pressure on the local authorities not to stand by Solomon b. Judah. Nathan describes this situation in a letter to the anonymous 'friend of the yeshiva'. The pressure consisted mainly of the threat (accompanied by an oath in the name of *mawlānā*, that is, the life of the caliph) that they would approach the *mishnē*, that is, the wazīr. Indeed, this pressure was effective and Nathan's followers took control of Jewish communal life in Ramla unhindered. The wazīr at the time of the dispute was Abū'l-Qā'im 'Alī b. Aḥmad al-Jarjarā'ī, who became wazīr in AH 418, that is AD 1027, and who remained in this post seventeen years, until his death on 7 Ramaḍān AH 436, that is 28 March AD 1045.

It seems that considerable weight was added to Nathan b. Abraham's camp by the support of the Tustaris, which was lent special substance as a result of the appointment of Ḥesed al-Tustarī, in the very midst of the dispute, to the position of *kātib al-amīr*, that is, the official in charge of the army on behalf of the Fatimid rulers. We know this from a fragment of a letter written by Nathan b. Abraham himself, in which this information is preserved. The term *al-amīr* is probably a shorter version of *amīr al-juyūsh*, the title of Anūshtakīn al-Dizbirī, commander of the Fatimid army. Nathan b. Abraham adds there that Ḥesed al-Tustarī 'looks after us and listens to what we tell him'. The addressee, whose identity we do not know, is asked to write Ḥesed al-Tustarī a letter of thanks, in which he is to be congratulated on his appointment.

The authorities' intervention is reflected also in letters written by supporters of Solomon b. Judah to the Nagid of Qayrawān, Jacob b. 'Amram, in the summer of 1039. He is asked to apply to the authorities. Something which it seems is not mentioned at all in the Arab chronicles, is implied in these letters; namely the close contact between the local Zīrid rulers in the Maghrib and the central Fatimid rule in Egypt, and the influence exercised by the ruler of Qayrawān on the central authority. From the first, or so the writers of the letter claim, Nathan b. Abraham wanted to get the assistance of the authorities and for this purpose used the two letters of recommendation that he received from the Nagid of Qayrawān to 'the elder Ibn al-Ukhuwwa', asking him to intervene on his behalf with the caliph. Now they ask the Nagid to make his amends and obtain a letter from *sayyidnā amīr al-umarā'* (our Lord the commander of the commanders) *sharaf al-dawla* and *tāj al-milla* (the glory of the kingdom and the crown of the religion), who is Mu'izz b. Bādīs, ruler of Qayrawān, to the (Fatimid) wazīr, *ṣafī amīr al-mu'minīn wa-khāliṣathu* (which is something like: 'the true and chosen friend of the caliph'), and to Abū'l-Qāsim (or al-Qasam) 'Alī ibn 'Abd al-'Azīz al-Ukhuwwa (who is the aforementioned Ibn al-Ukhuwwa) that they should support Solomon b. Judah. We do not know any further details concerning this Ibn al-Ukhuwwa, but he seems to have been a sort of representative of the ruler of Qayrawān at the Fatimid court.

The importance of the role played by the authorities' intervention in the dispute can also be seen in the petitions to the rulers, written by the supporters of Solomon b. Judah in Fustat; for instance, the draft of a petition to the caliph evidently written by Ephraim b. Shemaria. We find here a description of the dispute brought about by 'a man who came from the Maghrib', noting the fact that the synagogue of the 'Palestinians' was closed as a result of the dispute because the relatives and intimate friends of Nathan had exerted their considerable influence. Finally, the caliph is asked to send an order to one of his subordinates to open the synagogue. In this draft, there is also a request relating to al-Dizbirī (Muntakhab al-Dawla, 'the excellent of the kingdom'); we do not know the nature of this request though we can assume that it touched on the dispute, that is, the affairs of the Palestinian yeshiva. From the draft, we also learn of another interesting detail, namely that the caliph had already entered into the thick of the dispute and appointed a mediator to try to bring about a reconciliation of the two sides. This was David b. Isaac, one of the notables of Fustat, who was close to the Fatimid rulers, and on whom I have enlarged above. Here, David b. Isaac is accused of actually doing nothing to resolve the quarrel. We encounter David b. Isaac again in the drafts written by one of Solomon b. Judah's supporters, as well as in part of the final outcome of these drafts – a petition to the caliph. The time of the drafts and the petition is towards the end of 1041. Here, too, it is stated that David b. Isaac did nothing to put an end to the dispute and that he failed to fulfil his mission. In the final version, we first find a general summary of the dispute, where it clearly states that it is a division over leadership, between two authorities (*riyāsatayn*); while in the continuation there is also the matter of the synagogue in Fustat and its closure. Apparently, close to the date of the writing of the letter (perhaps during the holidays in Tishri, that is, the autumn of 1041) the people of Nathan b. Abraham's faction suceeded in opening the synagogue with the help of the regime's soldiers (*al-rajjāla*); they also made use of the foundations (heqdēsh) in Fustat as they saw fit. We gather further details from the drafts, which were omitted from the final text because they were evidently thought to be too sensitive. In the drafts, it says that the caliph should no longer suffer the domination of one faction over another. It is also stated that the person behind the forceful takeover of the synagogue was Faḍl (Ḥesed) b. Sahl al-Tustarī, with the help of the *kātib al-ṣināʿa*', the chief official of the Nile harbour in Fustat, a certain Abū'l-Mand. These people used their high rank and large sums of money in order to obtain what they wanted. In the final draft, the *amīr* Muntakhab al-Dawla, that is al-Dizbirī, is also mentioned, and the caliph is requested to order him to treat both factions with impartiality with regard to the synagogues and that neither faction should dominate the other and that no one should enforce religious matters by sending armed units to the synagogues on the sabbath and holidays.[155]

[883] Apparently, it was the intervention of the authorities which finally put an end to the dispute. Solomon b. Judah explicitly says as much in a letter written immediately after a reconciliation was arrived at and at which he expresses his pleasure. Peace, he writes, which really meant the capitulation of Nathan b. Abraham, was obtained through the efforts of the governor of Jerusalem; by what God has put 'in the heart of the governor of the Holy City' and thanks to the other grandees of the city ('the big ones of the city'), by order of the governor of jund Filasṭīn ('and over everyone the great ruler in Ramla'); and on the basis of the order issued to the latter by the caliph and the wazīr ('the great king', 'the *mishnē*'). The letter also mentions several figures who also evidently put pressure on the rulers in this matter, such as 'the splendid prince, *sar menūḥā*, whom I have already tried to identify with that anonymous Rawḥ who supported the Gaon; Mawhūb b. Yefet; the father of Mawhūb (evidently) Yefet 'head of the congregation'; and Abraham, who is apparently Abraham b. Mevassēr.

The nature of the peace itself becomes clear to us from a very special document in the form of a memorandum written in Jerusalem. The main points of the agreement were as follows: (1) Nathan b. Abraham would forego the titles he bestowed on himself and others; in other words, he would no longer be called Gaon and his appointment of judges and ḥavērīm and other titles which he conferred during the dispute would be invalid. (2) He would not grant any titles in the future (literally: he would not pray over anyone) unless it was with the agreement of the four: the Gaon, Tobiah 'the third' b. Daniel, Joseph and Elijah sons of Solomon ha-Kohen Gaon ('the fourth' and 'the fifth'). On the other hand, the

[155] The *tawqī'*: **182**, at the beginning. The letter to 'the friend of the yeshiva': **187**, lines 16ff; Mann, *Jews*, II, 171, n. 1, understood *mawlānā* (our master) in whose name they take the oath – as God, but it is clear that they mean the caliph, cf. Goitein's note in the Preface to the aforementioned book by Mann. Al-Jarjarā'ī: Ibn al-Ṣayrafī, 37f; Ibn al-Qalānisī, 84; Ibn Khallikān, III, 408; cf. the article al-Djardjarā'ī (by D. Sourdel) in *EI*². The matter of Ḥesed al-Tustarī: TS AS 157.231, 232. Apparently, it is impossible to be certain whether the reference is still to al-Dizbirī, since at this time, someone else may have held the position of *amīr al-juyūsh*; but in the drafts of the petition addressed to the caliph, they refer to an order to be given by the caliph to Muntakhab al-Dawla al-Dizbirī. The Nagid of Qayrawān: **191**, lines 33–35; 53; **192**, lines 24–31, 40, see also in the notes to these letters; Mu'izz b. Bādīs, head of the Banū Ṣinhāja, who rose to prominence in the days of al-Ḥākim, and received from him the title *sharaf al-dawla*, see Ibn al-Athīr, *Kāmil*, IX, 258; cf. Idris, *La Berbérie*, I, 149; Cohen, *AJSR*, 1(1976), 16f; 32, nn. 118, 119; Goitein, *Letters*, 309, n. 16. The first draft: **196**; the seven drafts and the petition: **197**, and see the notes to these documents.

appointments made by Solomon b. Judah would remain in force. Nathan b. Abraham promises to support actions against those who take on titles or appointments without the agreement of the five (that is, himself and the aforementioned four), which form the only authoritative body to confirm appointments, and no other person is to be appended to it. (3) The prerogative of sitting in judgment and of supervising the foundations (*heqdēshīm*) and the ritual slaughter in Ramla will rest with Joseph ha-Kohen 'the fourth'. If another of the yeshiva's personalities happens to be in Ramla, he will only be able to receive the right to make decisions with Solomon b. Judah's agreement. (4) If Nathan is moved to another position in the yeshiva – a hint that after Solomon b. Judah's death, he will become the Gaon – he will not be able to change the accepted order of advance in the yeshiva; that is, he would not be able to appoint additional people to the ranks of *av-bēt-dīn*, 'the third', etc. (5) Nathan can sit in judgment in Ramla only if the people to be judged have not been formerly judged by Joseph ha-Kohen; in other words, though he is *av-bēt-dīn* of the yeshiva, cases which Joseph ha-Kohen had already begun to deal with would not be passed on to him. It is stressed there that this clause only applies to him, that is to say that anyone appointed by the Gaon would have the right to sit on such court cases. The date of the agreement is Hosha'na rabbā AM 4803, that is 8 October AD 1042 (a Friday). The agreement was then signed on the seventh day of the holiday, perhaps during the mass congregation on the Mount of Olives. Thus the dispute which had lasted for four whole years came to an end. The signatories to the agreement were Solomon b. Judah, who naturally signed 'head of yeshiva Ge'ōn Ya'aqōv; Nathan, who signed: '*av-bēt-dīn* of all Israel'; Tobiah 'the third' b. Daniel; Joseph 'the fourth' and Elijah 'the fifth', sons of Solomon Gaon; and apart from these, Hezekiah the *nāsī* b. Solomon (the Karaite *nāsī*) and Mevorakh b. 'Allūn b. Moses, about whom we have no further information. A few days later, on Marḥeshwan 1354 Sel., October–November AD 1042, Solomon b. Judah writes to Ephraim b. Shemaria, and after summing up the motives which led to the dispute, he points out that there were still some who would not agree to the peace, for selfish reasons ('who only quarelled for their own needs'). It emerges that he had written a letter on the subject of the reconciliation to the Fustat congregation before that, but as the letter was addressed to Ephraim b. Shemaria, the congregation would not accept it and he was obliged to write another letter, which was explicitly addressed to the 'Palestinian' congregation. He also considered having Nathan sign the letter, with his title 'Nathan *av-bēt-dīn* of all Israel' and even sent it to Ramla for this purpose, but Nathan had left for Damascus in the meantime.[156]

[156] Solomon b. Judah's letter: **132**. The Jerusalem agreement: **199**. There will be a separate

[884] It is clear that the dispute ended in Nathan b. Abraham's downfall. Although he retained his status as *av-bēt-dīn*, the second rank in the yeshiva, all his actions and decisions made during the dispute were totally invalidated, and the position of the priestly brothers, Joseph and Elijah, was strengthened by their becoming 'the fourth' and 'the fifth' in the yeshiva. The name of Abraham 'the fourth' b. Samuel b. Hosha'na is missing, which may be due to the fact that he did not remain loyal to the winning side, or that he may have been ill or had even died around the time of the conclusion of the dispute. Tobiah b. Daniel, the son of Shemaiah Gaon's sister, continued, as formerly, as 'third' in the yeshiva. He died a short time afterward, evidence of which can be seen in drafts of letters of condolence written in Fustat by Ephraim b. Shemaria to Nathan b. Abraham and to Elijah ha-Kohen b. Solomon, on 21 February 1043. In the letter of condolence addressed to Nathan b. Abraham, Ephraim b. Shemaria added something about a court document (*shimmūsh*) which was validated in Jerusalem, an indication that Nathan b. Abraham was once again engaged in legal affairs. After the death of Tobiah b. Daniel, the priestly brothers Joseph and Elijah became 'third' and 'fourth' in the yeshiva, as we have seen. Indeed, we have the signature of Elijah ha-Kohen as 'the fourth of the *ḥavūrā,* son of a Gaon, of righteous memory' on a deed from the year 1045. From this, we can also conclude that in 1045, Nathan b. Abraham was still alive and active as *av-bēt-dīn* in the yeshiva. It appears that he died some time shortly afterward, for in a letter written by Abraham son of the Gaon (when Solomon b. Judah was still alive) to Sahlān b. Abraham, about what had happened during the month of Tishri in the Jerusalem yeshiva, he mentions the *av-bēt-dīn* and his brother 'the third'. These could only have been the priesty brothers, Joseph and Elijah, the one having become *av-bēt-dīn* and the other 'the third', which would only have become possible after the passing of Nathan b. Abraham, which occurred sometime between 1045 and 1051.

discussion on the Karaite nesī'īm; at any rate, the signature of the Karaite Nāsī is something of a puzzle, although it is clear that in the eyes of the Fatimid rulers the head of the Jerusalem yeshiva was the representative of all the Jews, including the Karaites. Nathan also wrote on the peace: **200**, lines 7–8; the letter was intended evidently for Fustat, and he writes of his intention to visit there, 'to enjoy seeing you and renew the covenant of your love'; Isaiah Nufūsī, who is mentioned there, is perhaps the father of Joseph b. al-Nufūsī, a Karaite of Fustat, mentioned in ULC Or 1080 J 167 in the upper margin, line 2; see Udovitch, in: *Individualism*, etc., 77 (a letter from Mūsā b. Abī'l-Ḥayy Khalīla to Nehorai b. Nissim). That is, it is possible that Nathan continued to maintain friendly relations with the Karaites. The additional letter of Solomon b. Judah: **133**; see also **134**, with remaining details on the dispute after it ended; and his letters to Sahlān b. Abraham, also written about the same time: **136**, **137**. To the letters Solomon b. Judah wrote after the dispute one should also add **137a**, which is perhaps a fragment of a letter to the 'Palestinian' congregation in Fustat. All he hoped for was 'Israel's peace', he writes there of himself; further on, he speaks of *ha'ataqat avōt* and it is difficult to know whether

Nathan b. Abraham is credited with an Arabic commentary on the Mishnā, which is included (all or partly) in a manuscript preserved in Yemen, copied by Yaḥyā and Joseph b. David (the grandson of the former) Qāfiḥ, and which is now in printed form. It mainly deals with the meaning of words. Formularies of letters in Nathan's handwriting have been preserved in the Geniza – letters intended to be sent on behalf of the yeshiva and which he seems to have prepared for his own use during his reign as head of the yeshiva. An elegy in his handwriting has also been preserved. Below we shall encounter his only son, Abraham, who was also involved in the enormous dispute between Abiathar ha-Kohen and David b. Daniel.[157]

Daniel b. Azariah

[885] The successor to Solomon b. Judah was Daniel b. Azariah, who was a descendant of the Babylonian exilarch. After Mar Zūṭrā in the sixth century, and Jehoshaphat and Ṣemaḥ, the nesī'īm and heads of the yeshiva in the ninth century, he was the fourth to unite in his person the two supreme ranks, that of *nāsī* and Gaon. He was an offspring of Zakkai, the father of David, the Babylonian exilarch during the first half of the

he meant by this the tradition of the forefathers, or perhaps he was referring to the *avōt bēt-dīn*, that is the inclination (that had existed) to oust Nathan b. Abraham from his post.

157 Tobiah b. Daniel was not a cousin of the priestly brothers, Joseph and Elijah, as Mann assumed, basing his assumption on **147**, b (Solomon b. Judah's letter), where the 'third' is mentioned; see his *Texts*, I, 326; and following him also Gil, *Perāqīm* (1979), 65, n. 38; the 'third' mentioned there is Elijah ha-Kohen, and thus the relationship did not exist. Letters of condolence: **333** (Gil, *Perāqīm, ibid.*: 'in the handwriting of Yefet b. David' which should be emended); Mann, *Jews*, I, 193f, erred in his interpretation of these letters; see the introduction and notes of **333**; the matter of the *shimmūsh* there, lines 19ff; Ephraim calls himself (*ibid.*, line 9) Nathan's pupil; Nathan is 'the voluntary teacher of whoever he meets' (line 6). **341** is a note in Sahlān b. Abraham's handwriting, in which he asks Aaron the cantor b. Ephraim to tend to Aaron he-ḥaver b. Tobiah, 'the third, of blessed memory', hence we understand that his son, Aaron, went to Egypt sometime after the death of his father; and he was also mentioned by Manasseh b. Joshua in his letters from Tyre to Shemaiah he-ḥāvēr b. Joshua in Jerusalem (a relative of Tobiah 'the third', from the family of Shemaiah Gaon); see the Hebrew Index. Elijah ha-Kohen 'the fourth': **564**, line 22. The letter of Abraham son of the Gaon: **141**. The Mishnā Commentary: Supplement to the Mishnā in the edition *el ha-meqōrōt*, Jerusalem 1954/5; see Assaf, *Teqūfat ha-ge'ōnīm*, 294ff (printed before that in *Kiryat Sefer*, 10, 1932/4); in the footsteps of Mann, who was mistaken about the descendants of Nathan b. Abraham, and invented a grandson named Nathan b. Abraham, Assaf placed the Commentary at the end of the eleventh century, but we have seen that Nathan b. Abraham died in about the middle of the century. It is therefore evident that it is not likely that his commentary would have included the sayings of a number of geonim and scholars to be found in the aforementioned manuscript and listed by Assaf in his article. It emerges, then, that only a part (and perhaps a small part) of the Commentary is, in fact, the work of Nathan b. Abraham, and the matter requires further study. The formularies of the letters, ENA 223, can be recognised as being in his handwriting, and here and there they have supra-linear vocalisation, with which he would amuse himself. The elegy: ENA 2924, f. 9.

tenth century, from the branch of the son of Zakkai, Josiah (Ḥasan), brother of David, as can be seen from their lineage tree in sec. 774.

As we have seen, Daniel's grandfather, Solomon b. Josiah, was exilarch, but after him, this branch of the family was excluded from the exilarchate and Hezekiah, the grandson of David b. Zakkai, became exilarch. Nevertheless, Daniel's father, Azariah, still called himself 'the exilarch of all Israel'. Apparently, the family was proud of its descent from Bustanai, the exilarch at the time of the Muslim conquest, despite the aspersions against him for having had children by a Persian captive (the fact that she was the Persian king's daughter meant little to the Jews of that time). Daniel's lineage, however, continued to Barādai b. Bustanai, who according to the geonic responsa was the son of Bustanai by his Jewish wife. In a *qaṣīda* written in his honour by a certain 'Eli ha-Kohen, Daniel is called *shevīv Bustānī*, ('a spark from Bustanai'). His *'alāma* was *yeshū'ā* (deliverance; like that of Saadia Gaon).

Daniel b. Azariah's brother Zakkai was involved in Daniel's affairs to a certain extent. During the latter's period as Gaon, he stayed in Fustat, where he quarrelled with the local ḥāvēr, 'Eli b. 'Amram. In one of Daniel's letters, he expresses his satisfaction over the fact that the quarrel has ended. One feels that he is very critical of his brother, who had evidently tried to organise a sort of separate authority within Fustat and who enjoyed the income from ritual slaughter ('he made himself a market') and set up his own faction. Daniel stood aloof from all this and points out that although most people know that he is not involved in this matter, it creates a great deal of slanderous gossip. At the same time, he warns 'Eli against any abuse of his brother, 'for he is my brother and the son of my father and mother'. In the same letter, Daniel mentions that his brother has crossed the Euphrates (apparently not long before), that is, he seems to have arrived in Fustat from Iraq after Daniel became Gaon.

Daniel's attitude to his brother is also revealed in a letter he wrote to the *māsōs*, who is evidently Abraham b. David ibn Sughmār. In this letter, he thanks the *māsōs* for caring for someone very close to him during the latter's illness, of whom he says 'for he is my brother and flesh and blood'; obviously speaking of his brother Zakkai. Apparently, after his arrival in Egypt, Zakkai was in the habit of travelling from Fustat, perhaps to Palestine, as one gathers from a letter of Daniel b. Azariah and also from a letter of Israel b. Sahlūn from Jerusalem, written on 29 November 1061, in which he mentions the return of 'Zakkai the *nāsī* and his son' to Fustat.[158]

[886] Daniel b. Azariah evidently had four sons. The youngest, David,

[158] See the family tree of the offspring of Zakkai, above on p. 545. In my collection, there are some sixty letters and fragments of letters and court documents, etc. written by Daniel b. Azariah and his scribe, or written to Daniel. For earlier surveys of information on him,

was born in 1058, four years before the death of his father. In some of the letters to him, the writers mention his three sons and send them greetings. In the *qaṣīda* mentioned above, written on 22 March 1057, it appears that only two of his sons are mentioned, Samuel and Jehoshaphat. Samuel's name is also found in a deed drawn up on 25 Tishri AM 1386, 19 October AD 1074, in Damascus. The court of 'Samuel the *nāsī* the third of the ḥavūrā son of R. Daniel *nāsī* and Gaon, of blessed memory' is mentioned

see Mann, *Jews*, I, 182–185, and see his Geniza sources pertaining to Daniel, *ibid.*, II, 218–221; 457–461; Goitein, *Shalem*, 2 (1975/6), 41ff, edited in full or partly, 25 additional documents, and discussed the information they contained; he ascribed **356** to Daniel's brother Zakkai, which was written by Daniel, a matter on which I disagree with him; cf. *ha-Yishuv*, 132ff, where he added another six documents. See Dropsie 462, which contains the lineage of Zakkai, Daniel's brother, written by Abraham ha-Levi b. Tamīm al-Raḥbī (evidently at the beginning of the twelfth century), cf. Mann, *Poznanski Jubilee Volume*, 19f; Mann read in the aforementioned list: b. Dādoy, and commented there, n. 9, that it should be – Barādoy; but this is in fact written this way in the MS. One should note that it emerges from the list that Barādoy (the correct spelling should be 'Barādai') had a son named Ḥasdai, whereas according to the responsum of the Gaon, Barādai and Ḥasdai were brothers, sons of Bustanai from his Jewish wife. (The nesī'īm of the Karaites, whom I shall discuss below, claimed descent from Ḥasdai, unlike Daniel's family, who claimed descent from Barādai, as mentioned above.) See details on the geonic responsa concerning Bustanai in: Gil, *Tarbiz*, 48 (1978/9), 36f, and the table *ibid.*, 44. The family tree in TS 8 K 22, f. 5, edited by Mann, *Jews*, II, 357, is not credible, as Daniel's grandfather is called there Joseph, while we know for certain that his name was Solomon, see **191**, lines 15–17, where he is mentioned with this lineage; see also Goode, *JQR*, NS 31(1940/1), 163f. See the *qaṣīda* BM Or 5557 K, f. 8, edited by Fleischer, *Shalem*, 1(1973/4), 70, line 162; in the Hebrew version of the present book there are a few completions to this edition, see vol. I, 584, and in the note. One verse apparently praises Daniel for having restored the Damascus community to the *rāshūt* (authority) of the Jerusalem yeshiva. TS Box K 16, f. 36 is written in the same handwriting as that of the aforementioned *qaṣīda*, and it is interesting that there is an anti-Babylonian verse there. We have no further information on Zakkai, Daniel's brother. Something of a myth was created around him – that he had settled in Mosul. Actually we have no proof of this; this grew out of what Mann said as an assumption, relying mainly on a Geniza fragment with the opening of a letter, 'from Zakkai b. Azariah Nāsī of the diaspora of all Israel' to the elders of Damascus. While there is some basis to believe that the writer is the brother of Daniel b. Azariah and belongs to the branch of Josiah b. Zakkai, one must bear in mind that the nesī'īm of Mosul are only mentioned at the end of the twelfth century (1174). Thus, what I have written in the Hebrew version of the present book, has to be rectified. See also Assaf, *Teqūfat ha-ge'ōnīm*, 35. Goode, *JQR*, 31(1940/1), 166, circumvented this problem, making Samuel of Mosul (1174–1195) a nephew of Daniel b. Ḥasdai, that is, of the branch of David b. Zakkai, and ignoring what Mann writes in the *Poznanski Jubilee Volume*, 23, on the basis of the lineage lists, that he was the descendant of the other branch, that of Josiah b. Zakkai. Bodl MS Heb e 101, f. 18 is a fragment of a letter 'from Zakkai b. Azariah, *nāsī* of the diaspora of all Israel, to all the mighty elders, our friends, in the city of Damascus'; Mann assumed (*Jews*, I, 175f; II, 208) that it is from the second half of the twelfth century; but *ibid.*, MS, he corrected this, noting that it was probably written by Zakkai, the brother of Daniel. Daniel on his brother: **356**, a, lines 5ff; b, lines 11ff. The letter to the *māsōs*: **378**. TS NS 338.94, a small fragment, written by Daniel b. Azariah, also contains thanks to someone who treated his brother (*mawlā'ī al-nāsī*) well. In the continuation he says as usual: 'since his honour is my honour and his rank is my rank'. The letter of Israel b Sahlūn: **479**, b, line 17.

there. Possibly Daniel's third son died before 1057, when the *qaṣīda* was written. As to David, he was born a year later. Daniel's son-in-law (or perhaps his brother-in-law? – *ṣihr*) Abū'l-Sarī (or: Abū'l-Surrī) Barhūn (Abraham) is also mentioned, but we have no details about him, except for the fact that after Daniel's death, he is to be found in Damascus.

Daniel hailed from Baghdad. This is clearly stated in the Scroll of Abiathar: 'He came up above them ['above' Joseph and Elijah, sons of Solomon ha-Kohen Gaon] from Babylonia'. A letter written by Daniel from al-Mahdiyya to Sahlān b. Abraham, on Tuesday 11 Tishri AM 4799, 12 September AD 1038, has been preserved. One can discern from the letter that there was an earlier correspondence between the two and that Daniel has been writing to him since they parted. From this we understand that before his arrival in the Maghrib, in the autumn of 1038, Daniel had stayed in Fustat. He notes in his letter, the marriage of Sahlān, which we know took place on 9 September 1037. Hence we may assume that his earlier arrival in Fustat probably occurred around 1036. In this letter, Daniel expresses his sorrow over the troubles which befell the Fustat community, noting however with satisfaction that things had now changed for the better, thanks to Abū Naṣr, that is Ḥesed al-Tustarī. Naturally, he is referring to the 'Babylonian' congregation in Fustat, where there seems to have been some tension related to the dispute which had begun to develop at that time between the Palestinian yeshiva and Nathan b. Abraham.

From al-Mahdiyya, Daniel returned to Fustat. We find him there in the summer of 1039, when Abraham b. David ibn Sughmār begins his letter to the Nagid of Qayrawān with enthusiastic comments on Daniel's personality and his activities in Fustat. His arrival there has produced a real change in the life of the community. He has restored the congregation, issued regulations concerning family matters (relations with female slaves), forbidden the participation in sensual parties with musicians. This may have been where the relationship between Daniel and the 'Palestinian' congregation first began, and as a result, his support for Solomon b. Judah (as evidently shown by most of this congregation), while the 'Babylonians' were then in favour of Nathan b. Abraham, which created a certain distance between Daniel and the latter congregation. Daniel remained in Fustat until after 1045, that is at least for six to seven years. This we learn from the letter written by 'Eli ha-Mumḥē – the son of Abraham 'the fourth', the grandson of Samuel 'the third' b. Hosha'na – to Ephraim b. Shemaria, in which he asks for news of 'Daniel al-Nāsī', and 'Eli sends regards on behalf of 'the *av* and his brother', that is Joseph ha-Kohen and his brother Elijah. As we have seen, Joseph ha-Kohen became *av-bēt-dīn* some time after 1045, upon the death of Nathan b. Abraham.[159]

[887] At this point, we are dealing with the period prior to Daniel b. Azariah's becoming Gaon. Apart from his communal activities, we now find him engaged in trade. A letter concerning his commercial ventures has been preserved, evidently written from Damascus to someone in Fustat. He speaks there in detail about various merchandise which he purchased and the payment of rather large sums, generally tens of dinars, to different people. He also deals in silk. His business connections are centred in Egypt. Tinnīs, the port in the Delta, and Fustat, are mentioned there. Despite the fact that his commercial ventures are not on a small scale, he complains of his straitened circumstances. Apparently, at the same time he wrote to a member of his family (at any rate, someone from the exilarchic family), deploring the limited means with which he and his large household must contend. In a fragment of another letter, he speaks of a deal of 200 dinars executed by a certain Abū'l-'Alā al-Mubārak b. Isḥaq, and Daniel asks the addressee to pay him 50 dinars for a *suftaja* (money order), which was evidently his own share of the partnership with this man. Another letter which he wrote from Tyre contains details of prices there and discusses textiles, oil, timber, and indigo. The addressee is a Palestinian staying in Fustat, who is about to return to his family in Palestine. Daniel encourages him on his objective and promises that he too will come to Ramla to enjoy himself in his company. The two people closest to Daniel b. Azariah were Abū Sa'd Josiah ha-Kohen b. Azariah,

[159] The three sons of Daniel: **386**, line 3; **397**, line 5; **400**, a, line 8; cf. Mann, *Jews*, I, 175, 185; II, 219–221. The *qaṣīda*: BM Or 5557 K, f. 8, lines 228–234; Cohen, *Self-Government*, 185, n. 16, with a correction of the date in the Damascene deed there: Bodl MS Heb d 75, f.11; see in Mann, *ibid.*, II, 221 (who read there 1396 instead of 1386). Mann, *Jews*, II, 221, speaks about Daniel's third son, who was allegedly called Josiah, but in the MS *ibid.*, I, 185, he emended and wrote: Azariah; but what he wrote there is based on the incorrect reading of **181**, which speaks of Tobiah b. Daniel, 'the son of the Gaon's sister', whereas Mann followed Schwab, *REJ*, 64 (1912), 120 (1934) who read *Ahwath* instead of *aḥōt* (sister), hence the incorrect interpretation. Abū'l-Sarī: see the Hebrew Index; David in Damascus: **500**, margin right. From Babylonia: **559**, b, line 9. The letter to Sahlān: **344**, see the notes there; Goitein, *Shalem*, 2 (1975/6), 47 (= *ha-Yishuv*, 137), assumed that the exilarch mentioned there was Zakkai, Daniel's brother. Ibn Sughmār: **191**, lines 13ff. 'Eli ha-mumḥē: **231**. Goitein, *Shalem*, 2 (1975/6), 55f (= *ha-Yishuv*, 143), assumed that in **565** there was evidence that Daniel settled in Palestine in 1046; but the letter speaks of someone from an important family in a distant country (Spain?) who came to Jerusalem and died there after some time; Daniel b. Azariah would not have been written about in this manner. Mann, *Jews*, II, 360, ascribes TS 16.128 to Daniel b. Azariah, which is a letter of recommendation, evidently from a Babylonian personality, for someone travelling to Palestine, dated 1031; probably because of the *'alāma – yeshū'ā*. For the same reason, he even suggested correcting the date there in order to place this document in the time when Daniel was still in Iraq; but the handwriting is not Daniel's, contrary to what Mann claims, and this was already realised by Goitein in *Shalem*, 2 (1975/6), 43 (= *ha-Yishuv*, 133).

the son of Daniel's sister, and Abraham ha-Kohen b. Isaac ibn Furāt. Josiah ha-Kohen was the son of the head of the Sura yeshiva; his father Azariah ha-Kohen, Daniel's brother-in-law, was the son of Israel ha-Kohen b. Samuel b. Ḥofni (the brother of Nehemiah) b. Kohen Ṣedeq. Israel and Samuel had also been geonim in Sura, while Kohen Ṣedeq and his son Nehemiah, the brother of Ḥofni, had been geonim in Pumbedita. One can assume that Josiah was to be found together with Daniel when the latter was Gaon in Jerusalem, for his signature is found on a deed written in the court of the yeshiva. Israel b. Nathan, writing from Jerusalem in the summer of 1060, asks Nehorai b. Nissim to arrange something for Josiah in Fustat, indicating that he was staying in Jerusalem at the time. Apparently Josiah ha-Kohen moved to Fustat in the autumn of 1061, and this, too, we learn from one of Israel b. Nathan's letters to Nehorai.

A letter that evidently contains a description of Josiah ha-Kohen's flight from Iraq and his journey to Palestine was written by Daniel b. Azariah before he had become Gaon. Josiah's name is not mentioned, but from the tone of the letter it can be seen that he is speaking of someone very close, and one senses that it is Josiah. Owing to the custom sometimes practised by the people of those times, of summarising in their letters the major points of the letter they are answering, we can understand what Josiah wrote (if indeed it is Josiah to whom he is writing) to Daniel about the vicissitudes of his journey. Josiah's letter was sent from Tripoli in Syria, where he arrived after managing to escape from al-Ma'arra (which is Ma'arrat Nu'mān) and from wicked men who had taken him from Aleppo (where he was in 'the hands of the enemy' – perhaps the Byzantines?) to Fāmiya. From there, he succeeded in getting away and reached Salūq, whence he also escaped and somehow made his way through the impassable mountains. Knowledge of his arrival in Tripoli reached (Jerusalem?) during a fast day (we do not know which one) and aroused rejoicing in the community. Everyone came to congratulate Daniel and even the fast was discontinued.[160]

[888] As to Abraham ha-Kohen b. Isaac ibn Furāt, I have already surveyed his special connections with the Fatimid rulers in general, and in

[160] The business letter: **345**. The letter from a member of the exilarchic family: **343**, lines 4–5. The fragment: **346**. The letter from Tyre: **347**; the addressee is perhaps Abraham ha-Kohen b. Isaac ibn Furāt. Josiah ha-Kohen b. Azariah, see the Hebrew Index. The deed of the yeshiva: **392**, line 36. Israel b. Sahlūn: **473**, b, lines 4–5. Josiah arrived in Fustat: **479**, b, lines 17ff. The description of the journey: **348**. See on Ma'arrat Nu'mān: Dussaud, *Topographie*, 188f; Salūq is Seleucia, see: Yāqūt, *Buldān*, III, 126; Fāmiya is Apamea of ancient times, see the entry Afāmiya (by H. A. R. Gibb) in *EI*². Josiah's journey evidently went from Aleppo, some 50 kilometres to the southwest to Ma'arrat Nu'mān, and from there still going southwest to Fāmiya, and from there some fifty kilometres northwest (through the mountains) to Seleucia on the Orontes (which is the 'Āṣī) and from there, evidently by sea to Tripoli.

particular with the governor of jund Filasṭīn, whose seat was in Ramla, where Abraham ha-Kohen was a physician and lived for many years. The close relationship with Solomon b. Judah has also been reviewed, as have other similar relations with Daniel b. Azariah. We find a note written by Daniel in Ramla, apparently, in which he invites Abraham ha-Kohen to honour him with his presence and to pray in the synagogue of the 'Palestinians', and he asks that he should not be forced to come and get Abraham from his house. Daniel even granted him an additional title, that of *hōd ha-zeqēnīm*, 'splendour of the elders'. In his letter, he informs him that since the title was bestowed on Abū 'Alī b. Faḍlān in Baghdad, no other person had been granted this honour. It is implied that the granting of the title was announced in the synagogue and that a prayer was said 'in memory (*tarḥīm*) of his forefathers the princes'; and that afterwards, benedictions were said for him. Daniel continued to display consideration for Abraham ha-Kohen even after he went down to Egypt. The latter had a financial claim against someone in Palestine, and Daniel (when he was already Gaon) suggests that he have someone appointed trustee to apply to the court and see to it that justice is carried out. Daniel also wrote from Damascus to Abraham ha-Kohen in Fustat. Eleven letters out of Daniel b. Azariah's documents were written to Abraham ha-Kohen, and it seems that one of Abraham's letters to him was also preserved in the Geniza. Abraham ha-Kohen's move to Egypt saddened the Gaon immensely, and he expressed this in one of his letters. He turned to Abraham ha-Kohen when one of his intimate circle ('the best of men') travelled to Egypt and needed help there. The only letter which is evidently in Abraham ha-Kohen's handwriting, to Daniel b. Azariah, contains expressions of extreme loyalty and promises of collaboration and assistance. It confirms having received Daniel's letter, in which there was information about the death of an important woman in Jerusalem, and continues with expressions of condolence and much praise for Daniel for having dealt with her burial, which he likens to the care 'the two masters took for our mother, their sister Miriam', that is Moses and Aaron. Below we shall see how Abraham ha-Kohen exerted all his influence on the authorities in order to help Daniel b. Azariah obtain the appointment of Gaon, throughout his struggle with Joseph ha-Kohen b. Solomon Gaon, even though there was a family relationship between Abraham and Joseph (they were cousins).[161]

161 The note from Ramla: **349**. 'The splendour of the elders': **354**; Abū 'Alī b. Faḍlān was one of the wealthy men of Baghdad, who refused to lend money to the amīr Bahā' al-Dawla in 998, which aroused anti-Jewish riots, see Fischel, *Jews*, 33, n. 1; Goitein, *Mediterranean Society*, II, 525, n. 6; that is, Daniel here cites a precedent from some two generations earlier. Ibn al-Jawzī, *Muntaẓam*, V, 190, mentions Abū 'Alī ibn Faḍlān *al-yahūdī*, in the events of 450, in Ramaḍān of that same year, that is, October 1058; there were then riots

[889] I shall now discuss the affair of the dispute over the office of Gaon following the death of Solomon b. Judah. The historical sequence in the Scroll of Abiathar begins with this affair. Daniel was backed by the Karaites ('and was strengthened by the sect of the *ṣela'*'; see sec. 848) and other elements whose nature cannot be defined, and also by the authorities ('the hand of the rulers'). He did not hesitate to use soldiers (*gūlīyērīm*), 'in order to seize houses of learning and completely close them' (that is, arrange for the closing of the synagogues of those who did not support him), 'on any holiday [*miqrā qodesh*], sabbath and [rōsh] *ḥōdesh*' (first of the month), and bring about the arrest of the priestly family (Joseph and Elijah, sons of Solomon Gaon, who 'were hastened to the dungeon').

Indeed, this dispute over the office of the Gaon between Daniel b. Azariah and Joseph ha-Kohen b. Solomon Gaon, who was the older of the two priestly brothers, is confirmed by a number of sources. It seems clear that Daniel indeed made every effort to achieve the status of Gaon in Jerusalem and that this aspiration was already implanted during the lifetime of the former Gaon, Solomon b. Judah. We have seen that Daniel was one of the leaders of the Gaon's supporters during the dispute with Nathan b. Abraham, and one can assume that there existed both understanding and friendship between Solomon and Daniel. Apparently, still in Solomon b. Judah's day, Daniel had already expressed his anger towards Joseph ha-Kohen, who took every opportunity to malign him. One cannot doubt that this was indeed the case, for even then, Joseph saw in Daniel a potential rival for the longed-for office.

To a large extent, the dispute was carried on with the active involvement of the authorities, and Daniel resorted to their help frequently, with the support of his good friend Abraham ha-Kohen. The *amīr* Ḥassām al-Dawla, who maintained contact with Daniel through an emissary, and the *qā'id* Abū Shujā', are explicitly mentioned in the course of the dispute. The wazīr, *al-ḥaḍra al-sāmiya* (his majestic honour) in Daniel's letters, was evidently one of Daniel's supporters. He even mentions that with Abraham's help, he received an official robe (*khal'a*) from the wazīr. However, there was also strong pressure against him. Daniel requested that Abraham be his champion and advocate, that he uncover whatever his rivals

against the Jews and the Christians (*ahl al-dhimma*) and an attempt to oust them from positions in the administration. This Ibn Faḍlān seems to have been the grandson of the one mentioned by Daniel b. Azariah, and it says that he was the secretary (*kātib*) of Khatūn, probably the wife of the Saljūq ruler of Baghdad (Ṭughril Beg). The matter of the claim: **355**, a, lines 2–16. The letter from Damascus: **357**. The letter from Abraham ha-Kohen is (evidently) **399**, and see there the note to line 9. The regret at Abraham ha-Kohen's leaving: Palestine is like a deserted place after his departure, see: **355**, a, lines 19–25. The request for help: **360** (although Abraham's name is not mentioned there, it appears that the reference is to him).

were plotting against him and that he broadcast his virtues. Indeed, the wazīr also issued a *manshūr* in Daniel's favour, that is, an official document of appointment, which was publicly proclaimed. Daniel also asked that, with the help of these eminent connections, he should be guaranteed a friendly attitude on the part of '*al-qāṣīn* (the chief) who is in Jerusalem'. Abū Muḥammad, the cadi mentioned in the letter, is none other than the wazīr Abū Muḥammad al-Ḥasan ibn 'Alī b. Abd al-Raḥmān al-Yāzūrī (whom I have discussed in sec. 598). He seems to have been a friend of Abraham ha-Kohen, for they both lived in Ramla for many years. In one of his letters to Abraham ha-Kohen, Daniel writes that the local *amīr*, the aforementioned Ḥassām al-Dawla, was trying to scheme against him in spite of the *manshūr* of appointment which was already in his hands. Daniel wrote to him, attaching to his letter another from one of the important intimates of the *amīr*, as well as a copy of the *manshūr*. Nevertheless, the *rayyis*, evidently his rival Joseph ha-Kohen, at the very time this letter was being written, was being invited by a number of notables to Dājūn (Bēt Dagan today; evidently the headquarters of the Fatimid army in Palestine was stationed there). It appears that the local authorities were inclined to support Joseph, preferring him to Daniel. Hence, Daniel asks Abraham ha-Kohen to intervene urgently, implying that he is very much afraid that Ḥassām al-Dawla will discriminate against him, the latter's judgment also being highly thought of by the wazīr. Indirectly, we learn that the other party, the priestly faction, did not hesitate to use the same means, trying hard to gain the Muslim rulers' support. The Scroll of Abiathar naturally does not touch on this aspect of the affair.[162]

[890] Further interesting allusions to the internal Jewish aspects of the dispute are to be found in letters from Daniel b. Azariah himself, and from his contemporaries. In December 1051, Daniel wrote a letter to one of the personalities of the Maghrib which reveals something of the ideological background to his struggle, with its rancour directed against the priestly family. It is the exilarchs who are worthy of leading 'our western

162 The Scroll of Abiathar: **559**, b, lines 8ff. Goitein, *Shalem*, 2(1975/6), 51–55 (= *Ha-yishuv*, 139–143), tried to find proof in **213** that Solomon b. Judah was the one who appointed Daniel as his successor; but this document is in the handwriting of Zadok ha-Levi b. Levi and hence was written in *ca.* 1030 and has no connection to our present matter, which occurred some twenty years later. Daniel's anger with Joseph ha-Kohen: **363**. Hints on the approaching struggle are evidently to be found also in **350**, a fragment of a letter to Abraham ha-Kohen, which speaks of some decision to be taken on the sabbath; Daniel does not dare do anything in the absence of Abraham. Ḥassām al-Dawla and the rest: **352**, **353**, **355**, b, lines 3–19; **357**, b; Goitein, *Shalem*, 2(1975/6), 81ff (*Ha-yishuv*, 163) assumed that this figure – *al-ḥaḍra al-sāmiya* – was the Nagid, Judah b. Saadia. Above we have seen that in one of his latters, Daniel speaks of the cadi Abū Muḥammad, who is evidently the ship-owning cadi of Tyre, Ibn Abī 'Aqīl; but there is no certain evidence of this, and it is possible that the reference is to the wazīr al-Yāzūrī, as they both had the same *kunya*: Abū Muḥammad.

brethren'; it is they who 'possess the authority over them and who are leading them'; this is a prerogative received from the Bible, 'and we have not seen in the Torah or the Prophets or the Hagiographa any command on authority but of our forefathers'. Therefore, there is no validity to any leadership of the Jews unless it stems from the House of David, that is, from the exilarchic family. In the same letter, Daniel extols the success of the pilgrimage in that year, which goes to prove that the authority over the Jews of Jerusalem was in fact already in his hands. At about the same time, Israel b. Nathan, Nehorai b. Nissim's cousin, wrote from Jerusalem. He lived, as we have seen, in Jerusalem, and his letters to Nehorai were at times interspersed with descriptions of public events there. We have seen above that Solomon b. Judah died in April 1051. On 20 December 1051, that is, when eight months had gone by without a Gaon heading the yeshiva, Israel wrote that on that very day, two emissaries had come from Ramla to *al-rayyis al-Da'ūdī* (the Davidian chief, who was Daniel, for the exilarchs claimed they originated from the House of David) and to *al-rayyis* R. Joseph, to take them to the governor in Ramla in order to settle the dispute between them. Daniel had only arrived in Jerusalem four days earlier, on 16 December, and on the 23rd there was to be a meeting in Ramla with the governor. Other notables were to accompany the two to Ramla: Elijah ha-Kohen, Joseph's brother, Mevorakh 'the sixth' b. Solomon; the ḥavēr Abū'l-Munajjā, the physician, and the ḥāvēr Ḥayyim (b. Solomon). Joseph ha-Kohen claimed that all he wanted now was to be appointed *av-bēt-dīn*, while his brother Elijah was a lover of peace and wanted no rank at all, promising to pray for both Daniel and Joseph. It seems that afterward, however, Joseph became stubborn and was not satisfied with the role of *av-bēt-dīn*, demanding that they both be called heads of the yeshiva – the title of Daniel would be 'head of the yeshiva Ge'ōn Ya'aqōv', whereas he would be called 'head of the yeshiva'. Daniel rejected this proposal out of hand and was not prepared to compromise in any way. While writing the second letter, on 11 January 1052, attempts were again being made to mediate, but these met with no success. It is implied in that letter that the Maghribis were on Daniel's side, conducting fervent discussions in Jerusalem, with the participation of people who came from various cities. On 24 August, we find Israel writing again about the main protagonists of the dispute. *Sayyidnā al-rayyis*, that is Daniel b. Azariah, arrived in Jerusalem via Nābulus (perhaps coming from Damascus), and Elijah ha-Kohen went to welcome him. Not so his brother Joseph, who was then staying in Ramla. It is implied that the letter was written after an agreement had already been reached between the parties. This is in keeping with a letter written by the Jerusalem parnās,

'Eli ha-Kohen b. Ezekiel, on 27 September 1052. The letter is in 'Eli's handwriting but it was written on behalf of a certain Ḥasan b. Mu'ammal, of Ramla, to Abū Naṣr al-Aḥwal ('the cross-eyed') in Fustat. The date noted in the letter is the last day of Tishri, and Ḥasan depicts there what happened in Jerusalem in Tishri during the pilgrimage. According to him, 'the Davidian', that is, Daniel b. Azariah, enquired about the addressee (Abū Naṣr), and Ḥasan explained that he could not come because of the dispute. It is obvious that the writer is not one of Daniel's admirers. He describes the events in Jerusalem in a disparaging manner; things were done that should not have been done and a squabble broke out between people from Tyre and the Tiberians, and they were obliged to call in the chief of police. Evidently, in the face of such hooliganism and humiliating occurrences, the two sides came to the conclusion that the dispute must come to an end. Thus, during the congregation on the Mount of Olives 'Joseph ha-Kohen prayed for Daniel, head of the yeshiva, while Daniel prayed for Joseph, *av-bēt-dīn*, father of the court and of the *methīvā*' (the Aramaic word for yeshiva). One can understand from this that the two camps reached an agreement in principle in August 1052, while the official announcement of the agreement took place on Hosha'na rabbā, that is, 18 September 1052. Hence, the yeshiva had been without a Gaon for sixteen months, from April 1051 until September 1052.[163]

[891] The rise of Daniel b. Azariah to the rank of Gaon was not a simple matter. On the contrary, it was an unusual event, for according to the regulations for advancing in the yeshiva, this position was due to Joseph ha-Kohen, who was *av-bēt-dīn*, that is, he occupied the place which was second in importance when the former Gaon died. In fact, Daniel's ascendancy to this office was the result of a well-planned campaign. Apparently the initiative for this campaign came from among the Maghribi

163 Daniel b. Azariah's letter: **365**, lines 5ff. The letters of Israel b. Nathan: **466**, a, lines 8ff; **467**, a, lines 11–17; b, line 6; **468**, a, lines 10ff and margin top; b, lines 1–2. Before this, I had a different view of the dates of these letters and hence about the length of the dispute altogether; see Gil, *Perāqīm*, 45, 74, see the introductions and notes to these letters in my collection. It is clear that the dispute was not ended before the winter of 4812 (1051/2), for the letters of Israel b. Nathan dealing with the matter were written in Tevet and Shevat, and the third was written in Elul. Ḥasan b. Mu'ammal: **436**; *ibid.*, in line 14, it says that Daniel prayed on Joseph 'father of the court and the *methīvā*'; it seems therefore that after all there was some concession on Daniel's part regarding Joseph's title. A document from the interim period in which the dispute over the office of Gaon was in process is a marriage deed from Ramla, **566**, written on 29 December 1051; it lacks the customary signature of one of the people of the yeshiva, the most important signature there being apparently that of Joshua the cantor b. 'Eli he-ḥāvēr. It is possible that a fragment of a letter from Jerusalem, **563**, belongs to the same period; the Jerusalemites complaining there of the mismanagement of Jewish affairs in Jerusalem; the writer expresses his loyalty to the 'House of David', which here means his loyalty to Daniel b. Azariah. One can assume that Abū Isḥaq, whom the writer is addressing, is Abraham ha-Kohen b. Isaac ibn Furāt; but naturally this is only an assumption.

circles in Fustat. They may have been striving to achieve a sort of mixture of the authority to which they belonged, that is, the Palestinian authority, to which the Egyptian Jewry was also subordinate, with the authority to which they had a special emotional link, the family of the exilarchs. This special relationship was undoubtedly a legacy going back for ages, from the forefathers of these merchants who had come from Babylonia. Allusions to this campaign, particularly to its outset, are to be found in the letter of some unnamed person in Fustat, writing to Daniel b. Azariah; one may guess that it is Abraham ha-Kohen b. Isaac ibn Furāt. The writer recalls Daniel's arrival 'in this land', and the meeting which took place at the house of a certain 'al-Damsīsī'. Even then, the writer knew that it was Divine Providence which sent Daniel (that is, from Baghdad to Egypt and to Palestine). It seems that the writer had experienced some sharp opposition and bitter altercations in the past, with one of the notables of the community in Fustat, probably 'Eli b. 'Amram, *he-ḥāvēr ha-me'ullē*, the successor to Ephraim b. Shemaria's status and office. 'Eli credited himself with all the achievements of Daniel b. Azariah', but it was the writer who made the effort and struggled. It was 'the Rav', the leader of the Maghribis (whom we know well from sec. 378), who persistently supported Daniel. He was the man who should have succeeded Ephraim b. Shemaria as head of the 'Palestinians' in Fustat, and the writer regrets that he did not back him instead of his rival (that is 'Eli b. 'Amram). Now 'Eli behaves arrogantly, abuses the people of the congregation, and even the memory of his predecessor, Ephraim b. Shemaria, which upsets the latter's son-in-law, Ghālib ha-Kohen b. Moses. He also offended some of the eminent Maghribis in Fustat, such as Abū'l-Surūr (*surūr* = *simḥā*, joy, and he is evidently the *māsōs* Abraham b. David ibn Sughmār). Now 'Eli fears that he will be ousted from his post and that the 'Rav' will be appointed in his stead, so he has started to scheme together with Ḥunayn, his brother-in-law (Abū'l-Ṭayyib Ḥanania ha-Levi, the father-in-law of Abraham b. Isaac *ha-talmīd*). They are impugning the 'Rav' with false charges, that of allegedly having converted to Islam (*pāsha'*) when he was in Palestine, and then presenting himself as a Jew when he came to Fustat. These are strange accusations which give us some indication of the persistent tense atmosphere of local community quarrels, and also of the influence of factional plotting on the central institution of leadership, the Palestinian yeshiva. An echo of this can be heard from Jerusalem, in a letter from Avon b. Ṣedaqa to Nehorai b. Nissim, written two years after the death of Daniel b. Azariah, in which he charges Nehorai's cousin, Israel b. Nathan, with some sort of madness: that he goes about and complains to whoever will listen to him that Nehorai is busy in Fustat making propaganda and collecting money for 'the Rav' (perhaps in order to install him in 'Eli b. 'Amram's place? It is difficult to know the true reason for this).[164]

[892] The period during which Daniel b. Azariah held the office of Gaon was a difficult one; it was marked by economic distress and the political instability of the Fatimid regime. It was during this time that the Jerusalem wall was constructed with the funds of its inhabitants, and that the Christians were enclosed in a wall within their part of the city, an episode that has been discussed earlier. Daniel b. Azariah mentions this event in one of his letters, speaking of the wall as if it were a decree imposed on the Jews of Jerusalem as well, in about the mid-fifties. A note which he wrote at the same time also contains mysterious hints at severe difficulties in Ramla and in other places. Indeed, he was visiting Ramla in May 1054, as emerges from the letter of Salāma ha-Kohen b. Joseph from Ramla to Shemaiah he-ḥāvēr b. Joshua in Jerusalem. The writer had asked Daniel to assist in some matter relating to Shemaiah, but Daniel evaded doing so out of fear. The same ambiance of vicious decrees and fears pervades Daniel's letter to one of the personalities of Fustat relating to some decree, about which we know nothing.

According to the Scroll of Abiathar, Daniel b. Azariah took ill some six years after the death of Joseph ha-Kohen (who died on Hanukkah 1365 Sel., that is mid-December, AD 1053), that is at the end of 1059. He 'was taken [*nikhpē*] every year for six months'. This expression was usually interpreted as meaning that he was an epileptic, but this is not certain. The regular cycles point to some kind of emotional disturbance, such as depression, and according to the Scroll, this was but one of the ills he suffered from towards the end of his life. There is no indication of illness in his letters, however. 'Eli ha-Kohen b. Ezekiel mentions in two letters, evidently written in about 1060, Daniel b. Azariah's visit to Fustat. Only in the third letter does he mention Daniel's return to Jerusalem.

During his absence, Jerusalem was in a sorry plight: merchants did not arrive and the poor of Jerusalem were suffering from severe distress, for they had not received their allowance from Fustat. In addition, the burden of taxes was very heavy. In 1059, Israel b. Nathan is engaged in passing on queries – put by his cousin Nehorai b. Nissim – to Daniel b. Azariah. He notes that Daniel is very busy, for most of his responsibilities fall in Tishri. Later, on 14 March 1062, Israel returns to the matter of the queries to the *nāsī*. Daniel b. Azariah was staying in Ramla and Israel has sent him

[164] The letter ascribed to Abraham ha-Kohen: **399**, a, lines 18ff; see the notes to this document. On Ḥunayn see Gil, *Michael*, 7(1981/2), 247, n. 5. Avon's letter: **500**, b, lines 21ff. On the struggles in Fustat during this period, see also the letter of 'Eli ha-Kohen b. Ezekiel: **444**, lines 13–15 (*ca.*1060), in which the writer expresses concern for 'my Master the *māsōs* and his son'; he hopes that Dōsā al-Lādhiqī and his son Joshua are helping them; evidently he is referring to Abraham b. David b. Sughmār.

Nehorai's letter via a messenger. He promises that Daniel will send the responsum to Fustat with a shipment of mail he is sending to Abū Sa'd (who is Josiah ha-Kohen b. Azariah, Daniel's sister's son).

The people of the West, who from the outset had a positive attitude to Daniel for his extraction from the House of David, the exilarchic family, undoubtedly derived a great deal of satisfaction from his elevated status as Gaon. This was expressed by Samuel, the Spanish Nagid, in one of the poems he sent to Daniel: 'tell anyone asking of Daniel, that he is a wide sea, with no shores . . . since the day he took over rule Truth stepped in instead of Lie . . . like a cedar of wisdom . . . Oh that I had wings, for then would I fly to the House of God, to look at the scion of David'. There was evidently a very strong link between Daniel b. Azariah and the Spanish negidim, Samuel, and Samuel's son Joseph, and Daniel even granted them titles (it is not clear which titles) on behalf of the yeshiva. It is possible that it was Daniel who granted Joseph b. Samuel the title Nagid that was also held by his father.

We do not have much knowledge of what went on at the yeshiva during Daniel's term of office. An interesting document is an anonymous letter informing Daniel that a certain Nathan 'the money-changer' and his son are about to arrive, suggesting that Daniel receive them with great courtesy and try to win their approval, because they are his devoted followers and the important thing is that 'they are loaded with dinars [*zehūvīm*]'.

We know who was the scribe of the yeshiva in Daniel b. Azariah's day – Abū'l-Faraj Ṣemaḥ b. Eleazar. Daniel calls him 'Ṣemaḥ, our scribe' (*sāfrā dīlānā*). 'Eli ha-Kohen b. Ezekiel recommends this Ṣemaḥ to 'Eli ha-Kohen b. Ḥayyim, the Fustat parnās, in one of his letters. He is expected to arrive in Fustat, and to fulfil certain expectations that are not clarified in the letter. He will stay with *sayyidnā al-nāsī* Abū'l-Riḍā, that is, a member of the exilarchic family whose name is Abū'l-Riḍā. We do not know who bore this by-name and it is not unlikely that it was Daniel himself, for he was also staying in Fustat at the time. It is also worth noting that during Daniel b. Azariah's time, we find a number of Jerusalem Maghribis suddenly bearing the title *ḥāvēr*, which seems to have been granted to them by Daniel, as in the case of Shemaiah he-ḥāvēr b. Yeshū'ā, Abraham he-ḥāvēr b. 'Amram and Moses he-ḥāvēr b. Jacob.[165]

[893] To what extent Daniel b. Azariah was involved in the life of the

[165] The matter of the wall: **357**, b, lines 9–10. The note: **364**. Salāma's letter: **525**, a, lines 11–15 (he calls him 'the head' there, clearly speaking of Daniel). The decree: **381**. Daniel's illness: **599**, b, lines 12ff. 'Eli ha-Kohen's letters: **442**, a, lines 13–15 (implying that Daniel – 'our Master the Nāsī' – is in Fustat); **443**, a, lines 7, 14, 18–19; **444**, a, line 5. The letters of Israel b. Nathan: **469**, a, lines 22-24; **482**, a, lines 5–8. Document **353a** is a fragment of a letter from Daniel, evidently to Abraham ha-Kohen b. Isaac ibn Furāt, written shortly after the end of the dispute over the office of Gaon, that is, towards the end of 1052; the *av*,

communities under his jurisdiction, we can learn from the information we have on Fustat. The letters to Fustat in particular (apparently similar letters were despatched to the rest of the communities) reveal Daniel's true character, the decisiveness and cleverness with which he managed affairs – qualities which were suited to a man who was probably a shrewd man of business before he became Gaon. The changes in the personnel of the yeshiva which took place after the death of Solomon b. Judah were more or less parallel in time to the changes in Fustat, when both Ephraim b. Shemaria, leader of the 'Palestinians', and Sahlān b. Abraham, leader of the 'Babylonians' died apparently at about the same time (we do not have the dates of their deaths). Owing to the Geniza, we know what was occurring among the 'Palestinians', whose new leader was 'Eli b. 'Amram.

Above, I have already mentioned the letter of condolence from Daniel b. Azariah to Ghālib ha-Kohen b. Moses, on the death of his father-in-law, Ephraim b. Shemaria, which has been preserved. We have also noted the meeting in the house of al-Damsīsī, and how Daniel's supporters were organised in the Egyptian capital. In general, one gets the impression that there were factions amongst the 'Palestinians' in Egypt, but 'Eli b. 'Amram's position seems to have been especially solid and the Gaon preferred him to the Maghribis and their leader, the 'Rav'. Some reservations concerning local appointments are revealed in the above-mentioned note,

that is, *av-bēt-dīn*, who is Joseph ha-Kohen b. Solomon, intends leaving for Ramla; an order arrived from the caliph, containing the appointment of the new Gaon, but as it was written in the midst of the dispute, when the matter was still undecided, the name of the Gaon was lacking. Hence, Daniel requests that a new and proper *sijill* be sent. Apart from ornately framed claims of friendship for Abraham ha-Kohen, similar to those Daniel had used in other letters to him, the copying of a prayer book for Abraham is also mentioned. The Jerusalem paper, writes Daniel, is not good enough, and paper has been ordered from Tyre; the work has been assigned to the best of copyists. A poem in the handwriting of 'Eli ha-Kohen b. Ezekiel, of which only a small part can be made out, was written in honour of Daniel b. Azariah, containing a new element, mention of 'the fourth' of the yeshiva, Mevorakh, and 'the fifth', Abraham. We have no further details on them nor do we have any further sources on the subject of titles of this kind in the yeshiva during Daniel's day, for the time being. See TS NS 149.43, to which Prof. E. Fleischer drew my attention. Samuel ha-Nagid, see the *Dīwān*, Sasson ed., 103f; Yarden ed., 139–142. On the connection between 'Eli b. 'Amram, the Fustat ḥāvēr, and the son of Samuel the Nagid, Joseph, see: Mann, *Jews*, I, 183f; II, 221f, 459–462 (Mann erred at first in identifying Joseph, but afterwards realised that it was the Spanish Nagid who was being referred to); *Texts*, I, 386, n. 2; in the letter ENA 3765, f. 8 (Mann, *ibid.*, 460f) it is implied that Joseph received 'the proper name and titles called and applied by our Lord Daniel': cf Ashtor, *Qōrōt*, II, 82f; Goitein, *Mediterranean Society*, II, 525, n. 13, where the conclusion is that it was Daniel b. Azariah who granted Joseph the title Nagid, and on the same page there are further references. Moses ibn Ezra wrote, some eighty years later, on the link between Samuel ha-Nagid the Spaniard and 'the leaders of Babylonia and the scholars of Palestine', see *al-Muḥāḍara*, 62. Nathan the money-changer: **386**. 'Eli b. Ezekiel on Ṣemaḥ: **441**, see also **443**, b, Daniel on him: **374**, line 10. I have already discussed above the matter of the Maghribis entitled ḥāvēr, see in particular: **519**.

which speaks of 'our honourable R. Samuel he-ḥāvēr ha-me'ullē, who may be Samuel ha-Kohen b. Avṭalyon of Fustat, certainly a very old man by this time, or perhaps Samuel b. Moses of Tyre. The Gaon mentions in the note that he has refrained from going to the synagogue for two days because someone was demanding a certain rank which he opposed. From another letter, we learn that 'Eli b. 'Amram was at a certain stage apparently tired of the tension and assaults on him, and resigned from his position. In a fragment remaining from this letter, it appears that Daniel is requesting the addressee to intervene in the division. Daniel's frank letter to 'Eli b. 'Amram is particularly interesting – it is a supportive letter in which he tries to appease him and promises that he will stand behind him, in terms of affection and respect. He recalls the support he has received from 'Eli and pledges to repay him for this in full. Also, the time would come when those who had been insolent towards him would be called to account.

We have seen in the discussion on the relationship between Daniel and Abraham b. Isaac ibn Furāt that the latter was considered a figure of the greatest importance in Fustat and that in fact, Daniel asked the Fustat ḥavēr, 'Eli b. 'Amram, to obey him. Evidently this was also a source of 'Eli's bitterness. Owing to the scarcity of information at this point, we cannot say anything precise about 'Eli's character but it seems that he knew how to defend his position in a restrained and almost diplomatic manner. We find a short letter he wrote to Abraham ha-Kohen, in which after some flowery opening phrases, as was common among learned and honourable men ('Abraham, prince of the congregation . . . son of his great honourable Sanctity, our Lord and Master Perāt, like Pōrāt') he writes that he regrets that he cannot accept the invitation to visit him, because he cannot be absent from his shop (*dukkān*). The letter mentions 'the synagogue of our Lord, the light of Israel, Daniel the great *nāsī* and head of the yeshiva Ge'ōn Ya'aqōv'.[166]

[166] The letter of condolence: **362**. In **356**, b, margin, Daniel writes about a house that had belonged to Ṣemaḥ, a matter connected with the old sister of Abū Kathīr, who is perhaps Ephraim b. Shemaria (whose *kunya* it was). We also find in this letter details on the ritual slaughtering in Fustat, from which one can sense Daniel's determined attitude in such matters, see b, lines 19ff. The meeting in al-Damsīsī's house: **399**. The note: **364**; cf. Goitein, *Mediterranean Society*, II, 511, sec. 5. 'Eli b. 'Amram resigns: **366**. Goitein, *Shalem*, 2(1975/6), 63 (= *ha-Yishuv*, 149) interpreted the account as speaking unfavourably of 'Eli, concluding that he failed in his office as leader of the congregation, and that he was among the harshest opponents of Daniel; my own interpretation is otherwise, as can be seen above. The letter of support: **368**; see also the beginning of a letter to 'Eli b. 'Amram, **369**, where some dispute is implied and there are condolences on someone's death. The letter of 'Eli to Abraham ha-Kohen: TS 13 J 31, f. 5, cf. Goitein, *Shalem*, 2 (1975/6), 64 (= *ha-Yishuv*, 93, nn. 18, 19, 157, n. 84), who assumed that an uncle of Abraham ha-Kohen b. Isaac ibn Furāt was intended there, but abandoned this idea; indeed, it was only natural to call Abraham in a shortened fashion: Ben Perāt or Ibn Furāt.

[894] The main focus of the division in Fustat at this time, seems to have been Yefet b. David, of whom I have already spoken in some detail. He evidently headed a sort of rebellion against ʿEli b. ʿAmram, and as a result, Daniel empowered ʿEli to proclaim the excommunication of Yefet, and even tried to convince ʿEli that he should not hesitate to do so. Daniel also wrote harsh things about ʿEli b. ʿAmram's other rivals. Nevertheless, we have seen that Yefet succeeded in obtaining part of the income from slaughtering in Fustat, with the help of Abraham ha-Kohen b. Isaac ibn Furāt, who approached the Gaon on this matter.

Apart from these stormy instances, Daniel b. Azariah's letters to ʿEli b. ʿAmram generally deal with routine matters. There is no doubt that their relationship differered from that of Daniel b. Azariah with Abraham ha-Kohen b. Isaac ibn Furāt. This is displayed even in the fact that while all of Daniel b. Azariah's letters to the latter are in his own handwriting, the letters to ʿEli b. ʿAmram (with the exception of two) are written by the scribe of the yeshiva, Ṣemaḥ b. Eleazar. We find a letter in which he asks ʿEli to try to help to collect funds for someone from a family of geonim (the name is not preserved), who was forced to come to Egypt (evidently from Palestine) because of the harsh poverty and certain 'heart-breaking' matters. In another letter, ʿEli is asked to help Marwān b. Suqayr to obtain money owed him by a certain Joseph b. Jacob, because this Marwān is about to arrive in Fustat from Palestine. The link between ʿEli b. ʿAmram and the Gaon seems therefore to have been a working relationship, concerned with everyday affairs. ʿEli b. ʿAmram was the representative of the Fustat community towards the Gaon, and vice versa – the Gaon's representative towards the community. The affair of a *ṭārima* built by some unknown person is characteristic, and the problem involved is not clear, as I have already mentioned. This person had written a letter to the Gaon in which he answered all the claims against him, but he seems to have given the letter to ʿEli b. ʿAmram first of all, out of a sense of loyalty, in order that ʿEli should know what is being discussed, but ʿEli kept the letter and worded it anew, which angered the owner of the *ṭārima*, who subsequently wrote to the Gaon.[167]

167 The matter of the excommunication: **342**, **370**, **371**; additional data on the affairs of Yefet are to be found in the letters: **355–358**; **342** opens with florid phrases of friendship to the addressee, who is evidently ʿEli b. ʿAmram; afterwards he goes over to Yefet b. David's affairs: 'the damnable actions of b. Shekhaniah'. Daniel notes that he wrote a letter to the community, in which he censured these actions and even announced a ban on him and the prohibition on eating the meat of his slaughtering. Goitein, *ha-Yishuv*, 182, 183, 187, attributes the quarrels on slaughtering to Manṣūr, Yefet's brother, basing this mainly on **319**, line 15, where Yefet b. David was warned not to involve his brother in the slaughtering affairs; but we find that Yefet is constantly in charge of the slaughtering and the affair of the excommunication and the sharp quarrel was apparently merely a passing episode, explained by his bad relations with ʿEli b. ʿAmram; and perhaps there were

[895] Money from the slaughtering in Fustat due to the Palestinian yeshiva is mentioned in another letter to 'Eli b. 'Amram. He is asked to give a certain emissary of the Gaon, a certain b. Moses, 'all that was collected in the market from the beginning of Elul until the end of Kislev, such is the account'. Evidently the dire straits drove Daniel to send another emissary to Fustat, on this occasion the veteran parnās 'Eli ha-Kohen b. Ezekiel. According to the Gaon in his letter to 'Eli b. 'Amram, this mission was successful. A letter arrived from 'Eli ha-Kohen, giving details of the help promised by the people of Fustat, 'a righteous act which our honourable he-ḥāvēr ha-me'ullē has done to us and the elders of Jerusalem, telling that [our] letter was read out [publicly] and also of his recommendation'.

Apparently, 'Eli ha-Kohen b. Ezekiel and 'Eli ha-Kohen b. Ḥayyim, who was evidently a family relative in Fustat, were a kind of advisers and mediators on behalf of Daniel b. Azariah in matters concerning the

financial matters and accounts with the yeshiva as well, on which we have insufficient data. The matter of the help: **372**. Marwān: **373**; on him and his father, we do have information: his father Suqayr (diminutive of Saqar, or Ṣaqar) received a ceremonial robe (*khal'a*), was led mounted on a mule through the streets as a sign of honour, received large grants, and was appointed physician to the caliph al-Ḥākim instead of the Christian Ibn Nasṭās, who died in Rabī' II 400, December 1009; see Maqrīzī, *Itti'āẓ*, II, 73, 83; in *Mughrib*, V, 62, he is called Shuqayr al-Yahūdī; al-Ḥākim bought him a house that cost 4,000 dinars, equipped with the best of furnishings and housewares; he would receive 10,000 dinars for one hour, money which al-Ḥākim confiscated from the Christians (all of which should be taken with a degree of scepticism, naturally). Marwān himself is mentioned in a colophon in MS Firkovitch II, No. 1283, see: Kahle, *Masoreten des Westens*, I, 70: 'This *maḥzor* was bought, containing the last four books . . . by the elder Marwān . . . son of Sūqayr . . . in the city of Jerusalem . . . in the year 4818', that is AD 1058 (i.e., during Daniel b. Azariah's day); his two sons are mentioned: David and Solomon. The *ṭārima*: **397**. The matter of queries sent from Fustat (Nehorai b. Nissim) to Daniel b. Azariah (sec. 892) is again repeated in **468a**. It appears that Daniel b. Azariah, whom we found so occupied in Tishri, is still as busy in Tammuz. For general information on what was happening in Jerusalem towards the end of the life of 'the Nāsī and Gaon' (*ibid.*), one should add what is contained in **449a**. This letter was written close to 1060, and is preserved in a very poor state. One cannot discern with any certitude the nature of the dispute described there. The writer is evidently in Alexandria and he is writing to a Jerusalemite who is visiting Fustat together with his family. The writer would stay with this family during his visits to Jerusalem and he intends doing so in the future. The main subject of the letter is a certain Surūr ibn Sabra, who slanders the writer and other notables of Fustat in every possible manner. This Surūr ibn Sabra is a Maghribi by origin and the writer accuses him of converting to Islam when he was still in the Maghrib. The writer and his faction are about to appeal to the *av-bēt-dīn* in Jerusalem (Elijah ha-Kohen b. Solomon?) and demand that he is banned. The Gaon is not mentioned in the letter at all, and perhaps this is a confirmation of what is said in the Scroll of Abiathar about Daniel's illness during the last years of his life. There is additional information concerning the relationship between Daniel b. Azariah and the people of Fustat, particularly 'Eli b. 'Amram, in **377a**. It deals with a court case concerning the collection of a debt, mentioning a certain b. Mukhtār, who is evidently Ṣedaqa b. Muvḥār (= Mukhtār), noted a number of times in my collection. He seems to have been a financier from Tyre, who moved to Fustat, who had special ties with Daniel b. Azariah (see also *infra*, secs. 903, 905).

community in Fustat. These two parnāsīm carried on a constant correspondence and one can see that they tried to do their best to maintain proper order and peace in Fustat. During the late fifties, a quarrel arose in Fustat between two ḥavērīm: Abū Zikrī Judah he-ḥāvēr b. Saadia (afterwards known by the title Nagid) and Joshua he-ḥāvēr b. Dōsā. A reconciliation was achieved through the efforts of 'Eli ha-Kohen b. Ḥayyim, when Daniel b. Azariah was also staying in Fustat. 'Eli ha-Koen b. Ezekiel writes of the joy the people of Jerusalem felt about this peaceful outcome, and also that 'the *nāsī*' (Daniel b. Azariah) was extremely happy. We also find Daniel directly approaching 'Eli, the parnās of Fustat, referring undoubtedly to the above-mentioned 'Eli ha-Kohen b. Ḥayyim, concerning aid for a poor man, Wahb of the city of Raqqa.[168]

[896] Some of Daniel b. Azariah's writings in the field of law have been preserved. His interest in the writings of the early geonim can be discerned from one of his letters to 'Eli b. Amram, from which it emerges that he sent quires of the queries and responsa of several geonim to Fustat. From these geonim only the name of 'Rabbēnū Samuel Gaon' remains, who we may assume was Samuel ha-Kohen b. Ḥofni, head of the Sura yeshiva, the grandfather of Daniel's brother-in-law Azariah (his sister's husband). The reason for sending them to Fustat was to have them copied there. It seems that Daniel had borrowed them from one of that priestly family, perhaps from his sister's son Josiah ha-Kohen (the great-grandson of Samuel b. Ḥofni). We have already seen that the people of Fustat – as we know from the instance of Nehorai b. Nissim – were directing queries to Daniel on matters of law and were anticipating his responsa. We find Abū Sa'd Josiah ha-Kohen, the Gaon's nephew, and his son-in-law Abū Sarī Barhūn, occupied with a legacy of books he had bequeathed. There was a complaint that the tractate *Bava qamma* was missing, but they found the Gaon's *tadhkira*, a sort of diary, where it was written that the missing book was in Jerusalem, with Israel b. Nathan. In addition, we find instructions to 'Eli b. 'Amram on matters of law; outlining how to summon people to court, as I have mentioned above. I have also noted the *shimmūsh* which Daniel wrote on the matter of Ḥayyim b. Hārūn of Ṣahrajt and the vow made by this Ḥayyim, to pay a fine should it be found that he had a wife in Fustat before marrying another. In my collection, there are ten documents which are remains of Daniel's responsa and deeds written in his court. There are four queries and one responsum copied by the Gaon in his own handwriting, and it is not clear whether they are the work of one of his

[168] The money from slaughtering: **374**. The mission of 'Eli ha-Kohen: **376**; mentioned *ibid.* is also the matter of a deserted wife, but no details have been preserved. 'Eli b. Ezekiel on peace in Fustat: **440**, **443**. Help for Wahb: **385**; see also **382**, a fragment from the opening of a letter, evidently also to Fustat, in which thanks for a gift have been preserved, and a beginning of expressions of anxiety over an unclear subject.

forefathers or whether they are his own. One query deals with the guarding of an orphan's inheritance, and the responsum is also preserved. Further, there are queries about the promise of money without a written deed; about a man who cast aspersions on his wife and about how to treat her son; on a vow to dedicate property to the heqdēsh and whether the responsibility to carry it out applies to the heirs. Deeds and fragments of deeds drawn up in his court have also been preserved. As I have already noted, these deeds were formulated according to the Babylonian tradition and generally conformed to the formulary of Hayy Gaon's Book of Deeds. In one of his letters, Daniel sharply criticises a responsum on a matter of law, and expresses disdain for its author; perhaps a Babylonian Gaon, the Gaon of Pumbedita, whose identity we do not know (Israel, according to Mann), or Hezekiah, the exilarch b. David.

The Scroll of Abiathar notes the date of Daniel's death, Elul 1373 Sel., August 1062. His funeral is mentioned in one of the letters of Avon b. Ṣedaqa, the Maghribi merchant who lived in Jerusalem, to Nehorai b. Nissim, dated 11 October 1064. A record of evidence in a court in Alexandria, from 14 May 1079, speaks of two men upon whom Daniel b. Azariah had placed a ban, for some reason unknown to us, and says that they cursed 'our Master Daniel the *nāsī* head of the yeshiva Ge'on Ya'aqōv, of blessed, holy [*qādōsh*] and pure memory'. Are we to understand from this formula (*qādōsh*) that he was murdered? This possibility is hinted at in a passage in a letter written by Daniel b. Ḥasdai, the Baghdadi exilarch, in the year AM 4922 (AD 1161). According to him, there was an interruption in the chain of ordination after the death of 'our Master our *nāsī* Daniel head of the yeshiva Ge'ōn Ya'aqōv of blessed holy (*qādōsh*) memory'. However, we do not know whether those generations were in the habit of using the term 'holy' for someone who was murdered by the gentiles. The passage in a dirge written on his death 'alas for he ailed and was exiled', is also unexplained. As to his illness, we do not know its nature, just as we do not know how to understand the passage in the Scroll of Abiathar quoted above, regarding the sickness from which he suffered during the last four years of his life. As to exile, it seems that he apparently had to leave Jerusalem for some unknown reason, although from Avon b. Ṣedaqa's letter, we are aware that he was buried in Jerusalem.

Daniel b. Azariah was Gaon for nearly ten years. He encompassed in his personality two ideals that were close to the hearts of the Jewish masses: the heritage of the Palestinian Sanhedrin with that of the legend of the House of David, from which the exilarchs claimed descent. He was the first protagonist of a new kind of division among the Jews, between the House of David and the House of Aaron, as exemplified by the propaganda he used during the dispute over the office of the Gaon against Joseph ha-Kohen b. Solomon Gaon. Although relative calm reigned after Daniel's victory, the division was likely to break out with even greater vigour, and this time, in utter opposition to the idea of the Palestinian Sanhedrin, when Daniel's son David, reached maturity. Today, it is rather difficult to grasp the significance of the antagonism between the two Houses, and it seems somewhat trivial to us, but the writings of the period prove to what extent people's feelings were divided and how great were the storms aroused by this antagonism.[169]

The priestly geonim: Joseph, Elijah and Abiathar, the yeshiva in exile

[897] Joseph ha-Kohen b. Solomon Gaon did not last long after the victory of his rival. He died about a year and a half after the end of the dispute, on Hanukkah, that is, in mid-December 1053, after he was obliged to be content with the role of *av-bēt-dīn* under Daniel b. Azariah. The Scroll of Abiathar, which provides us with these details, calls the two brothers Joseph and Elijah, 'Joseph ha-Kohen and Elijah ha-Kohen, two geonim'. These were only words used for their effect, and it is clear that Joseph ha-Kohen never rose to the seat of Gaon at all. The writer of the Scroll drops rather broad hints to the effect that Joseph's death was caused by Daniel b. Azariah, both because he was excluded from the gaonate and because of the suffering and persecution he endured as a consequence of the dispute. Towards the end of his life, Joseph sought revenge: 'The Lord will see and judge', and therefore the illness of Daniel b. Azariah described there in the continuation was – it implies – a sort of punishment from heaven. There is no doubt that the priestly family saw it as such and there

169 Quires of responsa: **371**. Queries to Daniel from Fustat: **469**. Daniel's books: **500**, a, margin, right. A summons to court: **375**. Ḥayyim b. Hārūn: **389**, cf. Friedman, *Tarbiz*, 43 (1973/4), 176; Goitein, *Mediterranean Society*, III, 148. Daniel's responsa and legal deeds: **387–396**. On the Babylonian character of the deeds, see: Assaf, *Tarbiz*, 9(1937/8), 17. The criticism of a responsum: **356**, b, lines 24ff, margin; Goitein, *Shalem*, 2(1975/6), 68 (= *ha-Yishuv*, 148), who ascribed this letter to Zakkai, Daniel's brother, assumed that the criticism was aimed at 'Eli b. 'Amram, but this does not seem likely. Cf. on the matter of the Babylonian geonim during the fifties: Mann, *Texts*, I, 202ff. To the deeds from Daniel's court, one should add the deed of release of a slave-girl edited by Blau, *Die jüdische Ehescheidung*, 102 (No. 11): in Jerusalem, on Friday, 28 Tishri 1369 Sel., 29 September AD 1057, Abraham b. R. Isaac, nicknamed 'the cousin' releases the slave-girl Ẓarā'if. Signed by the scribe Ṣemaḥ b. Eleazar, the witness being 'Daniel ha-Nāsī head of the yeshiva Ge'ōn Ya'aqōv'. The reading and the date in Blau's version should be corrected. The 'cousin' there is none other than Abraham b. Isaac ibn Furāt, whose nickname was *ibn al-'amm* in Arabic; we have here evidence that he visited Jerusalem in that year, 1057; he certainly made a pilgrimage in Tishri; the editor could not identify him, of course, nor could Poznanskxi, *REJ*, 65 (1913), 45. The death of Daniel: **559**, b, line 15. Avon's letter: **500**, a, lines 7–8. The passage of Daniel b. Ḥasdai: Assaf, *Tarbiz*, 1 (3;1929/30), 69. Cf. Mann, *Texts*, I, 230f. The dirge: Assaf, *Zlotnik Jubilee Volume*, 166f.

was blazing hatred between the two sides, despite the fact that they had to settle their differences with one another and even work together.

A letter of condolence has been preserved, written by Daniel b. Azariah upon the death of 'his honourable great Sanctity, our Lord and Master Joseph ha-Kohen *av-bēt-dīn* of all Israel'. It was apparently sent to members of the latter's family, that is from Jerusalem to Ramla, evidently, or perhaps Daniel was staying in Fustat and wrote to them from there. He points out that it was he who eulogised the deceased. Evidently the letter quoted a passage (only preserved in part) from the Babylonian Talmud (Mo'ed qaṭan, 25a): 'whoever weeps and mourns over a proper man will be forgiven all his transgressions for the honour paid him' (i.e., to the deceased). Although these are expressions of courtesy, they seem to imply a very slight admission of guilt.

We do not know much about Joseph ha-Kohen. For many years, he was active together with Solomon b. Judah and his son Abraham, for they were related and worked jointly on matters of the yeshiva. There is a letter from Solomon b. Judah remaining in the Geniza, written on behalf of the Gaon in Joseph's handwriting. He was taken to jail in Damascus together with his brother Elijah as a consequence of the episode of the excommunication of the Karaites described above. I have also surveyed his special connections with Ephraim b. Shemaria. At times, Joseph would use the *'alāma* which was characteristic of his father – *yesha' yuḥāsh*. It seems that he was an extremist both by nature and in his aspirations and it was he who banished the cantor 'Solomon who is called Sābiq', as I described earlier. Evidently, Solomon b. Judah suffered immensely from Joseph's fanaticism and contentiousness and he writes about this in one of his letters, written apparently near the end of his life. Joseph ha-Kohen was then *av-bēt-dīn*, and according to the Gaon, he automatically rejected his opinions. One can feel the Gaon's marked reservation regarding Joseph's character and he seems to be trying to explain to the addressee the reasons for his aversion to Joseph. It seems then that Solomon b. Judah had a hand in creating the conditions which led to Joseph ha-Kohen being deprived of the longed-for status of head of the yeshiva, mainly, it seems, by drawing Daniel b. Azariah nearer, and perhaps by preparing the ground among the people for his advancement. On the other hand, he expresses a very positive opinion of the younger brother, Elijah ha-Kohen, who, he says, does not follow in his elder brother's footsteps.

In the affair of Nathan b. Abraham, Joseph ha-Kohen also played a major role and added fuel to the fire by his fanaticism. This was also connected, evidently, to his uncompromising attitude to the Karaites, and we have seen how he initiated the pronouncement of a twofold excommunication on them, on the last two days of Succoth, both on the matter of the holidays and on the matter of meat and milk. 'Eli ha-mumḥē b. Abraham wrote to Ephraim b. Shemaria in *ca.* 1045 about a personal matter concerning Joseph ha-Kohen. Joseph was staying in Jerusalem continuously, because the ruin he had bought near his house in Ramla was being renovated.

When he was still *av-bēt-dīn*, in Daniel b. Azariah's day, he seems to have maintained personal contact with the people of Fustat. A letter of the emissary of the yeshiva appears to be evidence of this, as it contains a most depressing account of what is going on among the 'Palestinian' congregation in Fustat and the dispute there. It seems that the mission of the writer was to a large extent a mission of the priestly family and not necessarily that of the yeshiva or the head of the yeshiva, Daniel b. Azariah.

After the death of Joseph ha-Kohen, Israel b. Nathan, in a letter from Tyre to Nehorai b. Nissim, mentions quires left by the deceased. The writer met with Elijah ha-Kohen, Joseph's brother, and discussed the matter with him. It transpires that the sons of the deceased wanted to sell the quires. There is a fragment in the Geniza in his handwriting, of what seems to be his commentary to the tractate Ketubbot (17b), in which he deals with the chapter on the woman who became a widow.

We have information on Joseph ha-Kohen's son, Abū'l-Bayān Solomon, who emigrated to Egypt in about the year 1060, some seven years after the death of his father. 'Eli ha-Kohen b. Ezekiel enquires after him and asks whether he is still in Alexandria or whether he has already arrived in Fustat. Afterwards, 'Eli writes that in the meantime he has learned of his safe arrival in Fustat, and that the ḥavēr Abū Zikrī, who is Judah b. Saadia, afterwards called the Nagid, is looking after him, as I have already mentioned. Another Jerusalemite, the Maghribi Israel b. Nathan, was also interested in learning at the time whether it was true that Solomon b. Joseph *bēt-dīn* had married.[170]

[898] A few facts about Elijah ha-Kohen Gaon can be found in the Scroll

[170] The Scroll of Abiathar: **559**, b, lines 8–12; his brother, Elijah ha-Kohen, did not try to describe Joseph after his death, as if he had been Gaon; in his letter to a trustee of the yeshiva (whose name and place we do not know), he speaks of a certain person who has something in writing from 'our Master Joseph av (bēt-dīn) our brother, of blessed memory', see **419**. The letter of condolence: **384**. The letter written by Joseph for Solomon b. Judah: **173**; he also wrote **405**, on behalf of the Jerusalemites, on the subject of aid for the poor of Jerusalem, to Ephraim b. Shemaria; also **406–411** are letters in his handwriting, and they all deal with public affairs and matters concerning the court. Document **410a** is a fragment of the ending of a letter written by Joseph ha-Kohen b. Solomon Gaon when he was already *av-bēt-dīn* in the yeshiva, at the beginning of 1048, still during the gaonate of Solomon b. Judah. As in two other letters (**411**, **420**), we also find here ornate phrases based on verses in the Bible. *Yesha' yuḥāsh*, see **407**, b. The excommunication of the cantor: **334**. Solomon b. Judah on Joseph: **149**. There is also an apologetic tone here and the Gaon points out that he is grateful to Joseph's father, Solomon ha-Kohen Gaon. In another letter, much earlier than this, Solomon b. Judah

of Abiathar. After the death of his brother Joseph, he became *av-bēt-dīn* of the Palestinian yeshiva, until the death of Daniel b. Azariah. According to the Scroll, the period of his gaonate lasted for twenty-three years. Actually, Elijah served for twenty-one years and three months: from August 1062 until November 1083, but in his Scroll, Abiathar reckoned from Elul AM 4822, until Kislev AM 4843, and as was customary in those early times, he added the marginal years as well. Abiathar completely overlooks those years in which the yeshiva was still located in Jerusalem, when his father Elijah was Gaon (before it moved to Tyre). Some documents preserved in the Geniza round out our information on Elijah ha-Kohen. In my collection, there are eleven documents in his handwriting, and he is mentioned frequently in the letters of his contemporaries.

In a deed written when he was in Damascus, on 5 May 1031, he signed: Elijah ha-Kohen he-ḥāvēr in the Great Sanhedrin', etc. He apparently stayed there after he and his brother were released from jail, after having been involved in the affair of the excommunication of the Karaites. In a deed written by Solomon b. Judah, on 31 October 1036, Elijah is mentioned when he was already 'the sixth of the ḥavūrā'. We have already seen that during the dispute with Nathan b. Abraham, he was 'fifth', as was also laid down in the conditions of the agreement after the dispute.

After the death of Tobiah b. Daniel, Elijah became 'the fourth', and after Nathan b. Abraham's demise, 'the third'. We have found one of his letters from that time, written to the exilarch David b. Hezekiah. Ephraim b. Shemaria's letter, written near the end of his life in *ca.* 1055, when Elijah was *av-bēt-dīn*, is of particular interest. During this period, he also wrote a letter to Abū Sa'd Ḥalfon b. Solomon (whose father, Solomon b. Nathan, was one of Nathan b. Abraham's supporters), in which he describes the rumour that Abraham b. Isaac ha-Talmīd took a second wife in Ascalon. On the face of it, it is an innocent letter, in which he disengages himself from the rumours that were spread about, but one should note that Ḥalfon b. Solomon (or perhaps his father) and also Abraham b. ha-Talmīd

expresses a critical opinion of the two priestly brothers: they are only prepared to make an effort when there is something they could gain from it (hence they do not come to Ramla). See **80**, a, lines 8–9. Joseph and the ban on the Karaites: **182**. Restoration of the ruin: **231**. Letter of the emissary: **398**. Israel b. Nathan's letter: **475**. The fragment of the commentary: TS Arabic Box 18(1), f. 58; where there is a sentence also used by Hayy Gaon in his book 'of purchases and sales', end of ch. xxxviii. The letters of 'Eli ha-Kohen: **450**, line 15; **451**, a, lines 2ff; in **452**, a, line 8, 'Eli ha-Kohen sends regards to Solomon ha-Kohen b. Joseph and asks what is happening to him. Israel b. Nathan: **479**, b, line 12. On Passover of the year AM 4819, AD 1059, Solomon was still in Ramla, see the letter of Avon b. Ṣedaqa, **498**, a, lines 11–12. It seems that he visited Palestine in 1065, when he signed a deed drawn up in the court of the yeshiva: **425**, line 18. TS NS J 379 is a fragment of a deed relating to 'Eli ('Ūla) ha-Levi b. Joseph, with the signature, 'Solomon ha-Kohen b. Joseph *av* great-grandson of Solom[on Gaon]'.

belonged to the faction opposing the priestly family and were partisans of their rivals, at first of Nathan b. Abraham and afterwards of David b. Daniel, as we shall observe in the continuation.

When he became Gaon after the death of Daniel b. Azariah, Elijah evidently managed to establish good relations with the Maghribis, who stood by Daniel b. Azariah during the dispute over the gaonate, and afterwards supported Daniel's son David in his struggle against the priestly family. Avon b. Ṣedaqa describes in one of his letters a visit with the Gaon in October 1064. Avon reminded him that Nehorai b. Nissim (to whom he writes) was fond of him even before he became *av-bēt-dīn*. It is implied there that the Maghribis exercised their influence with the Fatimid authorities and managed to get him a *sijill*, certainly meaning here an official appointment. Elijah thanked him for this, although the *sijill* had not arrived in Jerusalem as yet. At the same meeting, Avon told him about the suffering endured by the Maghribi merchants who are being mistreated, and especially about the fire which destroyed their ships. Another Maghribi merchant, Ismā'īl b. Isaac al-Andalusī, also mentions Elijah ha-Kohen Gaon. According to him, the Gaon expressed his dissatisfaction with the contacts maintained by Ismā'īl with two members of the Kashkīl family, Spanish scholars who settled in Acre.

I have already noted the difference between the two brothers, Joseph and Elijah, and we have seen that Solomon b. Judah pointed out that he did not find in Elijah those faults of character which he found in his older brother. However, the tension and rivalry seem to have hardened Elijah as well and he treated his rivals vigorously and harshly. A letter written in his name by his son Abiathar in about 1065, warns the Fustat parnās, 'Eli ha-Kohen b. Ḥayyim, that a certain Shemaria b. Meshullam is about to arrive there. It seems that this man offended the priestly family in some manner, and the Gaon demands that they make his life a misery – 'to reward him according to his wickedness and to unveil his disgrace' – and also to bring this to the attention of the two brothers, Judah and Mevorakh, sons of Saadia: 'Judah, the dear ḥāvēr, *rōsh kallā, ha-me'ullē* of the *ḥavūrā*, and his brother, *alūf ha-bīnōt*' (Judah is still not called Nagid here), and also 'to the attention of all our brethren in Egypt'. The last deed written by Elijah ha-Kohen Gaon in Jerusalem (to the extent that deeds were preserved) dates from the summer of 1071.[171]

171 The Scroll of Abiathar on Elijah ha-Kohen: **559**, b, lines 15ff. Documents written by Elijah: **412–422**. The deed from Damascus: **415**; this is a receipt from Khibā', daughter of Abraham al-Ḥazzām al-Rūshtābī, to Solomon b. Musāfir; signed by nine witnesses; al-Ḥazzām al-Rūshtābī – 'the rustic packer' (*rūstābī*, in Persian, rustic); *ḥazzām*, see Dozy, s.v., and also Qāsimī, I, 96f. Solomon b. Judah's deed: **124**; see also **127**, line 18, where Elijah is still 'the sixth'. In one of his letters written when he was still young, which is a letter of condolence to his cousin Abraham ha-Kohen b. Isaac b. Furāt on the death of his father, Elijah writes around his signature the formula: '*he-'aṣūr mi-penē sha'ōn*', probably

[899] We now turn to the transfer of the yeshiva to Tyre. Above, I have described the Turcomans' conquest of Palestine and their conquest of Jerusalem in 1073. We have no exact information about the transfer of the yeshiva to Tyre, nor do we know whether this took place before or after the conquest of Jerusalem. Apparently, it is not fortuitous that it is to Tyre that the yeshiva moved from Jerusalem. Firstly, Tyre was close to the border of Palestine. Secondly, it had a large and organised Jewish congregation, which for generations was both attached and subordinate to the Palestinian yeshiva. Thirdly, as a port city, it offered possibilities of maintaining contact with Jewish communities living in other countries on the shores of the Mediterranean, Egypt in particular, when overland routes were endangered by warfare. Fourthly, as we have observed, Tyre had its own local ruler, from whom one could expect a more tolerant and even benevolent approach. We do not know how things really were, as for twenty years, before the Turcomans' conquest and afterward, almost nothing was said of these matters in the letters of the yeshiva. We find a fragment of a letter written by the Gaon Elijah ha-Kohen, from which only a request from the addressee to help the congregation in Ascalon could be read, and two fragments from another letter, which speaks of 'repairing the house' and 'the courtyards of the Lord's Temple'. Ezekiel ha-Kohen b. 'Eli left for Fustat (like his father, he was frequently on journeys on behalf of the yeshiva, and we shall find him on a similar mission below, during the gaonate of Abiathar ha-Kohen). He was entrusted with the task of explaining the situation of the yeshiva and collecting money due to the Jerusalemites from the income of the *heqdēsh* and from donations from people in Fustat. We can only assume that the letters were written in Tyre, in about 1080.

The first hint of the yeshiva's being situated in Tyre is perhaps a fragment from a power-of-attorney deed drawn up in Tripoli. A certain Yeshū'ā, 'pride of the congregation', appoints 'Ūla ha-Levi as trustee. Signatories to the deed are Solomon b. Isaac, who calls himself 'great-grandson of Meir Gaon'; Naḥum b. Yannai, of the Baradānī family (who lived in Tyre, as we have seen), and a further six witnesses. The deed was

meaning: 'who avoids uproar': **414**, and see also the note there. The letter to David b. Ezekiel: **416**. To Ephraim b. Shemaria: **418**, of which I have already quoted the main points above. Avon's letter: **500**, a, lines 18ff. Ismā'īl b. Isaac: **511**, upper margin. The matter of Abraham b. ha-Talmīd: **421**, an episode already mentioned above. On Elijah ha-Kohen's visit to Ascalon, when he is already Gaon, we learn from TS Box Misc. 27, f. 23, see: Friedman, *Gratz College Annual*, 1 (1972), 58 f; this is a court deed from Fustat (15 December 1094) concerning 'Eli b. Yefet who had bought a Nubian slave-girl in Ascalon at one time, set her free, married her and had a daughter by this marriage; the *muqaddam* (the appointee over the community) in Ascalon and Elijah ha-Kohen, head of the yeshiva Ge'ōn Ya'aqōv, who was then staying in Ascalon, dealt with the matter of this marriage. The matter of Shemaria b. Meshullam: **423**. The deed from 1071: **428**. Of much interest is

written on Monday, 9 Sivan AM 4839, that is 13 May AD 1079. We find a more explicit confirmation in a marriage deed written in Tyre on Thursday, 7 Elul AM 4839, that is 8 August AD 1079. Ḥalfon b. Aaron marries Ghāliya, daughter of Musāfir. Among the signatories, we find ʻAmram ha-Kohen b. Aaron, the son-in-law of Abiathar, son of the Gaon. At about the same time, another marriage deed was written by ʻAmram ha-Kohen himself, from which a fragment has been preserved. We find that a third of a new house in the western part of Tyre (evidently in the vicinity of the port) was included in the bride's dowry.

Two years before his death in AM 4842 (AD 1081) Elijah ha-Kohen organised a large assembly of community representatives ('all Israel') in Tyre, on Succoth. This was in line with the tradition of assembling on the Mount of Olives on Hoshaʻna rabbā, which that year fell on 28 September. The rulers of Tyre at the time were Nafīs and his brother, the sons of the cadi Ibn Abī ʻAqīl. They may have succeeded in maintaining a position of neutrality towards the two opponents, the Fatimids and the Turcomans. At any rate, it seems that people from communities in the various regions were able to reach the assembly despite the fighting. It was at this gathering that Elijah ha-Kohen proclaimed Abiathar as his successor as Gaon; Abiathar's brother Solomon ha-Kohen, was appointed *av-bēt-dīn* on the same occasion, and Zadok b. Josiah, the 'third' in the yeshiva. It was said of Josiah (b. Aaron b. Josiah b. Abraham), the father of Zadok, that he had been *av-bēt-dīn*, probably under Elijah ha-Kohen. Be that as it may, the members of this family were not the offspring of Josiah Gaon b. Aaron. Abiathar points out in his scroll that this was the accepted and normal advancement, for he had served as *av-bēt-dīn* before this, his brother Solomon was the 'third', and Zadok was the 'fourth'. The pronouncement of these appointments is confirmed in a letter from Saadia he-ḥavēr b. Abraham, of Hebron, to Abiathar. He calls Abiathar 'head of the yeshiva Ge'ōn Yaʻaqōv' (when his father, Elijah Gaon, was still alive), and expresses his happiness on the fact that 'our Lord the Gaon, may God preserve him' was lucky to live long enough 'to see his son occupying his seat'; they 'pray for Abiathar every day in the Cave of Machpelah', and on the Day of Atonement they did this even before they received confirmation of his appointment. The writer learned of the appointment from a letter he received from Abiathar himself, who had sent it to him together with a gift of one dinar (evidently it was the custom to allocate money to the Hebronites). Abiathar himself was then in Fustat, it seems, and thus the letter reached the Geniza. The letter itself does not make the impression of having been written in Tyre.

the very special formula used by Elijah Gaon in his signature (and also by his offspring), 'called the Gaon of God'; see the discussion on it: Friedman, *Marriage*, II, 153ff.

One year later, probably again on Hosha'na rabbā, that is, 18 September 1082, an event occurred which made a tremendous impression at the time. This was an assembly on actual Palestinian soil, in Haifa. There the year was 'sanctified' and the gaonate and the ordination renewed, 'in the house of the congregation' (*bēt ha-wa'ad*, by which the local synagogue was meant, apparently). The little that Abiathar tells us of this gathering is enough for us to understand its real intention – to alert the Jewish congregations against the seizure of leadership by David b. Daniel b. Azariah. He writes of appointments of ḥavērīm being ordained by the yeshiva (or the Great Sanhedrin, as they called themselves) from among the notables of the communities in order that they may serve as judges in their localities. We read between the lines that certain suitable figures were appointed, whose loyalty to the Palestinian yeshiva and the priestly family were not in doubt. This assembly was in fact a familiar ceremony, except that this time it was not held on the Mount of Olives but in Haifa. As the yeshiva and its head were already under considerable pressure from David b. Daniel's faction, which had by this time achieved a certain foothold in Egypt, it is not surprising that Elijah ha-Kohen Gaon pronounced an excommunication in Haifa 'on anyone who opposes and differs and on every usurper and trespasser', and it is clear who this was aimed at. The ban was also legally entered in 'a book', that is, a deed, as were the decisions concerning appointments, 'signed by the hand of all the scholars therein'. In other words, all those present signed that deed, or at any rate, the most notable among them did so. One should bear in mind that these events occurred one year before the death of Elijah ha-Kohen. He died in Kislev 1395 Sel. (which began on 14 November AD 1083).

Direct evidence of one of the participants in the assembly in Haifa can be found in a letter-treatise written by Shelah 'the sixth' b. Naḥum, which deals with the question of which coastal towns belong to Palestine, a subject which assumed special significance during the struggle with David b. Daniel. He writes there, among other things: 'and I came to Haifa, where they also prayed over me [that is, appointed me] as "sixth"'[172]

[900] Elijah ha-Kohen was buried in Daltūn in the Upper Galilee, and

172 The fragments relating to Tyre: **429**, **431**; see the details on matters relating to Tyre above, secs. 298–300, in the discussion on the city itself, on events there, and on the cadi Ibn Abī 'Aqīl and his family and connections with the Jewish Maghribi merchants. The deed of trusteeship: **604**; Solomon b. Isaac great-grandson of Meir Gaon is perhaps the son of Isaac *he-ḥāvēr ha-rōsh* who was listed above with the offspring of Meir Gaon. The marriage deed from Tyre: **600**. The fragment of a marriage deed: **601**; 'Amram ha-Kohen b. Aaron, Abiathar's son-in-law, was the son of a branch of this priestly family, as can be seen from his signature in TS 28.5 (edited by Friedman, *Dīnē Israel*, 5[1973/4], 211–216): "Amram ha-Kohen b. R. Aaron, may he have a good end, b. R. 'Amram of blessed memory, great-grandson of Elijah ha-Kohen . . . grandson of Aaron the Chief Priest, the Saint of God, of blessed memory'. The assembly in Tyre: **559**, b, lines 16–19; Josiah and

how this was achieved while the Turcomans controlled the entire surrounding area we do not know. Perhaps one of their commanders was bribed, or perhaps it was made possible owing to the good relationship between the Turcomans and the rulers of Tyre.

Abiathar inherited his father's seat and saw himself appointed to this high office by Divine Providence. As the yeshiva was cut off from the source of its vitality and prestige, situated outside of Palestine and no longer in Jerusalem, Abiathar and those around him clung to the principles of the ideology of consanguinity, of the vocation of the *kōhanīm* and of the centrality of the Sanhedrin in Palestine. This was the focus of their self-consciousness. Abiathar refers to himself in his Scroll and also in other documents as 'Abiathar ha-Kohen called by the name of God, son of a Gaon great-grandson (thus it should be read) of a Gaon'.

Abiathar Gaon was one of the four sons of the Gaon Elijah ha-Kohen. Apart from Solomon, whom I have already mentioned as having now become *av-bēt-dīn* in the yeshiva, Elijah had two other sons, Zadok and Eleazar. A letter from Zadok written in Jerusalem on 28 June 1056 has been preserved, evidently to his brother Abiathar, who was then staying in Fustat, concerning a debt due to their relative Mevorakh for a shipment of scented oil. Zadok died in 1094, probably, and a draft of a letter of condolence on his death written to his brother, the Gaon Abiathar ha-Kohen, by Ḥalfon and Joseph, evidently from Ascalon, has been preserved. As to Eleazar, his name is clearly written on the reverse side of a Geniza fragment, evidently a commentary to the book of Hosea: 'Eleazar ha-Kohen son of Elijah ha-Kohen of holy blessed memory; his brother Abiathar ha-Kohen, called by the name of God, son of a Gaon great-grandson of a Gaon, of blessed holy memory'. The aforementioned letter from Saadia he-ḥāvēr of Hebron to Abiathar ha-Kohen, contains expressions of sympathy on the death of Eleazar, and it is now clear to us that he meant this brother. It is also clear, therefore, that he died at about the

Zadok, his son, evidently lived in Acre earlier on, see **599**, line 28. **574** is a letter written by Zadok b. Josiah after the Crusaders' conquest of Palestine, concerning members of the family who had been taken captive; from which it is possible to understand that his family may have continued to live in Acre, while he himself lived in Tyre; see above, sec. 301. Contrary to what was written by Mann, *Jews*, I, 193f, Zadok never became *av-bēt-dīn*, and what he wrote was based on an error regarding document **568** (*ibid.*, II, 200f), of which he assumed that it was from 1096, whereas actually it was from 1076; as to Abraham b. Nathan 'av of the yeshiva', he was not *av-bēt-dīn*, and the title 'av of the yeshiva' relates to his father, Nathan b. Abraham. The letter from Hebron: **614**, a, lines 7ff. The alarm caused by David b. Daniel can be seen in the above-mentioned letter (**614**) of Saadia he-ḥāvēr the Hebronite, to Abiathar, who is in Egypt, in the opening of his letter, where he wrote in praise of Abiathar and his priority over someone who is not of priestly descent, clearly referring to David b. Daniel, as was also understood by Braslavi, *Eretz-Israel*, 5(1958/9), 221. Shelah b. Nahum: **550**, b, line 39, where the reference is certainly to this assembly in Haifa.

same time as his brother Abiathar was proclaimed Gaon, towards the end of 1081.[173]

[901] The first information we have on Abiathar ha-Kohen dates from the period when his father was already Gaon. On 16 July 1067, he was in Fustat signing his name on a colophon written entirely in his own hand, on the first page of a quire containing Hayy Gaon's commentary to the tractate Ḥagiga, together with the *sefer ha-dīnīn* (book of laws) of Rabbēnū Ḥananel and with 'gleanings and queries' which he copied for himself in Fustat. There he calls himself: 'Abiathar ha-Kohen the fourth of the ḥavūrā'. If we assume that he was then twenty-five years old (this is an assumption that has no further foundation than that he was relatively young at the time), then he was born in 1042.

After some three years or more, on 14 November 1070, Abiathar wrote a letter from Jerusalem, to the parnās 'Eli ha-Kohen b. Ḥayyim, in which he speaks mainly of a man who came from 'the land of the Franks' and of the affairs of Judah b. Saadia, 'the Nagid'. From this letter, it appears that Abiathar is still very young and he treats the addressee as if he were his father, for he insists that he should not be addressed as 'your servant' in his letters. He also apologises for having written letters to 'Eli b. 'Amram, *he-ḥavēr ha-me'ullē*, and not to the addressee, but these were merely deeds of trusteeship. It was his father, the Gaon, who wrote to the congregation in Fustat and to the *me'ullē*. Here too, Abiathar is still calling himself 'the fourth'.

Apparently, at about the same time, Abiathar became his father's chief aide, which was customary – as we have seen – with regard to the eldest son of a Gaon. On 15 April 1071, 'Eli ha-Kohen b. Ezekiel, the Jerusalem parnās, wrote to Abiathar, 'the fourth of the ḥavūrā'. The latter was then in Fustat, and from the deed I shall forthwith mention, it emerges that he was about to return home. I have already mentioned this letter, which contains news of the Turcomans' invasion of Palestine, the disrupted

173 The burial of Elijah ha-Kohen: **559**, b, lines 23ff; we find here the expression 'Eleazar b. Azariah his ancestor' (alongside whose grave Elijah was buried), apparently being evidence that this priestly family claimed descent from Eleazar b. Azariah, a matter I have already mentioned above. As to the burial of the ancient Jewish sages mentioned in the Scroll of Abiathar, there are similar accounts some seventy-five years later in Benjamin of Tudela: 'Meron . . . where there are the graves of Hillel and Shammai . . .; Qedesh Naphtali . . . where there are the graves of R. Eliezer b. 'Arākh and R. Eleazar b. Azariah . . . and R. Yose the Galilean'. 'Abiathar who is called by the name of God': **559**, a, line 1; as he also signs in other places. Mann, *Jews*, I, 187, speaks only of three sons of Elijah ha-Kohen: Abiathar, Solomon and Zadok. The letter of Zadok ha-Kohen b. Elijah: **432**; it seems that he is also mentioned in the colophon: **221**, line 9; in both places he calls himself: 'the smallest of the pupils in Shalem' (i.e. Jerusalem). The letter of condolence on the death of Zadok ha-Kohen: **554**. Eleazar ha-Kohen: ULC Or 1081 Box 1, f. 24; the condolences of Saadia he-ḥāvēr on the death of Eleazar ha-Kohen: **614**, b, lines 1–6; see the doubts of Braslavi, *Eretz-Israel*, 5(1958/9), 221.

roads, the rulers' mistreatment of the people in Jaffa and the rebellion in Tyre. Abiathar is staying in Fustat with Judah the Nagid b. Saadia and his brother Mevorakh. 'Eli asks Abiathar to look into the affairs (in Fustat) of his son-in-law Hiba (Nathan) b. Israel (or perhaps he meant his brother-in-law, *ṣihr*) who abandoned his wife and children in Jerusalem two years earlier (that is, in 1069). From this letter we also learn that Abiathar's *kunya* was Abū'l-Faḍl.

In Jerusalem in Tammuz AM 4831, that is, May or June AD 1071, Abiathar is a signatory to a deed referring to a claim of alimony, written by his father Elijah Gaon. Alongside his father's signature, he signed: 'Abiathar ha-Kohen son of the Gaon'. There is a similar signature in a fragment of a deed evidently written at about the same time, also in the handwriting of Elijah Gaon. Abiathar collaborated with his father in writing the responsa to the queries of Meshullam b. Moses of Mainz, where it is possible to read his signature: 'Abiathar ha-Kohen the fourth in the ḥavūrā.' Apparently at the same time, in 1071, he wrote his letter to Mevorakh, evidently b. Saadia, that is, the brother of Judah, who became the Nagid on the death of the latter. The letter describes the ill-treatment of the owners of *dukkān al-ḥarīr* (the silk shop) in Alexandria. We also find a colophon in Abiathar's hand, written on what was the title-page of the Talmudic tractate Bava qamma, dated AM 4832, that is AD 1071/2, in Jerusalem. It seems that even before the yeshiva moved from Jerusalem, Abiathar had risen to the status of 'third in the yeshiva', as is evidenced by a fragment of a court document written in Fustat in which a letter is mentioned as having been received from 'our Master, his great honour, our Lord and Master Abiathar the third of the ḥavūrā'. It speaks of a legacy of one of Fustat's notables who was also a parnās, Abraham 'known as b. al-Zayyāt' (dealer in oil). Thus we learn that Abiathar was in Fustat on a mission for the yeshiva during the Turcomans' invasion and that he succeeded in returning to Jerusalem safely, despite the considerable danger encountered on the roads.

In 1077 we again find him in Fustat, where he is a signatory on a court document written by Abraham b. Nathan, concerning an inheritance which mentions 'the trustworthy parnās b. Ya'īsh', who is undoubtedly 'Eli ha-Kohen b. Ḥayyim. Apart from 'Abraham b. R. Nathan *av* of the yeshiva, of blessed righteous memory', we also find there the signatures of Abraham b. R. Isaac of blessed memory (who is 'b. ha-Talmīd') as well as of 'Abiathar [son of the Gaon great-] grandson of a Gaon of blessed memory'. The date is Thursday, 3 Nisan 1388 Sel., 30 March AD 1077. It should be noted that the date is a little more than a month after the warding off of the Turcomans' offensive in Egypt (19 February 1077). At about the same time that Abiathar was staying in Fustat, Atsiz carried out the massacre in Jerusalem, mentioned earlier. We do not know to what extent the Jews of Jerusalem were affected by this, nor do we know whether Abiathar reached Fustat via Jerusalem or via Tyre – in other words, we do not know where the yeshiva was situated at the time.[174]

The affair of David b. Daniel

[902] Once again, the Jewish world was shaken by the fury of a dispute over its leadership, and this lasted for some fifteen years. This time, it was not a dispute over the position of head of the Palestinian yeshiva, but a struggle between the yeshiva and a new force, which called for a renewed exilarchate, this time with its centre in Egypt. In principle, this struggle was made possible by the decline in the status and vitality of the yeshiva, as a result of having to leave Jerusalem and thus losing much of its prestige and attraction for the Jews of the diaspora. Pilgrimages to Jerusalem were undoubtedly interrupted and what remained was a mere shadow of its past glory. The income of the yeshiva had certainly been considerably reduced.

[174] The colophon: **545**. Abiathar's letter to 'Eli ha-Kohen: **547** a, lines 13, 31ff. 'Eli ha-Kohen b. Ezekiel: **455**; the deed of alimony: **428**; Hiba b. Isrā'īl (Nathan b. Israel) is perhaps identical with Hiba al-Baṣrī al-A'raj who, according to **425**, asked to bring his wife al-Ḥasana from Egypt to Ramla. The other fragment: **427**. The responsa to Meshullam b. Moses: Bodl MS Heb c 23, f. 42. The matter of Alexandria: **548**. The colophon: **549**. The court document: TS Box K 24, f. 25. Cohen, *Self-Government*, 162, writes with an inexplicable amount of certainty: 'Doubtless Elijah hoped that Evyatar's presence in the Egyptian capital would make it difficult for the new negid to subvert the gaonate' (referring to the suspicion that Judah b. Saadia may have intended to compete with the Palestinian yeshiva). This has no foundation, however; for we have seen that it was the Gaon who granted the title Nagid to the brothers, Saadia's sons, one after the other; and in what follows, we shall realise that there was cooperation and solidarity between them, and during the dispute with David b. Daniel, the Gaon and the Nagid even shared the same fate, which I shall describe below. The court document from 1077: ULC Or 1080 J 9, and cf. Cohen, *ibid.*, 108, 122, 162. A poem written by Abiathar contains expressions of longing for Jerusalem, while he was staying in Egypt, first in Fustat, then in Alexandria, where he was warmly received by 'westerners' who were his faithful followers. It is not possible to determine the time of its writing, it may have been written when he was already Gaon (this may be the reason why he does not call himself 'fourth' or something similar, in the signature). The yeshiva was then in Tyre and his yearning for Jerusalem is therefore understandable; it is also possible that he came to Egypt on behalf of the yeshiva at a much earlier stage. The nature of his embroilment in Egypt mentioned in the poem is not explained either. See the poem, TS NS 193.32, ed. Fleischer, *Zion*, 49(1984), 396f. Abiathar is also mentioned in a letter from Ḥayy (?) b. Sa'āda to Abū Naṣr Judah b. . . . al-Dimashqī who was then in the port of Tyre; the writer paid, as requested, nineteen dinars which he had from the addressee, fourteen for *sayyidnā ra's al-mathība* (head of the yeshiva; evidently: Daniel b. Azariah) and five for *sayyidnā av bēt dīn*. The payment was made through Abū 'Alī Ḥusayn b. Muslim. The writer was asked to welcome '*al-rayyis* Abū'l-Faḍl, son of our Master av-bēt-dīn', that is, Abiathar b. Elijah, in Tyre; but times were hard and the writer tries to avoid it. This letter: TS 10 J 13, f. 21, mentioned also by Goitein, *Mediterranean Society*, I, 268, who assumed that it was written in Ascalon.

This was the background to the appearance of a young and vigorous man, a descendant of exilarchs, one of the *nesī'īm*, bearing the insignia of the House of David.

Most of the information on the outset of David b. Daniel's route is drawn from the Scroll of Abiathar. It begins with the data on his genealogy, which in fact goes back to the House of David, though to those of its bad kings, such as Ahaz and his ilk. He was also related to the family of *bīsh na'ar*, which is unexplained, but one can assume here that Bustanai was perhaps written in the original, a matter which I have discussed. The copyist of the Scroll evidently was not acquainted with the story of Bustanai and Daniel's relationship to it. Therefore, he could not decipher the name, or there may have been a play on words here which we cannot fathom.

In my collection there is a letter from David b. Daniel to some unidentified personality in Fustat, which sheds light on the chronological aspect of David's history. In this letter, he announces that he is about to arrive in Fustat 'to renew the alliance with its people'. He asks that the reply to his letter be sent to Tinnīs (the port city) in order that it reach him more quickly, which implies that he intended to come from Damīga, as it is called in the Scroll, which is Damīra (where he was staying), to Fustat via Tinnīs. The date of the letter is 18 Kislev 1391 Sel., that is 15 November AD 1079. The letter was written by someone else (probably his scribe) and at the end of the letter, David added regards to the son of the addressee in his own handwriting, the date, and the *'alāma*, his identifying formula (which was also that of his father, Daniel b. Azariah): *yeshū'ā*. We now return to the Scroll's version, with the words 'and three years before that', by which Abiathar means three years before what he considered the most important event of all those described by him until then, that is, the pronouncement of his succession to the seat of Gaon by his father, in September 1081. From this we understand that David set out on his way in 1078. Abiathar tells us further that David was then twenty years old, which means that he was born in 1058, a year before his father took ill, and that he was four when his father Daniel b. Azariah died, in 1062. Hence, when he was about to arrive in Tinnīs (15 November 1079), David was twenty-one.[175]

[903] We have no information about David's childhood and

[175] The Scroll of Abiathar: **559**, b, lines 27ff, and continued on c; Bornstein suggested that *bīsh na'ar* should be read: *be-shin'ār*, i.e. in Babylonia, see the *Sokolow Jubilee Volume*, 48, n. 5. David's letter: **532**; Marx, *JQR*, NS 1 (1910/1), 74ff refers the interval of the three years to Elijah ha-Kohen's death (November 1083) mentioned in the Scroll shortly before that, and concludes that David set out (from Iraq!) in 1081, arriving in Egypt only in 1083 (two years after his emigration, according to the Scroll); here he finds a contradiction between what is said in the Scroll and the marriage deed of David's wife, which has been

adolescence. As we have seen, he was four when his father died, and we can surmise that it was his older brothers who raised him. We already know that Samuel b. Daniel, the eldest, was one of the leaders of the congregation in Damascus, according to a document dated October 1074, when David was sixteen. Or perhaps he was reared by his sister, for we know that Abū'l-Sarī Barhūn, Daniel b. Azariah's son-in-law, evidently lived in Damascus as well. It is therefore likely that David grew up in Damascus, and left there, as we have seen, in 1078, at the age of twenty. Palestine was then under Turcoman rule, as was Damascus. It appears that the yeshiva was already in Tyre then. We have no idea whether, on setting out on his way, David already harboured the intention of struggling for the leadership of the Jewish diaspora. One could assume from the fact that he spent two years in a comparatively out-of-way place such as Damīra, that this was not the case, and that only in the course of his stay in Egypt did this ambition awaken within him, the impulse being aroused in him by others as well. David remained in Damīra for two years after reaching it in 1078, probably close to the beginning of the year. He stayed with a Damascene who had settled there (undoubtedly one of the close friends of David's family in Damascus), Maṣlīaḥ b. Yefet b. Zub'a. David even became engaged to his host Maṣlīaḥ's daughter, Abiathar tells us. We know that Maṣlīaḥ was one of two brothers, sons of Yefet, and that his brother's name was 'Uthmān.

In November 1079 David left the home of his benefactor (and also of his fiancee) and abandoned Damīra. We may assume that his departure was preceded by a sort of campaign to win over the devotees of the house of the *nesī'īm*, as well as those who cherished the memory of his father, Daniel b. Azariah. There is some indication of this in a record of evidence before a court in Alexandria from 14 May 1079, written by Hillel b. 'Eli, who afterwards became one of David's chief supporters. We find here the evidence of Muvḥār (*mukhtār* in Arabic) the elder b. Ṣedaqa, who is apparently identical with Mukhtār al-'Aṭṭār (perfume dealer), father of Ṣedaqa (i.e., the grandson of the former Ṣedaqa), apparently one of the wealthy men of the time, who conducted business in Tyre, Fustat and

preserved, in which it says that they were married in Fustat in 1082! He tried to extricate himself from this complication by suggesting reading 'six' instead of 'three' in the Scroll, that is, that he set out on his way in 1078 and reached Egypt in 1080. Bacher claimed (illogically) that if David really set out in 1081, and was then aged twenty, as the Scroll states, he could not have been Daniel b. Azariah's son, for the latter died in August 1062: Bacher, *JQR*, 15(1902/3), 86, n. 6; there he differs utterly with the (correct) opinion of Schechter, the first editor of the Scroll, that the David of the Scroll was the son of Daniel b. Azariah, see *Saadyana*, 81; see also the reservations of Cohen, *Self-Government*, 186, n. 18, regarding my chronological reconstruction, reservations which I consider unjustified, as they are founded on the (incorrect) claim that it was not David b. Daniel who wrote the additional part in **532**.

Palestine, and was afterwards granted the title 'ḥavēr' by David. Muvḥār states in his evidence that 'Imrān and Ezra, sons of Bashīr b. Naḥum, who were adversaries of Daniel b. Azariah and had even been excommunicated by him previously, were having a stormy argument with Muvḥār in the foyer of the house of a certain Za'īm al-Mulk, pouring vile curses on Daniel's head. We may assume that this evidence (seventeen years after the death of Daniel b. Azariah!) was somehow connected with the manner in which David, his son, organised his followers, and perhaps even expressed the desire to win his approval.[176]

[904] David reached Fustat near the close of the year 1079, and there he was warmly welcomed by Mevorakh b. Saadia (the Nagid) and the son of David's aunt (his father's sister), whom we already know as Abū Sā'd Josiah ha-Kohen b. Azariah.

The Scroll of Abiathar mentions the breaking off of David's engagement to the daughter of Maṣlīah b. Yefet. This occurred on Purim, evidently in the year AM 4841, or 26 February AD 1081. At the instigation of his cousin Josiah ha-Kohen, he afterwards married 'the daughter of the prince of the time'. The marriage deed of this woman has been preserved in the Geniza and we learn from it that her name was Nāshiya, that she came from a Karaite family, and that she was the daughter of Moses ha-Kohen b. Aaron. The date of the marriage deed: 23 Shevat 1393 Sel., Sunday 15 January AD 1082, that is, less than a year after breaking off his engagement with his fiancee from Damīra. Fourteen people signed the marriage deed, among them Ezekiel ha-Kohen b. 'Eli (who is 'Eli ha-Kohen the Jerusalemite, b. Ezekiel, the well-known parnās); the cantor and scribe Hillel b. 'Eli; Abraham b. Isaac ha-Talmīd; and of particular interest, Abiathar's cousin, Solomon ha-Kohen b. Joseph *av-bēt-dīn*, who afterwards was also a signatory on a document from David's court. Apparently the relationship between the two cousins, Solomon and Abiathar, was marred for some reason. As to the father of the bride, Moses ha-Kohen b. Aaron, 'prince of the time', he was one of the Karaite notables and wealthy men of Fustat. In his daughter's marriage deed, he is

[176] On Maṣlīaḥ b. Yefet, the Damascene in Damīra, see: Goitein, *Eretz-Israel*, 8(1966/7), 288f. The document from Alexandria: **531**; Ṣedaqa he-ḥāvēr b. Mukhtār, see the deed of partnership to which he is a party, in the handwriting of David b. Daniel: **541**, autumn 1086; see Ṣedaqa b. Muvḥār in the Hebrew Index. On the life of David in Fustat, see the Scroll of Abiathar: **559**, c, lines 5ff. A special relationship may have grown between David and the 'Babylonian' congregation in Fustat, as one can deduce from what is said in TS 10 J 7, f. 10, a document which contains a description of the affair of Wuḥsha, a woman who gave birth out of wedlock, see: Goitein, *JQR Anniversary Volume*, 241f; in lines 10–11 it is said that she went to the synagogue of the 'Babylonians' on the Day of Atonement, and when the *nāsī* saw her, he threw her out. This occurred in about 1080, probably David b. Daniel being referred to, as is also assumed by Goitein, *Mediterranean Society*, III, 280, 489, n. 19.

called 'banner of the Jews and joy of their splendour'. In a Karaite memorial list, he is called 'our crown, diadem of our heads . . . the honourable, mighty and noble prince'. This marriage seems to have been contracted with an eye to the public. Apparently there was support for the exilarchic family among the Karaites. As we have seen, similar things were also said in the Scroll about Daniel b. Azariah, that 'he was supported by the sect of the *ṣela'*', and it seems that the marriage of his son was an indication of this same connection. David's marriage thus took place slightly more than two years after his arrival in Fustat. In the continuation, Abiathar's Scroll describes briefly the quarrel which broke out between David b. Daniel and his cousin and benefactor, Josiah ha-Kohen. It is not accidental that David's rival, Abiathar, speaks respectfully of Josiah ha-Kohen and of his father Azariah as well. There could be no more likely reason for this quarrel than Josiah's rejection of the idea of a rebellion against the Palestinian yeshiva.[177]

[905] The rift between David and the Nagid Mevorakh b. Saadia becomes understandable when seen against the same background, that is their attitude towards the Palestinian yeshiva, for the physicians sons of Saadia were closely connected with the priestly family which headed the Palestinian yeshiva at that time. The dispute between David and Mevorakh first broke out, it emerges from the Scroll, after 1082, and it immediately took on a severe turn, with the consequent need for the intervention of the rulers. In his Scroll, Abiathar points to three stages in the dispute: the expulsion of Mevorakh to the Fayyūm for one year; the permission granted him to return to Lower Egypt, to Alexandria; and his return to his post. There is not the slightest hint in the Scroll as to the cause of the dispute; to the reader of the Scroll at the time, however, this silence in itself was proof of the fact that the dispute stemmed from the struggle

[177] The breaking-off of the engagement and the marriage: **559**, c, lines 7ff; according to what is said there, David sent the *gēṭ*, the deed of his breaking off the engagement, via Ṣedaqa b. Nufay', who is evidently the son of Solomon (Salāma) b. Saadia (Sa'īd) b. Ṣaghīr b. Nufay', mentioned in letters in my collection, see the Hebrew Index; see the appellation of b. Nufay' in **602**, b, and cf.: Goitein, *BJRL*, 54(1971/2), 100, n. 1. Document **602** is a letter from Ṣedaqa, writing from Tyre to his father on 28 October 1090. We find details about Ṣedaqa b. Nufay', the envoy of David b. Daniel, and about his father, in a short letter in the handwriting of Hillel b. 'Eli, saying that they were people who needed aid from the charity chest. Hillel writes to '*al-parnās al-ne'emān reṣūy* (the trustworthy and beloved one) of the yeshiva' asking for help for the two, 'since they are of the town's poor people'. See: TS NS J 294. Also Abū'l-Khayr *ha-gēr* (the proselyte; Abū'l-Khayr, which is correct, not Ben al-Khayr, as in the Scroll of Abiathar in its extant version), is mentioned there in the continuation (see *infra*, sec. 905), and also in the Geniza fragment: TS 8 J 24, f. 7, a, lines 10ff: 'As soon as you read my letter, give Zayn b. Abū'l Khayr *ha-gēr* forty *manns* of cedar resin'. It is a fragment of a merchant's letter dated *ca.* 1100. The marriage deed: TS 24.1, edited (in part) by Schechter, *JQR*, 13(1900/1), 220f. On Moses ha-Kohen b. Aaron see: Mann, *Jews*, I, 176f, 187, n. 2, 188; see also the memorial list: TS 8 K 22, f. 2, b, *ibid.*, II, 211; see also Goitein, *Mediterranean Society*, III, 136, 456, n. 95, who notes that

for the leadership of the diaspora which had begun to forge ahead. The man who helped David get the Nagid Mevorakh out of his way is said to have been a certain Ben al-Khayr *al-gēr* (the proselyte). We have no idea who this proselyte was. As noted above, his correct by-name was Abū'l-Khayr, a frequent *kunya* among the Jews during that period. The family of Saadia, who were close to the rulers, probably had quite a few opponents and even enemies. Abiathar had already written to the Fustat parnās 'Eli ha-Kohen b. Ḥayyim, some ten years before the dispute began (14 November 1071), telling of his anxiety for the Nagid (then Judah b. Saadia): 'Let there be deliverance for our Nagid and may the Lord's will save him from all terror'. Here there is a clear hint of the distress which had befallen Judah b. Saadia.

From here onward, Abiathar enumerates David b. Daniel's deeds, aberrant in his opinion, in the period from 1082 through 1094, twelve years in which he apparently enjoyed the unwavering support of the Jewish leadership in Fustat and the other communities of Egypt and its surroundings, and apparently also that of the authorities. Many letters and documents written by David b. Daniel have been preserved in the Geniza. A formula which is repeated in some of them is, 'and may your well-being, our dear one [or, our honourable one] increase' [or, 'increase forever'], together with the *'alāma, yeshū'ā*. Some of them bear the heading 'son of the exilarch'. In others, he calls himself 'David the *nāsī* b. Daniel the *nāsī* and Gaon'. According to the Scroll, he was given to bullying the cantors and even punishing them by flogging. Some letters also provide evidence of David b. Daniel's manner of imposing his dominion over the cantors and the slaughterers, such as his Arabic letter to Aaron the cantor, who is evidently 'Aaron the *mumḥē* and cantor b. Ephraim of Zoan', that is, of Fustat. He informs him there of the banning of a father and son (the father's name is Saul) for some sin they committed with regard to the slaughtering; the cantor is therefore asked to publicise the matter and to renew the ban until they mend their ways.

David ruled in Alexandria (*Nō' Ammōn*), in Tinnīs ('the Isle of *Ḥanēs'*), in Damietta ('the Isle of *Kaftōr*') and in Fustat (*Shafrīr nīlūs*), and collected taxes from all these communities, a practice previously unheard of. These taxes, mentioned by Abiathar in his Scroll, evidently came from the money for the slaughtering which previously had been set aside for the Palestinian yeshiva. We are well aware of the fact that David dominated the legal system and established his own court. A draft of a deed of partnership in his handwriting, dated Elul AM 4846, that is August–September AD 1086, has been preserved. The deed deals with a part-

the dowry amounted to an enormous sum, some 900 dinars. The quarrel with Josiah ha-Kohen: **559**, c, lines 9–11, and see also *ibid.*, line 6.

nership between Ṣedaqa he-ḥāvēr b. Muvḥār (Mukhtār) and the Jerusalemite Nethanel Hibat Allah b. Yeshū'ā, an expert weaver.[178]

[906] Another letter which bears witness to David's authoritative

[178] The rift with Mevorakh: **559**, c, lines 11ff. Abū'l Khayr, see the previous note. Abiathar's letter: **547**, a, upper margin, lines 10ff. The process of dominating the communities: **559**, c, lines 15ff; d, lines 1–4. The letters of David b. Daniel are collected in my corpus, **532–543**; among the writings in the Geniza, there are additional documents in the handwriting of David b. Daniel. Also in **532** is the characteristic greeting 'and your well-being, dear one, shoud increase', this being further proof that David dictated it and added some lines, which are certainly in his handwriting. Cohen, *Self-Government*, 191, notes that he assembled sixteen documents which mention David, calling him by the title *nāsī*, see *ibid.*, in the note. The deed written by David b. Daniel: **541**. To Aaron the cantor: **538**. Cohen, *ibid.*, 198, hastened to reject the identity I suggested (Gil, *Perāqīm*, 58) for the writer of six of the letters (included in my collection), namely David b. Daniel; he bases his claim on the comparison of the signature of David in **540** and the writing of **538**, which in his opinion are not from the same hand; but he is undoubtedly mistaken, evidently because of the difference in the shape of the *gimmel*. One cannot make decisions on matters of handwriting on the basis of signatures alone, for these are sometimes different from the usual handwriting; as to the *gimmel*, David was in the habit of writing it in two ways, and both can be seen in his letter **536**; the influence of the pen on the handwriting should also be taken into consideration, and David used pens of varying thickness. To the documents written by David, TS 20.162 should be added, which is the draft (or copy) of a court document concerning an inheritance, in which the first nineteen lines are in David's handwriting (a hurried and careless handwriting), after which Hillel b. 'Eli continued (evidently due to David's obvious nervousness). David's identity can also be felt from the contents and style of his letters: **533**, an invitation to one of the people of Fustat to take the trouble and appear before him; **534**, in which he agrees to meet with some unidentified person, while he himself is staying with Abū'l-Barakāt, who swears he will not let him go out of his house; **535**, advising someone not to be bitter; **536**, an episode of two girls, one too young to marry who is an orphan, and the other also too young, but her father married her off, hence the marriage is valid; **537**, instructions to a parnās to execute the payment of alimony to the divorcee of a certain Abū'l-Baqā' Samuel, for their daughter; the payment will be made by Abū'l-Riḍā Solomon b. Mevorakh (cf. on him: Goitein, *Shalem*, 3[1975/6], 95 [= *ha-Yishuv*, 173). The matter of **542** is very clear, which is a fragment from the opening of a letter in the handwriting of David b. Daniel; the style is lofty: 'we wish you much peace, we, our scholars and our judges who sit before us, and the Cherethites and Pelethites (2 Sam., xv:18; meaning – according to the midrash – the Sanhedrin!), for, by the grace of the God of David, our father (i.e. King David), we are at peace'. He further thanks God, 'who lifted up our heads against our enemies, to smite through the loins of them who rise against us, to beam down our foes' and see the notes to this fragment, cf. Scheiber, *Acta Orientalia* (BP), 17(1964), 219, n. 5; **539**, to *rabbēnū* (Nehorai b. Nissim?), about a family quarrel between Mufarrij b. Sulaymān and his wife, with the brother-in-law intervening. The two consider divorcing and David asks the addressee to summon them to the court; from line 4, it emerges that David lives in al-Qāhira, not in Fustat; **543** is a letter of condolence from David to Abū'l-Munā, on the death of his uncle, his father's brother; this Abū'l-Munā is perhaps David's aide and representative, mentioned in the letter of Tobiah ha-Kohen b. 'Eli of Bāniyās, Bodl MS Heb b. 13, f. 15, margin: 'we have learned from Muslims who arrived from Ascalon that Abū'l-Munā, the servant of our Master, has arrived in Ascalon'. Another letter with the heading 'David son of the exilarch' was preserved in the Geniza collection in Paris (Consist. isr. VII A 39), but it has been lost (according to information from the Director of the Library of the Alliance israélite universelle in Paris, from 18 April, 1978); see: Schwab, *REJ*, 64(1912), 120. Two brief letters written by David b. Daniel, **536a**, **536b**, in his characteristic style, addressed to Nehorai b. Nissim, deal with

methods is from the 'Rav', Judah ha-Kohen b. Joseph, the spiritual leader of the Maghribis in Egypt, to Nehorai b. Nissim. The writer tells Nehorai that David b. Daniel had demanded that the cantor Hillel b. 'Eli inform Nehorai that an excommunication of Joseph b. Eleazar al-Ḥarīrī ('the silk merchant'), of Tinnīs, who calls himself ḥāvēr, was to be proclaimed. The reason for this was that David had learned that this man has been calling for prayer for the well-being of someone whom the authorities have not recognised as 'head'. Obviously, the man in question was Abiathar ha-Kohen; his name was being mentioned in the prayer, as was customary in the synagogues in Egypt with regard to the Palestinian Gaon. This was a custom which David b. Daniel naturally tried to root out, for he was the 'head' from then on and it was his authority that should be mentioned in prayer. For the time being, various people intervened in the matter and obtained David's agreement to postpone the excommunication until Joseph b. Eleazar answered the warning letter that was written to him. Therefore, the 'Rav' writes, the proclamation of the excommunication had to be postponed. Indirectly, we learn how great was David b. Daniel's influence on much older, experienced and respected men, such as 'the Rav' and Nehorai b. Nissim, despite his youth and lack of experience. This undoubtedly expressed their adherence to the ideal David stood for, as they saw it: the unification of the entire nation and the entire diaspora, around a scion of the House of King David.

We have a comparatively large amount of information from Ascalon, which ties in with the details quoted by Abiathar in his Scroll. According to the Scroll, David controlled the communities of Ascalon, Caesarea, Haifa, Beirut, and Jubayl. And here we find Nathan ha-Kohen b. Mevorakh, leader of the community in Ascalon, writing (in Arabic) to 'Eli ha-Kohen b. Ḥayyim in Fustat, asking him to find some fine fabric, woven of silk and cotton, for a special outfit for the *nāsī*. The weave would cost 42 dinars. Two dinars had been received from the people of Fustat as their donation; the remainder would be collected from donations from the people of Ascalon. Nathan prays to God 'that he glorify the leadership of the nation by [lengthening] his days [of David] and enabling him to see the days of Redemption'. This seems to be more than the usual ornate phraseology. In another letter, written by Nathan ha-Kohen b. Mevorakh for another Ascalonian, Abraham b. Ḥalfon, on 3 November 1090, one can feel, beyond the compexities of local politics, the extent of David's influence on the communities. It is he who appoints dayyānīm and cantors or

help for two needy people, one whose name is Wahb and the other's Samuel the cantor and *mēvīn* (probably court assessor). From these we can also see to what extent David controlled his followers in Fustat.

dismisses them without much ado. It seems that in the fervour of his control over Ascalon and the other coastal cities mentioned above, David and his retainers also used the pretext that Ascalon was actually not part of Palestine. The answer to this claim was written by Shelah 'the sixth' b. Naḥum, in a draft of a letter to Ephraim Abū'l-Khayr. He has discussed the matter with the Gaon, he writes, who utterly refutes this opinion, on the basis of specific passages from the Book of Judges and Chronicles and by analogy with the other coastal cities and even with Jerusalem, which was only conquered in the days of King David.[179]

[907] In another letter, apparently written in the autumn of 1092, for Daniel is already called there 'our Master the Exilarch' (the timing of this title shall be discussed below), Nathan ha-Kohen b. Mevorakh mentions two notables in Ascalon who sent gifts to *sayyidnā rōsh ha-gōlā*: 4¹/₃ *raṭl*s of wax and green dates. David did not confirm their receipt; therefore the donors are worried, as is the community, for they assumed that he had refrained from writing to them because he believed the Gazans living in Ascalon, evidently refugees from the Turcomans' invasion, who were slandering them. The community threatened to remain in their homes and not to go to the synagogue (a form of protest which was customary among the Jewish communities, and in Ascalon in particular; there are characteristic examples of this in the Geniza). In another fragment in the handwriting of Nathan ha-Kohen b. Mevorakh, the appointment of a cantor from among the Gazans is mentioned, Ibrahīm b. Khalaf, who was not at all suited to this position, hence they asked of the *sayyidnā al-nāsī* to appoint another. This appears to be the onset of the enmity between the Gazans and the local people. In another fragment written by Nathan, he also mentions the *sayyidnā al-nāsī*, and there he speaks of the closing of the synagogue, evidently as a result of this internal quarrel. In a letter he wrote on 26 October 1093, to 'Eli ha-Kohen b. Ḥayyim in Fustat, Nathan ha-Kohen b. Mevorakh apparently began to rid himself of some of his public functions. It is obvious from the letter that he had been David's most trusted retainer in Ascalon for some years, but he had had to endure many hardships, while many hated him because of his status. Evidently, in order to embellish the phrase, he adds that he bears no grudge against

[179] The letter of 'the Rav': TS 12.657; see the English translation in Goitein, *Letters*, 173f; see *idem*, *Mediterranean Society*, II, 332. Cohen (*ibid.*, 108, 176) assumes that it refers to public prayers for the persecuted Nagid, Mevorakh b. Saadia. The domination of Ascalon and other communities in the coastal area: **559**, c, lines 18–20. Nathan ha-Kohen's letter: **585**; see the prayer in the margin right, lines 7ff. Abraham b. Ḥalfon: **584**. Shelah b. Naḥum: **550**; Abū'l-Khayr is perhaps identical with the person the surviving version of the Scroll refers to as 'Ben al-Khayr the proselyte', see **559**, c, line 12, and note 177, above.

David; on the contrary he is convinced that he has done his best for his communities.[180]

[908] From what has been said, it is clear that David had no desire to replace Abiathar in the leadership of the Palestinian yeshiva, which was then in Tyre. From the very outset, he denied the superiority of this institution and its authority. The status of exilarch was what seemed to him the appropriate status for the leadership of the diaspora, now that it was decreed that the Palestinian yeshiva was to be in exile, and the Jewish population in Palestine was being threatened with extinction because of the unceasing warfare and the ruthlessness of both the Turcomans and the Arabs. It was the exilarch, the embodiment of the regal concept of the exiled House of King David, from the time of Jehoiachin and onward, who would inaugurate changes in the nation's conditions in the diaspora and perhaps even lead to the awaited complete redemption. David did not start to call himself exilarch immediately. For some twelve years after his arrival in Egypt, he was content with the title *nāsī* which his father had borne, while at times (apparently mainly during the first years) he called himself 'son of the exilarch'. A letter dealing with the transfer of money to the Jerusalemites from the rent from the house in Fustat, which was a foundation (*heqdēsh*) for their welfare, dated 4 Adar II AM 4845, that is 3 March AD 1085, bears the signature 'David the *nāsī* b. Daniel the *nāsī* Gaon'; in Tammuz 1399 Sel., July AD 1088, in the court of 'our Master David *ha-nāsī* the great *nāsī* of all Israel' a deed of evidence was drawn up; on 23 Iyar 1400 Sel., that is 6 May AD 1089, in a court document written in Fustat, David is called '. . . our *nāsī* David the *nāsī* of all Israel'. In the draft of a record of evidence concerning a divorce, written by Abraham b. Isaac ha-Talmīd and bearing the date Monday, 26 Marḥeshwan 1403 Sel. (10 November AD 1091), it is stated: 'David the great *nāsī rōsh gālūyōt* [head of the diasporas] of all Israel, may our God destroy his foes, son of his honour, his great Sanctity, our Lord and Master Daniel, the great *nāsī*, head of the yeshiva Ge'ōn Ya'aqōv, may he rest in peace'. In a record of evidence written on 'Monday, 25 Kislev', a date which in that period was possible only in AM 4852, that is 8 December AD 1091, it says it was written in 'the council of the Grand Court of *sayyidnā ha-nāsī ha-gādōl nesī gālūyōt* (our Lord the great *nāsī, nāsī* of the diaporas) of all Israel, may his glory increase'.

180 The gifts from Ascalon: **587**; cf. also what is said in the letter of another Ascalonian, Abraham b. Ḥalfon: **584** a, lines 20–21, that the community threatens to remain in their homes if a certain appointment is imposed on them; also **595**, lines 10ff; cf. Goitein, *Mediterranean Society*, II, 65. The appointment of the cantor: Mosseri II 124.1 (L 126), see in Cohen, *Shalem*, 3(1980/81), 103f. The closing of the synagogue: ENA NS 63, f. 16, in Cohen, *ibid.*, 105. Giving up public functions: **586**. Another fragment in the handwriting

The next document at our disposal is dated 12 February 1092. It is a deed written by David's aide and scribe, the Maghribi Abraham b. Isaac ha-Talmīd, and drawn up in the court 'appointed by the Grand Court, may Heaven preserve it, of his honour, his great Sanctity, our Lord and Master David, the great *nāsī, rōsh gālūyōt* of all Israel, son of our Lord and Master Daniel the great *nāsī*, head of the yeshiva Ge'ōn Ya'aqōv, may he rest in peace'. The validation of the deed was written by David himself: 'this deed was validated before us in the Grand Court of our Lord David the exilarch, son of our Lord Daniel, Gaon and *nāsī* of all Israel'. Among the signatories, we find Abraham b. Shemaiah he-ḥāvēr, great-grandson of Shemaiah Gaon, and 'Ūla ha-Levi b. Joseph (the parnās from Fustat). Again, curiously enough, we find Abiathar's cousin, Solomon ha-Kohen b. Joseph *av-bēt-dīn*, signing this deed, in the company of Abiathar's rival, David. At this point, I may summarise and say that David's decision to be called exilarch was made in the autumn of 1091. Close to that time, apparently, Nathan ha-Kohen b. Mevorakh also wrote his letter dealing with the gifts to *sayyidnā rōsh ha-gōlā*, which I have already mentioned. This was also how he addressed David in a letter written about a year and a half later, on 26 October 1093, while on 13 November 1090 he was still calling David *sayyidnā al-nāsī*.[181]

[909] In the autumn of 1093, David tried to extend his authority to Tyre. In the Scroll of Abiathar, we are given to understand that a sort of assembly of Rabbanites and Karaites (*benē 'ōnenā*) took place jointly in Tyre on the eve of Rōsh ha-shānā, 23 September 1093. Near this date, we find a deed of betrothal written in Fustat on Sunday, 12 Kislev 1045 Sel., that is 4 December AD 1093. It is written by Abraham b. Isaac ha-Talmīd 'in the court which was appointed by the House of the *rēsh gālūtā*, may

of Nathan ha-Kohen of Ascalon, has been preserved: TS 8 J 39, f. 1, in which he sends regards to 'his excellency, our Lord the Exilarch', see in Cohen, *ibid.*, 114.

181 The letter from March 1085: **540**. The record of evidence: TS 20.116; on the verso there is a list of chattels and other details of a marriage deed, in the handwriting of David. The matter of the divorce: ENA 4020, f. 47*r*. Another fragment from the Geniza in which he is called, *ha-nāsī ha-gādōl rōsh gālūyōt kol Israel*, etc. is TS 8 J 7, f. 4, the opening of a letter to him, in which the writer informs him that he has arrived in Alexandria. The court document: BM Or 5545, f. 7. Cf. Goitein, *Mediterranean Society*, II, 523, n. 48. The record of evidence: ENA 4010, f. 31 – dealing with the collection of a joint debt in the name of the daughter of a deceased partner; the deed of partnership had been validated by '*ra's al-mathība* (head of the yeshiva) Elijah ha-Kohen of blessed memory', and was written in Tyre on a piece of paper that was cut from a letter dated 14 Kislev (that is eleven days earlier), which was sent from Alexandria and mentioned a shipment of a *jarra zayt ḥalāl* (a jar of kosher oil), perhaps for David b. Daniel. TS 20.162 is also connected with this matter, cf. Goitein, *Mediterranean Society*, III, 280, 489, n. 19. The deed from 12 February 1092: TS 20.31; a fragment of which was edited by Schechter, *Saadyana*, 81, n. 2 (the formula of the validation there is the usual one in deeds of the period, containing a confirmation of the identity of the witnesses, and there was no reason for Schechter's amazement, *ibid.*); the form *mārūtā* (Master) so-and-so was evidently commonly applied to the exilarch. Cf.: 'at the gate (i.e. court) of *mārūtā* David *rōsh gālūtā*' (who is David b.

Heaven guard him'. Apart from that of the writer, the signatures there are of Ezekiel ha-Kohen he-ḥavēr b. 'Eli he-ḥāvēr, of blessed memory (the father was 'Eli ha-Kohen b. Ezekiel, the Jerusalem parnās), and 'Eli ha-Kohen b. Yaḥyā (b. Ḥayyim, the Fustat parnās). Abraham b. Isaac ha-Talmīd also wrote a court document dealing with a case of the marriage to a Nubian slave-girl in Ascalon, which was written on 23 Kislev, of the same year (that is eleven days after the former document), that is 15 December, where the formula is as follows: 'David, [the great *nāsī*, *rōsh gālūyōt* of all Israel, son of his great honour] and Sanctity, our Lord and Master Daniel', etc; the reconstruction is beyond doubt. In the same hand, that of Abraham b. Isaac ha-Talmīd, there is also a deed of dedication of a house in Damascus, to the synagogue there. The deed was also written in Fustat 'in the Grand Court . . . of his great honour and Sanctity, our Lord and Master, David the great *nāsī rōsh gālūyōt* of all Israel'; however the date has not been preserved. In a letter of complaint sent from Tyre to David b. Daniel, to which we shall return below, he is called 'our Lord, *nāsī* of this generation, *rōsh gālūyōt*'; 'our Lord and Master, the great *nāsī*, *rōsh ha-gōlā*'; and there is also a prayer that 'he may be granted a worthy descendant', from which we understand that David was still childless, after ten years of marriage. The formula *sayyidnā ha-nāsī ha-gādōl rōsh gālūyōt kol Israel* is also to be found in a letter from the Jerusalemite Joseph b. Moses, writing from Fustat to Yefet b. Eleazer in al-Maḥalla.

It is now quite clear that what we are witnessing is the formation of two competing centres of leadership struggling with one another – the exilarch in Egypt (which had not existed until then) and the Palestinian yeshiva, in exile in Tyre. If we look at the general political scene at the time, we shall find a strong connection between the political and military events and those dramatic developments occurring within the Jewish context and dividing the Jewish communities. The Scroll of Abiathar also hints at this link without saying anything explicit. It states the facts one after the other: 'and Tyre was conquered', which is clearly a hint at the Fatimid conquest of the city and the liquidation of the rule of the sons of the cadi Ibn Abī 'Aqīl in AH 482, which began on 6 March AD 1089. Jubayl, Sidon and Acre were also conquered at the time by the Fatimid army, bringing an end to Saljūq control over these cities. As David was dependant largely on the patronage of the Fatimid rullers, both he and his followers once again had great hopes that it would be easy to degrade the yeshiva, which had enjoyed the protection of the cadi's family in Tyre. These hopes increased towards the end of 1091, and we have seen that at that time, David was already called exilarch. In Tyre itself, however, an entirely new situation

Zakkai), see Harkavy, *Teshūvōt*, No. 555, p. 296. Nathan ha-Kohen b. Mevorakh, the gifts: **587**. October 1093: **586**, a, lines 7, 12. November 1090: **584**, a, line 13.

arose for the time being, when the Fatimid army commander there, Munīr (or Naṣīr) al-Dawla al-Juyūshī, shook off the yoke of the central authorities, to the dissatisfaction of the local population. Only on 12 July 1093 did the Fatimid army suppress this local uprising, and it seems that as a consequence, David's authority in Tyre was strengthened and he was pronounced exilarch there as well, on the eve of Rōsh ha-shānā.[182]

[910] As to Abiathar ha-Kohen, who had now served as head of the yeshiva for some ten years, it was certainly not pleasant for him to remain in Tyre under Fatimid rule, and the same applied to all the people of the yeshiva. Nevertheless, it seems that the Fatimid authorities did not heavily interfere in public Jewish affairs in this region. As we have seen, contact with Egypt was again discontinued as a result of the rebellion of the local commander. On 4 July 1091, Abiathar was still in Tyre, writing letters from there, from which it emerges that he was still holding on to his status. One of his letters was written to Isaac b. Samuel the Spaniard, one of the devotees of the Palestinian yeshiva in Fustat. The bearer of the letter was Ezekiel ha-Kohen b. 'Eli, of Jerusalem, whom we have already encountered. He travelled to Egypt in order to get help on behalf of the yeshiva: 'we are all obliged to help those who are impoverished and destitute, the more so in the City of our Lord'. Jerusalem then became a key-word in Abiathar's counter-propaganda. Indeed, Ezekiel left for Fustat immediately after reaching Tyre from Jerusalem. Another letter was sent to Baghdad in which the writer describes himself and his circle as 'the geonic refugees of the land of Palestine', referring to his brother Solomon ha-Kohen b. Elijah, Abiathar's two sons, Elijah and Zadok, his son-in-law 'Amram ha-Kohen b. Aaron 'he-ḥāvēr ha-me'ullē the foundation of the yeshiva, of Jerusalem'. The letter deals with a matter of *ḥalīṣā* and contains some details on the state of insecurity. A large army is said to be stationed around Tyre. The distress returned with even greater severity, according to the Scroll, when 'Tyre returned to normality', 'in the year 1404 Sel., that is AD 1093, when the Fatimid army suppressed the rebellion, in the summer, and resumed its dominion over the city. The link with Egypt was renewed, and with it, the oppression of the yeshiva, this time with greater vigour.

Now (presumably August 1093) the emissaries of David arrived in Tyre

[182] The assembly in Tyre: **559**, d, lines 1–3; the year, 1404 Sel., is mentioned *ibid.*, c, line 25. The deed of betrothal: TS 13 J 2, f. 3; cf. Goitein, *Mediterranean Society*, II, 528, n. 51. The Nubian slave-girl: TS Box Misc. 27, f. 23, edited by Friedman, *Gratz College Annual*, 1(1972), 58f. The deed of dedication: BM Or 5566 B, f. 7, edited in Gil, *Documents*, 214f. (No. 33, where I erroneously stated that it is the handwriting of Abraham b. Nathan). The letter of complaint: **603**, a, lines 5–6; c, lines 1–8; see in this letter the florid praises of David and his forefathers, and the expression of joy that 'he was prayed on as exilarch'. Joseph ha-Levi: TS 13 J 19, f. 6.

with the intention of inaugurating an order preferable to him among the communities of Palestine and Syria. The Scroll calls them 'bums, vagrants, people with issues, lepers, vile'. In Tyre, one of the envoys attacked Abiathar directly: 'and he dismissed the head of the yeshiva and put him under heavy pressure'. Abiathar calls him *nōgēsh* (oppressor). This emissary evidently exploited his master's influence with the Fatimid authorities 'and turned over the Lord's people to the rulers'. These are very blunt statements, indeed. In addition, 'he misinterpreted the Torah and was biassed in his judgment', expressions which perhaps hint at the connection between David's emissary and the Karaites, a subject to which we shall return. This emissary also took over the court; 'he pointed his tongue against many honourable people' that is, he acted as an informant to the authorities. He 'put the children of the *av* of the yeshiva under pressure', speaking of the family of Solomon, Abiathar's brother, 'until they were forced to flee their homes, to desert their nest, he made their Creator angry, prevented them from studying the Torah, and it was found that some of them met their death' (this seems to be a reference to the confiscation of a house belonging to the family, placing severe blame on that emissary, as if he were responsible for a fatal incident within the family of Solomon, Abiathar's brother. It also speaks of preventing the priestly family from teaching the Torah, which apparently meant from earning their living).

A confirmation of these claims can also be found in the letter of 'Amram ha-Kohen b. Aaron, Abiathar's son-in-law, written in Damascus and evidently addressed to Zadok b. Josiah, which implies that they were undergoing terrible financial hardship. He intended to stay in Damascus in order to earn some money from the community there (apparently as a cantor, or scribe, or by collecting donations or the like), but the people of Damascus were under pressure because of the Jewish captives who fell into the hands of the Saljūqs. For the first four months, his income was minimal, but he decided to remain in Damascus because of the dire situation in Tyre and the dispute, as well as the straitened circumstances of his father-in-law, the Gaon. The letter also includes the matter of a family squabble between the writer and his wife and her father, concerning their son (the eldest, apparently). The family's situation was very bad for they were obliged to sell the entire contents of their house in Tyre and 'Amram had to see to the maintenance of six souls. He demands that his eldest son come to Damascus, so that they may both set out for Egypt and from there to Ascalon, to find some means of livelihood. If his son is not sent to him, he will leave for a distant land and this will mean the end of the family.[183]

[183] Abiathar's letters: **553**; see especially a, lines 8–13; b, lines 17–21; c, lines 15–16. See the Scroll of Abiathar: **559**, c, lines 19–25. On Isaac b. Samuel the Spaniard, see what is said

[911] We can identify the most eminent of David b. Daniel's emissaries and even enlarge on some of their activities. 'The oppressor' of which the Scroll speaks (in its words) is Aviram b. Dathan. One can easily see who is behind these Biblical names: Aviram is none other than Abraham, Dathan is Nathan, hence he is Abraham b. Nathan, the son of Nathan b. Abraham, Solomon b. Judah's rival, known to us from the dispute over the gaonate in Jerusalem. We know that this Abraham was the only son of Nathan. In a letter which he wrote to Nethanel b. Rawḥ, probably in 1038 while *en route* to Palestine, Nathan mentions him, implying that he was still a baby at the time. In a letter he wrote from Jerusalem fourteen years later, in the autumn of 1042, he mentions 'our son Abraham'. We first read about him again in a letter written some twenty years afterward by Labrāṭ b. Moses ibn Sughmār of al-Mahdiyya, to Nehorai b. Nissim, in August 1061. We understand from the letter that among the Maghribi circles in Fustat, there is great admiration and respect for Abraham's erudition and talent. We already know that Abraham's grandfather on his mother's side, Mevorakh b. 'Eli, was one of the heads of the 'Babylonian' congregation in Fustat, and he would stay with him when he visited Egypt, thus becoming acquainted with the Maghribis, whose notables (such as Nehorai) were among the most eminent of the 'Babylonian' congregation. We find a deed of sale written in Jerusalem on 8 March 1066 in which a woman named Sittūna, daughter of Yefet, sells a quarter of two shops, evidently in Ramla, to Abraham b. Nathan. The deed of sale is in the handwriting of Abiathar ha-Kohen b. Elijah Gaon; the validation of the deed was effected in Fustat, perhaps already after the Turcomans' conquest of Jerusalem, and this is in the handwriting of Hillel b. 'Eli, and also signed by 'Eli he-ḥāvēr b. 'Amram. In 1076, Abraham was in Ramla and there signed a deed written on Wednesday, 8 Elul 4836, 10 August 1076: 'Abraham b. R. Nathan *av ha-yeshīvā,* of blessed righteous memory.' As we are aware, Palestine was then in the hands of the Turcomans. Some half a year later, Abraham is in Fustat, and on Thursday, 3 Nisan Sel. 1388, that is 30 March AD 1077, we find him there signing a court document together with Abiathar ha-Kohen. It seems that when David b. Daniel started to organise his faction, Abraham b. Nathan was among the first to join him, a fact we can easily understand when taking into consideration the rivalry between his late father and the priestly family, whose son Abiathar was now head of the yeshiva in Tyre. The Scroll notes Aviram b. Dathan's mission to Tyre to establish David's authority there. We have also seen how, according to the Scroll, he maltreated the family of the Gaon. Some

above, sec. 315, in the note. The letter of 'Amram ha-Kohen: **552**; it is interesting that he wants to travel to Ascalon, which was definitely David b. Daniel's sphere of influence, which may have been the source of the dispute between him and his wife's family.

of Abraham b. Nathan's letters from that period have been preserved. In one of them, written from Tyre to Nehorai b. Nissim, evidently, he complains about someone named b. Elḥanan and he asks that the man be excommunicated, as he is hindering him and causing his *pesīqōt* (the allowances) to dwindle. He has already complained about him to *sayyidnā* (our Master), undoubtedly meaning David b. Daniel. He also asks that letters of recommendation be sent from the central authority in Egypt (*kutub sulṭāniyya*). In another letter, evidently also written in Tyre, to the 'Rav', he complains about the troubles caused him in the districts in which he is staying at the time (certainly Tyre and its surroundings), and cites an episode concerning a shop and the apartment above it – perhaps referring to the requisition hinted at in the Scroll at Abiathar. The third letter is also from Tyre, and was sent to Nehorai, evidently only in 1094, after the downfall of David b. Daniel. Abraham describes there his difficult circumstances after having backed the wrong side. He expresses his unhappiness at the resulting hardship he is enduring and his fear that there will be more to come. He also depicts in detail his economic distress and how he was forced to sell some of his quires and to squander money that had accumulated from rent (perhaps from the aforementioned houses in Ramla) which he had been receiving for a number of years. He asks about the possibility of moving to Egypt in order to find a livelihood there. There is also veiled news of gory events in Tyre (probably in 1093) and of the bitter fate of the Karaites (*benē ha-ṣōle'ā*) there, of whom only three remain.

Further light is shed on the events in Tyre and the activities of Abraham b. Nathan there, in a letter from one of David b. Daniel's followers, writing to David from Tyre, evidently in 1093. The writer resents the fact that he has received no backing from *al-rayyis* Abū Isḥaq; Abū Isḥaq is a common *kunya* for Abraham and there is almost no doubt that he is referring to Abraham b. Nathan. On the other hand, the writer complains, he helps the 'Rūm, the Ifranj (that is, the Jews who come from Byzantium and from Western European countries, whom he calls the Franks), and the proselytes' (evidently Christians who converted to Judaism in Christian countries and found refuge in Tyre). He provides them with *fasā'iq* (the plural form in Arabic of the Hebrew word *pesīqā*, which means a regular allowance) and food, and even appoints them to posts.

Eventually Abraham b. Nathan was reconciled with the adversaries of David b. Daniel, that is, Abiathar and the Palestinian yeshiva, and the Nagid. This is apparently borne out by a fragment of a letter from the Nagid, Mevorakh b. Saadia, to Abraham, from which it is only possible to make out that he is speaking of people from the Fayyūm and the mediation of some quarrel. It seems that through support from Nehorai and other eminent Maghribis, Abraham was given the position of dayyān in al-Qāhira, and he remained at this post until his death in *ca.* 1115. He merited a number of excellent titles: '*yesōd* (foundation of) the yeshiva', *rēsh bē rabbānān* (probably, head of the house of learning), *rōsh ha-seder.*[184]

[912] According to the Scroll, Abraham had to flee from Tyre during the uprising of Munīr (or Naṣīr) al-Dawla, and he returned there in 1404 Sel., that is 1093, evidently in August, when 'Tyre returned to normality', that is when the Fatimid army suppressed Munīr al-Dawla's rebellion. Before returning to Tyre, Abraham managed to be active on behalf of David b. Daniel in *Nō' Ammōn*, which is Alexandria, and in al-Maḥalla. When he returned to Tyre, he obtained a foothold in Acre as well and, as we have seen, he afterwards organised the great assembly in Tyre, at which he informed the people of Tyre of the decision taken in Fustat to proclaim David b. Daniel exilarch. In this connection the Scroll mentions his special relationship to the 'sons of 'ōnenā', the Karaites. Above we have seen a description of their end in Tyre according to Abraham b. Nathan's own letter. The proclamation of David as exilarch was made, according to Abiathar, with the consent of two notables: Ibn Sa'd (which should perhaps be Abū Sa'd) al-Razzāq and Abū Naṣr b. Shu'ayb. For the time being, we do not know the identity of this al-Razzāq (or his son). If his *kunya* was Abū Sa'd, it should be noted that Josiah ha-Kohen b. Azariah, a relative of David b. Daniel, had this *kunya*. However, we should bear in

184 Aviram b. Dathan: **559**, c, lines 21, 25, 29; Marx. *PAAJR*, 16(1946/7), 198, n. 71, already understood the meaning of these Biblical names in the Scroll, but did not attribute it to this Abraham b. Nathan, cf.: Cohen, *Self Government*, 123, n. 76. The letters of Nathan b. Abraham: **180**, line 7; **200**, line 3. Labrāṭ's letter: INA d 55, f. 13, lines 35–36; cf. Goitein, *Tarbiz*, 36(1966/7), 62f. The deed of sale: **544**. The deed from Ramla: **568**. Fustat in 1077: ULC Or 1080 J 9. The letters of Abraham b. Nathan: **555–557**. The complaint from Tyre: **603**. The Nagid's letter: TS NS J 131. **610**, the letter of Tobiah ha-Kohen of Bāniyās, contains information on the plague in AH 505, AD 1111, when Abraham b. Nathan also fell ill but recovered (the Nagid, Mevorakh b. Saadia, also fell ill of the plague and died from it); see on this plague Ibn al-Qalānisī, 181. For further details on Abraham b. Nathan, see: Goitein, *Mediterranean Society*, II, 512 f. He was probably about eighty when he died. In TS 18 J 1, f. 18, written in March 1116, Abraham b. Nathan's widow confirms having received what was due to her from her husband's property; cf. Goitein, *Mediterranean Society*, III, 483, n. 45. In TS 8 J 38, f. 11, a fragment of a letter, we find the *'alāma* of Nathan b. Abraham (and of his son Abraham), *yesha' yeqārēv*, and 'Abraham b. R. Nathan *av-bēt-dīn* of all Israel, of blessed memory', is mentioned there; TS AS 145.8 is a deed in the handwriting of Abraham b. Nathan, bearing his signature; ULC Or 1080 J 131 is a fragment from the opening of a letter from Mevorakh b. Isaac, of Aleppo, to 'the council of the splendour of the Torah and the arm of its magnificence, his great honour and sanctity, our Lord and Master Abraham, glory of the scholars, top of the learned, son of his great honour and sanctity, our Lord and Master Nathan, *av-bēt-dīn* of all Israel'. TS 13 J 6, f. 21 is a letter from Manasseh b. Saadia, to 'the council of our Master, crown and diadem of our heads, the excellent Master, foundation of the yeshiva and its deputy, great-grandson of his great honour and sanctity, our Lord and Master Nathan b. Abraham, of blessed righteous memory'; cf. Mann, *Jews*, II, 232 (its shelf-mark there: TS 13 J 5, f. 21); *nīn* here means son. TS 6 J 11, f. 8 is a fragment of a deed in the handwriting of Abraham with the remnant of his signature and also *yesha' yeqārēv*; TS 8 J 7, f. 11, is a

mind that a quarrel broke out between David and Josiah. As to Abū Naṣr b. Shu'ayb, also called Muslim (Meshullam) b. Shu'ayb, he is mentioned in a letter of Daniel b. Azariah, from which it emerges that he was one of the eminent figures of the community in Tyre. Perhaps he is 'Meshullam, known as ibn Shurayq al-Dimashqī', who dedicates his house in Damascus to the *heqdēsh* before the court of David b. Daniel in Fustat. When they learned that David b. Daniel was proclaimed exilarch, the devotees of the Palestinian yeshiva in Tyre organised an assembly of opponents, at which Zadok b. Josiah preached a sermon, which is preserved in the Scroll.

Another emissary of David b. Daniel to Tyre was Hillel b. al-Jāsūs (jāsūs: spy). Like Abraham b. Nathan, he also ill-treated Abiathar's brother Solomon, and even tried to kill him! Only that: 'the Lord saved him from his hands' and 'they [only] dispossessed him of his house and grounds'. Solomon and his family had to flee to the districts of Asher and Naphtali (apparently Haifa and Tiberias). The 'third', Zadok b. Josiah, was also abused by this Hillel. We know of the latter that he was a pupil of Rabbēnū Nissim. Maimonides mentions him in one of his responsa (not by the name of Hillel) and mentions 'the book he wrote on prayer'.

At the same time, Ṣedaqa b. Nufay' is also to be found in the region of Tyre. The Scroll mentions him as having been helpful to David b. Daniel (he was the bearer of the *gēṭ*, the deed breaking off David's engagement to his betrothed in Damīra). In a letter written to his father on 28 October 1090, Ṣedaqa informs him that he is about to be granted a post in Jubayl, evidently on behalf of David b. Daniel. He intends to travel to Acre to collect a debt and then to return to Tyre, where he will wed an orphan from a poor family, whom he will then bring with him to Fustat. (Apparently the Fatimids still ruled Tyre in the autumn of 1090, and Munīr al-Dawla had not yet rebelled against them.)

Hillel b. 'Eli was also a member of David b. Daniel's retinue, apparently having become his scribe; he was staying there at the time the Fatimids took over Tyre. A draft of a letter has been preserved, which he wrote from Tyre to Mevorakh b. Saadia, the Nagid, after the victory of Abiathar and Mevorakh, that is, apparently in the summer of 1094. It is obvious from the letter that Hillel had stayed in Tyre for some months prior to the victory. He describes the difficult days he endured in Tyre, where he witnessed a great deal of bloodshed. The major burden of the letter consists of his joy at Mevorakh's return to his former status and a vindication of his own behaviour, as he attempts to convince the addressee that he had never been one of David b. Daniel's followers. He calls the rule of the

confirmation that cheese being sent for sale is kosher, in his handwriting and with his signature, and *yesha' yeqārēv* is also added here.

Fatimids, the rule of righteousness, whereas the rebels were the forces of evil. Nevertheless, he admits to a modicum of error, 'for is there a man who has not erred?' and intends to come to Fustat and serve Mevorakh [which indeed occurred] – as he had promised his late brother, that is, Judah b. Saadia.[185]

[913] The subsequent events and the complete reversal in the status of the Palestinian yeshiva and of Abiathar ha-Kohen, its head, is described at the end of the Scroll. The turnabout was naturally the result of Divine intervention, and the man who executed the will of God was Mevorakh b. Saadia, the 'Nagid of God's nation, prince of princes, the might of the House of Israel'. 'He assembled all of Israel'; in other words, it seems that indeed, an assembly of representatives of all the communities convened, which 'restored the crown to its original condition like in the days of Ezra their forefather, to be maintained in the hands of his progeny'. (That is to say, this priestly family claims descent from Ezra the scribe and priest, who was also one of the greatest sages of Israel.) Palestine and all the countries to its west returned to the authority of the yeshiva, including Syria apparently, although the name was not preserved in the manuscript. The change for the better in Mevorakh b. Saadia's standing is already described in the first part of the Scroll. The ruler changed his mind and Mevorakh was reinstated in his former position: that is, he once more became the physician at court. We may assume that both events, the return of Mevorakh the Nagid to his former high rank and 'the restoration of the yeshiva's crown to its former condition' (and the deposal of David b. Daniel, about whom we have no detail from this point onwards), occurred within a very short span of time, as Mann also assumed. The date of what the Scroll calls 'the miracle' is Iyar 1405 Sel., that is, approximately May

[185] The flight of Abraham b. Nathan from Tyre and his return, and the other matters concerning Tyre: **559**, c, lines 25–30; d, lines 3–4. Daniel b. Azariah's letter: **347**, a, line 10. The document of the heqdēsh: BM Or 5566 B, f. 7; perhaps that Meshullam is the same as Meshullam b. Solomon, mentioned in the letter written by Daniel b. Azariah's scribe: **383**, line 8. 'Naphtali': see Mann, *Texts*, I, 249, n. 3: Rakkath in the portion of Naphtali, Joshua, xix:35; BT, Meg. 5b, 6a; 'Asher', see Joshua, xix:26: Carmel, the portion of Asher; on Hillel ibn al-Jāsūs see Poznanski, *Harkavy Jubilee Volume*, 183f; Maimonides, *Responsa*, II, 582, and see editor's note 25; Jāsūs al-Maghribī, evidently his father, is mentioned in **80**, a, line 24, which is a letter of Solomon b. Judah from 1037. See further mention of the name Jāsūs (Gāsūs) in Abramson, *Nissim Gaon*, in the introduction, 25; *idem*, *'Inyānōt*, 267. It should be read Gāsūs in every instance, not Gāsūm. The letter of Ṣedaqa b. Nufay': **602**; it seems that the *rayyis* mentioned there is not Abiathar as is the view of Goitein, *BJRL*, 54 (1971/2), 101, n. 5, but Abraham b. Nathan, for Ṣedaqa belonged to David b. Daniel's camp. The late G. Weiss wrote his Master's thesis on Hillel b. 'Eli, Univ. of Pennsylvania, Philadelphia 1967, which includes fifty-seven documents written by 'Eli in his own handwriting. Another Hillel, evidently his grandfather, was called 'the great cantor, crown of the cantors, al-Baghdādī'. See: TS AS 161.45, a fragment of a letter from the daughter of this Hillel (i.e., the aunt of our Hillel) to her brother 'Eli; the letter of Hillel b. 'Eli: **558**.

1094. Evidently the change of heart is connected with the illness of Badr al-Jamālī, who handed over the affairs of state to his son al-Afḍal in March or April, 1094. The friendship between the latter and Mevorakh is known from one of Geniza texts: 'Mevorakh . . . a Hebrew righteous and pious and physician and scholar and advisor to the king (that is, to al-Afḍal) . . . since his youth . . . and he gave him the title: prince of princes, and made him prince over all the children of Israel in his kingdom, and he cherished him enormously, and he became like a fortified wall for Israel'. Thus, the period of the worst distress for Abiathar and the priestly family lasted for some twenty months, from June 1093, when the Fatimids conquered Tyre, until April 1094, when al-Afḍal became wazīr in Egypt.

A very interesting document has been preserved, which begins shortly before David b. Daniel's downfall and ends after it. This is evidence concerning the despatch of a deed of divorce, written in 'al-Qāhira, near Zoan of Egypt', on Tuesday, 18 Shevat 1405 Sel., 7 February 1094, or two-and-a-half months before the collapse of David b. Daniel. The statement of evidence is followed by the validation, which is undoubtedly in the handwriting of David b. Daniel, without a signature, but with his *'alāma, yeshū'ā*. Further on, on the same sheet, we find an assessment written by 'Amram ha-Kohen b. R. Aaron s.ṭ. (*sāfēh ṭāv*, 'may he have a good end', indicating that his father is still alive) b. 'Amram great-grandson of Elijah ha-Kohen *bēt-dīn*. This is Abiathar's son-in-law 'Amram, who, as we see, returned from Damascus and was reconciled with his family. He ridicules the formulation in which the evidence was written, especially the validation that figures there. This was undoubtedly written a short time after the deposal of David b. Daniel in the summer of 1094. Hence, we have a document which clearly reflects the Jewish public's change of heart at that time. The reins of leadership and judgment were once again in the hands of the Palestinian yeshiva.[186]

[186] The reversal: **559**, j, lines 7ff. Mevorakh b. Saadia returns to his former status: *ibid.*, c, lines 14–15; see Mann, *Jews*, I, 187–193. Al-Afḍal and Mevorakh, see ULC Add 3335, edited by Neubauer, *JQR*, 9(1897), 35f; on al-Afḍal's appointment see: Ibn Khallikān, II, 450: in the month of Rabī' I, 487, March–April 1094; Sāwīrūs, II, 243 (and see the translation on p. 389); Ibn al-Ṣayrafī, 57f; Ibn Ẓāfir, 17. The renewal of the connection between the house of the negidim and the Palestinian localities is obvious from **569**, the letter from Joshua he-ḥāvēr b. 'Eli, who is in Caesarea from *ca.* 1098, to Mevorakh b. Saadia, in which he asks for his help with the local rulers in order that he may move to Ascalon: '*he-ḥāvēr ha-me'ullē, sanhedrā rabbā, alūf ha-bīnōt*, Nagid of God's nation, prince of princes, full of all wisdom, banner of God's nation'. Also mentioned is his late brother 'Judah the Nagid of God's nation'. The record of evidence: TS 28.5. To the documents from the period shortly after David's downfall, one should also add a court document which is torn into two fragments: Bodl MS Heb b 13, f. 19, and ENA 2805, f. 15. Abraham b. Isaac ha-Talmīd is still writing court documents in his own hand; apart from his signature, there are those of Nissim b. R. Nehorai the Rav; Isaac ha-melammēd b. R. Ḥayyim

[914] On 1 Tevet, December 1094 (apparently), eight months after the reversal, Mūsā b. Abī'l-Ḥayy Khalīla, a business partner of Nehorai b. Nissim, wrote a letter of congratulations to Abiathar, in which he expresses his joy at the renewal of Abiathar's status and appreciation of the backing he gets from the major figures in Fustat: the Nagid Mevorakh b. Saadia, Nehorai b. Nissim and his son Nissim. Apart from the usual ornate phrases, such as 'may God grant a crown to the nation through [preserving] your life', and the like, we find details of the praises which the Nagid pours forth regarding Abiathar and his brother, Solomon, the *av-bēt-dīn*. The letter, which was sent by Abiathar to al-Qāhira, was read out in the synagogue there and in the synagogue of the 'Palestinians' in Fustat, and the congregations were delighted with it. The writer of the letter was one of the Maghribi merchants, and this also serves as evidence that the Maghribis had gone over to Abiathar's side and had completely abandoned David b. Daniel.

Evidently, the draft of a letter of condolence written by two people of Ascalon, Ḥalfon and Joseph, to Abiathar's son, Elijah ha-Kohen 'the fourth', in Tyre, also belongs to this period. The expression of condolence was over the death of his uncle, his father's brother, Zadok ha-Kohen b. Elijah Gaon. In the letter, not only Abiathar is mentioned but also his grandson, son of Elijah 'the fourth', as well as 'Amram ha-Kohen 'the seventh', Abiathar's son-in-law. On the verso, Abiathar's brother, Solomon ha-Kohen, *av* of the yeshiva, is also mentioned.

At about the same time, a query was addressed to Nehorai b. Nissim, evidently from Malīj, in which he is asked to give his opinion on the matter of a deed of divorce that has gone astray; in the meantime, however, the divorcer has died. The letter mentions applying to the *alūf ha-bīnōt* (the Nagid Mevorakh b. Saadia), and to the head of the Palestinian yeshiva, and suggests that they should look for documents on the divorce in the archives of the yeshiva; the archives are in Tyre, however. The court in Acre is also mentioned in the letter.

The events surrounding 'the miracle' are very inadequately explained in the sources at our disposal and the matter is still extremely obscure. We would particularly like to know whether the change of heart was only due to the change of rulers or whether there was some internal factor which brought about the reversal. Did David b. Daniel fail as the result of some crude mistake, or did something happen to him? Perhaps he was forced to flee from Egypt and seek refuge in one of the Christian countries, perhaps Byzantium? For the time being, we have no answers to these questions,

Nufūsī; 'Eli ha-Kohen b. R. Yaḥyā. David b. Daniel is not mentioned any longer. The date is Tishri, 1406 Sel., that is, September–October AD 1094.

for David has utterly disappeared from the sources, at the age of about thirty-six.[187]

[915] I shall now summarise the major points of the dispute surveyed above and try to give some meaning to their contents, principally on the basis of that extraordinary document, the Scroll of Abiathar. Naturally, this document reflects the spiritual and ideological world of its author, Abiathar ha-Kohen. The target of his fire is the exilarchic house. They are unsuited to serve as the leaders of the Jews. We find this idea at the beginning of the Scroll, presenting the members of that family as 'sons of 'ōnenā', a hint of their linkage with 'Anan and the Karaites, 'forbidden idols', 'wicked people' 'disobeying the Torah', 'transgressors', etc. The House of King David, from which the exilarchs claim descent, has profaned its tradition and majesty. This decline of the House of David had already occurred in the days of the corrupt kings of Judah, such as Ahaz, Manasseh, and the like. The true son of David, the King and Messiah, was already born on the day of the destruction of Jerusalem. Contrary to all this, the position of the priesthood is preserved in the leadership of the nation, according to the highest tradition.

These arguments, with various additions, are repeated in the Scroll in the homily of 'the third', Zadok b. Josiah. Egypt is not a *gōlā* (exile), and was never called *gōlā*, and there was never an exilarch in Egypt. The only place where the terms *gōlā* and *rōsh gōlā* were used was Babylonia, and this has been true since the days of Nehemiah. This is followed by a homily on the verse: 'the sceptre shall not depart from Judah'. The true exilarch, who is in Babylonia, has no authority in Palestine. Proof of this is the story of Rabba bar-bar Ḥana. Palestine is no *gōlā* and it is impossible to ordain an exilarch there, evidently a hint that Daniel, David's father, could not have

[187] The letter of Mūsā b. Abī'l-Ḥayy: **551**; he is 'Abū 'Imrān, our Lord and Master Moses *segullat ha-yeshīvā*, son of our Master Abū'l-Ḥayy, of blessed memory', in a court document from 1089, in David b. Daniel's court: BM Or 5545, f. 7. The letter of condolence: **554**. The query to Nehorai: **560**; it seems that TS 13 J 8, f. 19 belongs to this matter (also in the view of Goitein, *Mediterranean Society*, III, 196f), which is a letter containing complaints of Hayfā' daughter of Sulaymān, of Acre, appealing to the ḥāvēr in Malīj about her husband Sa'īd b. Mu'ammar (Saadia b. Ḥayyim) al-Qazzāz (the silk merchant), who abandoned her and their children; she was forced to flee from Acre to Jaffa, whence she reached Egypt, where she learned that her husband was in Malīj with his brother; but on arriving in Malīj, she found that he has returned to Palestine; her request is that the ḥāvēr in Malīj write to Palestine and demand that her husband either return to her and their son, or give her a divorce. A *piyyūṭ* ascribed to 'David the Nāsī' is perhaps the work of David b. Daniel, see Bodl MS Heb f 56, f. 35*v*: 'Woe to my soul, for I have so many complaints ... therefore, instead of elevating me, He changed my honour into shame, and prescribed bitterness for me, of a harsh kind, with a style of iron, with a pen of flint', etc., verses of bitterness and disappointment; which end: 'my anger is overcome by pain, for I was inclined to conflict'; cf. Mann. *Jews*, II, 224f; Davidson, *Ōṣar*, IV, 377; also belonging to David b. Daniel, are perhaps three piyyūṭīm from the Yemenite manuscripts edited by Raẓhabi, *Tarbiz*, 14(1942/3), 204ff.

been an exilarch, because he sat in Palestine, in its yeshiva. There is also a hint here that it was improper for David to call himself 'son of the exilarch'. The *nāsī* in Palestine is the one who has the right to decide on the calendar order. To prove this, 'the third' takes the trouble to survey in his homily the history of intercalation from the creation of the world on 25 Elul, and from the creation of the luminaries on the night before Wednesday (the fourth day), 28 Elul. The tradition of intercalation continues, in his words, from Adam – Enoch – Noah – Shem (who is also the first of the priests, Melchizedek) – Abraham – Isaac. Jacob was at first not permitted the intercalation, as he was staying outside Palestine. When he returned to Palestine he intercalated. Joseph and his brothers also intercalated, in Palestine. When they went down to Egypt, the intercalations diminished. Between Nisan and Tishri, Moses appointed the Sanhedrin. Moses, head of the Sanhedrin, knew the secret of intercalation and passed it on: Moses – Joshua – the elders – Othniel b. Kenaz – Pinḥas – 'Eli – Samuel – Gad – Nathan – Ahiah of Shiloh – Elijah – Elisha – Amos – Isaiah – Joel – Jeremiah and Zephaniah – Ezekiel and Baruch – Haggai, Zechariah and Malachi (who is Ezra the scribe, head of the Great Assembly) – Simon the Righteous – Antigonos of Sōkhō – Yōsē b. Yō'ezer of Ṣerēdā – Joseph b. Yōḥānān of Jerusalem – Joshua b. Peraḥya and Nitai of Arbel – Judah b. Ṭabai and Simon b. Shaṭṭāḥ – Shemaiah and Avṭalyōn – Yōḥānān b. Zakkai, in whose day the temple was destroyed, in the year AM 4000 minus 172 (that is, AD 68). From Moses until Rabbān Yoḥānān b. Zakkai, the secret of intercalation was only held by the head of the Sanhedrin, and so it has been up until the days of our holy Rabbēnū (i.e. Judah ha-Nāsī). For instance: Joshua b. Ḥanania did not know the secret of intercalation, although he was *av-bēt-dīn* of Rabbān Gamaliel. In his desire to sum up all that was said, Zadok again stresses the fact that the computation of intercalation stretches from the six days of the creation, from Adam. The *nāsī* in Palestine is the one who decides on matters of intercalation, and Zadok explains: the nesī'īm of Palestine are but the heads of its yeshiva. It was only since the scattering of the nation to a diaspora caused so many divisions, and the appearance of 'trespassers and ignorant youths' (such as David b. Daniel, he implies), that the secret of intercalation had to be passed on to 'all the sages and the Sanhedrin', in the days of our holy Rabbēnū; it is nevertheless the head of the yeshiva, that is, the head of the Sanhedrin, who maintains the prerogative to sanctify the year.

The homily of 'the third' was a direct attack on the ideas by which David b. Daniel sought to achieve the status of world leader of the Jewish communities everywhere, namely: (1) the unification around the living descendant of King David, during a period when Palestine was at a low ebb due to military events and the Saljūqs' domination of the Holy City;

and (2) the depreciation of the Palestinian yeshiva and its special status, and the removal of the priestly family from the leadership. The attack of the 'third' focuses on the prerogative to intercalate and to sanctify the year publicly, which symbolises more than anything else, the legitimacy of the Palestinian leadership. The claim of descent from the House of David, on the other hand, is absurd, for the entire dynasty of the exilarchs is utterly invalid and the true son of David is being kept with God until the right moment.

The Karaites were another objective of the attack. Things were not said specifically but by implication. The Scroll mentions the connections between Daniel b. Azariah and the 'sect of the *ṣela*' '; his son David proclaims himself exilarch in collusion with 'the sons of 'ōnenā', and with their support. More than that, David married the daughter of one of the Karaite leaders. It would not be too far-fetched, then, to assume that his aspirations were to bring the Karaites closer and that they already sided with him. He may even have been inclined to make serious concessions in their favour. His emissary, Abraham b. Nathan, who seems to have had a special relationship with the Karaites, 'misinterpreted the Torah'. David himself is 'an illiterate, who does not know the secret behind what he tried to take upon himself... nor does he know of what he is plotting to eradicate, whether it is a fundamental principle on which the entire Torah is depending or, as seen in the eyes of the fool and ignoramus that he is, it is something trivial'. It seems that the reference is mainly to the calendar order, that is determining the beginning of the month according to the sighting of the new moon, and the leap year according to the *avīv* (the ripeness of the grain), as was the Karaite custom. This may have been the reason why the 'third' devoted a considerable part of his homily to this subject. In the main, he discusses the matter for its own sake, as stated, and not only to establish proof of the authority of the Palestinian yeshiva. It is obvious that implicitly he sought to deny the Karaite argumentation on the subject of the calendar, and indirectly also to stifle the tendency to compromise with the Karaites in these matters.

There is no doubt that the extent of the dispute was very widespread and that it enthralled many communities. Today, it is difficult to envisage its extent and significance. The subject of the exilarchic house, of the strong feelings for the alleged scion of the House of King David and the struggle against the priestly family who happened to stand at the head of the Palestinian yeshiva at the time, all these had no meaning to subsequent generations – from then until the present. One can still detect echoes of the principles and ideological essence of the dispute in the twelfth century, but the matter ended there. Contrary to other subjects of principle pertaining to the religion of the Jews, which were entirely relevant throughout the generations, these subjects were completely erased from the nation's conscience and even the researcher who studies these worn pages needs to make a special mental effort in order to fully grasp their enormous significance in those days. Although we must not hasten to see the movement led by David b. Daniel as a messianic one, there were in the struggle raging around it, the major elements of the polemics between messianism and anti-messianism, especially in the claim to the crown of the House of King David and in the denial of this claim. However, we do not know whether the followers of David b. Daniel attributed messianic qualities to him or whether they believed that he was destined to bring about the redemption of the Jews in those times of war and sweeping changes. As we have seen, it seems that at any rate the outcome of the struggle was not decided by ideological argument or successful propaganda, but by entirely mundane circumstances.[188]

The yeshiva, last pages

[916] Apparently, Abiathar ha-Kohen Gaon and the Palestinian yeshiva eventually had to leave Tyre behind, close to the time of the Crusaders' conquest. Their move from Tyre is perhaps connected with the events of the autumn of 1097 mentioned above. Afterwards, we find Abiathar in Tripoli. In a letter dealing with the messianic movement that was stirring in Salonika during the first crusade, a letter written by Abiathar to the community in Constantinople is mentioned. Was David b. Daniel perhaps involved in this movement? Unfortunately we have no details concerning it. A financial account written in Fustat in Shevat 1416 Sel., January–February AD 1105, recorded the transfer to Abiathar of ninety dinars, of which seventy-five were from goods which were sold, and fifteen from the income from the house in Fustat which was *heqdēsh* for the Jerusa-

188 See **559**, a; b, lines 1–8. The homily: *ibid.*, from d, lines 4ff, and see the notes there. The connection with the Karaites: *ibid.*, b, line 9; d, line 1; the innovations of Abraham b. Nathan: c, line 22; innovations of David: 9, lines 20–21. The intercalation: d, lines 21ff; f, lines 7ff. A delayed echo of the polemics on the authority of the Palestinian yeshiva can be found in the letter of Daniel b. Ḥasdai, the exilarch in Baghdad, written in Tishri AM 4922 (AD 1161); according to him, there was an interruption in the chain of ordainings since the death of 'our Master, our Nāsī Daniel head of the yeshiva Ge'ōn Ya'aqōv, of blessed holy [qādōsh!] memory'; 'the kōhanīm appointed after him [that is: Elijah, Abiathar] behaved light-heartedly in their ways'. His view is based on the claim that 'since our ancient forefathers' time, the Palestinian yeshiva had no rights in the land of Egypt, for Egypt is foreign land, exactly like Babylonia'. Unlike Daniel b. Azariah, who was 'in his generation like our holy Rabbēnū', those who followed him were intruders; see in Assaf, *Tarbiz*, 1 (3;1929/30), 68-77; cf. Mann, *Texts*, I, 230f; *idem, Jews*, I, 190f, ascribed these remarks to David b. Daniel, but he later rectified it, see *Texts*, I, 255. It is interesting that this dispute still continues in the ideological arena, in the twelfth century, whereas on the other hand we see that they were still copying the Scroll of Abiathar at the time (see the introduction to **559**).

lemites. This document is evidence of how extensive the financial aid was that was being sent to the yeshiva. The money was intended for 'his great honour and Sanctity, our Lord and Master Abiathar ha-Kohen, head of the yeshiva Ge'ōn Ya'aqōv'. It is not clear where a deed for alimony dated September 1102 was written, except for the fact that it was 'in the council of the Grand Court', which is in the handwriting of 'Amram ha-Kohen, Abiathar's son-in-law. The name of the city has not been preserved, only the words 'the city situated on the shore of the Great Sea', and one can fill in Tyre or also Tripoli: Sīnīm). We do not know the date of Abiathar's death. But we do know that he died before the end of 1112, for in a letter to his son Elijah, written on '13 Marheshwan 1424 Sel.', Monday, that is 4 November AD 1112, it refers to him 'of blessed righteous memory'.

From this point onward, news of the yeshiva shrinks to what is contained in two letters. The one, from which a fragment remains, is from Abiathar's successor to the gaonate, his brother Solomon, son of Elijah. It deals with the affairs of an abandoned wife. It is dated 23 February 1116, and was sent to 'Ūla ha-Levi b. Joseph in Fustat. This 'Ūla, who was a well-known parnās in Fustat, was appointed a sort of representative of the yeshiva in Fustat. The other letter was written by Meir ha-Kohen b. 'Eli to his brother Tobiah in Egypt. This was a family from Bāniyās, known to us mainly from the letters of Tobiah ha-Kohen b. 'Eli. The date of the letter is the beginning of September 1127, that is eleven years after the former letter. We learn from it that the Gaon (who is Maṣlīaḥ ha-Kohen b. Solomon) is in Fustat ('our Master Gaon' is mentioned in the letter a number of times); possibly this is the first mention of the Gaon staying in Fustat, indicating the transfer of the yeshiva. Both letters speak of Ḥadrak: Solomon ha-Kohen marks the end of his letter with the words 'Ḥadrak Syria', indicating that he writes from there and that the yeshiva was then in Ḥadrak. Meir ha-Kohen b. 'Eli also ends his letters with 'Ḥadrak, Syria', from which we learn that the yeshiva moved from Tyre to Ḥadrak. Where is Ḥadrak? It is mentioned in the Bible: '. . . the land of Hadrack and Damascus' (Zech., ix:1), and in the Sifrē on Deuteronomy, the saying of R. Yose b. Dormasqīt: 'Heaven and Earth are my witnesses that I am from Damascus and that there is a place there named Ḥadrak.' The riddle is solved with the help of Meir ha-Kohen's letter, for the writer says explicitly that he is staying in Damascus (where he has no livelihood), whereas at the end of the letter he states, as aforementioned, that he writes from 'Ḥadrak Syria'. We therefore understand that Ḥadrak is merely a nickname for Damascus. Implicitly, the view that there was a locality named Ḥadrak where the yeshiva was located, becomes void. The yeshiva was situated in Damascus and remained there until *ca.* 1120. We find Maṣlīaḥ ha-Kohen b. Solomon Gaon b. Elijah Gaon heading the yeshiva in

Fustat in the twenties of the century. We have witnessed then, from the beginning of the seventies of the eleventh century, the decline and fall of the Sanhedrin of Palestine, the central institution of Jewish leadership in the countries surrounding the Mediterranean. This process was the unavoidable result of the destruction and annihilation of the Jewish population in Palestine as a result of the political and military events of the period. On foreign soil, the Palestinian yeshiva could not continue to preserve its status for very long. Apart from Egypt, the diaspora discontinued its connections with it. It is also possible that its decline was caused by the quality of the people at its head, the sons of the priestly family, whose annals I have surveyed here.[189]

[189] Abiathar's letter: Bodl MS Heb a 3, f. 27, edited by Neubauer, *JQR*, 9 (1897), 28, and re-edited by Mann, *Hatequfa*, 23 (1924/5), 253–259. The account: **561**, and the matter has already been mentioned above. The deed from 1102: **606**. At about the same time, TS 13 J 2, f. 7 was written, a fragment from a record of evidence signed by 'Abiathar ha-Kohen called by the name of God, son of a Gaon great-grandson of a Gaon', and 'Ūlā ha-Levi b. Joseph, parnās of Fustat (who is Sa'īd b. Munajjā) who hailed from Damascus, see on him Goitein, *Mediterranean Society*, II, 78, 81; it was he who is the addressee of **611**, discussed here below. Abiathar, of righteous blessed memory: **589**. Abiathar's daughter, Sitt al-Sāda, is mentioned in TS 10 J 4, f. 17, lines 16–17, a deed dated Shevat 1429 Sel., January AD 1118; she was married to a certain Abū'l-Makārim, in Fustat. The two letters from Damascus: **611**, **612**. See Sifrē on Deuteronomy (Ish Shalom), 65a; (Horowitz-Finklestein), 7; Neubauer, *La géographie*, 297, translated with his own interpretation: une localité près de Damas qui s'appelle Hadrakh; 'there', not 'near', was what R. Yose said, that is, in Damascus. Meir ha-Kohen in Damascus: **612**, a, line 31. See further discussion on these letters: Poznanski, *Rivista israelitica*, 7(1911), 222, n. 3; *idem, Babylonische Geonim*, 102, n. 2. Mann, *Jews*, I, 196, says that Solomon ha-Kohen fled, according to the Scroll of Abiathar, to the 'estate of Asher and Naphtali', and concluded that the intention was Ḥadrak; see also the formula in Samuel b. 'Eli's letter: 'the holy community who live [in the city] of Damascus Ḥadrak', in Assaf, *Tarbiz*, 1 (2–1929/30), 80 (fol. 18a, lines 16–17); *ibid.*, (1), 115, 117. Assaf interprets: he speaks about the communities (plural) of Damascus and Ḥadrak', for he himself completed the missing part of the formula by 'in the cities' instead of 'in the city', also adding 'and'.

9

Karaites and Samaritans

The house of ʿAnan and the beginning of Karaism

[917] The Karaites have left a rather substantial record in the sources of the period, considering that they were a numerically small segment within the Jewish population of Palestine. From the moment they began to arrive in Palestine and build their quarter in Jerusalem, they were a constant challenge to the Jewish population which preceded them, in Jerusalem and in Palestine as a whole. Their drive to convert others to their views placed the Rabbanite leaders in a defensive position to such an extent that they were annually excommunicating them on the Mount of Olives (as I have described in sec. 833). On the other hand, however, despite the sharp differences, there was collaboration on matters of shared interest, especially those relating to taxes. There were also mixed marriages between Rabbanites and Karaites. As to the Palestinian yeshiva and the Jewish population of Jerusalem, they had to turn for political and economic aid to eminent Karaites in Egypt, who were close to the rulers, especially the Tustaris.

The origins of the Karaites and their early development are shrouded in obscurity. The sources which describe these beginnings single out the figure of ʿAnan, who is considered the founder of Karaism. He is first mentioned in a passage of Naṭronai b. Hilai, Gaon of Sura (around 865), which is included in the *Seder* of ʿAmram Gaon b. Sheshnā, written some time after Naṭronai Gaon's time, and quoted in connection with the Passover Seder. It speaks there of *mīnīm* (heretics), the pupils of ʿAnan and the pupils of his grandson Daniel, who (it is not clear which of them: ʿAnan or Daniel, but we shall see in what follows that it seems to have been Daniel) induced them to relinquish the Mishnā and the Talmud for a Talmud which he himself compiled for them. The existence of a Book of Precepts (by ʿAnan?) is quoted there in the name of a certain Eleazar *alūf*. In some of the versions of the *Letter* of Sherira Gaon, we find that ʿAnan's defection occurred during the days of Yehudai Gaon b. Naḥman, that is 757–761; it was then that '*nefaq* 'Anan', meaning that 'Anan made his appearance, which is about a decade after the Abbasid revolution. Abraham ibn Da'ūd, who wrote during the middle of the twelfth century, added that 'Anan stemmed from the exilarchic house and his defection came about because he was denied the office of exilarch.

As to the Karaite sources themselves, Qirqisānī says that 'Anan lived in the days of the second Abbasid caliph, the founder of Baghdad, Abū Ja'far al-Manṣūr (754–775), which fits what has been said above. He stresses the conformity between the teachings of 'Anan and those of the Rabbanites, even when he wrote things not based 'in the teachings of the Rabbanites', that is, in the Mishnā and the Talmud, and it was found that he had taken them from the *ḥizāna* (that is, the *piyyūṭīm*) of Yannai. He emphasises that 'Anan had been exilarch and mentions that the Rabbanites tried to kill him. Late Karaite tradition preserved 'Anan's memory as the founder of Karaism and notes that he had been an exilarch. Ibn al-Hītī, in the fifteenth century, makes such statements about 'Anan as: he was the first to reveal the truth, and exilarch of all the House of Israel.

We find a more detailed account by a Rabbanite included in the Karaite treatise, it is 'the *ḥillūq* [controversy] between the Karaites and the Rabbanites', written by the Karaite Elijah b. Abraham in the first half of the twelfth century. Here we learn that 'Anan was excluded from the exilarchate in favour of his younger brother Ḥanania because of his wayward views. This Rabbanite ascribes 'Anan's views and those of his followers to Zadok and Baitos. His faction recognised him as exilarch. The rulers then had him imprisoned and he was to be executed, but a fellow-prisoner, a Muslim who was jailed because of his deviation from Islam, advised him to proclaim that his movement was a separate religion and hence he would not be considered a rebel against the laws of the realm. He followed this advice, even resorting to the claim that his computation of the calendar was similar to that of the Muslims (the first day of the month defined by sighting of the new moon). This, in addition to an enormous bribe, saved his life. A fragment from an anonymous Karaite treatise also adds the name of that Muslim who advised 'Anan so shrewdly: Abū Ḥanīfa, al-Nu'man b. Thābit, the famous Muslim jurist, the founder of the rite of Muslim law called by his name. Indeed, there is one principle in his teaching, the importance of the *ra'y*, that is, individual judgment, based on analogy and common sense, which is also one of the principles of Karaism.[1]

[1] See: *Seder 'Amram Gaon*, II, 206f. See the matter of the Rabbanite sources on the beginning of Karaism: Poznanski, *REJ*, 45:176, 1902; see *ibid.*, 191ff, the supplement with the sources: Naṭronai Gaon, Saadia Gaon, Dūnash b. Labrāṭ, Sherira Gaon, Samuel Gaon b. Ḥofnī, and

[918] That there was a strong Muslim influence on the beginnings (attributed to 'Anan) of early Karaism is not in doubt. M. Zucker points to a number of common grounds: prayer that was entirely benedictions and readings from the Pentateuch and the Psalms, containing no prayers of supplication or personal requests for oneself or others; the abolition of the idea of impurity of the dead in the diaspora (although later Karaite personalities objected to this), as compared with the Muslim belief that a Muslim does not defile in his life nor in his death; the prohibition on the drinking of wine and other alcoholic beverages in the diaspora; similarity in the commandments against incest, in the laws of inheritance and other such matters.

These indications of Muslim influence provoke the need to examine the question more profoundly. Did Karaism develop out of the schismatic sects which preceded it, with their ancient ideological principles being adopted by the Karaites and the Muslims simultaneously, or was this a new departure, influenced by the Muslim environment but with motives which were intrinsic to Jewish society? This latter view was held by I. Friedländer, who considered the upholders of the early Jewish dissident sects to be naive and uneducated people who were easily taken in by false Messiahs and influenced by the non-Jewish environment, while Karaism evolved from learned circles and was essentially an internal Jewish movement, although it was also influenced by the *zeitgeist* of Muslim society,

others. From the lists of Karaite *nesī'īm* (to be discussed below) we know that Daniel was 'Anan's grandson and that he had a son named 'Anan. Mann, *JQR*, NS 10 (1919/20), 354, has shown that Naṭronai Gaon refers to the same heretics also in his responsum in *Sha'arē teshūvā*, No. 34: *mīnīm* who on Saturday do not eat *ḥamīn* (stew cooked and preserved for the sabbath). See the Letter of Sherira Gaon in Neubauaer, *Mediaeval Jewish Chronicles*, I, 37; Lewin, 107 ('Anan is missing in the Neubauer edition): see Harkavy, in Graetz (Hebrew), III, 186f., Abraham ibn Da'ud (Cohen), 37f. Qirqisānī, I, 2, 14. See the *Siddūr* (Karaite), I, 399. Ibn al-Hītī, 432. The *ḥillūq*, in Pinsker, *Liqqūṭē qadmōniyōt*, I, 103; Pinsker, Harkavy, and also Zucker assumed that this account was by Saadia Gaon; see: Poznanski, *JQR* 10(1898), 242; Zucker, *Targum*, 147. See the matter of Abū Ḥanīfa: Harkavy, *JJGL*, 2(1899), 109f; Goldziher, *Ẓāhiriten*, 3f; *idem, Muhammedanische Studien*, II, 76f. See the anonymous fragment: MS Firkovitch II, No. 3799, fol. 2a, in Mann, *Texts*, II, 108. Utter reservation regarding the sources on 'Anan is expressed by Nemoy, *Löw Memorial Volume*, 239; here are his main points: it is difficult to view it as accidental that neither Naṭronai Gaon nor Qirqisānī mention that 'Anan was exilarch or even from the exilarchic family; the account about him in the *ḥillūq* is not by Saadia Gaon, but by a contemporary of the writer of the treatise, in the twelfth century. The stories about 'Anan's arrest, about his brother Ḥanania, and similar stories, are merely fiction and illogical; Abraham ibn Da'ūd's account is based precisely on these stories in his *Sefer ha-qabbālā*; see especially Nemoy's reservations towards Qirqisānī, *ibid.*, 248 and n. 42; according to him the only source that may contain some real evidence concerning 'Anan is the Book of Precepts ascribed to him; from which it is only possible to learn that 'Anan demanded asceticism and radical austerity but there is nothing in his views directed against the Rabbanites; nevertheless 'Anan's teachings are not entirely in accord with the thinking of the yeshiva scholars, therefore Nemoy assumes that this was the reason why the Karaites adopted him and made him 'father of their creed'.

especially by its inclination to scepticism and excessive separatism. Poznanski, in particular, opposed this claim and argued on the basis of Qirqisānī's account, that 'Anan was but a link in a chain, preceded by people of earlier dissenting sects, such as the messianic movement in Iṣfahān, and by Abū 'Īsā (in 'Abd al-Malik's time: 685–705) and his pupil, Yudghān. They recognised Jesus and Muḥammad as prophets sent to the gentiles, and the Arab sources state that 'Anan also followed in their footsteps in this respect.

Here we must take a closer look at the Muslim sources. A Muslim writer who was a contemporary of Qirqisānī, Mas'ūdī, spoke of the 'Ananites as variants of Mu'tazilites among the Jews, people of *al-'adl wa'l-tawḥīd*; that is, they stood for the principle of Divine justice (God is good and just, whereas evil stems from man, who is responsible for it) and the principle of the absolute unity of God. They only accept the Bible (the *tawrāh* and the Prophets and *al-zubūr* [Psalms], which constitue twenty-four books). He also knows that a faction of the 'Ananites – who are the followers of 'Anan, one of the exilarchs in Babylonia – and the Karaites as well, are setting the date of Passover according to the ripeness of the grain, which they call *abīb*. Some of them also accept a partial ripening of the grain. Here we already find a distinction between diverse Karaite factions, and especially between 'Ananites and Karaites.

Bīrūnī, writing in *ca.* 1000, informs us that the Karaites are also called *mīlādiyya* (people of the new moon) or *ashma'iyya* (people of the tradition) for they are meticulous about starting the month with the appearance of the new moon (he meant: on sighting the new moon) and because they only obey the text of the Bible (*al-nuṣūṣ*). Among them, there is a faction called the 'Ananites, after 'Anan the exilarch, who lived a little more than a century earlier. Here Bīrūnī quotes 'Anan's lineage: b. Daniel b. Saul b. 'Anan b. David b. Ḥasdai b. Qafnai b. Bustanai, etc.; he was therefore of the sixth generation after Bustanai. (Qafnai, who is Kafnai, was, according to all exilarch lists, the father of Bustanai, and not his son.) Bīrūnī also does not know anything substantial about 'Anan's beliefs except that he adhered to Muslim custom with regard to the months (the sighting of the moon) and intercalated according to the *abīb*. He further adds details about the gravity with which the 'Ananites keep the sabbath, which according to them, takes precedent even over circumcision.

In Shahrastānī (who wrote in the first half of the twelfth century but used older sources) there are details on 'Anan the exilarch, concerning the differences in the calendar and the laws regarding food. In addition, he describes the way the 'Ananites slaughter: by killing the animal at the back of the neck. He also mentions their attitude to Jesus, whom they consider a righteous man but not a prophet; further, they deny that the Gospels were books that were handed down from Heaven, as they were compiled by four of Jesus' own disciples.

Maqrīzī, who wrote his great book on Egypt at the beginning of the fifteenth century, knew the Karaites in Egypt, but he also had before him the writings of his predecessors, hence his account is a mixture of personal knowledge and information copied from earlier sources. The essence of his account can be summed up as follows: The Karaites do not accept the Talmud but only the Bible, as they were taught by ʿAnan the exilarch. They are called people of the Bible as well as 'people of the beginnings' (he seems to have read *mabādiyya* instead of *mīlādiyya*, people of the new moon, as in Bīrūnī); and also 'people of the tradition' (*al-asmaʿiyya*, as in Bīrūnī). He presents the ʿAnanites, undoubtedly under the influence of his early sources, as a sect which differs from the Karaites. They are so-called after ʿAnan, the exilarch, who lived at the time of al-Manṣūr (754–775; the same information is found in Qirqisānī). He argued that the beginning of the month should be fixed by the sighting of the new moon, and the intercalation, according to the state of the barley grains; he spoke well of Jesus and recognised Muḥammad as a prophet sent to the Arabs; he states that the ʿAnanites are people of *ʿadl* and *tawḥīd* (like the Muʿtazilites, as Masʿūdi also writes) and they reject anthropomorphism (*tashbīh*).

One may sum up the information in the Arab sources in ten main points: (1) in general, they speak of ʿAnanites, not of Karaites; Masʿūdī and Maqrīzī divide them into two separate sects altogether; (2) ʿAnan was exilarch, and Bīrūnī even sets the time during which he held office; (3) they only recognise the Bible; (4) they resemble the Muʿtazilites (*ʿadl, tawḥīd*); (5) they fix the beginning of the month only according to the sighting of the new moon; (6) they intercalate according to the state of the *abīb*; (7) they have their own laws regarding food and slaughtering; (8) they have a positive attitude towards Jesus, but he is not a prophet in their view; (9) they recognise Muḥammad as a prophet sent to the Arabs; and (10) they reject anthropomorphism.[2]

[2] On the common elements of Islam and Karaism: Zucker, *Targum*, 144ff; *idem.*, *Sura*, 2(1954/6), 324–331, where there is a discussion on the Karaite use of the Islamic *ta'wīl* and *qiyās*; Poznanski, *REJ*, 44(1902), 178; Friedländer, *JQR*, NS 1(1910/1), 214; see Masʿūdī, *Tanbīh*, 112f, 219; Bīrūnī, 58f, 283; perhaps the ʿAnan he mentions, who he says lived in the ninth century, is ʿAnan II, b. Daniel, the great-grandson of ʿAnan I. ʿAnan II was the cousin (and contemporary) of the *nesīʾīm* Jehoshaphat and Ṣemaḥ who headed the Palestinian yeshiva. See the genealogical list below, in the note to sec. 927. See Shahrastānī, 167; his account was copied by Abū'l-Fidā', *Mukhtaṣar*, I, 86f. Maqrīzī, *Khiṭaṭ*, III, 326, mentions the dayyān (*qāḍī*) of the Karaites in his day: Ibrāhīm b. Faraj Allah b. ʿAbd al-Kāfī; he was from the House of David (*Da'ūdī*), i.e. belonged to the exilarchic house, being a descendant of ʿAnan (*ʿAnānī*); he mentions these details in the chapter on the mosque of Ibn al-Bannā', near the Zuwayla Gate in al-Qāhira, which according to the Karaites had formerly been their synagogue, but al-Ḥākim had confiscated it during the persecution; the synagogue was called after Shem the son of Noah, who according to Karaite tradition, was buried

[919] Above we have seen the continual distinction between the 'Ananites and the Karaites in the Muslim sources. A similar distinction is also adopted in Qirqisānī's account. He states that there were Karaites who called 'Anan 'head of the fools' (*kesīlīm* – a pun on the Hebrew word for learned: *maskīlīm*) and viewed his teaching as if it were the same as that of the Rabbanites. Not only was he not a prophet, but he was mistaken in many things; from the very outset, his path was that of the Rabbanites. This is said more explicitly by Salmon b. Yeruḥim in his commentary to Psalms (lxix:1). According to him, the Karaites appeared on the scene only after Benjamin al-Nihāwandī, that is, more than a century after 'Anan. Harkavy has already pointed out that the only Gaon (as far as writings of the geonim have been preserved) who mentions 'Anan, before Saadia Gaon, is Naṭronai Gaon in the latter half of the ninth century, more than a hundred years after 'Anan. To this Bīrūnī's account should be added, that 'Anan lived somewhat more than a century earlier, that is, in the latter half of the ninth century; as well as the fact that (according to our information) two of 'Anan's descendants, Jehoshaphat and Ṣemaḥ, sons of Josiah, headed the Palestinian yeshiva until some 100 years after 'Anan (until the sons of Ṣemaḥ were deposed). The conclusion one may arrive at, at least in the form of a working hypothesis, is that the formative stage of the Karaite movement only began in the latter half of the ninth century and that it was only during that period that the Karaites and the descendants of 'Anan, the nesī'īm, became associated with one another. From then onward, things were projected backwards, the new movement discovering an early founder in 'Anan who may have been a deposed exilarch of the eighth century. This crystallisation was preceded by the secession of another descendant of 'Anan's family, Daniel, mentioned by Naṭronai Gaon, evidently 'Anan's grandson, who lived in the first half of the ninth century. Apparently, he is the same Daniel of whom Sherira Gaon says in his Letter that he was the rival of David over the office of exilarch, the latter being the victor. He is also the Daniel of whom Dionysius of Tel Maḥrē (copied by Michael the Syrian and Bar Hebraeus) says that the Babylonians wanted as exilarch, in opposition to David, who was supported by the Palestinians (the 'Tiberians'); and further that Daniel stemmed from the 'Ananites, who sanctified

there; Maqrīzī notes that this is a folk legend which is not true. The mosque of Ibn al-Bannā' and its Karaite connections also drew the attention of Goldziher. He even notes in one of his articles that this mosque was a relatively late structure, built in around 1800; the Jews of Cairo did not know, writes Goldziher, that there was a Karaite synagogue there at one time; see his paper in *Globus*, 71(1897), 235f; see in Maqrīzī, on the Karaites and 'Ananites, *Khiṭaṭ*, III, 370ff, 375. Different information on the Karaite attitude to Muḥammad is found in Abū Bakr ibn al-'Arabī, who took it from his contemporary, a member of the Tustari family, who was evidently Sahl b. Faḍl (Yāshār b. Ḥesed), the Karaite writer who described it to him in Jerusalem, *ca.* 1095; it emerges that Sahl denied that Muḥammad was a prophet altogether; see *Riḥla*, 81f.

Wednesday instead of Saturday. It was due to this dispute, according to him, that al-Ma'mūn decreed that the Jews (and the Christians and the Zoroastrians as well) be permitted to secede from the main body of their persuasion and establish a separate congregation, even if this consisted of only ten souls. Apparently, one cannot rely on the account of Dionysius concerning the division between the two camps (Palestine versus Babylonia) or the sanctification of Wednesday which he attributes to the 'Ananites. We should also bear in mind that my present discussion is necessarily brief and that there remains ample reason to probe deeeper into further and more detailed aspects of the subject, such as the matter of the Book of Precepts ascribed to 'Anan, for instance.[3]

[920] If indeed Karaism – as it is known to us from tenth and eleventh century sources – was born out of the fusion of two elements, a dissident sect which held different views from those of the majority of the Jews, and a branch of the exilarchic family, the question is still unanswered as to what was the nature of this dissenting sect and where did it begin. This is a subject that is still clouded and this is not the place to enlarge on it. It is worth noting, however, that the early formulation of Karaite teaching took place in the Persian areas of the caliphate. Some hundred years after 'Anan, Benjamin al-Nihāwandī (Nihāwand, some forty miles south of Hamadān), was active. It is this period, the latter half of the ninth century, which was evidently the genuine period of Karaite formation. One should recall that this was the period in which the Jewish population of Palestine was struggling over the gaonate and the forefathers of Aaron b. Meir

[3] Qirqisānī, 3, 5, 624. Salmon b. Yeruḥim (Marwick), 98. The matter of the history of the Karaites and the place occupied by 'Anan has been widely discussed in the research literature. See Harkavy, *REJ*, 5(1882), 209; *idem* in Graetz (Hebrew), III, 187f; Poznanski, *REJ*, 45(1902), 50, and see *ibid.*, 191; where he quotes examples from an anonymous polemical anti-Karaite treatise on the conformity between the view of 'Anan and Rabbanite halakha. See also: Markon, *Festschrift M. Schaeffer*: 130, and see there references to earlier studies; Klar, *Tarbiz*, 15(1943/4), 36ff, who also has a discussion on 'Anan's Book of Precepts; on the same matter, see Epstein, *Tarbiz*, 7(1935/6): 283; see the discussion in Mann, *Texts*, II, 129-132. The matter of the dispute between David and Daniel: Sherira Gaon, *Letter*, 110f; Dionysius, copied by Michael the Syrian, 517 (text); III, 65 (translation); and by Bar Hebraeus (Abbeloos), 366. See *supra*, sec. 732. Bīrūnī, 283, ascribes the sanctification of Wednesday to 'the sect of the caves' (*al-maghāriyya*, which is the correct reading) which is also mentioned by Qirqisānī, see his Index. Cf. Ben-Sasson, *Zion*, 15 (1950), 42ff, who also stressed the difference between 'Anan and the Karaites, but his view of the four stages of development of Karaism is somewhat shaky, as the Arabic source (Salmon b. Yeruḥim) which he quotes, does not use 'revealed' as distinct from 'appeared', the distinction being only the product of Pinsker's Hebrew translation; the original text says throughout: *ẓaharū*. A book which is a monograph on Karaism was written by R. Mahler: *Di Karaimer* (Yiddish), N.Y. 1947, also extant in Hebrew: *ha-qārā'īm*, Merhavia 1949; a thorough and basic work of research, however, which should carry on a more profound study on the Karaites, must be based as far as possible on a thorough knowledge of the Arab sources, both of the Karaites themselves and of the Muslims. Information on sources and research on Karaism and on Karaite personalities can be found

fought with 'the sons of 'Anan', that is Jehoshaphat and Ṣemaḥ, sons of Josiah, and the sons of Ṣemaḥ, who as we have seen were deposed. This was also the juncture at which the Ismā'īlī movement in Islam was formed and in which the Qarmaṭīs and the Fatimids first appeared on the historical horizon. I have already reviewed (secs. 462–466) the rise of these two dissident movements, particularly during the last decade of the ninth century. Evidently it was also the period which witnessed the rise of the Karaites in Palestine.[4]

Karaism in Palestine in the tenth century

[921] The central Karaite figure at that time was Daniel al-Qūmisī. This was the period of flourishing Karaite propaganda, which tried to make converts everywhere, arousing opposition to the point of being excommunicated. It seems that following the example of the Ismā'īlīs, there evolved the figure of the preacher trying to convert souls to the true path. Among the Ismā'īlīs, these missionaries were called *dā'ī*, and it is reasonable to assume that the designation Karaites had a similar meaning, for *qārā* (*nomen agentis*) is the translation of *dā'ī*, 'the caller'. Ismā'īlī influence on Daniel al-Qūmisī can be clearly seen in a passage from his commentary on Leviticus: 'know ye, that God's Torah is likened to water, and those who taught knowledge (*maskīlīm*) were the prophets, who possessed knowledge, knowing the Bible in all its aspects, why such a thing is written as it is, and not otherwise. Therefore, it is to them that God gave the Torah, some of which is overt and explicit, but some is hidden and unseen'. This is in fact the very theory of *ẓāhir* and *bāṭin*, the overt and the covert, which the Ismā'īlīs held with regard to the Koran.

Very few details are known about Daniel al-Qūmisī. He was born in Dāmghān, a city in the district of Qūmis, in the Ṭabaristān province of northern Persia (the area of the Caspian Sea). He apparently stayed for some time in Khurāsān and afterwards emigrated to Palestine and settled in Jerusalem. His commentary to the Book of Daniel contains a description of the events of the latter half of the ninth century, especially those connected with the Ṣaffārid dynasty, which ruled Khurāsān and other parts of Persia. These events occurred before 875. He also mentions Qārin,

in Ankori, *Karaites in Byzantium*, using the detailed Index at the end of the volume. See the total reservations concerning 'Anan's Karaism: Nemoy, *Löw Memorial Volume*: 239.

[4] On Nihāwand, see: Le Strange, *Lands*, 196. Yefet b. 'Ali speaks in his commentary to the Song of Sol., ii:15 (little foxes), on new Muslim rulers who would arise in the realm of Islam, who will send *du'āh* – 'callers', i.e. preachers, missionaries; these rulers would decimate the Children of Israel – by which it seems that he means the Karaites; see BM Or 2520, 60a. See also Hirschfeld, in his introduction to the commentary on Nahum by Yefet b. 'Alī, 8ff, who points to the messianic hopes expressed by Yefet, evidently in connection with the rise of the Qarmaṭīs.

a local ruler in Ṭabaristān, who was involved in these events. On the basis of these facts, H. Ben-Shammai assumes that Daniel al-Qūmisī arrived in Palestine in about the year 880. It was Daniel al-Qūmisī who rendered Karaism the character it assumed from then onward, which can be summed up in three principles, as M. Zucker proposed: the utter exclusion of all Rabbanite teachings, the actual return to Palestine, and accepting ways of asceticism and mourning. Mas'ūdī mentions a Jewish scholar named David al-Qūmisī, who lived in Jerusalem and died there in AH 334 (which began on 13 August AD 945). If we assume that David is Abū Sulaymān (which is almost certain) we shall find the same David al-Qūmisī mentioned in two Karaite Bible commentaries (one of them by Yefet b. 'Alī). He may have been Daniel's son. Daniel al-Qūmisī is worth recalling here in particular, because of his propaganda for emigrating to Palestine, which expressed the aspiration to establish and consolidate a Karaite settlement in Jerusalem (a matter I have discussed in secs. 824–827).

It is likely that the close contact with Palestine, and the formation of the Karaite sect there, had a very profound influence on the ideo-theological contents of Karaism. According to the assumption proposed by the French scholar, P. André, the first Karaites who came to Palestine were deeply affected by the writings of the Judaean Desert sect which they found in Jerusalem. We learn about the finding of these writings at that time in Jerusalem, from a letter of the Nestorian catholicus of Baghdad, Timotheus, to Sergius, the priest in charge of the Elam area, from about 815. In that letter, he tells about a discovery 'ten years earlier' of books in a cave near Jericho. A Bedouin hunter's dog was chasing after some animal, followed it into a cave and did not return. Its owner followed it into the cave and found a little room hewn out of the rock, containing many books. The hunter told this to the Jews of Jerusalem, who came there *en masse* and found books of the Bible, as well as other books written in Hebrew script. The Jew who told this to Timotheus was a learned and erudite man and Timotheus was in the habit of questioning him about passages in the New Testament which are said to be in the Bible, but which are not to be found there, either in the Christian version, or in that of the Jews. The Jew would tell him in such instances, that such passages were to be found in the writings discovered in the cave. From this story, one can understand that the Jews of Jerusalem rejected those writings, which were evidently part of the literature of the Judaean Desert sect, which is now known to us. One may assume that with the arrival of the first Karaites in Jerusalem, they found these books, which they then adopted, copied and distributed. In particular, they seem to have taken the book of the Damascus Covenant for their own, and it was evidently through the Karaites that this treatise, found in the Judaean Desert, reached the Cairo Geniza. This may be the possible explanation for the presence of ideas and concepts from the literature of the Judaean Desert sect in the writings of Daniel al-Qūmisī and other early Karaite writers, like the use of such expressions and terms as: covert and overt Torah (we have seen that this idea may have stemmed from the Ismāʻīlīs), *dōrēsh ha-tōrā, shūv el tōrat Moshē, maskīl, mōrē ṣedeq, derekh emet, ʻaniyē ha-ṣo'n*, the two messiahs, *temīmē derekh*. These and other analogies are mentioned in the studies of N. Wieder, especially with regard to the attitude to adversaries: *sārē ha-derekh, dōreshē ḥalāqōt, massīgē gevūl, mateʻē Isrā'ēl*, and so on.[5]

[5] See the detailed survey on Daniel al-Qūmisī and his writings in Mann, *Texts*, II, 8ff; see Ben-Shammai, *Shalem*, 3 (1980/81), 295–305; Zucker, *Albeck Jubilee Volume*, 378ff. See Masʻūdī, *Tanbīh*, 113; Abū Sulaymān: Poznanski, *JQR*, 8(1896), 681. See fragments from Daniel's commentaries: Markon, *Korespondenzblatt*, 1927, 26–29; see Daniel al-Qūmisī's *Pitron*; see the article on Daniel al-Qūmisī's propaganda, by Zucker, *Targum*, 168ff. See *ibid.*, 176ff, Daniel al-Qūmisī's Arabic letter from the Geniza, which contains mainly the themes of the uniqueness of God, reward and penance, and the matter of the *ʻadl* and *tawḥīd*, the principles of the Muʻtazilites; and *ibid.*, 184ff, fragments of Daniel al-Qūmisī's commentaries. Concerning the matter of overt and covert Torah, see a fragment from Daniel's commentary to Leviticus, in Wieder, *Judean Scrolls*, 59f. (TS Loan 199, edited earlier by Ginzberg, *Ginzē Schechter*, II, 471ff, and see *ibid.*, 473f); see arguments against ascribing the *Pitron* to Daniel al-Qūmisī: Marwick, *SBB*, 5(1961), 42ff, and the answer: Wieder, *Judean Scrolls*, 265ff; and see on Daniel al-Qūmisī also: Nemoy, *Karaite Anthology*, 30–41. His letter which urges the Karaites to emigrate to Palestine, was first edited by Mann, *JQR*, NS 12(1921/2), 257–298, where he did not identify the author at first, but after studying Daniel's *Pitron*, he recognised that he was the author of the letter, see *idem, Texts*, II, 5. Timotheus' letter: Braun, *Oriens Christianus*, 1(1901), 299–313; cf. Paul, *Ecrits*, 94ff; and on this matter, of early discoveries of the writings of the Judaean Desert sect, see also: Eissfeldt, *TLZ*, 74(1949), 597ff, who, apart from the matter of Timotheus' letter, also quotes a fragment of Eusebius' *Ecclesiasticae historiae* (IV, 16), relating to the year AD 217 and referring to the translation of Psalms which Origenes appended to his Hexapla, which was found in an urn in Jericho. See also: De Vaux, *RB*, 57(1950), 417ff (I shall not enter into a detailed discussion here on the question of the 'sect of the caves' [*al-maghāriyya*] mentioned by Qirqisānī and some Arab writers, which is an important subject on its own). Regarding the matter of the impact of the Judaean Desert scrolls on the moulding of Karaite thought in the ninth and tenth centuries, there are some remote echoes in this passage of the Rabbanite Moses b. Ḥasdai Taku, written about the middle of the thirteenth century: 'and we have already heard from our scholars that 'Anan the heretic and his friends were writing heretic things and lies and burying them in the earth and afterwards they would dig them up and say: this is what we found in ancient books'. It is impossible to identify the channels through which such accounts moved down the centuries, but at any rate, they are noteworthy. See Kirchheim, *Ōṣar neḥmād*, 3(1859/60), 62. Rabin, *Qumran Studies*, 112, totally rejects the information in Timotheus' letter, because the matter of the books in the cave is not mentioned in any Jewish source; obviously this kind of argument cannot stand up to criticism. Some years before the publication of Paul's book, Naphtali Wieder wrote in his book *The Judean Scrolls and Karaism* similar things about the analogous views and concepts in the writings of the Judaean Desert sect and in Karaite literature. Although it is clear from Paul's bibliographical notes that he was acquainted with Wieder's book (which was published in 1962, while Paul's book was published in 1967), he does not mention it in his discussion on the analogies.

[922] Daniel al-Qūmisī, on occasion, mentions in his writings that the Muslims help the Karaites and that it was due to them that the Karaites were given the opportunity to rise and go to establish a foothold in Jerusalem. One should perhaps take these words at their face value; with the view that whereas this was not possible during the reign of the former rulers, the Christians, Jerusalem was now open to them: 'the kingdom of Ishmael . . . always helps the Karaites to keep [the precepts] as in the Torah of Moses, therefore we have to say benedictions for them'; 'they love those who guard [the custom of] fixing the months according to the moon; why, therefore, should you fear the Rabbanites?'. Mann assumed that one can learn from these sayings, that Karaite propaganda to establish a community of their own in Jerusalem moved forward at full swing with the advent of the Ṭūlūnids' control of Palestine, for it is they who were willing to help the Karaites. These are things that are difficult to prove or deny, however. Mann adds that afterwards, when the Abbasids returned and once again took over Palestine, the people of the Palestinian yeshiva hastened to apply to Baghdad in order to obtain the caliph's backing in their opposition to the Karaites, being assisted by the Jewish notables in Baghdad, as mentioned in the letter of the Palestinian Gaon during the calendar dispute. In this matter, it is also impossible to find confirmation in the sources of any real connection between the political and military changes in Palestine and the 'Jewish wars' waged at the time. Moreover, according to the information at our disposal concerning similar situations during the eleventh century, it seems that both sides were all too familiar with the ways and means of influencing the rulers, both in Egypt and in Baghdad.[6]

[923] In the tenth century, there were a number of Karaite personalities who lived and were active in Palestine, becoming famous mainly for their Bible commentaries. The first of these was Salmon b. Yeruḥim (Sulaym b. Ruḥaym). The fact that he was an inhabitant of Jerusalem is conspicuous in a number of passages in his commentaries, especially in his reactions to the scheming of the Byzantines and the Arabs and his complaints against the defilers of Jerusalem. According to the chronicle of Ibn al-Hītī, however, he was one of the Karaite scholars of Babylonia and lived in Aleppo, where he indulged in theological controversies with Saadia Gaon. Ibn al-Hītī also mentions that Saadia Gaon participated in his funeral and that his grave is well known in Aleppo 'to this very day'. Poznanski and Mann treated this information concerning Aleppo and Saadia Gaon very sceptically; but Mann was prepared to accept the possibility that Salmon

[6] See in Daniel al-Qūmisī's letter: Mann, *JQR*, NS 12 (1921/2), 285f; see Mann's assumptions regarding the Tulunids: *Jews*, I, 62f. The Gaon's letter: Guillaume, *JQR*, NS 5(1914/5), 554f; Bornstein, *Sokolow Jubilee Volume*, 63.

had lived in Aleppo towards the end of his life. Apart from his Bible commentaries, Salmon wrote a polemical work against Saadia Gaon – in rhyme – known as the Book of the Wars of the Lord. His commentaries also contain sharp attacks on Saadia Gaon, and he speaks of him disdainfully: 'I knew in the days of my life a man known by the nickname al-Fayyūmī'.[7]

[924] Abu Surrī Sahl ha-Kohen b. Maṣlīaḥ was a contemporary of Salmon b. Yeruḥim, though somewhat younger. He also wrote Bible commentaries, a book of precepts, remnants of which have been preserved, especially the introduction written in Hebrew, a book of laws (which has been lost), and a grammar. His 'epistle of rebuke', also in Hebrew, is of particular significance. This is a disputatious treatise against Jacob b. Samuel, who may have been a pupil of Saadia Gaon (Sahl calls him: 'Your Master Saadia the Pithomite', but one cannot say whether he meant an actual pupil). In this epistle Sahl twice stresses that he stemmed from *bēt-ha-miqdāsh*, meaning Palestine. Apparently he came to Fustat to convert people to Karaism: 'to caution my nation'. Evidently that Jacob b. Samuel was one of the Jewish leaders in Fustat. Apart from the latter, Sahl came up against the resistance of another Fustat personality whose name is not mentioned, merely: 'the enemy who angers'. Sahl was evidently the author of 'the answers to Jacob b. Samuel, the obstinate', a treatise in rhyme which the Karaite copyist ascribes to Yefet b. 'Alī; a fact which Mann has proven by the similarity of expressions in the 'epistle of rebuke' and in this work.[8]

[925] Yefet ha-Levi b. 'Alī, who is Abū 'Alī al-Ḥasan ibn 'Alī al-Baṣrī (that is, he hailed from Baṣra in Iraq), wrote in the latter half of the tenth century, and also mainly produced Bible commentaries. He was the most

[7] On Salmon see: Poznanski, *Encyclopaedia Oṣar Isrā'ēl*, s.v.; *idem, Yerushalayim* (Luncz), 10(1913/4), 95; Ibn al-Hītī, 434, 441; Mann, *Texts*, II, 18ff.; see Feuerstein's introduction to the edition of Salmon's commentary on Lament.; see further Steinschneider, *Polemische und apologetische Lit.*, 346; Harkavy, *ZAW*, 1(1881), 157; Poznanski, *JQR*, 8(1896), 689 (he shows that Salmon was much younger than Saadia Gaon, thus suggesting that it was not likely that Saadia was his pupil, as some Karaite sources claim). His knowledge of the surroundings of Jerusalem and the Dead Sea, which I mentioned (on the basis of his commentary on Eccl., above, in sec. 311) also goes to prove that he was a denizen of Jerusalem. On his writings see: Poznanski, *JQR*, 18(1905/6), 220; his *Book of the Wars of the Lord* was edited by Davidson, NY 1934, see *ibid.*, in the introduction, some details on Salmon's life. The piyyūṭīm at the beginning of the book are defined by Fleischer, *Settimane* (Spoleto 1978), 840, as being of the *musammaṭ* type. See on Salmon also: Nemoy, *Karaite Anthology*, 68.

[8] On Sahl b. Maṣlīaḥ see Poznanski, *Yerushalayim* (Luncz), 10(1913/4), 97–100; Mann, *Texts*, II, 22–29. His introduction to the Book of Precepts was edited by Harkavy, *Me'assēf*, I, No. 13. The 'epistle of rebuke': Pinsker, *Liqqūṭē qadmōniyōt*, II, 24ff; see the detailed discussion on the epistle: Harkavy, *ZAW*, 1(1881), 157; see also: Poznanski, *JQR*, 18(1906), 238; Nemoy, *PAAJR*, 38–39:145, 1972. On 'the enemy who angers', see the discussion in

prolific of the Karaite Bible commentators. His works also include a literal Arabic translation of the Bible, and a book of precepts, which has not been preserved. On the basis of the colophon at the beginning of a manuscript containing his commentaries of the Song of Solomon and Ruth, Nemoy assumed that he was still alive in the year 1005. This colophon states that it is the work of Abū 'Alī al-Ḥasan (Yefet) b. 'Alī al-Baṣrī, and adds after his name the blessing 'May the Lord give him His support' (*ayyadahu Allah*), indicating that he was still alive. The date was read as 395 but it seems to me that it should be read as *wa-sab'īn* (not *wa-tis'īn*), that is AH 375, which is AD 985/6. Another of Yefet's treatises was a polemical work against Saadia Gaon, a work he mentions in his commentary to Exodus, xxxv:3. Apparently Yefet lived in Jerusalem most of his life and one can assume that he also died there.

His son, Abū Sa'īd Levi ha-Levi, also lived in Jerusalem. He too wrote a book of precepts, which has been preserved in a Hebrew version. We know the names of his three sons, Isaiah, Azariah and Ḥananiah. Levi b. Yefet lived and worked at the beginning of the eleventh century. The year 397 'of the little horn', that is, of the Muslim era, which began on 27 September 1006, is noted in his book of precepts. His name is also to be found in several colophons in his father's Bible commentaries, stating that his son Levi dedicated them to the Karaite congregation (in Ramla or Jerusalem), and they also mention Sha'yā b. Ṣalaḥ (Ṣāliḥ?) b. Azariah (perhaps the great-grandson of Levi b. Yefet).

Other contemporaries of Yefet b. 'Alī and his son Levi were the Bible commentators Joseph b. Bakhtawayh and his pupil, the grammarian Sa'īd Shīrān. Joseph b. Bakhtawayh was evidently one of the heads of the Karaite congregation in Jerusalem; he was a wealthy man, and there is mention of his *ḥāṣēr*, that is a housing compound, which he owned in Jerusalem.

From what has been said until now, it emerges that from the end of the ninth century, with the arrival of Daniel al-Qūmisī in Palestine, until the end of the tenth century, Palestine served as a spiritual centre for the Karaites. Apparently this was where the fundamental principles of their teachings and views crystallised. The greatest and most important of their spiritual leaders, Bible interpreters and grammarians lived and worked in Palestine. There is no doubt that this fact proves that the Karaites succeeded in reaching the target they set for themselves when first advocating emigration to Palestine – to set up a strong Karaite community there, particularly in Jerusalem. This community was indeed established, with

Mann, *Texts*, 23, n. 42. The treatise in rhyme: Pinsker, *Liqqūṭē qadmōniyōt*, II, 18–24; Mann, *Texts*, 26f.

the best of the Karaite figures centred there. It was from Jerusalem that their teachings went forth to the entire Karaite diaspora.[9]

The Karaite *nesīʾīm*

[926] We have seen that in the latter half of the ninth century, a schism developed between the branch of the exilarchic family who were ʿAnan's descendants, and the yeshivot, particularly the Palestinian yeshiva. From then onward, the Karaites adopted this branch as their own, considering ʿAnan their founding father. We have seen the lineage of Jehoshaphat and Ṣemaḥ, who were both *nesīʾīm* (that is, they were counted among the exilarchic family) and geonim of Palestine. The first systematic list of Karaite *nesīʾīm* was compiled by Poznanski. As we have already taken note of Jehoshaphat and Ṣemaḥ, sons of the ninth century, I shall recount what we know about those who followed them.

Jehoshaphat's son was Boaz. He is mentioned in the story of Bustanai found in the Geniza and ascribed to Nathan b. Abraham, which disparages the exilarchs, claiming that they all stemmed from the Persian princess given to Bustanai by the caliph. The text there speaks of all those named

[9] See: Nemoy, *Karaite Anthology*, 83, n. 1; the commentary to the Song of Solomon: BM Or 2554, see: Margoliouth, *Catalogue*, I, 223f (No. 301); microfilm No. 6330 at the Institute of Microfilmed Hebrew MSS, at the National Library, Jerusalem; Assaf, *Sefer ha-yishuv*, 63: 'the year 395' which he says was the year AM 4844, AD 1084 (it is not clear why), which would take us as far as the Saljūq period! See the description of this MS: Hörning, *Six Karaite Manuscripts*, viii; see *ibid.*, in the previous pages, details about Yefet's other Bible commentaries, and see *ibid.*, 21, 27; see further: Harkavy, *ZAW*, 1(1881), 228. The Commentary to Exodus: Pinsker, *Liqqūṭē qadmōniyōt*, II, 20. On Yefet's writings, see also: Neubauer, *Aus der Petersburger Bibl.*, 15ff. The sons of Levi b. Yefet: Pinsker, *Liqqūṭē qadmōniyōt*, 106; see Mann, *Texts*, II, 32f, and *ibid.*, also the information on a treatise he wrote, which lists the differences between Ben Asher and Ben Naphtali (this is TS Box K 27, f. 36). Hananiah b. Levi b. Yefet is mentioned in **302**, a, line 20; Ṣalaḥ b. Azariah, who is mentioned there in line 23 is evidently the grandson of Yefet b. ʿAli. The book of precepts of Levi b. Yefet: MS Leiden, Or 4760, and at the Institute of Microfilmed Hebrew MSS at the National Library, Jerusalem: microfilm No. 28065; it can be seen from the language that it is a translation from the Arabic; see the date there: fol. 34a. See colophons with Levi's name: BM Or 2556, fol. 87a; BM Or 2558, fol. 166a, cf. Hörning, *Six Karaite Manuscripts*, 35. On Joseph b. Bakhtawayh and his pupil Saʿīd Shīrān see: Mann, *Texts*, II, 29f. Joseph ibn Noah and Abū'l-Surrī ʿAlī (?) ibn Zūṭā (or Zīṭā) were also contemporaries of Sahl b. Maṣlīaḥ and Yefet b. ʿAli. A Karaite source (a commentary on the Book of Samuel, by ʿAlī b. Israel *alūf*) calls them the teachers of the Jerusalemites (*muʿallimī al-maqādisa*). As to Abū'l-Surrī ibn Zūṭā, Mann has shown that he settled in Jerusalem evidently after 942, see *Texts*, II, 33, and more references there. In the Karaite marriage deed, **305**, line 35, Joshua ha-Kohen b. ʿAlī b. Zīṭā signed, perhaps his son; another of his relatives was perhaps Ṣedaqa b. Ṣāliḥ b. Sahl b. Zīṭā, who is the first of the signatories on a record on the state of the *avīv*, see **302**, a, line 19; after the Crusaders' conquest (Summer 1100), we find Shelah ha-Kohen b. Zadok b. Maṣlīaḥ b. Zīṭā, who is certainly the son of the former, see **577**, b, margin. The family of b. Zīṭā was then apparently an eminent and widely ramified Jerusalem Karaite family. See further on the commentaries of Yefet: Ben-Shammai, *Alei Sefer*, 2:17, 1975/6.

Boaz and 'the sons of Zakkai'; the entire dynasty of 'Anan on the one hand and the entire dynasty from which David and Josiah, the sons of Zakkai and their descendants (among them Hezekiah and his son David, and also Daniel b. Azariah – contemporaries of Nathan b. Abraham), all of them, it claims, are not proper Jews but the offspring of the Persian woman who had not converted to Judaism. In fact, we know that 'Anan's descendants claimed descent from Ḥasdai, while the offspring of Zakkai claimed descent from Barādai, the two sons of Bustanai from his Jewish wife. We know of two sons of Boaz, Abū Sa'īd David and Josiah. A fragment from a polemical work written by the Gaon of Pumbedita, Aaron ha-Kohen b. Joseph (who is Khalaf b. Sarjāda) against Saadia Gaon, lists the 'sons of Boaz', that is (as it should be understood) David and Josiah, as supporters of Saadia. It therefore becomes clear that they lived in the first half of the tenth century. According to Ibn al-Hītī, David b. Boaz wrote a commentary on Ecclesiastes in AH 383, that is, in 993, which means that he was probably in his eighties at the time, but it is also possible that there was an error in al-Hītī's version. David b. Boaz is credited with having written a commentary to the Pentateuch and a book on the principles of the religion (*kitāb al-uṣūl*). In his commentaries of the Pentateuch, there are arguments with Saadia Gaon, written with restraint and to the point. Apparently David lived in Jerusalem, and he was possibly an adversary of Meir Gaon and his son Aaron, because of whom and against whom they had to appeal to the notables of Baghdad and ask for assistance in the period before the calendar dispute. It is also possible (as Mann assumed) that it was his animosity towards the Palestinian Gaon which caused David and his brother Josiah to later side with Saadia Gaon, the tenacious adversary of Meir Gaon and his son Aaron in the calendar dispute. One may even assume that the Palestinian Gaon sided at that time with David b. Zakkai, Saadia Gaon's rival. However, we have no evidence that during these complicated events, the Karaites took part in the struggles. All sources merely refer to the descendants of 'Anan, a branch of the exilarchic family, the *nesī'īm*, the extent of whose connections with the Karaites cannot as yet be determined, although the later Karaite sources see David b. Boaz as a distinctly Karaite personality.[10]

10 See Poznanski, *Babylonische Geonim*, 128ff. The nesī'īm in the story of Bustanai, see Gil, *Tarbiz*, 48 (1978/9), 67. The matter of Ḥasdai and Barādai: *ibid.*, 44, 62f, based on the geonic responsa. On David b. Boaz see: Poznanski, *JQR*, 18(1906), 226f. The supporters of Saadia: in Harkavy, *Zikkārōn*, V, 227 (line 13); Khalaf b. Sarjāda adds the following nicknames for the sons of Boaz: 'the children of slave girls and camel flesh', meaning the same claim about their Persian ancestress, and also a hint (unexplained and certainly not true) at some descent from Arabs. Apparently their support of Saadia contradicts the polemics conducted by David (in his old age?) against him in his commentaries of the Pentateuch, in which he is called *hādhā al-rajul* (this man); see Harkavy, *ZAW*, 1(1881), 157, and also Poznanski (above in this note). See on David b. Boaz, Mann, *Texts*, II, according

[927] The son of David b. Boaz was Solomon, who was an inhabitant of Jerusalem, as is shown by an inscription of dedication at the head of a manuscript of the Bible in the Firkovitch collection. Ḥusn (or Ḥasūn), daughter of Jacob b. Joseph b. Kūshnām, dedicated the Bible to the Karaite congregation in Jerusalem 'through our Master the *nāsī* Solomon b. David b. Boaz'. It also contains a blessing for Solomon's two sons, Hezekiah and Josiah. The date of the dedication is Monday, 5 Tishri 1328 Sel., 10 September AD 1016 (the Karaite Rōsh ha-shānā that year fell on the same day as that of the Rabbanites).

Josiah and Hezekiah evidently lived most of their lives in Fustat, but they were in contact with the Palestinian yeshiva. The Karaite rank of *nāsī* was preserved for the offspring of Ṣemaḥ b. Josiah (of the ninth century, as we have seen) while Josiah and Hezekiah stemmed from his brother Jehoshaphat b. Josiah. It seems that after the death of David b. Ṣemaḥ (b. Asa b. Ṣemaḥ b. Josiah), however, when Fustat remained without a *nāsī*, it is Hezekiah b. Solomon b. David b. Boaz b. Jehoshaphat who succeeded to this rank, as did his offspring after him.

The two brothers, the *nesī'īm* Josiah and Hezekiah, the sons of Solomon, are mentioned in the colophon of the *Keter* of Aleppo, dedicated by Israel of Baṣra b. Simḥa b. Saadia b. Ephraim to the Karaites of Jerusalem, with the provision that it be kept by the 'two *nesī'īm*', Josiah and Hezekiah, the sons of Solomon. Hezekiah b. Solomon maintained a relationship with the Jerusalem Gaon Solomon b. Judah. In a letter written for him by his son Abraham but which he himself signed, in *ca.* 1026, the Gaon expresses his desire that the *nāsī* come to Jerusalem before Rōsh ha-shānā, and he hopes that the *nāsī* will bring with him a letter from the authorities in Egypt (implying that he will obtain this letter with the help of the Tustaris), which will reinforce the prerogative of the *nāsī*: 'to strengthen him against the provokers of quarrels'. Solomon b. Judah also expressed his willingness to grant the *nāsī* a very high rank in Jerusalem, 'to be a captain over God's nation' (2 Sam., v:4). In a letter written some years later, he mentions that the *nāsī* was a guarantor for large sums of money (a matter probably related to the Jerusalemites imprisoned because of their debts – an affair that has been enlarged on above). It seems that considerable sums of money were at the disposal of these *nesī'īm*, for in another letter the Gaon notes that while the Rabbanites still owe 900 dinars, some of them having been taken to prison, the Karaites ('the sect of the ṣela'') owed 800, despite the fact that they are given considerable help by the *nesī'īm*. At about the same time, the Gaon wrote a letter to Sahlān b. Abraham, in

to the Index, particularly 132ff, and *ibid.* also on the support of the sons of Boaz for Saadia Gaon. One can also get an idea of David b. Boaz' attitude to the Karaites and their views, from his opposition to the theory of *rikkūv*, that is, the extension of the incest regulations

which he mentioned the *nāsī* by name: 'our *nāsī*, his honour, our Master Hezekiah'.

In the days of these *nesī'īm* Josiah and Hezekiah, marriage ties were contracted between the *nesī'īm* and the Tustaris: Yefet (Ḥasan) the son of Abū Sa'd Abraham b. Yāshār (Sahl) al-Tustarī, became betrothed to the daughter of one of the *nesī'īm*. In the deed of betrothal, only the name of the grandfather, Solomon b. David, has been preserved. The deed was written in the presence of the Karaite *nāsī* in Fustat, 'the great *nāsī* David . . . son of Ṣemaḥ the *nāsī*', who is David b. Ṣemaḥ b. Asa b. Ṣemaḥ, from the other branch of the family of the *nesī'īm*. It is also likely that the uncle of Yefet al-Tustarī, Abū Manṣūr Aaron (Hārūn), the youngest of the Tustari brothers, married the daughter of one of these *nesī'īm*, for Solomon b. Judah mentions 'Aaron, the son-in-law of the *nāsī*' who happens to be in Jerusalem, perhaps referring to the Tustari. The relationship with the Tustaris is also evident from a letter of complaint written by Solomon b. Judah to Abraham ha-Kohen b. Isaac ibn Furāt, with claims against people who are scheming against him and his son Abraham. These people (perhaps the Shuway' family) wrote letters incriminating him 'to our *nāsī* Abū'l-Ḥasan Josiah', before his meeting with 'my Master, the grandee' (*ha-gevīr*) that is, with Ḥesed b. Yāshār the Tustari. Possibly related to this matter is another letter from the Gaon, perhaps written to the *nāsī* directly, which speaks of the appointment of a ḥāvēr in the yeshiva from among the people of Fustat, also containing his reaction to complaints about the Gaon, which reached the addressee from some unworthy person: 'but how can such a person be worthy of writing to your honour'. From all that has been said above, one may conclude that during Solomon b. Judah's day, friendly and collaborative relations developed between the Palestinian yeshiva and the Karaite nesī'īm of Jehoshaphat's family. The Tustari family, who, as we have seen, were connected by marriage to the nesī'īm, comprised a third party to this relationship, while a fourth party was the 'Babylonian' congregation in Fustat and its leaders, Abraham b. Sahlān and his son Sahlān. They were the bond which linked this alliance by virtue of their special connections with the Tustaris. This four-sided alliance disassembled during the dispute with Nathan b. Abraham. The 'Babylonians' in Fustat and the Tustaris sided with the rival Gaon. On the other hand, it seems that the nesī'īm of the house of Jehoshaphat maintained their friendship and relations with the old Gaon. One may even assume that due to their relationship with the other parties, they played an important role in the settling of the dispute, hence it is not accidental that we find the signature of 'Hezekiah the *nāsī* b. Solomon the *nāsī* b. David

to all relatives of the mate, where there are no blood-relations. See Mann, *ibid.*, 140, n. 290, and see also p. 1470.

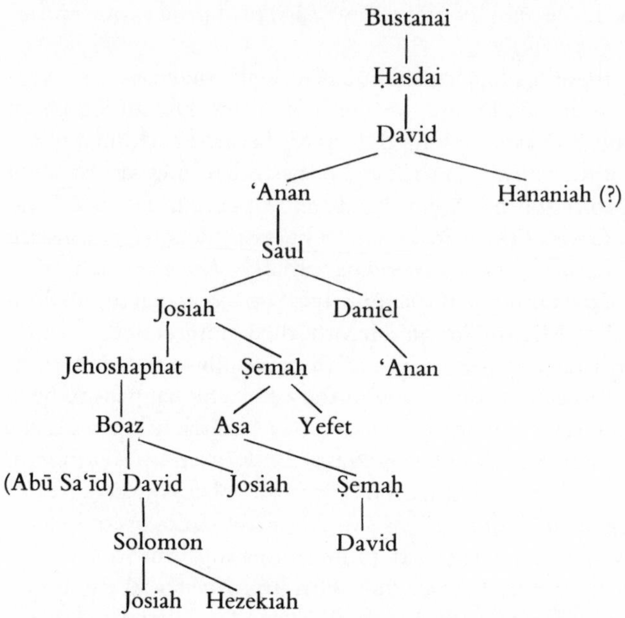

Family tree of the Karaite nesīʼīm

the *nāsī*, of blessed memory' in the written agreement which put an end to the dispute.[11]

Beliefs and opinions

[928] I shall now discuss something of the views of the Karaites on various subjects, especially as they are expressed in the writings of some of

[11] See the colophon: Kahle, *Masoreten des Westens*, I, 67, and in Mann, *Texts*, II, 134f, and see the notes there; the writer of the colophon signed in *atbash* (a system of cryptography), and he is Nissi b. Aaron b. Bakhtaway; see also: Poznanki, *Babylonische Geonim*, 129; Mann (*ibid.*, 46) assumed that Solomon b. David b. Boaz is the mysterious figure ('son-in-law of Sheshach') against whom Josiah Gaon came out in his epistle, **29**; the two *nesīʼīm* in the colophon: Harkavy, *Ḥadāshīm*, 104ff. Solomon b. Judah on the *nāsī*: **64**; cf. Mann, *Texts*, II, 46. The guarantee: **82**, lines 16ff. The aid: **84**, lines 12–13. 'Our Nāsī': **86**, line 15. The deed of betrothal: TS 16.50, cf. Goitein, *Mediterranean Society*, III, 135; 455, n. 92; this family relationship is also implied in ʻEli ha-Kohen b. Ezekiel's letter, from 17 July 1060, in which he asks the people of Fustat to obtain a reduction in his taxes for his shop in Jerusalem, suggesting that for this purpose, they ask 'our Master, the honoured Nāsī Hezekiah, may God preserve him, to speak to our Master Abū Manṣūr', etc.; it is quite clear that they are referring to the Nāsī Hezekiah b. Solomon, and evidently to Abū Manṣūr Aaron the Tustari, his son-in-law. See **446**, lines 27–28. David the Nāsī b. Ṣemaḥ (b. Asa) is also mentioned in **307**, lines 11, 16 (the year is 1051, when he is still the Karaite Nāsī in Fustat); cf. Gil, *ha-Tustarīm*, 58. Aaron the son-in-law of the Nāsī: **120**, a, line 9; there, too, money needed to ransom the Jerusalemite prisoners is mentioned. The

those figures who lived in Palestine, and in letters from the eleventh century, for this is not intended as an all-inclusive and comprehensive survey of the history of the Karaites and their ways of thinking, but mainly as a discussion focusing on the Palestinian sources.

One of the prominent issues in the lives of the Karaites, from which there were important projections with regard to their relationship with the Rabbanites, was that of the calendar. As they used to determine the beginning of the month by the actual sighting of the new moon, and the intercalation by an examination of the state of the grain in Palestine, it is understandable that there were differences between them and the Rabbanites over the days on which the holidays should be celebrated.

Observance of the moon is mentioned in Karaite marriage deeds as one of the characteristic principles of the sect. Whereas from a passage in Benjamin al-Nihāwandī, one gets the impression that the matter of fixing

complaints to Josiah: **142**, line 31. The letter to the Nāsī (?) Josiah (?): **152**; my view of this letter is merely an assumption; Mann, *Jews*, I, 131f, assumed that it was written to the *av-bēt-dīn* of the yeshiva who was then in Egypt. The record of agreement: **199**, b, line 4; in 1043, Solomon b. Judah wrote to Sahlān b. Abraham and expressed interest in 'the two books *pitrōn qōhelet* (commentary on Ecclesiastes) of the Nāsī, of blessed memory', which Solomon b. Judah had sent to Fustat, see **137**, b, lines 4–80. We know that Hezekiah lived a long time, until the sixties of the century, whereas Josiah is mentioned in a court document in Fustat, dated Thursday, 15 Tammuz 1366 Sel., 13 July AD 1055; hence we learn that the late *nāsī* mentioned in Solomon b. Judah's letter cannot be Josiah, contrary to Mann's assumption, and not even Hezekiah. See Mann, *Texts*, II, 48; Mann himself edited a fragment from a court document from 1055, in which Josiah is mentioned, see his *Jews*, II, 453. 'Hezekiah the great Nāsī, Nāsī of the Land of Israel and Judah . . . son of . . . Solomon the great Nāsī, of blessed memory', is mentioned in a fragment of a Karaite marriage deed, TS 20.42, dated Thursday, 9 Adar ('Shevat according to the Karaites'; thus it says in the deed) 1373 Sel., 21 February AD 1062, see in Mann, *Texts*, II, 173f. To this subject of the *nesī'īm*, **288** should also be considered, a letter from a Karaite who was requested 'to go up to the *bēt ha-miqdāsh* (i.e. Jerusalem) and meet with my Master the Nāsī'. The letter also contains news of the arrival of Abū Naṣr David b. Isaac ha-Levi, one of the Karaite leaders in Egypt (discussed above), at the writer's place (Ramla?); Abū Sulaymān David b. Bāpshād was also staying there then; he was probably the son of Bābshād ha-Kohen b. David, mentioned by Mann, *Texts*, I, 151 (*ibid.*, in n. 7 one should read: Abū Sulaymān instead of Sulaymān); *ibid.*, 163f, there is a fragment of a letter from the Gaon Samuel b. Ḥofnī, with regards to Abū Sulaymān b. Bābshād in the margin; see *ibid.*, n. 44b, on Bābshād ha-Kohen b. David and on the name Bābshād (Bāpshād). See: Justi, *Iranisches Namenbuch*, 55: Bābshādh. The Karaite of Fustat David b. Bāpshād evidently converted to Islam, according to information about a personality who was evidently his son, mentioned by al-Khaṭīb al-Baghdādī, *Ta'rīkh*, VII, 307: al-Ḥasan b. Da'ūd b. Bābshād b. Da'ūd b. Sulaymān; whose by-name was Abū Sa'īd al-Miṣrī. He was from a family who came from Persia. He arrived in Baghdad, and studied law according to Abū Ḥanīfa with the cadi Abū 'Abdallah al-Ṣaymarī. He was a very gifted pupil and particularly excelled in his knowledge of the Koran by heart in various reading versions; he was also learned in literature, mathematics and grammar. He also possessed a profound knowledge of traditions (ḥadīth), which he both studied and taught. Al-Khaṭīb al-Baghdādī knew him personally and studied with him, and he praises his keen mind; his father, he writes, was a Jew who converted to Islam, a genuine conversion. The son (Abū Sa'īd) lived in Baghdad until the end of his life, and died on Saturday, 14 Dhū'l-Qa'da AH 439 (1 May, AD 1048).

the first day of the month on the basis of the appearance of the new moon only related to Nisan and Tishri, Daniel al-Qūmisī explicitly states in his book of precepts that it is forbidden to compute on the basis of the movement of the celestial bodies: 'we are not permitted to deduce [the fixing of] the months of God and his holidays from the computation of sorcerers and astrologers'. In the same passage in which he speaks of the fixing of the new month, Benjamin al-Nihāwandī also formulates the rule relating to the intercalation: 'if the barley grain is ripe enough for harvesting in the month of Nisan to be used for the *'omer* offering during the seven days of Passover, the year is normal. But if the grain is not ripe enough for harvesting . . . that entire year is a leap year'. Later, we find Qirqisānī basing this rule on 'observe the month of Avīv' (Deut., xvi:1), which, he says, is referring to the ripeness of the grains – of barley, not wheat. Some say, he writes, that it is permissible to take moist ears for the *'omer*, but this contradicts 'and you shall reap the harvest thereof' (Lev., xxiii:10), for one did not harvest the ears when they were wet.

Salmon b. Yeruḥim blames the Rabbanites: 'they do not say anything of sighting the moon or looking for the *avīv*'. Evidently, ascertaining the leap year on the basis of the *avīv* was an innovation introduced by the Karaites from the time they settled in Palestine, as we are clearly told by Levi b. Yefet in his book of precepts: 'the Karaites living in the land of *Shin'ār* [which is Babylonia] and other remote places, were imitating the Rabbanites, since they saw that their [computation of the] leap years is, in most cases, perfect'; that is, as long as the Karaites lived in Babylonia and Persia, and so on, they abided by the calendar of the Rabbanites, which seemed to them good enough at the time; 'but the people [living] in Palestine contradicted them, for in their opinion, it sufficed to see the state of the *avīv* in order to fix [a leap year]'; that is, when they settled in Palestine, the settlers had the possibility of observing the state of the grain there, and this was sufficient for them to know when to fix a leap year. He continues with detailing the signs (of the *avīv*): the barley must be 'strong and hard'; the upper part must be dark green and the lower part, yellow, and so on. He also discusses the borders of Palestine with regard to the *avīv*, for example, 'Gaza is the extremity of Palestine, as it is said: . . . as thou comest to Gerar, unto Gaza' [Gen., x:19], by which he meant that Gaza is the border. The proper *avīv* should appear all over – in the Galilee and the *Dārōm* and the Sea of Galilee.[12]

[12] The sighting of the moon: **304**, c, line 14; **305**, line 31; **308**, line 3 (reconstructed); Saadia Gaon ascribes to 'Anan the matter of fixing the new month by sighting the new moon; according to him, after 'Anan was excluded from the exilarchate, he was helped by Muslims and imitated their customs in order to gain their good will, such as fixing of the new month by sighting the new moon; he first made his decision and then sought for proof in the scripture, see Zucker, *Targum*, 144ff. It should be noted here that whereas the fixing

[929] Now we can easily understand what is written in some of the documents in my collection. The Karaite Moses b. Isaac writes from Jerusalem, apparently in 1044, to one of the leaders of the Karaites in Fustat, informing him of the state of the *avīv*. He points out that at the beginning of Sha'bān, which is when the letter was written, the grain in the *al-dārūm* region was mostly a mottled green (*mujabban*), by which he evidently means yellowish, while less of it was dark green: *dajan*. In the regions of Rafaḥ (Rafiaḥ), the Ghawr (Jordan valley), Zughar (Zoar), and the surrounding areas, the situation was similar. The examination was being organised by *mawlā'ī al-rayyis*, 'my Master the chief', who is not known to us. In a document written in March 1052, we find a record compiled by a Karaite delegation, made up of Jerusalemites and Gazans. They went out to Sūq Māzin (described in sec. 310), near Gaza. The survey was partly carried out on the property of the cadi Salāma b. Maḥmūd, and they also examined a plot of land belonging to Ibrahīm b. al-Khūfyānī, and apparently still another – that of the cadi al-Ṣabgha (his name is not preserved in full). They established the state of the grain on the basis of the evidence of the *fallāḥīn*. The delegates remained in the fields for two days, Thursday and Friday, and examined a number of fields. Apparently, the delegation consisted of twelve participants, who signed at the end of the document. This document is evidently a copy of the original, for apart from some signatures which are not clear, the remainder is in the handwriting of the scribe.

Apparently it was the *nesī'īm* who made the decision when to fix the leap year, and this may have been the purpose of the letter from Moses b. Isaac of Fustat, that is, to inform the *nesī'īm* of the facts, in order that they may decide how to proceed. On this matter we have no clear information, however, and it is possible that in fact the decision would be made in Jerusalem and sent from there to all the Karaite congregations, as we learn from the letter of Eliah of Salonika, in which he expresses bitterness at the fact that the Karaites 'desecrated the sacred feasts of the Lord and celebrated Rōsh ha-shānā in the eighth month, for they had received letters from Palestine that the *avīv* was not to be seen in Nisan, and Passover was held in Iyar'.

Muslim writers were also aware of the Karaites' method of determining a leap year. Mas'ūdī mentions that the 'Ananites fix Passover according to

of the month according to the sighting of the moon and not according to computation, seemed to the Karaites a means of gaining the favour of the Muslims, we know that the Fatimids used to fix the new month by computation, not by sighting the moon. See: Canard, *AIEO*, 10(1952), 376. See Benjamin al-Nihāwandī in Harkavy, *Zikkārōn*, 8, 176; Daniel al-Qūmisī, *ibid.*, 189. Qirqisānī, 836, 843, 850. Salmon b. Yeruḥim, *Sefer Milḥamōt*, 82. Levi b. Yefet, MS Leiden Or 4760, 22a–b; 23b; 24a; 26a, ff. From the language, it is obvious that this is a translation from the Arabic, and that the translator did not know

the ripeness of the grain; there are even those for whom a partial ripeness is sufficient. Bīrūnī writes in the same vein: the fixing of the new month according to the sighting of the new moon, and the leap year according to the state of the barley in Iraq (!) and in Palestine. If the grain is easily husked and is ready for harvesting and the awns developed, a leap year is not in the offing. Their people go out to examine the fields for this purpose when there are still seven days left in the month of Shevat. Some add another month of Shevat (II) while others add Adar (II), but most prefer Shevat, in order to be different from the Rabbanites. Bīrūnī adds a critical remark to the description of this method, namely that it is unstable and lacks uniformity, and that it would be advisable to have such things regulated by law (*qānūn*).

There were differences of opinion and varied calendar systems amongst the Karaites themselves. We now know of one faction among the Karaites whose calendar system was different from that of the rest of the Karaites – that of the Tustaris. This can be seen in fragments of an eleventh century Karaite calendar, apparently belonging to the Tustaris, in which the dates of the Rabbanites, the Karaites and the Tustaris are listed side by side. This can also be observed in a Karaite deed from 26 July 1032, relating to a deal between Abū'l-Ḥasan Da'ūd b. al-Faraj and 'Imrān b. Levi ha-Kohen, where we find in Arabic script: 'Wednesday eve, the 15th of Av, which is Av for most of the Karaites and Elul for some of them, and is the month of Sha'bān for the gentiles, in the year one thousand and three hundred and forty-four of Alexander's era.'

As to the use of eras, we find in Karaite deeds and even letters, the frequent use of the Muslim hijra year. Sometimes the Seleucid era is used. An unusual method is their computation from the exile of Jehoiachin. We find this in fragments of a Karaite formulary, and also in one of the Karaite marriage deeds in my collection. An explicit clue to this era can be found in that same formulary, in which the year 1321 Sel. is listed as against 1484 of the exile of Jehoiachin, that is, the year was AD 1009/10, which shows that according to their reckoning, the exile of Jehoiachin occurred in 435–434 BC. It is also worth quoting what Salmon b. Yeruḥim says in his commentary to Lam., iii:6 (He hath set me in dark places, as they that be dead of old): 'as is known, 1385 years have now passed from the exile of Jehoiachin, and 885 from the destruction of the second Temple'. In view of what has been said above, this was, according to the era of the exile of Jehoiachin, AD 951. We must therefore deduce from this that they reckoned the date of the destruction of the second Temple as having occurred

how to translate the words relating to the details of the *avīv* discussed above; cf. Pinsker, *Liqqūṭē qadmōniyōt*, II, 90.

in the year 66, and not 68, which was the year generally accepted by the Jews.[13]

[930] Another domain in which the Karaites had their own laws, was that of food. One may find evidence of this in Daniel al-Qūmisī's commentary to Hosea, viii:11 (Because Ephraim hath made many altars to sin): 'altars mean the basins of the slaughterers'; 'basins of the butchers'; and further, to Hosea, x:1 (he hath increased the altars): 'to buy meat from the altars of the slaughterers and idol-worshippers'; and to Hosea, xiii:12 (the iniquity of Ephraim is bound up) '[these are] the altars in [the period of] the exile, basins of the butchers, to eat meat at a time when there are no sacrifices'. This clearly implies that the writer sees it as a sin to eat meat when there are no sacrifices, and in his book of precepts, Daniel says: 'know ye now that it is not permitted to any God-fearing person to eat fowl, but doves ... until the teacher of righteousness will come'.

Qirqisānī cites the Karaite ban on eating meat in Jerusalem and this was deduced from the expression 'without the camp' (Ex., xxix:14 and elsewhere); Jerusalem is the camp, hence consuming 'meat for lust' is only permitted outside Jerusalem. In an anonymous Karaite halakhic treatise we find: 'the more so, when the City of your Holy Mount is destroyed, nor do you have your priests, while dumb and blind dogs are observing

[13] Moses b. Isaac: **301**. The record: **302**; a remnant of a similar record is TS AS 158.147; it has a series of similar terms; it speaks there of two surveys, in Dhū'l-Qa'da and Dhū'l-Ḥijja, and of the varied hues of the ears; see also *ibid.* evidence of the exact time of the new moon (on the fourth hour on the ... day of Dhū'l-Ḥijja). The letter of Eliah from Salonika: TS 20.45, edited by Mann, *Texts*, I, 48f, lines 32ff. See Mas'ūdī, *Tanbīh*, 219; Bīrūnī, 59, 283. See the discussion in Bornstein, *Hatequfa*, 14–15 (1921/2), 365ff, on the matter of intercalation in Karaite sources. Fragments of the calendar: TS NS J 609; ENA 4010, f. 35; 4196, f. 15, in Gil, *ha-Tustarīm*, 86ff. The deed from 1032: TS Box J 3, f. 47*v* (formerly TS 13 J 32), in Assaf, *Klausner Jubilee Volume*, 230; see what Assaf quotes from *Aderet Eliyāhū* (relating to 1336/7), and from the letter of Obadiah of Bertinoro, with evidence on the differences between the Karaites themselves regarding the calendar in later generations. Ankori, *Karaites in Byzantium*, 317, n. 51, refers to this matter the passage of Levi b. Yefet quoted above, about the Karaites 'in the land of Shin'ār and other remote places', who followed the Rabbanite calendar, unlike their brethren in Palestine; but as I have stated above, this was how the Karaite writer described the process of detachment from the Rabbanite calendar after the establishment of the Karaite community in Palestine; in other words, in early Karaism, they followed the Rabbanite calendar; once they had established their community in Palestine, they adopted new calendar regulations. The era of Jehoiachin, see: **303**, 1 (a), lines 6, 14; **304**, I, lines 2–3; Salmon b. Yeruḥim: MS Paris 295, 71a; cf. Mann, *Texts*, II, 158, who assumes that this reckoning from the exile of Jehoiachin was peculiar to the people of Ramla, see in the document he edits, *ibid.*, 191 (BM Or 2538, f. 89*v*); the date of the copy he quotes there, 192, is 1334/5, not 1424, for 'of the little horn' means AH, not Sel. We have evidence from the tenth century regarding the difference (which we do not find in the eleventh century) in the reckoning of the years since the creation; Qirqisānī, writing in AM 4697 (AD 937) notes that according to the Karaite reckoning, that year was 4724 of the creation, that is, a difference of 27 years; see this passage in Neubauer, *Mediaeval Jewish Chronicles*, II, 249, and cf. Mann, *Texts*, II, 78, n. 33 (where there is a misprint, apparently, 997 instead of 937).

you, and menstruating women, and men with issues, and lepers, and uncircumcised Christians enter the shrine of the elevated 'Ofel . . . it is forbidden to eat meat and to drink wine'. There he also adds the ban on slaughtering pregnant animals, which he deduces from 'whether it be a cow or ewe, ye shall not kill it and her young both in one day' (Lev., xxii:28), and concludes: 'whoever slaughters or eats of a pregnant animal in the [during the] exile [!] is a transgressor and wicked person'. Sahl b. Maṣlīaḥ complains in his 'letter of rebuke' that the Rabbanites buy – after reading the megillā – in the 'gentile market', 'all sorts of sweets that are made from their [the gentiles'] fat and sweetened by them'; apart from this, 'they eat the animals they immolate after alien gentiles flay them'; 'and the essence of all this is: it is forbidden [to eat] meat of cattle or sheep in exile . . . cooked with the forbidden fat-tail . . . they eat stew which is placed on the eve of the sabbath on a kindled fire'. Apart from the matter of the fat-tail of the sheep and the stew kept warm from Friday, which is clear, it seems that the matter of 'it is forbidden in exile' needs interpretation; it probably means: when there is no Temple, and is not meant to discriminate between Palestine and other countries.

They were also pedantic about baking *maṣṣā* from barley flour, not wheat flour, which they attributed to 'Anan, who interpreted it from the expression 'the bread of affliction' (Dt., xvi:3). What we have not found stated explicitly in the writings of the Karaite figures I have mentioned here, is the permission to eat meat with milk. Karaite evidence of this exists only in comparatively later sources, but in the eleventh century Solomon b. Judah explicitly wrote in one of his letters that the Karaites ate meat with milk. He claimed that this is no reason to excommunicate them. In another of his letters, however, it emerges that a quarrel broke out in Ramla between the Rabbanites and the Karaites because of the latter's refusal to accept the Rabbanite supervision of their slaughtering. The Karaite customs in the eleventh century with regard to meat are not made quite clear in the Geniza documents. While on the one hand, we hear about the eating of meat with milk, on the other hand, we also read about a total ban on the eating of meat, in Jerusalem, at any rate. A Karaite marriage deed from Jerusalem, dated January 1028, contains the following prohibition: 'and without eating beef and mutton in Jerusalem'; which implies that they only ate fowl. As against this, the Karaite Maḥbūb b. Nissīm writes: 'I did not eat [in Jerusalem] either meat or fowl, out of fear of God'. Another document specifically relating to dietary laws of the Karaites at that time is a Rabbanite record of evidence concerning cheese made by the Karaites (of Samaritiqā) 'produced on the Mount of Olives', which was kosher. Three witnesses are signatories there, among them Aaron ha-

Kohen b. ʿAmram (undoubtedly the in-law of the Gaon Abiathar ha-Kohen b. Elijah, the father of his son-in-law ʿAmram). The confirmation of *kashrūt* is only granted after 'we acquired it from him according to their ways of purchase, which is from hand to hand' (that is, with a handshake), 'and we made him take an oath on the Holy Torah'.[14]

[931] There is a very interesting document in my collection dealing with Karaite matrimonial laws and incest regulations, which is a letter written by Simon b. Saul of Ṭulayṭula (Toledo) from Jerusalem, to his sister Ballūṭa in October 1057. He writes to her of the case of Abraham b. Fadānj, who arrived in Palestine with his wife and children after a difficult journey from Spain, via Byzantium, and was in very reduced circumstances. The Karaites learned that he had married the sister of his late first wife after her death. The writer tried at first to keep the matter from the Karaites but the women from Ṭulayṭula who lived in Ramla could not restrain from telling the Karaites about it. In the continuation, he describes the tragic situation that developed after the family settled in Jerusalem, in Samareitikē. The Karaite elders demanded that the couple separate. The writer intervened in the matter, holding forth on the case of one of the heads of the Karaites, Jacob, evidently also from Ṭulayṭula, who also had a wife who should be forbidden to him, because he was one of two brothers who had married two sisters. Indeed, as a result of this claim, Jacob divorced his wife. Simon b. Saul, the writer, then went to the trouble of applying to 'our Master *av-bēt-dīn*' (Elijah ha-Kohen b. Solomon, at the time), who interceded in the matter and insisted that Jacob return the bridal money to his wife, because their marriage had been concluded before a Rabbanite court (the woman may have been a Rabbanite

[14] See Daniel al-Qūmisī, *Pitrōn*, 13; The Book of Precepts, in Harkavy, *Zikkārōn*, VIII, 187ff; *gornā*, certainly the Arabic *jurn*, which means basin. Qirqisānī, 1243f. The anonymous: JTS Schechter Geniza, fs, 17a–18b; a similar ban on the eating of meat and drinking wine was declared by Abū ʿĪsā al-Iṣfahānī, who did this on his own, basing the ban on the prophets and not on the Pentateuch; see Qirqisānī, 51; Shahrastānī, 168. Sahl b. Maṣlīaḥ, in Pinsker, *Liqqūṭē qadmōniyōt*, II, 32; see similar things also in Levi b. Yefet, in his book of precepts, MS Leiden Or 4760, 109a, ff; see in Poznanski, *REJ*, 45(1902), 181, a passage by an unknown Karaite, referring the ban on meat 'in exile' to ʿAnan, who followed the ways of the Pharisees, deducing it from 'thou shalt eat it within thy gates' (Deut., xv:22). Tobiah b. Moses, in the eleventh century, complains in *Ōṣar neḥmād* about the Rabbanites, who permit the 'defiled foods' (see Poznanski, *ibid.*, 186). It is worth noting the opinion of Friedländer, *JQR*, NS 3(1912/3), 296, who assumes that the origin of the prohibitions on eating meat is in Manichaean influence, especially of the Persian Manichaean movement of Mazdaq. The matter of the *maṣṣā*: Levi b. Yefet, Book of Precepts, in Harkavy, *Zikkārōn*, VIII, 133. Solomon b. Judah: **121**, lines 9–10, 12; see Karaite sources on this matter in Mann, *Jews*, II, 156, n. 4 (from *Eshkōl ha-kofer* and others). The quarrel in Ramla: **122**, line 27. The marriage deed: **305**, lines 31–32. Maḥbūb: **292**, a, lines 17–18. The cheese: **309**. Cf. on the matter of dietary laws and the ban on eating meat also in Mann, *Texts*, II, 65f; and see the treatise on the ban on eating meat in Jerusalem, from the fourteenth century, which he edited *ibid.*, 108ff.

originally). As to Abraham ibn Fadānj, he and his wife and their four children, through the efforts of this Simon, were received back by the Rabbanites, although at first the latter were reluctant to do so because they had lived within the Karaite fold for two years, although they were Rabbanites by origin. A livelihood was even arranged for them in the form of a shop in one of the villages (in the neighbourhood of Jerusalem). In the letter, there is a description of the Karaite principle of the *rikkūv*: 'they have a law prohibiting marriage with a sister of a deceased wife, for which none of their learned people can find any reference, except that they say that this is what they received from 'Anan, the chief and founder of the Karaites'. Finally, he writes, the Karaites learned their lesson from the episode of Abraham ibn Fadānj and gave in to Jacob, that is, they compromised with him and agreed that he should not divorce his wife but he had to swear not to have intercourse with her. This, too, aroused the writer's gall. It is difficult to say – perhaps the tragic situations described here and their outcome is what influenced the spiritual leader of the Karaites at the time, the Jerusalemite Yeshū'ā b. Judah, to formulate his amendments to the *rikkūv*. These amendments and concessions aroused some opposition a generation later, on the part of one of the offspring of the Tustari family, Sahl b. al-Faḍl b. Sahl (Yāshār b. Ḥesed b. Yāshār), who lived in Jerusalem. In the spring of 1096, he felt the need to express his arguments in favour of the *rikkūv* in writing, rebuking Yeshū'ā b. Judah (Abū'l-Faraj Furqān b. Asad) for marrying a woman who was a relative of the family of his brother-in-law, his sister's husband.[15]

[15] The letter of Simon b. Saul: **457**. We find this matter of two sisters in the 'book of precepts' of Daniel al-Qūmisī, according to whom the sister of the wife, if she is a half-sister (that is, from another father or mother), is forbidden to her brother-in-law during the wife's lifetime, but permitted after her death; but if they are full sisters 'they are forbidden both in life and in death'; 'Anan is not mentioned there at all, and this seems to be one of the Karaite innovations introduced during their settlement in Palestine, evidently initiated by al-Qūmisī himself, as is also stated by Qirqisānī, 1144. See the statements of Daniel al-Qūmisī in Pinsker, *Liqqūṭē qadmōniyōt*, II, 188f., and in Harkavy, *Zikkārōn*, VIII, 190f; which are an interpretation of Lev., xviii:18, 'a wife to her sister'. See the matter of the ban on marrying two sisters to two brothers, in Qirqisānī, 1145f. See Sahl b. Maṣlīaḥ's 'letter of rebuke' in Pinsker, II, 33; Sahl boasts that many of the Rabbanites 'at the Holy Mount (i.e. Jerusalem) and in Ramla' behave in the Karaite manner both regarding the dietary laws (they do not eat mutton or beef in Jerusalem) and in the prohibitions of incest, and particularly do not marry daughters of their brothers or sisters; we do not have documents which would confirm his statements. Friedman, *Te'uda*, I, 76, n. 82, deduces from the Damascus Covenant and from the Qumrānic 'Scroll of the Temple', which contain the ban on such marriages, that this is an ancient ban, and that the Karaites took it from 'the Qumrānic Rabbanite *'am ha-areṣ* in Palestine'; but I do not think that the writings reflect any Rabbanite view, not even of the lay people but merely the attitudes of the Judaean Desert sect, by whom the Karaites were evidently influenced, as stated above. See the passage of Sahl b. Faḍl b. Sahl al-Tustarī, MS Firkovitch II, No. 3950, in Mann, *Texts*, 99f; see on him: Gil, *ha-Tustarīm*, 65f; it seems that it is this Sahl b. Faḍl with whom the Spanish Arab writer Abū Bakr ibn al-'Arabī met and argued, as mentioned *ibid.*

[932] There were also differences between the Rabbanites and the Karaites in matters of inheritance, especially with regard to the rights of the daughters. According to Daniel al-Qūmisī, the daughter should receive a third of the inheritance, for only on landed property in Palestine did the Torah rule that the son precedes the daughter. Qirqisānī attributes this approach to 'people of the 'Ananites'. There is no doubt that this view was not acceptable to all the Karaites, perhaps borne out by a fragment of a court document from Fustat, from Josiah Gaon's time, which I have mentioned above. It refers to a woman named Mubāraka, who applied to the Muslim 'judge of judges', that is the *qāḍī'l-quḍāh*, demanding that she receive the part of her father's inheritance which had been appropriated by her brother. The matter was forwarded to the Jerusalem Gaon, who was the representative of the Jews recognised by the authorities and whose opinion was considered decisive. It is not unlikely that this woman was a Karaite, a possibility supported by the fact that we find Joseph b. Israel the Tustari (*al-Dustarī*) among the signatories (the Tustaris being Karaites), as well as Faraḥ b. Mu'ammal, who was perhaps a Karaite as well, or who at least had special connections with them. We also find Karaite customs regarding inheritance in Karaite marriage deeds, such as in the marriage deed which stipulates that if the woman Ḥusn should die childless, all the property she brought with her to her husband's house (that is, her dowry) must be returned to her paternal family. This is indeed consistent with the ancient Jewish halakha, as it is recorded in the Palestinian Talmud (Ket. ix, 33a), but different from the usage among the Rabbanites in the period under discussion, to apportion only half the woman's property to her paternal family.[16]

[16] See what Jacob b. Reuven says about Daniel al-Qūmisī on this matter in Pinsker, *Liqqūṭē qadmōniyōt*, II, 85: 'this he has taken from the Arabs' and see the fragment from Daniel's commentary on Leviticus: TS Loan 199. See Qirqisānī, 1269–1272; as to him, he rejects the view that the daughter inherits at the same time as the son. Mubāraka: **44**. The marriage deeds: **304–306**. The matter of the dowry is extensively discussed in research, see references: Assaf, *Tarbiz*, 9(1937/8), 29, n. 1; Friedman, *Marriage*, I, 400, 415ff. The Karaite formulary and marriage deeds **303–308** are undoubtedly an interesting source for the study of the deeds, especially marriage deeds, of the Karaites. The deeds there mention 'Jerusalem the Holy City' and 'Ramla in the Sharon, which is near Lod', from which we may deduce that these were the main Karaite congregations, or perhaps the only ones in Palestine in that period. One should also take note of the formula of 'the 50 pieces of silver, bridal money for virginity', which we also find in the Karaite formulary, as well as in marriage deeds; of the term *darkemōnīm*, dinars, common in these documents (also used by the Rabbanites, however: see the Hebrew Index); of the matter of the *muqdām* (early) and *me'uḥār* (final) bridal money, also customary among them; and of the note at the end of the divorce form (**303**, 3), that the divorce document has to be given to the wife in the presence of two witnesses, and that among the Rabbanites, the wife's confirmation was required (here they evidently were thinking about mixed marriages). Generally, it can be seen that the Karaite deeds were imitations of Rabbanite deeds, translated from Aramaic to Hebrew, with certain improvements, mostly in a not polished language; they do not display a high standard of learning or knowledge of the language. One should also note the

[933] The Karaites held themselves in great esteem. This was undoubtedly linked with their missionary character and their efforts to make converts to their beliefs among the Rabbanites. Their major claim was that they were *maskīlē ha-rabbīm* (instruct the many) and *maṣdīqē ha-rabbīm* (turn many to righteousness), expressions taken from the book of Daniel, which were interpreted, naturally, as meaning imparting knowledge and guidance (*maskīl* being understood as the participle of the causative pattern, and not as it is meant today). As we have already seen, they referred to themselves as *shōshānīm* from the 'chief musician on the shoshanim' in the Psalms, chapter 45. Daniel al-Qūmisī and the Bible commentators of the tenth century, such as Salmon b. Yeruḥim, Sahl b. Maṣlīaḥ and Yefet b. 'Alī attached these labels to the Karaites as tokens of self-esteem. Sahl b. Maṣlīaḥ, in his epistle, expounds on the 'threescore valiant men' of the Song of Solomon (iii:7), referring to the Karaites: 'they are the sixty wise men . . . *maskīlīm*, who admonish and teach Israel'. Yefet b. 'Alī expounds on the *maṣdīqē ha-rabbīm* as relating to the Karaites (though he does not call them by name, it is impossible to mistake his meaning) as those who would replace corruption with faith, as it is said in Malachi, ii:6: 'and did turn many away from iniquity'; those who mourn over the exile while others feed the people with *al-khurāfāt* (fairy tales). He also interprets the 'threescore valiant men' of Solomon as the sixty *maskīlīm*, that is, the Karaites who would come from the diaspora to Jerusalem, who are the pride and glory of the nation. In his commentary to Isaiah, lv:2 ('hearken diligently unto me, and eat ye that which is good'), Yefet divides the nation into four categories: (1) the exilarchs, who claim that they are the 'people of knowledge'; (2) the ignorant masses who 'lack knowledge' and do not want to know, and all they know and have reverence for is coming to the synagogue on the sabbath and saying *amen* and *shema' isrā'ēl*; (3) those people who want to learn but seek knowledge from the exilarchs, who stuff them with fiction from the Talmud and magic, while taking considerable sums of money from them but not teaching them anything useful; (4) the *maskīlīm* and the *maṣdīqē ha-rabbīm* who are absorbed in their studies and do not accept payment; who are the Karaites, of course.

In principle, the Karaites were primarily 'hasteners of the coming of the Messiah', assuming that by increasing their activities, they would bring about the redemption. From this aspect, it appears that there was actually some kind of continuity between them and the messianic sects mentioned in earlier generations of the Muslim period. In this respect, the statements

appointment of a trustee, that is, a representative of the bride, found in Karaite marriage deeds, and this seems to be the result of Muslim influence (the *walī*); cf. Goitein, *Mediterranean Society*, III, 104, who also raises the possibility that this is an ancient Palestinian custom, which is less likely; see on this matter also: Friedman, *Marriage*, I, pp. 229ff.

of a Karaite Bible commentator of the time are particularly characteristic, according to whom 'the breaker is come up before them' (Micah, ii:13), is intended as breaking out of the prison, which is the exile, by virtue of the *maskīlīm*, the *shōshānīm*, who would bring about salvation through their piety and endless prayers. To this end, the Karaites made their computations of the End of Days, such as the computation of one Karaite commentator on Psalms, who evidently wrote at the beginning of the year 1335/6 Sel., that is, the autumn of AD 1024. This computation is based on Psalms, xc:4. The copy is faded and it is impossible to make out the details of his computation; only the principle is discernible. True, nine years had passed since the anticipated year of redemption, but one has to increase the number of years because of the length of 'the night watches', and in any case, redemption is at hand, owing to the prayers of the *maskīlīm*.

The Gaon Solomon b. Judah was infuriated by the vain pretensions of the Karaites, clearly expressing the accepted opinion of the Jewish public at the time. They consider themselves lilies (*shōshānīm*) and their fellowmen thorns, calling themselves *maskīlīm*, even though 'there is no agreement among them as to who is a *maskīl*'. Actually, the Rabbanites were also given to applying to themselves such terms as *maskīlīm* and *maṣdīqīm*. This is the case, for instance, in Abraham b. David ibn Sughmār's letter to the Nagid of Qayrawān, Jacob b. 'Amram. Solomon b. Judah himself, in a letter to Ephraim b. Shemaria, writes in favour of scholars who are content with little: 'and they should be considered as belonging to the *maskīlīm* and *maṣdīqīm* in the eternal nation, and made to shine as the brightness of the firmament' (Dan., xii:3), etc. Daniel b. Azariah calls someone he is writing to, evidently one of the notables of Fustat, 'the elder, the *maskīl*'. In a letter from the yeshiva written (evidently) by Elijah ha-Kohen b. Solomon, we find him complaining that 'there are no more any *maskīlīm* or *maṣdīqīm*, those who recognise the truth'. Also, someone addressing a query to Daniel b. Azariah wishes that God 'may make your face shine, like the light of the *maṣdīqē ha-rabbīm*, like the stars'. There is nothing surprising in this, for all these terms are taken from the Bible, from Isaiah and from Daniel, and the Rabbanites did not refrain from using them even though they were certainly aware of their peculiar semantic usage by the Karaites.[17]

[17] See the matter of the *maskīlīm*: Wieder, *Judean Scrolls*, 105–177. Shōshānīm: see for instance Salmon b. Yeruḥim, *Sefer Milḥamōt*, 57–65; Daniel al-Qūmisī, in Marmorstein, *Zion* (ha-me'assēf), 3(1928/9), 37, 39, 40; and see in Schechter, *Saadyana*, 41ff, TS 8 K 3, which is evidently a fragment of a polemical work of Saadia Gaon against Daniel al-Qūmisī, which mentions the book the latter wrote '*le-haskīl* [to teach] the nation about inheritance'. Sahl b. Maṣlīaḥ, in Pinsker, *Liqqūṭē qadmōniyōt*, II, 36. Ben-Sasson, *Shalem*, 2(1975/6), 3, tried to deduce from the homily on the 'threescore valiant men', that there was indeed such a group of 60 Karaites, but this is obviously merely theological construction. Yefet b. 'Alī, *Commentary on Daniel*, 140; see also his commentary on Psalms, xlii:1

[934] Whereas they were familiar with the Islamic world, having come from the East, principally from Persia, the Karaites' first encounter with the Christians in Jerusalem must have been something of a novelty to them. We come across indications of this here and there, particularly during the Byzantines' drive and advance in the tenth century, as we have seen above (sec. 550) in the discussion on the events of that period. We find Salmon b. Yeruḥim complaining about the Christians' claim that the time of the Jews had passed, that God had had enough of them, and that from then onward, the Christians were the chosen and a new era had come. In his comments on the parable of the chariots in Zechariah, vi:1–7, he states that the first represented idol-worshippers; the second, the believers in two authorities, the light and the darkness, who are the Zoroastrians (*al-mājūs*) – called 'the black'; the third, the philosophers seeking knowledge, while the fourth represented those who deny everything, i.e. Ishmael, the Muslims, who pretend to believe in the unity of God, and Edom (the Christians), who believe in the Trinity. As to Islam, while we find Daniel al-Qūmisī relying on its favours, there is an attitude of bitterness and resentment among the Bible commentators of the mid-tenth century. Salmon expresses this in his comments on Ps., xliii:1 (deliver me from the deceitful and unjust man): 'by which he means the realm of the son of Hagar, as it is said "through his policy also he shall cause craft to prosper in his hand" [Dan., viii:25] . . . the kingdom of the son of the slave-girl, which is the most severe and depressing among all of them, as is said in the scripture: "dreadful and terrible and strong exceedingly" [Dan., vii:7];

(as the hart panteth after the water brooks): 'these are the *maskīlīm* that came from the exile' etc.; and his commentary to Zech., xi:4–14, in Wieder, *Judean Scrolls*, 119, n. 1 (BM Or 2401, f. 214*b*), and see Wieder's discussion there, and the parallel in Pinsker, *Liqqūṭē qadmōniyōt*, II, 36. Yefet's commentary on Isaiah: Neubauer, *Aus der Petersburger Bibl.* 112, n. XII; it is somewhat strange that Yefet, who lived in Jerusalem, speaks of the exilarchs as representing the sages of Israel, but it seems that he wrote it when he was still in Babylonia; cf. Klar, *Tarbiz*, 15(1943/4), 43ff, who has a comparison between Yefet's statements and the Damascus covenant: 'and the sons of Zadok are the elect of Israel . . . and they will cause the righteous to be righteous' (*yaṣdīqū*), etc. See the chapter 'Messianism' in Wieder, *Judean Scrolls*, 95ff and see the quotation from the commentary *ibid.*, 102, n. 2, BM Or 2401, f. 29b. See the commentary on Psalms, MS Firkovitch I, No. 587, in Mann, *Texts*, 100ff. See also what I have said above, sec. 328, about the Karaite messianic movement which had its centre in Bāniyās in the twenties of the twelfth century. Solomon b. Judah: **92**, a, lines 18–19; to the Nagid of Qayrawān: **191**, line 26. Solomon b. Judah to Ephraim: **68**, lines 11–12. Daniel b. Azariah's letter: **343**, line 19; however the addressee may have been one of the Karaite *nesī'īm*. The letter of the yeshiva: **420**, b, line 27. The query to Daniel b. Azariah: **396**, line 41. (See in the BT, Bava batra, 8b: 'and *maṣdiqē ha-rabbīm*; they are those who teach little children'.) See the view of Mann on this matter in: *Jews*, I, 49, n. 2, who goes as far as to claim that there is no reason to assume that *maskīl* became a peculiarly Karaite term, basing his view on an incorrect reading of the Scroll of Aḥīma'aṣ (*ha-maskīlīm* instead of *ha-miskēnīm*), which I have already pointed out above; see also what he writes in *JQR*, NS 9(1918/9), 162, n. 156, where he quotes TS 12.194, b, lines 20–21 (the responsum of Elḥanan b. Ḥushiel which he prints there, 174): 'our Rock shall have

and it also says: "woe is me, that I sojourn in Mesech"' (Ps., cxx:5). Expressions of disdain for the Christians and the Muslims can also be found in Yefet b. 'Alī, such as in his commentary to Ps., v:5 (the foolish shall not stand in thy sight): 'the foolish are the Christians who are addicted to eating and drinking and constant merriment and as it is also said of them, "of mirth, what doeth it?" (Eccl., ii:2); whereas the workers of iniquity are Ishmael, people of deceit and depravity'. On the other hand, he still recalls the benefit of legitimacy which Islam accorded Karaism, unlike former regimes, 'and it is to this period that the scripture was referring, I will rise now and go about the streets' (Song of Sol., iii:2).[18]

The social structure of the Karaites

[935] This subject of the Karaite social structure came to the fore with the publication of Raphael Mahler's book on the Karaites. In his opinion, the Karaites could be regarded, over a period of several centuries, as a national and social liberation movement. The abysmal situation of the Jewish masses living in the lands of the caliphate, the taxes and tithes demanded of them by the authorities on the one hand, and by their own institutions of leadership on the other, the wrongs done by the exilarchs, the geonim and the upper class of the learned to the masses – all the oppression and discrimination they were subjected to, were in his view what nurtured the messianic movements at the beginning of the eighth century, and their heirs, the Karaite sect, as well.

Counter to Mahler's view was that of Ben-Sasson, who raised certain objections in a critical review of Mahler's book. He pointed to the severe set of laws of the early Karaites, especially those of Benjamin al-Nihāwandī, derived from the very nature of Karaism, including its social nature, which was influenced by the Muslim *Weltanschauung*. This set of laws is in no way consistent with the ideas of those whom Mahler considered the precursors of socialism and democracy among Jews. It is a legal system which essentially respects property and property-owners. As to Karaite society in general, it consisted of varied elements; there were substantial merchants and slave-owners, perhaps even slave-traders (in this respect, Ben-Sasson was correct, the proof of which are the Tustaris), shop-keepers and craftsmen, and also the poor. They also imposed taxes and tithes on their people, even a tithe on the women. They were very

mercy on us and make us *maskīlīm*, to teach truth, and equitable justice'; and see also Zucker, *Albeck Jubilee Volume*, 385, n. 26, with counter-arguments to Mann.

18 Salmon b. Yeruḥim: see his commentary of Lamentations (MS Paris 295), 51a; the parable of Zechariah, in his *Commentary on Psalms*, lxv:31 (according to the Heb. Bible: Marwick), 95; on the realm of Ishmael: the commentary on Lamentations (MS Paris 295), 75b. Yefet b. 'Alī: MS Paris 286, 32a; the commentary on the Song of Solomon, BM Or 2520, 65a.

strict about loans and their repayment – the lender preceded orphans in their right to have debts repaid, and was even permitted to enslave someone who did not repay his debt.

It is possible that the ascetic way of life that developed among the Karaites created the impression of a new direction in social thinking, from the days of Daniel al-Qūmisī onward, which found its expression in demonstrations of mourning customs and refraining from eating meat or drinking wine (at least in Jerusalem). It is clear, however, that these customs were not observed by all the Karaites, and it is doubtful whether they were kept outside of Jerusalem altogether. Hand in hand with advancing the cause of asceticism, Daniel al-Qūmisī set himself against the charitable system created by the Rabbanites, which was based on the foundations of the *heqdēsh*. In his commentary on Hosea, viii:13 (the sacrifices of mine offerings) he explains that it means gifts which (the Rabbanites) in exile (that is, after the destruction of the Temple) give to the poor, seeing them as replacing the sacrifices, something which 'the Lord accepteth them not'. Salmon b. Yeruḥim praises the 'poor of Israel' who seek the protection of God, according to Ps., lxxi:1 (In thee, O Lord, do I put my trust). However, this is merely a theological construction based on passages in the Bible, the likes of which we find in the New Testament and the literature of the Judaean Desert sect. And yet we can recognise, to a certain extent, the influence which the actual living conditions of the first Karaites in Jerusalem had on these writings. Some of the Karaites did indeed live in conditions of poverty and distress, after having left their homes and property behind, as Sahl b. Maṣlīaḥ says in his letter, and were subjected to persecution on the part of the Rabbanites in Jerusalem (probably because of their eagerness to win them over to Karaism). Sahl is particularly vehement against the leaders of the Jewish population in Jerusalem, the Rabbanites, who wanted the Karaites, even the poor among them, to participate in paying the tax imposed on the Jews of Jerusalem (a question I have dealt with in detail in secs. 246–254): 'and they force them to take [money] against interest and give it to them, and they take it from them and give it to the rulers, so that they give them support [i.e. to the Rabbanites], against them'. It emerges from what Sahl himself says, however, that most of the Karaite immigrants came from the merchant class.

In Egypt, there were some enormously wealthy people, as well as some who were also close to the rulers, among the Karaites who left Persia and Iraq; most outstanding among these were the Tustaris. There were others, too, however. Goitein states that the Karaites, on the basis of what we know about them from the Geniza, were in general wealthier than the Rabbanites. Two of their marriage deeds from Palestine, which are included in my collection, are evidence of great riches. On the other hand, we also find in the documents of the period, Karaites who were making cheese on the Mount of Olives, a Damascene weaver whom the authorities had enslaved in a workshop, and Moses b. Isaac, the Spanish immigrant who lived in Jerusalem on the bounty of donations from his congregation in Spain.[19]

The Karaites and their leaders in the eleventh century

[936] I have already discussed extensively the matter of the immigration of the Karaites and their settlement in Jerusalem, as well as of the Karaite quarter there, the Samareitikē (secs. 824–827; 848). The only Karaite congregation we have some substantive knowledge of, apart from that of Jerusalem, was the congregation in Ramla. We have already encountered the mention of the Karaite congregation in a number of places, in Solomon b. Judah's letters, in the letters relating to the dispute with Nathan b. Abraham, and elsewhere. There is an interesting colophon in a book of the Bible found by a certain 'Azriqam the scribe in the synagogue 'of the Prophet Samuel', 'kept by our brethren the Karaites . . . and dedicated by him to the Karaite congregation in Ramla'. It is dated 407 'of the little horn' (AH 407 began on 10 April AD 1016), on Monday, the first of 'the first month', evidently meaning Nisan, and hence, they are referring to the spring of 1017. That book of the Bible was left with a certain Mevassēr b. Isaac. In another colophon, the library of a certain Abū'l-Faraj Ya'qūb is

19 Mahler, *Karaimer*, 21 (and in Hebrew: 17); Ben-Sasson, *Zion* 15(1958), 42–54. Daniel al-Qūmisī, *Pitrōn*, 13. Salmon, *Commentary on Psalms* (Marwick), 107. See *ibid.*, 117, his commentary to Ps., lxxii:4: 'these good tidings were brought by the prophets to the exiles *ahl al-jāliya*, the poor and destitute . . . know ye that the Messiah, when he comes, will seek justice for these poor'; it is clear that here he is calling the entire Jewish nation 'the poor'. On the matter of 'the poor' in Karaite writings, cf.: Wieder, *Judean Scrolls*, 121f, 125ff, 204. The letter of Sahl b. Maṣlīaḥ, in Pinsker, *Liqqūṭē qadmōniyōt*; II, 31f; see also what he says, in Harkavy, *Me'assēf*, No. 13, 198: 'they left their business, forgot their families, rejected their homeland'. See on the economic status of the Tustaris and their circle: Gil, *ha-Tustarīm*, 29ff; see Goitein, *Mediterranean Society*, II, 7; III, 52, 101. See the Rabbanite-Karaite marriage deed from Fustat dated Elul 1428 Sel., August AD 1117, Bodl MS Heb a 3, f. 42: the Rabbanite Yaḥyā son of 'the important physician Abraham' marries the Karaite widow Rayyisa daughter of Saadia b. David; her dowry is worth 719 dinars, an enormous sum by any standard. Also in the Karaite marriage deed **304**, from the year 1009, Ramla, the sum mentioned is 200 dinars, a very pretty sum indeed; the details of the dowry have only been partly preserved, but it contained a number of very valuable objects, and also two houses in Ramla worth 400 dinars. Similarly **305**, from Jerusalem, 1028, in which the amounts are more modest, yet also greater than was customary. An interesting addition to all this is the fragment **305a**. We learn from this that the Karaite David ha-Levi b. Isaac also had a house in Tyre, where the document was written. Another of his daughters was married to 'Adī b. Manasseh b. al-Qazzāz (see on the father, Manasseh, and on the son: *supra*, sec. 560).

mentioned, for whom Yefet b. ʿAlī's commentary on Ruth and the Song of Solomon were copied, most likely in *ca.* 1000.

It is uncertain whether the Karaites had a synagogue in Jerusalem during this period. In the sources, only a *majlis* is mentioned, which may have been a hall in the home of one of the Karaites. In a colophon in a Bible from the Firkovitch collection mentioned above, it says that the Bible would be kept in 'the compound of Joseph b. Bakhtaway'. Nathan b. Isaac, a Karaite who lived in Jersualem, mentions the *majlis* of the Karaites there and whenever he passes it, he writes, he is stricken with yearning. In this *majlis*, the lessons of Yeshūʿā b. Judah (Abū'l-Faraj Furqān b. Asad) were held. It was also the address to which Karaites sent money for Jerusalem, or so it is implied from what he writes. There seems to have been a difference between the *majlis* and a synagogue, for there is mention of a Karaite synagogue in Ramla and we also know of their synagogue in Fustat. At the same time, Solomon b. Ṣemaḥ writes from Ramla about rumours concerning people who abandon the synagogue of the Palestinians in Fustat and go over to the *majālis al-qarā'iyīn*, and one must admit that this matter is not at all clear. Nor do we find among the Karaites during this period, those titles that were customary among the Rabbanites, such as *rōsh yeshīvā, av-bēt-dīn, rōsh kallā*, and so on. I ascribed above the mention of such titles in earlier generations to the fact that they preceded the final secession of the house of ʿAnan (such as the matter of the heads of the yeshiva, Jehoshaphat and Ṣemaḥ); one cannot consider anyone bearing these Rabbanite titles as Karaites; they were merely descendants of the exilarchic family, the progeny of ʿAnan.[20]

[20] At this juncture, one should note that the letter: JNUL 4°577.3, No. 11, edited by Yellin, *Kiryat Sefer*, 1(1924), 56–59; and also in his article in English: *JPOS*, 4(1924), 124–127, is from the fourteenth century and it is difficult to understand how the editor ascribed it to the 12th century, when there were almost no Jews in Jerusalem; and there is certainly no foundation to what is said in the *Sefer ha-yishuv*, 47, n. 39, that it is from the eleventh century. Aaron (Hārūn) ibn Ṣaghīr of al-Qāhira, who is mentioned there on verso, line 1, is mentioned in a memorial list – TS 8 K 22, f. 2: 'Aaron the honoured prince', etc.; he was a contemporary of the Karaite writer Yefet b. Ṣaʿīr (perhaps his brother) known from the fourteenth century; see Mann, *Texts*, II, 211, n. 20. Another assumption lacking any foundation is that of Kook, *Ginzē qedem*, 4(1930), 107–110, about three Karaite localities in the Jerusalem area: Givʿā, Rama, Barqa. Only the title of his article: 'An unknown Karaite centre', is correct. The dedication in Ramla: from a Bible MS which belonged to Firkovitch, in Poznanski, *Yerushalayim* (Luncz), 10(1914), 115. The Karaite synagogue 'of the Prophet Samuel' was evidently in Ramla; in this colophon there is also the date AM 4373, but it is not consistent with that of the AH, and it seems that the Karaites in Ramla used a different era of the creation (the differences in the computation of the era of the creation I have already dealt with above); a Mevassēr b. Isaac is mentioned in a marriage deed edited by Assaf, *Tarbiz*, 9(1937/8), 26ff, from a locality in Egypt, the name of which has not been preserved; it is very doubtful whether he is the same person to whom Poznanski is referring there; see the marriage deed (with the addition of some related fragments which were unknown to Assaf): Friedman, *Marriage*, II, 5–11 and see *ibid.*, 2f. The library of Abū'l-Faraj Yaʿqūb: BM Or 2554, in Hörning, *Six Karaite Manuscripts*, 27. The compound

[937] We have already witnessed something of the relationship between the Karaites and the Rabbanites, in the discussion on their contacts with the rulers, for as we have seen, both communities were requesting the intervention of the authorities in their quarrels. Obviously, the Karaites' attitude to the Rabbanites was critical in the extreme. Possibly the most apt expression of this attitude can be found in Sahl b. Maṣlīaḥ's 'letter of rebuke'; apart from his denouncement of their worshipping graves and their consumption of forbidden foods, which I have already mentioned, he claims that they pretend they are the Sanhedrin; they desecrate the sabbath and pay mutual visits 'to eat and to drink' on the sabbath; they invite gentiles to share their meals; they 'carry the coffins of the dead in the gentile fashion, nor do they sit the proscribed seven days in mourning'. True, there were some Rabbanites in Ramla, he writes, who learned from the Karaites, by which he may have meant that their propaganda had borne fruit and they had succeeded in winning them over to their teachings, a situation which enables us to understand the sharp reaction of the Rabbanites. The traditionists among the Rabbanites (those engaged in *taqlīd*, a term taken from the Muslims), such as Saadia Gaon (al-Fayyūmī) and others 'had brought perdition on Israel', says Yefet b. 'Alī, in his commentary on Ps., xxv:14 (The secret of the Lord is with them that fear him). Comparatively early evidence of the Palestinian Rabbanites' attitude to all this can be found perhaps in the Scroll of Aḥīm'aṣ, in the story of the excommunication of Silano, a man of Venosa in southern Italy who ridiculed the preacher who came to the town. The people of the Palestinian yeshiva cancelled the ban, however, because of an innovation which

of b. Bakhtaway, see in Kahle, *Masoreten des Westens*, 67, and in Mann, *Texts*, II, 134; Ankori, *Karaites in Byzantium*, translates *ḥaṣēr*: courtyard, which is not correct. Nathan b. Isaac: **297**. Solomon b. Ṣemaḥ: **205**. Pinkerfeld, *Luncz Memorial Volume*, 215, assumed that there were hints that the Karaite synagogue in Jerusalem was built in the eleventh century or the beginning of the twelfth. As to the first possibility, this is not likely, as there is no information on a Karaite synagogue in Jerusalem during that period; the second possibility is out of the question, because the Crusaders then controlled Jerusalem. What is said here about the lack of Rabbanite titles among the Karaites contradicts the view of Wieder, *Judean Scrolls*, 90f; Goitein, *Mediterranean Society*, II, 166; 555, n. 44, assumed that the *majlis* of the Karaites was actually a synagogue, but that they preferred not to call it so in order to evade the Muslim ban on erecting places of prayer on sites where they had not existed before the Muslim conquest. It is worth quoting here Sahl b. Maṣlīaḥ's epistle, where he mentions as one of the changes for the better brought about by Islam, the permission to 'His nation', that is the Karaites, to build 'places' in Jerusalem for 'reading and expounding and praying at any time and setting up night-watches'; see in Harkavy, *Me'assēf*, No. 13, p. 199, and see the commentary of Wieder, *ibid.*, 103, n. 2. It is also typical that in the colophons of the Bible belonging to the Karaites of Jerusalem which have reached us, it says in general, that the Bible is dedicated 'to the Karaite congregation' or only 'to the Karaites', not to the synagogue. See for instance the colophon in the Bible in the Karaite synagogue in Cairo: Gottheil, *JQR*, 17(1905), 639f, No. 34: 'to the Karaites in Jerusalem the Holy City'; and only in a later period is it inscribed: 'in the synagogue of al-Qāhira'.

Silano had introduced into one of the *piyyūṭīm*, which were evidently part of the prayers for the Day of Atonement. These were changes in praise of the Rabbanites, placing blame on the *mīnīm*, possibly meaning the Karaites. This seems to have occurred towards the end of the ninth century, when the Karaites were arriving and settling in Jerusalem.

More basic information concerning the conflict between the Rabbanites and the Karaites in Jerusalem is to be found primarily from the beginning of the thirties of the eleventh century, after the continuous warfare between the Fatimids and the Palestinian tribes had ceased. A strong faction in the yeshiva, headed by the priestly brothers, Joseph and Elijah, sons of Solomon Gaon, tried to renew the tradition of proclaiming a ban on the Karaites on Hosha'na rabbā, during the assembly on the Mount of Olives. The formula of the ban was apparently: 'on the eaters of meat with milk'. Solomon b. Judah objected to the renewal of this custom, undoubtedly because he was a restrained and peace-loving man, but probably also out of concern for the distressing state that existed at the time, and the dependence on the goodwill of the Tustari brothers, who were Karaites. The question of the ban held the masses spellbound, and they even refrained from throwing their contributions 'on the robe' as was customary, for they were too occupied with the thought of the excommunication. 'The third', Tobiah b. Daniel, also tried to influence the people to accept the Gaon's opinion, but to no avail. The two priestly brothers, together with Abraham, the son of the Gaon, proclaimed the ban, and the rest is known: the two brothers were arrested and taken to prison in Damascus.

The resentment and rivalry led to the Karaites libelling the Rabbanites, saying that some of them had made three figures (evidently drawings) and burnt them. There were consultations over this matter in the *majlis* situated in the Jewish market (apparently they are referring to the site of the yeshiva in Jerusalem, probably meaning: a hall); those present pressed the Gaon to declare a ban on the libellers and he was forced, it is implied, to submit to their demands. Solomon b. Judah displays a great deal of restraint in the letter in which he describes this, and although he has much to complain of in terms of the Karaites' behaviour and their arrogance, he does not think they should be excommunicated and cut off from the Rabbanites entirely. He also stresses the fact of the mixed marriages between the two communities, which are mainly to the advantage of the Karaites. They multiply, says the Gaon, with the help of the Rabbanites, who give their daughters in marriage to them; and he recalls that this was how the tribe of Judah had behaved, when they did not prevent their daughters from marrying into other tribes of Israel, even when the latter worshipped idols. Indeed, these mixed marriages were an indication of the link that still existed between the two communities despite the differences. (There are quite a few documents in the Geniza which give evidence of mixed marriages; we have seen above the matter of the marriage of David b. Daniel to the daughter of a Karaite, for instance. Generally, the 'mixed' marriage deed contained provision about the mutual respect for the other's customs with regard to holidays and foods, such as the fragment of a marriage deed in which the woman undertakes not to feed her husband meat 'not slaughtered by the Rabbanites' and not 'to desecrate his holidays'.)

In the continuation of his letter, Solomon b. Judah mentions the serious affliction caused by the custom of proclaiming these excommunications, for it brings about the intervention of the authorities, as we have seen. Strained relations between Rabbanites and Karaites are also felt in the letter of the Damascene weaver, who complains that the Rabbanite Jews (who dominate the entire branch of weaving) denounced him to the authorities.

On the other hand, there was also a certain degree of collaboration. Solomon b. Judah tells how he fulfilled the role of cantor for the Karaites in Ramla – before he became Gaon, naturally – and that he would pray on one day with the Rabbanites and on the other, with the Karaites. He himself treats this information jestingly. The ties and the mutual involvement are mainly revealed during the internal struggles in the yeshiva, when each of the parties tries to attract the Karaites to their side. We have seen that Nathan b. Abraham succeeded in this, owing to his personal contacts, particularly with the Tustaris. This also applies to Daniel b. Azariah in his struggle with Joseph ha-Kohen b. Solomon, and also to David, the son of Daniel, in his struggle against the Palestinian yeshiva and its head, Abiathar ha-Kohen.[21]

21 Sahl b. Maṣlīaḥ, in Pinsker, *Liqqūṭē qadmōniyōt*, II, 32f. Yefet b. 'Alī, *Commentary on Daniel*, 141; see the Scroll of Aḥīma'aṣ, 16f; see the original *piyyūṭ*: Marcus, *PAAJR*, 5(1933–4), 85–91, see also Davidson, *Ōṣar*, I, 311 (No. 6844). Cf. Starr, *Jews*, 102. The matter of the ban: **85**. The burning of the images: **92**, a, lines 30ff; the matter of the libel is not clear; what these three images depicted or represented, we do not know, but it seems to have been clear to the people at the time, for Solomon b. Judah, writing about it, does not think it necessary to go into details. See the matter of the excommunication of the Karaites also in **122**. Also **327**, to the extent that it can be read, speaks of the opposition of the Gaon to the excommunication of the Karaites; it mentions that the Karaites desecrate the Day of Atonement (by fixing its date differently from the Rabbanites), and also speaks of matters concerning meat with milk. The ban and its dire results are also described in **433**. The letter of the Damascene Karaite: **291**. Solomon b. Judah as cantor: **75**, a, lines 2–6. A general survey of the points on which the early Karaite leaders attacked the Rabbanites can be found in Mann, *Texts*, II, 49ff. He covers there matters of ritual, folk customs, dietary rules, superstitions and mystic beliefs. See what Solomon b. Judah writes on marriage with the Karaites: **92**, a, lines 24ff. See the fragment of the marriage deed: TS 8.223; it is signed by ''Eli ha-Kohen the cantor b. R. Hezekiah ha-Kohen he-ḥāvēr in the Great Sanhedrin'; from which we learn that it is a Jerusalem marriage deed, dated about the mid-eleventh century. Cf. Golb, in *Jewish Medieval and Renaissance Studies*, 11; see dis-

[938] Jerusalem continued to be the most important centre for the Karaites in the eleventh century as well. Their major figure at the start of the century was Abū Ya'qūb Joseph ha-Kohen b. Abraham, who is al-Baṣīr ('the seer'; this is of course of a euphemism; in Hebrew: ha-Rō'ē; that is, he was blind). He had a house in Jerusalem, where he expounded his teaching. Joseph al-Baṣīr was one of the pupils of Joseph ibn Noah. He wrote many treatises, among them a book of precepts (*kitāb al-istibsạār*), which he completed, according to Ibn al-Hītī, in AH 428, that is AD 1036/7; as well as philosophical works, such as 'the comprehensive book' (*al-muḥtawī*), which was translated by his pupil Tobiah b. Moses as *sefer ha-ne'īmōt*, of which we know of a chapter entitled *sefer ha-mō'adīm*; the book of discrimination (*kitāb al-tamyīz*), also translated by Tobiah and entitled *maḥkīmat petī* ('making wise the simple', Ps., xix:7); and other writings which have not been preserved. In his book of precepts, Joseph al-Baṣīr, was the first to oppose the excessive severity of the Karaites with regard to incest regulations. According to Poznanski, he died in *ca*. 1040.

A contemporary of Joseph al-Baṣīr was Abū'l-Faraj Hārūn b. al-Faraj, a grammarian and Bible commentator, mentioned by subsequent grammarians as 'the Jerusalemite grammarian'. His major work: 'The comprehensive book of roots and derivations in the Hebrew language', was completed in Rajab AH 417 (July AD 1026). Apart from this, he wrote *al-kitāb al-kāfī* ('the sufficient book'), which was considered a continuation (the eighth part) of the former work. Two pages of another of his grammatical works have been preserved and edited by Hirschfeld, namely from 'the book of strings in Hebrew usage'. He also wrote a book on the Aramaic of the Bible. He was still alive in 1048, as we can see from Tobiah b. Moses' letter.

Tobiah b. Moses was evidently one of Joseph al-Baṣīr's pupils. He came from Constantinople to Jerusalem to study with the Karaite personalities there, and was known by the nicknames *ha-ma'atīq* ('the copier'; because of his translations and being a scribe), *ha-bāqī* ('the erudite'), *ha-'ōvēd*, (or:*ha-'eved*; 'the worshipper', or: 'the slave').

We find references to him in *Eshkōl ha-kofer*, where it is said that Tobiah *ha-maskīl*, and other Karaite scholars from Constantinople addressed queries to the Jerusalemite Karaite scholars, the *avēlē maskīlē* ('the mourners among the *maskīlīm*') of the Holy City of Jerusalem. From what is known from Karaite sources, he went up to Jerusalem and studied there, and above we have seen that he translated some treatises of his master, Joseph al-Baṣīr, from Arabic into Hebrew. He also wrote a number of

cussions on the subject in Assaf, *Be-oholē ya'aqōv*, 182ff; Friedman, *Marriage*, II, 3, 290f, notes that he has identified fifteen marriage deeds and other documents which relate to marriages between Rabbanites and Karaites.

books: *Ōṣār neḥmād*, which is a discussion on the book of Leviticus, in which he also included quotations from other writers, such as the *nāsī* David b. Boaz and Yefet b. 'Alī; *Yehī me'ōrōt*, a treatise which has been lost and about which we know nothing; and *piyyūṭīm*, two of which were known and included in the Karaite prayer book. He is also credited with having written a philosophical work, *Meshīvat nefesh*, but Vajda has established that it is not Tobiah who wrote it.

Following on an account by Elijah Bashyatchi, in his epistle *gīd ha-nāshē*, there were some who assumed that Tobiah was the pupil of Yeshū'ā b. Judah (Abū'l-Faraj Furqān b. Asad), for the aforementioned speaks of 'our Master Tobiah the copier' who went to 'our Master Yeshū'ā and studied there and transcribed his books from the Arabic language to the holy tongue and brought them to Constandina' (which is Constantinople). The Geniza documents show that Tobiah was a contemporary of Yeshū'ā, and perhaps even somewhat older.[22]

[939] As I have mentioned, there are writings in the Geniza by Tobiah b. Moses which shed light on the period of his stays in Palestine and Egypt. It seems that he spent a considerable amount of time in the Muslim lands, and one can go even further and assume that he came from a family which had emigrated from a Muslim country to Constantinople, because of the distinctive Arabic influence which is very obvious in his Hebrew letters, and also because he wrote in Arabic.

Out of the four letters which have been preserved in the Geniza, the first is in fact written in Arabic. He wrote it in Jerusalem in the spring of 1040 or thereabouts and it is addressed to his daughter. And therein lies his

[22] On Joseph al-Baṣīr: Poznanski, *Yerushalayim* (Luncz), 10(1913/4), 102ff; *idem, JQR*, 19(1906/7), 63ff; see Hirschfeld, *JQR*, NS 8(1917/8), 167ff, who quotes a fragment dealing with the defence of the method of analogy (*qiyās*): BM Or 2580, fs. 44ff, which he ascribes to Joseph al-Baṣīr; see Skoss, in his edition of 'Alī b. Sulaymān, 7, n. 35; see further references: Ankori, *Karaites in Byzantium*, 81, n. 65; and see *idem, JJS*, 8:71, 1957, where he defends Poznanski's opinion that Joseph al-Baṣīr died in *ca.* 1040, not in 1048 as Alexander Marx claimed; his reliance on the silence of Tobiah b. Moses in his letter, **295**, does not support his claim, for the letter dates from 1048, not 1041 as he assumed. It is possible that Joseph al-Baṣīr is identical with Joseph b. Abraham ha-Kohen, who was appointed trustee by the Karaite marriage deed **305**, dated January 1028; and it is also possible that a certain ha-Kohen b. Joseph in the fragment of the marriage deed **308**, line 9, is the son of al-Baṣīr. On Abū'l-Faraj Hārūn: Harkavy, *ZAW*, 1(1881), 158; Poznanski, *Yerushalayim* (Luncz), 10(1913/4), 104ff; Poznanski, *REJ*, 33:24, 197, 1896; *ibid.*, 56:42, 1908; Hirschfeld, *JQR*, NS 13:1, 1922/3; *idem, Literary History*, 50–53; see further references: Ankori, *Karaites in Byzantium*, 185, n. 64. On Tobiah b. Moses see *Eshkōl ha-kofer*, 76a (alphabetically, 187); the version is not at all clear, and one may also understand that it is the sages of Constantinople who asked Tobiah; see Poznanski's article in *Encyclopaedia Ōṣar Isrā'ēl* s.v., and details there on his writings and piyyūṭīm; see Vajda, *Baneth Memorial Volume*, 103; see notes on his piyyūṭīm in Neubauer, *Aus der Petersburger Bibliothek*, 147; *Ankori*, S. W. *Baron Presentation Volume*: 1; *idem, Karaites in Byzantium*, according to the Index. See Elijah Bashyatchi, *Aderet*, at the beginning of the book. On the matter of the time of Tobiah, see also Ankori, *Tarbiz*, 25(1956/7), 44ff.

singular personal story. He had married a Christian woman who bore him a daughter, to whom he is writing this letter. The daughter is having a difficult time, he says, and suffers and is even begging for her bread because of the mother. His own situation is excellent, with ample finances, in view of his post as supervisor of the state's estates in Palestine (it seems that this is how we are to understand his text). As we know from his other letters about his contacts with the Tustari brothers, we may assume that it was due to the latter that he obtained such a post. He ponders over his daughter's state of mind – does she see herself as a Jewess or as a Christian? In the letter, his wife's sister is also mentioned. He expresses the desire to ransom his daughter, and it is naturally difficult to understand what he means by this; it is possible that both his wife and his daughter were enslaved to someone. He writes that he is intending to travel to his Byzantine homeland, 'to the Byzantine lands, to my country and family'.

The next letter is to Abū Sa'd Abraham al-Tustarī, in which Tobiah calls himself 'your servant Tobiah, the thin'. He writes out of distress, for he has undergone many troubles. Apparently his relationship with the Tustaris has deteriorated, but he nevertheless turns to them. This letter was written in Egypt, that is (it seems) he has lost his post in Palestine, which need not surprise us, as such things must have been everyday occurrences as a result of the constant reversals within the Fatimid court. He has with him in Egypt another two people, members of his family evidently, but he does not go into any detail about them. A certain Abū'l-Faraj Hiba, apparently one of the intimates of the Tustaris, told him that Abraham al-Tustarī is angry with him 'because I dwelt among you'; he therefore surmises that his coming to Fustat was a burden to his benefactors and that his presence is not wanted. He thus decided to return 'to my country and homeland and family' (exactly as he wrote to his daughter in the above-mentioned letter). The only reason for his coming to Fustat was his fear of the tax authorities. Therefore he asks the Tustari to obtain an authorisation (*ketāv*) for him, in order that he should not experience once again what he had suffered in Tinnīs (*Ḥanēs*), when he needed the intervention of the Tustaris after he was put in prison. Then he still had the money to pay bribes, but now he had none. We may assume that this is how he recalls his arrival in Egypt for the first time, perhaps as many as fifteen years earlier, when he was greeted with the reception usually reserved for people coming to Egypt from one of the Christian countries (see sec. 721, the story of the Christian traveller, the monk Bernard). Here too we find evidence of his Byzantine origin. He expresses gratitude and adds greetings to Abraham al-Tustarī for 'everything that was done with me and with everyone in all the congregations of the land of Edom, near and far'. He also promises that he will see to it that blessings are said over the

Tustari in the synagogues (in Byzantium) on every Monday and Thursday, which is an indication that Tobiah occupied a respected status among the Byzantine Karaites. He notes that he spent a 'whole year in the service of my illustrious master' – perhaps referring to his former position of supervisor of estates in Palestine. He sees himself as a priest ('ordained to be a priest: *ha-husmākh lihyōt mazzē*) among the Karaites, probably not meaning a priest by virtue of his lineage, but a spiritual leader, due to his teaching, unlike those claiming descent from Aaron, who are like the idol-worshippers, and in order to differentiate him from those claiming descent from the House of King David.

In 1048, Tobiah writes from Jerusalem to Peraḥia b. Mu'ammal, in Fustat, formerly one of the followers of Nathan b. Abraham. We find in this letter echoes of the terrible events occurring in Egypt, the internal wars during which Abraham al-Tustarī was murdered. Indeed, Abraham is referred to in this letter with the expression 'May God have mercy on him', and Tobiah speaks of the terrible calamity ('a breakdown for all of Israel'). In addition, Tobiah suffered a number of family tragedies and he is in great distress. No one cares for him apart from a few Byzantine (?) people who happen to be in Jerusalem. The Karaites do not support him, except for Abū'l-Faraj Aaron, who sometimes shows some interest; he probably means Abū'l-Faraj Hārūn, the aforementioned grammarian and Bible commentator. Money arrived from Ramla but Tobiah was not given any of it. Substantial sums of money (*darkemōnīm*) also arrived from the Tustaris, from Ḥesed b. Yāshār and Yefet b. Abraham; it was distributed to everyone but only he was denied any part of it. In this letter, too, he writes about setting off on a journey he intends to make, 'to my home and patrimony' and with this in mind, he asks Peraḥia to inform him as to whom he can leave money which he owes him, before he sets out on his way. He also mentions his daughter in the letter, who 'will not leave my heart', and who is still with her mother, his Christian wife; it would be better that the daughter die than to stay 'with that adulterous woman'.

The background to Tobiah's family affairs and his status among the Karaites in Jerusalem, who deprived him of all support, as we have seen, becomes clear from a fragment of one of his letters, to an addressee not known to us. In the interim, there had been dramatic developments – his Christian wife ('the daughter of Edom') returned to him after cutting off her ties with the Church. She left behind her motherland and moved to a Muslim land in order to be able to become a Jewess. God must have had a hand in the matter, for her family tried to molest her and even to kill her. They even slandered and fabricated libels against her. 'And now she is bereaved', he writes, apparently speaking of the death of the daughter. This tragedy is the apparent explanation for her conversion and devotion to Judaism; she was prepared to sacrifice herself, despite coaxing and threats on the part of her family and the authorities. She then returned to Tobiah ('my first husband'), to *ha-shāfālā* (the low city: Ezek., Heb., xxi:31), that is, to Jerusalem. At the end of the fragment, it is implied that one of the Christian priests (in Jerusalem?) tried to conspire against Tobiah.

If we summarise the information supplied in these letters, we can say that: (1) Tobiah married a Christian Byzantine who bore him a daughter; (2) this woman abandoned him; perhaps for this reason or perhaps because of plots against him in Byzantium, he came to Palestine (and not only because of his thirst for knowledge); (3) on his way to Palestine he was assisted by the Tustaris (in Tinnīs), established a relationship with them, and apparently obtained the appointment as supervisor of the state's estates in Palestine through them; (4) his ties with the Tustaris, and also with the Karaites in Jerusalem, were ambivalent, and there were moments of anger and rupture, perhaps because of the Christian wife or his opposition to the Karaite nesī'īm, which is implied in one of his letters; and (5) after some time, evidently after the death of his daughter, his wife returned to him, coming to Jerusalem after converting to Judaism. From all this we can conclude that Tobiah did not return to Byzantium, for his proselyte wife had fled from there.[23]

[940] One of Tobiah b. Moses' contemporaries was Abū'l-Faraj Furqān b. Asad, who is Yeshū'ā b. Judah, also a pupil of Joseph al-Baṣīr. Ibn al-Hītī mentions his Bible commentary; he says he was the pupil of Levi b. Yefet ha-Levi and of Abū'l-Faraj Hārūn. Abraham b. Da'ūd also mentions him in his *Sefer ha-qabbālā*, implying that he was the leader of the Karaites in Palestine and the teacher and friend of Ibn al-Tarās (or Abū'l-Tarās), who, together with his wife ('the teacher' – *al-mu'allima*) were the leaders of the Karaites in Castile. Under Yeshū'ā b. Judah's guidance, he writes, Ibn al-Tarās wrote 'a book of incitement and misguidance' and took it

[23] The letters of Tobiah b. Moses: **293–296**. Arabic forms of syntax, see for instance: **294**, b, line 19; he considers himself a priest: **294**, a, lines 21–23, see in the notes *ibid*. Echoes of the events: **295**, lines 10–14; the death of Abraham al-Tustarī: *ibid*., lines 6–8, 25–27; his distress: *ibid*., 18–21; money from Ramla and Fustat: *ibid*., 21–22, 24–27. Mann, *Texts*, I, 373, and also Ankori, in his abovementioned article (in the *Baron Presentation Volume*), did not identify Abū 'Alī Yefet b. Abraham al-Tustarī, mentioned there in line 25, although it is quite clear, cf. Gil, *ha-Tustarīm*, 43f; the money and starting on the journey: in the same letter, 30–34; in the margin there are additional greetings for Abū 'Alī Ḥasan, who is Yefet b. Abraham al-Tustarī; see on him Gil, *ibid*., 58. The above summary is essentially different from that of Ankori in his aforementioned article; also what he writes there on the schism among the Karaites does not have sufficient foundation. Tobiah evidently made his living also by copying books, and indeed he had a fine square script, comparatively easy to identify. He is the one who copied 'the ancient questions', the rhymed treatise, mentioned above several times, as noted also by Fleischer, and see his article: *Kiryat Sefer*, 55(1979/80): 183. See also the article of Scheiber, *Kiryat Sefer*, 55:791, 1979/80, where he

with him to Castile. Yeshū'ā b. Judah was the most outstanding and important of the Karaite spiritual leaders at that time. Apart from his Bible commentary, he also translated the Bible into Arabic and supplemented a short commentary to it. He wrote a treatise of a philosophical homiletic nature on the two first pericopes of Genesis, entitled *Berēshīt rabbā*. In the sphere of the law, his book on incest regulations has been preserved, which may have been part of a more comprehensive work, which he called *Sefer ha-yāshār*. He tried to abolish the severe laws of the Karaite *rikkūv* mentioned earlier. Those of his works which have been preserved in Hebrew are translations from the Arabic, carried out by his contemporary Jacob b. Simon, who stemmed from Byzantium, and they contain a great many Greek expressions.

Yeshū'ā b. Judah is mentioned in some Geniza documents in my collection. The Karaite Nathan b. Isaac, writing in Jerusalem in *ca.* 1050, mentions 'the lesson of Master Abū'l-Faraj b. Asad, who is none other than Yeshū'ā b. Judah. In November 1064, Avon b. Ṣedaqa mentions him, implying that the Gaon Elijah ha-Kohen b. Solomon sent a letter to Nehorai b. Nissim via Abū'l-Faraj b. Asad (that is, he included his letter in a package of letters sent by Abū'l-Faraj to Fustat). This is apparently evidence of the ties between the Gaon and the man who was then unquestionably the most important figure among the Karaites of Jersualem. In August 1065, in another letter from Jerusalem, Avon again mentions the letters of Abū'l-Faraj and it seems that here, too, Yeshū'ā b. Judah is meant. Abū'l-Faraj happens to be in Tyre, accompanied by the *ṣabī* (a youth or clerk) Asher (or perhaps one should read: Asad, with a 'left-hand' *sīn*, often replacing a *samekh*; if this is so, perhaps he is referring to the son of Yeshū'ā, probably called Asad, after his grandfather). From what has been said until now, it is clear that Yeshū'ā was a contemporary of Tobiah b. Moses and apparently outlived him.

We also have to mention Abū'l-Ḥasan 'Alī b. Sulaymān, who lived in Jerusalem towards the end of the century. He introduced into his treatises parts of the works of Karaite writers who had preceded him. He wrote an abridged version of the *Egron* of Abū Sulaymān David b. Abraham al-Fāsī, on the basis of an earlier compendium by Levi b. Yefet ha-Levi. He also wrote a commentary on the Pentateuch, which is merely an adaptation based on the abridged version of the commentary of Joseph ibn Noah, a compendium written by Abū'l-Faraj Hārūn, in which we find extracts of the commentaries of the *nāsī* David b. Boaz. Remnants of his commentary to the book of Psalms have been preserved, which he compiled from the commentaries of the *nāsī* David b. Boaz and Abū'l-Ṭayyib al-Tinnīsī (a

edited TS Box K 17, f. 6, a fragment in Tobiah's handwriting, dealing with Karaite prayer customs (during persecution?).

man of Tinnīs in Egypt). Another contemporary who lived in Jerusalem until close to the Crusaders' conquest was Sahl b. Faḍl al-Tustarī, who is Yāshār b. Ḥesed b. Yāshār b. Ḥesed, the great-grandson of Ḥesed al-Tustarī, Abraham's brother. We have seen that his stay in Jerusalem during the nineties of the century is confirmed by Abū Bakr ibn al-'Arabī, the Spanish Arab writer. Sahl b. Faḍl wrote a commentary to the Pentateuch and also halakhic and philosophical treatises. Abu Sa'd, a youth who was said to be 'the son of the Tustari's wife', apparently Sahl's wife, was one of the Karaite Jerusalemites taken captive by the Crusaders, of whom I shall speak in due course.[24]

The Samaritans

[941] There is no doubt that considering their assumed share of the population of Palestine during this period, the Samaritans are worthy of a chapter of their own. Unfortunately the sources on them are few and far between, and the history of the Samaritan population is almost unknown. In the Samaritan chronicles themselves, very little has been preserved concerning the period under discussion, apart from lists of high priests, which are very inexact and which contribute nothing to the annals of this community. According to a Samaritan chronicle, the high priest at the

[24] See Harkavy, *ZAW*, 1(1881), 158, who notes that Abraham ibn Ezra mentions Yeshū'ā b. Judah frequently in his Bible commentary. See Ibn al-Hītī, 434; Abraham b. Da'ūd, *S. ha-qabbālā*, 69; Poznanski, *JQR*, 19(1906/7), 65ff; MS Leiden Or 4779 is a collection of Karaite writings, where Yeshu'ā's book on incest regulations is included, and also: 'The responsa of fundamental law of R. Yeshū'ā *ha-melammēd*, of blessed memory, on restrictions concerning incest.' The book on incest regulations was edited by I. Markon, *Das Buch von den verbotenen Verwandschaftsgraden* (St Petersburg 1908); cf. Mann, *Texts*, II, 39. A comprehensive study of Yeshū'ā b. Judah's works and thought: M. Schreiner, *Studien über Jeschu'a ben Jehuda* (Berlin 1900); see a chapter on him: Husik, *History of Mediaeval Jewish Philosophy*, 55–58, based mainly on the aforementioned work of Schreiner; also Guttmann, *ha-Filōsōfya*, 77–80. Nathan b. Isaac: **297**, line 8. Avon b. Ṣedaqa: **500**, a, line 24; **501**, b, lines 16–17. See further on Yeshū'ā b. Judah: Ankori, *Karaites in Byzantium*, according to the Index, especially pp. 81f, on the *rikkūv*. On the preservation of the commentary to the Pentateuch of Yeshū'ā b. Judah in a Samaritan commentary see: Loewenstamm, *Tarbiz*, 41:183, 1971/2; *ibid.*, 187, she mentions the Samaritan Abū Sa'īd (the twelfth century), who called Yeshū'ā 'the greatest of the Karaite commentators'; on the matter of Tobiah b. Moses and Jacob b. Simon, one finds there the usual error, that they were allegedly pupils of Yeshū'ā b. Judah, whereas in fact they were his contemporaries. On 'Alī b. Sulaymān see Mann, *Texts*, II, 41, and see Skoss' introduction to his edition of the commentary to Gen. of the aforementioned, and the account of his life: *Tarbiz*, 2(1930/31), 510–513, where he proves that 'Alī was active from 1072–1103. On Yāshār b. Ḥesed al-Tustarī, the Karaite writer, see: Poznanski, *JQR*, 19(1906/7), 70ff; Mann, *Texts*, II, 39f; Gil, *ha-Tustarīm*, 63ff; there I still hesitated whether to identify him with the Tustari who was met by Ibn al-'Arabī, but this now seems to be almost certain; see the text of Yāshār in MS Firkovitch II, No. 3950, in Mann, *ibid.*, 100: 'Sahl b. al-Faḍl b. Sahl al-Tustarī concluded the copying of this his treatise in Muḥarram of the year 489', i.e. January AD 1095; the contents of the fragment imply that it was written in Jerusalem, at the very time Ibn al-'Arabī was staying there.

time of the Muslim conquest was Nethanel (when 'the Ishmaelites came and took over the land of the Philistines'). The priest who succeeded him was 'Eleazar, in whose day . . . Abū Bakr died', which is an indication of the reliability of this chronicle, for Abū Bakr died a short time after the beginning of the Muslim invasion. According to Balādhurī, whom I have already quoted, particularly heavy taxes were imposed on the Samaritans, from the time of Yazīd b. Mu'āwiya onward. In Urdunn (that is, the region of northern Samaria), they had to pay a poll-tax of two dinars per male, apart from the land tax (*kharāj*), whereas in Filasṭīn (probably referring to the neighbourhood of Shechem), a poll-tax of five dinars was collected from every Samaritan male. Ya'qūbī, who wrote during the latter half of the ninth century, notes that Yavne was a locality whose inhabitants were Samaritans. He notes that in Ramla the dhimmīs were Samaritans, and as has already been stated above, it is clear that there is some distortion in this version; however it does imply that there was indeed a Samaritan population in Ramla. Ibn Ḥawqal, who wrote in the mid-tenth century, mentions a Samaritan population in Ramla amounting to some 500 tax-payers; that is to say, Ramla had a Samaritan population of some 2,000 to 3,000 souls. The Samaritan centre, however, was obviously Nābulus, which is Shechem; 'the people of Palestine claim that every Samaritan in the world hails from there', says Ibn Ḥawkal.

A very close relationship seems to have developed between the Samaritans and the Muslims, and the process whereby the Samaritans lent themselves to the influence of Muslim culture was swifter than that of the rest of the population. To a certain extent, evidence of their influence can be seen in Islamic tradition. The Koran mentions the Samaritans in the sūra – ṭ.h. (xx:90–97), noting the fear of defilement as one of their marked characteristics. They had taken part in the episode of the golden calf, and were therefore punished by constantly having to say 'do not touch me' (*lā misāsa*). Ibn al-Jawzī, towards the end of the twelfth century, mentions that the Samaritans who were left in Palestine say this 'until today'. A tradition in the name of the Prophet, ascribed to Ka'b al-Aḥbār says: 'The place most beloved by God is al-Shām; the most beloved by God in al-Shām is Palestine (*al-Quds*; here meaning Palestine); and the most beloved by God in Palestine is the Mount Gerizim' (*jabal Nābulus*, the mountain of Shechem). According to al-Dimashqī (writing in *ca.* 1300) 'some say that if a Muslim and a Jew and a Samaritan and a Christian meet on the road, the Samaritan will join the Muslim'. The Muslim writers mention that the Samaritans are divided into two sects, the Dositheans (*Dustāniyya*) and the Kūshānīs, evidently information which they found in pre-Islamic sources. The name Kūshānīs can only be found in Arab writers; it seems to be a transformation of the Hebrew *Kūtīm*. According to the Samaritan chronicle of Abū'l-Fatḥ, it seems that there were still synagogues of the Dositheans in the ninth century. One should bear in mind that the name Dositheus corresponds to the Hebrew name Nethanel, which was the name of several of their high priests.

Mas'ūdi, as well as other Muslim writers, mention the Mount Gerizim, which is the sacred mountain of the Samaritans, and we know that the Samaritans called it *ṭūr berīk* (distorted in some versions). Mas'ūdi also notes their custom of blowing on silver *shofar*s in their prayers.

Bīrūnī informs us that in his time (the first half of the eleventh century) the Samaritans were called *lāmisāsiyya*, which was based on the version of 'do not touch me', *lā misāsa* of the Koran. According to him, their religion was a mixture of Judaism and the Persian religion. Maqrīzī has a passage which explains that the Samaritans are not really related to the Children of Israel and that their origin is in fact Persian.

As I have already stated, the Samaritans were subjected to terrible persecution in the days of the Abbasids, according to the chronicle of Abū'l-Fatḥ, which contains a general survey of their history in that period. It states the following details: many were forced to leave their homes, some converting to Islam. It was said that during al-Amīn's day, their synagogues were burnt down in Zaytā, in (Kafr) Sālim (evidently Kafr Salām), and in Arsūf. The governor of Shechem, Masrūr ibn Abī 'Āmir, sided with the Samaritans, and the Muslims executed him as a result, in *ca.* 815. In 818, al-Ma'mūn sent Khālid ibn Yazīd to fight the rebels in Palestine, and after him 'Abdallah ibn Ṭāhir, in 822. The latter came to Palestine heading a large army, and defended the Samaritans against the rebels. When he went on his way and moved to Egypt, however, the Samaritans were left without anyone to defend them, and the leader of the rebels, Ibn Firāsa, tried by force to get them to convert to Islam. Many then went into exile in order to evade persecution. After the insurgents assassinated the governor of Jericho, the caliph himself came to Palestine. The caliph's brother Ibrahīm (?) then conquered Bet Guvrin and caught the leader of the rebels. After the suppression of the rebellion, however, there followed a period of great hardship for the Samaritans because of the heavy taxes which the governor Abū'l-Jārūd imposed on them. In al-Mu'taṣim's time (833–842), the unbelievers (that is, the rebels) again took control of Shechem, setting fire to the synagogues of the Samaritans and the Dositheans. The two commanders sent by the caliph, Ṣāliḥ and Ja'far, overcame the insurgents in the Valley of Jā'ib (?), and once again, the Samaritans were secure, except for the heavy burden of taxes. Pinḥas b. Nethanel and Dartha (?) then restored the synagogue in Shechem. As I have already mentioned, Shechem was taken by the rebels of Tamīm Abū Ḥarb and the population fled. The high priest was wounded on the way to

Hebron and died of his wounds. At the same time, the division between the Samaritans and the Dositheans became very acute. After the suppression of the uprising of Abū Ḥarb (842), the Samaritans returned to their homes. In the days of al-Mutawakkil (847–861) the Samaritans again suffered severe persecution; the tomb of Nethanel, the high priest, was destroyed and the Samaritans had to abide by dress regulations imposed by Islam. Ja'far (evidently the governor of the area) tried to prohibit Samaritan rituals altogether, but Joseph ibn Dāsī, the governor of Palestine, limited this to the Dositheans only, exempting the rest of the Samaritans. The Ikhshīd Ibn Ṭughj also tyrannised the Samaritans harshly.

An important detail concerning the background to the difficult conditions under which the Samaritans laboured in the ninth century, as described by Abū'l-Fatḥ, is added by Balādhurī. According to him, Hārūn al-Rashīd (786–809) turned Samaritan lands into a caliph's estate. It is not clear from his text whether this meant that they were completely deprived of their property, or whether the caliph merely appropriated their land taxes (*kharāj*). Evidently the latter is correct, for if he was referring to the confiscation of land, we should have found some indication of this in Abū'l-Fatḥ, when he is markedly complaining about the heavy taxes, which was certainly true of the situation. The caliph needed large sums of money and his appointees undoubtedly laid their heavy hands on the Samaritans, being a rural population whose taxes went straight into the caliph's treasury from then on. According to Balādhurī, who lived close to that time (for he wrote towards the end of the ninth century), the Samaritans' complaints bore fruit and al-Mutawakkil eased the burden of taxes on them; at any rate, he reduced the poll-tax from five to three dinars, mainly as a result of the complaints of the Samaritans who lived in Bēt Māmā (the exact place is not identified).

The Samaritan chronicles tell us that Kāfūr was favourably inclined towards the Samaritans. They also tell of a certain Abū 'Abdallah (probably his name, not 'Abdallah) of the same period, who came from a city called Qnt (?), and who dealt very fairly with them. There was a man in his service 'from the house of Ephraim', that is, a Samaritan, whose name was ha-Taqwī b. Isaac, whom his Samaritan contemporaries called 'the saviour'. It is not unlikely that they are describing here the rule of the Qarmaṭīs in Palestine, while Abū 'Abdallah is perhaps Abū 'Abdallah Muḥammad b. Aḥmad ibn al-Nābulusī, a retainer of the Qarmaṭis and an enemy of the Fatimids (mentioned in sec. 555). This Abū 'Abdallah afterwards moved 'to the city of Pāsūn [or Pāsṭūn, i.e. Filasṭīn] which is Ramla' – which is also consistent with what we know about Ibn al-Nābulusī. This is all very unclear, however, and any interpretation would be based merely on assumptions. The chronicles also say that the base of this al-Taqwī was Sepphoris, and they also mention his son, Rawḥ.

Musabbiḥī, who served in the Fatimid court, tells in his chronicle of an incident in Ramla in the spring of 1024, that is, shortly after its conquest by al-Dizbirī, between a certain Abū Sa'd, who was the official in charge of the Fatimid army's administration, and a Samaritan named Sayf, who had received an official order (*sijill*) from the caliph, reprimanding Abū Sa'd (the reason is not explained). After Abū Sa'd refused to listen to the Samaritan's complaints, despite his efforts to convince him, the Samaritan stabbed him with a knife while they were arguing in one of the streets of Ramla. The Samaritan fled, taking Abū Sa'd's horse with him. He was caught, and al-Dizbirī had him imprisoned and the details of the incident were passed on to the caliph, who ordered the Samaritan to be executed, and this was done. We also know of a Samaritan who was in the service of the Fatimid authorities, perhaps as a tax collector, whom 'Eli ha-Kohen b. Ezekiel mentions in a letter written in connection with taxes on his shop, in which he describes the bribing of 'the Samaritan'.

The sources do not tell us anything about links between the Jewish and the Samaritan populations, and we get the impression that there was no contact between them – unlike the continuous co-existence marked by rifts and quarrels that was maintained between the Rabbanites and the Karaites. Apparently, the attitude of the Muslim rulers towards the Samaritans was also ambivalent, and they certainly had doubts as to their genuinely being what was called *ahl al-kitāb* (people of the book). This attitude was probably influenced by the Jews and their claim that the Samaritans were not genuine Children of Israel but Persians by origin, and we find indications of this in Muslim literature, as we have seen. It is possible that the authorities used this as a pretext for, and possibly also the background to, the persecution referred to in Abū'l-Fatḥ's chronicle, in which the main target was probably the Dositheans, a sect of which there are no remnants. Apparently, the Crusaders' conquest did not displace the Samaritans, but we have no information about what happened to them during the Crusaders' rule. However, the Samaritan chronicle written in 1149, the *Tōlīdā*, is in itself evidence of their survival. This chronicle also speaks of Samaritans in Gaza, all of them belonging to the tribe of Benjamin, except for one person who stemmed from the tribe of Ephraim. Mas'ūdī already noted the fact of the Samaritans' dispersal throughout Palestine, apart from their centres in Samaria and Shechem. He mentions *'Ārā* in particular, and he apparently means the present-day

ʻĀra. (Masʻūdī notes that he writes these things in AH 332, which began in September AD 943.)[25]

[25] See the anonymous chronicle: Adler et Seligsohn, *REJ*, 45(1902), 241; Balādhurī, *Futūḥ*, 158; Yaʻqūbī, *Buldān*, 328, 329; Ibn Ḥawqal, 172; Ibn al-Jawzī, *Zād*, V, 319; Kaʻb al-Aḥbār: Ibn ʻAsākir, I, 110; al-Dimashqī, 201. The division into sects: Balādhurī, *ibid.*; Masʻūdī, *Murūj*, I, 114f; *Tanbīh*, 213; Abū'l-Fidā', *Mukhtaṣar*, I, 88 (according to him, the difference between the two was that the Dositheans do not accept the idea of the world to come and of reward and penance, unlike the *kūshāniyya*); see Maqrīzī, *Khiṭaṭ*, III, 372ff, who has a history of the Samaritans starting from the Biblical period, and what he copied from Masʻūdī and Bīrūnī; see Bīrūnī, 21; Shahrastānī, 170f. Fragments from the Arabic sources in an English translation: Isser, *The Dositheans*, 69–73. See the chronicle of Abū'l-Fatḥ (Vilmar), pp. lxxx ff; there is a grain of truth in this chronicle but much of it is incorrect. The matter of taxes: Balādhurī, *ibid.*; cf. Lammens, *Yazīd*, 391; Yāqūt, *Buldān*, I, 781: al-Mutawakkil decreased the tax from ten dinars to three; ha-Taqwī: see the chronicle edited by Neubauer (the *Tōlīdā*), 24; Adler et Seligsohn, *ibid.*, 253, cf. Mann, *Jews*, I, 18f, n. 2. The matter of Sayf the Samaritan: Musabbiḥī, 94. ʻEli ha-Kohen: **446**, line 31. Samaritans in Gaza: in Neubauer, *ibid.*, 26.

10

The Crusaders' conquest and the fate of Palestinian Jewry

[942] In 1099, the curtain fell on the period of Muslim rule in Palestine, which had lasted for 465 years. For the Jewish population, the Crusaders' conquest was a mortal blow; it was almost completely uprooted and this marked the end of an uninterrupted history of a continuous Israelite and Jewish entity in Palestine for a period of some hundred generations, starting from Joshua bin Nun. For other sectors of the population as well, it was also a revolutionary change in every sense of the word. A new society arose, the kingdom of the Crusaders, which was altogether different from what Palestine had known hitherto.

The major setting for the circumstances which enabled the Crusaders to make headway in this part of the world is to be sought in the weakness of the Muslim world and its schisms. We have seen some of the facts above, in connection with the Turcomans' conquest. One must add something about the conditions in Egypt, the country which ruled Palestine at the time of the Crusaders' invasion. After the death of al-Mustanṣir in 1094, Egypt was torn by the war between his two sons, al-Musta'lī and Nizār. Al-Musta'lī was declared the successor to the throne, while Nizār aimed at replacing him. He fled to Alexandria, where Nāṣir al-Dawla Aftakīn, the governor of the city and leader of his faction, was in control. The latter's intention was to succeed to the post of al-Afḍal, son of Badr al-Jamālī, and become wazīr and chief commander of the army. The people of Alexandria stood behind him and Nizār. Al-Afḍal, however, hastened to besiege Alexandria, with little success at first, but after tightening the siege by organising additional forces, he managed to conquer the city. Nāṣir al-Dawla was executed, and Nizār was also caught and condemned to death. Together with a group of his supporters, he was put into a wall which was then sealed and built over. To this civil war which enfeebled Egypt's power, was added a terrible plague in 1097, which cost the lives of an enormous number of people. Nevertheless, al-Afḍal succeeded in gathering together an army which took Palestine from the Saljūqs, as we have seen. On 26 August 1098, Jerusalem was once more under the control of the Fatimids – for a period of less than a year before the Crusaders took it.[1]

[943] In the same year, as we know, the Crusaders took Antioch. From there, they launched an advance southward, along the coast, via Beirut, Sidon (Sagitta in the Latin sources), Tyre, Acre, Haifa and Caesarea. They avoided the fortified towns in the coastal area, and only Caesarea was taken at this stage, where they celebrated Pentecost in 1099. Immediately afterwards, the Crusaders entered Ramla, which they found empty of its inhabitants, who had all fled. They installed a bishop there, and gave the lands of the area to the Christians. From a description of the events, it seems clear that the Crusaders were impatient to get to Jerusalem. According to Ibn al-Athīr, they tried to attack Acre but were driven back, and gave up the attempt for the time being. Jerusalem came under siege at the beginning of June. Ibn al-Athīr tells that the Crusaders put up two towers for the siege, one to the south in the direction of Mount Zion, which the Muslims succeeded in setting on fire and killing the soldiers who manned it. According to Ibn al-Qalānisī, the Crusaders conquered the city by trickery. They attacked during the day but withdrew towards evening, announcing loudly that they intended to return on the morrow to launch another attack. The defenders then scattered to rest for the night, but on that same night, the Crusaders attacked again when the wall was undefended. This time they succeeded in penetrating the city. The siege lasted for some six weeks and the city was conquered on Friday, 23 Sha'bān AH 492 (15 July AD 1099). Apparently, most of the Crusader forces entered the city in the afternoon of that same day. Their major breakthrough was in the northern part of the city, in the neighbourhood of *bāb al-asbāṭ*.

All the sources, Muslim, Christian and Jewish, agree on the unprecedented amount of bloodshed that accompanied the conquest of the city. The principal Christian sources on this subject are the texts of Balderic, bishop of Dol (Baudry de Bourgueil), who wrote a treatise entitled The History of Jerusalem at the beginning of the twelfth century, that is quite near the time these events occurred, and Albert of Aachen, in his treatise on the conquest of Jerusalem. According to Balderic, most of the inhabitants of Jerusalem escaped to the area of the Temple Mount (templum Salomonis). The Christians violated their promise to the inhabitants that they would be left alive, and slaughtered some 20,000 to 30,000 people, a number which may be an exaggeration, although the Muslim sources

[1] The civil war: Ibn al-Qalānisī, 128f; Ibn al-Athīr, *Kāmil*, X, 238; Ibn Taghrī Bardī, under the year 487; Maqrīzī, *Khiṭaṭ*, II, 164f (which also discusses the plague), 276f.

speak of even 70,000. One must take into account that Jerusalem, which normally had a much smaller population, was then evidently full of refugees who had fled from other places. Apparently, the Fatimid army stationed in the city left unharmed, after their commander, Iftikhār al-Dawla, agreed to surrender, on condition that he and his forces would be permitted to leave the city without arms and without food. They actually did leave for Ascalon, and were accompanied by some of Jerusalem's inhabitants who managed to leave. Abū Bakr ibn al-'Arabī, a contemporary who remained in Jerusalem for a few years, until 1095, and who evidently also had reliable information on the conquest, notes that the Muslims all fled to the *miḥrāb Da'ūd*, obviously meaning the Temple Mount. According to him, they all remained alive and unharmed, on the condition that they surrender and hand over the citadel. Apparently Ibn al-Athīr also copied these details from him. Later Arab sources, beginning with Ibn al-Jawzī, as mentioned, speak of the slaughter of 70,000 people and the plunder of the mosques on the Temple Mount. From the Dome of the Rock, some 40 or more silver lamps were robbed, each of which weighed 3,600 dirhams (apparently *ca.* ten kilograms), a lighting fixture made of silver which weighed 40 *raṭls shāmī* (*ca.* 67 kilograms, evidently), gold lamps, and innumerable pieces of clothing, fabrics and precious objects. In addition, according to the Muslim sources, they destroyed the Cave of the Machpelah. The Arab sources stress in particular the killing of Abū'l-Qāsim Makkī b. 'Abd al-Salām al-Maqdisī al-Rumaylī, the Muslim writer mentioned above. As to the fate of the Jews, the version in most of the Muslim sources is that the Jews were gathered together in the synagogue, which was then set on fire. The Christian sources differ; they say that most of the Jews were taken captive, which is also borne out in the Geniza documents to be discussed below. According to Balderic, the Jews were forced to participate in clearing away the corpses, together with the local Christians (only the latter were paid for their labours). Afterwards the captives were sold on Tancred's orders, at the rate of thirty per *aureus* (dinar). A great many were taken by sea to southern Italy (Apulia); some were drowned in the sea and others were beheaded.

Both a Christian and a Muslim source tell of the plague which broke out immediately after the conquest. According to the Christian source, this was caused by 'the Barbarians', who poisoned the wells and other water sources. There are also those who say, according to the Christian source, that the plague broke out because of the many corpses that remained unburied.[2]

[944] As to Hebron, we have seen that according to the Arab sources, it

[2] On the matter of the conquest of Jerusalem see the detailed description in Ibn al-Qalānisī, 137; Ibn al-Athīr, *Kāmil*, X, 283f; Ibn Taghrī Bardī, V, 150; Ibn Khallikān, I, 161f (the

was taken at about the same time as Jerusalem, for they mentioned the destruction in the Cave of Machpelah. Albert of Aachen, however, says that Hebron was conquered in the summer of the following year, that is 1100, by Godfrey of Bouillon. The Crusaders turned the synagogue in Hebron into a church, as described by the Hebronite monk in his story quoted above (sec. 315) in the discussion on Hebron, which is also confirmed by Benjamin of Tudela, who notes that the church in Hebron, which was called 'the church of St Abraham' when he visited there (*ca.* 1170), had been a synagogue during the period of Muslim rule.

Haifa was taken two years later, in August 1100 or June 1101, according to Muslim sources which contradict one another. Albert of Aachen does not mention the date in a clear manner either. From what he says, it appears that it was mainly the Jewish inhabitants of the city who defended the fortress of Haifa. In his rather strange Latin style, he mentions that there was a Jewish population in Haifa, and that they fought bravely on the walls of the city. He explains that the Jews there were protected people of the Muslims (the Fatimids). They fought side by side with units of the Fatimid army, striking back at Tancred's army from above the walls of the citadel (... *Judaei cives commixtis Sarracenorum turmis*) until the Crusaders overcame them and they were forced to abandon the walls. The Muslims and the Jews then managed to escape from the fortress with their lives, while the rest of the population fled the city *en masse*. Whoever remained was slaughtered, and huge quantities of spoils were taken. According to the Muslim sources, the Crusaders also entered Arsūf at the same time, after granting an *amān* (a letter of security).[3]

article on Abū'l-Qāsim Aḥmad al-Musta'lī b. al-Mustanṣir); Sibṭ ibn al-Jawzī, *Mir'āh*, MS Leiden Or 88, fols. 56a–57b; Yāqūt, *Buldān*, II, 824; IV, 599 (*ibid.* on the breakthrough in the north of the city); Ibn al-Jawzī, *Muntaẓam*, IX, 108; Ibn Kathīr, *Bidāya*, XII, 106; Dhahabī, *'Ibar*, III, 332; Baldricus Dolensis, 102; Albert of Aachen (Albericus), 482f, and see version G of Balderic (MS Paris 5513), 103; Ibn al-'Arabī, *Aḥkām*, 1586; on the surrender of Iftikhār al-Dawla see also: Petri Tudebodi, *Historia*, 109f. On the matter of the date, there are contradictions in the Muslim sources, but as all are agreed that it was on a Friday, it is clear that 15 July is intended. Only one source, Gilo of Paris, lists the Jews among the defenders of Jerusalem against the Crusaders, which is not confirmed in any of the Muslim sources, nor in the Jewish sources. In Tudebotus abbreviatus in the *Gesta Francorum*, 161, it states that only Muslims (Sarraceni) were forced to clear away the corpses. On the price of the captives, see below what it says in the Geniza sources. On the plague, see Annalista Saxo, 733; Maqrīzī, *Khiṭaṭ*, II, 165; according to him the plague spread to Egypt as well and a great many people in Fustat succumbed, which is borne out by a letter in the Geniza, quoted below. A description of the First Crusade and the conquest of Jerusalem can be read in any book dealing with the history of the Crusades; cf. Dinur, *Zion* (ha-me'assēf), 2(1926/7), 40–54; Grousset, I, 157–163; Runciman, I, 279ff; Prawer, *Tōledōt*, I, 134ff; *idem, Ha-ṣalvānīm*, 31; and Goitein's articles: *Zion*, 17:129 1952; *JJS*, 3:162, 1952; *Yerushalayim*, 1955:54; *Eretz-Israel*, 4:147, 1955/6; see these articles, together with a general introduction and various additions: *idem, Ha-yishuv*, 229–305.

3 Hebron: Albert of Aachen (see previous note), 523; Benjamin of Tudela (Adler), 26f; cf. Dinur, *Zion* (ha-me'assēf), 2(1925/6) 54ff; Vincent, *Hébron*, 163f, n. 5, who quotes a source

[945] From here onward, I shall be referring to data contained in the Geniza documents belonging to the period of the Crusaders' dominion over Palestine. These documents can naturally serve as a source of information, particularly with regard to the fate of the Jewish population, although here and there they contain details on the general events of the time, and it is always interesting to compare them with the information we have gathered from Christian and Muslim sources.

Roughly about the same time that the news of the fall of Jerusalem to the Crusaders reached Fustat, evidence is to be found in two fragments of drafts of a letter intended for the Ascalon congregation, on behalf of the three congregations – the two congregations of Fustat, the 'Palestinian' and the 'Babylonian' as well as the congregation of al-Qāhira. The writer of the drafts is the cantor and scribe Hillel b. 'Eli, who can be recognised by his handwriting. From what has been preserved from the drafts, we read about an emergency assembly held by the Jews of Fustat and al-Qāhira at

which says that in 1100 assistance is already being requested for the *castrum Sancti Abrahae*, 'the citadel of St Abraham'. Haifa: Albert of Aachen, 521ff; he describes the Jews of Haifa as citizens (*cives*) who lived in the city by favour of and with the agreement of the King of Babylonia (*regis Babyloniae*), in exchange for the payment of taxes – this was in fact the status of every Jew of the Muslim world (Babylonia there meant Egypt), and nothing out of the ordinary. See Dhahabī, *'Ibar*, III, 338: Haifa was conquered in AḤ 494 (AD 1101) together with Arsūf; Ibn Khallikān, I, 179: in Shawwāl AH 493 (August AD 1100); and similarly Ibn Ẓāfir (print), 83 (= MS 75a); whereas Maqrīzī, *Itti'āẓ*, III, 261: the end of Rajab AH 494, that is, the beginning of June AD 1101; cf. Prawer, *Tōlēdōt*, I, 169f; in n. 15, the reference to Albert of Aachen has to be corrected: it should read vol. IV, also in *EI*², in the article Ḥayfā (by the editor) where there is also an incorrect interpretation of Albert of Aachen's passage about the status of the Jews, as if he were speaking of some special grant given them by the caliph, which is not said there; nor does it refer to any 'special privilege' (as assumed by Prawer, *Latin Kingdom*, 236). Albert writes: 'cives ex genere Judaeorum qui hanc inhabitabant dono et consensu regis Babyloniae in redditione tributorum', 'citizens of the Jewish nation, who lived there by the favour and with the agreement of the King of Babylonia [as they called the ruler of Egypt at the time], in exchange for the payment of taxes'. Common sense tells us that this is merely Albert's style and that all he wished to say was that the Jews of Haifa were *ahl al-dhimma*, i.e. protected people. It is worth adding some references to Arab sources: Ibn al-Shaddād (MS), 107a: Bet Shean was conquered at the same time as Jerusalem. The conquest of Caesarea: Ibn Khallikān, *ibid.*: in AH 494, that is AD 1101. Acre: Dhahabī, *'Ibar*, III, 345: in AH 497, i.e. AD 1104 (which began on 5 October 1103); and also in: Ibn Khallikān, V, 300; Ibn Taghrī Bardī, V, 170; on p. 188 he says that Acre was attacked by Baldwin (Baghdawīn) on land, and from the sea by more than ninety ships. He laid a siege on the city from every side. The governor, Zahr al-Dawla al-Juyūshī, asked for a pact for himself and the Muslims, but the Crusaders refused, for they knew that no one would come to their aid from Egypt; the city was then taken 'by the sword', in Ramaḍān AH 497 (June AD 1104). Bāniyās: Ibn Taghrī Bardī, V, 170: in AH 502, which began on 11 August AD 1108; similarly in Ibn Khallikān, V, 300; there is no information on the situation in Bāniyās from this date onward, and according to what I wrote above in sec. 328, it seems to have changed hands a number of times before the Crusaders finally took it in 1129. As to Tyre, the accepted date is Tuesday, 23 Jumādā I AH 518, 8 July AD 1124, see: Ibn al-Athīr, *Kāmil* X, 621f; Ibn Khallikān, V, 300; according to the surrender agreement, the population was permitted to leave the city with whatever they could carry, and indeed whoever was capable of it, left.

the home of Mevorakh b. Saadia, the Nagid. Mevorakh himself adopted mourning customs and when the people assembled there, they found him 'in torn clothes, sitting on the ground, weeping over that' (which had happened). The main subject dealt with at that meeting was the ransoming of the scrolls of the Torah and the captives (the Torah came before the captives!). A sum of 123 dinars was collected on the spot for this purpose and the money was sent with an emissary to Ascalon. The name of the emissary was Manṣūr. At the time the drafts were written, they did not know the name of his father, only his by-name, 'b. al-Mu'allima' (the woman teacher).[4]

[946] We also find details relating to the period of the Crusaders' conquest in a letter written by a Maghribi merchant to his cousin. After years of trading and eventually losing his fortune, the writer's only remaining ambition was to go on a pilgrimage to Jerusalem. *En route*, he first stopped in Alexandria, where he remained for some time. In the meantime, winter had set in, accompanied by storms at sea, while in Palestine, wars were raging and the country was completely disrupted by the armies. All roads leading to Jerusalem were hazardous. There were also riots in Egypt at the time; Alexandria was besieged time and again and partly destroyed in the process. Eventually it was taken by 'the Sultan' who imposed a regime of justice. In his description, the writer was obviously referring to the events which took place after al-Mustanṣir's death and the war between his two sons, Nizār and al-Musta'lī. The benign Sultan was naturally al-Afḍal. The writer was now hoping for better times, which would enable him to reach his destination, Jerusalem, in safety. Indeed, al-Afḍal's army conquered Jerusalem, but only for a very limited time (in the autumn of 1098, when travelling on the high seas was impossible due to storms; in the spring of 1099, the Crusaders were already in Palestine). He refers to the invasion of the Crusaders (*al-Ifranj*) and the conquest of Jerusalem, and to the fact that the Muslim and Jewish inhabitants were all killed, except for the few who were taken captive, some of whom were still in captivity in various places or had been ransomed in the interim. To the writer, these events seemed an ephemeral episode and he expresses the hope that the wheels of fortune would soon turn and that al-Afḍal would shortly, in that same year, take Jerusalem from the Crusaders. Then he would go up to the Holy City and afterwards return home. In continuation, he mentions the dreadful, drawn-out plague which claimed so many victims – as we have already heard.

Zadok b. Josiah, known to us as the 'third' in the Scrolls of Abiathar,

[4] The drafts: **573**; Goitein, *Mediterranean Society*, III, 356, assumed that this Manṣūr was identical to Abū Manṣūr, to whom the letter (requesting aid): ENA NS 2, f. 17, was written; Goitein writes that the letter was sent to *kanīsat al-mu'allima* ('the synagogue of the

writing to Joseph *ha-shōfēṭ* ('the judge') b. Abraham in Fustat, also deals at length with the matter of the captives. He speaks of family members who are in captivity. In order to deal with the release of members of his family, he seems to be in a place we cannot identify, near the area under Crusaders' occupation, while members of his family are in captivity in Antioch. His daughter was the only one he managed to redeem, while his son and son-in-law were still in captivity. Apparently this son-in-law was a man of considerable status and lineage, for he refers to him as 'his excellency, our mighty prince, our son-in-law, the prince of the House of Israel'. Although he has evidently arranged the ransom payment for his son, it is actually the son-in-law about whom he is most concerned. We do not know how members of Zadok's family were taken captive by the Crusaders, as they lived in Tyre, which was only conquered in 1124. They may have been on a pilgrimage to Jerusalem after the Fatimids took it in 1098. What is clearly evident from the letter is that the writer had also approached the Nagid, Mevorakh b. Saadia, about the ransom money and that he anticipates his active support in the matter of his family's redemption. As Goitein points out, although the writer held an important position in the Palestinian yeshiva, the letter itself is highly personal and his anxiety for his family overrides his concern for the other captives. Apparently from the same time, there is a letter which some member of the Palestinian yeshiva, staying in Tyre, wrote to one of the followers of the Nagid in Fustat. The writer wants to come to Fustat, hoping the Nagid would provide him with a livelihood. He cannot leave for Fustat himself, as he does not want to leave his family in Tyre in such uncertain conditions, referring to 'the child who was left behind'. Evidently, here too he was speaking of a son in captivity.[5]

[947] A letter from a group of Karaite refugees from Jerusalem is of particular interest. They are staying in Egypt, evidently Alexandria, and the letter is written to the Karaite congregation in Fustat, less than a year after the fall of Jerusalem. The letter deals mainly with the ransoming of captives. The writers acknowledge the receipt of a money order – and with

woman teacher'), but I read it: *kanīsat al-Maḥalla* ('the synagogue in al-Maḥalla'), and it was sent: *ilā al-shaykh abī Manṣūr bni'l-mu'allim* (to Mr. Abū Manṣūr, son of the teacher'); therefore it seems that these were two different people.

[5] The letter of the Maghribi: **575**. The letter of Zadok b. Josiah: **574**, and see Goitein's assumption, in *Eretz-Israel*, 4(1956/7), 147 (= Ha-yishuv, 283f), that his son-in-law was 'the son of the wife of the Tustari' mentioned in **577**; which does not seem to be based on sufficient evidence, for this was a child of eight to ten, and see below. Zadok b. Josiah did not become *av-bēt-dīn*, contrary to what Mann says in *Jews*, I, 193f, and also what he writes there on Nathan b. Abraham who was allegedly the grandson of Nathan *av-bēt-dīn* (the rival of Solomon b. Judah) and became *av-bēt-dīn* after Zadok, is incorrect, as I have shown above; and also what Goitein writes in his wake on this matter in the aforementioned place. The letter from Tyre: **576**, and see the matter of the son in line 10.

the money they received for it they have already redeemed some of the captives. The letter also includes a description of the conditions in which the ransomed Karaite captives live; they stay in Ascalon for the time being, in dire straits, and from day to day, some of them die of hunger. As to the captives who are still in the hands of the Crusaders, distressing news is arriving about them, telling of cruel executions, and they fear that the Crusaders intend to wipe out all the captives. Some of the Karaite refugees escaped from captivity, mostly with the help of Abū'l-Faḍl Sahl b. Yūsha' b. Sha'yā (evidently a Karaite from Ascalon) who had good connections with the Sultan (that is: al-Afḍal), and due to these connections, he had considerable influence in the port of Ascalon, succeeding in freeing many of the captives in ways which were only known to him. Among the captives still in the hands of the Crusaders is a child of eight to tẹn years of age, named Abū Sa'd, 'son of the wife of the Tustari'. This 'wife of the Tustari' was evidently the widow of the Karaite writer Sahl b. Faḍl (Yāshār b. Ḥesed) al-Tustarī, the great-grandson of Ḥesed al-Tustarī. We have seen that this Sahl lived in Jerusalem in the nineties, and we do not know the circumstances of his death; perhaps he was killed during the Crusaders' conquest. Nor do we know why the child is called 'the son of the wife of al-Tustarī' and not 'the son of al-Tustarī', and naturally there may be many explanations for this. His captors, the Crusaders, are trying to persuade him to convert to Christianity but he refuses and claims that it is unheard of for a priest to become a Christian. It appears that they are hoping to receive a particularly large sum in ransom money for him, as they are aware of his lineage. Some of the captives were taken to Antioch (we have seen confirmation of this also in Zadok b. Josiah's letter). We have heard, notes the writer, of no instances of 'the cursed Ashkenaz' (it is not clear which Crusaders were being referred to, nor who were the Crusaders who were holding the captives) raping the women in captivity. Another important detail that he mentions is the fact that some of the Jerusalem Karaites succeeded in leaving Jerusalem together with the governor, on the basis of an *amān*. This corresponds to what I have written above concerning Iftikhār al-Dawla, who handed over the Temple Mount (*miḥrāb Da'ūd*) to the Crusaders by a capitulation agreement. Some of the ransomed captives moved to Egypt without sufficient means to maintain themselves or adequate clothing, and many died on the way from the bitter cold and starvation. Many of those who left by sea also died. As to the cost of ransoming a captive, although they did not speak of thirty captives per dinar as in the Crusader source I quoted above, it does say in this letter, that it is fortunate for the captives that the Crusaders did not know what was the usual price, which was three Jewish captives for 100 dinars, and therefore, it implies, the ransom price was much lower than that. An account of the expenses, up until the writing of the letter, had reached 700 dinars, of which 200 was a debt. More money was needed, it says in the letter, to ensure the lives of some twenty ransomed captives who were left in Ascalon and to move them to Egypt. A special instance was that of Abū'l-Khayr Mubārak b. ha-melammēd Hiba b. Nisan (Mubārak = Mevorakh; Hiba = Nathan; that is, Mevorakh b. Nathan), who pledged an oath not to take any public money except that which the donors had specifically intended for him personally. In the continuation of the letter, there is an appeal that money from pledges and the income from the heqdēsh foundations be reserved for the rescuing of captives and of those redeemed from captivity. The redemption of books is another matter: 230 Bibles, 100 quires, 28 Torah scrolls were redeemed; all are considered *qōdesh* (= *heqdēsh*) and are being kept in Ascalon, and money must be found in order to transfer them to Egypt. There is no doubt that this letter is of a purely Karaite nature, as can be seen by its writers, its signatories, and its contents. Thus, even in these terrible hours of destruction and annihilation which befell the Jews of Palestine, it is obvious that the Karaites acted on their own and not together with the Rabbanites.[6]

[948] On the matter of redeeming the books from the Crusaders, it is worth noting the Karaite colophon copied by Harkavy in 1875 from a Torah scroll kept by a Karaite in Petersburg (received from Firkovitch), in which it says that God brought 'our master Solomon the *nāsī* into grace and favour and tender love in the sight of the Master Bālduwīn who reigned after his brother . . . and they returned to us all our holy books, among them this Torah scroll . . . on Friday, the fast of 10 Av, the first day of the year 1037 of the destruction of the second [Temple], 1416 Sel. (that is, in the summer of AD 1105). It also says there: 'we assembled in the synagogue of our *nāsī* 'Anan'. Firkovitch claimed (quoted by Harkavy)

[6] The letter of the Karaites: **577**, and see there in the note to a, line 28, remarks about where it was being written. As to Abū'l-Faḍl Sahl b. Yeshū'ā b. Sha'yā, Goitein, *ha-Yishuv*, 236, assumed that he is identical with Shelah, who married Sitt al-Dallāl in Ascalon in January 1100 (misprinted there as 1110), see **594**. On the matter of Abū Sa'd, son of the wife of the Tustari, cf. Gil, *ha-Tustarīm*, 65. Goitein, *JQR*, NS 45 (1954/5), 36f, n. 1, already stated his opinion that this boy was the son of Yāshār b. Ḥesed (should be: Yāshār the great-grandson of Ḥesed), and deduced from this that Yāshār, the Karaite writer, lived in Jerusalem until the Crusaders' conquest. As we have seen above, the fact that he lived in Jerusalem has additional proof. On the subject of the identity of the 'Ashkenaz', see Kedar, *Tarbiz*, 42 (1972/3), 407, n. 36; Goitein, *Zion*, 17 (1952), 133, n. 16 (= Ha-yishuv), 235, n. 17): 'probably meaning the Lotharingians'. See the discussion in Goitein, *ha-Yishuv*, 235, on the huge number of books and quires, compared with the inventory lists from the Geniza of books which belonged to the synagogues in Fustat in the eleventh and twelfth centuries. Baron, *SRHJ*, IV, 111f made a comparison between the matter of the ransom payment for the books of the Bible and the colophons of Bible manuscripts which were preserved and provide evidence that they are from Jerusalem, and correctly concluded that the letter was a Karaite one. Not so Prawer, in *ha-Ṣalvānīm*, 268, n. 42, who expresses his feeling that the letter is 'not Karaite but Jewish' (meaning: Rabbanite, naturally).

that this proves that the Karaites were not affected by the conquest of Jerusalem and that even their synagogue in Jerusalem remained intact. The first statement is completely contradicted by the above letter. As to the synagogue, we have already seen that there is no information on a Karaite synagogue in Jerusalem during this period, hence the synagogue in the name of 'Anan (if this is not one of Firkovitch' forgeries) was apparently the name of the Karaite synagogue in Fustat, or perhaps in another city, such as Damascus. The colophon in a commentary to the book of Isaiah written by Josiah b. Aaron he-ḥāvēr of Acre (which I have already mentioned above, sec. 301, and which is included in my collection) is also evidence of the redemption of books taken as spoils in Jerusalem and Palestine. The Latin inscription in this colophon is an indication that the book was taken as spoils by the Crusaders, who took the trouble to discover its value; only then could it be redeemed by the Jews. Similarly, the *Keter* of Aleppo mentioned above, is said to have been redeemed from the spoils of Jerusalem.[7]

[949] Another letter dealing with the captives is from one of the Palestinian refugees, sent from somewhere in the neighbourhood of Tyre or Damascus. He escaped to this place and was making every effort to free his family from captivity. With singular difficulty, he managed to redeem his mother, his brother, and young sister. The letter only provides us with the name of the writer's father, R. Kōkhāv, who he says died seven years earlier. One of his relatives is also mentioned, 'Petaḥia b. al-mu'allim Maḥāsin', that is, the son of a teacher, who asked the writer to add something in his name as well. It is obvious that the writer is a young man, for he writes that when his father died, 'we, the children remained'. One of the daughters of the family is still in captivity and they need a large sum of money for her redemption. The writer refrains from asking for money directly but seems to harbour resentment towards his relatives in Egypt who are well-off but who do not seem to care about the terrible distress of their relations. He calls Egypt 'the kingdom you live in', for apparently everyone hoped that it would be the source of their salvation. The refugees saw themselves as 'a posterity in the earth' which God had left in order to 'save your lives by a great deliverance' (Gen., xlv:7); which again goes to show that they considered what had occurred to be a passing episode.

Abū Sa'd b. Ghanā'im wrote from Ascalon to his brother Abū'l-Bahā' in Bilbays, about a woman captive who had been released from captivity. Goitein, the first editor of the letter, assumed that it was written after the

[7] See Harkavy, *ha-Ṣefīrā*, 1874/5, 47f; the dating is according to the Karaite calendar, and we do not know when their month of Av began in that year. Solomon the Nāsī is evidently the son of Ezekiel b. Solomon b. David; cf. Mann, *Jews*, I, 199f, and n. 1 (he copied 1417 Sel. instead of 1416). The colophon in the book of Isaiah: **221**.

Crusaders' conquest of Ascalon (1153), for we know that a remnant of the community remained there. His opinion probably stemmed from the supposition that there was no possibility of maintaining contact between Ascalon and the region seized by the Crusaders, as long as Ascalon was under Muslim control. It seems to me that this supposition is not necessarily so, however, and we may assume that the letter dates from the beginning of the twelfth century. This same Abū Sa'd writes in his letter that he visited Shechem (that is, the region occupied by the Crusaders) together with a certain Muslim (= Meshullām) ibn Abī Sahl, where they ransomed the latter's sister from the Crusaders' captivity. Muslim still owed sixty dinars from this transaction (twice the usual price for ransoming a prisoner). Abū Sa'd had succumbed to Muslim's entreaties and stood as his guarantor with 'the Frank', probably one of the Crusader commanders with whom he maintained contact. Quite some time has passed since then and the Frank is putting pressure on him to pay the money. The writer therefore asks his brother to obtain the money from the captive's father, who it is implied also lives in Bilbays. If he has no money, he will return the sister (this sounds like bluster), and if necessary, he would even get a decision from the judges. The writer cannot obtain the money despite all his efforts, for no one is ready to lend it to him, although he has offered interest and even his son as deposit (this also seems rather exaggerated). It is also worth noting Muslim's argument that if his sister is free, she will be able to recruit some of the ransom money herself.

A direct appeal to the congregation from a woman captive (evidently after she was redeemed) can be seen in a version of a request from a woman 'from among the captives of Palestine'. She has just reached Sunbāṭ in Egypt, and in her appeal says she has no clothing and that she has a small child to care for. She asks for help, and blesses those that would help with God's granting them a double reward, adding: 'may He not dislodge you from your retreat'. Another woman captive whose redemption is being dealt with at about the same time is also mentioned in a letter from the Jewish leader of Ascalon, Nathan ha-Kohen b. Mevorakh to the parnās of Fustat, 'Ūla ha-Levi b. Joseph. He promises him that the people of Ascalon are looking after the affairs of the woman, 'may our God unchain her fetters and the captives of His nation Israel'.[8]

[950] And so ends the period which began with the suffering attendant on the conquest of Palestine by the nomadic tribes which united round the vision of Islam. This period brought about an essential change in the status of Palestine. Jerusalem became a holy city to the Muslims, while at the same time a Jewish community returned to the city, which became the

[8] The refugee's letter: **578**. The letter from Ascalon: **579**, see Goitein, *Tarbiz*, 31(1961/2), 287ff (= ha-Yishuv, 306f). The captive's appeal: **580**. Ascalon: **588**, margin, top.

centre of the diaspora and the seat of the yeshiva Ge'ōn Ya'aqōv. The Christians, the former rulers of Palestine, became dhimmīs lacking political rights, like the Jews. To the two ancient components of the population in Palestine, another was added: the Muslims – their tribes, armies, theologians and scholars, and their mosques. At the end of this period, Islam could no longer hold Palestine, as a result of the internal division and unceasing warfare which it experienced, and it slipped out of its hands. The outcome was the destruction of the Jewish population in Palestine by the Crusaders. At the outset of this period, the Jews of Palestine heard the footsteps of the Messiah in the stamping of the horses' hooves of the Muslim conquerers; the finale of this era marked their annihilation and destruction.

Some indication of what had occurred can be found in a letter of the leader of the Aleppo Jews at the time, Baruch b. Isaac. In a letter which is mainly a recommendation for Obadiah, a Norman proselyte, he included rhymed expressions of mourning (mostly in Biblical terms) on the destruction of Palestine and Jerusalem, on the slaughter, on captivity, and on the total annihilation of the Jewish population. He writes about 'the daughter of Jeshurun [whose] . . . restorers who were strengthening her [house] became powerless'; about 'their despairing of the soul because of the fury of the oppressor'; 'the terrible famine'; about Jerusalem – 'it became abhorred by the nation'; 'for a child to be hired out and a girl to be given for a price'; 'those who dwell in the midst of the land were defiled'; 'their blood was shed like rivulets'; 'their houses were handed over to those who despoiled them'; 'they were thrown away from a holy place, to breathe the dust of a foreign land'. He sums up the annihilation of the entire Jewish population of Palestine by saying that 'everyone who believes in the uniqueness of God, was banished from every corner of the holy soil'.[9]

[9] Baruch b. Isaac's letter: Bodl MS Heb a 3, f. 1, edited by Wertheimer, *Ginzē Yerūshālayim* 2(1901), 16f; its verso was quoted by Mann, *Jews*, II, 236, and the last part, which Wertheimer did not edit, with details on Obadiah, was edited by him in *REJ*, 89 (1930), 247ff; cf. Dinur, *Zion* (ha-me'assēf) 2(1926/7), 51; see the corrections and discussion on the letter in Golb, *Goitein Jubilee Volume*, 90–94, and his new edition of the entire letter, *ibid.*, 103–106, and also references to all earlier discussions on Obadiah the proselyte.

Chronology

610	Heraclius is crowned emperor of Byzantium
611	the Persians start their offensive against Byzantium
614	Jerusalem is conquered by the Persians
619	Sophronius arrives in Palestine
622–628	the Byzantines fight back against the Persians
622, end of September	the hijra
628, end of summer	conquest of Khaybar
629, September	raid on Mu'ta
630, October–December	the Tabūk expedition
631, 12 March	the Holy Cross is returned to Jerusalem
632, 8 June	death of Muḥammad
633, spring	suppression of the *ridda*
633, autumn	Sophronius is appointed patriarch of Jerusalem
634, February–March	the invasion of Palestine begins
634, beginning of May	Khālid b. al-Walīd arrives in Palestine
634, summer	defeat of the Muslims at Marj Ṣuffar
634, 30 July	battle of Ijnādayn
634, 23 August	death of the caliph Abū Bakr; he is succeeded by 'Umar ibn al-Khaṭṭāb
634, 25 December	sermon of Sophronius in Jerusalem
635, 12 March	siege of Damascus begins
635, 10 September	conquest of Damascus
636, 23 July (or 13 August)	battle of the Yarmūk
638	Emperor Heraclius proclaims his new religious programme (monotheletism)
638 (probably at the beginning of the year)	conquest of Jerusalem
639	the plague of 'Imwās
640, October	conquest of Caesarea
641	'Umar ibn al-Khaṭṭāb introduces a new order in the grants for the Muslims

644, November	murder of the caliph ʿUmar; he is succeeded by ʿUthmān b. ʿAffān
647	the Muslim fleet sets sail from Acre to the conquest of Cyprus
652	death of Aws b. al-Ṣāmit, in Ramla (?)
654/5	death of ʿUbāda b. al-Ṣāmit, in Ramla (?)
658/9	Shumayr al-Khathʿamī is appointed as governor of jund Filasṭīn
659, 9 June	earthquake in Palestine
661	Muʿāwiya is proclaimed caliph in Jerusalem
674	death of Thawbān b. Yamrud
677	death of Kaʿb b. Murra al-Bahzī, in Tiberias
677	death of Abū Muḥammad ʿAbdallah b. al-Saʿdī
678	death of ʿAbdallah b. Ḥawāla, in Tiberias
680, April	death of the caliph Muʿāwiya; Yazīd b. Muʿāwiya succeeds him, coming from Jerusalem
680, 10 October	murder of al-Ḥusayn b. ʿAlī ibn Abī Ṭalib, in Karbalā
682	Ṭarīf b. Ḥābis, who is Ibn Khushkhāsh al-Hilālī, is appointed as chief of the tribes in jund Filasṭīn
683/4	mention of Abū Rāshid, governor of Nessana
683, November	death of Yazīd b. Muʿāwiya; Muʿāwiya II, b. Yazīd, succeeds him as caliph
684	death of Ḥubaysh b. Dalaja, chief of the Banū Quḍāʿa in Palestine
684, June	Marwān b. al-Ḥakam becomes caliph
684, July	victory of the supporters of the Umayyads at Marj Rāhiṭ
685, April	ʿAbd al-Malik b. Marwān becomes caliph
685/6	death of Nātil b. Qays, chief of the Banū Judhām
686 (?)	destruction of Caesarea and Ascalon by the Byzantines and deportation of their populations
688	beginning of the construction of the Dome of the Rock
ca. 690	ʿAlī b. ʿAbdallah b. ʿAbbās settles in Ḥumayma
691	Anastasius is appointed patriarch of Jerusalem
692	the construction of the Dome of the Rock is completed
692, October	final defeat of ʿAbdallah b. al-Zubayr
695	first Muslim dinars are minted
696/7	death of ʿAbd al-Raḥmān b. Ghanm
699/700	severe plague in Palestine
700	the Dome of the Rock is hit by lightning
704	death of Abu Qirṣāfa Wāthila b. al-Asqaʿ
705	plague 'of the girls'
705, 14 September	death of the caliph ʿAbd al-Malik; he is succeeded by his son, al-Walīd

706	John (V) is appointed patriarch of Jerusalem
708	death of Abū Bishr ʻAbdallah b. Fayrūz, in Jerusalem
713, 13 January	Petrus of Capitolias (Bayt Ra's) is executed by the Arabs
ca. 714	foundation of Ramla
715, 24 February	death of the caliph al-Walīd; he is succeeded by Sulaymān b. ʻAbd al-Malik, who is brought from Ramla
717, September	death of the caliph Sulaymān; he is succeeded by ʻUmar b. ʻAbd al-ʻAzīz
718	death of Maḥmūd b. al-Rabīʻ b. Surāqa al-Madanī, in Jerusalem
719/729	the church in Māʻin is reconstructed
720, February	death of the caliph ʻUmar b. ʻAbd al-ʻAzīz; he is succeeded by Yazīd b. ʻAbd al-Malik
723	Willibald visits Tiberias
724	death of the caliph Yazīd b. ʻAbd al-Malik; his brother Hishām succeeds him
728	death of al-Qāsim b. ʻAbd al-Raḥmān b. ʻAbdallah b. Masʻūd
730/1	death of Rajā' b. Ḥayawa
ca. 732	John of Damascus joins the monastery of Mar Saba
733/4	plagues in Palestine
736	death of ʻUbāda b. Nussay
737	the tribes of jund Filasṭīn fight the Turks in Central Asia
738, 18 January	earthquake
742	death of Muḥammad b. Muslim b. Shihāb al-Zuhrī
743	an irrigation channel is dug in the Jordan Valley
743, February	death of the caliph Hishām b. ʻAbd al-Malik; he is succeeded by al-Walīd b. Yazīd b. ʻAbd al-Malik
744, spring	beginning of wide-spread mutinies against the Umayyads
744, April	the murder of the caliph al-Walīd b. Yazīd, he is succeeded by Yazīd b. al-Walīd b. ʻAbd al-Malik
744, October	the murder of the caliph Yazīd; he is succeeded by Ibrahīm b. al-Walīd b. ʻAbd al-Malik
744, November	the caliph Ibrahīm is defeated; Marwān b. Muḥammad b. Marwān becomes caliph
745	Theodore (I) is appointed as patriarch of Jerusalem
748, 28 January	a strong earthquake, mainly in Tiberias
750, January	defeat of the Umayyads, on the Great Zāb
751, 4 March	Ṣāliḥ b. ʻAlī is appointed governor of jund Filasṭīn
752/3	ʻAṭā' b. Abī Muslim dies in Jericho
753, 8 October	Ṣāliḥ b. ʻAlī's appointment is extended also to Trans-Jordan

754, 9 June	death of the caliph Abū'l-'Abbās al-Saffāḥ; he is succeeded by his brother Abū Ja'far al-Manṣūr
758	Jerusalem is visited by the caliph al-Manṣūr
764	Theodore, patriarch of Jerusalem, proclaims a ban against Cosmas, the iconoclast
765	death of Abū Zur'a Yaḥyā b. Abī 'Amr al-Saybānī, in Ramla
768	death of the poet Ibrahīm b. Abī 'Abla (Abū 'Abla: Shamir b. Yaqẓān), in Jerusalem
770	Elias (II) is appointed patriarch of Jerusalem
770	death of Thawr b. Yazīd
771	Jerusalem is visited by the caliph al-Manṣūr
772, beginning	al-Mahdī orders a mosque to be built in Ascalon
773	death of 'Abdallah b. Shawdhib
775	death of 'Abd al-Wahhāb b. Ibrahīm, the governor of jund Filasṭīn
775, October	death of the caliph al-Manṣūr; he is succeeded by his son, al-Mahdī
778	Ibrahīm b. Adham falls in battle with the Byzantines
778	death of Rajā' b. Mihrān
780	the caliph al-Mahdī visits Jerusalem
780	Ibrahīm b. Ṣāliḥ, the governor of jund Filasṭīn, is removed from office by the caliph al-Mahdī
785, 4 August	death of the caliph al-Mahdī; he is succeeded by his son, al-Hādī
786, 13 September	death of the caliph al-Hādī; he is succeeded by his brother, Hārūn al-Rashīd
786/7	death of the Ascalonian Abū Ghassān Muḥammad b. Muṭarrif
787	Ibrahīm b. Ṣāliḥ is reinstated as governor of jund Filasṭīn instead of Rawḥ b. Ḥātim
788–790	the rebellion of Yaḥyā b. Irmiyā
789, 14 April	Christoforos, a Muslim who converted to Christianity, is executed
789, May	inscription in the pool of Ramla
792/3	war between the tribes in Palestine
793, 29 December	end of the war of the tribes
796	Harthama b. A'yun is removed from his office as governor of jund Filasṭīn
796, 13–20 March	Arabs attack the monastery of Mar Saba
796/7	death of Abū Shihāb Aḥmad al-'Aqrabānī, in 'Aqraba
797	George is appointed patriarch of Jerusalem
797	embassy of Charlemagne to Hārūn al-Rashīd
797	death of Ḥafṣ b. Maysara, in Ascalon

797, November	death of 'Abd al-Rahmān 'Abdallah b. al-Mubārak b. Wāḍiḥ al-Ḥanẓalī al-Tamīmī, in Eilat
798	death of al-Walīd b. Muḥammad al-Muwaqqarī, in Trans-Jordan
799	a monk from Jerusalem visits Charlemagne
801	embassy from Hārūn al-Rashīd to Charlemagne
801	death of Rābi'a b. Isma'īl, Umm al-Khayr, in Jerusalem
ca. 805	writings of the Judaean Desert sect are found in a cave near Jericho
806, December	death of 'Abd al-Raḥmān b. al-Qāsim al-'Utaqī, Ramla
807	Thomas (I) is appointed patriarch of Jerusalem
807	Caliph Hārūn al-Rashīd orders the destruction of the non-Muslim prayer houses; destruction of the church of Mary Magdalene in Jerusalem
807	exchange of embassies between Charlemagne and Hārūn al-Rashīd
807	rebellion of Abū'l-Nidā'
809	rebellion of the tribes in jund Filasṭīn
809, March	death of the caliph Hārūn al-Rashīd; he is succeeded by his son, al-Amīn; his struggle with his brother al-Ma'mūn starts in the same year
810	decree of Charlemagne regarding gifts for Jerusalem
810	rebellions in Palestine, lead by 'Umar
811, September	anti-Abbasid rebellion in Damascus
812, 20 September	death of Abū Sufyān Wakī' b. al-Jarrāḥ b. Māliḥ al-Rawāsī in Jerusalem
813	Christians in Palestine are attacked; many flee the country
813, April	death of Abū Kharbaq Salāma b. Rawḥ, in Eilat
813, September	murder of the caliph al-Amīn; his brother al-Ma'mūn becomes caliph; victory of the 'northern' tribes over the 'southerners'; beginning of the rebellion of Naṣr b. Shabath
814 (?)	famine, caused by locusts, in Palestine
814, January	death of Abū 'Uthmān 'Anbasa b. Khālid b. Yazīd b. Abī'l-Najjād, in Eilat
ca. 815	Masrūr ibn Abī 'Āmir, governor of Nābulus, is executed for having sided with the Samaritans
817	death of Abū Zakkariyyā' Yaḥyā b. 'Īsā b. 'Abd al-Raḥmān al-Nahshalī, in Ramla
817, March	death of Abū 'Abdallah Ḍamra b. Rabī'a al-Qurashī, in Ramla
819, 25 August	death of Abū 'Abdallah Muḥammad b. Idrīs al-Shāfi'ī
820	Basil is appointed patriarch of Jerusalem

ca. 820	repair of the church of the Holy Sepulchre
824, April	death of Abū Ya'qūb Isḥāq b. Ismā'īl b. 'Abd al-A'lā b. 'Abd al-Ḥamīd, in Eilat
ca. 825	severe dispute over the exilarchate
827	'Abdallah b. Ṭāhir, the Abbasid commander, is in Jerusalem
ca. 830	torture of the Graptoi brothers in Constantinople
830/1	al-Ma'mūn stays in al-Shām during the war with the Byzantines; his visit in Jerusalem (?)
831, May–June	al-Ma'mūn's name is inscribed in the Dome of the Rock
833, August	death of the caliph al-Ma'mūn; he is succeeded by his brother al-Mu'taṣim
835	a Nestorian bishop is appointed in Jerusalem
835	the exilarch's letter on matters of the calendar
835	death of al-Ḥasan b. Wāqi', in Ramla
835, June	death of Abū'l-Ḥasan Ādam b. Abī Iyās, in Ascalon
836	Basil, patriarch of Jerusalem, convenes a council of the Church in Jerusalem in order to combat the iconoclastic policy
837	death of Khālid b. Nizār b. al-Mughīra b. Salīm, in Eilat
838	John (VI) is appointed patriarch of Jerusalem
841	'Alī b. Ishāq b. Yahyā b. Mu'ādh al-Dārikānī rebels against Rajā' b. Abī'l-Ḍaḥḥāk, the governor of Damascus and Urdunn
842, January	death of the caliph al-Mu'taṣim; he is succeeded by his son, al-Wāthiq
842	Sergius (I) is appointed patriarch of Jerusalem
842	the rebellion of Abū Ḥarb Tamīm al-Mubarqa'
847	death of the caliph al-Wāthiq; he is succeeded by his brother, al-Mutawakkil
847 (?)	death, in Ramla, of Abū Khālid Yazīd b. Khālid b. Yazīd al-Hamadānī
850	the caliph al-Mutawakkil orders the destruction of the non-Muslims' prayer houses
851/2	a big fire in Ascalon
852/3	death, in Ramla, of Abū'l-Aṣbagh Muḥammad b. Simā'a
853, January	death, in Ascalon, of Muḥammad b. al-Mutawakkil b. Abī'l-Surrī
855	Solomon is appointed patriarch of Jerusalem
855, October	revolt of the Christians in Ḥimṣ
856/7	earthquake in Palestine
858	Frotmund, a French aristocrat, makes a pilgrimage to Jerusalem

859, December	death of the cadi Abu Sa'īd 'Abd al-Raḥmān b. Ibrahīm b. 'Amr b. Maymūn al-Qurashī (who is Duḥaym b. al-Yatīm)
ca. 860	works of broadening the mountain passage, 'Aqaba, near Eilat
860	Theodosius is appointed patriarch of Jerusalem
ca. 860	death of Jehoshaphat b. Josiah, *nāsī* and head of the Palestinian yeshiva; he is succeeded by his brother, Ṣemaḥ
861, December	murder of the caliph al-Mutawakkil; he is succeeded by his son, al-Muntaṣir
862	death of the caliph al-Muntaṣir; he is succeeded by his cousin, al-Musta'īn b. Muḥammad b. al-Mu'taṣim
862	the deacon Theodore copies an uncial codex in Tiberias
864	death of the cadi Abū Bakr Muḥammad b. al-Ḥārith b. al-Nu'mān al-Iyādī
866, end	the caliph al-Mu'tazz appoints 'Īsā b. al-Shaykh as governor in Ramla
866, February (?)	the caliph al-Musta'īn is removed from the throne; he is succeeded by al-Mu'tazz b. al-Mutawakkil
866–868	the Bedouin are in control of Palestine
867, 16 March	death of Hārūn b. Sa'īd b. al-Haytham, in Eilat
ca. 868	the monk Bernard visits Palestine
868, 1 July	death of Abū 'Abd al-Raḥmān Mu'ammal b. Ihāb, in Ramla
868, September	Aḥmad ibn Ṭūlūn arrives in Egypt
869	Elias, the Jerusalemite synkellos, is at the Council of the Church in Constantinople
869, June	the caliph al-Mu'tazz is murdered; he is succeeded by al-Mu'tamid b. al-Mutawakkil
869, 16 December	death of Abū 'Umayr 'Īsā b. Muḥammad b. Isḥāq (who is Ibn al-Naḥḥās)
870, January	death of Muḥammad ibn Karrām, in Jerusalem
870, June	the caliph al-Muhtadī is murdered; he is succeeded by al-Mu'tamid b. al-Mutawakkil
871, May	'Īsā b. Shaykh leaves Palestine; the Turk Amājūr becomes its governor
872/3	Ḥanīnā b. Yannai, of Baghdad, divorces his wife, in Jerusalem
874, 7 February	death of Abū Sulaymān Ayyūb b. Isḥāq b. Ibrahīm b. Sāfārī, in Ramla
876, February	death of Abū 'Imrān Mūsā b. Sahl b. Qādim, in Ramla
877, December	Stephen ibn Ḥakam completes the copying of a treatise by Theodore Abū Qurra, in Ramla
878	Elias (III) is appointed patriarch of Jerusalem

878, May	Aḥmad ibn Ṭūlūn enters Ramla, at the head of his army
879, May	Pope John VIII writes to Elias III, patriarch of Jerusalem
ca. 880	Daniel al-Qūmisī arrives in Palestine
880/81	death of Abū 'Abdallah Muḥammad b. 'Azīz b. 'Abdallah b. Ziyād b. Khālid b. 'Uqayl b. Khālid
881	the appointment of a Christian governor in Ramla is mentioned by the patriarch Elias
884, May	death of Aḥmad ibn Ṭūlūn; he is succeeded by his son, Khumārawayh
884, 16 October	death of Muḥammad b. Ḥammād al-Rāzī al-Ṭabarānī, in Ascalon
885, February	Ibn al-Muwaffaq enters Damascus
885, 5 April	battle of al-Ṭawāḥīn, between Khumārawayh and Ibn al-Muwaffaq
887	death, in Ramla, of the Jerusalemite Aḥmad b. Zakariyyā' b. Yaḥyā
887/8	death of Aḥmad b. Mas'ūd al-Khayyāṭ, in Jerusalem
888, June	Khumārawayh visits Ramla during his military expedition to Syria
888/9	Aḥmad b. 'Abdallah al-Liḥyānī stays in Acre and teaches there
892, January–February	death of 'Abd al-Raḥmān b. Hārūn b. Sa'īd b. al-Haytham, in Ramla
892, October	death of the caliph al-Mu'tamid; he is succeeded by his brother's son, al-Mu'taḍid b. al-Muwaffaq
893	Abū 'Abdallah, the emissary of the Fatimids, arrives in North Africa
893	the Nestorian bishop of Jerusalem is appointed metropolitan of Damascus
ca. 893	Aaron b. Moses b. Meir becomes head of the Palestinian yeshiva
893, November	death of Abū Ḥāmid Ḥamdān b. Ghārim al-Zandī
895	death of Abū Shu'ayb Ṣāliḥ ibn Yūsuf (al-Muqanna'), in Ramla
896	Stephen ibn al-Ḥakam copies the four gospels, in Ramla
897	Hārūn b. Khumārawayh appoints Abu Zur'a Muḥammad b. 'Uthmān as chief cadi of Palestine
901	*anbā* Mūsā b. Ḥakīm al-Qasīs does copying work in Adhruḥ
902, 5 April	death of the caliph al-Mu'taḍid; he is succeeded by his son, al-Muktafī
902, July	'Ubaydallah the Fatimid *mahdī* and his retinue watch falling stars, in Ramla

904, February	death of Aḥmad b. ʻAmr, al-Bazzār al-ʻAtakī, in Ramla
904, end of December	Khumārawayh the Ṭūlūnid is murdered
905, June	al-Khalanjī conquers Ramla
905, December	Aḥmad b. Kayghalagh is defeated by al-Khalanjī, near al-ʻArīsh
906, 4 April	Elias, the patriarch of Jerusalem, annoints Christodulos of Aleppo, as patriarch of Alexandria
906, April-May (?)	Tiberias is conquered by the Qarmaṭīs
906, May	al-Khalanjī is defeated by the Abbasid army
906, 16 June	the Qarmaṭīs raid Hīt (on the Euphrates), after their retreat from Palestine
906/7	death of ʻAbd al-Ṣamad b. Muḥammad b. Abī ʻImrān (Abū Muḥammad al-Hamadānī), in ʻAynūn
908	Sergius (II) is appointed patriarch of Jerusalem
908, August	death of the caliph al-Muktafī; he is succeeded by his brother, al-Muqtadir
ca. 910	Isaac becomes head of the Palestinian yeshiva
912	Leo (I) is appointed as patriarch of Jerusalem
ca. 912	Meir b. Aaron b. Moses becomes head of the Palestinian yeshiva; he is assisted by his son Aaron, who succeeds him after his death (date unknown)
913	*Waqf* inscriptions of a *funduq* in Ramla
913/4	the caliph al-Muqtadir appoints his son Abū'l-ʻAbbās as governor of al-Shām
914/5	death of Aḥmad ibn ʻAlī ibn Shuʻayb al-Nasā'ī, in Ramla
914/5	death of Abū Zurʻa Muḥammad b. ʻUthmān, former chief cadi of Palestine, in Damascus
915/6	death of Abū Bakr Yamūt b. al-Muzarraʻ, in Tiberias
917, October	Funerary inscription on the Temple Mount: Hiba b. Sulaymān and Salāma b. Hiba
918, October	death of Abū'l-Ḥasan Manṣūr b. Ismāʻīl al-Ḍarīr, of Ramla
918, December	death of Abū ʻAbdallah Aḥmad b. Yaḥyā, Ibn al-Jallā', in Ramla
918/9	the Abbasid army passes through Palestine on its way to Egypt
920	death of Abū ʻAbdallah al-Tawwazī, in Tiberias
921, summer	beginning of the calendar dispute between Babylonia and Palestine
922, September	Meir Gaon sends his son Aaron to Jerusalem, to proclaim the calendar order for the next year
923, 3 January	Saadia Gaon writes his third letter on the calendar dispute

ca. 926	Abraham b. Aaron b. Meir becomes head of the Palestinian yeshiva
927	death of Abū'l-Qāsim ʻAbdallah b. Muḥammad b. Jaʻfar al-Qazwīnī, cadi of Ramla
928	Muḥammad ibn Tughj (the Ikhshīd) becomes governor of jund Filasṭīn
929	Athanasius (I) is appointed patriarch of Jerusalem
ca. 930	Abū'l-Hawā' Nasīm b. ʻAbdallah is appointed governor of Jerusalem
931, July	Muḥammad ibn Tughj (the Ikhshīd) is appointed governor of Damascus; al-Rashīdī is appointed as governor of jund Filasṭīn in his stead
932, 31 October	the caliph al-Muqtadir is murdered; he is succeeded by his brother, al-Qāhir
ca. 933	Aaron ha-Kohen becomes head of the Palestinian yeshiva
933, March	funeral of Takīn, governor of Egypt, in Jerusalem
934, 24 April	the caliph al-Qāhir is removed from his throne; he is succeeded by al-Rāḍī b. al-Muqtadir
935, July	Mufliḥ the black is appointed as governor of Jerusalem instead of Nasīm b. ʻAbdallah
935, 9 December	death of Abū'l-Qāsim Muḥammad ibn al-Ḥasan al-Nakhāʻī, Ibn Ka's, in Ramla
936	al-Masʻūdī visits Tiberias
936, February	death of Abū Bakr Muḥammad b. Aḥmad b. ʻUmar (al-Ḍarīr), in Ramla
937	the Ikhshīd writes to Emperor Romanus boasting about his control of the holy places
937	Christodulus (I) is appointed patriarch of Jerusalem
937	death of Ismāʻīl b. ʻAbd al-Wāḥid al-Rabaʻī al-Maqdisī, in Ramla
937	death of Abū Bakr al-Khiḍr b. Muḥammad al-Tanūkhī, in Acre
937, 26 March	the church of the Resurrection is burnt down by Muslims; more churches in Jerusalem are attacked
939, January	death of Abū Nuʻaym Muḥammad b. Jaʻfar al-Kharāʻiṭī
939, 4 March	death of Faḍl b. Jaʻfar ibn al-Furāt, in Ramla
939, 17 October	Ramla is conquered by Ibn Rā'iq
939, end	battle of al-ʻArīsh, between Ibn Rā'iq and the Ikhshīd
ca. 940	Ikhshīdid pressure on Byzantium, through the patriarch of Jerusalem, to stop the maltreatment of Muslim prisoners
940, 24 June	the battle of Lajjūn, between Ibn Rā'iq and the Ikhshīd
943, 14 April	funerary inscription of Jabūr, a Christian of Ramla
945	death of David (b. Daniel?) al-Qūmisī, in Jerusalem

946, July	Palestine is invaded by Sayf al-Dawla, the Ḥamdānid
946, July	funeral of the Ikhshīd, Muḥammad ibn Tughj, in Jerusalem
946, August	the emperor's emissary to jund Filasṭīn travels to Egypt in the company of Kāfūr
946, 22 December	the battle of Iksāl; the Ikhshīdid army defeats the Ḥamdānid Sayf al-Dawla
947	description of the Paschal fire by Nicetas, a Byzantine official
948	death of the cadi of Ramla, Abū'l-Ṭayyib Muḥammad b. Muḥammad al-Ḥanẓalī
950	Agathon is appointed patriarch of Jerusalem
951/2	inaugural inscription of a building in Jerusalem: Aḥmad ibn Abī Karāsa
952, February	death of the grammarian Abū'l-Qāsim 'Abd al-Raḥmān ibn Isḥāq al-Zajjājī al-Nihāwandī
953/4	death of al-Ḥasan ibn Ṭughj, the Ikhshīd's brother, in Ramla
958/9	death of al-Ḥasan b. Ḥajjāj b. Ghālib (Abū 'Alī ibn Ḥaydara al-Zayyāt), of Tiberias
959, 20 January	funeral of Anūjūr, son of the Ikhshīd, in Jerusalem
960	query of the communities of the Rhine to the Palestinian yeshiva
961/2	inscription of the Temple Mount, about the building of a wall to the order of 'Alī, son of the Ikhshīd, and Kāfūr
962	conquest of Aleppo by the Byzantines
962	rebellion in Trans-Jordan, lead by Muḥammad b. Aḥmad al-Sulamī
962, 5 December	Muḥammad b. Aḥmad al-Sulamī, leader of the rebellion in Trans-Jordan, is exhibited before the people of Fustat
963	death of the Jerusalemite Abū'l-Ḥusayn Aḥmad ibn Maḥmūd al-Shama'ī
964	John (VII) is appointed as patriarch of Jerusalem
964, May	Tiberias is raided by the Qarmaṭīs
ca. 965	death of the cadi of Ramla, 'Uthmān b. Muḥammad b. Shādhān
966, 8 January	funeral of 'Alī, son of the Ikhshīd, in Jerusalem
966, end of May	anti-Christian riots in Jerusalem
966, June (?)	Christodulus (II) is appointed patriarch of Jerusalem
967	al-Ḥasan al-A'ṣam, leader of the Qarmaṭīs, is in Ramla
967, 30 July	Ya'qūb ibn Killis' conversion to Islam
968	conquest of Ṭarsūs by the Byzantines
968, April	death of Kāfūr, ruler of Egypt; his funeral takes place in Jerusalem

968, 28 October	battle (in Ramla?) between the Qarmaṭīs and the Ikhshīdids; defeat of al-Ḥasan the Ikhshīdid
968, 23 December	death of Christodulus II, patriarch of Jerusalem, in Egypt
969	Thomas (II) is appointed patriarch of Jerusalem
969, 22 (or 24) February	al-Ḥasan b. 'Ubaydallah the Ikhshīdid leaves Egypt for Ramla
969, 5 August	the Fatimid army enters Fustat
969, October–November	Ramla is besieged by the Qarmaṭīs
970	Judith, grandmother of the emperor Henry II, makes a pilgrimage to Jerusalem
970, beginning of summer	the Fatimid army is sent to Palestine
ca. 970	'Ezrūn ha-Kohen becomes head of the Palestinian yeshiva
970, 24 May	conquest of Ramla by the Fatimid army
970, middle of October	conquest of Damascus by the Fatimid army
971, August	Sa'āda b. Ḥiyān is appointed as governor of Ramla by Jawhar
971, August–September	conquest of Damascus by the Qarmaṭīs and the Banū 'Uqayl
971, 5 September	conquest of Ramla by the Qarmaṭīs
971, 12 October	death of the Tiberian writer Abū'l-Qāsim Sulaymān b. Aḥmad al-Ṭabarānī
971, end of December	the Qarmaṭī invasion of Egypt is repelled by Jawhar
972	conquest of Nisibis by the Byzantines
972/3	al-Ḥasan al-A'ṣam becomes the exclusive leader of the Qarmaṭīs
973, April	Aḥmad b. al-Musawwir, governor of Damascus, is removed from office by the Fatimids
973, May	al-Mu'izz, the Fatimid caliph, arrives in Egypt
973, summer	Palestine and southern Syria are again conquered by the Fatimids
973, October	Ya'qūb ibn Killis is entrusted by the caliph al-Mu'izz with the internal affairs and the taxes
974, spring	the Qarmaṭīs and their allies attack Egypt
975, end of the winter	the northern coastal area of Palestine is attacked by Alptakīn
975, April	Damascus is conquered by Alptakīn
975, 24 December	death of al-Mu'izz, the Fatimid caliph; he is succeeded by his son, al-'Azīz
976, May	a Fatimid army sets out northwards and conquers Palestine

976, 1 July	the Fatimid army reaches Damascus
977, January	retreat of the Fatimid army from Damascus
977, 12 March	Ramla is conquered by the Qarmaṭīs
977, 17 March	death of al-Ḥasan al-A'ṣam, leader of the Qarmaṭīs, in Ramla
978	Joseph (II) is appointed patriarch of Jerusalem
978, beginning of April	Jawhar and the remnants of his army hand over Ascalon to Alptakīn
978, June	al-'Azīz leads a huge army into Palestine
978, 15 August	battle of al-Ṭawāḥīn, between the Fatimid army and Alptakīn with his allies; victory of the Fatimids
978, 31 August	Alptakīn is caught by al-Mufarrij b. Daghfal
978, 28 October	al-'Azīz arrives in Egypt after the victory
978/9, winter	Faḍl b. Ṣāliḥ conducts negotiations with Abū Taghlib, the Ḥamdānid
979, 3 May	Abū Taghlib the Ḥamdānid is informed that he is invited to Egypt, by al-'Azīz
979, August	Abū Taghlib the Ḥamdānid sets out to attack Ramla
979, 29 August	Abū Taghlib the Ḥamdānid is defeated by the Fatimid army commanded by Faḍl b. Ṣāliḥ, near Ramla
979, end of August	an expeditionary army is sent by al-'Azīz to Damascus
980, July	death of Aḥmad b. 'Aṭā' al-Rūdhbādī, in Tyre
980, 29 November	a marriage deed from Damascus, apparently the marriage of 'Adī b. Manasse ibn al-Qazzāz: TS 8.129
981, June	Damascus is besieged by a Fatimid army under the command of Subuktakīn
981, summer	rebellion of the Bedouin in Palestine, led by the Banū Jarrāḥ
982/3, summer	death of Abū Bakr Muḥammad b. al-'Abbās b. Waṣīf, in Gaza (?)
983	Agapius is appointed patriarch of Jerusalem
983, 5 July	conquest of Damascus by the Fatimid army
983, autumn	al-Mufarrij b. Daghfal takes part in the Byzantine siege of Aleppo
983, December	the Fatimid administration hands over Damascus to Bakjūr
984	Orestes is appointed patriarch of Jerusalem
984	death of 'Abd al-Raḥīm b. Muḥammad al-Fāriqī, a preacher, in Ramla
ca. 985	Shams al-Dīn al-Muqaddasī writes his book on the Muslim lands
987/8	death of Abū'l-Ḥusayn Muḥammad b. Aḥmad al-Malaṭī, in Ascalon (?)
988	Faḍl b. Ṣāliḥ suppresses a rebellion in the Delta region
988	pilgrimage to Jerusalem of Gontier, abbot of the monastery of St Aubain in Angers

988, May	a Fatimid army sets out to conquer Damascus and is encamped in Ramla
988, 29 October	Bakjūr leaves Damascus
989	Joseph b. Isaac ibn Abītūr writes to Samuel ha-Kohen Gaon b. Joseph
989	Joseph b. Jacob ha-Ma'arāvī in Jerusalem copies the book of the first prophets
989, 18 July	Sherira and Hayy write to Samuel ha-Kohen Gaon b. Joseph
990	Adalpert, bishop of the Slavs, performs a pilgrimage to Jerusalem
991	'Amīd al-Dawla Abū Muḥammad al-Ḥasan b. Ṣāliḥ al-Rūdhbādī is appointed commander of the army in al-Shām
991, 24 February	death of the wazīr Ya'qūb ibn Killis
992	pilgrimage to Jerusalem of Adso, abbot of the Benedictine monastery in Lotharingia
993	Faḍl b. Ṣālih is put in charge of the finances of the Fatimid regime
993	David b. Boaz b. Jehoshaphat, a Karaite *nāsī*, writes a commentary on Ecclesiastes
993, May	'Īsā b. Nestorius is appointed wazīr
993, 29 October	Hugo of Tuscany donates property to the Holy Sepulchre
994	death of Abū'l-'Abbās 'Ubaydallah b. Muḥammad al-Bustī
995	Orestes, patriarch of Jerusalem, sends an embassy to the Pope
996	Rebellion in Tyre, led by 'Allāqa, a mariner
996, 14 October	death of the caliph al-'Azīz; he is succeeded by his son, al-Ḥākim
997, March	'Īsā b. Nestorius is put to death, on the order of al-Ḥākim
997, April	the battle of Ascalon, between the Berber and the Turk unities of the Fatimid army; victory of the Berbers
997, summer (?)	Jaysh ibn Ṣamṣāma attacks the Bedouin in Palestine
998, May	a Fatimid army takes control of Tyre
998, end (?)	a Byzantine embassy arrives in Egypt for negotiations
999	Fatimid victory over the Byzantines
999	Barjawān is put to death, on the order of al-Ḥākim
1000, 14 January	Bishāra is appointed as governor of Tiberias by al-Ḥākim
1001, 28 April	Isaac he-ḥāvēr b. Solomon he-ḥāvēr b. Meir Gaon completes the copying of *sefer ha-dīnīm* (book of laws), in Acre (?)

1002	Stephen, king of Hungary, founds a monastery in Jerusalem
1002, beginning	Samuel b. Hosha'nā describes the sufferings of the Palestinian Jewish communities
1002, 8 July	a Christian funerary inscription in Jerusalem
1003	first persecutions by al-Ḥākim; the church of St Mark in Fustat is destroyed
1004	Sahl ibn Killis (Ya'qūb's brother) is put to death, on the order of al-Ḥākim
ca. 1005	Abū'l-Ẓahir Maḥmūd b. Muḥammad al-Naḥwī, a high official of the Fatimids, is put to death on the order of al-Ḥākim
1006	the rebel Abū Rakwa is defeated by Faḍl b. Ṣāliḥ
1006, 18 July	'Alī b. Mufarrij, the Jarrāḥid, is given a ceremonial dress by al-Ḥākim
1007	al-Ḥākim hands over seven villages in Palestine to the ruler of Aleppo
1007, spring	conflict among the Christians in Egypt and in Palestine over the date of Easter
1007, 24 June	Samuel 'the third' b. Hosha'nā is in Damascus
1007, 1 September	Ḥanania ha-Kohen *av-bēt-dīn* b. Joseph Gaon is in Fustat
1008	Foulque Nerra, Count of Anjou, goes on pilgrimage to Jerusalem
1008, 15 November	death of Abū Aḥmad 'Abdallah b. Bakr, in Tiberias (?)
1009, 17 July	Faḍl b. Ṣāliḥ is put to death on the order of al-Ḥākim
1009, 28 September	destruction of the church of the Resurrection
ca. 1010	death of 'Abdallah b. al-Walīd al-Anṣārī, in Jerusalem
1010/11	flight of Abū'l-Qāsim al-Ḥusayn b. 'Ali *al-wazīr al-maghribī*, from Egypt to Palestine
1011, 21 January	Ismā'īl b. Ṣāliḥ (Faḍl's brother), al-Ḥusayn b. Jawhar, and 'Abd al-'Azīz b. al-Nu'mān, are put to death on al-Ḥākim's order
1011, February	uprising of the Bedouin in Palestine begins
1011, end	death of Shĕmaria b. Elḥanan
1011, 31 December	Jews in Fustat are attacked during the funeral of the cantor Palṭī'ēl
1012	beginning of al-Ḥākim's oppressive decrees against Christians and Jews
1012, April	al-Mufarrij b. Daghfal appoints Theophilus patriarch of Jerusalem
1012, 13 September	Abū'l-Futūḥ al-Ḥasan b. Ja'far is proclaimed caliph by the tribes of Palestine (al-Rāshid bi'llāh), in Ramla
1013, July	a Fatimid army under 'Alī b. Ja'far ibn Fallāḥ sets out for Palestine

1014/5	destruction of the synagogues in Fustat
1014/5	a fragment of a deed from Ramla
1015, 4 September	earthquake in Palestine; the dome of the Dome of the Rock collapses
1016, 10 September	Ḥusn, daughter of Kūshnām, dedicates a Bible to the Karaite congregation in Jerusalem
1016/7	Mukhtār al-Dawla ibn Nizāl al-Kitāmī is appointed by al-Ḥākim as governor of Tripoli
1017, spring	ʻAzrīqām the scribe dedicates a Bible to the Karaite synagogue in Ramla
1018/9	death of Abū'l-Fatḥ Muḥammad b. Ibrahīm al-Bazzāz al-Ṭarsūsī (Ibn al-Baṣrī), in Jerusalem
1019/20	Abū Bakr al-Wāsiṭī writes his book on the praises of Jerusalem
1020, January	death of Theophilus, patriarch of Jerusalem
1020, 10 July	Nicephorus is appointed patriarch of Jerusalem
1020, November–December	a decree regarding the protection of churches and monasteries is issued by al-Ḥākim
1021, 13 February	the caliph al-Ḥākim is murdered; he is succeeded by his son, al-Ẓāhir
1021, September	al-Karājilī meets Abū'l-Qasam ʻĪsā b. ʻAlī al-ʻUmarī in Ramla
1021, 24 November	Samuel b. Jacob receives payment for copying the books of the prophets
1022/3	inscription on the Temple Mount: construction works ordered by the caliph al-Ẓāhir
1023	Anūshtakīn al-Dizbirī is appointed as governor of jund Filasṭīn
1023, 10 February	David ha-Levi b. Isaac is put in charge of the Fatimid finances
1023, 21 August	a son of al-Mufarrij the Jarrāḥid visits Fustat and is received with great honours
1023, 28 November	the marriage deed of the wife of Nathan ha-Kohen ha-Ṣefātī b. Solomon (Tyre?)
1024	Abū'l-ʻAssāf al-Kabbāshī becomes cadi of Ramla
1024, April	the pilgrims' caravan from Khurāsān passes through Palestine
1024, 18 May	Muḥassin b. Badūs is appointed to supervise the revenue from Palestine
1024, May–July (September?)	Ramla is taken by the Bedouin
1024, June	ʻAbdallah b. Idrīs al-Jaʻfarī and the Bedouin raid Eilat
1024, 12 June	Abū Ṭālib al-Gharābilī is appointed collector of the *kharāj* in Ramla, instead of ʻUbaydallah b. Yūnus

1024, 24 October	Muḥassin b. Badūs, the Fatimid treasurer, is executed for his ties with the tribes of Palestine
1024, November	al-Ḥassān b. al-Mufarrij the Jarrāḥid writes to the Fatimid caliph about his conditions for peace
1024, November	battle between Anūshtakīn al-Dizbirī and al-Ḥassān the Jarrāḥid, near Ascalon
1024, 26 November	Anūshtakīn al-Dizbirī receives the title *amīr al-umarā'*
1024, end	Aleppo is attacked by Ṣāliḥ b. Mirdās
1024/5, winter	severe famine in Egypt
1025, beginning	the Bedouin abscond with a transport of apples from the Lebanon to Egypt
1025, January	al-'Arīsh and al-Faramā are attacked by the Bedouin
1025, 16 January	Aleppo is conquered by Ṣāliḥ b. Mirdās
1025, 24 January	the road to Eilat is obstructed and the Egyptian pilgrims are forced to return home
1025, February	beginning of al-Dizbirī's offensive in Palestine
1025, 14 February (10 Dhū'l-Ḥijja, *'īd al-aḍḥā*)	Anūshtakīn al-Dizbirī prays in the Ramla mosque
1025, end of February	Ramla is retaken by al-Ḥassān the Jarrāḥid
1025, spring	death of Josiah Gaon b. Aaron
1025, spring	liquidation of remaining Jarrāḥid units in Palestine, by al-Dizbirī; al-Ḥassān the Jarrāḥid flees to the Byzantines
1025, 13 March	the fortress of Aleppo is conquered by Ṣāliḥ b. Mirdās
1025, 21 August	death of Solomon ha-Kohen Gaon b. Joseph; he is succeeded by Solomon b. Judah
1026	Anūshtakīn al-Dizbirī is imprisoned in Ascalon
1026	death of Elḥanan b. Shemaria
1026, 11 March	death of Josiah, the son of the *ḥāvēr* of Gaza Yeshū'ā b. Nathan
1026, April–May	Abraham b. Solomon b. Judah is in Fustat
1026, July	Abū'l-Faraj Hārūn completes his book *al-mushtamil*, in Jerusalem
1027	armistice agreement between the Fatimids and the Byzantines
1027, March	William of Angoulême and a group of pilgrims arrive in Jerusalem
1028, 15 January	the court in Fustat deals with the inheritance of Khalaf b. Isaac, of Acre
1028, July	death of Sinān b. 'Ulayyān, leader of the Banū Kalb, allies of the Jarrāḥids
1028, 20 December	arrival in Palestine of a Fatimid army, under al-Dizbirī
1029, 12 May	the Bedouin of Ṣāliḥ b. Mirdās (the Banū 'Uqayl) are defeated by the Fatimid army at Uqḥuwāna

1029, summer	Abraham b. Solomon b. Judah travels to Tyre and Aleppo
1029, 9 June	a ban is proclaimed in 'the cave' in Jerusalem, against the ('Babylonian') adversary of Ephraim b. Shemaria
1030	Nicephorus (I) is appointed patriarch of Jerusalem
1032	inscription in the Dome of the Rock: the reconstruction was completed on Caliph al-Ẓāhir's orders
1032	death of Abū Muḥammad Ismā'īl b. Rajā' b. Sa'īd, in Ramla
1033, 5–6 December	earthquakes in Ramla and various regions of Palestine
1034	inscription on the Temple Mount: construction works ordered by the caliph al-Ẓāhir
1034	pilgrimage to Jerusalem of Adhémar de Chabannes
1034, 3 April	a decree in favour of the Karaites is issued by al-Ẓāhir
1034, 7 April	collapse of a wall close to 'the cave', the synagogue of the Jerusalem Jews
1035	death of Joseph the scribe, son-in-law of Ephraim b. Shemaria
1035, 6 October	inscription on the Temple Mount: completion of a dome, on the order of the wazīr al-Jarjarā'ī
1035, 15 October	a copy of the introduction to the Talmud by Samuel b. Ḥofni is completed, in Jerusalem
1036	Ioannikos is appointed patriarch of Jerusalem
1036	the church of the Resurrection is reconstructed
1036, June	death of the caliph al-Ẓāhir; he is succeeded by his son, al-Mustanṣir
1036/7	Joseph ha-Kohen al-Baṣīr finishes the writing of his 'book of precepts', in Jerusalem
1037	power of attorney from Aleppo
1037, 9 September	marriage of Sahlān b. Abraham
1037/8	an armistice is agreed between the Fatimids and the Byzantines
1038, 18 April	death of Hayy Gaon
1038, autumn	Daniel b. Azariah is in the Maghrib
1038, 23 October	beginning of the conflict between Solomon b. Judah and Nathan b. Abraham
1038, 24 October	Nathan b. Abraham is proclaimed Gaon by his followers
1039, 12 February	mass gathering of Nathan b. Abraham's followers in Ramla, during the reading of the *megillā*
1039, spring and summer	news of the strength of Nathan b. Abraham's followers in Ramla
1039, summer	Jacob b. 'Amram, the Nagid of Qayrawān, is requested by the followers of Solomon b. Judah to intervene in the conflict

1039, 12 October	gathering on the Mount of Olives, on *hosha'nā rabbā*, with many of Nathan b. Abraham's supporters taking part; Solomon b. Judah is taken ill
1039, middle of November	the synagogue of 'the Palestinians' in Fustat is closed
1039, December–1040, March	Nathan b. Abraham is in Fustat
ca. 1040	Ḥesed b. Sahl al-Tustarī is appointed chief official of al-Dizbirī
1041, 20 February	the synagogue of 'the Palestinians' in Ramla is closed for several days
1041, 27 March	a *rōsh kallā* from Mosul arrives in Ramla
1041, 8 May	Joseph b. Kulayb writes an account on matters related to the conflict, from Ramla, to Nathan b. Abraham, who is (probably) in Tyre
1041, autumn	the synagogue of 'the Palestinians' in Fustat is opened by Nathan b. Abraham's faction, for themselves
1041, end (?)	a petition to the caliph, by the supporters of Solomon b. Judah
1042 (?)	al-Dizbirī quarrels with the wazīr al-Jarjarā'ī and flees to Aleppo
1042, 8 October	agreement concluded between Solomon b. Judah and Nathan b. Abraham
1043, beginning	death of Tobiah b. Daniel, 'the third' of the yeshiva
1044	Georgius Mtzamindeli, one of the saints of the Church of Georgia, visits Palestine
1044, summer	Abraham b. Sahl al-Tustarī is appointed as *wāsiṭa*
1045, spring	Naṣr Khusraw is in Jerusalem
1047, February	Naṣr Khusraw is in Tyre
1047, 1 March	Naṣr Khusraw visits Ramla
1047, 25 October	murder of Abraham b. Sahl al-Tustarī
1048	the reconstruction of the church of the Resurrection is completed
1049	an order of Georgian monks is founded at the church of the Holy Sepulchre
1049, summer	a Fatimid army under Rifq is encamped in Ramla, on its way to Damascus
1049 (or 1050), summer	Ḥesed b. Sahl al-Tustarī is executed
1049, September (?)	rebellion of the Bedouin in Palestine
1050, 1 June	the cadi Abū Muḥammad al-Ḥasan b. 'Alī is appointed wazīr
1051, April	death of the Gaon Solomon b. Judah
1051, 20 December	efforts to reach a compromise between Daniel b. Azariah and Joseph ha-Kohen b. Solomon Gaon

1052, March	a Karaite delegation examines the state of the grain in the Gaza region
1052, 19 April	beginning of the tribes' taking control of Qayrawān
1052, August	agreement between Daniel b. Azariah and Joseph ha-Kohen b. Solomon Gaon
1052, 18 September	gathering on *hosha'nā rabbā* on the Mount of Olives; Daniel b. Azariah is proclaimed Gaon
1053	Odilus of Rouergue dedicates property to the church of the Holy Sepulchre
1053, middle of December	death of Joseph ha-Kohen *av-bēt-dīn* b. Solomon Gaon
1055	Conquest of Baghdad by the Saljūqs
1055, December	death of Abū'l-Faraj 'Abd al-Wahhāb b. al-Ḥusayn al-Ghazzāl, in Tyre
1055–1059	drought and plagues in Egypt, Palestine, Syria and Iraq
1055/6	conflict between the Fatimids and the Byzantines; confiscation of property of the church of the Resurrection
1056	Georgius Mtzamindeli visits Palestine again
1057, 21 March	'Eli ha-Kohen writes a piyyūṭ honouring Daniel b. Azariah
1057, May	death of Muḥammad b. 'Alī al-Karājikī, in Tyre
1057, September	Abraham ha-Kohen b. Isaac b. Furāt is in Jerusalem
1057, November	destruction of Qayrawān
1057, 17 December	Mūsā b. Jacob writes from Damascus on business matters, to Abū'l-A'lā Joseph b. Da'ūd b. Sha'yā in Fustat
1058	Menas is appointed patriarch of Jerusalem
1058	birth of David b. Daniel b. Azariah
1058, March	execution of Abū Muḥammad al-Yāzūrī
1059	Israel b. Nathan (Sahlūn) copies the mishnā orders *nāshīm* and *nezīqīn*, in Jerusalem
1059	Sophronius (II) is appointed patriarch of Jerusalem
1059	death of Judah ibn al-'Uṣfūra
1059	long stay of Daniel b. Azariah in Fustat
1059, end	beginning of Daniel b. Azariah's illness
1060	collapse of the lighting system of the Dome of the Rock
1062	Makīn al-Dawla al-Ḥasan b. Mulham is appointed governor of Tiberias and Acre by al-Mustanṣir
1062, March	queries from Fustat to the Gaon Daniel b. Azariah
1062, August	death of the Gaon Daniel b. Azariah
1063	the wall around the Christian quarter of Jerusalem is completed
1063	the cadi Abū Muḥammad ibn 'Alī ibn Abī 'Aqīl is in control of Tyre

1064 (?)	Ingulph visits Jaffa
1065–1072	drought in Egypt
1065	the head of the Nestorians in Jerusalem gets the rank of metropolitan
1065, 15 March	the pilgrims headed by Gunther, bishop of Bamberg, are attacked by Bedouin
1067, summer	Abiathar ha-Kohen b. Solomon Gaon is in Fustat
1067, November	the Turks in the Fatimid army raid Ramla
1068, 18 March	Eilat destroyed by earthquake
1068, 29 May	severe earthquake in Palestine
1070	Mark (II) is appointed patriarch of Jerusalem
1070, summer	a Fatimid army under Badr al-Jamālī attacks Tyre
1071	Saljūq victory over the Byzantines at Manzikert
1071	Ṭāhir b. Muḥammad b. Salāma al-Quḍā'ī al-Miṣrī teaches traditions in Jerusalem
1071, spring	Abiathar ha-Kohen b. Elijah Gaon is in Fustat
1071, end	the Turcomans invade Palestine, under Atsiz b. Uwaq
1071/2	death in Damascus of Aḥmad b. Muḥammad al-Kattānī, of Ramla
1072, 5 July	deathbed will of Maymūn b. Khalfa al-Maghribī
1073	death of the cadi Abū Muḥammad ibn Abī 'Aqīl, master of Tyre
1073, June–July	conquest of Jerusalem by the Turcomans
1073/4	death of Abū 'Abdallah Muḥammad b. Muḥammad al-Ṭāliqānī, in Tyre (?)
1074	conquest of Acre and Tiberias by the Turcomans
1075, April–May	Shuklī is driven out of Acre by the army of Atsiz, which also conquers Tiberias, and slaughters its inhabitants
1076, 10 August	Abraham b. Nathan is in Ramla
1076, 2 October	beginning of Atsiz' expedition against Egypt
1077, 22 January	Solomon ha-Kohen b. Joseph *av-bēt-dīn* writes a piyyūṭ on the events in Palestine
1077, 19 February	defeat of Atsiz in Egypt
1077, March	Abiathar ha-Kohen b. Elijah Gaon and Abraham b. Nathan are in Fustat
1077, 12 June	deed of divorce from Ramla: Yefet b. Abraham divorces Sitt al-Ḥusn
1077/8	Saadia *he-ḥāvēr* b. Israel writes a responsum on calendar matters, in Acre
1078	rebellion of the Muslims in Jerusalem against the Turcomans
ca. 1078	death of the nagid Judah b. Saadia
1078	David b. Daniel b. Azariah departs for Egypt

1078/9 (?)	the Palestinian yeshiva is transferred to Tyre
1078/9	Abū'l-Fatḥ Naṣr b. Ibrahīm al-Maqdisī al-Nābulusī, leader of the Shāfi'ites, leaves Jerusalem to live in Damascus
1078/9	execution of Atsiz; Tutush and Artuq take control of Palestine
1079, summer	first evidence of the Palestinian yeshiva being in Tyre
1079, 13 May	Solomon and Isaac, great-grandchildren of Meir Gaon, sign as witnesses a court document in Tripoli (Syria)
1079, 15 November	David b. Daniel writes that he intends to set out from Damīra to Fustat
1079, end	David b. Daniel arrives in Fustat
1080	Abū Muḥammad Hiyāj b. 'Ubayd, of Ḥiṭṭīn, is killed in Mecca
1081, 28 September	gathering in Tyre, on Hosha'nā rabbā
1082, 15 January	David b. Daniel marries Nāshiya, daughter of Moses ha-Kohen b. Aaron
1082, 18 September	gathering in Haifa, on Hosha'nā rabbā; sanctification of the year, proclamation of the calendar order
1082/3	Jerusalem is handed over to Artuq, by Turmush, Atsiz' appointee (?)
1083, November	death of Elijah ha-Kohen Gaon b. Solomon
1084	Simon (II) is appointed patriarch of Jerusalem
1085	Solomon b. Ḥayyim, 'the seventh', in Fustat, is paid back 20 dinars which he had transferred to the Rabbanite Jews remaining in Jerusalem
1085, April	the Saljūqs try to conquer Ascalon from the Fatimids
1086	Palestine is handed over by Tutush to Artuq
1087	death of Salāma b. Ismā'īl al-Maqdisī al-Ḍarīr, in Jerusalem
1087/8	pilgrimage of Urso, archbishop of Bari
1089	Tyre, Sidon, Beirut, Jubayl, Acre, are conquered by a Fatimid army under Munīr (or: Naṣīr) al-Dawla al-Juyūshī, who rebels against the Fatimids
1091	death of Artuq the Saljūqid
1091	Abū 'Alī Jamīl b. Yūsuf b. Ismā'īl al-Mardānī, of Bāniyās, dies in Damascus
1091, autumn	David b. Daniel starts calling himself exilarch
1092	Mālik b. Aḥmad al-Bāniyāsī is killed in Baghdad (in the big fire)
1092–1095	Abū Bakr ibn al-'Arabī stays in Jerusalem
1093	Muslims in the coastal cities of Palestine bar Christian pilgrims from entering the country
1093	Abū 'Alī al-Ḥasan b. 'Abd al-Ṣamad b. Abī'l-Shiḥna, of Ascalon, is killed

1093, 12 July	suppression of Munīr al-Dawla's rebellion in Tyre
1093, August (approximately)	Abraham b. Nathan and other emissaries of David b. Daniel arrive in Tyre
1093, 23 September	a gathering of Rabbanites and Karaites in Tyre joins the acceptance of David b. Daniel as exilarch
1094 (?)	rebellion of al-Katīla, governor of Tyre, against the Fatimids
1094, 19 January	death of Abū'l-Faraj 'Abd al-Wāḥid b. Aḥmad al-Shīrāzī al-Anṣārī, in Damascus
1094, March	Badr al-Jamālī is taken ill; he is succeeded by his son, al-Afḍal
1094, May	Mevorakh b. Saadia is reinstated; end of the affair of David b. Daniel
1095, January	Yashar b. Ḥesed al-Tustarī finishes the copying of a treatise on incest regulations
1095, 26 February	Tutush is killed in battle
1096	al-Ghazālī arrives in Jerusalem
1096	Euthymius is appointed patriarch of Jerusalem
1096, 26 December	death of Abū'l-Fatḥ Naṣr b. Ibrahīm al-Maqdisī al-Nābulusī, in Damascus
1097, August–September	suppression of Katīla's rebellion in Tyre by a Fatimid army
1097, 21 October–1098, 2 June	siege of Antioch by the Crusaders
1098	death of Ṣamdūn b. Ḥusayn, in Bāniyās
1098, 26 August	al-Afḍal captures Jerusalem from the Saljūqs
1099, May	conquest of Caesarea by the Crusaders
1099, 15 July	conquest of Jerusalem by the Crusaders
1104	conquest of Acre by the Crusaders
1105, beginning	revenue of the *heqdēsh* for the poor of Jerusalem is transferred from Fustat to Abiathar ha-Kohen in Tyre
1110/11	death of Abū'l-Ḥasan Idrīs b. Ḥamza, who had been head of the Shāfi'ites in Jerusalem, in Samarqand
1111	siege of Damascus by the Crusaders
1111, 2 December	death of the nagid Mevorakh b. Saadia
1112, December	death of the Jerusalemite cadi Muḥammad b. al-Ḥasan al-Balāshā'ūnī, in Damascus
1124	death of the Shāfi'ite scholar Abū'l-Fatḥ Sulṭān b. Ibrahīm, of Jerusalem
1124, 8 July	conquest of Tyre by the Crusaders
1126	the *hashīshiyya* (the Assassins) conquer Bāniyās
1129, September	conquest of Bāniyās by the Crusaders
1130	Abū Isḥāq Ibrahīm b. Yaḥyā b. 'Uthmān, of Gaza, dies in Khurāsān
1144	death of Nathan ha-Kohen b. Mevorakh, of Ascalon
1153, 31 August	the head of al-Ḥusayn b. 'Alī is transferred from Ascalon to Fustat

BIBLIOGRAPHICAL INDEX

Entries are indexed by section numbers (inclusive of the notes) rather than page numbers

Hebrew, Aramaic, Syriac, Judaeo-Arabic

Abraham Ibn Da'ūd, *Sefer ha-qabbālā* (the Book of Tradition), ed. G. D. Cohen, Philadelphia 1967 773, 833, 917

Abraham Ibn Ezra, *Commentary* (as printed in the editions of the Hebrew Bible) 827, 940

Abraham b. Moses Maimonides (Maimuni) *Commentary on Genesis and Exodus*, ed. E. Wiesenberg, London 1959 337, 338

Abraham b. Moses Maimonides (Maimuni), *Teshūvōt* (*Responsa*), ed. A. H. Freimann, transl. S. D. Goitein, Jerusalem 1937 853

Abraham Zacuto, *Sefer ha-yuḥasīn*, ed. H. Filipowski, London 1857 729

Abramson, S., *Ba-merkāzīm u-va-tefūṣōt*, Jerusalem 1965 298, 572, 784, 795, 796, 798, 800, 850, 852, 854, 871

'Inyānōt be-sifrūt ha-ge'ōnīm, Jerusalem 1974 347, 810, 912

Qeṭa' ḥādāsh min ha-sefer essā meshālī, *Tarbiz*, 32:160, 1962/3 733

Rav Nissim Gaon, Jerusalem 1964/6 384, 912

Abū'l-Fatḥ, *The Chronicle*, ed. E. Vilmar, Gotha 1865 410–414, 941

Aḥīma'aṣ of Oria, *ha-Megillā*², ed. B. Klar, Jerusalem 1974 561, 734, 741, 776, 809, 827–828, 844, 937

Alder, I., Ha-omnām nimṣe'ū ba-genīzā, *Alei Sefer*, 12:51, 1986 286

'Alī Ibn Sulaymān, *The Commentary on Genesis*, ed. S. L. Skoss, Philadelphia 1928 835, 938, 940

Allony, N., 'Alī b. Yehūdā ha-nāzīr we-ḥibbūrō, *Leshonenu* 34:75, 187, 1969/70 286

Dūnash we-adōnīm, *Sinai*, 43:385, 1957/8 13

Kitāb al-sab'īn lafẓa, *I. Goldziher Memorial Volume* (Hebrew part), Jerusalem 1958:1 123

Shetē reshīmōt, *Kiryat Sefer*, 38:531, 1962/3 378

Allony, N. and Scheiber, A., Reshīmat sefārīm, *Kiryat Sefer*, 48:152, 1972/3 378

Alon, G., *Studies* (*Meḥqārīm*), Tel Aviv 1957 2

The Chronicle, ed. Bedjan 1890; ed. and transl. E. A. W. Budge, Oxford 1932   50, 65, 69, 72, 81, 376, 410, 414, 420, 482, 550, 560, 565, 571, 597, 606, 701, 716

Bareket, E., Elḥānān b. shemaryā we-sahlān b. avrāhām (MA thesis), Tel Aviv Univ. 1979/80   795, 806, 808

Sahlān b. avrāhām, *Tarbiz*, 52:17, 1982/3   795

Beit-Arie, M., ha-Pale'ōgrafiya shel qiṭ'ē ha-genīzā, *Te'uda*, 1:193, 1980   193, 342

Ben Horin, Review of Prawer's *Mamlekhet Yerūshālayim ha-ṣalvānīt, Kiryat Sefer*, 24:108, 1947/8   330, 603, 839

Ben-Sasson, Ḥ. H., Demūtāh shel 'adat ha-shōshānīm, *Shalem*, 2:1, 1975/6   933

Ri'shōnē ha-qārā'īm, *Zion*, 15:42, 1950   919, 935

Ben-Sasson, M., Ge'ōnūtō shel shemū'ēl ha-kohen, *Zion*, 51:379, 1985   797, 828, 854

Ben-Shammai, H., Dānī'ēl al-qūmisī we-tōlodēt E. I., *Shalem*, 3:295, 1980/81   11, 669, 921

Ha'aliyya le-E. I., *Cathedra*, 8:145, 1977/8   824

Mahadūrā we-nusḥā'ōt mi-pērūshē yefet ben 'alī, *Alei Sefer*, 2:17, 1975/6   925

Ben-Zvi, I., Keter ha-tōrā, *Sinai*, 43:5, 1957/8   289

Benjamin b. Jonah of Tudela, *Sefer massā'ōt*, ed. Asher, London 1840; ed. Adler, London 1907   308, 325, 330, 360, 746, 790, 900, 944

Benjamin al-Nihāwandī, *Masse'at benyāmīn*, Eupatoria 1835   274

Blau, J., *Diqdūq ha-'arāvīt ha-yehūdīt*, Jerusalem 1961

Bornstein, Ḥ. J., Divrē yemē ha-'ibbūr, *Hatequfa*, 14–15:321; 16:228, 1921/2   785–788, 929

Maḥalōqet rav se'adyā gā'ōn, *N. Sokolow Jubilee Volume*, Warsaw 1904:19   738, 784–789, 828, 831, 840, 849, 852, 902, 922

Braslavi, J., 'Aliyōt regālīm, *Ha-kinnūs* (xxv), *Yerushālayim le-dōrōtēhā*: 120   841

Le-ḥeqer arṣēnū, Tel Aviv 1954   119, 255, 301, 307, 319, 324, 325–329, 828

Le-minnūyō shel rabbī evyātār, *Eretz-Israel*, 5:220, 1959   302, 899, 900

Li-meqōmōt ha-yishūv ha-yehūdī, *BJPES*, 5:27, 1936/8   840, 848

Madrīkh E. I. min ha-genīzā, *Eretz-Israel*, 7:69, 1963/4   840

Qīnā 'al rabbī ṣādōq, *Tarbiz*, 32:174, 1962/3   772

Brawer, A. J., Ha-yesōd ha-yehūdī she-be-'arvīyē E. I., *Molad*, 24:424, 1966/8   334

Cassuto, M. D., 'Al ma neḥleqū, etc., *Sefer rav se'adyā gā'ōn*: 333, Jerusalem 1942   787

Chapira, E. D. (B.), Mikhtāv mē-ramlā lirūshālayim, *Yerushalayim*, 4:118, 1952/3   383, 879

Chronicon anonymum ad A. C. 1234 pertinens, ed. J. B. Chabot, *CSCO* (Syri) nos. 36, 37 (transl. by J. B. Chabot, further by A. Abouna, *ibid.*, nos. 36, 154)   46, 58, 62, 69, 607

Shiv'atōt ḥadāshōt..., *Sinai*, 61:30, 1966/7 287
Frenkel, J., Ḥadīrātām shel ha-badawīm le-ereṣ isrā'ēl, *Cathedra*, 11:86, 1978/9 589, 591
Ha-saljūqīm be-ereṣ isrā'ēl, *Cathedra*, 21:49, 1981/2 603, 609
Friedman, M. A., Ha-ketubbōt ha-ereṣ-isre'ēliyōt..., *Te'uda*, 1:57, 1979/80 931
'Ha-ṣarī eyn be-miṣrayim'..., *Dīnē isrā'ēl*, 5:205, 1973/4 899
'Ōd 'al'iṭṭūr'..., *Tarbiz*, 49:202, 1979/80 779
Ōnō, yedi'ot ḥadāshōt..., in: D. Grossmann, ed., *Beyn yarqōn wa-ayalōn*, Ramat Gan 1983:75 332
Pōlīgāmiya..., *Tarbiz*, 43:166, 1973/4 896
Ribbūy nāshīm be-isrā'ēl, Jerusalem 1986 285, 754
Ribbūy nāshīm be-mismekhē ha-genīzā, *Tarbiz*, 40:320, 1980/81 823
Shenē qeṭa'īm mi-sefer ha-ma'asīm, *Sinai*, 74:14, 1973/4 823
Gartner, I., Hashpa'atām... *Bar Ilan Univ. Annual*, 20:128, 1983 826
Geiger, A., *Qevūṣat ma'amārīm*, Warsaw 1910 286
Ge'ōnē mizrāḥ ū-ma'arāv, Responsa, ed. J. Muller, reprint 1958/9 273, 739
Gil, M., 'Aliyā wa-'aliyā la-regel, *Cathedra*, 8:124, 1977/8 823
Ereṣ isrā'ēl..., *Te'uda*, 7:281, 1990 269, 779, 797
Megillat evyātār..., *Perāqīm be-tōledōt yerūshālayim bīmē ha-beynayim*, ed. B. Z. Kedar, Jerusalem 1979:39 811, 884, 890, 905
ha-Mōkhēr et he-ḥāsēr, *Tarbiz*, 46:17, 1976/7 843
Le-tōledōt ge'ōnē ereṣ isrā'ēl, *Tarbiz*, 44:144, 1974/5 851–852
ha-Mifgāsh ha-bavlī, *Tarbiz*, 48:35, 1978/9 241, 774, 806, 852, 870
Mikhtāv shel isrā'ēl b. nātān, *Michael*, 7:244, 1981/2 376, 891
Milḥemet shishshīm ha-shānīm, *Shalem*, 3:1, 1980/81 564
Rav aharōn gā'ōn b. yōsēf, *Sefunot*, NS 1(16):9, 1979/80 488, 797, 853
Shekhūnōt ha-yehūdīm bīrūshālayim, *Shalem*, 2:19, 1975/6 668, 842, 845
ha-Tustarīm, Tel Aviv 1981 78, 255, 274, 285, 350, 357–358, 364, 370, 560, 590, 598, 609, 764, 773, 780, 803, 880, 927, 929, 931, 935, 939, 940, 947
Ginzberg, L., *Ginzē Schechter*, New York 1927/9 76, 808, 821, 826, 921, 932
Goitein, S. D., 'Al shemōtēhā ha'arviyīm shel yerūshālayim, *J. L. Zlotnick Jubilee Volume*, Jerusalem 1950:62 125
Arba' ketubbōt, *Leshonenu*, 30:197, 1965/6 123, 775
Battē yehūdīm be-'ārīm damesseq we-ṣōr, *Eretz-Israel*, 8:288, 1966/7 903
Bēt ha-keneset we-ṣiyyūdō, *Eretz-Israel*, 7:81, 1963/4 769
Dānī'ēl b. 'azaryā, nāsī we-gā'ōn, *Shalem*, 2:41, 1975/6 738, 773–774, 779, 801–802, 809, 822, 857, 885–886, 889, 893, 896, 905
ha-Hitmōdedūt beyn bēt-ha-keneset le-veyn ha-qehillā, *H. Schirmann Jubilee Volume*, Jerusalem 1970:69 767
Ha-omnām āsar ha-khalīfa 'umar 'al ha-yehūdīm la-shevet bīrūshālayim, *Melila*, 3–4:156, 1949/50 69
Iggeret labrāṭ b. mōshē, *Tarbiz*, 36:59, 1966/7 376, 879
Kitāb dhimmat al-nabī, *Kiryat Sefer*, 9:507, 1931/33 255

Le-tōledōt ha-ge'ōnūt, *Shalem*, 1:15, 1973/4 742, 753, 793, 802, 857, 859, 862
Ma'asē bēt-dīn, *Eretz Israel*, 12:200, 1974/5 311
Meqōrōt ḥadāshīm al gōral ha-yehūdīm, *Zion*, 17:129, 1952 943, 947
Mikhtāvīm mē-ereṣ isrā'ēl, *Yerushālayim*, 1955:54 943
Misḥar ha-yehūdīm ba-yam ha-tīkhōn, *Tarbiz*, 36:366, 1966/7 339
'Ōlālōt..., *Tarbiz*, 38:18, 1968/9 856
Pe'ūlātō ha-ṣibbūrīt shel r. elḥānān b. shemaryā, *J. Finkel Jubilee Volume*, New York 1974 (Hebrew part):117 252, 795, 796, 798
Pidyōn shevūyā be-nābulus..., *Tarbiz*, 31:287, 1961/2 949
Qedūshātāh shel ereṣ-isrā'ēl ba-ḥasīdūt ha-muslimīt, *BJPES*, 12:120, 1945/6 109, 181, 389
Ha-rav, bērūr parāshā setūmā, *Tarbiz*, 45:64, 1975/6 374, 378, 861, 864
Rōsh yeshīvat ereṣ-isrā'ēl..., *Eretz-Israel*, 10:100, 1970/71 877
Ṣawwa'ōt mi-miṣrayim, *Sefunot*, 8:107, 1963/4 598, 835
Shālōsh iggārōt, *Tarbiz*, 34:162, 1964/5 835, 856
Shemaryā birrabī elḥānān, *Tarbiz*, 32:266, 1962/3 795, 798
Yedī'ōt ḥadāshōt 'al ereṣ isrā'ēl, *Eretz-Israel*, 4:147, 1955/6 328, 943, 946
Yedi'ōt ḥadāshōt 'al negīdē qayrawān, *Zion*, 27:11, 1962 809
Yerūshālayim ba-teqūfā ha-'arāvīt, *Yerūshālayim*, 4:82, 1952/3 66, 69, 105, 157, 414, 456, 624
ha-Yishūv be-ereṣ isrā'ēl..., Jerusalem 1979/80 66, 311, 609, 624–626, 634, 773–774, 779, 793, 822, 856, 859, 885–886, 889, 893–894, 896, 905, 946–947, 949
Golb, N., Gēr ṣedeq she-bāraḥ le-miṣrayim, *Sefunot*, 8:85, 1963/4 278
Megillat 'ōvadyā ha-gēr, *S. D. Goitein Jubilee Volume*, Jerusalem 1981:77 328, 950
Tōledōt ha-yehūdīm ba'īr Rouen bīmē ha-beynayim, Tel Aviv 1976 777
Grabois, A., ha-Ṣalyānūt ha-nōṣerīt..., *Ha-yam ha-tīkhōn ū-meqōmō...*, (kenes ha-ḥevrā ha-hisṭōrīt), Jerusalem:68 719
Graetz, H. H., *Divrē yemē isrā'ēl* (transl. S. P. Rabbinowitz), Warsaw 1890 *et sqq.* 76, 119, 728, 732
Grossman, A., ha-'Aliyā le-ereṣ-isrā'ēl, *Cathedra*, 8:136, 1977/8 821, 827
Ḥakhmē ashkenāz ha-ri'shōnīm, Jerusalem 1981 777
Zīqātāh shel yahadūt ashkenāz..., *Shalem*, 3:57, 1980/81 574, 777
Guttmann, J., *Ha-fīlōsōfya shel ha-yahadūt*, Jerusalem 1951 940
Habermann, A. M., Qerōvā le-ḥanukkā, *Sinai*, 53:183, 1962/3 810, 867
Hadāsī, Judah, *Eshkōl ha-kofer*, Goslow 1836 286
Halper, B., 'Alīm bālīm (v), *Hatequfā*, 20:261, 1922/3 786
Ha-yehūdīm taḥat shilṭōn ha-khalīfīm ha-fāṭimiyīm, *Hatequfa*, 18:175, 1922/3 560, 779, 808, 857, 860
Harkavy, A., Divrē avrāhām, *Hamagid*, 21:134, 1877 301
Ḥadāshīm gam yeshānīm, reprint, Jerusalem 1969/70 289, 309, 927
He'ārōt ūmillū'īm, in: Grätz, *Divrē yemē isrā'ēl* (transl. S. P. Rabbinowitz), vol. III 917, 919

Me'assēf niddāḥīm, reprint, Jerusalem 1969/70 83, 87, 824, 826, 832, 834, 837, 924, 935
Teshūvōt ha-ge'ōnīm (Responsa), Berlin 1887 34, 273, 728, 770, 800, 908
Zikkārōn la-ri'shōnīm, V, Berlin 1891 286
Zikkārōn la-ri'shōnīm, VIII, Petersburg 1903 286
Hecker, M., Haspāqat mayim..., *Sefer Yerushālayim*, 1:191, 1955/6 847
Hayy Gaon, *Sefer ha-meqqaḥ we-ha-mimkār*, Venice 1602 897
Heilprin, Y., *Seder ha-dōrōt*, Warsaw 1877 325
Heinemann, J., Yaḥasō shel rav Se'adyā gā'ōn..., *Bar-Ilan Univ. Annual*, 1 (= *P. Churgin Memorial Volume*): 220, 1962/3 820
Hirschberg, H. Z., 'Al r. zekharyā aghmātī, *Tarbiz*, 42:379, 1972/3 835
'Arkhā'ōt shel goyīm..., *I. Herzog Memorial Volume*, Jerusalem 1961/2:493 273
'Inyenē har ha-zeytīm, *BJPES*, 13:156, 1946/7 246, 771, 831, 840
'Iqevōt ha-māshīaḥ be-ereṣ 'arāv, *Vienna Rabbinical Seminary Memorial Volume*, Jerusalem 1946:112 730
Isrā'ēl ba-'arāv, Tel Aviv 1946 38, 730
Qehillōt isrā'ēl..., *Sinai Jubilee Volume*, Jerusalem 1958:344 827
Ha-qeshārīm beyn yehūdē ha-maghrib..., *Eretz-Israel*, 5:213, 1958/9 342, 350, 795, 828
Hirschman, M., Sha'ar ha-kōhēn..., *Tarbiz*, 55:217, 1985/6 840
Horowitz, H. M., *Bēt 'eqed ha-agādōt*, Frankfurt 1881 76
Iṣḥāq Ibn Ghayyāth, *Sha'arē simḥā*, Fürth 1860/62 739
Ibn al-Hītī, The Chronicle, ed. G. Margoliouth, Arabic Chronicles, *JQR*, 9:429, 1897 917, 923, 940
Ish Shalom, M., 'Al yishshūvē ha-shefēlā, in: *Ḥafīrōt ū-meḥqārīm*, Tel Aviv 1973 116
Masse'ē nōṣerīm, Tel Aviv 1966 664
Jellinek, A., *Bēt ha-midrāsh*, Leipzig 1853/7 76, 84, 103, 119, 412
Jonah Ibn Janāḥ, *Sefer ha-riqmā*, (1) ed. J. Derenbourg, Paris 1886, (2) ed. M. Wilensky and D. Tenne, Jerusalem 1964 293, 829
Sefer ha-shorāshīm, ed. A. Neubauer, reprint, Amsterdam 1968 338, 346, 350, 368
Joseph b. Judah Ibn 'Aqnīn, *Pērūsh shīr ha-shīrīm*, ed. A. S. Halkin, Jerusalem 1964 776
Judah al-Ḥarīzī, *Taḥkemōnī*, ed. J. Toporowski, Tel Aviv 1952 330
Karmon, Y., ha-Tenā'īm ha-fisiyōgrāfiyīm..., *BJPES*, 23:111, 1958/9 275
Kedar, B. Z., Le-tōledōt ha-yishūv ha-yehūdī be-ereṣ isrā'ēl bīmē ha-beynayim, *Tarbiz*, 42:401, 1972/3 309, 564, 947
ha-Yishūv ha-yehūdī bīrūshālayim..., *Tarbiz*, 41:82, 1971/2 835
Ketāvā de-ḥimyarē, ed. A. Moberg, Lund 1924 730
Kirchheim, R., Sefer ketāv tamīm, *Ōṣar neḥmād*, 3:54, 1859/60 634
Kister, M. J. and M., 'Al yehūdē 'arāv, *Tarbiz*, 48:231, 1978/9 295
Klar, B., Ben-ashēr, *Tarbiz*, 14:156, 1942/3; 15:36, 1943/4 734, 745, 919, 933
Meḥqārīm we-'iyyūnīm, Tel Aviv 1954 291, 294, 852

Klein, S., Asiya ('asiya), *J. Freimann Jubilee Volume*, Berlin 1937:116 2
Kochavi, M., ed., *Yehūdā shōmrōn we-gōlān*, Jerusalem 1972 275
Kook, S. H., Merkāz qārā'ī biltī yādū'a, *Ginzē qedem*, 4:107, 1929/30 936
Krauss, S., ha-Teḥuqqā ha-nōṣerīt . . ., *Melila*, 3–4:77, 1949/50 269
Wikkūaḥ dātī . . ., *Zion* (ha-me'assēf), 2:28, 1926/7 52, 731
Lazarus-Yafeh, Ḥ., *Abū ḥāmid al-ghazālī, ha-pōdē* . . ., Tel Aviv 1965 633
Beyn halākhā ba-yahadūt la-halākhā ba-islām, *Tarbiz*, 51:207, 1981/2 246
Qedūshat yerūshālayim . . ., *J. Herzog Memorial Volume*, Jerusalem 1979 109
Levi (Abu Sa'īd) b. Yefet ha-Levi, Sefer ha-miṣwōt, MS Leiden 4760 (Cat. Warner no. 22) 925, 928–930
Lewin, B. M., Essā meshālī, *Sefer rav se'adyā gā'ōn*, Jerusalem 1942:481 294
Ma'asīm livnē ereṣ isrā'ēl, *Tarbiz*, 1(1):79, 1929/30 367
Mi-serīdē ha-genīzā, *Tarbiz*, 2:383, 1930/31 728, 821
Teshūvōt anshē ereṣ isrā'ēl, *Ginzē qedem*, 4:50, 1929/30 736, 828, 854
Lewin B. M. (ed.), *Ōṣar ḥillūf minhāgīm*, Jerusalem 1944 739
Linder, A., Yerushālayim ke-mōqēd shel 'immūt, *Perāqīm be-tōledōt yerūshālayim bīmē ha-beynayim*, ed. B. Z. Kedar, Jerusalem 1979 665, 700
Loewenstamm, A., ha-Qārā'ī yeshū'ā bar yehūdā, *Tarbiz*, 41:183, 1971/2 940
Luncz, A. M., Kotel ha-ma'arāvī, *Yerūshālayim* (Luncz), 10:1, 1913/14 840
Mahler, R., *ha-Qārā'īm*, Merhavia 1949 919, 935
Maḥzōr witrī, ed. S. Hurwitz, reprint, Jerusalem 1963 733, 777
Mann, J., 'Inyānīm shōnīm . . ., *Tarbiz*, 5:148, 1933/4 741
Misrat rōsh ha-gōlā we-hista'afūtāh, *S. Poznanski Jubilee Volume*, Warsaw 1927 (Hebrew part): 18 773, 885
Ha-tenū'ōt ha-meshīḥiyōt . . ., *Hatequfa*, 24:335, 1925/6 300, 916
Margaliot, M., *Hilekhōt ereṣ isrā'ēl min ha-genīzā*, Jerusalem 1974 331, 821
Ha-ḥillūqīm . . ., Jerusalem 1938 739
Li-qevī'at zemānō shel ra'ash shevī'īt, *BJPES*, 8:97, 1980/81 102
Te'ūdā ḥadāshā 'al ṣōm ha-ra'ash, *Tarbiz*, 29:339, 1959/60 102
Marmorstein, A., Derāshōt dānī'ēl al-qūmisī, *Zion* (ha-me'assēf), 3:26, 1928/9 807, 826, 933
Marmorstein, A., ed. *Midrash ḥasērōt wītērōt*, London 1917 807
Mayer, L. A., 'Emdat ha-yehūdīm bīmē ha-mamlūkīm, *J. L. Magnes Jubilee Volume*, Jerusalem 1938 238
Ketōvōt yehūdiyōt, *Zion* (ha-me'assēf), 3:22, 1928/9 839
Aṣ-ṣinnabra, *Eretz-Israel*, 1:169, 1980/81 92
Megillat Aḥīma'as, see Aḥīma'aṣ
Michael the Syrian, *The Chronicle*, ed. J. B. Chabot, Paris 1899–1910 5, 50, 69, 87–88, 97, 102, 333, 414, 550, 678, 919
Michaeli, M. A., Arkhiyōnō shel Nahrai b. Nissim . . ., (PhD dissertation), the Hebrew Univ., Jerusalem 1968 371, 372
Moses Maimonides, *Responsa*, ed. J. Blau, Jerusalem 1957/61 835, 912
Sharḥ asmā' al-uqqār, ed. M. Meyerhof, Cairo 1940 337, 346, 353
Moses Ibn Ezra, *Kitāb al-muḥāḍara wa'l-mudhākara*, ed. A. S. Halkin, Jerusalem 1975 892

Nathan b. Abraham, *Pērūsh la-mishnā* (ascribed to him), suppl. to the *mishnā* edition, el-ha-meqōrōt, Jerusalem 1955 337, 353, 884

Neubauer, A., *Mediaeval Jewish Chronicles*, Oxford 1888–93 728–729, 732, 741–742, 773, 849, 859–860, 929

Neubauer, A., ed. The *Tōlīdā (Chronique samaritaine)*, Paris 1873 10, 116, 941

Ōṣar ha-ge'ōnīm, ed. B. M. Lewin, Haifa 1928 *et sqq.* 123, 273, 350, 735, 739, 741, 777, 835

Ha-Pardēs (ascribed to Rashi), ed. Ehrenreich, Budapest 1924 777

Pinkerfeld, J., Bēt ha-keneset la-'adat ha-qārā'īm bīrushālayim, *A. M. Luncz Memorial Volume*, Jerusalem 1928:205 936

Pinsker, S., *Liqqūṭe qadmōniyōt*, Vienna 1860 125, 263, 286, 741, 786, 824–825, 829, 842, 848, 852, 917, 924, 925, 928, 930–933, 935, 937

Pirqē r. elī'ezer, ed. M. Higger, *Ḥōrēv*, 8:82; 9:94; 10:185, 1943/48 739, 784

Pitrōn tōrā, ed. E. E. Urbach, Jerusalem 1978 293

Poliak, A., Even shetiyā, *B. Dinaburg* (Dinur) *Jubilee Volume*, Jerusalem 1949:165 105, 418

Mōṣā'ām shel 'arviyē ha-areṣ, *Molad*, 24:297, 1966/8 334

Ha-yehūdīm u-vēt ha-miṭbā'ōt be-miṣrayim, *Zion*, 1:24, 1936 746

Poznanski, S., Anshē qayrawān, *A. Harkavy Presentation Volume*, Petersburg 1909:175 347, 376, 741, 871, 912

'Inyānīm shōnīm..., *Hakedem*, 1:133, 1906–1908; 2:24, 29, 1907/8 763

Rēshīt hityashvūt ha-qārā'īm bīrūshālayim, *Yerushālayim* (Luncz), 10:83, 1913/4 825, 848, 923–924, 936, 938

Salmon ben yerūḥam, *Encyclopaedia Ōṣar isrā'ēl*, VII:208 923

Ṭuviyāhū ben mōshē ha-ma'atīq, *Encyclopaedia Ōṣar isrā'ēl*, V:12 938

Prawer, J., Ha-auṭōbiyōgrāfiya shel 'ōvadya ha-gēr ha-nōrmānī, *Tarbiz*, 45:272, 1975/6 727

Gilgūlē ha-shekhūnā ha-yehūdīt, *Zion*, 12:136, 1947 839, 841, 848

ha-Ṣalvānīm, Jerusalem 1975 360, 677, 947

Tōledōt mamlekhet ha-ṣalvānīm[3], Jerusalem 1971 276, 328, 553, 943–944

ha-Yehūdīm be-malkhūt yerūshālayim ha-ṣalvānīt, *Zion*, 11:38, 1946 315, 839

Yerushālayim bi-tefīsat ha-naṣrūt we-ha-yahadūt bīmē ha-beynayim ha-muqdāmīm, *Cathedra*, 17:40, 1980/81 81

al-Qirqisānī, Ya'qūb, *Kitāb al-anwār wa'l marāqib*, ed. L. Nemoy, New York 1939/43 76, 287, 291, 367, 740, 826, 917, 919, 928–930, 931

Rapoport, S., He'ārā gedōlā..., *Kerem ḥemed*, 4:204, 1838/9 728

Raẓhabi, J., Gimel piyyūṭīm le-rabbī dawīd ben nāsī, *Tarbiz*, 14:204, 1942/3 914

Saadia Gaon, Commentary on the Book of Isaiah, ed. J. Derenbourg, reprint, in: *Qoveṣ pērūshīm*, Jerusalem 1981, I 820

The *Siddūr*, ed. I. Davidson *et al.*, Jerusalem 1981 820

Ha-egrōn, ed. N. Allony, Jerusalem 1969 287

Safrai, S., ha'Aliyā la-regel..., *Perāqīm be-tōledōt yerūshālayim bīmē bayit shēnī*, ed.

A. Oppenheimer *et al.* (= *A. Schalit Memorial Volume*) Jerusalem 1981:376 81

Sahl b. Maṣlīah, Introduction to Sefer ha-miṣwōt, ed. A. Harkavy, *Ha-mēlīṣ* 1879 = *Me'assēf niddāḥīm* No. 13 81, 83, 87

Salmon Ben Yeruḥim, *Commentary on the Book of Lamentations,* (1) ed. S. Feuerstein, Krakau 1898; (2) MS Paris, Bibliothèque nationale, 295 86, 825, 837, 829, 934

Commentary on the Book of Psalms, ed. L. Marwick, Philadelphia 1956 123, 252, 728, 825, 919, 934–935

Commentary on the Book of Qōhelet, MS BM Or 2517 311, 825, 837

Sefer milḥamōt, ed. I. Davidson, New York 1934 825, 923, 928

al-Sam'ānī = J. S. Assemani, *Bibliotheca Orientalis,* Roma 1719–28 679

Samuel Ibn Naghrila, ha-Nagid, *The Dīwān* (1) ed. D. S. Sassoon, London 1934; (2) ed. D. Yarden, Jerusalem 1966 773–774, 892

Schechter, S., ed. *Saadyana,* Cambridge 1903 298, 793, 852, 859, 902, 908, 933

Genizah Manuscripts, *Festschrift A. Berliner,* Frankfurt am Main, 1903:108 773

Scheiber, A., Iggartō shel ēliyāhū ha-kōhēn, *Tarbiz,* 32:273, 1962/3 380

Leaves from she'ēlōt 'atīqōt, *HUCA,* 27:291, 1956 745, 827

Li-fe'īlūtō shel ṭūviyā ha-qārā'ī, *Kiryat Sefer,* 55:791, 1979/80 939

Shīr tehillā..., *Sefunot,* NS 1:59, 1979/80 298

Schirmann, Ḥ., Shīr 'al meṣūqātān shel qehillōt, *Yedī'ōt ha-mākhōn la-ḥeqer ha-shīra ha'ivrīt,* 7:157, 1957/8 564

Shīrīm ḥadāshīm min ha-genīzā, Jerusalem 1966 808, 857

Schwabe, M., Ha-yehūdīm we-har ha-bayit, *Zion* (ha-me'assēf), 2:90, 1926/7 87

Sefer ha-eshkōl (of Abraham b. Isaac of Narbonne), Halberstadt 1868 763

Sefer ha-ḥasīdīm, ed. J. Wistinetzki, Frankfurt 1924 353, 561, 828

Sefer ha-yishūv, ed. S. Assaf and L. A. Mayer, Jerusalem 1944 70, 102, 284, 330–331, 599, 780, 827, 829, 835, 925, 936

Ṣemaḥ, M., Battē ha-keneset be-miṣrayim, *Mizrāḥ* u-ma'arāv, 1:358, 1919/20 331

Sha'arē ṣedeq (Responsa), ed. H. Mōdā'ī, Salonica 1792 273, 823

Sha'arē teshūvā (Responsa), New York 1946 917

Sharon, M., Shabbāt ha-gādōl..., *Shalem,* 1:1, 1973/4 282

Sherira Gaon, *The Letter,* (1) ed. A. Neubauer, *Mediaeval Jewish Chronicles,* I; (2) ed. B. M. Lewin, Haifa 1921 773, 789, 821, 852, 917, 919

Siddūr ha-tefillōt ke-minhag ha-qārā'īm, Wilno 1890/92 917

Skoss, S. L., Li-qevī'at..., *Tarbiz,* 2:510, 1930/31 940

Slouschz, N., ha-Ḥafīrōt..., *Qoveṣ* (JPES), I (2):5, 1924/5 668

Solomon ben ha-yātōm, *Pērūsh massekhet mashqīn,* ed. H. P. Chajes, Berlin 1910 346, 773, 835

Spiegel, S., Le-fārāshat ha-pulmūs, *Wolfson Jubilee Volume,* Jerusalem 1965:243 821

Starr, J., Le-tōledōt nehōray b. nissīm, *Zion,* 1:436, 1936 376

Stern, M., Memorbuch ha-yāshān..., *A. Berliner Jubilee Volume*, Berlin 1903:113 733
Stern, S. M., Qeṭa‘ ḥādāsh mi-sefer ha-gālūy, *Melila*, 5:133, 1954/5 797
Ṭa‘am zeqēnīm (ed. E. Ashkenazi), Frankfurt 1915 741
Tanḥūm Ha-yerūshalmī, *Commentary on the Book of Joshua*, ed. T. Haarbrücker, Berlin 1862 330
Toledano, J. M., Mi-serīdē ha-genīzā be-miṣrayim, *Mizrāḥ u-ma‘arāv*, 1:344, 1919/20 805, 813
Urbach, E. E., Midrash ge'ūlā, *Eretz Israel*, 10:58, 1970/71 76
Vajda, G., Shenē qiṣṣūrīm..., *D. H. Baneth Memorial Volume*, Jerusalem 1979 938
Vilnay, Z., Shēmōt ‘arviyīm..., *Zion*, 5:73, 1940 123, 125, 330, 839
Wertheimer, S., *Battē midrāshōt*, Jerusalem 1894, 1953, 1968 104, 412, 596
Ginzē yerūshālayim, II, 1901; III, 1902 950
Yaari, A., *Iggerōt ereṣ isrā'ēl*, Ramat Gan 1971 846
Yefet b. ‘Alī, *Commentary on the Book of Daniel*, ed. D. S. Margoliouth, Oxford 1889 60, 933, 937
Commentary on the Book of Nahum, ed. H. Hirschfeld, London 1911 481, 920
Commentary on Psalms, MS Paris, Bibl. nat., 286–289 275, 551, 824, 837, 842, 934
Commentary on the Song of Solomon, MS BM Or 2520, 2554 826, 920, 925, 934
Yehuda, Y., Ha-kotel ha-ma‘arāvī, *Zion* (ha-me'assēf), 3:95, 1928/9 840, 844
Yellin, A., Mi-ginzē bēt ha-sefārīm, *Kiryat Sefer*, 1:55, 1923/4 936
Zohary, M., *‘Ōlam ha-ṣemāḥīm*, Tel Aviv 1963 346, 353
Zucker, M., *‘Al targūm rasag la-tōrā*, New York 1959 917–918, 921, 928
Mi-pērūshō shel rasag la-tōrā, *Sura*, 2:313, 1954/7 918
Neged mī kātav rav se‘adyā gā'ōn et ha-piyyūṭ essā meshālī? *Tarbiz*, 27:61, 1957/8 294
Tegūvōt li-tenū‘at avēlē ṣiyōn, *H. Albeck Jubilee Volume*, Jerusalem 1963:378 827, 921, 933
Zulay, M., Ereṣ isrā'ēl we-‘aliyat regālīm..., *Yerushalayim*, 1:51, 1952/3 287, 311
Le-tōledōt ha-piyyūṭ be-ereṣ isrā'ēl, *Yedī‘ōt ha-mākhōn le-ḥeqer ha-shīrā ha-‘ivrīt*, 5:107, 1938/9 309, 851
Māqōr we-ḥiqqūy ba-piyyūṭ, *Sinai*, 25:32, 1948/9 867
Piyyūṭīm le-zekher me'ōrā‘ōt shōnīm, *Yedī‘ōt ha-mākhōn le-ḥeqer ha-shīrā ha-‘ivrīt*, 3:153, 1936/7 102, 309, 564

Arabic, Persian

‘Abd al-Jabbār b. Aḥmad al-Asadābādī, *Sharḥ al-uṣūl al-khamsa*, Cairo 1960 76
Tathbīt dalā'il al-mubuwwa, Beirut 1386 63, 465, 482, 702
‘Abd al-Laṭīf al-Baghdādī, Muwaffaq al-Dīn, *Kitāb al-ifāda wa'l-i‘tibār*, ed. Silvestre de Sacy, Paris 1810 561

al-'Abdarī, Muḥammad b. Muḥammad, *al-Riḥla al-maghribiyya*, Rabat 1968 304
Abū'l-Fidā', 'Imād al-Dīn Ismā'īl b. 'Alī, *al-Mukhtaṣar fī akhbār al-bashar*, Cairo 1325 64, 81, 98–99, 125, 232, 388, 393, 422, 424, 460, 463–464, 473–474, 522, 545, 548, 550, 552–553, 557–558, 560, 592, 918, 941
Abū Nu'aym al-Iṣbahānī, Aḥmad b. 'Abdallah, *Akhbār iṣbahān*, Leiden 1931/4 492, 513
Ḥilyat al-awliyā', Beirut 1387 162, 181
Abū Ṣāliḥ al-Armanī, *Kitāb al-diyārāt*, ed. Butler, Oxford 1895 561
Abu Shujā', Muḥammad b. al-Ḥusayn al-Rudhdrāwarī, *Dhayl tajārib al-umam*, in *The Eclipse of the 'Abbāsid Caliphate*, H. F. Amedroz and D. S. Margoliouth eds., Oxford 1920/21, Vol. III 549, 560, 563–564, 577
Abū'l-Su'ūd b. Muḥammad al-'Imādī, *Tafsīr*, Riyāḍ 1974 843
Abū 'Ubayd, al-Qāsim b. Sallām, *Kitāb al-amwāl*, Cairo 1353 36, 64, 81, 86
Abū 'Ubayda, Ma'mar b. al-Muthannā, *Majāz al-qur'ān*, Cairo 1954/5 843
Abū Yūsuf, Ya'qūb b. Ibrahīm al-Anṣārī al-Kūfī, *Kitāb al-kharāj*, Cairo 1346 60, 224–225, 267, 269
Abū Zur'a, 'Abd al-Raḥmān b. 'Abdallah al-Dimashqī, Ta'rikh, MS Muḥammad Fātik (Istanbul) no. 4210, in: L. Manṣūr (MA thesis), Bar-Ilan Univ. 1976 64, 150, 153, 165
Agapius, *see* Maḥbūb
al-'Ajlūnī, Ismā'īl b. Muḥammad, *Kashf al-khafā' wa-muzīl al-ilbās*, Cairo 1351/2 111, 226, 284
Akhbār al-dawla al-'abbāsiyya, Beirut 1971 95, 100, 137
'Arīb b. Sa'd al-Qurṭubī, *Ṣilat ta'rikh al-ṭabarī*, Leiden 1897 468, 473
'Ārif al-'Ārif, *al-Mūjaz fī ta'rīkh 'asqalān*, Jerusalem 1362 304
al-Azdī, Yazīd b. Muḥammad, *Ta'rīkh al-Mawṣil*, Cairo 1967 418
al-'Aẓīmī: C. Cahen, La chronique abrégée d'al-'Aẓīmī, *JA*, 230:353, 1938 602–603, 606–608, 610–611, 727
al-'Azīzī, 'Alī b. Aḥmad, *al-Sirāj al-munīr*, Cairo 1957 63, 80, 107, 111, 113, 116, 226, 228–229, 236, 259, 346
al-Azraqī, Muḥammad b. 'Abd Allah, *Akhbār makka*, ed. F. Wüstenfeld, Leipzig 1858 2
al-Badrī, 'Abd Allah b. Muḥammad al-Miṣrī al-Dimashqī, *Nuzhat al-ānām fī maḥāsin al-shām*, Cairo 1341 58, 123, 269
al-Bakrī, 'Abd Allah b. 'Abd al-'Azīz, *Mu'jam ma'sta'jama*, ed. al-Saqqā', Cairo 1959 81, 122, 125, 201, 337
al-Balādhurī, Aḥmad b. Yaḥyā, *Ansāb al-ashrāf*, I, ed. M. Hamidullah, Cairo 1959; IV (A) ed. M. Schloessinger, revised by M. J. Kister, Jerusalem 1971; IV (B) ed. M. Schloessinger, Jerusalem 1939; V ed. S. D. Goitein, Jerusalem 1936 18, 44, 81, 94, 126, 129, 141, 157–158, 161, 179, 182, 266
al-Balādhurī, Aḥmad b. Yaḥyā, *Futūḥ al-buldān*, Leiden 1866 36, 38, 44–45, 49, 50, 54–55, 57–62, 64–66, 69, 71–74, 93, 99, 116–117, 122, 236, 238, 240–241, 243, 269–270, 411, 941

al-Fīrūzābādī, Majd al-Dīn Muḥammad b. Ya'qūb, *al-Qāmūs al-muḥīṭ*, Cairo 1371 99

Futūḥ al-shām (ascribed to al-Wāqidī), Beirut 1966 61, 65–66, 69, 81, 116

al-Ghāfiqī, Aḥmad b. Muḥammad, *al-Jāmi' fi'l-ṭibb fi'l-adwiya al-mufrada*, ed. M. Meyerhof and G. P. Sobhy, Cairo 1937 346

al-Ghazālī, Muḥammad b. Muḥammad, *al-Munqidh min al-ḍalāl*, Cairo 1973 314

Ghāzī Ibn al-Wāsiṭī, Radd 'alā ahl al-dhimma, ed. R. Gottheil, *JAOS*, 41:389, 1921 270, 569

al-Ḥalabī, Nūr al-Dīn b. 'Alī, *Insān al-'uyūn fi sīrat al-amīn al-ma'mūn*, Cairo 1320 38, 79, 201

al-Hamdānī, *Ṣifat jazīrat al-'arab*, Leiden 1884/91 21

al-Hamadhānī, Aḥmad b. 'Abd al-Malik, *Takmilat ta'rīkh al-ṭabari*, Beirut 1961 475–476, 482, 552

Hammām b. Munabbih, Ṣaḥīfa (3), ed. M. Hamidullah, *RAAD*, 28:443, 1953 843

al-Harawī, 'Alī b. Abī Bakr, *al-Ishārāt ilā ma'rifat al-ziyārāt*, ed. J. Sourdel Thomine, Damascus 1953 304, 668

Ḥasan, I. H., *Ta'rīkh al-islām al-siyāsī wa'l-dīnī wa'l-thaqafī wa'l-ijtimā'ī*, Cairo 1964/8 422

Ḥassān b. Thābit. *al-Dīwān*, London 1971 232

Hilāl al-Ṣābī', *Kitāb al-wuzarā'*, ed. H. F. Amedroz, Leiden 1904 357, 470

al-Ḥimyarī, Ibn 'Abd al-Mun'im, al-Rawḍ al-mi'ṭār fī khabar al-aqṭār, ed. S. K. Hamarneh, *Folia Orientalia*, 11:145, 1969 69, 81, 86

Ibn 'Abd al-Barr al-Qurṭubī, Yūsuf b. 'Abdallah, *al-Intiqā' fi faḍā'il al-thalātha al-a'imma al-fuqahā'*, Cairo 1350 451

Ibn 'Abd al-Barr al-Qurṭubī, Yūsuf b. 'Abdallah, *al-Istī'āb fi ma'rifat al-aṣḥāb*, Cairo 1957 54, 169–170, 232

Ibn 'Abd al-Ḥakam, 'Abd al-Raḥmān, *Futūḥ miṣr*, Leiden 1920 72, 235, 239, 242, 255, 268

Ibn 'Abd Rabbihi, Aḥmad b. Muḥammad, *al-'Iqd al-farīd*, Cairo 1953/65 100, 115, 122, 842–843

Ibn Abī'l-Ḥadīd, *Sharḥ nahj al-balāgha*, Beirut 1963 88, 93, 131

Ibn Abī Shayba, Abū Bakr 'Abdallah b. Muḥammad, *al-Muṣannaf fi'l-aḥādīth wa'l-āthār*, Ḥaydarabad 1967/71 224, 236, 246

Ibn Abī Uṣaybi'a, Aḥmad b. al-Qāsim, *'Uyūn al-anbā' fi ṭabaqāt al-alibbā'*, Cairo 1882 556, 702, 720

Ibn Abī Ya'lā, Muḥammad b. 'Umar al-Farrā', *Ṭabaqāt al-ḥanābila*, Cairo 1952 433, 492, 625

Ibn al-'Adīm, Kamāl al-Dīn Abū'l-Qāsim 'Umar, *Zubdat al-ḥalab fi ta'rīkh ḥalab*, Damascus 1951/4 101, 115, 300, 460, 476–477, 482, 548, 553, 560, 564, 567, 585, 592, 603, 610

Bughyat al-ṭalab fi ta'rīkh ḥalab, ed. 'Ali Suwaym, Ankara 1976 606

Ibn Khaldūn, ʿAbd al-Raḥmān b. Muḥammad, *Kitāb al-ʿibar*, Cairo 1284 10, 18, 65, 94, 98–99, 101, 104, 130, 153, 191, 393–394, 414, 422, 456, 457, 459–460, 463, 475–476, 545, 548, 550, 552, 565, 603

Ibn Khallikān, Aḥmad b. Muḥammad, *Wafayāt al-aʿyān*, Beirut 1969 100, 114, 153, 162, 216, 233, 255, 300–304, 387, 390, 402, 409, 417, 473–474, 476, 481, 486, 490–492, 496, 514, 544–545, 549, 553, 557, 561, 571, 577, 588, 592, 596, 607, 629, 632, 653, 836, 842, 882, 913, 943–944

Ibn Khurdādhbih, *Kitāb al-masālik wa'l-mamālik*, Leiden 1889 54, 122, 241

Ibn Māja, Muḥammad b. Yazīd, *al-Sunan*, Cairo 1953 107

Ibn Mākūlā, ʿAlī b. Hibat Allah, *Ikmāl al-ikmāl*, Ḥaydarabad 1962/7 447

Ibn Mammātī, Asʿad, *Qawānīn al-dawāwīn*, Cairo 1943 346, 353

Ibn Manẓūr, Muḥammad b. Mukarram, *Lisān al-ʿarab*, Beirut 1955 606

Ibn Māsawayh Abū Zakkarīya, Yuḥanna (Yaḥya?), *Kitāb al-azmina*, Cairo 1933 352, 700

Iba Miskawayh, Aḥmad b. Muḥammad, *Tajārib al-umam*, in: *The Eclipse of the ʿAbbāsid Caliphate*, H. F. Amedroz and D. S. Margoliouth eds., Oxford 1920/21 476, 481, 557

Ibn Muyassar, Muḥammad b. ʿAlī, *Akhbār miṣr*, ed. H. Massé, Cairo 1919 304, 549, 564, 596, 598–599, 603, 605, 607, 610–611, 650

Ibn al-Qalānisī, Ḥamza, *Dhayl ta'rīkh dimashq*, ed. H. F. Amedroz, Beirut 1908 550, 553, 557–560, 562, 564–565, 568–569, 577, 584, 592, 596, 599, 600, 603, 605, 608, 610–611, 625, 701, 811, 882, 911, 943

Ibn Qayyim al-Jawziyya, Muḥammad b. Abī Bakr, *Badāʾiʿ al-fawāʾid*, Cairo n.d. 81

al-Manār al-munīf fi'l-ṣaḥīḥ wa'l-ḍaʿīf, Ḥalab 1970 39, 114

Ibn al-Qifṭī, ʿAlī b. Yūsuf, *Ta'rīkh al-ḥukamā'*, Leipzig 1903 393, 556, 561, 720, 848

Ibn Qudāma al-Maqdisī, ʿAbdallah b. Aḥmad, *al-Istibṣār fī nasab al-ṣaḥāba min al-anṣār*, Beirut 1392 74, 141, 158

Ibn Qutayba, ʿAbdallah b. Muslim, *al-Maʿārif*, Cairo 1969 2, 18, 89, 101, 126, 140–141, 153, 158, 161, 179, 389–390, 439

al-Qirṭayn, Cairo 1355 843

Tafsīr gharīb al-qur'ān, Cairo 1958 843

ʿUyūn al-akhbār, Cairo 1943/9 270

Ibn al-Rāhib, Buṭrus, *Ta'rīkh*, ed. L. Cheikho, Beirut 1903 10, 576

Ibn Rajab, Abū'l-Faraj ʿAbd al-Raḥmān b. Shihāb al-Din Aḥmad. *Dhayl ṭabaqāt al-ḥanābila*, Damascus 1951 625

Ibn Rusta, Aḥmad b. ʿUmar, *al-Aʿlāq al-nafīsa*, Leiden 1891 455

Ibn Saʿd, Muḥammad, *Kitāb al-ṭabaqāt*, Leiden 1905 18, 22, 29, 36–39, 57, 81, 88, 95, 98, 111, 122, 141, 143, 153, 155, 158–159, 161–162, 167, 169–170, 173, 176–177, 181, 185, 197, 201, 229, 241, 255, 266, 313, 405, 425, 428, 440, 443, 446, 448–449, 452

Ibn Saʿīd, ʿAlī b. Mūsā, *al-Mughrib fī ḥulā al-maghrib*, IV, Leiden 1899 473, 475–476, 484, 487–488, 500, 836

Ibn al-Ṣayrafī, ʿAlī b. Munjib, *al-Ishāra ilā man nāla'l-wizāra*, Cairo 1924 549, 561, 577, 594, 598, 803, 882, 913

Ibn Sayyid al-Nās, Muḥammad b. Muḥammad, *'Uyūn al-athar fī funūn al-maghāzī wa'l-shamā'il wa'l-siyar*, Cairo 1356 29, 81

Ibn al-Shaddād, Muḥammad b. ʿAlī al-Ḥalabī, Barq al-sha'm fi maḥāsin iqlīm al-sha'm, MS Leiden Or 3076 71, 122, 297, 260, 467–468, 470, 476, 565, 602, 610, 944

Ibn al-Shiḥna, Muḥibb al-Dīn al-Ḥalabī, *al-Durr al-muntakhab fi takmilat ta'rīkh ḥalab*, (1) ed. J. Sarkis 1909; (2) transl. J. Sauvaget, *Les perles choisies*, Beirut 1933 300

Ibn Taghrī Bardī, Abū'l-Maḥāsin Yūsuf, *al-Nujūm al-zāhira fī mulūk miṣr wa'l-qāhira*, Cairo 1929/56 101–102, 116, 121–122, 136, 141, 179, 213, 303, 339, 387, 388, 393–394, 410, 414, 417–418, 420, 433, 456, 460–461, 469–470, 475–476, 477, 481, 491–492, 496–497, 545, 548, 552–553, 560, 580, 588, 592, 595–596, 599, 602–603, 606–608, 610–611, 645, 700, 836, 942–944

Ibn Taymiyya, Aḥmad b. ʿAbd al-Ḥalīm, *Majmū'at al-rasā'il al-kubrā*, Beirut 1972 105, 114

Tafsīr sūrat al-ikhlāṣ, Cairo 1323 114

Ibn al-Ṭayyib, *Commentaire sur la genèse*, ed. J. C. J. Sanders, *CSCO* 274, Louvain 1967 679

Ibn Ṭiqṭaqā Muḥammad b. ʿAlī, *al-Fakhrī fī'l-ādāb al-sulṭāniyya*, ed. H. Derenbourg, Paris 1895 399

Ibn Ṭūlūn, Muḥammad, *Umarā' miṣr fī'l-islām*, Beirut n.d. 179

Ibn Ẓafar al-Siqillī, Muḥammad b. ʿAlī, *Khayr al-bishr fī khayr al-bashar*, Cairo 1280 77

Ibn Ẓāfir, Jamāl al-Dīn ʿAlī al-Azdī, *Akhbār al-zamān fī ta'rīkh banī'l-'abbās (= al duwal al-munqaṭi'a)*, (1) MS BM Or 3685; (2) ed. A. Ferré, Paris 1971 357, 552, 561, 577, 592, 598, 860, 913, 944

al-Idrīsī, Muḥammad b. Muḥammad, *Nuzhat al-mushtāq fī iḥtirāq al-āfāq*, ed. E. Cerulli *et al.*, Neapoli 1970 *et sqq.* 297, 311, 337, 348, 350, 606, 874

ʿImād al-Dīn b. Muḥammad al-Ḥanafī, Tadhkirat al-ʿimād fī faḍā'il dimashq wa'l-shām, MS Cambridge Or 742 269

ʿInān, Muḥammad ʿAbdallah, al-Ḥākim bi-amri 'llāh, Cairo n.d. 569

al-Iṣbahānī, Abū'l-Faraj ʿAlī b. al-Ḥusayn, *Kitāb al-aghānī* (the Bulaq edition), Beirut 1970 10, 18, 89, 93, 175, 313, 345, 399, 418

Maqātil al-ṭālibiyīn, Cairo 1368 460

al-Ishbīlī, Muḥammad b. Khayr, *Fahrasa*, Saraqusṭa 1894/5 492, 513, 624

al-Iṣṭakhrī, Ibrahīm b. Muḥammad, *Masālik al-mamālik*, Leiden 1967 122, 276, 311, 314, 317, 337

ʿIyāḍ (al-qāḍī) b. Mūsā, *Tartīb al-madārik wa-taqrīb al-masālik li-ma'rifat a'lām madhhab mālik*, Beirut 1387 178, 400, 402, 481, 555

al-Jāḥiẓ, ʿAmr b. Baḥr, *Kitāb al-ḥayawān*, ed. ʿAbd al-Salām Hārūn, Cairo 1938/45 701, 757, 797

Kitāb al-tabaṣṣur bi'l-tijāra, ed. Ḥasan Ḥusni ʿAbd al-Wahhāb, *Majallat al-majma' al-'ilmī al-'arabī bi-dimashq*, 12:321, 1932 354, 355

al-Jāḥiẓ, ʿAmr b. Baḥr, *Rasā'il*, Cairo 1964/5 835

al-Qalqashandī, Aḥmad b. ʻAbdallah, *Ma'āthir al-ināfa fī ma'rifat al-khilāfa*, Kuwayt 1964 482, 543
Ṣubḥ al-a'shā', Cairo 1913/19 201, 238, 259, 549, 746
al-Qaramānī, Aḥmad b. Yūsuf, *Akhbār al-duwal*, Baghdad 1282 92
Qārī, Niẓām al-Dīn Maḥmūd, *Dīwān albisa*, Constantinople 1303 357
al-Qāsimī, Muḥammad Sa'īd, *Qāmūs al-ṣinā'āt al-shāmiya*, Paris 1960 898
al-Qazwīnī, Zakariyyā b. Muḥammad, *'Ajā'ib al-makhlūqāt*, on margin of al-Damīrī's *Kitāb al-Ḥayawān*, Cairo 1383 233
al-Quḍā'ī, Muḥammad b. Salāma, 'Uyūn al-ma'ārif wa-funūn akhbār al-khalā'if, MS Bodl Pockok 270 549, 563, 571, 576
al-Qurashī, Muḥammad b. Yūsuf, *Kifāyat al-ṭālib*, Najaf 1390 80
al-Qurṭubī, Muḥammad b. Aḥmad, *al-Jāmi' li-aḥkām al-qur'ān*, Cairo 1387 9
al-Razzāz al-Wāsiṭi, Aslam b. Sahl, *Ta'rīkh wāsiṭ*, Baghdad 1967 432
al-Ṣafadī, Khalīl b. Aybak, *al-Wāfī bi'l-wafayāt*, ed. H. Ritter, Wiesbaden 1959 *et sqq*. 255, 400, 424, 439, 441–442, 460, 476, 489, 524, 556, 624, 641, 643, 653–654, 656–657, 836
al-Sahmī, Ḥamza b. Yūsuf, *Ta'rīkh jurjān*, Ḥaydarabad 1950 129, 646
Sa'īd Ibn Biṭrīq, *Ta'rīkh*, ed. L. Cheikho, *CSCO* (Ar.), ser. III, vols. VI, VII, Leipzig 1906, 1909 4, 8, 44, 48–49, 58, 61–62, 65, 69, 72–73, 81–82, 104–105, 116, 413, 468–469, 665, 669–670, 686, 688–696, 710, 714, 718
al-Sam'ānī, 'Abd al-Karīm b. Muḥammad, *al-Ansāb*, (1) Ḥaydarabad 1963/6; (2) facsimile edition by D. S. Margoliouth: BM Add. 23,355 113, 176–177, 297, 328, 389, 403–404, 407, 426, 450, 453, 511, 520, 540, 630, 658
al-Samarqandī, Naṣr b. Muḥammad, *Bustān al-'ārifīn*, on margin of *Tanbīh al-ghāfiqīn*, Cairo 1347 80, 201
al-Samhūdī, 'Alī b. 'Abdallah, *Wafā' al-wafā' bi-akhbār dār al-muṣṭafā*, Cairo 1980 69, 80–81, 109, 120–122, 255, 575, 841
Sāwīrūs b. al-Muqaffa', *Siyar al-ābā al-baṭārika, ta'rīkh baṭārika miṣr*, ed. B. Evetts, C. F. Seybold, A. Khater, O. H. E. Burmester, 1904 *et sqq* 102, 338, 456, 479, 549, 551, 569, 608, 678, 704, 913
al-Shabushtī, 'Alī b. Muḥammad, *al-Diyārāt*, Baghdad 1951 673–674
al-Shāfi'ī, Muḥammad b. Idrīs, *Kitāb al-Umm*, Cairo 1968 238
al-Shahrastānī, Muḥammad 'Abd al-Karīm, *Kitāb al-milal wa'l-niḥal*, London 1846 918, 930, 941
al-Sha'rānī, 'Abd al-Wahhāb b. Aḥmad, *Mukhtaṣar tadhkirat al-qurṭubī bi-aḥwāl al-mawtā wa-umūr al-ākhira*, Cairo 1388 80
al-Shayzarī, 'Abd al-Raḥmān b. Naṣr, *Nihāyat al-rutba fī ṭalab al-ḥisba*, Cairo 1946 238, 346
al-Shazarī, 'Alī b. Ja'far, Kitāb al-buldān, MS BM Add 7496 111, 116
al-Shiblī, Muḥammad b. 'Abdallah, Maḥāsin al-wasā'il, MS BM Or 1530 111, 201
Sibṭ Ibn al-Jawzī, Yūsuf b. Qaza'ūghlū, *Kanz al-mulūk fī kayfiyyat al-sulūk*, ed. G. Witestam, Lund 1970 89, 93, 605
Mir'āt al-zamān, (1) MS BM Or 4215, 4618–9; (2) ed. A. Suwaym; (3) MS Leiden

C. D. Matthews, *JPOS*, 17:108, 1937 112, 230, 518, 541, 835
al-Tanūkhī, Abū 'Alī al-Muḥassin, *Nishwār al-muḥāḍara*, ed. D. S. Margoliouth, London 1921 357, 702
al-Ṭayālisī, Abū Da'ūd Sulaymān b. Da'ūd, *al-Musnad*, Ḥaydarabad 1321 80, 201, 271
al-Tha'ālibī, 'Abd al-Malik b. Muḥammad, *Laṭā'if al-ma'ārif*, Cairo 1960 94, 233, 357–358, 414
Thimār al-qulūb fi'l-muḍāf wa'l-mansūb, Cairo 1965 74, 337, 345, 348
Yatīmat al-dahr fi shu'arā' ahl al-'aṣr, Damascus 1304 560
Thābit b. Sinān b. Qurra al-Ṣābī' (wa-Ibn al-'Adīm). *Ta'rīkh akhbār al-qarāmiṭa*, Beirut 1971 468, 550, 552–553, 555
al-Ṭiḥāwī, Aḥmad b. Muḥammad, *Sharḥ ma'ānī al-āthār*, Cairo 1388 76
al-Tirmidhī, Muḥammad b. 'Īsā, *Sunan*, al-Madīna 1964/67 417
al-Ṭurṭūshī, Abū Bakr Muḥammad b. al-Walīd, *Kitāb al-ḥawādith wa'l-bida'*, ed. M. al-Talibi, Tunis 1959 229, 629, 843
al-Ṭūsī, Muḥammad b. Ja'far, *Āmālī*, Baghdad 1964 636
al-'Ulaymī, Abū'l-Yumn Mujīr al-Dīn, *al-Uns al-jalīl bi-ta'rīkh al-quds wa'l-khalīl*, Cairo 1866 69, 81, 86, 104–105, 112, 114–115, 127, 141, 159, 164, 166, 183, 184, 190, 201, 229, 304, 389, 405, 409, 418, 509, 569, 580, 595, 600, 602, 616, 619, 620–621, 623–625, 628–631, 634, 678, 832, 836, 838, 842–844, 848
al-'Uyūn wa'l-ḥadā'iq fi akhbār al-haqā'iq, (1) ed. M. J. De Geoeje, *Fragm. Historicorum Arabicorum*, Leiden 1871; (2) MS Berlin Wetzstein II 342 101, 367, 399–410, 460, 468, 472, 475, 477
al-Wāqidī, Muḥammad b. 'Umar, *Kitāb al-maghāzī*, London 1966 21, 28–29, 33, 35, 37, 41, 46, 109
Warrām b. Abī Firās al-Ashtarī, *Tanbīh al-khawāṭir wa-nuzhat al-nawāẓir*, Najaf 1964 843
al-Wāsiṭī, Abū Bakr Muḥammad b. Aḥmad, *Faḍā'il al-bayt al-muqaddas*, ed. I. Hasson, Jerusalem 1979 81–82, 86, 102, 104, 107, 125, 228, 417–418, 441, 614, 617, 836
al-Yāfi'ī, 'Abdallah b. As'ad, *Mir'at al-janān wa-'ibrat al-yaqẓān*, Ḥaydarabad 1337/9 66, 94, 417, 439, 460, 474, 477, 549, 553, 563, 569, 571, 580, 624, 836
Yaḥyā b. Ādam, *Kitāb al-kharāj*, ed. A. Ben Shemesh, Leiden 1967 238, 241
Yaḥyā Ibn Sa'īd al-Anṭakī, *Ta'rīkh*, (1) ed. L. Cheikho, *CSCO* (Ar.) ser. III, vol. VII, pp. 91 *et sqq*. (2) ed. J. Kratschkovsky et A. Vasiliev, *PO* XVIII (5), XXIII (2) 246, 255, 477, 480–481, 483, 485, 545, 548–549, 552–553, 557–560, 563, 565–566, 569–570, 577–578, 585, 592, 594–595, 597, 696–700, 716, 746
al-Ya'qūbī, Ibn Wāḍiḥ, *Kitāb al-buldān*, Leiden 1892 21, 41, 57, 122, 223, 282, 297, 298, 320–321, 326, 328, 331, 941
Ta'rīkh, Leiden 1883 23, 29, 46, 53–54, 57, 61, 63, 66, 69, 72–74, 88–89, 92–93, 101, 105, 114, 116, 132, 140, 149, 241, 244, 388, 399, 410, 414, 421, 422
Yāqūt, b. 'Abdallah al-Ḥamawī, *Mu'jam al-buldān*, ed. F. Wüstenfeld, Leipzig 1866 17, 21, 54, 57, 72, 80, 92, 107, 111, 113, 116, 122, 125, 162, 185, 190, 212, 241, 277, 301, 302, 312, 319, 362, 426, 429, 430, 431, 440, 492, 497, 501,

European languages

Allony, N., An Autograph of Sa'īd b. Farjoi of the Ninth Century, *Textus*, 6:106, 1968 290

Alt, A., Die Bistümer der alten Kirche Palästinas, *Palästinajahrbuch*, 29:67, 1933 310

Amann, E., Jérusalem (Église de), *DTC*, VIII:997 663, 685, 699
Silvestre II, *DTC*, XIV 682

Amari, M., *Storia dei musulmani di Sicilia*², I, Catania 1933 695

Amedroz, H. F., Tales of Official Life from the 'Tadhkira' of Ibn Hamdun... *JRAS*, 1804:409 746

Anawati et Jomier, Un papyrus chrétien en arabe, *Mélanges islamologiques*, 2:91, 1954 720

Andrae, T., *Mohammed, the Man and His Faith*, London 1956 109

Ankori, Z., The Correspondence of Tobias Ben Moses the Karaite of Constantinople, *S. W. Baron Presentation Volume*, New York 1959:1 938, 939
Karaites in Byzantium, New York 1959 919, 929, 936, 938, 940

Annales Altahenses Maiores, ed. E. L. B. Oefele, Hannover 1891 726

Annales Augustani, in: *MGH* (SS), III 712, 726

Annales Cavenses, in *MGH* (SS), III 65

Annales Hildesheimenses, in: *MGH* (SS), III 726

Annales Juvavenses maiores, in: *MGH* (SS), I 396

Annales Ottenburani, in: *MGH* (SS), V 726

Annales Wirziburgenses, in *MGH* (SS), II 726

Annalista Saxo, in: *MGH* (SS), VI 709, 722–723

Antoninus Placentinus, *Itinerarium*, ed. T. Tobler et A. Molinier, *Itinera Hierosolymitana*, Genève 1879:92 21, 847

Aptowitzer, V., Formularies of Decrees and Documents from a Gaonic Court, *JQR*, NS 4:23, 1913/4 757

Aronius, J., *Regesten*, Berlin 1902 351, 574, 579

Ashtor, E., The Diet of Salaried Classes in the Medieval Near East, *JAH*, 4:1, 1970 337–338
Histoire des prix et des salaires dans l'Orient médiéval, Paris 1969 338
Migrations de l'Iraq vers les pays méditerranéens dans le haut Moyen Age, *AESC*, 27:185, 1972 282, 424, 836
Républiques urbaines dans le Proche-Orient à l'époque des croisades? *CCM* 118:117, 1975 344, 348, 360, 611
A Social and Economic History of the Near East in the Middle Ages, London 1976 23, 275, 611

Atiya, A. S., *A History of Eastern Christianity*, London 1968 679

Bacharach, J. L., The Career of Muhammad Ibn Tughj al-Ikhshid, a Tenth Century Governor of Egypt, *Speculum*, 50:586, 1975 367, 473, 475–477

Bacher, W., La bibliothèque d'un médecin juif, *REJ*, 40:55, 1900 750
Ein neuerschlossenes Capitel der jüdischen Geschichte, *JQR*, 15:79, 1902/3 859, 902
Schām als Name Palästina's, *JQR*, 18:564, 1905/6 123

Baedeker, K., *Palestine and Syria*, London 1876 80

New Light on the Conflict over the Palestinian Gaonate, 1038–1042 and on Daniel b. 'Azarya, *AJSR*, 1:1, 1976 774, 877, 882

Combe, E., Natte de Tibériade au musée Benaki a Athènes, *Mélanges R. Dussaud*, Paris 1939:841 339

Constantelos, D. J., The Moslem Conquests of the Near East as Revealed in the Greek Sources of the Seventh and the Eighth Centuries, *Byzantion*, 42:325, 1972 19, 52, 392, 687, 706, 708

Constantinus Porphyrogenitus, *De administrando imperio*, (I) ed. I. Bekker, Bonn 1840 (*CSHB*); (II) *MPG* 113: (III) ed. G. Moravcsik, Dumbarton Oaks 1967 66–67, 81

Conybeare, F. C., Antiochus Strategos' Account of the Sack of Jerusalem in AD 614, *EHR*, 25:502, 1910 7, 668

Coüasnon, C., *The Church of the Holy Sepulchre in Jerusalem*, London 1974 665

Couret, A., *La Palestine sous les empereurs grecs*, Grenoble 1869 2, 18–19, 80, 107, 297, 353, 661, 669, 680, 847

La prise de Jérusalem par les Perses, *ROC*, 2:125, 1897 7, 65, 668

Cowley, A., Bodleian Geniza Fragments, *JQR*, 18:399, 1906; 19:104, 1907 868

Cozza-Luzi, I., ed., *Historia et laudes SS. Sabae et Macarii*, auctore Oreste Patriarcha Hierosolymitano, Roma 1893 699

Creswell, K. A. C., *Early Muslim Architecture*², vol. I (1–2), Oxford 1969 102, 104–106, 108, 669

The Origin of the Plan of the Dome of the Rock, *British School of Archaeology in Jerusalem, Supplementary Papers*, 2 (1924) 106

A Short Account of Early Muslim Architecture, London 1958 116

Crone, P., Islam, Judeo-Christianity and Byzantine Iconoclasm, *JSAI*, 2:59, 1980 97

Crone, P., and M. Cook, *Hagarism*, Cambridge 1977 52, 76, 85, 105

Crowfoot, J. W., Ophel again, *PEFQ*, 77:66, 1945 847

Daniel the Monk, *Vie et pèlerinage*, in: *Itinéraires russes en Orient*, ed. B. Khitrowo, Genève 1889 311, 666, 673

Davidson, I., Poetic Fragments from the Genizah, *JQR*, 2:221, 1911/2 854

De Funes, J. A., *Coronica de la ilustrissima milicia y sagrada religion de San Juan Bavtista de Jerusalem*, l, Valencia 1626 718

De Goeje, M. J., *Indices, glossarium et addenda et emendanda*, *BGA* IV, Leiden 1879 337

Mémoire sur la conquête de la Syrie, Leiden 1900 30, 41, 42, 44, 46–50, 53–54, 56–58, 60, 63, 65, 67, 69

Paltiel – Djauhar, *ZDMG*, 52:75, 1898 561

De Prima institutione, in: *RHC* (Occid.), V:401 250, 718

De Vaux, R., A propos des manuscrits de la Mer morte, *RB*, 57:417, 1950 921

Une mosaïque byzantine a Ma'in, *RB*, 47:227, 1938 674

Delaborde, H. F., *Notre Dame de Josaphat*, Paris 1880 839

Delehaye, H., ed., Passio sanctorum sexaginta martyrum, *Analecta Bollandiana*, 23:289, 1904 703

Demetrius Martyr, *Acta, MPG* 116 4

Dieterich, K., *Byzantinische Quellen zur Länder u. Völkerkunde*, Leipzig 1912 673
Diptykha tēs en Hierosolymois ekklēsias, in: Papadopoulos-Kerameos, I 683–684, 691
von Dobschütz, E., Methodios und die Studiten, *BZ*, 18:41, 1909 687, 689
Dölger, F., Besprechung: Ostrogorski, Die Chronologie d. Theophanes, *BZ*, 31:350, 1931 87
Regesten der Kaiserkunden des oströmischen Reiches, München 1924–65 562, 597, 672
Donner, H., Der Felsen und der Tempel, *ZDPV*, 93:1, 1977 104
Dositheos, *Paraleipomena ek tēs historias peri tōn en Hierosolymois patriarkheusantōn*, in Papadopoulos-Kerameos, I:23 485, 663, 683–686, 690, 694–695
Dotan, A., *Ben Asher's Creed*, Missoula 1977 294
Douglas, D., The Earliest Norman Counts, *EHR*, 61:129, 1946 723
Some Problems of Early Norman Chronology, *EHR*, 56:289, 1950 723
Dowling, [T. E.], The Episcopal Succession in Jerusalem, *PEFQ*, 1913:164 683
The Georgian Church in Jerusalem, *PEFQ*, 1911:181 680
Dozy, R., *Dictionnaire des noms des vêtements*, Amsterdam 1845 112
Supplément aux dictionnaires arabes, Leiden 1881 358, 376
Dressaire, L., La basilique de Sainte Marie la Neuve à Jérusalem, *EO*, 15:234, 1912 662
Dubeer, C. E., Sobre la crónica arabigo-bizantina de 741, *Andalus*, 11:300, 1946 333
Du Cange, C., *Glossarium Mediae and Infimae Latinitatis*, reprint, Graz 1954 52, 59
Ducros, A. H., *Essai sur le droguier populaire arabe des pharmacies du Caire*, Cairo 1929 (*MIE*, t. 14) 346, 353, 379
Dümmler, E., Ekkehart IV von St. Gallen, *Zeitschrift für deutsches Altertum*, 14:1, 1869 579
Duri, A., The Origins of Iqṭā‘ in Islam, *Abḥāth*, 22:3, 1969 335
Al-Zuhrī, *BSOAS*, 19:1, 1957 162
Duschinsky, C., The Yekum Purkan, *S. Poznanski Jubilee Volume*, Warsaw 1927:182 733
Dussaud, R., *Topographie historique de la Syrie*, Paris 1927 44, 297, 301, 330, 550, 558, 562, 686, 887
Échouard, M., A propos du dôme du rocher et d'un article de M. Oleg Grabar, *BEO*, 25:37, 1972 106
Edelby, N., La Transjordanie chrétienne des origines aux Croisades, *Proche-Orient chrétien*, 6:97, 1956 19
Ehrhardt, A., Das griechische Kloster Mar-Saba in Palaestina, *Römische Quartalschrift*, 7:32, 1893 672, 689
Die griechische Patriarchal-Bibliothek von Jerusalem, *Römische Quartalschrift*, 5:217, 1891 674
Eickhoff, E., *Seekrieg und Seepolitik zwischen Islam und Abendland* (650–1040), Berlin 1966 117

Ghévond, *Histoire des guerres et des conquêtes des Arabes en Arménie*, transl. G. V. Shahnazarian, Paris 1856 75

Gibb, H. A. R., Abū 'Ubayda b. al-Djarrāh, *EI²* 44, 63

Afamiya, *EI²* 887

The Fiscal Rescript of 'Umar II, *Arabica*, 2:1, 1955 238

Gil, M., The Constitution of Medina, *IOS*, 4:44, 1974 266

Documents of the Jewish Pious Foundations from the Cairo Geniza, Leiden 1976 245, 283, 309, 311, 315, 339, 341, 363, 572, 601, 739, 751, 755, 769, 775, 782, 793–794, 804–805, 807, 814–815, 835, 851, 877, 909

The Jews in Sicily under Muslim Rule, *Italia Judaica*, Rome 1983:87 776

The Origin of the Jews of Yathrib, *JSAI*, 4:203, 1984 12, 21, 69, 76

The Rādhānite Merchants and the Land of Rādhān, *JESHO*, 17:299, 1974 298, 350, 370

Supplies of Oil in Medieval Egypt, *JNES*, 34:63, 1975 345, 355

Gildemeister, J., Beiträge zur Palästinakunde aus arabischen Quellen, *ZDPV*, 4:85, 1881:8, 117, 1885 842–843, 874

Gilo, *Ad historiam gestorum*, in: *RHC* (Occ.), V 839, 943

Ginsburg, C. D., *Introduction to the Massoretic Critical Edition of the Hebrew Bible*, reprint: New York 1966 295

Ginzberg, L., Genizah Studies (IV), *JQR*, 17:263, 1905 736

Geonica, New York 1909 347, 736, 770

The Legends of the Jews, Philadephia 1909 *et sqq.* 21

Glabri Rudolphi, *Historiarum liber*, in: *RHFG* X 574

Goffart, W., The Fredegar Problem Reconsidered, *Speculum*, 38:206, 1963 10

Goitein, S. D., Contemporary Letters on the Capture of Jerusalem by the Crusaders, *JJS*, 3:162, 1952 943

An Eleventh-Century Letter from Tyre in the John Rylands Library, *BJRL*, 54:94, 1971–2 904, 912

Evidence on the Muslim Poll Tax from Non-Muslim Sources, *JESHO*, 6:278, 1963 257

The Historical Background of the Erection of the Dome of the Rock, *JAORS*, 70:104, 1950 105

A Jewish Business Woman, *JQR 75th Anniversary Volume*, Philadelphia 1967:225 845, 903

Jews and Arabs, New York 1964 236

Judaeo-Arabic Letters from Spain (Early 11th Century), *F. M. Pareja Jubilee Volume*, I. Leiden 1974:331 353

Letters of Medieval Jewish Traders, Princeton 1973 328, 337, 350, 356, 364, 375, 377, 380, 382, 384, 753, 823, 882, 906

A Mediterranean Society, Berkeley 1967 *et sqq.* 249, 252, 255, 257, 261, 270, 274, 283, 298, 301, 305, 307, 309, 315, 328, 329, 341–344, 353, 355–356, 358–359, 361, 363–365, 366, 370, 372, 374, 377, 380, 383, 385, 560–561, 572, 600, 624, 700, 733, 744, 746, 750, 752, 756, 760, 776, 778–779, 781, 786, 792–796, 809–811, 816, 823, 839, 845, 855, 860, 866, 870–871, 875, 881, 888, 892–893, 896, 901, 903–904, 907–909, 911, 914, 916, 927, 932, 935, 936, 945

Greenstone, J. H., The Turkoman Defeat at Cairo, *AJSLL*, 22:144, 1905/6 603, 609
Grégoire, H. and A. M. Kugener, eds., Marc le diacre, *Vie de Porphyre*, Paris 1930 337, 676
Grohmann, A., ed., *Arabic Papyri from Ḫirbet El-Mird*, Louvain 1963 122
Grousset, *Histoire des croisades*, I, Paris 1934 943
Gruber, E. A., *Verdienst und Rang*, Freiburg 1975 113, 185
Grumel, V., *La chronologie*, Paris 1958 683
Jérusalem entre Rome et Byzance, *EO*, 38:104, 1939 699
Guarmani, C., *Gl'Italiani in Terra Santa*, Bologna 1872 601, 682, 718
Guérin, V. H., *Description géographique, historique et archéologique de la Palestine*, Paris 1868 *et sqq.* 392
Guilland, R., *Recherches sur les institutions byzantines*, Berlin 1967 54, 59
Guillaume, A., Further Documents on the Ben Meir Controversy, *JQR*, NS 5:543, 1914/5 784–785, 787–789, 849, 852, 922
Where Was al-Masjid al-Aqṣā, *Andalus*, 18:323, 1953 109
von Gutschmid, A., Kleine Schriften, II, III, Leipzig 1890, 1892 80, 695
Guy, P. L. O., Archaeological Evidence of Soil Erosion, *IEJ*, 4:77, 1954 275
Haarmann, U., Khumārawayh, *EI²* 460
Hage, W., *Die syrisch-jakobitische Kirche in frühislamischer Zeit*, Wiesbaden 1966 8, 679
Halphen, L., *Le comté d'Anjou au XIᵉ siècle*, Paris 1906 722–724
Hamdani, A., Byzantine-Fāṭimid Relations before the Battle of Manzikert, *Byzantine Studies*, 1:169, 1974 566
A Possible Fāṭimid Background to the Battle of Manzikert, *Ankara Univ. Tarih . . . Dergisi*, 6:1, 1968 596, 598
Hamilton, R. W., *Khirbet al-Mafjar*, Oxford 1959 117
The Structural History of the Aqsa Mosque, Oxford 1949 108
Harkavy, A., Additions et rectifications à l'histoire des Juifs, de Graetz, *REJ*, 5:199, 1882 919
Anan, der Stifter der Karäischen Secte, *JJGL*, 2:107, 1899 917
Mittheilungen aus Petersburger Handschriften, *ZAW*, 1:150, 1881; 2:73, 1882 923–925, 926, 938, 940
Hartmann, R., 'Asḳalān, *EI²* (with additions by B. Lewis) 113
Hassan, Z. M., Aḥmad b. Ṭūlūn, *EI²* 456
Les Tulunides, Paris 1933 456
von Hefele, C. J., *Conciliengeschichte*, III, Freiburg 1877 681
Henning, W., Arabisch *ḫarāǧ, Orientalia*, NS 4:291, 1935 241
Heraeus, W., *Silviae vel potius Aetheriae peregrinatio*, Heidelberg 1929 676
Heyd, W., *Histoire du commerce du Levant au moyen-âge*, reprint, Amsterdam 1967 348, 717
Hierocles, *Synecdemus*, Berlin 1866 310
(Eusebii) Hieronymi, *Opera Omnia*, in *MPL*, 24–25 21, 81–82, 751
Hinds, M., The Banners and Battle Cries of the Arabs at Ṣiffīn (657 AD), *Al-abḥāth*, 23:3, 1971 222

Janin, R., Basile, patriarche de Jérusalem, in: *DHGE*, VI, 1141 690
Les Géorgiens à Jérusalem (I), *EO*, 16:32, 1913 680
Élie III, patriarche de Jérusalem, in: *DHGE*, XV, 191 695
Jarry, J., L'Égypte et l'invasion musulmane, *Annales islamologiques*, 6:1, 1966 26
Hérésies et factions en Égypte byzantine, *BIFAO*, 62:173, 1964 26
Jastrow, M., *A Dictionary of the Targumim . . .*, New York 1943 367
Jaussen, A., Noms relevés au Nedjeb, *RB*, 3:602, 1906 310
Jeffery, A., Ghevond's Text of the Correspondence between 'Umar II and Leo III, *HTR*, 37:269, 1944 77, 706
Jeremias, J., *Heiligengräber in Jesu Umwelt*, Göttingen 1958 668
Johns, C. N., The Citadel, Jerusalem, *QDAP*, 14:121, 1950 606
Joranson, E., The Alleged Frankish Protectorate on Palestine, *AHR*, 32:241, 1927 398
The Great German Pilgrimage of 1064–1065, in: *D. C. Munroe Presentation Volume*, New York 1928:3 726
Josephus Flavius, *Antiquitates Judaicae*, Loeb Classical Library, London 1966 *et sqq*. 844
Jugie, M., Une nouvelle vie et un nouvel écrit de saint Jean Damascène, *EO*, 28:35, 1929 672
La vie de St Jean Damascène, *EO*, 23:137, 1924 672
Juster, J., *Les Juifs dans l'Empire romain*, New York 1914 269
Justi, F., *Iranisches Namenbuch*, Marburg 1895 927
Kafesoğlu, I., A propos du nom Türkmen, *Oriens*, 11:146, 1958 603
Kahle, P. E., *The Cairo Geniza*, Oxford 1959 294
Masoreten des Westens, Stuttgart 1927–1930 289, 342, 894, 927, 936
Kamenetzky, A. S., Deux lettres de l'époque du dernier exilarque, *REJ*, 55:48; 56:254, 1908 784
Kandel, S., *Genizai kéziratok*, Budapest 1909 612
Karabacek, J., Bericht über zwei kufische Münzfunde, *ZDMG*, 21:618, 1867 367
ed., Papyrus Erzherzog Rainer – *Führer durch die Ausstellung*, Wien 1894 600
Karlin-Hayter, P., Arethas' Letter to the Emir at Damascus, *Byzantion*, 29/30:281, 1959/60 701
Kaufmann, D., Beiträge zur Geschichte Ägyptens aus jüdischen Quellen, *ZDMG*, 51:436, 1897 561, 572
Die Chronik des Achimaaz von Oria, *MGWJ*, 40:462, 496, 529, 1896 561
Kawerau, P., *Die jakobitische Kirche im Zeitalter der syrischen Renaissance*², Berlin 1960 678
Kazimirski, A. (de Biberstein), *Dictionnaire arabe-français*, Paris 1860 346
Kessler, C., Above the Ceiling of the Outer Ambulatory in the Dome of the Rock in Jerusalem, *JRAS*, 1964:83 104, 470
Kister, M. J., ''An yadin', *Arabica*, 11:272, 1964 39, 239
The Battle of the Ḥarra, *G. Wiet Memorial Volume*, Jerusalem 1977:33 231
A Booth like the Booth of Moses, *BSOAS*, 25:150, 1962 103

Mabillon, J., *Annales ordinis S. Benedicti*, I, Paris 1703 10
McLaughlin, M. M., *The Portable Medieval Reader*, New York 1949 726
Macler, F., Les Arméniens en Syrie et en Palestine, *Congrès français de la Syrie*, II, Paris 1919:151 680
Histoire d'Héraclius (Sebeus), Paris 1904 75
Macpherson, J. R., The Church of the Resurrection, *EHR*, 7:417, 669, 1892 665
Madelung, W., Fatimiden und Baḥrainqarmaten, *Der Islam*, 34:34, 1959 481, 545, 548
Ismāʿīliyya, *EI*2 462
Ḳarmaṭī, *EI*2 463
Malter, H., *Saadia Gaon, His Life and Works*, Philadelphia 1921 471, 784
Manitius, M., *Geschichte der lateinischen Literatur des Mittelalters*, reprint, München 1959 396
Mann, J., Les chapitres de Ben Bāboï, *REJ*, 70:113, 1920 343, 741, 821
Early Karaite Bible Commentaries, *JQR*, NS 12:435, 1921–22 11, 669
Gaonic Studies, *Hebrew Union College Jubilee Volume*, Cincinnati 1925:248, 849 559
Genizah Studies, *AJSLL*, 46:263, 1929–30 745
*The Jews in Egypt and in Palestine under the Fatimid Caliphs*2, New York 1970 83, 274, 288, 296, 299, 301, 305, 307, 309, 315, 323–324, 328, 330, 339, 378, 380, 383, 551, 560–561, 572, 575, 579, 589, 595, 729, 738, 745, 763, 765, 769, 774–777, 779–780, 788, 790, 793, 795–796, 798, 800–810, 815, 817, 827–829, 833–834, 848–849, 851–855, 857, 859–860, 864, 866, 871, 875–876, 881–882, 884–886, 892, 899–900, 904, 911, 913–916, 922, 927, 930, 933, 941, 946, 948–950
Jews (MS), meaning the copy of the previously mentioned book with the author's emendations, kept at the Ben-Zvi Institute, Jerusalem 307, 876, 885–886
Listes des livres provenant de la Gueniza, *REJ*, 72:163, 1921 293
New Studies in Karaism, *Yearbook of the Central Conference of American Rabbis*, 44:220, 1934 852
Note on Solomon b. Judah and Some of His Contemporaries, *JQR*, NS 9:409, 1918/9 856, 859
Obadya, prosélyte normand, etc., *REJ*, 89:245, 1930 950
The Responsa of the Babylonian Geonim as a Source of Jewish History, *JQR*, NS 7:457, 1916/7; 8:339, 1917/8; 9:139, 1918/9; 10:121, 309, 1919/20; 11:433, 1920/1 (=Addenda) 273, 298, 745, 750, 757, 760, 762, 764, 800, 867, 881, 917, 933
Texts and Studies in Jewish History and Literature, Cincinnati 1931 11, 83, 86, 249, 274, 292, 298, 301, 315, 325, 378, 551, 564, 608, 745, 762, 764, 766, 773–774, 783–784, 795, 797–798, 802, 806, 809, 817, 835, 841–842, 844, 848, 852, 855, 859, 868, 870–871, 874, 876–877, 879, 881, 884, 892, 896, 912, 915, 917, 919, 921, 923–927, 929–931, 933, 936–937, 939–940
A Tract by an Early Karaite Settler in Jerusalem, *JQR*, NS 12:257, 1921/2 819, 921–922

La topographie de Jérusalem vers la fin de l'époque byzantine, *MUSJ*, 37:127, 1961 665, 668
Millàs y Vallicrosa, J., *Memoris*, I(3), *Documents Hebraics*, Barcelona 1927 868
Mingana, A., A Charter of Protection granted to the Nestorian Church in AD 1138, by Muktafi II, Caliph of Baghdad, *BJRL*, 10:127, 1926 746
Miquel, A., *La géographie humaine du monde musulman*, Paris 1973 455
Mitchell, H. W. and S. Levy, A Hoard of Gold Dinars from Ramleh, *INJ*, 3:37, 1965/6 486, 548, 562
Mommert, C., Die Grabeskirche des Modestus nach Arkulfs Bericht, *ZDPV*, 20:34, 1897 665
Monachi Sangallensis *de gestis Karoli imperatoris*, libri duo, *MGH* (SS), II, 726–763 (=Notker Balbulus of St Gallen) 396
Monés, H., Djawhar al-Siḳillī, *EI*[2] 545
Monete cufiche, Museo di Milano, Milano 1819 121
Morrisson, C., *Catalogue des monnaies byzantines de la Bibliothèque nationale*, II, Paris 1970 369
Moscati, S., Abū 'Ubayd Allāh, *EI*[2] 399
Nuovi studi storici sul califfato di al-Mahdi, *Orientalia*, NS 15:155, 1946 101, 399
Le massacre des Umayyads dans l'histoire et dans les fragments poétiques, *Archiv Orientalni*, 18(3):88, 1950 972
Muir, W., *The Caliphate, Its Rise, Decline, and Fall*, Edinburgh 1924 418
Munk, S., Notice sur Abou'l-Walid (I), *JA*, 4e série, t. 15:297, 1850 848
Musca, G., *Carlo Magno ed Harun al Rashid*, Bari 1963 398
Musil, A., *Edom (Arabia Petraea*, vol. II), Vienna 1907/8 310
Musset, H., *Histoire du Christianisme, spécialement en Orient.*, Harissa 1948/9 682, 686, 688–690, 694, 707–708
Nagel, T., *Untersuchungen zur Entstehung des abbasidischen Kalifates*, Bonn 1972 99
Nassar, N. G., The Arabic Mints in Palestine and Trans-Jordan, *QDAP*, 13:121, 1948 121, 548
Nau, F., Lettre de Jacques d'Édesse, *ROC*, 6:512, 1901 80
La didascalie de Jacob, *PO*, vol. 8(v), 1912 8
Opuscules maronites, *ROC*, 4:318, 1899 92, 676
Sur quelques autographes de Michel le Syrien, *ROC*, 19:378, 1914 678
Nemoy, L., Anan b. David, *I. Löw Memorial Volume*, Budapest 1947:239 917, 919
The Epistle of Sahl ben Maṣlīah, *PAAJR*, 38–39:145, 1972 924
Karaite Anthology, Yale Univ. Press, 1952
Nessana: C. J. Kraemer Jr. ed., *Excavations at Nessana*, vol. III; *Non-Literary Papyri*, Princeton 1958 36, 88, 122, 131, 135, 223, 243, 275, 310, 676
Neubauer, A., *Aus der Petersburger Bibliothek*, Leipzig 1966 83, 551, 925, 933
Egyptian Fragments, *JQR*, 8:541, 1896; 9:24, 1897 913, 916
Elhanan, Son of Shemariah ben Elhanan, *JQR*, 6:222, 1894 745
La géographie du Talmud, Paris 1868 916

Neumann, C., *Die Weltstellung des byzantinischen Reiches*, Leipzig 1894 571

Nicephori Patriarchae Constantinopolitani, *Breviarium* (ed. Bekker), Bonn 1837 38

Nicephorus Callistus Xanthopulus, *Historia ecclesiastica* (II), in: *MPG* 146 847

Nilus, *Epistula*, in: *MPG* 79 109

Nöldeke, T., Die von Guidi herausgegebene syrische Chronik, Akademie d. Wissenschaften Wien, *Sitzungsberichte*, 128 (1893), no. 9 8, 80

Zur Geschichte der Araber im l. Jahrh, a. H. aus syrischen Quellen, *ZDMG*, 29:76, 1875 58, 60, 61, 92

Zur Topographie und Geschichte des Damascenischen Gebietes und der Haurāngegend, *ZDMG*, 29:419, 1876 44

Norberti Abbatis, *Vita Bennonis II* (Osnabrück) in: *Lebensbeschreibungen einiger Bischöfe*, ed. and transl. H. Kallfelz, Darmstadt 1973 724

Noth, A., *Quellenkritische Studien zu Themen, Formen und Tendenzen frühislamischer Geschichtsüberlieferung*, Bonn 1973 66, 69, 72

Oestrup, J., Über zwei arabische Codices sinaitici, *ZDMG*, 51:453, 1897 100, 674

Ostrogorsky, G., *History of the Byzantine State*, New Brunswick 1957 87

Padwick, C. E., al-Ghazali and the Arabic Versions of the Gospels, *MW*, 29:130, 1939 674

Palmieri, A., Filioque, in *DTC*, VIII 681

Papadopoulos-Kerameos, A., *Analekta Hierosolymitikēs Stakhyologias* (reprint), Bruxelles 1963 102, 413, 574, 683, 704, 707, 709, 714

Historia tēs ekklēsias Hierosolymōn, Jerusalem 1900 683–685, 694, 706

Pargoire, J., *L'église byzantine*, Paris 1905 661, 663, 669, 681, 684, 687, 689, 700

Les LX soldats martyrs de Gaza, *EO*, 8:40, 1905 703

Paul, A., *Écrits de Qumran et sectes juives aux premiers siècles de l'Islam*, Paris 1969 921

Peeters, P., La prise de Jérusalem par les Perses, *Mélanges de l'Université Saint Joseph*, 9:3, 1923/4 7

Un nouveau manuscrit arabe du récit de la prise de Jérusalem par les Perses en 614, *Anal. Boll.*, 38:137, 1920 7

La passion de S. Pierre de Capitolias, *Anal. Boll.*, 57:299, 1939 705

Le tréfonds oriental de l'hagiographie byzantine, Bruxelles 1950 7, 668, 676, 680, 696, 706

Pellat, C., Harthama b. A'yan, *EI*[2] 394

Peradze, G., An Account of the Georgian Monks and Monasteries in Palestine, *Georgica*, 4–5:181, 1937 680

Perles, J., Die Berner Handschrift des Kleinen Aruch, *H. Graetz Jubelschrift*, Breslau 1887:1 736

Pernice, A., *L'imperatore Eraclio*, Firenze 1905 51, 53

Pertusi, A., La Persia nelle fonti bizantine . . ., in *La Persia nel medioevo*, Roma 1971 8

Petit, L., Jean de Jérusalem, in: *DTC*, VIII 687

Reifenberg, A., Caesarea, a Study in the Decline of a Town, *IEJ*, 1:20, 1950/1 330
Renaudot, E., *Historia patriarcharum Alexandrinorum Jacobitarum*, Paris 1713 569
Répertoire chronologique d'épigraphie arabe, Cairo: IFAO, 1931, *et sqq.* 120, 246, 303, 304, 314, 358, 392, 419, 470, 487, 505, 508, 594
Rey, E., Les dignitaires de la principauté d'Antioche, *ROL*, 8:116, 1900/1 676, 678
Riant, M., La donation de Hugues . . ., *MAIBL*, 31 (2):151, 1884 395, 398, 484–485, 717–718, 722
Inventaire critique des lettres historiques des croisades, *AOL*, 1:1, 1881/3 398, 574, 663, 681–682, 694, 697, 699, 701, 715–716, 726
Invention de la sépulture des patriarches Abraham, Isaac et Jacob à Hebron, *AOL*, 2:411, 1884 70
Richard, J., Quelques textes sur les premiers temps de l'église latine de Jérusalem, *Mélanges Clovis Brunel*, Paris 1955, II:420 670, 680
Riess, Zur Baugeschichte des Felsendomes in Jerusalem, *ZDPV*, 11:197, 1888 103
Riley-Smith, J., *The Knights of St. John in Jerusalem and Cyprus*, London 1967 718
Röhricht, R., *Die Deutschen im Heiligen Lande*, Innsbruck 1894 719
Rosen-Ayalon, M. and A. Eitan, Ramlah (excavations), *IEJ*, 16:148, 1966 116, 339
Rosenthal, F., *A History of Muslim Historiography*², Leiden 1968 630
Ibn Ḥamdūn, *EI*² 746
Rotter, G., Abū Zur'a ad-Dimašqī . . . *Welt des Orients*, 6:80, 1970/1 434
Rudolph, W., *Die Abhängigkeit des Qorans von Judentum und Christentum*, Stuttgart 1922 843
Runciman, S., Charlemagne and Palestine, *EHR*, 50:601, 1935 398
A History of the Crusades, London 1965 943
The Pilgrimages to Palestine before 1095, in: *A History of the Crusades*, ed. K. M. Setton, Madison 1969, I:68 663, 719, 721, 722
Saige, G., De l'ancienneté de l'hôpital S. Jean de Jérusalem, *Bibliothèque de l'école des chartes*, 25:552, 1864 717, 718
Saller, S. J., An Eighth-Century Christian Inscription at Quweisme, near Amman, Trans-Jordan, *JPOS*, 21:138, 1948 674
Samōnas, Dialexis pros Akhmed ton Sarakēnon, in: *MPG*, 120:821 674
Scanlon, G. T., Leadership in the Qarmaṭian Sect, *BIFAO*, 59:29, 1960 548, 553
Schacht, J., Amān, *EI*² 228
al-Awzā'ī, *EI*² 114
Ibn al-Qaysarānī, *EI*² 634
An Introduction to Islamic Law, Oxford 1964 40
Schechter, S., Geniza Specimens, *JQR*, 13:218, 1901 745, 848, 904
Schefer, C., in: Documents divers, *AOL*, 1:587, 1881–83 668

Sobhy, G., *Common Words in the Spoken Arabic of Egypt of Greek or Coptic Origin*, Cairo 1950 338

Sophocles, E. A., *Greek Lexicon of the Roman and Byzantine Periods*, Harvard 1914 54, 59

Sourdel, D., Bughā al-Sharābī, *EI*[2] 422

al-Djardjarā'ī, *EI*[2] 592, 882

Dulūk, *EI*[2] 297

Ḥumayma, *EI*[2] 100

Le vizirat 'abbāside, II, Damas 1960 475

Sourdel-Thomine, J., Buzā'a, *EI*[2] 300

Sperber, J., Die Schreiben Muḥammads an die Stämme Arabiens, *Mitteilungen des Seminars für orientalische Sprachen zu Berlin*, 19(2): 1, 1916

Spuler, B., *Die morgenländischen Kirchen*, Leiden 1964 679

Starr, J., An Iconodulic Legend and Its Historical Basis, *Speculum*, 8:500, 1933 97

The Jews in the Byzantine Empire, Athens 1939 269, 355, 376, 484, 829, 937

Notes on the Byzantine Incursions into Syria and Palestine, *Archiv Orientalni*, 8:91, 1936 550

Steinschneider, M., Apocalypsen mit polemischer Tendenz, *ZDMG*, 28, 627, 1874 76, 80, 119, 596

An Introduction to the Arabic Literature of the Jews, *JQR*, 13:92, 296, 446, 1900/1901 286

Polemische und apologetische Literatur in arabischer Sprache, Leipzig 1877 (*Abhandlungen für die Kunde des Morgenlandes herausgegeben von der deutschen morgenländischen Gesellschaft* VI, no. 3) 923

Stern, S. M., 'Abdallāh b. Maymūn, *EI*[2] 462

An Embassy of the Byzantine Emperor to the Fatimid Caliph al-Mu'izz, *Byzantion*, 20:239, 1950 239, 241

Fāṭimid Decrees, London 1964 783

A Petition to the Fāṭimid Caliph al-Mustanṣir Concerning a Conflict within the Jewish Community, *REJ*, 128:203, 1969 877, 880

Stickel, J. G., Ergänzungen . . ., *ZDMG*, 39:17, 1885; 40:81, 1886 121

Stratos, A. N., *Byzantium in the Seventh Century*, II, Amsterdam 1972 44, 58, 69, 72

Strauss, (Ashtor), E., The Social Isolation of Ahl adh-Dhimma, *Études orientales à la mémoire de Paul Hirschler*, Budapest 1950:73 236

Strehlke, E., Über byzantinische Erzthüren des xi. Jahrhunderts in Italien, *Zeitschrift für christliche Archäologie und Kunst* 2:100, 1858 718

Strika, V., Qaṣr aṭ-Ṭūbah. Considerazioni sull'abitazione ommiade, Accademia nazionale dei Lincei, *Rendiconti*, ser. 8, vol. 23:69, 1968 117

Strzygowski, J., Felsendom und Aksamoschee, *Der Islam*, 2:79, 1911 106

Sukenik, E. L., The Ancient Synagogue of el-Ḥammah, *JPOS*, 15:101, 1935 367

Le synaxaire arabe jacobite, in *PO* vols. I, III, XI, XVI, XVII, XX 10, 572

Theophanes Confessor, *Chronographia* (ed. C. De Boor) Leipzig 1883 4, 7, 30,

The rise of Extremist Sects and the Dissolution of the Fatimid Empire in Egypt, *IC*, 31:17, 1957 464
Veccia Vaglieri, L., The Patriarchal and Umayyad Caliphates, in: *The Cambridge History of Islam*, I (P. M. Holt *et al.*, eds.; Cambridge 1970):57 12
Vidal, F. S., Ḥasā, *EI*² 550
Vincent, H., Notes d'épigraphie palestinienne, *RB*, 12:271, 1903 120
Vincent, L. H. and F. M. Abel, *Jérusalem*, vol. II, Paris 1914–22 398, 483, 665, 668, 678, 701, 706, 841
Emmaüs, Paris 1932 55, 74
Vincent, L. H., E. J. H. Mackay, and F. M. Abel, *Hébron, le ḥaram al-khalīl*, Paris 1923 304, 944
Vita S. Gregorii Chozebitae – auctore Antonio eius discipulo, *Analecta Bollandiana*, 7:95, 1888 19
Vogt, E., Vom Tempel zum Felsendom, *Biblica*, 55:23, 1974 81
de Vogue, M., *Les églises de la Terre Sainte*, Paris 1860 678, 712, 839
Von Grunebaum, G. E., *Classical Islam*, London 1970 396, 603
*Medieval Islam*², Chicago 1969 77
Vööbus, A., *History of Asceticism in the Syrian Orient*, Louvain 1958 126
Walker, J., *A Catalogue of the Arab-Byzantine and Post-Reform Umaiyad Coins*, London 1956 121
Walker, P. E., A Byzantine Victory over the Fatimids at Alexandretta (971), *Byzantion*, 42:431, 1972 547, 550
The 'Crusade' of John Tsimisces in the Light of New Arabic Evidence, *Byzanion*, 47:301, 1977 553
Walzer, R., al-Fārābī, *EI*² 478
Watt, W. M., Abū Bakr, *EI*² 43
Economic and Social Aspects of the Origin of Islam, *IQ*, 1:90, 1954 13
al-Ghazālī, *EI*² 633
Muhammad at Medina, Oxford 1962 204, 209, 211, 213–214, 216–217, 219, 221–222
Weiss, G., Hillel b. Eli (MA thesis), University of Pennsylvania, Philadelphia 1967 912
Weisz, M., *Geniza-Fragmente*, Budapest 1924 853
Wensinck, A. J., al-Nasā'ī, *EI*¹ 490
White, L., Jr., A Forged Letter on Latin Monks at St Mary's Jehoshaphat, *Speculum*, 9:404, 1934 667
Widrici *Vita S. Gerardi episcopi*, in: *MGH* (SS), IV 722
Wieder, N., *The Judean Scrolls and Karaism*, London 1962 83, 820, 824, 826, 921, 933, 935–936
Wiet, G., *L'Égypte arabe*, Paris n.d. 569, 574, 578, 588, 594, 597
Un proconsul fatimide de Syrie: Anushtakin Dizbiri, *MUSJ*, 46:385, 1970 584, 592
Wild, S., *Libanesische Ortsnamen*, Wiesbaden, 1973 874
Willermus Tyrensis, Archiepiscopus, *Historiae*, in: *RHC*, (Occid.), I 250, 330, 397, 569, 597, 601, 677, 712, 716, 718

General index

Entries are indexed by section numbers (inclusive of the notes) rather than page numbers

Numbers in italics refer to sections in which a more substantial discussion or information is found

Abraham b. David al-Kafrmandī, Ramla 329, 823
Abraham b. David b. Labrāṭ 750
Abraham b. David b. Sughmār (see also: *mesōs ha-yeshīvā*) 331, 383, 384, *750*, 790, 792, 805, 845, 871, 876, *881*, 885, 886, 891, 933
Abraham b. Eleazar, Fustat 307
Abraham the physician b. 'Eli, Qayrawān 871
Abraham b. Fadānj 827, 931
Abraham b. Furāt, masorete 288
Abraham b. Ḥabashī, Tyre 348
Abraham ha-Kohen b. Haggai, Fustat (brother of Isaac, see also: Haggai ha-Kohen b. Joseph) 311, 342, 353, 821, 857, 862
Abraham b. Ḥalfōn b. Naḥum, Ascalon 315, 906, 907
Abraham b. al-Hārūnī al-Andalusī, Jerusalem 827
Abraham b. Isaac al-Andalusī, (= Ibn Sughmār, see also: Abraham b. David b. Sughmār; Isaac b. David b. Sughmār) 350, 355, 356, 376, 381, 385, 596, 820
Abraham b. Isaac *ha-talmīd* 306, 346, 376, 378, *380*, 382, 609, 891, *898*, 904, 908, *909*
Abraham ha-Kohen b. Isaac b. Furāt, (see also: Isaac ha-Kohen b. Abraham, Isaac ha-Kohen b. Furāt) 247, 264, 274, 283, 315, 360, 600, 601, 751, *779*, 781, 782, 791, 801, 802, 805, 809, 810, 812, 813, 814, 851, 858, 862, 865, 866, 875, 887, *888*, 890, 891, 893, 894, 896, 898, 927
Abraham b. Isaac al-Tāhirtī 372
Abraham b. Jacob, a Karaite 827
Abraham b. Judah The Spaniard, from Jī'ān 829
Abraham (Ibrahīm) b. Khalaf, Gaza-Ascalon
Abraham b. Manṣūr, Rafīaḥ (brother of Mūsā and Sahlān) 274
Abraham b. Meir al-Andalusī (a man of Alīsāna, who is b. Qālūs) 311, 365, 753
Abraham b. Mevassēr, Tinnīs 311
Abraham b. Mevassēr, *parnās* in Fustat (see also: Jacob b. Mevassēr) 793, 805, 813
Abraham b. Mevassēr (father of Solomon *ha-gizbār*) 861, 883
(Abū Isḥaq) Abraham (Barhūn) b. Moses al-Tāhirtī, cousin and partner of Nehorai b. Nissim 315, 346, 355, 358, 360, 363, *374*, 381
Abraham b. Naḥum Ṭulayṭulī 817
Abraham b. Nathan *av* b. Abraham 609, 757, 879, 884, 899, 901, 909, *911–912*, 915
Abraham b. Qurdūsī, see: Turayk daughter of Abraham
Abraham b. Rīqāt, masorete 288
Abraham b. Saadia the *ḥāvēr*, Hebron, Bilbays 315
Abraham b. Sahlān ibn Sunbāṭ 318, 564, 579, 762, *763*, *764*, *766*, *767*, 768, 769, 770, 781, 783, 797, *806*, 864, 865, 927
Abraham b. Salmān, Tiberias 285
Abraham 'the fourth' b. Samuel, 'the third' (see also: Samuel 'the third' b. Hosha'na – his father; 'Eli *ha-mumḥē* b. Abraham – his son; Joshua *he-ḥāvēr* b. 'Eli – his grandson) 283, 353, 753, *857*, 874, 877, 884
Abraham b. Saul, father of Nathan 870, 871
Abraham b. Ṣedaqa, Ramla 283
Abraham b. Ṣedaqa al-'Aṭṭār, Ascalon 307
Abraham b. Shelah 876
Abraham *he-ḥāvēr* b. Shemaiah *he-ḥāvēr*, great-grandson of Shemaiah Gaon 305, 383, 855, 908
Abraham b. Solomon 818
Abraham b. Solomon b. Judah 252, 258, 274, 301, 339, 341, 590, 596, 748, 749, 754, 757, 758, 760, 761,762, 772, 774, 775, 777, 780, 784, 793, 796, 804, 808, 812, 818, 819, 828, 833, 838, 845, 858, 860, 861, 862, 863, 864, 865, 866, 867, *868–869*, 874, 877, 882, 884, 897, 927, 937
(Abū Sa'd) Abraham b. Yāshār (Sahl) al-Tustarī 255, 301, 364, *598*, 780, 851, 939, 940
Abraham b. Al-Zayyāt, Fustat 901
Absalom's Monument 668
Abū'l-'Abbas, see: Ibn al-Muwaffaq; Muḥammad b. al-Ḥasan; Muḥammad b. Isḥaq; 'Ubaydallah b. Muḥammad
Abū 'Abdallah, see: Aḥmad b. Yaḥyā; Ḍamra b. Rabī'a; al-Ḥusayn b. Nāṣir al-dawla; Muḥammad b. 'Abd al-'Azīz; Muḥammad b. Abū Bakr; Muḥammad b. 'Azīz; Muḥammad b. Ibrāhīm; Muḥammad b. Idrīs; Muḥammad b. Muḥammad; Muḥammad b. Naṣr; Mu'āwiya b. Yāshār
Abū 'Abdallah al-Aylī (Muḥammad b. 'Azīz?) 18, 445
Abū 'Abdallah, the Fatimids' emissary 464

ghazl (spun yarn) 339, 350, 350
al-Ghazzāl, see: 'Abd al-Wahhāb b. Ḥusayn
ghirāra, measure of volume 608
ghiṭāra, a kind of head covering 869
Ghulayb, see: Moses b. Ghulayb
Ghulayb ha-Kohen b. Moses (b. Ghulayb) 368
Gisla, Charlemagne's sister 396
Gispert, a monk of Jerusalem 682
glass 348, 351
glue 350, 377
the Golan 57, 58, 61, 328, 393, 557
Gontier, abbot of the monastery of St Aubin 722
grapes 337, 385
the Graptoi (the brothers Theodore and Theophanes) 689, 690
Grave of St Mary 92, 667
Grave of St Stephen 669
Grave of Umm al-Khayr, on the Mount of Olives 832
Graves of the patriarchs (see also: Hebron) 112, 314, 315, 829, 830, 833, 879
Graves of the prophets 424
Greece, Greek, 2, 676, 702, 707, 713, 721, 776
Gregorius, abbot of a monastery 19
Gregorius I, Pope 718
Gunther, bishop of Bamberg 726, 834
Gūriyā, one of Mar Zūṭrā's descendants 849
Gūsh (= Gūsh Ḥālāv) 298, *324*, 329, 342, 344, 376

al-Ḥabashī, see: Mamṭūr al-Dimashqī
Ḥadrak 916
Ḥaḍramawt 183, 406
Hadrian, Pope 687
at Ḥaffāẓ, see: Shemaria ha-Kohen; Abū'l-A'lā b. Mevorakh ha-Kohen; Shemaria ha-Kohen
(Abū 'Umar) Ḥafṣ b. Maysara 388
Haggai ha-Kohen b. Joseph (see also: Abraham ha-Kohen b. Haggai; Isaac ha-Kohen b. Haggai) 865
Haifa (see also: Fortress of Haifa; Sykamina) 2, 276, *302*, 329, 339, 464, 595, *658*, 784, *899*, 906, 912, 943, *944*
ḥājib, manager of the caliph's court 390
al-Ḥajjāj b. Yūsuf 57, 96, 121, 126, 137, 216
al-Ḥakam, the Spanish caliph 561
al-Ḥakam b. Ḍib'ān b. Rawḥ 101, 139
al-Ḥakam b. Maymūn 345
al-Ḥākim, caliph 255, 267, 267, 269, *333*, 334, 364, 367, 560, 561, *563–581*, 584, 589, 667, 670, 699, 700, 701, 710, 712, 716, 746, 769, 800, 865, 882, 894
Ḥalfon, Ascalon 914
Ḥalfon, Fustat 879
Ḥalfon the elder, Fustat, see: Nethanel ha-Levi b. Ḥalfon
(the son of) Ḥalfon al-Ramlī, Caesarea 330, 747
Ḥalfon ha-Kohen b. Aaron, Tyre (see also: Ghāliya daughter of Musāfir) 899
Ḥalfon (Khalfon) b. Benāyā 376
Ḥalfon ha-Kohen b. Eleazar, Ascalon 305
Ḥalfon b. Manasseh, scribe of the community in Fustat 308
Ḥalfon b. Jacob b. Mevassēr, Fustat (see also: Jacob b. Mevassēr) 793, 861
(Ibn Abī Qīda) Ḥalfon b. Moses b. Aaron, representative of the merchants in Tyre (see also: Dara daughter of Solomon, his wife) 348 359, 580
Ḥalfon b. Naḥum, see: Abraham b. Naḥum
(Abū Sa'd) Ḥalfon b. Solomon b. Nathan (see also: Solomon b. Nathan) 380, 398
Ḥalfon (Khalaf) b. Tha'lab, Tyre 812
Ḥalfon ha-Levi b. Yefet, Tyre, representative of the merchants 812
halīlaj (myrobalan) 346, 353, 379
halīlaj kābilī 355
ḥallāl, supervisor of ritual slaughtering 805
Hamadān 504
Ḥamāh, in Syria 307, 477
Ḥamat-Gādēr (see also: Jadariyya) 296, 341, 352
al-Hamadānī, see: 'Abd al-Ṣamad b. Muḥammad; Ḥamza b. Mālik; Yazīd b. Khālid
(Abū Ḥāmid) Ḥamdān b. Ghārim b. Yanār (or Nayār) al-Zandī, Ascalon 526
Ḥamīd, one of al-Qassām's men, Damascus 558
Ḥāmid b. al-Ḥasan al-Bazzār al-Mu'addal, Tiberias 437, 495
ḥammām al-fa'r, Fustat (see also: *sūq ḥammām al-fa'r*) 805
Hammath and Rakkath (= Tiberias) 285
Ḥamza b. Mālik al-Hamadānī 88
the Ḥanafites 609, 628
R. Ḥananel 339, 901
Ḥanania, 'Anan's brother, exilarch 917
Ḥanania, Qayrawān 871
(Abū'l-Ṭayyib) Ḥanania ha-Levi (= Ḥunayn), father of Sitt al-Dār 380, 891